# DISCOVER YOUR DESTINY

## Your Future Revealed!

HEE YIN FAN

TIMES BOOKS INTERNATIONAL
*Singapore • Kuala Lumpur*

## Acknowledgements

I would like to express my thanks and gratitude to Master Raymond Lo who generously imparted his knowledge to me, patiently teaching me the mysterious art of the Four Pillars of Destiny.

My special thanks also to the following at Times Editions: Shirley Hew and Shova Loh for believing in me, Tan Jin Hock for his fine editing work and Loo Chuan Ming for putting together the graphics.

I dedicate this book to my mother, who sacrificed many years of her life so that I could have a bright future, and who moulded me into a person with perseverance and determination.





Reprinted 1996

Published by Times Books International
an imprint of Times Editions Pte Ltd
Times Centre
1 New Industrial Road
Singapore 536196

Times Subang
Lot 46, Subang Hi-Tech Industrial Park
Batu Tiga
40000 Shah Alam
Selangor Darul Ehsan
Malaysia





Printed in Singapore

ISBN 981 204 670 4

# CONTENTS

Foreword ***5***

Preface ***7***

Introduction ***9***

The Five Elements ***13***

How To Derive The Pillars Of Destiny And Luck Pillars ***24***

A Look At Some Famous Destinies ***39***

Clashes And Combinations ***58***

Symbolic Stars ***74***

Hidden Heavenly Stems ***81***

Face Reading, Punishment Symbols And Labels ***90***

House Of Conception And House Of Life ***101***

The Thousand Year Calendar ***118***

# FOREWORD

The Four Pillars of Destiny is an ancient Chinese art which allows us to delve into the great mysteries of life through our birth data.

Man is an intellectual animal. As soon as he can think, he starts to wonder. What is the meaning of life? Is life on earth governed by any comprehensive plan? After thousands of years of such contemplation and observation, the Chinese have now accumulated a vast body of knowledge linking human life to the universe.

Understanding this link gives us a powerful tool to uncover our destiny. This tool is the Four Pillars of Destiny. By reducing our birth data into basic elements and analysing the interaction of these elements with the cyclical changes in the universe, our destiny can be revealed.

After 10 years of practising and studying the Four Pillars of Destiny, I am fully convinced of its power to analyse relationships and forecast the future. This intellectually stimulating subject also generated so much personal joy and excitement that I soon began to share my knowledge with others by conducting courses and seminars.

Yin Fan has not only mastered the technique. Because she also shares my belief that such wisdom should be made available to anyone who is interested, she has devoted considerable time and effort to write this book – perhaps the very first to introduce the subject step-by-step in English.

It has always been my desire to reach out to those who do not speak Chinese. This is no easy task given the obstacles imposed by the language barrier and differences in culture and traditions. However, I believe I have discovered a universal language that both Chinese and non-Chinese can embrace – "logic". Yin Fan, I'm pleased to see, has adopted this method.

I congratulate Yin Fan for her worthy accomplishment in putting together this work on the Four Pillars of Destiny.

Raymond Lo
Hong Kong

# PREFACE

When I was a little girl, my mother used to tell me of the various fortunes and misfortunes of relatives and families in my neighbourhood which matched predictions made by "*feng shui* experts". I was fascinated by the mystery of Chinese metaphysics then but could not understand its logic.

As I studied in English-medium schools, I only had access to English books on this subject, which were usually written by Western authors. It was frustrating to find that there seemed to be hardly any Asian authors of *feng shui*. Little did I realise that I was wrong. For there are numerous books authored by Asians – only they were written in Chinese.

In February 1993, I attended a course conducted in English by a *feng shui* expert from Hong Kong, Master Raymond Lo. The short course wheted my appetite. I persuaded Master Lo to conduct more and more courses until he advised me that he had taught me all the fundamental principles of the subject and that it was time to apply them, as otherwise it would only remain a theoretical subject. Over many weekends the following two years, I analysed the destinies of friends, colleagues, relatives, and anyone else I came across, as long as their date of birth was available and the significant events that had taken place in their lives were disclosed. Master Lo patiently guided me and taught me more advanced techniques on how to handle each case.

I have written this book to share what I've learned with readers who are more comfortable with English than Chinese. Written with beginners in mind, this is a complete book on the fundamental principles of the Four Pillars of Destiny. Once readers have completed reading this book, I would recommend that they go on to books by Master Lo, such as *Feng-shui and Destiny*,

*Feng Shui: The Pillars Of Destiny* and *Feng Shui & Destiny For Managers*. I have also translated 120 years of the Thousand Year Calendar so that readers can practise deriving their own Four Pillars of Destiny. This way, readers will be able to relate to the subject better.

As the main objective of this book is to provide a step-by-step guide on how to derive the Four Pillars of Destiny, I have included examples from Master Lo's books for illustration. Where relevant, I have incorporated common Chinese beliefs, tradition and culture to provide some "basis" for these examples.

Since the subject of destiny originated more than 3,000 years ago, some of the terminology and Chinese characters are no longer in common use today. Although no knowledge of Chinese is required of readers, I have included Chinese characters with the phonetics (in Hanyu Pinyin) for the benefit of those interested.

It is my hope that with this book, more people will be able to appreciate some of the aspects of Chinese metaphysics, which, though ancient, remains relevant to our daily lives.

# INTRODUCTION

## General

The analysis of destiny is a form of fortune telling based on the Four Pillars of Destiny, which is regarded by many as one of the most accurate. This technique involves the translation of each of the four components of a person's birth data – year, month, day and hour – into a pair of Chinese characters. Each pair is called a "pillar". These four pairs of pillars are commonly known as the Eight Characters in Chinese.

There are five factors which purport to determine our fate and fortune. They are:

- Destiny – what we are born with
- Luck – which appears during the various phases of our lives
- *Feng shui* – remedial steps to enhance our fortune or alleviate the severity of misfortune
- Our virtues, philanthropic attitudes and deeds towards mankind
- Education, exposure and experience in life from which we can draw wisdom

## Why Study Destiny?

- To become more knowledgeable, so as not to be easily influenced by superstitions or predictions based merely on the year element (animal sign).
- As a guide in decision making to determine whether we are presently in good or bad luck. If you are in good luck, chances are that you will make decisions that will bring benefit to you. For example, if our luck is good,

we can take on investments with greater risks. If our luck is against us, we should exercise caution in financial and health matters.

- To give us additional insight into our relationships with others.
- In the choice of auspicious days for special events, such as a wedding, celebration or commencement of business, this knowledge will be extremely useful when applied with reference to the Chinese Almanac (or 通胜 tōng shèng ).
- When at the crossroads in our career, such knowledge can help guide our decisions.

## Is Destiny A Difficult Subject?

Deriving the Four Pillars of Destiny is not difficult. The difficulty lies in the interpretation and analysis of the pillars. We should not expect the subject to be easily mastered as it deals with the intricacies of life. There are basic rules but there are also numerous exceptions. At times, other methods of fortune telling, such as the Chinese art of face reading, palmistry, astrology and even investigating a person's past, are needed before a more accurate analysis can be made.

## The Four Pillars Of Destiny

The ancient Chinese believed that the universe is made up of five basic elements – metal, wood, water, fire and earth. Each character of the four pillars represents an element and good fortune follows a well-balanced interrelationship between the five elements. Upsetting this balance will bring misfortune and degrade the quality of life. An expert in this art of fortune telling can describe, with a high degree of accuracy, a person's character, behaviour, family and social relationship, potential and achievements, physique and health, and link these to his path of fortune (also known as his luck pillars).

The first three sets of pillars can be obtained by looking up a book called the Thousand Year Calendar. This book links the dates of the Western calendar to the Lunar and Xia ( 夏 历 xìa lì ) calendars, the latter being the calendar used in the analysis of destiny.

The last set of pillars is worked out, based on certain rules, which will be explained later in the book.

Sometimes a fairly accurate analysis can be made with just three sets of pillars (where only the time of birth is not known). There are, however, situations where the hour pillar is the deciding factor. If the hour information is not available, we will need details of past significant events to deduce the hour of birth. This can only be done by an expert.

## Two More Pillars Of Destiny

In addition to the Four Pillars of Destiny, there are two other pillars, known as:

House of Conception ( 胎元 tāi yúan ), and

House of Life ( 命宫 mìng gōng )

These pillars are usually derived in the following circumstances:

- To help evaluate the strength of the self element if the Four Pillars of Destiny show that the self element is very weak and may not be able to "survive" without supporting elements.
- To determine the number of siblings or children in the family. However, this method is no longer accurate today because of the widespread use of modern contraceptive devices.

We will learn how to calculate these two sets of pillars later in this book.

## Luck Pillars

If destiny is our car or mode of transport, then our luck pillars can be thought of as our journey through life. Life, as we all know, can be smooth or bumpy with winding, hilly roads.

If we have a good, strong destiny, entering a phase with bad luck pillars need not be devastating. However, those of us with weak elements will need other elements to strengthen ourselves. While it is possible for a person to enjoy 40 years of good luck, there could still be a complete reversal of fortune at some point in his life. Each luck pillar lasts ten years, with stronger influence from each element for five of those years.

## Year And Month Influences

Besides destiny and the luck pillars, which are derived from a person's birth data, the year and various months of the year also have an impact on our destiny. However, if a person is in a period of good luck, then a year which is not favourable to him will not have any serious implications.

As a year is divided into four seasons, the influence of certain elements will be greater during certain months. For example, in 1995, a year of wood over water, 乙 *yin* wood 亥 *yin* water, that is, strong wood, the wood influence is stronger during the spring months of February, March and April. If wood is unfavourable, more problems could arise during these months.

## Can We Change Our Destiny?

Destiny and luck rank highly as factors determining the quality of our lives. Although we can enhance the other three factors – *feng shui*, our virtues and education – we cannot change our destiny and luck. Knowing this, some sceptics might be tempted to put their supposed good fortune to the test and just lie back, waiting for fortune to literally drop from the sky. Such an attitude, however, is not advisable as our overall fortune can be affected if we do not apply the wisdom of our education and experience.

## Conclusion

Analyse our destiny only as a guide. Do not be obsessed with the subject. After all, we are only human and cannot play God. Instead, we can learn to appreciate the wisdom of those who had taken the pains to record their great discoveries – some records were deliberately burnt during times of war but were subsequently reconstructed – more than 3,000 years ago.

# THE FIVE ELEMENTS

Ancient Chinese metaphysics is based on the theory that everything in the universe (material or abstract) is made up of five elements – metal, wood, water, fire and earth. These elements are the symbols of the five fundamental forces or types of energy which are governed by the Cycles of Birth and Destruction. These two cycles or laws are believed to regulate all motion and activity in the universe, based on the following interrelationships between the elements.

## Cycle Of Birth

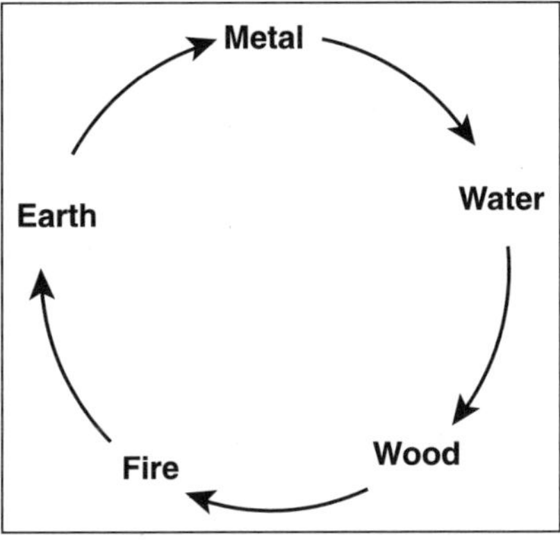


The Cycle of Birth is also known as the Cycle of Harmony or the Cycle of Mother and Child Relationship. According to the Cycle of Birth:

- Metal generates water (comparable to molten metal melting)
- Water gives rise to wood (comparable to plants or trees needing water for nourishment)
- Wood generates fire (comparable to the adding of wood to increase a fire's strength)
- Fire produces earth (comparable to things turning to ashes and forming part of the earth after being burnt)
- Earth generates metal (from earth, minerals such as gold and diamond are derived) and completes the cycle

## Cycle Of Destruction

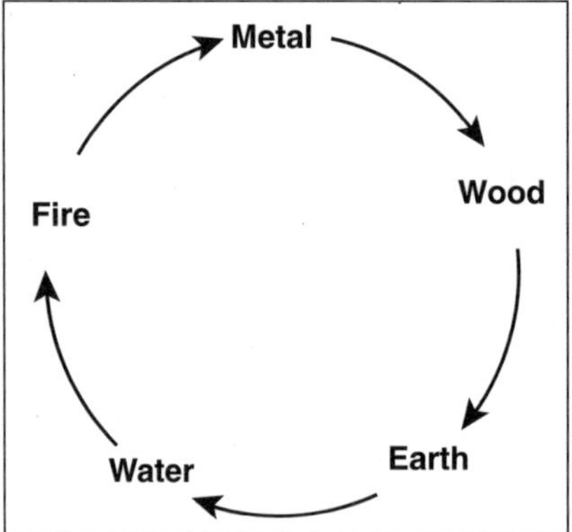


This cycle is also known as the Cycle of Conflicting and Antagonistic Relationships. According to the Cycle of Destruction:

- Metal suppresses wood (similar to an axe chopping firewood)
- Wood conquers earth (for example, a sharp, wooden pole piercing the ground)
- Earth stops the flow of water (for example, a dam)
- Water douses fire
- Fire melts metal

All five elements are capable of dynamic interaction and it is this interaction which forms the force behind life, activity and changes in the universe.

The Xia calendar can also be expressed in terms of the five elements, with each item of year, month, day and hour represented by two Chinese characters. For example, the year 1995 (Year of the Pig) can be expressed as follows:

| 乙<br>*Yin* Wood | Heavenly stem |
|---|---|
| 亥<br>*Yin* Water | Earthly branch |

The Chinese character on top is known as the "heavenly stem" while the character at the bottom is the "earthly branch". Altogether, there are 10 heavenly stems and 12 earthly branches. The table below lists all the stems and branches.

| **Heavenly Stems** | | | **Earthly Branches** | | |
|---|---|---|---|---|---|
| 甲 | (jiă) | *Yang* Wood | 子 | (zĭ) | *Yang* Water (Rat) |
| 乙 | (yĭ) | *Yin* Wood | 丑 | (chŏu) | *Yin* Earth (Ox) |
| 丙 | (bĭng) | *Yang* Fire | 寅 | (yín) | *Yang* Wood (Tiger) |
| 丁 | (dīng) | *Yin* Fire | 卯 | (măo) | *Yin* Wood (Rabbit) |
| 戊 | (wù) | *Yang* Earth | 辰 | (chén) | *Yang* Earth (Dragon) |
| 己 | (jĭ) | *Yin* Earth | 巳 | (sì) | *Yin* Fire (Snake) |
| 庚 | (gēng) | *Yang* Metal | 午 | (wŭ) | *Yang* Fire (Horse) |
| 辛 | (xīn) | *Yin* Metal | 未 | (wèi) | *Yin* Earth (Goat) |
| 壬 | (rén) | *Yang* Water | 申 | (shēn) | *Yang* Metal (Monkey) |
| 癸 | (gŭi) | *Yin* Water | 酉 | (yŏu) | *Yin* Metal (Rooster) |
| | | | 戌 | (xū) | *Yang* Earth (Dog) |
| | | | 亥 | (hài) | *Yin* Water (Pig) |

From this table, we can see that the year 1995 represents the influence of wood (heavenly stem) and water (earthly branch).

A person's birth data comprises the year, month, day and hour. The moment of birth can be translated into a combination of elements, referred to as the Four Pillars of Destiny. From these pillars, we can evaluate a person's background, potential, character, talents, relationships with family members, health and physical appearance and predict his future.

## Animal Signs

According to legend, before the Lord Buddha departed from the world, he summoned all the animals on earth to him. Only 12 completed the journey successfully and in gratitude, the Lord Buddha named a year after each of them in the sequence of their arrival. This sequence became the basis for the Chinese system of naming the 12 earthly branches according to the 12 animal signs.

## *Yin* And *Yang* (Negative And Positive)

According to the concept of *yin* and *yang*, the world is in a constant state of change, alternating between action and rest. *Yang* represents the active force while *yin* is the passive force. *Yang* describes the masculine side of human while *yin* is the feminine side of existence.

Each of the five elements has a *yang* (positive) or *yin* (negative) expression. Of the 12 animal signs, six are *yang* and six are *yin*. The Rat, Tiger, Dragon, Horse, Monkey and Dog are *yang* while the Ox, Rabbit, Snake, Goat, Rooster and Pig are *yin*. In general, *yang* and *yin* is used to distinguish between stronger and weaker characters. For example, *yang* wood is often compared to a tall, thick tree while *yin* wood is the flower, grass or branch of a tree. *Yang* fire symbolises sunlight while *yin* fire represents a candle flame.

## Seasons

The 12 earthly branches also form the various seasons in a year. As nature on earth changes according to the four seasons, the prosperity and strength of the elements also change with this natural cycle. The relationship between the Xia calendar (the calendar used in the analysis of destiny) and the Western calendar is shown below:

| Xia Months | | | Element | Season | Western Months |
|---|---|---|---|---|---|
| 1 | 寅 | (yín) | *Yang* Wood | Spring | 4, 5 Feb – 4, 5 Mar |
| 2 | 卯 | (mǎo) | *Yin* Wood | Spring | 5, 6 Mar – 3, 4 Apr |
| 3 | 辰 | (chén) | *Yang* Earth | Spring | 4, 5 Apr – 4, 5 May |
| 4 | 巳 | (sì) | *Yin* Fire | Summer | 5, 6 May – 4, 5 June |
| 5 | 午 | (wǔ) | *Yang* Fire | Summer | 5, 6 June – 6, 7 July |
| 6 | 未 | (wèi) | *Yin* Earth | Summer | 7, 8 July – 6, 7 Aug |
| 7 | 申 | (shēn) | *Yang* Metal | Autumn | 7, 8 Aug – 6, 7 Sep |
| 8 | 酉 | (yǒu) | *Yin* Metal | Autumn | 7, 8 Sep – 7, 8 Oct |
| 9 | 戌 | (xū) | *Yang* Earth | Autumn | 8, 9 Oct – 6, 7 Nov |
| 10 | 亥 | (hài) | *Yin* Water | Winter | 7, 8 Nov – 6, 7 Dec |
| 11 | 子 | (zǐ) | *Yang* Water | Winter | 7, 8 Dec – 4, 5 Jan |
| 12 | 丑 | (chǒu) | *Yin* Earth | Winter | 5, 6 Jan – 3, 4 Feb |

According to the Xia calendar, the year begins with spring, which is the most prosperous season for wood as all plant life thrive in spring. During the summer months of May, June and July, fire, being associated with summer, is most prosperous. The autumn months of August, September and October are when leaves fall (i.e. the wood element weakens) and metal, which destroys wood, becomes strongest. Finally, during the winter months of November, December and January, with ice and snow reigning, water is the strongest element.

| | **Metal** | **Wood** | **Water** | **Fire** |
|---|---|---|---|---|
| **Spring** | die | prosper | weak | born |
| **Summer** | born | weak | die | prosper |
| **Autumn** | prosper | die | born | weak |
| **Winter** | weak | born | prosper | die |

The above table shows the strength of the five elements during the various seasons. The fifth element of earth is neutral and its presence is felt throughout the year. However, earth's influence is felt most strongly during the last month of each season, during the transition into the next season.

During spring when wood is strongest, metal cannot "survive" as, according to the Cycle of Destruction, wood exhausts the conflicting energy of metal. Thus metal characteristics will not be able to manifest themselves during this season. Water influence is weak during spring as water is needed to nourish the abundance of wood, trees and plants while the fire element, which "died" in the winter season of strong water, is rekindled with the help of strong wood.

## How To Interpret Elemental Relationships

Now that we have some theoretical background, we need a tool to convert the five elements into matters relating to our complex daily lives. We start by defining the element on the heavenly stem of the day of birth as the "self" element ( 自元 zì yuán ) and then apply the Cycles of Birth and Destruction to derive the various relationships between the "self" element and other aspects of life.

For example, if a person is born on a day of wood as the heavenly stem, then this person is, by definition, a wood person. As water gives birth to wood, water is the symbol of a wood person's mother. Water also symbolises the resources and knowledge of a wood person as it supports the growth of wood.

According to the Cycle of Destruction, wood conquers earth. Thus, to a wood person, earth is the symbol of wealth – his reward and achievement. Earth also represents his wife as in ancient times of traditional Chinese culture, woman was the weaker sex and was "conquered" by the male. So the element which the "self" conquers represents the wife. This rule, however, only applies to a male person.

The following table lists out all the interrelationships for a male wood person:

| Element | Persons | Areas of Life |
|---|---|---|
| Wood | Self | Friends/colleagues, competitors |
| Water | Mother | Resources, support |
| Earth | Wife, father | Wealth, money |
| Metal | Son | Status, pressure, power |
| Fire | – | Intelligence, expression, freedom |

Earth symbolises the father to a wood man since earth is the element that conquers a wood person's mother, water. Therefore, metal is a wood man's child as it is the element generated by earth (the element of a wood person's wife), according to the Cycle of Birth.

Based on the chain of logical deduction, we can use the five elements to represent all complicated human relationships and areas of life. The complete table showing the various relationships for all five elements is shown opposite. It will be a good exercise for readers to try to deduce the relationships for persons of various elements as this is fundamental in the analysis of destiny.

## Elemental Relationships For Persons Of Various Elements

1. **Metal Man**

| Element | Persons | Areas of Life |
|---|---|---|
| Metal | Self | Friends/colleagues, competitors |
| Earth | Mother | Resources, support |
| Wood | Wife, father | Wealth, money |
| Fire | Child | Status, pressure, power |
| Water | – | Intelligence, expression, freedom |

2. **Water Man**

| Element | Persons | Areas of Life |
|---|---|---|
| Water | Self | Friends/colleagues, competitors |
| Metal | Mother | Resources, support |
| Fire | Wife, father | Wealth, money |
| Earth | Child | Status, pressure, power |
| Wood | – | Intelligence, expression, freedom |

3. **Wood Man**

| Element | Persons | Areas of Life |
|---|---|---|
| Wood | Self | Friends/colleagues, competitors |
| Water | Mother | Resources, support |
| Earth | Wife, father | Wealth, money |
| Metal | Child | Status, pressure, power |
| Fire | – | Intelligence, expression, freedom |

4. **Fire Man**

| Element | Persons | Areas of Life |
|---|---|---|
| Fire | Self | Friends/colleagues, competitors |
| Wood | Mother | Resources, support |
| Metal | Wife, father | Wealth, money |
| Water | Child | Status, pressure, power |
| Earth | – | Intelligence, expression, freedom |

5. **Earth Man**

| Element | Persons | Areas of Life |
|---|---|---|
| Earth | Self | Friends/colleagues, competitors |
| Fire | Mother | Resources, support |
| Water | Wife, father | Wealth, money |
| Wood | Child | Status, pressure, power |
| Metal | – | Intelligence, expression, freedom |

The previous table shows the relationships for a male person only. For a female, the relationships with her husband and child differ. The following table shows the spouse and child elements for each female self-sign:

| Self | Child | Husband |
|---|---|---|
| Metal woman | Water | Fire |
| Wood woman | Fire | Metal |
| Water woman | Wood | Earth |
| Fire woman | Earth | Water |
| Earth woman | Metal | Wood |

Since a woman gives birth to her child, the element of her child is the element which her self-sign gives birth to. The element that conquers the self symbolises her husband. In all other aspects the elemental relationships follow the pattern for a male person.

## Thousand Year Calendar

For the purpose of deriving the Four Pillars of Destiny, there are basically three types of calendars: Western, Lunar and Xia.

The Xia calendar ( 夏历 xìa lì ) existed as early as the Xia Dynasty (c. 2200 B.C.). It is a solar calendar, closely related to the movement of the earth around the sun on the imaginary circle called the ecliptic. The year commences on the first day of spring, which usually falls on 4 or 5 February in the Western calendar and ends on the last day of winter when the earth completes its cycle. The 12 months of the year are formed by dividing the ecliptic into 12 portions which are named according to the 12 earthly branches. For example, the first day of the first month of the year (also known as the first day of spring 立春 lì chūn ), around 4 February, is expressed by the earthly branch symbolising the wood element. The relationship between the Xia and Western calendars for all the 12 months has been shown earlier on page 16.

The original Thousand Year Calendar contains tables with the Lunar calendar shown against the Western calendar and Xia calendar elements. Because most Chinese follow the Lunar calendar, the point of reference is the Lunar calendar. The Thousand Year Calendar can therefore be confusing for someone who needs to determine a Xia calendar month. The Lunar calendar also needs some explaining to those not familiar with it. For instance, the start of the Lunar year is the first day of Chinese New Year. There is also an additional month every two to three years when a Lunar Leap Year (the additional month is needed to keep the shorter lunar calendar in line with the solar calendar) and "Blind Year" (i.e when the Lunar Year commences after the first day of spring – after the first day of the Xia calendar) occurs.

For this book, I have therefore simplified the format of the Thousand Year Calendar by using the Xia calendar as the base and cross-referencing it to the Western calendar. I have not incorporated the Lunar calendar as birth data expressed in the Western calendar is readily available today. This way, readers will be able to appreciate the subject of destiny without needing to understand the Lunar calendar.

The present version of the Thousand Year Calendar covers a period of 120 years from 1912 to 2031. The first year for each 12-year cycle is as follows:

| 1912 | 1924 | 1936 | 1948 | 1960 |
|---|---|---|---|---|
| 壬<br>*Yang* Water<br>子<br>*Yang* Water | 甲<br>*Yang* Wood<br>子<br>*Yang* Water | 丙<br>*Yang* Fire<br>子<br>*Yang* Water | 戊<br>*Yang* Earth<br>子<br>*Yang* Water | 庚<br>*Yang* Metal<br>子<br>*Yang* Water |
| **1972** | **1984** | **1996** | **2008** | **2020** |
| 壬<br>*Yang* Water<br>子<br>*Yang* Water | 甲<br>*Yang* Wood<br>子<br>*Yang* Water | 丙<br>*Yang* Fire<br>子<br>*Yang* Water | 戊<br>*Yang* Earth<br>子<br>*Yang* Water | 庚<br>*Yang* Metal<br>子<br>*Yang* Water |

The sequence for each year of the 12-year period starting 1924 is:

| 1924 | 1925 | 1926 | 1927 | 1928 | 1929 |
|---|---|---|---|---|---|
| 甲 | 乙 | 丙 | 丁 | 戊 | 己 |
| *Yang* Wood | *Yin* Wood | *Yang* Fire | *Yin* Fire | *Yang* Earth | *Yin* Earth |
| 子 | 丑 | 寅 | 卯 | 辰 | 巳 |
| *Yang* Water | *Yin* Earth | *Yang* Wood | *Yin* Wood | *Yang* Earth | *Yin* Fire |
| **1930** | **1931** | **1932** | **1933** | **1934** | **1935** |
| 庚 | 辛 | 壬 | 癸 | 甲 | 乙 |
| *Yang* Metal | *Yin* Metal | *Yang* Water | *Yin* Water | *Yang* Wood | *Yin* Wood |
| 午 | 未 | 申 | 酉 | 戌 | 亥 |
| *Yang* Fire | *Yin* Earth | *Yang* Metal | *Yin* Metal | *Yang* Earth | *Yin* Water |

Note that the sequences of both the heavenly stems and earthly branches follow the table on page 15.

## Possible Combinations

Because of the numerous possible combinations, it takes 60 years for the same set of year pillars to repeat itself (by comparison, a set of month pillars repeats itself after just five years). Therefore, if you have a certain day and time, the set of four pillars will repeat itself in 60 years. However, since the same day may not appear in exactly the same month – and even if it is in the same month, the day may not be found in the same half month (whether the day falls before or after the mid-month will make a difference to the derivation of the House of Life) – it takes 240 years before the identical four pillars appear again.

## Commencement Date And Time Of A Xia Month

How each month is divided in the Xia calendar is determined by the position of the sun on the ecliptic. Therefore the exact time when the sun is located at a certain position can be calculated to the nearest minute. For example, in the year 1995, the Year of the Pig began at 1524 hours or 24 minutes past 3 in the afternoon of 4 February 1995 while the second month of 卯 (*yin* wood earthly branch) began at 0934 hours or 34 minutes after nine on the morning of 6 March 1995. The exact times for all the months from 1912 to 2031 are shown in the Thousand Year Calendar at the back of this book.

## Mid-Point Of A Xia Month

The dates of the mid-months are outlined in the Thousand Year Calendar. This information is needed to calculate the House of Life.

# HOW TO DERIVE THE PILLARS OF DESTINY AND LUCK PILLARS

## How To Derive The First Three Pillars Of Destiny

Here, I will be using the birth data of well-known personalities to illustrate how we can derive and analyse the first three pillars of destiny.

### *(a) Bruce Lee (born 27 November 1940)*

From the Thousand Year Calendar, extract the elements for the year, month and day of the date of birth.

| Day | Month | Year |
|---|---|---|
| 甲 | 丁 | 庚 |
| *Yang* Wood | *Yin* Fire | *Yang* Metal |
| 戌 | 亥 | 辰 |
| *Yang* Earth | *Yin* Water | *Yang* Earth |

Bruce Lee was a *yang* wood person 甲, born in the winter season 亥 (*yin* water is in the winter season – refer to page 16) when water is most prosperous (see page 17 for the strength of the elements during the various seasons). According to the Cycle of Birth, water provides nourishment to wood. However, wood is surrounded by earth which hinders free flow of water and is thus unfavourable (according to the Cycle of Destruction). Therefore, he is considered a person of weak wood.

**Favourable And Unfavourable Elements**

Fire, which provides warmth essential to prevent wood from decaying during winter, is a favourable element. Fire also helps wood control the unfavourable element metal (which is a threat to wood) by destroying metal. Any element that supports fire will bring Bruce Lee good fortune. On the other hand, any element that suppresses fire will bring misfortune.

### *(b) Mike Tyson (30 June 1966)*

| Day | Month | Year |
|---|---|---|
| 庚 | 甲 | 丙 |
| *Yang* Metal | *Yang* Wood | *Yang* Fire |
| 申 | 午 | 午 |
| *Yang* Metal | *Yang* Fire | *Yang* Fire |

Mike Tyson is a *yang* metal person 庚 , born in the summer season of *yang* fire 午 when fire is strongest. In the Cycle of Destruction, fire melts metal, so the summer fire is not favourable to him. Mike Tyson is thus a person of weak metal.

**Favourable Elements**

Earth which provides nourishment and metal which provides support.

**Unfavourable Elements**

Fire and wood, both of which support fire, are unfavourable elements.

### *(c) President Richard Nixon (9 January 1913)*

| Day | Month | Year |
|---|---|---|
| 庚 | 癸 | 壬 |
| *Yang* Metal | *Yin* Water | *Yang* Water |
| 寅 | 丑 | 子 |
| *Yang* Wood | *Yin* Earth | *Yang* Water |

(Note: President Nixon's date of birth is still within the Year of the Rat even though it is another year according to the Western calendar.)

President Nixon was a *yang* metal person, born in the winter season month of *yin* earth 丑. The water element has the strongest influence in winter and there are three water elements – in the year and month pillars – in his destiny. There is, therefore, too much water. According to the Cycle of Birth, metal gives rise to water, so these water elements draw energy from metal. His metal is hence very weak.

**Favourable Elements**

Earth, which generates metal to strengthen him and fire, which helps provide warmth in the cold winter and nourishes the earth.

**Unfavourable Elements**

Water which suppresses fire (a favourable element) and exhausts the energy of metal (which is already weak).

### *(d) A Baby Born On 5 February 1994*

(This example highlights to readers that the Xia calendar does not begin on the first day of Chinese New Year.)

| Day | Month | Year |
|---|---|---|
| 壬<br>*Yang* Water | 丙<br>*Yang* Fire | 甲<br>*Yang* Wood |
| 戌<br>*Yang* Earth | 寅<br>*Yang* Wood | 戌<br>*Yang* Earth |

In 1994, the first day of spring (i.e. the commencement of the Xia calendar) was on 4 February 1994 (when the year 甲 *yang* wood 戌 *yang* earth began). This child was therefore born in the Year of the Dog 戌 *yang* earth and not Rooster 酉 *yin* metal. Note that the Year of the Rooster ended on 3 February 1994.

The year 1994 is called a "blind year" because the first day of the Lunar calendar (Chinese New Year) was on 10 February – six days after 4 February. In other words, the Lunar Year did not "see" the first day of spring.

Furthermore, 1994 is considered a "doubly blind year" as it did not get to "see" the first day of spring the following year either. The next "doubly blind year" is 1997, followed by 2000, i.e. every third year.

Traditionally, a "blind year" is supposed to be inauspicious for marriage but there is no evidence to substantiate this. Whether a year is good for marriage depends on the compatibility of the year with the Four Pillars of Destiny of the couple.

## Hour Pillar

The Xia calendar expresses the 24 hours of the day in terms of elements represented by the heavenly stems and earthly branches. Since there are only 12 earthly branches, under the Xia calendar each of the 12 hours is equivalent to two hours of Western time.

The following table shows the 12-hour system of a day in the Xia calendar as represented by the earthly branches:

| Xia Hours | Animal Sign | Element | Western Time |
|---|---|---|---|
| 1. 子 | Rat | *Yang* Water | 2300-0100 |
| 2. 丑 | Ox | *Yin* Earth | 0100-0300 |
| 3. 寅 | Tiger | *Yang* Wood | 0300-0500 |
| 4. 卯 | Rabbit | *Yin* Wood | 0500-0700 |
| 5. 辰 | Dragon | *Yang* Earth | 0700-0900 |
| 6. 巳 | Snake | *Yin* Fire | 0900-1100 |
| 7. 午 | Horse | *Yang* Fire | 1100-1300 |
| 8. 未 | Goat | *Yin* Earth | 1300-1500 |
| 9. 申 | Monkey | *Yang* Metal | 1500-1700 |
| 10. 酉 | Rooster | *Yin* Metal | 1700-1900 |
| 11. 戌 | Dog | *Yang* Earth | 1900-2100 |
| 12. 亥 | Pig | *Yin* Water | 2100-2300 |

## How To Derive The Heavenly Stem Of The Hour Pillar

There is a correlation between the heavenly stem of the day pillar (the self-sign) and the heavenly stem of the hour pillar.

The following table shows the count commencing hour for the heavenly stems of the day pillar that is needed to arrive at the heavenly stem of the hour pillar:

| Day Heavenly Stem | | | Count Commencing Hour |
|---|---|---|---|
| 甲<br>*Yang* Wood | or | 己<br>*Yin* Earth | 甲<br>*Yang* Wood |
| 乙<br>*Yin* Wood | or | 庚<br>*Yang* Metal | 丙<br>*Yang* Fire |
| 丙<br>*Yang* Fire | or | 辛<br>*Yin* Metal | 戊<br>*Yang* Earth |
| 丁<br>*Yin* Fire | or | 壬<br>*Yang* Water | 庚<br>*Yang* Metal |
| 戊<br>*Yang* Earth | or | 癸<br>*Yin* Water | 壬<br>*Yang* Water |

The following are examples of how to derive the heavenly stem of the hour pillar.

***(a) Bruce Lee (born 7–9 am, 27 November 1940)***

| Hour | Day | Month | Year |
|---|---|---|---|
| 戊<br>*Yang* Earth | 甲<br>*Yang* Wood | 丁<br>*Yin* Fire | 庚<br>*Yang* Metal |
| 辰<br>*Yang* Earth | 戌<br>*Yang* Earth | 亥<br>*Yin* Water | 辰<br>*Yang* Earth |

| Heavenly Stems | | Count Position |
|---|---|---|
| 甲 | *Yang* Wood | 1 |
| 乙 | *Yin* Wood | 2 |
| 丙 | *Yang* Fire | 3 |
| 丁 | *Yin* Fire | 4 |
| 戊 | *Yang* Earth ← | 5 |
| 己 | *Yin* Earth | |
| 庚 | *Yang* Metal | |
| 辛 | *Yin* Metal | |
| 壬 | *Yang* Water | |
| 癸 | *Yin* Water | |

**Step 1** Determine the earthly branch of the hour of birth from the table on page 27. We see that 0700–0900, being the 5th hour, is 辰 *yang* earth.

**Step 2** Determine the heavenly stem of the hour pillar:

(a) The day heavenly stem is 甲 *yang* wood. Therefore, the count commencement hour is 甲 (see page 28).

(b) Starting from heavenly stem 甲 in the sequence of heavenly stems (page 15), count to the fifth position in a downward movement ( 甲 being position 1) to arrive at 戊 *yang* earth.

### *(b) Anita Mui (5–7 pm, 10 October 1963)*

| Hour | Day | Month | Year |
|---|---|---|---|
| 丁<br>*Yin* Fire | 丙<br>*Yang* Fire | 壬<br>*Yang* Water | 癸<br>*Yin* Water |
| 酉<br>*Yin* Metal | 戌<br>*Yang* Earth | 戌<br>*Yang* Earth | 卯<br>*Yin* Wood |

| Heavenly Stems | | Count Position |
|---|---|---|
| 甲 | *Yang* Wood | 7 |
| 乙 | *Yin* Wood | 8 |
| 丙 | *Yang* Fire | 9 |
| 丁 | *Yin* Fire ◄- - - - - - - - - - - - | 10 |
| 戊 | *Yang* Earth | 1 |
| 己 | *Yin* Earth | 2 |
| 庚 | *Yang* Metal | 3 |
| 辛 | *Yin* Metal | 4 |
| 壬 | *Yang* Water | 5 |
| 癸 | *Yin* Water | 6 |

**Step 1** Determine the earthly branch of the hour of birth. We find that 1700–1900, the 10th hour, is 酉 *yin* metal.

**Step 2** Determine the heavenly stem of the hour pillar:

(a) The day heavenly stem is 丙 *yang* fire. Therefore, the count commencement hour is 戊 *yang* earth (see page 28).

(b) In the sequence of heavenly stems (see page 15), starting from heavenly stem 戊, count to the 10th position in a downward movement ( 戊 *yang* earth being position 1). You will arrive at 丁 *yin* fire.

## How To Derive The Luck Pillars

Each luck pillar governs a period of 10 years. The heavenly stem covers the first five years while the earthly branch covers the period from the sixth to tenth year. After setting up of the Four Pillars of Destiny, we can now derive a set of luck pillars:

**Step 1** Determine whether the earthly branch of the year pillar is *yin* or *yang* (see page 15).

For example:

(a) Bruce Lee's birth year of 1940 is 辰, *yang* earth, Dragon.
(b) Anita Mui's birth year of 1963 is 卯, *yin* wood, Rabbit.
(c) Madonna's birth year of 1958 is 戌, *yang* earth, Dog.
(d) John F. Kennedy's birth year of 1917 is 巳, *yin* fire, Snake.

**Step 2** Determine the type of sequence: Forward or Reverse

*Situation (a)*

If the person is male, born in a *yang* year OR if the person is female, born in *yin* year, the sequence movement is forward. Examples are Bruce Lee and Anita Mui.

*Situation (b)*

If the person is male but born in a *yin* year OR if person is female, born in a *yang* year, the sequence movement is reverse. Examples are Madonna and John F. Kennedy.

**Step 3** Derivation of Sequence

The sequence of the luck pillar is based on the month pillar.

Examples of luck pillars in forward sequence:

***(a) Bruce Lee (born 27 November 1940)***

| Day | Month | Year |
|---|---|---|
| 甲 | 丁 | 庚 |
| *Yang* Wood | *Yin* Fire | *Yang* Metal |
| 戌 | 亥 | 辰 |
| *Yang* Earth | *Yin* Water | *Yang* Earth |

Bruce Lee is a male born in a *yang* year, so this is a forward sequence. Based on the month pillar heavenly stem 丁 *yin* fire, write down the elements in a forward (downward) sequence. You can refer to the sequence of the heavenly stem on page 15. Repeat the procedure for the month pillar earthly branch 亥 *yin* water.

You should arrive at the following sequence:

| Month Pillar | Luck Pillars | | | | | |
|---|---|---|---|---|---|---|
| | 1st | 2nd | 3rd | 4th | 5th | 6th |
| 丁<br>*Yin* Fire | 戊<br>*Yang* Earth | 己<br>*Yin* Earth | 庚<br>*Yang* Metal | 辛<br>*Yin* Metal | 壬<br>*Yang* Water | 癸<br>*Yin* Water |
| 亥<br>*Yin* Water | 子<br>*Yang* Water | 丑<br>*Yin* Earth | 寅<br>*Yang* Wood | 卯<br>*Yin* Wood | 辰<br>*Yang* Earth | 巳<br>*Yin* Fire |

***(b) Anita Mui (born 10 October 1963)***

| Day | Month | Year |
|---|---|---|
| 丙 | 壬 | 癸 |
| *Yang* Fire | *Yang* Water | *Yin* Water |
| 戌 | 戌 | 卯 |
| *Yang* Earth | *Yang* Earth | *Yin* Wood |

Anita Mui is a female born in a *yin* year of 卯 *yin* wood, so this is a forward sequence. Based on the month pillar heavenly stem and earthly branch, write down the elements in a forward (downward) sequence in the order shown on page 15. The resulting sequence should be:

| Month Pillar | Luck Pillars | | | | | |
|---|---|---|---|---|---|---|
| | 1st | 2nd | 3rd | 4th | 5th | 6th |
| 壬<br>*Yang* Water | 癸<br>*Yin* Water | 甲<br>*Yang* Wood | 乙<br>*Yin* Wood | 丙<br>*Yang* Fire | 丁<br>*Yin* Fire | 戊<br>*Yang* Earth |
| 戌<br>*Yang* Earth | 亥<br>*Yin* Water | 子<br>*Yang* Water | 丑<br>*Yin* Earth | 寅<br>*Yang* Wood | 卯<br>*Yin* Wood | 辰<br>*Yang* Earth |

Note: The luck pillar sequence is actually written from right to left (this practice follows Chinese writing which is written from right to left). The above illustration is written from left to right to help readers understand how the sequence is derived.

Examples of luck pillars in reverse sequence:

### *(c) Madonna (born 16 August 1958)*

| Day | Month | Year |
|---|---|---|
| 乙<br>*Yin* Wood | 庚<br>*Yang* Metal | 戊<br>*Yang* Earth |
| 丑<br>*Yin* Earth | 申<br>*Yang* Metal | 戌<br>*Yang* Earth |

| Month Pillar | Luck Pillars | | | | | |
|---|---|---|---|---|---|---|
| | 1st | 2nd | 3rd | 4th | 5th | 6th |
| 庚<br>*Yang* Metal | 己<br>*Yin* Earth | 戊<br>*Yang* Earth | 丁<br>*Yin* Fire | 丙<br>*Yang* Fire | 乙<br>*Yin* Wood | 甲<br>*Yang* Wood |
| 申<br>*Yang* Metal | 未<br>*Yin* Earth | 午<br>*Yang* Fire | 巳<br>*Yin* Fire | 辰<br>*Yang* Earth | 卯<br>*Yin* Wood | 寅<br>*Yang* Wood |

### *(d) President John F. Kennedy (born 29 May 1917)*

| Day | Month | Year |
|---|---|---|
| 辛 | 乙 | 丁 |
| *Yin* Metal | *Yin* Wood | *Yin* Fire |
| 未 | 巳 | 巳 |
| *Yin* Earth | *Yin* Fire | *Yin* Fire |

| Month Pillar | Luck Pillars | | | |
|---|---|---|---|---|
| | 1st | 2nd | 3rd | 4th |
| 乙 | 甲 | 癸 | 壬 | 辛 |
| *Yin* Wood | *Yang* Wood | *Yin* Water | *Yang* Water | *Yin* Metal |
| 巳 | 辰 | 卯 | 寅 | 丑 |
| *Yin* Fire | *Yang* Earth | *Yin* Wood | *Yang* Wood | *Yin* Earth |

## How To Derive The Commencing Age of Luck Pillars

The luck pillars, which cover a span of 10 years each, are linked to the person's age. If the commencing age is 2, then the luck pillars are from age 2 to 11, 12 to 21, 22 to 31 and so on.

Again, the relationship of the male and female to the *yin* and *yang* year of birth must be taken into account. For a male person born in a *yang* year and a female person born in a *yin* year, the sequence is forward while for a male person born in a *yin* year and a female person born in a *yang* year, the sequence is reversed.

The sequence of the count to calculate the starting age of the luck pillars is based on the date of birth with reference to the Thousand Year Calendar.

Let us look at the following examples:

***(a) Bruce Lee (born 7–9 am, 27 November 1940)***

| Hour | Day | Month | Year |
|---|---|---|---|
| 戊 | 甲 | 丁 | 庚 |
| *Yang* Earth | *Yang* Wood | *Yin* Fire | *Yang* Metal |
| 辰 | 戌 | 亥 | 辰 |
| *Yang* Earth | *Yang* Earth | *Yin* Water | *Yang* Earth |

**Steps** (1) As he is a male born in a *yang* year 辰 of *yang* earth, the sequence is forward.

(2) Look up the relevant page of the Thousand Year Calendar for his date of birth.

(3) Find the position of 27 November and count, starting from 27 November, the number of days to the first day of the next month 戊 *yang* earth 子 *yang* water (that is, to 7 December in a forward sequence). This adds up to 10.

(4) Divide 10 by 3 and round up to the nearest number, which is 3. (The reason for using the factor 3 is because the 30 days in each Xia month can only be represented by 10 heavenly stems.) 3 is thus the commencing age.

| Luck Pillars | | | | | |
|---|---|---|---|---|---|
| 53 | 43 | 33 | 23 | 13 | 3 |
| 癸 | 壬 | 辛 | 庚 | 己 | 戊 |
| *Yin* Water | *Yang* Water | *Yin* Metal | *Yang* Metal | *Yin* Earth | *Yang* Earth |
| 巳 | 辰 | 卯 | 寅 | 丑 | 子 |
| *Yin* Fire | *Yang* Earth | *Yin* Wood | *Yang* Wood | *Yin* Earth | *Yang* Water |

### *(b) Anita Mui (5–7 pm, 10 October 1963)*

| Hour | Day | Month | Year |
|---|---|---|---|
| 丁 | 丙 | 壬 | 癸 |
| *Yin* Fire | *Yang* Fire | *Yang* Water | *Yin* Water |
| 酉 | 戌 | 戌 | 卯 |
| *Yin* Metal | *Yang* Earth | *Yang* Earth | *Yin* Wood |

| Luck Pillars | | | | |
|---|---|---|---|---|
| 50 | 40 | 30 | 20 | 10 |
| 丁<br>*Yin* Fire | 丙<br>*Yang* Fire | 乙<br>*Yin* Wood | 甲<br>*Yang* Wood | 癸<br>*Yin* Water |
| 卯<br>*Yin* Wood | 寅<br>*Yang* Wood | 丑<br>*Yin* Earth | 子<br>*Yang* Water | 亥<br>*Yin* Water |

Being a female born in a *yin* wood year 卯 of *yin* wood, the sequence is forward. The number of days from 10 October 1963 to 8 November is 29. And 29 divided by 3 is almost 10.

### *(c) Madonna (born 11 am–1 pm, 16 August 1958)*

| Hour | Day | Month | Year |
|---|---|---|---|
| 壬 | 乙 | 庚 | 戊 |
| *Yang* Water | *Yin* Wood | *Yang* Metal | *Yang* Earth |
| 午 | 丑 | 申 | 戌 |
| *Yang* Fire | *Yin* Earth | *Yang* Metal | *Yang* Earth |

| Luck Pillars | | | | |
|---|---|---|---|---|
| 43 | 33 | 23 | 13 | 3 |
| 乙<br>*Yin* Wood<br>卯<br>*Yin* Wood | 丙<br>*Yang* Fire<br>辰<br>*Yang* Earth | 丁<br>*Yin* Fire<br>巳<br>*Yin* Fire | 戊<br>*Yang* Earth<br>午<br>*Yang* Fire | 己<br>*Yin* Earth<br>未<br>*Yin* Earth |

Madonna is a female born in a *yang* year so this is a reverse sequence. The number of days from 16 August to the first day of the month 庚 *yang* metal 申 *yang* metal (i.e. 8 August) is 8 days. Divided by 3, this gives us almost 3.

### *(d) President John F. Kennedy (born 29 May 1917)*

| Hour | Day | Month | Year |
|---|---|---|---|
| ? | 辛<br>*Yin* Metal | 乙<br>*Yin* Wood | 丁<br>*Yin* Fire |
| ? | 未<br>*Yin* Earth | 巳<br>*Yin* Fire | 巳<br>*Yin* Fire |

| Luck Pillars | | | |
|---|---|---|---|
| 38 | 28 | 18 | 8 |
| 辛<br>*Yin* Metal<br>丑<br>*Yin* Earth | 壬<br>*Yang* Water<br>寅<br>*Yang* Wood | 癸<br>*Yin* Water<br>卯<br>*Yin* Wood | 甲<br>*Yang* Wood<br>辰<br>*Yang* Earth |

John F. Kennedy was a male born in a *yin* year 巳 of *yin* fire, so the sequence is reversed. The number of days from 29 May to 6 May is 23 and 23 divided by 3 is almost 8. Hence, the commencing age of his luck pillars is 8.

## What The Four Pillars Mean

Each pillar of the Four Pillars of Destiny also represents the various stages of our life and family members.

Stages Of Life

| **Hour** | **Day** | **Month** | **Year** |
|---|---|---|---|
| *Heavenly Stem* | *Heavenly Stem* | *Heavenly Stem* | *Heavenly Stem* |
| *Earthly Branch* | *Earthly Branch* | *Earthly Branch* | *Earthly Branch* |
| **Old Age** | **Middle Age** | **Youth** | **Childhood** |

Family Grouping

| **Hour** | **Day** | **Month** | **Year** |
|---|---|---|---|
| *Heavenly Stem* | *Heavenly Stem -Self* | *Heavenly Stem -Father* | *Heavenly Stem* |
| *Earthly Branch* | *Earthly Branch -House of Spouse* | *Earthly Branch -Mother* | *Earthly Branch* |
| **Children** | **Self & Spouse** | **Parents** | **Grandparents** |

While these tables can serve as a guide, it is best to analyse them together with the luck pillars (which indicate the various stages in our life) for the various interpersonal relationships with family members.

# A LOOK AT SOME FAMOUS DESTINIES

When analysing the pillars of destiny, the first rule to remember is that the element on the heavenly stem of the day when a person was born symbolises the person himself, while the other elements refer to other people and aspects of life.

The philosophy behind the Four Pillars of Destiny is harmony and balance. It is generally undesirable for any element in a set of pillars to be either too weak or too strong. If a person is of an element which is very weak, the element's strength must then be improved with the other supportive elements. Otherwise he will encounter good fortune only during the luck pillars with these supportive elements. On the other hand, if an element is too strong, its excessive energy should be controlled or diluted.

## Case Studies

***(a)*** ***Li Ka-Shing****, Hong Kong's richest man: a person of weak wood but the favourable influence of consecutive good luck pillars provided him with the resources and strength to control his wealth. Born 13 June 1928.*

| Hour | Day | Month | Year |
|---|---|---|---|
| ? | 甲<br>*Yang* Wood | 戊<br>*Yang* Earth | 戊<br>*Yang* Earth |
| ? | 申<br>*Yang* Metal | 午<br>*Yang* Fire | 辰<br>*Yang* Earth |

| Luck Pillars | | | | | | |
|---|---|---|---|---|---|---|
| 68 | 58 | 48 | 38 | 28 | 18 | 8 |
| 乙 *Yin* Wood | 甲 *Yang* Wood | 癸 *Yin* Water | 壬 *Yang* Water | 辛 *Yin* Metal | 庚 *Yang* Metal | 己 *Yin* Earth |
| 丑 *Yin* Earth | 子 *Yang* Water | 亥 *Yin* Water | 戌 *Yang* Earth | 酉 *Yin* Metal | 申 *Yang* Metal | 未 *Yin* Earth |

Li is a *yang* wood 甲 person born in the summer season month of *yang* fire 午. Therefore the fire influence is very strong. Since wood generates fire, fire in the month earthly branch exhausts wood energy. He is, therefore, a weak wood person.

**Favourable Elements**

His favourable elements are water, which provide wood with the necessary nourishment, and metal, which generates water.

**Unfavourable Elements**

His unfavourable elements are fire and earth, which are antagonistic elements. Wood gives rise to fire (i.e. fire draws energy from wood) in the Cycle of Birth. Wood also destroys earth in the Cycle of Destruction. However, a weak wood does not have the strength to conquer earth. Instead, earth weakens wood further.

**Family Background**

The month pillar symbolises a person's parents and family background (see page 38). In Li Ka-Shing's month pillar, the heavenly stem is *yang* earth 戊 sitting on *yang* fire 午 earthly branch, neither of which support wood. He was born in China and his first luck pillar (age 8 to 17) of *yin* earth 己未 influence explains his family's poverty. At 14, he left school when his schoolteacher father died.

**Luck Pillars**

Seven years after he arrived in Hong Kong, his fortune improved considerably. At the age of 18, he had entered the luck pillar of metal 庚 *yang* metal 申 *yang* metal.

***Luck Pillar 18 (age 18 to 27)***

| 庚 Yang Metal<br>申 Yang Metal | Some significant events which took place during this period:<br>Age 18: He worked as a salesman in a small machine factory.<br>Age 20: In 1948, a year of water, he was promoted to manager.<br>Age 22: In 1950, a wood year, he made his first million and opened his own plastics factory, manufacturing plastic flowers.<br>Age 27: He set up his flagship company, Cheung Kong. |
|---|---|

***Luck Pillar 38 (age 38 to 47)***

| 壬 Yang Water<br>戌 Yang Earth | Age 38: He entered another favourable luck pillar of water and invested in property.<br>Age 43: In 1971, his Cheung Kong company was listed in the Hong Kong stock exchange. |
|---|---|

***Luck Pillar 48 (age 48 to 57)***

Age 48: He entered a luck pillar of pure water, by which time he was already a property tycoon.

Age 51: A turning point in Li's fortune came in 1979 when the Hong Kong Bank sold him its 22.8% stake in Hutchison, enabling him to become the first Chinese to control one of five traditionally British *hongs* in Hong Kong.

***Luck Pillar 58 (age 58 to 67)***

Age 58: Another 10 years of great success awaited him.

**Spouse**

The earthly branch of the day pillar, often referred to as the "House of Spouse", symbolises a person's relationship with his or her spouse. In Li

Ka-Shing's destiny, the element in the House of Spouse is metal, a favourable element. Indeed he received strong support from his wife – the late Mrs Li was a well-educated and capable lady who gave him invaluable encouragement during his early years in business.

**Talent And Wealth**

Born in the summer month of fire, fire is his strongest element in his Four Pillars of Destiny. To a wood person, fire represents his aspirations and intelligence (see page 19).

Fire gives birth to earth and there are three earth elements in the year and month pillars. Earth (the element that the self-sign wood destroys) is the symbol of wealth to a wood person. To a weak person, wealth elements only indicate financial burden as he is not strong enough to control the wealth.

During Mr Li's era of success, he was in metal and water luck pillars, which strengthened the wood. The strong wood in turn fed and generated fire which resulted in earth. The strong presence of fire and earth in this configuration shows that he possesses great talent in generating wealth out of earth. However, only the consecutive luck pillars of favourable elements (which strengthened his originally weak wood) enabled him to manipulate earth (his symbol of wealth) and fire (his symbol of intelligence). All these factors constitute the destiny of a great business man.

*(b)* ***Anita Mui**, a famous Hong Kong singer: a person of weak fire who became a superstar during favourable luck pillars but encountered problems during periods under the influence of unfavourable elements. Born 5–7 pm, 10 October 1963.*

| Hour | Day | Month | Year |
|---|---|---|---|
| 丁 | 丙 | 壬 | 癸 |
| *Yin* Fire | *Yang* Fire | *Yang* Water | *Yin* Water |
| 酉 | 戌 | 戌 | 卯 |
| *Yin* Metal | *Yang* Earth | *Yang* Earth | *Yin* Wood |

| Luck Pillars | | | | |
|---|---|---|---|---|
| 50 | 40 | 30 | 20 | 10 |
| 丁<br>*Yin* Fire | 丙<br>*Yang* Fire | 乙<br>*Yin* Wood | 甲<br>*Yang* Wood | 癸<br>*Yin* Water |
| 卯<br>*Yin* Wood | 寅<br>*Yang* Wood | 丑<br>*Yin* Earth | 子<br>*Yang* Water | 亥<br>*Yin* Water |

Anita Mui is a *yang* fire 丙 person born in the autumn month of earth 戌 .

**Why Is Her Self-Sign Weak?**

Earth, in the earthly branch of the month pillar, exhausts the energy of the self-sign fire (according to the Cycle of Birth, fire generates earth). Moreover, she is sitting on another *yang* earth element 戌 , the earthly branch of the day pillar.

**Favourable Elements**

- Wood which generates fire
- Fire – friends who provide support

**Unfavourable Elements**

- Water which conquers fire in the Cycle of Destruction
- Metal (fire destroys metal in the Cycle of Destruction)
- Earth (fire gives rise to earth in the Cycle of Birth)

**Childhood**

The month pillar represents her family background and the first luck pillar, her childhood. Her month pillar of *yang* water and *yang* earth elements is not supportive. Her luck pillar up to the age 19 is also pure water. The luck pillar only reinforces her unfavourable month pillar. During her childhood, Anita Mui was very poor. She stopped school early and followed her sister, singing and dancing for a living while travelling.

***Luck Pillar 20 (age 20 to 29)***

| 甲<br>*Yang* Wood<br>子<br>*Yang* Water |
|---|

Age 20: She won a singing contest after entering a luck pillar of strong wood. Her popularity then grew rapidly. This luck pillar of *yang* wood 甲 heavenly stem and *yang* water 子 earthly branch is a period of strong wood as the earthly branch of the water nourishes the wood heavenly stem.

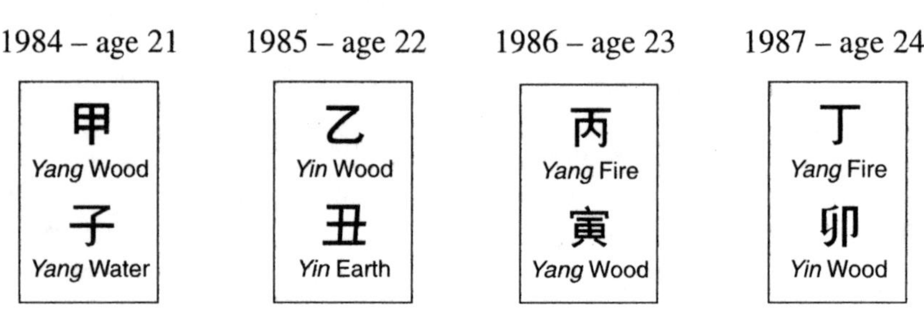


These four years of strong wood and fire during the luck pillar of strong wood were her best years.

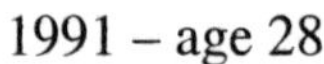
1991 – age 28

Anita Mui retired from singing in 1991 just before she entered the less favourable luck pillar of *yin* weak wood 乙.

***Luck Pillar 30 (age 30 to 39)***

1992 – age 29

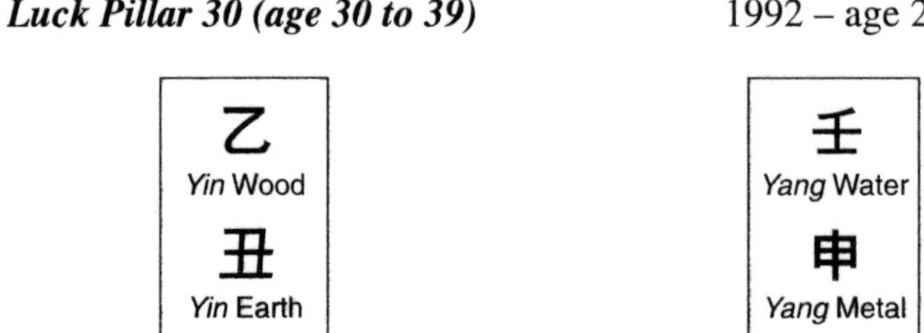


Wood destroys earth in the Cycle of Destruction. As earth exhausts the energy of wood, this luck pillar has weak wood influence.

In 1992, a year of strong water (metal generates water), trouble struck when she was linked to the death of an underworld gangster. However, as she was approaching her luck pillar of wood (which, though weak, is still favourable), only the year's influence caused problems. She was able to settle the matter by paying a large sum of money. [Note: On page 36, we determined the commencing age of her luck pillar as 10. Since 29 divided by 3 is actually less than 10, the change in her fortune occurs between the ages of 29 to 30.]

***Luck Pillar 40 (age 40 to 49)***

In this luck pillar, the fire 丙 heavenly stem is sitting on the wood earthly branch 寅 . Since wood generates fire, this is a luck pillar of strong fire.

This period of fire and wood is favourable to her and she can become famous again. However the presence of another fire element in the luck pillar symbolises a strong competitor in her singing career. (When a person is a weak fire, the presence of another fire symbolises a friend who provides support. But when a person is a strong fire, the presence of another fire is not desirable as it symbolises a competitor.)

(c) ***Margaret Thatcher**, a former British Prime Minister: a person of excessively strong metal who needs fire, representing power and status, to control and dilute the strong metal. Born 13 October 1925.*

| Hour | Day | Month | Year |
|---|---|---|---|
| ? | 庚<br>*Yang* Metal | 丙<br>*Yang* Fire | 乙<br>*Yin* Wood |
| ? | 午<br>*Yang* Fire | 戌<br>*Yang* Earth | 丑<br>*Yin* Earth |

| Luck Pillars | | | | | | | |
|---|---|---|---|---|---|---|---|
| 79 | 69 | 59 | 49 | 39 | 29 | 19 | 9 |
| 甲 *Yang* Wood | 癸 *Yin* Water | 壬 *Yang* Water | 辛 *Yin* Metal | 庚 *Yang* Metal | 己 *Yin* Earth | 戊 *Yang* Earth | 丁 *Yin* Fire |
| 午 *Yang* Fire | 巳 *Yin* Fire | 辰 *Yang* Earth | 卯 *Yin* Wood | 寅 *Yang* Wood | 丑 *Yin* Earth | 子 *Yang* Water | 亥 *Yin* Water |

Margaret Thatcher is a *yang* metal person 庚 born in autumn 戌 when metal is most prosperous. *Yang* earth in the month earthly branch also supports metal as earth generates metal. The metal is thus too strong since it is further supported by earth in the year pillar.

**Favourable Elements**

- Fire which will control and dilute the excessive energy of metal (fire destroys metal in the Cycle of Destruction). Fire to a metal person is power and status. A simple analogy is that metal needs fire to transform it into useful tools – for example, fire turns iron into steel.
- Wood which generates fire (her favourable element) and also draws away excessive metal energy (metal destroys wood). Wood also represents her wealth, the element destroyed by the self-sign.
- Water which generates wood and exhausts the energy of metal (metal gives rise to water in the Cycle of Birth). However, in the absence of wood, strong water may exhaust the energy of fire, which will then be unfavourable. Water is thus a double-edged sword.

**Unfavourable Elements**

- Earth
- Metal

Since Margaret Thatcher is a strong metal person, the presence of another metal represents competition. Earth generates metal which will only further strengthen someone already with too much metal.

**Fire In Month Pillar And House Of Spouse**

Fire, her favourable element, is present in the month pillar heavenly stem and House of Spouse (earthly branch of the day pillar), symbolising close and harmonious relationships with her father and husband (see page 38 for the location of family members in the Four Pillars of Destiny).

### Father's Wealth

Her father is the fire heavenly stem in the month pillar; metal is his wealth (fire destroys metal). Since there is only one metal element in this configuration, her father is not a very wealthy person.

(Note that we use a combination of methods here to analyse the month heavenly stem representing her father, the elemental relationship of her father and his wealth element.)

### Evaluation

Margaret Thatcher is a strong metal person. Her metal is refined and controlled by the presence of prominent fire elements. Her four pillars are well balanced. Fire, wood and water are favourable elements while metal and earth are bad influences. However, since she is strong and well balanced, the impact of these five elements is not obvious. Standing on firm ground, she apparently finds it easier to maintain her balance.

***Luck Pillar 19 (age 19 to 28)*** 1951 – age 26

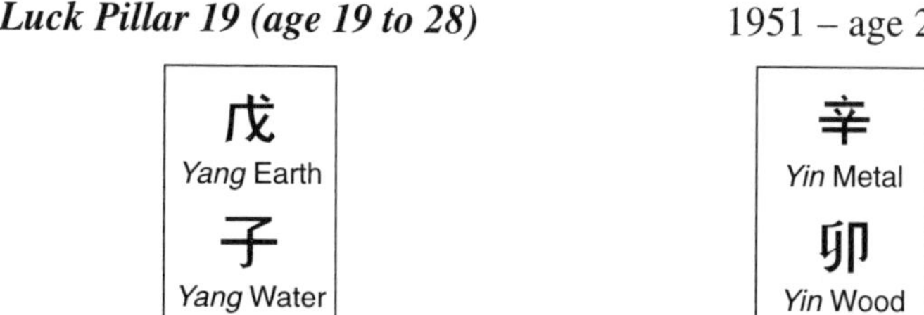


1951 was a year of wood, which allowed the fire in the four pillars to prosper. Fire is also the element of her spouse (fire destroys metal). She married in 1951.

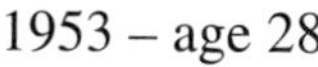
1953 – age 28

In 1953, a year of water, she gave birth to a pair of twins. As she was in the luck pillar of water, the water year 1953 therefore represents two water elements. Water is the offspring of metal and for a metal lady, this timing was favourable for children.

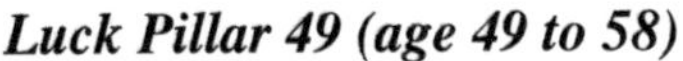

***Luck Pillar 49 (age 49 to 58)***

1975 – age 50

The wood year of 1975 generated fire which is power and status to a metal person. This gave her political career a vital boost and she was elected leader of the Conservative Party.

1979 – age 54

1979 was the Year of the Goat and the goat is known as the "storage of wood" (for further explanation, see page 61). At the time she had just entered the luck pillar of strong wood. This heavy wood configuration enhanced the strength of fire – her power. In May, a month of fire, she was elected Prime Minister.

***Luck Pillar 59 (age 59 to 68)***

At the age of 65 in 1990, she was in the luck pillar of *yang* water and *yang* earth. However, the strong earth reduced the influence of the water (the earth earthly branch destroys water in the heavenly stem).

1990

1990 was a year of metal over fire. The metal element strengthened the water element in the luck pillar (metal generates water), resulting in strong water influence. This strong water posed a strong threat to her power, symbolised by the fire element.

In November, the fire element of the Year of the Horse 午 faded. Being a winter month, the water influence was very strong. As a result, the *yin* fire sitting over *yin* water in November 丁 亥 was very weak.

*Configuration for 22 November 1990*

| Day | Month | Year |
|---|---|---|
| 辛 | 丁 | 庚 |
| *Yin* Metal | *Yin* Fire | *Yang* Metal |
| 卯 | 亥 | 午 |
| *Yin* Wood | *Yin* Water | *Yang* Fire |

On 22 November, after fending off strong opposition on two previous occasions the same month, she announced her resignation.

Now, advanced theories of the Four Pillars of Destiny postulate that the *yang* fire 丙 in the month pillar combines with the *yin* metal 辛 of the day to become water.

| 丙 | + | 辛 | = WATER |
|---|---|---|---|
| *Yang* Fire<br>Heavenly Stem of Month Pillar of her destiny | | *Yin* Metal<br>Heavenly Stem of Day Pillar of 22.11.90 | |

In other words, both fire and metal lose their characteristics to become water, which is devastating to her power element, fire. And so it was on this day that she resigned. (The combination of heavenly stems is further explained on page 58.)

*(d)* ***Chris Patten*** *was appointed the Governor of Hong Kong in April 1992. He is a person of excessively strong fire, with metal and water his favourable elements. Water symbolises his status and power. Born on 12 May 1944.*

| Hour | Day | Month | Year |
|---|---|---|---|
| ? | 丙 | 己 | 甲 |
| | *Yang* Fire | *Yin* Earth | *Yang* Wood |
| ? | 子 | 巳 | 申 |
| | *Yang* Water | *Yin* Fire | *Yang* Metal |

| Luck Pillars | | | | | | |
|---|---|---|---|---|---|---|
| 68 | 58 | 48 | 38 | 28 | 18 | 8 |
| 丙<br>*Yang* Fire<br>子<br>*Yang* Water | 乙<br>*Yin* Wood<br>亥<br>*Yin* Water | 甲<br>*Yang* Wood<br>戌<br>*Yang* Earth | 癸<br>*Yin* Water<br>酉<br>*Yin* Metal | 壬<br>*Yang* Water<br>申<br>*Yang* Metal | 辛<br>*Yin* Metal<br>未<br>*Yin* Earth | 庚<br>*Yang* Metal<br>午<br>*Yang* Fire |

Chris Patten is a fire person 丙 born in summer 巳 when fire has the strongest influence. His fire is further strengthened by the presence of wood in the year heavenly stem 甲. A strong *yang* fire person usually has a strong, aggressive character and may be occasionally hot-tempered.

**Favourable Elements**

According to the philosophy of balance and harmony, anything excessive is against the cosmic order and some action has to be taken to restore the balance. As a general rule, weak fire needs wood and fire whereas strong fire needs water to control (water destroys fire) and metal (fire destroys metal) to release its excess energy.

Thus, water and metal temper his strong fire. Water, to a fire person, symbolises power and status; metal, his achievements and rewards. Earth is fairly favourable as it helps to generate metal (metal is the money element to a fire person). Earth is also his outlet element – his aspirations, creativity and intelligence.

**Unfavourable Elements**

His unfavourable elements are wood and fire, both of which only aggravate the excessive fire energy and thus generate strong competition (the presence of an element similar to the self symbolises a competitor if the self-sign is strong).

***Luck Pillar 28 (age 28 to 37)***

This is a luck pillar of water and metal, his favourable elements. Some significant events that took place during this period are:

Age 30: He became the youngest ever Director of Research for the Conservative Party.

Age 35: He was elected Member of Parliament for Bath.

***Luck Pillar 38 (age 38 to 47)***

*Yin* Water

*Yin* Metal

During this period of another 10 years of metal and water influence, he found further success in British politics.

1990

*Yang* Metal

午

*Yang* Fire

In the autumn of 1990, a year of strong metal influence, he was appointed Chairman of the Conservative Party.

1992

*Yang* Water

申

*Yang* Metal

Chris Patten was appointed Governor of Hong Kong in April 1992, a year of water and metal.

***Luck Pillar 48 (age 48 to 57)***

*Yang* Wood

戌

*Yang* Earth

This luck pillar of wood over earth is not too favourable. The wood suppresses the earth which is his creativity and aspirations. As a result, he is not able to express himself as freely as before.

1994

The political friction with China began in early 1993 when he entered this luck pillar. The year 1994 of *yang* wood over *yang* earth strengthened the elements appearing in his luck pillar (also *yang* wood over *yang* earth) causing him to experience even further constraints.

***Luck Pillar 58 (age 58 to 67)***

This luck pillar is of wood and water. The beneficial water element, his symbol of power, will give him the opportunity to make a triumphant return to British politics after completing his term as Governor of Hong Kong.

**House Of Spouse**

The House of Spouse (earthly branch of the day pillar) is water, his power element, thus revealing a high-profiled woman for a wife. Indeed, his wife is a barrister-of-law.

*(e)* ***Deng Xiaoping****, the paramount Chinese leader: an earth person of the category "Follow the Leader" metal-and-water. That is, any element which supports these metal and water will bring him good fortune while any element which suppresses them will bring bad luck. Born 3–5 am, 22 August 1904.*

| Hour | Day | Month | Year |
|---|---|---|---|
| 甲 | 戊 | 壬 | 甲 |
| *Yang* Wood | *Yang* Earth | *Yang* Water | *Yang* Wood |
| 寅 | 子 | 申 | 辰 |
| *Yang* Wood | *Yang* Water | *Yang* Metal | *Yang* Earth |

| Luck Pillars | | | | | | | |
|---|---|---|---|---|---|---|---|
| 86 | 76 | 66 | 56 | 46 | 36 | 26 | 16 |
| 辛<br>*Yin* Metal | 庚<br>*Yang* Metal | 己<br>*Yin* Earth | 戊<br>*Yang* Earth | 丁<br>*Yin* Fire | 丙<br>*Yang* Fire | 乙<br>*Yin* Wood | 甲<br>*Yang* Wood |
| 巳<br>*Yin* Fire | 辰<br>*Yang* Earth | 卯<br>*Yin* Wood | 寅<br>*Yang* Wood | 丑<br>*Yin* Earth | 子<br>*Yang* Water | 亥<br>*Yin* Water | 戌<br>*Yang* Earth |

Deng is a *yang* earth person 戊 born in the autumn month of *yang* metal 申 , when metal is strongest. Metal draws energy from earth (according to the Cycle of Birth). There are also three wood elements, in the heavenly stem 甲 *yang* wood in the year and hour pillars and in the 寅 *yang* wood earthly branch in the hour pillar, to suppress the earth element. Fire, which may otherwise provide support to the earth, is totally absent in this configuration.

The *yang* earth in the earthly branch in the year pillar 辰 cannot provide support because according to advanced theories of the Pillars of Destiny (explained further on page 63), the elements in the earthly branches of the day, month and year pillars will combine to become water. Therefore, the *yang* earth 辰 earthly branch in the year pillar cannot offer any support to the earth in the day heavenly stem.

According to the theory of "Follow the Leader," if the self is very weak, it will submit completely to the strongest element and adopt the characteristics of this strong element. In this case, the earth is so weak, it has absolutely no chance of survival. To recap, this is due to:

- The total absence of fire which can otherwise provide nourishment.
- The strong metal of autumn which draws energy from earth (Cycle of Birth).
- The presence of strong wood which suppresses and destroys the earth (Cycle of Destruction).

**Favourable Elements**

The metal in the month earthly branch is very strong as it can draw on the earth energy from the day heavenly stem. As mentioned earlier, the earthly branches in the year, month and day pillars will combine, resulting in water. Therefore, in this configuration, the strongest "Follow the Leader" elements are metal and water. Any element that supports metal and water will bring him good fortune.

**Unfavourable Elements**
According to the "Follow the Leader" theory, the "leader" will not allow the self-sign to become strong. Therefore, any element which helps the earth and stimulates its revival (fire and earth) will bring him bad luck.

***Luck Pillar 56 (age 56 to 65)***

The *yang* wood 寅 earthly branch in this luck pillar helped strengthen the fire of the years 1966 and 1967.

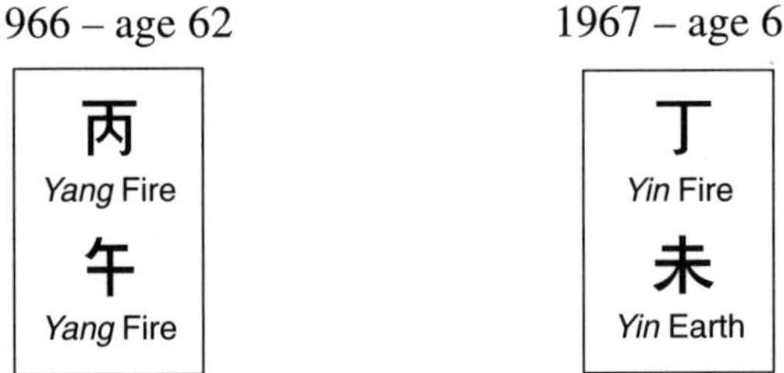


These two years of fire and earth brought him misfortune during the Cultural Revolution.

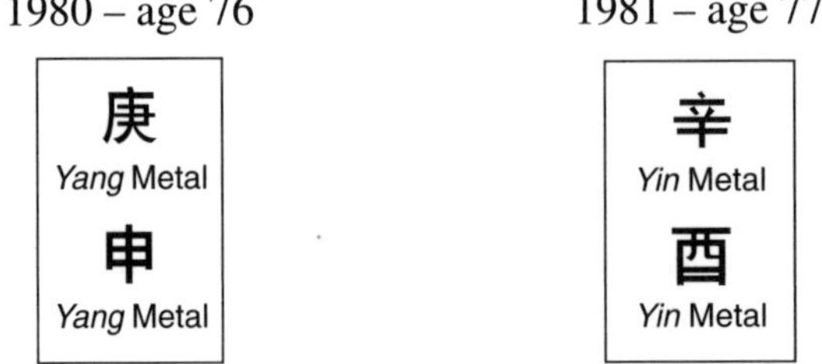


The years 1980 and 1981 were years of metal, his favourable element, and helped propel him back into power.

*Tiananmen Square Incident – 4 June 1989*

| Day | Month | Year |
| --- | --- | --- |
| 乙 *Yin* Wood | 己 *Yin* Earth | 己 *Yin* Earth |
| 未 *Yin* Earth | 巳 *Yin* Fire | 巳 *Yin* Fire |

The Tiananmen Square incident took place on 4 June 1989, a day of strong earth and fire – his unfavourable elements. That year of *yin* earth 己 over *yin* fire 巳 proved an uncomfortable year for him. Deng was then also under the influence of the unfavourable *yang* earth 辰 luck pillar.

(f) ***John Lennon****, a member of the famous Beatles pop group, was shot dead by a fan at the age of 40. He was a wood person in the "Follow the Leader" category of earth and metal. That is, elements that support earth and metal will bring him good fortune while elements that suppress them will bring bad luck. Born 7–9 am, 9 October 1940.*

| Hour | Day | Month | Year |
| --- | --- | --- | --- |
| 庚 *Yang* Metal | 乙 *Yin* Wood | 丙 *Yang* Fire | 庚 *Yang* Metal |
| 辰 *Yang* Earth | 酉 *Yin* Metal | 戌 *Yang* Earth | 辰 *Yang* Earth |

| Luck Pillars | | | |
| --- | --- | --- | --- |
| 40 | 30 | 20 | 10 |
| 庚 *Yang* Metal | 己 *Yin* Earth | 戊 *Yang* Earth | 丁 *Yin* Fire |
| 寅 *Yang* Wood | 丑 *Yin* Earth | 子 *Yang* Water | 亥 *Yin* Water |

John Lennon is a *yin* wood person 乙 born in autumn when metal is most prosperous, in the month of *yang* earth 戌. As wood destroys earth, the self-sign wood is weak. Note that the wood is also surrounded by three metal elements (in the heavenly stem of the year pillar 庚, the earthly branch of the day pillar 酉 and the heavenly stem of the hour pillar 庚), which are strongly reinforced by three prominent earth elements (in the earthly branch of the year pillar 辰, the earthly branch of the month pillar 戌 and the earthly branch of the hour pillar 辰). Remember, according to the Cycle of Birth, earth gives birth to metal.

Water, the element that can otherwise provide nourishment to the self-sign *yin* wood 乙, is totally absent. Wood has therefore no chance of "surviving" and has to surrender its property to the strongest elements – earth and metal. Thus, John Lennon is a "Follow the Leader" person.

**Favourable Elements**

Any element which supports the "leaders" of earth and metal is favourable. Hence, fire, which gives birth to earth, is favourable.

**Unfavourable Elements**

Any element which supports the weak self is unfavourable as it upsets the equilibrium. Examples of unfavourable elements are water and wood.

***Luck Pillar 20 (age 20 to 29)***

Even though there is water (an unfavourable element) in the earthly branch of this luck pillar, this water is weak because the *yang* earth in the heavenly stem destroys water (the Cycle of Destruction).

1960

In 1960 (a year of metal), a 20-year-old John Lennon formed the pop group, the Beatles. The group would soon take the world by storm.

His good fortune lasted for 20 years (from 1960 to 1980) while he was in the luck pillar of earth.

### *Luck Pillar 40 (age 40 to 49)*

Immediately after entering the luck pillar of *yang* metal over *yang* wood, John Lennon was assassinated. He had just turned 40. The *yang* wood 寅 in the luck pillar tried to revive the self wood 乙, antagonising the strong metal elements surrounding him. The self-sign wood 乙 was immediately crushed by the overwhelming metal power. He died on 8 December 1980 – a day of wood ( 乙 *yin* wood over 卯 *yin* wood), intensified by the month of *yang* water.

| Day | Month | Year |
|---|---|---|
| 乙 | 戊 | 庚 |
| *Yin* Wood | *Yang* Earth | *Yang* Metal |
| 卯 | 子 | 申 |
| *Yin* Wood | *Yang* Water | *Yang* Metal |

# CLASHES AND COMBINATIONS

## Heavenly Stem Combinations

The element in position 1 of the heavenly stem sequence can combine with the element in the sixth position in the sequence (see page 15 for the heavenly stem sequence), position 2 with position 7, and so on. When the elements combine, the individual characteristics do not manifest themselves. Instead the characteristics of the resultant element take over.

| *Sequence position* | Element | | *Sequence position* | Element | | Resultant Element |
|---|---|---|---|---|---|---|
| 1 | 甲 *Yang* Wood | + | 6 | 己 *Yin* Earth | = | **EARTH** |
| 2 | 乙 *Yin* Wood | + | 7 | 庚 *Yang* Metal | = | **METAL** |
| 3 | 丙 *Yang* Fire | + | 8 | 辛 *Yin* Metal | = | **WATER** |
| 4 | 丁 *Yin* Fire | + | 9 | 壬 *Yang* Water | = | **WOOD** |
| 5 | 戊 *Yang* Earth | + | 10 | 癸 *Yin* Water | = | **FIRE** |

## Heavenly Stem Clashes

Just as there are combinations, there are also clashes between the elements in the heavenly stems. These clashes are:

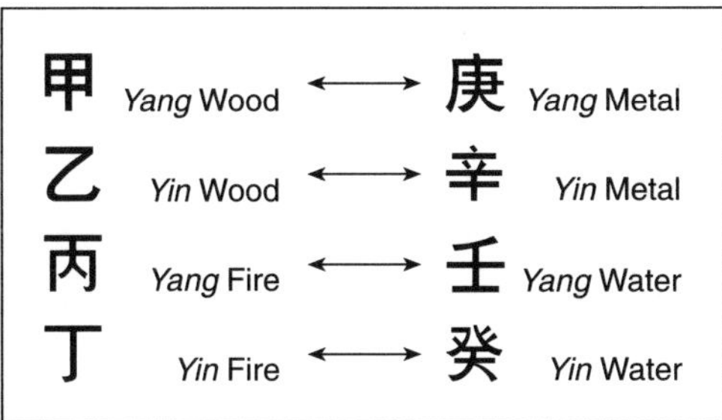

| | | | | |
|---|---|---|---|---|
| 甲 | *Yang* Wood | ⟷ | 庚 | *Yang* Metal |
| 乙 | *Yin* Wood | ⟷ | 辛 | *Yin* Metal |
| 丙 | *Yang* Fire | ⟷ | 壬 | *Yang* Water |
| 丁 | *Yin* Fire | ⟷ | 癸 | *Yin* Water |

Note that the earth heavenly stems do not clash with other heavenly stems.

## Earthly Branch Combinations

There are six combinations of the elements in the earthly branches.

| | | | | | | |
|---|---|---|---|---|---|---|
| 午 | *Yang* Fire (Horse) | + | 未 | *Yin* Earth (Goat) | = | **FIRE** |
| 子 | *Yang* Water (Rat) | + | 丑 | *Yin* Earth (Ox) | = | **EARTH** |
| 寅 | *Yang* Wood (Tiger) | + | 亥 | *Yin* Water (Pig) | = | **WOOD** |
| 卯 | *Yin* Wood (Rabbit) | + | 戌 | *Yang* Earth (Dog) | = | **FIRE** |
| 辰 | *Yang* Earth (Dragon) | + | 酉 | *Yin* Metal (Rooster) | = | **METAL** |
| 巳 | *Yin* Fire (Snake) | + | 申 | *Yang* Metal (Monkey) | = | **WATER** |

Since each earthly branch is assigned with an animal sign, the combinations in the earthly branches are more commonly known as the compatibility of animal signs. It is said that if you were born in the Year of the Horse 午, for example, your compatible companion will be someone born in the Year of the Goat 未. However this is a very general assumption as it only reflects the combinations of earthly branches of the year pillar and disregards the other pillars of destiny. Neither does this evaluate the strength of the self-sign to determine the favourable and unfavourable elements.

In Chinese wedding ceremonies, it is common to find drawings of the Dragon and the Phoenix in invitation cards and in the house. The Dragon (辰 *yang* earth) signifies the male (*yang* is associated with the man) while the Phoenix, the mythical bird (酉 *yin* metal), represents the female (*yin* is associated with the lady). This reflects the strong belief among the Chinese in the compatibility of animal signs.

## Earthly Branch Clashes

| | | | | |
|---|---|---|---|---|
| 子 | *Yang* Water (Rat) | ⟷ | 午 | *Yang* Fire (Horse) |
| 丑 | *Yin* Earth (Ox) | ⟷ | 未 | *Yin* Earth (Goat) |
| 寅 | *Yang* Wood (Tiger) | ⟷ | 申 | *Yang* Metal (Monkey) |
| 卯 | *Yin* Wood (Rabbit) | ⟷ | 酉 | *Yin* Metal (Rooster) |
| 辰 | *Yang* Earth (Dragon) | ⟷ | 戌 | *Yang* Earth (Dog) |
| 巳 | *Yin* Fire (Snake) | ⟷ | 亥 | *Yin* Water (Pig) |

This set of clashes of the earthly branches is more commonly known as the incompatibility of the animal signs. As the animal ruling the year in which you are born exercises some influence on your character, this may explain why you cannot get along with someone else.

## Earthly Branch Three-Element Combinations

Although there are hidden elements in each earthly branch, some elements are purer than others, without other hidden elements. Most of these pure elements are elements in the second month of each season. For example, pure water is found in the second month of winter when water is strongest.

The earth element is more complex as it buries everything. If a person has several earth elements in his earthly branches, he will probably have many interests. Each earth element in the earthly branch contains three hidden elements (see page 81 for the hidden heavenly stems in the earthly branches). The set of three-element combinations among the elements in the earthly branches is derived from the various stages of "growth" of an element during the four seasons.

| Germinating stage of resultant element *1st mth of season* | Month when resultant element is strongest *2nd mth of season* | Month when resultant element is at its dying stage *3rd mth of season* | Resultant element |
|---|---|---|---|
| 寅 *Yang* Wood (Spring) | 午 *Yang* Fire (Summer) | 戌 *Yang* Earth (Autumn) | = **FIRE** |
| 巳 *Yin* Fire (Summer) | 酉 *Yin* Metal (Autumn) | 丑 *Yin* Earth (Winter) | = **METAL** |
| 申 *Yang* Metal (Autumn) | 子 *Yang* Water (Winter) | 辰 *Yang* Earth (Spring) | = **WATER** |
| 亥 *Yin* Water (Winter) | 卯 *Yin* Wood (Spring) | 未 *Yin* Earth (Summer) | = **WOOD** |

In the first set of combination, fire begins its cycle in spring in the first month ( 寅 *yang* wood) of spring and becomes strongest during the second month ( 午 *yang* fire) in summer. Fire begins dying during the third month ( 戌 *yang* earth) of autumn, when it hibernates (see page 17 for the strength of each element during the various seasons).

The third month, which is a month of earth before the season changes to the next, is also known as the "grave " or "storage" of the resultant element. Hence, the *yang* earth Dog 戌 is the "storage" of fire while the Dragon 辰 *yang* earth is the "grave" of water. Similarly, the Ox 丑 *yin* earth is the "storage" of metal while wood hibernates in the Goat 未 *yin* earth.

## What Combinations And Clashes Mean

### *Combinations*

- The rule is that the elements combine before they clash with other elements in the Four Pillars of Destiny.
- The elements lose their individual characteristics when they are combined. Instead, the characteristics of the resultant element take over. Therefore, if a much needed element combines with other elements and the resultant element is not favourable, the person may be adversely affected.

The resultant element reinforces the strength of a similar element in the Four Pillars of Destiny. For example, if a fire person has the elements 寅 , 午 and 戌 in the earthly branches in his Four Pillars of Destiny, a three-element combination of the earthly branches will result in fire. Since his self-sign is fire, the resultant fire from the combination will strengthen his fire in the day pillar.

### *Clashes*

Like the clashes of the heavenly stems, the elements in the earthly branch also follow a sequence. That is, Rat *yang* water in position 1, clashes with Horse *yang* fire, in position 7 while Ox *yin* earth, in position 2, clashes with Goat *yin* earth, in position 8. This accounts for the common Chinese belief that a couple's age gap should not be six years as it infers incompatible personalities.

Clashes in the earthly branches are more serious than clashes in the heavenly stems, especially in the year and day pillars. When choosing an auspicious date for a wedding, we should avoid any clash in the earthly branches in the couple's Four Pillars of Destiny.

### *"Good Clash"*

When a favourable element clashes with the Four Pillars of Destiny, it is considered a good clash. The impact will be good.

Take, for example, a person whose self-sign is weak wood with the House of Spouse as Snake 巳 *yin* fire. When he or she enters a luck pillar of Pig 亥 *yin* water or is in a favourable luck pillar as the year of Pig *yin* water approaches, he or she, if of marriageable age, is highly likely to marry suddenly. This is because the Pig clashes with the House of Spouse Snake *yin* fire 巳 and water is a favourable element to a weak wood person.

## Combinations: More Examples

(a) *As we saw earlier in the analysis of* ***Deng Xiaoping's*** *destiny, a combination of the year, month and day earthly branches made him a "Follow the Leader" person. His set of Four Pillars of Destiny is shown again here.*

| Hour | Day | Month | Year |
|---|---|---|---|
| 甲 | 戊 | 壬 | 甲 |
| *Yang* Wood | *Yang* Earth | *Yang* Water | *Yang* Wood |
| 寅 | 子 | 申 | 辰 |
| *Yang* Wood | *Yang* Water | *Yang* Metal | *Yang* Earth |

Factors that categorised him as "Follow the Leader" (metal and water) are:

- The absence of a fire element in the configuration to support and nourish the extremely weak earth.
- The earth self-sign is exhausted by the metal month.
- The earth self-sign is attacked by strong wood (which is nourished by water).
- His only possible source of support is the earth in the year pillar. However, because it combines with the month and day pillars, the earth in the year pillar loses its characteristics and can no longer help support the self-sign.

*(b) A person with the following birth data is also categorised as "Follow the Leader" because of the combination of elements.*

| Hour | Day | Month | Year |
|---|---|---|---|
| 戊<br>*Yang* Earth | 癸<br>*Yin* Water | 壬<br>*Yang* Water | 壬<br>*Yang* Water |
| 午<br>*Yang* Fire | 未<br>*Yin* Earth | 寅<br>*Yang* Wood | 寅<br>*Yang* Wood |

This person is a water person 癸 born in the spring month of wood 寅, when wood is most prosperous.

He is a "Follow the Leader" type because:

- There is no metal to help support the self-sign *yin* water. Thus his water has no root.
- The heavenly stems of the day and hour pillars combine to become fire.

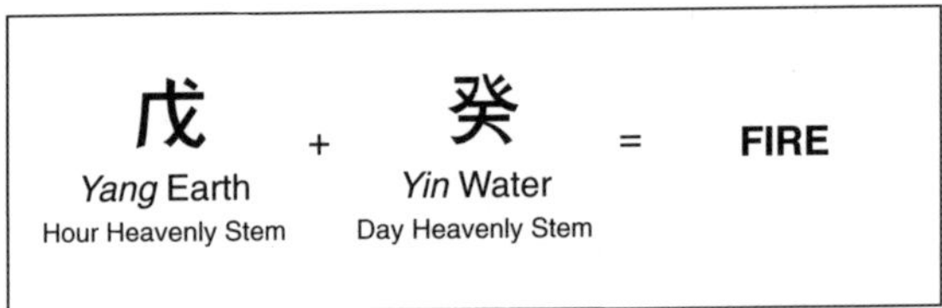


- The earthly branches of the day and hour pillars also combine to become fire.

午 *Yang* Fire (Hour Earthly Branch) + 未 *Yin* Earth (Day Earthly Branch) = **FIRE**

- The strong 寅 *yang* wood in the year and month pillars strengthen the resultant element of fire in the heavenly stem and earthly branch combinations, thus destroying the self element, 癸 *yin* water.

This person therefore follows the leader of fire.

*(c) Male Person (born 10 am, 13 November 1993)*

| Hour | Day | Month | Year |
|---|---|---|---|
| 丁 | 戊 | 癸 | 癸 |
| *Yin* Fire | *Yang* Earth | *Yin* Water | *Yin* Water |
| 巳 | 戌 | 亥 | 酉 |
| *Yin* Fire | *Yang* Earth | *Yin* Water | *Yin* Metal |

| Luck Pillars | | | | | | |
|---|---|---|---|---|---|---|
| 62 | 52 | 42 | 32 | 22 | 12 | 2 |
| 丙 | 丁 | 戊 | 己 | 庚 | 辛 | 壬 |
| *Yang* Fire | *Yin* Fire | *Yang* Earth | *Yin* Earth | *Yang* Metal | *Yin* Metal | *Yang* Water |
| 辰 | 巳 | 午 | 未 | 申 | 酉 | 戌 |
| *Yang* Earth | *Yin* Fire | *Yang* Fire | *Yin* Earth | *Yang* Metal | *Yin* Metal | *Yang* Earth |

He is a 戊 *yang* earth person born in the winter season 亥 when water is strongest. There are also strong water elements in the year and month pillars. Being winter, the abundance of water creates a "cold configuration". His favourable element is therefore fire.

**Combination**

The month heavenly stem of water combines with the heavenly stem of the day pillar to become fire.

| 戊<br>*Yang* Earth<br>Day Heavenly Stem | + | 癸<br>*Yin* Water<br>Month Heavenly Stem | = | **FIRE** |
|---|---|---|---|---|

Water is money to an earth person while fire (which he needs) is his mother and resources. His mother will provide support but the strong influence of water (his father element) exhausts the earth. Money to a water person is fire, which is also the resultant element of the combination. A combination means a close association of elements, so this combination not only implies that the man has a harmonious relationship with his father but that he is merrily spending his father's money!

The combination also shows that he is closely associated with money (water) and may even be a calculating person. Although he needs fire, he turns his back on that element and turns towards money, i.e. he combines with water instead of looking to fire for support. He is likely to be a mean person.

**Father**

His father's money (fire) element is not strong because:

- The strong water influence weakens the strength of the fire.
- Fire is weakened further by the presence of strong earth in the day pillar.
- Fire is shared by many water elements.

Therefore his father is not rich, probably middle class.

The earth element is fairly strong, implying that his father has some status. His father is likely to be an employee with some authority and status.

**Luck Pillar 2 (age 2 to 11)**

During his first luck pillar, the water heavenly stem of the luck pillar combines with fire in the hour pillar. In such a combination, the characteristics of fire is destroyed. This means that he will have a difficult childhood as water destroys the fire that he needs.

| 壬<br>*Yang* Water<br>Luck Pillar | + | 丁<br>*Yin* Fire<br>Hour Pillar | = | **WOOD** |
|---|---|---|---|---|

It can also mean that during this period, his mother (fire) is attracted to another man (water) or encounters health problems (because the fire is very weak). Since fire is also his resource, weak fire in his destiny and the lack of fire (or elements that support fire) in his early luck pillars imply that he will not fare well in his studies. Metal is intelligence to an earth person and since there is only one metal in his destiny, he is of average intelligence.

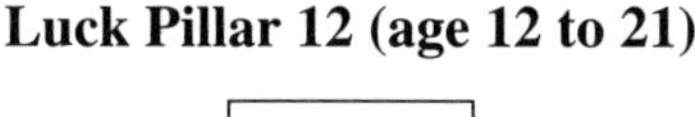

**Luck Pillar 12 (age 12 to 21)**

**Luck Pillar 22 (age 22 to 31)**

During these 20 years, the metal element is very strong. As this intelligence is too powerful for a weak earth person to handle, he may become a rebellious or even a crafty person. Metal generates water which is his money. The earthly branch *yin* fire in the hour pillar also combines with *yang* metal in the luck pillar of 22 to become water (money).

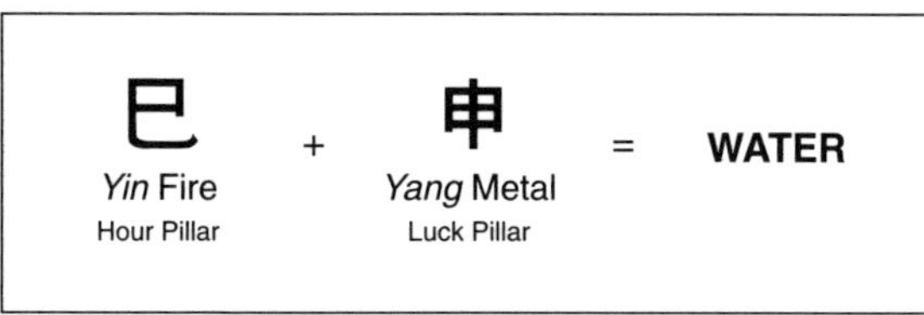


During this period, there will be much money. But since he is too weak to control it, he may misuse his wealth through gambling or other vices.

**Luck Pillar 32 (age 32 to 41)**

On turning 32, he will have the support of strong earth luck pillars (thereby strengthening the self element) and will now be in a position to control his money.

**Status And Power**

His status and power element is wood but wood is absent in his destiny. As such, he is unlikely to become an administrator, only a low ranking employee.

**Luck Pillar 42 (age 42 to 51)**

Another earth element (similar to the self-sign earth) in the luck pillar reveals that he may team up with another person in a business venture.

**Resources**

His resource element is fire. This comes late in life, around the age of 47, and lasts until his old age. This means that he will acquire knowledge late in life.

## Clashes: More Examples

(a) ***Ronald Li****, former chairman of the Hong Kong Stock Exchange, decided to shut down the Hong Kong stock market for four days in 1987, which later caused the Hang Seng index to drop over 1,000 points. He was later arrested on bribery charges in early 1988.*

*Born 10 February 1929*

| Hour | Day | Month | Year |
|---|---|---|---|
| ? | 丙 *Yang* Fire | 丙 *Yang* Fire | 己 *Yin* Earth |
| ? | 戌 *Yang* Earth | 寅 *Yang* Wood | 巳 *Yin* Fire |

| Luck Pillars | | | | | | |
|---|---|---|---|---|---|---|
| 62 | 52 | 42 | 32 | 22 | 12 | 2 |
| 己 *Yin* Earth | 庚 *Yang* Metal | 辛 *Yin* Metal | 壬 *Yang* Water | 癸 *Yin* Water | 甲 *Yang* Wood | 乙 *Yin* Wood |
| 未 *Yin* Earth | 申 *Yang* Metal | 酉 *Yin* Metal | 戌 *Yang* Earth | 亥 *Yin* Water | 子 *Yang* Water | 丑 *Yin* Earth |

Ronald Li is a *yang* fire person, born in spring in the first wood month of 寅 *yang* wood when wood is strongest. More fire elements can be found in the year 巳 *yin* fire and month 丙 *yang* fire pillars. The strong early spring wood further strengthens the fire, making fire very prominent in all three known pillars. He is, therefore, a very strong fire person. His business successes are in finance and the stock market, which are associated with the fire element.

**Wealth**

Money to a fire person is metal (fire destroys metal). However, metal is not prominent in Ronald Li's known pillars of destiny. Nevertheless, there is a great potential to produce wealth. As earth generates metal, the earth element represents his wisdom to generate wealth. There are two earth elements in the year and day pillars and both are nourished by the fire element which is very strong in this set of pillars.

To be rich, a person must be strong enough to control the money elements in his pillars of destiny, otherwise the presence of these elements merely represents a financial burden to him. In Li's case, as he is a very strong fire person, he has the capacity to gain and control wealth once he encounters his favourable luck pillars with money elements.

**Favourable Elements**

Li relies very much on the fire influence and the support of wood for his success in the stock market. Continual years of wood and fire will boost his success to greater heights.

His set of pillars of destiny is balanced: he has strong resources from the strong spring wood and intelligence as represented by the strong earth wealth-generating abilities. Therefore, his favourable element is metal – the money element.

**Unfavourable Elements**

As the fire element is a symbol of the stock market, in the past, years of prosperous fire often brought about a "bullish" market. The fire influence peaked in 1986, a year of strong wood and fire, which brought boom times to most industries and their stocks. The run continued in 1987, again a year of fire. The change of fortune came in October 1987, as this dominant fire influence was transiting into the following year of strong earth (Year of Dragon). The global stock market nose-dived. This loss of fire influence in the autumn of 1987 caused the stock market to collapse and brought a dramatic change in fortune for Li who had relied on the strength of the fire element for his success.

Thus his unfavourable elements are elements that weaken fire and wood. Clashes with these elements are also unfavourable.

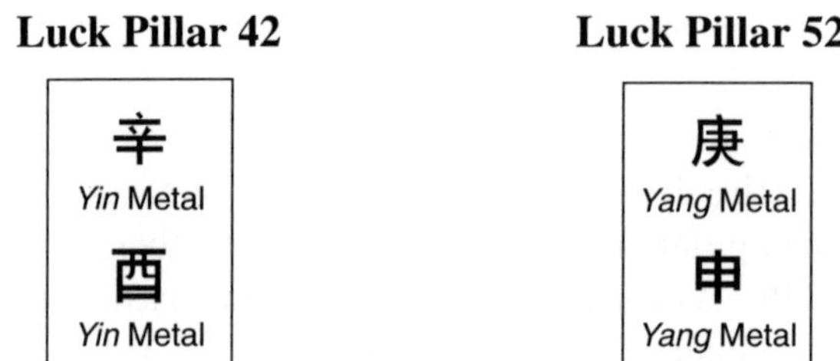


During his luck pillars of 42 and 52, there were strong metal elements, elements that symbolise wealth to him, a fire person.

**Clash In Luck Pillar 52**

When he turned 57, the influence of 申 *yang* metal took stronger effect. Even though metal should be favourable to him, there is a clash between the *yang* metal in the luck pillar and the *yang* wood in the earthly branch of the month pillar.

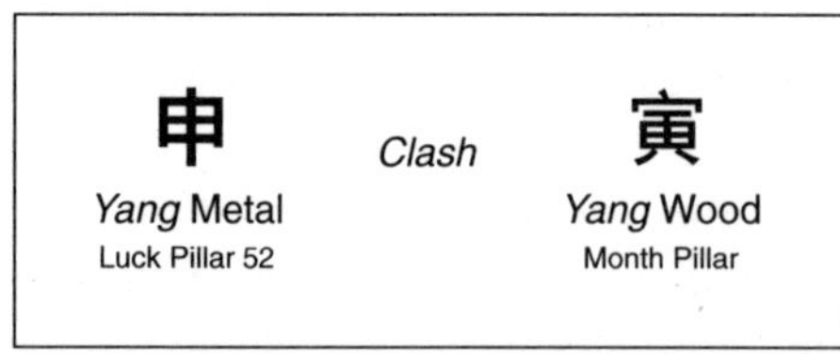


This clash destroyed his life-supporting wood, thus weakening his fire influence and incapacitating his ability to manipulate wealth (metal). This unfortunate clash did not take effect immediately when he was 57 as he could still rely on the external fire of the years of 1986 and 1987.

| 1986 | 1987 |
|---|---|
| 丙 | 丁 |
| *Yang* Fire | *Yin* Fire |
| 寅 | 卯 |
| *Yang* Wood | *Yin* Wood |

Eventually, the demise of the fire compelled him to close the Hong Kong Stock Exchange for four days. This took place in late 1987 when autumn was turning to winter (when water is strong) before transiting into 1988, a year of strong earth which has an even greater adverse impact on his fire self-sign.

| 1988 | 1989 | 1990 | 1991 |
|---|---|---|---|
| 戊 | 己 | 庚 | 辛 |
| *Yang* Earth | *Yin* Earth | *Yang* Metal | *Yin* Metal |
| 辰 | 巳 | 午 | 未 |
| *Yang* Earth | *Yin* Fire | *Yang* Fire | *Yin* Earth |

Li was arrested on bribery charges in early 1988, a year of strong earth which further exhausted his fire's strength. As the years of 1989 and early 1990 (periods of fire) arrived, his situation appeared to improve. It seemed probable then that the charges against him might be dropped. However, when the cyclical change from fire influence to metal took place (1991 was a strong year of metal, especially since the earthly branch of 未 *yin* earth supports the heavenly stem of 辛 *yin* metal), he could no longer be rescued. The year fire influence of 1990 waned, turning into metal influence the following year. Li was then imprisoned.

(b) ***Wong Kar Kwui**, lead singer of Hong Kong rock and roll group **Beyond**, died when he fell from the stage during a rehearsal in Japan. He was a well-known composer, singer and guitarist.*

*Born 5–7 am, 10 June 1962*

| Hour | Day | Month | Year |
|---|---|---|---|
| 丁 | 己 | 丙 | 壬 |
| *Yin* Fire | *Yin* Earth | *Yang* Fire | *Yang* Water |
| 卯 | 卯 | 午 | 寅 |
| *Yin* Wood | *Yin* Wood | *Yang* Fire | *Yang* Wood |

| 39 | 29 | 19 | 9 |
|---|---|---|---|
| 庚 | 己 | 戊 | 丁 |
| *Yang* Metal | *Yin* Earth | *Yang* Earth | *Yin* Fire |
| 戌 | 酉 | 申 | 未 |
| *Yang* Earth | *Yin* Metal | *Yang* Metal | *Yin* Earth |

Date of accident: Midnight of 24 June 1993

| Hour | Day | Month | Year |
|---|---|---|---|
| 戊 | 丙 | 戊 | 癸 |
| *Yang* Earth | *Yang* Fire | *Yang* Earth | *Yin* Water |
| 子 | 子 | 午 | 酉 |
| *Yang* Water | *Yang* Water | *Yang* Fire | *Yin* Metal |

Wong was a 己 *yin* earth person, born in summer 午 when fire has the strongest influence. As fire supports earth, his earth self-sign is strong. In addition, there is strong wood support in the year pillar. The month pillar is strong fire while the hour pillar is another pillar of strong fire. He was thus a very strong earth person. His favourable element is metal which serves as an outlet for his excessive energy.

**Clash In His Luck Pillar**

As his favourable element is metal, the luck pillar of 29 was a good period for him. However, there is a clash between the 卯 *yin* wood in the earthly branch of the day and hour pillars and the 酉 *yin* metal in the earthly branch of the luck pillar 29.

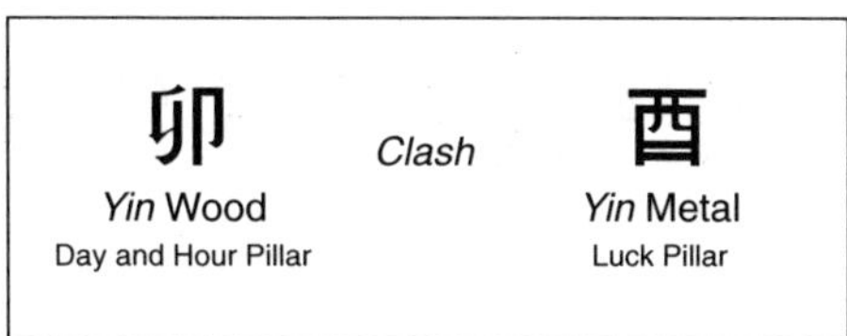


These double clashes destroyed the wood that supported the fire needed to nourish the self-sign, earth.

**Clashes On The Day Of The Accident**

The year 1993 was a Year of the Rooster (*yin* metal), the same element as the metal in the luck pillar under the clash influence. The fire in the month pillar also clashes with the day and the hour of the date of the accident. Moreover, because this fire is the earthly branch of the month pillar, the clash is even more serious.

**Why Did He Die If He Was In A Good Luck Pillar?**

- The clash in the luck pillar was intensified by the year earthly branch. He should have avoided travelling in an East–West direction (representing the directions of wood and metal in *feng shui* theory) to avoid activating a further clash (travelling to Japan from Hong Kong is travelling towards the East).
- There was no water in the earthly branch to reduce the energy of metal in the luck and year pillars. (Even though water was found in the heavenly stem of the year pillar, it was weakened by the surrounding elements. Also, the influence of elements in the earthly branches is stronger than those of the heavenly stems.)
- Possible unknown adverse effects from the *feng shui* of his house.

This case shows that even a person in good luck can still encounter misfortune because of clashes between elements, especially if the affected elements are crucial to the self-sign. After all, the next luck pillar of 39 of strong metal is another good luck pillar for him.

# SYMBOLIC STARS

Most experts analyse the Four Pillars of Destiny using the elemental relationships between the heavenly stems and the earthly branches, and logical deduction. This method is believed to be the most accurate.

There is another method, based on symbolic stars, which is less accurate. This method can be used to complement the first method, but should not be used solely. For example, the "Flower of Romance" may not be suitable unless the element of the Flower of Romance is favourable to you.

Hour
Day
Month
Year
甲
癸
庚
丙
Yang Wood
Yin Water
Yang Metal
Yang Fire
寅
卯
寅
申
Yang Wood
Yin Wood
Yang Wood
Yang Metal


To determine the symbolic stars in the Four Pillars of Destiny, we look up the earthly branch of the year or day pillar. Exceptions are the academic and nobleman stars, where the point of reference is the heavenly stem of the year and day pillar. If the earthly branch year or day pillar is, for example, Monkey, Rat or Dragon, then the Flower of Romance is the Rooster. This Rooster may appear in other pillars of destiny, the luck pillar or the Xia calendar year pillar (see page 15 for the animal signs and the elements).

## (a) Flower Of Romance

This symbolic star refers to romance and social life.

| Earthly branch of Year or Day pillar | | | Flower of Romance |
|---|---|---|---|
| 申 **Monkey** (*Yang* Metal) | 子 **Rat** (*Yang* Water) | 辰 **Dragon** (*Yang* Earth) | 酉 **Rooster** (*Yin* Metal) |
| 亥 **Pig** (*Yin* Water) | 卯 **Rabbit** (*Yin* Wood) | 未 **Goat** (*Yin* Earth) | 子 **Rat** (*Yang* Water) |
| 寅 **Tiger** (*Yang* Wood) | 午 **Horse** (*Yang* Fire) | 戌 **Dog** (*Yang* Earth) | 卯 **Rabbit** (*Yin* Wood) |
| 巳 **Snake** (*Yin* Fire) | 酉 **Rooster** (*Yin* Metal) | 丑 **Ox** (*Yin* Earth) | 午 **Horse** (*Yang* Fire) |

## (b) Horse

The Horse symbolic star refers to travel and movement.

| Earthly branch of Year or Day pillar | | | Horse Star |
|---|---|---|---|
| 申 **Monkey** (*Yang* Metal) | 子 **Rat** (*Yang* Water) | 辰 **Dragon** (*Yang* Earth) | 寅 **Tiger** (*Yang* Wood) |
| 亥 **Pig** (*Yin* Water) | 卯 **Rabbit** (*Yin* Wood) | 未 **Goat** (*Yin* Earth) | 巳 **Snake** (*Yin* Fire) |
| 寅 **Tiger** (*Yang* Wood) | 午 **Horse** (*Yang* Fire) | 戌 **Dog** (*Yang* Earth) | 申 **Monkey** (*Yang* Metal) |
| 巳 **Snake** (*Yin* Fire) | 酉 **Rooster** (*Yin* Metal) | 丑 **Ox** (*Yin* Earth) | 亥 **Pig** (*Yin* Water) |

## (c) Nobleman ( 贵人 gùi rén )

The Nobleman is a helpful person.

| Heavenly stem of Year or Day pillar | | | Nobleman Star | |
|---|---|---|---|---|
| 甲 *Yang* Wood | 戊 *Yang* Earth | 庚 *Yang* Metal | 丑 **Ox** (*Yin* Earth) | 未 **Goat** (*Yin* Earth) |
| 乙 *Yin* Water | 己 *Yin* Earth | | 子 **Rat** (*Yang* Water) | 申 **Monkey** (*Yang* Metal) |
| 丙 *Yang* Fire | 丁 *Yin* Fire | | 亥 **Pig** (*Yin* Water) | 酉 **Rooster** (*Yin* Metal) |
| 壬 *Yang* Water | 癸 *Yin* Water | | 卯 **Rabbit** (*Yin* Wood) | 巳 **Snake** (*Yin* Fire) |
| 辛 *Yin* Metal | | | 午 **Horse** (*Yang* Fire) | 寅 **Tiger** (*Yang* Wood) |

## (d) Academic Stars

Academic Stars refer to excellence in studies. Authors often have two Academic Stars in their Four Pillars of Destiny.

| Heavenly stem of Year or Day pillar | | Academic Star |
|---|---|---|
| 甲 *Yang* Wood | | 巳 **Snake** (*Yin* Fire) |
| 乙 *Yin* Wood | | 午 **Horse** (*Yang* Fire) |
| 丙 *Yang* Fire | 戊 *Yang* Earth | 申 **Monkey** (*Yang* Metal) |
| 丁 *Yin* Fire | 己 *Yin* Earth | 酉 **Rooster** (*Yin* Metal) |
| 庚 *Yang* Metal | | 亥 **Pig** (*Yin* Water) |
| 辛 *Yin* Metal | | 子 **Rat** (*Yang* Water) |
| 壬 *Yang* Water | | 寅 **Tiger** (*Yang* Wood) |
| 癸 *Yin* Water | | 卯 **Rabbit** (*Yin* Wood) |

## (e) Star Of Arts

The Star of Arts can refer to interest in arts or to loneliness in a person.

| Earthly branch of Year or Day pillar | | | Star of Arts |
|---|---|---|---|
| 申 **Monkey** (*Yang* Metal) | 子 **Rat** (*Yang* Water) | 辰 **Dragon** (*Yang* Earth) | 辰 **Dragon** (*Yang* Earth) |
| 亥 **Pig** (*Yin* Water) | 卯 **Rabbit** (*Yin* Wood) | 未 **Goat** (*Yin* Earth) | 未 **Goat** (*Yin* Earth) |
| 寅 **Tiger** (*Yang* Wood) | 午 **Horse** (*Yang* Fire) | 戌 **Dog** (*Yang* Earth) | 戌 **Dog** (*Yang* Earth) |
| 巳 **Snake** (*Yin* Fire) | 酉 **Rooster** (*Yin* Metal) | 丑 **Ox** (*Yin* Earth) | 丑 **Ox** (*Yin* Earth) |

## Flower Of Romance

If the earthly branch of your year or day pillar is either 申 *yang* metal, 子 *yang* water or 辰 *yang* earth, you will encounter romance in a year of 酉 *yin* metal. But if the earthly branch of the day or year pillar has the same animal sign, only one romance will occur every 12 years. Otherwise, there will be two romances every 12 years. However, the Flower of Romance only symbolises romance or social events, and does not necessarily imply a relationship leading to marriage.

If the element is favourable (after evaluating the self-sign), then the romance will be good. Whether the Flower of Romance affects your marriage depends on its relationship with the earthly branch of your day pillar, also known as the House of Spouse. For example, if the earthly branch of your day pillar is Rabbit 卯 *yin* wood and you are born in the Year of the Monkey 申 *yang* metal, you will encounter a Flower of Romance in the year 1993 酉 *yin* metal. If we look up the clashes of the elements in the earthly branches on page 60, we will see that 卯 *yin* wood clashes with 酉 *yin* metal. This Flower of Romance 酉 *yin* metal thus clashes with your House of Spouse 卯 *yin* wood and may create marital difficulties if you are married.

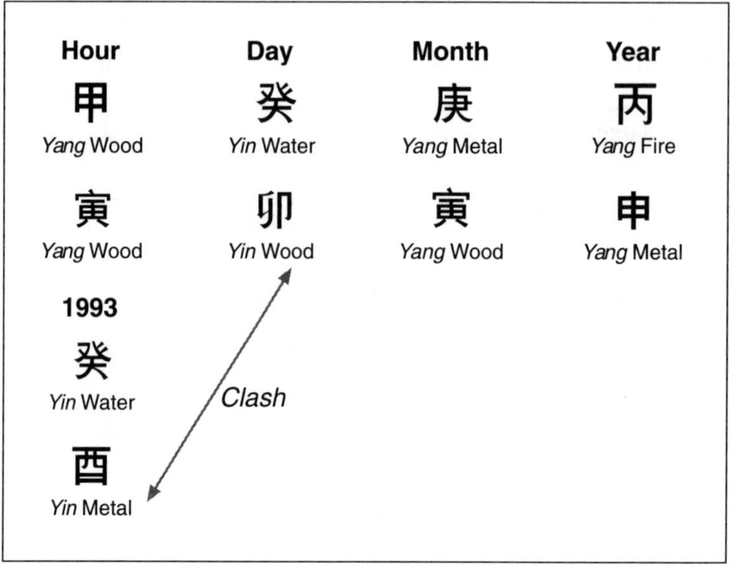


In the example above, if you are single, there is still a chance for marriage even though the Flower of Romance 酉 *yin* metal clashes with the House of Spouse 卯 *yin* wood as metal is favourable to a weak water person.

## Four Flowers of Romance – Emperor Qian Long

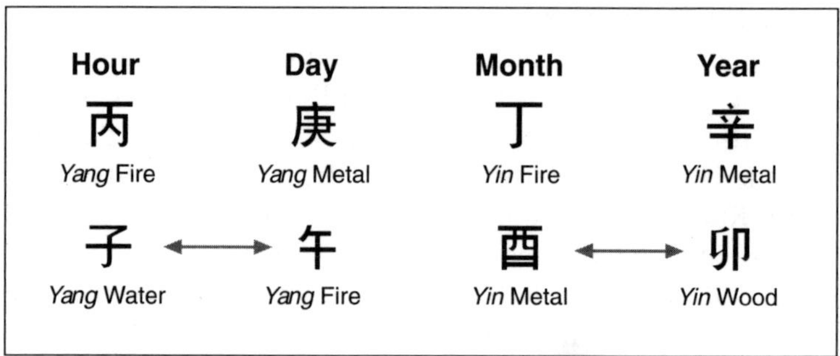

Hour
丙
Yang Fire
子
Yang Water
Day
庚
Yang Metal
午
Yang Fire
Month
丁
Yin Fire
酉
Yin Metal
Year
辛
Yin Metal
卯
Yin Wood

| Luck Pillars | | | | | |
|---|---|---|---|---|---|
| 辛<br>*Yin* Metal | 壬<br>*Yang* Water | 癸<br>*Yin* Water | 甲<br>*Yang* Wood | 乙<br>*Yin* Wood | 丙<br>*Yang* Fire |
| 卯<br>*Yin* Wood | 辰<br>*Yang* Earth | 巳<br>*Yin* Fire | 午<br>*Yang* Fire | 未<br>*Yin* Earth | 申<br>*Yang* Metal |

Emperor Qian Long of the Qing Dynasty was a metal person 庚 born in the autumn season 酉 when metal is strongest. Uniquely, he had all four Flowers of Romance in his earthly branches.

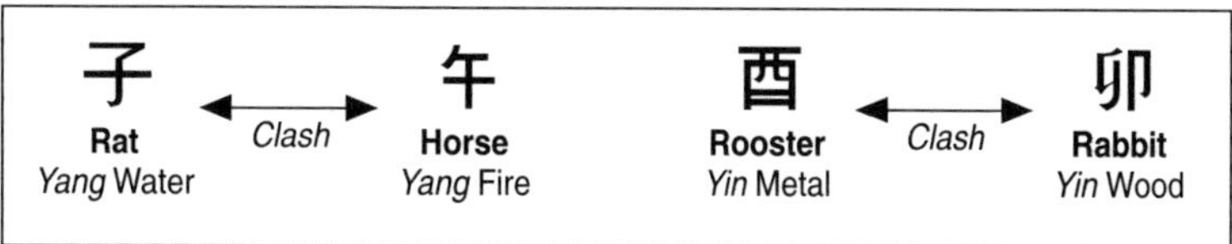


Note that all four elements are strong elements as they are at their most prosperous (all are second month elements of each season). Moreover, these elements are in clash positions, i.e. the Rat 子 clashes with the Horse 午 while the Rooster 酉 clashes with the Rabbit 卯. However, being an emperor, he can handle them all!

His Four Pillars of Destiny has no earth, the resource element to a metal person. But as an emperor, he did not need resources! Besides being capable, he was famous for his charm and charisma (which many women found attractive). He was, however, not known for his academic achievement. Emperor Qian Long died at the ripe old age of 85 after living life to the fullest. It was said that he had the best set of pillars in the world. All he needed was fire, which is power to a metal person.

## Horse

The Horse symbolic star indicates movement. Depending on what the element represents to a person, it can mean a change of house, job or travel. If the horse is your resource element, this represents a change of house; if the horse is your status element, it means a change of job. For example:

| Hour | Day | Month | Year |
|---|---|---|---|
| 甲 | 癸 | 庚 | 丙 |
| *Yang* Wood | *Yin* Water | *Yang* Metal | *Yang* Fire |
| *Travel Horse* 寅 | 卯 | 寅 | 申 *Travel Horse* |
| *Yang* Wood | *Yin* Wood | *Yang* Wood | *Yang* Metal |

The person with this set of Four Pillars of Destiny has a horse star in the hour pillar, 寅 *yang* wood, for 申 *yang* metal in the year pillar, which itself is another horse star. This configuration shows a very mobile person, perhaps an airline pilot. If you wish to find out if a friend is likely to migrate, look for the horse star in the four pillars or in the luck pillars. But you will still need to check if the element is favourable to determine whether this move will turn out well.

# HIDDEN HEAVENLY STEMS

According to the ancient Chinese, sandwiched between the heavenly stems and earthly branches, are we humans on earth. With so much complexity in our lives, it has been said that there are hidden elements in the earthly branches, especially for the earth elements. There are four earth elements, which symbolise the diverse interests of mankind. The three categories of earthly branches with hidden heavenly stems are:

## (a) The Earth Month (Last Month Of Each Season)

| Earthly Branch | | | Hidden Heavenly Stems | | |
|---|---|---|---|---|---|
| **Spring** | 辰 | *Yang* Earth | 戊 *Yang* Earth | 乙 *Yin* Wood | 癸 *Yin* Water |
| **Summer** | 未 | *Yin* Earth | 丁 *Yin* Fire | 己 *Yin* Earth | 乙 *Yin* Wood |
| **Autumn** | 戌 | *Yang* Earth | 戊 *Yang* Earth | 辛 *Yin* Metal | 丁 *Yin* Fire |
| **Winter** | 丑 | *Yin* Earth | 己 *Yin* Earth | 辛 *Yin* Metal | 癸 *Yin* Water |

## (b) The First Earthly Branch Of The Season Containing Hidden *Yang* Heavenly Stems

| Earthly Branch | | | Hidden Heavenly Stems | | |
|---|---|---|---|---|---|
| Spring | 寅 | *Yang* Wood | 甲 *Yang* Wood | 丙 *Yang* Fire | 戊 *Yang* Earth |
| Summer | 巳 | *Yin* Fire | 庚 *Yang* Metal | 丙 *Yang* Fire | 戊 *Yang* Earth |
| Autumn | 申 | *Yang* Metal | 戊 *Yang* Earth | 庚 *Yang* Metal | 壬 *Yang* Water |
| Winter | 亥 | *Yin* Water | 壬 *Yang* Water | 甲 *Yang* Wood | |

## (c) The Second Earthly Branch Of The Season (The Most Prosperous Month As The Element Is Usually Pure)

| Earthly Branch | | | Hidden Heavenly Stems | |
|---|---|---|---|---|
| Spring | 卯 | *Yin* Wood | 乙 *Yin* Wood | |
| Summer | 午 | *Yang* Fire | 丁 *Yin* Fire | 己 *Yin* Earth |
| Autumn | 酉 | *Yin* Metal | 辛 *Yin* Metal | |
| Winter | 子 | *Yang* Water | 癸 *Yin* Water | |

Table Of Hidden Heavenly Stems In Earthly Branches

| Earthly Branch | | Hidden Heavenly Stems | | |
|---|---|---|---|---|
| **Rat** | 子 *Yang* Water | 癸 *Yin* Water | | |
| **Ox** | 丑 *Yin* Earth | 己 *Yin* Earth | 辛 *Yin* Metal | 癸 *Yin* Water |
| **Tiger** | 寅 *Yang* Wood | 甲 *Yang* Wood | 丙 *Yang* Fire | 戊 *Yang* Earth |
| **Rabbit** | 卯 *Yin* Wood | 乙 *Yin* Wood | | |
| **Dragon** | 辰 *Yang* Earth | 戊 *Yang* Earth | 乙 *Yin* Wood | 癸 *Yin* Water |
| **Snake** | 巳 *Yin* Fire | 庚 *Yang* Metal | 丙 *Yang* Fire | 戊 *Yang* Earth |
| **Horse** | 午 *Yang* Fire | 丁 *Yin* Fire | 己 *Yin* Earth | |
| **Goat** | 未 *Yin* Earth | 丁 *Yin* Fire | 己 *Yin* Earth | 乙 *Yin* Wood |
| **Monkey** | 申 *Yang* Metal | 戊 *Yang* Earth | 庚 *Yang* Metal | 壬 *Yang* Water |
| **Rooster** | 酉 *Yin* Metal | 辛 *Yin* Metal | | |
| **Dog** | 戌 *Yang* Earth | 戊 *Yang* Earth | 辛 *Yin* Metal | 丁 *Yin* Fire |
| **Pig** | 亥 *Yin* Water | 壬 *Yang* Water | 甲 *Yang* Wood | |

## What The Hidden Heavenly Stems Mean

Some elements are only present implicitly, being hidden in the earthly branches. These hidden heavenly stems can influence events considerably. For example, if the self element is in season (born in the month when the element is most prosperous), then all the hidden heavenly stems in the earthly branch of the month pillar will exert a stronger influence. If elements similar to these hidden heavenly stems also appear in the four pillars, it means that they have taken deeper root in the earthly branch and will appear as vital qualities of the person. In other words, if these hidden heavenly stems represent power, status, authority or money, then these people may become very successful. If an element similar to the self-sign is hidden in the House of Spouse, it symbolises a competitor and means that the spouse has a strong tendency to have illicit affairs.

## Case Studies

### *(a) General Chiang Kai-Shek, Taiwan Nationalist Leader*

His Four Pillars of Destiny are as follows:

| Hour | Day | Month | Year |
|---|---|---|---|
| 庚<br>*Yang* Metal | 己<br>*Yin* Earth | 庚<br>*Yang* Metal | 丁<br>*Yin* Fire |
| 午<br>*Yang* Horse | 巳<br>*Yin* Fire | 戌<br>*Yang* Earth | 亥<br>*Yin* Water |

| Luck Pillars | | | | | | |
|---|---|---|---|---|---|---|
| 68 | 58 | 48 | 38 | 28 | 18 | 8 |
| 癸<br>*Yin* Water | 甲<br>*Yang* Wood | 乙<br>*Yin* Wood | 丙<br>*Yang* Fire | 丁<br>*Yin* Fire | 戊<br>*Yang* Earth | 己<br>*Yin* Earth |
| 卯<br>*Yin* Wood | 辰<br>*Yang* Earth | 巳<br>*Yin* Fire | 午<br>*Yang* Fire | 未<br>*Yin* Earth | 申<br>*Yang* Metal | 酉<br>*Yin* Metal |

General Chiang is a *yin* earth person 己 born in the autumn season of *yang* earth 戌. Therefore, his earth is in season. The hidden heavenly stems in the earthly branch earth are:

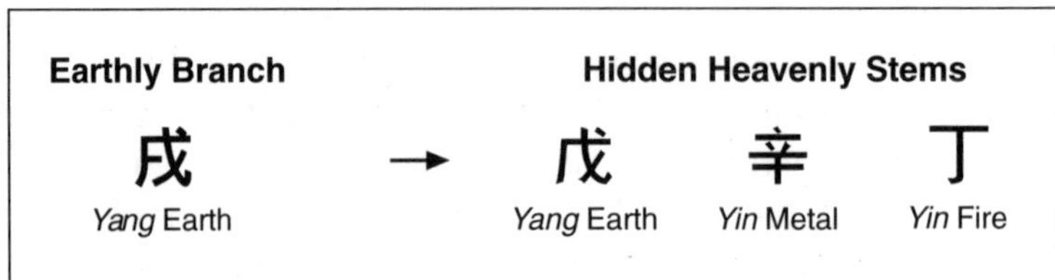

| Earthly Branch | | Hidden Heavenly Stems | | |
|---|---|---|---|---|
| 戌<br>*Yang* Earth | → | 戊<br>*Yang* Earth | 辛<br>*Yin* Metal | 丁<br>*Yin* Fire |

Since these hidden heavenly stems of earth, metal and fire are also found in the Four Pillars of Destiny (i.e. metal in the month and hour pillar heavenly stems and fire in the year pillar heavenly stem and in the day and hour pillar earthly branches), this shows that the elements of metal and fire are very strong. These elements, when translated, represent his intelligence and expression (metal) and resources (fire), while earth are his supporters, friends and colleagues.

### *(b) Cherry Chung, Hong Kong Actress (born 3–5 am, 16 February 1960)*

| Hour | Day | Month | Year |
|---|---|---|---|
| 丙 | 甲 | 戊 | 庚 |
| *Yang* Fire | *Yang* Wood | *Yang* Earth | *Yang* Metal |
| 寅 | 戌 | 寅 | 子 |
| *Yang* Wood | *Yang* Earth | *Yang* Wood | *Yang* Water |

| Luck Pillars | | | | | |
|---|---|---|---|---|---|
| 54 | 44 | 34 | 24 | 14 | 4 |
| 壬 | 癸 | 甲 | 乙 | 丙 | 丁 |
| *Yang* Water | *Yin* Water | *Yang* Wood | *Yin* Wood | *Yang* Fire | *Yin* Fire |
| 申 | 酉 | 戌 | 亥 | 子 | 丑 |
| *Yang* Metal | *Yin* Metal | *Yang* Earth | *Yin* Water | *Yang* Water | *Yin* Earth |

Cherry Chung is a *yang* wood 甲 person born in the spring season month of *yang* wood 寅, when wood is in season. The hidden heavenly stems in the earthly branch of the month pillar, *yang* wood 寅, are:

| Earthly Branch | | Hidden Heavenly Stems | | |
|---|---|---|---|---|
| 寅 | → | 甲 | 丙 | 戊 |
| *Yang* Wood | | *Yang* Wood | *Yang* Fire | *Yang* Earth |

Other similar elements of fire, earth and wood in her Four Pillars of Destiny are:

| Heavenly Stems | | | Earthly Branches | |
|---|---|---|---|---|
| Hour Pillar | Day Pillar | Month Pillar | Hour Pillar | Day Pillar |
| 丙 | 甲 | 戊 | 寅 | 戌 |
| *Yang* Fire | *Yang* Wood | *Yang* Earth | *Yang* Wood | *Yang* Earth |

The elements of fire, earth and wood play a important role in her life. Fire is her element for expression and intelligence – important qualities for an actress –while earth is her money element. As a strong wood person, she can manage the money element.

### *(c) Jet Li, Chinese Martial Arts Expert (born 7–9 pm, 26 April 1963)*

| Hour | Day | Month | Year |
|---|---|---|---|
| 甲 | 己 | 丙 | 癸 |
| *Yang* Wood | *Yin* Earth | *Yang* Fire | *Yin* Water |
| 戌 | 亥 | 辰 | 卯 |
| *Yang* Earth | *Yin* Water | *Yang* Earth | *Yin* Wood |

| Luck Pillars | | | | | |
|---|---|---|---|---|---|
| 57 | 47 | 37 | 27 | 17 | 7 |
| 庚 | 辛 | 壬 | 癸 | 甲 | 乙 |
| *Yang* Metal | *Yin* Metal | *Yang* Water | *Yin* Water | *Yang* Wood | *Yin* Wood |
| 戌 | 亥 | 子 | 丑 | 寅 | 卯 |
| *Yang* Earth | *Yin* Water | *Yang* Water | *Yin* Earth | *Yang* Wood | *Yin* Wood |

Jet Li is a *yin* earth person 己 , born in the spring month of *yang* earth 辰 , with the support of *yang* fire 丙 in the month pillar. As he was born in a month of the same element (strong earth), his self-sign *yin* earth is in season.

**Favourable Elements**

His favourable elements are wood (to suppress the strong earth) and water which, according to the Cycle of Destruction, exhausts the energy of earth.

**Unfavourable Elements**

As earth is already strong, further nourishment is not necessary. Hence, fire and earth are unfavourable elements. The earthly branch of the month pillar contains the hidden elements of the wood, earth and water heavenly stems.

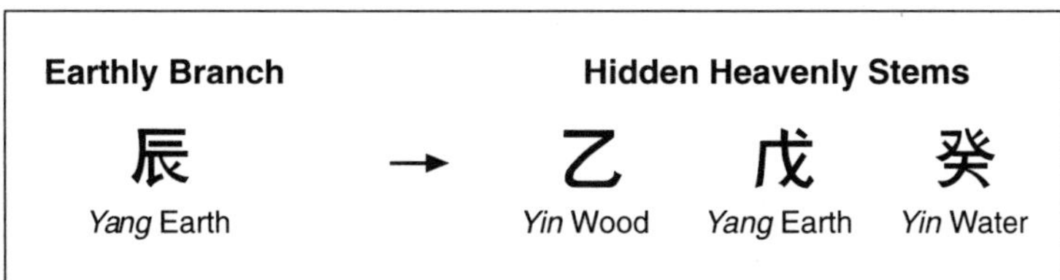

| Earthly Branch | | Hidden Heavenly Stems | | |
|---|---|---|---|---|
| 辰 | → | 乙 | 戊 | 癸 |
| *Yang* Earth | | *Yin* Wood | *Yang* Earth | *Yin* Water |

In situations where the self element is in season, those with elements similar to the hidden heavenly stems in the earthly branch of the month pillar in the four pillars are often said to have excellent destiny as these elements have strong roots in the earthly branch. Good examples are General Chiang Kai-Shek, Cherry Chung and Jet Li.

In the case of Jet Li, his heavenly stems represent the following areas in his life:

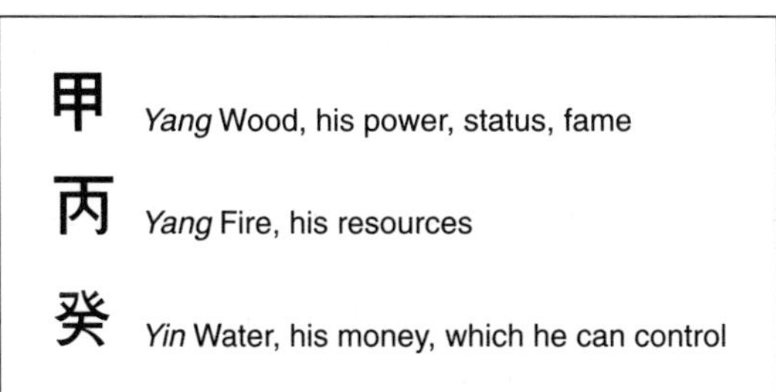

| | |
|---|---|
| 甲 | *Yang* Wood, his power, status, fame |
| 丙 | *Yang* Fire, his resources |
| 癸 | *Yin* Water, his money, which he can control |

Being an earth person, wood symbolises his power and status. During his first luck pillar (age 7 to 16) of *yin* wood, this power is harsher as he is a person of *yin* earth, according to the "Label" Theory (explained further on pages 96 and 97). In the eyes of the Chinese, he is said to have "fighting spirit," a vital quality in martial arts exponents.

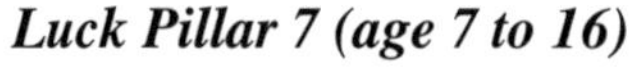

***Luck Pillar 7 (age 7 to 16)*** Self element

Wood is his power and status element.

In 1974, a year of

Jet Li received great acclaim when he won a National Martial Arts Championship.

In 1980, at 17, he made his first movie which brought him fame: "少林寺," *The Shaolin Temple*. 1980 was a year of

Metal, symbolising talent to an earth person, helped Jet Li express his capabilities well.

Before the age of 28, he had only his reputation, with wood elements dominating his luck pillars. Being a martial arts champion, the element of power is more prominent than the aspirations and talent element usually found in the destiny of movie stars. As he was from China, the money element was not strong.

After age 28, he moved to Hong Kong and starred in the movie *Wong Fei Hong*, which attracted huge audiences. As a result, his wealth increased spectacularly. Money, to an earth person, is symbolised by water; after the age of 27, Jet Li entered a luck pillar of water.

**Marriage**

He married in the luck pillar of

but divorced in 1991, a year of

when he was 28 years old.

**Why Jet Li's Marriage Failed**

A combination of elements conspired to produce discord in his marriage: 未 *yin* earth in the year 1991, *yin* wood 卯 in the earthly branch of the year pillar and the House of Spouse, 亥 *yin* water.

| 未 | + | 卯 | + | 亥 | = | WOOD |
|---|---|---|---|---|---|---|
| *Yin* Earth<br>1991 | | *Yin* Wood<br>Year Pillar | | *Yin* Water<br>House of Spouse | | |

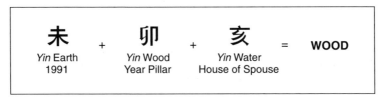

Wood, the resultant element of this three-element combination, is not supportive of water, his spouse element.

***Luck Pillar 27 (age 27 to 36)***

Water symbolises an earth man's wife (according to the Cycle of Destruction, earth conquers water) and this luck pillar has water. Thus, he very likely found a female friend outside his marriage. In fact, he had three chances of romance: 亥 *yin* water in the House of Spouse, 癸 *yin* water in the luck pillar and 癸 *yin* water hidden in the earthly branch of the month pillar.

# FACE READING, PUNISHMENT SYMBOLS AND LABELS

## The Five Elements And Your Face

According to Chinese metaphysics, everything in the universe can be represented by the five elements. Therefore, the five elements set out in the Four Pillars of Destiny can influence the facial appearance of a person. The shape and form of the various features is determined by the relative strength and weakness of each element. The facial features as symbolised by the five elements are:

Facial Representations Of The Five Elements

| Element | Shape of Face | Facial Features |
|---|---|---|
| Metal | Oval | Teeth, Skin |
| Wood | Triangular | Chin, Hair, Ear, Mole |
| Water | Round | Eyes |
| Fire | Rectangular | Eyes, Lips |
| Earth | Square | Nose, Cheek |

### Hair

A weak wood person can expect grey hair at a relatively young age. It is also believed that excessive fire and earth, coupled with a lack of water, will cause a person to start to bald early.

**Eyes**
Strong water influence in the Four Pillars of Destiny often result in large, round eyes while those with strong fire influence have large, piercing eyes.

**Mole**
The mole is reflected by the wood heavenly stem sitting on the earth earthly branch. An analogy is to imagine a wooden pole piercing the ground, leaving a mark which can be translated as a mole on the face.

Essential Representations Of The Five Elements

| Type | Metal | Wood | Water | Fire | Earth |
|---|---|---|---|---|---|
| **Season** | Autumn | Spring | Winter | Summer | 3rd Month |
| **Shape** | Round | Long | Irregular | Sharp | Square |
| **Direction** | West | East | North | South | Centre |
| **Colour** | White, Gold | Green | Black, Grey | Red, Purple Orange | Yellow, Brown |
| **Body** | Lung, Breathing Organs | Liver | Kidney, Bones, Body fluids | Heart, Blood | Stomach, Body tissues |

**Body Parts**
Based on the principle that the five elements must be balanced harmoniously, our body will be healthy if the balance is good. Otherwise, we will suffer from illness of that body part if it is weak or under attack by another element in the Cycle of Destruction.

**Direction**
This is more relevant in the study of *feng shui*. The idea is to enhance the balance of our Four Pillars of Destiny by analysing of the *feng shui* of our house or office.

## Punishment Symbols

### "Punishment" Triple Symbol ( 三刑 sān xíng )

Sometimes, when a certain triplet of earthly branches come together, trouble, regardless of the person's self-sign, will arise. We call these configurations "punishment" triple symbols.

For instance, if the three elements shown above (from the Four Pillars of Destiny together with the luck or year pillars) appear together, then the person with this "punishment" symbol will encounter trouble.

Take another case: if earth is not a favourable element for a person and the elements above come together, then some "punishment" can be expected, including the possibility of death.

Let us look at someone with the following pillars of destiny:

In 1994 甲 戌 , this person's mother may be affected as the mother's location (the earthly branch of the month pillar – see page 38 for the various locations of family members) is in a "punishment" position with the year pillar, especially in the month of 丑 *yin* earth, January 1995.

**"Punishment" Double Symbol (** 双 刑 shūang xíng **)**
Like the "punishment" triple symbol, the "punishment" double symbol occurs when certain two elements coming together.

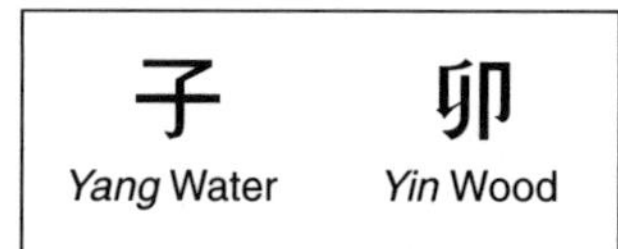


This is an example of a pair of "punishment" symbol elements.

**Self "Punishment" Symbol ( 自刑 zì xíng )**
When these symbols come together, a period of wasted effort, where nothing is achieved, can be expected.

For example, if your day pillar is

and you encounter a day of 亥 *yin* water you may end up not accomplishing anything useful.

If these symbols appear in your Four Pillars of Destiny, you could even find yourself doing silly things all through your life.

## Labels

When *yin/yang* or *yang/yang* elements representing the various aspects of life combine, these combinations can be labelled opposite or same genders. A combination of *yin* and *yang* is said to be an opposite gender combination and usually signifies harmony, whereas a combination of *yin* with *yin* or *yang* with *yang* is termed a same gender combination, and usually signifies a harsher, more extreme situation. An exception is the area of intelligence. An opposite gender combination for intelligence suppresses the power and status element or the element that exerts control over oneself. Thus the opposite gender combination for intelligence usually shows someone with a rebellious nature. This is explained further on page 99.

The harmony of *yin* and *yang* elements is in line with the concept of *yin* and *yang* being the duality of everything in the universe. Very few things in life are completely *yin* or *yang* because most things are in transition, composed of a little of both elements. For example, electricity has positive and negative electrical pulses while male and female hormones are found in everyone, man or woman.

## *(a) Money And Wife*

| **Opposite gender** | **Same gender** |
|---|---|
| 正财 | 偏财 |
| direct wealth<br>zhèng cái | unexpected wealth<br>pīan cái |

A 壬 *yang* water man's money or wife is symbolised by fire. If his set of Four Pillars of Destiny has *yin* fire and *yang* fire, he will very likely have a main source of income as well as other supplementary sources, and perhaps more than one wife, as bigamy was acceptable in olden days.

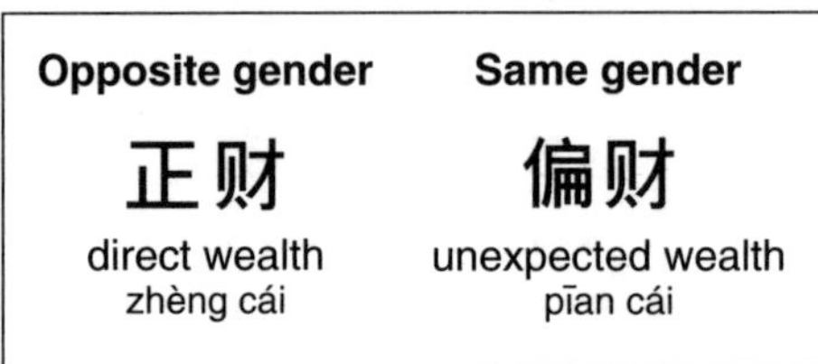

| **Opposite gender** | | **Same gender** | |
|---|---|---|---|
| 壬 | 丁 | 壬 | 丙 |
| *Yang* Water<br>Self Sign | *Yin* Fire<br>Other Pillars | *Yang* Water<br>Self Sign | *Yang* Fire<br>Other Pillars |

Take, for example, a person with the following Four Pillars of Destiny:

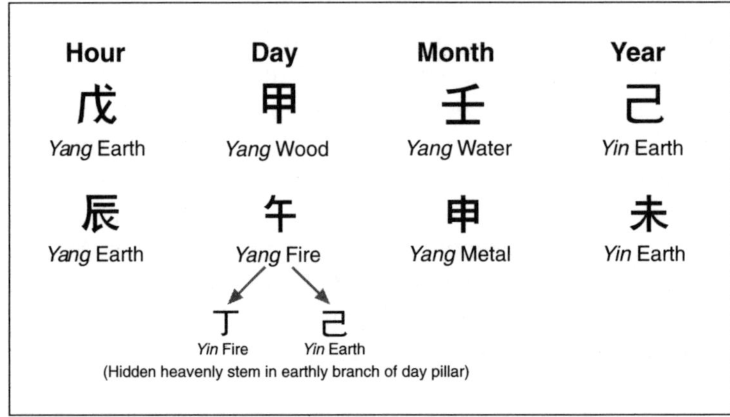

| **Hour** | **Day** | **Month** | **Year** |
|---|---|---|---|
| 戊<br>*Yang* Earth | 甲<br>*Yang* Wood | 壬<br>*Yang* Water | 己<br>*Yin* Earth |
| 辰<br>*Yang* Earth | 午<br>*Yang* Fire | 申<br>*Yang* Metal | 未<br>*Yin* Earth |
| | 丁 *Yin* Fire / 己 *Yin* Earth | | |

(Hidden heavenly stem in earthly branch of day pillar)

This wood person's direct wealth (main source of income) combination is:

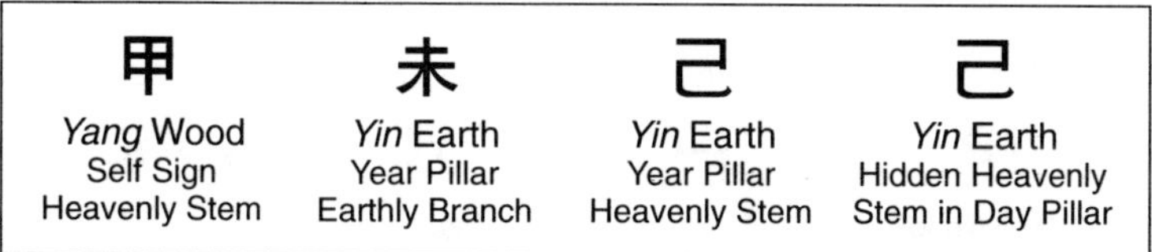

| 甲 | 未 | 己 | 己 |
|---|---|---|---|
| *Yang* Wood<br>Self Sign<br>Heavenly Stem | *Yin* Earth<br>Year Pillar<br>Earthly Branch | *Yin* Earth<br>Year Pillar<br>Heavenly Stem | *Yin* Earth<br>Hidden Heavenly<br>Stem in Day Pillar |

whereas his same gender combination for other wealth (other source of income) is:

| 甲 | 戊 | 辰 |
|---|---|---|
| *Yang* Wood<br>Self Sign | *Yang* Earth<br>Heavenly Stem hour pillar | *Yang* Earth<br>Earthly Branch hour pillar |

This man may have two wives or else have an extramarital affair.

### *(b) Power And Status*

| **Opposite gender** | **Same gender** |
|---|---|
| 正官<br>authority<br>zhèng gūan | 七杀<br>fighting spirit<br>qī shā |

The element of power, status and fame (see page 19 for the elemental relationships) is the element that destroys the self-sign. To a water person, earth is the power element. A *yin* and *yang* combination shows a person with authority in an organisation whereas a *yang* and *yang* or *yin* and *yin* same gender combination reveals someone who displays his authority in other ways (for example, Jet Li has a combination which symbolises his power or fighting spirit in the martial arts).

For a *yang* water person, these represent his authority and fighting spirit:

| **Authority** | | **Fighting spirit** | |
|---|---|---|---|
| 壬 | 己 | 壬 | 戊 |
| *Yang* Water<br>Self Sign | *Yin* Earth<br>Other Pillars | *Yang* Water<br>Self Sign | *Yang* Earth<br>Other Pillars |

Jet Li's Four Pillars of Destiny are:

| Hour | Day | Month | Year |
|---|---|---|---|
| 甲<br>*Yang* Wood | 己<br>*Yin* Earth | 丙<br>*Yang* Fire | 癸<br>*Yin* Water |
| 戌<br>*Yang* Earth | 亥<br>*Yin* Water | 辰<br>*Yang* Earth | 卯<br>*Yin* Wood |

| Luck Pillars | | | | | |
|---|---|---|---|---|---|
| 57 | 47 | 37 | 27 | 17 | 7 |
| 庚<br>*Yang* Metal | 辛<br>*Yin* Metal | 壬<br>*Yang* Water | 癸<br>*Yin* Water | 甲<br>*Yang* Wood | 乙<br>*Yin* Wood |
| 戌<br>*Yang* Earth | 亥<br>*Yin* Water | 子<br>*Yang* Water | 丑<br>*Yin* Earth | 寅<br>*Yang* Wood | 卯<br>*Yin* Wood |

| Earthly Branch | | Hidden Heavenly Stems | | |
|---|---|---|---|---|
| 辰<br>*Yang* Earth | → | 乙<br>*Yin* Wood | 戊<br>*Yang* Earth | 癸<br>*Yin* Water |

His power element is wood and there is 甲 *yang* wood in the heavenly stem of the hour pillar, 卯 *yin* wood in the earthly branch of the year pillar and a hidden 乙 *yin* wood in the earthly branch of the month pillar. His luck pillar of age 7 to 16 comprises of the 乙 卯 *yin* wood element in both the heavenly stem and earthly branch. Being a 己 *yin* earth person, this re-occurrence of same gender combinations helped him excel in the martial arts. The fighting spirit (same gender combination of *yin* and *yin*) in his pillars of destiny is:

| Self Sign | Other *Yin* Wood Elements | | | |
|---|---|---|---|---|
| 己<br>*Yin* Earth<br>Heavenly Stem of day pillar | 乙<br>*Yin* Wood<br>Hidden heavenly stem in month earthly branch | 卯<br>*Yin* Wood<br>Earthly branch of year pillar | 乙<br>*Yin* Wood<br>Heavenly stem of luck pillar 7 | 卯<br>*Yin* Wood<br>Earthly branch of luck pillar 7 |

[Note: The same gender combination for power can often be found in the destiny of policemen and senior military officers.]

The wood in Jet Li's luck pillar of 17 to 26 is 甲 *yang* wood over 寅 *yang* wood. With a *yin* and *yang* combination, he no longer has a strong fighting spirit. Instead, he amassed great popularity and fame when he moved to Hong Kong to act in movies.

| Self Sign | Other *Yang* Wood Elements | | |
|---|---|---|---|
| 己<br>*Yin* Earth<br>Heavenly Stem of day pillar | 甲<br>*Yang* Wood<br>Heavenly stem of hour pillar | 甲<br>*Yang* Wood<br>Heavenly stem of luck pillar 17 | 寅<br>*Yang* Wood<br>Earthly branch of luck pillar 1 7 |

As another example, let us look at the pillars of Mike Tyson, the former World Heavyweight Boxing Champion, who was born on 30 June 1966:

| Hour | Day | Month | Year |
|---|---|---|---|
| ? | 庚<br>*Yang* Metal | 甲<br>*Yang* Wood | 丙<br>*Yang* Fire |
| ? | 申<br>*Yang* Metal | 午<br>*Yang* Fire | 午<br>*Yang* Fire |

His power element is fire and there are three *yang* fire elements to complement his *yang* metal self-sign. These three sets of same gender combinations created a more aggressive power and contributed to his great success in the boxing ring.

### *(c) Resources*

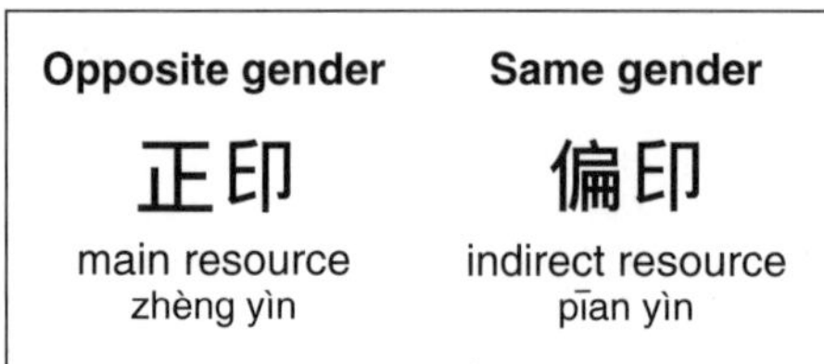

| Opposite gender | Same gender |
|---|---|
| 正印 | 偏印 |
| main resource<br>zhèng yìn | indirect resource<br>pīan yìn |

A water person's resource element is metal:

| Main resource | | Indirect resource | |
|---|---|---|---|
| 壬 | 辛 | 壬 | 庚 |
| *Yang* Water<br>Self Sign | *Yin* Metal<br>Other Pillars | *Yang* Water<br>Self Sign | *Yang* Metal<br>Other Pillars |

Same gender combinations can mean a person is interested in unconventional studies, such as *feng shui*. In ancient times, if a person had both main and indirect resources, it suggested that he or she had two mothers (the mother is also the resource element).

### *(d) Intelligence*

| Opposite gender | Same gender |
|---|---|
| 伤官 | 食神 |
| intelligence<br>shāng gūan | unconventional intelligence<br>shí shén |

A water person's intelligence is symbolised by wood.

| Intelligence | | Unconventional intelligence | |
|---|---|---|---|
| 壬 | 乙 | 壬 | 申 |
| *Yang* Water<br>Self Sign | *Yin* Wood<br>Other Pillars | *Yang* Water<br>Self Sign | *Yang* Wood<br>Other Pillars |

In olden days, many people believed that an "intelligent" lady would not make a good wife as she could not be totally submissive. Today, intelligence is more sought after. But if a lady has both opposite and same gender combinations, the intelligence element (symbolised by wood in a water lady) could overpower her husband (symbolised by earth), causing an imbalance in the marriage. [Strong wood destroys earth.]

Fortunately, if a lady is *yang* water and her husband is *yin* earth, a harmonious relationship is still possible as her intelligence of *yang* wood combines with his *yin* earth.

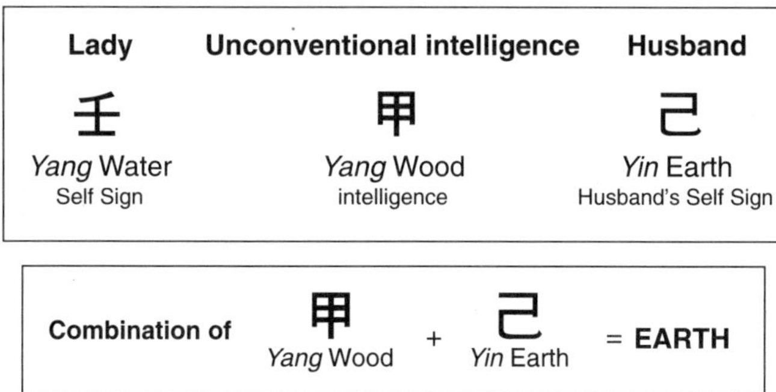


Opposite gender combinations for intelligence suppress power, status and the element that controls the self. A person with an opposite gender combination for intelligence may become rebellious or misuse his intelligence. Same gender combinations are more harmonious.

For example, for a 壬 *yang* water person, opposite gender combinations with elements symbolising intelligence, such as 乙 *yin* wood, will be strong and harmonious.

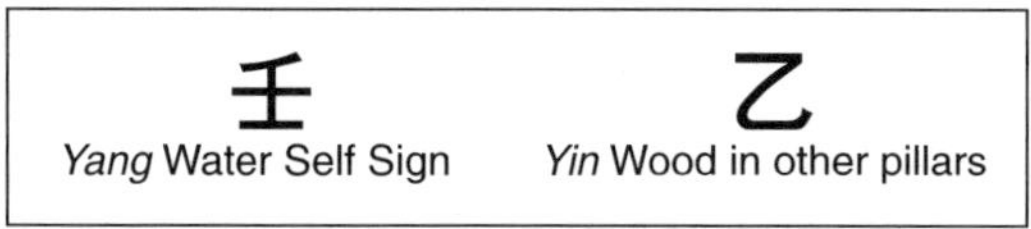


This combination can destroy power, status or the element that controls the self (earth, in this case). According to the Cycle of Destruction, since wood destroys earth, the intelligence element suppresses the power element. Hence, if the element that exerts control over the self, earth, is weak, this person may become rebellious.

### *(e) Friends*

As mentioned previously, a similar element can be either a friend, colleague, supporter or competitor, depending on the strength of the person at that particular point in time. According to label theory, the same gender indicates a friend while the opposite gender symbolises a competitor.

| Opposite gender | Same gender |
|---|---|
| 劫财 | 比肩 |
| competitor<br>jíe cái | friend<br>bǐ jīan |

To a *yang* water person, for example, another water element could signify either a friend or a competitor.

| Competitor | | Friend | |
|---|---|---|---|
| 壬 | 癸 | 壬 | 壬 |
| *Yang* Water<br>Self Sign | *Yin* Water<br>Other Pillars | *Yang* Water<br>Self Sign | *Yang* Water<br>Other Pillars |

# HOUSE OF CONCEPTION AND HOUSE OF LIFE

## House of Conception (胎元 tāi yúan)

This pillar refers to the month of conception which usually occurs about nine months before the month of birth. The House of Conception is a useful supplement to the Four Pillars of Destiny for determining the number of siblings or children in a family. We can also use it to help evaluate the strength of the self-sign.

This pillar can be derived from the earthly branch of the month pillar (the month of birth) by counting nine months backwards in the sequence of the earthly branches (see page 15).

A simpler method is shown here:

- Heavenly stem: From the month of birth, move one month forward
- Earthly branch: From the month of birth, move three months forward

The count positions differ because there are only 10 heavenly stems as opposed to 12 earthly branches.

For example:

| | Month Pillar | | House of Conception |
|---|---|---|---|
| Heavenly Stem | 壬 *Yang* Water | Move one position to | 癸 *Yin* Water |
| Earthly Branch | 戌 *Yang* Earth | Move three positions to | 丑 *Yin* Earth |

## House Of Life ( 命宫 mìng gōng )

The House of Life reflects our ancestors' influence in our Four Pillars of Destiny. Like the House of Conception, this pillar helps determine the number of siblings and children in a family as well as helps evaluate the strength of the self-sign. In astrological terms, the House of Life is the position of the sun at the time of birth of a person.

There are two ways to set up the House of Life, which is derived from the month and hour pillars.

### Position Of The Month Of Birth

Before we start to derive the House of Life, we must first check the sequence number of the month of birth. Readers can refer to page 16 for the positions of each month of the Xia calendar.

The mid-month day of each Xia month (equivalent to the Western date between 18th and the 24th) is outlined in the Thousand Year Calendar. If the date of birth is after the middle of the month, then for the purpose of the counting the month's position, the following month should be taken.

For example, let's take a date of birth, 8 pm, 24 May 1964. The month of birth (with reference to the earthly branch) is 巳 *yin* fire, the fourth month of the Xia year (see page 16). If we look up the Thousand Year Calendar, we will see that the middle of that month is 21 May. Since the date of birth is after the middle of the month, we should pick the following month, i.e. the fifth month, as the month of birth for our purpose.

| Hour | Day | Month | Year |
|---|---|---|---|
| 壬 | 癸 | 己 | 甲 |
| *Yang* Water | *Yin* Water | *Yin* Earth | *Yang* Wood |
| 戌 | 酉 | 巳 | 辰 |
| *Yang* Earth | *Yin* Metal | *Yin* Fire | *Yang* Earth |

The hour of birth (earthly branch of the hour pillar) is 戌 Dog *yang* earth. This is the 11th hour (see page 27).

## Method One

Look up the tables on pages 104 and 105. On the top row (which shows the month of birth), find the fifth month, the month of Horse 午 *yang* fire (YgF). Now look up the right hand column for the hour of birth – the 11th hour, the hour of Dog 戌 *yang* earth (YgE3). The resulting cross-referenced earthly branch is *yin* earth (YnE4) 丑 the Ox earth, which is the 12th month in the Xia year sequence (see page 16).

| | Month of birth | House of Life |
|---|---|---|
| **Earthly branch** | 巳<br>*Yin* Fire | 丑<br>*Yin* Earth<br>(12th month of the Xia year) |

Now let us derive the heavenly stem of the House of Life. Beginning with 甲 *yang* wood (the starting element in the heavenly stem sequence on page 15), move to the 12th position in the sequence (the same position number as the earthly branch of the House of Life *yin* earth derived earlier). We thus arrive at 乙 *yin* wood.

| | Month of birth | House of Life |
|---|---|---|
| **Heavenly stem** | 己<br>*Yin* Earth | 乙<br>*Yin* Wood<br>(equivalent 12th position in the sequence of the heavenly stems) |

The complete set of pillars of destiny together with the House of Conception and House of Life for a person born on 8 pm, 24 May 1964 is therefore:

| House of Conception | Hour | Day | Month | Year | House of Life |
|---|---|---|---|---|---|
| 庚<br>*Yang* Metal | 壬<br>*Yang* Water | 癸<br>*Yin* Water | 己<br>*Yin* Earth | 甲<br>*Yang* Wood | 乙<br>*Yin* Wood |
| 申<br>*Yang* Metal | 戌<br>*Yang* Earth | 酉<br>*Yin* Metal | 巳<br>*Yin* Fire | 辰<br>*Yang* Earth | 丑<br>*Yin* Earth |

The House of Conception has been derived as follows:

| | Month Pillar | | House of Conception |
|---|---|---|---|
| Heavenly Stem | 己<br>*Yin* Earth | Move one position to | 庚<br>*Yang* Metal |
| Earthly Branch | 巳<br>*Yin* Fire | Move three positions to | 申<br>*Yang* Metal |

Table For Deriving The Earthly Branch Of The House Of Life

| 12 丑 | 11 子 | 10 亥 | 9 戌 | 8 酉 | 7 申 | 6 未 | 5 午 | 4 巳 | 3 辰 | 2 卯 | 1 寅 | Month<br>House of Life<br>Birth Hour |
|---|---|---|---|---|---|---|---|---|---|---|---|---|
| 辰 | 巳 | 午 | 未 | 申 | 酉 | 戌 | 亥 | 子 | 丑 | 寅 | 卯 | 1 Rat 子 |
| 卯 | 辰 | 巳 | 午 | 未 | 申 | 酉 | 戌 | 亥 | 子 | 丑 | 寅 | 2 Ox 丑 |
| 寅 | 卯 | 辰 | 巳 | 午 | 未 | 申 | 酉 | 戌 | 亥 | 子 | 丑 | 3 Tiger 寅 |
| 丑 | 寅 | 卯 | 辰 | 巳 | 午 | 未 | 申 | 酉 | 戌 | 亥 | 子 | 4 Rabbit 卯 |
| 子 | 丑 | 寅 | 卯 | 辰 | 巳 | 午 | 未 | 申 | 酉 | 戌 | 亥 | 5 Dragon 辰 |
| 亥 | 子 | 丑 | 寅 | 卯 | 辰 | 巳 | 午 | 未 | 申 | 酉 | 戌 | 6 Snake 巳 |
| 戌 | 亥 | 子 | 丑 | 寅 | 卯 | 辰 | 巳 | 午 | 未 | 申 | 酉 | 7 Horse 午 |
| 酉 | 戌 | 亥 | 子 | 丑 | 寅 | 卯 | 辰 | 巳 | 午 | 未 | 申 | 8 Goat 未 |
| 申 | 酉 | 戌 | 亥 | 子 | 丑 | 寅 | 卯 | 辰 | 巳 | 午 | 未 | 9 Monkey 申 |
| 未 | 申 | 酉 | 戌 | 亥 | 子 | 丑 | 寅 | 卯 | 辰 | 巳 | 午 | 10 Rooster 酉 |
| 午 | 未 | 申 | 酉 | 戌 | 亥 | 子 | 丑 | 寅 | 卯 | 辰 | 巳 | 11 Dog 戌 |
| 巳 | 午 | 未 | 申 | 酉 | 戌 | 亥 | 子 | 丑 | 寅 | 卯 | 辰 | 12 Pig 亥 |

## Table For Deriving The Earthly Branch Of The House Of Life

| 12<br>YnE4 | 11<br>YgW | 10<br>YnW | 9<br>YgE3 | 8<br>YnM | 7<br>YgM | 6<br>YnE2 | 5<br>YgF | 4<br>YnF | 3<br>YgE1 | 2<br>YnWd | 1<br>YgWd | **Month**<br>**House of Life**<br>**Birth Hour** |
|---|---|---|---|---|---|---|---|---|---|---|---|---|
| YgE1 | YnF | YgF | YnE2 | YgM | YnM | YgE3 | YnW | YgW | YnE4 | YgWd | YnWd | **1 Rat**<br>**YgW** |
| YnWd | YgE1 | YnF | YgF | YnE2 | YgM | YnM | YgE3 | YnW | YgW | YnE4 | YgWd | **2 Ox**<br>**YnE4** |
| YgWd | YnWd | YgE1 | YnF | YgF | YnE2 | YgM | YnM | YgE3 | YnW | YgW | YnE4 | **3 Tiger**<br>**YgWd** |
| YnE4 | YgWd | YnWd | YgE1 | YnF | YgF | YnE2 | YgM | YnM | YgE3 | YnW | YgW | **4 Rabbit**<br>**YnWd** |
| YgW | YnE4 | YgWd | YnWd | YgE1 | YnF | YgF | YnE2 | YgM | YnM | YgE3 | YnW | **5 Dragon**<br>**YgE1** |
| YnW | YgW | YnE4 | YgWd | YnWd | YgE1 | YnF | YgF | YnE2 | YgM | YnM | YgE3 | **6 Snake**<br>**YnF** |
| YgE3 | YnW | YgW | YnE4 | YgWd | YnWd | YgE1 | YnF | YgF | YnE2 | YgM | YnM | **7 Horse**<br>**YgF** |
| YnM | YgE3 | YnW | YgW | YnE4 | YgWd | YnWd | YgE1 | YnF | YgF | YnE2 | YgM | **8 Goat**<br>**YnE2** |
| YgM | YnM | YgE3 | YnW | YgW | YnE4 | YgWd | YnWd | YgE1 | YnF | YgF | YnE2 | **9 Monkey**<br>**YgM** |
| YnE2 | YgM | YnM | YgE3 | YnW | YgW | YnE4 | YgWd | YnWd | YgE1 | YnF | YgF | **10 Rooster**<br>**YnM** |
| YgF | YnE2 | YgM | YnM | YgE3 | YnW | YgW | YnE4 | YgWd | YnWd | YgE1 | YnF | **11 Dog**<br>**YgE3** |
| YnF | YgF | YnE2 | YgM | YnM | YgE3 | YnW | YgW | YnE4 | YgWd | YnWd | YgE1 | **12 Pig**<br>**YnW** |

Note: The index for the abbreviations used is listed in the Thousand Year Calendar (page 118).

## Method Two

In this method, we use the sequence of the earthly branches on the palm as shown here:

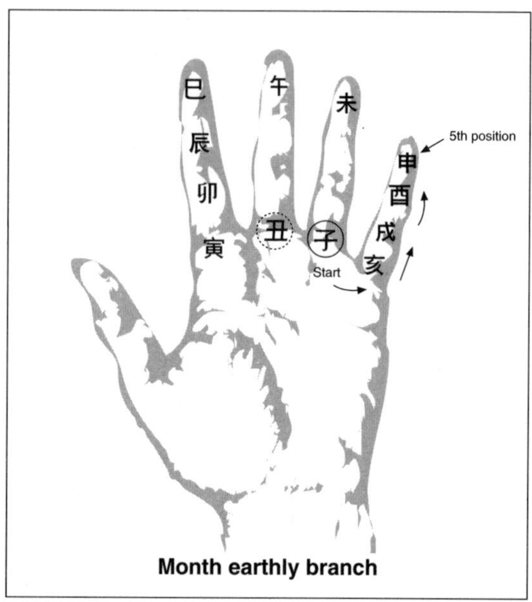


**Month earthly branch**

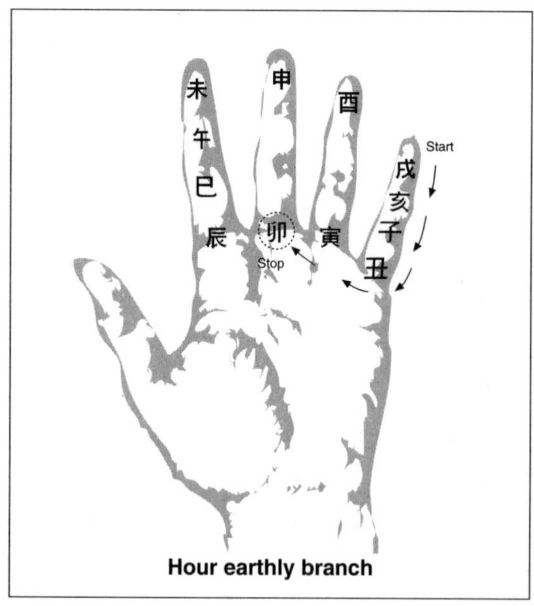


**Hour earthly branch**

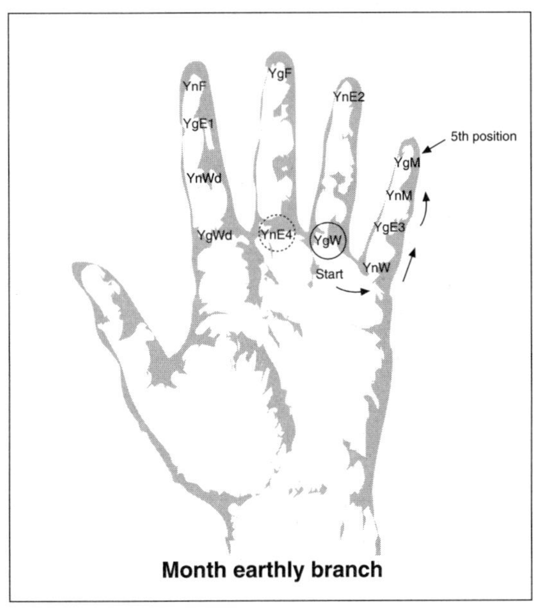

Month earthly branch

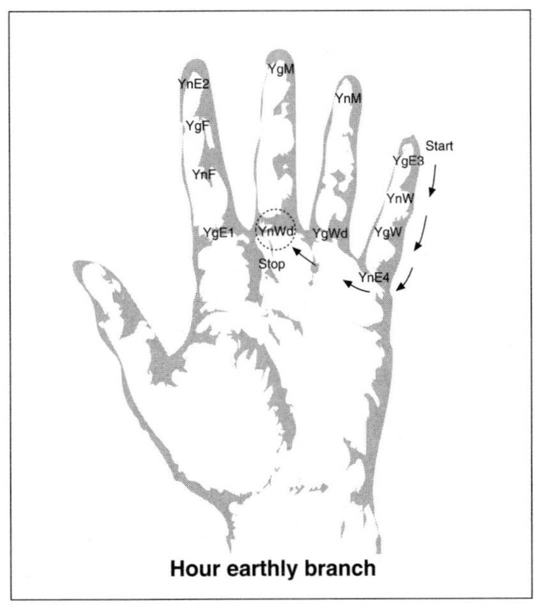

Hour earthly branch

Let us look at the same birth data of 8 pm, 24 May 1964:

| Hour | Day | Month | Year |
|---|---|---|---|
| 壬 | 癸 | 己 | 甲 |
| *Yang* Water | *Yin* Water | *Yin* Earth | *Yang* Wood |
| 戌 | 酉 | 巳 | 辰 |
| *Yang* Earth | *Yin* Metal | *Yin* Fire | *Yang* Earth |

**Step 1** Determine the sequence position for the month of birth (earthly branch of month pillar). For this example, we have already confirmed it to be the 5th month.

**Step 2** Refer to the month earthly branch palm drawings on pages 106 and 107. The earthly branches are located at various positions around the fingers. Start counting anticlockwise from the earthly branch 子 Rat *yang* water (YgW) at the base of the fourth finger to position 5. We thus arrive at the earthly branch 申 Monkey *yang* metal (YgM) at the tip of the little finger. Note that the starting point is always at 子 Rat *yang* water (YgW) as this is where the earthly branch sequence begins (see page 15 for the sequence).

**Step 3** Look up the hour earthly branch palm drawing. We will be using the location we derived in Step 2 as the starting point for another count. Our location at the tip of the little finger is now the site of the earthly branch 戌 *yang* earth (YgE3) of the person's hour pillar.

**Step 4** In a clockwise motion, label each finger according to the sequence of the earthly branches. The tip of the last finger is 戌 Dog *yang* earth (YgE3), the second position is 亥 Pig *yin* water (YnW), the third position 子 Rat *yang* water (YgW), and so on. Then, starting from 戌 *yang* earth (YgE3), count clockwise in the order of the earthly branches until you reach the hour of 卯 Rabbit *yin* wood (YnWd), i.e. 5 to 7 am, the dawn of day. Stop here and look up the month earthly branch palm to obtain the equivalent month in the same position of the palm. [Note: We stop at the hour of dawn because the House of Life, as mentioned earlier, is the position of the sun at the time of birth.]

The count from the hour of Dog 戌 *yang* earth (YgE3) to the hour of Rabbit 卯 *yin* wood (YnWd) is six spaces. This is the location of the base of the middle finger. In the month earthly branch palm, this position is 丑 *yin* earth (YnE4).

**Step 5** As in Method 1, find the equivalent for the House of Life heavenly stem.

## Case Studies

### *(a) John Lennon (born 7–9 am, 9 October 1940)*

| House of Conception | Hour | Day | Month | Year | House of Life |
|---|---|---|---|---|---|
| 丁 *Yin* Fire | 庚 *Yang* Metal | 乙 *Yin* Wood | 丙 *Yang* Fire | 庚 *Yang* Metal | 乙 *Yin* Wood |
| 丑 *Yin* Earth | 辰 *Yang* Earth | 酉 *Yin* Metal | 戌 *Yang* Earth | 辰 *Yang* Earth | 卯 *Yin* Wood |

**House Of Conception**

From the sequence of heavenly stems and earthly branches, we can obtain his House of Conception:

| | Month of birth | | House of Conception |
|---|---|---|---|
| Heavenly stem | 丙 *Yang* Fire | Move one position to | 丁 *Yin* Fire |
| Earthly Branch | 戌 *Yang* Earth | Move three positions to | 丑 *Yin* Earth |

**House Of Life (Palm Method)**

**Step 1** His month of birth is the ninth month of the Xia year (see page 16). From the Thousand Year Calendar, we see that 9 October is the second day of the ninth month and is therefore not affected by the mid-month point.

**Step 2** Refer to the drawings of the month earthly branch palm on pages 111 and 112. Starting from the earthly branch 子 Rat *yang* water (YgW), count anticlockwise to position 9 – the 9th month.

**Step 3** Position 9 is the earthly branch 辰 Dragon *yang* earth (YgE1) at the second position from the tip of the index finger.

**Step 4** Now let the position we derived in Step 3 be the hour of birth. From the hour earthly branch palm drawing, we see that it is also 辰 Dragon *yang* earth (YgE1). Label, in a clockwise direction, the sequence of the earthly branches on each of the finger markings. Thus 辰 *yang* earth (YgE1) becomes sequence number 1 on the second marking from the tip of the index finger, followed by 巳 *yin* fire (YnF) on the tip of the index finger, and so on.

Start counting in a clockwise direction until the hour of 卯 Rabbit *yin* wood (YnWd). The count from the hour of Dragon 辰 to the hour of Rabbit involves 12 spaces. In the hour palm, this is the location of the third position of the index finger. This location in the month palm is equivalent to 卯 Rabbit *yin* wood (YnWd). Thus the earthly branch of the House of Life is 卯 *yin* wood.

**Step 5** Derive the heavenly stem of the House of Life:

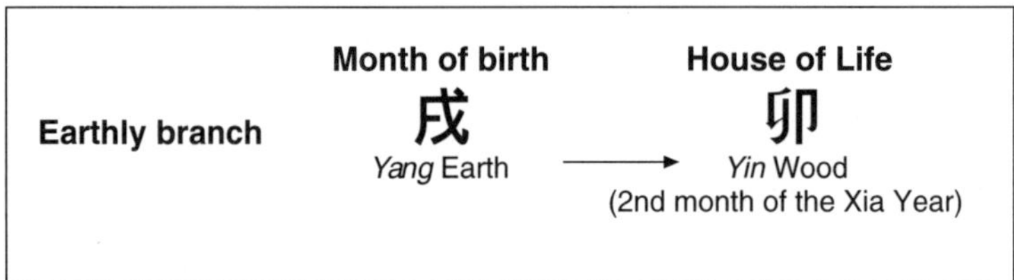

| | Month of birth | | House of Life |
|---|---|---|---|
| Earthly branch | 戌<br>*Yang* Earth | → | 卯<br>*Yin* Wood<br>(2nd month of the Xia Year) |

The heavenly stem is thus:

| | | | |
|---|---|---|---|
| Heavenly stem | 丙<br>*Yang* Fire | → | 乙<br>*Yin* Wood<br>(equivalent 2nd position from 甲 *Yang* Wood, the commencement of the heavenly sequence) |

## Evaluating The Self-Sign

John Lennon belongs to the "Follow the Leader" category of earth and metal. As mentioned earlier, we can use the House of Conception and House of Life to evaluate the strength of the self. In this case, the House of Conception is fire and earth (i.e. a pillar of strong earth). Both elements are destructive to the self-sign wood.

There, however, appears to be some weak support in the House of Life as the elements of the heavenly stem and earthly branch are both wood. Nevertheless, this weak House of Life is not strong enough to suppress the powerful destructive elements in the four pillars. Hence, by analysing the House of Conception and House of Life, we can confirm that he is a "Follow the Leader" type since the self-sign wood is too weak to "survive" on its own.

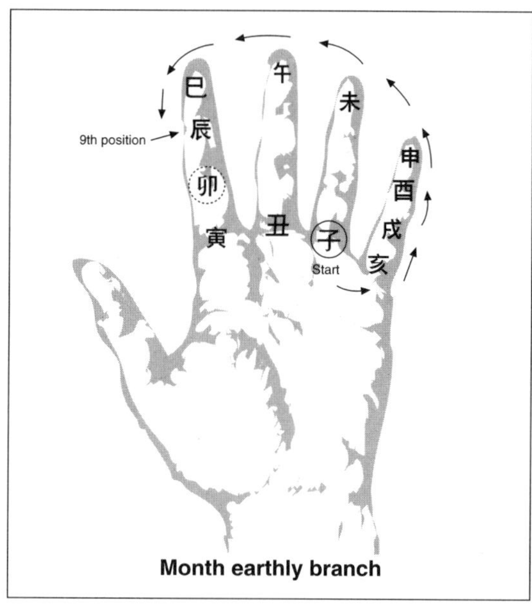


**Month earthly branch**

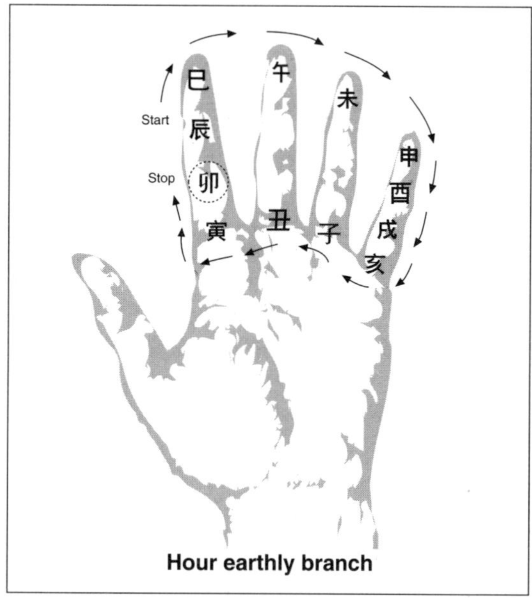


**Hour earthly branch**

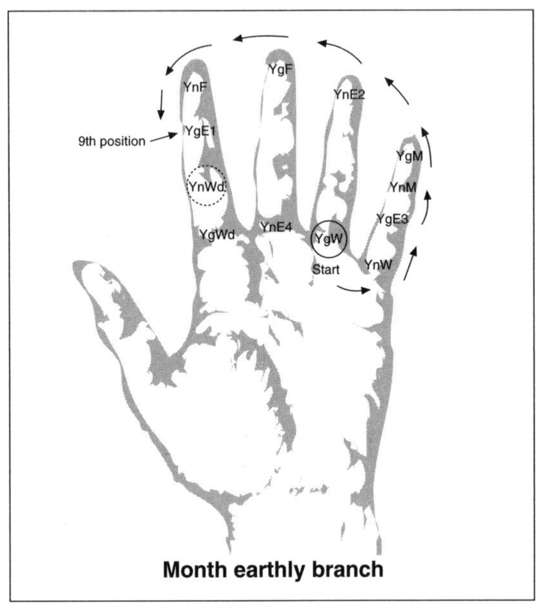

Month earthly branch

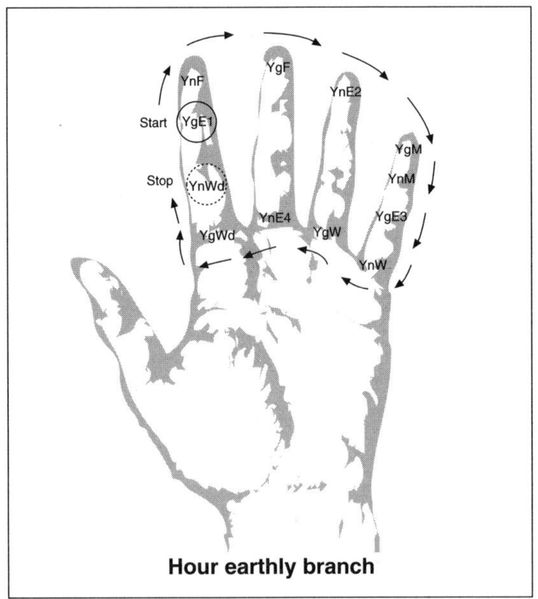

Hour earthly branch

## *(b) Male, born 10 am, 13 November 1993*

| House of Conception | Hour | Day | Month | Year | House of Life |
|---|---|---|---|---|---|
| 甲 *Yang* Wood | 丁 *Yin* Fire | 戊 *Yang* Earth | 癸 *Yin* Water | 癸 *Yin* Water | 乙 *Yin* Wood |
| 寅 *Yang* Wood | 巳 *Yin* Fire | 戌 *Yang* Earth | 亥 *Yin* Water | 酉 *Yin* Metal | 丑 *Yin* Earth |

### House of Conception

| | Month of birth | | House of Conception |
|---|---|---|---|
| Heavenly Stem | 癸 *Yin* Water | Move one position to | 甲 *Yang* Wood |
| Earthly Branch | 亥 *Yin* Water | Move three positions to | 寅 *Yang* Wood |

### House Of Life (Palm Method)

**Step 1** The month of birth is the 10th month of the Xia year (see page 16).

**Step 2** See the drawings of the month earthly branch palm on pages 114 to 116. Starting from earthly branch 子 Rat *yang* water (YgW), count anticlockwise to position 10.

**Step 3** Position 10, at the third position from the tip of the index finger, is earthly branch Rabbit 卯 *yin* wood (YnWd).

**Step 4** The location we derived in Step 3 is now the hour of birth in the Four Pillars of Destiny, i.e. 巳 Snake *yin* fire (YnF). In the hour palm drawing, label the finger markings according to the earthly branch sequence, with Snake *yin* fire (YnF), the first earthly branch. Start counting in a clockwise direction until the hour of Rabbit 卯 *yin* wood (YnWd). The count from the hour of Snake 巳 *yin* fire (YnF) to the hour of Rabbit *yin* wood (YnWd) is 11 spaces. In the hour palm, the hour of Rabbit *yin* wood (YnWd) is the base of the middle finger. In the month earthly branch palm drawing, this location is equivalent to 丑 *yin* earth (YnE4), the Ox.

Thus the earthly branch of the House of Life is the Ox, *yin* earth (YnE4), which, according to the Xia year, is the 12th month.

**Step 5** Derive the heavenly stem of the House of Life:

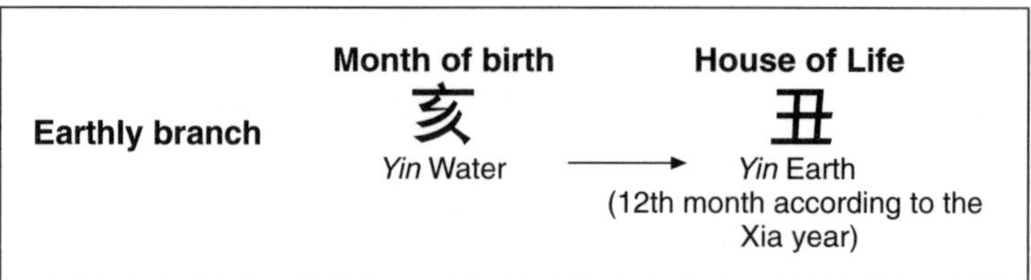

| | Month of birth | | House of Life |
|---|---|---|---|
| **Earthly branch** | 亥<br>*Yin* Water | → | 丑<br>*Yin* Earth<br>(12th month according to the Xia year) |

The heavenly stem of the House of Life is thus:

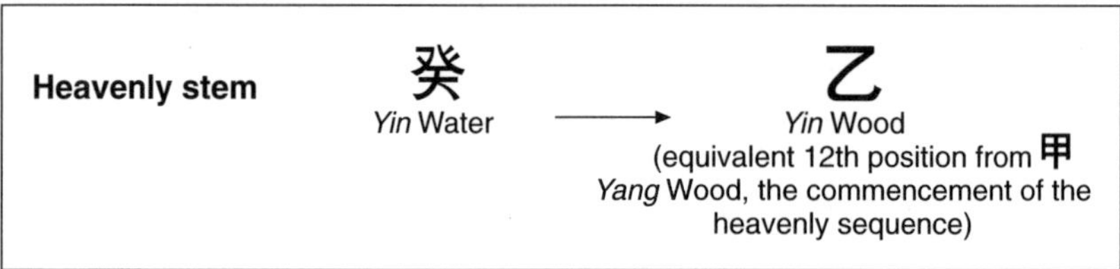

| | | | |
|---|---|---|---|
| **Heavenly stem** | 癸<br>*Yin* Water | → | 乙<br>*Yin* Wood<br>(equivalent 12th position from 甲 *Yang* Wood, the commencement of the heavenly sequence) |

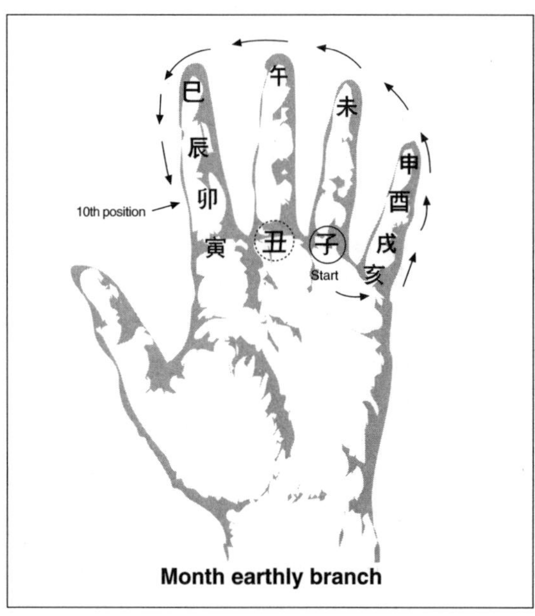


**Month earthly branch**

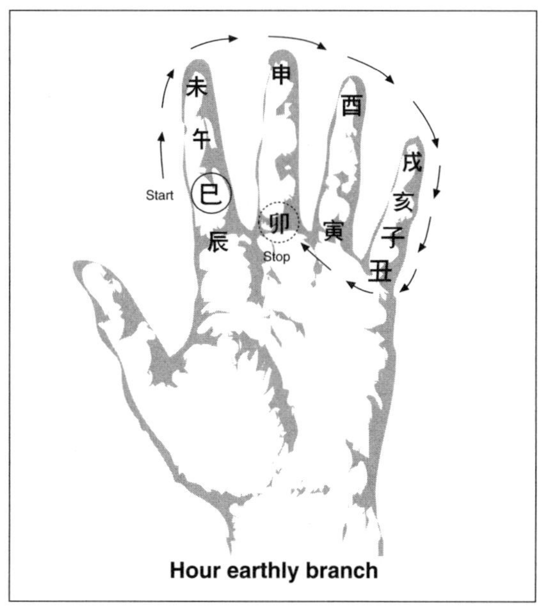

Hour earthly branch

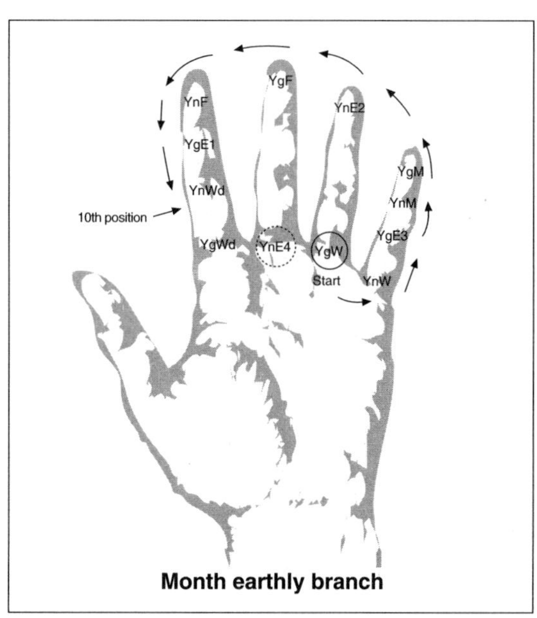

Month earthly branch

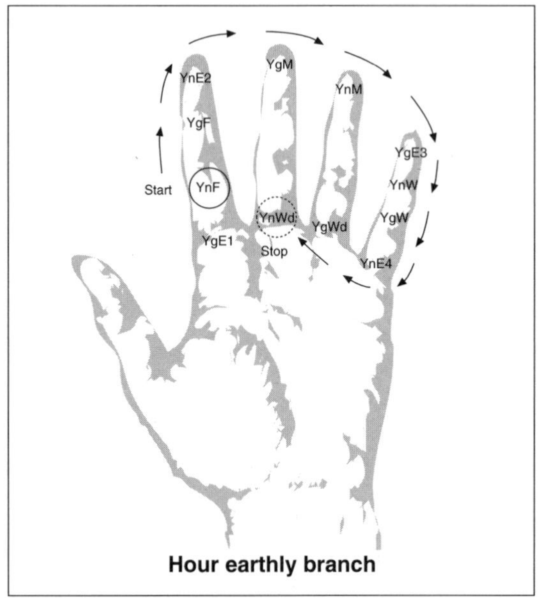

Hour earthly branch

**Evaluation**

This *yang* earth person was born in the winter month of 亥 *yin* water when water is strongest. Strong water influence can be found in the year and month pillars. Fortunately, there is fire support from the hour pillar. This person is, therefore, a weak earth person.

**Favourable Elements**

Fire, earth and wood (to strengthen the fire).

**Unfavourable Elements**

Water, which is already too strong and metal, which will generate more water and draw energy from earth.

**House Of Conception**

This pillar of wood for both the heavenly stem and the earthly branch indicates that the man will have one child (wood is an earth man's child).

If this person is a lady, she may encounter difficulty during the birth. This is because the pillar of conception is strong wood which destroys her self element of earth.

**Month Pillar**

The heavenly stem and earthly branch of the month pillar are of the same element, indicating the same person. In other words, his father is strong as he is in season (water is strong in winter).

**Day Pillar**

The day pillar is also of the same element. This means that he and his spouse will enjoy good fortune together and have a close, harmonious relationship, especially since earth is a favourable element to him.

**Hour Pillar**

This pillar of fire is excellent for him. His children (the hour pillar represents children) will be filial. Because fire is the symbol for an earth person's mother, fire over fire in the hour pillar means that he has a strong mother. The symbol of mother in his hour pillar also means that his mother will live to a ripe old age.

# THE THOUSAND YEAR CALENDAR

## Index For Abbreviations Used

| HEAVENLY STEM (H) | | | | EARTHLY BRANCH (E) | | | | | |
|---|---|---|---|---|---|---|---|---|---|---|
| Abbr. | Element | Chinese Character | | Month | Abbr. | Element | Chinese Character | | Animal Sign |
| Yg Wd | *Yang* Wood | 甲 | jǐa | Feb/Mar | Yg Wd | *Yang* Wood | 寅 | yín | Tiger |
| Yn Wd | *Yin* Wood | 乙 | yǐ | Mar/April | Yn Wd | *Yin* Wood | 卯 | mǎo | Rabbit |
| Yg F | *Yang* Fire | 丙 | bǐng | April/May | Yg E1 | *Yang* Earth | 辰 | chén | Dragon |
| Yn F | *Yin* Fire | 丁 | dīng | May/June | Yn F | *Yin* Fire | 巳 | sì | Snake |
| Yg E | *Yang* Earth | 戊 | wù | June/July | Yg F | *Yang* Fire | 午 | wǔ | Horse |
| Yn E | *Yin* Earth | 己 | jǐ | July/Aug | Yn E2 | *Yin* Earth | 未 | wèi | Goat |
| Yg M | *Yang* Metal | 庚 | gēng | Aug/Sept | Yg M | *Yang* Metal | 申 | shēn | Monkey |
| Yn M | *Yin* Metal | 辛 | xīn | Sept/Oct | Yn M | *Yin* Metal | 酉 | yǒu | Rooster |
| Yg W | *Yang* Water | 壬 | rén | Oct/Nov | Yg E3 | *Yang* Earth | 戌 | xū | Dog |
| Yn W | *Yin* Water | 癸 | guǐ | Nov/Dec | Yn W | *Yin* Water | 亥 | hài | Pig |
| | | | | Dec/Jan | Yg W | *Yang* Water | 子 | zǐ | Rat |
| | | | | Jan/Feb | Yn E4 | *Yin* Earth | 丑 | chǒu | Ox |

# YEAR OF THE RAT

| | H | E | H | E | H | E | H | E | H | E | H | E | H | E | H | E | H | E | H | E | H | E | H | E | |
|---|---|---|---|---|---|---|---|---|---|---|---|---|---|---|---|---|---|---|---|---|---|---|---|---|---|
| YEAR | YEAR | | 1912 | | | | | | | | | | | | | | | | | | 1913 | | | | |
| | Yg W | Yg W | | | | | | | | | | | | | | | | | | | | | | | |
| MONTH | 5 Feb - 5 Mar | | 6 Mar - 4 Apr | | 5 Apr - 5 May | | 6 May - 5 June | | 6 June - 6 Jul | | 7 Jul - 7 Aug | | 8 Aug - 7 Sep | | 8 Sep - 8 Oct | | 9 Oct - 7 Nov | | 8 Nov- 6 Dec | | 7 Dec - 5 Jan | | 6 Jan -3 Feb | | |
| | Yg W | Yg Wd | Yn W | Yn Wd | Yg Wd | Yg E1 | Yn Wd | Yn F | Yg F | Yg F | Yn F | Yn E2 | Yg E | Yg M | Yn E | Yn M | Yg M | Yg E3 | Yn M | Yn W | Yg W | Yg W | Yn W | Yn E4 | |
| Starting time | 1st day | Mid-pt | 1st day | Mid-pt | 1st day | Mid-pt | 1st day | Mid-pt | 1st day | Mid-pt | 1st day | Mid-pt | 1st day | Mid-pt | 1st day | Mid-pt | 1st day | Mid-pt | 1st day | Mid-pt | 1st day | Mid-pt | 1st day | Mid-pt | |
| Date | 5 | 20 | 6 | 21 | 5 | 20 | 6 | 21 | 6 | 22 | 7 | 23 | 8 | 23 | 8 | 23 | 9 | 24 | 8 | 22 | 7 | 22 | 6 | 20 | |
| Hour | | 0756 | 0621 | 0729 | 1148 | 1919 | 0547 | 1857 | 1028 | 0317 | 2057 | 1414 | 0637 | 2102 | 0906 | 1808 | 0007 | 0250 | 0239 | 2348 | 1859 | 1245 | 0558 | 2319 | |
| DATE 4 | | | | | | | | | | | | | | | | | | | | | | | | | 4 |
| 5 | Yn M | Yn W | | | Yn M | Yn W | | | | | | | | | | | | | | | | | | | 5 |
| 6 | Yg W | Yg W | Yn M | Yn F | Yg W | Yg W | Yg W | Yg F | Yn W | Yn E4 | | | | | | | | | | | | | Yn F | Yn W | 6 |
| 7 | Yn W | Yn E4 | Yg W | Yg F | Yn W | Yn E4 | Yn W | Yn E2 | Yg Wd | Yg Wd | Yg Wd | Yg M | | | | | | | | | Yn F | Yn F | Yg E | Yg W | 7 |
| 8 | Yg Wd | Yg Wd | Yn W | Yn E2 | Yg Wd | Yg Wd | Yg Wd | Yg M | Yn Wd | Yn Wd | Yn Wd | Yn M | Yg F | Yg E1 | Yn F | Yn W | | | Yg E | Yg W | Yg E | Yg F | Yn E | Yn E4 | 8 |
| 9 | Yn Wd | Yn Wd | Yg Wd | Yg M | Yn Wd | Yn Wd | Yn Wd | Yn M | Yg F | Yg E1 | Yg F | Yg E3 | Yn F | Yn F | Yg E | Yg W | Yg E | Yg F | Yn E | Yn E4 | Yn E | Yn E2 | Yg M | Yg Wd | 9 |
| 10 | Yg F | Yg E1 | Yn Wd | Yn M | Yg F | Yg E1 | Yg F | Yg E3 | Yn F | Yn F | Yn F | Yn W | Yg E | Yg F | Yn E | Yn E4 | Yn E | Yn E2 | Yg M | Yg Wd | Yg M | Yg M | Yn M | Yn Wd | 10 |
| 11 | Yn F | Yn F | Yg F | Yg E3 | Yn F | Yn F | Yn F | Yn W | Yg E | Yg F | Yg E | Yg W | Yn E | Yn E2 | Yg M | Yg Wd | Yg M | Yg M | Yn M | Yn Wd | Yn M | Yn M | Yg W | Yg E1 | 11 |
| 12 | Yg E | Yg F | Yn F | Yn W | Yg E | Yg F | Yg E | Yg W | Yn E | Yn E2 | Yn E | Yn E4 | Yg M | Yg M | Yn M | Yn Wd | Yn M | Yn M | Yg W | Yg E1 | Yg W | Yg E3 | Yn W | Yn F | 12 |
| 13 | Yn E | Yn E2 | Yg E | Yg W | Yn E | Yn E2 | Yn E | Yn E4 | Yg M | Yg M | Yg M | Yg Wd | Yn M | Yn M | Yg W | Yg E1 | Yg W | Yg E3 | Yn W | Yn F | Yn W | Yn W | Yg Wd | Yg F | 13 |
| 14 | Yg M | Yg M | Yn E | Yn E4 | Yg M | Yg M | Yg M | Yg Wd | Yn M | Yn M | Yn M | Yn Wd | Yg W | Yg E3 | Yn W | Yn F | Yn W | Yn W | Yg Wd | Yg F | Yg Wd | Yg W | Yn Wd | Yn E2 | 14 |
| 15 | Yn M | Yn M | Yg M | Yg Wd | Yn M | Yn M | Yn M | Yn Wd | Yg W | Yg E3 | Yg W | Yg E1 | Yn W | Yn W | Yg Wd | Yg F | Yg Wd | Yg W | Yn Wd | Yn E2 | Yn Wd | Yn E4 | Yg F | Yg M | 15 |
| 16 | Yg W | Yg E3 | Yn M | Yn Wd | Yg W | Yg E3 | Yg W | Yg E1 | Yn W | Yn W | Yn W | Yn F | Yg Wd | Yg W | Yn Wd | Yn E2 | Yn Wd | Yn E4 | Yg F | Yg M | Yg F | Yg Wd | Yn F | Yn M | 16 |
| 17 | Yn W | Yn W | Yg W | Yg E1 | Yn W | Yn W | Yn W | Yn F | Yg Wd | Yg W | Yg Wd | Yg F | Yn Wd | Yn E4 | Yg F | Yg M | Yg F | Yg Wd | Yn F | Yn M | Yn F | Yn Wd | Yg E | Yg E3 | 17 |
| 18 | Yg Wd | Yg W | Yn W | Yn F | Yg Wd | Yg W | Yg Wd | Yg F | Yn Wd | Yn E4 | Yn Wd | Yn E2 | Yg F | Yg Wd | Yn F | Yn M | Yn F | Yn Wd | Yg E | Yg E3 | Yg E | Yg E1 | Yn E | Yn W | 18 |
| 19 | Yn Wd | Yn E4 | Yg Wd | Yg F | Yn Wd | Yn E4 | Yn Wd | Yn E2 | Yg F | Yg Wd | Yg F | Yg M | Yn F | Yn Wd | Yg E | Yg E3 | Yg E | Yg E1 | Yn E | Yn W | Yn E | Yn F | Yg M | Yg W | 19 |
| 20 | Yg F | Yg Wd | Yn Wd | Yn E2 | Yg F | Yg Wd | Yg F | Yg M | Yn F | Yn Wd | Yn F | Yn M | Yg E | Yg E1 | Yn E | Yn W | Yn E | Yn F | Yg M | Yg W | Yg M | Yg F | Yn M | Yn E4 | 20 |
| 21 | Yn F | Yn Wd | Yg F | Yg M | Yn F | Yn Wd | Yn F | Yn M | Yg E | Yg E1 | Yg E | Yg E3 | Yn E | Yn F | Yg M | Yg W | Yg M | Yg F | Yn M | Yn E4 | Yn M | Yn E2 | Yg W | Yg Wd | 21 |
| 22 | Yg E | Yg E1 | Yn F | Yn M | Yg E | Yg E1 | Yg E | Yg E3 | Yn E | Yn F | Yn E | Yn W | Yg M | Yg F | Yn M | Yn E4 | Yn M | Yn E2 | Yg W | Yg Wd | Yg W | Yg M | Yn W | Yn Wd | 22 |
| 23 | Yn E | Yn F | Yg E | Yg E3 | Yn E | Yn F | Yn E | Yn W | Yg M | Yg F | Yg M | Yg W | Yn M | Yn E2 | Yg W | Yg Wd | Yg W | Yg M | Yn W | Yn Wd | Yn W | Yn M | Yg Wd | Yg E1 | 23 |
| 24 | Yg M | Yg F | Yn E | Yn W | Yg M | Yg F | Yg M | Yg W | Yn M | Yn E2 | Yn M | Yn E4 | Yg W | Yg M | Yn W | Yn Wd | Yn W | Yn M | Yg Wd | Yg E1 | Yg Wd | Yg E3 | Yn Wd | Yn F | 24 |
| 25 | Yn M | Yn E2 | Yg M | Yg W | Yn M | Yn E2 | Yn M | Yn E4 | Yg W | Yg M | Yg W | Yg Wd | Yn W | Yn M | Yg Wd | Yg E1 | Yg Wd | Yg E3 | Yn Wd | Yn F | Yn Wd | Yn W | Yg F | Yg F | 25 |
| 26 | Yg W | Yg M | Yn M | Yn E4 | Yg W | Yg M | Yg W | Yg Wd | Yn W | Yn M | Yn W | Yn Wd | Yg Wd | Yg E3 | Yn Wd | Yn F | Yn Wd | Yn W | Yg F | Yg F | Yg F | Yg W | Yn F | Yn E2 | 26 |
| 27 | Yn W | Yn M | Yg W | Yg Wd | Yn W | Yn M | Yn W | Yn Wd | Yg Wd | Yg E3 | Yg Wd | Yg E1 | Yn Wd | Yn W | Yg F | Yg F | Yg F | Yg W | Yn F | Yn E2 | Yn F | Yn E4 | Yg E | Yg M | 27 |
| 28 | Yg Wd | Yg E3 | Yn W | Yn Wd | Yg Wd | Yg E3 | Yg Wd | Yg E1 | Yn Wd | Yn W | Yn Wd | Yn F | Yg F | Yg W | Yn F | Yn E2 | Yn F | Yn E4 | Yg E | Yg M | Yg E | Yg Wd | Yn E | Yn M | 28 |
| 29 | Yn Wd | Yn W | Yg Wd | Yg E1 | Yn Wd | Yn W | Yn Wd | Yn F | Yg F | Yg W | Yg F | Yg F | Yn F | Yn E4 | Yg E | Yg M | Yg E | Yg Wd | Yn E | Yn M | Yn E | Yn Wd | Yg M | Yg E3 | 29 |
| 30 | | | Yn Wd | Yn F | Yg F | Yg W | Yg F | Yg F | Yn F | Yn E4 | Yn F | Yn E2 | Yg E | Yg Wd | Yn E | Yn M | Yn E | Yn Wd | Yg M | Yg E3 | Yg M | Yg E1 | Yn M | Yn W | 30 |
| 31 | | | Yg F | Yg F | | | Yn F | Yn E2 | | | Yg E | Yg M | Yn E | Yn Wd | | | Yg M | Yg E1 | | | Yn M | Yn F | Yg W | Yg W | 31 |
| 1 | Yg F | Yg W | Yn F | Yn E2 | Yn F | Yn E4 | Yg E | Yg M | Yg E | Yg Wd | Yn E | Yn M | Yg M | Yg E1 | Yg M | Yg E3 | Yn M | Yn F | Yn M | Yn W | Yg W | Yg F | Yn W | Yn E4 | 1 |
| 2 | Yn F | Yn E4 | Yg E | Yg M | Yg E | Yg Wd | Yn E | Yn M | Yn E | Yn Wd | Yg M | Yg E3 | Yn M | Yn F | Yn M | Yn W | Yg W | Yg F | Yg W | Yg W | Yn W | Yn E2 | Yg Wd | Yg Wd | 2 |
| 3 | Yg E | Yg Wd | Yn E | Yn M | Yn E | Yn Wd | Yg M | Yg E3 | Yg M | Yg E1 | Yn M | Yn W | Yg W | Yg F | Yg W | Yg W | Yn W | Yn E2 | Yn W | Yn E4 | Yg Wd | Yg M | Yn Wd | Yn Wd | 3 |
| 4 | Yn E | Yn Wd | Yg M | Yg E3 | Yg M | Yg E1 | Yn M | Yn W | Yn M | Yn F | Yg W | Yg W | Yn W | Yn E2 | Yn W | Yn E4 | Yg Wd | Yg M | Yg Wd | Yg Wd | Yn Wd | Yn M | | | 4 |
| 5 | Yg M | Yg E1 | | | Yn M | Yn F | Yg W | Yg W | Yg W | Yg F | Yn W | Yn E4 | Yg Wd | Yg M | Yg Wd | Yg Wd | Yn Wd | Yn M | Yn Wd | Yn Wd | Yg F | Yg E3 | | | 5 |
| 6 | | | | | | | | | Yn W | Yn E2 | Yg Wd | Yg Wd | Yn Wd | Yn M | Yn Wd | Yn Wd | Yg F | Yg E3 | Yg F | Yg E1 | | | | | 6 |
| 7 | | | | | | | | | | | Yn Wd | Yn Wd | Yg F | Yg E3 | Yg F | Yg E1 | Yn F | Yn W | | | | | | | 7 |
| 8 | | | | | | | | | | | | | | | Yn F | Yn F | | | | | | | | | 8 |

# YEAR OF THE OX

| | H | E | H | E | H | E | H | E | H | E | H | E | H | E | H | E | H | E | H | E | H | E | H | E | |
|---|---|---|---|---|---|---|---|---|---|---|---|---|---|---|---|---|---|---|---|---|---|---|---|---|---|
| YEAR | YEAR | | 1913 | | | | | | | | | | | | | | | | | | | 1914 | | | |
| | Yn W | Yn E4 | | | | | | | | | | | | | | | | | | | | | | | |
| MONTH | 4 Feb - 5 Mar | | 6 Mar - 4 Apr | | 5 Apr - 5 May | | 6 May - 5 June | | 6 June - 7 Jul | | 8 Jul - 7 Aug | | 8 Aug - 7 Sep | | 8 Sep - 8 Oct | | 9 Oct - 7 Nov | | 8 Nov- 7 Dec | | 8 Dec - 5 Jan | | 6 Jan -3 Feb | | |
| | Yg Wd | Yg Wd | Yn Wd | Yn Wd | Yg F | Yg E1 | Yn F | Yn F | Yg E | Yg F | Yn E | Yn E2 | Yg M | Yg M | Yn M | Yn M | Yg W | Yg E3 | Yn W | Yn W | Yg Wd | Yg W | Yn Wd | Yn E4 | |
| Starting time | 1st day | Mid-pt | 1st day | Mid-pt | 1st day | Mid-pt | 1st day | Mid-pt | 1st day | Mid-pt | 1st day | Mid-pt | 1st day | Mid-pt | 1st day | Mid-pt | 1st day | Mid-pt | 1st day | Mid-pt | 1st day | Mid-pt | 1st day | Mid-pt | |
| Date | 4 | 19 | 6 | 21 | 5 | 21 | 6 | 22 | 6 | 22 | 8 | 23 | 8 | 24 | 8 | 23 | 9 | 24 | 8 | 23 | 8 | 22 | 6 | 21 | |
| Hour | 1743 | 1345 | 1209 | 1318 | 1736 | 0105 | 1135 | 0050 | 1614 | 0910 | 0239 | 2004 | 1216 | 0248 | 1443 | 2353 | 0544 | 0935 | 0818 | 0535 | 0041 | 1835 | 1143 | 0512 | |
| DATE 4 | Yg F | Yg E1 | | | | | | | | | | | | | | | | | | | | | | | 4 |
| 5 | Yn F | Yn F | | | Yg F | Yg E1 | | | | | | | | | | | | | | | | | | | 5 |
| 6 | Yg E | Yg F | Yg F | Yg E3 | Yn F | Yn F | Yn F | Yn W | Yg E | Yg F | | | | | | | | | | | | | Yg W | Yg E1 | 6 |
| 7 | Yn E | Yn E2 | Yn F | Yn W | Yg E | Yg F | Yg E | Yg W | Yn E | Yn E2 | | | | | | | | | | | | | Yn W | Yn F | 7 |
| 8 | Yg M | Yg M | Yg E | Yg W | Yn E | Yn E2 | Yn E | Yn E4 | Yg M | Yg M | Yg M | Yg Wd | Yn M | Yn M | Yg W | Yg E1 | | | Yn W | Yn F | Yn W | Yn W | Yg Wd | Yg F | 8 |
| 9 | Yn M | Yn M | Yn E | Yn E4 | Yg M | Yg M | Yg M | Yg Wd | Yn M | Yn M | Yn M | Yn Wd | Yg W | Yg E3 | Yn W | Yn F | Yn W | Yn W | Yg Wd | Yg F | Yg Wd | Yg W | Yn Wd | Yn E2 | 9 |
| 10 | Yg W | Yg E3 | Yg M | Yg Wd | Yn M | Yn M | Yn M | Yn Wd | Yg W | Yg E3 | Yg W | Yg E1 | Yn W | Yn W | Yg Wd | Yg F | Yg Wd | Yg W | Yn Wd | Yn E2 | Yn Wd | Yn E4 | Yg F | Yg M | 10 |
| 11 | Yn W | Yn W | Yn M | Yn Wd | Yg W | Yg E3 | Yg W | Yg E1 | Yn W | Yn W | Yn W | Yn F | Yg Wd | Yg W | Yn Wd | Yn E2 | Yn Wd | Yn E4 | Yg F | Yg M | Yg F | Yg Wd | Yn F | Yn M | 11 |
| 12 | Yg Wd | Yg W | Yg W | Yg E1 | Yn W | Yn W | Yn W | Yn F | Yg Wd | Yg W | Yg Wd | Yg F | Yn Wd | Yn E4 | Yg F | Yg M | Yg F | Yg Wd | Yn F | Yn M | Yn F | Yn Wd | Yg E | Yg E3 | 12 |
| 13 | Yn Wd | Yn E4 | Yn W | Yn F | Yg Wd | Yg W | Yg Wd | Yg F | Yn Wd | Yn E4 | Yn Wd | Yn E2 | Yg F | Yg Wd | Yn F | Yn M | Yn F | Yn Wd | Yg E | Yg E3 | Yg E | Yg E1 | Yn E | Yn W | 13 |
| 14 | Yg F | Yg Wd | Yg Wd | Yg F | Yn Wd | Yn E4 | Yn Wd | Yn E2 | Yg F | Yg Wd | Yg F | Yg M | Yn F | Yn Wd | Yg E | Yg E3 | Yg E | Yg E1 | Yn E | Yn W | Yn E | Yn F | Yg M | Yg W | 14 |
| 15 | Yn F | Yn Wd | Yn Wd | Yn E2 | Yg F | Yg Wd | Yg F | Yg M | Yn F | Yn Wd | Yn F | Yn M | Yg E | Yg E1 | Yn E | Yn W | Yn E | Yn F | Yg M | Yg W | Yg M | Yg F | Yn M | Yn E4 | 15 |
| 16 | Yg E | Yg E1 | Yg F | Yg M | Yn F | Yn Wd | Yn F | Yn M | Yg E | Yg E1 | Yg E | Yg E3 | Yn E | Yn F | Yg M | Yg W | Yg M | Yg F | Yn M | Yn E4 | Yn M | Yn E2 | Yg W | Yg Wd | 16 |
| 17 | Yn E | Yn F | Yn F | Yn M | Yg E | Yg E1 | Yg E | Yg E3 | Yn E | Yn F | Yn E | Yn W | Yg M | Yg F | Yn M | Yn E4 | Yn M | Yn E2 | Yg W | Yg Wd | Yg W | Yg M | Yn W | Yn Wd | 17 |
| 18 | Yg M | Yg F | Yg E | Yg E3 | Yn E | Yn F | Yn E | Yn W | Yg M | Yg F | Yg M | Yg W | Yn M | Yn E2 | Yg W | Yg Wd | Yg W | Yg M | Yn W | Yn Wd | Yn W | Yn M | Yg Wd | Yg E1 | 18 |
| 19 | Yn M | Yn E2 | Yn E | Yn W | Yg M | Yg F | Yg M | Yg W | Yn M | Yn E2 | Yn M | Yn E4 | Yg W | Yg M | Yn W | Yn Wd | Yn W | Yn M | Yg Wd | Yg E1 | Yg Wd | Yg E3 | Yn Wd | Yn F | 19 |
| 20 | Yg W | Yg M | Yg M | Yg W | Yn M | Yn E2 | Yn M | Yn E4 | Yg W | Yg M | Yg W | Yg Wd | Yn W | Yn M | Yg Wd | Yg E1 | Yg Wd | Yg E3 | Yn Wd | Yn F | Yn Wd | Yn W | Yg F | Yg F | 20 |
| 21 | Yn W | Yn M | Yn M | Yn E4 | Yg W | Yg M | Yg W | Yg Wd | Yn W | Yn M | Yn W | Yn Wd | Yg Wd | Yg E3 | Yn Wd | Yn F | Yn Wd | Yn W | Yg F | Yg F | Yg F | Yg W | Yn F | Yn E2 | 21 |
| 22 | Yg Wd | Yg E3 | Yg W | Yg Wd | Yn W | Yn M | Yn W | Yn Wd | Yg Wd | Yg E3 | Yg Wd | Yg E1 | Yn Wd | Yn W | Yg F | Yg F | Yg F | Yg W | Yn F | Yn E2 | Yn F | Yn E4 | Yg E | Yg M | 22 |
| 23 | Yn Wd | Yn W | Yn W | Yn Wd | Yg Wd | Yg E3 | Yg Wd | Yg E1 | Yn Wd | Yn W | Yn Wd | Yn F | Yg F | Yg W | Yn F | Yn E2 | Yn F | Yn E4 | Yg E | Yg M | Yg E | Yg Wd | Yn E | Yn M | 23 |
| 24 | Yg F | Yg W | Yg Wd | Yg E1 | Yn Wd | Yn W | Yn Wd | Yn F | Yg F | Yg W | Yg F | Yg F | Yn F | Yn E4 | Yg E | Yg M | Yg E | Yg Wd | Yn E | Yn M | Yn E | Yn Wd | Yg M | Yg E3 | 24 |
| 25 | Yn F | Yn E4 | Yn Wd | Yn F | Yg F | Yg W | Yg F | Yg F | Yn F | Yn E4 | Yn F | Yn E2 | Yg E | Yg Wd | Yn E | Yn M | Yn E | Yn Wd | Yg M | Yg E3 | Yg M | Yg E1 | Yn M | Yn W | 25 |
| 26 | Yg E | Yg Wd | Yg F | Yg F | Yn F | Yn E4 | Yn F | Yn E2 | Yg E | Yg Wd | Yg E | Yg M | Yn E | Yn Wd | Yg M | Yg E3 | Yg M | Yg E1 | Yn M | Yn W | Yn M | Yn F | Yg W | Yg W | 26 |
| 27 | Yn E | Yn Wd | Yn F | Yn E2 | Yg E | Yg Wd | Yg E | Yg M | Yn E | Yn Wd | Yn E | Yn M | Yg M | Yg E1 | Yn M | Yn W | Yn M | Yn F | Yg W | Yg W | Yg W | Yg F | Yn W | Yn E4 | 27 |
| 28 | Yg M | Yg E1 | Yg E | Yg M | Yn E | Yn Wd | Yn E | Yn M | Yg M | Yg E1 | Yg M | Yg E3 | Yn M | Yn F | Yg W | Yg W | Yg W | Yg F | Yn W | Yn E4 | Yn W | Yn E2 | Yg Wd | Yg Wd | 28 |
| 29 | | | Yn E | Yn M | Yg M | Yg E1 | Yg M | Yg E3 | Yn M | Yn F | Yn M | Yn W | Yg W | Yg F | Yn W | Yn E4 | Yn W | Yn E2 | Yg Wd | Yg Wd | Yg Wd | Yg M | Yn Wd | Yn Wd | 29 |
| 30 | | | Yg M | Yg E3 | Yn M | Yn F | Yn M | Yn W | Yg W | Yg F | Yg W | Yg W | Yn W | Yn E2 | Yg Wd | Yg Wd | Yg Wd | Yg M | Yn Wd | Yn Wd | Yn Wd | Yn M | Yg F | Yg E1 | 30 |
| 31 | | | Yn M | Yn W | | | Yg W | Yg W | | | Yn W | Yn E4 | Yg Wd | Yg M | | | Yn Wd | Yn M | | | Yg F | Yg E3 | Yn F | Yn F | 31 |
| 1 | Yn M | Yn F | Yg W | Yg W | Yg W | Yg F | Yn W | Yn E4 | Yn W | Yn E2 | Yg Wd | Yg Wd | Yn Wd | Yn M | Yn Wd | Yn Wd | Yg F | Yg E3 | Yg F | Yg E1 | Yn F | Yn W | Yg E | Yg F | 1 |
| 2 | Yg W | Yg F | Yn W | Yn E4 | Yn W | Yn E2 | Yg Wd | Yg Wd | Yg Wd | Yg M | Yn Wd | Yn Wd | Yg F | Yg E3 | Yg F | Yg E1 | Yn F | Yn W | Yn F | Yn F | Yg E | Yg W | Yn E | Yn E2 | 2 |
| 3 | Yn W | Yn E2 | Yg Wd | Yg Wd | Yg Wd | Yg M | Yn Wd | Yn Wd | Yn Wd | Yn M | Yg F | Yg E1 | Yn F | Yn W | Yn F | Yn F | Yg E | Yg W | Yg E | Yg F | Yn E | Yn E4 | Yg M | Yg M | 3 |
| 4 | Yg Wd | Yg M | Yn Wd | Yn Wd | Yn Wd | Yn M | Yg F | Yg E1 | Yg F | Yg E3 | Yn F | Yn F | Yg E | Yg W | Yg E | Yg F | Yn E | Yn E4 | Yn E | Yn E2 | Yg M | Yg Wd | | | 4 |
| 5 | Yn Wd | Yn M | | | Yg F | Yg E3 | Yn F | Yn F | Yn F | Yn W | Yg E | Yg F | Yn E | Yn E4 | Yn E | Yn E2 | Yg M | Yg Wd | Yg M | Yg M | Yn M | Yn Wd | | | 5 |
| 6 | | | | | | | | | Yg E | Yg W | Yn E | Yn E2 | Yg M | Yg Wd | Yg M | Yg M | Yn M | Yn Wd | Yn M | Yn M | | | | | 6 |
| 7 | | | | | | | | | Yn E | Yn E4 | Yg M | Yg M | Yn M | Yn Wd | Yn M | Yn M | Yg W | Yg E1 | Yg W | Yg E3 | | | | | 7 |
| 8 | | | | | | | | | | | | | | | Yg W | Yg E3 | | | | | | | | | 8 |

# YEAR OF THE TIGER

| YEAR | H | E | H | E | H | E | H | E | H | E | H | E | H | E | H | E | H | E | H | E | H | E | H | E | |
|---|---|---|---|---|---|---|---|---|---|---|---|---|---|---|---|---|---|---|---|---|---|---|---|---|---|
| | YEAR | | 1914 | | | | | | | | | | | | | | | | | | 1915 | | | | |
| | Yg Wd | Yg Wd | | | | | | | | | | | | | | | | | | | | | | | |
| MONTH | 4 Feb - 5 Mar | | 6 Mar - 4 Apr | | 5 Apr - 5 May | | 6 May - 5 June | | 6 June - 7 Jul | | 8 Jul - 7 Aug | | 8 Aug - 7 Sep | | 8 Sep - 8 Oct | | 9 Oct - 7 Nov | | 8 Nov- 6 Dec | | 7 Dec - 5 Jan | | 6 Jan -4 Feb | | |
| | Yg F | Yg Wd | Yn F | Yn Wd | Yg E | Yg E1 | Yn E | Yn F | Yg M | Yg F | Yn M | Yn E2 | Yg W | Yg M | Yn W | Yn M | Yg Wd | Yg E3 | Yn Wd | Yn W | Yg F | Yg W | Yn F | Yn E4 | |
| Starting time | 1st day | Mid-pt | 1st day | Mid-pt | 1st day | Mid-pt | 1st day | Mid-pt | 1st day | Mid-pt | 1st day | Mid-pt | 1st day | Mid-pt | 1st day | Mid-pt | 1st day | Mid-pt | 1st day | Mid-pt | 1st day | Mid-pt | 1st day | Mid-pt | |
| Date | 4 | 19 | 6 | 21 | 5 | 21 | 6 | 22 | 6 | 22 | 8 | 24 | 8 | 24 | 8 | 24 | 9 | 24 | 8 | 22 | 7 | 23 | 6 | 21 | |
| Hour | 2329 | 1938 | 1756 | 1911 | 2322 | 0653 | 1720 | 0638 | 2200 | 1455 | 0828 | 0147 | 1806 | 0830 | 2033 | 0534 | 1135 | 1418 | 1411 | 1121 | 0637 | 0023 | 1741 | 1100 | |
| DATE 4 | Yn M | Yn M | | | | | | | | | | | | | | | | | | | | | | | 4 |
| 5 | Yg W | Yg E3 | | | Yn M | Yn M | | | | | | | | | | | | | | | | | | | 5 |
| 6 | Yn W | Yn W | Yn M | Yn Wd | Yg W | Yg E3 | Yg W | Yg E1 | Yn W | Yn W | | | | | | | | | | | | | Yn F | Yn M | 6 |
| 7 | Yg Wd | Yg W | Yg W | Yg E1 | Yn W | Yn W | Yn W | Yn F | Yg Wd | Yg W | | | | | | | | | | | Yn F | Yn Wd | Yg E | Yg E3 | 7 |
| 8 | Yn Wd | Yn E4 | Yn W | Yn F | Yg Wd | Yg W | Yg Wd | Yg F | Yn Wd | Yn E4 | Yn Wd | Yn E2 | Yg F | Yg Wd | Yn F | Yn M | | | Yg E | Yg E3 | Yg E | Yg E1 | Yn E | Yn W | 8 |
| 9 | Yg F | Yg Wd | Yg Wd | Yg F | Yn Wd | Yn E4 | Yn Wd | Yn E2 | Yg F | Yg Wd | Yg F | Yg M | Yn F | Yn Wd | Yg E | Yg E3 | Yg E | Yg E1 | Yn E | Yn W | Yn E | Yn F | Yg M | Yg W | 9 |
| 10 | Yn F | Yn Wd | Yn Wd | Yn E2 | Yg F | Yg Wd | Yg F | Yg M | Yn F | Yn Wd | Yn F | Yn M | Yg E | Yg E1 | Yn E | Yn W | Yn E | Yn F | Yg M | Yg W | Yg M | Yg F | Yn M | Yn E4 | 10 |
| 11 | Yg E | Yg E1 | Yg F | Yg M | Yn F | Yn Wd | Yn F | Yn M | Yg E | Yg E1 | Yg E | Yg E3 | Yn E | Yn F | Yg M | Yg W | Yg M | Yg F | Yn M | Yn E4 | Yn M | Yn E2 | Yg W | Yg Wd | 11 |
| 12 | Yn E | Yn F | Yn F | Yn M | Yg E | Yg E1 | Yg E | Yg E3 | Yn E | Yn F | Yn E | Yn W | Yg M | Yg F | Yn M | Yn E4 | Yn M | Yn E2 | Yg W | Yg Wd | Yg W | Yg M | Yn W | Yn Wd | 12 |
| 13 | Yg M | Yg F | Yg E | Yg E3 | Yn E | Yn F | Yn E | Yn W | Yg M | Yg F | Yg M | Yg W | Yn M | Yn E2 | Yg W | Yg Wd | Yg W | Yg M | Yn W | Yn Wd | Yn W | Yn M | Yg Wd | Yg E1 | 13 |
| 14 | Yn M | Yn E2 | Yn E | Yn W | Yg M | Yg F | Yg M | Yg W | Yn M | Yn E2 | Yn M | Yn E4 | Yg W | Yg M | Yn W | Yn Wd | Yn W | Yn M | Yg Wd | Yg E1 | Yg Wd | Yg E3 | Yn Wd | Yn F | 14 |
| 15 | Yg W | Yg M | Yg M | Yg W | Yn M | Yn E2 | Yn M | Yn E4 | Yg W | Yg M | Yg W | Yg Wd | Yn W | Yn M | Yg Wd | Yg E1 | Yg Wd | Yg E3 | Yn Wd | Yn F | Yn Wd | Yn W | Yg F | Yg F | 15 |
| 16 | Yn W | Yn M | Yn M | Yn E4 | Yg W | Yg M | Yg W | Yg Wd | Yn W | Yn M | Yn W | Yn Wd | Yg Wd | Yg E3 | Yn Wd | Yn F | Yn Wd | Yn W | Yg F | Yg F | Yg F | Yg W | Yn F | Yn E2 | 16 |
| 17 | Yg Wd | Yg E3 | Yg W | Yg Wd | Yn W | Yn M | Yn W | Yn Wd | Yg Wd | Yg E3 | Yg Wd | Yg E1 | Yn Wd | Yn W | Yg F | Yg F | Yg F | Yg W | Yn F | Yn E2 | Yn F | Yn E4 | Yg E | Yg M | 17 |
| 18 | Yn Wd | Yn W | Yn W | Yn Wd | Yg Wd | Yg E3 | Yg Wd | Yg E1 | Yn Wd | Yn W | Yn Wd | Yn F | Yg F | Yg W | Yn F | Yn E2 | Yn F | Yn E4 | Yg E | Yg M | Yg E | Yg Wd | Yn E | Yn M | 18 |
| 19 | Yg F | Yg W | Yg Wd | Yg E1 | Yn Wd | Yn W | Yn Wd | Yn F | Yg F | Yg W | Yg F | Yg F | Yn F | Yn E4 | Yg E | Yg M | Yg E | Yg Wd | Yn E | Yn M | Yn E | Yn Wd | Yg M | Yg E3 | 19 |
| 20 | Yn F | Yn E4 | Yn Wd | Yn F | Yg F | Yg W | Yg F | Yg F | Yn F | Yn E4 | Yn F | Yn E2 | Yg E | Yg Wd | Yn E | Yn M | Yn E | Yn Wd | Yg M | Yg E3 | Yg M | Yg E1 | Yn M | Yn W | 20 |
| 21 | Yg E | Yg Wd | Yg F | Yg F | Yn F | Yn E4 | Yn F | Yn E2 | Yg E | Yg Wd | Yg E | Yg M | Yn E | Yn Wd | Yg M | Yg E3 | Yg M | Yg E1 | Yn M | Yn W | Yn M | Yn F | Yg W | Yg W | 21 |
| 22 | Yn E | Yn Wd | Yn F | Yn E2 | Yg E | Yg Wd | Yg E | Yg M | Yn E | Yn Wd | Yn E | Yn M | Yg M | Yg E1 | Yn M | Yn W | Yn M | Yn F | Yg W | Yg W | Yg W | Yg F | Yn W | Yn E4 | 22 |
| 23 | Yg M | Yg E1 | Yg E | Yg M | Yn E | Yn Wd | Yn E | Yn M | Yg M | Yg E1 | Yg M | Yg E3 | Yn M | Yn F | Yg W | Yg W | Yg W | Yg F | Yn W | Yn E4 | Yn W | Yn E2 | Yg Wd | Yg Wd | 23 |
| 24 | Yn M | Yn F | Yn E | Yn M | Yg M | Yg E1 | Yg M | Yg E3 | Yn M | Yn F | Yn M | Yn W | Yg W | Yg F | Yn W | Yn E4 | Yn W | Yn E2 | Yg Wd | Yg Wd | Yg Wd | Yg M | Yn Wd | Yn Wd | 24 |
| 25 | Yg W | Yg F | Yg M | Yg E3 | Yn M | Yn F | Yn M | Yn W | Yg W | Yg F | Yg W | Yg W | Yn W | Yn E2 | Yg Wd | Yg Wd | Yg Wd | Yg M | Yn Wd | Yn Wd | Yn Wd | Yn M | Yg F | Yg E1 | 25 |
| 26 | Yn W | Yn E2 | Yn M | Yn W | Yg W | Yg F | Yg W | Yg W | Yn W | Yn E2 | Yn W | Yn E4 | Yg Wd | Yg M | Yn Wd | Yn Wd | Yn Wd | Yn M | Yg F | Yg E1 | Yg F | Yg E3 | Yn F | Yn F | 26 |
| 27 | Yg Wd | Yg M | Yg W | Yg W | Yn W | Yn E2 | Yn W | Yn E4 | Yg Wd | Yg M | Yg Wd | Yg Wd | Yn Wd | Yn M | Yg F | Yg E1 | Yg F | Yg E3 | Yn F | Yn F | Yn F | Yn W | Yg E | Yg F | 27 |
| 28 | Yn Wd | Yn M | Yn W | Yn E4 | Yg Wd | Yg M | Yg Wd | Yg Wd | Yn Wd | Yn M | Yn Wd | Yn Wd | Yg F | Yg E3 | Yn F | Yn F | Yn F | Yn W | Yg E | Yg F | Yg E | Yg W | Yn E | Yn E2 | 28 |
| 29 | | | Yg Wd | Yg Wd | Yn Wd | Yn M | Yn Wd | Yn Wd | Yg F | Yg E3 | Yg F | Yg E1 | Yn F | Yn W | Yg E | Yg F | Yg E | Yg W | Yn E | Yn E2 | Yn E | Yn E4 | Yg M | Yg M | 29 |
| 30 | | | Yn Wd | Yn Wd | Yg F | Yg E3 | Yg F | Yg E1 | Yn F | Yn W | Yn F | Yn F | Yg E | Yg W | Yn E | Yn E2 | Yn E | Yn E4 | Yg M | Yg M | Yg M | Yg Wd | Yn M | Yn M | 30 |
| 31 | | | Yg F | Yg E1 | | | Yn F | Yn F | | | Yg E | Yg F | Yn E | Yn E4 | | | Yg M | Yg Wd | | | Yn M | Yn Wd | Yg W | Yg E3 | 31 |
| 1 | Yg F | Yg E3 | Yn F | Yn F | Yn F | Yn W | Yg E | Yg F | Yg E | Yg W | Yn E | Yn E2 | Yg M | Yg M | Yg M | Yg M | Yn M | Yn Wd | Yn M | Yn M | Yg W | Yg E1 | Yn W | Yn W | 1 |
| 2 | Yn F | Yn W | Yg E | Yg F | Yg E | Yg W | Yn E | Yn E2 | Yn E | Yn E4 | Yg M | Yg M | Yn M | Yn Wd | Yn M | Yn M | Yg W | Yg E1 | Yg W | Yg E3 | Yn W | Yn F | Yg Wd | Yg W | 2 |
| 3 | Yg E | Yg W | Yn E | Yn E2 | Yn E | Yn E4 | Yg M | Yg M | Yg M | Yg Wd | Yn M | Yn M | Yg W | Yg E1 | Yg W | Yg E3 | Yn W | Yn F | Yn W | Yn W | Yg Wd | Yg F | Yn Wd | Yn E4 | 3 |
| 4 | Yn E | Yn E4 | Yg M | Yg M | Yg M | Yg Wd | Yn M | Yn M | Yn M | Yn Wd | Yg W | Yg E3 | Yn W | Yn F | Yn W | Yn W | Yg Wd | Yg F | Yg Wd | Yg W | Yn Wd | Yn E2 | Yg F | Yg Wd | 4 |
| 5 | Yg M | Yg Wd | | | Yg M | Yn Wd | Yg W | Yg E3 | Yg W | Yg E1 | Yn W | Yn W | Yg Wd | Yg F | Yg Wd | Yg W | Yn Wd | Yn E2 | Yn Wd | Yn E4 | Yg F | Yg M | | | 5 |
| 6 | | | | | | | | | Yn W | Yn F | Yg Wd | Yg W | Yn Wd | Yn E2 | Yn Wd | Yn E4 | Yg F | Yg M | Yg F | Yg Wd | | | | | 6 |
| 7 | | | | | | | | | Yg Wd | Yg F | Yn Wd | Yn E4 | Yg F | Yg M | Yg F | Yg Wd | Yn F | Yn M | | | | | | | 7 |
| 8 | | | | | | | | | | | | | | | Yn F | Yn Wd | | | | | | | | | 8 |

# YEAR OF THE RABBIT

| | H | E | H | E | H | E | H | E | H | E | H | E | H | E | H | E | H | E | H | E | H | E | H | E | |
|---|---|---|---|---|---|---|---|---|---|---|---|---|---|---|---|---|---|---|---|---|---|---|---|---|---|
| YEAR | YEAR Yn Wd | Yn Wd | 1915 | | | | | | | | | | | | | | | | | | | | 1916 | | |
| MONTH | 5 Feb - 5 Mar | | 6 Mar - 5 Apr | | 6 Apr - 5 May | | 6 May - 6 June | | 7 June - 7 Jul | | 8 Jul - 7 Aug | | 8 Aug - 8 Sep | | 9 Sep - 8 Oct | | 9 Oct - 7 Nov | | 8 Nov- 7 Dec | | 8 Dec - 5 Jan | | 6 Jan -4 Feb | | |
| | Yg E | Yg Wd | Yn E | Yn Wd | Yg M | Yg E1 | Yn M | Yn F | Yg W | Yg F | Yn W | Yn E2 | Yg Wd | Yg M | Yn Wd | Yn M | Yg F | Yg E3 | Yn F | Yn W | Yg E | Yg W | Yn E | Yn E4 | |
| Starting time | 1st day | Mid-pt | 1st day | Mid-pt | 1st day | Mid-pt | 1st day | Mid-pt | 1st day | Mid-pt | 1st day | Mid-pt | 1st day | Mid-pt | 1st day | Mid-pt | 1st day | Mid-pt | 1st day | Mid-pt | 1st day | Mid-pt | 1st day | Mid-pt | |
| Date | 5 | 20 | 6 | 22 | 6 | 21 | 6 | 22 | 7 | 22 | 8 | 24 | 8 | 24 | 9 | 24 | 9 | 24 | 8 | 23 | 8 | 23 | 6 | 21 | |
| Hour | 0526 | 0123 | 2348 | 0051 | 0510 | 1229 | 2303 | 1211 | 0340 | 2029 | 1408 | 0727 | 2348 | 1419 | 0217 | 1124 | 1721 | 2014 | 1958 | 1714 | 1224 | 0616 | 2328 | 1654 | |
| DATE 4 | | | | | | | | | | | | | | | | | | | | | | | | | 4 |
| 5 | Yn F | Yn Wd | | | | | | | | | | | | | | | | | | | | | | | 5 |
| 6 | Yg E | Yg E1 | Yg F | Yg M | Yn F | Yn Wd | Yn F | Yn M | | | | | | | | | | | | | | | Yg W | Yg Wd | 6 |
| 7 | Yn E | Yn F | Yn F | Yn M | Yg E | Yg E1 | Yg E | Yg E3 | Yn E | Yn F | | | | | | | | | | | | | Yn W | Yn Wd | 7 |
| 8 | Yg M | Yg F | Yg E | Yg E3 | Yn E | Yn F | Yn E | Yn W | Yg M | Yg F | Yg M | Yg W | Yn M | Yn E2 | | | | | Yn W | Yn Wd | Yn W | Yn M | Yg Wd | Yg E1 | 8 |
| 9 | Yn M | Yn E2 | Yn E | Yn W | Yg M | Yg F | Yg M | Yg W | Yn M | Yn E2 | Yn M | Yn E4 | Yg W | Yg M | Yn W | Yn Wd | Yn W | Yn M | Yg Wd | Yg E1 | Yg Wd | Yg E3 | Yn Wd | Yn F | 9 |
| 10 | Yg W | Yg M | Yg M | Yg W | Yn M | Yn E2 | Yn M | Yn E4 | Yg W | Yg M | Yg W | Yg Wd | Yn W | Yn M | Yg Wd | Yg E1 | Yg Wd | Yg E3 | Yn Wd | Yn F | Yn Wd | Yn W | Yg F | Yg F | 10 |
| 11 | Yn W | Yn M | Yn M | Yn E4 | Yg W | Yg M | Yg W | Yg Wd | Yn W | Yn M | Yn W | Yn Wd | Yg Wd | Yg E3 | Yn Wd | Yn F | Yn Wd | Yn W | Yg F | Yg F | Yg F | Yg W | Yn F | Yn E2 | 11 |
| 12 | Yg Wd | Yg E3 | Yg W | Yg Wd | Yn W | Yn M | Yn W | Yn Wd | Yg Wd | Yg E3 | Yg Wd | Yg E1 | Yn Wd | Yn W | Yg F | Yg F | Yg F | Yg W | Yn F | Yn E2 | Yn F | Yn E4 | Yg E | Yg M | 12 |
| 13 | Yn Wd | Yn W | Yn W | Yn Wd | Yg Wd | Yg E3 | Yg Wd | Yg E1 | Yn Wd | Yn W | Yn Wd | Yn F | Yg F | Yg W | Yn F | Yn E2 | Yn F | Yn E4 | Yg E | Yg M | Yg E | Yg Wd | Yn E | Yn M | 13 |
| 14 | Yg F | Yg W | Yg Wd | Yg E1 | Yn Wd | Yn W | Yn Wd | Yn F | Yg F | Yg W | Yg F | Yg F | Yn F | Yn E4 | Yg E | Yg M | Yg E | Yg Wd | Yn E | Yn M | Yn E | Yn Wd | Yg M | Yg E3 | 14 |
| 15 | Yn F | Yn E4 | Yn Wd | Yn F | Yg F | Yg W | Yg F | Yg F | Yn F | Yn E4 | Yn F | Yn E2 | Yg E | Yg Wd | Yn E | Yn M | Yn E | Yn Wd | Yg M | Yg E3 | Yg M | Yg E1 | Yn M | Yn W | 15 |
| 16 | Yg E | Yg Wd | Yg F | Yg F | Yn F | Yn E4 | Yn F | Yn E2 | Yg E | Yg Wd | Yg E | Yg M | Yn E | Yn Wd | Yg M | Yg E3 | Yg M | Yg E1 | Yn M | Yn W | Yn M | Yn F | Yg W | Yg W | 16 |
| 17 | Yn E | Yn Wd | Yn F | Yn E2 | Yg E | Yg Wd | Yg E | Yg M | Yn E | Yn Wd | Yn E | Yn M | Yg M | Yg E1 | Yn M | Yn W | Yn M | Yn F | Yg W | Yg W | Yg W | Yg F | Yn W | Yn E4 | 17 |
| 18 | Yg M | Yg E1 | Yg E | Yg M | Yn E | Yn Wd | Yn E | Yn M | Yg M | Yg E1 | Yg M | Yg E3 | Yn M | Yn F | Yg W | Yg W | Yg W | Yg F | Yn W | Yn E4 | Yn W | Yn E2 | Yg Wd | Yg Wd | 18 |
| 19 | Yn M | Yn F | Yn E | Yn M | Yg M | Yg E1 | Yg M | Yg E3 | Yn M | Yn F | Yn M | Yn W | Yg W | Yg F | Yn W | Yn E4 | Yn W | Yn E2 | Yg Wd | Yg Wd | Yg Wd | Yg M | Yn Wd | Yn Wd | 19 |
| 20 | Yg W | Yg F | Yg M | Yg E3 | Yn M | Yn F | Yn M | Yn W | Yg W | Yg F | Yg W | Yg W | Yn W | Yn E2 | Yg Wd | Yg Wd | Yg Wd | Yg M | Yn Wd | Yn Wd | Yn Wd | Yn M | Yg F | Yg E1 | 20 |
| 21 | Yn W | Yn E2 | Yn M | Yn W | Yg W | Yg F | Yg W | Yg W | Yn W | Yn E2 | Yn W | Yn E4 | Yg Wd | Yg M | Yn Wd | Yn Wd | Yn Wd | Yn M | Yg F | Yg E1 | Yg F | Yg E3 | Yn F | Yn F | 21 |
| 22 | Yg Wd | Yg M | Yg W | Yg W | Yn W | Yn E2 | Yn W | Yn E4 | Yg Wd | Yg M | Yg Wd | Yg Wd | Yn Wd | Yn M | Yg F | Yg E1 | Yg F | Yg E3 | Yn F | Yn F | Yn F | Yn W | Yg E | Yg F | 22 |
| 23 | Yn Wd | Yn M | Yn W | Yn E4 | Yg Wd | Yg M | Yg Wd | Yg Wd | Yn Wd | Yn M | Yn Wd | Yn Wd | Yg F | Yg E3 | Yn F | Yn F | Yn F | Yn W | Yg E | Yg F | Yg E | Yg W | Yn E | Yn E2 | 23 |
| 24 | Yg F | Yg E3 | Yg Wd | Yg Wd | Yn Wd | Yn M | Yn Wd | Yn Wd | Yg F | Yg E3 | Yg F | Yg E1 | Yn F | Yn W | Yg E | Yg F | Yg E | Yg W | Yn E | Yn E2 | Yn E | Yn E4 | Yg M | Yg M | 24 |
| 25 | Yn F | Yn W | Yn Wd | Yn Wd | Yg F | Yg E3 | Yg F | Yg E1 | Yn F | Yn W | Yn F | Yn F | Yg E | Yg W | Yn E | Yn E2 | Yn E | Yn E4 | Yg M | Yg M | Yg M | Yg Wd | Yn M | Yn M | 25 |
| 26 | Yg E | Yg W | Yg F | Yg E1 | Yn F | Yn W | Yn F | Yn F | Yg E | Yg W | Yg E | Yg F | Yn E | Yn E4 | Yg M | Yg M | Yg M | Yg Wd | Yn M | Yn M | Yn M | Yn Wd | Yg W | Yg E3 | 26 |
| 27 | Yn E | Yn E4 | Yn F | Yn F | Yg E | Yg W | Yg E | Yg F | Yn E | Yn E4 | Yn E | Yn E2 | Yg M | Yg Wd | Yn M | Yn M | Yn M | Yn Wd | Yg W | Yg E3 | Yg W | Yg E1 | Yn W | Yn W | 27 |
| 28 | Yg M | Yg Wd | Yg E | Yg F | Yn E | Yn E4 | Yn E | Yn E2 | Yg M | Yg Wd | Yg M | Yg M | Yn M | Yn Wd | Yg W | Yg E3 | Yg W | Yg E1 | Yn W | Yn W | Yn W | Yn F | Yg Wd | Yg W | 28 |
| 29 | | | Yn E | Yn E2 | Yg M | Yg Wd | Yg M | Yg M | Yn M | Yn Wd | Yn M | Yn M | Yg W | Yg E1 | Yn W | Yn W | Yn W | Yn F | Yg Wd | Yg W | Yg Wd | Yg F | Yn Wd | Yn E4 | 29 |
| 30 | | | Yg M | Yg M | Yn M | Yn Wd | Yn M | Yn M | Yg W | Yg E1 | Yg W | Yg E3 | Yn W | Yn F | Yg Wd | Yg W | Yg Wd | Yg F | Yn Wd | Yn E4 | Yn Wd | Yn E2 | Yg F | Yg Wd | 30 |
| 31 | | | Yn M | Yn M | | | Yg W | Yg E3 | | | Yn W | Yn W | Yg Wd | Yg F | | | Yn Wd | Yn E2 | | | Yg F | Yg M | Yn F | Yn Wd | 31 |
| 1 | Yn M | Yn Wd | Yg W | Yg E3 | Yg W | Yg E1 | Yn W | Yn W | Yn W | Yn F | Yg Wd | Yg W | Yn Wd | Yn E2 | Yn Wd | Yn E4 | Yg F | Yg M | Yg F | Yg Wd | Yn F | Yn M | Yg E | Yg E1 | 1 |
| 2 | Yg W | Yg E1 | Yn W | Yn W | Yn W | Yn F | Yg Wd | Yg W | Yg Wd | Yg F | Yn Wd | Yn E4 | Yg F | Yg M | Yg F | Yg Wd | Yn F | Yn M | Yn F | Yn Wd | Yg E | Yg E3 | Yn E | Yn F | 2 |
| 3 | Yn W | Yn F | Yg Wd | Yg W | Yg Wd | Yg F | Yn Wd | Yn E4 | Yn Wd | Yn E2 | Yg F | Yg Wd | Yn F | Yn M | Yn F | Yn Wd | Yg E | Yg E3 | Yg E | Yg E1 | Yn E | Yn W | Yg M | Yg F | 3 |
| 4 | Yg Wd | Yg F | Yn Wd | Yn E4 | Yn Wd | Yn E2 | Yg F | Yg Wd | Yg F | Yg M | Yn F | Yn Wd | Yg E | Yg E3 | Yg E | Yg E1 | Yn E | Yn W | Yn E | Yn F | Yg M | Yg W | Yn M | Yn E2 | 4 |
| 5 | Yn Wd | Yn E2 | Yg F | Yg Wd | Yg F | Yg M | Yn F | Yn Wd | Yn F | Yn M | Yg E | Yg E1 | Yn E | Yn W | Yn E | Yn F | Yg M | Yg W | Yg M | Yg F | Yn M | Yn E4 | | | 5 |
| 6 | | | | | | | Yg E | Yg E1 | Yg E | Yg E3 | Yn E | Yn F | Yg M | Yg W | Yg M | Yg F | Yn M | Yn E4 | Yn M | Yn E2 | | | | | 6 |
| 7 | | | | | | | | | Yn E | Yn W | Yg M | Yg F | Yn M | Yn E4 | Yn M | Yn E2 | Yg W | Yg Wd | Yg W | Yg M | | | | | 7 |
| 8 | | | | | | | | | | | | | Yg W | Yg Wd | Yg W | Yg M | | | | | | | | | 8 |

# YEAR OF THE DRAGON

| | H | E | H | E | H | E | H | E | H | E | H | E | H | E | H | E | H | E | H | E | H | E | H | E | |
|---|---|---|---|---|---|---|---|---|---|---|---|---|---|---|---|---|---|---|---|---|---|---|---|---|---|
| YEAR | YEAR Yg F | Yg E1 | 1916 | | | | | | | | | | | | | | | | | | 1917 | | | | |
| MONTH | 5 Feb - 5 Mar | | 6 Mar - 4 Apr | | 5 Apr - 5 May | | 6 May - 5 June | | 6 June - 6 Jul | | 7 Jul - 7 Aug | | 8 Aug - 7 Sep | | 8 Sep - 7 Oct | | 8 Oct - 7 Nov | | 8 Nov- 5 Dec | | 6 Dec - 5 Jan | | 6 Jan -3 Feb | | |
| | Yg M | Yg Wd | Yn M | Yn Wd | Yg W | Yg E1 | Yn W | Yn F | Yg Wd | Yg F | Yn Wd | Yn E2 | Yg F | Yg M | Yn F | Yn M | Yg E | Yg E3 | Yn E | Yn W | Yg M | Yg W | Yn M | Yn E4 | |
| Starting time | 1st day | Mid-pt | 1st day | Mid-pt | 1st day | Mid-pt | 1st day | Mid-pt | 1st day | Mid-pt | 1st day | Mid-pt | 1st day | Mid-pt | 1st day | Mid-pt | 1st day | Mid-pt | 1st day | Mid-pt | 1st day | Mid-pt | 1st day | Mid-pt | |
| Date | 5 | 20 | 6 | 21 | 5 | 20 | 6 | 21 | 6 | 22 | 7 | 23 | 8 | 23 | 8 | 23 | 8 | 24 | 8 | 22 | 6 | 22 | 6 | 20 | |
| Hour | 1114 | 0718 | 0538 | 0647 | 1058 | 1825 | 0450 | 1806 | 0926 | 0225 | 1954 | 1321 | 0535 | 2009 | 0805 | 1715 | 2308 | 0157 | 0143 | 2258 | 1806 | 1159 | 0510 | 2238 | |
| DATE 4 | | | | | | | | | | | | | | | | | | | | | | | | | 4 |
| 5 | Yg W | Yg M | | | Yg W | Yg M | | | | | | | | | | | | | | | | | | | 5 |
| 6 | Yn W | Yn M | Yg W | Yg Wd | Yn W | Yn M | Yn W | Yn Wd | Yg Wd | Yg E3 | | | | | | | | | | | Yn F | Yn E4 | Yg E | Yg M | 6 |
| 7 | Yg Wd | Yg E3 | Yn W | Yn Wd | Yg Wd | Yg E3 | Yg Wd | Yg E1 | Yn Wd | Yn W | Yn Wd | Yn F | | | | | | | | | Yg E | Yg Wd | Yn E | Yn M | 7 |
| 8 | Yn Wd | Yn W | Yg Wd | Yg E1 | Yn Wd | Yn W | Yn Wd | Yn F | Yg F | Yg W | Yg F | Yg F | Yn F | Yn E4 | Yg E | Yg M | Yg E | Yg Wd | Yn E | Yn M | Yn E | Yn Wd | Yg M | Yg E3 | 8 |
| 9 | Yg F | Yg W | Yn Wd | Yn F | Yg F | Yg W | Yg F | Yg F | Yn F | Yn E4 | Yn F | Yn E2 | Yg E | Yg Wd | Yn E | Yn M | Yn E | Yn Wd | Yg M | Yg E3 | Yg M | Yg E1 | Yn M | Yn W | 9 |
| 10 | Yn F | Yn E4 | Yg F | Yg F | Yn F | Yn E4 | Yn F | Yn E2 | Yg E | Yg Wd | Yg E | Yg M | Yn E | Yn Wd | Yg M | Yg E3 | Yg M | Yg E1 | Yn M | Yn W | Yn M | Yn F | Yg W | Yg W | 10 |
| 11 | Yg E | Yg Wd | Yn F | Yn E2 | Yg E | Yg Wd | Yg E | Yg M | Yn E | Yn Wd | Yn E | Yn M | Yg M | Yg E1 | Yn M | Yn W | Yn M | Yn F | Yg W | Yg W | Yg W | Yg F | Yn W | Yn E4 | 11 |
| 12 | Yn E | Yn Wd | Yg E | Yg M | Yn E | Yn Wd | Yn E | Yn M | Yg M | Yg E1 | Yg M | Yg E3 | Yn M | Yn F | Yg W | Yg W | Yg W | Yg F | Yn W | Yn E4 | Yn W | Yn E2 | Yg Wd | Yg Wd | 12 |
| 13 | Yg M | Yg E1 | Yn E | Yn M | Yg M | Yg E1 | Yg M | Yg E3 | Yn M | Yn F | Yn M | Yn W | Yg W | Yg F | Yn W | Yn E4 | Yn W | Yn E2 | Yg Wd | Yg Wd | Yg Wd | Yg M | Yn Wd | Yn Wd | 13 |
| 14 | Yn M | Yn F | Yg M | Yg E3 | Yn M | Yn F | Yn M | Yn W | Yg W | Yg F | Yg W | Yg W | Yn W | Yn E2 | Yg Wd | Yg Wd | Yg Wd | Yg M | Yn Wd | Yn Wd | Yn Wd | Yn M | Yg F | Yg E1 | 14 |
| 15 | Yg W | Yg F | Yn M | Yn W | Yg W | Yg F | Yg W | Yg W | Yn W | Yn E2 | Yn W | Yn E4 | Yg Wd | Yg M | Yn Wd | Yn Wd | Yn Wd | Yn M | Yg F | Yg E1 | Yg F | Yg E3 | Yn F | Yn F | 15 |
| 16 | Yn W | Yn E2 | Yg W | Yg W | Yn W | Yn E2 | Yn W | Yn E4 | Yg Wd | Yg M | Yg Wd | Yg Wd | Yn Wd | Yn M | Yg F | Yg E1 | Yg F | Yg E3 | Yn F | Yn F | Yn F | Yn W | Yg E | Yg F | 16 |
| 17 | Yg Wd | Yg M | Yn W | Yn E4 | Yg Wd | Yg M | Yg Wd | Yg Wd | Yn Wd | Yn M | Yn Wd | Yn Wd | Yg F | Yg E3 | Yn F | Yn F | Yn F | Yn W | Yg E | Yg F | Yg E | Yg W | Yn E | Yn E2 | 17 |
| 18 | Yn Wd | Yn M | Yg Wd | Yg Wd | Yn Wd | Yn M | Yn Wd | Yn Wd | Yg F | Yg E3 | Yg F | Yg E1 | Yn F | Yn W | Yg E | Yg F | Yg E | Yg W | Yn E | Yn E2 | Yn E | Yn E4 | Yg M | Yg M | 18 |
| 19 | Yg F | Yg E3 | Yn Wd | Yn Wd | Yg F | Yg E3 | Yg F | Yg E1 | Yn F | Yn W | Yn F | Yn F | Yg E | Yg W | Yn E | Yn E2 | Yn E | Yn E4 | Yg M | Yg M | Yg M | Yg Wd | Yn M | Yn M | 19 |
| 20 | Yn F | Yn W | Yg F | Yg E1 | Yn F | Yn W | Yn F | Yn F | Yg E | Yg W | Yg E | Yg F | Yn E | Yn E4 | Yg M | Yg M | Yg M | Yg Wd | Yn M | Yn M | Yn M | Yn Wd | Yg W | Yg E3 | 20 |
| 21 | Yg E | Yg W | Yn F | Yn F | Yg E | Yg W | Yg E | Yg F | Yn E | Yn E4 | Yn E | Yn E2 | Yg M | Yg Wd | Yn M | Yn M | Yn M | Yn Wd | Yg W | Yg E3 | Yg W | Yg E1 | Yn W | Yn W | 21 |
| 22 | Yn E | Yn E4 | Yg E | Yg F | Yn E | Yn E4 | Yn E | Yn E2 | Yg M | Yg Wd | Yg M | Yg M | Yn M | Yn Wd | Yg W | Yg E3 | Yg W | Yg E1 | Yn W | Yn W | Yn W | Yn F | Yg Wd | Yg W | 22 |
| 23 | Yg M | Yg Wd | Yn E | Yn E2 | Yg M | Yg Wd | Yg M | Yg M | Yn M | Yn Wd | Yn M | Yn M | Yg W | Yg E1 | Yn W | Yn W | Yn W | Yn F | Yg Wd | Yg W | Yg Wd | Yg F | Yn Wd | Yn E4 | 23 |
| 24 | Yn M | Yn Wd | Yg M | Yg M | Yn M | Yn Wd | Yn M | Yn M | Yg W | Yg E1 | Yg W | Yg E3 | Yn W | Yn F | Yg Wd | Yg W | Yg Wd | Yg F | Yn Wd | Yn E4 | Yn Wd | Yn E2 | Yg F | Yg Wd | 24 |
| 25 | Yg W | Yg E1 | Yn M | Yn M | Yg W | Yg E1 | Yg W | Yg E3 | Yn W | Yn F | Yn W | Yn W | Yg Wd | Yg F | Yn Wd | Yn E4 | Yn Wd | Yn E2 | Yg F | Yg Wd | Yg F | Yg M | Yn F | Yn Wd | 25 |
| 26 | Yn W | Yn F | Yg W | Yg E3 | Yn W | Yn F | Yn W | Yn W | Yg Wd | Yg F | Yg Wd | Yg W | Yn Wd | Yn E2 | Yg F | Yg Wd | Yg F | Yg M | Yn F | Yn Wd | Yn F | Yn M | Yg E | Yg E1 | 26 |
| 27 | Yg Wd | Yg F | Yn W | Yn W | Yg Wd | Yg F | Yg Wd | Yg W | Yn Wd | Yn E2 | Yn Wd | Yn E4 | Yg F | Yg M | Yn F | Yn Wd | Yn F | Yn M | Yg E | Yg E1 | Yg E | Yg E3 | Yn E | Yn F | 27 |
| 28 | Yn Wd | Yn E2 | Yg Wd | Yg W | Yn Wd | Yn E2 | Yn Wd | Yn E4 | Yg F | Yg M | Yg F | Yg Wd | Yn F | Yn M | Yg E | Yg E1 | Yg E | Yg E3 | Yn E | Yn F | Yn E | Yn W | Yg M | Yg F | 28 |
| 29 | Yg F | Yg M | Yn Wd | Yn E4 | Yg F | Yg M | Yg F | Yg Wd | Yn F | Yn M | Yn F | Yn Wd | Yg E | Yg E3 | Yn E | Yn F | Yn E | Yn W | Yg M | Yg F | Yg M | Yg W | Yn M | Yn E2 | 29 |
| 30 | | | Yg F | Yg Wd | Yn F | Yn M | Yn F | Yn Wd | Yg E | Yg E3 | Yg E | Yg E1 | Yn E | Yn W | Yg M | Yg F | Yg M | Yg W | Yn M | Yn E2 | Yn M | Yn E4 | Yg W | Yg M | 30 |
| 31 | | | Yn F | Yn Wd | | | Yg E | Yg E1 | | | Yn E | Yn F | Yg M | Yg W | | | Yn M | Yn E4 | | | Yg W | Yg Wd | Yn W | Yn M | 31 |
| 1 | Yn F | Yn M | Yg E | Yg E1 | Yg E | Yg E3 | Yn E | Yn F | Yn E | Yn W | Yg M | Yg F | Yn M | Yn E4 | Yn M | Yn E2 | Yg W | Yg Wd | Yg W | Yg M | Yn W | Yn Wd | Yg Wd | Yg E3 | 1 |
| 2 | Yg E | Yg E3 | Yn E | Yn F | Yn E | Yn W | Yg M | Yg F | Yg M | Yg W | Yn M | Yn E2 | Yg W | Yg Wd | Yg W | Yg M | Yn W | Yn Wd | Yn W | Yn M | Yg Wd | Yg E1 | Yn Wd | Yn W | 2 |
| 3 | Yn E | Yn W | Yg M | Yn E2 | Yg M | Yg W | Yn M | Yn E2 | Yn M | Yn E4 | Yg W | Yg M | Yn W | Yn Wd | Yn W | Yn M | Yg Wd | Yg E1 | Yg Wd | Yg E3 | Yn Wd | Yn F | Yg F | Yg W | 3 |
| 4 | Yg M | Yg W | Yn M | Yn E2 | Yn M | Yn E4 | Yg W | Yg M | Yg W | Yg Wd | Yn W | Yn M | Yg Wd | Yg E1 | Yg Wd | Yg E3 | Yn Wd | Yn F | Yn Wd | Yn W | Yg F | Yg F | | | 4 |
| 5 | Yn M | Yn E4 | | | Yg W | Yg Wd | Yn W | Yn M | Yn W | Yn Wd | Yg Wd | Yg E3 | Yn Wd | Yn F | Yn Wd | Yn W | Yg F | Yg F | Yg F | Yg W | Yn F | Yn E2 | | | 5 |
| 6 | | | | | | | | | Yg Wd | Yg E1 | Yn Wd | Yn W | Yg F | Yg F | Yg F | Yg W | Yn F | Yn E2 | | | | | | | 6 |
| 7 | | | | | | | | | | | Yg F | Yg W | Yn F | Yn E2 | Yn F | Yn E4 | Yg E | Yg M | | | | | | | 7 |
| 8 | | | | | | | | | | | | | | | | | | | | | | | | | 8 |

# YEAR OF THE SNAKE

| | H | E | H | E | H | E | H | E | H | E | H | E | H | E | H | E | H | E | H | E | H | E | H | E | |
|---|---|---|---|---|---|---|---|---|---|---|---|---|---|---|---|---|---|---|---|---|---|---|---|---|---|
| YEAR | YEAR Yn F | Yn F | 1917 | | | | | | | | | | | | | | | | | | | | 1918 | | |
| MONTH | 4 Feb - 5 Mar | | 6 Mar - 4 Apr | | 5 Apr - 5 May | | 6 May - 5 June | | 6 June - 7 Jul | | 8 Jul - 7 Aug | | 8 Aug - 7 Sep | | 8 Sep - 8 Oct | | 9 Oct - 7 Nov | | 8 Nov - 7 Dec | | 8 Dec - 5 Jan | | 6 Jan - 3 Feb | | |
| | Yg W | Yg Wd | Yn W | Yn Wd | Yg Wd | Yg E1 | Yn Wd | Yn F | Yg F | Yg F | Yn F | Yn E2 | Yg E | Yg M | Yn E | Yn M | Yg M | Yg E3 | Yn M | Yn W | Yg W | Yg W | Yn W | Yn E4 | |
| Starting time | 1st day | Mid-pt | 1st day | Mid-pt | 1st day | Mid-pt | 1st day | Mid-pt | 1st day | Mid-pt | 1st day | Mid-pt | 1st day | Mid-pt | 1st day | Mid-pt | 1st day | Mid-pt | 1st day | Mid-pt | 1st day | Mid-pt | 1st day | Mid-pt | |
| Date | 4 | 19 | 6 | 21 | 5 | 21 | 6 | 21 | 6 | 22 | 8 | 23 | 8 | 24 | 8 | 23 | 9 | 24 | 8 | 23 | 8 | 22 | 6 | 21 | |
| Hour | 1658 | 1305 | 1125 | 1238 | 1650 | 0018 | 1046 | 2359 | 1523 | 0815 | 0151 | 1908 | 1130 | 0154 | 1400 | 2300 | 0503 | 0744 | 0737 | 0445 | 0001 | 1746 | 1105 | 0425 | |
| DATE 4 | Yn F | Yn E4 | | | | | | | | | | | | | | | | | | | | | | | 4 |
| 5 | Yg E | Yg Wd | | | Yn F | Yn E4 | | | | | | | | | | | | | | | | | | | 5 |
| 6 | Yn E | Yn Wd | Yn F | Yn E2 | Yg E | Yg Wd | Yg E | Yg M | Yn E | Yn Wd | | | | | | | | | | | | | Yn W | Yn E4 | 6 |
| 7 | Yg M | Yg E1 | Yg E | Yg M | Yn E | Yn Wd | Yn E | Yn M | Yg M | Yg E1 | | | | | | | | | | | | | Yg Wd | Yg Wd | 7 |
| 8 | Yn M | Yn F | Yn E | Yn M | Yg M | Yg E1 | Yg M | Yg E3 | Yn M | Yn F | Yn M | Yn W | Yg W | Yg F | Yn W | Yn E4 | | | Yg Wd | Yg Wd | Yg Wd | Yg M | Yn Wd | Yn Wd | 8 |
| 9 | Yg W | Yg F | Yg M | Yg E3 | Yn M | Yn F | Yn M | Yn W | Yg W | Yg F | Yg W | Yg W | Yn W | Yn E2 | Yg Wd | Yg Wd | Yg Wd | Yg M | Yn Wd | Yn Wd | Yn Wd | Yn M | Yg F | Yg E1 | 9 |
| 10 | Yn W | Yn E2 | Yn M | Yn W | Yg W | Yg F | Yg W | Yg W | Yn W | Yn E2 | Yn W | Yn E4 | Yg Wd | Yg M | Yn Wd | Yn Wd | Yn Wd | Yn M | Yg F | Yg E1 | Yg F | Yg E3 | Yn F | Yn F | 10 |
| 11 | Yg Wd | Yg M | Yg W | Yg W | Yn W | Yn E2 | Yn W | Yn E4 | Yg Wd | Yg M | Yg Wd | Yg Wd | Yn Wd | Yn M | Yg F | Yg E1 | Yg F | Yg E3 | Yn F | Yn F | Yn F | Yn W | Yg E | Yg F | 11 |
| 12 | Yn Wd | Yn M | Yn W | Yn E4 | Yg Wd | Yg M | Yg Wd | Yg Wd | Yn Wd | Yn M | Yn Wd | Yn Wd | Yg F | Yg E3 | Yn F | Yn F | Yn F | Yn W | Yg E | Yg F | Yg E | Yg W | Yn E | Yn E2 | 12 |
| 13 | Yg F | Yg E3 | Yg Wd | Yg Wd | Yn Wd | Yn M | Yn Wd | Yn Wd | Yg F | Yg E3 | Yg F | Yg E1 | Yn F | Yn W | Yg E | Yg F | Yg E | Yg W | Yn E | Yn E2 | Yn E | Yn E4 | Yg M | Yg M | 13 |
| 14 | Yn F | Yn W | Yn Wd | Yn Wd | Yg F | Yg E3 | Yg F | Yg E1 | Yn F | Yn W | Yn F | Yn F | Yg E | Yg W | Yn E | Yn E2 | Yn E | Yn E4 | Yg M | Yg M | Yg M | Yg Wd | Yn M | Yn M | 14 |
| 15 | Yg E | Yg W | Yg F | Yg E1 | Yn F | Yn W | Yn F | Yn F | Yg E | Yg W | Yg E | Yg F | Yn E | Yn E4 | Yg M | Yg M | Yg M | Yg Wd | Yn M | Yn M | Yn M | Yn Wd | Yg W | Yg E3 | 15 |
| 16 | Yn E | Yn E4 | Yn F | Yn F | Yg E | Yg W | Yg E | Yg F | Yn E | Yn E4 | Yn E | Yn E2 | Yg M | Yg Wd | Yn M | Yn M | Yn M | Yn Wd | Yg W | Yg E3 | Yg W | Yg E1 | Yn W | Yn W | 16 |
| 17 | Yg M | Yg Wd | Yg E | Yg F | Yn E | Yn E4 | Yn E | Yn E2 | Yg M | Yg Wd | Yg M | Yg M | Yn M | Yn Wd | Yg W | Yg E3 | Yg W | Yg E1 | Yn W | Yn W | Yn W | Yn F | Yg Wd | Yg W | 17 |
| 18 | Yn M | Yn Wd | Yn E | Yn E2 | Yg M | Yg Wd | Yg M | Yg M | Yn M | Yn Wd | Yn M | Yn M | Yg W | Yg E1 | Yn W | Yn W | Yn W | Yn F | Yg Wd | Yg W | Yg Wd | Yg F | Yn Wd | Yn E4 | 18 |
| 19 | Yg W | Yg E1 | Yg M | Yg M | Yn M | Yn Wd | Yn M | Yn M | Yg W | Yg E1 | Yg W | Yg E3 | Yn W | Yn F | Yg Wd | Yg W | Yg Wd | Yg F | Yn Wd | Yn E4 | Yn Wd | Yn E2 | Yg F | Yg Wd | 19 |
| 20 | Yn W | Yn F | Yn M | Yn M | Yg W | Yg E1 | Yg W | Yg E3 | Yn W | Yn F | Yn W | Yn W | Yg Wd | Yg F | Yn Wd | Yn E4 | Yn Wd | Yn E2 | Yg F | Yg Wd | Yg F | Yg M | Yn F | Yn Wd | 20 |
| 21 | Yg Wd | Yg F | Yg W | Yg E3 | Yn W | Yn F | Yn W | Yn W | Yg Wd | Yg F | Yg Wd | Yg W | Yn Wd | Yn E2 | Yg F | Yg Wd | Yg F | Yg M | Yn F | Yn Wd | Yn F | Yn M | Yg E | Yg E1 | 21 |
| 22 | Yn Wd | Yn E2 | Yn W | Yn W | Yg Wd | Yg F | Yg Wd | Yg W | Yn Wd | Yn E2 | Yn Wd | Yn E4 | Yg F | Yg M | Yn F | Yn Wd | Yn F | Yn M | Yg E | Yg E1 | Yg E | Yg E3 | Yn E | Yn F | 22 |
| 23 | Yg F | Yg M | Yg Wd | Yg W | Yn Wd | Yn E2 | Yn Wd | Yn E4 | Yg F | Yg M | Yg F | Yg Wd | Yn F | Yn M | Yg E | Yg E1 | Yg E | Yg E3 | Yn E | Yn F | Yn E | Yn W | Yg M | Yg F | 23 |
| 24 | Yn F | Yn M | Yn Wd | Yn E4 | Yg F | Yg M | Yg F | Yg Wd | Yn F | Yn M | Yn F | Yn Wd | Yg E | Yg E3 | Yn E | Yn F | Yn E | Yn W | Yg M | Yg F | Yg M | Yg W | Yn M | Yn E2 | 24 |
| 25 | Yg E | Yg E3 | Yg F | Yg Wd | Yn F | Yn M | Yn F | Yn Wd | Yg E | Yg E3 | Yg E | Yg E1 | Yn E | Yn W | Yg M | Yg F | Yg M | Yg W | Yn M | Yn E2 | Yn M | Yn E4 | Yg W | Yg M | 25 |
| 26 | Yn E | Yn W | Yn F | Yn Wd | Yg E | Yg E3 | Yg E | Yg E1 | Yn E | Yn W | Yn E | Yn F | Yg M | Yg W | Yn M | Yn E2 | Yn M | Yn E4 | Yg W | Yg M | Yg W | Yg Wd | Yn W | Yn M | 26 |
| 27 | Yg M | Yg W | Yg E | Yg E1 | Yn E | Yn W | Yn E | Yn F | Yg M | Yg W | Yg M | Yg F | Yn M | Yn E4 | Yg W | Yg M | Yg W | Yg Wd | Yn W | Yn M | Yn W | Yn Wd | Yg Wd | Yg E3 | 27 |
| 28 | Yn M | Yn E4 | Yn E | Yn F | Yg M | Yg W | Yg M | Yg F | Yn M | Yn E4 | Yn M | Yn E2 | Yg W | Yg Wd | Yn W | Yn M | Yn W | Yn Wd | Yg Wd | Yg E3 | Yg Wd | Yg E1 | Yn Wd | Yn W | 28 |
| 29 | | | Yg M | Yg F | Yn M | Yn E4 | Yn M | Yn E2 | Yg W | Yg Wd | Yg W | Yg M | Yn W | Yn Wd | Yg Wd | Yg E3 | Yg Wd | Yg E1 | Yn Wd | Yn W | Yn Wd | Yn F | Yg F | Yg W | 29 |
| 30 | | | Yn M | Yn E2 | Yg W | Yg Wd | Yg W | Yg M | Yn W | Yn Wd | Yn W | Yn M | Yg Wd | Yg E1 | Yn Wd | Yn W | Yn Wd | Yn F | Yg F | Yg W | Yg F | Yg F | Yn F | Yn E4 | 30 |
| 31 | | | Yg W | Yg M | | | Yn W | Yn M | | | Yg Wd | Yg E3 | Yn Wd | Yn F | | | Yg F | Yg F | | | Yn F | Yn E2 | Yg E | Yg Wd | 31 |
| 1 | Yg W | Yg Wd | Yn W | Yn M | Yn W | Yn Wd | Yg Wd | Yg E3 | Yg Wd | Yg E1 | Yn Wd | Yn W | Yg F | Yg F | Yg F | Yg W | Yn F | Yn E2 | Yn F | Yn E4 | Yg E | Yg M | Yn E | Yn Wd | 1 |
| 2 | Yn W | Yn Wd | Yg Wd | Yg E3 | Yg Wd | Yg E1 | Yn Wd | Yn W | Yn Wd | Yn F | Yg F | Yg W | Yn F | Yn E2 | Yn F | Yn E4 | Yg E | Yg M | Yg E | Yg Wd | Yn E | Yn M | Yg M | Yg E1 | 2 |
| 3 | Yg Wd | Yg E1 | Yn Wd | Yn W | Yn Wd | Yn F | Yg F | Yg W | Yg F | Yg F | Yn F | Yn E4 | Yg E | Yg M | Yg E | Yg Wd | Yn E | Yn M | Yn E | Yn Wd | Yg M | Yg E3 | Yn M | Yn F | 3 |
| 4 | Yn Wd | Yn F | Yg F | Yg W | Yg F | Yg F | Yn F | Yn E4 | Yn F | Yn E2 | Yg E | Yg Wd | Yn E | Yn M | Yn E | Yn Wd | Yg M | Yg E3 | Yg M | Yg E1 | Yn M | Yn W | | | 4 |
| 5 | Yg F | Yg F | | | Yn F | Yn E2 | Yg E | Yg Wd | Yg E | Yg M | Yn E | Yn Wd | Yg M | Yg E3 | Yg M | Yg E1 | Yn M | Yn W | Yn M | Yn F | Yg W | Yg W | | | 5 |
| 6 | | | | | | | | | Yn E | Yn M | Yg M | Yg E1 | Yn M | Yn W | Yn M | Yn F | Yg W | Yg W | Yg W | Yg F | | | | | 6 |
| 7 | | | | | | | | | Yg M | Yg E3 | Yn M | Yn F | Yg W | Yg W | Yg W | Yg F | Yn W | Yn E4 | Yn W | Yn E2 | | | | | 7 |
| 8 | | | | | | | | | | | | | | | Yn W | Yn E2 | | | | | | | | | 8 |

# YEAR OF THE HORSE

| | H | E | H | E | H | E | H | E | H | E | H | E | H | E | H | E | H | E | H | E | H | E | H | E | |
|---|---|---|---|---|---|---|---|---|---|---|---|---|---|---|---|---|---|---|---|---|---|---|---|---|---|
| YEAR | YEAR YgE | YgF | 1918 | | | | | | | | | | | | | | | | | | | | 1919 | | |
| MONTH | 4 Feb - 5 Mar | | 6 Mar - 4 Apr | | 5 Apr - 5 May | | 6 May - 5 June | | 6 June - 7 Jul | | 8 Jul - 7 Aug | | 8 Aug - 7 Sep | | 8 Sep - 8 Oct | | 9 Oct - 7 Nov | | 8 Nov- 7 Dec | | 8 Dec - 5 Jan | | 6 Jan - 4 Feb | | |
| | Yg Wd | Yg Wd | Yn Wd | Yn Wd | Yg F | Yg E1 | Yn F | Yn F | Yg E | Yg F | Yn E | Yn E2 | Yg M | Yg M | Yn M | Yn M | Yg W | Yg E3 | Yn W | Yn W | Yg Wd | Yg W | Yn Wd | Yn E4 | |
| Starting time | 1st day | Mid-pt | 1st day | Mid-pt | 1st day | Mid-pt | 1st day | Mid-pt | 1st day | Mid-pt | 1st day | Mid-pt | 1st day | Mid-pt | 1st day | Mid-pt | 1st day | Mid-pt | 1st day | Mid-pt | 1st day | Mid-pt | 1st day | Mid-pt | |
| Date | 4 | 19 | 6 | 21 | 5 | 21 | 6 | 22 | 6 | 22 | 8 | 24 | 8 | 24 | 8 | 24 | 9 | 24 | 8 | 23 | 8 | 22 | 6 | 21 | |
| Hour | 2253 | 1853 | 1721 | 1826 | 2246 | 0606 | 1638 | 0546 | 2111 | 1400 | 0732 | 0052 | 1708 | 0737 | 1936 | 0446 | 1048 | 1333 | 1319 | 1039 | 0547 | 2342 | 1728 | 1021 | |
| DATE 4 | Yg W | Yg F | | | | | | | | | | | | | | | | | | | | | | | 4 |
| 5 | Yn W | Yn E2 | | | Yg W | Yg F | | | | | | | | | | | | | | | | | | | 5 |
| 6 | Yg Wd | Yg M | Yg W | Yg W | Yn W | Yn E2 | Yn W | Yn E4 | Yg Wd | Yg M | | | | | | | | | | | | | Yg E | Yg F | 6 |
| 7 | Yn Wd | Yn M | Yn W | Yn E4 | Yg Wd | Yg M | Yg Wd | Yg Wd | Yn Wd | Yn M | | | | | | | | | | | | | Yn E | Yn E2 | 7 |
| 8 | Yg F | Yg E3 | Yg Wd | Yg Wd | Yn Wd | Yn M | Yn Wd | Yn Wd | Yg F | Yg E3 | Yg F | Yg E1 | Yn F | Yn W | Yg E | Yg F | | | Yn E | Yn E2 | Yn E | Yn E4 | Yg M | Yg M | 8 |
| 9 | Yn F | Yn W | Yn Wd | Yn Wd | Yg F | Yg E3 | Yg F | Yg E1 | Yn F | Yn W | Yn F | Yn F | Yg E | Yg W | Yn E | Yn E2 | Yn E | Yn E4 | Yg M | Yg M | Yg M | Yg Wd | Yn M | Yn M | 9 |
| 10 | Yg E | Yg W | Yg F | Yg E1 | Yn F | Yn W | Yn F | Yn F | Yg E | Yg W | Yg E | Yg F | Yn E | Yn E4 | Yg M | Yg M | Yg M | Yg Wd | Yn M | Yn M | Yn M | Yn Wd | Yg W | Yg E3 | 10 |
| 11 | Yn E | Yn E4 | Yn F | Yn F | Yg E | Yg W | Yg E | Yg F | Yn E | Yn E4 | Yn E | Yn E2 | Yg M | Yg Wd | Yn M | Yn M | Yn M | Yn Wd | Yg W | Yg E3 | Yg W | Yg E1 | Yn W | Yn W | 11 |
| 12 | Yg M | Yg Wd | Yg E | Yg F | Yn E | Yn E4 | Yn E | Yn E2 | Yg M | Yg Wd | Yg M | Yg M | Yn M | Yn Wd | Yg W | Yg E3 | Yg W | Yg E1 | Yn W | Yn W | Yn W | Yn F | Yg Wd | Yg W | 12 |
| 13 | Yn M | Yn Wd | Yn E | Yn E2 | Yg M | Yg Wd | Yg M | Yg M | Yn M | Yn Wd | Yn M | Yn M | Yg W | Yg E1 | Yn W | Yn W | Yn W | Yn F | Yg Wd | Yg W | Yg Wd | Yg F | Yn Wd | Yn E4 | 13 |
| 14 | Yg W | Yg E1 | Yg M | Yg M | Yn M | Yn Wd | Yn M | Yn M | Yg W | Yg E1 | Yg W | Yg E3 | Yn W | Yn F | Yg Wd | Yg W | Yg Wd | Yg F | Yn Wd | Yn E4 | Yn Wd | Yn E2 | Yg F | Yg Wd | 14 |
| 15 | Yn W | Yn F | Yn M | Yn M | Yg W | Yg E1 | Yg W | Yg E3 | Yn W | Yn F | Yn W | Yn W | Yg Wd | Yg F | Yn Wd | Yn E4 | Yn Wd | Yn E2 | Yg F | Yg Wd | Yg F | Yg M | Yn F | Yn Wd | 15 |
| 16 | Yg Wd | Yg F | Yg W | Yg E3 | Yn W | Yn F | Yn W | Yn W | Yg Wd | Yg F | Yg Wd | Yg W | Yn Wd | Yn E2 | Yg F | Yg Wd | Yg F | Yg M | Yn F | Yn Wd | Yn F | Yn M | Yg E | Yg E1 | 16 |
| 17 | Yn Wd | Yn E2 | Yn W | Yn W | Yg Wd | Yg F | Yg Wd | Yg W | Yn Wd | Yn E2 | Yn Wd | Yn E4 | Yg F | Yg M | Yn F | Yn Wd | Yn F | Yn M | Yg E | Yg E1 | Yg E | Yg E3 | Yn E | Yn F | 17 |
| 18 | Yg F | Yg M | Yg Wd | Yg W | Yn Wd | Yn E2 | Yn Wd | Yn E4 | Yg F | Yg M | Yg F | Yg Wd | Yn F | Yn M | Yg E | Yg E1 | Yg E | Yg E3 | Yn E | Yn F | Yn E | Yn W | Yg M | Yg F | 18 |
| 19 | Yn F | Yn M | Yn Wd | Yn E4 | Yg F | Yg M | Yg F | Yg Wd | Yn F | Yn M | Yn F | Yn Wd | Yg E | Yg E3 | Yn E | Yn F | Yn E | Yn W | Yg M | Yg F | Yg M | Yg W | Yn M | Yn E2 | 19 |
| 20 | Yg E | Yg E3 | Yg F | Yg Wd | Yn F | Yn M | Yn F | Yn Wd | Yg E | Yg E3 | Yg E | Yg E1 | Yn E | Yn W | Yg M | Yg F | Yg M | Yg W | Yn M | Yn E2 | Yn M | Yn E4 | Yg W | Yg M | 20 |
| 21 | Yn E | Yn W | Yn F | Yn Wd | Yg E | Yg E3 | Yg E | Yg E1 | Yn E | Yn W | Yn E | Yn F | Yg M | Yg W | Yn M | Yn E2 | Yn M | Yn E4 | Yg W | Yg M | Yg W | Yg Wd | Yn W | Yn M | 21 |
| 22 | Yg M | Yg W | Yg E | Yg E1 | Yn E | Yn W | Yn E | Yn F | Yg M | Yg W | Yg M | Yg F | Yn M | Yn E4 | Yg W | Yg M | Yg W | Yg Wd | Yn W | Yn M | Yn W | Yn Wd | Yg Wd | Yg E3 | 22 |
| 23 | Yn M | Yn E4 | Yn E | Yn F | Yg M | Yg W | Yg M | Yg F | Yn M | Yn E4 | Yn M | Yn E2 | Yg W | Yg Wd | Yn W | Yn M | Yn W | Yn Wd | Yg Wd | Yg E3 | Yg Wd | Yg E1 | Yn Wd | Yn W | 23 |
| 24 | Yg W | Yg Wd | Yg M | Yg F | Yn M | Yn E4 | Yn M | Yn E2 | Yg W | Yg Wd | Yg W | Yg M | Yn W | Yn Wd | Yg Wd | Yg E3 | Yg Wd | Yg E1 | Yn Wd | Yn W | Yn Wd | Yn F | Yg F | Yg W | 24 |
| 25 | Yn W | Yn Wd | Yn M | Yn E2 | Yg W | Yg Wd | Yg W | Yg M | Yn W | Yn Wd | Yn W | Yn M | Yg Wd | Yg E1 | Yn Wd | Yn W | Yn Wd | Yn F | Yg F | Yg W | Yg F | Yg F | Yn F | Yn E4 | 25 |
| 26 | Yg Wd | Yg E1 | Yg W | Yg M | Yn W | Yn Wd | Yn W | Yn M | Yg Wd | Yg E1 | Yg Wd | Yg E3 | Yn Wd | Yn F | Yg F | Yg W | Yg F | Yg F | Yn F | Yn E4 | Yn F | Yn E2 | Yg E | Yg Wd | 26 |
| 27 | Yn Wd | Yn F | Yn W | Yn M | Yg Wd | Yg E1 | Yg Wd | Yg E3 | Yn Wd | Yn F | Yn Wd | Yn W | Yg F | Yg F | Yn F | Yn E4 | Yn F | Yn E2 | Yg E | Yg Wd | Yg E | Yg M | Yn E | Yn Wd | 27 |
| 28 | Yg F | Yg F | Yg Wd | Yg E3 | Yn Wd | Yn F | Yn Wd | Yn W | Yg F | Yg F | Yg F | Yg W | Yn F | Yn E2 | Yg E | Yg Wd | Yg E | Yg M | Yn E | Yn Wd | Yn E | Yn M | Yg M | Yg E1 | 28 |
| 29 | | | Yn Wd | Yn W | Yg F | Yg F | Yg F | Yg W | Yn F | Yn E2 | Yn F | Yn E4 | Yg E | Yg M | Yn E | Yn Wd | Yn E | Yn M | Yg M | Yg E1 | Yg M | Yg E3 | Yn M | Yn F | 29 |
| 30 | | | Yg F | Yg W | Yn F | Yn E2 | Yn F | Yn E4 | Yg E | Yg M | Yg E | Yg Wd | Yn E | Yn M | Yg M | Yg E1 | Yg M | Yg E3 | Yn M | Yn F | Yn M | Yn W | Yg W | Yg F | 30 |
| 31 | | | Yn F | Yn E4 | | | Yg E | Yg Wd | | | Yn E | Yn Wd | Yg M | Yg E3 | | | Yn M | Yn W | | | Yg W | Yg W | Yn W | Yn E2 | 31 |
| 1 | Yn F | Yn E2 | Yg E | Yg Wd | Yg E | Yg M | Yn E | Yn Wd | Yn E | Yn M | Yg M | Yg E1 | Yn M | Yn W | Yn M | Yn F | Yg W | Yg W | Yg W | Yg F | Yn W | Yn E4 | Yg Wd | Yg M | 1 |
| 2 | Yg E | Yg M | Yn E | Yn Wd | Yn E | Yn M | Yg M | Yg E1 | Yg M | Yg E3 | Yn M | Yn F | Yg W | Yg W | Yg W | Yg F | Yn W | Yn E4 | Yn W | Yn E2 | Yg Wd | Yg Wd | Yn Wd | Yn M | 2 |
| 3 | Yn E | Yn M | Yg M | Yg E1 | Yg M | Yg E3 | Yn M | Yn F | Yn M | Yn W | Yg W | Yg F | Yn W | Yn E4 | Yn W | Yn E2 | Yg Wd | Yg Wd | Yg Wd | Yg M | Yn Wd | Yn Wd | Yg F | Yg E3 | 3 |
| 4 | Yg M | Yg E3 | Yn M | Yn F | Yn M | Yn W | Yg W | Yg F | Yg W | Yg W | Yn W | Yn E2 | Yg Wd | Yg Wd | Yg Wd | Yg M | Yn Wd | Yn Wd | Yn Wd | Yn M | Yg F | Yg E1 | Yn F | Yn W | 4 |
| 5 | Yn M | Yn W | | | Yg W | Yg W | Yn W | Yn E2 | Yn W | Yn E4 | Yg Wd | Yg M | Yn Wd | Yn Wd | Yn Wd | Yn M | Yg F | Yg E1 | Yg F | Yg E3 | Yn F | Yn F | | | 5 |
| 6 | | | | | | | | | Yg Wd | Yg Wd | Yn Wd | Yn M | Yg F | Yg E1 | Yg F | Yg E3 | Yn F | Yn F | Yn F | Yn W | | | | | 6 |
| 7 | | | | | | | | | Yn Wd | Yn Wd | Yg F | Yg E3 | Yn F | Yn F | Yn F | Yn W | Yg E | Yg F | Yg E | Yg W | | | | | 7 |
| 8 | | | | | | | | | | | | | | | Yg E | Yg W | | | | | | | | | 8 |

# YEAR OF THE GOAT

| | H | E | H | E | H | E | H | E | H | E | H | E | H | E | H | E | H | E | H | E | H | E | H | E | |
|---|---|---|---|---|---|---|---|---|---|---|---|---|---|---|---|---|---|---|---|---|---|---|---|---|---|
| YEAR | YEAR YnE | YnE2 | 1919 | | | | | | | | | | | | | | | | | | | | 1920 | | |
| MONTH | 5 Feb - 5 Mar | | 6 Mar - 5 Apr | | 6 Apr - 5 May | | 6 May - 6 June | | 7 June - 7 Jul | | 8 Jul - 7 Aug | | 8 Aug - 8 Sep | | 9 Sep - 8 Oct | | 9 Oct - 7 Nov | | 8 Nov- 7 Dec | | 8 Dec - 5 Jan | | 6 Jan - 4 Feb | | |
| | YgF | YgWd | YnF | YnWd | YgE | YgE1 | YnE | YnF | YgM | YgF | YnM | YnE2 | YgW | YgM | YnW | YnM | YgWd | YgE3 | YnWd | YnW | YgF | YgW | YnF | YnE4 | |
| Starting time | 1st day | Mid-pt | 1st day | Mid-pt | 1st day | Mid-pt | 1st day | Mid-pt | 1st day | Mid-pt | 1st day | Mid-pt | 1st day | Mid-pt | 1st day | Mid-pt | 1st day | Mid-pt | 1st day | Mid-pt | 1st day | Mid-pt | 1st day | Mid-pt | |
| Date | 5 | 20 | 6 | 22 | 6 | 21 | 6 | 22 | 7 | 22 | 8 | 24 | 8 | 24 | 9 | 24 | 9 | 24 | 8 | 23 | 8 | 23 | 6 | 21 | |
| Hour | 0440 | 0048 | 2306 | 0019 | 0429 | 1159 | 2222 | 1139 | 0257 | 1954 | 1321 | 0645 | 2258 | 1329 | 0128 | 1036 | 1634 | 1922 | 1912 | 1626 | 1138 | 0527 | 2241 | 1605 | |
| DATE 4 | | | | | | | | | | | | | | | | | | | | | | | | | 4 |
| 5 | YgE | YgW | | | | | | | | | | | | | | | | | | | | | | | 5 |
| 6 | YnE | YnE4 | YnF | YnF | YgE | YgW | YgE | YgF | | | | | | | | | | | | | | | YnW | YnW | 6 |
| 7 | YgM | YgWd | YgE | YgF | YnE | YnE4 | YnE | YnE2 | YgM | YgWd | | | | | | | | | | | | | YgWd | YgW | 7 |
| 8 | YnM | YnWd | YnE | YnE2 | YgM | YgWd | YgM | YgM | YnM | YnWd | YnM | YnM | YgW | YgE1 | | | | | YgWd | YgW | YgWd | YgF | YnWd | YnE4 | 8 |
| 9 | YgW | YgE1 | YgM | YgM | YnM | YnWd | YnM | YnM | YgW | YgE1 | YgW | YgE3 | YnW | YnF | YgWd | YgW | YgWd | YgF | YnWd | YnE4 | YnWd | YnE2 | YgF | YgWd | 9 |
| 10 | YnW | YnF | YnM | YnM | YgW | YgE1 | YgW | YgE3 | YnW | YnF | YnW | YnW | YgWd | YgF | YnWd | YnE4 | YnWd | YnE2 | YgF | YgWd | YgF | YgM | YnF | YnWd | 10 |
| 11 | YgWd | YgF | YgW | YgE3 | YnW | YnF | YnW | YnW | YgWd | YgF | YgWd | YgW | YnWd | YnE2 | YgF | YgWd | YgF | YgM | YnF | YnWd | YnF | YnM | YgE | YgE1 | 11 |
| 12 | YnWd | YnE2 | YnW | YnW | YgWd | YgF | YgWd | YgW | YnWd | YnE2 | YnWd | YnE4 | YgF | YgM | YnF | YnWd | YnF | YnM | YgE | YgE1 | YgE | YgE3 | YnE | YnF | 12 |
| 13 | YgF | YgM | YgWd | YgW | YnWd | YnE2 | YnWd | YnE4 | YgF | YgM | YgF | YgWd | YnF | YnM | YgE | YgE1 | YgE | YgE3 | YnE | YnF | YnE | YnW | YgM | YgF | 13 |
| 14 | YnF | YnM | YnWd | YnE4 | YgF | YgM | YgF | YgWd | YnF | YnM | YnF | YnWd | YgE | YgE3 | YnE | YnF | YnE | YnW | YgM | YgF | YgM | YgW | YnM | YnE2 | 14 |
| 15 | YgE | YgE3 | YgF | YgWd | YnF | YnM | YnF | YnWd | YgE | YgE3 | YgE | YgE1 | YnE | YnW | YgM | YgF | YgM | YgW | YnM | YnE2 | YnM | YnE4 | YgW | YgM | 15 |
| 16 | YnE | YnW | YnF | YnWd | YgE | YgE3 | YgE | YgE1 | YnE | YnW | YnE | YnF | YgM | YgW | YnM | YnE2 | YnM | YnE4 | YgW | YgM | YgW | YgWd | YnW | YnM | 16 |
| 17 | YgM | YgW | YgE | YgE1 | YnE | YnW | YnE | YnF | YgM | YgW | YgM | YgF | YnM | YnE4 | YgW | YgM | YgW | YgWd | YnW | YnM | YnW | YnWd | YgWd | YgE3 | 17 |
| 18 | YnM | YnE4 | YnE | YnF | YgM | YgW | YgM | YgF | YnM | YnE4 | YnM | YnE2 | YgW | YgWd | YnW | YnM | YnW | YnWd | YgWd | YgE3 | YgWd | YgE1 | YnWd | YnW | 18 |
| 19 | YgW | YgWd | YgM | YgF | YnM | YnE4 | YnM | YnE2 | YgW | YgWd | YgW | YgM | YnW | YnWd | YgWd | YgE3 | YgWd | YgE1 | YnWd | YnW | YnWd | YnF | YgF | YgW | 19 |
| 20 | YnW | YnWd | YnM | YnE2 | YgW | YgWd | YgW | YgM | YnW | YnWd | YnW | YnM | YgWd | YgE1 | YnWd | YnW | YnWd | YnF | YgF | YgW | YgF | YgF | YnF | YnE4 | 20 |
| 21 | YgWd | YgE1 | YgW | YgM | YnW | YnWd | YnW | YnM | YgWd | YgE1 | YgWd | YgE3 | YnWd | YnF | YgF | YgW | YgF | YgF | YnF | YnE4 | YnF | YnE2 | YgE | YgWd | 21 |
| 22 | YnWd | YnF | YnW | YnM | YgWd | YgE1 | YgWd | YgE3 | YnWd | YnF | YnWd | YnW | YgF | YgF | YnF | YnE4 | YnF | YnE2 | YgE | YgWd | YgE | YgM | YnE | YnWd | 22 |
| 23 | YgF | YgF | YgWd | YgE3 | YnWd | YnF | YnWd | YnW | YgF | YgF | YgF | YgW | YnF | YnE2 | YgE | YgWd | YgE | YgM | YnE | YnWd | YnE | YnM | YgM | YgE1 | 23 |
| 24 | YnF | YnE2 | YnWd | YnW | YgF | YgF | YgF | YgW | YnF | YnE2 | YnF | YnE4 | YgE | YgM | YnE | YnWd | YnE | YnM | YgM | YgE1 | YgM | YgE3 | YnM | YnF | 24 |
| 25 | YgE | YgM | YgF | YgW | YnF | YnE2 | YnF | YnE4 | YgE | YgM | YgE | YgWd | YnE | YnM | YgM | YgE1 | YgM | YgE3 | YnM | YnF | YnM | YnW | YgW | YgF | 25 |
| 26 | YnE | YnM | YnF | YnE4 | YgE | YgM | YgE | YgWd | YnE | YnM | YnE | YnWd | YgM | YgE3 | YnM | YnF | YnM | YnW | YgW | YgF | YgW | YgW | YnW | YnE2 | 26 |
| 27 | YgM | YgE3 | YgE | YgWd | YnE | YnM | YnE | YnWd | YgM | YgE3 | YgM | YgE1 | YnM | YnW | YgW | YgF | YgW | YgW | YnW | YnE2 | YnW | YnE4 | YgWd | YgM | 27 |
| 28 | YnM | YnW | YnE | YnWd | YgM | YgE3 | YgM | YgE1 | YnM | YnW | YnM | YnF | YgW | YgW | YnW | YnE2 | YnW | YnE4 | YgWd | YgM | YgWd | YgWd | YnWd | YnM | 28 |
| 29 | | | YgM | YgE1 | YnM | YnW | YnM | YnF | YgW | YgW | YgW | YgF | YnW | YnE4 | YgWd | YgM | YgWd | YgWd | YnWd | YnM | YnWd | YnWd | YgF | YgE3 | 29 |
| 30 | | | YnM | YnF | YgW | YgW | YgW | YgF | YnW | YnE4 | YnW | YnE2 | YgWd | YgWd | YnWd | YnM | YnWd | YnWd | YgF | YgE3 | YgF | YgE1 | YnF | YnW | 30 |
| 31 | | | YgW | YgF | | | YnW | YnE2 | | | YgWd | YgM | YnWd | YnWd | | | YgF | YgE1 | | | YnF | YnF | YgE | YgW | 31 |
| 1 | YgW | YgW | YnW | YnE2 | YnW | YnE4 | YgWd | YgM | YgWd | YgWd | YnWd | YnM | YgF | YgE1 | YgF | YgE3 | YnF | YnF | YnF | YnW | YgE | YgF | YnE | YnE4 | 1 |
| 2 | YnW | YnE4 | YgWd | YgM | YgWd | YgWd | YnWd | YnM | YnWd | YnWd | YgF | YgE3 | YnF | YnF | YnF | YnW | YgE | YgF | YgE | YgW | YnE | YnE2 | YgM | YgWd | 2 |
| 3 | YgWd | YgWd | YnWd | YnM | YnWd | YnWd | YgF | YgE3 | YgF | YgE1 | YnF | YnW | YgE | YgF | YgE | YgW | YnE | YnE2 | YnE | YnE4 | YgM | YgM | YnM | YnWd | 3 |
| 4 | YnWd | YnWd | YgF | YgE3 | YgF | YgE1 | YnF | YnW | YnF | YnF | YgE | YgW | YnE | YnE2 | YnE | YnE4 | YgM | YgM | YgM | YgWd | YnM | YnM | YgW | YgE1 | 4 |
| 5 | YgF | YgE1 | YnF | YnW | YnF | YnF | YgE | YgW | YgE | YgF | YnE | YnE4 | YgM | YgM | YgM | YgWd | YnM | YnM | YnM | YnWd | YgW | YgE3 | | | 5 |
| 6 | | | | | | | YnE | YnE4 | YnE | YnE2 | YgM | YgWd | YnM | YnM | YnM | YnWd | YgW | YgE3 | YgW | YgE1 | | | | | 6 |
| 7 | | | | | | | | | YgM | YgM | YnM | YnWd | YgW | YgE3 | YgW | YgE1 | YnW | YnW | YnW | YnF | | | | | 7 |
| 8 | | | | | | | | | | | | | YnW | YnW | YnW | YnF | | | | | | | | | 8 |

# YEAR OF THE MONKEY

| | H | E | H | E | H | E | H | E | H | E | H | E | H | E | H | E | H | E | H | E | H | E | H | E | |
|---|---|---|---|---|---|---|---|---|---|---|---|---|---|---|---|---|---|---|---|---|---|---|---|---|---|
| YEAR | YEAR YgM | YgM | 1920 | | | | | | | | | | | | | | | | | | 1921 | | | | |
| MONTH | 5 Feb - 5 Mar | | 6 Mar - 4 Apr | | 5 Apr - 5 May | | 6 May - 5 June | | 6 June - 6 Jul | | 7 Jul - 7 Aug | | 8 Aug - 7 Sep | | 8 Sep - 7 Oct | | 8 Oct - 7 Nov | | 8 Nov - 6 Dec | | 7 Dec - 5 Jan | | 6 Jan - 3 Feb | | |
| | YgE | YgWd | YnE | YnWd | YgM | YgE1 | YnM | YnF | YgW | YgF | YnW | YnE2 | YgWd | YgM | YnWd | YnM | YgF | YgE3 | YnF | YnW | YgE | YgW | YnE | YnE4 | |
| Starting time | 1st day | Mid-pt | 1st day | Mid-pt | 1st day | Mid-pt | 1st day | Mid-pt | 1st day | Mid-pt | 1st day | Mid-pt | 1st day | Mid-pt | 1st day | Mid-pt | 1st day | Mid-pt | 1st day | Mid-pt | 1st day | Mid-pt | 1st day | Mid-pt | |
| Date | 5 | 20 | 6 | 21 | 5 | 20 | 6 | 21 | 6 | 22 | 7 | 23 | 8 | 23 | 8 | 23 | 8 | 24 | 8 | 22 | 7 | 22 | 6 | 20 | |
| Hour | 1027 | 0629 | 0451 | 0600 | 1015 | 1739 | 0412 | 1722 | 0851 | 0140 | 1919 | 1235 | 0458 | 1922 | 0727 | 1629 | 2230 | 0113 | 0105 | 2216 | 1731 | 1117 | 0434 | 2155 | |
| DATE 4 | | | | | | | | | | | | | | | | | | | | | | | | | 4 |
| 5 | YnW | YnF | | | YnW | YnF | | | | | | | | | | | | | | | | | | | 5 |
| 6 | YgWd | YgF | YnW | YnW | YgWd | YgF | YgWd | YgW | YnWd | YnE2 | | | | | | | | | | | | | YnE | YnF | 6 |
| 7 | YnWd | YnE2 | YgWd | YgW | YnWd | YnE2 | YnWd | YnE4 | YgF | YgM | YgF | YgWd | | | | | | | | | YnE | YnW | YgM | YgF | 7 |
| 8 | YgF | YgM | YnWd | YnE4 | YgF | YgM | YgF | YgWd | YnF | YnM | YnF | YnWd | YgE | YgE3 | YnE | YnF | YnE | YnW | YgM | YgF | YgM | YgW | YnM | YnE2 | 8 |
| 9 | YnF | YnM | YgF | YgWd | YnF | YnM | YnF | YnWd | YgE | YgE3 | YgE | YgE1 | YnE | YnW | YgM | YgF | YgM | YgW | YnM | YnE2 | YnM | YnE4 | YgW | YgM | 9 |
| 10 | YgE | YgE3 | YnF | YnWd | YgE | YgE3 | YgE | YgE1 | YnE | YnW | YnE | YnF | YgM | YgW | YnM | YnE2 | YnM | YnE4 | YgW | YgM | YgW | YgWd | YnW | YnM | 10 |
| 11 | YnE | YnW | YgE | YgE1 | YnE | YnW | YnE | YnF | YgM | YgW | YgM | YgF | YnM | YnE4 | YgW | YgM | YgW | YgWd | YnW | YnM | YnW | YnWd | YgWd | YgE3 | 11 |
| 12 | YgM | YgW | YnE | YnF | YgM | YgW | YgM | YgF | YnM | YnE4 | YnM | YnE2 | YgW | YgWd | YnW | YnM | YnW | YnWd | YgWd | YgE3 | YgWd | YgE1 | YnWd | YnW | 12 |
| 13 | YnM | YnE4 | YgM | YgF | YnM | YnE4 | YnM | YnE2 | YgW | YgWd | YgW | YgM | YnW | YnWd | YgWd | YgE3 | YgWd | YgE1 | YnWd | YnW | YnWd | YnF | YgF | YgW | 13 |
| 14 | YgW | YgWd | YnM | YnE2 | YgW | YgWd | YgW | YgM | YnW | YnWd | YnW | YnM | YgWd | YgE1 | YnWd | YnW | YnWd | YnF | YgF | YgW | YgF | YgF | YnF | YnE4 | 14 |
| 15 | YnW | YnWd | YgW | YgM | YnW | YnWd | YnW | YnM | YgWd | YgE1 | YgWd | YgE3 | YnWd | YnF | YgF | YgW | YgF | YgF | YnF | YnE4 | YnF | YnE2 | YgE | YgWd | 15 |
| 16 | YgWd | YgE1 | YnW | YnM | YgWd | YgE1 | YgWd | YgE3 | YnWd | YnF | YnWd | YnW | YgF | YgF | YnF | YnE4 | YnF | YnE2 | YgE | YgWd | YgE | YgM | YnE | YnWd | 16 |
| 17 | YnWd | YnF | YgWd | YgE3 | YnWd | YnF | YnWd | YnW | YgF | YgF | YgF | YgW | YnF | YnE2 | YgE | YgWd | YgE | YgM | YnE | YnWd | YnE | YnM | YgM | YgE1 | 17 |
| 18 | YgF | YgF | YnWd | YnW | YgF | YgF | YgF | YgW | YnF | YnE2 | YnF | YnE4 | YgE | YgM | YnE | YnWd | YnE | YnM | YgM | YgE1 | YgM | YgE3 | YnM | YnF | 18 |
| 19 | YnF | YnE2 | YgF | YgW | YnF | YnE2 | YnF | YnE4 | YgE | YgM | YgE | YgWd | YnE | YnM | YgM | YgE1 | YgM | YgE3 | YnM | YnF | YnM | YnW | YgW | YgF | 19 |
| 20 | YgE | YgM | YnF | YnE4 | YgE | YgM | YgE | YgWd | YnE | YnM | YnE | YnWd | YgM | YgE3 | YnM | YnF | YnM | YnW | YgW | YgF | YgW | YgW | YnW | YnE2 | 20 |
| 21 | YnE | YnM | YgE | YgWd | YnE | YnM | YnE | YnWd | YgM | YgE3 | YgM | YgE1 | YnM | YnW | YgW | YgF | YgW | YgW | YnW | YnE2 | YnW | YnE4 | YgWd | YgM | 21 |
| 22 | YgM | YgE3 | YnE | YnWd | YgM | YgE3 | YgM | YgE1 | YnM | YnW | YnM | YnF | YgW | YgW | YnW | YnE2 | YnW | YnE4 | YgWd | YgM | YgWd | YgWd | YnWd | YnM | 22 |
| 23 | YnM | YnW | YgM | YgE1 | YnM | YnW | YnM | YnF | YgW | YgW | YgW | YgF | YnW | YnE4 | YgWd | YgM | YgWd | YgWd | YnWd | YnM | YnWd | YnWd | YgF | YgE3 | 23 |
| 24 | YgW | YgW | YnM | YnF | YgW | YgW | YgW | YgF | YnW | YnE4 | YnW | YnE2 | YgWd | YgWd | YnWd | YnM | YnWd | YnWd | YgF | YgE3 | YgF | YgE1 | YnF | YnW | 24 |
| 25 | YnW | YnE4 | YgW | YgF | YnW | YnE4 | YnW | YnE2 | YgWd | YgWd | YgWd | YgM | YnWd | YnWd | YgF | YgE3 | YgF | YgE1 | YnF | YnW | YnF | YnF | YgE | YgW | 25 |
| 26 | YgWd | YgWd | YnW | YnE2 | YgWd | YgWd | YgWd | YgM | YnWd | YnWd | YnWd | YnM | YgF | YgE1 | YnF | YnW | YnF | YnF | YgE | YgW | YgE | YgF | YnE | YnE4 | 26 |
| 27 | YnWd | YnWd | YgWd | YgM | YnWd | YnWd | YnWd | YnM | YgF | YgE1 | YgF | YgE3 | YnF | YnF | YgE | YgW | YgE | YgF | YnE | YnE4 | YnE | YnE2 | YgM | YgWd | 27 |
| 28 | YgF | YgE1 | YnWd | YnM | YgF | YgE1 | YgF | YgE3 | YnF | YnF | YnF | YnW | YgE | YgF | YnE | YnE4 | YnE | YnE2 | YgM | YgWd | YgM | YgM | YnM | YnWd | 28 |
| 29 | YnF | YnF | YgF | YgE3 | YnF | YnF | YnF | YnW | YgE | YgF | YgE | YgW | YnE | YnE2 | YgM | YgWd | YgM | YgM | YnM | YnWd | YnM | YnM | YgW | YgE1 | 29 |
| 30 | | | YnF | YnW | YgE | YgF | YgE | YgW | YnE | YnE2 | YnE | YnE4 | YgM | YgM | YnM | YnWd | YnM | YnM | YgW | YgE1 | YgW | YgE3 | YnW | YnF | 30 |
| 31 | | | YgE | YgW | | | YnE | YnE4 | | | YgM | YgWd | YnM | YnM | | | YgW | YgE3 | | | YnW | YnW | YgWd | YgF | 31 |
| 1 | YgE | YgF | YnE | YnE4 | YnE | YnE2 | YgM | YgWd | YgM | YgM | YnM | YnWd | YgW | YgE3 | YgW | YgE1 | YnW | YnW | YnW | YnF | YgWd | YgW | YnWd | YnE2 | 1 |
| 2 | YnE | YnE2 | YgM | YgWd | YgM | YgM | YnM | YnWd | YnM | YnM | YgW | YgE1 | YnW | YnW | YnW | YnF | YgWd | YgW | YgWd | YgF | YnWd | YnE4 | YgF | YgM | 2 |
| 3 | YgM | YgM | YnM | YnWd | YnM | YnM | YgW | YgE1 | YgW | YgE3 | YnW | YnF | YgWd | YgW | YgWd | YgF | YnWd | YnE4 | YnWd | YnE2 | YgF | YgWd | YnF | YnM | 3 |
| 4 | YnM | YnM | YgW | YgE1 | YgW | YgE3 | YnW | YnF | YnW | YnW | YgWd | YgF | YnWd | YnE4 | YnWd | YnE2 | YgF | YgWd | YgF | YgM | YnF | YnWd | | | 4 |
| 5 | YgW | YgE3 | | | YnW | YnW | YgWd | YgF | YgWd | YgW | YnWd | YnE2 | YgF | YgWd | YgF | YgM | YnF | YnWd | YnF | YnM | YgE | YgE1 | | | 5 |
| 6 | | | | | | | | | YnWd | YnE4 | YgF | YgM | YnF | YnWd | YnF | YnM | YgE | YgE1 | YgE | YgE3 | | | | | 6 |
| 7 | | | | | | | | | | | YnF | YnM | YgE | YgE1 | YgE | YgE3 | YnE | YnF | | | | | | | 7 |
| 8 | | | | | | | | | | | | | | | | | | | | | | | | | 8 |

# YEAR OF THE ROOSTER

| | H | E | H | E | H | E | H | E | H | E | H | E | H | E | H | E | H | E | H | E | H | E | H | E | |
|---|---|---|---|---|---|---|---|---|---|---|---|---|---|---|---|---|---|---|---|---|---|---|---|---|---|
| **YEAR** | **YEAR** | | 1921 | | | | | | | | | | | | | | | | | | | | 1922 | | |
| | YnM | YnM | | | | | | | | | | | | | | | | | | | | | | | |
| **MONTH** | 4 Feb - 5 Mar | | 6 Mar - 4 Apr | | 5 Apr - 5 May | | 6 May - 5 June | | 6 June - 7 Jul | | 8 Jul - 7 Aug | | 8 Aug - 7 Sep | | 8 Sep - 8 Oct | | 9 Oct - 7 Nov | | 8 Nov - 6 Dec | | 7 Dec - 5 Jan | | 6 Jan - 3 Feb | | |
| | Yg M | Yg Wd | Yn M | Yn Wd | Yg W | Yg E1 | Yn W | Yn F | YgWd | Yg F | Yn Wd | Yn E2 | Yg F | Yg M | Yn F | Yn M | Yg E | Yg E3 | Yn E | Yn W | Yg M | Yg W | Yn M | Yn E4 | |
| **Starting time** | 1st day | Mid-pt | 1st day | Mid-pt | 1st day | Mid-pt | 1st day | Mid-pt | 1st day | Mid-pt | 1st day | Mid-pt | 1st day | Mid-pt | 1st day | Mid-pt | 1st day | Mid-pt | 1st day | Mid-pt | 1st day | Mid-pt | 1st day | Mid-pt | |
| Date | 4 | 19 | 6 | 21 | 5 | 20 | 6 | 21 | 6 | 22 | 8 | 23 | 8 | 24 | 8 | 23 | 9 | 24 | 8 | 23 | 7 | 22 | 6 | 21 | |
| Hour | 1621 | 1220 | 1046 | 1151 | 1609 | 2333 | 1005 | 2319 | 1442 | 0736 | 0107 | 1831 | 1044 | 0115 | 1310 | 2220 | 0411 | 0703 | 0646 | 0405 | 2312 | 1708 | 1017 | 0348 | |
| **DATE** 4 | Yg E | Yg E3 | | | | | | | | | | | | | | | | | | | | | | | 4 |
| 5 | Yn E | Yn W | | | Yg E | Yg E3 | | | | | | | | | | | | | | | | | | | 5 |
| 6 | Yg M | Yg W | Yg E | Yg E1 | Yn E | Yn W | Yn E | Yn F | Yg M | Yg W | | | | | | | | | | | | | Yg Wd | Yg E3 | 6 |
| 7 | Yn M | Yn E4 | Yn E | Yn F | Yg M | Yg W | Yg M | Yg F | Yn M | Yn E4 | | | | | | | | | | | Yg Wd | Yg E1 | Yn Wd | Yn W | 7 |
| 8 | Yg W | Yg Wd | Yg M | Yg F | Yn M | Yn E4 | Yn M | Yn E2 | Yg W | Yg Wd | Yg W | Yg M | Yn W | Yn Wd | Yg Wd | Yg E3 | | | Yn Wd | Yn W | Yn Wd | Yn F | Yg F | Yg W | 8 |
| 9 | Yn W | Yn Wd | Yn M | Yn E2 | Yg W | Yg Wd | Yg W | Yg M | Yn W | Yn Wd | Yn W | Yn M | Yg Wd | Yg E1 | Yn Wd | Yn W | Yn Wd | Yn F | Yg F | Yg W | Yg F | Yg F | Yn F | Yn E4 | 9 |
| 10 | Yg Wd | Yg E1 | Yg W | Yg M | Yn W | Yn Wd | Yn W | Yn M | Yg Wd | Yg E1 | Yg Wd | Yg E3 | Yn Wd | Yn F | Yg F | Yg W | Yg F | Yg F | Yn F | Yn E4 | Yn F | Yn E2 | Yg E | Yg Wd | 10 |
| 11 | Yn Wd | Yn F | Yn W | Yn M | Yg Wd | Yg E1 | Yg Wd | Yg E3 | Yn Wd | Yn F | Yn Wd | Yn W | Yg F | Yg F | Yn F | Yn E4 | Yn F | Yn E2 | Yg E | Yg Wd | Yg E | Yg M | Yn E | Yn Wd | 11 |
| 12 | Yg F | Yg F | Yg Wd | Yg E3 | Yn Wd | Yn F | Yn Wd | Yn W | Yg F | Yg F | Yg F | Yg W | Yn F | Yn E2 | Yg E | Yg Wd | Yg E | Yg M | Yn E | Yn Wd | Yn E | Yn M | Yg M | Yg E1 | 12 |
| 13 | Yn F | Yn E2 | Yn Wd | Yn W | Yg F | Yg F | Yg F | Yg W | Yn F | Yn E2 | Yn F | Yn E4 | Yg E | Yg M | Yn E | Yn Wd | Yn E | Yn M | Yg M | Yg E1 | Yg M | Yg E3 | Yn M | Yn F | 13 |
| 14 | Yg E | Yg M | Yg F | Yg W | Yn F | Yn E2 | Yn F | Yn E4 | Yg E | Yg M | Yg E | Yg Wd | Yn E | Yn M | Yg M | Yg E1 | Yg M | Yg E3 | Yn M | Yn F | Yn M | Yn W | Yg W | Yg F | 14 |
| 15 | Yn E | Yn M | Yn F | Yn E4 | Yg E | Yg M | Yg E | Yg Wd | Yn E | Yn M | Yn E | Yn Wd | Yg M | Yg E3 | Yn M | Yn F | Yn M | Yn W | Yg W | Yg F | Yg W | Yg W | Yn W | Yn E2 | 15 |
| 16 | Yg M | Yg E3 | Yg E | Yg Wd | Yn E | Yn M | Yn E | Yn Wd | Yg M | Yg E3 | Yg M | Yg E1 | Yn M | Yn W | Yg W | Yg F | Yg W | Yg W | Yn W | Yn E2 | Yn W | Yn E4 | Yg Wd | Yg M | 16 |
| 17 | Yn M | Yn W | Yn E | Yn Wd | Yg M | Yg E3 | Yg M | Yg E1 | Yn M | Yn W | Yn M | Yn F | Yg W | Yg W | Yn W | Yn E2 | Yn W | Yn E4 | Yg Wd | Yg M | Yg Wd | Yg Wd | Yn Wd | Yn M | 17 |
| 18 | Yg W | Yg W | Yg M | Yg E1 | Yn M | Yn W | Yn M | Yn F | Yg W | Yg W | Yg W | Yg F | Yn W | Yn E4 | Yg Wd | Yg M | Yg Wd | Yg Wd | Yn Wd | Yn M | Yn Wd | Yn Wd | Yg F | Yg E3 | 18 |
| 19 | Yn W | Yn E4 | Yn M | Yn F | Yg W | Yg W | Yg W | Yg F | Yn W | Yn E4 | Yn W | Yn E2 | Yg Wd | Yg Wd | Yn Wd | Yn M | Yn Wd | Yn Wd | Yg F | Yg E3 | Yg F | Yg E1 | Yn F | Yn W | 19 |
| 20 | Yg Wd | Yg Wd | Yg W | Yg F | Yn W | Yn E4 | Yn W | Yn E2 | Yg Wd | Yg Wd | Yg Wd | Yg M | Yn Wd | Yn Wd | Yg F | Yg E3 | Yg F | Yg E1 | Yn F | Yn W | Yn F | Yn F | Yg E | Yg W | 20 |
| 21 | Yn Wd | Yn Wd | Yn W | Yn E2 | Yg Wd | Yg Wd | Yg Wd | Yg M | Yn Wd | Yn Wd | Yn Wd | Yn M | Yg F | Yg E1 | Yn F | Yn W | Yn F | Yn F | Yg E | Yg W | Yg E | Yg F | Yn E | Yn E4 | 21 |
| 22 | Yg F | Yg E1 | Yg Wd | Yg M | Yn Wd | Yn Wd | Yn Wd | Yn M | Yg F | Yg E1 | Yg F | Yg E3 | Yn F | Yn F | Yg E | Yg W | Yg E | Yg F | Yn E | Yn E4 | Yn E | Yn E2 | Yg M | Yg Wd | 22 |
| 23 | Yn F | Yn F | Yn Wd | Yn M | Yg F | Yg E1 | Yg F | Yg E3 | Yn F | Yn F | Yn F | Yn W | Yg E | Yg F | Yn E | Yn E4 | Yn E | Yn E2 | Yg M | Yg Wd | Yg M | Yg M | Yn M | Yn Wd | 23 |
| 24 | Yg E | Yg F | Yg F | Yg E3 | Yn F | Yn F | Yn F | Yn W | Yg E | Yg F | Yg E | Yg W | Yn E | Yn E2 | Yg M | Yg Wd | Yg M | Yg M | Yn M | Yn Wd | Yn M | Yn M | Yg W | Yg E1 | 24 |
| 25 | Yn E | Yn E2 | Yn F | Yn W | Yg E | Yg F | Yg E | Yg W | Yn E | Yn E2 | Yn E | Yn E4 | Yg M | Yg M | Yn M | Yn Wd | Yn M | Yn M | Yg W | Yg E1 | Yg W | Yg E3 | Yn W | Yn F | 25 |
| 26 | Yg M | Yg M | Yg E | Yg W | Yn E | Yn E2 | Yn E | Yn E4 | Yg M | Yg M | Yg M | Yg Wd | Yn M | Yn M | Yg W | Yg E1 | Yg W | Yg E3 | Yn W | Yn F | Yn W | Yn W | Yg Wd | Yg F | 26 |
| 27 | Yn M | Yn M | Yn E | Yn E4 | Yg M | Yg M | Yg M | Yg Wd | Yn M | Yn M | Yn M | Yn Wd | Yg W | Yg E3 | Yn W | Yn F | Yn W | Yn W | Yg Wd | Yg F | Yg Wd | Yg W | Yn Wd | Yn E2 | 27 |
| 28 | Yg W | Yg E3 | Yg M | Yg Wd | Yn M | Yn M | Yn M | Yn Wd | Yg W | Yg E3 | Yg W | Yg E1 | Yn W | Yn W | Yg Wd | Yg F | Yg Wd | Yg W | Yn Wd | Yn E2 | Yn Wd | Yn E4 | Yg F | Yg M | 28 |
| 29 | | | Yn M | Yn Wd | Yg W | Yg E3 | Yg W | Yg E1 | Yn W | Yn W | Yn W | Yn F | Yg Wd | Yg W | Yn Wd | Yn E2 | Yn Wd | Yn E4 | Yg F | Yg M | Yg F | Yg Wd | Yn F | Yn M | 29 |
| 30 | | | Yg W | Yg E1 | Yn W | Yn W | Yn W | Yn F | Yg Wd | Yg W | Yg Wd | Yg F | Yn Wd | Yn E4 | Yg F | Yg M | Yg F | Yg Wd | Yn F | Yn M | Yn F | Yn Wd | Yg E | Yg E3 | 30 |
| 31 | | | Yn W | Yn F | | | Yg Wd | Yg F | | | Yn Wd | Yn E2 | Yg F | Yg Wd | | | Yn F | Yn Wd | | | Yg E | Yg E1 | Yn E | Yn W | 31 |
| 1 | Yn W | Yn W | Yg Wd | Yg F | Yg Wd | Yg W | Yn Wd | Yn E2 | Yn Wd | Yn E4 | Yg F | Yg M | Yn F | Yn Wd | Yn F | Yn M | Yg E | Yg E1 | Yg E | Yg E3 | Yn E | Yn F | Yg M | Yg W | 1 |
| 2 | Yg Wd | Yg W | Yn Wd | Yn E2 | Yn Wd | Yn E4 | Yg F | Yg M | Yg F | Yg Wd | Yn F | Yn M | Yg E | Yg E1 | Yg E | Yg E3 | Yn E | Yn F | Yn E | Yn W | Yg M | Yg F | Yn M | Yn E4 | 2 |
| 3 | Yn Wd | Yn E4 | Yg F | Yg M | Yg F | Yg Wd | Yn F | Yn M | Yn F | Yn Wd | Yg E | Yg E3 | Yn E | Yn F | Yn E | Yn W | Yg M | Yg F | Yg M | Yg W | Yn M | Yn E2 | Yg W | Yg Wd | 3 |
| 4 | Yg F | Yg Wd | Yn F | Yn M | Yn F | Yn Wd | Yg E | Yg E3 | Yg E | Yg E1 | Yn E | Yn W | Yg M | Yg F | Yg M | Yg W | Yn M | Yn E2 | Yn M | Yn E4 | Yg W | Yg M | | | 4 |
| 5 | Yn F | Yn Wd | | | Yg E | Yg E1 | Yn E | Yn W | Yn E | Yn F | Yg M | Yg W | Yn M | Yn E2 | Yn M | Yn E4 | Yg W | Yg M | Yg W | Yg Wd | Yn W | Yn M | | | 5 |
| 6 | | | | | | | | | Yg M | Yg F | Yn M | Yn E4 | Yg W | Yg M | Yg W | Yg Wd | Yn W | Yn M | Yn W | Yn Wd | | | | | 6 |
| 7 | | | | | | | | | Yn M | Yn E2 | Yg W | Yg Wd | Yn W | Yn M | Yn W | Yn Wd | Yg Wd | Yg E3 | | | | | | | 7 |
| 8 | | | | | | | | | | | | | | | Yg Wd | Yg E1 | | | | | | | | | 8 |

# YEAR OF THE DOG

| | H | E | H | E | H | E | H | E | H | E | H | E | H | E | H | E | H | E | H | E | H | E | H | E | |
|---|---|---|---|---|---|---|---|---|---|---|---|---|---|---|---|---|---|---|---|---|---|---|---|---|---|
| YEAR | YEAR Yg W | Yg E3 | 1922 | | | | | | | | | | | | | | | | | | | | 1923 | | |
| MONTH | 4 Feb - 5 Mar | | 6 Mar - 4 Apr | | 5 Apr - 5 May | | 6 May - 5 June | | 6 June - 7 Jul | | 8 Jul - 7 Aug | | 8 Aug - 7 Sep | | 8 Sep - 8 Oct | | 9 Oct - 7 Nov | | 8 Nov - 7 Dec | | 8 Dec - 5 Jan | | 6 Jan - 4 Feb | | |
| | Yg W | Yg Wd | Yn W | Yn Wd | Yg Wd | Yg E1 | Yn Wd | Yn F | Yg F | Yg F | Yn F | Yn E2 | Yg E | Yg M | Yn E | Yn M | Yg M | Yg E3 | Yn M | Yn W | Yg W | Yg W | Yn W | Yn E4 | |
| Starting time | 1st day | Mid-pt | 1st day | Mid-pt | 1st day | Mid-pt | 1st day | Mid-pt | 1st day | Mid-pt | 1st day | Mid-pt | 1st day | Mid-pt | 1st day | Mid-pt | 1st day | Mid-pt | 1st day | Mid-pt | 1st day | Mid-pt | 1st day | Mid-pt | |
| Date | 4 | 19 | 6 | 21 | 5 | 21 | 6 | 22 | 6 | 22 | 8 | 24 | 8 | 24 | 8 | 24 | 9 | 24 | 8 | 23 | 8 | 22 | 6 | 21 | |
| Hour | 2207 | 1816 | 1634 | 1749 | 2158 | 0529 | 1553 | 0503 | 2030 | 1327 | 0654 | 0020 | 1638 | 0705 | 1907 | 0410 | 1010 | 1253 | 1246 | 0956 | 0511 | 2257 | 1615 | 0935 | |
| DATE 4 | Yn W | Yn Wd | | | | | | | | | | | | | | | | | | | | | | | 4 |
| 5 | Yg Wd | Yg E1 | | | Yn W | Yn Wd | | | | | | | | | | | | | | | | | | | 5 |
| 6 | Yn Wd | Yn F | Yn W | Yn M | Yg Wd | Yg E1 | Yg Wd | Yg E3 | Yn Wd | Yn F | | | | | | | | | | | | | Yn E | Yn Wd | 6 |
| 7 | Yg F | Yg F | Yg Wd | Yg E3 | Yn Wd | Yn F | Yn Wd | Yn W | Yg F | Yg F | | | | | | | | | | | | | Yg M | Yg E1 | 7 |
| 8 | Yn F | Yn E2 | Yn Wd | Yn W | Yg F | Yg F | Yg F | Yg W | Yn F | Yn E2 | Yn F | Yn E4 | Yg E | Yg M | Yn E | Yn Wd | | | Yg M | Yg E1 | Yg M | Yg E3 | Yn M | Yn F | 8 |
| 9 | Yg E | Yg M | Yg F | Yg W | Yn F | Yn E2 | Yn F | Yn E4 | Yg E | Yg M | Yg E | Yg Wd | Yn E | Yn M | Yg M | Yg E1 | Yg M | Yg E3 | Yn M | Yn F | Yn M | Yn W | Yg W | Yg F | 9 |
| 10 | Yn E | Yn M | Yn F | Yn E4 | Yg E | Yg M | Yg E | Yg Wd | Yn E | Yn M | Yn E | Yn Wd | Yg M | Yg E3 | Yn M | Yn F | Yn M | Yn W | Yg W | Yg F | Yg W | Yg W | Yn W | Yn E2 | 10 |
| 11 | Yg M | Yg E3 | Yg E | Yg Wd | Yn E | Yn M | Yn E | Yn Wd | Yg M | Yg E3 | Yg M | Yg E1 | Yn M | Yn W | Yg W | Yg F | Yg W | Yg W | Yn W | Yn E2 | Yn W | Yn E4 | Yg Wd | Yg M | 11 |
| 12 | Yn M | Yn W | Yn E | Yn Wd | Yg M | Yg E3 | Yg M | Yg E1 | Yn M | Yn W | Yn M | Yn F | Yg W | Yg W | Yn W | Yn E2 | Yn W | Yn E4 | Yg Wd | Yg M | Yg Wd | Yg Wd | Yn Wd | Yn M | 12 |
| 13 | Yg W | Yg W | Yg M | Yg E1 | Yn M | Yn W | Yn M | Yn F | Yg W | Yg W | Yg W | Yg F | Yn W | Yn E4 | Yg Wd | Yg M | Yg Wd | Yg Wd | Yn Wd | Yn M | Yn Wd | Yn Wd | Yg F | Yg E3 | 13 |
| 14 | Yn W | Yn E4 | Yn M | Yn F | Yg W | Yg W | Yg W | Yg F | Yn W | Yn E4 | Yn W | Yn E2 | Yg Wd | Yg Wd | Yn Wd | Yn M | Yn Wd | Yn Wd | Yg F | Yg E3 | Yg F | Yg E1 | Yn F | Yn W | 14 |
| 15 | Yg Wd | Yg Wd | Yg W | Yg F | Yn W | Yn E4 | Yn W | Yn E2 | Yg Wd | Yg Wd | Yg Wd | Yg M | Yn Wd | Yn Wd | Yg F | Yg E3 | Yg F | Yg E1 | Yn F | Yn W | Yn F | Yn F | Yg E | Yg W | 15 |
| 16 | Yn Wd | Yn Wd | Yn W | Yn E2 | Yg Wd | Yg Wd | Yg Wd | Yg M | Yn Wd | Yn Wd | Yn Wd | Yn M | Yg F | Yg E1 | Yn F | Yn W | Yn F | Yn F | Yg E | Yg W | Yg E | Yg F | Yn E | Yn E4 | 16 |
| 17 | Yg F | Yg E1 | Yg Wd | Yg M | Yn Wd | Yn Wd | Yn Wd | Yn M | Yg F | Yg E1 | Yg F | Yg E3 | Yn F | Yn F | Yg E | Yg W | Yg E | Yg F | Yn E | Yn E4 | Yn E | Yn E2 | Yg M | Yg Wd | 17 |
| 18 | Yn F | Yn F | Yn Wd | Yn M | Yg F | Yg E1 | Yg F | Yg E3 | Yn F | Yn F | Yn F | Yn W | Yg E | Yg F | Yn E | Yn E4 | Yn E | Yn E2 | Yg M | Yg Wd | Yg M | Yg M | Yn M | Yn Wd | 18 |
| 19 | Yg E | Yg F | Yg F | Yg E3 | Yn F | Yn F | Yn F | Yn W | Yg E | Yg F | Yg E | Yg W | Yn E | Yn E2 | Yg M | Yg Wd | Yg M | Yg M | Yn M | Yn Wd | Yn M | Yn M | Yg W | Yg E1 | 19 |
| 20 | Yn E | Yn E2 | Yn F | Yn W | Yg E | Yg F | Yg E | Yg W | Yn E | Yn E2 | Yn E | Yn E4 | Yg M | Yg M | Yn M | Yn Wd | Yn M | Yn M | Yg W | Yg E1 | Yg W | Yg E3 | Yn W | Yn F | 20 |
| 21 | Yg M | Yg M | Yg E | Yg W | Yn E | Yn E2 | Yn E | Yn E4 | Yg M | Yg M | Yg M | Yg Wd | Yn M | Yn M | Yg W | Yg E1 | Yg W | Yg E3 | Yn W | Yn F | Yn W | Yn W | Yg Wd | Yg F | 21 |
| 22 | Yn M | Yn M | Yn E | Yn E4 | Yg M | Yg M | Yg M | Yg Wd | Yn M | Yn M | Yn M | Yn Wd | Yg W | Yg E3 | Yn W | Yn F | Yn W | Yn W | Yg Wd | Yg F | Yg Wd | Yg W | Yn Wd | Yn E2 | 22 |
| 23 | Yg W | Yg E3 | Yg M | Yg Wd | Yn M | Yn M | Yn M | Yn Wd | Yg W | Yg E3 | Yg W | Yg E1 | Yn W | Yn W | Yg Wd | Yg F | Yg Wd | Yg W | Yn Wd | Yn E2 | Yn Wd | Yn E4 | Yg F | Yg M | 23 |
| 24 | Yn W | Yn W | Yn M | Yn Wd | Yg W | Yg E3 | Yg W | Yg E1 | Yn W | Yn W | Yn W | Yn F | Yg Wd | Yg W | Yn Wd | Yn E2 | Yn Wd | Yn E4 | Yg F | Yg M | Yg F | Yg Wd | Yn F | Yn M | 24 |
| 25 | Yg Wd | Yg W | Yg W | Yg E1 | Yn W | Yn W | Yn W | Yn F | Yg Wd | Yg W | Yg Wd | Yg F | Yn Wd | Yn E4 | Yg F | Yg M | Yg F | Yg Wd | Yn F | Yn M | Yn F | Yn Wd | Yg E | Yg E3 | 25 |
| 26 | Yn Wd | Yn E4 | Yn W | Yn F | Yg Wd | Yg W | Yg Wd | Yg F | Yn Wd | Yn E4 | Yn Wd | Yn E2 | Yg F | Yg Wd | Yn F | Yn M | Yn F | Yn Wd | Yg E | Yg E3 | Yg E | Yg E1 | Yn E | Yn W | 26 |
| 27 | Yg F | Yg Wd | Yg Wd | Yg F | Yn Wd | Yn E4 | Yn Wd | Yn E2 | Yg F | Yg Wd | Yg F | Yg M | Yn F | Yn Wd | Yg E | Yg E3 | Yg E | Yg E1 | Yn E | Yn W | Yn E | Yn F | Yg M | Yg W | 27 |
| 28 | Yn F | Yn Wd | Yn Wd | Yn E2 | Yg F | Yg Wd | Yg F | Yg M | Yn F | Yn Wd | Yn F | Yn M | Yg E | Yg E1 | Yn E | Yn W | Yn E | Yn F | Yg M | Yg W | Yg M | Yg F | Yn M | Yn E4 | 28 |
| 29 | | | Yg F | Yg M | Yn F | Yn Wd | Yn F | Yn M | Yg E | Yg E1 | Yg E | Yg E3 | Yn E | Yn F | Yg M | Yg W | Yg M | Yg F | Yn M | Yn E4 | Yn M | Yn E2 | Yg W | Yg Wd | 29 |
| 30 | | | Yn F | Yn M | Yg E | Yg E1 | Yg E | Yg E3 | Yn E | Yn F | Yn E | Yn W | Yg M | Yg F | Yn M | Yn E4 | Yn M | Yn E2 | Yg W | Yg Wd | Yg W | Yg M | Yn W | Yn Wd | 30 |
| 31 | | | Yg E | Yg E3 | | | Yn E | Yn W | | | Yg M | Yg W | Yn M | Yn E2 | | | Yg W | Yg M | | | Yn W | Yn M | Yg Wd | Yg E1 | 31 |
| 1 | Yg E | Yg E1 | Yn E | Yn W | Yn E | Yn F | Yg M | Yg W | Yg M | Yg F | Yn M | Yn E4 | Yg W | Yg M | Yg W | Yg Wd | Yn W | Yn M | Yn W | Yn Wd | Yg Wd | Yg E3 | Yn Wd | Yn F | 1 |
| 2 | Yn E | Yn F | Yg M | Yg W | Yg M | Yg F | Yn M | Yn E4 | Yn M | Yn E2 | Yg W | Yg Wd | Yn W | Yn M | Yn W | Yn Wd | Yg Wd | Yg E3 | Yg Wd | Yg E1 | Yn Wd | Yn W | Yg F | Yg F | 2 |
| 3 | Yg M | Yg F | Yn M | Yn E4 | Yn M | Yn E2 | Yg W | Yg Wd | Yg W | Yg M | Yn W | Yn Wd | Yg Wd | Yg E3 | Yg Wd | Yg E1 | Yn Wd | Yn W | Yn Wd | Yn F | Yg F | Yg W | Yn F | Yn E2 | 3 |
| 4 | Yn M | Yn E2 | Yg W | Yg Wd | Yg W | Yg M | Yn W | Yn Wd | Yn W | Yn M | Yg Wd | Yg E1 | Yn Wd | Yn W | Yn Wd | Yn F | Yg F | Yg W | Yg F | Yg F | Yn F | Yn E4 | Yg E | Yg M | 4 |
| 5 | Yg W | Yg M | | | Yn W | Yn M | Yg Wd | Yg E1 | Yg Wd | Yg E3 | Yn Wd | Yn F | Yg F | Yg W | Yg F | Yg F | Yn F | Yn E4 | Yn F | Yn E2 | Yg E | Yg Wd | | | 5 |
| 6 | | | | | | | | | Yn Wd | Yn W | Yg F | Yg F | Yn F | Yn E4 | Yn F | Yn E2 | Yg E | Yg Wd | Yg E | Yg M | | | | | 6 |
| 7 | | | | | | | | | Yg F | Yg W | Yn F | Yn E2 | Yg E | Yg Wd | Yg E | Yg M | Yn E | Yn Wd | Yn E | Yn M | | | | | 7 |
| 8 | | | | | | | | | | | | | | | Yn E | Yn M | | | | | | | | | 8 |

# YEAR OF THE PIG

| | H | E | H | E | H | E | H | E | H | E | H | E | H | E | H | E | H | E | H | E | H | E | H | E | |
|---|---|---|---|---|---|---|---|---|---|---|---|---|---|---|---|---|---|---|---|---|---|---|---|---|---|
| YEAR | YEAR<br>Yn W | Yn W | 1923 | | | | | | | | | | | | | | | | | | | | 1924 | | |
| MONTH | 5 Feb - 5 Mar | | 6 Mar - 5 Apr | | 6 Apr - 5 May | | 6 May - 6 June | | 7 June - 7 Jul | | 8 Jul - 7 Aug | | 8 Aug - 8 Sep | | 9 Sep - 8 Oct | | 9 Oct - 7 Nov | | 8 Nov - 7 Dec | | 8 Dec - 5 Jan | | 6 Jan - 4 Feb | | |
| | Yg Wd | Yg Wd | Yn Wd | Yn Wd | Yg F | Yg E1 | Yn F | Yn F | Yg E | Yg F | Yn E | Yn E2 | Yg M | Yg M | Yn M | Yn M | Yg W | Yg E3 | Yn W | Yn W | Yg Wd | Yg W | Yn Wd | Yn E4 | |
| Starting time | 1st day | Mid-pt | 1st day | Mid-pt | 1st day | Mid-pt | 1st day | Mid-pt | 1st day | Mid-pt | 1st day | Mid-pt | 1st day | Mid-pt | 1st day | Mid-pt | 1st day | Mid-pt | 1st day | Mid-pt | 1st day | Mid-pt | 1st day | Mid-pt | |
| Date | 5 | 20 | 6 | 21 | 6 | 21 | 6 | 22 | 7 | 22 | 8 | 24 | 8 | 24 | 9 | 24 | 9 | 24 | 8 | 23 | 8 | 23 | 6 | 21 | |
| Hour | 0401 | 0000 | 2225 | 2329 | 0346 | 1106 | 2139 | 1046 | 0215 | 1908 | 1242 | 0601 | 2225 | 1252 | 0058 | 1004 | 1604 | 1851 | 1841 | 1554 | 1105 | 0454 | 2206 | 1529 | |
| DATE 4 | | | | | | | | | | | | | | | | | | | | | | | | | 4 |
| 5 | Yn E | Yn M | | | | | | | | | | | | | | | | | | | | | | | 5 |
| 6 | Yg M | Yg E3 | Yg E | Yg Wd | Yn E | Yn M | Yn E | Yn Wd | | | | | | | | | | | | | | | Yg Wd | Yg M | 6 |
| 7 | Yn M | Yn W | Yn E | Yn Wd | Yg M | Yg E3 | Yg M | Yg E1 | Yn M | Yn W | | | | | | | | | | | | | Yn Wd | Yn M | 7 |
| 8 | Yg W | Yg W | Yg M | Yg E1 | Yn M | Yn W | Yn M | Yn F | Yg W | Yg W | Yg W | Yg F | Yn W | Yn E4 | | | | | Yn Wd | Yn M | Yn Wd | Yn Wd | Yg F | Yg E3 | 8 |
| 9 | Yn W | Yn E4 | Yn M | Yn F | Yg W | Yg W | Yg W | Yg F | Yn W | Yn E4 | Yn W | Yn E2 | Yg Wd | Yg Wd | Yn Wd | Yn M | Yn Wd | Yn Wd | Yg F | Yg E3 | Yg F | Yg E1 | Yn F | Yn W | 9 |
| 10 | Yg Wd | Yg Wd | Yg W | Yg F | Yn W | Yn E4 | Yn W | Yn E2 | Yg Wd | Yg Wd | Yg Wd | Yg M | Yn Wd | Yn Wd | Yg F | Yg E3 | Yg F | Yg E1 | Yn F | Yn W | Yn F | Yn F | Yg E | Yg W | 10 |
| 11 | Yn Wd | Yn Wd | Yn W | Yn E2 | Yg Wd | Yg Wd | Yg Wd | Yg M | Yn Wd | Yn Wd | Yn Wd | Yn M | Yg F | Yg E1 | Yn F | Yn W | Yn F | Yn F | Yg E | Yg W | Yg E | Yg F | Yn E | Yn E4 | 11 |
| 12 | Yg F | Yg E1 | Yg Wd | Yg M | Yn Wd | Yn Wd | Yn Wd | Yn M | Yg F | Yg E1 | Yg F | Yg E3 | Yn F | Yn F | Yg E | Yg W | Yg E | Yg F | Yn E | Yn E4 | Yn E | Yn E2 | Yg M | Yg Wd | 12 |
| 13 | Yn F | Yn F | Yn Wd | Yn M | Yg F | Yg E1 | Yg F | Yg E3 | Yn F | Yn F | Yn F | Yn W | Yg E | Yg F | Yn E | Yn E4 | Yn E | Yn E2 | Yg M | Yg Wd | Yg M | Yg M | Yn M | Yn Wd | 13 |
| 14 | Yg E | Yg F | Yg F | Yg E3 | Yn F | Yn F | Yn F | Yn W | Yg E | Yg F | Yg E | Yg W | Yn E | Yn E2 | Yg M | Yg Wd | Yg M | Yg M | Yn M | Yn Wd | Yn M | Yn M | Yg W | Yg E1 | 14 |
| 15 | Yn E | Yn E2 | Yn F | Yn W | Yg E | Yg F | Yg E | Yg W | Yn E | Yn E2 | Yn E | Yn E4 | Yg M | Yg M | Yn M | Yn Wd | Yn M | Yn M | Yg W | Yg E1 | Yg W | Yg E3 | Yn W | Yn F | 15 |
| 16 | Yg M | Yg M | Yg E | Yg W | Yn E | Yn E2 | Yn E | Yn E4 | Yg M | Yg M | Yg M | Yg Wd | Yn M | Yn M | Yg W | Yg E1 | Yg W | Yg E3 | Yn W | Yn F | Yn W | Yn W | Yg Wd | Yg F | 16 |
| 17 | Yn M | Yn M | Yn E | Yn E4 | Yg M | Yg M | Yg M | Yg Wd | Yn M | Yn M | Yn M | Yn Wd | Yg W | Yg E3 | Yn W | Yn F | Yn W | Yn W | Yg Wd | Yg F | Yg Wd | Yg W | Yn Wd | Yn E2 | 17 |
| 18 | Yg W | Yg E3 | Yg M | Yg Wd | Yn M | Yn M | Yn M | Yn Wd | Yg W | Yg E3 | Yg W | Yg E1 | Yn W | Yn W | Yg Wd | Yg F | Yg Wd | Yg W | Yn Wd | Yn E2 | Yn Wd | Yn E4 | Yg F | Yg M | 18 |
| 19 | Yn W | Yn W | Yn M | Yn Wd | Yg W | Yg E3 | Yg W | Yg E1 | Yn W | Yn W | Yn W | Yn F | Yg Wd | Yg W | Yn Wd | Yn E2 | Yn Wd | Yn E4 | Yg F | Yg M | Yg F | Yg Wd | Yn F | Yn M | 19 |
| 20 | Yg Wd | Yg W | Yg W | Yg E1 | Yn W | Yn W | Yn W | Yn F | Yg Wd | Yg W | Yg Wd | Yg F | Yn Wd | Yn E4 | Yg F | Yg M | Yg F | Yg Wd | Yn F | Yn M | Yn F | Yn Wd | Yg E | Yg E3 | 20 |
| 21 | Yn Wd | Yn E4 | Yn W | Yn F | Yg Wd | Yg W | Yg Wd | Yg F | Yn Wd | Yn E4 | Yn Wd | Yn E2 | Yg F | Yg Wd | Yn F | Yn M | Yn F | Yn Wd | Yg E | Yg E3 | Yg E | Yg E1 | Yn E | Yn W | 21 |
| 22 | Yg F | Yg Wd | Yg Wd | Yg F | Yn Wd | Yn E4 | Yn Wd | Yn E2 | Yg F | Yg Wd | Yg F | Yg M | Yn F | Yn Wd | Yg E | Yg E3 | Yg E | Yg E1 | Yn E | Yn W | Yn E | Yn F | Yg M | Yg W | 22 |
| 23 | Yn F | Yn Wd | Yn Wd | Yn E2 | Yg F | Yg Wd | Yg F | Yg M | Yn F | Yn Wd | Yn F | Yn M | Yg E | Yg E1 | Yn E | Yn W | Yn E | Yn F | Yg M | Yg W | Yg M | Yg F | Yn M | Yn E4 | 23 |
| 24 | Yg E | Yg E1 | Yg F | Yg M | Yn F | Yn Wd | Yn F | Yn M | Yg E | Yg E1 | Yg E | Yg E3 | Yn E | Yn F | Yg M | Yg W | Yg M | Yg F | Yn M | Yn E4 | Yn M | Yn E2 | Yg W | Yg Wd | 24 |
| 25 | Yn E | Yn F | Yn F | Yn M | Yg E | Yg E1 | Yg E | Yg E3 | Yn E | Yn F | Yn E | Yn W | Yg M | Yg F | Yn M | Yn E4 | Yn M | Yn E2 | Yg W | Yg Wd | Yg W | Yg M | Yn W | Yn Wd | 25 |
| 26 | Yg M | Yg F | Yg E | Yg E3 | Yn E | Yn F | Yn E | Yn W | Yg M | Yg F | Yg M | Yg W | Yn M | Yn E2 | Yg W | Yg Wd | Yg W | Yg M | Yn W | Yn Wd | Yn W | Yn M | Yg Wd | Yg E1 | 26 |
| 27 | Yn M | Yn E2 | Yn E | Yn W | Yg M | Yg F | Yg M | Yg W | Yn M | Yn E2 | Yn M | Yn E4 | Yg W | Yg M | Yn W | Yn Wd | Yn W | Yn M | Yg Wd | Yg E1 | Yg Wd | Yg E3 | Yn Wd | Yn F | 27 |
| 28 | Yg W | Yg M | Yg M | Yg W | Yn M | Yn E2 | Yn M | Yn E4 | Yg W | Yg M | Yg W | Yg Wd | Yn W | Yn M | Yg Wd | Yg E1 | Yg Wd | Yg E3 | Yn Wd | Yn F | Yn Wd | Yn W | Yg F | Yg F | 28 |
| 29 | | | Yn M | Yn E4 | Yg W | Yg M | Yg W | Yg Wd | Yn W | Yn M | Yn W | Yn Wd | Yg Wd | Yg E3 | Yn Wd | Yn F | Yn Wd | Yn W | Yg F | Yg F | Yg F | Yg W | Yn F | Yn E2 | 29 |
| 30 | | | Yg W | Yg Wd | Yn W | Yn M | Yn W | Yn Wd | Yg Wd | Yg E3 | Yg Wd | Yg E1 | Yn Wd | Yn W | Yg F | Yg F | Yg F | Yg W | Yn F | Yn E2 | Yn F | Yn E4 | Yg E | Yg M | 30 |
| 31 | | | Yn W | Yn Wd | | | Yg Wd | Yg E1 | | | Yn Wd | Yn F | Yg F | Yg W | | | Yn F | Yn E4 | | | Yg E | Yg Wd | Yn E | Yn M | 31 |
| 1 | Yn W | Yn M | Yg Wd | Yg E1 | Yg Wd | Yg E3 | Yn Wd | Yn F | Yn Wd | Yn W | Yg F | Yg F | Yn F | Yn E4 | Yn F | Yn E2 | Yg E | Yg Wd | Yg E | Yg M | Yn E | Yn Wd | Yg M | Yg E3 | 1 |
| 2 | Yg Wd | Yg E3 | Yn Wd | Yn F | Yn Wd | Yn W | Yg F | Yg F | Yg F | Yg W | Yn F | Yn E2 | Yg E | Yg Wd | Yg E | Yg M | Yn E | Yn Wd | Yn E | Yn M | Yg M | Yg E1 | Yn M | Yn W | 2 |
| 3 | Yn Wd | Yn W | Yg F | Yg F | Yg F | Yg W | Yn F | Yn E2 | Yn F | Yn E4 | Yg E | Yg M | Yn E | Yn Wd | Yn E | Yn M | Yg M | Yg E1 | Yg M | Yg E3 | Yn M | Yn F | Yg W | Yg W | 3 |
| 4 | Yg F | Yg W | Yn F | Yn E2 | Yn F | Yn E4 | Yg E | Yg M | Yg E | Yg Wd | Yn E | Yn M | Yg M | Yg E1 | Yg M | Yg E3 | Yn M | Yn F | Yn M | Yn W | Yg W | Yg F | Yn W | Yn E4 | 4 |
| 5 | Yn F | Yn E4 | Yg E | Yg M | Yg E | Yg Wd | Yn E | Yn M | Yn E | Yn Wd | Yg M | Yg E3 | Yn M | Yn F | Yn M | Yn W | Yg W | Yg F | Yg W | Yg W | Yn W | Yn E2 | | | 5 |
| 6 | | | | | | | Yg M | Yg E3 | Yg M | Yg E1 | Yn M | Yn W | Yg W | Yg F | Yg W | Yg W | Yn W | Yn E2 | Yn W | Yn E4 | | | | | 6 |
| 7 | | | | | | | | | Yn M | Yn F | Yg W | Yg W | Yn W | Yn E2 | Yn W | Yn E4 | Yg Wd | Yg M | Yg Wd | Yg Wd | | | | | 7 |
| 8 | | | | | | | | | | | | | Yg Wd | Yg M | Yg Wd | Yg Wd | | | | | | | | | 8 |

# YEAR OF THE RAT

| | H | E | H | E | H | E | H | E | H | E | H | E |
|---|---|---|---|---|---|---|---|---|---|---|---|---|
| YEAR | YEAR<br>Yg Wd | <br>Yg W | 1924 | | | | | | | | | |
| MONTH | 5 Feb - 5 Mar | | 6 Mar - 4 Apr | | 5 Apr - 5 May | | 6 May - 5 June | | 6 June - 6 Jul | | 7 Jul - 7 Aug | |
| | Yg F | Yg Wd | Yn F | Yn Wd | Yg E | Yg E1 | Yn E | Yn F | Yg M | Yg F | Yn M | Yn E2 |
| Starting time | 1st day | Mid-pt | 1st day | Mid-pt | 1st day | Mid-pt | 1st day | Mid-pt | 1st day | Mid-pt | 1st day | Mid-pt |
| Date | 5 | 20 | 6 | 21 | 5 | 20 | 6 | 21 | 6 | 22 | 7 | 23 |
| Hour | 0950 | 0552 | 0413 | 0521 | 0934 | 1659 | 0326 | 1641 | 0802 | 0100 | 1830 | 1158 |
| DATE 4 | | | | | | | | | | | | |
| 5 | Yg Wd | Yg Wd | | | Yg Wd | Yg Wd | | | | | | |
| 6 | Yn Wd | Yn Wd | Yg Wd | Yg M | Yn Wd | Yn Wd | Yn Wd | Yn M | Yg F | Yg E1 | | |
| 7 | Yg F | Yg E1 | Yn Wd | Yn M | Yg F | Yg E1 | Yg F | Yg E3 | Yn F | Yn F | Yn F | Yn W |
| 8 | Yn F | Yn F | Yg F | Yg E3 | Yn F | Yn F | Yn F | Yn W | Yg E | Yg F | Yg E | Yg W |
| 9 | Yg E | Yg F | Yn F | Yn W | Yg E | Yg F | Yg E | Yg W | Yn E | Yn E2 | Yn E | Yn E4 |
| 10 | Yn E | Yn E2 | Yg E | Yg W | Yn E | Yn E2 | Yn E | Yn E4 | Yg M | Yg M | Yg M | Yg Wd |
| 11 | Yg M | Yg M | Yn E | Yn E4 | Yg M | Yg M | Yg M | Yg Wd | Yn M | Yn M | Yn M | Yn Wd |
| 12 | Yn M | Yn M | Yg M | Yg Wd | Yn M | Yn M | Yn M | Yn Wd | Yg W | Yg E3 | Yg W | Yg E1 |
| 13 | Yg W | Yg E3 | Yn M | Yn Wd | Yg W | Yg E3 | Yg W | Yg E1 | Yn W | Yn W | Yn W | Yn F |
| 14 | Yn W | Yn W | Yg W | Yg E1 | Yn W | Yn W | Yn W | Yn F | Yg Wd | Yg W | Yg Wd | Yg F |
| 15 | Yg Wd | Yg W | Yn W | Yn F | Yg Wd | Yg W | Yg Wd | Yg F | Yn Wd | Yn E4 | Yn Wd | Yn E2 |
| 16 | Yn Wd | Yn E4 | Yg Wd | Yg F | Yn Wd | Yn E4 | Yn Wd | Yn E2 | Yg F | Yg Wd | Yg F | Yg M |
| 17 | Yg F | Yg Wd | Yn Wd | Yn E2 | Yg F | Yg Wd | Yg F | Yg M | Yn F | Yn Wd | Yn F | Yn M |
| 18 | Yn F | Yn Wd | Yg F | Yg M | Yn F | Yn Wd | Yn F | Yn M | Yg E | Yg E1 | Yg E | Yg E3 |
| 19 | Yg E | Yg E1 | Yn F | Yn M | Yg E | Yg E1 | Yg E | Yg E3 | Yn E | Yn F | Yn E | Yn W |
| 20 | Yn E | Yn F | Yg E | Yg E3 | Yn E | Yn F | Yn E | Yn W | Yg M | Yg F | Yg M | Yg W |
| 21 | Yg M | Yg F | Yn E | Yn W | Yg M | Yg F | Yg M | Yg W | Yn M | Yn E2 | Yn M | Yn E4 |
| 22 | Yn M | Yn E2 | Yg M | Yg W | Yn M | Yn E2 | Yn M | Yn E4 | Yg W | Yg M | Yg W | Yg Wd |
| 23 | Yg W | Yg M | Yn M | Yn E4 | Yg W | Yg M | Yg W | Yg Wd | Yn W | Yn M | Yn W | Yn Wd |
| 24 | Yn W | Yn M | Yg W | Yg Wd | Yn W | Yn M | Yn W | Yn Wd | Yg Wd | Yg E3 | Yg Wd | Yg E1 |
| 25 | Yg Wd | Yg E3 | Yn W | Yn Wd | Yg Wd | Yg E3 | Yg Wd | Yg E1 | Yn Wd | Yn W | Yn Wd | Yn F |
| 26 | Yn Wd | Yn W | Yg Wd | Yg E1 | Yn Wd | Yn W | Yn Wd | Yn F | Yg F | Yg W | Yg F | Yg F |
| 27 | Yg F | Yg W | Yn Wd | Yn F | Yg F | Yg W | Yg F | Yg F | Yn F | Yn E4 | Yn F | Yn E2 |
| 28 | Yn F | Yn E4 | Yg F | Yg F | Yn F | Yn E4 | Yn F | Yn E2 | Yg E | Yg Wd | Yg E | Yg M |
| 29 | Yg E | Yg Wd | Yn F | Yn E2 | Yg E | Yg Wd | Yg E | Yg M | Yn E | Yn Wd | Yn E | Yn M |
| 30 | | | Yg E | Yg M | Yn E | Yn Wd | Yn E | Yn M | Yg M | Yg E1 | Yg M | Yg E3 |
| 31 | | | Yn E | Yn M | | | Yg M | Yg E3 | | | Yn M | Yn W |
| 1 | Yn E | Yn Wd | Yg M | Yg E3 | Yg M | Yg E1 | Yn M | Yn W | Yn M | Yn F | Yg W | Yg W |
| 2 | Yg M | Yg E1 | Yn M | Yn W | Yn M | Yn F | Yg W | Yg W | Yg W | Yg F | Yn W | Yn E4 |
| 3 | Yn M | Yn F | Yg W | Yg W | Yg W | Yg F | Yn W | Yn E4 | Yn W | Yn E2 | Yg Wd | Yg Wd |
| 4 | Yg W | Yg F | Yn W | Yn E4 | Yn W | Yn E2 | Yg Wd | Yg Wd | Yg Wd | Yg M | Yn Wd | Yn Wd |
| 5 | Yn W | Yn E2 | | | Yg Wd | Yg M | Yn Wd | Yn Wd | Yn Wd | Yn M | Yg F | Yg E1 |
| 6 | | | | | | | | | Yg F | Yg E3 | Yn F | Yn F |
| 7 | | | | | | | | | | | Yg E | Yg F |
| 8 | | | | | | | | | | | | |

| | H | E | H | E | H | E | H | E | H | E | H | E | |
|---|---|---|---|---|---|---|---|---|---|---|---|---|---|
| YEAR | 1924 | | | | | | | | | | 1925 | | |
| MONTH | 8 Aug - 7 Sep | | 8 Sep - 7 Oct | | 8 Oct - 7 Nov | | 8 Nov - 6 Dec | | 7 Dec - 5 Jan | | 6 Jan - 3 Feb | | |
| | Yg W | Yg M | Yn W | Yn M | Yg Wd | Yg E3 | Yn Wd | Yn W | Yg F | Yg W | Yn F | Yn E4 | |
| Starting time | 1st day | Mid-pt | 1st day | Mid-pt | 1st day | Mid-pt | 1st day | Mid-pt | 1st day | Mid-pt | 1st day | Mid-pt | |
| Date | 8 | 23 | 8 | 23 | 8 | 24 | 8 | 22 | 7 | 22 | 6 | 20 | |
| Hour | 0413 | 1848 | 0646 | 1559 | 2153 | 0045 | 0017 | 2147 | 1654 | 1046 | 0354 | 2121 | |
| DATE 4 | | | | | | | | | | | | | 4 |
| 5 | | | | | | | | | | | | | 5 |
| 6 | | | | | | | | | | | Yg M | Yg Wd | 6 |
| 7 | | | | | | | | | Yg M | Yg M | Yn M | Yn Wd | 7 |
| 8 | Yn E | Yn E2 | Yg M | Yg Wd | Yg M | Yg M | Yn M | Yn Wd | Yn M | Yn M | Yg W | Yg E1 | 8 |
| 9 | Yg M | Yg M | Yn M | Yn Wd | Yn M | Yn M | Yg W | Yg E1 | Yg W | Yg E3 | Yn W | Yn F | 9 |
| 10 | Yn M | Yn M | Yg W | Yg E1 | Yg W | Yg E3 | Yn W | Yn F | Yn W | Yn W | Yg Wd | Yg F | 10 |
| 11 | Yg W | Yg E3 | Yn W | Yn F | Yn W | Yn W | Yg Wd | Yg F | Yg Wd | Yg W | Yn Wd | Yn E2 | 11 |
| 12 | Yn W | Yn W | Yg Wd | Yg F | Yg Wd | Yg W | Yn Wd | Yn E2 | Yn Wd | Yn E4 | Yg F | Yg M | 12 |
| 13 | Yg Wd | Yg W | Yn Wd | Yn E2 | Yn Wd | Yn E4 | Yg F | Yg M | Yg F | Yg Wd | Yn F | Yn M | 13 |
| 14 | Yn Wd | Yn E4 | Yg F | Yg M | Yg F | Yg Wd | Yn F | Yn M | Yn F | Yn Wd | Yg E | Yg E3 | 14 |
| 15 | Yg F | Yg Wd | Yn F | Yn M | Yn F | Yn Wd | Yg E | Yg E3 | Yg E | Yg E1 | Yn E | Yn W | 15 |
| 16 | Yn F | Yn Wd | Yg E | Yg E3 | Yg E | Yg E1 | Yn E | Yn W | Yn E | Yn F | Yg M | Yg W | 16 |
| 17 | Yg E | Yg E1 | Yn E | Yn W | Yn E | Yn F | Yg M | Yg W | Yg M | Yg F | Yn M | Yn E4 | 17 |
| 18 | Yn E | Yn F | Yg M | Yg W | Yg M | Yg F | Yn M | Yn E4 | Yn M | Yn E2 | Yg W | Yg Wd | 18 |
| 19 | Yg M | Yg F | Yn M | Yn E4 | Yn M | Yn E2 | Yg W | Yg Wd | Yg W | Yg M | Yn W | Yn Wd | 19 |
| 20 | Yn M | Yn E2 | Yg W | Yg Wd | Yg W | Yg M | Yn W | Yn Wd | Yn W | Yn M | Yg Wd | Yg E1 | 20 |
| 21 | Yg W | Yg M | Yn W | Yn Wd | Yn W | Yn M | Yg Wd | Yg E1 | Yg Wd | Yg E3 | Yn Wd | Yn F | 21 |
| 22 | Yn W | Yn M | Yg Wd | Yg E1 | Yg Wd | Yg E3 | Yn Wd | Yn F | Yn Wd | Yn W | Yg F | Yg F | 22 |
| 23 | Yg Wd | Yg E3 | Yn Wd | Yn F | Yn Wd | Yn W | Yg F | Yg F | Yg F | Yg W | Yn F | Yn E2 | 23 |
| 24 | Yn Wd | Yn W | Yg F | Yg F | Yg F | Yg W | Yn F | Yn E2 | Yn F | Yn E4 | Yg E | Yg M | 24 |
| 25 | Yg F | Yg W | Yn F | Yn E2 | Yn F | Yn E4 | Yg E | Yg M | Yg E | Yg Wd | Yn E | Yn M | 25 |
| 26 | Yn F | Yn E4 | Yg E | Yg M | Yg E | Yg Wd | Yn E | Yn M | Yn E | Yn Wd | Yg M | Yg E3 | 26 |
| 27 | Yg E | Yg Wd | Yn E | Yn M | Yn E | Yn Wd | Yg M | Yg E3 | Yg M | Yg E1 | Yn M | Yn W | 27 |
| 28 | Yn E | Yn Wd | Yg M | Yg E3 | Yg M | Yg E1 | Yn M | Yn W | Yn M | Yn F | Yg W | Yg W | 28 |
| 29 | Yg M | Yg E1 | Yn M | Yn W | Yn M | Yn F | Yg W | Yg W | Yg W | Yg F | Yn W | Yn E4 | 29 |
| 30 | Yn M | Yn F | Yg W | Yg W | Yg W | Yg F | Yn W | Yn E4 | Yn W | Yn E2 | Yg Wd | Yg Wd | 30 |
| 31 | Yg W | Yg F | | | Yn W | Yn E2 | | | Yg Wd | Yg M | Yn Wd | Yn Wd | 31 |
| 1 | Yn W | Yn E2 | Yn W | Yn E4 | Yg Wd | Yg M | Yg Wd | Yg Wd | Yn Wd | Yn M | Yg F | Yg E1 | 1 |
| 2 | Yg Wd | Yg M | Yg Wd | Yg Wd | Yn Wd | Yn M | Yn Wd | Yn Wd | Yg F | Yg E3 | Yn F | Yn F | 2 |
| 3 | Yn Wd | Yn M | Yn Wd | Yn Wd | Yg F | Yg E3 | Yg F | Yg E1 | Yn F | Yn W | Yg E | Yg F | 3 |
| 4 | Yg F | Yg E3 | Yg F | Yg E1 | Yn F | Yn W | Yn F | Yn F | Yg E | Yg W | | | 4 |
| 5 | Yn F | Yn W | Yn F | Yn F | Yg E | Yg W | Yg E | Yg F | Yn E | Yn E4 | | | 5 |
| 6 | Yg E | Yg W | Yg E | Yg F | Yn E | Yn E4 | Yn E | Yn E2 | | | | | 6 |
| 7 | Yn E | Yn E4 | Yn E | Yn E2 | Yg M | Yg Wd | | | | | | | 7 |
| 8 | | | | | | | | | | | | | 8 |

# YEAR OF THE OX

| | H | E | H | E | H | E | H | E | H | E | H | E | H | E | H | E | H | E | H | E | H | E | H | E | |
|---|---|---|---|---|---|---|---|---|---|---|---|---|---|---|---|---|---|---|---|---|---|---|---|---|---|
| YEAR | YEAR<br>Yn Wd | Yn E4 | 1925 | | | | | | | | | | | | | | | | | | 1926 | | | | |
| MONTH | 4 Feb - 5 Mar<br>Yg E | Yg Wd | 6 Mar - 4 Apr<br>Yn E | Yn Wd | 5 Apr - 5 May<br>Yg M | Yg E1 | 6 May - 5 June<br>Yn M | Yn F | 6 June - 7 Jul<br>Yg W | Yg F | 8 Jul - 7 Aug<br>Yn W | Yn E2 | 8 Aug - 7 Sep<br>Yg Wd | Yg M | 8 Sep - 8 Oct<br>Yn Wd | Yn M | 9 Oct - 7 Nov<br>Yg F | Yg E3 | 8 Nov - 6 Dec<br>Yn F | Yn W | 7 Dec - 5 Jan<br>Yg E | Yg W | 6 Jan - 3 Feb<br>Yn E | Yn E4 | |
| Starting time | 1st day | Mid-pt | 1st day | Mid-pt | 1st day | Mid-pt | 1st day | Mid-pt | 1st day | Mid-pt | 1st day | Mid-pt | 1st day | Mid-pt | 1st day | Mid-pt | 1st day | Mid-pt | 1st day | Mid-pt | 1st day | Mid-pt | 1st day | Mid-pt | |
| Date | 4 | 19 | 6 | 21 | 5 | 20 | 6 | 21 | 6 | 22 | 8 | 23 | 8 | 24 | 8 | 23 | 9 | 24 | 8 | 23 | 7 | 22 | 6 | 21 | |
| Hour | 1537 | 1143 | 1000 | 1113 | 1523 | 2252 | 0918 | 2233 | 1355 | 0650 | 0025 | 1745 | 1008 | 0033 | 1240 | 2144 | 0348 | 0632 | 0627 | 0336 | 2253 | 1637 | 0955 | 0313 | |
| DATE 4 | Yn E | Yn E2 | | | | | | | | | | | | | | | | | | | | | | | 4 |
| 5 | Yg M | Yg M | | | Yn E | Yn E2 | | | | | | | | | | | | | | | | | | | 5 |
| 6 | Yn M | Yn M | Yn E | Yn E4 | Yg M | Yg M | Yg M | Yg Wd | Yn M | Yn M | | | | | | | | | | | | | Yn Wd | Yn E2 | 6 |
| 7 | Yg W | Yg E3 | Yg M | Yg Wd | Yn M | Yn M | Yn M | Yn Wd | Yg W | Yg E3 | | | | | | | | | | | Yn Wd | Yn E4 | Yg F | Yg M | 7 |
| 8 | Yn W | Yn W | Yn M | Yn Wd | Yg W | Yg E3 | Yg W | Yg E1 | Yn W | Yn W | Yn W | Yn F | Yg Wd | Yg W | Yn Wd | Yn E2 | | | Yg F | Yg M | Yg F | Yg Wd | Yn F | Yn M | 8 |
| 9 | Yg Wd | Yg W | Yg W | Yg E1 | Yn W | Yn W | Yn W | Yn F | Yg Wd | Yg W | Yg Wd | Yg F | Yn Wd | Yn E4 | Yg F | Yg M | Yg F | Yg Wd | Yn F | Yn M | Yn F | Yn Wd | Yg E | Yg E3 | 9 |
| 10 | Yn Wd | Yn E4 | Yn W | Yn F | Yg Wd | Yg W | Yg Wd | Yg F | Yn Wd | Yn E4 | Yn Wd | Yn E2 | Yg F | Yg Wd | Yn F | Yn M | Yn F | Yn Wd | Yg E | Yg E3 | Yg E | Yg E1 | Yn E | Yn W | 10 |
| 11 | Yg F | Yg Wd | Yg Wd | Yg F | Yn Wd | Yn E4 | Yn Wd | Yn E2 | Yg F | Yg Wd | Yg F | Yg M | Yn F | Yn Wd | Yg E | Yg E3 | Yg E | Yg E1 | Yn E | Yn W | Yn E | Yn F | Yg M | Yg W | 11 |
| 12 | Yn F | Yn Wd | Yn Wd | Yn E2 | Yg F | Yg Wd | Yg F | Yg M | Yn F | Yn Wd | Yn F | Yn M | Yg E | Yg E1 | Yn E | Yn W | Yn E | Yn F | Yg M | Yg W | Yg M | Yg F | Yn M | Yn E4 | 12 |
| 13 | Yg E | Yg E1 | Yg F | Yg M | Yn F | Yn Wd | Yn F | Yn M | Yg E | Yg E1 | Yg E | Yg E3 | Yn E | Yn F | Yg M | Yg W | Yg M | Yg F | Yn M | Yn E4 | Yn M | Yn E2 | Yg W | Yg Wd | 13 |
| 14 | Yn E | Yn F | Yn F | Yn M | Yg E | Yg E1 | Yg E | Yg E3 | Yn E | Yn F | Yn E | Yn W | Yg M | Yg F | Yn M | Yn E4 | Yn M | Yn E2 | Yg W | Yg Wd | Yg W | Yg M | Yn W | Yn Wd | 14 |
| 15 | Yg M | Yg F | Yg E | Yg E3 | Yn E | Yn F | Yn E | Yn W | Yg M | Yg F | Yg M | Yg W | Yn M | Yn E2 | Yg W | Yg Wd | Yg W | Yg M | Yn W | Yn Wd | Yn W | Yn M | Yg Wd | Yg E1 | 15 |
| 16 | Yn M | Yn E2 | Yn E | Yn W | Yg M | Yg F | Yg M | Yg W | Yn M | Yn E2 | Yn M | Yn E4 | Yg W | Yg M | Yn W | Yn Wd | Yn W | Yn M | Yg Wd | Yg E1 | Yg Wd | Yg E3 | Yn Wd | Yn F | 16 |
| 17 | Yg W | Yg M | Yg M | Yg W | Yn M | Yn E2 | Yn M | Yn E4 | Yg W | Yg M | Yg W | Yg Wd | Yn W | Yn M | Yg Wd | Yg E1 | Yg Wd | Yg E3 | Yn Wd | Yn F | Yn Wd | Yn W | Yg F | Yg F | 17 |
| 18 | Yn W | Yn M | Yn M | Yn E4 | Yg W | Yg M | Yg W | Yg Wd | Yn W | Yn M | Yn W | Yn Wd | Yg Wd | Yg E3 | Yn Wd | Yn F | Yn Wd | Yn W | Yg F | Yg F | Yg F | Yg W | Yn F | Yn E2 | 18 |
| 19 | Yg Wd | Yg E3 | Yg W | Yg Wd | Yn W | Yn M | Yn W | Yn Wd | Yg Wd | Yg E3 | Yg Wd | Yg E1 | Yn Wd | Yn W | Yg F | Yg F | Yg F | Yg W | Yn F | Yn E2 | Yn F | Yn E4 | Yg E | Yg M | 19 |
| 20 | Yn Wd | Yn W | Yn W | Yn Wd | Yg Wd | Yg E3 | Yg Wd | Yg E1 | Yn Wd | Yn W | Yn Wd | Yn F | Yg F | Yg W | Yn F | Yn E2 | Yn F | Yn E4 | Yg E | Yg M | Yg E | Yg Wd | Yn E | Yn M | 20 |
| 21 | Yg F | Yg W | Yg Wd | Yg E1 | Yn Wd | Yn W | Yn Wd | Yn F | Yg F | Yg W | Yg F | Yg F | Yn F | Yn E4 | Yg E | Yg M | Yg E | Yg Wd | Yn E | Yn M | Yn E | Yn Wd | Yg M | Yg E3 | 21 |
| 22 | Yn F | Yn E4 | Yn Wd | Yn F | Yg F | Yg W | Yg F | Yg F | Yn F | Yn E4 | Yn F | Yn E2 | Yg E | Yg Wd | Yn E | Yn M | Yn E | Yn Wd | Yg M | Yg E3 | Yg M | Yg E1 | Yn M | Yn W | 22 |
| 23 | Yg E | Yg Wd | Yg F | Yg F | Yn F | Yn E4 | Yn F | Yn E2 | Yg E | Yg Wd | Yg E | Yg M | Yn E | Yn Wd | Yg M | Yg E3 | Yg M | Yg E1 | Yn M | Yn W | Yn M | Yn F | Yg W | Yg W | 23 |
| 24 | Yn E | Yn Wd | Yn F | Yn E2 | Yg E | Yg Wd | Yg E | Yg M | Yn E | Yn Wd | Yn E | Yn M | Yg M | Yg E1 | Yn M | Yn W | Yn M | Yn F | Yg W | Yg W | Yg W | Yg F | Yn W | Yn E4 | 24 |
| 25 | Yg M | Yg E1 | Yg E | Yg M | Yn E | Yn Wd | Yn E | Yn M | Yg M | Yg E1 | Yg M | Yg E3 | Yn M | Yn F | Yg W | Yg W | Yg W | Yg F | Yn W | Yn E4 | Yn W | Yn E2 | Yg Wd | Yg Wd | 25 |
| 26 | Yn M | Yn F | Yn E | Yn M | Yg M | Yg E1 | Yg M | Yg E3 | Yn M | Yn F | Yn M | Yn W | Yg W | Yg F | Yn W | Yn E4 | Yn W | Yn E2 | Yg Wd | Yg Wd | Yg Wd | Yg M | Yn Wd | Yn Wd | 26 |
| 27 | Yg W | Yg F | Yg M | Yg E3 | Yn M | Yn F | Yn M | Yn W | Yg W | Yg F | Yg W | Yg W | Yn W | Yn E2 | Yg Wd | Yg Wd | Yg Wd | Yg M | Yn Wd | Yn Wd | Yn Wd | Yn M | Yg F | Yg E1 | 27 |
| 28 | Yn W | Yn E2 | Yn M | Yn W | Yg W | Yg F | Yg W | Yg W | Yn W | Yn E2 | Yn W | Yn E4 | Yg Wd | Yg M | Yn Wd | Yn Wd | Yn Wd | Yn M | Yg F | Yg E1 | Yg F | Yg E3 | Yn F | Yn F | 28 |
| 29 | | | Yg W | Yg W | Yn W | Yn E2 | Yn W | Yn E4 | Yg Wd | Yg M | Yg Wd | Yg Wd | Yn Wd | Yn M | Yg F | Yg E1 | Yg F | Yg E3 | Yn F | Yn F | Yn F | Yn W | Yg E | Yg F | 29 |
| 30 | | | Yn W | Yn E4 | Yg Wd | Yg M | Yg Wd | Yg Wd | Yn Wd | Yn M | Yn Wd | Yn Wd | Yg F | Yg E3 | Yn F | Yn F | Yn F | Yn W | Yg E | Yg F | Yg E | Yg W | Yn E | Yn E2 | 30 |
| 31 | | | Yg Wd | Yg Wd | | | Yn Wd | Yn Wd | | | Yg F | Yg E1 | Yn F | Yn W | | | Yg E | Yg W | | | Yn E | Yn E4 | Yg M | Yg M | 31 |
| 1 | Yg Wd | Yg M | Yn Wd | Yn Wd | Yn Wd | Yn M | Yg F | Yg E1 | Yg F | Yg E3 | Yn F | Yn F | Yg E | Yg W | Yg E | Yg F | Yn E | Yn E4 | Yn E | Yn E2 | Yg M | Yg Wd | Yn M | Yn M | 1 |
| 2 | Yn Wd | Yn M | Yg F | Yg E1 | Yg F | Yg E3 | Yn F | Yn F | Yn F | Yn W | Yg E | Yg F | Yn E | Yn E4 | Yn E | Yn E2 | Yg M | Yg Wd | Yg M | Yg M | Yn M | Yn Wd | Yg W | Yg E3 | 2 |
| 3 | Yg F | Yg E3 | Yn F | Yn F | Yn F | Yn W | Yg E | Yg F | Yg E | Yg W | Yn E | Yn E2 | Yg M | Yg Wd | Yg M | Yg M | Yn M | Yn Wd | Yn M | Yn M | Yg W | Yg E1 | Yn W | Yn W | 3 |
| 4 | Yn F | Yn W | Yg E | Yg F | Yg E | Yg W | Yn E | Yn E2 | Yn E | Yn E4 | Yg M | Yg M | Yn M | Yn Wd | Yn M | Yn M | Yg W | Yg E1 | Yg W | Yg E3 | Yn W | Yn F | | | 4 |
| 5 | Yg E | Yg W | | | Yn E | Yn E4 | Yg M | Yg M | Yg M | Yg Wd | Yn M | Yn M | Yg W | Yg E1 | Yg W | Yg E3 | Yn W | Yn F | Yn W | Yn W | Yg Wd | Yg F | | | 5 |
| 6 | | | | | | | | | Yn M | Yn Wd | Yg W | Yg E3 | Yn W | Yn F | Yn W | Yn W | Yg Wd | Yg F | Yg Wd | Yg W | | | | | 6 |
| 7 | | | | | | | | | Yg W | Yg E1 | Yn W | Yn W | Yg Wd | Yg F | Yg Wd | Yg W | Yn Wd | Yn E2 | | | | | | | 7 |
| 8 | | | | | | | | | | | | | | | Yn Wd | Yn E4 | | | | | | | | | 8 |

# YEAR OF THE TIGER

| | H | E | H | E | H | E | H | E | H | E | H | E | H | E | H | E | H | E | H | E | H | E | H | E | |
|---|---|---|---|---|---|---|---|---|---|---|---|---|---|---|---|---|---|---|---|---|---|---|---|---|---|
| YEAR | YEAR<br>Yg F | Yg Wd | 1926 | | | | | | | | | | | | | | | | | | | | 1927 | | |
| MONTH | 4 Feb - 5 Mar | | 6 Mar - 4 Apr | | 5 Apr - 5 May | | 6 May - 5 June | | 6 June - 7 Jul | | 8 Jul - 7 Aug | | 8 Aug - 7 Sep | | 8 Sep - 8 Oct | | 9 Oct - 7 Nov | | 8 Nov - 7 Dec | | 8 Dec - 5 Jan | | 6 Jan - 4 Feb | | |
| | Yg M | Yg Wd | Yn M | Yn Wd | Yg W | Yg E1 | Yn W | Yn F | Yg Wd | Yg F | Yn Wd | Yn E2 | Yg F | Yg M | Yn F | Yn M | Yg E | Yg E3 | Yn E | Yn W | Yg M | Yg W | Yn M | Yn E4 | |
| Starting time | 1st day | Mid-pt | 1st day | Mid-pt | 1st day | Mid-pt | 1st day | Mid-pt | 1st day | Mid-pt | 1st day | Mid-pt | 1st day | Mid-pt | 1st day | Mid-pt | 1st day | Mid-pt | 1st day | Mid-pt | 1st day | Mid-pt | 1st day | Mid-pt | |
| Date | 4 | 19 | 6 | 21 | 5 | 21 | 6 | 22 | 6 | 22 | 8 | 23 | 8 | 24 | 8 | 24 | 9 | 24 | 8 | 23 | 8 | 22 | 6 | 21 | |
| Hour | 2139 | 1735 | 1600 | 1701 | 2119 | 0437 | 1509 | 0415 | 1942 | 1230 | 0606 | 2325 | 1545 | 0614 | 1816 | 0327 | 0925 | 1219 | 1208 | 0928 | 0439 | 2234 | 1545 | 0912 | |
| DATE 4 | Yg Wd | Yg W | | | | | | | | | | | | | | | | | | | | | | | 4 |
| 5 | Yn Wd | Yn E4 | | | Yg Wd | Yg W | | | | | | | | | | | | | | | | | | | 5 |
| 6 | Yg F | Yg Wd | Yg Wd | Yg F | Yn Wd | Yn E4 | Yn Wd | Yn E2 | Yg F | Yg Wd | | | | | | | | | | | | | Yg M | Yg W | 6 |
| 7 | Yn F | Yn Wd | Yn Wd | Yn E2 | Yg F | Yg Wd | Yg F | Yg M | Yn F | Yn Wd | | | | | | | | | | | | | Yn M | Yn E4 | 7 |
| 8 | Yg E | Yg E1 | Yg F | Yg M | Yn F | Yn Wd | Yn F | Yn M | Yg E | Yg E1 | Yg E | Yg E3 | Yn E | Yn F | Yg M | Yg W | | | Yn M | Yn E4 | Yn M | Yn E2 | Yg W | Yg Wd | 8 |
| 9 | Yn E | Yn F | Yn F | Yn M | Yg E | Yg E1 | Yg E | Yg E3 | Yn E | Yn F | Yn E | Yn W | Yg M | Yg F | Yn M | Yn E4 | Yn M | Yn E2 | Yg W | Yg Wd | Yg W | Yg M | Yn W | Yn Wd | 9 |
| 10 | Yg M | Yg F | Yg E | Yg E3 | Yn E | Yn F | Yn E | Yn W | Yg M | Yg F | Yg M | Yg W | Yn M | Yn E2 | Yg W | Yg Wd | Yg W | Yg M | Yn W | Yn Wd | Yn W | Yn M | Yg Wd | Yg E1 | 10 |
| 11 | Yn M | Yn E2 | Yn E | Yn W | Yg M | Yg F | Yg M | Yg W | Yn M | Yn E2 | Yn M | Yn E4 | Yg W | Yg M | Yn W | Yn Wd | Yn W | Yn M | Yg Wd | Yg E1 | Yg Wd | Yg E3 | Yn Wd | Yn F | 11 |
| 12 | Yg W | Yg M | Yg M | Yg W | Yn M | Yn E2 | Yn M | Yn E4 | Yg W | Yg M | Yg W | Yg Wd | Yn W | Yn M | Yg Wd | Yg E1 | Yg Wd | Yg E3 | Yn Wd | Yn F | Yn Wd | Yn W | Yg F | Yg F | 12 |
| 13 | Yn W | Yn M | Yn M | Yn E4 | Yg W | Yg M | Yg W | Yg Wd | Yn W | Yn M | Yn W | Yn Wd | Yg Wd | Yg E3 | Yn Wd | Yn F | Yn Wd | Yn W | Yg F | Yg F | Yg F | Yg W | Yn F | Yn E2 | 13 |
| 14 | Yg Wd | Yg E3 | Yg W | Yg Wd | Yn W | Yn M | Yn W | Yn Wd | Yg Wd | Yg E3 | Yg Wd | Yg E1 | Yn Wd | Yn W | Yg F | Yg F | Yg F | Yg W | Yn F | Yn E2 | Yn F | Yn E4 | Yg E | Yg M | 14 |
| 15 | Yn Wd | Yn W | Yn W | Yn Wd | Yg Wd | Yg E3 | Yg Wd | Yg E1 | Yn Wd | Yn W | Yn Wd | Yn F | Yg F | Yg W | Yn F | Yn E2 | Yn F | Yn E4 | Yg E | Yg M | Yg E | Yg Wd | Yn E | Yn M | 15 |
| 16 | Yg F | Yg W | Yg Wd | Yg E1 | Yn Wd | Yn W | Yn Wd | Yn F | Yg F | Yg W | Yg F | Yg F | Yn F | Yn E4 | Yg E | Yg M | Yg E | Yg Wd | Yn E | Yn M | Yn E | Yn Wd | Yg M | Yg E3 | 16 |
| 17 | Yn F | Yn E4 | Yn Wd | Yn F | Yg F | Yg W | Yg F | Yg F | Yn F | Yn E4 | Yn F | Yn E2 | Yg E | Yg Wd | Yn E | Yn M | Yn E | Yn Wd | Yg M | Yg E3 | Yg M | Yg E1 | Yn M | Yn W | 17 |
| 18 | Yg E | Yg Wd | Yg F | Yg F | Yn F | Yn E4 | Yn F | Yn E2 | Yg E | Yg Wd | Yg E | Yg M | Yn E | Yn Wd | Yg M | Yg E3 | Yg M | Yg E1 | Yn M | Yn W | Yn M | Yn F | Yg W | Yg W | 18 |
| 19 | Yn E | Yn Wd | Yn F | Yn E2 | Yg E | Yg Wd | Yg E | Yg M | Yn E | Yn Wd | Yn E | Yn M | Yg M | Yg E1 | Yn M | Yn W | Yn M | Yn F | Yg W | Yg W | Yg W | Yg F | Yn W | Yn E4 | 19 |
| 20 | Yg M | Yg E1 | Yg E | Yg M | Yn E | Yn Wd | Yn E | Yn M | Yg M | Yg E1 | Yg M | Yg E3 | Yn M | Yn F | Yg W | Yg W | Yg W | Yg F | Yn W | Yn E4 | Yn W | Yn E2 | Yg Wd | Yg Wd | 20 |
| 21 | Yn M | Yn F | Yn E | Yn M | Yg M | Yg E1 | Yg M | Yg E3 | Yn M | Yn F | Yn M | Yn W | Yg W | Yg F | Yn W | Yn E4 | Yn W | Yn E2 | Yg Wd | Yg Wd | Yg Wd | Yg M | Yn Wd | Yn Wd | 21 |
| 22 | Yg W | Yg F | Yg M | Yg E3 | Yn M | Yn F | Yn M | Yn W | Yg W | Yg F | Yg W | Yg W | Yn W | Yn E2 | Yg Wd | Yg Wd | Yg Wd | Yg M | Yn Wd | Yn Wd | Yn Wd | Yn M | Yg F | Yg E1 | 22 |
| 23 | Yn W | Yn E2 | Yn M | Yn W | Yg W | Yg F | Yg W | Yg W | Yn W | Yn E2 | Yn W | Yn E4 | Yg Wd | Yg M | Yn Wd | Yn Wd | Yn Wd | Yn M | Yg F | Yg E1 | Yg F | Yg E3 | Yn F | Yn F | 23 |
| 24 | Yg Wd | Yg M | Yg W | Yg W | Yn W | Yn E2 | Yn W | Yn E4 | Yg Wd | Yg M | Yg Wd | Yg Wd | Yn Wd | Yn M | Yg F | Yg E1 | Yg F | Yg E3 | Yn F | Yn F | Yn F | Yn W | Yg E | Yg F | 24 |
| 25 | Yn Wd | Yn M | Yn W | Yn E4 | Yg Wd | Yg M | Yg Wd | Yg Wd | Yn Wd | Yn M | Yn Wd | Yn Wd | Yg F | Yg E3 | Yn F | Yn F | Yn F | Yn W | Yg E | Yg F | Yg E | Yg W | Yn E | Yn E2 | 25 |
| 26 | Yg F | Yg E3 | Yg Wd | Yg Wd | Yn Wd | Yn M | Yn Wd | Yn Wd | Yg F | Yg E3 | Yg F | Yg E1 | Yn F | Yn W | Yg E | Yg F | Yg E | Yg W | Yn E | Yn E2 | Yn E | Yn E4 | Yg M | Yg M | 26 |
| 27 | Yn F | Yn W | Yn Wd | Yn Wd | Yg F | Yg E3 | Yg F | Yg E1 | Yn F | Yn W | Yn F | Yn F | Yg E | Yg W | Yn E | Yn E2 | Yn E | Yn E4 | Yg M | Yg M | Yg M | Yg Wd | Yn M | Yn M | 27 |
| 28 | Yg E | Yg W | Yg F | Yg E1 | Yn F | Yn W | Yn F | Yn F | Yg E | Yg W | Yg E | Yg F | Yn E | Yn E4 | Yg M | Yg M | Yg M | Yg Wd | Yn M | Yn M | Yn M | Yn Wd | Yg W | Yg E3 | 28 |
| 29 | | | Yn F | Yn F | Yg E | Yg W | Yg E | Yg F | Yn E | Yn E4 | Yn E | Yn E2 | Yg M | Yg Wd | Yn M | Yn M | Yn M | Yn Wd | Yg W | Yg E3 | Yg W | Yg E1 | Yn W | Yn W | 29 |
| 30 | | | Yg E | Yg F | Yn E | Yn E4 | Yn E | Yn E2 | Yg M | Yg Wd | Yg M | Yg M | Yn M | Yn Wd | Yg W | Yg E3 | Yg W | Yg E1 | Yn W | Yn W | Yn W | Yn F | Yg Wd | Yg W | 30 |
| 31 | | | Yn E | Yn E2 | | | Yg M | Yg M | | | Yn M | Yn M | Yg W | Yg E1 | | | Yn W | Yn F | | | Yg Wd | Yg F | Yn Wd | Yn E4 | 31 |
| 1 | Yn E | Yn E4 | Yg M | Yg M | Yg M | Yg Wd | Yn M | Yn M | Yn M | Yn Wd | Yg W | Yg E3 | Yn W | Yn F | Yn W | Yn W | Yg Wd | Yg F | Yg Wd | Yg W | Yn Wd | Yn E2 | Yg F | Yg Wd | 1 |
| 2 | Yg M | Yg Wd | Yn M | Yn M | Yn M | Yn Wd | Yg W | Yg E3 | Yg W | Yg E1 | Yn W | Yn W | Yg Wd | Yg F | Yg Wd | Yg W | Yn Wd | Yn E2 | Yn Wd | Yn E4 | Yg F | Yg M | Yn F | Yn Wd | 2 |
| 3 | Yn M | Yn Wd | Yg W | Yg E3 | Yg W | Yg E1 | Yn W | Yn W | Yn W | Yn F | Yg Wd | Yg W | Yn Wd | Yn E2 | Yn Wd | Yn E4 | Yg F | Yg M | Yg F | Yg Wd | Yn F | Yn M | Yg E | Yg E1 | 3 |
| 4 | Yg W | Yg E1 | Yn W | Yn W | Yn W | Yn F | Yg Wd | Yg W | Yg Wd | Yg F | Yn Wd | Yn E4 | Yg F | Yg M | Yg F | Yg Wd | Yn F | Yn M | Yn F | Yn Wd | Yg E | Yg E3 | Yn E | Yn F | 4 |
| 5 | Yn W | Yn F | | | Yg Wd | Yg F | Yn Wd | Yn E4 | Yn Wd | Yn E2 | Yg F | Yg Wd | Yn F | Yn M | Yn F | Yn Wd | Yg E | Yg E3 | Yg E | Yg E1 | Yn E | Yn W | | | 5 |
| 6 | | | | | | | | | Yg F | Yg M | Yn F | Yn Wd | Yg E | Yg E3 | Yg E | Yg E1 | Yn E | Yn W | Yn E | Yn F | | | | | 6 |
| 7 | | | | | | | | | Yn F | Yn M | Yg E | Yg E1 | Yn E | Yn W | Yn E | Yn F | Yg M | Yg W | Yg M | Yg F | | | | | 7 |
| 8 | | | | | | | | | | | | | | | Yg M | Yg F | | | | | | | | | 8 |

# YEAR OF THE RABBIT

| | H | E | H | E | H | E | H | E | H | E | H | E | H | E | H | E | H | E | H | E | H | E | H | E | |
|---|---|---|---|---|---|---|---|---|---|---|---|---|---|---|---|---|---|---|---|---|---|---|---|---|---|
| YEAR | YEAR<br>Yn F | Yn Wd | 1927 | | | | | | | | | | | | | | | | | | | | 1928 | | |
| MONTH | 5 Feb - 5 Mar<br>Yg W | Yg Wd | 6 Mar - 5 Apr<br>Yn W | Yn Wd | 6 Apr - 5 May<br>Yg Wd | Yg E1 | 6 May - 6 June<br>Yn Wd | Yn F | 7 June - 7 Jul<br>Yg F | Yg F | 8 Jul - 7 Aug<br>Yn F | Yn E2 | 8 Aug - 8 Sep<br>Yg E | Yg M | 9 Sep - 8 Oct<br>Yn E | Yn M | 9 Oct - 7 Nov<br>Yg M | Yg E3 | 8 Nov - 7 Dec<br>Yn M | Yn W | 8 Dec - 5 Jan<br>Yg W | Yg W | 6 Jan - 4 Feb<br>Yn W | Yn E4 | |
| Starting time | 1st day | Mid-pt | 1st day | Mid-pt | 1st day | Mid-pt | 1st day | Mid-pt | 1st day | Mid-pt | 1st day | Mid-pt | 1st day | Mid-pt | 1st day | Mid-pt | 1st day | Mid-pt | 1st day | Mid-pt | 1st day | Mid-pt | 1st day | Mid-pt | |
| Date | 5 | 19 | 6 | 21 | 6 | 21 | 6 | 22 | 7 | 22 | 8 | 24 | 8 | 24 | 9 | 24 | 9 | 24 | 8 | 23 | 8 | 23 | 6 | 21 | |
| Hour | 0331 | 2335 | 2151 | 2259 | 0307 | 1019 | 2054 | 1008 | 0125 | 1823 | 1150 | 0517 | 2132 | 1206 | 0006 | 0917 | 1516 | 1807 | 1757 | 1514 | 1027 | 0419 | 2132 | 1455 | |
| DATE 4 | | | | | | | | | | | | | | | | | | | | | | | | | 4 |
| 5 | Yg M | Yg F | | | | | | | | | | | | | | | | | | | | | | | 5 |
| 6 | Yn M | Yn E2 | Yn E | Yn W | Yg M | Yg F | Yg M | Yg W | | | | | | | | | | | | | | | Yn Wd | Yn F | 6 |
| 7 | Yg W | Yg M | Yg M | Yg W | Yn M | Yn E2 | Yn M | Yn E4 | Yg W | Yg M | | | | | | | | | | | | | Yg F | Yg F | 7 |
| 8 | Yn W | Yn M | Yn M | Yn E4 | Yg W | Yg M | Yg W | Yg Wd | Yn W | Yn M | Yn W | Yn Wd | Yg Wd | Yg E3 | | | | | Yg F | Yg F | Yg F | Yg W | Yn F | Yn E2 | 8 |
| 9 | Yg Wd | Yg E3 | Yg W | Yg Wd | Yn W | Yn M | Yn W | Yn Wd | Yg Wd | Yg E3 | Yg Wd | Yg E1 | Yn Wd | Yn W | Yg F | Yg F | Yg F | Yg W | Yn F | Yn E2 | Yn F | Yn E4 | Yg E | Yg M | 9 |
| 10 | Yn Wd | Yn W | Yn W | Yn Wd | Yg Wd | Yg E3 | Yg Wd | Yg E1 | Yn Wd | Yn W | Yn Wd | Yn F | Yg F | Yg W | Yn F | Yn E2 | Yn F | Yn E4 | Yg E | Yg M | Yg E | Yg Wd | Yn E | Yn M | 10 |
| 11 | Yg F | Yg W | Yg Wd | Yg E1 | Yn Wd | Yn W | Yn Wd | Yn F | Yg F | Yg W | Yg F | Yg F | Yn F | Yn E4 | Yg E | Yg M | Yg E | Yg Wd | Yn E | Yn M | Yn E | Yn Wd | Yg M | Yg E3 | 11 |
| 12 | Yn F | Yn E4 | Yn Wd | Yn F | Yg F | Yg W | Yg F | Yg F | Yn F | Yn E4 | Yn F | Yn E2 | Yg E | Yg Wd | Yn E | Yn M | Yn E | Yn Wd | Yg M | Yg E3 | Yg M | Yg E1 | Yn M | Yn W | 12 |
| 13 | Yg E | Yg Wd | Yg F | Yg F | Yn F | Yn E4 | Yn F | Yn E2 | Yg E | Yg Wd | Yg E | Yg M | Yn E | Yn Wd | Yg M | Yg E3 | Yg M | Yg E1 | Yn M | Yn W | Yn M | Yn F | Yg W | Yg W | 13 |
| 14 | Yn E | Yn Wd | Yn F | Yn E2 | Yg E | Yg Wd | Yg E | Yg M | Yn E | Yn Wd | Yn E | Yn M | Yg M | Yg E1 | Yn M | Yn W | Yn M | Yn F | Yg W | Yg W | Yg W | Yg F | Yn W | Yn E4 | 14 |
| 15 | Yg M | Yg E1 | Yg E | Yg M | Yn E | Yn Wd | Yn E | Yn M | Yg M | Yg E1 | Yg M | Yg E3 | Yn M | Yn F | Yg W | Yg W | Yg W | Yg F | Yn W | Yn E4 | Yn W | Yn E2 | Yg Wd | Yg Wd | 15 |
| 16 | Yn M | Yn F | Yn E | Yn M | Yg M | Yg E1 | Yg M | Yg E3 | Yn M | Yn F | Yn M | Yn W | Yg W | Yg F | Yn W | Yn E4 | Yn W | Yn E2 | Yg Wd | Yg Wd | Yg Wd | Yg M | Yn Wd | Yn Wd | 16 |
| 17 | Yg W | Yg F | Yg M | Yg E3 | Yn M | Yn F | Yn M | Yn W | Yg W | Yg F | Yg W | Yg W | Yn W | Yn E2 | Yg Wd | Yg Wd | Yg Wd | Yg M | Yn Wd | Yn Wd | Yn Wd | Yn M | Yg F | Yg E1 | 17 |
| 18 | Yn W | Yn E2 | Yn M | Yn W | Yg W | Yg F | Yg W | Yg W | Yn W | Yn E2 | Yn W | Yn E4 | Yg Wd | Yg M | Yn Wd | Yn Wd | Yn Wd | Yn M | Yg F | Yg E1 | Yg F | Yg E3 | Yn F | Yn F | 18 |
| 19 | Yg Wd | Yg M | Yg W | Yg W | Yn W | Yn E2 | Yn W | Yn E4 | Yg Wd | Yg M | Yg Wd | Yg Wd | Yn Wd | Yn M | Yg F | Yg E1 | Yg F | Yg E3 | Yn F | Yn F | Yn F | Yn W | Yg E | Yg F | 19 |
| 20 | Yn Wd | Yn M | Yn W | Yn E4 | Yg Wd | Yg M | Yg Wd | Yg Wd | Yn Wd | Yn M | Yn Wd | Yn Wd | Yg F | Yg E3 | Yn F | Yn F | Yn F | Yn W | Yg E | Yg F | Yg E | Yg W | Yn E | Yn E2 | 20 |
| 21 | Yg F | Yg E3 | Yg Wd | Yg Wd | Yn Wd | Yn M | Yn Wd | Yn Wd | Yg F | Yg E3 | Yg F | Yg E1 | Yn F | Yn W | Yg E | Yg F | Yg E | Yg W | Yn E | Yn E2 | Yn E | Yn E4 | Yg M | Yg M | 21 |
| 22 | Yn F | Yn W | Yn Wd | Yn Wd | Yg F | Yg E3 | Yg F | Yg E1 | Yn F | Yn W | Yn F | Yn F | Yg E | Yg W | Yn E | Yn E2 | Yn E | Yn E4 | Yg M | Yg M | Yg M | Yg Wd | Yn M | Yn M | 22 |
| 23 | Yg E | Yg W | Yg F | Yg E1 | Yn F | Yn W | Yn F | Yn F | Yg E | Yg W | Yg E | Yg F | Yn E | Yn E4 | Yg M | Yg M | Yg M | Yg Wd | Yn M | Yn M | Yn M | Yn Wd | Yg W | Yg E3 | 23 |
| 24 | Yn E | Yn E4 | Yn F | Yn F | Yg E | Yg W | Yg E | Yg F | Yn E | Yn E4 | Yn E | Yn E2 | Yg M | Yg Wd | Yn M | Yn M | Yn M | Yn Wd | Yg W | Yg E3 | Yg W | Yg E1 | Yn W | Yn W | 24 |
| 25 | Yg M | Yg Wd | Yg E | Yg F | Yn E | Yn E4 | Yn E | Yn E2 | Yg M | Yg Wd | Yg M | Yg M | Yn M | Yn Wd | Yg W | Yg E3 | Yg W | Yg E1 | Yn W | Yn W | Yn W | Yn F | Yg Wd | Yg W | 25 |
| 26 | Yn M | Yn Wd | Yn E | Yn E2 | Yg M | Yg Wd | Yg M | Yg M | Yn M | Yn Wd | Yn M | Yn M | Yg W | Yg E1 | Yn W | Yn W | Yn W | Yn F | Yg Wd | Yg W | Yg Wd | Yg F | Yn Wd | Yn E4 | 26 |
| 27 | Yg W | Yg E1 | Yg M | Yg M | Yn M | Yn Wd | Yn M | Yn M | Yg W | Yg E1 | Yg W | Yg E3 | Yn W | Yn F | Yg Wd | Yg W | Yg Wd | Yg F | Yn Wd | Yn E4 | Yn Wd | Yn E2 | Yg F | Yg Wd | 27 |
| 28 | Yn W | Yn F | Yn M | Yn M | Yg W | Yg E1 | Yg W | Yg E3 | Yn W | Yn F | Yn W | Yn W | Yg Wd | Yg F | Yn Wd | Yn E4 | Yn Wd | Yn E2 | Yg F | Yg Wd | Yg F | Yg M | Yn F | Yn Wd | 28 |
| 29 | | | Yg W | Yg E3 | Yn W | Yn F | Yn W | Yn W | Yg Wd | Yg F | Yg Wd | Yg W | Yn Wd | Yn E2 | Yg F | Yg Wd | Yg F | Yg M | Yn F | Yn Wd | Yn F | Yn M | Yg E | Yg E1 | 29 |
| 30 | | | Yn W | Yn W | Yg Wd | Yg F | Yg Wd | Yg W | Yn Wd | Yn E2 | Yn Wd | Yn E4 | Yg F | Yg M | Yn F | Yn Wd | Yn F | Yn M | Yg E | Yg E1 | Yg E | Yg E3 | Yn E | Yn F | 30 |
| 31 | | | Yg Wd | Yg W | | | Yn Wd | Yn E4 | | | Yg F | Yg Wd | Yn F | Yn M | | | Yg E | Yg E3 | | | Yn E | Yn W | Yg M | Yg F | 31 |
| 1 | Yg Wd | Yg F | Yn Wd | Yn E4 | Yn Wd | Yn E2 | Yg F | Yg Wd | Yg F | Yg M | Yn F | Yn Wd | Yg E | Yg E3 | Yg E | Yg E1 | Yn E | Yn W | Yn E | Yn F | Yg M | Yg W | Yn M | Yn E2 | 1 |
| 2 | Yn Wd | Yn E2 | Yg F | Yg Wd | Yg F | Yg M | Yn F | Yn Wd | Yn F | Yn M | Yg E | Yg E1 | Yn E | Yn W | Yn E | Yn F | Yg M | Yg W | Yg M | Yg F | Yn M | Yn E4 | Yg W | Yg M | 2 |
| 3 | Yg F | Yg M | Yn F | Yn Wd | Yn F | Yn M | Yg E | Yg E1 | Yg E | Yg E3 | Yn E | Yn F | Yg M | Yg W | Yg M | Yg F | Yn M | Yn E4 | Yn M | Yn E2 | Yg W | Yg Wd | Yn W | Yn M | 3 |
| 4 | Yn F | Yn M | Yg E | Yg E1 | Yg E | Yg E3 | Yn E | Yn F | Yn E | Yn W | Yg M | Yg F | Yn M | Yn E4 | Yn M | Yn E2 | Yg W | Yg Wd | Yg W | Yg M | Yn W | Yn Wd | Yg Wd | Yg E3 | 4 |
| 5 | Yg E | Yg E3 | Yn E | Yn F | Yn E | Yn W | Yg M | Yg F | Yg M | Yg W | Yn M | Yn E2 | Yg W | Yg Wd | Yg W | Yg M | Yn W | Yn Wd | Yn W | Yn M | Yg Wd | Yg E1 | | | 5 |
| 6 | | | | | | | Yn M | Yn E2 | Yn M | Yn E4 | Yg W | Yg M | Yn W | Yn Wd | Yn W | Yn M | Yg Wd | Yg E1 | Yg Wd | Yg E3 | | | | | 6 |
| 7 | | | | | | | | | Yg W | Yg Wd | Yn W | Yn M | Yg Wd | Yg E1 | Yg Wd | Yg E3 | Yn Wd | Yn F | Yn Wd | Yn W | | | | | 7 |
| 8 | | | | | | | | | | | | | Yn Wd | Yn F | Yn Wd | Yn W | | | | | | | | | 8 |

# YEAR OF THE DRAGON

| | H | E | H | E | H | E | H | E | H | E | H | E | H | E | H | E | H | E | H | E | H | E | H | E |
|---|---|---|---|---|---|---|---|---|---|---|---|---|---|---|---|---|---|---|---|---|---|---|---|---|
| YEAR | YEAR<br>Yg E | Yg E1 | 1928 | | | | | | | | | | | | | | | | | | | | 1929 | |
| MONTH | 5 Feb - 5 Mar<br>Yg Wd | Yg Wd | 6 Mar - 4 Apr<br>Yn Wd | Yn Wd | 5 Apr - 5 May<br>Yg F | Yg E1 | 6 May - 5 June<br>Yn F | Yn F | 6 June - 6 Jul<br>Yg E | Yg F | 7 Jul - 7 Aug<br>Yn E | Yn E2 | 8 Aug - 7 Sep<br>Yg M | Yg M | 8 Sep - 7 Oct<br>Yn M | Yn M | 8 Oct - 6 Nov<br>Yg W | Yg E3 | 7 Nov - 6 Dec<br>Yn W | Yn W | 7 Dec - 5 Jan<br>Yg Wd | Yg W | 6 Jan - 3 Feb<br>Yn Wd | Yn E4 |
| Starting time | 1st day | Mid-pt | 1st day | Mid-pt | 1st day | Mid-pt | 1st day | Mid-pt | 1st day | Mid-pt | 1st day | Mid-pt | 1st day | Mid-pt | 1st day | Mid-pt | 1st day | Mid-pt | 1st day | Mid-pt | 1st day | Mid-pt | 1st day | Mid-pt |
| Date | 5 | 20 | 6 | 21 | 5 | 20 | 6 | 21 | 6 | 22 | 7 | 23 | 8 | 23 | 8 | 23 | 8 | 23 | 7 | 22 | 7 | 22 | 6 | 20 |
| Hour | 0917 | 0520 | 0338 | 0445 | 0855 | 1617 | 0244 | 1553 | 0718 | 0007 | 1745 | 1103 | 0328 | 1754 | 0602 | 1506 | 2111 | 2355 | 2350 | 2110 | 1618 | 1004 | 0323 | 2043 |
| DATE 4 | | | | | | | | | | | | | | | | | | | | | | | | |
| 5 | Yn Wd | Yn W | | | Yn Wd | Yn W | | | | | | | | | | | | | | | | | | |
| 6 | Yg F | Yg W | Yn Wd | Yn F | Yg F | Yg W | Yg F | Yg F | Yn F | Yn E4 | | | | | | | | | | | | | Yn M | Yn W |
| 7 | Yn F | Yn E4 | Yg F | Yg F | Yn F | Yn E4 | Yn F | Yn E2 | Yg E | Yg Wd | Yg E | Yg M | | | | | | | Yn M | Yn W | Yn M | Yn F | Yg W | Yg W |
| 8 | Yg E | Yg Wd | Yn F | Yn E2 | Yg E | Yg Wd | Yg E | Yg M | Yn E | Yn Wd | Yn E | Yn M | Yg M | Yg E1 | Yn M | Yn W | Yn M | Yn F | Yg W | Yg W | Yg W | Yg F | Yn W | Yn E4 |
| 9 | Yn E | Yn Wd | Yg E | Yg M | Yn E | Yn Wd | Yn E | Yn M | Yg M | Yg E1 | Yg M | Yg E3 | Yn M | Yn F | Yg W | Yg W | Yg W | Yg F | Yn W | Yn E4 | Yn W | Yn E2 | Yg Wd | Yg Wd |
| 10 | Yg M | Yg E1 | Yn E | Yn M | Yg M | Yg E1 | Yg M | Yg E3 | Yn M | Yn F | Yn M | Yn W | Yg W | Yg F | Yn W | Yn E4 | Yn W | Yn E2 | Yg Wd | Yg Wd | Yg Wd | Yg M | Yn Wd | Yn Wd |
| 11 | Yn M | Yn F | Yg M | Yg E3 | Yn M | Yn F | Yn M | Yn W | Yg W | Yg F | Yg W | Yg W | Yn W | Yn E2 | Yg Wd | Yg Wd | Yg Wd | Yg M | Yn Wd | Yn Wd | Yn Wd | Yn M | Yg F | Yg E1 |
| 12 | Yg W | Yg F | Yn M | Yn W | Yg W | Yg F | Yg W | Yg W | Yn W | Yn E2 | Yn W | Yn E4 | Yg Wd | Yg M | Yn Wd | Yn Wd | Yn Wd | Yn M | Yg F | Yg E1 | Yg F | Yg E3 | Yn F | Yn F |
| 13 | Yn W | Yn E2 | Yg W | Yg W | Yn W | Yn E2 | Yn W | Yn E4 | Yg Wd | Yg M | Yg Wd | Yg Wd | Yn Wd | Yn M | Yg F | Yg E1 | Yg F | Yg E3 | Yn F | Yn F | Yn F | Yn W | Yg E | Yg F |
| 14 | Yg Wd | Yg M | Yn W | Yn E4 | Yg Wd | Yg M | Yg Wd | Yg Wd | Yn Wd | Yn M | Yn Wd | Yn Wd | Yg F | Yg E3 | Yn F | Yn F | Yn F | Yn W | Yg E | Yg F | Yg E | Yg W | Yn E | Yn E2 |
| 15 | Yn Wd | Yn M | Yg Wd | Yg Wd | Yn Wd | Yn M | Yn Wd | Yn Wd | Yg F | Yg E3 | Yg F | Yg E1 | Yn F | Yn W | Yg E | Yg F | Yg E | Yg W | Yn E | Yn E2 | Yn E | Yn E4 | Yg M | Yg M |
| 16 | Yg F | Yg E3 | Yn Wd | Yn Wd | Yg F | Yg E3 | Yg F | Yg E1 | Yn F | Yn W | Yn F | Yn F | Yg E | Yg W | Yn E | Yn E2 | Yn E | Yn E4 | Yg M | Yg M | Yg M | Yg Wd | Yn M | Yn M |
| 17 | Yn F | Yn W | Yg F | Yg E1 | Yn F | Yn W | Yn F | Yn F | Yg E | Yg W | Yg E | Yg F | Yn E | Yn E4 | Yg M | Yg M | Yg M | Yg Wd | Yn M | Yn M | Yn M | Yn Wd | Yg W | Yg E3 |
| 18 | Yg E | Yg W | Yn F | Yn F | Yg E | Yg W | Yg E | Yg F | Yn E | Yn E4 | Yn E | Yn E2 | Yg M | Yg Wd | Yn M | Yn M | Yn M | Yn Wd | Yg W | Yg E3 | Yg W | Yg E1 | Yn W | Yn W |
| 19 | Yn E | Yn E4 | Yg E | Yg F | Yn E | Yn E4 | Yn E | Yn E2 | Yg M | Yg Wd | Yg M | Yg M | Yn M | Yn Wd | Yg W | Yg E3 | Yg W | Yg E1 | Yn W | Yn W | Yn W | Yn F | Yg Wd | Yg W |
| 20 | Yg M | Yg Wd | Yn E | Yn E2 | Yg M | Yg Wd | Yg M | Yg M | Yn M | Yn Wd | Yn M | Yn M | Yg W | Yg E1 | Yn W | Yn W | Yn W | Yn F | Yg Wd | Yg W | Yg Wd | Yg F | Yn Wd | Yn E4 |
| 21 | Yn M | Yn Wd | Yg M | Yg M | Yn M | Yn Wd | Yn M | Yn M | Yg W | Yg E1 | Yg W | Yg E3 | Yn W | Yn F | Yg Wd | Yg W | Yg Wd | Yg F | Yn Wd | Yn E4 | Yn Wd | Yn E2 | Yg F | Yg Wd |
| 22 | Yg W | Yg E1 | Yn M | Yn M | Yg W | Yg E1 | Yg W | Yg E3 | Yn W | Yn F | Yn W | Yn W | Yg Wd | Yg F | Yn Wd | Yn E4 | Yn Wd | Yn E2 | Yg F | Yg Wd | Yg F | Yg M | Yn F | Yn Wd |
| 23 | Yn W | Yn F | Yg W | Yg E3 | Yn W | Yn F | Yn W | Yn W | Yg Wd | Yg F | Yg Wd | Yg W | Yn Wd | Yn E2 | Yg F | Yg Wd | Yg F | Yg M | Yn F | Yn Wd | Yn F | Yn M | Yg E | Yg E1 |
| 24 | Yg Wd | Yg F | Yn W | Yn W | Yg Wd | Yg F | Yg Wd | Yg W | Yn Wd | Yn E2 | Yn Wd | Yn E4 | Yg F | Yg M | Yn F | Yn Wd | Yn F | Yn M | Yg E | Yg E1 | Yg E | Yg E3 | Yn E | Yn F |
| 25 | Yn Wd | Yn E2 | Yg Wd | Yg W | Yn Wd | Yn E2 | Yn Wd | Yn E4 | Yg F | Yg M | Yg F | Yg Wd | Yn F | Yn M | Yg E | Yg E1 | Yg E | Yg E3 | Yn E | Yn F | Yn E | Yn W | Yg M | Yg F |
| 26 | Yg F | Yg M | Yn Wd | Yn E4 | Yg F | Yg M | Yg F | Yg Wd | Yn F | Yn M | Yn F | Yn Wd | Yg E | Yg E3 | Yn E | Yn F | Yn E | Yn W | Yg M | Yg F | Yg M | Yg W | Yn M | Yn E2 |
| 27 | Yn F | Yn M | Yg F | Yg Wd | Yn F | Yn M | Yn F | Yn Wd | Yg E | Yg E3 | Yg E | Yg E1 | Yn E | Yn W | Yg M | Yg F | Yg M | Yg W | Yn M | Yn E2 | Yn M | Yn E4 | Yg W | Yg M |
| 28 | Yg E | Yg E3 | Yn F | Yn Wd | Yg E | Yg E3 | Yg E | Yg E1 | Yn E | Yn W | Yn E | Yn F | Yg M | Yg W | Yn M | Yn E2 | Yn M | Yn E4 | Yg W | Yg M | Yg W | Yg Wd | Yn W | Yn M |
| 29 | Yn E | Yn W | Yg E | Yg E1 | Yn E | Yn W | Yn E | Yn F | Yg M | Yg W | Yg M | Yg F | Yn M | Yn E4 | Yg W | Yg M | Yg W | Yg Wd | Yn W | Yn M | Yn W | Yn Wd | Yg Wd | Yg E3 |
| 30 | | | Yn E | Yn F | Yg M | Yg W | Yg M | Yg F | Yn M | Yn E4 | Yn M | Yn E2 | Yg W | Yg Wd | Yn W | Yn M | Yn W | Yn Wd | Yg Wd | Yg E3 | Yg Wd | Yg E1 | Yn Wd | Yn W |
| 31 | | | Yg M | Yg F | | | Yn M | Yn E2 | | | Yg W | Yg M | Yn W | Yn Wd | | | Yg Wd | Yg E1 | | | Yn Wd | Yn F | Yg F | Yg W |
| 1 | Yg M | Yg W | Yn M | Yn E2 | Yn M | Yn E4 | Yg W | Yg M | Yg W | Yg Wd | Yn W | Yn M | Yg Wd | Yg E1 | Yg Wd | Yg E3 | Yn Wd | Yn F | Yn Wd | Yn W | Yg F | Yg F | Yn F | Yn E4 |
| 2 | Yn M | Yn E4 | Yg W | Yg M | Yg W | Yg Wd | Yn W | Yn M | Yn W | Yn Wd | Yg Wd | Yg E3 | Yn Wd | Yn F | Yn Wd | Yn W | Yg F | Yg F | Yg F | Yg W | Yn F | Yn E2 | Yg E | Yg Wd |
| 3 | Yg W | Yg Wd | Yn W | Yn M | Yn W | Yn Wd | Yg Wd | Yg E3 | Yg Wd | Yg E1 | Yn Wd | Yn W | Yg F | Yg F | Yg F | Yg W | Yn F | Yn E2 | Yn F | Yn E4 | Yg E | Yg M | Yn E | Yn Wd |
| 4 | Yn W | Yn Wd | Yg Wd | Yg E3 | Yg Wd | Yg E1 | Yn Wd | Yn W | Yn Wd | Yn F | Yg F | Yg W | Yn F | Yn E2 | Yn F | Yn E4 | Yg E | Yg M | Yg E | Yg Wd | Yn E | Yn M | | |
| 5 | Yg Wd | Yg E1 | | | Yn Wd | Yn F | Yg F | Yg W | Yg F | Yg F | Yn F | Yn E4 | Yg E | Yg M | Yg E | Yg Wd | Yn E | Yn M | Yn E | Yn Wd | Yg M | Yg E3 | | |
| 6 | | | | | | | | | Yn F | Yn E2 | Yg E | Yg Wd | Yn E | Yn M | Yn E | Yn Wd | Yg M | Yg E3 | Yg M | Yg E1 | | | | |
| 7 | | | | | | | | | | | Yn E | Yn Wd | Yg M | Yg E3 | Yg M | Yg E1 | | | | | | | | |
| 8 | | | | | | | | | | | | | | | | | | | | | | | | |

# YEAR OF THE SNAKE

| | H | E | H | E | H | E | H | E | H | E | H | E | H | E | H | E | H | E | H | E | H | E | H | E | |
|---|---|---|---|---|---|---|---|---|---|---|---|---|---|---|---|---|---|---|---|---|---|---|---|---|---|
| YEAR | YEAR<br>YnE | YnF | 1929 | | | | | | | | | | | | | | | | | | | | 1930 | | |
| MONTH | 4 Feb - 5 Mar<br>Yg F | Yg Wd | 6 Mar - 4 Apr<br>Yn F | Yn Wd | 5 Apr - 5 May<br>Yg E | Yg E1 | 6 May - 5 June<br>Yn E | Yn F | 6 June - 6 Jul<br>Yg M | Yg F | 7 Jul - 7 Aug<br>Yn M | Yn E2 | 8 Aug - 7 Sep<br>Yg W | Yg M | 8 Sep - 8 Oct<br>Yn W | Yn M | 9 Oct - 7 Nov<br>Yg Wd | Yg E3 | 8 Nov - 6 Dec<br>Yn Wd | Yn W | 7 Dec - 5 Jan<br>Yg F | Yg W | 6 Jan - 3 Feb<br>Yn F | Yn E4 | |
| Starting time | 1st day | Mid-pt | 1st day | Mid-pt | 1st day | Mid-pt | 1st day | Mid-pt | 1st day | Mid-pt | 1st day | Mid-pt | 1st day | Mid-pt | 1st day | Mid-pt | 1st day | Mid-pt | 1st day | Mid-pt | 1st day | Mid-pt | 1st day | Mid-pt | |
| Date | 4 | 19 | 6 | 21 | 5 | 20 | 6 | 21 | 6 | 22 | 7 | 23 | 8 | 23 | 8 | 23 | 9 | 24 | 8 | 23 | 7 | 22 | 6 | 21 | |
| Hour | 1509 | 1107 | 0932 | 1035 | 1452 | 2211 | 0841 | 2148 | 1311 | 0604 | 2332 | 1654 | 0909 | 2342 | 1140 | 2053 | 0248 | 0542 | 0528 | 0249 | 2157 | 1553 | 0903 | 0233 | |
| DATE 4 | Yg M | Yg E1 | | | | | | | | | | | | | | | | | | | | | | | 4 |
| 5 | Yn M | Yn F | | | Yg M | Yg E1 | | | | | | | | | | | | | | | | | | | 5 |
| 6 | Yg W | Yg F | Yg M | Yg E3 | Yn M | Yn F | Yn M | Yn W | Yg W | Yg F | | | | | | | | | | | | | Yg F | Yg E1 | 6 |
| 7 | Yn W | Yn E2 | Yn M | Yn W | Yg W | Yg F | Yg W | Yg W | Yn W | Yn E2 | Yn W | Yn E4 | | | | | | | | | Yg F | Yg E3 | Yn F | Yn F | 7 |
| 8 | Yg Wd | Yg M | Yg W | Yg W | Yn W | Yn E2 | Yn W | Yn E4 | Yg Wd | Yg M | Yg Wd | Yg Wd | Yn Wd | Yn M | Yg F | Yg E1 | | | Yn F | Yn F | Yn F | Yn W | Yg E | Yg F | 8 |
| 9 | Yn Wd | Yn M | Yn W | Yn E4 | Yg Wd | Yg M | Yg Wd | Yg Wd | Yn Wd | Yn M | Yn Wd | Yn Wd | Yg F | Yg E3 | Yn F | Yn F | Yn F | Yn W | Yg E | Yg F | Yg E | Yg W | Yn E | Yn E2 | 9 |
| 10 | Yg F | Yg E3 | Yg Wd | Yg Wd | Yn Wd | Yn M | Yn Wd | Yn Wd | Yg F | Yg E3 | Yg F | Yg E1 | Yn F | Yn W | Yg E | Yg F | Yg E | Yg W | Yn E | Yn E2 | Yn E | Yn E4 | Yg M | Yg M | 10 |
| 11 | Yn F | Yn W | Yn Wd | Yn Wd | Yg F | Yg E3 | Yg F | Yg E1 | Yn F | Yn W | Yn F | Yn F | Yg E | Yg W | Yn E | Yn E2 | Yn E | Yn E4 | Yg M | Yg M | Yg M | Yg Wd | Yn M | Yn M | 11 |
| 12 | Yg E | Yg W | Yg F | Yg E1 | Yn F | Yn W | Yn F | Yn F | Yg E | Yg W | Yg E | Yg F | Yn E | Yn E4 | Yg M | Yg M | Yg M | Yg Wd | Yn M | Yn M | Yn M | Yn Wd | Yg W | Yg E3 | 12 |
| 13 | Yn E | Yn E4 | Yn F | Yn F | Yg E | Yg W | Yg E | Yg F | Yn E | Yn E4 | Yn E | Yn E2 | Yg M | Yg Wd | Yn M | Yn M | Yn M | Yn Wd | Yg W | Yg E3 | Yg W | Yg E1 | Yn W | Yn W | 13 |
| 14 | Yg M | Yg Wd | Yg E | Yg F | Yn E | Yn E4 | Yn E | Yn E2 | Yg M | Yg Wd | Yg M | Yg M | Yn M | Yn Wd | Yg W | Yg E3 | Yg W | Yg E1 | Yn W | Yn W | Yn W | Yn F | Yg Wd | Yg W | 14 |
| 15 | Yn M | Yn Wd | Yn E | Yn E2 | Yg M | Yg Wd | Yg M | Yg M | Yn M | Yn Wd | Yn M | Yn M | Yg W | Yg E1 | Yn W | Yn W | Yn W | Yn F | Yg Wd | Yg W | Yg Wd | Yg F | Yn Wd | Yn E4 | 15 |
| 16 | Yg W | Yg E1 | Yg M | Yg M | Yn M | Yn Wd | Yn M | Yn M | Yg W | Yg E1 | Yg W | Yg E3 | Yn W | Yn F | Yg Wd | Yg W | Yg Wd | Yg F | Yn Wd | Yn E4 | Yn Wd | Yn E2 | Yg F | Yg Wd | 16 |
| 17 | Yn W | Yn F | Yn M | Yn M | Yg W | Yg E1 | Yg W | Yg E3 | Yn W | Yn F | Yn W | Yn W | Yg Wd | Yg F | Yn Wd | Yn E4 | Yn Wd | Yn E2 | Yg F | Yg Wd | Yg F | Yg M | Yn F | Yn Wd | 17 |
| 18 | Yg Wd | Yg F | Yg W | Yg E3 | Yn W | Yn F | Yn W | Yn W | Yg Wd | Yg F | Yg Wd | Yg W | Yn Wd | Yn E2 | Yg F | Yg Wd | Yg F | Yg M | Yn F | Yn Wd | Yn F | Yn M | Yg E | Yg E1 | 18 |
| 19 | Yn Wd | Yn E2 | Yn W | Yn W | Yg Wd | Yg F | Yg Wd | Yg W | Yn Wd | Yn E2 | Yn Wd | Yn E4 | Yg F | Yg M | Yn F | Yn Wd | Yn F | Yn M | Yg E | Yg E1 | Yg E | Yg E3 | Yn E | Yn F | 19 |
| 20 | Yg F | Yg M | Yg Wd | Yg W | Yn Wd | Yn E2 | Yn Wd | Yn E4 | Yg F | Yg M | Yg F | Yg Wd | Yn F | Yn M | Yg E | Yg E1 | Yg E | Yg E3 | Yn E | Yn F | Yn E | Yn W | Yg M | Yg F | 20 |
| 21 | Yn F | Yn M | Yn Wd | Yn E4 | Yg F | Yg M | Yg F | Yg Wd | Yn F | Yn M | Yn F | Yn Wd | Yg E | Yg E3 | Yn E | Yn F | Yn E | Yn W | Yg M | Yg F | Yg M | Yg W | Yn M | Yn E2 | 21 |
| 22 | Yg E | Yg E3 | Yg F | Yg Wd | Yn F | Yn M | Yn F | Yn Wd | Yg E | Yg E3 | Yg E | Yg E1 | Yn E | Yn W | Yg M | Yg F | Yg M | Yg W | Yn M | Yn E2 | Yn M | Yn E4 | Yg W | Yg M | 22 |
| 23 | Yn E | Yn W | Yn F | Yn Wd | Yg E | Yg E3 | Yg E | Yg E1 | Yn E | Yn W | Yn E | Yn F | Yg M | Yg W | Yn M | Yn E2 | Yn M | Yn E4 | Yg W | Yg M | Yg W | Yg Wd | Yn W | Yn M | 23 |
| 24 | Yg M | Yg W | Yg E | Yg E1 | Yn E | Yn W | Yn E | Yn F | Yg M | Yg W | Yg M | Yg F | Yn M | Yn E4 | Yg W | Yg M | Yg W | Yg Wd | Yn W | Yn M | Yn W | Yn Wd | Yg Wd | Yg E3 | 24 |
| 25 | Yn M | Yn E4 | Yn E | Yn F | Yg M | Yg W | Yg M | Yg F | Yn M | Yn E4 | Yn M | Yn E2 | Yg W | Yg Wd | Yn W | Yn M | Yn W | Yn Wd | Yg Wd | Yg E3 | Yg Wd | Yg E1 | Yn Wd | Yn W | 25 |
| 26 | Yg W | Yg Wd | Yg M | Yg F | Yn M | Yn E4 | Yn M | Yn E2 | Yg W | Yg Wd | Yg W | Yg M | Yn W | Yn Wd | Yg Wd | Yg E3 | Yg Wd | Yg E1 | Yn Wd | Yn W | Yn Wd | Yn F | Yg F | Yg W | 26 |
| 27 | Yn W | Yn Wd | Yn M | Yn E2 | Yg W | Yg Wd | Yg W | Yg M | Yn W | Yn Wd | Yn W | Yn M | Yg Wd | Yg E1 | Yn Wd | Yn W | Yn Wd | Yn F | Yg F | Yg W | Yg F | Yg F | Yn F | Yn E4 | 27 |
| 28 | Yg Wd | Yg E1 | Yg W | Yg M | Yn W | Yn Wd | Yn W | Yn M | Yg Wd | Yg E1 | Yg Wd | Yg E3 | Yn Wd | Yn F | Yg F | Yg W | Yg F | Yg F | Yn F | Yn E4 | Yn F | Yn E2 | Yg E | Yg Wd | 28 |
| 29 | | | Yn W | Yn M | Yg Wd | Yg E1 | Yg Wd | Yg E3 | Yn Wd | Yn F | Yn Wd | Yn W | Yg F | Yg F | Yn F | Yn E4 | Yn F | Yn E2 | Yg E | Yg Wd | Yg E | Yg M | Yn E | Yn Wd | 29 |
| 30 | | | Yg Wd | Yg E3 | Yn Wd | Yn F | Yn Wd | Yn W | Yg F | Yg F | Yg F | Yg W | Yn F | Yn E2 | Yg E | Yg Wd | Yg E | Yg M | Yn E | Yn Wd | Yn E | Yn M | Yg M | Yg E1 | 30 |
| 31 | | | Yn Wd | Yn W | | | Yg F | Yg W | | | Yn F | Yn E4 | Yg E | Yg M | | | Yn E | Yn M | | | Yg M | Yg E3 | Yn M | Yn F | 31 |
| 1 | Yn Wd | Yn F | Yg F | Yg W | Yg F | Yg F | Yn F | Yn E4 | Yn F | Yn E2 | Yg E | Yg Wd | Yn E | Yn M | Yn E | Yn Wd | Yg M | Yg E3 | Yg M | Yg E1 | Yn M | Yn W | Yg W | Yg F | 1 |
| 2 | Yg F | Yg F | Yn F | Yn E4 | Yn F | Yn E2 | Yg E | Yg Wd | Yg E | Yg M | Yn E | Yn Wd | Yg M | Yg E3 | Yg M | Yg E1 | Yn M | Yn W | Yn M | Yn F | Yg W | Yg W | Yn W | Yn E2 | 2 |
| 3 | Yn F | Yn E2 | Yg E | Yg Wd | Yg E | Yg M | Yn E | Yn Wd | Yn E | Yn M | Yg M | Yg E1 | Yn M | Yn W | Yn M | Yn F | Yg W | Yg W | Yg W | Yg F | Yn W | Yn E4 | Yg Wd | Yg M | 3 |
| 4 | Yg E | Yg M | Yn E | Yn Wd | Yn E | Yn M | Yg M | Yg E1 | Yg M | Yg E3 | Yn M | Yn F | Yg W | Yg W | Yg W | Yg F | Yn W | Yn E4 | Yn W | Yn E2 | Yg Wd | Yg Wd | | | 4 |
| 5 | Yn E | Yn M | | | Yg M | Yg E3 | Yn M | Yn F | Yn M | Yn W | Yg W | Yg F | Yn W | Yn E4 | Yn W | Yn E2 | Yg Wd | Yg Wd | Yg Wd | Yg M | Yn Wd | Yn Wd | | | 5 |
| 6 | | | | | | | | | Yg W | Yg W | Yn W | Yn E2 | Yg Wd | Yg Wd | Yg Wd | Yg M | Yn Wd | Yn Wd | Yn Wd | Yn M | | | | | 6 |
| 7 | | | | | | | | | | | Yg Wd | Yg M | Yn Wd | Yn Wd | Yn Wd | Yn M | Yg F | Yg E1 | | | | | | | 7 |
| 8 | | | | | | | | | | | | | | | Yg F | Yg E3 | | | | | | | | | 8 |

# YEAR OF THE HORSE

| | H | E | H | E | H | E | H | E | H | E | H | E | H | E | H | E | H | E | H | E | H | E | H | E | |
|---|---|---|---|---|---|---|---|---|---|---|---|---|---|---|---|---|---|---|---|---|---|---|---|---|---|
| YEAR | YEAR<br>Yg M | <br>Yg F | 1930 | | | | | | | | | | | | | | | | | | | | 1931 | | |
| MONTH | 4 Feb - 5 Mar | | 6 Mar - 4 Apr | | 5 Apr - 5 May | | 6 May - 5 June | | 6 June - 7 Jul | | 8 Jul - 7 Aug | | 8 Aug - 7 Sep | | 8 Sep - 8 Oct | | 9 Oct - 7 Nov | | 8 Nov - 7 Dec | | 8 Dec - 5 Jan | | 6 Jan - 4 Feb | | |
| | Yg E | Yg Wd | Yn E | Yn Wd | Yg M | Yg E1 | Yn M | Yn F | Yg W | Yg F | Yn W | Yn E2 | Yg Wd | Yg M | Yn Wd | Yn M | Yg F | Yg E3 | Yn F | Yn W | Yg E | Yg W | Yn E | Yn E4 | |
| Starting time | 1st day | Mid-pt | 1st day | Mid-pt | 1st day | Mid-pt | 1st day | Mid-pt | 1st day | Mid-pt | 1st day | Mid-pt | 1st day | Mid-pt | 1st day | Mid-pt | 1st day | Mid-pt | 1st day | Mid-pt | 1st day | Mid-pt | 1st day | Mid-pt | |
| Date | 4 | 19 | 6 | 21 | 5 | 21 | 6 | 22 | 6 | 22 | 8 | 23 | 8 | 24 | 8 | 24 | 9 | 24 | 8 | 23 | 8 | 22 | 6 | 21 | |
| Hour | 2052 | 1700 | 1517 | 1630 | 2038 | 0406 | 1428 | 0342 | 1858 | 1153 | 0520 | 2242 | 1458 | 0527 | 1729 | 0236 | 0838 | 1126 | 1121 | 0835 | 0351 | 2115 | 1456 | 0818 | |
| DATE 4 | Yn Wd | Yn M | | | | | | | | | | | | | | | | | | | | | | | 4 |
| 5 | Yg F | Yg E3 | | | Yn Wd | Yn M | | | | | | | | | | | | | | | | | | | 5 |
| 6 | Yn F | Yn W | Yn Wd | Yn Wd | Yg F | Yg E3 | Yg F | Yg E1 | Yn F | Yn W | | | | | | | | | | | | | Yn M | Yn M | 6 |
| 7 | Yg E | Yg W | Yg F | Yg E1 | Yn F | Yn W | Yn F | Yn F | Yg E | Yg W | | | | | | | | | | | | | Yg W | Yg E3 | 7 |
| 8 | Yn E | Yn E4 | Yn F | Yn F | Yg E | Yg W | Yg E | Yg F | Yn E | Yn E4 | Yn E | Yn E2 | Yg M | Yg Wd | Yn M | Yn M | | | Yg W | Yg E3 | Yg W | Yg E1 | Yn W | Yn W | 8 |
| 9 | Yg M | Yg Wd | Yg E | Yg F | Yn E | Yn E4 | Yn E | Yn E2 | Yg M | Yg Wd | Yg M | Yg M | Yn M | Yn Wd | Yg W | Yg E3 | Yg W | Yg E1 | Yn W | Yn W | Yn W | Yn F | Yg Wd | Yg W | 9 |
| 10 | Yn M | Yn Wd | Yn E | Yn E2 | Yg M | Yg Wd | Yg M | Yg M | Yn M | Yn Wd | Yn M | Yn M | Yg W | Yg E1 | Yn W | Yn W | Yn W | Yn F | Yg Wd | Yg W | Yg Wd | Yg F | Yn Wd | Yn E4 | 10 |
| 11 | Yg W | Yg E1 | Yg M | Yg M | Yn M | Yn Wd | Yn M | Yn M | Yg W | Yg E1 | Yg W | Yg E3 | Yn W | Yn F | Yg Wd | Yg W | Yg Wd | Yg F | Yn Wd | Yn E4 | Yn Wd | Yn E2 | Yg F | Yg Wd | 11 |
| 12 | Yn W | Yn F | Yn M | Yn M | Yg W | Yg E1 | Yg W | Yg E3 | Yn W | Yn F | Yn W | Yn W | Yg Wd | Yg F | Yn Wd | Yn E4 | Yn Wd | Yn E2 | Yg F | Yg Wd | Yg F | Yg M | Yn F | Yn Wd | 12 |
| 13 | Yg Wd | Yg F | Yg W | Yg E3 | Yn W | Yn F | Yn W | Yn W | Yg Wd | Yg F | Yg Wd | Yg W | Yn Wd | Yn E2 | Yg F | Yg Wd | Yg F | Yg M | Yn F | Yn Wd | Yn F | Yn M | Yg E | Yg E1 | 13 |
| 14 | Yn Wd | Yn E2 | Yn W | Yn W | Yg Wd | Yg F | Yg Wd | Yg W | Yn Wd | Yn E2 | Yn Wd | Yn E4 | Yg F | Yg M | Yn F | Yn Wd | Yn F | Yn M | Yg E | Yg E1 | Yg E | Yg E3 | Yn E | Yn F | 14 |
| 15 | Yg F | Yg M | Yg Wd | Yg W | Yn Wd | Yn E2 | Yn Wd | Yn E4 | Yg F | Yg M | Yg F | Yg Wd | Yn F | Yn M | Yg E | Yg E1 | Yg E | Yg E3 | Yn E | Yn F | Yn E | Yn W | Yg M | Yg F | 15 |
| 16 | Yn F | Yn M | Yn Wd | Yn E4 | Yg F | Yg M | Yg F | Yg Wd | Yn F | Yn M | Yn F | Yn Wd | Yg E | Yg E3 | Yn E | Yn F | Yn E | Yn W | Yg M | Yg F | Yg M | Yg W | Yn M | Yn E2 | 16 |
| 17 | Yg E | Yg E3 | Yg F | Yg Wd | Yn F | Yn M | Yn F | Yn Wd | Yg E | Yg E3 | Yg E | Yg E1 | Yn E | Yn W | Yg M | Yg F | Yg M | Yg W | Yn M | Yn E2 | Yn M | Yn E4 | Yg W | Yg M | 17 |
| 18 | Yn E | Yn W | Yn F | Yn Wd | Yg E | Yg E3 | Yg E | Yg E1 | Yn E | Yn W | Yn E | Yn F | Yg M | Yg W | Yn M | Yn E2 | Yn M | Yn E4 | Yg W | Yg M | Yg W | Yg Wd | Yn W | Yn M | 18 |
| 19 | Yg M | Yg W | Yg E | Yg E1 | Yn E | Yn W | Yn E | Yn F | Yg M | Yg W | Yg M | Yg F | Yn M | Yn E4 | Yg W | Yg M | Yg W | Yg Wd | Yn W | Yn M | Yn W | Yn Wd | Yg Wd | Yg E3 | 19 |
| 20 | Yn M | Yn E4 | Yn E | Yn F | Yg M | Yg W | Yg M | Yg F | Yn M | Yn E4 | Yn M | Yn E2 | Yg W | Yg Wd | Yn W | Yn M | Yn W | Yn Wd | Yg Wd | Yg E3 | Yg Wd | Yg E1 | Yn Wd | Yn W | 20 |
| 21 | Yg W | Yg Wd | Yg M | Yg F | Yn M | Yn E4 | Yn M | Yn E2 | Yg W | Yg Wd | Yg W | Yg M | Yn W | Yn Wd | Yg Wd | Yg E3 | Yg Wd | Yg E1 | Yn Wd | Yn W | Yn Wd | Yn F | Yg F | Yg W | 21 |
| 22 | Yn W | Yn Wd | Yn M | Yn E2 | Yg W | Yg Wd | Yg W | Yg M | Yn W | Yn Wd | Yn W | Yn M | Yg Wd | Yg E1 | Yn Wd | Yn W | Yn Wd | Yn F | Yg F | Yg W | Yg F | Yg F | Yn F | Yn E4 | 22 |
| 23 | Yg Wd | Yg E1 | Yg W | Yg M | Yn W | Yn Wd | Yn W | Yn M | Yg Wd | Yg E1 | Yg Wd | Yg E3 | Yn Wd | Yn F | Yg F | Yg W | Yg F | Yg F | Yn F | Yn E4 | Yn F | Yn E2 | Yg E | Yg Wd | 23 |
| 24 | Yn Wd | Yn F | Yn W | Yn M | Yg Wd | Yg E1 | Yg Wd | Yg E3 | Yn Wd | Yn F | Yn Wd | Yn W | Yg F | Yg F | Yn F | Yn E4 | Yn F | Yn E2 | Yg E | Yg Wd | Yg E | Yg M | Yn E | Yn Wd | 24 |
| 25 | Yg F | Yg F | Yg Wd | Yg E3 | Yn Wd | Yn F | Yn Wd | Yn W | Yg F | Yg F | Yg F | Yg W | Yn F | Yn E2 | Yg E | Yg Wd | Yg E | Yg M | Yn E | Yn Wd | Yn E | Yn M | Yg M | Yg E1 | 25 |
| 26 | Yn F | Yn E2 | Yn Wd | Yn W | Yg F | Yg F | Yg F | Yg W | Yn F | Yn E2 | Yn F | Yn E4 | Yg E | Yg M | Yn E | Yn Wd | Yn E | Yn M | Yg M | Yg E1 | Yg M | Yg E3 | Yn M | Yn F | 26 |
| 27 | Yg E | Yg M | Yg F | Yg W | Yn F | Yn E2 | Yn F | Yn E4 | Yg E | Yg M | Yg E | Yg Wd | Yn E | Yn M | Yg M | Yg E1 | Yg M | Yg E3 | Yn M | Yn F | Yn M | Yn W | Yg W | Yg F | 27 |
| 28 | Yn E | Yn M | Yn F | Yn E4 | Yg E | Yg M | Yg E | Yg Wd | Yn E | Yn M | Yn E | Yn Wd | Yg M | Yg E3 | Yn M | Yn F | Yn M | Yn W | Yg W | Yg F | Yg W | Yg W | Yn W | Yn E2 | 28 |
| 29 | | | Yg E | Yg Wd | Yn E | Yn M | Yn E | Yn Wd | Yg M | Yg E3 | Yg M | Yg E1 | Yn M | Yn W | Yg W | Yg F | Yg W | Yg W | Yn W | Yn E2 | Yn W | Yn E4 | Yg Wd | Yg M | 29 |
| 30 | | | Yn E | Yn Wd | Yg M | Yg E3 | Yg M | Yg E1 | Yn M | Yn W | Yn M | Yn F | Yg W | Yg W | Yn W | Yn E2 | Yn W | Yn E4 | Yg Wd | Yg M | Yg Wd | Yg Wd | Yn Wd | Yn M | 30 |
| 31 | | | Yg M | Yg E1 | | | Yn M | Yn F | | | Yg W | Yg F | Yn W | Yn E4 | | | Yg Wd | Yg Wd | | | Yn Wd | Yn Wd | Yg F | Yg E3 | 31 |
| 1 | Yg M | Yg E3 | Yn M | Yn F | Yn M | Yn W | Yg W | Yg F | Yg W | Yg W | Yn W | Yn E2 | Yg Wd | Yg Wd | Yg Wd | Yg M | Yn Wd | Yn Wd | Yn Wd | Yn M | Yg F | Yg E1 | Yn F | Yn W | 1 |
| 2 | Yn M | Yn W | Yg W | Yg F | Yg W | Yg W | Yn W | Yn E2 | Yn W | Yn E4 | Yg Wd | Yg M | Yn Wd | Yn Wd | Yn Wd | Yn M | Yg F | Yg E1 | Yg F | Yg E3 | Yn F | Yn F | Yg E | Yg W | 2 |
| 3 | Yg W | Yg W | Yn W | Yn E2 | Yn W | Yn E4 | Yg Wd | Yg M | Yg Wd | Yg Wd | Yn Wd | Yn M | Yg F | Yg E1 | Yg F | Yg E3 | Yn F | Yn F | Yn F | Yn W | Yg E | Yg F | Yn E | Yn E4 | 3 |
| 4 | Yn W | Yn E4 | Yg Wd | Yg M | Yg Wd | Yg Wd | Yn Wd | Yn M | Yn Wd | Yn Wd | Yg F | Yg E3 | Yn F | Yn F | Yn F | Yn W | Yg E | Yg F | Yg E | Yg W | Yn E | Yn E2 | Yg M | Yg Wd | 4 |
| 5 | Yg Wd | Yg Wd | | | Yn Wd | Yn Wd | Yg F | Yg E3 | Yg F | Yg E1 | Yn F | Yn W | Yg E | Yg F | Yg E | Yg W | Yn E | Yn E2 | Yn E | Yn E4 | Yg M | Yg M | | | 5 |
| 6 | | | | | | | | | Yn F | Yn F | Yg E | Yg W | Yn E | Yn E2 | Yn E | Yn E4 | Yg M | Yg M | Yg M | Yg Wd | | | | | 6 |
| 7 | | | | | | | | | Yg E | Yg F | Yn E | Yn E4 | Yg M | Yg M | Yg M | Yg Wd | Yn M | Yn M | Yn M | Yn Wd | | | | | 7 |
| 8 | | | | | | | | | | | | | | | Yn M | Yn Wd | | | | | | | | | 8 |

# YEAR OF THE GOAT

| | H | E | H | E | H | E | H | E | H | E | H | E | H | E | H | E | H | E | H | E | H | E | H | E | |
|---|---|---|---|---|---|---|---|---|---|---|---|---|---|---|---|---|---|---|---|---|---|---|---|---|---|
| YEAR | YEAR | | 1931 | | | | | | | | | | | | | | | | | | | | 1932 | | |
| | YnM | Yn E2 | | | | | | | | | | | | | | | | | | | | | | | |
| MONTH | 5 Feb - 5 Mar | | 6 Mar - 5 Apr | | 6 Apr - 5 May | | 6 May - 6 June | | 7 June - 7 Jul | | 8 Jul - 7 Aug | | 8 Aug - 7 Sep | | 8 Sep - 8 Oct | | 9 Oct - 7 Nov | | 8 Nov - 7 Dec | | 8 Dec - 5 Jan | | 6 Jan - 4 Feb | | |
| | Yg M | Yg Wd | Yn M | Yn Wd | Yg W | Yg E1 | Yn W | Yn F | Yg Wd | Yg F | Yn Wd | Yn E2 | Yg F | Yg M | Yn F | Yn M | Yg E | Yg E3 | Yn E | Yn W | Yg M | Yg W | Yn M | Yn E4 | |
| Starting time | 1st day | Mid-pt | 1st day | Mid-pt | 1st day | Mid-pt | 1st day | Mid-pt | 1st day | Mid-pt | 1st day | Mid-pt | 1st day | Mid-pt | 1st day | Mid-pt | 1st day | Mid-pt | 1st day | Mid-pt | 1st day | Mid-pt | 1st day | Mid-pt | |
| Date | 5 | 19 | 6 | 21 | 6 | 21 | 6 | 22 | 7 | 22 | 8 | 24 | 8 | 24 | 8 | 24 | 9 | 24 | 8 | 23 | 8 | 23 | 6 | 21 | |
| Hour | 0241 | 2241 | 2103 | 2207 | 0221 | 0940 | 2010 | 0916 | 0042 | 1728 | 1106 | 0422 | 2045 | 1111 | 2318 | 0824 | 1427 | 1716 | 1714 | 1425 | 0941 | 0330 | 2046 | 1407 | |
| DATE 4 | | | | | | | | | | | | | | | | | | | | | | | | | 4 |
| 5 | Yn M | Yn Wd | | | | | | | | | | | | | | | | | | | | | | | 5 |
| 6 | Yg W | Yg E1 | Yg M | Yg M | Yn M | Yn Wd | Yn M | Yn M | | | | | | | | | | | | | | | Yg F | Yg Wd | 6 |
| 7 | Yn W | Yn F | Yn M | Yn M | Yg W | Yg E1 | Yg W | Yg E3 | Yn W | Yn F | | | | | | | | | | | | | Yn F | Yn Wd | 7 |
| 8 | Yg Wd | Yg F | Yg W | Yg E3 | Yn W | Yn F | Yn W | Yn W | Yg Wd | Yg F | Yg Wd | Yg W | Yn Wd | Yn E2 | Yg F | Yg Wd | | | Yn F | Yn Wd | Yn F | Yn M | Yg E | Yg E1 | 8 |
| 9 | Yn Wd | Yn E2 | Yn W | Yn W | Yg Wd | Yg F | Yg Wd | Yg W | Yn Wd | Yn E2 | Yn Wd | Yn E4 | Yg F | Yg M | Yn F | Yn Wd | Yn F | Yn M | Yg E | Yg E1 | Yg E | Yg E3 | Yn E | Yn F | 9 |
| 10 | Yg F | Yg M | Yg Wd | Yg W | Yn Wd | Yn E2 | Yn Wd | Yn E4 | Yg F | Yg M | Yg F | Yg Wd | Yn F | Yn M | Yg E | Yg E1 | Yg E | Yg E3 | Yn E | Yn F | Yn E | Yn W | Yg M | Yg F | 10 |
| 11 | Yn F | Yn M | Yn Wd | Yn E4 | Yg F | Yg M | Yg F | Yg Wd | Yn F | Yn M | Yn F | Yn Wd | Yg E | Yg E3 | Yn E | Yn F | Yn E | Yn W | Yg M | Yg F | Yg M | Yg W | Yn M | Yn E2 | 11 |
| 12 | Yg E | Yg E3 | Yg F | Yg Wd | Yn F | Yn M | Yn F | Yn Wd | Yg E | Yg E3 | Yg E | Yg E1 | Yn E | Yn W | Yg M | Yg F | Yg M | Yg W | Yn M | Yn E2 | Yn M | Yn E4 | Yg W | Yg M | 12 |
| 13 | Yn E | Yn W | Yn F | Yn Wd | Yg E | Yg E3 | Yg E | Yg E1 | Yn E | Yn W | Yn E | Yn F | Yg M | Yg W | Yn M | Yn E2 | Yn M | Yn E4 | Yg W | Yg M | Yg W | Yg Wd | Yn W | Yn M | 13 |
| 14 | Yg M | Yg W | Yg E | Yg E1 | Yn E | Yn W | Yn E | Yn F | Yg M | Yg W | Yg M | Yg F | Yn M | Yn E4 | Yg W | Yg M | Yg W | Yg Wd | Yn W | Yn M | Yn W | Yn Wd | Yg Wd | Yg E3 | 14 |
| 15 | Yn M | Yn E4 | Yn E | Yn F | Yg M | Yg W | Yg M | Yg F | Yn M | Yn E4 | Yn M | Yn E2 | Yg W | Yg Wd | Yn W | Yn M | Yn W | Yn Wd | Yg Wd | Yg E3 | Yg Wd | Yg E1 | Yn Wd | Yn W | 15 |
| 16 | Yg W | Yg Wd | Yg M | Yg F | Yn M | Yn E4 | Yn M | Yn E2 | Yg W | Yg Wd | Yg W | Yg M | Yn W | Yn Wd | Yg Wd | Yg E3 | Yg Wd | Yg E1 | Yn Wd | Yn W | Yn Wd | Yn F | Yg F | Yg W | 16 |
| 17 | Yn W | Yn Wd | Yn M | Yn E2 | Yg W | Yg Wd | Yg W | Yg M | Yn W | Yn Wd | Yn W | Yn M | Yg Wd | Yg E1 | Yn Wd | Yn W | Yn Wd | Yn F | Yg F | Yg W | Yg F | Yg F | Yn F | Yn E4 | 17 |
| 18 | Yg Wd | Yg E1 | Yg W | Yg M | Yn W | Yn Wd | Yn W | Yn M | Yg Wd | Yg E1 | Yg Wd | Yg E3 | Yn Wd | Yn F | Yg F | Yg W | Yg F | Yg F | Yn F | Yn E4 | Yn F | Yn E2 | Yg E | Yg Wd | 18 |
| 19 | Yn Wd | Yn F | Yn W | Yn M | Yg Wd | Yg E1 | Yg Wd | Yg E3 | Yn Wd | Yn F | Yn Wd | Yn W | Yg F | Yg F | Yn F | Yn E4 | Yn F | Yn E2 | Yg E | Yg Wd | Yg E | Yg M | Yn E | Yn Wd | 19 |
| 20 | Yg F | Yg F | Yg Wd | Yg E3 | Yn Wd | Yn F | Yn Wd | Yn W | Yg F | Yg F | Yg F | Yg W | Yn F | Yn E2 | Yg E | Yg Wd | Yg E | Yg M | Yn E | Yn Wd | Yn E | Yn M | Yg M | Yg E1 | 20 |
| 21 | Yn F | Yn E2 | Yn Wd | Yn W | Yg F | Yg F | Yg F | Yg W | Yn F | Yn E2 | Yn F | Yn E4 | Yg E | Yg M | Yn E | Yn Wd | Yn E | Yn M | Yg M | Yg E1 | Yg M | Yg E3 | Yn M | Yn F | 21 |
| 22 | Yg E | Yg M | Yg F | Yg W | Yn F | Yn E2 | Yn F | Yn E4 | Yg E | Yg M | Yg E | Yg Wd | Yn E | Yn M | Yg M | Yg E1 | Yg M | Yg E3 | Yn M | Yn F | Yn M | Yn W | Yg W | Yg F | 22 |
| 23 | Yn E | Yn M | Yn F | Yn E4 | Yg E | Yg M | Yg E | Yg Wd | Yn E | Yn M | Yn E | Yn Wd | Yg M | Yg E3 | Yn M | Yn F | Yn M | Yn W | Yg W | Yg F | Yg W | Yg W | Yn W | Yn E2 | 23 |
| 24 | Yg M | Yg E3 | Yg E | Yg Wd | Yn E | Yn M | Yn E | Yn Wd | Yg M | Yg E3 | Yg M | Yg E1 | Yn M | Yn W | Yg W | Yg F | Yg W | Yg W | Yn W | Yn E2 | Yn W | Yn E4 | Yg Wd | Yg M | 24 |
| 25 | Yn M | Yn W | Yn E | Yn Wd | Yg M | Yg E3 | Yg M | Yg E1 | Yn M | Yn W | Yn M | Yn F | Yg W | Yg W | Yn W | Yn E2 | Yn W | Yn E4 | Yg Wd | Yg M | Yg Wd | Yg Wd | Yn Wd | Yn M | 25 |
| 26 | Yg W | Yg W | Yg M | Yg E1 | Yn M | Yn W | Yn M | Yn F | Yg W | Yg W | Yg W | Yg F | Yn W | Yn E4 | Yg Wd | Yg M | Yg Wd | Yg Wd | Yn Wd | Yn M | Yn Wd | Yn Wd | Yg F | Yg E3 | 26 |
| 27 | Yn W | Yn E4 | Yn M | Yn F | Yg W | Yg W | Yg W | Yg F | Yn W | Yn E4 | Yn W | Yn E2 | Yg Wd | Yg Wd | Yn Wd | Yn M | Yn Wd | Yn Wd | Yg F | Yg E3 | Yg F | Yg E1 | Yn F | Yn W | 27 |
| 28 | Yg Wd | Yg Wd | Yg W | Yg F | Yn W | Yn E4 | Yn W | Yn E2 | Yg Wd | Yg Wd | Yg Wd | Yg M | Yn Wd | Yn Wd | Yg F | Yg E3 | Yg F | Yg E1 | Yn F | Yn W | Yn F | Yn F | Yg E | Yg W | 28 |
| 29 | | | Yn W | Yn E2 | Yg Wd | Yg Wd | Yg Wd | Yg M | Yn Wd | Yn Wd | Yn Wd | Yn M | Yg F | Yg E1 | Yn F | Yn W | Yn F | Yn F | Yg E | Yg W | Yg E | Yg F | Yn E | Yn E4 | 29 |
| 30 | | | Yg Wd | Yg M | Yn Wd | Yn Wd | Yn Wd | Yn M | Yg F | Yg E1 | Yg F | Yg E3 | Yn F | Yn F | Yg E | Yg W | Yg E | Yg F | Yn E | Yn E4 | Yn E | Yn E2 | Yg M | Yg Wd | 30 |
| 31 | | | Yn Wd | Yn M | | | Yg F | Yg E3 | | | Yn F | Yn W | Yg E | Yg F | | | Yn E | Yn E2 | | | Yg M | Yg M | Yn M | Yn Wd | 31 |
| 1 | Yn Wd | Yn Wd | Yg F | Yg E3 | Yg F | Yg E1 | Yn F | Yn W | Yn F | Yn F | Yg E | Yg W | Yn E | Yn E2 | Yn E | Yn E4 | Yg M | Yg M | Yg M | Yg Wd | Yn M | Yn M | Yg W | Yg E1 | 1 |
| 2 | Yg F | Yg E1 | Yn F | Yn W | Yn F | Yn F | Yg E | Yg W | Yg E | Yg F | Yn E | Yn E4 | Yg M | Yg M | Yg M | Yg Wd | Yn M | Yn M | Yn M | Yn Wd | Yg W | Yg E3 | Yn W | Yn F | 2 |
| 3 | Yn F | Yn F | Yg E | Yg W | Yg E | Yg F | Yn E | Yn E4 | Yn E | Yn E2 | Yg M | Yg Wd | Yn M | Yn M | Yn M | Yn Wd | Yg W | Yg E3 | Yg W | Yg E1 | Yn W | Yn W | Yg Wd | Yg F | 3 |
| 4 | Yg E | Yg F | Yn E | Yn E4 | Yn E | Yn E2 | Yg M | Yg Wd | Yg M | Yg M | Yn M | Yn Wd | Yg W | Yg E3 | Yg W | Yg E1 | Yn W | Yn W | Yn W | Yn F | Yg Wd | Yg W | Yn Wd | Yn E2 | 4 |
| 5 | Yn E | Yn E2 | Yg M | Yg Wd | Yg M | Yg M | Yn M | Yn Wd | Yn M | Yn M | Yg W | Yg E1 | Yn W | Yn W | Yn W | Yn F | Yg Wd | Yg W | Yg Wd | Yg F | Yn Wd | Yn E4 | | | 5 |
| 6 | | | | | | | Yg W | Yg E1 | Yg W | Yg E3 | Yn W | Yn F | Yg Wd | Yg W | Yg Wd | Yg F | Yn Wd | Yn E4 | Yn Wd | Yn E2 | | | | | 6 |
| 7 | | | | | | | | | Yn W | Yn W | Yg Wd | Yg F | Yn Wd | Yn E4 | Yn Wd | Yn E2 | Yg F | Yg Wd | Yg F | Yg M | | | | | 7 |
| 8 | | | | | | | | | | | | | | | Yg F | Yg M | | | | | | | | | 8 |

# YEAR OF THE MONKEY

| | H | E | H | E | H | E | H | E | H | E | H | E | H | E | H | E | H | E | H | E | H | E | H | E | |
|---|---|---|---|---|---|---|---|---|---|---|---|---|---|---|---|---|---|---|---|---|---|---|---|---|---|
| YEAR | YEAR Yg W | Yg M | 1932 | | | | | | | | | | | | | | | | | | | | 1933 | | |
| MONTH | 5 Feb - 5 Mar | | 6 Mar - 4 Apr | | 5 Apr - 5 May | | 6 May - 5 June | | 6 June - 6 Jul | | 7 Jul - 7 Aug | | 8 Aug - 7 Sep | | 8 Sep - 7 Oct | | 8 Oct - 6 Nov | | 7 Nov - 6 Dec | | 7 Dec - 5 Jan | | 6 Jan - 3 Feb | | |
| | Yg W | Yg Wd | Yn W | Yn Wd | Yg Wd | Yg E1 | Yn Wd | Yn F | Yg F | Yg F | Yn F | Yn E2 | Yg E | Yg M | Yn E | Yn M | Yg M | Yg E3 | Yn M | Yn W | Yg W | Yg W | Yn W | Yn E4 | |
| Starting time | 1st day | Mid-pt | 1st day | Mid-pt | 1st day | Mid-pt | 1st day | Mid-pt | 1st day | Mid-pt | 1st day | Mid-pt | 1st day | Mid-pt | 1st day | Mid-pt | 1st day | Mid-pt | 1st day | Mid-pt | 1st day | Mid-pt | 1st day | Mid-pt | |
| Date | 5 | 20 | 6 | 21 | 5 | 20 | 6 | 21 | 6 | 21 | 7 | 23 | 8 | 23 | 8 | 23 | 8 | 23 | 7 | 22 | 7 | 22 | 6 | 20 | |
| Hour | 0830 | 0429 | 0250 | 0354 | 0807 | 1528 | 0155 | 1507 | 0628 | 2323 | 1653 | 1018 | 0232 | 1706 | 0503 | 1416 | 2010 | 2302 | 2250 | 2011 | 1519 | 0915 | 0224 | 1953 | |
| DATE 4 | | | | | | | | | | | | | | | | | | | | | | | | | 4 |
| 5 | Yg F | Yg M | | | Yg F | Yg M | | | | | | | | | | | | | | | | | | | 5 |
| 6 | Yn F | Yn M | Yg F | Yg Wd | Yn F | Yn M | Yn F | Yn Wd | Yg E | Yg E3 | | | | | | | | | | | | | Yg W | Yg M | 6 |
| 7 | Yg E | Yg E3 | Yn F | Yn Wd | Yg E | Yg E3 | Yg E | Yg E1 | Yn E | Yn W | Yn E | Yn F | | | | | | | Yg W | Yg M | Yg W | Yg Wd | Yn W | Yn M | 7 |
| 8 | Yn E | Yn W | Yg E | Yg E1 | Yn E | Yn W | Yn E | Yn F | Yg M | Yg W | Yg M | Yg F | Yn M | Yn E4 | Yg W | Yg M | Yg W | Yg Wd | Yn W | Yn M | Yn W | Yn Wd | Yg Wd | Yg E3 | 8 |
| 9 | Yg M | Yg W | Yn E | Yn F | Yg M | Yg W | Yg M | Yg F | Yn M | Yn E4 | Yn M | Yn E2 | Yg W | Yg Wd | Yn W | Yn M | Yn W | Yn Wd | Yg Wd | Yg E3 | Yg Wd | Yg E1 | Yn Wd | Yn W | 9 |
| 10 | Yn M | Yn E4 | Yg M | Yg F | Yn M | Yn E4 | Yn M | Yn E2 | Yg W | Yg Wd | Yg W | Yg M | Yn W | Yn Wd | Yg Wd | Yg E3 | Yg Wd | Yg E1 | Yn Wd | Yn W | Yn Wd | Yn F | Yg F | Yg W | 10 |
| 11 | Yg W | Yg Wd | Yn M | Yn E2 | Yg W | Yg Wd | Yg W | Yg M | Yn W | Yn Wd | Yn W | Yn M | Yg Wd | Yg E1 | Yn Wd | Yn W | Yn Wd | Yn F | Yg F | Yg W | Yg F | Yg F | Yn F | Yn E4 | 11 |
| 12 | Yn W | Yn Wd | Yg W | Yg M | Yn W | Yn Wd | Yn W | Yn M | Yg Wd | Yg E1 | Yg Wd | Yg E3 | Yn Wd | Yn F | Yg F | Yg W | Yg F | Yg F | Yn F | Yn E4 | Yn F | Yn E2 | Yg E | Yg Wd | 12 |
| 13 | Yg Wd | Yg E1 | Yn W | Yn M | Yg Wd | Yg E1 | Yg Wd | Yg E3 | Yn Wd | Yn F | Yn Wd | Yn W | Yg F | Yg F | Yn F | Yn E4 | Yn F | Yn E2 | Yg E | Yg Wd | Yg E | Yg M | Yn E | Yn Wd | 13 |
| 14 | Yn Wd | Yn F | Yg Wd | Yg E3 | Yn Wd | Yn F | Yn Wd | Yn W | Yg F | Yg F | Yg F | Yg W | Yn F | Yn E2 | Yg E | Yg Wd | Yg E | Yg M | Yn E | Yn Wd | Yn E | Yn M | Yg M | Yg E1 | 14 |
| 15 | Yg F | Yg F | Yn Wd | Yn W | Yg F | Yg F | Yg F | Yg W | Yn F | Yn E2 | Yn F | Yn E4 | Yg E | Yg M | Yn E | Yn Wd | Yn E | Yn M | Yg M | Yg E1 | Yg M | Yg E3 | Yn M | Yn F | 15 |
| 16 | Yn F | Yn E2 | Yg F | Yg W | Yn F | Yn E2 | Yn F | Yn E4 | Yg E | Yg M | Yg E | Yg Wd | Yn E | Yn M | Yg M | Yg E1 | Yg M | Yg E3 | Yn M | Yn F | Yn M | Yn W | Yg W | Yg F | 16 |
| 17 | Yg E | Yg M | Yn F | Yn E4 | Yg E | Yg M | Yg E | Yg Wd | Yn E | Yn M | Yn E | Yn Wd | Yg M | Yg E3 | Yn M | Yn F | Yn M | Yn W | Yg W | Yg F | Yg W | Yg W | Yn W | Yn E2 | 17 |
| 18 | Yn E | Yn M | Yg E | Yg Wd | Yn E | Yn M | Yn E | Yn Wd | Yg M | Yg E3 | Yg M | Yg E1 | Yn M | Yn W | Yg W | Yg F | Yg W | Yg W | Yn W | Yn E2 | Yn W | Yn E4 | Yg Wd | Yg M | 18 |
| 19 | Yg M | Yg E3 | Yn E | Yn Wd | Yg M | Yg E3 | Yg M | Yg E1 | Yn M | Yn W | Yn M | Yn F | Yg W | Yg W | Yn W | Yn E2 | Yn W | Yn E4 | Yg Wd | Yg M | Yg Wd | Yg Wd | Yn Wd | Yn M | 19 |
| 20 | Yn M | Yn W | Yg M | Yg E1 | Yn M | Yn W | Yn M | Yn F | Yg W | Yg W | Yg W | Yg F | Yn W | Yn E4 | Yg Wd | Yg M | Yg Wd | Yg Wd | Yn Wd | Yn M | Yn Wd | Yn Wd | Yg F | Yg E3 | 20 |
| 21 | Yg W | Yg W | Yn M | Yn F | Yg W | Yg W | Yg W | Yg F | Yn W | Yn E4 | Yn W | Yn E2 | Yg Wd | Yg Wd | Yn Wd | Yn M | Yn Wd | Yn Wd | Yg F | Yg E3 | Yg F | Yg E1 | Yn F | Yn W | 21 |
| 22 | Yn W | Yn E4 | Yg W | Yg F | Yn W | Yn E4 | Yn W | Yn E2 | Yg Wd | Yg Wd | Yg Wd | Yg M | Yn Wd | Yn Wd | Yg F | Yg E3 | Yg F | Yg E1 | Yn F | Yn W | Yn F | Yn F | Yg E | Yg W | 22 |
| 23 | Yg Wd | Yg Wd | Yn W | Yn E2 | Yg Wd | Yg Wd | Yg Wd | Yg M | Yn Wd | Yn Wd | Yn Wd | Yn M | Yg F | Yg E1 | Yn F | Yn W | Yn F | Yn F | Yg E | Yg W | Yg E | Yg F | Yn E | Yn E4 | 23 |
| 24 | Yn Wd | Yn Wd | Yg Wd | Yg M | Yn Wd | Yn Wd | Yn Wd | Yn M | Yg F | Yg E1 | Yg F | Yg E3 | Yn F | Yn F | Yg E | Yg W | Yg E | Yg F | Yn E | Yn E4 | Yn E | Yn E2 | Yg M | Yg Wd | 24 |
| 25 | Yg F | Yg E1 | Yn Wd | Yn M | Yg F | Yg E1 | Yg F | Yg E3 | Yn F | Yn F | Yn F | Yn W | Yg E | Yg F | Yn E | Yn E4 | Yn E | Yn E2 | Yg M | Yg Wd | Yg M | Yg M | Yn M | Yn Wd | 25 |
| 26 | Yn F | Yn F | Yg F | Yg E3 | Yn F | Yn F | Yn F | Yn W | Yg E | Yg F | Yg E | Yg W | Yn E | Yn E2 | Yg M | Yg Wd | Yg M | Yg M | Yn M | Yn Wd | Yn M | Yn M | Yg W | Yg E1 | 26 |
| 27 | Yg E | Yg F | Yn F | Yn W | Yg E | Yg F | Yg E | Yg W | Yn E | Yn E2 | Yn E | Yn E4 | Yg M | Yg M | Yn M | Yn Wd | Yn M | Yn M | Yg W | Yg E1 | Yg W | Yg E3 | Yn W | Yn F | 27 |
| 28 | Yn E | Yn E2 | Yg E | Yg W | Yn E | Yn E2 | Yn E | Yn E4 | Yg M | Yg M | Yg M | Yg Wd | Yn M | Yn M | Yg W | Yg E1 | Yg W | Yg E3 | Yn W | Yn F | Yn W | Yn W | Yg Wd | Yg F | 28 |
| 29 | Yg M | Yg M | Yn E | Yn E4 | Yg M | Yg M | Yg M | Yg Wd | Yn M | Yn M | Yn M | Yn Wd | Yg W | Yg E3 | Yn W | Yn F | Yn W | Yn W | Yg Wd | Yg F | Yg Wd | Yg W | Yn Wd | Yn E2 | 29 |
| 30 | | | Yg M | Yg Wd | Yn M | Yn M | Yn M | Yn Wd | Yg W | Yg E3 | Yg W | Yg E1 | Yn W | Yn W | Yg Wd | Yg F | Yg Wd | Yg W | Yn Wd | Yn E2 | Yn Wd | Yn E4 | Yg F | Yg M | 30 |
| 31 | | | Yn M | Yn Wd | | | Yg W | Yg E1 | | | Yn W | Yn F | Yg Wd | Yg W | | | Yn Wd | Yn E4 | | | Yg F | Yg Wd | Yn F | Yn M | 31 |
| 1 | Yn M | Yn M | Yg W | Yg E1 | Yg W | Yg E3 | Yn W | Yn F | Yn W | Yn W | Yg Wd | Yg F | Yn Wd | Yn E4 | Yn Wd | Yn E2 | Yg F | Yg Wd | Yg F | Yg M | Yn F | Yn Wd | Yg E | Yg E3 | 1 |
| 2 | Yg W | Yg E3 | Yn W | Yn F | Yn W | Yn W | Yg Wd | Yg F | Yg Wd | Yg W | Yn Wd | Yn E2 | Yg F | Yg Wd | Yg F | Yg M | Yn F | Yn Wd | Yn F | Yn M | Yg E | Yg E1 | Yn E | Yn W | 2 |
| 3 | Yn W | Yn W | Yg Wd | Yg F | Yg Wd | Yg W | Yn Wd | Yn E2 | Yn Wd | Yn E4 | Yg F | Yg M | Yn F | Yn Wd | Yn F | Yn M | Yg E | Yg E1 | Yg E | Yg E3 | Yn E | Yn F | Yg M | Yg W | 3 |
| 4 | Yg Wd | Yg W | Yn Wd | Yn E2 | Yn Wd | Yn E4 | Yg F | Yg M | Yg F | Yg Wd | Yn F | Yn M | Yg E | Yg E1 | Yg E | Yg E3 | Yn E | Yn F | Yn E | Yn W | Yg M | Yg F | | | 4 |
| 5 | Yn Wd | Yn E4 | | | Yg F | Yg Wd | Yn F | Yn M | Yn F | Yn Wd | Yg E | Yg E3 | Yn E | Yn F | Yn E | Yn W | Yg M | Yg F | Yg M | Yg W | Yn M | Yn E2 | | | 5 |
| 6 | | | | | | | | | Yg E | Yg E1 | Yn E | Yn W | Yg M | Yg F | Yg M | Yg W | Yn M | Yn E2 | Yn M | Yn E4 | | | | | 6 |
| 7 | | | | | | | | | | | Yg M | Yg W | Yn M | Yn E2 | Yn M | Yn E4 | | | | | | | | | 7 |
| 8 | | | | | | | | | | | | | | | | | | | | | | | | | 8 |

# YEAR OF THE ROOSTER

| | H | E | H | E | H | E | H | E | H | E | H | E | H | E | H | E | H | E | H | E | H | E | H | E | |
|---|---|---|---|---|---|---|---|---|---|---|---|---|---|---|---|---|---|---|---|---|---|---|---|---|---|
| YEAR | YEAR<br>Yn W | <br>Yn M | 1933 | | | | | | | | | | | | | | | | | | 1934 | | | | |
| MONTH | 4 Feb - 5 Mar | | 6 Mar - 4 Apr | | 5 Apr - 5 May | | 6 May - 5 June | | 6 June - 6 Jul | | 7 Jul - 6 Aug | | 7 Aug - 7 Sep | | 8 Sep - 8 Oct | | 9 Oct - 7 Nov | | 8 Nov - 6 Dec | | 7 Dec - 5 Jan | | 6 Jan - 3 Feb | | |
| | Yg Wd | Yg Wd | Yn Wd | Yn Wd | Yg F | Yg E1 | Yn F | Yn F | Yg E | Yg F | Yn E | Yn E2 | Yg M | Yg M | Yn M | Yn M | Yg W | Yg E3 | Yn W | Yn W | Yg Wd | Yg W | Yn Wd | Yn E4 | |
| Starting time | 1st day | Mid-pt | 1st day | Mid-pt | 1st day | Mid-pt | 1st day | Mid-pt | 1st day | Mid-pt | 1st day | Mid-pt | 1st day | Mid-pt | 1st day | Mid-pt | 1st day | Mid-pt | 1st day | Mid-pt | 1st day | Mid-pt | 1st day | Mid-pt | |
| Date | 4 | 19 | 6 | 21 | 5 | 20 | 6 | 21 | 6 | 22 | 7 | 22 | 7 | 23 | 8 | 23 | 9 | 24 | 8 | 23 | 7 | 22 | 6 | 21 | |
| Hour | 1410 | 1017 | 0830 | 0944 | 1351 | 2119 | 0716 | 2057 | 1218 | 0512 | 2245 | 1606 | 0826 | 2253 | 1058 | 2001 | 0205 | 0449 | 0444 | 0155 | 2112 | 1458 | 0817 | 0126 | |
| DATE 4 | Yn M | Yn E4 | | | | | | | | | | | | | | | | | | | | | | | 4 |
| 5 | Yg W | Yg Wd | | | Yn M | Yn E4 | | | | | | | | | | | | | | | | | | | 5 |
| 6 | Yn W | Yn Wd | Yn M | Yn E2 | Yg W | Yg Wd | Yg W | Yg M | Yn W | Yn Wd | | | | | | | | | | | | | Yn F | Yn E4 | 6 |
| 7 | Yg Wd | Yg E1 | Yg W | Yg M | Yn W | Yn Wd | Yn W | Yn M | Yg Wd | Yg E1 | Yg Wd | Yg E3 | Yn Wd | Yn F | | | | | | | Yn F | Yn E2 | Yg E | Yg Wd | 7 |
| 8 | Yn Wd | Yn F | Yn W | Yn M | Yg Wd | Yg E1 | Yg Wd | Yg E3 | Yn Wd | Yn F | Yn Wd | Yn W | Yg F | Yg F | Yn F | Yn E4 | | | Yg E | Yg Wd | Yg E | Yg M | Yn E | Yn Wd | 8 |
| 9 | Yg F | Yg F | Yg Wd | Yg E3 | Yn Wd | Yn F | Yn Wd | Yn W | Yg F | Yg F | Yg F | Yg W | Yn F | Yn E2 | Yg E | Yg Wd | Yg E | Yg M | Yn E | Yn Wd | Yn E | Yn M | Yg M | Yg E1 | 9 |
| 10 | Yn F | Yn E2 | Yn Wd | Yn W | Yg F | Yg F | Yg F | Yg W | Yn F | Yn E2 | Yn F | Yn E4 | Yg E | Yg M | Yn E | Yn Wd | Yn E | Yn M | Yg M | Yg E1 | Yg M | Yg E3 | Yn M | Yn F | 10 |
| 11 | Yg E | Yg M | Yg F | Yg W | Yn F | Yn E2 | Yn F | Yn E4 | Yg E | Yg M | Yg E | Yg Wd | Yn E | Yn M | Yg M | Yg E1 | Yg M | Yg E3 | Yn M | Yn F | Yn M | Yn W | Yg W | Yg F | 11 |
| 12 | Yn E | Yn M | Yn F | Yn E4 | Yg E | Yg M | Yg E | Yg Wd | Yn E | Yn M | Yn E | Yn Wd | Yg M | Yg E3 | Yn M | Yn F | Yn M | Yn W | Yg W | Yg F | Yg W | Yg W | Yn W | Yn E2 | 12 |
| 13 | Yg M | Yg E3 | Yg E | Yg Wd | Yn E | Yn M | Yn E | Yn Wd | Yg M | Yg E3 | Yg M | Yg E1 | Yn M | Yn W | Yg W | Yg F | Yg W | Yg W | Yn W | Yn E2 | Yn W | Yn E4 | Yg Wd | Yg M | 13 |
| 14 | Yn M | Yn W | Yn E | Yn Wd | Yg M | Yg E3 | Yg M | Yg E1 | Yn M | Yn W | Yn M | Yn F | Yg W | Yg W | Yn W | Yn E2 | Yn W | Yn E4 | Yg Wd | Yg M | Yg Wd | Yg Wd | Yn Wd | Yn M | 14 |
| 15 | Yg W | Yg W | Yg M | Yg E1 | Yn M | Yn W | Yn M | Yn F | Yg W | Yg W | Yg W | Yg F | Yn W | Yn E4 | Yg Wd | Yg M | Yg Wd | Yg Wd | Yn Wd | Yn M | Yn Wd | Yn Wd | Yg F | Yg E3 | 15 |
| 16 | Yn W | Yn E4 | Yn M | Yn F | Yg W | Yg W | Yg W | Yg F | Yn W | Yn E4 | Yn W | Yn E2 | Yg Wd | Yg Wd | Yn Wd | Yn M | Yn Wd | Yn Wd | Yg F | Yg E3 | Yg F | Yg E1 | Yn F | Yn W | 16 |
| 17 | Yg Wd | Yg Wd | Yg W | Yg F | Yn W | Yn E4 | Yn W | Yn E2 | Yg Wd | Yg Wd | Yg Wd | Yg M | Yn Wd | Yn Wd | Yg F | Yg E3 | Yg F | Yg E1 | Yn F | Yn W | Yn F | Yn F | Yg E | Yg W | 17 |
| 18 | Yn Wd | Yn Wd | Yn W | Yn E2 | Yg Wd | Yg Wd | Yg Wd | Yg M | Yn Wd | Yn Wd | Yn Wd | Yn M | Yg F | Yg E1 | Yn F | Yn W | Yn F | Yn F | Yg E | Yg W | Yg E | Yg F | Yn E | Yn E4 | 18 |
| 19 | Yg F | Yg E1 | Yg Wd | Yg M | Yn Wd | Yn Wd | Yn Wd | Yn M | Yg F | Yg E1 | Yg F | Yg E3 | Yn F | Yn F | Yg E | Yg W | Yg E | Yg F | Yn E | Yn E4 | Yn E | Yn E2 | Yg M | Yg Wd | 19 |
| 20 | Yn F | Yn F | Yn Wd | Yn M | Yg F | Yg E1 | Yg F | Yg E3 | Yn F | Yn F | Yn F | Yn W | Yg E | Yg F | Yn E | Yn E4 | Yn E | Yn E2 | Yg M | Yg Wd | Yg M | Yg M | Yn M | Yn Wd | 20 |
| 21 | Yg E | Yg F | Yg F | Yg E3 | Yn F | Yn F | Yn F | Yn W | Yg E | Yg F | Yg E | Yg W | Yn E | Yn E2 | Yg M | Yg Wd | Yg M | Yg M | Yn M | Yn Wd | Yn M | Yn M | Yg W | Yg E1 | 21 |
| 22 | Yn E | Yn E2 | Yn F | Yn W | Yg E | Yg F | Yg E | Yg W | Yn E | Yn E2 | Yn E | Yn E4 | Yg M | Yg M | Yn M | Yn Wd | Yn M | Yn M | Yg W | Yg E1 | Yg W | Yg E3 | Yn W | Yn F | 22 |
| 23 | Yg M | Yg M | Yg E | Yg W | Yn E | Yn E2 | Yn E | Yn E4 | Yg M | Yg M | Yg M | Yg Wd | Yn M | Yn M | Yg W | Yg E1 | Yg W | Yg E3 | Yn W | Yn F | Yn W | Yn W | Yg Wd | Yg F | 23 |
| 24 | Yn M | Yn M | Yn E | Yn E4 | Yg M | Yg M | Yg M | Yg Wd | Yn M | Yn M | Yn M | Yn Wd | Yg W | Yg E3 | Yn W | Yn F | Yn W | Yn W | Yg Wd | Yg F | Yg Wd | Yg W | Yn Wd | Yn E2 | 24 |
| 25 | Yg W | Yg E3 | Yg M | Yg Wd | Yn M | Yn M | Yn M | Yn Wd | Yg W | Yg E3 | Yg W | Yg E1 | Yn W | Yn W | Yg Wd | Yg F | Yg Wd | Yg W | Yn Wd | Yn E2 | Yn Wd | Yn E4 | Yg F | Yg M | 25 |
| 26 | Yn W | Yn W | Yn M | Yn Wd | Yg W | Yg E3 | Yg W | Yg E1 | Yn W | Yn W | Yn W | Yn F | Yg Wd | Yg W | Yn Wd | Yn E2 | Yn Wd | Yn E4 | Yg F | Yg M | Yg F | Yg Wd | Yn F | Yn M | 26 |
| 27 | Yg Wd | Yg W | Yg W | Yg E1 | Yn W | Yn W | Yn W | Yn F | Yg Wd | Yg W | Yg Wd | Yg F | Yn Wd | Yn E4 | Yg F | Yg M | Yg F | Yg Wd | Yn F | Yn M | Yn F | Yn Wd | Yg E | Yg E3 | 27 |
| 28 | Yn Wd | Yn E4 | Yn W | Yn F | Yg Wd | Yg W | Yg Wd | Yg F | Yn Wd | Yn E4 | Yn Wd | Yn E2 | Yg F | Yg Wd | Yn F | Yn M | Yn F | Yn Wd | Yg E | Yg E3 | Yg E | Yg E1 | Yn E | Yn W | 28 |
| 29 | | | Yg Wd | Yg F | Yn Wd | Yn E4 | Yn Wd | Yn E2 | Yg F | Yg Wd | Yg F | Yg M | Yn F | Yn Wd | Yg E | Yg E3 | Yg E | Yg E1 | Yn E | Yn W | Yn E | Yn F | Yg M | Yg W | 29 |
| 30 | | | Yn Wd | Yn E2 | Yg F | Yg Wd | Yg F | Yg M | Yn F | Yn Wd | Yn F | Yn M | Yg E | Yg E1 | Yn E | Yn W | Yn E | Yn F | Yg M | Yg W | Yg M | Yg F | Yn M | Yn E4 | 30 |
| 31 | | | Yg F | Yg M | | | Yn F | Yn M | | | Yg E | Yg E3 | Yn E | Yn F | | | Yg M | Yg F | | | Yn M | Yn E2 | Yg W | Yg Wd | 31 |
| 1 | Yg F | Yg Wd | Yn F | Yn M | Yn F | Yn Wd | Yg E | Yg E3 | Yg E | Yg E1 | Yn E | Yn W | Yg M | Yg F | Yg M | Yg W | Yn M | Yn E2 | Yn M | Yn E4 | Yg W | Yg M | Yn W | Yn Wd | 1 |
| 2 | Yn F | Yn Wd | Yg E | Yg E3 | Yg E | Yg E1 | Yn E | Yn W | Yn E | Yn F | Yg M | Yg W | Yn M | Yn E2 | Yn M | Yn E4 | Yg W | Yg M | Yg W | Yg Wd | Yn W | Yn M | Yg Wd | Yg E1 | 2 |
| 3 | Yg E | Yg E1 | Yn E | Yn W | Yn E | Yn F | Yg M | Yg W | Yg M | Yg F | Yn M | Yn E4 | Yg W | Yg M | Yg W | Yg Wd | Yn W | Yn M | Yn W | Yn Wd | Yg Wd | Yg E3 | Yn Wd | Yn F | 3 |
| 4 | Yn E | Yn F | Yg M | Yg W | Yg M | Yg F | Yn M | Yn E4 | Yn M | Yn E2 | Yg W | Yg Wd | Yn W | Yn M | Yn W | Yn Wd | Yg Wd | Yg E3 | Yg Wd | Yg E1 | Yn Wd | Yn W | | | 4 |
| 5 | Yg M | Yg F | | | Yn M | Yn E2 | Yg W | Yg Wd | Yg W | Yg M | Yn W | Yn Wd | Yg Wd | Yg E3 | Yg Wd | Yg E1 | Yn Wd | Yn W | Yn Wd | Yn F | Yg F | Yg W | | | 5 |
| 6 | | | | | | | | | Yn W | Yn M | Yg Wd | Yg E1 | Yn Wd | Yn W | Yn Wd | Yn F | Yg F | Yg W | Yg F | Yg F | | | | | 6 |
| 7 | | | | | | | | | | | | | Yg F | Yg W | Yg F | Yg F | Yn F | Yn E4 | | | | | | | 7 |
| 8 | | | | | | | | | | | | | | | Yn F | Yn E2 | | | | | | | | | 8 |

# YEAR OF THE DOG

| | H | E | H | E | H | E | H | E | H | E | H | E | H | E | H | E | H | E | H | E | H | E | H | E | |
|---|---|---|---|---|---|---|---|---|---|---|---|---|---|---|---|---|---|---|---|---|---|---|---|---|---|
| YEAR | YEAR<br>Yg Wd | Yg E3 | 1934 | | | | | | | | | | | | | | | | | | | | 1935 | | |
| MONTH | 4 Feb - 5 Mar | | 6 Mar - 4 Apr | | 5 Apr - 5 May | | 6 May - 5 June | | 6 June - 7 Jul | | 8 Jul - 7 Aug | | 8 Aug - 7 Sep | | 8 Sep - 8 Oct | | 9 Oct - 7 Nov | | 8 Nov - 7 Dec | | 8 Dec - 5 Jan | | 6 Jan - 4 Feb | | |
| | Yg F | Yg Wd | Yn F | Yn Wd | Yg E | Yg E1 | Yn E | Yn F | Yg M | Yg F | Yn M | Yn E2 | Yg W | Yg M | Yn W | Yn M | Yg Wd | Yg E3 | Yn Wd | Yn W | Yg F | Yg W | Yn F | Yn E4 | |
| Starting time | 1st day | Mid-pt | 1st day | Mid-pt | 1st day | Mid-pt | 1st day | Mid-pt | 1st day | Mid-pt | 1st day | Mid-pt | 1st day | Mid-pt | 1st day | Mid-pt | 1st day | Mid-pt | 1st day | Mid-pt | 1st day | Mid-pt | 1st day | Mid-pt | |
| Date | 4 | 19 | 6 | 21 | 5 | 21 | 6 | 22 | 6 | 22 | 8 | 23 | 8 | 24 | 8 | 24 | 9 | 24 | 8 | 23 | 8 | 22 | 6 | 21 | |
| Hour | 2004 | 1602 | 1427 | 1528 | 1944 | 0301 | 1331 | 0235 | 1802 | 1048 | 0425 | 2144 | 1404 | 0433 | 1637 | 0138 | 0745 | 1037 | 1027 | 0745 | 0257 | 2050 | 1403 | 0729 | |
| DATE 4 | Yg F | Yg F | | | | | | | | | | | | | | | | | | | | | | | 4 |
| 5 | Yn F | Yn E2 | | | Yg F | Yg F | | | | | | | | | | | | | | | | | | | 5 |
| 6 | Yg E | Yg M | Yg F | Yg W | Yn F | Yn E2 | Yn F | Yn E4 | Yg E | Yg M | | | | | | | | | | | | | Yg W | Yg F | 6 |
| 7 | Yn E | Yn M | Yn F | Yn E4 | Yg E | Yg M | Yg E | Yg Wd | Yn E | Yn M | | | | | | | | | | | | | Yn W | Yn E2 | 7 |
| 8 | Yg M | Yg E3 | Yg E | Yg Wd | Yn E | Yn M | Yn E | Yn Wd | Yg M | Yg E3 | Yg M | Yg E1 | Yn M | Yn W | Yg W | Yg F | | | Yn W | Yn E2 | Yn W | Yn E4 | Yg Wd | Yg M | 8 |
| 9 | Yn M | Yn W | Yn E | Yn Wd | Yg M | Yg E3 | Yg M | Yg E1 | Yn M | Yn W | Yn M | Yn F | Yg W | Yg W | Yn W | Yn E2 | Yn W | Yn E4 | Yg Wd | Yg M | Yg Wd | Yg Wd | Yn Wd | Yn M | 9 |
| 10 | Yg W | Yg W | Yg M | Yg E1 | Yn M | Yn W | Yn M | Yn F | Yg W | Yg W | Yg W | Yg F | Yn W | Yn E4 | Yg Wd | Yg M | Yg Wd | Yg Wd | Yn Wd | Yn M | Yn Wd | Yn Wd | Yg F | Yg E3 | 10 |
| 11 | Yn W | Yn E4 | Yn M | Yn F | Yg W | Yg W | Yg W | Yg F | Yn W | Yn E4 | Yn W | Yn E2 | Yg Wd | Yg Wd | Yn Wd | Yn M | Yn Wd | Yn Wd | Yg F | Yg E3 | Yg F | Yg E1 | Yn F | Yn W | 11 |
| 12 | Yg Wd | Yg Wd | Yg W | Yg F | Yn W | Yn E4 | Yn W | Yn E2 | Yg Wd | Yg Wd | Yg Wd | Yg M | Yn Wd | Yn Wd | Yg F | Yg E3 | Yg F | Yg E1 | Yn F | Yn W | Yn F | Yn F | Yg E | Yg W | 12 |
| 13 | Yn Wd | Yn Wd | Yn W | Yn E2 | Yg Wd | Yg Wd | Yg Wd | Yg M | Yn Wd | Yn Wd | Yn Wd | Yn M | Yg F | Yg E1 | Yn F | Yn W | Yn F | Yn F | Yg E | Yg W | Yg E | Yg F | Yn E | Yn E4 | 13 |
| 14 | Yg F | Yg E1 | Yg Wd | Yg M | Yn Wd | Yn Wd | Yn Wd | Yn M | Yg F | Yg E1 | Yg F | Yg E3 | Yn F | Yn F | Yg E | Yg W | Yg E | Yg F | Yn E | Yn E4 | Yn E | Yn E2 | Yg M | Yg Wd | 14 |
| 15 | Yn F | Yn F | Yn Wd | Yn M | Yg F | Yg E1 | Yg F | Yg E3 | Yn F | Yn F | Yn F | Yn W | Yg E | Yg F | Yn E | Yn E4 | Yn E | Yn E2 | Yg M | Yg Wd | Yg M | Yg M | Yn M | Yn Wd | 15 |
| 16 | Yg E | Yg F | Yg F | Yg E3 | Yn F | Yn F | Yn F | Yn W | Yg E | Yg F | Yg E | Yg W | Yn E | Yn E2 | Yg M | Yg Wd | Yg M | Yg M | Yn M | Yn Wd | Yn M | Yn M | Yg W | Yg E1 | 16 |
| 17 | Yn E | Yn E2 | Yn F | Yn W | Yg E | Yg F | Yg E | Yg W | Yn E | Yn E2 | Yn E | Yn E4 | Yg M | Yg M | Yn M | Yn Wd | Yn M | Yn M | Yg W | Yg E1 | Yg W | Yg E3 | Yn W | Yn F | 17 |
| 18 | Yg M | Yg M | Yg E | Yg W | Yn E | Yn E2 | Yn E | Yn E4 | Yg M | Yg M | Yg M | Yg Wd | Yn M | Yn M | Yg W | Yg E1 | Yg W | Yg E3 | Yn W | Yn F | Yn W | Yn W | Yg Wd | Yg F | 18 |
| 19 | Yn M | Yn M | Yn E | Yn E4 | Yg M | Yg M | Yg M | Yg Wd | Yn M | Yn M | Yn M | Yn Wd | Yg W | Yg E3 | Yn W | Yn F | Yn W | Yn W | Yg Wd | Yg F | Yg Wd | Yg W | Yn Wd | Yn E2 | 19 |
| 20 | Yg W | Yg E3 | Yg M | Yg Wd | Yn M | Yn M | Yn M | Yn Wd | Yg W | Yg E3 | Yg W | Yg E1 | Yn W | Yn W | Yg Wd | Yg F | Yg Wd | Yg W | Yn Wd | Yn E2 | Yn Wd | Yn E4 | Yg F | Yg M | 20 |
| 21 | Yn W | Yn W | Yn M | Yn Wd | Yg W | Yg E3 | Yg W | Yg E1 | Yn W | Yn W | Yn W | Yn F | Yg Wd | Yg W | Yn Wd | Yn E2 | Yn Wd | Yn E4 | Yg F | Yg M | Yg F | Yg Wd | Yn F | Yn M | 21 |
| 22 | Yg Wd | Yg W | Yg W | Yg E1 | Yn W | Yn W | Yn W | Yn F | Yg Wd | Yg W | Yg Wd | Yg F | Yn Wd | Yn E4 | Yg F | Yg M | Yg F | Yg Wd | Yn F | Yn M | Yn F | Yn Wd | Yg E | Yg E3 | 22 |
| 23 | Yn Wd | Yn E4 | Yn W | Yn F | Yg Wd | Yg W | Yg Wd | Yg F | Yn Wd | Yn E4 | Yn Wd | Yn E2 | Yg F | Yg Wd | Yn F | Yn M | Yn F | Yn Wd | Yg E | Yg E3 | Yg E | Yg E1 | Yn E | Yn W | 23 |
| 24 | Yg F | Yg Wd | Yg Wd | Yg F | Yn Wd | Yn E4 | Yn Wd | Yn E2 | Yg F | Yg Wd | Yg F | Yg M | Yn F | Yn Wd | Yg E | Yg E3 | Yg E | Yg E1 | Yn E | Yn W | Yn E | Yn F | Yg M | Yg W | 24 |
| 25 | Yn F | Yn Wd | Yn Wd | Yn E2 | Yg F | Yg Wd | Yg F | Yg M | Yn F | Yn Wd | Yn F | Yn M | Yg E | Yg E1 | Yn E | Yn W | Yn E | Yn F | Yg M | Yg W | Yg M | Yg F | Yn M | Yn E4 | 25 |
| 26 | Yg E | Yg E1 | Yg F | Yg M | Yn F | Yn Wd | Yn F | Yn M | Yg E | Yg E1 | Yg E | Yg E3 | Yn E | Yn F | Yg M | Yg W | Yg M | Yg F | Yn M | Yn E4 | Yn M | Yn E2 | Yg W | Yg Wd | 26 |
| 27 | Yn E | Yn F | Yn F | Yn M | Yg E | Yg E1 | Yg E | Yg E3 | Yn E | Yn F | Yn E | Yn W | Yg M | Yg F | Yn M | Yn E4 | Yn M | Yn E2 | Yg W | Yg Wd | Yg W | Yg M | Yn W | Yn Wd | 27 |
| 28 | Yg M | Yg F | Yg E | Yg E3 | Yn E | Yn F | Yn E | Yn W | Yg M | Yg F | Yg M | Yg W | Yn M | Yn E2 | Yg W | Yg Wd | Yg W | Yg M | Yn W | Yn Wd | Yn W | Yn M | Yg Wd | Yg E1 | 28 |
| 29 | | | Yn E | Yn W | Yg M | Yg F | Yg M | Yg W | Yn M | Yn E2 | Yn M | Yn E4 | Yg W | Yg M | Yn W | Yn Wd | Yn W | Yn M | Yg Wd | Yg E1 | Yg Wd | Yg E3 | Yn Wd | Yn F | 29 |
| 30 | | | Yg M | Yg W | Yn M | Yn E2 | Yn M | Yn E4 | Yg W | Yg M | Yg W | Yg Wd | Yn W | Yn M | Yg Wd | Yg E1 | Yg Wd | Yg E3 | Yn Wd | Yn F | Yn Wd | Yn W | Yg F | Yg F | 30 |
| 31 | | | Yn M | Yn E4 | | | Yg W | Yg Wd | | | Yn W | Yn Wd | Yg Wd | Yg E3 | | | Yn Wd | Yn W | | | Yg F | Yg W | Yn F | Yn E2 | 31 |
| 1 | Yn M | Yn E2 | Yg W | Yg Wd | Yg W | Yg M | Yn W | Yn Wd | Yn W | Yn M | Yg Wd | Yg E1 | Yn Wd | Yn W | Yn Wd | Yn F | Yg F | Yg W | Yg F | Yg F | Yn F | Yn E4 | Yg E | Yg M | 1 |
| 2 | Yg W | Yg M | Yn W | Yn Wd | Yn W | Yn M | Yg Wd | Yg E1 | Yg Wd | Yg E3 | Yn Wd | Yn F | Yg F | Yg W | Yg F | Yg F | Yn F | Yn E4 | Yn F | Yn E2 | Yg E | Yg Wd | Yn E | Yn M | 2 |
| 3 | Yn W | Yn M | Yg Wd | Yg E1 | Yg Wd | Yg E3 | Yn Wd | Yn F | Yn Wd | Yn W | Yg F | Yg F | Yn F | Yn E4 | Yn F | Yn E2 | Yg E | Yg Wd | Yg E | Yg M | Yn E | Yn Wd | Yg M | Yg E3 | 3 |
| 4 | Yg Wd | Yg E3 | Yn Wd | Yn F | Yn Wd | Yn W | Yg F | Yg F | Yg F | Yg W | Yn F | Yn E2 | Yg E | Yg Wd | Yg E | Yg M | Yn E | Yn Wd | Yn E | Yn M | Yg M | Yg E1 | Yn M | Yn W | 4 |
| 5 | Yn Wd | Yn W | | | Yg F | Yg W | Yn F | Yn E2 | Yn F | Yn E4 | Yg E | Yg M | Yn E | Yn Wd | Yn E | Yn M | Yg M | Yg E1 | Yg M | Yg E3 | Yn M | Yn F | | | 5 |
| 6 | | | | | | | | | Yg E | Yg Wd | Yn E | Yn M | Yg M | Yg E1 | Yg M | Yg E3 | Yn M | Yn F | Yn M | Yn W | | | | | 6 |
| 7 | | | | | | | | | Yn E | Yn Wd | Yg M | Yg E3 | Yn M | Yn F | Yn M | Yn W | Yg W | Yg F | Yg W | Yg W | | | | | 7 |
| 8 | | | | | | | | | | | | | | | Yg W | Yg W | | | | | | | | | 8 |

# YEAR OF THE PIG

| | H | E | H | E | H | E | H | E | H | E | H | E | H | E | H | E | H | E | H | E | H | E | H | E | |
|---|---|---|---|---|---|---|---|---|---|---|---|---|---|---|---|---|---|---|---|---|---|---|---|---|---|
| YEAR | YEAR Yn Wd | Yn W | 1935 | | | | | | | | | | | | | | | | | | | | 1936 | | |
| MONTH | 5 Feb - 5 Mar | | 6 Mar - 5 Apr | | 6 Apr - 5 May | | 6 May - 5 June | | 6 June - 7 Jul | | 8 Jul - 7 Aug | | 8 Aug - 7 Sep | | 8 Sep - 8 Oct | | 9 Oct - 7 Nov | | 8 Nov - 7 Dec | | 8 Dec - 5 Jan | | 6 Jan - 4 Feb | | |
| | Yg E | Yg Wd | Yn E | Yn Wd | Yg M | Yg E1 | Yn M | Yn F | Yg W | Yg F | Yn W | Yn E2 | Yg Wd | Yg M | Yn Wd | Yn M | Yg F | Yg E3 | Yn F | Yn W | Yg E | Yg W | Yn E | Yn E4 | |
| Starting time | 1st day | Mid-pt | 1st day | Mid-pt | 1st day | Mid-pt | 1st day | Mid-pt | 1st day | Mid-pt | 1st day | Mid-pt | 1st day | Mid-pt | 1st day | Mid-pt | 1st day | Mid-pt | 1st day | Mid-pt | 1st day | Mid-pt | 1st day | Mid-pt | |
| Date | 5 | 19 | 6 | 21 | 6 | 21 | 6 | 22 | 6 | 22 | 8 | 24 | 8 | 24 | 8 | 24 | 9 | 24 | 8 | 23 | 8 | 23 | 6 | 21 | |
| Hour | 0149 | .2152 | 2011 | 2118 | 0127 | 0850 | 1912 | 0825 | 2342 | 1638 | 1006 | 0333 | 1948 | 1024 | 2225 | 0739 | 1336 | 1630 | 1618 | 1336 | 0845 | 0237 | 1947 | 1313 | |
| DATE 4 | | | | | | | | | | | | | | | | | | | | | | | | | 4 |
| 5 | Yg W | Yg W | | | | | | | | | | | | | | | | | | | | | | | 5 |
| 6 | Yn W | Yn E4 | Yn M | Yn F | Yg W | Yg W | Yg W | Yg F | Yn W | Yn E4 | | | | | | | | | | | | | Yn F | Yn W | 6 |
| 7 | Yg Wd | Yg Wd | Yg W | Yg F | Yn W | Yn E4 | Yn W | Yn E2 | Yg Wd | Yg Wd | | | | | | | | | | | | | Yg E | Yg W | 7 |
| 8 | Yn Wd | Yn Wd | Yn W | Yn E2 | Yg Wd | Yg Wd | Yg Wd | Yg M | Yn Wd | Yn Wd | Yn Wd | Yn M | Yg F | Yg E1 | Yn F | Yn W | | | Yg E | Yg W | Yg E | Yg F | Yn E | Yn E4 | 8 |
| 9 | Yg F | Yg E1 | Yg Wd | Yg M | Yn Wd | Yn Wd | Yn Wd | Yn M | Yg F | Yg E1 | Yg F | Yg E3 | Yn F | Yn F | Yg E | Yg W | Yg E | Yg F | Yn E | Yn E4 | Yn E | Yn E2 | Yg M | Yg Wd | 9 |
| 10 | Yn F | Yn F | Yn Wd | Yn M | Yg F | Yg E1 | Yg F | Yg E3 | Yn F | Yn F | Yn F | Yn W | Yg E | Yg F | Yn E | Yn E4 | Yn E | Yn E2 | Yg M | Yg Wd | Yg M | Yg M | Yn M | Yn Wd | 10 |
| 11 | Yg E | Yg F | Yg F | Yg E3 | Yn F | Yn F | Yn F | Yn W | Yg E | Yg F | Yg E | Yg W | Yn E | Yn E2 | Yg M | Yg Wd | Yg M | Yg M | Yn M | Yn Wd | Yn M | Yn M | Yg W | Yg E1 | 11 |
| 12 | Yn E | Yn E2 | Yn F | Yn W | Yg E | Yg F | Yg E | Yg W | Yn E | Yn E2 | Yn E | Yn E4 | Yg M | Yg M | Yn M | Yn Wd | Yn M | Yn M | Yg W | Yg E1 | Yg W | Yg E3 | Yn W | Yn F | 12 |
| 13 | Yg M | Yg M | Yg E | Yg W | Yn E | Yn E2 | Yn E | Yn E4 | Yg M | Yg M | Yg M | Yg Wd | Yn M | Yn M | Yg W | Yg E1 | Yg W | Yg E3 | Yn W | Yn F | Yn W | Yn W | Yg Wd | Yg F | 13 |
| 14 | Yn M | Yn M | Yn E | Yn E4 | Yg M | Yg M | Yg M | Yg Wd | Yn M | Yn M | Yn M | Yn Wd | Yg W | Yg E3 | Yn W | Yn F | Yn W | Yn W | Yg Wd | Yg F | Yg Wd | Yg W | Yn Wd | Yn E2 | 14 |
| 15 | Yg W | Yg E3 | Yg M | Yg Wd | Yn M | Yn M | Yn M | Yn Wd | Yg W | Yg E3 | Yg W | Yg E1 | Yn W | Yn W | Yg Wd | Yg F | Yg Wd | Yg W | Yn Wd | Yn E2 | Yn Wd | Yn E4 | Yg F | Yg M | 15 |
| 16 | Yn W | Yn W | Yn M | Yn Wd | Yg W | Yg E3 | Yg W | Yg E1 | Yn W | Yn W | Yn W | Yn F | Yg Wd | Yg W | Yn Wd | Yn E2 | Yn Wd | Yn E4 | Yg F | Yg M | Yg F | Yg Wd | Yn F | Yn M | 16 |
| 17 | Yg Wd | Yg W | Yg W | Yg E1 | Yn W | Yn W | Yn W | Yn F | Yg Wd | Yg W | Yg Wd | Yg F | Yn Wd | Yn E4 | Yg F | Yg M | Yg F | Yg Wd | Yn F | Yn M | Yn F | Yn Wd | Yg E | Yg E3 | 17 |
| 18 | Yn Wd | Yn E4 | Yn W | Yn F | Yg Wd | Yg W | Yg Wd | Yg F | Yn Wd | Yn E4 | Yn Wd | Yn E2 | Yg F | Yg Wd | Yn F | Yn M | Yn F | Yn Wd | Yg E | Yg E3 | Yg E | Yg E1 | Yn E | Yn W | 18 |
| 19 | Yg F | Yg Wd | Yg Wd | Yg F | Yn Wd | Yn E4 | Yn Wd | Yn E2 | Yg F | Yg Wd | Yg F | Yg M | Yn F | Yn Wd | Yg E | Yg E3 | Yg E | Yg E1 | Yn E | Yn W | Yn E | Yn F | Yg M | Yg W | 19 |
| 20 | Yn F | Yn Wd | Yn Wd | Yn E2 | Yg F | Yg Wd | Yg F | Yg M | Yn F | Yn Wd | Yn F | Yn M | Yg E | Yg E1 | Yn E | Yn W | Yn E | Yn F | Yg M | Yg W | Yg M | Yg F | Yn M | Yn E4 | 20 |
| 21 | Yg E | Yg E1 | Yg F | Yg M | Yn F | Yn Wd | Yn F | Yn M | Yg E | Yg E1 | Yg E | Yg E3 | Yn E | Yn F | Yg M | Yg W | Yg M | Yg F | Yn M | Yn E4 | Yn M | Yn E2 | Yg W | Yg Wd | 21 |
| 22 | Yn E | Yn F | Yn F | Yn M | Yg E | Yg E1 | Yg E | Yg E3 | Yn E | Yn F | Yn E | Yn W | Yg M | Yg F | Yn M | Yn E4 | Yn M | Yn E2 | Yg W | Yg Wd | Yg W | Yg M | Yn W | Yn Wd | 22 |
| 23 | Yg M | Yg F | Yg E | Yg E3 | Yn E | Yn F | Yn E | Yn W | Yg M | Yg F | Yg M | Yg W | Yn M | Yn E2 | Yg W | Yg Wd | Yg W | Yg M | Yn W | Yn Wd | Yn W | Yn M | Yg Wd | Yg E1 | 23 |
| 24 | Yn M | Yn E2 | Yn E | Yn W | Yg M | Yg F | Yg M | Yg W | Yn M | Yn E2 | Yn M | Yn E4 | Yg W | Yg M | Yn W | Yn Wd | Yn W | Yn M | Yg Wd | Yg E1 | Yg Wd | Yg E3 | Yn Wd | Yn F | 24 |
| 25 | Yg W | Yg M | Yg M | Yg W | Yn M | Yn E2 | Yn M | Yn E4 | Yg W | Yg M | Yg W | Yg Wd | Yn W | Yn M | Yg Wd | Yg E1 | Yg Wd | Yg E3 | Yn Wd | Yn F | Yn Wd | Yn W | Yg F | Yg F | 25 |
| 26 | Yn W | Yn M | Yn M | Yn E4 | Yg W | Yg M | Yg W | Yg Wd | Yn W | Yn M | Yn W | Yn Wd | Yg Wd | Yg E3 | Yn Wd | Yn F | Yn Wd | Yn W | Yg F | Yg F | Yg F | Yg W | Yn F | Yn E2 | 26 |
| 27 | Yg Wd | Yg E3 | Yg W | Yg Wd | Yn W | Yn M | Yn W | Yn Wd | Yg Wd | Yg E3 | Yg Wd | Yg E1 | Yn Wd | Yn W | Yg F | Yg F | Yg F | Yg W | Yn F | Yn E2 | Yn F | Yn E4 | Yg E | Yg M | 27 |
| 28 | Yn Wd | Yn W | Yn W | Yn Wd | Yg Wd | Yg E3 | Yg Wd | Yg E1 | Yn Wd | Yn W | Yn Wd | Yn F | Yg F | Yg W | Yn F | Yn E2 | Yn F | Yn E4 | Yg E | Yg M | Yg E | Yg Wd | Yn E | Yn M | 28 |
| 29 | | | Yg Wd | Yg E1 | Yn Wd | Yn W | Yn Wd | Yn F | Yg F | Yg W | Yg F | Yg F | Yn F | Yn E4 | Yg E | Yg M | Yg E | Yg Wd | Yn E | Yn M | Yn E | Yn Wd | Yg M | Yg E3 | 29 |
| 30 | | | Yn Wd | Yn F | Yg F | Yg W | Yg F | Yg F | Yn F | Yn E4 | Yn F | Yn E2 | Yg E | Yg Wd | Yn E | Yn M | Yn E | Yn Wd | Yg M | Yg E3 | Yg M | Yg E1 | Yn M | Yn W | 30 |
| 31 | | | Yg F | Yg F | | | Yn F | Yn E2 | | | Yg E | Yg M | Yn E | Yn Wd | | | Yg M | Yg E1 | | | Yn M | Yn F | Yg W | Yg W | 31 |
| 1 | Yg F | Yg W | Yn F | Yn E2 | Yn F | Yn E4 | Yg E | Yg M | Yg E | Yg Wd | Yn E | Yn M | Yg M | Yg E1 | Yg M | Yg E3 | Yn M | Yn F | Yn M | Yn W | Yg W | Yg F | Yn W | Yn E4 | 1 |
| 2 | Yn F | Yn E4 | Yg E | Yg M | Yg E | Yg Wd | Yn E | Yn M | Yn E | Yn Wd | Yg M | Yg E3 | Yn M | Yn F | Yn M | Yn W | Yg W | Yg F | Yg W | Yg W | Yn W | Yn E2 | Yg Wd | Yg Wd | 2 |
| 3 | Yg E | Yg Wd | Yn E | Yn M | Yn E | Yn Wd | Yg M | Yg E3 | Yg M | Yg E1 | Yn M | Yn W | Yg W | Yg F | Yg W | Yg W | Yn W | Yn E2 | Yn W | Yn E4 | Yg Wd | Yg M | Yn Wd | Yn Wd | 3 |
| 4 | Yn E | Yn Wd | Yg M | Yg E3 | Yg M | Yg E1 | Yn M | Yn W | Yn M | Yn F | Yg W | Yg W | Yn W | Yn E2 | Yn W | Yn E4 | Yg Wd | Yg M | Yg Wd | Yg Wd | Yn Wd | Yn M | Yg F | Yg E1 | 4 |
| 5 | Yg M | Yg E1 | Yn M | Yn W | Yn M | Yn F | Yg W | Yg W | Yg W | Yg F | Yn W | Yn E4 | Yg Wd | Yg M | Yg Wd | Yg Wd | Yn Wd | Yn M | Yn Wd | Yn Wd | Yg F | Yg E3 | | | 5 |
| 6 | | | | | | | | | Yn W | Yn E2 | Yg Wd | Yg Wd | Yn Wd | Yn M | Yn Wd | Yn Wd | Yg F | Yg E3 | Yg F | Yg E1 | | | | | 6 |
| 7 | | | | | | | | | Yg Wd | Yg M | Yn Wd | Yn Wd | Yg F | Yg E3 | Yg F | Yg E1 | Yn F | Yn W | Yn F | Yn F | | | | | 7 |
| 8 | | | | | | | | | | | | | | | Yn F | Yn F | | | | | | | | | 8 |

# YEAR OF THE RAT

| | H | E | H | E | H | E | H | E | H | E | H | E | H | E | H | E | H | E | H | E | H | E | H | E | |
|---|---|---|---|---|---|---|---|---|---|---|---|---|---|---|---|---|---|---|---|---|---|---|---|---|---|
| YEAR | YEAR Yg F | Yg W | 1936 | | | | | | | | | | | | | | | | | | | | 1937 | | |
| MONTH | 5 Feb - 5 Mar | | 6 Mar - 4 Apr | | 5 Apr - 5 May | | 6 May - 5 June | | 6 June - 6 Jul | | 7 Jul - 7 Aug | | 8 Aug - 7 Sep | | 8 Sep - 7 Oct | | 8 Oct - 6 Nov | | 7 Nov - 6 Dec | | 7 Dec - 5 Jan | | 6 Jan - 3 Feb | | |
| | Yg M | Yg Wd | Yn M | Yn Wd | Yg W | Yg E1 | Yn W | Yn F | Yg Wd | Yg F | Yn Wd | Yn E2 | Yg F | Yg M | Yn F | Yn M | Yg E | Yg E3 | Yn E | Yn W | Yg M | Yg W | Yn M | Yn E4 | |
| Starting time | 1st day | Mid-pt | 1st day | Mid-pt | 1st day | Mid-pt | 1st day | Mid-pt | 1st day | Mid-pt | 1st day | Mid-pt | 1st day | Mid-pt | 1st day | Mid-pt | 1st day | Mid-pt | 1st day | Mid-pt | 1st day | Mid-pt | 1st day | Mid-pt | |
| Date | 5 | 20 | 6 | 21 | 5 | 20 | 6 | 21 | 6 | 21 | 7 | 23 | 8 | 23 | 8 | 23 | 8 | 23 | 7 | 22 | 7 | 22 | 6 | 20 | |
| Hour | 0730 | 0334 | 0150 | 0258 | 0709 | 1431 | 0014 | 1408 | 0531 | 2222 | 1559 | 0918 | 0143 | 1611 | 0421 | 1326 | 1933 | 2219 | 2215 | 1924 | 1443 | 0827 | 0144 | 1901 | |
| DATE 4 | | | | | | | | | | | | | | | | | | | | | | | | | 4 |
| 5 | Yn F | Yn F | | | Yn F | Yn F | | | | | | | | | | | | | | | | | | | 5 |
| 6 | Yg E | Yg F | Yn F | Yn W | Yg E | Yg F | Yg E | Yg W | Yn E | Yn E2 | | | | | | | | | | | | | Yn W | Yn F | 6 |
| 7 | Yn E | Yn E2 | Yg E | Yg W | Yn E | Yn E2 | Yn E | Yn E4 | Yg M | Yg M | Yg M | Yg Wd | | | | | | | Yn W | Yn F | Yn W | Yn W | Yg Wd | Yg F | 7 |
| 8 | Yg M | Yg M | Yn E | Yn E4 | Yg M | Yg M | Yg M | Yg Wd | Yn M | Yn M | Yn M | Yn Wd | Yg W | Yg E3 | Yn W | Yn F | Yn W | Yn W | Yg Wd | Yg F | Yg Wd | Yg W | Yn Wd | Yn E2 | 8 |
| 9 | Yn M | Yn M | Yg M | Yg Wd | Yn M | Yn M | Yn M | Yn Wd | Yg W | Yg E3 | Yg W | Yg E1 | Yn W | Yn W | Yg Wd | Yg F | Yg Wd | Yg W | Yn Wd | Yn E2 | Yn Wd | Yn E4 | Yg F | Yg M | 9 |
| 10 | Yg W | Yg E3 | Yn M | Yn Wd | Yg W | Yg E3 | Yg W | Yg E1 | Yn W | Yn W | Yn W | Yn F | Yg Wd | Yg W | Yn Wd | Yn E2 | Yn Wd | Yn E4 | Yg F | Yg M | Yg F | Yg Wd | Yn F | Yn M | 10 |
| 11 | Yn W | Yn W | Yg W | Yg E1 | Yn W | Yn W | Yn W | Yn F | Yg Wd | Yg W | Yg Wd | Yg F | Yn Wd | Yn E4 | Yg F | Yg M | Yg F | Yg Wd | Yn F | Yn M | Yn F | Yn Wd | Yg E | Yg E3 | 11 |
| 12 | Yg Wd | Yg W | Yn W | Yn F | Yg Wd | Yg W | Yg Wd | Yg F | Yn Wd | Yn E4 | Yn Wd | Yn E2 | Yg F | Yg Wd | Yn F | Yn M | Yn F | Yn Wd | Yg E | Yg E3 | Yg E | Yg E1 | Yn E | Yn W | 12 |
| 13 | Yn Wd | Yn E4 | Yg Wd | Yg F | Yn Wd | Yn E4 | Yn Wd | Yn E2 | Yg F | Yg Wd | Yg F | Yg M | Yn F | Yn Wd | Yg E | Yg E3 | Yg E | Yg E1 | Yn E | Yn W | Yn E | Yn F | Yg M | Yg W | 13 |
| 14 | Yg F | Yg Wd | Yn Wd | Yn E2 | Yg F | Yg Wd | Yg F | Yg M | Yn F | Yn Wd | Yn F | Yn M | Yg E | Yg E1 | Yn E | Yn W | Yn E | Yn F | Yg M | Yg W | Yg M | Yg F | Yn M | Yn E4 | 14 |
| 15 | Yn F | Yn Wd | Yg F | Yg M | Yn F | Yn Wd | Yn F | Yn M | Yg E | Yg E1 | Yg E | Yg E3 | Yn E | Yn F | Yg M | Yg W | Yg M | Yg F | Yn M | Yn E4 | Yn M | Yn E2 | Yg W | Yg Wd | 15 |
| 16 | Yg E | Yg E1 | Yn F | Yn M | Yg E | Yg E1 | Yg E | Yg E3 | Yn E | Yn F | Yn E | Yn W | Yg M | Yg F | Yn M | Yn E4 | Yn M | Yn E2 | Yg W | Yg Wd | Yg W | Yg M | Yn W | Yn Wd | 16 |
| 17 | Yn E | Yn F | Yg E | Yg E3 | Yn E | Yn F | Yn E | Yn W | Yg M | Yg F | Yg M | Yg W | Yn M | Yn E2 | Yg W | Yg Wd | Yg W | Yg M | Yn W | Yn Wd | Yn W | Yn M | Yg Wd | Yg E1 | 17 |
| 18 | Yg M | Yg F | Yn E | Yn W | Yg M | Yg F | Yg M | Yg W | Yn M | Yn E2 | Yn M | Yn E4 | Yg W | Yg M | Yn W | Yn Wd | Yn W | Yn M | Yg Wd | Yg E1 | Yg Wd | Yg E3 | Yn Wd | Yn F | 18 |
| 19 | Yn M | Yn E2 | Yg M | Yg W | Yn M | Yn E2 | Yn M | Yn E4 | Yg W | Yg M | Yg W | Yg Wd | Yn W | Yn M | Yg Wd | Yg E1 | Yg Wd | Yg E3 | Yn Wd | Yn F | Yn Wd | Yn W | Yg F | Yg F | 19 |
| 20 | Yg W | Yg M | Yn M | Yn E4 | Yg W | Yg M | Yg W | Yg Wd | Yn W | Yn M | Yn W | Yn Wd | Yg Wd | Yg E3 | Yn Wd | Yn F | Yn Wd | Yn W | Yg F | Yg F | Yg F | Yg W | Yn F | Yn E2 | 20 |
| 21 | Yn W | Yn M | Yg W | Yg Wd | Yn W | Yn M | Yn W | Yn Wd | Yg Wd | Yg E3 | Yg Wd | Yg E1 | Yn Wd | Yn W | Yg F | Yg F | Yg F | Yg W | Yn F | Yn E2 | Yn F | Yn E4 | Yg E | Yg M | 21 |
| 22 | Yg Wd | Yg E3 | Yn W | Yn Wd | Yg Wd | Yg E3 | Yg Wd | Yg E1 | Yn Wd | Yn W | Yn Wd | Yn F | Yg F | Yg W | Yn F | Yn E2 | Yn F | Yn E4 | Yg E | Yg M | Yg E | Yg Wd | Yn E | Yn M | 22 |
| 23 | Yn Wd | Yn W | Yg Wd | Yg E1 | Yn Wd | Yn W | Yn Wd | Yn F | Yg F | Yg W | Yg F | Yg F | Yn F | Yn E4 | Yg E | Yg M | Yg E | Yg Wd | Yn E | Yn M | Yn E | Yn Wd | Yg M | Yg E3 | 23 |
| 24 | Yg F | Yg W | Yn Wd | Yn F | Yg F | Yg W | Yg F | Yg F | Yn F | Yn E4 | Yn F | Yn E2 | Yg E | Yg Wd | Yn E | Yn M | Yn E | Yn Wd | Yg M | Yg E3 | Yg M | Yg E1 | Yn M | Yn W | 24 |
| 25 | Yn F | Yn E4 | Yg F | Yg F | Yn F | Yn E4 | Yn F | Yn E2 | Yg E | Yg Wd | Yg E | Yg M | Yn E | Yn Wd | Yg M | Yg E3 | Yg M | Yg E1 | Yn M | Yn W | Yn M | Yn F | Yg W | Yg W | 25 |
| 26 | Yg E | Yg Wd | Yn F | Yn E2 | Yg E | Yg Wd | Yg E | Yg M | Yn E | Yn Wd | Yn E | Yn M | Yg M | Yg E1 | Yn M | Yn W | Yn M | Yn F | Yg W | Yg W | Yg W | Yg F | Yn W | Yn E4 | 26 |
| 27 | Yn E | Yn Wd | Yg E | Yg M | Yn E | Yn Wd | Yn E | Yn M | Yg M | Yg E1 | Yg M | Yg E3 | Yn M | Yn F | Yg W | Yg W | Yg W | Yg F | Yn W | Yn E4 | Yn W | Yn E2 | Yg Wd | Yg Wd | 27 |
| 28 | Yg M | Yg E1 | Yn E | Yn M | Yg M | Yg E1 | Yg M | Yg E3 | Yn M | Yn F | Yn M | Yn W | Yg W | Yg F | Yn W | Yn E4 | Yn W | Yn E2 | Yg Wd | Yg Wd | Yg Wd | Yg M | Yn Wd | Yn Wd | 28 |
| 29 | Yn M | Yn F | Yg M | Yg E3 | Yn M | Yn F | Yn M | Yn W | Yg W | Yg F | Yg W | Yg W | Yn W | Yn E2 | Yg Wd | Yg Wd | Yg Wd | Yg M | Yn Wd | Yn Wd | Yn Wd | Yn M | Yg F | Yg E1 | 29 |
| 30 | | | Yn M | Yn W | Yg W | Yg F | Yg W | Yg W | Yn W | Yn E2 | Yn W | Yn E4 | Yg Wd | Yg M | Yn Wd | Yn Wd | Yn Wd | Yn M | Yg F | Yg E1 | Yg F | Yg E3 | Yn F | Yn F | 30 |
| 31 | | | Yg W | Yg W | | | Yn W | Yn E4 | | | Yg Wd | Yg Wd | Yn Wd | Yn M | | | Yg F | Yg E3 | | | Yn F | Yn W | Yg E | Yg F | 31 |
| 1 | Yg W | Yg F | Yn W | Yn E4 | Yn W | Yn E2 | Yg Wd | Yg Wd | Yg Wd | Yg M | Yn Wd | Yn Wd | Yg F | Yg E3 | Yg F | Yg E1 | Yn F | Yn W | Yn F | Yn F | Yg E | Yg W | Yn E | Yn E2 | 1 |
| 2 | Yn W | Yn E2 | Yg Wd | Yg Wd | Yg Wd | Yg M | Yn Wd | Yn Wd | Yn Wd | Yn M | Yg F | Yg E1 | Yn F | Yn W | Yn F | Yn F | Yg E | Yg W | Yg E | Yg F | Yn E | Yn E4 | Yg M | Yg M | 2 |
| 3 | Yg Wd | Yg M | Yn Wd | Yn Wd | Yn Wd | Yn M | Yg F | Yg E1 | Yg F | Yg E3 | Yn F | Yn F | Yg E | Yg W | Yg E | Yg F | Yn E | Yn E4 | Yn E | Yn E2 | Yg M | Yg Wd | Yn M | Yn M | 3 |
| 4 | Yn Wd | Yn M | Yg F | Yg E1 | Yg F | Yg E3 | Yn F | Yn F | Yn F | Yn W | Yg E | Yg F | Yn E | Yn E4 | Yn E | Yn E2 | Yg M | Yg Wd | Yg M | Yg M | Yn M | Yn Wd | | | 4 |
| 5 | Yg F | Yg E3 | | | Yn F | Yn W | Yg E | Yg F | Yg E | Yg W | Yn E | Yn E2 | Yg M | Yg Wd | Yg M | Yg M | Yn M | Yn Wd | Yn M | Yn M | Yg W | Yg E1 | | | 5 |
| 6 | | | | | | | | | Yn E | Yn E4 | Yg M | Yg M | Yn M | Yn Wd | Yn M | Yn M | Yg W | Yg E1 | Yg W | Yg E3 | | | | | 6 |
| 7 | | | | | | | | | | | Yn M | Yn M | Yg W | Yg E1 | Yg W | Yg E3 | | | | | | | | | 7 |
| 8 | | | | | | | | | | | | | | | | | | | | | | | | | 8 |

# YEAR OF THE OX

| | H | E | H | E | H | E | H | E | H | E | H | E | H | E | H | E | H | E | H | E | H | E | H | E | |
|---|---|---|---|---|---|---|---|---|---|---|---|---|---|---|---|---|---|---|---|---|---|---|---|---|---|
| YEAR | YEAR<br>Yn F | Yn E4 | 1937 | | | | | | | | | | | | | | | | | | | | 1938 | | |
| MONTH | 4 Feb - 5 Mar<br>Yg W | Yg Wd | 6 Mar - 4 Apr<br>Yn W | Yn Wd | 5 Apr - 5 May<br>Yg Wd | Yg E1 | 6 May - 5 June<br>Yn Wd | Yn F | 6 June - 6 Jul<br>Yg F | Yg F | 7 Jul - 7 Aug<br>Yn F | Yn E2 | 8 Aug - 7 Sep<br>Yg E | Yg M | 8 Sep - 8 Oct<br>Yn E | Yn M | 9 Oct - 7 Nov<br>Yg M | Yg E3 | 8 Nov - 6 Dec<br>Yn M | Yn W | 7 Dec - 5 Jan<br>Yg W | Yg W | 6 Jan - 3 Feb<br>Yn W | Yn E4 | |
| Starting time | 1st day | Mid-pt | 1st day | Mid-pt | 1st day | Mid-pt | 1st day | Mid-pt | 1st day | Mid-pt | 1st day | Mid-pt | 1st day | Mid-pt | 1st day | Mid-pt | 1st day | Mid-pt | 1st day | Mid-pt | 1st day | Mid-pt | 1st day | Mid-pt | |
| Date | 4 | 19 | 6 | 21 | 5 | 20 | 6 | 21 | 6 | 22 | 7 | 23 | 8 | 23 | 8 | 23 | 9 | 24 | 8 | 23 | 7 | 22 | 6 | 21 | |
| Hour | 1326 | 0921 | 0745 | 0846 | 1302 | 2020 | 0651 | 1957 | 1123 | 0412 | 1246 | 1507 | 0726 | 2158 | 1000 | 1913 | 0111 | 0407 | 0356 | 0117 | 2027 | 1422 | 0732 | 0059 | |
| DATE 4 | Yg W | Yg E3 | | | | | | | | | | | | | | | | | | | | | | | 4 |
| 5 | Yn W | Yn W | | | Yg W | Yg E3 | | | | | | | | | | | | | | | | | | | 5 |
| 6 | Yg Wd | Yg W | Yg W | Yg E1 | Yn W | Yn W | Yn W | Yn F | Yg Wd | Yg W | | | | | | | | | | | | | Yg E | Yg E3 | 6 |
| 7 | Yn Wd | Yn E4 | Yn W | Yn F | Yg Wd | Yg W | Yg Wd | Yg F | Yn Wd | Yn E4 | Yn Wd | Yn E2 | | | | | | | | | Yg E | Yg E1 | Yn E | Yn W | 7 |
| 8 | Yg F | Yg Wd | Yg Wd | Yg F | Yn Wd | Yn E4 | Yn Wd | Yn E2 | Yg F | Yg Wd | Yg F | Yg M | Yn F | Yn Wd | Yg E | Yg E3 | | | Yn E | Yn W | Yn E | Yn F | Yg M | Yg W | 8 |
| 9 | Yn F | Yn Wd | Yn Wd | Yn E2 | Yg F | Yg Wd | Yg F | Yg M | Yn F | Yn Wd | Yn F | Yn M | Yg E | Yg E1 | Yn E | Yn W | Yn E | Yn F | Yg M | Yg W | Yg M | Yg F | Yn M | Yn E4 | 9 |
| 10 | Yg E | Yg E1 | Yg F | Yg M | Yn F | Yn Wd | Yn F | Yn M | Yg E | Yg E1 | Yg E | Yg E3 | Yn E | Yn F | Yg M | Yg W | Yg M | Yg F | Yn M | Yn E4 | Yn M | Yn E2 | Yg W | Yg Wd | 10 |
| 11 | Yn E | Yn F | Yn F | Yn M | Yg E | Yg E1 | Yg E | Yg E3 | Yn E | Yn F | Yn E | Yn W | Yg M | Yg F | Yn M | Yn E4 | Yn M | Yn E2 | Yg W | Yg Wd | Yg W | Yg M | Yn W | Yn Wd | 11 |
| 12 | Yg M | Yg F | Yg E | Yg E3 | Yn E | Yn F | Yn E | Yn W | Yg M | Yg F | Yg M | Yg W | Yn M | Yn E2 | Yg W | Yg Wd | Yg W | Yg M | Yn W | Yn Wd | Yn W | Yn M | Yg Wd | Yg E1 | 12 |
| 13 | Yn M | Yn E2 | Yn E | Yn W | Yg M | Yg F | Yg M | Yg W | Yn M | Yn E2 | Yn M | Yn E4 | Yg W | Yg M | Yn W | Yn Wd | Yn W | Yn M | Yg Wd | Yg E1 | Yg Wd | Yg E3 | Yn Wd | Yn F | 13 |
| 14 | Yg W | Yg M | Yg M | Yg W | Yn M | Yn E2 | Yn M | Yn E4 | Yg W | Yg M | Yg W | Yg Wd | Yn W | Yn M | Yg Wd | Yg E1 | Yg Wd | Yg E3 | Yn Wd | Yn F | Yn Wd | Yn W | Yg F | Yg F | 14 |
| 15 | Yn W | Yn M | Yn M | Yn E4 | Yg W | Yg M | Yg W | Yg Wd | Yn W | Yn M | Yn W | Yn Wd | Yg Wd | Yg E3 | Yn Wd | Yn F | Yn Wd | Yn W | Yg F | Yg F | Yg F | Yg W | Yn F | Yn E2 | 15 |
| 16 | Yg Wd | Yg E3 | Yg W | Yg Wd | Yn W | Yn M | Yn W | Yn Wd | Yg Wd | Yg E3 | Yg Wd | Yg E1 | Yn Wd | Yn W | Yg F | Yg F | Yg F | Yg W | Yn F | Yn E2 | Yn F | Yn E4 | Yg E | Yg M | 16 |
| 17 | Yn Wd | Yn W | Yn W | Yn Wd | Yg Wd | Yg E3 | Yg Wd | Yg E1 | Yn Wd | Yn W | Yn Wd | Yn F | Yg F | Yg W | Yn F | Yn E2 | Yn F | Yn E4 | Yg E | Yg M | Yg E | Yg Wd | Yn E | Yn M | 17 |
| 18 | Yg F | Yg W | Yg Wd | Yg E1 | Yn Wd | Yn W | Yn Wd | Yn F | Yg F | Yg W | Yg F | Yg F | Yn F | Yn E4 | Yg E | Yg M | Yg E | Yg Wd | Yn E | Yn M | Yn E | Yn Wd | Yg M | Yg E3 | 18 |
| 19 | Yn F | Yn E4 | Yn Wd | Yn F | Yg F | Yg W | Yg F | Yg F | Yn F | Yn E4 | Yn F | Yn E2 | Yg E | Yg Wd | Yn E | Yn M | Yn E | Yn Wd | Yg M | Yg E3 | Yg M | Yg E1 | Yn M | Yn W | 19 |
| 20 | Yg E | Yg Wd | Yg F | Yg F | Yn F | Yn E4 | Yn F | Yn E2 | Yg E | Yg Wd | Yg E | Yg M | Yn E | Yn Wd | Yg M | Yg E3 | Yg M | Yg E1 | Yn M | Yn W | Yn M | Yn F | Yg W | Yg W | 20 |
| 21 | Yn E | Yn Wd | Yn F | Yn E2 | Yg E | Yg Wd | Yg E | Yg M | Yn E | Yn Wd | Yn E | Yn M | Yg M | Yg E1 | Yn M | Yn W | Yn M | Yn F | Yg W | Yg W | Yg W | Yg F | Yn W | Yn E4 | 21 |
| 22 | Yg M | Yg E1 | Yg E | Yg M | Yn E | Yn Wd | Yn E | Yn M | Yg M | Yg E1 | Yg M | Yg E3 | Yn M | Yn F | Yg W | Yg W | Yg W | Yg F | Yn W | Yn E4 | Yn W | Yn E2 | Yg Wd | Yg Wd | 22 |
| 23 | Yn M | Yn F | Yn E | Yn M | Yg M | Yg E1 | Yg M | Yg E3 | Yn M | Yn F | Yn M | Yn W | Yg W | Yg F | Yn W | Yn E4 | Yn W | Yn E2 | Yg Wd | Yg Wd | Yg Wd | Yg M | Yn Wd | Yn Wd | 23 |
| 24 | Yg W | Yg F | Yg M | Yg E3 | Yn M | Yn F | Yn M | Yn W | Yg W | Yg F | Yg W | Yg W | Yn W | Yn E2 | Yg Wd | Yg Wd | Yg Wd | Yg M | Yn Wd | Yn Wd | Yn Wd | Yn M | Yg F | Yg E1 | 24 |
| 25 | Yn W | Yn E2 | Yn M | Yn W | Yg W | Yg F | Yg W | Yg W | Yn W | Yn E2 | Yn W | Yn E4 | Yg Wd | Yg M | Yn Wd | Yn Wd | Yn Wd | Yn M | Yg F | Yg E1 | Yg F | Yg E3 | Yn F | Yn F | 25 |
| 26 | Yg Wd | Yg M | Yg W | Yg W | Yn W | Yn E2 | Yn W | Yn E4 | Yg Wd | Yg M | Yg Wd | Yg Wd | Yn Wd | Yn M | Yg F | Yg E1 | Yg F | Yg E3 | Yn F | Yn F | Yn F | Yn W | Yg E | Yg F | 26 |
| 27 | Yn Wd | Yn M | Yn W | Yn E4 | Yg Wd | Yg M | Yg Wd | Yg Wd | Yn Wd | Yn M | Yn Wd | Yn Wd | Yg F | Yg E3 | Yn F | Yn F | Yn F | Yn W | Yg E | Yg F | Yg E | Yg W | Yn E | Yn E2 | 27 |
| 28 | Yg F | Yg E3 | Yg Wd | Yg Wd | Yn Wd | Yn M | Yn Wd | Yn Wd | Yg F | Yg E3 | Yg F | Yg E1 | Yn F | Yn W | Yg E | Yg F | Yg E | Yg W | Yn E | Yn E2 | Yn E | Yn E4 | Yg M | Yg M | 28 |
| 29 | | | Yn Wd | Yn Wd | Yg F | Yg E3 | Yg F | Yg E1 | Yn F | Yn W | Yn F | Yn F | Yg E | Yg W | Yn E | Yn E2 | Yn E | Yn E4 | Yg M | Yg M | Yg M | Yg Wd | Yn M | Yn M | 29 |
| 30 | | | Yg F | Yg E1 | Yn F | Yn W | Yn F | Yn F | Yg E | Yg W | Yg E | Yg F | Yn E | Yn E4 | Yg M | Yg M | Yg M | Yg Wd | Yn M | Yn M | Yn M | Yn Wd | Yg W | Yg E3 | 30 |
| 31 | | | Yn F | Yn F | | | Yg E | Yg F | | | Yn E | Yn E2 | Yg M | Yg Wd | | | Yn M | Yn Wd | | | Yg W | Yg E1 | Yn W | Yn W | 31 |
| 1 | Yn F | Yn W | Yg E | Yg F | Yg E | Yg W | Yn E | Yn E2 | Yn E | Yn E4 | Yg M | Yg M | Yn M | Yn Wd | Yn M | Yn M | Yg W | Yg E1 | Yg W | Yg E3 | Yn W | Yn F | Yg Wd | Yg W | 1 |
| 2 | Yg E | Yg W | Yn E | Yn E2 | Yn E | Yn E4 | Yg M | Yg M | Yg M | Yg Wd | Yn M | Yn M | Yg W | Yg E1 | Yg W | Yg E3 | Yn W | Yn F | Yn W | Yn W | Yg Wd | Yg F | Yn Wd | Yn E4 | 2 |
| 3 | Yn E | Yn E4 | Yg M | Yg M | Yg M | Yg Wd | Yn M | Yn M | Yn M | Yn Wd | Yg W | Yg E3 | Yn W | Yn F | Yn W | Yn W | Yg Wd | Yg F | Yg Wd | Yg W | Yn Wd | Yn E2 | Yg F | Yg Wd | 3 |
| 4 | Yg M | Yg Wd | Yn M | Yn M | Yn M | Yn Wd | Yg W | Yg E3 | Yg W | Yg E1 | Yn W | Yn W | Yg Wd | Yg F | Yg Wd | Yg W | Yn Wd | Yn E2 | Yn Wd | Yn E4 | Yg F | Yg M | | | 4 |
| 5 | Yn M | Yn Wd | | | Yg W | Yg E1 | Yn W | Yn W | Yn W | Yn F | Yg Wd | Yg W | Yn Wd | Yn E2 | Yn Wd | Yn E4 | Yg F | Yg M | Yg F | Yg Wd | Yn F | Yn M | | | 5 |
| 6 | | | | | | | | | Yg Wd | Yg F | Yn Wd | Yn E4 | Yg F | Yg M | Yg F | Yg Wd | Yn F | Yn M | Yn F | Yn Wd | | | | | 6 |
| 7 | | | | | | | | | | | Yg F | Yg Wd | Yn F | Yn M | Yn F | Yn Wd | Yg E | Yg E3 | | | | | | | 7 |
| 8 | | | | | | | | | | | | | | | Yg E | Yg E1 | | | | | | | | | 8 |

# YEAR OF THE TIGER

| YEAR | H | E | H | E | H | E | H | E | H | E | H | E | H | E | H | E | H | E | H | E | H | E | H | E | |
|---|---|---|---|---|---|---|---|---|---|---|---|---|---|---|---|---|---|---|---|---|---|---|---|---|---|
| YEAR | YEAR Yg E | Yg Wd | 1938 | | | | | | | | | | | | | | | | | | | | 1939 | | |
| MONTH | 4 Feb - 5 Mar | | 6 Mar - 4 Apr | | 5 Apr - 5 May | | 6 May - 5 June | | 6 June - 7 Jul | | 8 Jul - 7 Aug | | 8 Aug - 7 Sep | | 8 Sep - 8 Oct | | 9 Oct - 7 Nov | | 8 Nov - 7 Dec | | 8 Dec - 5 Jan | | 6 Jan - 4 Feb | | |
| | Yg Wd | Yg Wd | Yn Wd | Yn Wd | Yg F | Yg E1 | Yn F | Yn F | Yg E | Yg F | Yn E | Yn E2 | Yg M | Yg M | Yn M | Yn M | Yg W | Yg E3 | Yn W | Yn W | Yg Wd | Yg W | Yn Wd | Yn E4 | |
| Starting time | 1st day | Mid-pt | 1st day | Mid-pt | 1st day | Mid-pt | 1st day | Mid-pt | 1st day | Mid-pt | 1st day | Mid-pt | 1st day | Mid-pt | 1st day | Mid-pt | 1st day | Mid-pt | 1st day | Mid-pt | 1st day | Mid-pt | 1st day | Mid-pt | |
| Date | 4 | 19 | 6 | 21 | 5 | 21 | 6 | 22 | 6 | 22 | 8 | 23 | 8 | 24 | 8 | 24 | 9 | 24 | 8 | 23 | 8 | 22 | 6 | 21 | |
| Hour | 1915 | 1520 | 1334 | 1443 | 1849 | 0215 | 1236 | 0151 | 1707 | 1004 | 0332 | 2057 | 1313 | 0346 | 1549 | 0100 | 0702 | 0954 | 0949 | 0707 | 0223 | 2014 | 1328 | 0651 | |
| DATE 4 | Yn F | Yn Wd | | | | | | | | | | | | | | | | | | | | | | | 4 |
| 5 | Yg E | Yg E1 | | | Yn F | Yn Wd | | | | | | | | | | | | | | | | | | | 5 |
| 6 | Yn E | Yn F | Yn F | Yn M | Yg E | Yg E1 | Yg E | Yg E3 | Yn E | Yn F | | | | | | | | | | | | | Yn W | Yn Wd | 6 |
| 7 | Yg M | Yg F | Yg E | Yg E3 | Yn E | Yn F | Yn E | Yn W | Yg M | Yg F | | | | | | | | | | | | | Yg Wd | Yg E1 | 7 |
| 8 | Yn M | Yn E2 | Yn E | Yn W | Yg M | Yg F | Yg M | Yg W | Yn M | Yn E2 | Yn M | Yn E4 | Yg W | Yg M | Yn W | Yn Wd | | | Yg Wd | Yg E1 | Yg Wd | Yg E3 | Yn Wd | Yn F | 8 |
| 9 | Yg W | Yg M | Yg M | Yg W | Yn M | Yn E2 | Yn M | Yn E4 | Yg W | Yg M | Yg W | Yg Wd | Yn W | Yn M | Yg Wd | Yg E1 | Yg Wd | Yg E3 | Yn Wd | Yn F | Yn Wd | Yn W | Yg F | Yg F | 9 |
| 10 | Yn W | Yn M | Yn M | Yn E4 | Yg W | Yg M | Yg W | Yg Wd | Yn W | Yn M | Yn W | Yn Wd | Yg Wd | Yg E3 | Yn Wd | Yn F | Yn Wd | Yn W | Yg F | Yg F | Yg F | Yg W | Yn F | Yn E2 | 10 |
| 11 | Yg Wd | Yg E3 | Yg W | Yg Wd | Yn W | Yn M | Yn W | Yn Wd | Yg Wd | Yg E3 | Yg Wd | Yg E1 | Yn Wd | Yn W | Yg F | Yg F | Yg F | Yg W | Yn F | Yn E2 | Yn F | Yn E4 | Yg E | Yg M | 11 |
| 12 | Yn Wd | Yn W | Yn W | Yn Wd | Yg Wd | Yg E3 | Yg Wd | Yg E1 | Yn Wd | Yn W | Yn Wd | Yn F | Yg F | Yg W | Yn F | Yn E2 | Yn F | Yn E4 | Yg E | Yg M | Yg E | Yg Wd | Yn E | Yn M | 12 |
| 13 | Yg F | Yg W | Yg Wd | Yg E1 | Yn Wd | Yn W | Yn Wd | Yn F | Yg F | Yg W | Yg F | Yg F | Yn F | Yn E4 | Yg E | Yg M | Yg E | Yg Wd | Yn E | Yn M | Yn E | Yn Wd | Yg M | Yg E3 | 13 |
| 14 | Yn F | Yn E4 | Yn Wd | Yn F | Yg F | Yg W | Yg F | Yg F | Yn F | Yn E4 | Yn F | Yn E2 | Yg E | Yg Wd | Yn E | Yn M | Yn E | Yn Wd | Yg M | Yg E3 | Yg M | Yg E1 | Yn M | Yn W | 14 |
| 15 | Yg E | Yg Wd | Yg F | Yg F | Yn F | Yn E4 | Yn F | Yn E2 | Yg E | Yg Wd | Yg E | Yg M | Yn E | Yn Wd | Yg M | Yg E3 | Yg M | Yg E1 | Yn M | Yn W | Yn M | Yn F | Yg W | Yg W | 15 |
| 16 | Yn E | Yn Wd | Yn F | Yn E2 | Yg E | Yg Wd | Yg E | Yg M | Yn E | Yn Wd | Yn E | Yn M | Yg M | Yg E1 | Yn M | Yn W | Yn M | Yn F | Yg W | Yg W | Yg W | Yg F | Yn W | Yn E4 | 16 |
| 17 | Yg M | Yg E1 | Yg E | Yg M | Yn E | Yn Wd | Yn E | Yn M | Yg M | Yg E1 | Yg M | Yg E3 | Yn M | Yn F | Yg W | Yg W | Yg W | Yg F | Yn W | Yn E4 | Yn W | Yn E2 | Yg Wd | Yg Wd | 17 |
| 18 | Yn M | Yn F | Yn E | Yn M | Yg M | Yg E1 | Yg M | Yg E3 | Yn M | Yn F | Yn M | Yn W | Yg W | Yg F | Yn W | Yn E4 | Yn W | Yn E2 | Yg Wd | Yg Wd | Yg Wd | Yg M | Yn Wd | Yn Wd | 18 |
| 19 | Yg W | Yg F | Yg M | Yg E3 | Yn M | Yn F | Yn M | Yn W | Yg W | Yg F | Yg W | Yg W | Yn W | Yn E2 | Yg Wd | Yg Wd | Yg Wd | Yg M | Yn Wd | Yn Wd | Yn Wd | Yn M | Yg F | Yg E1 | 19 |
| 20 | Yn W | Yn E2 | Yn M | Yn W | Yg W | Yg F | Yg W | Yg W | Yn W | Yn E2 | Yn W | Yn E4 | Yg Wd | Yg M | Yn Wd | Yn Wd | Yn Wd | Yn M | Yg F | Yg E1 | Yg F | Yg E3 | Yn F | Yn F | 20 |
| 21 | Yg Wd | Yg M | Yg W | Yg W | Yn W | Yn E2 | Yn W | Yn E4 | Yg Wd | Yg M | Yg Wd | Yg Wd | Yn Wd | Yn M | Yg F | Yg E1 | Yg F | Yg E3 | Yn F | Yn F | Yn F | Yn W | Yg E | Yg F | 21 |
| 22 | Yn Wd | Yn M | Yn W | Yn E4 | Yg Wd | Yg M | Yg Wd | Yg Wd | Yn Wd | Yn M | Yn Wd | Yn Wd | Yg F | Yg E3 | Yn F | Yn F | Yn F | Yn W | Yg E | Yg F | Yg E | Yg W | Yn E | Yn E2 | 22 |
| 23 | Yg F | Yg E3 | Yg Wd | Yg Wd | Yn Wd | Yn M | Yn Wd | Yn Wd | Yg F | Yg E3 | Yg F | Yg E1 | Yn F | Yn W | Yg E | Yg F | Yg E | Yg W | Yn E | Yn E2 | Yn E | Yn E4 | Yg M | Yg M | 23 |
| 24 | Yn F | Yn W | Yn Wd | Yn Wd | Yg F | Yg E3 | Yg F | Yg E1 | Yn F | Yn W | Yn F | Yn F | Yg E | Yg W | Yn E | Yn E2 | Yn E | Yn E4 | Yg M | Yg M | Yg M | Yg Wd | Yn M | Yn M | 24 |
| 25 | Yg E | Yg W | Yg F | Yg E1 | Yn F | Yn W | Yn F | Yn F | Yg E | Yg W | Yg E | Yg F | Yn E | Yn E4 | Yg M | Yg M | Yg M | Yg Wd | Yn M | Yn M | Yn M | Yn Wd | Yg W | Yg E3 | 25 |
| 26 | Yn E | Yn E4 | Yn F | Yn F | Yg E | Yg W | Yg E | Yg F | Yn E | Yn E4 | Yn E | Yn E2 | Yg M | Yg Wd | Yn M | Yn M | Yn M | Yn Wd | Yg W | Yg E3 | Yg W | Yg E1 | Yn W | Yn W | 26 |
| 27 | Yg M | Yg Wd | Yg E | Yg F | Yn E | Yn E4 | Yn E | Yn E2 | Yg M | Yg Wd | Yg M | Yg M | Yn M | Yn Wd | Yg W | Yg E3 | Yg W | Yg E1 | Yn W | Yn W | Yn W | Yn F | Yg Wd | Yg W | 27 |
| 28 | Yn M | Yn Wd | Yn E | Yn E2 | Yg M | Yg Wd | Yg M | Yg M | Yn M | Yn Wd | Yn M | Yn M | Yg W | Yg E1 | Yn W | Yn W | Yn W | Yn F | Yg Wd | Yg W | Yg Wd | Yg F | Yn Wd | Yn E4 | 28 |
| 29 | | | Yg M | Yg M | Yn M | Yn Wd | Yn M | Yn M | Yg W | Yg E1 | Yg W | Yg E3 | Yn W | Yn F | Yg Wd | Yg W | Yg Wd | Yg F | Yn Wd | Yn E4 | Yn Wd | Yn E2 | Yg F | Yg Wd | 29 |
| 30 | | | Yn M | Yn M | Yg W | Yg E1 | Yg W | Yg E3 | Yn W | Yn F | Yn W | Yn W | Yg Wd | Yg F | Yn Wd | Yn E4 | Yn Wd | Yn E2 | Yg F | Yg Wd | Yg F | Yg M | Yn F | Yn Wd | 30 |
| 31 | | | Yg W | Yg E3 | | | Yn W | Yn W | | | Yg Wd | Yg W | Yn Wd | Yn E2 | | | Yg F | Yg M | | | Yn F | Yn M | Yg E | Yg E1 | 31 |
| 1 | Yg W | Yg E1 | Yn W | Yn W | Yn W | Yn F | Yg Wd | Yg W | Yg Wd | Yg F | Yn Wd | Yn E4 | Yg F | Yg M | Yg F | Yg Wd | Yn F | Yn M | Yn F | Yn Wd | Yg E | Yg E3 | Yn E | Yn F | 1 |
| 2 | Yn W | Yn F | Yg Wd | Yg W | Yg Wd | Yg F | Yn Wd | Yn E4 | Yn Wd | Yn E2 | Yg F | Yg Wd | Yn F | Yn M | Yn F | Yn Wd | Yg E | Yg E3 | Yg E | Yg E1 | Yn E | Yn W | Yg M | Yg F | 2 |
| 3 | Yg Wd | Yg F | Yn Wd | Yn E4 | Yn Wd | Yn E2 | Yg F | Yg Wd | Yg F | Yg M | Yn F | Yn Wd | Yg E | Yg E3 | Yg E | Yg E1 | Yn E | Yn W | Yn E | Yn F | Yg M | Yg W | Yn M | Yn E2 | 3 |
| 4 | Yn Wd | Yn E2 | Yg F | Yg Wd | Yg F | Yg M | Yn F | Yn Wd | Yn F | Yn M | Yg E | Yg E1 | Yn E | Yn W | Yn E | Yn F | Yg M | Yg W | Yg M | Yg F | Yn M | Yn E4 | Yg W | Yg M | 4 |
| 5 | Yg F | Yg M | | | Yn F | Yn M | Yg E | Yg E1 | Yg E | Yg E3 | Yn E | Yn F | Yg M | Yg W | Yg M | Yg F | Yn M | Yn E4 | Yn M | Yn E2 | Yg W | Yg Wd | | | 5 |
| 6 | | | | | | | | | Yn E | Yn W | Yg M | Yg F | Yn M | Yn E4 | Yn M | Yn E2 | Yg W | Yg Wd | Yg W | Yg M | | | | | 6 |
| 7 | | | | | | | | | Yg M | Yg W | Yn M | Yn E2 | Yg W | Yg Wd | Yg W | Yg M | Yn W | Yn Wd | Yn W | Yn M | | | | | 7 |
| 8 | | | | | | | | | | | | | | | Yn W | Yn M | | | | | | | | | 8 |

# YEAR OF THE RABBIT

| | H | E | H | E | H | E | H | E | H | E | H | E | H | E | H | E | H | E | H | E | H | E | H | E | |
|---|---|---|---|---|---|---|---|---|---|---|---|---|---|---|---|---|---|---|---|---|---|---|---|---|---|
| YEAR | YEAR<br>YnE | Yn Wd | 1939 | | | | | | | | | | | | | | | | | | | | 1940 | | |
| MONTH | 5 Feb - 5 Mar | | 6 Mar - 5 Apr | | 6 Apr - 5 May | | 6 May - 5 June | | 6 June - 7 Jul | | 8 Jul - 7 Aug | | 8 Aug - 7 Sep | | 8 Sep - 8 Oct | | 9 Oct - 7 Nov | | 8 Nov - 7 Dec | | 8 Dec - 5 Jan | | 6 Jan - 4 Feb | | |
| | Yg F | Yg Wd | Yn F | Yn Wd | Yg E | Yg E1 | Yn E | Yn F | Yg M | Yg F | Yn M | Yn E2 | Yg W | Yg M | Yn W | Yn M | Yg Wd | Yg E3 | Yn Wd | Yn W | Yg F | Yg W | Yn F | Yn E4 | |
| Starting time | 1st day | Mid-pt | 1st day | Mid-pt | 1st day | Mid-pt | 1st day | Mid-pt | 1st day | Mid-pt | 1st day | Mid-pt | 1st day | Mid-pt | 1st day | Mid-pt | 1st day | Mid-pt | 1st day | Mid-pt | 1st day | Mid-pt | 1st day | Mid-pt | |
| Date | 5 | 19 | 6 | 21 | 6 | 21 | 6 | 22 | 6 | 22 | 8 | 24 | 8 | 24 | 8 | 24 | 9 | 24 | 8 | 23 | 8 | 23 | 6 | 21 | |
| Hour | 0117 | 2110 | 1927 | 2029 | 0038 | 0755 | 1821 | 0727 | 2252 | 1538 | 0919 | 0237 | 1904 | 0932 | 2142 | 0650 | 1257 | 1542 | 1540 | 1259 | 0818 | 0206 | 1924 | 1244 | |
| DATE 4 | | | | | | | | | | | | | | | | | | | | | | | | | 4 |
| 5 | Yn W | Yn M | | | | | | | | | | | | | | | | | | | | | | | 5 |
| 6 | Yg Wd | Yg E3 | Yg W | Yg Wd | Yn W | Yn M | Yn W | Yn Wd | Yg Wd | Yg E3 | | | | | | | | | | | | | Yg E | Yg M | 6 |
| 7 | Yn Wd | Yn W | Yn W | Yn Wd | Yg Wd | Yg E3 | Yg Wd | Yg E1 | Yn Wd | Yn W | | | | | | | | | | | | | Yn E | Yn M | 7 |
| 8 | Yg F | Yg W | Yg Wd | Yg E1 | Yn Wd | Yn W | Yn Wd | Yn F | Yg F | Yg W | Yg F | Yg F | Yn F | Yn E4 | Yg E | Yg M | | | Yn E | Yn M | Yn E | Yn Wd | Yg M | Yg E3 | 8 |
| 9 | Yn F | Yn E4 | Yn Wd | Yn F | Yg F | Yg W | Yg F | Yg F | Yn F | Yn E4 | Yn F | Yn E2 | Yg E | Yg Wd | Yn E | Yn M | Yn E | Yn Wd | Yg M | Yg E3 | Yg M | Yg E1 | Yn M | Yn W | 9 |
| 10 | Yg E | Yg Wd | Yg F | Yg F | Yn F | Yn E4 | Yn F | Yn E2 | Yg E | Yg Wd | Yg E | Yg M | Yn E | Yn Wd | Yg M | Yg E3 | Yg M | Yg E1 | Yn M | Yn W | Yn M | Yn F | Yg W | Yg W | 10 |
| 11 | Yn E | Yn Wd | Yn F | Yn E2 | Yg E | Yg Wd | Yg E | Yg M | Yn E | Yn Wd | Yn E | Yn M | Yg M | Yg E1 | Yn M | Yn W | Yn M | Yn F | Yg W | Yg W | Yg W | Yg F | Yn W | Yn E4 | 11 |
| 12 | Yg M | Yg E1 | Yg E | Yg M | Yn E | Yn Wd | Yn E | Yn M | Yg M | Yg E1 | Yg M | Yg E3 | Yn M | Yn F | Yg W | Yg W | Yg W | Yg F | Yn W | Yn E4 | Yn W | Yn E2 | Yg Wd | Yg Wd | 12 |
| 13 | Yn M | Yn F | Yn E | Yn M | Yg M | Yg E1 | Yg M | Yg E3 | Yn M | Yn F | Yn M | Yn W | Yg W | Yg F | Yn W | Yn E4 | Yn W | Yn E2 | Yg Wd | Yg Wd | Yg Wd | Yg M | Yn Wd | Yn Wd | 13 |
| 14 | Yg W | Yg F | Yg M | Yg E3 | Yn M | Yn F | Yn M | Yn W | Yg W | Yg F | Yg W | Yg W | Yn W | Yn E2 | Yg Wd | Yg Wd | Yg Wd | Yg M | Yn Wd | Yn Wd | Yn Wd | Yn M | Yg F | Yg E1 | 14 |
| 15 | Yn W | Yn E2 | Yn M | Yn W | Yg W | Yg F | Yg W | Yg W | Yn W | Yn E2 | Yn W | Yn E4 | Yg Wd | Yg M | Yn Wd | Yn Wd | Yn Wd | Yn M | Yg F | Yg E1 | Yg F | Yg E3 | Yn F | Yn F | 15 |
| 16 | Yg Wd | Yg M | Yg W | Yg W | Yn W | Yn E2 | Yn W | Yn E4 | Yg Wd | Yg M | Yg Wd | Yg Wd | Yn Wd | Yn M | Yg F | Yg E1 | Yg F | Yg E3 | Yn F | Yn F | Yn F | Yn W | Yg E | Yg F | 16 |
| 17 | Yn Wd | Yn M | Yn W | Yn E4 | Yg Wd | Yg M | Yg Wd | Yg Wd | Yn Wd | Yn M | Yn Wd | Yn Wd | Yg F | Yg E3 | Yn F | Yn F | Yn F | Yn W | Yg E | Yg F | Yg E | Yg W | Yn E | Yn E2 | 17 |
| 18 | Yg F | Yg E3 | Yg Wd | Yg Wd | Yn Wd | Yn M | Yn Wd | Yn Wd | Yg F | Yg E3 | Yg F | Yg E1 | Yn F | Yn W | Yg E | Yg F | Yg E | Yg W | Yn E | Yn E2 | Yn E | Yn E4 | Yg M | Yg M | 18 |
| 19 | Yn F | Yn W | Yn Wd | Yn Wd | Yg F | Yg E3 | Yg F | Yg E1 | Yn F | Yn W | Yn F | Yn F | Yg E | Yg W | Yn E | Yn E2 | Yn E | Yn E4 | Yg M | Yg M | Yg M | Yg Wd | Yn M | Yn M | 19 |
| 20 | Yg E | Yg W | Yg F | Yg E1 | Yn F | Yn W | Yn F | Yn F | Yg E | Yg W | Yg E | Yg F | Yn E | Yn E4 | Yg M | Yg M | Yg M | Yg Wd | Yn M | Yn M | Yn M | Yn Wd | Yg W | Yg E3 | 20 |
| 21 | Yn E | Yn E4 | Yn F | Yn F | Yg E | Yg W | Yg E | Yg F | Yn E | Yn E4 | Yn E | Yn E2 | Yg M | Yg Wd | Yn M | Yn M | Yn M | Yn Wd | Yg W | Yg E3 | Yg W | Yg E1 | Yn W | Yn W | 21 |
| 22 | Yg M | Yg Wd | Yg E | Yg F | Yn E | Yn E4 | Yn E | Yn E2 | Yg M | Yg Wd | Yg M | Yg M | Yn M | Yn Wd | Yg W | Yg E3 | Yg W | Yg E1 | Yn W | Yn W | Yn W | Yn F | Yg Wd | Yg W | 22 |
| 23 | Yn M | Yn Wd | Yn E | Yn E2 | Yg M | Yg Wd | Yg M | Yg M | Yn M | Yn Wd | Yn M | Yn M | Yg W | Yg E1 | Yn W | Yn W | Yn W | Yn F | Yg Wd | Yg W | Yg Wd | Yg F | Yn Wd | Yn E4 | 23 |
| 24 | Yg W | Yg E1 | Yg M | Yg M | Yn M | Yn Wd | Yn M | Yn M | Yg W | Yg E1 | Yg W | Yg E3 | Yn W | Yn F | Yg Wd | Yg W | Yg Wd | Yg F | Yn Wd | Yn E4 | Yn Wd | Yn E2 | Yg F | Yg Wd | 24 |
| 25 | Yn W | Yn F | Yn M | Yn M | Yg W | Yg E1 | Yg W | Yg E3 | Yn W | Yn F | Yn W | Yn W | Yg Wd | Yg F | Yn Wd | Yn E4 | Yn Wd | Yn E2 | Yg F | Yg Wd | Yg F | Yg M | Yn F | Yn Wd | 25 |
| 26 | Yg Wd | Yg F | Yg W | Yg E3 | Yn W | Yn F | Yn W | Yn W | Yg Wd | Yg F | Yg Wd | Yg W | Yn Wd | Yn E2 | Yg F | Yg Wd | Yg F | Yg M | Yn F | Yn Wd | Yn F | Yn M | Yg E | Yg E1 | 26 |
| 27 | Yn Wd | Yn E2 | Yn W | Yn W | Yg Wd | Yg F | Yg Wd | Yg W | Yn Wd | Yn E2 | Yn Wd | Yn E4 | Yg F | Yg M | Yn F | Yn Wd | Yn F | Yn M | Yg E | Yg E1 | Yg E | Yg E3 | Yn E | Yn F | 27 |
| 28 | Yg F | Yg M | Yg Wd | Yg W | Yn Wd | Yn E2 | Yn Wd | Yn E4 | Yg F | Yg M | Yg F | Yg Wd | Yn F | Yn M | Yg E | Yg E1 | Yg E | Yg E3 | Yn E | Yn F | Yn E | Yn W | Yg M | Yg F | 28 |
| 29 | | | Yn Wd | Yn E4 | Yg F | Yg M | Yg F | Yg Wd | Yn F | Yn M | Yn F | Yn Wd | Yg E | Yg E3 | Yn E | Yn F | Yn E | Yn W | Yg M | Yg F | Yg M | Yg W | Yn M | Yn E2 | 29 |
| 30 | | | Yg F | Yg Wd | Yn F | Yn M | Yn F | Yn Wd | Yg E | Yg E3 | Yg E | Yg E1 | Yn E | Yn W | Yg M | Yg F | Yg M | Yg W | Yn M | Yn E2 | Yn M | Yn E4 | Yg W | Yg M | 30 |
| 31 | | | Yn F | Yn Wd | | | Yg E | Yg E1 | | | Yn E | Yn F | Yg M | Yg W | | | Yn M | Yn E4 | | | Yg W | Yg Wd | Yn W | Yn M | 31 |
| 1 | Yn F | Yn M | Yg E | Yg E1 | Yg E | Yg E3 | Yn E | Yn F | Yn E | Yn W | Yg M | Yg F | Yn M | Yn E4 | Yn M | Yn E2 | Yg W | Yg Wd | Yg W | Yg M | Yn W | Yn Wd | Yg Wd | Yg E3 | 1 |
| 2 | Yg E | Yg E3 | Yn E | Yn F | Yn E | Yn W | Yg M | Yg F | Yg M | Yg W | Yn M | Yn E2 | Yg W | Yg Wd | Yg W | Yg M | Yn W | Yn Wd | Yn W | Yn M | Yg Wd | Yg E1 | Yn Wd | Yn W | 2 |
| 3 | Yn E | Yn W | Yg M | Yg F | Yg M | Yg W | Yn M | Yn E2 | Yn M | Yn E4 | Yg W | Yg M | Yn W | Yn Wd | Yn W | Yn M | Yg Wd | Yg E1 | Yg Wd | Yg E3 | Yn Wd | Yn F | Yg F | Yg W | 3 |
| 4 | Yg M | Yg W | Yn M | Yn E2 | Yn M | Yn E4 | Yg W | Yg M | Yg W | Yg Wd | Yn W | Yn M | Yg Wd | Yg E1 | Yg Wd | Yg E3 | Yn Wd | Yn F | Yn Wd | Yn W | Yg F | Yg F | Yn F | Yn E4 | 4 |
| 5 | Yn M | Yn E4 | Yg W | Yg M | Yg W | Yg Wd | Yn W | Yn M | Yn W | Yn Wd | Yg Wd | Yg E3 | Yn Wd | Yn F | Yn Wd | Yn W | Yg F | Yg F | Yg F | Yg W | Yn F | Yn E2 | | | 5 |
| 6 | | | | | | | | | Yg Wd | Yg E1 | Yn Wd | Yn W | Yg F | Yg F | Yg F | Yg W | Yn F | Yn E2 | Yn F | Yn E4 | | | | | 6 |
| 7 | | | | | | | | | Yn Wd | Yn F | Yg F | Yg W | Yn F | Yn E2 | Yn F | Yn E4 | Yg E | Yg M | Yg E | Yg Wd | | | | | 7 |
| 8 | | | | | | | | | | | | | | | Yg E | Yg Wd | | | | | | | | | 8 |

# YEAR OF THE DRAGON

| | H | E | H | E | H | E | H | E | H | E | H | E | H | E | H | E | H | E | H | E | H | E | H | E | |
|---|---|---|---|---|---|---|---|---|---|---|---|---|---|---|---|---|---|---|---|---|---|---|---|---|---|
| YEAR | YEAR YgM | Yg E1 | 1940 | | | | | | | | | | | | | | | | | | | | 1941 | | |
| MONTH | 5 Feb - 5 Mar | | 6 Mar - 4 Apr | | 5 Apr - 5 May | | 6 May - 5 June | | 6 June - 6 Jul | | 7 Jul - 7 Aug | | 8 Aug - 7 Sep | | 8 Sep - 7 Oct | | 8 Oct - 6 Nov | | 7 Nov - 6 Dec | | 7 Dec - 5 Jan | | 6 Jan - 3 Feb | | |
| | Yg E | Yg Wd | Yn E | Yn Wd | Yg M | Yg E1 | Yn M | Yn F | Yg W | Yg F | Yn W | Yn E2 | Yg Wd | Yg M | Yn Wd | Yn M | Yg F | Yg E3 | Yn F | Yn W | Yg E | Yg W | Yn E | Yn E4 | |
| Starting time | 1st day | Mid-pt | 1st day | Mid-pt | 1st day | Mid-pt | 1st day | Mid-pt | 1st day | Mid-pt | 1st day | Mid-pt | 1st day | Mid-pt | 1st day | Mid-pt | 1st day | Mid-pt | 1st day | Mid-pt | 1st day | Mid-pt | 1st day | Mid-pt | |
| Date | 5 | 20 | 6 | 21 | 5 | 20 | 6 | 21 | 6 | 21 | 7 | 23 | 8 | 23 | 8 | 23 | 8 | 23 | 7 | 22 | 7 | 22 | 6 | 20 | |
| Hour | 0708 | 0304 | 0124 | 0224 | 0635 | 1350 | 0016 | 1323 | 0444 | 2137 | 1508 | 0835 | 0052 | 1529 | 0330 | 1246 | 1843 | 2140 | 2121 | 1849 | 1358 | 0755 | 0104 | 1834 | |
| DATE 4 | | | | | | | | | | | | | | | | | | | | | | | | | 4 |
| 5 | Yg E | Yg Wd | | | Yg E | Yg Wd | | | | | | | | | | | | | | | | | | | 5 |
| 6 | Yn E | Yn Wd | Yg E | Yg M | Yn E | Yn Wd | Yn E | Yn M | Yg M | Yg E1 | | | | | | | | | | | | | Yg Wd | Yg Wd | 6 |
| 7 | Yg M | Yg E1 | Yn E | Yn M | Yg M | Yg E1 | Yg M | Yg E3 | Yn M | Yn F | Yn M | Yn W | | | | | | | Yg Wd | Yg Wd | Yg Wd | Yg M | Yn Wd | Yn Wd | 7 |
| 8 | Yn M | Yn F | Yg M | Yg E3 | Yn M | Yn F | Yn M | Yn W | Yg W | Yg F | Yg W | Yg W | Yn W | Yn E2 | Yg Wd | Yg Wd | Yg Wd | Yg M | Yn Wd | Yn Wd | Yn Wd | Yn M | Yg F | Yg E1 | 8 |
| 9 | Yg W | Yg F | Yn M | Yn W | Yg W | Yg F | Yg W | Yg W | Yn W | Yn E2 | Yn W | Yn E4 | Yg Wd | Yg M | Yn Wd | Yn Wd | Yn Wd | Yn M | Yg F | Yg E1 | Yg F | Yg E3 | Yn F | Yn F | 9 |
| 10 | Yn W | Yn E2 | Yg W | Yg W | Yn W | Yn E2 | Yn W | Yn E4 | Yg Wd | Yg M | Yg Wd | Yg Wd | Yn Wd | Yn M | Yg F | Yg E1 | Yg F | Yg E3 | Yn F | Yn F | Yn F | Yn W | Yg E | Yg F | 10 |
| 11 | Yg Wd | Yg M | Yn W | Yn E4 | Yg Wd | Yg M | Yg Wd | Yg Wd | Yn Wd | Yn M | Yn Wd | Yn Wd | Yg F | Yg E3 | Yn F | Yn F | Yn F | Yn W | Yg E | Yg F | Yg E | Yg W | Yn E | Yn E2 | 11 |
| 12 | Yn Wd | Yn M | Yg Wd | Yg Wd | Yn Wd | Yn M | Yn Wd | Yn Wd | Yg F | Yg E3 | Yg F | Yg E1 | Yn F | Yn W | Yg E | Yg F | Yg E | Yg W | Yn E | Yn E2 | Yn E | Yn E4 | Yg M | Yg M | 12 |
| 13 | Yg F | Yg E3 | Yn Wd | Yn Wd | Yg F | Yg E3 | Yg F | Yg E1 | Yn F | Yn W | Yn F | Yn F | Yg E | Yg W | Yn E | Yn E2 | Yn E | Yn E4 | Yg M | Yg M | Yg M | Yg Wd | Yn M | Yn M | 13 |
| 14 | Yn F | Yn W | Yg F | Yg E1 | Yn F | Yn W | Yn F | Yn F | Yg E | Yg W | Yg E | Yg F | Yn E | Yn E4 | Yg M | Yg M | Yg M | Yg Wd | Yn M | Yn M | Yn M | Yn Wd | Yg W | Yg E3 | 14 |
| 15 | Yg E | Yg W | Yn F | Yn F | Yg E | Yg W | Yg E | Yg F | Yn E | Yn E4 | Yn E | Yn E2 | Yg M | Yg Wd | Yn M | Yn M | Yn M | Yn Wd | Yg W | Yg E3 | Yg W | Yg E1 | Yn W | Yn W | 15 |
| 16 | Yn E | Yn E4 | Yg E | Yg F | Yn E | Yn E4 | Yn E | Yn E2 | Yg M | Yg Wd | Yg M | Yg M | Yn M | Yn Wd | Yg W | Yg E3 | Yg W | Yg E1 | Yn W | Yn W | Yn W | Yn F | Yg Wd | Yg W | 16 |
| 17 | Yg M | Yg Wd | Yn E | Yn E2 | Yg M | Yg Wd | Yg M | Yg M | Yn M | Yn Wd | Yn M | Yn M | Yg W | Yg E1 | Yn W | Yn W | Yn W | Yn F | Yg Wd | Yg W | Yg Wd | Yg F | Yn Wd | Yn E4 | 17 |
| 18 | Yn M | Yn Wd | Yg M | Yg M | Yn M | Yn Wd | Yn M | Yn M | Yg W | Yg E1 | Yg W | Yg E3 | Yn W | Yn F | Yg Wd | Yg W | Yg Wd | Yg F | Yn Wd | Yn E4 | Yn Wd | Yn E2 | Yg F | Yg Wd | 18 |
| 19 | Yg W | Yg E1 | Yn M | Yn M | Yg W | Yg E1 | Yg W | Yg E3 | Yn W | Yn F | Yn W | Yn W | Yg Wd | Yg F | Yn Wd | Yn E4 | Yn Wd | Yn E2 | Yg F | Yg Wd | Yg F | Yg M | Yn F | Yn Wd | 19 |
| 20 | Yn W | Yn F | Yg W | Yg E3 | Yn W | Yn F | Yn W | Yn W | Yg Wd | Yg F | Yg Wd | Yg W | Yn Wd | Yn E2 | Yg F | Yg Wd | Yg F | Yg M | Yn F | Yn Wd | Yn F | Yn M | Yg E | Yg E1 | 20 |
| 21 | Yg Wd | Yg F | Yn W | Yn W | Yg Wd | Yg F | Yg Wd | Yg W | Yn Wd | Yn E2 | Yn Wd | Yn E4 | Yg F | Yg M | Yn F | Yn Wd | Yn F | Yn M | Yg E | Yg E1 | Yg E | Yg E3 | Yn E | Yn F | 21 |
| 22 | Yn Wd | Yn E2 | Yg Wd | Yg W | Yn Wd | Yn E2 | Yn Wd | Yn E4 | Yg F | Yg M | Yg F | Yg Wd | Yn F | Yn M | Yg E | Yg E1 | Yg E | Yg E3 | Yn E | Yn F | Yn E | Yn W | Yg M | Yg F | 22 |
| 23 | Yg F | Yg M | Yn Wd | Yn E4 | Yg F | Yg M | Yg F | Yg Wd | Yn F | Yn M | Yn F | Yn Wd | Yg E | Yg E3 | Yn E | Yn F | Yn E | Yn W | Yg M | Yg F | Yg M | Yg W | Yn M | Yn E2 | 23 |
| 24 | Yn F | Yn M | Yg F | Yg Wd | Yn F | Yn M | Yn F | Yn Wd | Yg E | Yg E3 | Yg E | Yg E1 | Yn E | Yn W | Yg M | Yg F | Yg M | Yg W | Yn M | Yn E2 | Yn M | Yn E4 | Yg W | Yg M | 24 |
| 25 | Yg E | Yg E3 | Yn F | Yn Wd | Yg E | Yg E3 | Yg E | Yg E1 | Yn E | Yn W | Yn E | Yn F | Yg M | Yg W | Yn M | Yn E2 | Yn M | Yn E4 | Yg W | Yg M | Yg W | Yg Wd | Yn W | Yn M | 25 |
| 26 | Yn E | Yn W | Yg E | Yg E1 | Yn E | Yn W | Yn E | Yn F | Yg M | Yg W | Yg M | Yg F | Yn M | Yn E4 | Yg W | Yg M | Yg W | Yg Wd | Yn W | Yn M | Yn W | Yn Wd | Yg Wd | Yg E3 | 26 |
| 27 | Yg M | Yg W | Yn E | Yn F | Yg M | Yg W | Yg M | Yg F | Yn M | Yn E4 | Yn M | Yn E2 | Yg W | Yg Wd | Yn W | Yn M | Yn W | Yn Wd | Yg Wd | Yg E3 | Yg Wd | Yg E1 | Yn Wd | Yn W | 27 |
| 28 | Yn M | Yn E4 | Yg M | Yg F | Yn M | Yn E4 | Yn M | Yn E2 | Yg W | Yg Wd | Yg W | Yg M | Yn W | Yn Wd | Yg Wd | Yg E3 | Yg Wd | Yg E1 | Yn Wd | Yn W | Yn Wd | Yn F | Yg F | Yg W | 28 |
| 29 | Yg W | Yg Wd | Yn M | Yn E2 | Yg W | Yg Wd | Yg W | Yg M | Yn W | Yn Wd | Yn W | Yn M | Yg Wd | Yg E1 | Yn Wd | Yn W | Yn Wd | Yn F | Yg F | Yg W | Yg F | Yg F | Yn F | Yn E4 | 29 |
| 30 | | | Yg W | Yg M | Yn W | Yn Wd | Yn W | Yn M | Yg Wd | Yg E1 | Yg Wd | Yg E3 | Yn Wd | Yn F | Yg F | Yg W | Yg F | Yg F | Yn F | Yn E4 | Yn F | Yn E2 | Yg E | Yg Wd | 30 |
| 31 | | | Yn W | Yn M | | | Yg Wd | Yg E3 | | | Yn Wd | Yn W | Yg F | Yg F | | | Yn F | Yn E2 | | | Yg E | Yg M | Yn E | Yn Wd | 31 |
| 1 | Yn W | Yn Wd | Yg Wd | Yg E3 | Yg Wd | Yg E1 | Yn Wd | Yn W | Yn Wd | Yn F | Yg F | Yg W | Yn F | Yn E2 | Yn F | Yn E4 | Yg E | Yg M | Yg E | Yg Wd | Yn E | Yn M | Yg M | Yg E1 | 1 |
| 2 | Yg Wd | Yg E1 | Yn Wd | Yn W | Yn Wd | Yn F | Yg F | Yg W | Yg F | Yg F | Yn F | Yn E4 | Yg E | Yg M | Yg E | Yg Wd | Yn E | Yn M | Yn E | Yn Wd | Yg M | Yg E3 | Yn M | Yn F | 2 |
| 3 | Yn Wd | Yn F | Yg F | Yg W | Yg F | Yg F | Yn F | Yn E4 | Yn F | Yn E2 | Yg E | Yg Wd | Yn E | Yn M | Yn E | Yn Wd | Yg M | Yg E3 | Yg M | Yg E1 | Yn M | Yn W | Yg W | Yg F | 3 |
| 4 | Yg F | Yg F | Yn F | Yn E4 | Yn F | Yn E2 | Yg E | Yg Wd | Yg E | Yg M | Yn E | Yn Wd | Yg M | Yg E3 | Yg M | Yg E1 | Yn M | Yn W | Yn M | Yn F | Yg W | Yg W | | | 4 |
| 5 | Yn F | Yn E2 | | | Yg E | Yg M | Yn E | Yn Wd | Yn E | Yn M | Yg M | Yg E1 | Yn M | Yn W | Yn M | Yn F | Yg W | Yg W | Yg W | Yg F | Yn W | Yn E4 | | | 5 |
| 6 | | | | | | | | | Yg M | Yg E3 | Yn M | Yn F | Yg W | Yg W | Yg W | Yg F | Yn W | Yn E4 | Yn W | Yn E2 | | | | | 6 |
| 7 | | | | | | | | | | | Yg W | Yg F | Yn W | Yn E4 | Yn W | Yn E2 | | | | | | | | | 7 |
| 8 | | | | | | | | | | | | | | | | | | | | | | | | | 8 |

# YEAR OF THE SNAKE

| | H | E | H | E | H | E | H | E | H | E | H | E | H | E | H | E | H | E | H | E | H | E | H | E | |
|---|---|---|---|---|---|---|---|---|---|---|---|---|---|---|---|---|---|---|---|---|---|---|---|---|---|
| YEAR | YEAR<br>Yn M | Yn F | 1941 | | | | | | | | | | | | | | | | | | | | 1942 | | |
| MONTH | 4 Feb - 5 Mar | | 6 Mar - 4 Apr | | 5 Apr - 5 May | | 6 May - 5 June | | 6 June - 6 Jul | | 7 Jul - 7 Aug | | 8 Aug - 7 Sep | | 8 Sep - 8 Oct | | 9 Oct - 7 Nov | | 8 Nov - 6 Dec | | 7 Dec - 5 Jan | | 6 Jan - 3 Feb | | |
| | Yg M | Yg Wd | Yn M | Yn Wd | Yg W | Yg E1 | Yn W | Yn F | Yg Wd | Yg F | Yn Wd | Yn E2 | Yg F | Yg M | Yn F | Yn M | Yg E | Yg E3 | Yn E | Yn W | Yg M | Yg W | Yn M | Yn E4 | |
| Starting time | 1st day | Mid-pt | 1st day | Mid-pt | 1st day | Mid-pt | 1st day | Mid-pt | 1st day | Mid-pt | 1st day | Mid-pt | 1st day | Mid-pt | 1st day | Mid-pt | 1st day | Mid-pt | 1st day | Mid-pt | 1st day | Mid-pt | 1st day | Mid-pt | |
| Date | 4 | 19 | 6 | 21 | 5 | 20 | 6 | 21 | 6 | 22 | 7 | 23 | 8 | 23 | 8 | 23 | 9 | 24 | 8 | 23 | 7 | 22 | 6 | 21 | |
| Hour | 1250 | 0857 | 0710 | 0821 | 1225 | 1951 | 0609 | 1923 | 1040 | 0334 | 2101 | 1427 | 0646 | 2121 | 0924 | 1833 | 0039 | 0328 | 0325 | 0038 | 1957 | 1345 | 0719 | 0024 | |
| DATE 4 | Yn W | Yn E2 | | | | | | | | | | | | | | | | | | | | | | | 4 |
| 5 | Yg Wd | Yg M | | | Yn W | Yn E2 | | | | | | | | | | | | | | | | | | | 5 |
| 6 | Yn Wd | Yn M | Yn W | Yn E4 | Yg Wd | Yg M | Yg Wd | Yg Wd | Yn Wd | Yn M | | | | | | | | | | | | | Yn E | Yn E2 | 6 |
| 7 | Yg F | Yg E3 | Yg Wd | Yg Wd | Yn Wd | Yn M | Yn Wd | Yn Wd | Yg F | Yg E3 | Yg F | Yg E1 | | | | | | | | | Yn E | Yn E4 | Yg M | Yg M | 7 |
| 8 | Yn F | Yn W | Yn Wd | Yn Wd | Yg F | Yg E3 | Yg F | Yg E1 | Yn F | Yn W | Yn F | Yn F | Yg E | Yg W | Yn E | Yn E2 | | | Yg M | Yg M | Yg M | Yg Wd | Yn M | Yn M | 8 |
| 9 | Yg E | Yg W | Yg F | Yg E1 | Yn F | Yn W | Yn F | Yn F | Yg E | Yg W | Yg E | Yg F | Yn E | Yn E4 | Yg M | Yg M | Yg M | Yg Wd | Yn M | Yn M | Yn M | Yn Wd | Yg W | Yg E3 | 9 |
| 10 | Yn E | Yn E4 | Yn F | Yn F | Yg E | Yg W | Yg E | Yg F | Yn E | Yn E4 | Yn E | Yn E2 | Yg M | Yg Wd | Yn M | Yn M | Yn M | Yn Wd | Yg W | Yg E3 | Yg W | Yg E1 | Yn W | Yn W | 10 |
| 11 | Yg M | Yg Wd | Yg E | Yg F | Yn E | Yn E4 | Yn E | Yn E2 | Yg M | Yg Wd | Yg M | Yg M | Yn M | Yn Wd | Yg W | Yg E3 | Yg W | Yg E1 | Yn W | Yn W | Yn W | Yn F | Yg Wd | Yg W | 11 |
| 12 | Yn M | Yn Wd | Yn E | Yn E2 | Yg M | Yg Wd | Yg M | Yg M | Yn M | Yn Wd | Yn M | Yn M | Yg W | Yg E1 | Yn W | Yn W | Yn W | Yn F | Yg Wd | Yg W | Yg Wd | Yg F | Yn Wd | Yn E4 | 12 |
| 13 | Yg W | Yg E1 | Yg M | Yg M | Yn M | Yn Wd | Yn M | Yn M | Yg W | Yg E1 | Yg W | Yg E3 | Yn W | Yn F | Yg Wd | Yg W | Yg Wd | Yg F | Yn Wd | Yn E4 | Yn Wd | Yn E2 | Yg F | Yg Wd | 13 |
| 14 | Yn W | Yn F | Yn M | Yn M | Yg W | Yg E1 | Yg W | Yg E3 | Yn W | Yn F | Yn W | Yn W | Yg Wd | Yg F | Yn Wd | Yn E4 | Yn Wd | Yn E2 | Yg F | Yg Wd | Yg F | Yg M | Yn F | Yn Wd | 14 |
| 15 | Yg Wd | Yg F | Yg W | Yg E3 | Yn W | Yn F | Yn W | Yn W | Yg Wd | Yg F | Yg Wd | Yg W | Yn Wd | Yn E2 | Yg F | Yg Wd | Yg F | Yg M | Yn F | Yn Wd | Yn F | Yn M | Yg E | Yg E1 | 15 |
| 16 | Yn Wd | Yn E2 | Yn W | Yn W | Yg Wd | Yg F | Yg Wd | Yg W | Yn Wd | Yn E2 | Yn Wd | Yn E4 | Yg F | Yg M | Yn F | Yn Wd | Yn F | Yn M | Yg E | Yg E1 | Yg E | Yg E3 | Yn E | Yn F | 16 |
| 17 | Yg F | Yg M | Yg Wd | Yg W | Yn Wd | Yn E2 | Yn Wd | Yn E4 | Yg F | Yg M | Yg F | Yg Wd | Yn F | Yn M | Yg E | Yg E1 | Yg E | Yg E3 | Yn E | Yn F | Yn E | Yn W | Yg M | Yg F | 17 |
| 18 | Yn F | Yn M | Yn Wd | Yn E4 | Yg F | Yg M | Yg F | Yg Wd | Yn F | Yn M | Yn F | Yn Wd | Yg E | Yg E3 | Yn E | Yn F | Yn E | Yn W | Yg M | Yg F | Yg M | Yg W | Yn M | Yn E2 | 18 |
| 19 | Yg E | Yg E3 | Yg F | Yg Wd | Yn F | Yn M | Yn F | Yn Wd | Yg E | Yg E3 | Yg E | Yg E1 | Yn E | Yn W | Yg M | Yg F | Yg M | Yg W | Yn M | Yn E2 | Yn M | Yn E4 | Yg W | Yg M | 19 |
| 20 | Yn E | Yn W | Yn F | Yn Wd | Yg E | Yg E3 | Yg E | Yg E1 | Yn E | Yn W | Yn E | Yn F | Yg M | Yg W | Yn M | Yn E2 | Yn M | Yn E4 | Yg W | Yg M | Yg W | Yg Wd | Yn W | Yn M | 20 |
| 21 | Yg M | Yg W | Yg E | Yg E1 | Yn E | Yn W | Yn E | Yn F | Yg M | Yg W | Yg M | Yg F | Yn M | Yn E4 | Yg W | Yg M | Yg W | Yg Wd | Yn W | Yn M | Yn W | Yn Wd | Yg Wd | Yg E3 | 21 |
| 22 | Yn M | Yn E4 | Yn E | Yn F | Yg M | Yg W | Yg M | Yg F | Yn M | Yn E4 | Yn M | Yn E2 | Yg W | Yg Wd | Yn W | Yn M | Yn W | Yn Wd | Yg Wd | Yg E3 | Yg Wd | Yg E1 | Yn Wd | Yn W | 22 |
| 23 | Yg W | Yg Wd | Yg M | Yg F | Yn M | Yn E4 | Yn M | Yn E2 | Yg W | Yg Wd | Yg W | Yg M | Yn W | Yn Wd | Yg Wd | Yg E3 | Yg Wd | Yg E1 | Yn Wd | Yn W | Yn Wd | Yn F | Yg F | Yg W | 23 |
| 24 | Yn W | Yn Wd | Yn M | Yn E2 | Yg W | Yg Wd | Yg W | Yg M | Yn W | Yn Wd | Yn W | Yn M | Yg Wd | Yg E1 | Yn Wd | Yn W | Yn Wd | Yn F | Yg F | Yg W | Yg F | Yg F | Yn F | Yn E4 | 24 |
| 25 | Yg Wd | Yg E1 | Yg W | Yg M | Yn W | Yn Wd | Yn W | Yn M | Yg Wd | Yg E1 | Yg Wd | Yg E3 | Yn Wd | Yn F | Yg F | Yg W | Yg F | Yg F | Yn F | Yn E4 | Yn F | Yn E2 | Yg E | Yg Wd | 25 |
| 26 | Yn Wd | Yn F | Yn W | Yn M | Yg Wd | Yg E1 | Yg Wd | Yg E3 | Yn Wd | Yn F | Yn Wd | Yn W | Yg F | Yg F | Yn F | Yn E4 | Yn F | Yn E2 | Yg E | Yg Wd | Yg E | Yg M | Yn E | Yn Wd | 26 |
| 27 | Yg F | Yg F | Yg Wd | Yg E3 | Yn Wd | Yn F | Yn Wd | Yn W | Yg F | Yg F | Yg F | Yg W | Yn F | Yn E2 | Yg E | Yg Wd | Yg E | Yg M | Yn E | Yn Wd | Yn E | Yn M | Yg M | Yg E1 | 27 |
| 28 | Yn F | Yn E2 | Yn Wd | Yn W | Yg F | Yg F | Yg F | Yg W | Yn F | Yn E2 | Yn F | Yn E4 | Yg E | Yg M | Yn E | Yn Wd | Yn E | Yn M | Yg M | Yg E1 | Yg M | Yg E3 | Yn M | Yn F | 28 |
| 29 | | | Yg F | Yg W | Yn F | Yn E2 | Yn F | Yn E4 | Yg E | Yg M | Yg E | Yg Wd | Yn E | Yn M | Yg M | Yg E1 | Yg M | Yg E3 | Yn M | Yn F | Yn M | Yn W | Yg W | Yg F | 29 |
| 30 | | | Yn F | Yn E4 | Yg E | Yg M | Yg E | Yg Wd | Yn E | Yn M | Yn E | Yn Wd | Yg M | Yg E3 | Yn M | Yn F | Yn M | Yn W | Yg W | Yg F | Yg W | Yg W | Yn W | Yn E2 | 30 |
| 31 | | | Yg E | Yg Wd | | | Yn E | Yn Wd | | | Yg M | Yg E1 | Yn M | Yn W | | | Yg W | Yg W | | | Yn W | Yn E4 | Yg Wd | Yg M | 31 |
| 1 | Yg E | Yg M | Yn E | Yn Wd | Yn E | Yn M | Yg M | Yg E1 | Yg M | Yg E3 | Yn M | Yn F | Yg W | Yg W | Yg W | Yg F | Yn W | Yn E4 | Yn W | Yn E2 | Yg Wd | Yg Wd | Yn Wd | Yn M | 1 |
| 2 | Yn E | Yn M | Yg M | Yg E1 | Yg M | Yg E3 | Yn M | Yn F | Yn M | Yn W | Yg W | Yg F | Yn W | Yn E4 | Yn W | Yn E2 | Yg Wd | Yg Wd | Yg Wd | Yg M | Yn Wd | Yn Wd | Yg F | Yg E3 | 2 |
| 3 | Yg M | Yg E3 | Yn M | Yn F | Yn M | Yn W | Yg W | Yg F | Yg W | Yg W | Yn W | Yn E2 | Yg Wd | Yg Wd | Yg Wd | Yg M | Yn Wd | Yn Wd | Yn Wd | Yn M | Yg F | Yg E1 | Yn F | Yn W | 3 |
| 4 | Yn M | Yn W | Yg W | Yg F | Yg W | Yg W | Yn W | Yn E2 | Yn W | Yn E4 | Yg Wd | Yg M | Yn Wd | Yn Wd | Yn Wd | Yn M | Yg F | Yg E1 | Yg F | Yg E3 | Yn F | Yn F | | | 4 |
| 5 | Yg W | Yg W | | | Yn W | Yn E4 | Yg Wd | Yg M | Yg Wd | Yg Wd | Yn Wd | Yn M | Yg F | Yg E1 | Yg F | Yg E3 | Yn F | Yn F | Yn F | Yn W | Yg E | Yg F | | | 5 |
| 6 | | | | | | | | | Yn Wd | Yn Wd | Yg F | Yg E3 | Yn F | Yn F | Yn F | Yn W | Yg E | Yg F | Yg E | Yg W | | | | | 6 |
| 7 | | | | | | | | | | | Yn F | Yn W | Yg E | Yg F | Yg E | Yg W | Yn E | Yn E2 | | | | | | | 7 |
| 8 | | | | | | | | | | | | | | | Yn E | Yn E4 | | | | | | | | | 8 |

# YEAR OF THE HORSE

| | H | E | H | E | H | E | H | E | H | E | H | E | H | E | H | E | H | E | H | E | H | E | H | E |
|---|---|---|---|---|---|---|---|---|---|---|---|---|---|---|---|---|---|---|---|---|---|---|---|---|
| **YEAR** | YEAR Yg W | Yg F | 1942 | | | | | | | | | | | | | | | | | | | | 1943 | |
| **MONTH** | 4 Feb - 5 Mar | | 6 Mar - 4 Apr | | 5 Apr - 5 May | | 6 May - 5 June | | 6 June - 7 Jul | | 8 Jul - 7 Aug | | 8 Aug - 7 Sep | | 8 Sep - 8 Oct | | 9 Oct - 7 Nov | | 8 Nov - 7 Dec | | 8 Dec - 5 Jan | | 6 Jan - 4 Feb | |
| | Yg W | Yg Wd | Yn W | Yn Wd | Yg Wd | Yg E1 | Yn Wd | Yn F | Yg F | Yg F | Yn F | Yn E2 | Yg E | Yg M | Yn E | Yn M | Yg M | Yg E3 | Yn M | Yn W | Yg W | Yg W | Yn W | Yn E4 |
| **Starting time** | 1st day | Mid-pt | 1st day | Mid-pt | 1st day | Mid-pt | 1st day | Mid-pt | 1st day | Mid-pt | 1st day | Mid-pt | 1st day | Mid-pt | 1st day | Mid-pt | 1st day | Mid-pt | 1st day | Mid-pt | 1st day | Mid-pt | 1st day | Mid-pt |
| Date | 4 | 19 | 6 | 21 | 5 | 21 | 6 | 22 | 6 | 22 | 8 | 23 | 8 | 24 | 8 | 24 | 9 | 24 | 8 | 23 | 8 | 22 | 6 | 21 |
| Hour | 1849 | 1447 | 1310 | 1411 | 1824 | 0138 | 1207 | 0109 | 1637 | 0917 | 0252 | 2008 | 1231 | 0259 | 1507 | 0017 | 0622 | 0916 | 0912 | 0631 | 0147 | 1940 | 1255 | 0619 |
| **DATE 4** | Yg E | Yg W | | | | | | | | | | | | | | | | | | | | | | |
| 5 | Yn E | Yn E4 | | | Yg E | Yg W | | | | | | | | | | | | | | | | | | |
| 6 | Yg M | Yg Wd | Yg E | Yg F | Yn E | Yn E4 | Yn E | Yn E2 | Yg M | Yg Wd | | | | | | | | | | | | | Yg Wd | Yg W |
| 7 | Yn M | Yn Wd | Yn E | Yn E2 | Yg M | Yg Wd | Yg M | Yg M | Yn M | Yn Wd | | | | | | | | | | | | | Yn Wd | Yn E4 |
| 8 | Yg W | Yg E1 | Yg M | Yg M | Yn M | Yn Wd | Yn M | Yn M | Yg W | Yg E1 | Yg W | Yg E3 | Yn W | Yn F | Yg Wd | Yg W | | | Yn Wd | Yn E4 | Yn Wd | Yn E2 | Yg F | Yg Wd |
| 9 | Yn W | Yn F | Yn M | Yn M | Yg W | Yg E1 | Yg W | Yg E3 | Yn W | Yn F | Yn W | Yn W | Yg Wd | Yg F | Yn Wd | Yn E4 | Yn Wd | Yn E2 | Yg F | Yg Wd | Yg F | Yg M | Yn F | Yn Wd |
| 10 | Yg Wd | Yg F | Yg W | Yg E3 | Yn W | Yn F | Yn W | Yn W | Yg Wd | Yg F | Yg Wd | Yg W | Yn Wd | Yn E2 | Yg F | Yg Wd | Yg F | Yg M | Yn F | Yn Wd | Yn F | Yn M | Yg E | Yg E1 |
| 11 | Yn Wd | Yn E2 | Yn W | Yn W | Yg Wd | Yg F | Yg Wd | Yg W | Yn Wd | Yn E2 | Yn Wd | Yn E4 | Yg F | Yg M | Yn F | Yn Wd | Yn F | Yn M | Yg E | Yg E1 | Yg E | Yg E3 | Yn E | Yn F |
| 12 | Yg F | Yg M | Yg Wd | Yg W | Yn Wd | Yn E2 | Yn Wd | Yn E4 | Yg F | Yg M | Yg F | Yg Wd | Yn F | Yn M | Yg E | Yg E1 | Yg E | Yg E3 | Yn E | Yn F | Yn E | Yn W | Yg M | Yg F |
| 13 | Yn F | Yn M | Yn Wd | Yn E4 | Yg F | Yg M | Yg F | Yg Wd | Yn F | Yn M | Yn F | Yn Wd | Yg E | Yg E3 | Yn E | Yn F | Yn E | Yn W | Yg M | Yg F | Yg M | Yg W | Yn M | Yn E2 |
| 14 | Yg E | Yg E3 | Yg F | Yg Wd | Yn F | Yn M | Yn F | Yn Wd | Yg E | Yg E3 | Yg E | Yg E1 | Yn E | Yn W | Yg M | Yg F | Yg M | Yg W | Yn M | Yn E2 | Yn M | Yn E4 | Yg W | Yg M |
| 15 | Yn E | Yn W | Yn F | Yn Wd | Yg E | Yg E3 | Yg E | Yg E1 | Yn E | Yn W | Yn E | Yn F | Yg M | Yg W | Yn M | Yn E2 | Yn M | Yn E4 | Yg W | Yg M | Yg W | Yg Wd | Yn W | Yn M |
| 16 | Yg M | Yg W | Yg E | Yg E1 | Yn E | Yn W | Yn E | Yn F | Yg M | Yg W | Yg M | Yg F | Yn M | Yn E4 | Yg W | Yg M | Yg W | Yg Wd | Yn W | Yn M | Yn W | Yn Wd | Yg Wd | Yg E3 |
| 17 | Yn M | Yn E4 | Yn E | Yn F | Yg M | Yg W | Yg M | Yg F | Yn M | Yn E4 | Yn M | Yn E2 | Yg W | Yg Wd | Yn W | Yn M | Yn W | Yn Wd | Yg Wd | Yg E3 | Yg Wd | Yg E1 | Yn Wd | Yn W |
| 18 | Yg W | Yg Wd | Yg M | Yg F | Yn M | Yn E4 | Yn M | Yn E2 | Yg W | Yg Wd | Yg W | Yg M | Yn W | Yn Wd | Yg Wd | Yg E3 | Yg Wd | Yg E1 | Yn Wd | Yn W | Yn Wd | Yn F | Yg F | Yg W |
| 19 | Yn W | Yn Wd | Yn M | Yn E2 | Yg W | Yg Wd | Yg W | Yg M | Yn W | Yn Wd | Yn W | Yn M | Yg Wd | Yg E1 | Yn Wd | Yn W | Yn Wd | Yn F | Yg F | Yg W | Yg F | Yg F | Yn F | Yn E4 |
| 20 | Yg Wd | Yg E1 | Yg W | Yg M | Yn W | Yn Wd | Yn W | Yn M | Yg Wd | Yg E1 | Yg Wd | Yg E3 | Yn Wd | Yn F | Yg F | Yg W | Yg F | Yg F | Yn F | Yn E4 | Yn F | Yn E2 | Yg E | Yg Wd |
| 21 | Yn Wd | Yn F | Yn W | Yn M | Yg Wd | Yg E1 | Yg Wd | Yg E3 | Yn Wd | Yn F | Yn Wd | Yn W | Yg F | Yg F | Yn F | Yn E4 | Yn F | Yn E2 | Yg E | Yg Wd | Yg E | Yg M | Yn E | Yn Wd |
| 22 | Yg F | Yg F | Yg Wd | Yg E3 | Yn Wd | Yn F | Yn Wd | Yn W | Yg F | Yg F | Yg F | Yg W | Yn F | Yn E2 | Yg E | Yg Wd | Yg E | Yg M | Yn E | Yn Wd | Yn E | Yn M | Yg M | Yg E1 |
| 23 | Yn F | Yn E2 | Yn Wd | Yn W | Yg F | Yg F | Yg F | Yg W | Yn F | Yn E2 | Yn F | Yn E4 | Yg E | Yg M | Yn E | Yn Wd | Yn E | Yn M | Yg M | Yg E1 | Yg M | Yg E3 | Yn M | Yn F |
| 24 | Yg E | Yg M | Yg F | Yg W | Yn F | Yn E2 | Yn F | Yn E4 | Yg E | Yg M | Yg E | Yg Wd | Yn E | Yn M | Yg M | Yg E1 | Yg M | Yg E3 | Yn M | Yn F | Yn M | Yn W | Yg W | Yg F |
| 25 | Yn E | Yn M | Yn F | Yn E4 | Yg E | Yg M | Yg E | Yg Wd | Yn E | Yn M | Yn E | Yn Wd | Yg M | Yg E3 | Yn M | Yn F | Yn M | Yn W | Yg W | Yg F | Yg W | Yg W | Yn W | Yn E2 |
| 26 | Yg M | Yg E3 | Yg E | Yg Wd | Yn E | Yn M | Yn E | Yn Wd | Yg M | Yg E3 | Yg M | Yg E1 | Yn M | Yn W | Yg W | Yg F | Yg W | Yg W | Yn W | Yn E2 | Yn W | Yn E4 | Yg Wd | Yg M |
| 27 | Yn M | Yn W | Yn E | Yn Wd | Yg M | Yg E3 | Yg M | Yg E1 | Yn M | Yn W | Yn M | Yn F | Yg W | Yg W | Yn W | Yn E2 | Yn W | Yn E4 | Yg Wd | Yg M | Yg Wd | Yg Wd | Yn Wd | Yn M |
| 28 | Yg W | Yg W | Yg M | Yg E1 | Yn M | Yn W | Yn M | Yn F | Yg W | Yg W | Yg W | Yg F | Yn W | Yn E4 | Yg Wd | Yg M | Yg Wd | Yg Wd | Yn Wd | Yn M | Yn Wd | Yn Wd | Yg F | Yg E3 |
| 29 | | | Yn M | Yn F | Yg W | Yg W | Yg W | Yg F | Yn W | Yn E4 | Yn W | Yn E2 | Yg Wd | Yg Wd | Yn Wd | Yn M | Yn Wd | Yn Wd | Yg F | Yg E3 | Yg F | Yg E1 | Yn F | Yn W |
| 30 | | | Yg W | Yg F | Yn W | Yn E4 | Yn W | Yn E2 | Yg Wd | Yg Wd | Yg Wd | Yg M | Yn Wd | Yn Wd | Yg F | Yg E3 | Yg F | Yg E1 | Yn F | Yn W | Yn F | Yn F | Yg E | Yg W |
| 31 | | | Yn W | Yn E2 | | | Yg Wd | Yg M | | | Yn Wd | Yn M | Yg F | Yg E1 | | | Yn F | Yn F | | | Yg E | Yg F | Yn E | Yn E4 |
| 1 | Yn W | Yn E4 | Yg Wd | Yg M | Yg Wd | Yg Wd | Yn Wd | Yn M | Yn Wd | Yn Wd | Yg F | Yg E3 | Yn F | Yn F | Yn F | Yn W | Yg E | Yg F | Yg E | Yg W | Yn E | Yn E2 | Yg M | Yg Wd |
| 2 | Yg Wd | Yg Wd | Yn Wd | Yn M | Yn Wd | Yn Wd | Yg F | Yg E3 | Yg F | Yg E1 | Yn F | Yn W | Yg E | Yg F | Yg E | Yg W | Yn E | Yn E2 | Yn E | Yn E4 | Yg M | Yg M | Yn M | Yn Wd |
| 3 | Yn Wd | Yn Wd | Yg F | Yg E3 | Yg F | Yg E1 | Yn F | Yn W | Yn F | Yn F | Yg E | Yg W | Yn E | Yn E2 | Yn E | Yn E4 | Yg M | Yg M | Yg M | Yg Wd | Yn M | Yn M | Yg W | Yg E1 |
| 4 | Yg F | Yg E1 | Yn F | Yn W | Yn F | Yn F | Yg E | Yg W | Yg E | Yg F | Yn E | Yn E4 | Yg M | Yg M | Yg M | Yg Wd | Yn M | Yn M | Yn M | Yn Wd | Yg W | Yg E3 | Yn W | Yn F |
| 5 | Yn F | Yn F | | | Yg E | Yg F | Yn E | Yn E4 | Yn E | Yn E2 | Yg M | Yg Wd | Yn M | Yn M | Yn M | Yn Wd | Yg W | Yg E3 | Yg W | Yg E1 | Yn W | Yn W | | |
| 6 | | | | | | | | | Yg M | Yg M | Yn M | Yn Wd | Yg W | Yg E3 | Yg W | Yg E1 | Yn W | Yn W | Yn W | Yn F | | | | |
| 7 | | | | | | | | | Yn M | Yn M | Yg W | Yg E1 | Yn W | Yn W | Yn W | Yn F | Yg Wd | Yg W | Yg Wd | Yg F | | | | |
| 8 | | | | | | | | | | | | | | | Yg Wd | Yg F | | | | | | | | |

# YEAR OF THE GOAT

| | H | E | H | E | H | E | H | E | H | E | H | E | H | E | H | E | H | E | H | E | H | E | H | E | |
|---|---|---|---|---|---|---|---|---|---|---|---|---|---|---|---|---|---|---|---|---|---|---|---|---|---|
| YEAR | YEAR<br>Yn W | Yn E2 | 1943 | | | | | | | | | | | | | | | | | | 1944 | | | | |
| MONTH | 5 Feb - 5 Mar<br>Yg Wd | Yg Wd | 6 Mar - 5 Apr<br>Yn Wd | Yn Wd | 6 Apr - 5 May<br>Yg F | Yg E1 | 6 May - 5 June<br>Yn F | Yn F | 6 June - 7 Jul<br>Yg E | Yg F | 8 Jul - 7 Aug<br>Yn E | Yn E2 | 8 Aug - 7 Sep<br>Yg M | Yg M | 8 Sep - 8 Oct<br>Yn M | Yn M | 9 Oct - 7 Nov<br>Yg W | Yg E3 | 8 Nov - 7 Dec<br>Yn W | Yn W | 8 Dec - 5 Jan<br>Yg Wd | Yg W | 6 Jan - 4 Feb<br>Yn Wd | Yn E4 | |
| Starting time | 1st day | Mid-pt | 1st day | Mid-pt | 1st day | Mid-pt | 1st day | Mid-pt | 1st day | Mid-pt | 1st day | Mid-pt | 1st day | Mid-pt | 1st day | Mid-pt | 1st day | Mid-pt | 1st day | Mid-pt | 1st day | Mid-pt | 1st day | Mid-pt | |
| Date | 5 | 19 | 6 | 21 | 6 | 21 | 6 | 22 | 6 | 22 | 8 | 24 | 8 | 24 | 8 | 24 | 9 | 24 | 8 | 23 | 8 | 23 | 6 | 21 | |
| Hour | 0041 | 2041 | 1859 | 2003 | 0012 | 0732 | 1754 | 0703 | 2219 | 1513 | 0839 | 0205 | 1819 | 0855 | 2056 | 0612 | 1211 | 1509 | 1459 | 1222 | 0733 | 0130 | 1840 | 1208 | |
| DATE 4 | | | | | | | | | | | | | | | | | | | | | | | | | 4 |
| 5 | Yg Wd | Yg F | | | | | | | | | | | | | | | | | | | | | | | 5 |
| 6 | Yn Wd | Yn E2 | Yn W | Yn W | Yg Wd | Yg F | Yg Wd | Yg W | Yn Wd | Yn E2 | | | | | | | | | | | | | Yn E | Yn F | 6 |
| 7 | Yg F | Yg M | Yg Wd | Yg W | Yn Wd | Yn E2 | Yn Wd | Yn E4 | Yg F | Yg M | | | | | | | | | | | | | Yg M | Yg F | 7 |
| 8 | Yn F | Yn M | Yn Wd | Yn E4 | Yg F | Yg M | Yg F | Yg Wd | Yn F | Yn M | Yn F | Yn Wd | Yg E | Yg E3 | Yn E | Yn F | | | Yg M | Yg F | Yg M | Yg W | Yn M | Yn E2 | 8 |
| 9 | Yg E | Yg E3 | Yg F | Yg Wd | Yn F | Yn M | Yn F | Yn Wd | Yg E | Yg E3 | Yg E | Yg E1 | Yn E | Yn W | Yg M | Yg F | Yg M | Yg W | Yn M | Yn E2 | Yn M | Yn E4 | Yg W | Yg M | 9 |
| 10 | Yn E | Yn W | Yn F | Yn Wd | Yg E | Yg E3 | Yg E | Yg E1 | Yn E | Yn W | Yn E | Yn F | Yg M | Yg W | Yn M | Yn E2 | Yn M | Yn E4 | Yg W | Yg M | Yg W | Yg Wd | Yn W | Yn M | 10 |
| 11 | Yg M | Yg W | Yg E | Yg E1 | Yn E | Yn W | Yn E | Yn F | Yg M | Yg W | Yg M | Yg F | Yn M | Yn E4 | Yg W | Yg M | Yg W | Yg Wd | Yn W | Yn M | Yn W | Yn Wd | Yg Wd | Yg E3 | 11 |
| 12 | Yn M | Yn E4 | Yn E | Yn F | Yg M | Yg W | Yg M | Yg F | Yn M | Yn E4 | Yn M | Yn E2 | Yg W | Yg Wd | Yn W | Yn M | Yn W | Yn Wd | Yg Wd | Yg E3 | Yg Wd | Yg E1 | Yn Wd | Yn W | 12 |
| 13 | Yg W | Yg Wd | Yg M | Yg F | Yn M | Yn E4 | Yn M | Yn E2 | Yg W | Yg Wd | Yg W | Yg M | Yn W | Yn Wd | Yg Wd | Yg E3 | Yg Wd | Yg E1 | Yn Wd | Yn W | Yn Wd | Yn F | Yg F | Yg W | 13 |
| 14 | Yn W | Yn Wd | Yn M | Yn E2 | Yg W | Yg Wd | Yg W | Yg M | Yn W | Yn Wd | Yn W | Yn M | Yg Wd | Yg E1 | Yn Wd | Yn W | Yn Wd | Yn F | Yg F | Yg W | Yg F | Yg F | Yn F | Yn E4 | 14 |
| 15 | Yg Wd | Yg E1 | Yg W | Yg M | Yn W | Yn Wd | Yn W | Yn M | Yg Wd | Yg E1 | Yg Wd | Yg E3 | Yn Wd | Yn F | Yg F | Yg W | Yg F | Yg F | Yn F | Yn E4 | Yn F | Yn E2 | Yg E | Yg Wd | 15 |
| 16 | Yn Wd | Yn F | Yn W | Yn M | Yg Wd | Yg E1 | Yg Wd | Yg E3 | Yn Wd | Yn F | Yn Wd | Yn W | Yg F | Yg F | Yn F | Yn E4 | Yn F | Yn E2 | Yg E | Yg Wd | Yg E | Yg M | Yn E | Yn Wd | 16 |
| 17 | Yg F | Yg F | Yg Wd | Yg E3 | Yn Wd | Yn F | Yn Wd | Yn W | Yg F | Yg F | Yg F | Yg W | Yn F | Yn E2 | Yg E | Yg Wd | Yg E | Yg M | Yn E | Yn Wd | Yn E | Yn M | Yg M | Yg E1 | 17 |
| 18 | Yn F | Yn E2 | Yn Wd | Yn W | Yg F | Yg F | Yg F | Yg W | Yn F | Yn E2 | Yn F | Yn E4 | Yg E | Yg M | Yn E | Yn Wd | Yn E | Yn M | Yg M | Yg E1 | Yg M | Yg E3 | Yn M | Yn F | 18 |
| 19 | Yg E | Yg M | Yg F | Yg W | Yn F | Yn E2 | Yn F | Yn E4 | Yg E | Yg M | Yg E | Yg Wd | Yn E | Yn M | Yg M | Yg E1 | Yg M | Yg E3 | Yn M | Yn F | Yn M | Yn W | Yg W | Yg F | 19 |
| 20 | Yn E | Yn M | Yn F | Yn E4 | Yg E | Yg M | Yg E | Yg Wd | Yn E | Yn M | Yn E | Yn Wd | Yg M | Yg E3 | Yn M | Yn F | Yn M | Yn W | Yg W | Yg F | Yg W | Yg W | Yn W | Yn E2 | 20 |
| 21 | Yg M | Yg E3 | Yg E | Yg Wd | Yn E | Yn M | Yn E | Yn Wd | Yg M | Yg E3 | Yg M | Yg E1 | Yn M | Yn W | Yg W | Yg F | Yg W | Yg W | Yn W | Yn E2 | Yn W | Yn E4 | Yg Wd | Yg M | 21 |
| 22 | Yn M | Yn W | Yn E | Yn Wd | Yg M | Yg E3 | Yg M | Yg E1 | Yn M | Yn W | Yn M | Yn F | Yg W | Yg W | Yn W | Yn E2 | Yn W | Yn E4 | Yg Wd | Yg M | Yg Wd | Yg Wd | Yn Wd | Yn M | 22 |
| 23 | Yg W | Yg W | Yg M | Yg F | Yn M | Yn W | Yn M | Yn F | Yg W | Yg W | Yg W | Yg F | Yn W | Yn E4 | Yg Wd | Yg M | Yg Wd | Yg Wd | Yn Wd | Yn M | Yn Wd | Yn Wd | Yg F | Yg E3 | 23 |
| 24 | Yn W | Yn E4 | Yn M | Yn F | Yg W | Yg W | Yg W | Yg F | Yn W | Yn E4 | Yn W | Yn E2 | Yg Wd | Yg Wd | Yn Wd | Yn M | Yn Wd | Yn Wd | Yg F | Yg E3 | Yg F | Yg E1 | Yn F | Yn W | 24 |
| 25 | Yg Wd | Yg Wd | Yg W | Yg E | Yn W | Yn E4 | Yn W | Yn E2 | Yg Wd | Yg Wd | Yg Wd | Yg M | Yn Wd | Yn Wd | Yg F | Yg E3 | Yg F | Yg E1 | Yn F | Yn W | Yn F | Yn F | Yg E | Yg W | 25 |
| 26 | Yn Wd | Yn Wd | Yn W | Yn E2 | Yg Wd | Yg Wd | Yg Wd | Yg M | Yn Wd | Yn Wd | Yn Wd | Yn M | Yg F | Yg E1 | Yn F | Yn W | Yn F | Yn F | Yg E | Yg W | Yg E | Yg F | Yn E | Yn E4 | 26 |
| 27 | Yg F | Yg E1 | Yg Wd | Yg M | Yn Wd | Yn Wd | Yn Wd | Yn M | Yg F | Yg E1 | Yg F | Yg E3 | Yn F | Yn F | Yg E | Yg W | Yg E | Yg F | Yn E | Yn E4 | Yn E | Yn E2 | Yg M | Yg Wd | 27 |
| 28 | Yn F | Yn F | Yn Wd | Yn M | Yg F | Yg E1 | Yg F | Yg E3 | Yn F | Yn F | Yn F | Yn W | Yg E | Yg F | Yn E | Yn E4 | Yn E | Yn E2 | Yg M | Yg Wd | Yg M | Yg M | Yn M | Yn Wd | 28 |
| 29 | | | Yg F | Yg E3 | Yn F | Yn F | Yn F | Yn W | Yg E | Yg F | Yg E | Yg W | Yn E | Yn E2 | Yg M | Yg Wd | Yg M | Yg M | Yn M | Yn Wd | Yn M | Yn M | Yg W | Yg E1 | 29 |
| 30 | | | Yn F | Yn W | Yg E | Yg F | Yg E | Yg W | Yn E | Yn E2 | Yn E | Yn E4 | Yg M | Yg M | Yn M | Yn Wd | Yn M | Yn M | Yg W | Yg E1 | Yg W | Yg E3 | Yn W | Yn F | 30 |
| 31 | | | Yg E | Yg W | | | Yn E | Yn E4 | | | Yg M | Yg Wd | Yn M | Yn M | | | Yg W | Yg E3 | | | Yn W | Yn W | Yg Wd | Yg F | 31 |
| 1 | Yg E | Yg F | Yn E | Yn E4 | Yn E | Yn E2 | Yg M | Yg Wd | Yg M | Yg M | Yn M | Yn Wd | Yg W | Yg E3 | Yg W | Yg E1 | Yn W | Yn W | Yn W | Yn F | Yg Wd | Yg W | Yn Wd | Yn E2 | 1 |
| 2 | Yn E | Yn E2 | Yg M | Yg Wd | Yg M | Yg M | Yn M | Yn Wd | Yn M | Yn M | Yg W | Yg E1 | Yn W | Yn W | Yn W | Yn F | Yg Wd | Yg W | Yg Wd | Yg F | Yn Wd | Yn E4 | Yg F | Yg M | 2 |
| 3 | Yg M | Yg M | Yn M | Yn Wd | Yn M | Yn M | Yg W | Yg E1 | Yg W | Yg E3 | Yn W | Yn F | Yg Wd | Yg W | Yg Wd | Yg F | Yn Wd | Yn E4 | Yn Wd | Yn E2 | Yg F | Yg Wd | Yn F | Yn M | 3 |
| 4 | Yn M | Yn M | Yg W | Yg F | Yg W | Yg E3 | Yn W | Yn F | Yn W | Yn W | Yg Wd | Yg F | Yn Wd | Yn E4 | Yn Wd | Yn E2 | Yg F | Yg Wd | Yg F | Yg M | Yn F | Yn Wd | Yg E | Yg E3 | 4 |
| 5 | Yg W | Yg E3 | Yn W | Yn F | Yn W | Yn W | Yg Wd | Yg F | Yg Wd | Yg W | Yn Wd | Yn E2 | Yg F | Yg Wd | Yg F | Yg M | Yn F | Yn Wd | Yn F | Yn M | Yg E | Yg E1 | | | 5 |
| 6 | | | | | | | | | Yn Wd | Yn E4 | Yg F | Yg M | Yn F | Yn Wd | Yn F | Yn M | Yg E | Yg E1 | Yg E | Yg E3 | | | | | 6 |
| 7 | | | | | | | | | Yg F | Yg Wd | Yn F | Yn M | Yg E | Yg E1 | Yg E | Yg E3 | Yn E | Yn F | Yn E | Yn W | | | | | 7 |
| 8 | | | | | | | | | | | | | | | Yn E | Yn W | | | | | | | | | 8 |

# YEAR OF THE MONKEY

| | H | E | H | E | H | E | H | E | H | E | H | E | H | E | H | E | H | E | H | E | H | E | H | E | |
|---|---|---|---|---|---|---|---|---|---|---|---|---|---|---|---|---|---|---|---|---|---|---|---|---|---|
| YEAR | YEAR Yg Wd | Yg M | 1944 | | | | | | | | | | | | | | | | | | | | 1945 | | |
| MONTH | 5 Feb - 5 Mar | | 6 Mar - 4 Apr | | 5 Apr - 4 May | | 5 May - 5 June | | 6 June - 6 Jul | | 7 Jul - 7 Aug | | 8 Aug - 7 Sep | | 8 Sep - 7 Oct | | 8 Oct - 6 Nov | | 7 Nov - 6 Dec | | 7 Dec - 5 Jan | | 6 Jan - 3 Feb | | |
| | Yg F | Yg Wd | Yn F | Yn Wd | Yg E | Yg E1 | Yn E | Yn F | Yg M | Yg F | Yn M | Yn E2 | Yg W | Yg M | Yn W | Yn M | Yg Wd | Yg E3 | Yn Wd | Yn W | Yg F | Yg W | Yn F | Yn E4 | |
| Starting time | 1st day | Mid-pt | 1st day | Mid-pt | 1st day | Mid-pt | 1st day | Mid-pt | 1st day | Mid-pt | 1st day | Mid-pt | 1st day | Mid-pt | 1st day | Mid-pt | 1st day | Mid-pt | 1st day | Mid-pt | 1st day | Mid-pt | 1st day | Mid-pt | |
| Date | 5 | 20 | 6 | 21 | 5 | 20 | 5 | 21 | 6 | 21 | 7 | 23 | 8 | 23 | 8 | 23 | 8 | 23 | 7 | 22 | 7 | 22 | 6 | 20 | |
| Hour | 0623 | 0228 | 0041 | 0149 | 0554 | 1218 | 2340 | 1251 | 0414 | 2103 | 1437 | 0756 | 0019 | 1447 | 0256 | 1202 | 1809 | 2057 | 2055 | 1808 | 1328 | 0715 | 0035 | 1754 | |
| DATE 4 | | | | | | | | | | | | | | | | | | | | | | | | | 4 |
| 5 | Yn E | Yn W | | | Yn E | Yn W | Yn E | Yn F | | | | | | | | | | | | | | | | | 5 |
| 6 | Yg M | Yg W | Yn E | Yn F | Yg M | Yg W | Yg M | Yg F | Yn M | Yn E4 | | | | | | | | | | | | | Yn Wd | Yn W | 6 |
| 7 | Yn M | Yn E4 | Yg M | Yg F | Yn M | Yn E4 | Yn M | Yn E2 | Yg W | Yg Wd | Yg W | Yg M | | | | | | | Yn Wd | Yn W | Yn Wd | Yn F | Yg F | Yg W | 7 |
| 8 | Yg W | Yg Wd | Yn M | Yn E2 | Yg W | Yg Wd | Yg W | Yg M | Yn W | Yn Wd | Yn W | Yn M | Yg Wd | Yg E1 | Yn Wd | Yn W | Yn Wd | Yn F | Yg F | Yg W | Yg F | Yg F | Yn F | Yn E4 | 8 |
| 9 | Yn W | Yn Wd | Yg W | Yg M | Yn W | Yn Wd | Yn W | Yn M | Yg Wd | Yg E1 | Yg Wd | Yg E3 | Yn Wd | Yn F | Yg F | Yg W | Yg F | Yg F | Yn F | Yn E4 | Yn F | Yn E2 | Yg E | Yg Wd | 9 |
| 10 | Yg Wd | Yg E1 | Yn W | Yn M | Yg Wd | Yg E1 | Yg Wd | Yg E3 | Yn Wd | Yn F | Yn Wd | Yn W | Yg F | Yg F | Yn F | Yn E4 | Yn F | Yn E2 | Yg E | Yg Wd | Yg E | Yg M | Yn E | Yn Wd | 10 |
| 11 | Yn Wd | Yn F | Yg Wd | Yg E3 | Yn Wd | Yn F | Yn Wd | Yn W | Yg F | Yg F | Yg F | Yg W | Yn F | Yn E2 | Yg E | Yg Wd | Yg E | Yg M | Yn E | Yn Wd | Yn E | Yn M | Yg M | Yg E1 | 11 |
| 12 | Yg F | Yg F | Yn Wd | Yn W | Yg F | Yg F | Yg F | Yg W | Yn F | Yn E2 | Yn F | Yn E4 | Yg E | Yg M | Yn E | Yn Wd | Yn E | Yn M | Yg M | Yg E1 | Yg M | Yg E3 | Yn M | Yn F | 12 |
| 13 | Yn F | Yn E2 | Yg F | Yg W | Yn F | Yn E2 | Yn F | Yn E4 | Yg E | Yg M | Yg E | Yg Wd | Yn E | Yn M | Yg M | Yg E1 | Yg M | Yg E3 | Yn M | Yn F | Yn M | Yn W | Yg W | Yg F | 13 |
| 14 | Yg E | Yg M | Yn F | Yn E4 | Yg E | Yg M | Yg E | Yg Wd | Yn E | Yn M | Yn E | Yn Wd | Yg M | Yg E3 | Yn M | Yn F | Yn M | Yn W | Yg W | Yg F | Yg W | Yg W | Yn W | Yn E2 | 14 |
| 15 | Yn E | Yn M | Yg E | Yg Wd | Yn E | Yn M | Yn E | Yn Wd | Yg M | Yg E3 | Yg M | Yg E1 | Yn M | Yn W | Yg W | Yg F | Yg W | Yg W | Yn W | Yn E2 | Yn W | Yn E4 | Yg Wd | Yg M | 15 |
| 16 | Yg M | Yg E3 | Yn E | Yn Wd | Yg M | Yg E3 | Yg M | Yg E1 | Yn M | Yn W | Yn M | Yn F | Yg W | Yg W | Yn W | Yn E2 | Yn W | Yn E4 | Yg Wd | Yg M | Yg Wd | Yg Wd | Yn Wd | Yn M | 16 |
| 17 | Yn M | Yn W | Yg M | Yg E1 | Yn M | Yn W | Yn M | Yn F | Yg W | Yg W | Yg W | Yg F | Yn W | Yn E4 | Yg Wd | Yg M | Yg Wd | Yg Wd | Yn Wd | Yn M | Yn Wd | Yn Wd | Yg F | Yg E3 | 17 |
| 18 | Yg W | Yg W | Yn M | Yn F | Yg W | Yg W | Yg W | Yg F | Yn W | Yn E4 | Yn W | Yn E2 | Yg Wd | Yg Wd | Yn Wd | Yn M | Yn Wd | Yn Wd | Yg F | Yg E3 | Yg F | Yg E1 | Yn F | Yn W | 18 |
| 19 | Yn W | Yn E4 | Yg W | Yg F | Yn W | Yn E4 | Yn W | Yn E2 | Yg Wd | Yg Wd | Yg Wd | Yg M | Yn Wd | Yn Wd | Yg F | Yg E3 | Yg F | Yg E1 | Yn F | Yn W | Yn F | Yn F | Yg E | Yg W | 19 |
| 20 | Yg Wd | Yg Wd | Yn W | Yn E2 | Yg Wd | Yg Wd | Yg Wd | Yg M | Yn Wd | Yn Wd | Yn Wd | Yn M | Yg F | Yg E1 | Yn F | Yn W | Yn F | Yn F | Yg E | Yg W | Yg E | Yg F | Yn E | Yn E4 | 20 |
| 21 | Yn Wd | Yn Wd | Yg Wd | Yg M | Yn Wd | Yn Wd | Yn Wd | Yn M | Yg F | Yg E1 | Yg F | Yg E3 | Yn F | Yn F | Yg E | Yg W | Yg E | Yg F | Yn E | Yn E4 | Yn E | Yn E2 | Yg M | Yg Wd | 21 |
| 22 | Yg F | Yg E1 | Yn Wd | Yn M | Yg F | Yg E1 | Yg F | Yg E3 | Yn F | Yn F | Yn F | Yn W | Yg E | Yg F | Yn E | Yn E4 | Yn E | Yn E2 | Yg M | Yg Wd | Yg M | Yg M | Yn M | Yn Wd | 22 |
| 23 | Yn F | Yn F | Yg F | Yg E3 | Yn F | Yn F | Yn F | Yn W | Yg E | Yg F | Yg E | Yg W | Yn E | Yn E2 | Yg M | Yg Wd | Yg M | Yg M | Yn M | Yn Wd | Yn M | Yn M | Yg W | Yg E1 | 23 |
| 24 | Yg E | Yg F | Yn F | Yn W | Yg E | Yg F | Yg E | Yg W | Yn E | Yn E2 | Yn E | Yn E4 | Yg M | Yg M | Yn M | Yn Wd | Yn M | Yn M | Yg W | Yg E1 | Yg W | Yg E3 | Yn W | Yn F | 24 |
| 25 | Yn E | Yn E2 | Yg E | Yg W | Yn E | Yn E2 | Yn E | Yn E4 | Yg M | Yg M | Yg M | Yg Wd | Yn M | Yn M | Yg W | Yg E1 | Yg W | Yg E3 | Yn W | Yn F | Yn W | Yn W | Yg Wd | Yg F | 25 |
| 26 | Yg M | Yg M | Yn E | Yn E4 | Yg M | Yg M | Yg M | Yg Wd | Yn M | Yn M | Yn M | Yn Wd | Yg W | Yg E3 | Yn W | Yn F | Yn W | Yn W | Yg Wd | Yg F | Yg Wd | Yg W | Yn Wd | Yn E2 | 26 |
| 27 | Yn M | Yn M | Yg M | Yg Wd | Yn M | Yn M | Yn M | Yn Wd | Yg W | Yg E3 | Yg W | Yg E1 | Yn W | Yn W | Yg Wd | Yg F | Yg Wd | Yg W | Yn Wd | Yn E2 | Yn Wd | Yn E4 | Yg F | Yg M | 27 |
| 28 | Yg W | Yg E3 | Yn M | Yn Wd | Yg W | Yg E3 | Yg W | Yg E1 | Yn W | Yn W | Yn W | Yn F | Yg Wd | Yg W | Yn Wd | Yn E2 | Yn Wd | Yn E4 | Yg F | Yg M | Yg F | Yg Wd | Yn F | Yn M | 28 |
| 29 | Yn W | Yn W | Yg W | Yg E1 | Yn W | Yn W | Yn W | Yn F | Yg Wd | Yg W | Yg Wd | Yg F | Yn Wd | Yn E4 | Yg F | Yg M | Yg F | Yg Wd | Yn F | Yn M | Yn F | Yn Wd | Yg E | Yg E3 | 29 |
| 30 | | | Yn W | Yn F | Yg Wd | Yg W | Yg Wd | Yg F | Yn Wd | Yn E4 | Yn Wd | Yn E2 | Yg F | Yg Wd | Yn F | Yn M | Yn F | Yn Wd | Yg E | Yg E3 | Yg E | Yg E1 | Yn E | Yn W | 30 |
| 31 | | | Yg Wd | Yg F | | | Yn Wd | Yn E2 | | | Yg F | Yg M | Yn F | Yn Wd | | | Yg E | Yg E1 | | | Yn E | Yn F | Yg M | Yg W | 31 |
| 1 | Yg Wd | Yg W | Yn Wd | Yn E2 | Yn Wd | Yn E4 | Yg F | Yg M | Yg F | Yg Wd | Yn F | Yn M | Yg E | Yg E1 | Yg E | Yg E3 | Yn E | Yn F | Yn E | Yn W | Yg M | Yg F | Yn M | Yn E4 | 1 |
| 2 | Yn Wd | Yn E4 | Yg F | Yg M | Yg F | Yg Wd | Yn F | Yn M | Yn F | Yn Wd | Yg E | Yg E3 | Yn E | Yn F | Yn E | Yn W | Yg M | Yg F | Yg M | Yg W | Yn M | Yn E2 | Yg W | Yg Wd | 2 |
| 3 | Yg F | Yg Wd | Yn F | Yn M | Yn F | Yn Wd | Yg E | Yg E3 | Yg E | Yg E1 | Yn E | Yn W | Yg M | Yg F | Yg M | Yg W | Yn M | Yn E2 | Yn M | Yn E4 | Yg W | Yg M | Yn W | Yn Wd | 3 |
| 4 | Yn F | Yn Wd | Yg E | Yg E3 | Yg E | Yg E1 | Yn E | Yn W | Yn E | Yn F | Yg M | Yg W | Yn M | Yn E2 | Yn M | Yn E4 | Yg W | Yg M | Yg W | Yg Wd | Yn W | Yn M | | | 4 |
| 5 | Yg E | Yg E1 | | | | | Yg M | Yg W | Yg M | Yg F | Yn M | Yn E4 | Yg W | Yg M | Yg W | Yg Wd | Yn W | Yn M | Yn W | Yn Wd | Yg Wd | Yg E3 | | | 5 |
| 6 | | | | | | | | | Yn M | Yn E2 | Yg W | Yg Wd | Yn W | Yn M | Yn W | Yn Wd | Yg Wd | Yg E3 | Yg Wd | Yg E1 | | | | | 6 |
| 7 | | | | | | | | | | | Yn W | Yn Wd | Yg Wd | Yg E3 | Yg Wd | Yg E1 | | | | | | | | | 7 |
| 8 | | | | | | | | | | | | | | | | | | | | | | | | | 8 |

# YEAR OF THE ROOSTER

| | H | E | H | E | H | E | H | E | H | E | H | E | H | E | H | E | H | E | H | E | H | E | H | E | |
|---|---|---|---|---|---|---|---|---|---|---|---|---|---|---|---|---|---|---|---|---|---|---|---|---|---|
| YEAR | YEAR<br>Yn Wd | <br>Yn M | 1945 | | | | | | | | | | | | | | | | | | 1946 | | | | |
| MONTH | 4 Feb - 5 Mar<br>Yg E | <br>Yg Wd | 6 Mar - 4 Apr<br>Yn E | <br>Yn Wd | 5 Apr - 5 May<br>Yg M | <br>Yg E1 | 6 May - 5 June<br>Yn M | <br>Yn F | 6 June - 6 Jul<br>Yg W | <br>Yg F | 7 Jul - 7 Aug<br>Yn W | <br>Yn E2 | 8 Aug - 7 Sep<br>Yg Wd | <br>Yg M | 8 Sep - 7 Oct<br>Yn Wd | <br>Yn M | 8 Oct - 7 Nov<br>Yg F | <br>Yg E3 | 8 Nov - 6 Dec<br>Yn F | <br>Yn W | 7 Dec - 5 Jan<br>Yg E | <br>Yg W | 6 Jan - 3 Feb<br>Yn E | <br>Yn E4 | |
| Starting time | 1st day | Mid-pt | 1st day | Mid-pt | 1st day | Mid-pt | 1st day | Mid-pt | 1st day | Mid-pt | 1st day | Mid-pt | 1st day | Mid-pt | 1st day | Mid-pt | 1st day | Mid-pt | 1st day | Mid-pt | 1st day | Mid-pt | 1st day | Mid-pt | |
| Date | 4 | 19 | 6 | 21 | 5 | 20 | 6 | 21 | 6 | 22 | 7 | 23 | 8 | 23 | 8 | 23 | 8 | 24 | 8 | 22 | 7 | 22 | 6 | 20 | |
| Hour | 2120 | 0815 | 0638 | 0738 | 1152 | 1909 | 0537 | 1841 | 1006 | 0252 | 2027 | 1346 | 0606 | 2036 | 0839 | 1750 | 2350 | 0244 | 0235 | 2356 | 1908 | 1304 | 0617 | 2345 | |
| DATE 4 | Yg Wd | Yg E1 | | | | | | | | | | | | | | | | | | | | | | | 4 |
| 5 | Yn Wd | Yn F | | | Yg Wd | Yg E1 | | | | | | | | | | | | | | | | | | | 5 |
| 6 | Yg F | Yg F | Yg Wd | Yg E3 | Yn Wd | Yn F | Yn Wd | Yn W | Yg F | Yg F | | | | | | | | | | | | | Yg M | Yg E1 | 6 |
| 7 | Yn F | Yn E2 | Yn Wd | Yn W | Yg F | Yg F | Yg F | Yg W | Yn F | Yn E2 | Yn F | Yn E4 | | | | | | | | | Yg M | Yg E3 | Yn M | Yn F | 7 |
| 8 | Yg E | Yg M | Yg F | Yg W | Yn F | Yn E2 | Yn F | Yn E4 | Yg E | Yg M | Yg E | Yg Wd | Yn E | Yn M | Yg M | Yg E1 | Yg M | Yg E3 | Yn M | Yn F | Yn M | Yn W | Yg W | Yg F | 8 |
| 9 | Yn E | Yn M | Yn F | Yn E4 | Yg E | Yg M | Yg E | Yg Wd | Yn E | Yn M | Yn E | Yn Wd | Yg M | Yg E3 | Yn M | Yn F | Yn M | Yn W | Yg W | Yg F | Yg W | Yg W | Yn W | Yn E2 | 9 |
| 10 | Yg M | Yg E3 | Yg E | Yg Wd | Yn E | Yn M | Yn E | Yn Wd | Yg M | Yg E3 | Yg M | Yg E1 | Yn M | Yn W | Yg W | Yg F | Yg W | Yg W | Yn W | Yn E2 | Yn W | Yn E4 | Yg Wd | Yg M | 10 |
| 11 | Yn M | Yn W | Yn E | Yn Wd | Yg M | Yg E3 | Yg M | Yg E1 | Yn M | Yn W | Yn M | Yn F | Yg W | Yg W | Yn W | Yn E2 | Yn W | Yn E4 | Yg Wd | Yg M | Yg Wd | Yg Wd | Yn Wd | Yn M | 11 |
| 12 | Yg W | Yg W | Yg M | Yg E1 | Yn M | Yn W | Yn M | Yn F | Yg W | Yg W | Yg W | Yg F | Yn W | Yn E4 | Yg Wd | Yg M | Yg Wd | Yg Wd | Yn Wd | Yn M | Yn Wd | Yn Wd | Yg F | Yg E3 | 12 |
| 13 | Yn W | Yn E4 | Yn M | Yn F | Yg W | Yg W | Yg W | Yg F | Yn W | Yn E4 | Yn W | Yn E2 | Yg Wd | Yg Wd | Yn Wd | Yn M | Yn Wd | Yn Wd | Yg F | Yg E3 | Yg F | Yg E1 | Yn F | Yn W | 13 |
| 14 | Yg Wd | Yg Wd | Yg W | Yg F | Yn W | Yn E4 | Yn W | Yn E2 | Yg Wd | Yg Wd | Yg Wd | Yg M | Yn Wd | Yn Wd | Yg F | Yg E3 | Yg F | Yg E1 | Yn F | Yn W | Yn F | Yn F | Yg E | Yg W | 14 |
| 15 | Yn Wd | Yn Wd | Yn W | Yn E2 | Yg Wd | Yg Wd | Yg Wd | Yg M | Yn Wd | Yn Wd | Yn Wd | Yn M | Yg F | Yg E1 | Yn F | Yn W | Yn F | Yn F | Yg E | Yg W | Yg E | Yg F | Yn E | Yn E4 | 15 |
| 16 | Yg F | Yg E1 | Yg Wd | Yg M | Yn Wd | Yn Wd | Yn Wd | Yn M | Yg F | Yg E1 | Yg F | Yg E3 | Yn F | Yn F | Yg E | Yg W | Yg E | Yg F | Yn E | Yn E4 | Yn E | Yn E2 | Yg M | Yg Wd | 16 |
| 17 | Yn F | Yn F | Yn Wd | Yn M | Yg F | Yg E1 | Yg F | Yg E3 | Yn F | Yn F | Yn F | Yn W | Yg E | Yg F | Yn E | Yn E4 | Yn E | Yn E2 | Yg M | Yg Wd | Yg M | Yg M | Yn M | Yn Wd | 17 |
| 18 | Yg E | Yg F | Yg F | Yg E3 | Yn F | Yn F | Yn F | Yn W | Yg E | Yg F | Yg E | Yg W | Yn E | Yn E2 | Yg M | Yg Wd | Yg M | Yg M | Yn M | Yn Wd | Yn M | Yn M | Yg W | Yg E1 | 18 |
| 19 | Yn E | Yn E2 | Yn F | Yn W | Yg E | Yg F | Yg E | Yg W | Yn E | Yn E2 | Yn E | Yn E4 | Yg M | Yg M | Yn M | Yn Wd | Yn M | Yn M | Yg W | Yg E1 | Yg W | Yg E3 | Yn W | Yn F | 19 |
| 20 | Yg M | Yg M | Yg E | Yg W | Yn E | Yn E2 | Yn E | Yn E4 | Yg M | Yg M | Yg M | Yg Wd | Yn M | Yn M | Yg W | Yg E1 | Yg W | Yg E3 | Yn W | Yn F | Yn W | Yn W | Yg Wd | Yg F | 20 |
| 21 | Yn M | Yn M | Yn E | Yn E4 | Yg M | Yg M | Yg M | Yg Wd | Yn M | Yn M | Yn M | Yn Wd | Yg W | Yg E3 | Yn W | Yn F | Yn W | Yn W | Yg Wd | Yg F | Yg Wd | Yg W | Yn Wd | Yn E2 | 21 |
| 22 | Yg W | Yg E3 | Yg M | Yg Wd | Yn M | Yn M | Yn M | Yn Wd | Yg W | Yg E3 | Yg W | Yg E1 | Yn W | Yn W | Yg Wd | Yg F | Yg Wd | Yg W | Yn Wd | Yn E2 | Yn Wd | Yn E4 | Yg F | Yg M | 22 |
| 23 | Yn W | Yn W | Yn M | Yn Wd | Yg W | Yg E3 | Yg W | Yg E1 | Yn W | Yn W | Yn W | Yn F | Yg Wd | Yg W | Yn Wd | Yn E2 | Yn Wd | Yn E4 | Yg F | Yg M | Yg F | Yg Wd | Yn F | Yn M | 23 |
| 24 | Yg Wd | Yg W | Yg W | Yg E1 | Yn W | Yn W | Yn W | Yn F | Yg Wd | Yg W | Yg Wd | Yg F | Yn Wd | Yn E4 | Yg F | Yg M | Yg F | Yg Wd | Yn F | Yn M | Yn F | Yn Wd | Yg E | Yg E3 | 24 |
| 25 | Yn Wd | Yn E4 | Yn W | Yn F | Yg Wd | Yg W | Yg Wd | Yg F | Yn Wd | Yn E4 | Yn Wd | Yn E2 | Yg F | Yg Wd | Yn F | Yn M | Yn F | Yn Wd | Yg E | Yg E3 | Yg E | Yg E1 | Yn E | Yn W | 25 |
| 26 | Yg F | Yg Wd | Yg Wd | Yg F | Yn Wd | Yn E4 | Yn Wd | Yn E2 | Yg F | Yg Wd | Yg F | Yg M | Yn F | Yn Wd | Yg E | Yg E3 | Yg E | Yg E1 | Yn E | Yn W | Yn E | Yn F | Yg M | Yg W | 26 |
| 27 | Yn F | Yn Wd | Yn Wd | Yn E2 | Yg F | Yg Wd | Yg F | Yg M | Yn F | Yn Wd | Yn F | Yn M | Yg E | Yg E1 | Yn E | Yn W | Yn E | Yn F | Yg M | Yg W | Yg M | Yg F | Yn M | Yn E4 | 27 |
| 28 | Yg E | Yg E1 | Yg F | Yg M | Yn F | Yn Wd | Yn F | Yn M | Yg E | Yg E1 | Yg E | Yg E3 | Yn E | Yn F | Yg M | Yg W | Yg M | Yg F | Yn M | Yn E4 | Yn M | Yn E2 | Yg W | Yg Wd | 28 |
| 29 | | | Yn F | Yn M | Yg E | Yg E1 | Yg E | Yg E3 | Yn E | Yn F | Yn E | Yn W | Yg M | Yg F | Yn M | Yn E4 | Yn M | Yn E2 | Yg W | Yg Wd | Yg W | Yg M | Yn W | Yn Wd | 29 |
| 30 | | | Yg E | Yg E3 | Yn E | Yn F | Yn E | Yn W | Yg M | Yg F | Yg M | Yg W | Yn M | Yn E2 | Yg W | Yg Wd | Yg W | Yg M | Yn W | Yn Wd | Yn W | Yn M | Yg Wd | Yg E1 | 30 |
| 31 | | | Yn E | Yn W | | | Yg M | Yg W | | | Yn M | Yn E4 | Yg W | Yg M | | | Yn W | Yn M | | | Yg Wd | Yg E3 | Yn Wd | Yn F | 31 |
| 1 | Yn E | Yn F | Yg M | Yg W | Yg M | Yg F | Yn M | Yn E4 | Yn M | Yn E2 | Yg W | Yg Wd | Yn W | Yn M | Yn W | Yn Wd | Yg Wd | Yg E3 | Yg Wd | Yg E1 | Yn Wd | Yn W | Yg F | Yg F | 1 |
| 2 | Yg M | Yg F | Yn M | Yn E4 | Yn M | Yn E2 | Yg W | Yg Wd | Yg W | Yg M | Yn W | Yn Wd | Yg Wd | Yg E3 | Yg Wd | Yg E1 | Yn Wd | Yn W | Yn Wd | Yn F | Yg F | Yg W | Yn F | Yn E2 | 2 |
| 3 | Yn M | Yn E2 | Yg W | Yg Wd | Yg W | Yg M | Yn W | Yn Wd | Yn W | Yn M | Yg Wd | Yg E1 | Yn Wd | Yn W | Yn Wd | Yn F | Yg F | Yg W | Yg F | Yg F | Yn F | Yn E4 | Yg E | Yg M | 3 |
| 4 | Yg W | Yg M | Yn W | Yn Wd | Yn W | Yn M | Yg Wd | Yg E1 | Yg Wd | Yg E3 | Yn Wd | Yn F | Yg F | Yg W | Yg F | Yg F | Yn F | Yn E4 | Yn F | Yn E2 | Yg E | Yg Wd | | | 4 |
| 5 | Yn W | Yn M | | | Yg Wd | Yg E3 | Yn Wd | Yn F | Yn Wd | Yn W | Yg F | Yg F | Yn F | Yn E4 | Yn F | Yn E2 | Yg E | Yg Wd | Yg E | Yg M | Yn E | Yn Wd | | | 5 |
| 6 | | | | | | | | | Yg F | Yg W | Yn F | Yn E2 | Yg E | Yg Wd | Yg E | Yg M | Yn E | Yn Wd | Yn E | Yn M | | | | | 6 |
| 7 | | | | | | | | | | | Yg E | Yg M | Yn E | Yn Wd | Yn E | Yn M | Yg M | Yg E1 | | | | | | | 7 |
| 8 | | | | | | | | | | | | | | | | | | | | | | | | | 8 |

# YEAR OF THE DOG

| | H | E | H | E | H | E | H | E | H | E | H | E | H | E | H | E | H | E | H | E | H | E | H | E | |
|---|---|---|---|---|---|---|---|---|---|---|---|---|---|---|---|---|---|---|---|---|---|---|---|---|---|
| **YEAR** | **YEAR** Yg F | Yg E3 | **1946** | | | | | | | | | | | | | | | | | | | **1947** | | | |
| **MONTH** | 4 Feb - 5 Mar | | 6 Mar - 4 Apr | | 5 Apr - 5 May | | 6 May - 5 June | | 6 June - 7 Jul | | 8 Jul - 7 Aug | | 8 Aug - 7 Sep | | 8 Sep - 8 Oct | | 9 Oct - 7 Nov | | 8 Nov - 7 Dec | | 8 Dec - 5 Jan | | 6 Jan - 3 Feb | | |
| | Yg M | Yg Wd | Yn M | Yn Wd | Yg W | Yg E1 | Yn W | Yn F | Yg Wd | Yg F | Yn Wd | Yn E2 | Yg F | Yg M | Yn F | Yn M | Yg E | Yg E3 | Yn E | Yn W | Yg M | Yg W | Yn M | Yn E4 | |
| **Starting time** | 1st day | Mid-pt | 1st day | Mid-pt | 1st day | Mid-pt | 1st day | Mid-pt | 1st day | Mid-pt | 1st day | Mid-pt | 1st day | Mid-pt | 1st day | Mid-pt | 1st day | Mid-pt | 1st day | Mid-pt | 1st day | Mid-pt | 1st day | Mid-pt | |
| Date | 4 | 19 | 6 | 21 | 5 | 21 | 6 | 22 | 6 | 22 | 8 | 23 | 8 | 24 | 8 | 23 | 9 | 24 | 8 | 23 | 8 | 22 | 6 | 21 | |
| Hour | 1805 | 1409 | 1225 | 1333 | 1739 | 0102 | 1122 | 0034 | 1549 | 0845 | 0211 | 1937 | 1152 | 0227 | 1428 | 2341 | 0542 | 0835 | 0828 | 0547 | 0101 | 1854 | 1211 | 0535 | |
| **DATE** 4 | Yn E | Yn M | | | | | | | | | | | | | | | | | | | | | | | 4 |
| 5 | Yg M | Yg E3 | | | Yn E | Yn M | | | | | | | | | | | | | | | | | | | 5 |
| 6 | Yn M | Yn W | Yn E | Yn Wd | Yg M | Yg E3 | Yg M | Yg E1 | Yn M | Yn W | | | | | | | | | | | | | Yn Wd | Yn M | 6 |
| 7 | Yg W | Yg W | Yg M | Yg E1 | Yn M | Yn W | Yn M | Yn F | Yg W | Yg W | | | | | | | | | | | | | Yg F | Yg E3 | 7 |
| 8 | Yn W | Yn E4 | Yn M | Yn F | Yg W | Yg W | Yg W | Yg F | Yn W | Yn E4 | Yn W | Yn E2 | Yg Wd | Yg Wd | Yn Wd | Yn M | | | Yg F | Yg E3 | Yg F | Yg E1 | Yn F | Yn W | 8 |
| 9 | Yg Wd | Yg Wd | Yg W | Yg F | Yn W | Yn E4 | Yn W | Yn E2 | Yg Wd | Yg Wd | Yg Wd | Yg M | Yn Wd | Yn Wd | Yg F | Yg E3 | Yg F | Yg E1 | Yn F | Yn W | Yn F | Yn F | Yg E | Yg W | 9 |
| 10 | Yn Wd | Yn Wd | Yn W | Yn E2 | Yg Wd | Yg Wd | Yg Wd | Yg M | Yn Wd | Yn Wd | Yn Wd | Yn M | Yg F | Yg E1 | Yn F | Yn W | Yn F | Yn F | Yg E | Yg W | Yg E | Yg F | Yn E | Yn E4 | 10 |
| 11 | Yg F | Yg E1 | Yg Wd | Yg M | Yn Wd | Yn Wd | Yn Wd | Yn M | Yg F | Yg E1 | Yg F | Yg E3 | Yn F | Yn F | Yg E | Yg W | Yg E | Yg F | Yn E | Yn E4 | Yn E | Yn E2 | Yg M | Yg Wd | 11 |
| 12 | Yn F | Yn F | Yn Wd | Yn M | Yg F | Yg E1 | Yg F | Yg E3 | Yn F | Yn F | Yn F | Yn W | Yg E | Yg F | Yn E | Yn E4 | Yn E | Yn E2 | Yg M | Yg Wd | Yg M | Yg M | Yn M | Yn Wd | 12 |
| 13 | Yg E | Yg F | Yg F | Yg E3 | Yn F | Yn F | Yn F | Yn W | Yg E | Yg F | Yg E | Yg W | Yn E | Yn E2 | Yg M | Yg Wd | Yg M | Yg M | Yn M | Yn Wd | Yn M | Yn M | Yg W | Yg E1 | 13 |
| 14 | Yn E | Yn E2 | Yn F | Yn W | Yg E | Yg F | Yg E | Yg W | Yn E | Yn E2 | Yn E | Yn E4 | Yg M | Yg M | Yn M | Yn Wd | Yn M | Yn M | Yg W | Yg E1 | Yg W | Yg E3 | Yn W | Yn F | 14 |
| 15 | Yg M | Yg M | Yg E | Yg W | Yn E | Yn E2 | Yn E | Yn E4 | Yg M | Yg M | Yg M | Yg Wd | Yn M | Yn M | Yg W | Yg E1 | Yg W | Yg E3 | Yn W | Yn F | Yn W | Yn W | Yg Wd | Yg F | 15 |
| 16 | Yn M | Yn M | Yn E | Yn E4 | Yg M | Yg M | Yg M | Yg Wd | Yn M | Yn M | Yn M | Yn Wd | Yg W | Yg E3 | Yn W | Yn F | Yn W | Yn W | Yg Wd | Yg F | Yg Wd | Yg W | Yn Wd | Yn E2 | 16 |
| 17 | Yg W | Yg E3 | Yg M | Yg Wd | Yn M | Yn M | Yn M | Yn Wd | Yg W | Yg E3 | Yg W | Yg E1 | Yn W | Yn W | Yg Wd | Yg F | Yg Wd | Yg W | Yn Wd | Yn E2 | Yn Wd | Yn E4 | Yg F | Yg M | 17 |
| 18 | Yn W | Yn W | Yn M | Yn Wd | Yg W | Yg E3 | Yg W | Yg E1 | Yn W | Yn W | Yn W | Yn F | Yg Wd | Yg W | Yn Wd | Yn E2 | Yn Wd | Yn E4 | Yg F | Yg M | Yg F | Yg Wd | Yn F | Yn M | 18 |
| 19 | Yg Wd | Yg W | Yg W | Yg E1 | Yn W | Yn W | Yn W | Yn F | Yg Wd | Yg W | Yg Wd | Yg F | Yn Wd | Yn E4 | Yg F | Yg M | Yg F | Yg Wd | Yn F | Yn M | Yn F | Yn Wd | Yg E | Yg E3 | 19 |
| 20 | Yn Wd | Yn E4 | Yn W | Yn F | Yg Wd | Yg W | Yg Wd | Yg F | Yn Wd | Yn E4 | Yn Wd | Yn E2 | Yg F | Yg Wd | Yn F | Yn M | Yn F | Yn Wd | Yg E | Yg E3 | Yg E | Yg E1 | Yn E | Yn W | 20 |
| 21 | Yg F | Yg Wd | Yg Wd | Yg F | Yn Wd | Yn E4 | Yn Wd | Yn E2 | Yg F | Yg Wd | Yg F | Yg M | Yn F | Yn Wd | Yg E | Yg E3 | Yg E | Yg E1 | Yn E | Yn W | Yn E | Yn F | Yg M | Yg W | 21 |
| 22 | Yn F | Yn Wd | Yn Wd | Yn E2 | Yg F | Yg Wd | Yg F | Yg M | Yn F | Yn Wd | Yn F | Yn M | Yg E | Yg E1 | Yn E | Yn W | Yn E | Yn F | Yg M | Yg W | Yg M | Yg F | Yn M | Yn E4 | 22 |
| 23 | Yg E | Yg E1 | Yg F | Yg M | Yn F | Yn Wd | Yn F | Yn M | Yg E | Yg E1 | Yg E | Yg E3 | Yn E | Yn F | Yg M | Yg W | Yg M | Yg F | Yn M | Yn E4 | Yn M | Yn E2 | Yg W | Yg Wd | 23 |
| 24 | Yn E | Yn F | Yn F | Yn M | Yg E | Yg E1 | Yg E | Yg E3 | Yn E | Yn F | Yn E | Yn W | Yg M | Yg F | Yn M | Yn E4 | Yn M | Yn E2 | Yg W | Yg Wd | Yg W | Yg M | Yn W | Yn Wd | 24 |
| 25 | Yg M | Yg F | Yg E | Yg E3 | Yn E | Yn F | Yn E | Yn W | Yg M | Yg F | Yg M | Yg W | Yn M | Yn E2 | Yg W | Yg Wd | Yg W | Yg M | Yn W | Yn Wd | Yn W | Yn M | Yg Wd | Yg E1 | 25 |
| 26 | Yn M | Yn E2 | Yn E | Yn W | Yg M | Yg F | Yg M | Yg W | Yn M | Yn E2 | Yn M | Yn E4 | Yg W | Yg M | Yn W | Yn Wd | Yn W | Yn M | Yg Wd | Yg E1 | Yg Wd | Yg E3 | Yn Wd | Yn F | 26 |
| 27 | Yg W | Yg M | Yg M | Yg W | Yn M | Yn E2 | Yn M | Yn E4 | Yg W | Yg M | Yg W | Yg Wd | Yn W | Yn M | Yg Wd | Yg E1 | Yg Wd | Yg E3 | Yn Wd | Yn F | Yn Wd | Yn W | Yg F | Yg F | 27 |
| 28 | Yn W | Yn M | Yn M | Yn E4 | Yg W | Yg M | Yg W | Yg Wd | Yn W | Yn M | Yn W | Yn Wd | Yg Wd | Yg E3 | Yn Wd | Yn F | Yn Wd | Yn W | Yg F | Yg F | Yg F | Yg W | Yn F | Yn E2 | 28 |
| 29 | | | Yg W | Yg Wd | Yn W | Yn M | Yn W | Yn Wd | Yg Wd | Yg E3 | Yg Wd | Yg E1 | Yn Wd | Yn W | Yg F | Yg F | Yg F | Yg W | Yn F | Yn E2 | Yn F | Yn E4 | Yg E | Yg M | 29 |
| 30 | | | Yn W | Yn Wd | Yg Wd | Yg E3 | Yg Wd | Yg E1 | Yn Wd | Yn W | Yn Wd | Yn F | Yg F | Yg W | Yn F | Yn E2 | Yn F | Yn E4 | Yg E | Yg M | Yg E | Yg Wd | Yn E | Yn M | 30 |
| 31 | | | Yg Wd | Yg E1 | | | Yn Wd | Yn F | | | Yg F | Yg F | Yn F | Yn E4 | | | Yg E | Yg Wd | | | Yn E | Yn Wd | Yg M | Yg E3 | 31 |
| 1 | Yg Wd | Yg E3 | Yn Wd | Yn F | Yn Wd | Yn W | Yg F | Yg F | Yg F | Yg W | Yn F | Yn E2 | Yg E | Yg Wd | Yg E | Yg M | Yn E | Yn Wd | Yn E | Yn M | Yg M | Yg E1 | Yn M | Yn W | 1 |
| 2 | Yn Wd | Yn W | Yg F | Yg F | Yg F | Yg W | Yn F | Yn E2 | Yn F | Yn E4 | Yg E | Yg M | Yn E | Yn Wd | Yn E | Yn M | Yg M | Yg E1 | Yg M | Yg E3 | Yn M | Yn F | Yg W | Yg W | 2 |
| 3 | Yg F | Yg W | Yn F | Yn E2 | Yn F | Yn E4 | Yg E | Yg M | Yg E | Yg Wd | Yn E | Yn M | Yg M | Yg E1 | Yg M | Yg E3 | Yn M | Yn F | Yn M | Yn W | Yg W | Yg F | Yn W | Yn E4 | 3 |
| 4 | Yn F | Yn E4 | Yg E | Yg M | Yg E | Yg Wd | Yn E | Yn M | Yn E | Yn Wd | Yg M | Yg E3 | Yn M | Yn F | Yn M | Yn W | Yg W | Yg F | Yg W | Yg W | Yn W | Yn E2 | | | 4 |
| 5 | Yg E | Yg Wd | | | Yn E | Yn Wd | Yg M | Yg E3 | Yg M | Yg E1 | Yn M | Yn W | Yg W | Yg F | Yg W | Yg W | Yn W | Yn E2 | Yn W | Yn E4 | Yg Wd | Yg M | | | 5 |
| 6 | | | | | | | | | Yn M | Yn F | Yg W | Yg W | Yn W | Yn E2 | Yn W | Yn E4 | Yg Wd | Yg M | Yg Wd | Yg Wd | | | | | 6 |
| 7 | | | | | | | | | Yg W | Yg F | Yn W | Yn E4 | Yg Wd | Yg M | Yg Wd | Yg Wd | Yn Wd | Yn M | Yn Wd | Yn Wd | | | | | 7 |
| 8 | | | | | | | | | | | | | | | Yn Wd | Yn Wd | | | | | | | | | 8 |

# YEAR OF THE PIG

| | H | E | H | E | H | E | H | E | H | E | H | E |
|---|---|---|---|---|---|---|---|---|---|---|---|---|
| YEAR | YEAR<br>Yn F Yn W | | 1947 | | | | | | | | | |
| MONTH | 4 Feb - 5 Mar | | 6 Mar - 4 Apr | | 5 Apr - 5 May | | 6 May - 5 June | | 6 June - 7 Jul | | 8 Jul - 7 Aug | |
| | Yg W | Yg Wd | Yn W | Yn Wd | Yg Wd | Yg E1 | Yn Wd | Yn F | Yg F | Yg F | Yn F | Yn E2 |
| Starting time | 1st day | Mid-pt | 1st day | Mid-pt | 1st day | Mid-pt | 1st day | Mid-pt | 1st day | Mid-pt | 1st day | Mid-pt |
| Date | 4 | 19 | 6 | 21 | 5 | 21 | 6 | 22 | 6 | 22 | 8 | 24 |
| Hour | 2327 | 1955 | 1812 | 1915 | 2319 | 0642 | 1705 | 0613 | 2133 | 1424 | 0756 | 0119 |
| DATE 4 | Yg Wd | Yg Wd | | | | | | | | | | |
| 5 | Yn Wd | Yn Wd | | | Yg Wd | Yg Wd | | | | | | |
| 6 | Yg F | Yg E1 | Yg Wd | Yg M | Yn Wd | Yn Wd | Yn Wd | Yn M | Yg F | Yg E1 | | |
| 7 | Yn F | Yn F | Yn Wd | Yn M | Yg F | Yg E1 | Yg F | Yg E3 | Yn F | Yn F | | |
| 8 | Yg E | Yg F | Yg F | Yg E3 | Yn F | Yn F | Yn F | Yn W | Yg E | Yg F | Yg E | Yg W |
| 9 | Yn E | Yn E2 | Yn F | Yn W | Yg E | Yg F | Yg E | Yg W | Yn E | Yn E2 | Yn E | Yn E4 |
| 10 | Yg M | Yg M | Yg E | Yg W | Yn E | Yn E2 | Yn E | Yn E4 | Yg M | Yg M | Yg M | Yg Wd |
| 11 | Yn M | Yn M | Yn E | Yn E4 | Yg M | Yg M | Yg M | Yg Wd | Yn M | Yn M | Yn M | Yn Wd |
| 12 | Yg W | Yg E3 | Yg M | Yg Wd | Yn M | Yn M | Yn M | Yn Wd | Yg W | Yg E3 | Yg W | Yg E1 |
| 13 | Yn W | Yn W | Yn M | Yn Wd | Yg W | Yg E3 | Yg W | Yg E1 | Yn W | Yn W | Yn W | Yn F |
| 14 | Yg Wd | Yg W | Yg W | Yg E1 | Yn W | Yn W | Yn W | Yn F | Yg Wd | Yg W | Yg Wd | Yg F |
| 15 | Yn Wd | Yn E4 | Yn W | Yn F | Yg Wd | Yg W | Yg Wd | Yg F | Yn Wd | Yn E4 | Yn Wd | Yn E2 |
| 16 | Yg F | Yg Wd | Yg Wd | Yg F | Yn Wd | Yn E4 | Yn Wd | Yn E2 | Yg F | Yg Wd | Yg F | Yg M |
| 17 | Yn F | Yn Wd | Yn Wd | Yn E2 | Yg F | Yg Wd | Yg F | Yg M | Yn F | Yn Wd | Yn F | Yn M |
| 18 | Yg E | Yg E1 | Yg F | Yg M | Yn F | Yn Wd | Yn F | Yn M | Yg E | Yg E1 | Yg E | Yg E3 |
| 19 | Yn E | Yn F | Yn F | Yn M | Yg E | Yg E1 | Yg E | Yg E3 | Yn E | Yn F | Yn E | Yn W |
| 20 | Yg M | Yg F | Yg E | Yg E3 | Yn E | Yn F | Yn E | Yn W | Yg M | Yg F | Yg M | Yg W |
| 21 | Yn M | Yn E2 | Yn E | Yn W | Yg M | Yg F | Yg M | Yg W | Yn M | Yn E2 | Yn M | Yn E4 |
| 22 | Yg W | Yg M | Yg M | Yg W | Yn M | Yn E2 | Yn M | Yn E4 | Yg W | Yg M | Yg W | Yg Wd |
| 23 | Yn W | Yn M | Yn M | Yn E4 | Yg W | Yg M | Yg W | Yg Wd | Yn W | Yn M | Yn W | Yn Wd |
| 24 | Yg Wd | Yg E3 | Yg W | Yg Wd | Yn W | Yn M | Yn W | Yn Wd | Yg Wd | Yg E3 | Yg Wd | Yg E1 |
| 25 | Yn Wd | Yn W | Yn W | Yn Wd | Yg Wd | Yg E3 | Yg Wd | Yg E1 | Yn Wd | Yn W | Yn Wd | Yn F |
| 26 | Yg F | Yg W | Yg Wd | Yg E1 | Yn Wd | Yn W | Yn Wd | Yn F | Yg F | Yg W | Yg F | Yg F |
| 27 | Yn F | Yn E4 | Yn Wd | Yn F | Yg F | Yg W | Yg F | Yg F | Yn F | Yn E4 | Yn F | Yn E2 |
| 28 | Yg E | Yg Wd | Yg F | Yg F | Yn F | Yn E4 | Yn F | Yn E2 | Yg E | Yg Wd | Yg E | Yg M |
| 29 | | | Yn F | Yn E2 | Yg E | Yg Wd | Yg E | Yg M | Yn E | Yn Wd | Yn E | Yn M |
| 30 | | | Yg E | Yg M | Yn E | Yn Wd | Yn E | Yn M | Yg M | Yg E1 | Yg M | Yg E3 |
| 31 | | | Yn E | Yn M | | | Yg M | Yg E3 | | | Yn M | Yn W |
| 1 | Yn E | Yn Wd | Yg M | Yg E3 | Yg M | Yg E1 | Yn M | Yn W | Yn M | Yn F | Yg W | Yg W |
| 2 | Yg M | Yg E1 | Yn M | Yn W | Yn M | Yn F | Yg W | Yg W | Yg W | Yg F | Yn W | Yn E4 |
| 3 | Yn M | Yn F | Yg W | Yg W | Yg W | Yg F | Yn W | Yn E4 | Yn W | Yn E2 | Yg Wd | Yg Wd |
| 4 | Yg W | Yg F | Yn W | Yn E4 | Yn W | Yn E2 | Yg Wd | Yg Wd | Yg Wd | Yg M | Yn Wd | Yn Wd |
| 5 | Yn W | Yn E2 | | | Yg Wd | Yg M | Yn Wd | Yn Wd | Yn Wd | Yn M | Yg F | Yg E1 |
| 6 | | | | | | | | | Yg F | Yg E3 | Yn F | Yn F |
| 7 | | | | | | | | | Yn F | Yn W | Yg E | Yg F |
| 8 | | | | | | | | | | | | |

| | H | E | H | E | H | E | H | E | H | E | H | E | |
|---|---|---|---|---|---|---|---|---|---|---|---|---|---|
| YEAR | 1947 | | | | | | | | | | 1948 | | |
| MONTH | 8 Aug - 7 Sep | | 8 Sep - 8 Oct | | 9 Oct - 7 Nov | | 8 Nov - 7 Dec | | 8 Dec - 5 Jan | | 6 Jan - 4 Feb | | |
| | Yg E | Yg M | Yn E | Yn M | Yg M | Yg E3 | Yn M | Yn W | Yg W | Yg W | Yn W | Yn E4 | |
| Starting time | 1st day | Mid-pt | 1st day | Mid-pt | 1st day | Mid-pt | 1st day | Mid-pt | 1st day | Mid-pt | 1st day | Mid-pt | |
| Date | 8 | 24 | 8 | 24 | 9 | 24 | 8 | 23 | 8 | 23 | 6 | 21 | |
| Hour | 1739 | 0811 | 2017 | 0528 | 1132 | 1424 | 1419 | 1137 | 0653 | 0045 | 1806 | 1119 | |
| DATE 4 | | | | | | | | | | | | | 4 |
| 5 | | | | | | | | | | | | | 5 |
| 6 | | | | | | | | | | | Yg M | Yg Wd | 6 |
| 7 | | | | | | | | | | | Yn M | Yn Wd | 7 |
| 8 | Yn E | Yn E2 | Yg M | Yg Wd | | | Yn M | Yn Wd | Yn M | Yn M | Yg W | Yg E1 | 8 |
| 9 | Yg M | Yg M | Yn M | Yn Wd | Yn M | Yn M | Yg W | Yg E1 | Yg W | Yg E3 | Yn W | Yn F | 9 |
| 10 | Yn M | Yn M | Yg W | Yg E1 | Yg W | Yg E3 | Yn W | Yn F | Yn W | Yn W | Yg Wd | Yg F | 10 |
| 11 | Yg W | Yg E3 | Yn W | Yn F | Yn W | Yn W | Yg Wd | Yg F | Yg Wd | Yg W | Yn Wd | Yn E2 | 11 |
| 12 | Yn W | Yn W | Yg Wd | Yg F | Yg Wd | Yg W | Yn Wd | Yn E2 | Yn Wd | Yn E4 | Yg F | Yg M | 12 |
| 13 | Yg Wd | Yg W | Yn Wd | Yn E2 | Yn Wd | Yn E4 | Yg F | Yg M | Yg F | Yg Wd | Yn F | Yn M | 13 |
| 14 | Yn Wd | Yn E4 | Yg F | Yg M | Yg F | Yg Wd | Yn F | Yn M | Yn F | Yn Wd | Yg E | Yg E3 | 14 |
| 15 | Yg F | Yg Wd | Yn F | Yn M | Yn F | Yn Wd | Yg E | Yg E3 | Yg E | Yg E1 | Yn E | Yn W | 15 |
| 16 | Yn F | Yn Wd | Yg E | Yg E3 | Yg E | Yg E1 | Yn E | Yn W | Yn E | Yn F | Yg M | Yg W | 16 |
| 17 | Yg E | Yg E1 | Yn E | Yn W | Yn E | Yn F | Yg M | Yg W | Yg M | Yg F | Yn M | Yn E4 | 17 |
| 18 | Yn E | Yn F | Yg M | Yg W | Yg M | Yg F | Yn M | Yn E4 | Yn M | Yn E2 | Yg W | Yg Wd | 18 |
| 19 | Yg M | Yg F | Yn M | Yn E4 | Yn M | Yn E2 | Yg W | Yg Wd | Yg W | Yg M | Yn W | Yn Wd | 19 |
| 20 | Yn M | Yn E2 | Yg W | Yg Wd | Yg W | Yg M | Yn W | Yn Wd | Yn W | Yn M | Yg Wd | Yg E1 | 20 |
| 21 | Yg W | Yg M | Yn W | Yn Wd | Yn W | Yn M | Yg Wd | Yg E1 | Yg Wd | Yg E3 | Yn Wd | Yn F | 21 |
| 22 | Yn W | Yn M | Yg Wd | Yg E1 | Yg Wd | Yg E3 | Yn Wd | Yn F | Yn Wd | Yn W | Yg F | Yg F | 22 |
| 23 | Yg Wd | Yg E3 | Yn Wd | Yn F | Yn Wd | Yn W | Yg F | Yg F | Yg F | Yg W | Yn F | Yn E2 | 23 |
| 24 | Yn Wd | Yn W | Yg F | Yg F | Yg F | Yg W | Yn F | Yn E2 | Yn F | Yn E4 | Yg E | Yg M | 24 |
| 25 | Yg F | Yg W | Yn F | Yn E2 | Yn F | Yn E4 | Yg E | Yg M | Yg E | Yg Wd | Yn E | Yn M | 25 |
| 26 | Yn F | Yn E4 | Yg E | Yg M | Yg E | Yg Wd | Yn E | Yn M | Yn E | Yn Wd | Yg M | Yg E3 | 26 |
| 27 | Yg E | Yg Wd | Yn E | Yn M | Yn E | Yn Wd | Yg M | Yg E3 | Yg M | Yg E1 | Yn M | Yn W | 27 |
| 28 | Yn E | Yn Wd | Yg M | Yg E3 | Yg M | Yg E1 | Yn M | Yn W | Yn M | Yn F | Yg W | Yg W | 28 |
| 29 | Yg M | Yg E1 | Yn M | Yn W | Yn M | Yn F | Yg W | Yg W | Yg W | Yg F | Yn W | Yn E4 | 29 |
| 30 | Yn M | Yn F | Yg W | Yg W | Yg W | Yg F | Yn W | Yn E4 | Yn W | Yn E2 | Yg Wd | Yg Wd | 30 |
| 31 | Yg W | Yg F | | | Yn W | Yn E2 | | | Yg Wd | Yg M | Yn Wd | Yn Wd | 31 |
| 1 | Yn W | Yn E2 | Yn W | Yn E4 | Yg Wd | Yg M | Yg Wd | Yg Wd | Yn Wd | Yn M | Yg F | Yg E1 | 1 |
| 2 | Yg Wd | Yg M | Yg Wd | Yg Wd | Yn Wd | Yn M | Yn Wd | Yn Wd | Yg F | Yg E3 | Yn F | Yn F | 2 |
| 3 | Yn Wd | Yn M | Yn Wd | Yn Wd | Yg F | Yg E3 | Yg F | Yg E1 | Yn F | Yn W | Yg E | Yg F | 3 |
| 4 | Yg F | Yg E3 | Yg F | Yg E1 | Yn F | Yn W | Yn F | Yn F | Yg E | Yg W | Yn E | Yn E2 | 4 |
| 5 | Yn F | Yn W | Yn F | Yn F | Yg E | Yg W | Yg E | Yg F | Yn E | Yn E4 | | | 5 |
| 6 | Yg E | Yg W | Yg E | Yg F | Yn E | Yn E4 | Yn E | Yn E2 | | | | | 6 |
| 7 | Yn E | Yn E4 | Yn E | Yn E2 | Yg M | Yg Wd | Yg M | Yg M | | | | | 7 |
| 8 | | | Yg M | Yg M | | | | | | | | | 8 |

# YEAR OF THE RAT

| | H | E | H | E | H | E | H | E | H | E | H | E | H | E | H | E | H | E | H | E | H | E | H | E | |
|---|---|---|---|---|---|---|---|---|---|---|---|---|---|---|---|---|---|---|---|---|---|---|---|---|---|
| YEAR | YEAR Yg E | Yg W | 1948 | | | | | | | | | | | | | | | | | | | | 1949 | | |
| MONTH | 5 Feb - 4 Mar | | 5 Mar - 4 Apr | | 5 Apr - 4 May | | 5 May - 5 June | | 6 June - 6 Jul | | 7 Jul - 6 Aug | | 7 Aug - 7 Sep | | 8 Sep - 7 Oct | | 8 Oct - 6 Nov | | 7 Nov - 6 Dec | | 7 Dec - 4 Jan | | 5 Jan - 3 Feb | | |
| | Yg Wd | Yg Wd | Yn Wd | Yn Wd | Yg F | Yg E1 | Yn F | Yn F | Yg E | Yg F | Yn E | Yn E2 | Yg M | Yg M | Yn M | Yn M | Yg W | Yg E3 | Yn W | Yn W | Yg Wd | Yg W | Yn Wd | Yn E4 | |
| Starting time | 1st day | Mid-pt | 1st day | Mid-pt | 1st day | Mid-pt | 1st day | Mid-pt | 1st day | Mid-pt | 1st day | Mid-pt | 1st day | Mid-pt | 1st day | Mid-pt | 1st day | Mid-pt | 1st day | Mid-pt | 1st day | Mid-pt | 1st day | Mid-pt | |
| Date | 5 | 20 | 5 | 21 | 5 | 20 | 5 | 21 | 6 | 21 | 7 | 23 | 7 | 23 | 8 | 23 | 8 | 23 | 7 | 22 | 7 | 22 | 5 | 20 | |
| Hour | 0543 | 0137 | 2358 | 0057 | 0510 | 1225 | 2253 | 1158 | 0321 | 2011 | 1344 | 0708 | 2327 | 1403 | 0206 | 1122 | 1721 | 2019 | 2007 | 1730 | 1238 | 0634 | 2342 | 1709 | |
| DATE 4 | | | | | | | | | | | | | | | | | | | | | | | | | 4 |
| 5 | Yg M | Yg M | Yn E | Yn E4 | Yg M | Yg M | Yg M | Yg Wd | | | | | | | | | | | | | | | Yn Wd | Yn E2 | 5 |
| 6 | Yn M | Yn M | Yg M | Yg Wd | Yn M | Yn M | Yn M | Yn Wd | Yg W | Yg E3 | | | | | | | | | | | | | Yg F | Yg M | 6 |
| 7 | Yg W | Yg E3 | Yn M | Yn Wd | Yg W | Yg E3 | Yg W | Yg E1 | Yn W | Yn W | Yn W | Yn F | Yg Wd | Yg W | | | | | Yg F | Yg M | Yg F | Yg Wd | Yn F | Yn M | 7 |
| 8 | Yn W | Yn W | Yg W | Yg E1 | Yn W | Yn W | Yn W | Yn F | Yg Wd | Yg W | Yg Wd | Yg F | Yn Wd | Yn E4 | Yg F | Yg M | Yg F | Yg Wd | Yn F | Yn M | Yn F | Yn Wd | Yg E | Yg E3 | 8 |
| 9 | Yg Wd | Yg W | Yn W | Yn F | Yg Wd | Yg W | Yg Wd | Yg F | Yn Wd | Yn E4 | Yn Wd | Yn E2 | Yg F | Yg Wd | Yn F | Yn M | Yn F | Yn Wd | Yg E | Yg E3 | Yg E | Yg E1 | Yn E | Yn W | 9 |
| 10 | Yn Wd | Yn E4 | Yg Wd | Yg F | Yn Wd | Yn E4 | Yn Wd | Yn E2 | Yg F | Yg Wd | Yg F | Yg M | Yn F | Yn Wd | Yg E | Yg E3 | Yg E | Yg E1 | Yn E | Yn W | Yn E | Yn F | Yg M | Yg W | 10 |
| 11 | Yg F | Yg Wd | Yn Wd | Yn E2 | Yg F | Yg Wd | Yg F | Yg M | Yn F | Yn Wd | Yn F | Yn M | Yg E | Yg E1 | Yn E | Yn W | Yn E | Yn F | Yg M | Yg W | Yg M | Yg F | Yn M | Yn E4 | 11 |
| 12 | Yn F | Yn Wd | Yg F | Yg M | Yn F | Yn Wd | Yn F | Yn M | Yg E | Yg E1 | Yg E | Yg E3 | Yn E | Yn F | Yg M | Yg W | Yg M | Yg F | Yn M | Yn E4 | Yn M | Yn E2 | Yg W | Yg Wd | 12 |
| 13 | Yg E | Yg E1 | Yn F | Yn M | Yg E | Yg E1 | Yg E | Yg E3 | Yn E | Yn F | Yn E | Yn W | Yg M | Yg F | Yn M | Yn E4 | Yn M | Yn E2 | Yg W | Yg Wd | Yg W | Yg M | Yn W | Yn Wd | 13 |
| 14 | Yn E | Yn F | Yg E | Yg E3 | Yn E | Yn F | Yn E | Yn W | Yg M | Yg F | Yg M | Yg W | Yn M | Yn E2 | Yg W | Yg Wd | Yg W | Yg M | Yn W | Yn Wd | Yn W | Yn M | Yg Wd | Yg E1 | 14 |
| 15 | Yg M | Yg F | Yn E | Yn W | Yg M | Yg F | Yg M | Yg W | Yn M | Yn E2 | Yn M | Yn E4 | Yg W | Yg M | Yn W | Yn Wd | Yn W | Yn M | Yg Wd | Yg E1 | Yg Wd | Yg E3 | Yn Wd | Yn F | 15 |
| 16 | Yn M | Yn E2 | Yg M | Yg W | Yn M | Yn E2 | Yn M | Yn E4 | Yg W | Yg M | Yg W | Yg Wd | Yn W | Yn M | Yg Wd | Yg E1 | Yg Wd | Yg E3 | Yn Wd | Yn F | Yn Wd | Yn W | Yg F | Yg F | 16 |
| 17 | Yg W | Yg M | Yn M | Yn E4 | Yg W | Yg M | Yg W | Yg Wd | Yn W | Yn M | Yn W | Yn Wd | Yg Wd | Yg E3 | Yn Wd | Yn F | Yn Wd | Yn W | Yg F | Yg F | Yg F | Yg W | Yn F | Yn E2 | 17 |
| 18 | Yn W | Yn M | Yg W | Yg Wd | Yn W | Yn M | Yn W | Yn Wd | Yg Wd | Yg E3 | Yg Wd | Yg E1 | Yn Wd | Yn W | Yg F | Yg F | Yg F | Yg W | Yn F | Yn E2 | Yn F | Yn E4 | Yg E | Yg M | 18 |
| 19 | Yg Wd | Yg E3 | Yn W | Yn Wd | Yg Wd | Yg E3 | Yg Wd | Yg E1 | Yn Wd | Yn W | Yn Wd | Yn F | Yg F | Yg W | Yn F | Yn E2 | Yn F | Yn E4 | Yg E | Yg M | Yg E | Yg Wd | Yn E | Yn M | 19 |
| 20 | Yn Wd | Yn W | Yg Wd | Yg E1 | Yn Wd | Yn W | Yn Wd | Yn F | Yg F | Yg W | Yg F | Yg F | Yn F | Yn E4 | Yg E | Yg M | Yg E | Yg Wd | Yn E | Yn M | Yn E | Yn Wd | Yg M | Yg E3 | 20 |
| 21 | Yg F | Yg W | Yn Wd | Yn F | Yg F | Yg W | Yg F | Yg F | Yn F | Yn E4 | Yn F | Yn E2 | Yg E | Yg Wd | Yn E | Yn M | Yn E | Yn Wd | Yg M | Yg E3 | Yg M | Yg E1 | Yn M | Yn W | 21 |
| 22 | Yn F | Yn E4 | Yg F | Yg F | Yn F | Yn E4 | Yn F | Yn E2 | Yg E | Yg Wd | Yg E | Yg M | Yn E | Yn Wd | Yg M | Yg E3 | Yg M | Yg E1 | Yn M | Yn W | Yn M | Yn F | Yg W | Yg W | 22 |
| 23 | Yg E | Yg Wd | Yn F | Yn E2 | Yg E | Yg Wd | Yg E | Yg M | Yn E | Yn Wd | Yn E | Yn M | Yg M | Yg E1 | Yn M | Yn W | Yn M | Yn F | Yg W | Yg W | Yg W | Yg F | Yn W | Yn E4 | 23 |
| 24 | Yn E | Yn Wd | Yg E | Yg M | Yn E | Yn Wd | Yn E | Yn M | Yg M | Yg E1 | Yg M | Yg E3 | Yn M | Yn F | Yg W | Yg W | Yg W | Yg F | Yn W | Yn E4 | Yn W | Yn E2 | Yg Wd | Yg Wd | 24 |
| 25 | Yg M | Yg E1 | Yn E | Yn M | Yg M | Yg E1 | Yg M | Yg E3 | Yn M | Yn F | Yn M | Yn W | Yg W | Yg F | Yn W | Yn E4 | Yn W | Yn E2 | Yg Wd | Yg Wd | Yg Wd | Yg M | Yn Wd | Yn Wd | 25 |
| 26 | Yn M | Yn F | Yg M | Yg E3 | Yn M | Yn F | Yn M | Yn W | Yg W | Yg F | Yg W | Yg W | Yn W | Yn E2 | Yg Wd | Yg Wd | Yg Wd | Yg M | Yn Wd | Yn Wd | Yn Wd | Yn M | Yg F | Yg E1 | 26 |
| 27 | Yg W | Yg F | Yn M | Yn W | Yg W | Yg F | Yg W | Yg W | Yn W | Yn E2 | Yn W | Yn E4 | Yg Wd | Yg M | Yn Wd | Yn Wd | Yn Wd | Yn M | Yg F | Yg E1 | Yg F | Yg E3 | Yn F | Yn F | 27 |
| 28 | Yn W | Yn E2 | Yg W | Yg W | Yn W | Yn E2 | Yn W | Yn E4 | Yg Wd | Yg M | Yg Wd | Yg Wd | Yn Wd | Yn M | Yg F | Yg E1 | Yg F | Yg E3 | Yn F | Yn F | Yn F | Yn W | Yg E | Yg F | 28 |
| 29 | Yg Wd | Yg M | Yn W | Yn E4 | Yg Wd | Yg M | Yg Wd | Yg Wd | Yn Wd | Yn M | Yn Wd | Yn Wd | Yg F | Yg E3 | Yn F | Yn F | Yn F | Yn W | Yg E | Yg F | Yg E | Yg W | Yn E | Yn E2 | 29 |
| 30 | | | Yg Wd | Yg Wd | Yn Wd | Yn M | Yn Wd | Yn Wd | Yg F | Yg E3 | Yg F | Yg E1 | Yn F | Yn W | Yg E | Yg F | Yg E | Yg W | Yn E | Yn E2 | Yn E | Yn E4 | Yg M | Yg M | 30 |
| 31 | | | Yn Wd | Yn Wd | | | Yg F | Yg E1 | | | Yn F | Yn F | Yg E | Yg W | | | Yn E | Yn E4 | | | Yg M | Yg Wd | Yn M | Yn M | 31 |
| 1 | Yn Wd | Yn M | Yg F | Yg E1 | Yg F | Yg E3 | Yn F | Yn F | Yn F | Yn W | Yg E | Yg F | Yn E | Yn E4 | Yn E | Yn E2 | Yg M | Yg Wd | Yg M | Yg M | Yn M | Yn Wd | Yg W | Yg E3 | 1 |
| 2 | Yg F | Yg E3 | Yn F | Yn F | Yn F | Yn W | Yg E | Yg F | Yg E | Yg W | Yn E | Yn E2 | Yg M | Yg Wd | Yg M | Yg M | Yn M | Yn Wd | Yn M | Yn M | Yg W | Yg E1 | Yn W | Yn W | 2 |
| 3 | Yn F | Yn W | Yg E | Yg F | Yg E | Yg W | Yn E | Yn E2 | Yn E | Yn E4 | Yg M | Yg M | Yn M | Yn Wd | Yn M | Yn M | Yg W | Yg E1 | Yg W | Yg E3 | Yn W | Yn F | Yg Wd | Yg W | 3 |
| 4 | Yg E | Yg W | Yn E | Yn E2 | Yn E | Yn E4 | Yg M | Yg M | Yg M | Yg Wd | Yn M | Yn M | Yg W | Yg E1 | Yg W | Yg E3 | Yn W | Yn F | Yn W | Yn W | Yg Wd | Yg F | | | 4 |
| 5 | | | | | | | Yn M | Yn M | Yn M | Yn Wd | Yg W | Yg E3 | Yn W | Yn F | Yn W | Yn W | Yg Wd | Yg F | Yg Wd | Yg W | | | | | 5 |
| 6 | | | | | | | | | Yg W | Yg E1 | Yn W | Yn W | Yg Wd | Yg F | Yg Wd | Yg W | Yn Wd | Yn E2 | Yn Wd | Yn E4 | | | | | 6 |
| 7 | | | | | | | | | | | | | Yn Wd | Yn E2 | Yn Wd | Yn E4 | | | | | | | | | 7 |
| 8 | | | | | | | | | | | | | | | | | | | | | | | | | 8 |

# YEAR OF THE OX

| | H | E | H | E | H | E | H | E | H | E | H | E | H | E | H | E | H | E | H | E | H | E | H | E | |
|---|---|---|---|---|---|---|---|---|---|---|---|---|---|---|---|---|---|---|---|---|---|---|---|---|---|
| **YEAR** | **YEAR** YnE | YnE4 | 1949 | | | | | | | | | | | | | | | | | | | | 1950 | | |
| **MONTH** | 4 Feb - 5 Mar | | 6 Mar - 4 Apr | | 5 Apr - 5 May | | 6 May - 5 June | | 6 June - 6 Jul | | 7 Jul - 7 Aug | | 8 Aug - 7 Sep | | 8 Sep - 7 Oct | | 8 Oct - 7 Nov | | 8 Nov - 6 Dec | | 7 Dec - 5 Jan | | 6 Jan - 3 Feb | | |
| | Yg F | Yg Wd | Yn F | Yn Wd | Yg E | Yg E1 | Yn E | Yn F | Yg M | Yg F | Yn M | Yn E2 | Yg W | Yg M | Yn W | Yn M | Yg Wd | Yg E3 | Yn Wd | Yn W | Yg F | Yg W | Yn F | Yn E4 | |
| **Starting time** | 1st day | Mid-pt | 1st day | Mid-pt | 1st day | Mid-pt | 1st day | Mid-pt | 1st day | Mid-pt | 1st day | Mid-pt | 1st day | Mid-pt | 1st day | Mid-pt | 1st day | Mid-pt | 1st day | Mid-pt | 1st day | Mid-pt | 1st day | Mid-pt | |
| Date | 4 | 19 | 6 | 21 | 5 | 20 | 6 | 21 | 6 | 22 | 7 | 23 | 8 | 23 | 8 | 23 | 8 | 24 | 8 | 22 | 7 | 22 | 6 | 20 | |
| Hour | 1123 | 0727 | 0540 | 0649 | 1052 | 1818 | 0437 | 1752 | 0907 | 0203 | 1932 | 1257 | 0516 | 1949 | 0755 | 1706 | 2312 | 0204 | 0200 | 2317 | 1834 | 1224 | 0539 | 2300 | |
| **DATE** 4 | Yn Wd | Yn E4 | | | | | | | | | | | | | | | | | | | | | | | 4 |
| 5 | Yg F | Yg Wd | | | Yn Wd | Yn E4 | | | | | | | | | | | | | | | | | | | 5 |
| 6 | Yn F | Yn Wd | Yn Wd | Yn E2 | Yg F | Yg Wd | Yg F | Yg M | Yn F | Yn Wd | | | | | | | | | | | | | Yn M | Yn E4 | 6 |
| 7 | Yg E | Yg E1 | Yg F | Yg M | Yn F | Yn Wd | Yn F | Yn M | Yg E | Yg E1 | Yg E | Yg E3 | | | | | | | | | Yn M | Yn E2 | Yg W | Yg Wd | 7 |
| 8 | Yn E | Yn F | Yn F | Yn M | Yg E | Yg E1 | Yg E | Yg E3 | Yn E | Yn F | Yn E | Yn W | Yg M | Yg F | Yn M | Yn E4 | Yn M | Yn E2 | Yg W | Yg Wd | Yg W | Yg M | Yn W | Yn Wd | 8 |
| 9 | Yg M | Yg F | Yg E | Yg E3 | Yn E | Yn F | Yn E | Yn W | Yg M | Yg F | Yg M | Yg W | Yn M | Yn E2 | Yg W | Yg Wd | Yg W | Yg M | Yn W | Yn Wd | Yn W | Yn M | Yg Wd | Yg E1 | 9 |
| 10 | Yn M | Yn E2 | Yn E | Yn W | Yg M | Yg F | Yg M | Yg W | Yn M | Yn E2 | Yn M | Yn E4 | Yg W | Yg M | Yn W | Yn Wd | Yn W | Yn M | Yg Wd | Yg E1 | Yg Wd | Yg E3 | Yn Wd | Yn F | 10 |
| 11 | Yg W | Yg M | Yg M | Yg W | Yn M | Yn E2 | Yn M | Yn E4 | Yg W | Yg M | Yg W | Yg Wd | Yn W | Yn M | Yg Wd | Yg E1 | Yg Wd | Yg E3 | Yn Wd | Yn F | Yn Wd | Yn W | Yg F | Yg F | 11 |
| 12 | Yn W | Yn M | Yn M | Yn E4 | Yg W | Yg M | Yg W | Yg Wd | Yn W | Yn M | Yn W | Yn Wd | Yg Wd | Yg E3 | Yn Wd | Yn F | Yn Wd | Yn W | Yg F | Yg F | Yg F | Yg W | Yn F | Yn E2 | 12 |
| 13 | Yg Wd | Yg E3 | Yg W | Yg Wd | Yn W | Yn M | Yn W | Yn Wd | Yg Wd | Yg E3 | Yg Wd | Yg E1 | Yn Wd | Yn W | Yg F | Yg F | Yg F | Yg W | Yn F | Yn E2 | Yn F | Yn E4 | Yg E | Yg M | 13 |
| 14 | Yn Wd | Yn W | Yn W | Yn Wd | Yg Wd | Yg E3 | Yg Wd | Yg E1 | Yn Wd | Yn W | Yn Wd | Yn F | Yg F | Yg W | Yn F | Yn E2 | Yn F | Yn E4 | Yg E | Yg M | Yg E | Yg Wd | Yn E | Yn M | 14 |
| 15 | Yg F | Yg W | Yg Wd | Yg E1 | Yn Wd | Yn W | Yn Wd | Yn F | Yg F | Yg W | Yg F | Yg F | Yn F | Yn E4 | Yg E | Yg M | Yg E | Yg Wd | Yn E | Yn M | Yn E | Yn Wd | Yg M | Yg E3 | 15 |
| 16 | Yn F | Yn E4 | Yn Wd | Yn F | Yg F | Yg W | Yg F | Yg F | Yn F | Yn E4 | Yn F | Yn E2 | Yg E | Yg Wd | Yn E | Yn M | Yn E | Yn Wd | Yg M | Yg E3 | Yg M | Yg E1 | Yn M | Yn W | 16 |
| 17 | Yg E | Yg Wd | Yg F | Yg F | Yn F | Yn E4 | Yn F | Yn E2 | Yg E | Yg Wd | Yg E | Yg M | Yn E | Yn Wd | Yg M | Yg E3 | Yg M | Yg E1 | Yn M | Yn W | Yn M | Yn F | Yg W | Yg W | 17 |
| 18 | Yn E | Yn Wd | Yn F | Yn E2 | Yg E | Yg Wd | Yg E | Yg M | Yn E | Yn Wd | Yn E | Yn M | Yg M | Yg E1 | Yn M | Yn W | Yn M | Yn F | Yg W | Yg W | Yg W | Yg F | Yn W | Yn E4 | 18 |
| 19 | Yg M | Yg E1 | Yg E | Yg M | Yn E | Yn Wd | Yn E | Yn M | Yg M | Yg E1 | Yg M | Yg E3 | Yn M | Yn F | Yg W | Yg W | Yg W | Yg F | Yn W | Yn E4 | Yn W | Yn E2 | Yg Wd | Yg Wd | 19 |
| 20 | Yn M | Yn F | Yn E | Yn M | Yg M | Yg E1 | Yg M | Yg E3 | Yn M | Yn F | Yn M | Yn W | Yg W | Yg F | Yn W | Yn E4 | Yn W | Yn E2 | Yg Wd | Yg Wd | Yg Wd | Yg M | Yn Wd | Yn Wd | 20 |
| 21 | Yg W | Yg F | Yg M | Yg E3 | Yn M | Yn F | Yn M | Yn W | Yg W | Yg F | Yg W | Yg W | Yn W | Yn E2 | Yg Wd | Yg Wd | Yg Wd | Yg M | Yn Wd | Yn Wd | Yn Wd | Yn M | Yg F | Yg E1 | 21 |
| 22 | Yn W | Yn E2 | Yn M | Yn W | Yg W | Yg F | Yg W | Yg W | Yn W | Yn E2 | Yn W | Yn E4 | Yg Wd | Yg M | Yn Wd | Yn Wd | Yn Wd | Yn M | Yg F | Yg E1 | Yg F | Yg E3 | Yn F | Yn F | 22 |
| 23 | Yg Wd | Yg M | Yg W | Yg W | Yn W | Yn E2 | Yn W | Yn E4 | Yg Wd | Yg M | Yg Wd | Yg Wd | Yn Wd | Yn M | Yg F | Yg E1 | Yg F | Yg E3 | Yn F | Yn F | Yn F | Yn W | Yg E | Yg F | 23 |
| 24 | Yn Wd | Yn M | Yn W | Yn E4 | Yg Wd | Yg M | Yg Wd | Yg Wd | Yn Wd | Yn M | Yn Wd | Yn Wd | Yg F | Yg E3 | Yn F | Yn F | Yn F | Yn W | Yg E | Yg F | Yg E | Yg W | Yn E | Yn E2 | 24 |
| 25 | Yg F | Yg E3 | Yg Wd | Yg Wd | Yn Wd | Yn M | Yn Wd | Yn Wd | Yg F | Yg E3 | Yg F | Yg E1 | Yn F | Yn W | Yg E | Yg F | Yg E | Yg W | Yn E | Yn E2 | Yn E | Yn E4 | Yg M | Yg M | 25 |
| 26 | Yn F | Yn W | Yn Wd | Yn Wd | Yg F | Yg E3 | Yg F | Yg E1 | Yn F | Yn W | Yn F | Yn F | Yg E | Yg W | Yn E | Yn E2 | Yn E | Yn E4 | Yg M | Yg M | Yg M | Yg Wd | Yn M | Yn M | 26 |
| 27 | Yg E | Yg W | Yg F | Yg E1 | Yn F | Yn W | Yn F | Yn F | Yg E | Yg W | Yg E | Yg F | Yn E | Yn E4 | Yg M | Yg M | Yg M | Yg Wd | Yn M | Yn M | Yn M | Yn Wd | Yg W | Yg E3 | 27 |
| 28 | Yn E | Yn E4 | Yn F | Yn F | Yg E | Yg W | Yg E | Yg F | Yn E | Yn E4 | Yn E | Yn E2 | Yg M | Yg Wd | Yn M | Yn M | Yn M | Yn Wd | Yg W | Yg E3 | Yg W | Yg E1 | Yn W | Yn W | 28 |
| 29 | | | Yg E | Yg F | Yn E | Yn E4 | Yn E | Yn E2 | Yg M | Yg Wd | Yg M | Yg M | Yn M | Yn Wd | Yg W | Yg E3 | Yg W | Yg E1 | Yn W | Yn W | Yn W | Yn F | Yg Wd | Yg W | 29 |
| 30 | | | Yn E | Yn E2 | Yg M | Yg Wd | Yg M | Yg M | Yn M | Yn Wd | Yn M | Yn M | Yg W | Yg E1 | Yn W | Yn W | Yn W | Yn F | Yg Wd | Yg W | Yg Wd | Yg F | Yn Wd | Yn E4 | 30 |
| 31 | | | Yg M | Yg M | | | Yn M | Yn M | | | Yg W | Yg E3 | Yn W | Yn F | | | Yg Wd | Yg F | | | Yn Wd | Yn E2 | Yg F | Yg Wd | 31 |
| 1 | Yg M | Yg Wd | Yn M | Yn M | Yn M | Yn Wd | Yg W | Yg E3 | Yg W | Yg E1 | Yn W | Yn W | Yg Wd | Yg F | Yg Wd | Yg W | Yn Wd | Yn E2 | Yn Wd | Yn E4 | Yg F | Yg M | Yn F | Yn Wd | 1 |
| 2 | Yn M | Yn Wd | Yg W | Yg E3 | Yg W | Yg E1 | Yn W | Yn W | Yn W | Yn F | Yg Wd | Yg W | Yn Wd | Yn E2 | Yn Wd | Yn E4 | Yg F | Yg M | Yg F | Yg Wd | Yn F | Yn M | Yg E | Yg E1 | 2 |
| 3 | Yg W | Yg E1 | Yn W | Yn W | Yn W | Yn F | Yg Wd | Yg W | Yg Wd | Yg F | Yn Wd | Yn E4 | Yg F | Yg M | Yg F | Yg Wd | Yn F | Yn M | Yn F | Yn Wd | Yg E | Yg E3 | Yn E | Yn F | 3 |
| 4 | Yn W | Yn F | Yg Wd | Yg W | Yg Wd | Yg F | Yn Wd | Yn E4 | Yn Wd | Yn E2 | Yg F | Yg Wd | Yn F | Yn M | Yn F | Yn Wd | Yg E | Yg E3 | Yg E | Yg E1 | Yn E | Yn W | | | 4 |
| 5 | Yg Wd | Yg F | | | Yn Wd | Yn E2 | Yg F | Yg Wd | Yg F | Yg M | Yn F | Yn Wd | Yg E | Yg E3 | Yg E | Yg E1 | Yn E | Yn W | Yn E | Yn F | Yg M | Yg W | | | 5 |
| 6 | | | | | | | | | Yn F | Yn M | Yg E | Yg E1 | Yn E | Yn W | Yn E | Yn F | Yg M | Yg W | Yg M | Yg F | | | | | 6 |
| 7 | | | | | | | | | | | Yn E | Yn F | Yg M | Yg W | Yg M | Yg F | Yn M | Yn E4 | | | | | | | 7 |
| 8 | | | | | | | | | | | | | | | | | | | | | | | | | 8 |

# YEAR OF THE TIGER

| | H | E | H | E | H | E | H | E | H | E | H | E | H | E | H | E | H | E | H | E | H | E | H | E | |
|---|---|---|---|---|---|---|---|---|---|---|---|---|---|---|---|---|---|---|---|---|---|---|---|---|---|
| YEAR | YEAR Yg M | Yg Wd | 1950 | | | | | | | | | | | | | | | | | | | | 1951 | | |
| MONTH | 4 Feb - 5 Mar | | 6 Mar - 4 Apr | | 5 Apr - 5 May | | 6 May - 5 June | | 6 June - 7 Jul | | 8 Jul - 7 Aug | | 8 Aug - 7 Sep | | 8 Sep - 8 Oct | | 9 Oct - 7 Nov | | 8 Nov - 7 Dec | | 8 Dec - 5 Jan | | 6 Jan - 3 Feb | | |
| | Yg E | Yg Wd | Yn E | Yn Wd | Yg M | Yg E1 | Yn M | Yn F | Yg W | Yg F | Yn W | Yn E2 | Yg Wd | Yg M | Yn Wd | Yn M | Yg F | Yg E3 | Yn F | Yn W | Yg E | Yg W | Yn E | Yn E4 | |
| Starting time | 1st day | Mid-pt | 1st day | Mid-pt | 1st day | Mid-pt | 1st day | Mid-pt | 1st day | Mid-pt | 1st day | Mid-pt | 1st day | Mid-pt | 1st day | Mid-pt | 1st day | Mid-pt | 1st day | Mid-pt | 1st day | Mid-pt | 1st day | Mid-pt | |
| Date | 4 | 19 | 6 | 21 | 5 | 21 | 6 | 21 | 6 | 22 | 8 | 23 | 8 | 24 | 8 | 23 | 9 | 24 | 8 | 23 | 8 | 22 | 6 | 21 | |
| Hour | 1721 | 1318 | 1136 | 1236 | 1645 | 0000 | 1025 | 2328 | 1452 | 0737 | 0114 | 1830 | 1056 | 0124 | 1334 | 2244 | 0452 | 0745 | 0744 | 0503 | 0022 | 1814 | 1131 | 0453 | |
| DATE 4 | Yg M | Yg F | | | | | | | | | | | | | | | | | | | | | | | 4 |
| 5 | Yn M | Yn E2 | | | Yg M | Yg F | | | | | | | | | | | | | | | | | | | 5 |
| 6 | Yg W | Yg M | Yg M | Yg W | Yn M | Yn E2 | Yn M | Yn E4 | Yg W | Yg M | | | | | | | | | | | | | Yg F | Yg F | 6 |
| 7 | Yn W | Yn M | Yn M | Yn E4 | Yg W | Yg M | Yg W | Yg Wd | Yn W | Yn M | | | | | | | | | | | | | Yn F | Yn E2 | 7 |
| 8 | Yg Wd | Yg E3 | Yg W | Yg Wd | Yn W | Yn M | Yn W | Yn Wd | Yg Wd | Yg E3 | Yg Wd | Yg E1 | Yn Wd | Yn W | Yg F | Yg F | | | Yn F | Yn E2 | Yn F | Yn E4 | Yg E | Yg M | 8 |
| 9 | Yn Wd | Yn W | Yn W | Yn Wd | Yg Wd | Yg E3 | Yg Wd | Yg E1 | Yn Wd | Yn W | Yn Wd | Yn F | Yg F | Yg W | Yn F | Yn E2 | Yn F | Yn E4 | Yg E | Yg M | Yg E | Yg Wd | Yn E | Yn M | 9 |
| 10 | Yg F | Yg W | Yg Wd | Yg E1 | Yn Wd | Yn W | Yn Wd | Yn F | Yg F | Yg W | Yg F | Yg F | Yn F | Yn E4 | Yg E | Yg M | Yg E | Yg Wd | Yn E | Yn M | Yn E | Yn Wd | Yg M | Yg E3 | 10 |
| 11 | Yn F | Yn E4 | Yn Wd | Yn F | Yg F | Yg W | Yg F | Yg F | Yn F | Yn E4 | Yn F | Yn E2 | Yg E | Yg Wd | Yn E | Yn M | Yn E | Yn Wd | Yg M | Yg E3 | Yg M | Yg E1 | Yn M | Yn W | 11 |
| 12 | Yg E | Yg Wd | Yg F | Yg F | Yn F | Yn E4 | Yn F | Yn E2 | Yg E | Yg Wd | Yg E | Yg M | Yn E | Yn Wd | Yg M | Yg E3 | Yg M | Yg E1 | Yn M | Yn W | Yn M | Yn F | Yg W | Yg W | 12 |
| 13 | Yn E | Yn Wd | Yn F | Yn E2 | Yg E | Yg Wd | Yg E | Yg M | Yn E | Yn Wd | Yn E | Yn M | Yg M | Yg E1 | Yn M | Yn W | Yn M | Yn F | Yg W | Yg W | Yg W | Yg F | Yn W | Yn E4 | 13 |
| 14 | Yg M | Yg E1 | Yg E | Yg M | Yn E | Yn Wd | Yn E | Yn M | Yg M | Yg E1 | Yg M | Yg E3 | Yn M | Yn F | Yg W | Yg W | Yg W | Yg F | Yn W | Yn E4 | Yn W | Yn E2 | Yg Wd | Yg Wd | 14 |
| 15 | Yn M | Yn F | Yn E | Yn M | Yg M | Yg E1 | Yg M | Yg E3 | Yn M | Yn F | Yn M | Yn W | Yg W | Yg F | Yn W | Yn E4 | Yn W | Yn E2 | Yg Wd | Yg Wd | Yg Wd | Yg M | Yn Wd | Yn Wd | 15 |
| 16 | Yg W | Yg F | Yg M | Yg E3 | Yn M | Yn F | Yn M | Yn W | Yg W | Yg F | Yg W | Yg W | Yn W | Yn E2 | Yg Wd | Yg Wd | Yg Wd | Yg M | Yn Wd | Yn Wd | Yn Wd | Yn M | Yg F | Yg E1 | 16 |
| 17 | Yn W | Yn E2 | Yn M | Yn W | Yg W | Yg F | Yg W | Yg W | Yn W | Yn E2 | Yn W | Yn E4 | Yg Wd | Yg M | Yn Wd | Yn Wd | Yn Wd | Yn M | Yg F | Yg E1 | Yg F | Yg E3 | Yn F | Yn F | 17 |
| 18 | Yg Wd | Yg M | Yg W | Yg W | Yn W | Yn E2 | Yn W | Yn E4 | Yg Wd | Yg M | Yg Wd | Yg Wd | Yn Wd | Yn M | Yg F | Yg E1 | Yg F | Yg E3 | Yn F | Yn F | Yn F | Yn W | Yg E | Yg F | 18 |
| 19 | Yn Wd | Yn M | Yn W | Yn E4 | Yg Wd | Yg M | Yg Wd | Yg Wd | Yn Wd | Yn M | Yn Wd | Yn Wd | Yg F | Yg E3 | Yn F | Yn F | Yn F | Yn W | Yg E | Yg F | Yg E | Yg W | Yn E | Yn E2 | 19 |
| 20 | Yg F | Yg E3 | Yg Wd | Yg Wd | Yn Wd | Yn M | Yn Wd | Yn Wd | Yg F | Yg E3 | Yg F | Yg E1 | Yn F | Yn W | Yg E | Yg F | Yg E | Yg W | Yn E | Yn E2 | Yn E | Yn E4 | Yg M | Yg M | 20 |
| 21 | Yn F | Yn W | Yn Wd | Yn Wd | Yg F | Yg E3 | Yg F | Yg E1 | Yn F | Yn W | Yn F | Yn F | Yg E | Yg W | Yn E | Yn E2 | Yn E | Yn E4 | Yg M | Yg M | Yg M | Yg Wd | Yn M | Yn M | 21 |
| 22 | Yg E | Yg W | Yg F | Yg E1 | Yn F | Yn W | Yn F | Yn F | Yg E | Yg W | Yg E | Yg F | Yn E | Yn E4 | Yg M | Yg M | Yg M | Yg Wd | Yn M | Yn M | Yn M | Yn Wd | Yg W | Yg E3 | 22 |
| 23 | Yn E | Yn E4 | Yn F | Yn F | Yg E | Yg W | Yg E | Yg F | Yn E | Yn E4 | Yn E | Yn E2 | Yg M | Yg Wd | Yn M | Yn M | Yn M | Yn Wd | Yg W | Yg E3 | Yg W | Yg E1 | Yn W | Yn W | 23 |
| 24 | Yg M | Yg Wd | Yg E | Yg F | Yn E | Yn E4 | Yn E | Yn E2 | Yg M | Yg Wd | Yg M | Yg M | Yn M | Yn Wd | Yg W | Yg E3 | Yg W | Yg E1 | Yn W | Yn W | Yn W | Yn F | Yg Wd | Yg W | 24 |
| 25 | Yn M | Yn Wd | Yn E | Yn E2 | Yg M | Yg Wd | Yg M | Yg M | Yn M | Yn Wd | Yn M | Yn M | Yg W | Yg E1 | Yn W | Yn W | Yn W | Yn F | Yg Wd | Yg W | Yg Wd | Yg F | Yn Wd | Yn E4 | 25 |
| 26 | Yg W | Yg E1 | Yg M | Yg M | Yn M | Yn Wd | Yn M | Yn M | Yg W | Yg E1 | Yg W | Yg E3 | Yn W | Yn F | Yg Wd | Yg W | Yg Wd | Yg F | Yn Wd | Yn E4 | Yn Wd | Yn E2 | Yg F | Yg Wd | 26 |
| 27 | Yn W | Yn F | Yn M | Yn M | Yg W | Yg E1 | Yg W | Yg E3 | Yn W | Yn F | Yn W | Yn W | Yg Wd | Yg F | Yn Wd | Yn E4 | Yn Wd | Yn E2 | Yg F | Yg Wd | Yg F | Yg M | Yn F | Yn Wd | 27 |
| 28 | Yg Wd | Yg F | Yg W | Yg E3 | Yn W | Yn F | Yn W | Yn W | Yg Wd | Yg F | Yg Wd | Yg W | Yn Wd | Yn E2 | Yg F | Yg Wd | Yg F | Yg M | Yn F | Yn Wd | Yn F | Yn M | Yg E | Yg E1 | 28 |
| 29 | | | Yn W | Yn W | Yg Wd | Yg F | Yg Wd | Yg W | Yn Wd | Yn E2 | Yn Wd | Yn E4 | Yg F | Yg M | Yn F | Yn Wd | Yn F | Yn M | Yg E | Yg E1 | Yg E | Yg E3 | Yn E | Yn F | 29 |
| 30 | | | Yg Wd | Yg W | Yn Wd | Yn E2 | Yn Wd | Yn E4 | Yg F | Yg M | Yg F | Yg Wd | Yn F | Yn M | Yg E | Yg E1 | Yg E | Yg E3 | Yn E | Yn F | Yn E | Yn W | Yg M | Yg F | 30 |
| 31 | | | Yn Wd | Yn E4 | | | Yg F | Yg Wd | | | Yn F | Yn Wd | Yg E | Yg E3 | | | Yn E | Yn W | | | Yg M | Yg W | Yn M | Yn E2 | 31 |
| 1 | Yn Wd | Yn E2 | Yg F | Yg Wd | Yg F | Yg M | Yn F | Yn Wd | Yn F | Yn M | Yg E | Yg E1 | Yn E | Yn W | Yn E | Yn F | Yg M | Yg W | Yg M | Yg F | Yn M | Yn E4 | Yg W | Yg M | 1 |
| 2 | Yg F | Yg M | Yn F | Yn Wd | Yn F | Yn M | Yg E | Yg E1 | Yg E | Yg E3 | Yn E | Yn F | Yg M | Yg W | Yg M | Yg F | Yn M | Yn E4 | Yn M | Yn E2 | Yg W | Yg Wd | Yn W | Yn M | 2 |
| 3 | Yn F | Yn M | Yg E | Yg E1 | Yg E | Yg E3 | Yn E | Yn F | Yn E | Yn W | Yg M | Yg F | Yn M | Yn E4 | Yn M | Yn E2 | Yg W | Yg Wd | Yg W | Yg M | Yn W | Yn Wd | Yg Wd | Yg E3 | 3 |
| 4 | Yg E | Yg E3 | Yn E | Yn F | Yn E | Yn W | Yg M | Yg F | Yg M | Yg W | Yn M | Yn E2 | Yg W | Yg Wd | Yg W | Yg M | Yn W | Yn Wd | Yn W | Yn M | Yg Wd | Yg E1 | | | 4 |
| 5 | Yn E | Yn W | | | Yg M | Yg W | Yn M | Yn E2 | Yn M | Yn E4 | Yg W | Yg M | Yn W | Yn Wd | Yn W | Yn M | Yg Wd | Yg E1 | Yg Wd | Yg E3 | Yn Wd | Yn F | | | 5 |
| 6 | | | | | | | | | Yg W | Yg Wd | Yn W | Yn M | Yg Wd | Yg E1 | Yg Wd | Yg E3 | Yn Wd | Yn F | Yn Wd | Yn W | | | | | 6 |
| 7 | | | | | | | | | Yn W | Yn Wd | Yg Wd | Yg E3 | Yn Wd | Yn F | Yn Wd | Yn W | Yg F | Yg F | Yg F | Yg W | | | | | 7 |
| 8 | | | | | | | | | | | | | | | Yg F | Yg W | | | | | | | | | 8 |

# YEAR OF THE RABBIT

| | H | E | H | E | H | E | H | E | H | E | H | E | H | E | H | E | H | E | H | E | H | E | H | E | |
|---|---|---|---|---|---|---|---|---|---|---|---|---|---|---|---|---|---|---|---|---|---|---|---|---|---|
| YEAR | YEAR<br>Yn M | Yn Wd | | | | | | | | | | 1951 | | | | | | | | | | | 1952 | | |
| MONTH | 4 Feb - 5 Mar<br>Yg M | Yg Wd | 6 Mar - 4 Apr<br>Yn M | Yn Wd | 5 Apr - 5 May<br>Yg W | Yg E1 | 6 May - 5 June<br>Yn W | Yn F | 6 June - 7 Jul<br>Yg Wd | Yg F | 8 Jul - 7 Aug<br>Yn Wd | Yn E2 | 8 Aug - 7 Sep<br>Yg F | Yg M | 8 Sep - 8 Oct<br>Yn F | Yn M | 9 Oct - 7 Nov<br>Yg E | Yg E3 | 8 Nov - 7 Dec<br>Yn E | Yn W | 8 Dec - 5 Jan<br>Yg M | Yg W | 6 Jan - 4 Feb<br>Yn M | Yn E4 | |
| Starting time | 1st day | Mid-pt | 1st day | Mid-pt | 1st day | Mid-pt | 1st day | Mid-pt | 1st day | Mid-pt | 1st day | Mid-pt | 1st day | Mid-pt | 1st day | Mid-pt | 1st day | Mid-pt | 1st day | Mid-pt | 1st day | Mid-pt | 1st day | Mid-pt | |
| Date | 4 | 19 | 6 | 21 | 5 | 21 | 6 | 22 | 6 | 22 | 8 | 24 | 8 | 24 | 8 | 24 | 9 | 24 | 8 | 23 | 8 | 23 | 6 | 21 | |
| Hour | 2314 | 1910 | 1727 | 1826 | 2233 | 0541 | 1610 | 0516 | 2033 | 1325 | 0654 | 0021 | 1638 | 0717 | 1919 | 0438 | 1037 | 1337 | 1327 | 1052 | 0603 | 0001 | 1710 | 1039 | |
| DATE 4 | Yn Wd | Yn W | | | | | | | | | | | | | | | | | | | | | | | 4 |
| 5 | Yg F | Yg W | | | Yn Wd | Yn W | | | | | | | | | | | | | | | | | | | 5 |
| 6 | Yn F | Yn E4 | Yn Wd | Yn F | Yg F | Yg W | Yg F | Yg F | Yn F | Yn E4 | | | | | | | | | | | | | Yn M | Yn W | 6 |
| 7 | Yg E | Yg Wd | Yg F | Yg F | Yn F | Yn E4 | Yn F | Yn E2 | Yg E | Yg Wd | | | | | | | | | | | | | Yg W | Yg W | 7 |
| 8 | Yn E | Yn Wd | Yn F | Yn E2 | Yg E | Yg Wd | Yg E | Yg M | Yn E | Yn Wd | Yn E | Yn M | Yg M | Yg E1 | Yn M | Yn W | | | Yg W | Yg W | Yg W | Yg F | Yn W | Yn E4 | 8 |
| 9 | Yg M | Yg E1 | Yg E | Yg M | Yn E | Yn Wd | Yn E | Yn M | Yg M | Yg E1 | Yg M | Yg E3 | Yn M | Yn F | Yg W | Yg W | Yg W | Yg F | Yn W | Yn E4 | Yn W | Yn E2 | Yg Wd | Yg Wd | 9 |
| 10 | Yn M | Yn F | Yn E | Yn M | Yg M | Yg E1 | Yg M | Yg E3 | Yn M | Yn F | Yn M | Yn W | Yg W | Yg F | Yn W | Yn E4 | Yn W | Yn E2 | Yg Wd | Yg Wd | Yg Wd | Yg M | Yn Wd | Yn Wd | 10 |
| 11 | Yg W | Yg F | Yg M | Yg E3 | Yn M | Yn F | Yn M | Yn W | Yg W | Yg F | Yg W | Yg W | Yn W | Yn E2 | Yg Wd | Yg Wd | Yg Wd | Yg M | Yn Wd | Yn Wd | Yn Wd | Yn M | Yg F | Yg E1 | 11 |
| 12 | Yn W | Yn E2 | Yn M | Yn W | Yg W | Yg F | Yg W | Yg W | Yn W | Yn E2 | Yn W | Yn E4 | Yg Wd | Yg M | Yn Wd | Yn Wd | Yn Wd | Yn M | Yg F | Yg E1 | Yg F | Yg E3 | Yn F | Yn F | 12 |
| 13 | Yg Wd | Yg M | Yg W | Yg W | Yn W | Yn E2 | Yn W | Yn E4 | Yg Wd | Yg M | Yg Wd | Yg Wd | Yn Wd | Yn M | Yg F | Yg E1 | Yg F | Yg E3 | Yn F | Yn F | Yn F | Yn W | Yg E | Yg F | 13 |
| 14 | Yn Wd | Yn M | Yn W | Yn E4 | Yg Wd | Yg M | Yg Wd | Yg Wd | Yn Wd | Yn M | Yn Wd | Yn Wd | Yg F | Yg E3 | Yn F | Yn F | Yn F | Yn W | Yg E | Yg F | Yg E | Yg W | Yn E | Yn E2 | 14 |
| 15 | Yg F | Yg E3 | Yg Wd | Yg Wd | Yn Wd | Yn M | Yn Wd | Yn Wd | Yg F | Yg E3 | Yg F | Yg E1 | Yn F | Yn W | Yg E | Yg F | Yg E | Yg W | Yn E | Yn E2 | Yn E | Yn E4 | Yg M | Yg M | 15 |
| 16 | Yn F | Yn W | Yn Wd | Yn Wd | Yg F | Yg E3 | Yg F | Yg E1 | Yn F | Yn W | Yn F | Yn F | Yg E | Yg W | Yn E | Yn E2 | Yn E | Yn E4 | Yg M | Yg M | Yg M | Yg Wd | Yn M | Yn M | 16 |
| 17 | Yg E | Yg W | Yg F | Yg E1 | Yn F | Yn W | Yn F | Yn F | Yg E | Yg W | Yg E | Yg F | Yn E | Yn E4 | Yg M | Yg M | Yg M | Yg Wd | Yn M | Yn M | Yn M | Yn Wd | Yg W | Yg E3 | 17 |
| 18 | Yn E | Yn E4 | Yn F | Yn F | Yg E | Yg W | Yg E | Yg F | Yn E | Yn E4 | Yn E | Yn E2 | Yg M | Yg Wd | Yn M | Yn M | Yn M | Yn Wd | Yg W | Yg E3 | Yg W | Yg E1 | Yn W | Yn W | 18 |
| 19 | Yg M | Yg Wd | Yg E | Yg F | Yn E | Yn E4 | Yn E | Yn E2 | Yg M | Yg Wd | Yg M | Yg M | Yn M | Yn Wd | Yg W | Yg E3 | Yg W | Yg E1 | Yn W | Yn W | Yn W | Yn F | Yg Wd | Yg W | 19 |
| 20 | Yn M | Yn Wd | Yn E | Yn E2 | Yg M | Yg Wd | Yg M | Yg M | Yn M | Yn Wd | Yn M | Yn M | Yg W | Yg E1 | Yn W | Yn W | Yn W | Yn F | Yg Wd | Yg W | Yg Wd | Yg F | Yn Wd | Yn E4 | 20 |
| 21 | Yg W | Yg E1 | Yg M | Yg M | Yn M | Yn Wd | Yn M | Yn M | Yg W | Yg E1 | Yg W | Yg E3 | Yn W | Yn F | Yg Wd | Yg W | Yg Wd | Yg F | Yn Wd | Yn E4 | Yn Wd | Yn E2 | Yg F | Yg Wd | 21 |
| 22 | Yn W | Yn F | Yn M | Yn M | Yg W | Yg E1 | Yg W | Yg E3 | Yn W | Yn F | Yn W | Yn W | Yg Wd | Yg F | Yn Wd | Yn E4 | Yn Wd | Yn E2 | Yg F | Yg Wd | Yg F | Yg M | Yn F | Yn Wd | 22 |
| 23 | Yg Wd | Yg F | Yg W | Yg E3 | Yn W | Yn F | Yn W | Yn W | Yg Wd | Yg F | Yg Wd | Yg W | Yn Wd | Yn E2 | Yg F | Yg Wd | Yg F | Yg M | Yn F | Yn Wd | Yn F | Yn M | Yg E | Yg E1 | 23 |
| 24 | Yn Wd | Yn E2 | Yn W | Yn W | Yg Wd | Yg F | Yg Wd | Yg W | Yn Wd | Yn E2 | Yn Wd | Yn E4 | Yg F | Yg M | Yn F | Yn Wd | Yn F | Yn M | Yg E | Yg E1 | Yg E | Yg E3 | Yn E | Yn F | 24 |
| 25 | Yg F | Yg M | Yg Wd | Yg W | Yn Wd | Yn E2 | Yn Wd | Yn E4 | Yg F | Yg M | Yg F | Yg Wd | Yn F | Yn M | Yg E | Yg E1 | Yg E | Yg E3 | Yn E | Yn F | Yn E | Yn W | Yg M | Yg F | 25 |
| 26 | Yn F | Yn M | Yn Wd | Yn E4 | Yg F | Yg M | Yg F | Yg Wd | Yn F | Yn M | Yn F | Yn Wd | Yg E | Yg E3 | Yn E | Yn F | Yn E | Yn W | Yg M | Yg F | Yg M | Yg W | Yn M | Yn E2 | 26 |
| 27 | Yg E | Yg E3 | Yg F | Yg Wd | Yn F | Yn M | Yn F | Yn Wd | Yg E | Yg E3 | Yg E | Yg E1 | Yn E | Yn W | Yg M | Yg F | Yg M | Yg W | Yn M | Yn E2 | Yn M | Yn E4 | Yg W | Yg M | 27 |
| 28 | Yn E | Yn W | Yn F | Yn Wd | Yg E | Yg E3 | Yg E | Yg E1 | Yn E | Yn W | Yn E | Yn F | Yg M | Yg W | Yn M | Yn E2 | Yn M | Yn E4 | Yg W | Yg M | Yg W | Yg Wd | Yn W | Yn M | 28 |
| 29 | | | Yg E | Yg E1 | Yn E | Yn W | Yn E | Yn F | Yg M | Yg W | Yg M | Yg F | Yn M | Yn E4 | Yg W | Yg M | Yg W | Yg Wd | Yn W | Yn M | Yn W | Yn Wd | Yg Wd | Yg E3 | 29 |
| 30 | | | Yn E | Yn F | Yg M | Yg W | Yg M | Yg F | Yn M | Yn E4 | Yn M | Yn E2 | Yg W | Yg Wd | Yn W | Yn M | Yn W | Yn Wd | Yg Wd | Yg E3 | Yg Wd | Yg E1 | Yn Wd | Yn W | 30 |
| 31 | | | Yg M | Yg F | | | Yn M | Yn E2 | | | Yg W | Yg M | Yn W | Yn Wd | | | Yg Wd | Yg E1 | | | Yn Wd | Yn F | Yg F | Yg W | 31 |
| 1 | Yg M | Yg W | Yn M | Yn E2 | Yn M | Yn E4 | Yg W | Yg M | Yg W | Yg Wd | Yn W | Yn M | Yg Wd | Yg E1 | Yg Wd | Yg E3 | Yn Wd | Yn F | Yn Wd | Yn W | Yg F | Yg F | Yn F | Yn E4 | 1 |
| 2 | Yn M | Yn E4 | Yg W | Yg M | Yg W | Yg Wd | Yn W | Yn M | Yn W | Yn Wd | Yg Wd | Yg E3 | Yn Wd | Yn F | Yn Wd | Yn W | Yg F | Yg F | Yg F | Yg W | Yn F | Yn E2 | Yg E | Yg Wd | 2 |
| 3 | Yg W | Yg Wd | Yn W | Yn M | Yn W | Yn Wd | Yg Wd | Yg E3 | Yg Wd | Yg E1 | Yn Wd | Yn W | Yg F | Yg F | Yg F | Yg W | Yn F | Yn E2 | Yn F | Yn E4 | Yg E | Yg M | Yn E | Yn Wd | 3 |
| 4 | Yn W | Yn Wd | Yg Wd | Yg E3 | Yg Wd | Yg E1 | Yn Wd | Yn W | Yn Wd | Yn F | Yg F | Yg W | Yn F | Yn E2 | Yn F | Yn E4 | Yg E | Yg M | Yg E | Yg Wd | Yn E | Yn M | Yg M | Yg E1 | 4 |
| 5 | Yg Wd | Yg E1 | | | Yn Wd | Yn F | Yg F | Yg W | Yg F | Yg F | Yn F | Yn E4 | Yg E | Yg M | Yg E | Yg Wd | Yn E | Yn M | Yn E | Yn Wd | Yg M | Yg E3 | | | 5 |
| 6 | | | | | | | | | Yn F | Yn E2 | Yg E | Yg Wd | Yn E | Yn M | Yn E | Yn Wd | Yg M | Yg E3 | Yg M | Yg E1 | | | | | 6 |
| 7 | | | | | | | | | Yg E | Yg M | Yn E | Yn Wd | Yg M | Yg E3 | Yg M | Yg E1 | Yn M | Yn W | Yn M | Yn F | | | | | 7 |
| 8 | | | | | | | | | | | | | | | Yn M | Yn F | | | | | | | | | 8 |

# YEAR OF THE DRAGON

| | H | E | H | E | H | E | H | E | H | E | H | E | H | E | H | E | H | E | H | E | H | E | H | E | |
|---|---|---|---|---|---|---|---|---|---|---|---|---|---|---|---|---|---|---|---|---|---|---|---|---|---|
| YEAR | YEAR Yg W | Yg E1 | 1952 | | | | | | | | | | | | | | | | | | | | 1953 | | |
| MONTH | 5 Feb - 4 Mar | | 5 Mar - 4 Apr | | 5 Apr - 4 May | | 5 May - 5 June | | 6 June - 6 Jul | | 7 Jul - 6 Aug | | 7 Aug - 7 Sep | | 8 Sep - 7 Oct | | 8 Oct - 6 Nov | | 7 Nov - 6 Dec | | 7 Dec - 4 Jan | | 5 Jan - 3 Feb | | |
| | Yg W | Yg Wd | Yn W | Yn Wd | Yg Wd | Yg E1 | Yn Wd | Yn F | Yg F | Yg F | Yn F | Yn E2 | Yg E | Yg M | Yn E | Yn M | Yg M | Yg E3 | Yn M | Yn W | Yg W | Yg W | Yn W | Yn E4 | |
| Starting time | 1st day | Mid-pt | 1st day | Mid-pt | 1st day | Mid-pt | 1st day | Mid-pt | 1st day | Mid-pt | 1st day | Mid-pt | 1st day | Mid-pt | 1st day | Mid-pt | 1st day | Mid-pt | 1st day | Mid-pt | 1st day | Mid-pt | 1st day | Mid-pt | |
| Date | 5 | 20 | 5 | 21 | 5 | 20 | 5 | 21 | 6 | 21 | 7 | 23 | 7 | 23 | 8 | 23 | 8 | 23 | 7 | 22 | 7 | 22 | 5 | 20 | |
| Hour | 0454 | 0057 | 2308 | 0014 | 0416 | 1137 | 2154 | 1104 | 0221 | 1913 | 1245 | 0608 | 2232 | 1303 | 0114 | 1024 | 1633 | 1923 | 1922 | 1636 | 1156 | 0544 | 2303 | 1622 | |
| DATE 4 | | | | | | | | | | | | | | | | | | | | | | | | | 4 |
| 5 | Yn M | Yn F | Yg M | Yg E3 | Yn M | Yn F | Yn M | Yn W | | | | | | | | | | | | | | | Yg F | Yg E1 | 5 |
| 6 | Yg W | Yg F | Yn M | Yn W | Yg W | Yg F | Yg W | Yg W | Yn W | Yn E2 | | | | | | | | | | | | | Yn F | Yn F | 6 |
| 7 | Yn W | Yn E2 | Yg W | Yg W | Yn W | Yn E2 | Yn W | Yn E4 | Yg Wd | Yg M | Yg Wd | Yg Wd | Yn Wd | Yn M | | | | | Yn F | Yn F | Yn F | Yn W | Yg E | Yg F | 7 |
| 8 | Yg Wd | Yg M | Yn W | Yn E4 | Yg Wd | Yg M | Yg Wd | Yg Wd | Yn Wd | Yn M | Yn Wd | Yn Wd | Yg F | Yg E3 | Yn F | Yn F | Yn F | Yn W | Yg E | Yg F | Yg E | Yg W | Yn E | Yn E2 | 8 |
| 9 | Yn Wd | Yn M | Yg Wd | Yg Wd | Yn Wd | Yn M | Yn Wd | Yn Wd | Yg F | Yg E3 | Yg F | Yg E1 | Yn F | Yn W | Yg E | Yg F | Yg E | Yg W | Yn E | Yn E2 | Yn E | Yn E4 | Yg M | Yg M | 9 |
| 10 | Yg F | Yg E3 | Yn Wd | Yn Wd | Yg F | Yg E3 | Yg F | Yg E1 | Yn F | Yn W | Yn F | Yn F | Yg E | Yg W | Yn E | Yn E2 | Yn E | Yn E4 | Yg M | Yg M | Yg M | Yg Wd | Yn M | Yn M | 10 |
| 11 | Yn F | Yn W | Yg F | Yg E1 | Yn F | Yn W | Yn F | Yn F | Yg E | Yg W | Yg E | Yg F | Yn E | Yn E4 | Yg M | Yg M | Yg M | Yg Wd | Yn M | Yn M | Yn M | Yn Wd | Yg W | Yg E3 | 11 |
| 12 | Yg E | Yg W | Yn F | Yn F | Yg E | Yg W | Yg E | Yg F | Yn E | Yn E4 | Yn E | Yn E2 | Yg M | Yg Wd | Yn M | Yn M | Yn M | Yn Wd | Yg W | Yg E3 | Yg W | Yg E1 | Yn W | Yn W | 12 |
| 13 | Yn E | Yn E4 | Yg E | Yg F | Yn E | Yn E4 | Yn E | Yn E2 | Yg M | Yg Wd | Yg M | Yg M | Yn M | Yn Wd | Yg W | Yg E3 | Yg W | Yg E1 | Yn W | Yn W | Yn W | Yn F | Yg Wd | Yg W | 13 |
| 14 | Yg M | Yg Wd | Yn E | Yn E2 | Yg M | Yg Wd | Yg M | Yg M | Yn M | Yn Wd | Yn M | Yn M | Yg W | Yg E1 | Yn W | Yn W | Yn W | Yn F | Yg Wd | Yg W | Yg Wd | Yg F | Yn Wd | Yn E4 | 14 |
| 15 | Yn M | Yn Wd | Yg M | Yg M | Yn M | Yn Wd | Yn M | Yn M | Yg W | Yg E1 | Yg W | Yg E3 | Yn W | Yn F | Yg Wd | Yg W | Yg Wd | Yg F | Yn Wd | Yn E4 | Yn Wd | Yn E2 | Yg F | Yg Wd | 15 |
| 16 | Yg W | Yg E1 | Yn M | Yn M | Yg W | Yg E1 | Yg W | Yg E3 | Yn W | Yn F | Yn W | Yn W | Yg Wd | Yg F | Yn Wd | Yn E4 | Yn Wd | Yn E2 | Yg F | Yg Wd | Yg F | Yg M | Yn F | Yn Wd | 16 |
| 17 | Yn W | Yn F | Yg W | Yg E3 | Yn W | Yn F | Yn W | Yn W | Yg Wd | Yg F | Yg Wd | Yg W | Yn Wd | Yn E2 | Yg F | Yg Wd | Yg F | Yg M | Yn F | Yn Wd | Yn F | Yn M | Yg E | Yg E1 | 17 |
| 18 | Yg Wd | Yg F | Yn W | Yn W | Yg Wd | Yg F | Yg Wd | Yg W | Yn Wd | Yn E2 | Yn Wd | Yn E4 | Yg F | Yg M | Yn F | Yn Wd | Yn F | Yn M | Yg E | Yg E1 | Yg E | Yg E3 | Yn E | Yn F | 18 |
| 19 | Yn Wd | Yn E2 | Yg Wd | Yg W | Yn Wd | Yn E2 | Yn Wd | Yn E4 | Yg F | Yg M | Yg F | Yg Wd | Yn F | Yn M | Yg E | Yg E1 | Yg E | Yg E3 | Yn E | Yn F | Yn E | Yn W | Yg M | Yg F | 19 |
| 20 | Yg F | Yg M | Yn Wd | Yn E4 | Yg F | Yg M | Yg F | Yg Wd | Yn F | Yn M | Yn F | Yn Wd | Yg E | Yg E3 | Yn E | Yn F | Yn E | Yn W | Yg M | Yg F | Yg M | Yg W | Yn M | Yn E2 | 20 |
| 21 | Yn F | Yn M | Yg F | Yg Wd | Yn F | Yn M | Yn F | Yn Wd | Yg E | Yg E3 | Yg E | Yg E1 | Yn E | Yn W | Yg M | Yg F | Yg M | Yg W | Yn M | Yn E2 | Yn M | Yn E4 | Yg W | Yg M | 21 |
| 22 | Yg E | Yg E3 | Yn F | Yn Wd | Yg E | Yg E3 | Yg E | Yg E1 | Yn E | Yn W | Yn E | Yn F | Yg M | Yg W | Yn M | Yn E2 | Yn M | Yn E4 | Yg W | Yg M | Yg W | Yg Wd | Yn W | Yn M | 22 |
| 23 | Yn E | Yn W | Yg E | Yg E1 | Yn E | Yn W | Yn E | Yn F | Yg M | Yg W | Yg M | Yg F | Yn M | Yn E4 | Yg W | Yg M | Yg W | Yg Wd | Yn W | Yn M | Yn W | Yn Wd | Yg Wd | Yg E3 | 23 |
| 24 | Yg M | Yg W | Yn E | Yn F | Yg M | Yg W | Yg M | Yg F | Yn M | Yn E4 | Yn M | Yn E2 | Yg W | Yg Wd | Yn W | Yn M | Yn W | Yn Wd | Yg Wd | Yg E3 | Yg Wd | Yg E1 | Yn Wd | Yn W | 24 |
| 25 | Yn M | Yn E4 | Yg M | Yg F | Yn M | Yn E4 | Yn M | Yn E2 | Yg W | Yg Wd | Yg W | Yg M | Yn W | Yn Wd | Yg Wd | Yg E3 | Yg Wd | Yg E1 | Yn Wd | Yn W | Yn Wd | Yn F | Yg F | Yg W | 25 |
| 26 | Yg W | Yg Wd | Yn M | Yn E2 | Yg W | Yg Wd | Yg W | Yg M | Yn W | Yn Wd | Yn W | Yn M | Yg Wd | Yg E1 | Yn Wd | Yn W | Yn Wd | Yn F | Yg F | Yg W | Yg F | Yg F | Yn F | Yn E4 | 26 |
| 27 | Yn W | Yn Wd | Yg W | Yg M | Yn W | Yn Wd | Yn W | Yn M | Yg Wd | Yg E1 | Yg Wd | Yg E3 | Yn Wd | Yn F | Yg F | Yg W | Yg F | Yg F | Yn F | Yn E4 | Yn F | Yn E2 | Yg E | Yg Wd | 27 |
| 28 | Yg Wd | Yg E1 | Yn W | Yn M | Yg Wd | Yg E1 | Yg Wd | Yg E3 | Yn Wd | Yn F | Yn Wd | Yn W | Yg F | Yg F | Yn F | Yn E4 | Yn F | Yn E2 | Yg E | Yg Wd | Yg E | Yg M | Yn E | Yn Wd | 28 |
| 29 | Yn Wd | Yn F | Yg Wd | Yg E3 | Yn Wd | Yn F | Yn Wd | Yn W | Yg F | Yg F | Yg F | Yg W | Yn F | Yn E2 | Yg E | Yg Wd | Yg E | Yg M | Yn E | Yn Wd | Yn E | Yn M | Yg M | Yg E1 | 29 |
| 30 | | | Yn Wd | Yn W | Yg F | Yg F | Yg F | Yg W | Yn F | Yn E2 | Yn F | Yn E4 | Yg E | Yg M | Yn E | Yn Wd | Yn E | Yn M | Yg M | Yg E1 | Yg M | Yg E3 | Yn M | Yn F | 30 |
| 31 | | | Yg F | Yg W | | | Yn F | Yn E4 | | | Yg E | Yg Wd | Yn E | Yn M | | | Yg M | Yg E3 | | | Yn M | Yn W | Yg W | Yg F | 31 |
| 1 | Yg F | Yg F | Yn F | Yn E4 | Yn F | Yn E2 | Yg E | Yg Wd | Yg E | Yg M | Yn E | Yn Wd | Yg M | Yg E3 | Yg M | Yg E1 | Yn M | Yn W | Yn M | Yn F | Yg W | Yg W | Yn W | Yn E2 | 1 |
| 2 | Yn F | Yn E2 | Yg E | Yg Wd | Yg E | Yg M | Yn E | Yn Wd | Yn E | Yn M | Yg M | Yg E1 | Yn M | Yn W | Yn M | Yn F | Yg W | Yg W | Yg W | Yg F | Yn W | Yn E4 | Yg Wd | Yg M | 2 |
| 3 | Yg E | Yg M | Yn E | Yn Wd | Yn E | Yn M | Yg M | Yg E1 | Yg M | Yg E3 | Yn M | Yn F | Yg W | Yg W | Yg W | Yg F | Yn W | Yn E4 | Yn W | Yn E2 | Yg Wd | Yg Wd | Yn Wd | Yn M | 3 |
| 4 | Yn E | Yn M | Yg M | Yg E1 | Yg M | Yg E3 | Yn M | Yn F | Yn M | Yn W | Yg W | Yg F | Yn W | Yn E4 | Yn W | Yn E2 | Yg Wd | Yg Wd | Yg Wd | Yg M | Yn Wd | Yn Wd | | | 4 |
| 5 | | | | | | | Yg W | Yg F | Yg W | Yg W | Yn W | Yn E2 | Yg Wd | Yg Wd | Yg Wd | Yg M | Yn Wd | Yn Wd | Yn Wd | Yn M | | | | | 5 |
| 6 | | | | | | | | | Yn W | Yn E4 | Yg Wd | Yg M | Yn Wd | Yn Wd | Yn Wd | Yn M | Yg F | Yg E1 | Yg F | Yg E3 | | | | | 6 |
| 7 | | | | | | | | | | | | | Yg F | Yg E1 | Yg F | Yg E3 | | | | | | | | | 7 |
| 8 | | | | | | | | | | | | | | | | | | | | | | | | | 8 |

# YEAR OF THE SNAKE

| | H | E | H | E | H | E | H | E | H | E | H | E | H | E | H | E | H | E | H | E | H | E | H | E | |
|---|---|---|---|---|---|---|---|---|---|---|---|---|---|---|---|---|---|---|---|---|---|---|---|---|---|
| YEAR | YEAR<br>Yn W | Yn F | 1953 | | | | | | | | | | | | | | | | | | 1954 | | | | |
| MONTH | 4 Feb - 5 Mar | | 6 Mar - 4 Apr | | 5 Apr - 5 May | | 6 May - 5 June | | 6 June - 6 Jul | | 7 Jul - 7 Aug | | 8 Aug - 7 Sep | | 8 Sep - 7 Oct | | 8 Oct - 7 Nov | | 8 Nov - 6 Dec | | 7 Dec - 5 Jan | | 6 Jan - 3 Feb | | |
| | Yg Wd | Yg Wd | Yn Wd | Yn Wd | Yg F | Yg E1 | Yn F | Yn F | Yg E | Yg F | Yn E | Yn E2 | Yg M | Yg M | Yn M | Yn M | Yg W | Yg E3 | Yn W | Yn W | Yg Wd | Yg W | Yn Wd | Yn E4 | |
| Starting time | 1st day | Mid-pt | 1st day | Mid-pt | 1st day | Mid-pt | 1st day | Mid-pt | 1st day | Mid-pt | 1st day | Mid-pt | 1st day | Mid-pt | 1st day | Mid-pt | 1st day | Mid-pt | 1st day | Mid-pt | 1st day | Mid-pt | 1st day | Mid-pt | |
| Date | 4 | 19 | 6 | 21 | 5 | 20 | 6 | 21 | 6 | 22 | 7 | 23 | 8 | 23 | 8 | 23 | 8 | 24 | 8 | 22 | 7 | 22 | 6 | 20 | |
| Hour | 1046 | 0642 | 0503 | 0609 | 1013 | 1726 | 0353 | 1654 | 0817 | 0100 | 1836 | 1153 | 0415 | 1846 | 0654 | 1607 | 2211 | 0107 | 0102 | 2223 | 1738 | 1132 | 0446 | 2212 | |
| DATE 4 | Yg F | Yg E3 | | | | | | | | | | | | | | | | | | | | | | | 4 |
| 5 | Yn F | Yn W | | | Yg F | Yg E3 | | | | | | | | | | | | | | | | | | | 5 |
| 6 | Yg E | Yg W | Yg F | Yg E1 | Yn F | Yn W | Yn F | Yn F | Yg E | Yg W | | | | | | | | | | | | | Yg W | Yg E3 | 6 |
| 7 | Yn E | Yn E4 | Yn F | Yn F | Yg E | Yg W | Yg E | Yg F | Yn E | Yn E4 | Yn E | Yn E2 | | | | | | | | | Yg W | Yg E1 | Yn W | Yn W | 7 |
| 8 | Yg M | Yg Wd | Yg E | Yg F | Yn E | Yn E4 | Yn E | Yn E2 | Yg M | Yg Wd | Yg M | Yg M | Yn M | Yn Wd | Yg W | Yg E3 | Yg W | Yg E1 | Yn W | Yn W | Yn W | Yn F | Yg Wd | Yg W | 8 |
| 9 | Yn M | Yn Wd | Yn E | Yn E2 | Yg M | Yg Wd | Yg M | Yg M | Yn M | Yn Wd | Yn M | Yn M | Yg W | Yg E1 | Yn W | Yn W | Yn W | Yn F | Yg Wd | Yg W | Yg Wd | Yg F | Yn Wd | Yn E4 | 9 |
| 10 | Yg W | Yg E1 | Yg M | Yg M | Yn M | Yn Wd | Yn M | Yn M | Yg W | Yg E1 | Yg W | Yg E3 | Yn W | Yn F | Yg Wd | Yg W | Yg Wd | Yg F | Yn Wd | Yn E4 | Yn Wd | Yn E2 | Yg F | Yg Wd | 10 |
| 11 | Yn W | Yn F | Yn M | Yn M | Yg W | Yg E1 | Yg W | Yg E3 | Yn W | Yn F | Yn W | Yn W | Yg Wd | Yg F | Yn Wd | Yn E4 | Yn Wd | Yn E2 | Yg F | Yg Wd | Yg F | Yg M | Yn F | Yn Wd | 11 |
| 12 | Yg Wd | Yg F | Yg W | Yg E3 | Yn W | Yn F | Yn W | Yn W | Yg Wd | Yg F | Yg Wd | Yg W | Yn Wd | Yn E2 | Yg F | Yg Wd | Yg F | Yg M | Yn F | Yn Wd | Yn F | Yn M | Yg E | Yg E1 | 12 |
| 13 | Yn Wd | Yn E2 | Yn W | Yn W | Yg Wd | Yg F | Yg Wd | Yg W | Yn Wd | Yn E2 | Yn Wd | Yn E4 | Yg F | Yg M | Yn F | Yn Wd | Yn F | Yn M | Yg E | Yg E1 | Yg E | Yg E3 | Yn E | Yn F | 13 |
| 14 | Yg F | Yg M | Yg Wd | Yg W | Yn Wd | Yn E2 | Yn Wd | Yn E4 | Yg F | Yg M | Yg F | Yg Wd | Yn F | Yn M | Yg E | Yg E1 | Yg E | Yg E3 | Yn E | Yn F | Yn E | Yn W | Yg M | Yg F | 14 |
| 15 | Yn F | Yn M | Yn Wd | Yn E4 | Yg F | Yg M | Yg F | Yg Wd | Yn F | Yn M | Yn F | Yn Wd | Yg E | Yg E3 | Yn E | Yn F | Yn E | Yn W | Yg M | Yg F | Yg M | Yg W | Yn M | Yn E2 | 15 |
| 16 | Yg E | Yg E3 | Yg F | Yg Wd | Yn F | Yn M | Yn F | Yn Wd | Yg E | Yg E3 | Yg E | Yg E1 | Yn E | Yn W | Yg M | Yg F | Yg M | Yg W | Yn M | Yn E2 | Yn M | Yn E4 | Yg W | Yg M | 16 |
| 17 | Yn E | Yn W | Yn F | Yn Wd | Yg E | Yg E3 | Yg E | Yg E1 | Yn E | Yn W | Yn E | Yn F | Yg M | Yg W | Yn M | Yn E2 | Yn M | Yn E4 | Yg W | Yg M | Yg W | Yg Wd | Yn W | Yn M | 17 |
| 18 | Yg M | Yg W | Yg E | Yg E1 | Yn E | Yn W | Yn E | Yn F | Yg M | Yg W | Yg M | Yg F | Yn M | Yn E4 | Yg W | Yg M | Yg W | Yg Wd | Yn W | Yn M | Yn W | Yn Wd | Yg Wd | Yg E3 | 18 |
| 19 | Yn M | Yn E4 | Yn E | Yn F | Yg M | Yg W | Yg M | Yg F | Yn M | Yn E4 | Yn M | Yn E2 | Yg W | Yg Wd | Yn W | Yn M | Yn W | Yn Wd | Yg Wd | Yg E3 | Yg Wd | Yg E1 | Yn Wd | Yn W | 19 |
| 20 | Yg W | Yg Wd | Yg M | Yg F | Yn M | Yn E4 | Yn M | Yn E2 | Yg W | Yg Wd | Yg W | Yg M | Yn W | Yn Wd | Yg Wd | Yg E3 | Yg Wd | Yg E1 | Yn Wd | Yn W | Yn Wd | Yn F | Yg F | Yg W | 20 |
| 21 | Yn W | Yn Wd | Yn M | Yn E2 | Yg W | Yg Wd | Yg W | Yg M | Yn W | Yn Wd | Yn W | Yn M | Yg Wd | Yg E1 | Yn Wd | Yn W | Yn Wd | Yn F | Yg F | Yg W | Yg F | Yg F | Yn F | Yn E4 | 21 |
| 22 | Yg Wd | Yg E1 | Yg W | Yg M | Yn W | Yn Wd | Yn W | Yn M | Yg Wd | Yg E1 | Yg Wd | Yg E3 | Yn Wd | Yn F | Yg F | Yg W | Yg F | Yg F | Yn F | Yn E4 | Yn F | Yn E2 | Yg E | Yg Wd | 22 |
| 23 | Yn Wd | Yn F | Yn W | Yn M | Yg Wd | Yg E1 | Yg Wd | Yg E3 | Yn Wd | Yn F | Yn Wd | Yn W | Yg F | Yg F | Yn F | Yn E4 | Yn F | Yn E2 | Yg E | Yg Wd | Yg E | Yg M | Yn E | Yn Wd | 23 |
| 24 | Yg F | Yg F | Yg Wd | Yg E3 | Yn Wd | Yn F | Yn Wd | Yn W | Yg F | Yg F | Yg F | Yg W | Yn F | Yn E2 | Yg E | Yg Wd | Yg E | Yg M | Yn E | Yn Wd | Yn E | Yn M | Yg M | Yg E1 | 24 |
| 25 | Yn F | Yn E2 | Yn Wd | Yn W | Yg F | Yg F | Yg F | Yg W | Yn F | Yn E2 | Yn F | Yn E4 | Yg E | Yg M | Yn E | Yn Wd | Yn E | Yn M | Yg M | Yg E1 | Yg M | Yg E3 | Yn M | Yn F | 25 |
| 26 | Yg E | Yg M | Yg F | Yg W | Yn F | Yn E2 | Yn F | Yn E4 | Yg E | Yg M | Yg E | Yg Wd | Yn E | Yn M | Yg M | Yg E1 | Yg M | Yg E3 | Yn M | Yn F | Yn M | Yn W | Yg W | Yg F | 26 |
| 27 | Yn E | Yn M | Yn F | Yn E4 | Yg E | Yg M | Yg E | Yg Wd | Yn E | Yn M | Yn E | Yn Wd | Yg M | Yg E3 | Yn M | Yn F | Yn M | Yn W | Yg W | Yg F | Yg W | Yg W | Yn W | Yn E2 | 27 |
| 28 | Yg M | Yg E3 | Yg E | Yg Wd | Yn E | Yn M | Yn E | Yn Wd | Yg M | Yg E3 | Yg M | Yg E1 | Yn M | Yn W | Yg W | Yg F | Yg W | Yg W | Yn W | Yn E2 | Yn W | Yn E4 | Yg Wd | Yg M | 28 |
| 29 | | | Yn E | Yn Wd | Yg M | Yg E3 | Yg M | Yg E1 | Yn M | Yn W | Yn M | Yn F | Yg W | Yg W | Yn W | Yn E2 | Yn W | Yn E4 | Yg Wd | Yg M | Yg Wd | Yg Wd | Yn Wd | Yn M | 29 |
| 30 | | | Yg M | Yg E1 | Yn M | Yn W | Yn M | Yn F | Yg W | Yg W | Yg W | Yg F | Yn W | Yn E4 | Yg Wd | Yg M | Yg Wd | Yg Wd | Yn Wd | Yn M | Yn Wd | Yn Wd | Yg F | Yg E3 | 30 |
| 31 | | | Yn M | Yn F | | | Yg W | Yg F | | | Yn W | Yn E2 | Yg Wd | Yg Wd | | | Yn Wd | Yn Wd | | | Yg F | Yg E1 | Yn F | Yn W | 31 |
| 1 | Yn M | Yn W | Yg W | Yg F | Yg W | Yg W | Yn W | Yn E2 | Yn W | Yn E4 | Yg Wd | Yg M | Yn Wd | Yn Wd | Yn Wd | Yn M | Yg F | Yg E1 | Yg F | Yg E3 | Yn F | Yn F | Yg E | Yg W | 1 |
| 2 | Yg W | Yg W | Yn W | Yn E2 | Yn W | Yn E4 | Yg Wd | Yg M | Yg Wd | Yg Wd | Yn Wd | Yn M | Yg F | Yg E1 | Yg F | Yg E3 | Yn F | Yn F | Yn F | Yn W | Yg E | Yg F | Yn E | Yn E4 | 2 |
| 3 | Yn W | Yn E4 | Yg Wd | Yg M | Yg Wd | Yg Wd | Yn Wd | Yn M | Yn Wd | Yn Wd | Yg F | Yg E3 | Yn F | Yn F | Yn F | Yn W | Yg E | Yg F | Yg E | Yg W | Yn E | Yn E2 | Yg M | Yg Wd | 3 |
| 4 | Yg Wd | Yg Wd | Yn Wd | Yn M | Yn Wd | Yn Wd | Yg F | Yg E3 | Yg F | Yg E1 | Yn F | Yn W | Yg E | Yg F | Yg E | Yg W | Yn E | Yn E2 | Yn E | Yn E4 | Yg M | Yg M | | | 4 |
| 5 | Yn Wd | Yn Wd | | | Yg F | Yg E1 | Yn F | Yn W | Yn F | Yn F | Yg E | Yg W | Yn E | Yn E2 | Yn E | Yn E4 | Yg M | Yg M | Yg M | Yg Wd | Yn M | Yn M | | | 5 |
| 6 | | | | | | | | | Yg E | Yg F | Yn E | Yn E4 | Yg M | Yg M | Yg M | Yg Wd | Yn M | Yn M | Yn M | Yn Wd | | | | | 6 |
| 7 | | | | | | | | | | | Yg M | Yg Wd | Yn M | Yn M | Yn M | Yn Wd | Yg W | Yg E3 | | | | | | | 7 |
| 8 | | | | | | | | | | | | | | | | | | | | | | | | | 8 |

# YEAR OF THE HORSE

| | H | E | H | E | H | E | H | E | H | E | H | E | H | E | H | E | H | E | H | E | H | E | H | E | |
|---|---|---|---|---|---|---|---|---|---|---|---|---|---|---|---|---|---|---|---|---|---|---|---|---|---|
| YEAR | YEAR Yg Wd | Yg F | 1954 | | | | | | | | | | | | | | | | | | 1955 | | | | |
| MONTH | 4 Feb - 5 Mar | | 6 Mar - 4 Apr | | 5 Apr - 5 May | | 6 May - 5 June | | 6 June - 7 Jul | | 8 Jul - 7 Aug | | 8 Aug - 7 Sep | | 8 Sep - 8 Oct | | 9 Oct - 7 Nov | | 8 Nov - 6 Dec | | 7 Dec - 5 Jan | | 6 Jan - 3 Feb | | |
| | Yg F | Yg Wd | Yn F | Yn Wd | Yg E | Yg E1 | Yn E | Yn F | Yg M | Yg F | Yn M | Yn E2 | Yg W | Yg M | Yn W | Yn M | Yg Wd | Yg E3 | Yn Wd | Yn W | Yg F | Yg W | Yn F | Yn E4 | |
| Starting time | 1st day | Mid-pt | 1st day | Mid-pt | 1st day | Mid-pt | 1st day | Mid-pt | 1st day | Mid-pt | 1st day | Mid-pt | 1st day | Mid-pt | 1st day | Mid-pt | 1st day | Mid-pt | 1st day | Mid-pt | 1st day | Mid-pt | 1st day | Mid-pt | |
| Date | 4 | 19 | 6 | 21 | 5 | 20 | 6 | 21 | 6 | 22 | 8 | 23 | 8 | 24 | 8 | 23 | 9 | 24 | 8 | 23 | 7 | 22 | 6 | 21 | |
| Hour | 1631 | 1233 | 1049 | 1154 | 1600 | 2320 | 0934 | 2248 | 1402 | 0655 | 0020 | 1745 | 1000 | 0037 | 1239 | 2156 | 0358 | 0657 | 0651 | 0415 | 2329 | 1725 | 1036 | 0402 | |
| DATE 4 | Yn M | Yn Wd | | | | | | | | | | | | | | | | | | | | | | | 4 |
| 5 | Yg W | Yg E1 | | | Yn M | Yn Wd | | | | | | | | | | | | | | | | | | | 5 |
| 6 | Yn W | Yn F | Yn M | Yn M | Yg W | Yg E1 | Yg W | Yg E3 | Yn W | Yn F | | | | | | | | | | | | | Yn F | Yn Wd | 6 |
| 7 | Yg Wd | Yg F | Yg W | Yg E3 | Yn W | Yn F | Yn W | Yn W | Yg Wd | Yg F | | | | | | | | | | | Yn F | Yn M | Yg E | Yg E1 | 7 |
| 8 | Yn Wd | Yn E2 | Yn W | Yn W | Yg Wd | Yg F | Yg Wd | Yg W | Yn Wd | Yn E2 | Yn Wd | Yn E4 | Yg F | Yg M | Yn F | Yn Wd | | | Yg E | Yg E1 | Yg E | Yg E3 | Yn E | Yn F | 8 |
| 9 | Yg F | Yg M | Yg Wd | Yg W | Yn Wd | Yn E2 | Yn Wd | Yn E4 | Yg F | Yg M | Yg F | Yg Wd | Yn F | Yn M | Yg E | Yg E1 | Yg E | Yg E3 | Yn E | Yn F | Yn E | Yn W | Yg M | Yg F | 9 |
| 10 | Yn F | Yn M | Yn Wd | Yn E4 | Yg F | Yg M | Yg F | Yg Wd | Yn F | Yn M | Yn F | Yn Wd | Yg E | Yg E3 | Yn E | Yn F | Yn E | Yn W | Yg M | Yg F | Yg M | Yg W | Yn M | Yn E2 | 10 |
| 11 | Yg E | Yg E3 | Yg F | Yg Wd | Yn F | Yn M | Yn F | Yn Wd | Yg E | Yg E3 | Yg E | Yg E1 | Yn E | Yn W | Yg M | Yg F | Yg M | Yg W | Yn M | Yn E2 | Yn M | Yn E4 | Yg W | Yg M | 11 |
| 12 | Yn E | Yn W | Yn F | Yn Wd | Yg E | Yg E3 | Yg E | Yg E1 | Yn E | Yn W | Yn E | Yn F | Yg M | Yg W | Yn M | Yn E2 | Yn M | Yn E4 | Yg W | Yg M | Yg W | Yg Wd | Yn W | Yn M | 12 |
| 13 | Yg M | Yg W | Yg E | Yg E1 | Yn E | Yn W | Yn E | Yn F | Yg M | Yg W | Yg M | Yg F | Yn M | Yn E4 | Yg W | Yg M | Yg W | Yg Wd | Yn W | Yn M | Yn W | Yn Wd | Yg Wd | Yg E3 | 13 |
| 14 | Yn M | Yn E4 | Yn E | Yn F | Yg M | Yg W | Yg M | Yg F | Yn M | Yn E4 | Yn M | Yn E2 | Yg W | Yg Wd | Yn W | Yn M | Yn W | Yn Wd | Yg Wd | Yg E3 | Yg Wd | Yg E1 | Yn Wd | Yn W | 14 |
| 15 | Yg W | Yg Wd | Yg M | Yg F | Yn M | Yn E4 | Yn M | Yn E2 | Yg W | Yg Wd | Yg W | Yg M | Yn W | Yn Wd | Yg Wd | Yg E3 | Yg Wd | Yg E1 | Yn Wd | Yn W | Yn Wd | Yn F | Yg F | Yg W | 15 |
| 16 | Yn W | Yn Wd | Yn M | Yn E2 | Yg W | Yg Wd | Yg W | Yg M | Yn W | Yn Wd | Yn W | Yn M | Yg Wd | Yg E1 | Yn Wd | Yn W | Yn Wd | Yn F | Yg F | Yg W | Yg F | Yg F | Yn F | Yn E4 | 16 |
| 17 | Yg Wd | Yg E1 | Yg W | Yg M | Yn W | Yn Wd | Yn W | Yn M | Yg Wd | Yg E1 | Yg Wd | Yg E3 | Yn Wd | Yn F | Yg F | Yg W | Yg F | Yg F | Yn F | Yn E4 | Yn F | Yn E2 | Yg E | Yg Wd | 17 |
| 18 | Yn Wd | Yn F | Yn W | Yn M | Yg Wd | Yg E1 | Yg Wd | Yg E3 | Yn Wd | Yn F | Yn Wd | Yn W | Yg F | Yg F | Yn F | Yn E4 | Yn F | Yn E2 | Yg E | Yg Wd | Yg E | Yg M | Yn E | Yn Wd | 18 |
| 19 | Yg F | Yg F | Yg Wd | Yg E3 | Yn Wd | Yn F | Yn Wd | Yn W | Yg F | Yg F | Yg F | Yg W | Yn F | Yn E2 | Yg E | Yg Wd | Yg E | Yg M | Yn E | Yn Wd | Yn E | Yn M | Yg M | Yg E1 | 19 |
| 20 | Yn F | Yn E2 | Yn Wd | Yn W | Yg F | Yg F | Yg F | Yg W | Yn F | Yn E2 | Yn F | Yn E4 | Yg E | Yg M | Yn E | Yn Wd | Yn E | Yn M | Yg M | Yg E1 | Yg M | Yg E3 | Yn M | Yn F | 20 |
| 21 | Yg E | Yg M | Yg F | Yg W | Yn F | Yn E2 | Yn F | Yn E4 | Yg E | Yg M | Yg E | Yg Wd | Yn E | Yn M | Yg M | Yg E1 | Yg M | Yg E3 | Yn M | Yn F | Yn M | Yn W | Yg W | Yg F | 21 |
| 22 | Yn E | Yn M | Yn F | Yn E4 | Yg E | Yg M | Yg E | Yg Wd | Yn E | Yn M | Yn E | Yn Wd | Yg M | Yg E3 | Yn M | Yn F | Yn M | Yn W | Yg W | Yg F | Yg W | Yg W | Yn W | Yn E2 | 22 |
| 23 | Yg M | Yg E3 | Yg E | Yg Wd | Yn E | Yn M | Yn E | Yn Wd | Yg M | Yg E3 | Yg M | Yg E1 | Yn M | Yn W | Yg W | Yg F | Yg W | Yg W | Yn W | Yn E2 | Yn W | Yn E4 | Yg Wd | Yg M | 23 |
| 24 | Yn M | Yn W | Yn E | Yn Wd | Yg M | Yg E3 | Yg M | Yg E1 | Yn M | Yn W | Yn M | Yn F | Yg W | Yg W | Yn W | Yn E2 | Yn W | Yn E4 | Yg Wd | Yg M | Yg Wd | Yg Wd | Yn Wd | Yn M | 24 |
| 25 | Yg W | Yg W | Yg M | Yg E1 | Yn M | Yn W | Yn M | Yn F | Yg W | Yg W | Yg W | Yg F | Yn W | Yn E4 | Yg Wd | Yg M | Yg Wd | Yg Wd | Yn Wd | Yn M | Yn Wd | Yn Wd | Yg F | Yg E3 | 25 |
| 26 | Yn W | Yn E4 | Yn M | Yn F | Yg W | Yg W | Yg W | Yg F | Yn W | Yn E4 | Yn W | Yn E2 | Yg Wd | Yg Wd | Yn Wd | Yn M | Yn Wd | Yn Wd | Yg F | Yg E3 | Yg F | Yg E1 | Yn F | Yn W | 26 |
| 27 | Yg Wd | Yg Wd | Yg W | Yg F | Yn W | Yn E4 | Yn W | Yn E2 | Yg Wd | Yg Wd | Yg Wd | Yg M | Yn Wd | Yn Wd | Yg F | Yg E3 | Yg F | Yg E1 | Yn F | Yn W | Yn F | Yn F | Yg E | Yg W | 27 |
| 28 | Yn Wd | Yn Wd | Yn W | Yn E2 | Yg Wd | Yg Wd | Yg Wd | Yg M | Yn Wd | Yn Wd | Yn Wd | Yn M | Yg F | Yg E1 | Yn F | Yn W | Yn F | Yn F | Yg E | Yg W | Yg E | Yg F | Yn E | Yn E4 | 28 |
| 29 | | | Yg Wd | Yg M | Yn Wd | Yn Wd | Yn Wd | Yn M | Yg F | Yg E1 | Yg F | Yg E3 | Yn F | Yn F | Yg E | Yg W | Yg E | Yg F | Yn E | Yn E4 | Yn E | Yn E2 | Yg M | Yg Wd | 29 |
| 30 | | | Yn Wd | Yn M | Yg F | Yg E1 | Yg F | Yg E3 | Yn F | Yn F | Yn F | Yn W | Yg E | Yg F | Yn E | Yn E4 | Yn E | Yn E2 | Yg M | Yg Wd | Yg M | Yg M | Yn M | Yn Wd | 30 |
| 31 | | | Yg F | Yg E3 | | | Yn F | Yn W | | | Yg E | Yg W | Yn E | Yn E2 | | | Yg M | Yg M | | | Yn M | Yn M | Yg W | Yg E1 | 31 |
| 1 | Yg F | Yg E1 | Yn F | Yn W | Yn F | Yn F | Yg E | Yg W | Yg E | Yg F | Yn E | Yn E4 | Yg M | Yg M | Yg M | Yg Wd | Yn M | Yn M | Yn M | Yn Wd | Yg W | Yg E3 | Yn W | Yn F | 1 |
| 2 | Yn F | Yn F | Yg E | Yg W | Yg E | Yg F | Yn E | Yn E4 | Yn E | Yn E2 | Yg M | Yg Wd | Yn M | Yn M | Yn M | Yn Wd | Yg W | Yg E3 | Yg W | Yg E1 | Yn W | Yn W | Yg Wd | Yg F | 2 |
| 3 | Yg E | Yg F | Yn E | Yn E4 | Yn E | Yn E2 | Yg M | Yg Wd | Yg M | Yg M | Yn M | Yn Wd | Yg W | Yg E3 | Yg W | Yg E1 | Yn W | Yn W | Yn W | Yn F | Yg Wd | Yg W | Yn Wd | Yn E2 | 3 |
| 4 | Yn E | Yn E2 | Yg M | Yg Wd | Yg M | Yg M | Yn M | Yn Wd | Yn M | Yn M | Yg W | Yg E1 | Yn W | Yn W | Yn W | Yn F | Yg Wd | Yg W | Yg Wd | Yg F | Yn Wd | Yn E4 | | | 4 |
| 5 | Yg M | Yg M | | | Yn M | Yn M | Yg W | Yg E1 | Yg W | Yg E3 | Yn W | Yn F | Yg Wd | Yg W | Yg Wd | Yg F | Yn Wd | Yn E4 | Yn Wd | Yn E2 | Yg F | Yg Wd | | | 5 |
| 6 | | | | | | | | | Yn W | Yn W | Yg Wd | Yg F | Yn Wd | Yn E4 | Yn Wd | Yn E2 | Yg F | Yg Wd | Yg F | Yg M | | | | | 6 |
| 7 | | | | | | | | | Yg Wd | Yg W | Yn Wd | Yn E2 | Yg F | Yg Wd | Yg F | Yg M | Yn F | Yn Wd | | | | | | | 7 |
| 8 | | | | | | | | | | | | | | | Yn F | Yn M | | | | | | | | | 8 |

# YEAR OF THE GOAT

| | H | E | H | E | H | E | H | E | H | E | H | E | H | E | H | E | H | E | H | E | H | E | H | E | |
|---|---|---|---|---|---|---|---|---|---|---|---|---|---|---|---|---|---|---|---|---|---|---|---|---|---|
| **YEAR** | **YEAR** Yn Wd | Yn E2 | **1955** | | | | | | | | | | | | | | | | | | | | **1956** | | |
| **MONTH** | 4 Feb - 5 Mar | | 6 Mar - 4 Apr | | 5 Apr - 5 May | | 6 May - 5 June | | 6 June - 7 Jul | | 8 Jul - 7 Aug | | 8 Aug - 7 Sep | | 8 Sep - 8 Oct | | 9 Oct - 7 Nov | | 8 Nov - 7 Dec | | 8 Dec - 5 Jan | | 6 Jan - 4 Feb | | |
| | Yg E | Yg Wd | Yn E | Yn Wd | Yg M | Yg E1 | Yn M | Yn F | Yg W | Yg F | Yn W | Yn E2 | Yg Wd | Yg M | Yn Wd | Yn M | Yg F | Yg E3 | Yn F | Yn W | Yg E | Yg W | Yn E | Yn E4 | |
| **Starting time** | 1st day | Mid-pt | 1st day | Mid-pt | 1st day | Mid-pt | 1st day | Mid-pt | 1st day | Mid-pt | 1st day | Mid-pt | 1st day | Mid-pt | 1st day | Mid-pt | 1st day | Mid-pt | 1st day | Mid-pt | 1st day | Mid-pt | 1st day | Mid-pt | |
| Date | 4 | 19 | 6 | 21 | 5 | 21 | 6 | 22 | 6 | 22 | 8 | 23 | 8 | 24 | 8 | 24 | 9 | 24 | 8 | 23 | 8 | 22 | 6 | 21 | |
| Hour | 2218 | 1819 | 1632 | 1736 | 2139 | 0458 | 1518 | 0425 | 1944 | 1232 | 0607 | 2325 | 1550 | 0620 | 1832 | 0342 | 0953 | 1244 | 1246 | 1002 | 0523 | 2312 | 1631 | 0919 | |
| **DATE** 4 | Yg F | Yg M | | | | | | | | | | | | | | | | | | | | | | | 4 |
| 5 | Yn F | Yn M | | | Yg F | Yg M | | | | | | | | | | | | | | | | | | | 5 |
| 6 | Yg E | Yg E3 | Yg F | Yg Wd | Yn F | Yn M | Yn F | Yn Wd | Yg E | Yg E3 | | | | | | | | | | | | | Yg W | Yg M | 6 |
| 7 | Yn E | Yn W | Yn F | Yn Wd | Yg E | Yg E3 | Yg E | Yg E1 | Yn E | Yn W | | | | | | | | | | | | | Yn W | Yn M | 7 |
| 8 | Yg M | Yg W | Yg E | Yg E1 | Yn E | Yn W | Yn E | Yn F | Yg M | Yg W | Yg M | Yg F | Yn M | Yn E4 | Yg W | Yg M | | | Yn W | Yn M | Yn W | Yn Wd | Yg Wd | Yg E3 | 8 |
| 9 | Yn M | Yn E4 | Yn E | Yn F | Yg M | Yg W | Yg M | Yg F | Yn M | Yn E4 | Yn M | Yn E2 | Yg W | Yg Wd | Yn W | Yn M | Yn W | Yn Wd | Yg Wd | Yg E3 | Yg Wd | Yg E1 | Yn Wd | Yn W | 9 |
| 10 | Yg W | Yg Wd | Yg M | Yg F | Yn M | Yn E4 | Yn M | Yn E2 | Yg W | Yg Wd | Yg W | Yg M | Yn W | Yn Wd | Yg Wd | Yg E3 | Yg Wd | Yg E1 | Yn Wd | Yn W | Yn Wd | Yn F | Yg F | Yg W | 10 |
| 11 | Yn W | Yn Wd | Yn M | Yn E2 | Yg W | Yg Wd | Yg W | Yg M | Yn W | Yn Wd | Yn W | Yn M | Yg Wd | Yg E1 | Yn Wd | Yn W | Yn Wd | Yn F | Yg F | Yg W | Yg F | Yg F | Yn F | Yn E4 | 11 |
| 12 | Yg Wd | Yg E1 | Yg W | Yg M | Yn W | Yn Wd | Yn W | Yn M | Yg Wd | Yg E1 | Yg Wd | Yg E3 | Yn Wd | Yn F | Yg F | Yg W | Yg F | Yg F | Yn F | Yn E4 | Yn F | Yn E2 | Yg E | Yg Wd | 12 |
| 13 | Yn Wd | Yn F | Yn W | Yn M | Yg Wd | Yg E1 | Yg Wd | Yg E3 | Yn Wd | Yn F | Yn Wd | Yn W | Yg F | Yg F | Yn F | Yn E4 | Yn F | Yn E2 | Yg E | Yg Wd | Yg E | Yg M | Yn E | Yn Wd | 13 |
| 14 | Yg F | Yg F | Yg Wd | Yg E3 | Yn Wd | Yn F | Yn Wd | Yn W | Yg F | Yg F | Yg F | Yg W | Yn F | Yn E2 | Yg E | Yg Wd | Yg E | Yg M | Yn E | Yn Wd | Yn E | Yn M | Yg M | Yg E1 | 14 |
| 15 | Yn F | Yn E2 | Yn Wd | Yn W | Yg F | Yg F | Yg F | Yg W | Yn F | Yn E2 | Yn F | Yn E4 | Yg E | Yg M | Yn E | Yn Wd | Yn E | Yn M | Yg M | Yg E1 | Yg M | Yg E3 | Yn M | Yn F | 15 |
| 16 | Yg E | Yg M | Yg F | Yg W | Yn F | Yn E2 | Yn F | Yn E4 | Yg E | Yg M | Yg E | Yg Wd | Yn E | Yn M | Yg M | Yg E1 | Yg M | Yg E3 | Yn M | Yn F | Yn M | Yn W | Yg W | Yg F | 16 |
| 17 | Yn E | Yn M | Yn F | Yn E4 | Yg E | Yg M | Yg E | Yg Wd | Yn E | Yn M | Yn E | Yn Wd | Yg M | Yg E3 | Yn M | Yn F | Yn M | Yn W | Yg W | Yg F | Yg W | Yg W | Yn W | Yn E2 | 17 |
| 18 | Yg M | Yg E3 | Yg E | Yg Wd | Yn E | Yn M | Yn E | Yn Wd | Yg M | Yg E3 | Yg M | Yg E1 | Yn M | Yn W | Yg W | Yg F | Yg W | Yg W | Yn W | Yn E2 | Yn W | Yn E4 | Yg Wd | Yg M | 18 |
| 19 | Yn M | Yn W | Yn E | Yn Wd | Yg M | Yg E3 | Yg M | Yg E1 | Yn M | Yn W | Yn M | Yn F | Yg W | Yg W | Yn W | Yn E2 | Yn W | Yn E4 | Yg Wd | Yg M | Yg Wd | Yg Wd | Yn Wd | Yn M | 19 |
| 20 | Yg W | Yg W | Yg M | Yg E1 | Yn M | Yn W | Yn M | Yn F | Yg W | Yg W | Yg W | Yg F | Yn W | Yn E4 | Yg Wd | Yg M | Yg Wd | Yg Wd | Yn Wd | Yn M | Yn Wd | Yn Wd | Yg F | Yg E3 | 20 |
| 21 | Yn W | Yn E4 | Yn M | Yn F | Yg W | Yg W | Yg W | Yg F | Yn W | Yn E4 | Yn W | Yn E2 | Yg Wd | Yg Wd | Yn Wd | Yn M | Yn Wd | Yn Wd | Yg F | Yg E3 | Yg F | Yg E1 | Yn F | Yn W | 21 |
| 22 | Yg Wd | Yg Wd | Yg W | Yg F | Yn W | Yn E4 | Yn W | Yn E2 | Yg Wd | Yg Wd | Yg Wd | Yg M | Yn Wd | Yn Wd | Yg F | Yg E3 | Yg F | Yg E1 | Yn F | Yn W | Yn F | Yn F | Yg E | Yg W | 22 |
| 23 | Yn Wd | Yn Wd | Yn W | Yn E2 | Yg Wd | Yg Wd | Yg Wd | Yg M | Yn Wd | Yn Wd | Yn Wd | Yn M | Yg F | Yg E1 | Yn F | Yn W | Yn F | Yn F | Yg E | Yg W | Yg E | Yg F | Yn E | Yn E4 | 23 |
| 24 | Yg F | Yg E1 | Yg Wd | Yg M | Yn Wd | Yn Wd | Yn Wd | Yn M | Yg F | Yg E1 | Yg F | Yg E3 | Yn F | Yn F | Yg E | Yg W | Yg E | Yg F | Yn E | Yn E4 | Yn E | Yn E2 | Yg M | Yg Wd | 24 |
| 25 | Yn F | Yn F | Yn Wd | Yn M | Yg F | Yg E1 | Yg F | Yg E3 | Yn F | Yn F | Yn F | Yn W | Yg E | Yg F | Yn E | Yn E4 | Yn E | Yn E2 | Yg M | Yg Wd | Yg M | Yg M | Yn M | Yn Wd | 25 |
| 26 | Yg E | Yg F | Yg F | Yg E3 | Yn F | Yn F | Yn F | Yn W | Yg E | Yg F | Yg E | Yg W | Yn E | Yn E2 | Yg M | Yg Wd | Yg M | Yg M | Yn M | Yn Wd | Yn M | Yn M | Yg W | Yg E1 | 26 |
| 27 | Yn E | Yn E2 | Yn F | Yn W | Yg E | Yg F | Yg E | Yg W | Yn E | Yn E2 | Yn E | Yn E4 | Yg M | Yg M | Yn M | Yn Wd | Yn M | Yn M | Yg W | Yg E1 | Yg W | Yg E3 | Yn W | Yn F | 27 |
| 28 | Yg M | Yg M | Yg E | Yg W | Yn E | Yn E2 | Yn E | Yn E4 | Yg M | Yg M | Yg M | Yg Wd | Yn M | Yn M | Yg W | Yg E1 | Yg W | Yg E3 | Yn W | Yn F | Yn W | Yn W | Yg Wd | Yg F | 28 |
| 29 | | | Yn E | Yn E4 | Yg M | Yg M | Yg M | Yg Wd | Yn M | Yn M | Yn M | Yn Wd | Yg W | Yg E3 | Yn W | Yn F | Yn W | Yn W | Yg Wd | Yg F | Yg Wd | Yg W | Yn Wd | Yn E2 | 29 |
| 30 | | | Yg M | Yg Wd | Yn M | Yn M | Yn M | Yn Wd | Yg W | Yg E3 | Yg W | Yg E1 | Yn W | Yn W | Yg Wd | Yg F | Yg Wd | Yg W | Yn Wd | Yn E2 | Yn Wd | Yn E4 | Yg F | Yg M | 30 |
| 31 | | | Yn M | Yn Wd | | | Yg W | Yg E1 | | | Yn W | Yn F | Yg Wd | Yg W | | | Yn Wd | Yn E4 | | | Yg F | Yg Wd | Yn F | Yn M | 31 |
| 1 | Yn M | Yn M | Yg W | Yg E1 | Yg W | Yg E3 | Yn W | Yn F | Yn W | Yn W | Yg Wd | Yg F | Yn Wd | Yn E4 | Yn Wd | Yn E2 | Yg F | Yg Wd | Yg F | Yg M | Yn F | Yn Wd | Yg E | Yg E3 | 1 |
| 2 | Yg W | Yg E3 | Yn W | Yn F | Yn W | Yn W | Yg Wd | Yg F | Yg Wd | Yg W | Yn Wd | Yn E2 | Yg F | Yg Wd | Yg F | Yg M | Yn F | Yn Wd | Yn F | Yn M | Yg E | Yg E1 | Yn E | Yn W | 2 |
| 3 | Yn W | Yn W | Yg Wd | Yg F | Yg Wd | Yg W | Yn Wd | Yn E2 | Yn Wd | Yn E4 | Yg F | Yg M | Yn F | Yn Wd | Yn F | Yn M | Yg E | Yg E1 | Yg E | Yg E3 | Yn E | Yn F | Yg M | Yg W | 3 |
| 4 | Yg Wd | Yg W | Yn Wd | Yn E2 | Yn Wd | Yn E4 | Yg F | Yg M | Yg F | Yg Wd | Yn F | Yn M | Yg E | Yg E1 | Yg E | Yg E3 | Yn E | Yn F | Yn E | Yn W | Yg M | Yg F | Yn M | Yn E4 | 4 |
| 5 | Yn Wd | Yn E4 | | | Yg F | Yg Wd | Yn F | Yn M | Yn F | Yn Wd | Yg E | Yg E3 | Yn E | Yn F | Yn E | Yn W | Yg M | Yg F | Yg M | Yg W | Yn M | Yn E2 | | | 5 |
| 6 | | | | | | | | | Yg E | Yg E1 | Yn E | Yn W | Yg M | Yg F | Yg M | Yg W | Yn M | Yn E2 | Yn M | Yn E4 | | | | | 6 |
| 7 | | | | | | | | | Yn E | Yn F | Yg M | Yg W | Yn M | Yn E2 | Yn M | Yn E4 | Yg W | Yg M | Yg W | Yg Wd | | | | | 7 |
| 8 | | | | | | | | | | | | | | | Yg W | Yg Wd | | | | | | | | | 8 |

# YEAR OF THE MONKEY

| | H | E | H | E | H | E | H | E | H | E | H | E | H | E | H | E | H | E | H | E | H | E | H | E | |
|---|---|---|---|---|---|---|---|---|---|---|---|---|---|---|---|---|---|---|---|---|---|---|---|---|---|
| YEAR | YEAR<br>Yg F | <br>Yg M | 1956 | | | | | | | | | | | | | | | | | | | | 1957 | | |
| MONTH | 5 Feb - 4 Mar<br>Yg M | <br>Yg Wd | 5 Mar - 4 Apr<br>Yn M | <br>Yn Wd | 5 Apr - 4 May<br>Yg W | <br>Yg E1 | 5 May - 5 June<br>Yn W | <br>Yn F | 6 June - 6 Jul<br>Yg Wd | <br>Yg F | 7 Jul - 6 Aug<br>Yn Wd | <br>Yn E2 | 7 Aug - 7 Sep<br>Yg F | <br>Yg M | 8 Sep - 7 Oct<br>Yn F | <br>Yn M | 8 Oct - 6 Nov<br>Yg E | <br>Yg E3 | 7 Nov - 6 Dec<br>Yn E | <br>Yn W | 7 Dec - 4 Jan<br>Yg M | <br>Yg W | 5 Jan - 3 Feb<br>Yn M | <br>Yn E4 | |
| Starting time | 1st day | Mid-pt | 1st day | Mid-pt | 1st day | Mid-pt | 1st day | Mid-pt | 1st day | Mid-pt | 1st day | Mid-pt | 1st day | Mid-pt | 1st day | Mid-pt | 1st day | Mid-pt | 1st day | Mid-pt | 1st day | Mid-pt | 1st day | Mid-pt | |
| Date | 5 | 20 | 5 | 20 | 5 | 20 | 5 | 21 | 6 | 21 | 7 | 23 | 7 | 23 | 8 | 23 | 8 | 23 | 7 | 22 | 7 | 22 | 5 | 20 | |
| Hour | 0413 | 0005 | 2225 | 2321 | 0332 | 1044 | 2111 | 1013 | 0136 | 1824 | 1159 | 0521 | 2141 | 1215 | 0020 | 0936 | 1537 | 1835 | 1827 | 1551 | 1103 | 0500 | 2211 | 1539 | |
| DATE 4 | | | | | | | | | | | | | | | | | | | | | | | | | 4 |
| 5 | Yg W | Yg Wd | Yn M | Yn E2 | Yg W | Yg Wd | Yg W | Yg M | | | | | | | | | | | | | | | Yn F | Yn E4 | 5 |
| 6 | Yn W | Yn Wd | Yg W | Yg M | Yn W | Yn Wd | Yn W | Yn M | Yg Wd | Yg E1 | | | | | | | | | | | | | Yg E | Yg Wd | 6 |
| 7 | Yg Wd | Yg E1 | Yn W | Yn M | Yg Wd | Yg E1 | Yg Wd | Yg E3 | Yn Wd | Yn F | Yn Wd | Yn W | Yg F | Yg F | | | | | Yg E | Yg Wd | Yg E | Yg M | Yn E | Yn Wd | 7 |
| 8 | Yn Wd | Yn F | Yg Wd | Yg E3 | Yn Wd | Yn F | Yn Wd | Yn W | Yg F | Yg F | Yg F | Yg W | Yn F | Yn E2 | Yg E | Yg Wd | Yg E | Yg M | Yn E | Yn Wd | Yn E | Yn M | Yg M | Yg E1 | 8 |
| 9 | Yg F | Yg F | Yn Wd | Yn W | Yg F | Yg F | Yg F | Yg W | Yn F | Yn E2 | Yn F | Yn E4 | Yg E | Yg M | Yn E | Yn Wd | Yn E | Yn M | Yg M | Yg E1 | Yg M | Yg E3 | Yn M | Yn F | 9 |
| 10 | Yn F | Yn E2 | Yg F | Yg W | Yn F | Yn E2 | Yn F | Yn E4 | Yg E | Yg M | Yg E | Yg Wd | Yn E | Yn M | Yg M | Yg E1 | Yg M | Yg E3 | Yn M | Yn F | Yn M | Yn W | Yg W | Yg F | 10 |
| 11 | Yg E | Yg M | Yn F | Yn E4 | Yg E | Yg M | Yg E | Yg Wd | Yn E | Yn M | Yn E | Yn Wd | Yg M | Yg E3 | Yn M | Yn F | Yn M | Yn W | Yg W | Yg F | Yg W | Yg W | Yn W | Yn E2 | 11 |
| 12 | Yn E | Yn M | Yg E | Yg Wd | Yn E | Yn M | Yn E | Yn Wd | Yg M | Yg E3 | Yg M | Yg E1 | Yn M | Yn W | Yg W | Yg F | Yg W | Yg W | Yn W | Yn E2 | Yn W | Yn E4 | Yg Wd | Yg M | 12 |
| 13 | Yg M | Yg E3 | Yn E | Yn Wd | Yg M | Yg E3 | Yg M | Yg E1 | Yn M | Yn W | Yn M | Yn F | Yg W | Yg W | Yn W | Yn E2 | Yn W | Yn E4 | Yg Wd | Yg M | Yg Wd | Yg Wd | Yn Wd | Yn M | 13 |
| 14 | Yn M | Yn W | Yg M | Yg E1 | Yn M | Yn W | Yn M | Yn F | Yg W | Yg W | Yg W | Yg F | Yn W | Yn E4 | Yg Wd | Yg M | Yg Wd | Yg Wd | Yn Wd | Yn M | Yn Wd | Yn Wd | Yg F | Yg E3 | 14 |
| 15 | Yg W | Yg W | Yn M | Yn F | Yg W | Yg W | Yg W | Yg F | Yn W | Yn E4 | Yn W | Yn E2 | Yg Wd | Yg Wd | Yn Wd | Yn M | Yn Wd | Yn Wd | Yg F | Yg E3 | Yg F | Yg E1 | Yn F | Yn W | 15 |
| 16 | Yn W | Yn E4 | Yg W | Yg F | Yn W | Yn E4 | Yn W | Yn E2 | Yg Wd | Yg Wd | Yg Wd | Yg M | Yn Wd | Yn Wd | Yg F | Yg E3 | Yg F | Yg E1 | Yn F | Yn W | Yn F | Yn F | Yg E | Yg W | 16 |
| 17 | Yg Wd | Yg Wd | Yn W | Yn E2 | Yg Wd | Yg Wd | Yg Wd | Yg M | Yn Wd | Yn Wd | Yn Wd | Yn M | Yg F | Yg E1 | Yn F | Yn W | Yn F | Yn F | Yg E | Yg W | Yg E | Yg F | Yn E | Yn E4 | 17 |
| 18 | Yn Wd | Yn Wd | Yg Wd | Yg M | Yn Wd | Yn Wd | Yn Wd | Yn M | Yg F | Yg E1 | Yg F | Yg E3 | Yn F | Yn F | Yg E | Yg W | Yg E | Yg F | Yn E | Yn E4 | Yn E | Yn E2 | Yg M | Yg Wd | 18 |
| 19 | Yg F | Yg E1 | Yn Wd | Yn M | Yg F | Yg E1 | Yg F | Yg E3 | Yn F | Yn F | Yn F | Yn W | Yg E | Yg F | Yn E | Yn E4 | Yn E | Yn E2 | Yg M | Yg Wd | Yg M | Yg M | Yn M | Yn Wd | 19 |
| 20 | Yn F | Yn F | Yg F | Yg E3 | Yn F | Yn F | Yn F | Yn W | Yg E | Yg F | Yg E | Yg W | Yn E | Yn E2 | Yg M | Yg Wd | Yg M | Yg M | Yn M | Yn Wd | Yn M | Yn M | Yg W | Yg E1 | 20 |
| 21 | Yg E | Yg F | Yn F | Yn W | Yg E | Yg F | Yg E | Yg W | Yn E | Yn E2 | Yn E | Yn E4 | Yg M | Yg M | Yn M | Yn Wd | Yn M | Yn M | Yg W | Yg E1 | Yg W | Yg E3 | Yn W | Yn F | 21 |
| 22 | Yn E | Yn E2 | Yg E | Yg W | Yn E | Yn E2 | Yn E | Yn E4 | Yg M | Yg M | Yg M | Yg Wd | Yn M | Yn M | Yg W | Yg E1 | Yg W | Yg E3 | Yn W | Yn F | Yn W | Yn W | Yg Wd | Yg F | 22 |
| 23 | Yg M | Yg M | Yn E | Yn E4 | Yg M | Yg M | Yg M | Yg Wd | Yn M | Yn M | Yn M | Yn Wd | Yg W | Yg E3 | Yn W | Yn F | Yn W | Yn W | Yg Wd | Yg F | Yg Wd | Yg W | Yn Wd | Yn E2 | 23 |
| 24 | Yn M | Yn M | Yg M | Yg Wd | Yn M | Yn M | Yn M | Yn Wd | Yg W | Yg E3 | Yg W | Yg E1 | Yn W | Yn W | Yg Wd | Yg F | Yg Wd | Yg W | Yn Wd | Yn E2 | Yn Wd | Yn E4 | Yg F | Yg M | 24 |
| 25 | Yg W | Yg E3 | Yn M | Yn Wd | Yg W | Yg E3 | Yg W | Yg E1 | Yn W | Yn W | Yn W | Yn F | Yg Wd | Yg W | Yn Wd | Yn E2 | Yn Wd | Yn E4 | Yg F | Yg M | Yg F | Yg Wd | Yn F | Yn M | 25 |
| 26 | Yn W | Yn W | Yg W | Yg E1 | Yn W | Yn W | Yn W | Yn F | Yg Wd | Yg W | Yg Wd | Yg F | Yn Wd | Yn E4 | Yg F | Yg M | Yg F | Yg Wd | Yn F | Yn M | Yn F | Yn Wd | Yg E | Yg E3 | 26 |
| 27 | Yg Wd | Yg W | Yn W | Yn F | Yg Wd | Yg W | Yg Wd | Yg F | Yn Wd | Yn E4 | Yn Wd | Yn E2 | Yg F | Yg Wd | Yn F | Yn M | Yn F | Yn Wd | Yg E | Yg E3 | Yg E | Yg E1 | Yn E | Yn W | 27 |
| 28 | Yn Wd | Yn E4 | Yg Wd | Yg F | Yn Wd | Yn E4 | Yn Wd | Yn E2 | Yg F | Yg Wd | Yg F | Yg M | Yn F | Yn Wd | Yg E | Yg E3 | Yg E | Yg E1 | Yn E | Yn W | Yn E | Yn F | Yg M | Yg W | 28 |
| 29 | Yg F | Yg Wd | Yn Wd | Yn E2 | Yg F | Yg Wd | Yg F | Yg M | Yn F | Yn Wd | Yn F | Yn M | Yg E | Yg E1 | Yn E | Yn W | Yn E | Yn F | Yg M | Yg W | Yg M | Yg F | Yn M | Yn E4 | 29 |
| 30 | | | Yg F | Yg M | Yn F | Yn Wd | Yn F | Yn M | Yg E | Yg E1 | Yg E | Yg E3 | Yn E | Yn F | Yg M | Yg W | Yg M | Yg F | Yn M | Yn E4 | Yn M | Yn E2 | Yg W | Yg Wd | 30 |
| 31 | | | Yn F | Yn M | | | Yg E | Yg E3 | | | Yn E | Yn W | Yg M | Yg F | | | Yn M | Yn E2 | | | Yg W | Yg M | Yn W | Yn Wd | 31 |
| 1 | Yn F | Yn Wd | Yg E | Yg E3 | Yg E | Yg E1 | Yn E | Yn W | Yn E | Yn F | Yg M | Yg W | Yn M | Yn E2 | Yn M | Yn E4 | Yg W | Yg M | Yg W | Yg Wd | Yn W | Yn M | Yg Wd | Yg E1 | 1 |
| 2 | Yg E | Yg E1 | Yn E | Yn W | Yn E | Yn F | Yg M | Yg W | Yg M | Yg F | Yn M | Yn E4 | Yg W | Yg M | Yg W | Yg Wd | Yn W | Yn M | Yn W | Yn Wd | Yg Wd | Yg E3 | Yn Wd | Yn F | 2 |
| 3 | Yn E | Yn F | Yg M | Yg W | Yg M | Yg F | Yn M | Yn E4 | Yn M | Yn E2 | Yg W | Yg Wd | Yn W | Yn M | Yn W | Yn Wd | Yg Wd | Yg E3 | Yg Wd | Yg E1 | Yn Wd | Yn W | Yg F | Yg F | 3 |
| 4 | Yg M | Yg F | Yn M | Yn E4 | Yn M | Yn E2 | Yg W | Yg Wd | Yg W | Yg M | Yn W | Yn Wd | Yg Wd | Yg E3 | Yg Wd | Yg E1 | Yn Wd | Yn W | Yn Wd | Yn F | Yg F | Yg W | | | 4 |
| 5 | | | | | | | Yn W | Yn Wd | Yn W | Yn M | Yg Wd | Yg E1 | Yn Wd | Yn W | Yn Wd | Yn F | Yg F | Yg W | Yg F | Yg F | | | | | 5 |
| 6 | | | | | | | | | Yg Wd | Yg E3 | Yn Wd | Yn F | Yg F | Yg W | Yg F | Yg F | Yn F | Yn E4 | Yn F | Yn E2 | | | | | 6 |
| 7 | | | | | | | | | | | | | Yn F | Yn E4 | Yn F | Yn E2 | | | | | | | | | 7 |
| 8 | | | | | | | | | | | | | | | | | | | | | | | | | 8 |

# YEAR OF THE ROOSTER

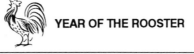

| | H | E | H | E | H | E | H | E | H | E | H | E | H | E | H | E | H | E | H | E | H | E | H | E | |
|---|---|---|---|---|---|---|---|---|---|---|---|---|---|---|---|---|---|---|---|---|---|---|---|---|---|
| YEAR | YEAR Yn F | Yn M | 1957 | | | | | | | | | | | | | | | | | | | | 1958 | | |
| MONTH | 4 Feb - 5 Mar | | 6 Mar - 4 Apr | | 5 Apr - 5 May | | 6 May - 5 June | | 6 June - 6 Jul | | 7 Jul - 7 Aug | | 8 Aug - 7 Sep | | 8 Sep - 7 Oct | | 8 Oct - 7 Nov | | 8 Nov - 6 Dec | | 7 Dec - 5 Jan | | 6 Jan - 3 Feb | | |
| | Yg W | Yg Wd | Yn W | Yn Wd | Yg Wd | Yg E1 | Yn Wd | Yn F | Yg F | Yg F | Yn F | Yn E2 | Yg E | Yg M | Yn E | Yn M | Yg M | Yg E3 | Yn M | Yn W | Yg W | Yg W | Yn W | Yn E4 | |
| Starting time | 1st day | Mid-pt | 1st day | Mid-pt | 1st day | Mid-pt | 1st day | Mid-pt | 1st day | Mid-pt | 1st day | Mid-pt | 1st day | Mid-pt | 1st day | Mid-pt | 1st day | Mid-pt | 1st day | Mid-pt | 1st day | Mid-pt | 1st day | Mid-pt | |
| Date | 4 | 19 | 6 | 21 | 5 | 20 | 6 | 21 | 6 | 22 | 7 | 23 | 8 | 23 | 8 | 23 | 8 | 24 | 8 | 22 | 7 | 22 | 6 | 20 | |
| Hour | 0955 | 0558 | 0411 | 0517 | 0919 | 1642 | 0259 | 1611 | 0725 | 0021 | 1749 | 1115 | 0333 | 1808 | 0613 | 1527 | 2131 | 0025 | 0021 | 2140 | 1657 | 1049 | 0405 | 2129 | |
| DATE 4 | Yn F | Yn E2 | | | | | | | | | | | | | | | | | | | | | | | 4 |
| 5 | Yg E | Yg M | | | Yn F | Yn E2 | | | | | | | | | | | | | | | | | | | 5 |
| 6 | Yn E | Yn M | Yn F | Yn E4 | Yg E | Yg M | Yg E | Yg Wd | Yn E | Yn M | | | | | | | | | | | | | Yn W | Yn E2 | 6 |
| 7 | Yg M | Yg E3 | Yg E | Yg Wd | Yn E | Yn M | Yn E | Yn Wd | Yg M | Yg E3 | Yg M | Yg E1 | | | | | | | | | Yn W | Yn E4 | Yg Wd | Yg M | 7 |
| 8 | Yn M | Yn W | Yn E | Yn Wd | Yg M | Yg E3 | Yg M | Yg E1 | Yn M | Yn W | Yn M | Yn F | Yg W | Yg W | Yn W | Yn E2 | Yn W | Yn E4 | Yg Wd | Yg M | Yg Wd | Yg Wd | Yn Wd | Yn M | 8 |
| 9 | Yg W | Yg W | Yg M | Yg E1 | Yn M | Yn W | Yn M | Yn F | Yg W | Yg W | Yg W | Yg F | Yn W | Yn E4 | Yg Wd | Yg M | Yg Wd | Yg Wd | Yn Wd | Yn M | Yn Wd | Yn Wd | Yg F | Yg E3 | 9 |
| 10 | Yn W | Yn E4 | Yn M | Yn F | Yg W | Yg W | Yg W | Yg F | Yn W | Yn E4 | Yn W | Yn E2 | Yg Wd | Yg Wd | Yn Wd | Yn M | Yn Wd | Yn Wd | Yg F | Yg E3 | Yg F | Yg E1 | Yn F | Yn W | 10 |
| 11 | Yg Wd | Yg Wd | Yg W | Yg F | Yn W | Yn E4 | Yn W | Yn E2 | Yg Wd | Yg Wd | Yg Wd | Yg M | Yn Wd | Yn Wd | Yg F | Yg E3 | Yg F | Yg E1 | Yn F | Yn W | Yn F | Yn F | Yg E | Yg W | 11 |
| 12 | Yn Wd | Yn Wd | Yn W | Yn E2 | Yg Wd | Yg Wd | Yg Wd | Yg M | Yn Wd | Yn Wd | Yn Wd | Yn M | Yg F | Yg E1 | Yn F | Yn W | Yn F | Yn F | Yg E | Yg W | Yg E | Yg F | Yn E | Yn E4 | 12 |
| 13 | Yg F | Yg E1 | Yg Wd | Yg M | Yn Wd | Yn Wd | Yn Wd | Yn M | Yg F | Yg E1 | Yg F | Yg E3 | Yn F | Yn F | Yg E | Yg W | Yg E | Yg F | Yn E | Yn E4 | Yn E | Yn E2 | Yg M | Yg Wd | 13 |
| 14 | Yn F | Yn F | Yn Wd | Yn M | Yg F | Yg E1 | Yg F | Yg E3 | Yn F | Yn F | Yn F | Yn W | Yg E | Yg F | Yn E | Yn E4 | Yn E | Yn E2 | Yg M | Yg Wd | Yg M | Yg M | Yn M | Yn Wd | 14 |
| 15 | Yg E | Yg F | Yg F | Yg E3 | Yn F | Yn F | Yn F | Yn W | Yg E | Yg F | Yg E | Yg W | Yn E | Yn E2 | Yg M | Yg Wd | Yg M | Yg M | Yn M | Yn Wd | Yn M | Yn M | Yg W | Yg E1 | 15 |
| 16 | Yn E | Yn E2 | Yn F | Yn W | Yg E | Yg F | Yg E | Yg W | Yn E | Yn E2 | Yn E | Yn E4 | Yg M | Yg M | Yn M | Yn Wd | Yn M | Yn M | Yg W | Yg E1 | Yg W | Yg E3 | Yn W | Yn F | 16 |
| 17 | Yg M | Yg M | Yg E | Yg W | Yn E | Yn E2 | Yn E | Yn E4 | Yg M | Yg M | Yg M | Yg Wd | Yn M | Yn M | Yg W | Yg E1 | Yg W | Yg E3 | Yn W | Yn F | Yn W | Yn W | Yg Wd | Yg F | 17 |
| 18 | Yn M | Yn M | Yn E | Yn E4 | Yg M | Yg M | Yg M | Yg Wd | Yn M | Yn M | Yn M | Yn Wd | Yg W | Yg E3 | Yn W | Yn F | Yn W | Yn W | Yg Wd | Yg F | Yg Wd | Yg W | Yn Wd | Yn E2 | 18 |
| 19 | Yg W | Yg E3 | Yg M | Yg Wd | Yn M | Yn M | Yn M | Yn Wd | Yg W | Yg E3 | Yg W | Yg E1 | Yn W | Yn W | Yg Wd | Yg F | Yg Wd | Yg W | Yn Wd | Yn E2 | Yn Wd | Yn E4 | Yg F | Yg M | 19 |
| 20 | Yn W | Yn W | Yn M | Yn Wd | Yg W | Yg E3 | Yg W | Yg E1 | Yn W | Yn W | Yn W | Yn F | Yg Wd | Yg W | Yn Wd | Yn E2 | Yn Wd | Yn E4 | Yg F | Yg M | Yg F | Yg Wd | Yn F | Yn M | 20 |
| 21 | Yg Wd | Yg W | Yg W | Yg E1 | Yn W | Yn W | Yn W | Yn F | Yg Wd | Yg W | Yg Wd | Yg F | Yn Wd | Yn E4 | Yg F | Yg M | Yg F | Yg Wd | Yn F | Yn M | Yn F | Yn Wd | Yg E | Yg E3 | 21 |
| 22 | Yn Wd | Yn E4 | Yn W | Yn F | Yg Wd | Yg W | Yg Wd | Yg F | Yn Wd | Yn E4 | Yn Wd | Yn E2 | Yg F | Yg Wd | Yn F | Yn M | Yn F | Yn Wd | Yg E | Yg E3 | Yg E | Yg E1 | Yn E | Yn W | 22 |
| 23 | Yg F | Yg Wd | Yg Wd | Yg F | Yn Wd | Yn E4 | Yn Wd | Yn E2 | Yg F | Yg Wd | Yg F | Yg M | Yn F | Yn Wd | Yg E | Yg E3 | Yg E | Yg E1 | Yn E | Yn W | Yn E | Yn F | Yg M | Yg W | 23 |
| 24 | Yn F | Yn Wd | Yn Wd | Yn E2 | Yg F | Yg Wd | Yg F | Yg M | Yn F | Yn Wd | Yn F | Yn M | Yg E | Yg E1 | Yn E | Yn W | Yn E | Yn F | Yg M | Yg W | Yg M | Yg F | Yn M | Yn E4 | 24 |
| 25 | Yg E | Yg E1 | Yg F | Yg M | Yn F | Yn Wd | Yn F | Yn M | Yg E | Yg E1 | Yg E | Yg E3 | Yn E | Yn F | Yg M | Yg W | Yg M | Yg F | Yn M | Yn E4 | Yn M | Yn E2 | Yg W | Yg Wd | 25 |
| 26 | Yn E | Yn F | Yn F | Yn M | Yg E | Yg E1 | Yg E | Yg E3 | Yn E | Yn F | Yn E | Yn W | Yg M | Yg F | Yn M | Yn E4 | Yn M | Yn E2 | Yg W | Yg Wd | Yg W | Yg M | Yn W | Yn Wd | 26 |
| 27 | Yg M | Yg F | Yg E | Yg E3 | Yn E | Yn F | Yn E | Yn W | Yg M | Yg F | Yg M | Yg W | Yn M | Yn E2 | Yg W | Yg Wd | Yg W | Yg M | Yn W | Yn Wd | Yn W | Yn M | Yg Wd | Yg E1 | 27 |
| 28 | Yn M | Yn E2 | Yn E | Yn W | Yg M | Yg F | Yg M | Yg W | Yn M | Yn E2 | Yn M | Yn E4 | Yg W | Yg M | Yn W | Yn Wd | Yn W | Yn M | Yg Wd | Yg E1 | Yg Wd | Yg E3 | Yn Wd | Yn F | 28 |
| 29 | | | Yg M | Yg W | Yn M | Yn E2 | Yn M | Yn E4 | Yg W | Yg M | Yg W | Yg Wd | Yn W | Yn M | Yg Wd | Yg E1 | Yg Wd | Yg E3 | Yn Wd | Yn F | Yn Wd | Yn W | Yg F | Yg F | 29 |
| 30 | | | Yn M | Yn E4 | Yg W | Yg M | Yg W | Yg Wd | Yn W | Yn M | Yn W | Yn Wd | Yg Wd | Yg E3 | Yn Wd | Yn F | Yn Wd | Yn W | Yg F | Yg F | Yg F | Yg W | Yn F | Yn E2 | 30 |
| 31 | | | Yg W | Yg Wd | | | Yn W | Yn Wd | | | Yg Wd | Yg E1 | Yn Wd | Yn W | | | Yg F | Yg W | | | Yn F | Yn E4 | Yg E | Yg M | 31 |
| 1 | Yg W | Yg M | Yn W | Yn Wd | Yn W | Yn M | Yg Wd | Yg E1 | Yg Wd | Yg E3 | Yn Wd | Yn F | Yg F | Yg W | Yg F | Yg F | Yn F | Yn E4 | Yn F | Yn E2 | Yg E | Yg Wd | Yn E | Yn M | 1 |
| 2 | Yn W | Yn M | Yg Wd | Yg E1 | Yg Wd | Yg E3 | Yn Wd | Yn F | Yn Wd | Yn W | Yg F | Yg F | Yn F | Yn E4 | Yn F | Yn E2 | Yg E | Yg Wd | Yg E | Yg M | Yn E | Yn Wd | Yg M | Yg E3 | 2 |
| 3 | Yg Wd | Yg E3 | Yn Wd | Yn F | Yn Wd | Yn W | Yg F | Yg F | Yg F | Yg W | Yn F | Yn E2 | Yg E | Yg Wd | Yg E | Yg M | Yn E | Yn Wd | Yn E | Yn M | Yg M | Yg E1 | Yn M | Yn W | 3 |
| 4 | Yn Wd | Yn W | Yg F | Yg F | Yg F | Yg W | Yn F | Yn E2 | Yn F | Yn E4 | Yg E | Yg M | Yn E | Yn Wd | Yn E | Yn M | Yg M | Yg E1 | Yg M | Yg E3 | Yn M | Yn F | | | 4 |
| 5 | Yg F | Yg W | | | Yn F | Yn E4 | Yg E | Yg M | Yg E | Yg Wd | Yn E | Yn M | Yg M | Yg E1 | Yg M | Yg E3 | Yn M | Yn F | Yn M | Yn W | Yg W | Yg F | | | 5 |
| 6 | | | | | | | | | Yn E | Yn Wd | Yg M | Yg E3 | Yn M | Yn F | Yn M | Yn W | Yg W | Yg F | Yg W | Yg W | | | | | 6 |
| 7 | | | | | | | | | | | Yn M | Yn W | Yg W | Yg F | Yg W | Yg W | Yn W | Yn E2 | | | | | | | 7 |
| 8 | | | | | | | | | | | | | | | | | | | | | | | | | 8 |

# YEAR OF THE DOG

| YEAR | YEAR | | 1958 | | | | | | | | | | | | | | | | | | | | 1959 | | |
|---|---|---|---|---|---|---|---|---|---|---|---|---|---|---|---|---|---|---|---|---|---|---|---|---|---|
| | H | E | H | E | H | E | H | E | H | E | H | E | H | E | H | E | H | E | H | E | H | E | H | E | |
| | YgE | YgE3 | | | | | | | | | | | | | | | | | | | | | | | |
| MONTH | 4 Feb - 5 Mar | | 6 Mar - 4 Apr | | 5 Apr - 5 May | | 6 May - 5 June | | 6 June - 6 Jul | | 7 Jul - 7 Aug | | 8 Aug - 7 Sep | | 8 Sep - 8 Oct | | 9 Oct - 7 Nov | | 8 Nov - 6 Dec | | 7 Dec - 5 Jan | | 6 Jan - 3 Feb | | |
| | Yg Wd | Yg Wd | Yn Wd | Yn Wd | Yg F | Yg E1 | Yn F | Yn F | Yg E | Yg F | Yn E | Yn E2 | Yg M | Yg M | Yn M | Yn M | Yg W | Yg E3 | Yn W | Yn W | Yg Wd | Yg W | Yn Wd | Yn E4 | |
| Starting time | 1st day | Mid-pt | 1st day | Mid-pt | 1st day | Mid-pt | 1st day | Mid-pt | 1st day | Mid-pt | 1st day | Mid-pt | 1st day | Mid-pt | 1st day | Mid-pt | 1st day | Mid-pt | 1st day | Mid-pt | 1st day | Mid-pt | 1st day | Mid-pt | |
| Date | 4 | 19 | 6 | 21 | 5 | 20 | 6 | 21 | 6 | 22 | 7 | 23 | 8 | 23 | 8 | 23 | 9 | 24 | 8 | 23 | 7 | 22 | 6 | 21 | |
| Hour | 1550 | 1149 | 1006 | 1106 | 1513 | 2228 | 0850 | 2152 | 1313 | 0558 | 2334 | 1651 | 0918 | 2347 | 1200 | 2110 | 0320 | 0612 | 0613 | 0330 | 2250 | 1640 | 0959 | 0320 | |
| DATE 4 | Yg W | Yg W | | | | | | | | | | | | | | | | | | | | | | | 4 |
| 5 | Yn W | Yn E4 | | | Yg W | Yg W | | | | | | | | | | | | | | | | | | | 5 |
| 6 | Yg Wd | Yg Wd | Yg W | Yg F | Yn W | Yn E4 | Yn W | Yn E2 | Yg Wd | Yg Wd | | | | | | | | | | | | | Yg E | Yg W | 6 |
| 7 | Yn Wd | Yn Wd | Yn W | Yn E2 | Yg Wd | Yg Wd | Yg Wd | Yg M | Yn Wd | Yn Wd | Yn Wd | Yn M | | | | | | | | | Yg E | Yg F | Yn E | Yn E4 | 7 |
| 8 | Yg F | Yg E1 | Yg Wd | Yg M | Yn Wd | Yn Wd | Yn Wd | Yn M | Yg F | Yg E1 | Yg F | Yg E3 | Yn F | Yn F | Yg E | Yg W | | | Yn E | Yn E4 | Yn E | Yn E2 | Yg M | Yg Wd | 8 |
| 9 | Yn F | Yn F | Yn Wd | Yn M | Yg F | Yg E1 | Yg F | Yg E3 | Yn F | Yn F | Yn F | Yn W | Yg E | Yg F | Yn E | Yn E4 | Yn E | Yn E2 | Yg M | Yg Wd | Yg M | Yg M | Yn M | Yn Wd | 9 |
| 10 | Yg E | Yg F | Yg F | Yg E3 | Yn F | Yn F | Yn F | Yn W | Yg E | Yg F | Yg E | Yg W | Yn E | Yn E2 | Yg M | Yg Wd | Yg M | Yg M | Yn M | Yn Wd | Yn M | Yn M | Yg W | Yg E1 | 10 |
| 11 | Yn E | Yn E2 | Yn F | Yn W | Yg E | Yg F | Yg E | Yg W | Yn E | Yn E2 | Yn E | Yn E4 | Yg M | Yg M | Yn M | Yn Wd | Yn M | Yn M | Yg W | Yg E1 | Yg W | Yg E3 | Yn W | Yn F | 11 |
| 12 | Yg M | Yg M | Yg E | Yg W | Yn E | Yn E2 | Yn E | Yn E4 | Yg M | Yg M | Yg M | Yg Wd | Yn M | Yn M | Yg W | Yg E1 | Yg W | Yg E3 | Yn W | Yn F | Yn W | Yn W | Yg Wd | Yg F | 12 |
| 13 | Yn M | Yn M | Yn E | Yn E4 | Yg M | Yg M | Yg M | Yg Wd | Yn M | Yn M | Yn M | Yn Wd | Yg W | Yg E3 | Yn W | Yn F | Yn W | Yn W | Yg Wd | Yg F | Yg Wd | Yg W | Yn Wd | Yn E2 | 13 |
| 14 | Yg W | Yg E3 | Yg M | Yg Wd | Yn M | Yn M | Yn M | Yn Wd | Yg W | Yg E3 | Yg W | Yg E1 | Yn W | Yn W | Yg Wd | Yg F | Yg Wd | Yg W | Yn Wd | Yn E2 | Yn Wd | Yn E4 | Yg F | Yg M | 14 |
| 15 | Yn W | Yn W | Yn M | Yn Wd | Yg W | Yg E3 | Yg W | Yg E1 | Yn W | Yn W | Yn W | Yn F | Yg Wd | Yg W | Yn Wd | Yn E2 | Yn Wd | Yn E4 | Yg F | Yg M | Yg F | Yg Wd | Yn F | Yn M | 15 |
| 16 | Yg Wd | Yg W | Yg W | Yg E1 | Yn W | Yn W | Yn W | Yn F | Yg Wd | Yg W | Yg Wd | Yg F | Yn Wd | Yn E4 | Yg F | Yg M | Yg F | Yg Wd | Yn F | Yn M | Yn F | Yn Wd | Yg E | Yg E3 | 16 |
| 17 | Yn Wd | Yn E4 | Yn W | Yn F | Yg Wd | Yg W | Yg Wd | Yg F | Yn Wd | Yn E4 | Yn Wd | Yn E2 | Yg F | Yg Wd | Yn F | Yn M | Yn F | Yn Wd | Yg E | Yg E3 | Yg E | Yg E1 | Yn E | Yn W | 17 |
| 18 | Yg F | Yg Wd | Yg Wd | Yg F | Yn Wd | Yn E4 | Yn Wd | Yn E2 | Yg F | Yg Wd | Yg F | Yg M | Yn F | Yn Wd | Yg E | Yg E3 | Yg E | Yg E1 | Yn E | Yn W | Yn E | Yn F | Yg M | Yg W | 18 |
| 19 | Yn F | Yn Wd | Yn Wd | Yn E2 | Yg F | Yg Wd | Yg F | Yg M | Yn F | Yn Wd | Yn F | Yn M | Yg E | Yg E1 | Yn E | Yn W | Yn E | Yn F | Yg M | Yg W | Yg M | Yg F | Yn M | Yn E4 | 19 |
| 20 | Yg E | Yg E1 | Yg F | Yg M | Yn F | Yn Wd | Yn F | Yn M | Yg E | Yg E1 | Yg E | Yg E3 | Yn E | Yn F | Yg M | Yg W | Yg M | Yg F | Yn M | Yn E4 | Yn M | Yn E2 | Yg W | Yg Wd | 20 |
| 21 | Yn E | Yn F | Yn F | Yn M | Yg E | Yg E1 | Yg E | Yg E3 | Yn E | Yn F | Yn E | Yn W | Yg M | Yg F | Yn M | Yn E4 | Yn M | Yn E2 | Yg W | Yg Wd | Yg W | Yg M | Yn W | Yn Wd | 21 |
| 22 | Yg M | Yg F | Yg E | Yg E3 | Yn E | Yn F | Yn E | Yn W | Yg M | Yg F | Yg M | Yg W | Yn M | Yn E2 | Yg W | Yg Wd | Yg W | Yg M | Yn W | Yn Wd | Yn W | Yn M | Yg Wd | Yg E1 | 22 |
| 23 | Yn M | Yn E2 | Yn E | Yn W | Yg M | Yg F | Yg M | Yg W | Yn M | Yn E2 | Yn M | Yn E4 | Yg W | Yg M | Yn W | Yn Wd | Yn W | Yn M | Yg Wd | Yg E1 | Yg Wd | Yg E3 | Yn Wd | Yn F | 23 |
| 24 | Yg W | Yg M | Yg M | Yg W | Yn M | Yn E2 | Yn M | Yn E4 | Yg W | Yg M | Yg W | Yg Wd | Yn W | Yn M | Yg Wd | Yg E1 | Yg Wd | Yg E3 | Yn Wd | Yn F | Yn Wd | Yn W | Yg F | Yg F | 24 |
| 25 | Yn W | Yn M | Yn M | Yn E4 | Yg W | Yg M | Yg W | Yg Wd | Yn W | Yn M | Yn W | Yn Wd | Yg Wd | Yg E3 | Yn Wd | Yn F | Yn Wd | Yn W | Yg F | Yg F | Yg F | Yg W | Yn F | Yn E2 | 25 |
| 26 | Yg Wd | Yg E3 | Yg W | Yg Wd | Yn W | Yn M | Yn W | Yn Wd | Yg Wd | Yg E3 | Yg Wd | Yg E1 | Yn Wd | Yn W | Yg F | Yg F | Yg F | Yg W | Yn F | Yn E2 | Yn F | Yn E4 | Yg E | Yg M | 26 |
| 27 | Yn Wd | Yn W | Yn W | Yn Wd | Yg Wd | Yg E3 | Yg Wd | Yg E1 | Yn Wd | Yn W | Yn Wd | Yn F | Yg F | Yg W | Yn F | Yn E2 | Yn F | Yn E4 | Yg E | Yg M | Yg E | Yg Wd | Yn E | Yn M | 27 |
| 28 | Yg F | Yg W | Yg Wd | Yg E1 | Yn Wd | Yn W | Yn Wd | Yn F | Yg F | Yg W | Yg F | Yg F | Yn F | Yn E4 | Yg E | Yg M | Yg E | Yg Wd | Yn E | Yn M | Yn E | Yn Wd | Yg M | Yg E3 | 28 |
| 29 | | | Yn Wd | Yn F | Yg F | Yg W | Yg F | Yg F | Yn F | Yn E4 | Yn F | Yn E2 | Yg E | Yg Wd | Yn E | Yn M | Yn E | Yn Wd | Yg M | Yg E3 | Yg M | Yg E1 | Yn M | Yn W | 29 |
| 30 | | | Yg F | Yg F | Yn F | Yn E4 | Yn F | Yn E2 | Yg E | Yg Wd | Yg E | Yg M | Yn E | Yn Wd | Yg M | Yg E3 | Yg M | Yg E1 | Yn M | Yn W | Yn M | Yn F | Yg W | Yg W | 30 |
| 31 | | | Yn F | Yn E2 | | | Yg E | Yg M | | | Yn E | Yn M | Yg M | Yg E1 | | | Yn M | Yn F | | | Yg W | Yg F | Yn W | Yn E4 | 31 |
| 1 | Yn F | Yn E4 | Yg E | Yg M | Yg E | Yg Wd | Yn E | Yn M | Yn E | Yn Wd | Yg M | Yg E3 | Yn M | Yn F | Yn M | Yn W | Yg W | Yg F | Yg W | Yg W | Yn W | Yn E2 | Yg Wd | Yg Wd | 1 |
| 2 | Yg E | Yg Wd | Yn E | Yn M | Yn E | Yn Wd | Yg M | Yg E3 | Yg M | Yg E1 | Yn M | Yn W | Yg W | Yg F | Yg W | Yg W | Yn W | Yn E2 | Yn W | Yn E4 | Yg Wd | Yg M | Yn Wd | Yn Wd | 2 |
| 3 | Yn E | Yn Wd | Yg M | Yg E3 | Yg M | Yg E1 | Yn M | Yn W | Yn M | Yn F | Yg W | Yg W | Yn W | Yn E2 | Yn W | Yn E4 | Yg Wd | Yg M | Yg Wd | Yg Wd | Yn Wd | Yn M | Yg F | Yg E1 | 3 |
| 4 | Yg M | Yg E1 | Yn M | Yn W | Yn M | Yn F | Yg W | Yg W | Yg W | Yg F | Yn W | Yn E4 | Yg Wd | Yg M | Yg Wd | Yg Wd | Yn Wd | Yn M | Yn Wd | Yn Wd | Yg F | Yg E3 | | | 4 |
| 5 | Yn M | Yn F | | | Yg W | Yg F | Yn W | Yn E4 | Yn W | Yn E2 | Yg Wd | Yg Wd | Yn Wd | Yn M | Yn Wd | Yn Wd | Yg F | Yg E3 | Yg F | Yg E1 | Yn F | Yn W | | | 5 |
| 6 | | | | | | | | | Yg Wd | Yg M | Yn Wd | Yn Wd | Yg F | Yg E3 | Yg F | Yg E1 | Yn F | Yn W | Yn F | Yn F | | | | | 6 |
| 7 | | | | | | | | | | | Yg F | Yg E1 | Yn F | Yn W | Yn F | Yn F | Yg E | Yg W | | | | | | | 7 |
| 8 | | | | | | | | | | | | | | | Yg E | Yg F | | | | | | | | | 8 |

# YEAR OF THE PIG

| | H | E | H | E | H | E | H | E | H | E | H | E | H | E | H | E | H | E | H | E | H | E | H | E | |
|---|---|---|---|---|---|---|---|---|---|---|---|---|---|---|---|---|---|---|---|---|---|---|---|---|---|
| **YEAR** | YEAR<br>Yn E | Yn W | 1959 | | | | | | | | | | | | | | | | | | | 1960 | | | |
| **MONTH** | 4 Feb - 5 Mar | | 6 Mar - 4 Apr | | 5 Apr - 5 May | | 6 May - 5 June | | 6 June - 7 Jul | | 8 Jul - 7 Aug | | 8 Aug - 7 Sep | | 8 Sep - 8 Oct | | 9 Oct - 7 Nov | | 8 Nov - 7 Dec | | 8 Dec - 5 Jan | | 6 Jan - 4 Feb | | |
| | Yg F | Yg Wd | Yn F | Yn Wd | Yg E | Yg E1 | Yn E | Yn F | Yg M | Yg F | Yn M | Yn E2 | Yg W | Yg M | Yn W | Yn M | Yg Wd | Yg E3 | Yn Wd | Yn W | Yg F | Yg W | Yn F | Yn E4 | |
| **Starting time** | 1st day | Mid-pt | 1st day | Mid-pt | 1st day | Mid-pt | 1st day | Mid-pt | 1st day | Mid-pt | 1st day | Mid-pt | 1st day | Mid-pt | 1st day | Mid-pt | 1st day | Mid-pt | 1st day | Mid-pt | 1st day | Mid-pt | 1st day | Mid-pt | |
| Date | 4 | 19 | 6 | 21 | 5 | 21 | 6 | 22 | 6 | 22 | 8 | 23 | 8 | 24 | 8 | 24 | 9 | 24 | 8 | 23 | 8 | 22 | 6 | 21 | |
| Hour | 2143 | 1738 | 1557 | 1655 | 2104 | 0417 | 1439 | 0343 | 1901 | 1151 | 0521 | 2246 | 1505 | 0544 | 1749 | 0309 | 0911 | 1212 | 1203 | 0928 | 0438 | 2235 | 1543 | 0910 | |
| **DATE** 4 | Yn F | Yn F | | | | | | | | | | | | | | | | | | | | | | | 4 |
| 5 | Yg E | Yg F | | | Yn F | Yn F | | | | | | | | | | | | | | | | | | | 5 |
| 6 | Yn E | Yn E2 | Yn F | Yn W | Yg E | Yg F | Yg E | Yg W | Yn E | Yn E2 | | | | | | | | | | | | | Yn W | Yn F | 6 |
| 7 | Yg M | Yg M | Yg E | Yg W | Yn E | Yn E2 | Yn E | Yn E4 | Yg M | Yg M | | | | | | | | | | | | | Yg Wd | Yg F | 7 |
| 8 | Yn M | Yn M | Yn E | Yn E4 | Yg M | Yg M | Yg M | Yg Wd | Yn M | Yn M | Yn M | Yn Wd | Yg W | Yg E3 | Yn W | Yn F | | | Yg Wd | Yg F | Yg Wd | Yg W | Yn Wd | Yn E2 | 8 |
| 9 | Yg W | Yg E3 | Yg M | Yg Wd | Yn M | Yn M | Yn M | Yn Wd | Yg W | Yg E3 | Yg W | Yg E1 | Yn W | Yn W | Yg Wd | Yg F | Yg Wd | Yg W | Yn Wd | Yn E2 | Yn Wd | Yn E4 | Yg F | Yg M | 9 |
| 10 | Yn W | Yn W | Yn M | Yn Wd | Yg W | Yg E3 | Yg W | Yg E1 | Yn W | Yn W | Yn W | Yn F | Yg Wd | Yg W | Yn Wd | Yn E2 | Yn Wd | Yn E4 | Yg F | Yg M | Yg F | Yg Wd | Yn F | Yn M | 10 |
| 11 | Yg Wd | Yg W | Yg W | Yg E1 | Yn W | Yn W | Yn W | Yn F | Yg Wd | Yg W | Yg Wd | Yg F | Yn Wd | Yn E4 | Yg F | Yg M | Yg F | Yg Wd | Yn F | Yn M | Yn F | Yn Wd | Yg E | Yg E3 | 11 |
| 12 | Yn Wd | Yn E4 | Yn W | Yn F | Yg Wd | Yg W | Yg Wd | Yg F | Yn Wd | Yn E4 | Yn Wd | Yn E2 | Yg F | Yg Wd | Yn F | Yn M | Yn F | Yn Wd | Yg E | Yg E3 | Yg E | Yg E1 | Yn E | Yn W | 12 |
| 13 | Yg F | Yg Wd | Yg Wd | Yg F | Yn Wd | Yn E4 | Yn Wd | Yn E2 | Yg F | Yg Wd | Yg F | Yg M | Yn F | Yn Wd | Yg E | Yg E3 | Yg E | Yg E1 | Yn E | Yn W | Yn E | Yn F | Yg M | Yg W | 13 |
| 14 | Yn F | Yn Wd | Yn Wd | Yn E2 | Yg F | Yg Wd | Yg F | Yg M | Yn F | Yn Wd | Yn F | Yn M | Yg E | Yg E1 | Yn E | Yn W | Yn E | Yn F | Yg M | Yg W | Yg M | Yg F | Yn M | Yn E4 | 14 |
| 15 | Yg E | Yg E1 | Yg F | Yg M | Yn F | Yn Wd | Yn F | Yn M | Yg E | Yg E1 | Yg E | Yg E3 | Yn E | Yn F | Yg M | Yg W | Yg M | Yg F | Yn M | Yn E4 | Yn M | Yn E2 | Yg W | Yg Wd | 15 |
| 16 | Yn E | Yn F | Yn F | Yn M | Yg E | Yg E1 | Yg E | Yg E3 | Yn E | Yn F | Yn E | Yn W | Yg M | Yg F | Yn M | Yn E4 | Yn M | Yn E2 | Yg W | Yg Wd | Yg W | Yg M | Yn W | Yn Wd | 16 |
| 17 | Yg M | Yg F | Yg E | Yg E3 | Yn E | Yn F | Yn E | Yn W | Yg M | Yg F | Yg M | Yg W | Yn M | Yn E2 | Yg W | Yg Wd | Yg W | Yg M | Yn W | Yn Wd | Yn W | Yn M | Yg Wd | Yg E1 | 17 |
| 18 | Yn M | Yn E2 | Yn E | Yn W | Yg M | Yg F | Yg M | Yg W | Yn M | Yn E2 | Yn M | Yn E4 | Yg W | Yg M | Yn W | Yn Wd | Yn W | Yn M | Yg Wd | Yg E1 | Yg Wd | Yg E3 | Yn Wd | Yn F | 18 |
| 19 | Yg W | Yg M | Yg M | Yg W | Yn M | Yn E2 | Yn M | Yn E4 | Yg W | Yg M | Yg W | Yg Wd | Yn W | Yn M | Yg Wd | Yg E1 | Yg Wd | Yg E3 | Yn Wd | Yn F | Yn Wd | Yn W | Yg F | Yg F | 19 |
| 20 | Yn W | Yn M | Yn M | Yn E4 | Yg W | Yg M | Yg W | Yg Wd | Yn W | Yn M | Yn W | Yn Wd | Yg Wd | Yg E3 | Yn Wd | Yn F | Yn Wd | Yn W | Yg F | Yg F | Yg F | Yg W | Yn F | Yn E2 | 20 |
| 21 | Yg Wd | Yg E3 | Yg W | Yg Wd | Yn W | Yn M | Yn W | Yn Wd | Yg Wd | Yg E3 | Yg Wd | Yg E1 | Yn Wd | Yn W | Yg F | Yg F | Yg F | Yg W | Yn F | Yn E2 | Yn F | Yn E4 | Yg E | Yg M | 21 |
| 22 | Yn Wd | Yn W | Yn W | Yn Wd | Yg Wd | Yg E3 | Yg Wd | Yg E1 | Yn Wd | Yn W | Yn Wd | Yn F | Yg F | Yg W | Yn F | Yn E2 | Yn F | Yn E4 | Yg E | Yg M | Yg E | Yg Wd | Yn E | Yn M | 22 |
| 23 | Yg F | Yg W | Yg Wd | Yg E1 | Yn Wd | Yn W | Yn Wd | Yn F | Yg F | Yg W | Yg F | Yg F | Yn F | Yn E4 | Yg E | Yg M | Yg E | Yg Wd | Yn E | Yn M | Yn E | Yn Wd | Yg M | Yg E3 | 23 |
| 24 | Yn F | Yn E4 | Yn Wd | Yn F | Yg F | Yg W | Yg F | Yg F | Yn F | Yn E4 | Yn F | Yn E2 | Yg E | Yg Wd | Yn E | Yn M | Yn E | Yn Wd | Yg M | Yg E3 | Yg M | Yg E1 | Yn M | Yn W | 24 |
| 25 | Yg E | Yg Wd | Yg F | Yg F | Yn F | Yn E4 | Yn F | Yn E2 | Yg E | Yg Wd | Yg E | Yg M | Yn E | Yn Wd | Yg M | Yg E3 | Yg M | Yg E1 | Yn M | Yn W | Yn M | Yn F | Yg W | Yg W | 25 |
| 26 | Yn E | Yn Wd | Yn F | Yn E2 | Yg E | Yg Wd | Yg E | Yg M | Yn E | Yn Wd | Yn E | Yn M | Yg M | Yg E1 | Yn M | Yn W | Yn M | Yn F | Yg W | Yg W | Yg W | Yg F | Yn W | Yn E4 | 26 |
| 27 | Yg M | Yg E1 | Yg E | Yg M | Yn E | Yn Wd | Yn E | Yn M | Yg M | Yg E1 | Yg M | Yg E3 | Yn M | Yn F | Yg W | Yg W | Yg W | Yg F | Yn W | Yn E4 | Yn W | Yn E2 | Yg Wd | Yg Wd | 27 |
| 28 | Yn M | Yn F | Yn E | Yn M | Yg M | Yg E1 | Yg M | Yg E3 | Yn M | Yn F | Yn M | Yn W | Yg W | Yg F | Yn W | Yn E4 | Yn W | Yn E2 | Yg Wd | Yg Wd | Yg Wd | Yg M | Yn Wd | Yn Wd | 28 |
| 29 | | | Yg M | Yg E3 | Yn M | Yn F | Yn M | Yn W | Yg W | Yg F | Yg W | Yg W | Yn W | Yn E2 | Yg Wd | Yg Wd | Yg Wd | Yg M | Yn Wd | Yn Wd | Yn Wd | Yn M | Yg F | Yg E1 | 29 |
| 30 | | | Yn M | Yn W | Yg W | Yg F | Yg W | Yg W | Yn W | Yn E2 | Yn W | Yn E4 | Yg Wd | Yg M | Yn Wd | Yn Wd | Yn Wd | Yn M | Yg F | Yg E1 | Yg F | Yg E3 | Yn F | Yn F | 30 |
| 31 | | | Yg W | Yg W | | | Yn W | Yn E4 | | | Yg Wd | Yg Wd | Yn Wd | Yn M | | | Yg F | Yg E3 | | | Yn F | Yn W | Yg E | Yg F | 31 |
| 1 | Yg W | Yg F | Yn W | Yn E4 | Yn W | Yn E2 | Yg Wd | Yg Wd | Yg Wd | Yg M | Yn Wd | Yn Wd | Yg F | Yg E3 | Yg F | Yg E1 | Yn F | Yn W | Yn F | Yn F | Yg E | Yg W | Yn E | Yn E2 | 1 |
| 2 | Yn W | Yn E2 | Yg Wd | Yg Wd | Yg Wd | Yg M | Yn Wd | Yn Wd | Yn Wd | Yn M | Yg F | Yg E1 | Yn F | Yn W | Yn F | Yn F | Yg E | Yg W | Yg E | Yg F | Yn E | Yn E4 | Yg M | Yg M | 2 |
| 3 | Yg Wd | Yg M | Yn Wd | Yn Wd | Yn Wd | Yn M | Yg F | Yg E1 | Yg F | Yg E3 | Yn F | Yn F | Yg E | Yg W | Yg E | Yg F | Yn E | Yn E4 | Yn E | Yn E2 | Yg M | Yg Wd | Yn M | Yn M | 3 |
| 4 | Yn Wd | Yn M | Yg F | Yg E1 | Yg F | Yg E3 | Yn F | Yn F | Yn F | Yn W | Yg E | Yg F | Yn E | Yn E4 | Yn E | Yn E2 | Yg M | Yg Wd | Yg M | Yg M | Yn M | Yn Wd | Yg W | Yg E3 | 4 |
| 5 | Yg F | Yg E3 | | | Yn F | Yn W | Yg E | Yg F | Yg E | Yg W | Yn E | Yn E2 | Yg M | Yg Wd | Yg M | Yg M | Yn M | Yn Wd | Yn M | Yn M | Yg W | Yg E1 | | | 5 |
| 6 | | | | | | | | | Yn E | Yn E4 | Yg M | Yg M | Yn M | Yn Wd | Yn M | Yn M | Yg W | Yg E1 | Yg W | Yg E3 | | | | | 6 |
| 7 | | | | | | | | | Yg M | Yg Wd | Yn M | Yn M | Yg W | Yg E1 | Yg W | Yg E3 | Yn W | Yn F | Yn W | Yn W | | | | | 7 |
| 8 | | | | | | | | | | | | | | | Yn W | Yn W | | | | | | | | | 8 |

# YEAR OF THE RAT

| | H | E | H | E | H | E | H | E | H | E | H | E |
|---|---|---|---|---|---|---|---|---|---|---|---|---|
| YEAR | YEAR Yg M | Yg W | 1960 | | | | | | | | | |
| MONTH | 5 Feb - 4 Mar | | 5 Mar - 4 Apr | | 5 Apr - 4 May | | 5 May - 5 June | | 6 June - 6 Jul | | 7 Jul - 6 Aug | |
| | Yg E | Yg Wd | Yn E | Yn Wd | Yg M | Yg E1 | Yn M | Yn F | Yg W | Yg F | Yn W | Yn E2 |
| Starting time | 1st day | Mid-pt | 1st day | Mid-pt | 1st day | Mid-pt | 1st day | Mid-pt | 1st day | Mid-pt | 1st day | Mid-pt |
| Date | 5 | 19 | 5 | 20 | 5 | 20 | 5 | 21 | 6 | 21 | 7 | 23 |
| Hour | 0323 | 2326 | 2136 | 2243 | 0244 | 1006 | 2023 | 0934 | 0049 | 1742 | 1113 | 0438 |
| DATE 4 | | | | | | | | | | | | |
| 5 | Yn W | Yn W | Yg W | Yg E1 | Yn W | Yn W | Yn W | Yn F | | | | |
| 6 | Yg Wd | Yg W | Yn W | Yn F | Yg Wd | Yg W | Yg Wd | Yg F | Yn Wd | Yn E4 | | |
| 7 | Yn Wd | Yn E4 | Yg Wd | Yg F | Yn Wd | Yn E4 | Yn Wd | Yn E2 | Yg F | Yg Wd | Yg F | Yg M |
| 8 | Yg F | Yg Wd | Yn Wd | Yn E2 | Yg F | Yg Wd | Yg F | Yg M | Yn F | Yn Wd | Yn F | Yn M |
| 9 | Yn F | Yn Wd | Yg F | Yg M | Yn F | Yn Wd | Yn F | Yn M | Yg E | Yg E1 | Yg E | Yg E3 |
| 10 | Yg E | Yg E1 | Yn F | Yn M | Yg E | Yg E1 | Yg E | Yg E3 | Yn E | Yn F | Yn E | Yn W |
| 11 | Yn E | Yn F | Yg E | Yg E3 | Yn E | Yn F | Yn E | Yn W | Yg M | Yg F | Yg M | Yg W |
| 12 | Yg M | Yg F | Yn E | Yn W | Yg M | Yg F | Yg M | Yg W | Yn M | Yn E2 | Yn M | Yn E4 |
| 13 | Yn M | Yn E2 | Yg M | Yg W | Yn M | Yn E2 | Yn M | Yn E4 | Yg W | Yg M | Yg W | Yg Wd |
| 14 | Yg W | Yg M | Yn M | Yn E4 | Yg W | Yg M | Yg W | Yg Wd | Yn W | Yn M | Yn W | Yn Wd |
| 15 | Yn W | Yn M | Yg W | Yg Wd | Yn W | Yn M | Yn W | Yn Wd | Yg Wd | Yg E3 | Yg Wd | Yg E1 |
| 16 | Yg Wd | Yg E3 | Yn W | Yn Wd | Yg Wd | Yg E3 | Yg Wd | Yg E1 | Yn Wd | Yn W | Yn Wd | Yn F |
| 17 | Yn Wd | Yn W | Yg Wd | Yg E1 | Yn Wd | Yn W | Yn Wd | Yn F | Yg F | Yg W | Yg F | Yg F |
| 18 | Yg F | Yg W | Yn Wd | Yn F | Yg F | Yg W | Yg F | Yg F | Yn F | Yn E4 | Yn F | Yn E2 |
| 19 | Yn F | Yn E4 | Yg F | Yg F | Yn F | Yn E4 | Yn F | Yn E2 | Yg E | Yg Wd | Yg E | Yg M |
| 20 | Yg E | Yg Wd | Yn F | Yn E2 | Yg E | Yg Wd | Yg E | Yg M | Yn E | Yn Wd | Yn E | Yn M |
| 21 | Yn E | Yn Wd | Yg E | Yg M | Yn E | Yn Wd | Yn E | Yn M | Yg M | Yg E1 | Yg M | Yg E3 |
| 22 | Yg M | Yg E1 | Yn E | Yn M | Yg M | Yg E1 | Yg M | Yg E3 | Yn M | Yn F | Yn M | Yn W |
| 23 | Yn M | Yn F | Yg M | Yg E3 | Yn M | Yn F | Yn M | Yn W | Yg W | Yg F | Yg W | Yg W |
| 24 | Yg W | Yg F | Yn M | Yn W | Yg W | Yg F | Yg W | Yg W | Yn W | Yn E2 | Yn W | Yn E4 |
| 25 | Yn W | Yn E2 | Yg W | Yg W | Yn W | Yn E2 | Yn W | Yn E4 | Yg Wd | Yg M | Yg Wd | Yg Wd |
| 26 | Yg Wd | Yg M | Yn W | Yn E4 | Yg Wd | Yg M | Yg Wd | Yg Wd | Yn Wd | Yn M | Yn Wd | Yn Wd |
| 27 | Yn Wd | Yn M | Yg Wd | Yg Wd | Yn Wd | Yn M | Yn Wd | Yn Wd | Yg F | Yg E3 | Yg F | Yg E1 |
| 28 | Yg F | Yg E3 | Yn Wd | Yn Wd | Yg F | Yg E3 | Yg F | Yg E1 | Yn F | Yn W | Yn F | Yn F |
| 29 | Yn F | Yn W | Yg F | Yg E1 | Yn F | Yn W | Yn F | Yn F | Yg E | Yg W | Yg E | Yg F |
| 30 | | | Yn F | Yn F | Yg E | Yg W | Yg E | Yg F | Yn E | Yn E4 | Yn E | Yn E2 |
| 31 | | | Yg E | Yg F | | | Yn E | Yn E2 | | | Yg M | Yg M |
| 1 | Yg E | Yg W | Yn E | Yn E2 | Yn E | Yn E4 | Yg M | Yg M | Yg M | Yg Wd | Yn M | Yn M |
| 2 | Yn E | Yn E4 | Yg M | Yg M | Yg M | Yg Wd | Yn M | Yn M | Yn M | Yn Wd | Yg W | Yg E3 |
| 3 | Yg M | Yg Wd | Yn M | Yn M | Yn M | Yn Wd | Yg W | Yg E3 | Yg W | Yg E1 | Yn W | Yn W |
| 4 | Yn M | Yn Wd | Yg W | Yg E3 | Yg W | Yg E1 | Yn W | Yn W | Yn W | Yn F | Yg Wd | Yg W |
| 5 | | | | | | | Yg Wd | Yg W | Yg Wd | Yg F | Yn Wd | Yn E4 |
| 6 | | | | | | | | | Yn Wd | Yn E2 | Yg F | Yg Wd |
| 7 | | | | | | | | | | | | |
| 8 | | | | | | | | | | | | |

| | H | E | H | E | H | E | H | E | H | E | H | E | |
|---|---|---|---|---|---|---|---|---|---|---|---|---|---|
| YEAR | 1960 | | | | | | | | | | 1961 | | |
| MONTH | 7 Aug - 6 Sep | | 7 Sep - 7 Oct | | 8 Oct - 6 Nov | | 7 Nov - 6 Dec | | 7 Dec - 4 Jan | | 5 Jan - 3 Feb | | |
| | Yg Wd | Yg M | Yn Wd | Yn M | Yg F | Yg E3 | Yn F | Yn W | Yg E | Yg W | Yn E | Yn E4 | |
| Starting time | 1st day | Mid-pt | 1st day | Mid-pt | 1st day | Mid-pt | 1st day | Mid-pt | 1st day | Mid-pt | 1st day | Mid-pt | |
| Date | 7 | 23 | 7 | 23 | 8 | 23 | 7 | 22 | 7 | 22 | 5 | 20 | |
| Hour | 2100 | 1135 | 2346 | 0859 | 1509 | 1802 | 1802 | 1518 | 1038 | 0426 | 2143 | 1501 | |
| DATE 4 | | | | | | | | | | | | | 4 |
| 5 | | | | | | | | | | | Yg E | Yg E3 | 5 |
| 6 | | | | | | | | | | | Yn E | Yn W | 6 |
| 7 | Yn F | Yn Wd | Yg E | Yg E3 | | | Yn E | Yn W | Yn E | Yn F | Yg M | Yg W | 7 |
| 8 | Yg E | Yg E1 | Yn E | Yn W | Yn E | Yn F | Yg M | Yg W | Yg M | Yg F | Yn M | Yn E4 | 8 |
| 9 | Yn E | Yn F | Yg M | Yg W | Yg M | Yg F | Yn M | Yn E4 | Yn M | Yn E2 | Yg W | Yg Wd | 9 |
| 10 | Yg M | Yg F | Yn M | Yn E4 | Yn M | Yn E2 | Yg W | Yg Wd | Yg W | Yg M | Yn W | Yn Wd | 10 |
| 11 | Yn M | Yn E2 | Yg W | Yg Wd | Yg W | Yg M | Yn W | Yn Wd | Yn W | Yn M | Yg Wd | Yg E1 | 11 |
| 12 | Yg W | Yg M | Yn W | Yn Wd | Yn W | Yn M | Yg Wd | Yg E1 | Yg Wd | Yg E3 | Yn Wd | Yn F | 12 |
| 13 | Yn W | Yn M | Yg Wd | Yg E1 | Yg Wd | Yg E3 | Yn Wd | Yn F | Yn Wd | Yn W | Yg F | Yg F | 13 |
| 14 | Yg Wd | Yg E3 | Yn Wd | Yn F | Yn Wd | Yn W | Yg F | Yg F | Yg F | Yg W | Yn F | Yn E2 | 14 |
| 15 | Yn Wd | Yn W | Yg F | Yg F | Yg F | Yg W | Yn F | Yn E2 | Yn F | Yn E4 | Yg E | Yg M | 15 |
| 16 | Yg F | Yg W | Yn F | Yn E2 | Yn F | Yn E4 | Yg E | Yg M | Yg E | Yg Wd | Yn E | Yn M | 16 |
| 17 | Yn F | Yn E4 | Yg E | Yg M | Yg E | Yg Wd | Yn E | Yn M | Yn E | Yn Wd | Yg M | Yg E3 | 17 |
| 18 | Yg E | Yg Wd | Yn E | Yn M | Yn E | Yn Wd | Yg M | Yg E3 | Yg M | Yg E1 | Yn M | Yn W | 18 |
| 19 | Yn E | Yn Wd | Yg M | Yg E3 | Yg M | Yg E1 | Yn M | Yn W | Yn M | Yn F | Yg W | Yg W | 19 |
| 20 | Yg M | Yg E1 | Yn M | Yn W | Yn M | Yn F | Yg W | Yg W | Yg W | Yg F | Yn W | Yn E4 | 20 |
| 21 | Yn M | Yn F | Yg W | Yg W | Yg W | Yg F | Yn W | Yn E4 | Yn W | Yn E2 | Yg Wd | Yg Wd | 21 |
| 22 | Yg W | Yg F | Yn W | Yn E4 | Yn W | Yn E2 | Yg Wd | Yg Wd | Yg Wd | Yg M | Yn Wd | Yn Wd | 22 |
| 23 | Yn W | Yn E2 | Yg Wd | Yg Wd | Yg Wd | Yg M | Yn Wd | Yn Wd | Yn Wd | Yn M | Yg F | Yg E1 | 23 |
| 24 | Yg Wd | Yg M | Yn Wd | Yn Wd | Yn Wd | Yn M | Yg F | Yg E1 | Yg F | Yg E3 | Yn F | Yn F | 24 |
| 25 | Yn Wd | Yn M | Yg F | Yg E1 | Yg F | Yg E3 | Yn F | Yn F | Yn F | Yn W | Yg E | Yg F | 25 |
| 26 | Yg F | Yg E3 | Yn F | Yn F | Yn F | Yn W | Yg E | Yg F | Yg E | Yg W | Yn E | Yn E2 | 26 |
| 27 | Yn F | Yn W | Yg E | Yg F | Yg E | Yg W | Yn E | Yn E2 | Yn E | Yn E4 | Yg M | Yg M | 27 |
| 28 | Yg E | Yg W | Yn E | Yn E2 | Yn E | Yn E4 | Yg M | Yg M | Yg M | Yg Wd | Yn M | Yn M | 28 |
| 29 | Yn E | Yn E4 | Yg M | Yg M | Yg M | Yg Wd | Yn M | Yn M | Yn M | Yn Wd | Yg W | Yg E3 | 29 |
| 30 | Yg M | Yg Wd | Yn M | Yn M | Yn M | Yn Wd | Yg W | Yg E3 | Yg W | Yg E1 | Yn W | Yn W | 30 |
| 31 | Yn M | Yn Wd | | | Yg W | Yg E1 | | | Yn W | Yn F | Yg Wd | Yg W | 31 |
| 1 | Yg W | Yg E1 | Yg W | Yg E3 | Yn W | Yn F | Yn W | Yn W | Yg Wd | Yg F | Yn Wd | Yn E4 | 1 |
| 2 | Yn W | Yn F | Yn W | Yn W | Yg Wd | Yg F | Yg Wd | Yg W | Yn Wd | Yn E2 | Yg F | Yg Wd | 2 |
| 3 | Yg Wd | Yg F | Yg Wd | Yg W | Yn Wd | Yn E2 | Yn Wd | Yn E4 | Yg F | Yg M | Yn F | Yn Wd | 3 |
| 4 | Yn Wd | Yn E2 | Yn Wd | Yn E4 | Yg F | Yg M | Yg F | Yg Wd | Yn F | Yn M | | | 4 |
| 5 | Yg F | Yg M | Yg F | Yg Wd | Yn F | Yn M | Yn F | Yn Wd | | | | | 5 |
| 6 | Yn F | Yn M | Yn F | Yn Wd | Yg E | Yg E3 | Yg E | Yg E1 | | | | | 6 |
| 7 | | | Yg E | Yg E1 | | | | | | | | | 7 |
| 8 | | | | | | | | | | | | | 8 |

# YEAR OF THE OX

| | H | E | H | E | H | E | H | E | H | E | H | E | H | E | H | E | H | E | H | E | H | E | H | E | |
|---|---|---|---|---|---|---|---|---|---|---|---|---|---|---|---|---|---|---|---|---|---|---|---|---|---|
| YEAR | YEAR<br>YnM | Yn E4 | 1961 | | | | | | | | | | | | | | | | | | 1962 | | | | |
| MONTH | 4 Feb - 5 Mar<br>Yg M | Yg Wd | 6 Mar - 4 Apr<br>Yn M | Yn Wd | 5 Apr - 5 May<br>Yg W | Yg E1 | 6 May - 5 June<br>Yn W | Yn F | 6 June - 6 Jul<br>Yg Wd | Yg F | 7 Jul - 7 Aug<br>Yn Wd | Yn E2 | 8 Aug - 7 Sep<br>Yg F | Yg M | 8 Sep - 7 Oct<br>Yn F | Yn M | 8 Oct - 6 Nov<br>Yg E | Yg E3 | 7 Nov - 6 Dec<br>Yn E | Yn W | 7 Dec - 5 Jan<br>Yg M | Yg W | 6 Jan - 3 Feb<br>Yn M | Yn E4 | |
| Starting time | 1st day | Mid-pt | 1st day | Mid-pt | 1st day | Mid-pt | 1st day | Mid-pt | 1st day | Mid-pt | 1st day | Mid-pt | 1st day | Mid-pt | 1st day | Mid-pt | 1st day | Mid-pt | 1st day | Mid-pt | 1st day | Mid-pt | 1st day | Mid-pt | |
| Date | 4 | 19 | 6 | 21 | 5 | 20 | 6 | 21 | 6 | 21 | 7 | 23 | 8 | 23 | 8 | 23 | 8 | 23 | 7 | 22 | 7 | 22 | 6 | 20 | |
| Hour | 0923 | 0517 | 0335 | 0432 | 0842 | 1555 | 0221 | 1522 | 0646 | 2330 | 1707 | 1024 | 0249 | 1719 | 0529 | 1443 | 2051 | 2347 | 2346 | 2108 | 1626 | 1020 | 0335 | 2058 | |
| DATE 4 | Yg E | Yg E1 | | | | | | | | | | | | | | | | | | | | | | | 4 |
| 5 | Yn E | Yn F | | | Yg E | Yg E1 | | | | | | | | | | | | | | | | | | | 5 |
| 6 | Yg M | Yg F | Yg E | Yg E3 | Yn E | Yn F | Yn E | Yn W | Yg M | Yg F | | | | | | | | | | | | | Yg Wd | Yg E1 | 6 |
| 7 | Yn M | Yn E2 | Yn E | Yn W | Yg M | Yg F | Yg M | Yg W | Yn M | Yn E2 | Yn M | Yn E4 | | | | | | | Yg Wd | Yg E1 | Yg Wd | Yg E3 | Yn Wd | Yn F | 7 |
| 8 | Yg W | Yg M | Yg M | Yg W | Yn M | Yn E2 | Yn M | Yn E4 | Yg W | Yg M | Yg W | Yg Wd | Yn W | Yn M | Yg Wd | Yg E1 | Yg Wd | Yg E3 | Yn Wd | Yn F | Yn Wd | Yn W | Yg F | Yg F | 8 |
| 9 | Yn W | Yn M | Yn M | Yn E4 | Yg W | Yg M | Yg W | Yg Wd | Yn W | Yn M | Yn W | Yn Wd | Yg Wd | Yg E3 | Yn Wd | Yn F | Yn Wd | Yn W | Yg F | Yg F | Yg F | Yg W | Yn F | Yn E2 | 9 |
| 10 | Yg Wd | Yg E3 | Yg W | Yg Wd | Yn W | Yn M | Yn W | Yn Wd | Yg Wd | Yg E3 | Yg Wd | Yg E1 | Yn Wd | Yn W | Yg F | Yg F | Yg F | Yg W | Yn F | Yn E2 | Yn F | Yn E4 | Yg E | Yg M | 10 |
| 11 | Yn Wd | Yn W | Yn W | Yn Wd | Yg Wd | Yg E3 | Yg Wd | Yg E1 | Yn Wd | Yn W | Yn Wd | Yn F | Yg F | Yg W | Yn F | Yn E2 | Yn F | Yn E4 | Yg E | Yg M | Yg E | Yg Wd | Yn E | Yn M | 11 |
| 12 | Yg F | Yg W | Yg Wd | Yg E1 | Yn Wd | Yn W | Yn Wd | Yn F | Yg F | Yg W | Yg F | Yg F | Yn F | Yn E4 | Yg E | Yg M | Yg E | Yg Wd | Yn E | Yn M | Yn E | Yn Wd | Yg M | Yg E3 | 12 |
| 13 | Yn F | Yn E4 | Yn Wd | Yn F | Yg F | Yg W | Yg F | Yg F | Yn F | Yn E4 | Yn F | Yn E2 | Yg E | Yg Wd | Yn E | Yn M | Yn E | Yn Wd | Yg M | Yg E3 | Yg M | Yg E1 | Yn M | Yn W | 13 |
| 14 | Yg E | Yg Wd | Yg F | Yg F | Yn F | Yn E4 | Yn F | Yn E2 | Yg E | Yg Wd | Yg E | Yg M | Yn E | Yn Wd | Yg M | Yg E3 | Yg M | Yg E1 | Yn M | Yn W | Yn M | Yn F | Yg W | Yg W | 14 |
| 15 | Yn E | Yn Wd | Yn F | Yn E2 | Yg E | Yg Wd | Yg E | Yg M | Yn E | Yn Wd | Yn E | Yn M | Yg M | Yg E1 | Yn M | Yn W | Yn M | Yn F | Yg W | Yg W | Yg W | Yg F | Yn W | Yn E4 | 15 |
| 16 | Yg M | Yg E1 | Yg E | Yg M | Yn E | Yn Wd | Yn E | Yn M | Yg M | Yg E1 | Yg M | Yg E3 | Yn M | Yn F | Yg W | Yg W | Yg W | Yg F | Yn W | Yn E4 | Yn W | Yn E2 | Yg Wd | Yg Wd | 16 |
| 17 | Yn M | Yn F | Yn E | Yn M | Yg M | Yg E1 | Yg M | Yg E3 | Yn M | Yn F | Yn M | Yn W | Yg W | Yg F | Yn W | Yn E4 | Yn W | Yn E2 | Yg Wd | Yg Wd | Yg Wd | Yg M | Yn Wd | Yn Wd | 17 |
| 18 | Yg W | Yg F | Yg M | Yg E3 | Yn M | Yn F | Yn M | Yn W | Yg W | Yg F | Yg W | Yg W | Yn W | Yn E2 | Yg Wd | Yg Wd | Yg Wd | Yg M | Yn Wd | Yn Wd | Yn Wd | Yn M | Yg F | Yg E1 | 18 |
| 19 | Yn W | Yn E2 | Yn M | Yn W | Yg W | Yg F | Yg W | Yg W | Yn W | Yn E2 | Yn W | Yn E4 | Yg Wd | Yg M | Yn Wd | Yn Wd | Yn Wd | Yn M | Yg F | Yg E1 | Yg F | Yg E3 | Yn F | Yn F | 19 |
| 20 | Yg Wd | Yg M | Yg W | Yg W | Yn W | Yn E2 | Yn W | Yn E4 | Yg Wd | Yg M | Yg Wd | Yg Wd | Yn Wd | Yn M | Yg F | Yg E1 | Yg F | Yg E3 | Yn F | Yn F | Yn F | Yn W | Yg E | Yg F | 20 |
| 21 | Yn Wd | Yn M | Yn W | Yn E4 | Yg Wd | Yg M | Yg Wd | Yg Wd | Yn Wd | Yn M | Yn Wd | Yn Wd | Yg F | Yg E3 | Yn F | Yn F | Yn F | Yn W | Yg E | Yg F | Yg E | Yg W | Yn E | Yn E2 | 21 |
| 22 | Yg F | Yg E3 | Yg Wd | Yg Wd | Yn Wd | Yn M | Yn Wd | Yn Wd | Yg F | Yg E3 | Yg F | Yg E1 | Yn F | Yn W | Yg E | Yg F | Yg E | Yg W | Yn E | Yn E2 | Yn E | Yn E4 | Yg M | Yg M | 22 |
| 23 | Yn F | Yn W | Yn Wd | Yn Wd | Yg F | Yg E3 | Yg F | Yg E1 | Yn F | Yn W | Yn F | Yn F | Yg E | Yg W | Yn E | Yn E2 | Yn E | Yn E4 | Yg M | Yg M | Yg M | Yg Wd | Yn M | Yn M | 23 |
| 24 | Yg E | Yg W | Yg F | Yg E1 | Yn F | Yn W | Yn F | Yn F | Yg E | Yg W | Yg E | Yg F | Yn E | Yn E4 | Yg M | Yg M | Yg M | Yg Wd | Yn M | Yn M | Yn M | Yn Wd | Yg W | Yg E3 | 24 |
| 25 | Yn E | Yn E4 | Yn F | Yn F | Yg E | Yg W | Yg E | Yg F | Yn E | Yn E4 | Yn E | Yn E2 | Yg M | Yg Wd | Yn M | Yn M | Yn M | Yn Wd | Yg W | Yg E3 | Yg W | Yg E1 | Yn W | Yn W | 25 |
| 26 | Yg M | Yg Wd | Yg E | Yg F | Yn E | Yn E4 | Yn E | Yn E2 | Yg M | Yg Wd | Yg M | Yg M | Yn M | Yn Wd | Yg W | Yg E3 | Yg W | Yg E1 | Yn W | Yn W | Yn W | Yn F | Yg Wd | Yg W | 26 |
| 27 | Yn M | Yn Wd | Yn E | Yn E2 | Yg M | Yg Wd | Yg M | Yg M | Yn M | Yn Wd | Yn M | Yn M | Yg W | Yg E1 | Yn W | Yn W | Yn W | Yn F | Yg Wd | Yg W | Yg Wd | Yg F | Yn Wd | Yn E4 | 27 |
| 28 | Yg W | Yg E1 | Yg M | Yg M | Yn M | Yn Wd | Yn M | Yn M | Yg W | Yg E1 | Yg W | Yg E3 | Yn W | Yn F | Yg Wd | Yg W | Yg Wd | Yg F | Yn Wd | Yn E4 | Yn Wd | Yn E2 | Yg F | Yg Wd | 28 |
| 29 | | | Yn M | Yn M | Yg W | Yg E1 | Yg W | Yg E3 | Yn W | Yn F | Yn W | Yn W | Yg Wd | Yg F | Yn Wd | Yn E4 | Yn Wd | Yn E2 | Yg F | Yg Wd | Yg F | Yg M | Yn F | Yn Wd | 29 |
| 30 | | | Yg W | Yg E3 | Yn W | Yn F | Yn W | Yn W | Yg Wd | Yg F | Yg Wd | Yg W | Yn Wd | Yn E2 | Yg F | Yg Wd | Yg F | Yg M | Yn F | Yn Wd | Yn F | Yn M | Yg E | Yg E1 | 30 |
| 31 | | | Yn W | Yn W | | | Yg Wd | Yg W | | | Yn Wd | Yn E4 | Yg F | Yg M | | | Yn F | Yn M | | | Yg E | Yg E3 | Yn E | Yn F | 31 |
| 1 | Yn W | Yn F | Yg Wd | Yg W | Yg Wd | Yg F | Yn Wd | Yn E4 | Yn Wd | Yn E2 | Yg F | Yg Wd | Yn F | Yn M | Yn F | Yn Wd | Yg E | Yg E3 | Yg E | Yg E1 | Yn E | Yn W | Yg M | Yg F | 1 |
| 2 | Yg Wd | Yg F | Yn Wd | Yn E4 | Yn Wd | Yn E2 | Yg F | Yg Wd | Yg F | Yg M | Yn F | Yn Wd | Yg E | Yg E3 | Yg E | Yg E1 | Yn E | Yn W | Yn E | Yn F | Yg M | Yg W | Yn M | Yn E2 | 2 |
| 3 | Yn Wd | Yn E2 | Yg F | Yg Wd | Yg F | Yg M | Yn F | Yn Wd | Yn F | Yn M | Yg E | Yg E1 | Yn E | Yn W | Yn E | Yn F | Yg M | Yg W | Yg M | Yg F | Yn M | Yn E4 | Yg W | Yg M | 3 |
| 4 | Yg F | Yg M | Yn F | Yn Wd | Yn F | Yn M | Yg E | Yg E1 | Yg E | Yg E3 | Yn E | Yn F | Yg M | Yg W | Yg M | Yg F | Yn M | Yn E4 | Yn M | Yn E2 | Yg W | Yg Wd | | | 4 |
| 5 | Yn F | Yn M | | | Yg E | Yg E3 | Yn E | Yn F | Yn E | Yn W | Yg M | Yg F | Yn M | Yn E4 | Yn M | Yn E2 | Yg W | Yg Wd | Yg W | Yg M | Yn W | Yn Wd | | | 5 |
| 6 | | | | | | | | | Yg M | Yg W | Yn M | Yn E2 | Yg W | Yg Wd | Yg W | Yg M | Yn W | Yn Wd | Yn W | Yn M | | | | | 6 |
| 7 | | | | | | | | | | | Yg W | Yg M | Yn W | Yn Wd | Yn W | Yn M | | | | | | | | | 7 |
| 8 | | | | | | | | | | | | | | | | | | | | | | | | | 8 |

# YEAR OF THE TIGER

| | H | E | H | E | H | E | H | E | H | E | H | E | H | E | H | E | H | E | H | E | H | E | H | E | |
|---|---|---|---|---|---|---|---|---|---|---|---|---|---|---|---|---|---|---|---|---|---|---|---|---|---|
| YEAR | YEAR<br>Yg W Yg Wd | | 1962 | | | | | | | | | | | | | | | | | | | | 1963 | | |
| MONTH | 4 Feb - 5 Mar | | 6 Mar - 4 Apr | | 5 Apr - 5 May | | 6 May - 5 June | | 6 June - 6 Jul | | 7 Jul - 7 Aug | | 8 Aug - 7 Sep | | 8 Sep - 8 Oct | | 9 Oct - 7 Nov | | 8 Nov - 6 Dec | | 7 Dec - 5 Jan | | 6 Jan - 3 Feb | | |
| | Yg W | Yg Wd | Yn W | Yn Wd | Yg Wd | Yg E1 | Yn Wd | Yn F | Yg F | Yg F | Yn F | Yn E2 | Yg E | Yg M | Yn E | Yn M | Yg M | Yg E3 | Yn M | Yn W | Yg W | Yg W | Yn W | Yn E4 | |
| Starting time | 1st day | Mid-pt | 1st day | Mid-pt | 1st day | Mid-pt | 1st day | Mid-pt | 1st day | Mid-pt | 1st day | Mid-pt | 1st day | Mid-pt | 1st day | Mid-pt | 1st day | Mid-pt | 1st day | Mid-pt | 1st day | Mid-pt | 1st day | Mid-pt | |
| Date | 4 | 19 | 6 | 21 | 5 | 20 | 6 | 21 | 6 | 22 | 7 | 23 | 8 | 23 | 8 | 23 | 9 | 24 | 8 | 23 | 7 | 22 | 6 | 21 | |
| Hour | 1518 | 1115 | 0930 | 1030 | 1434 | 2151 | 0810 | 2117 | 1231 | 0524 | 2251 | 1618 | 0834 | 2313 | 1116 | 2035 | 0238 | 0540 | 0535 | 0303 | 2217 | 1615 | 0927 | 0254 | |
| DATE 4 | Yn W | Yn M | | | | | | | | | | | | | | | | | | | | | | | 4 |
| 5 | Yg Wd | Yg E3 | | | Yn W | Yn M | | | | | | | | | | | | | | | | | | | 5 |
| 6 | Yn Wd | Yn W | Yn W | Yn Wd | Yg Wd | Yg E3 | Yg Wd | Yg E1 | Yn Wd | Yn W | | | | | | | | | | | | | Yn E | Yn M | 6 |
| 7 | Yg F | Yg W | Yg Wd | Yg E1 | Yn Wd | Yn W | Yn Wd | Yn F | Yg F | Yg W | Yg F | Yg F | | | | | | | | | Yn E | Yn Wd | Yg M | Yg E3 | 7 |
| 8 | Yn F | Yn E4 | Yn Wd | Yn F | Yg F | Yg W | Yg F | Yg F | Yn F | Yn E4 | Yn F | Yn E2 | Yg E | Yg Wd | Yn E | Yn M | | | Yg M | Yg E3 | Yg M | Yg E1 | Yn M | Yn W | 8 |
| 9 | Yg E | Yg Wd | Yg F | Yg F | Yn F | Yn E4 | Yn F | Yn E2 | Yg E | Yg Wd | Yg E | Yg M | Yn E | Yn Wd | Yg M | Yg E3 | Yg M | Yg E1 | Yn M | Yn W | Yn M | Yn F | Yg W | Yg W | 9 |
| 10 | Yn E | Yn Wd | Yn F | Yn E2 | Yg E | Yg Wd | Yg E | Yg M | Yn E | Yn Wd | Yn E | Yn M | Yg M | Yg E1 | Yn M | Yn W | Yn M | Yn F | Yg W | Yg W | Yg W | Yg F | Yn W | Yn E4 | 10 |
| 11 | Yg M | Yg E1 | Yg E | Yg M | Yn E | Yn Wd | Yn E | Yn M | Yg M | Yg E1 | Yg M | Yg E3 | Yn M | Yn F | Yg W | Yg W | Yg W | Yg F | Yn W | Yn E4 | Yn W | Yn E2 | Yg Wd | Yg Wd | 11 |
| 12 | Yn M | Yn F | Yn E | Yn M | Yg M | Yg E1 | Yg M | Yg E3 | Yn M | Yn F | Yn M | Yn W | Yg W | Yg F | Yn W | Yn E4 | Yn W | Yn E2 | Yg Wd | Yg Wd | Yg Wd | Yg M | Yn Wd | Yn Wd | 12 |
| 13 | Yg W | Yg F | Yg M | Yg E3 | Yn M | Yn F | Yn M | Yn W | Yg W | Yg F | Yg W | Yg W | Yn W | Yn E2 | Yg Wd | Yg Wd | Yg Wd | Yg M | Yn Wd | Yn Wd | Yn Wd | Yn M | Yg F | Yg E1 | 13 |
| 14 | Yn W | Yn E2 | Yn M | Yn W | Yg W | Yg F | Yg W | Yg W | Yn W | Yn E2 | Yn W | Yn E4 | Yg Wd | Yg M | Yn Wd | Yn Wd | Yn Wd | Yn M | Yg F | Yg E1 | Yg F | Yg E3 | Yn F | Yn F | 14 |
| 15 | Yg Wd | Yg M | Yg W | Yg W | Yn W | Yn E2 | Yn W | Yn E4 | Yg Wd | Yg M | Yg Wd | Yg Wd | Yn Wd | Yn M | Yg F | Yg E1 | Yg F | Yg E3 | Yn F | Yn F | Yn F | Yn W | Yg E | Yg F | 15 |
| 16 | Yn Wd | Yn M | Yn W | Yn E4 | Yg Wd | Yg M | Yg Wd | Yg Wd | Yn Wd | Yn M | Yn Wd | Yn Wd | Yg F | Yg E3 | Yn F | Yn F | Yn F | Yn W | Yg E | Yg F | Yg E | Yg W | Yn E | Yn E2 | 16 |
| 17 | Yg F | Yg E3 | Yg Wd | Yg Wd | Yn Wd | Yn M | Yn Wd | Yn Wd | Yg F | Yg E3 | Yg F | Yg E1 | Yn F | Yn W | Yg E | Yg F | Yg E | Yg W | Yn E | Yn E2 | Yn E | Yn E4 | Yg M | Yg M | 17 |
| 18 | Yn F | Yn W | Yn Wd | Yn Wd | Yg F | Yg E3 | Yg F | Yg E1 | Yn F | Yn W | Yn F | Yn F | Yg E | Yg W | Yn E | Yn E2 | Yn E | Yn E4 | Yg M | Yg M | Yg M | Yg Wd | Yn M | Yn M | 18 |
| 19 | Yg E | Yg W | Yg F | Yg E1 | Yn F | Yn W | Yn F | Yn F | Yg E | Yg W | Yg E | Yg F | Yn E | Yn E4 | Yg M | Yg M | Yg M | Yg Wd | Yn M | Yn M | Yn M | Yn Wd | Yg W | Yg E3 | 19 |
| 20 | Yn E | Yn E4 | Yn F | Yn F | Yg E | Yg W | Yg E | Yg F | Yn E | Yn E4 | Yn E | Yn E2 | Yg M | Yg Wd | Yn M | Yn M | Yn M | Yn Wd | Yg W | Yg E3 | Yg W | Yg E1 | Yn W | Yn W | 20 |
| 21 | Yg M | Yg Wd | Yg E | Yg F | Yn E | Yn E4 | Yn E | Yn E2 | Yg M | Yg Wd | Yg M | Yg M | Yn M | Yn Wd | Yg W | Yg E3 | Yg W | Yg E1 | Yn W | Yn W | Yn W | Yn F | Yg Wd | Yg W | 21 |
| 22 | Yn M | Yn Wd | Yn E | Yn E2 | Yg M | Yg Wd | Yg M | Yg M | Yn M | Yn Wd | Yn M | Yn M | Yg W | Yg E1 | Yn W | Yn W | Yn W | Yn F | Yg Wd | Yg W | Yg Wd | Yg F | Yn Wd | Yn E4 | 22 |
| 23 | Yg W | Yg E1 | Yg M | Yg M | Yn M | Yn Wd | Yn M | Yn M | Yg W | Yg E1 | Yg W | Yg E3 | Yn W | Yn F | Yg Wd | Yg W | Yg Wd | Yg F | Yn Wd | Yn E4 | Yn Wd | Yn E2 | Yg F | Yg Wd | 23 |
| 24 | Yn W | Yn F | Yn M | Yn M | Yg W | Yg E1 | Yg W | Yg E3 | Yn W | Yn F | Yn W | Yn W | Yg Wd | Yg F | Yn Wd | Yn E4 | Yn Wd | Yn E2 | Yg F | Yg Wd | Yg F | Yg M | Yn F | Yn Wd | 24 |
| 25 | Yg Wd | Yg F | Yg W | Yg E3 | Yn W | Yn F | Yn W | Yn W | Yg Wd | Yg F | Yg Wd | Yg W | Yn Wd | Yn E2 | Yg F | Yg Wd | Yg F | Yg M | Yn F | Yn Wd | Yn F | Yn M | Yg E | Yg E1 | 25 |
| 26 | Yn Wd | Yn E2 | Yn W | Yn W | Yg Wd | Yg F | Yg Wd | Yg W | Yn Wd | Yn E2 | Yn Wd | Yn E4 | Yg F | Yg M | Yn F | Yn Wd | Yn F | Yn M | Yg E | Yg E1 | Yg E | Yg E3 | Yn E | Yn F | 26 |
| 27 | Yg F | Yg M | Yg Wd | Yg W | Yn Wd | Yn E2 | Yn Wd | Yn E4 | Yg F | Yg M | Yg F | Yg Wd | Yn F | Yn M | Yg E | Yg E1 | Yg E | Yg E3 | Yn E | Yn F | Yn E | Yn W | Yg M | Yg F | 27 |
| 28 | Yn F | Yn M | Yn Wd | Yn E4 | Yg F | Yg M | Yg F | Yg Wd | Yn F | Yn M | Yn F | Yn Wd | Yg E | Yg E3 | Yn E | Yn F | Yn E | Yn W | Yg M | Yg F | Yg M | Yg W | Yn M | Yn E2 | 28 |
| 29 | | | Yg F | Yg Wd | Yn F | Yn M | Yn F | Yn Wd | Yg E | Yg E3 | Yg E | Yg E1 | Yn E | Yn W | Yg M | Yg F | Yg M | Yg W | Yn M | Yn E2 | Yn M | Yn E4 | Yg W | Yg M | 29 |
| 30 | | | Yn F | Yn Wd | Yg E | Yg E3 | Yg E | Yg E1 | Yn E | Yn W | Yn E | Yn F | Yg M | Yg W | Yn M | Yn E2 | Yn M | Yn E4 | Yg W | Yg M | Yg W | Yg Wd | Yn W | Yn M | 30 |
| 31 | | | Yg E | Yg E1 | | | Yn E | Yn F | | | Yg M | Yg F | Yn M | Yn E4 | | | Yg W | Yg Wd | | | Yn W | Yn Wd | Yg Wd | Yg E3 | 31 |
| 1 | Yg E | Yg E3 | Yn E | Yn F | Yn E | Yn W | Yg M | Yg F | Yg M | Yg W | Yn M | Yn E2 | Yg W | Yg Wd | Yg W | Yg M | Yn W | Yn Wd | Yn W | Yn M | Yg Wd | Yg E1 | Yn Wd | Yn W | 1 |
| 2 | Yn E | Yn W | Yg M | Yg F | Yg M | Yg W | Yn M | Yn E2 | Yn M | Yn E4 | Yg W | Yg M | Yn W | Yn Wd | Yn W | Yn M | Yg Wd | Yg E1 | Yg Wd | Yg E3 | Yn Wd | Yn F | Yg F | Yg W | 2 |
| 3 | Yg M | Yg W | Yn M | Yn E2 | Yn M | Yn E4 | Yg W | Yg M | Yg W | Yg Wd | Yn W | Yn M | Yg Wd | Yg E1 | Yg Wd | Yg E3 | Yn Wd | Yn F | Yn Wd | Yn W | Yg F | Yg F | Yn F | Yn E4 | 3 |
| 4 | Yn M | Yn E4 | Yg W | Yg M | Yg W | Yg Wd | Yn W | Yn M | Yn W | Yn Wd | Yg Wd | Yg E3 | Yn Wd | Yn F | Yn Wd | Yn W | Yg F | Yg F | Yg F | Yg W | Yn F | Yn E2 | | | 4 |
| 5 | Yg W | Yg Wd | | | Yn W | Yn Wd | Yg Wd | Yg E3 | Yg Wd | Yg E1 | Yn Wd | Yn W | Yg F | Yg F | Yg F | Yg W | Yn F | Yn E2 | Yn F | Yn E4 | Yg E | Yg M | | | 5 |
| 6 | | | | | | | | | Yn Wd | Yn F | Yg F | Yg W | Yn F | Yn E2 | Yn F | Yn E4 | Yg E | Yg M | Yg E | Yg Wd | | | | | 6 |
| 7 | | | | | | | | | | | Yn F | Yn E4 | Yg E | Yg M | Yg E | Yg Wd | Yn E | Yn M | | | | | | | 7 |
| 8 | | | | | | | | | | | | | | | Yn E | Yn Wd | | | | | | | | | 8 |

# YEAR OF THE RABBIT

| | H | E | H | E | H | E | H | E | H | E | H | E | H | E | H | E | H | E | H | E | H | E | H | E | |
|---|---|---|---|---|---|---|---|---|---|---|---|---|---|---|---|---|---|---|---|---|---|---|---|---|---|
| YEAR | YEAR Yn W | Yn Wd | 1963 | | | | | | | | | | | | | | | | | | | | 1964 | | |
| MONTH | 4 Feb - 5 Mar Yg Wd | Yg Wd | 6 Mar - 4 Apr Yn Wd | Yn Wd | 5 Apr - 5 May Yg F | Yg E1 | 6 May - 5 June Yn F | Yn F | 6 June - 7 Jul Yg E | Yg F | 8 Jul - 7 Aug Yn E | Yn E2 | 8 Aug - 7 Sep Yg M | Yg M | 8 Sep - 8 Oct Yn M | Yn M | 9 Oct - 7 Nov Yg W | Yg E3 | 8 Nov - 7 Dec Yn W | Yn W | 8 Dec - 5 Jan Yg Wd | Yg W | 6 Jan - 4 Feb Yn Wd | Yn E4 | |
| Starting time | 1st day | Mid-pt | 1st day | Mid-pt | 1st day | Mid-pt | 1st day | Mid-pt | 1st day | Mid-pt | 1st day | Mid-pt | 1st day | Mid-pt | 1st day | Mid-pt | 1st day | Mid-pt | 1st day | Mid-pt | 1st day | Mid-pt | 1st day | Mid-pt | |
| Date | 4 | 19 | 6 | 21 | 5 | 21 | 6 | 22 | 6 | 22 | 8 | 23 | 8 | 24 | 8 | 24 | 9 | 24 | 8 | 23 | 8 | 22 | 6 | 21 | |
| Hour | 2108 | 1709 | 1517 | 1620 | 2019 | 0336 | 1352 | 0258 | 1815 | 1104 | 0438 | 2159 | 1426 | 0458 | 1712 | 0224 | 0836 | 1129 | 1132 | 0850 | 0413 | 2202 | 1522 | 0841 | |
| DATE 4 | Yg E | Yg Wd | | | | | | | | | | | | | | | | | | | | | | | 4 |
| 5 | Yn E | Yn Wd | | | Yg E | Yg Wd | | | | | | | | | | | | | | | | | | | 5 |
| 6 | Yg M | Yg E1 | Yg E | Yg M | Yn E | Yn Wd | Yn E | Yn M | Yg M | Yg E1 | | | | | | | | | | | | | Yg Wd | Yg Wd | 6 |
| 7 | Yn M | Yn F | Yn E | Yn M | Yg M | Yg E1 | Yg M | Yg E3 | Yn M | Yn F | | | | | | | | | | | | | Yn Wd | Yn Wd | 7 |
| 8 | Yg W | Yg F | Yg M | Yg E3 | Yn M | Yn F | Yn M | Yn W | Yg W | Yg F | Yg W | Yg W | Yn W | Yn E2 | Yg Wd | Yg Wd | | | Yn Wd | Yn Wd | Yn Wd | Yn M | Yg F | Yg E1 | 8 |
| 9 | Yn W | Yn E2 | Yn M | Yn W | Yg W | Yg F | Yg W | Yg W | Yn W | Yn E2 | Yn W | Yn E4 | Yg Wd | Yg M | Yn Wd | Yn Wd | Yn Wd | Yn M | Yg F | Yg E1 | Yg F | Yg E3 | Yn F | Yn F | 9 |
| 10 | Yg Wd | Yg M | Yg W | Yg W | Yn W | Yn E2 | Yn W | Yn E4 | Yg Wd | Yg M | Yg Wd | Yg Wd | Yn Wd | Yn M | Yg F | Yg E1 | Yg F | Yg E3 | Yn F | Yn F | Yn F | Yn W | Yg E | Yg F | 10 |
| 11 | Yn Wd | Yn M | Yn W | Yn E4 | Yg Wd | Yg M | Yg Wd | Yg Wd | Yn Wd | Yn M | Yn Wd | Yn Wd | Yg F | Yg E3 | Yn F | Yn F | Yn F | Yn W | Yg E | Yg F | Yg E | Yg W | Yn E | Yn E2 | 11 |
| 12 | Yg F | Yg E3 | Yg Wd | Yg Wd | Yn Wd | Yn M | Yn Wd | Yn Wd | Yg F | Yg E3 | Yg F | Yg E1 | Yn F | Yn W | Yg E | Yg F | Yg E | Yg W | Yn E | Yn E2 | Yn E | Yn E4 | Yg M | Yg M | 12 |
| 13 | Yn F | Yn W | Yn Wd | Yn Wd | Yg F | Yg E3 | Yg F | Yg E1 | Yn F | Yn W | Yn F | Yn F | Yg E | Yg W | Yn E | Yn E2 | Yn E | Yn E4 | Yg M | Yg M | Yg M | Yg Wd | Yn M | Yn M | 13 |
| 14 | Yg E | Yg W | Yg F | Yg E1 | Yn F | Yn W | Yn F | Yn F | Yg E | Yg W | Yg E | Yg F | Yn E | Yn E4 | Yg M | Yg M | Yg M | Yg Wd | Yn M | Yn M | Yn M | Yn Wd | Yg W | Yg E3 | 14 |
| 15 | Yn E | Yn E4 | Yn F | Yn F | Yg E | Yg W | Yg E | Yg F | Yn E | Yn E4 | Yn E | Yn E2 | Yg M | Yg Wd | Yn M | Yn M | Yn M | Yn Wd | Yg W | Yg E3 | Yg W | Yg E1 | Yn W | Yn W | 15 |
| 16 | Yg M | Yg Wd | Yg E | Yg F | Yn E | Yn E4 | Yn E | Yn E2 | Yg M | Yg Wd | Yg M | Yg M | Yn M | Yn Wd | Yg W | Yg E3 | Yg W | Yg E1 | Yn W | Yn W | Yn W | Yn F | Yg Wd | Yg W | 16 |
| 17 | Yn M | Yn Wd | Yn E | Yn E2 | Yg M | Yg Wd | Yg M | Yg M | Yn M | Yn Wd | Yn M | Yn M | Yg W | Yg E1 | Yn W | Yn W | Yn W | Yn F | Yg Wd | Yg W | Yg Wd | Yg F | Yn Wd | Yn E4 | 17 |
| 18 | Yg W | Yg E1 | Yg M | Yg M | Yn M | Yn Wd | Yn M | Yn M | Yg W | Yg E1 | Yg W | Yg E3 | Yn W | Yn F | Yg Wd | Yg W | Yg Wd | Yg F | Yn Wd | Yn E4 | Yn Wd | Yn E2 | Yg F | Yg Wd | 18 |
| 19 | Yn W | Yn F | Yn M | Yn M | Yg W | Yg E1 | Yg W | Yg E3 | Yn W | Yn F | Yn W | Yn W | Yg Wd | Yg F | Yn Wd | Yn E4 | Yn Wd | Yn E2 | Yg F | Yg Wd | Yg F | Yg M | Yn F | Yn Wd | 19 |
| 20 | Yg Wd | Yg F | Yg W | Yg E3 | Yn W | Yn F | Yn W | Yn W | Yg Wd | Yg F | Yg Wd | Yg W | Yn Wd | Yn E2 | Yg F | Yg Wd | Yg F | Yg M | Yn F | Yn Wd | Yn F | Yn M | Yg E | Yg E1 | 20 |
| 21 | Yn Wd | Yn E2 | Yn W | Yn W | Yg Wd | Yg F | Yg Wd | Yg W | Yn Wd | Yn E2 | Yn Wd | Yn E4 | Yg F | Yg M | Yn F | Yn Wd | Yn F | Yn M | Yg E | Yg E1 | Yg E | Yg E3 | Yn E | Yn F | 21 |
| 22 | Yg F | Yg M | Yg Wd | Yg W | Yn Wd | Yn E2 | Yn Wd | Yn E4 | Yg F | Yg M | Yg F | Yg Wd | Yn F | Yn M | Yg E | Yg E1 | Yg E | Yg E3 | Yn E | Yn F | Yn E | Yn W | Yg M | Yg F | 22 |
| 23 | Yn F | Yn M | Yn Wd | Yn E4 | Yg F | Yg M | Yg F | Yg Wd | Yn F | Yn M | Yn F | Yn Wd | Yg E | Yg E3 | Yn E | Yn F | Yn E | Yn W | Yg M | Yg F | Yg M | Yg W | Yn M | Yn E2 | 23 |
| 24 | Yg E | Yg E3 | Yg F | Yg Wd | Yn F | Yn M | Yn F | Yn Wd | Yg E | Yg E3 | Yg E | Yg E1 | Yn E | Yn W | Yg M | Yg F | Yg M | Yg W | Yn M | Yn E2 | Yn M | Yn E4 | Yg W | Yg M | 24 |
| 25 | Yn E | Yn W | Yn F | Yn Wd | Yg E | Yg E3 | Yg E | Yg E1 | Yn E | Yn W | Yn E | Yn F | Yg M | Yg W | Yn M | Yn E2 | Yn M | Yn E4 | Yg W | Yg M | Yg W | Yg Wd | Yn W | Yn M | 25 |
| 26 | Yg M | Yg W | Yg E | Yg E1 | Yn E | Yn W | Yn E | Yn F | Yg M | Yg W | Yg M | Yg F | Yn M | Yn E4 | Yg W | Yg M | Yg W | Yg Wd | Yn W | Yn M | Yn W | Yn Wd | Yg Wd | Yg E3 | 26 |
| 27 | Yn M | Yn E4 | Yn E | Yn F | Yg M | Yg W | Yg M | Yg F | Yn M | Yn E4 | Yn M | Yn E2 | Yg W | Yg Wd | Yn W | Yn M | Yn W | Yn Wd | Yg Wd | Yg E3 | Yg Wd | Yg E1 | Yn Wd | Yn W | 27 |
| 28 | Yg W | Yg Wd | Yg M | Yg F | Yn M | Yn E4 | Yn M | Yn E2 | Yg W | Yg Wd | Yg W | Yg M | Yn W | Yn Wd | Yg Wd | Yg E3 | Yg Wd | Yg E1 | Yn Wd | Yn W | Yn Wd | Yn F | Yg F | Yg W | 28 |
| 29 | | | Yn M | Yn E2 | Yg W | Yg Wd | Yg W | Yg M | Yn W | Yn Wd | Yn W | Yn M | Yg Wd | Yg E1 | Yn Wd | Yn W | Yn Wd | Yn F | Yg F | Yg W | Yg F | Yg F | Yn F | Yn E4 | 29 |
| 30 | | | Yg W | Yg M | Yn W | Yn Wd | Yn W | Yn M | Yg Wd | Yg E1 | Yg Wd | Yg E3 | Yn Wd | Yn F | Yg F | Yg W | Yg F | Yg F | Yn F | Yn E4 | Yn F | Yn E2 | Yg E | Yg Wd | 30 |
| 31 | | | Yn W | Yn M | | | Yg Wd | Yg E3 | | | Yn Wd | Yn W | Yg F | Yg F | | | Yn F | Yn E2 | | | Yg E | Yg M | Yn E | Yn Wd | 31 |
| 1 | Yn W | Yn Wd | Yg Wd | Yg E3 | Yg Wd | Yg E1 | Yn Wd | Yn W | Yn Wd | Yn F | Yg F | Yg W | Yn F | Yn E2 | Yn F | Yn E4 | Yg E | Yg M | Yg E | Yg Wd | Yn E | Yn M | Yg M | Yg E1 | 1 |
| 2 | Yg Wd | Yg E1 | Yn Wd | Yn W | Yn Wd | Yn F | Yg F | Yg W | Yg F | Yg F | Yn F | Yn E4 | Yg E | Yg M | Yg E | Yg Wd | Yn E | Yn M | Yn E | Yn Wd | Yg M | Yg E3 | Yn M | Yn F | 2 |
| 3 | Yn Wd | Yn F | Yg F | Yg W | Yg F | Yg F | Yn F | Yn E4 | Yn F | Yn E2 | Yg E | Yg Wd | Yn E | Yn M | Yn E | Yn Wd | Yg M | Yg E3 | Yg M | Yg E1 | Yn M | Yn W | Yg W | Yg F | 3 |
| 4 | Yg F | Yg F | Yn F | Yn E4 | Yn F | Yn E2 | Yg E | Yg Wd | Yg E | Yg M | Yn E | Yn Wd | Yg M | Yg E3 | Yg M | Yg E1 | Yn M | Yn W | Yn M | Yn F | Yg W | Yg W | Yn W | Yn E2 | 4 |
| 5 | Yn F | Yn E2 | | | Yg E | Yg M | Yn E | Yn Wd | Yn E | Yn M | Yg M | Yg E1 | Yn M | Yn W | Yn M | Yn F | Yg W | Yg W | Yg W | Yg F | Yn W | Yn E4 | | | 5 |
| 6 | | | | | | | | | Yg M | Yg E3 | Yn M | Yn F | Yg W | Yg W | Yg W | Yg F | Yn W | Yn E4 | Yn W | Yn E2 | | | | | 6 |
| 7 | | | | | | | | | Yn M | Yn W | Yg W | Yg F | Yn W | Yn E4 | Yn W | Yn E2 | Yg Wd | Yg Wd | Yg Wd | Yg M | | | | | 7 |
| 8 | | | | | | | | | | | | | | | Yg Wd | Yg M | | | | | | | | | 8 |

# YEAR OF THE DRAGON

| | H | E | H | E | H | E | H | E | H | E | H | E | H | E | H | E | H | E | H | E | H | E | H | E |
|---|---|---|---|---|---|---|---|---|---|---|---|---|---|---|---|---|---|---|---|---|---|---|---|---|
| YEAR | YEAR Yg Wd | Yg E1 | 1964 | | | | | | | | | | | | | | | | | | | | 1965 | |
| MONTH | 5 Feb - 4 Mar | | 5 Mar - 4 Apr | | 5 Apr - 4 May | | 5 May - 5 June | | 6 June - 6 Jul | | 7 Jul - 6 Aug | | 7 Aug - 6 Sep | | 7 Sep - 7 Oct | | 8 Oct - 6 Nov | | 7 Nov - 6 Dec | | 7 Dec - 4 Jan | | 5 Jan - 3 Feb | |
| | Yg F | Yg Wd | Yn F | Yn Wd | Yg E | Yg E1 | Yn E | Yn F | Yg M | Yg F | Yn M | Yn E2 | Yg W | Yg M | Yn W | Yn M | Yg Wd | Yg E3 | Yn Wd | Yn W | Yg F | Yg W | Yn F | Yn E4 |
| Starting time | 1st day | Mid-pt | 1st day | Mid-pt | 1st day | Mid-pt | 1st day | Mid-pt | 1st day | Mid-pt | 1st day | Mid-pt | 1st day | Mid-pt | 1st day | Mid-pt | 1st day | Mid-pt | 1st day | Mid-pt | 1st day | Mid-pt | 1st day | Mid-pt |
| Date | 5 | 19 | 5 | 20 | 5 | 20 | 5 | 21 | 6 | 21 | 7 | 23 | 7 | 23 | 7 | 23 | 8 | 23 | 7 | 22 | 7 | 22 | 5 | 20 |
| Hour | 0305 | 2257 | 2116 | 2210 | 0218 | 0927 | 1951 | 0850 | 0012 | 1657 | 1032 | 0353 | 2016 | 1051 | 2300 | 0817 | 1422 | 1721 | 1715 | 1439 | 0953 | 0350 | 2102 | 1429 |
| DATE 4 | | | | | | | | | | | | | | | | | | | | | | | | |
| 5 | Yg Wd | Yg M | Yn W | Yn E4 | Yg Wd | Yg M | Yg Wd | Yg Wd | | | | | | | | | | | | | | | Yn E | Yn E2 |
| 6 | Yn Wd | Yn M | Yg Wd | Yg Wd | Yn Wd | Yn M | Yn Wd | Yn Wd | Yg F | Yg E3 | | | | | | | | | | | | | Yg M | Yg M |
| 7 | Yg F | Yg E3 | Yn Wd | Yn Wd | Yg F | Yg E3 | Yg F | Yg E1 | Yn F | Yn W | Yn F | Yn F | Yg E | Yg W | Yn E | Yn E2 | | | Yg M | Yg M | Yg M | Yg Wd | Yn M | Yn M |
| 8 | Yn F | Yn W | Yg F | Yg E1 | Yn F | Yn W | Yn F | Yn F | Yg E | Yg W | Yg E | Yg F | Yn E | Yn E4 | Yg M | Yg M | Yg M | Yg Wd | Yn M | Yn M | Yn M | Yn Wd | Yg W | Yg E3 |
| 9 | Yg E | Yg W | Yn F | Yn F | Yg E | Yg W | Yg E | Yg F | Yn E | Yn E4 | Yn E | Yn E2 | Yg M | Yg Wd | Yn M | Yn M | Yn M | Yn Wd | Yg W | Yg E3 | Yg W | Yg E1 | Yn W | Yn W |
| 10 | Yn E | Yn E4 | Yg E | Yg F | Yn E | Yn E4 | Yn E | Yn E2 | Yg M | Yg Wd | Yg M | Yg M | Yn M | Yn Wd | Yg W | Yg E3 | Yg W | Yg E1 | Yn W | Yn W | Yn W | Yn F | Yg Wd | Yg W |
| 11 | Yg M | Yg Wd | Yn E | Yn E2 | Yg M | Yg Wd | Yg M | Yg M | Yn M | Yn Wd | Yn M | Yn M | Yg W | Yg E1 | Yn W | Yn W | Yn W | Yn F | Yg Wd | Yg W | Yg Wd | Yg F | Yn Wd | Yn E4 |
| 12 | Yn M | Yn Wd | Yg M | Yg M | Yn M | Yn Wd | Yn M | Yn M | Yg W | Yg E1 | Yg W | Yg E3 | Yn W | Yn F | Yg Wd | Yg W | Yg Wd | Yg F | Yn Wd | Yn E4 | Yn Wd | Yn E2 | Yg F | Yg Wd |
| 13 | Yg W | Yg E1 | Yn M | Yn M | Yg W | Yg E1 | Yg W | Yg E3 | Yn W | Yn F | Yn W | Yn W | Yg Wd | Yg F | Yn Wd | Yn E4 | Yn Wd | Yn E2 | Yg F | Yg Wd | Yg F | Yg M | Yn F | Yn Wd |
| 14 | Yn W | Yn F | Yg W | Yg E3 | Yn W | Yn F | Yn W | Yn W | Yg Wd | Yg F | Yg Wd | Yg W | Yn Wd | Yn E2 | Yg F | Yg Wd | Yg F | Yg M | Yn F | Yn Wd | Yn F | Yn M | Yg E | Yg E1 |
| 15 | Yg Wd | Yg F | Yn W | Yn W | Yg Wd | Yg F | Yg Wd | Yg W | Yn Wd | Yn E2 | Yn Wd | Yn E4 | Yg F | Yg M | Yn F | Yn Wd | Yn F | Yn M | Yg E | Yg E1 | Yg E | Yg E3 | Yn E | Yn F |
| 16 | Yn Wd | Yn E2 | Yg Wd | Yg W | Yn Wd | Yn E2 | Yn Wd | Yn E4 | Yg F | Yg M | Yg F | Yg Wd | Yn F | Yn M | Yg E | Yg E1 | Yg E | Yg E3 | Yn E | Yn F | Yn E | Yn W | Yg M | Yg F |
| 17 | Yg F | Yg M | Yn Wd | Yn E4 | Yg F | Yg M | Yg F | Yg Wd | Yn F | Yn M | Yn F | Yn Wd | Yg E | Yg E3 | Yn E | Yn F | Yn E | Yn W | Yg M | Yg F | Yg M | Yg W | Yn M | Yn E2 |
| 18 | Yn F | Yn M | Yg F | Yg Wd | Yn F | Yn M | Yn F | Yn Wd | Yg E | Yg E3 | Yg E | Yg E1 | Yn E | Yn W | Yg M | Yg F | Yg M | Yg W | Yn M | Yn E2 | Yn M | Yn E4 | Yg W | Yg M |
| 19 | Yg E | Yg E3 | Yn F | Yn Wd | Yg E | Yg E3 | Yg E | Yg E1 | Yn E | Yn W | Yn E | Yn F | Yg M | Yg W | Yn M | Yn E2 | Yn M | Yn E4 | Yg W | Yg M | Yg W | Yg Wd | Yn W | Yn M |
| 20 | Yn E | Yn W | Yg E | Yg E1 | Yn E | Yn W | Yn E | Yn F | Yg M | Yg W | Yg M | Yg F | Yn M | Yn E4 | Yg W | Yg M | Yg W | Yg Wd | Yn W | Yn M | Yn W | Yn Wd | Yg Wd | Yg E3 |
| 21 | Yg M | Yg W | Yn E | Yn F | Yg M | Yg W | Yg M | Yg F | Yn M | Yn E4 | Yn M | Yn E2 | Yg W | Yg Wd | Yn W | Yn M | Yn W | Yn Wd | Yg Wd | Yg E3 | Yg Wd | Yg E1 | Yn Wd | Yn W |
| 22 | Yn M | Yn E4 | Yg M | Yg F | Yn M | Yn E4 | Yn M | Yn E2 | Yg W | Yg Wd | Yg W | Yg M | Yn W | Yn Wd | Yg Wd | Yg E3 | Yg Wd | Yg E1 | Yn Wd | Yn W | Yn Wd | Yn F | Yg F | Yg W |
| 23 | Yg W | Yg Wd | Yn M | Yn E2 | Yg W | Yg Wd | Yg W | Yg M | Yn W | Yn Wd | Yn W | Yn M | Yg Wd | Yg E1 | Yn Wd | Yn W | Yn Wd | Yn F | Yg F | Yg W | Yg F | Yg F | Yn F | Yn E4 |
| 24 | Yn W | Yn Wd | Yg W | Yg M | Yn W | Yn Wd | Yn W | Yn M | Yg Wd | Yg E1 | Yg Wd | Yg E3 | Yn Wd | Yn F | Yg F | Yg W | Yg F | Yg F | Yn F | Yn E4 | Yn F | Yn E2 | Yg E | Yg Wd |
| 25 | Yg Wd | Yg E1 | Yn W | Yn M | Yg Wd | Yg E1 | Yg Wd | Yg E3 | Yn Wd | Yn F | Yn Wd | Yn W | Yg F | Yg F | Yn F | Yn E4 | Yn F | Yn E2 | Yg E | Yg Wd | Yg E | Yg M | Yn E | Yn Wd |
| 26 | Yn Wd | Yn F | Yg Wd | Yg E3 | Yn Wd | Yn F | Yn Wd | Yn W | Yg F | Yg F | Yg F | Yg W | Yn F | Yn E2 | Yg E | Yg Wd | Yg E | Yg M | Yn E | Yn Wd | Yn E | Yn M | Yg M | Yg E1 |
| 27 | Yg F | Yg F | Yn Wd | Yn W | Yg F | Yg F | Yg F | Yg W | Yn F | Yn E2 | Yn F | Yn E4 | Yg E | Yg M | Yn E | Yn Wd | Yn E | Yn M | Yg M | Yg E1 | Yg M | Yg E3 | Yn M | Yn F |
| 28 | Yn F | Yn E2 | Yg F | Yg W | Yn F | Yn E2 | Yn F | Yn E4 | Yg E | Yg M | Yg E | Yg Wd | Yn E | Yn M | Yg M | Yg E1 | Yg M | Yg E3 | Yn M | Yn F | Yn M | Yn W | Yg W | Yg F |
| 29 | Yg E | Yg M | Yn F | Yn E4 | Yg E | Yg M | Yg E | Yg Wd | Yn E | Yn M | Yn E | Yn Wd | Yg M | Yg E3 | Yn M | Yn F | Yn M | Yn W | Yg W | Yg F | Yg W | Yg W | Yn W | Yn E2 |
| 30 | | | Yg E | Yg Wd | Yn E | Yn M | Yn E | Yn Wd | Yg M | Yg E3 | Yg M | Yg E1 | Yn M | Yn W | Yg W | Yg F | Yg W | Yg W | Yn W | Yn E2 | Yn W | Yn E4 | Yg Wd | Yg M |
| 31 | | | Yn E | Yn Wd | | | Yg M | Yg E1 | | | Yn M | Yn F | Yg W | Yg W | | | Yn W | Yn E4 | | | Yg Wd | Yg Wd | Yn Wd | Yn M |
| 1 | Yn E | Yn M | Yg M | Yg E1 | Yg M | Yg E3 | Yn M | Yn F | Yn M | Yn W | Yg W | Yg F | Yn W | Yn E4 | Yn W | Yn E2 | Yg Wd | Yg Wd | Yg Wd | Yg M | Yn Wd | Yn Wd | Yg F | Yg E3 |
| 2 | Yg M | Yg E3 | Yn M | Yn F | Yn M | Yn W | Yg W | Yg F | Yg W | Yg W | Yn W | Yn E2 | Yg Wd | Yg Wd | Yg Wd | Yg M | Yn Wd | Yn Wd | Yn Wd | Yn M | Yg F | Yg E1 | Yn F | Yn W |
| 3 | Yn M | Yn W | Yg W | Yg F | Yg W | Yg W | Yn W | Yn E2 | Yn W | Yn E4 | Yg Wd | Yg M | Yn Wd | Yn Wd | Yn Wd | Yn M | Yg F | Yg E1 | Yg F | Yg E3 | Yn F | Yn F | Yg E | Yg W |
| 4 | Yg W | Yg W | Yn W | Yn E2 | Yn W | Yn E4 | Yg Wd | Yg M | Yg Wd | Yg Wd | Yn Wd | Yn M | Yg F | Yg E1 | Yg F | Yg E3 | Yn F | Yn F | Yn F | Yn W | Yg E | Yg F | | |
| 5 | | | | | | | Yn Wd | Yn M | Yn Wd | Yn Wd | Yg F | Yg E3 | Yn F | Yn F | Yn F | Yn W | Yg E | Yg F | Yg E | Yg W | | | | |
| 6 | | | | | | | | | Yg F | Yg E1 | Yn F | Yn W | Yg E | Yg F | Yg E | Yg W | Yn E | Yn E2 | Yn E | Yn E4 | | | | |
| 7 | | | | | | | | | | | | | | | Yn E | Yn E4 | | | | | | | | |
| 8 | | | | | | | | | | | | | | | | | | | | | | | | |

# YEAR OF THE SNAKE

| | H | E | H | E | H | E | H | E | H | E | H | E | H | E | H | E | H | E | H | E | H | E | H | E | |
|---|---|---|---|---|---|---|---|---|---|---|---|---|---|---|---|---|---|---|---|---|---|---|---|---|---|
| YEAR | YEAR Yn Wd | Yn F | 1965 | | | | | | | | | | | | | | | | | | | | 1966 | | |
| MONTH | 4 Feb - 5 Mar | | 6 Mar - 4 Apr | | 5 Apr - 5 May | | 6 May - 5 June | | 6 June - 6 Jul | | 7 Jul - 7 Aug | | 8 Aug - 7 Sep | | 8 Sep - 7 Oct | | 8 Oct - 6 Nov | | 7 Nov - 6 Dec | | 7 Dec - 5 Jan | | 6 Jan - 3 Feb | | |
| | Yg E | Yg Wd | Yn E | Yn Wd | Yg M | Yg E1 | Yn M | Yn F | Yg W | Yg F | Yn W | Yn E2 | Yg Wd | Yg M | Yn Wd | Yn M | Yg F | Yg E3 | Yn F | Yn W | Yg E | Yg W | Yn E | Yn E4 | |
| Starting time | 1st day | Mid-pt | 1st day | Mid-pt | 1st day | Mid-pt | 1st day | Mid-pt | 1st day | Mid-pt | 1st day | Mid-pt | 1st day | Mid-pt | 1st day | Mid-pt | 1st day | Mid-pt | 1st day | Mid-pt | 1st day | Mid-pt | 1st day | Mid-pt | |
| Date | 4 | 19 | 6 | 21 | 5 | 20 | 6 | 21 | 6 | 21 | 7 | 23 | 8 | 23 | 8 | 23 | 8 | 23 | 7 | 22 | 7 | 22 | 6 | 20 | |
| Hour | 0846 | 0448 | 0301 | 0405 | 0807 | 1526 | 0142 | 1450 | 0602 | 2256 | 1622 | 0948 | 0205 | 1643 | 0448 | 1406 | 2011 | 2310 | 2307 | 2029 | 1546 | 0941 | 0255 | 2020 | |
| DATE 4 | Yn E | Yn E4 | | | | | | | | | | | | | | | | | | | | | | | 4 |
| 5 | Yg M | Yg Wd | | | Yn E | Yn E4 | | | | | | | | | | | | | | | | | | | 5 |
| 6 | Yn M | Yn Wd | Yn E | Yn E2 | Yg M | Yg Wd | Yg M | Yg M | Yn M | Yn Wd | | | | | | | | | | | | | Yn Wd | Yn E4 | 6 |
| 7 | Yg W | Yg E1 | Yg M | Yg M | Yn M | Yn Wd | Yn M | Yn M | Yg W | Yg E1 | Yg W | Yg E3 | | | | | | | Yn Wd | Yn E4 | Yn Wd | Yn E2 | Yg F | Yg Wd | 7 |
| 8 | Yn W | Yn F | Yn M | Yn M | Yg W | Yg E1 | Yg W | Yg E3 | Yn W | Yn F | Yn W | Yn W | Yg Wd | Yg F | Yn Wd | Yn E4 | Yn Wd | Yn E2 | Yg F | Yg Wd | Yg F | Yg M | Yn F | Yn Wd | 8 |
| 9 | Yg Wd | Yg F | Yg W | Yg E3 | Yn W | Yn F | Yn W | Yn W | Yg Wd | Yg F | Yg Wd | Yg W | Yn Wd | Yn E2 | Yg F | Yg Wd | Yg F | Yg M | Yn F | Yn Wd | Yn F | Yn M | Yg E | Yg E1 | 9 |
| 10 | Yn Wd | Yn E2 | Yn W | Yn W | Yg Wd | Yg F | Yg Wd | Yg W | Yn Wd | Yn E2 | Yn Wd | Yn E4 | Yg F | Yg M | Yn F | Yn Wd | Yn F | Yn M | Yg E | Yg E1 | Yg E | Yg E3 | Yn E | Yn F | 10 |
| 11 | Yg F | Yg M | Yg Wd | Yg W | Yn Wd | Yn E2 | Yn Wd | Yn E4 | Yg F | Yg M | Yg F | Yg Wd | Yn F | Yn M | Yg E | Yg E1 | Yg E | Yg E3 | Yn E | Yn F | Yn E | Yn W | Yg M | Yg F | 11 |
| 12 | Yn F | Yn M | Yn Wd | Yn E4 | Yg F | Yg M | Yg F | Yg Wd | Yn F | Yn M | Yn F | Yn Wd | Yg E | Yg E3 | Yn E | Yn F | Yn E | Yn W | Yg M | Yg F | Yg M | Yg W | Yn M | Yn E2 | 12 |
| 13 | Yg E | Yg E3 | Yg F | Yg Wd | Yn F | Yn M | Yn F | Yn Wd | Yg E | Yg E3 | Yg E | Yg E1 | Yn E | Yn W | Yg M | Yg F | Yg M | Yg W | Yn M | Yn E2 | Yn M | Yn E4 | Yg W | Yg M | 13 |
| 14 | Yn E | Yn W | Yn F | Yn Wd | Yg E | Yg E3 | Yg E | Yg E1 | Yn E | Yn W | Yn E | Yn F | Yg M | Yg W | Yn M | Yn E2 | Yn M | Yn E4 | Yg W | Yg M | Yg W | Yg Wd | Yn W | Yn M | 14 |
| 15 | Yg M | Yg W | Yg E | Yg E1 | Yn E | Yn W | Yn E | Yn F | Yg M | Yg W | Yg M | Yg F | Yn M | Yn E4 | Yg W | Yg M | Yg W | Yg Wd | Yn W | Yn M | Yn W | Yn Wd | Yg Wd | Yg E3 | 15 |
| 16 | Yn M | Yn E4 | Yn E | Yn F | Yg M | Yg W | Yg M | Yg F | Yn M | Yn E4 | Yn M | Yn E2 | Yg W | Yg Wd | Yn W | Yn M | Yn W | Yn Wd | Yg Wd | Yg E3 | Yg Wd | Yg E1 | Yn Wd | Yn W | 16 |
| 17 | Yg W | Yg Wd | Yg M | Yg F | Yn M | Yn E4 | Yn M | Yn E2 | Yg W | Yg Wd | Yg W | Yg M | Yn W | Yn Wd | Yg Wd | Yg E3 | Yg Wd | Yg E1 | Yn Wd | Yn W | Yn Wd | Yn F | Yg F | Yg W | 17 |
| 18 | Yn W | Yn Wd | Yn M | Yn E2 | Yg W | Yg Wd | Yg W | Yg M | Yn W | Yn Wd | Yn W | Yn M | Yg Wd | Yg E1 | Yn Wd | Yn W | Yn Wd | Yn F | Yg F | Yg W | Yg F | Yg F | Yn F | Yn E4 | 18 |
| 19 | Yg Wd | Yg E1 | Yg W | Yg M | Yn W | Yn Wd | Yn W | Yn M | Yg Wd | Yg E1 | Yg Wd | Yg E3 | Yn Wd | Yn F | Yg F | Yg W | Yg F | Yg F | Yn F | Yn E4 | Yn F | Yn E2 | Yg E | Yg Wd | 19 |
| 20 | Yn Wd | Yn F | Yn W | Yn M | Yg Wd | Yg E1 | Yg Wd | Yg E3 | Yn Wd | Yn F | Yn Wd | Yn W | Yg F | Yg F | Yn F | Yn E4 | Yn F | Yn E2 | Yg E | Yg Wd | Yg E | Yg M | Yn E | Yn Wd | 20 |
| 21 | Yg F | Yg F | Yg Wd | Yg E3 | Yn Wd | Yn F | Yn Wd | Yn W | Yg F | Yg F | Yg F | Yg W | Yn F | Yn E2 | Yg E | Yg Wd | Yg E | Yg M | Yn E | Yn Wd | Yn E | Yn M | Yg M | Yg E1 | 21 |
| 22 | Yn F | Yn E2 | Yn Wd | Yn W | Yg F | Yg F | Yg F | Yg W | Yn F | Yn E2 | Yn F | Yn E4 | Yg E | Yg M | Yn E | Yn Wd | Yn E | Yn M | Yg M | Yg E1 | Yg M | Yg E3 | Yn M | Yn F | 22 |
| 23 | Yg E | Yg M | Yg F | Yg W | Yn F | Yn E2 | Yn F | Yn E4 | Yg E | Yg M | Yg E | Yg Wd | Yn E | Yn M | Yg M | Yg E1 | Yg M | Yg E3 | Yn M | Yn F | Yn M | Yn W | Yg W | Yg F | 23 |
| 24 | Yn E | Yn M | Yn F | Yn E4 | Yg E | Yg M | Yg E | Yg Wd | Yn E | Yn M | Yn E | Yn Wd | Yg M | Yg E3 | Yn M | Yn F | Yn M | Yn W | Yg W | Yg F | Yg W | Yg W | Yn W | Yn E2 | 24 |
| 25 | Yg M | Yg E3 | Yg E | Yg Wd | Yn E | Yn M | Yn E | Yn Wd | Yg M | Yg E3 | Yg M | Yg E1 | Yn M | Yn W | Yg W | Yg F | Yg W | Yg W | Yn W | Yn E2 | Yn W | Yn E4 | Yg Wd | Yg M | 25 |
| 26 | Yn M | Yn W | Yn E | Yn Wd | Yg M | Yg E3 | Yg M | Yg E1 | Yn M | Yn W | Yn M | Yn F | Yg W | Yg W | Yn W | Yn E2 | Yn W | Yn E4 | Yg Wd | Yg M | Yg Wd | Yg Wd | Yn Wd | Yn M | 26 |
| 27 | Yg W | Yg W | Yg M | Yg E1 | Yn M | Yn W | Yn M | Yn F | Yg W | Yg W | Yg W | Yg F | Yn W | Yn E4 | Yg Wd | Yg M | Yg Wd | Yg Wd | Yn Wd | Yn M | Yn Wd | Yn Wd | Yg F | Yg E3 | 27 |
| 28 | Yn W | Yn E4 | Yn M | Yn F | Yg W | Yg W | Yg W | Yg F | Yn W | Yn E4 | Yn W | Yn E2 | Yg Wd | Yg Wd | Yn Wd | Yn M | Yn Wd | Yn Wd | Yg F | Yg E3 | Yg F | Yg E1 | Yn F | Yn W | 28 |
| 29 | | | Yg W | Yg F | Yn W | Yn E4 | Yn W | Yn E2 | Yg Wd | Yg Wd | Yg Wd | Yg M | Yn Wd | Yn Wd | Yg F | Yg E3 | Yg F | Yg E1 | Yn F | Yn W | Yn F | Yn F | Yg E | Yg W | 29 |
| 30 | | | Yn W | Yn E2 | Yg Wd | Yg Wd | Yg Wd | Yg M | Yn Wd | Yn Wd | Yn Wd | Yn M | Yg F | Yg E1 | Yn F | Yn W | Yn F | Yn F | Yg E | Yg W | Yg E | Yg F | Yn E | Yn E4 | 30 |
| 31 | | | Yg Wd | Yg M | | | Yn Wd | Yn M | | | Yg F | Yg E3 | Yn F | Yn F | | | Yg E | Yg F | | | Yn E | Yn E2 | Yg M | Yg Wd | 31 |
| 1 | Yg Wd | Yg Wd | Yn Wd | Yn M | Yn Wd | Yn Wd | Yg F | Yg E3 | Yg F | Yg E1 | Yn F | Yn W | Yg E | Yg F | Yg E | Yg W | Yn E | Yn E2 | Yn E | Yn E4 | Yg M | Yg M | Yn M | Yn Wd | 1 |
| 2 | Yn Wd | Yn Wd | Yg F | Yg E3 | Yg F | Yg E1 | Yn F | Yn W | Yn F | Yn F | Yg E | Yg W | Yn E | Yn E2 | Yn E | Yn E4 | Yg M | Yg M | Yg M | Yg Wd | Yn M | Yn M | Yg W | Yg E1 | 2 |
| 3 | Yg F | Yg E1 | Yn F | Yn W | Yn F | Yn F | Yg E | Yg W | Yg E | Yg F | Yn E | Yn E4 | Yg M | Yg M | Yg M | Yg Wd | Yn M | Yn M | Yn M | Yn Wd | Yg W | Yg E3 | Yn W | Yn F | 3 |
| 4 | Yn F | Yn F | Yg E | Yg W | Yg E | Yg F | Yn E | Yn E4 | Yn E | Yn E2 | Yg M | Yg Wd | Yn M | Yn M | Yn M | Yn Wd | Yg W | Yg E3 | Yg W | Yg E1 | Yn W | Yn W | | | 4 |
| 5 | Yg E | Yg F | | | Yn E | Yn E2 | Yg M | Yg Wd | Yg M | Yg M | Yn M | Yn Wd | Yg W | Yg E3 | Yg W | Yg E1 | Yn W | Yn W | Yn W | Yn F | Yg Wd | Yg W | | | 5 |
| 6 | | | | | | | | | Yn M | Yn M | Yg W | Yg E1 | Yn W | Yn W | Yn W | Yn F | Yg Wd | Yg W | Yg Wd | Yg F | | | | | 6 |
| 7 | | | | | | | | | | | Yn W | Yn F | Yg Wd | Yg W | Yg Wd | Yg F | | | | | | | | | 7 |
| 8 | | | | | | | | | | | | | | | | | | | | | | | | | 8 |

# YEAR OF THE HORSE

| | H | E | H | E | H | E | H | E | H | E | H | E | H | E | H | E | H | E | H | E | H | E | H | E | |
|---|---|---|---|---|---|---|---|---|---|---|---|---|---|---|---|---|---|---|---|---|---|---|---|---|---|
| YEAR | YEAR | | 1966 | | | | | | | | | | | | | | | | | | | | 1967 | | |
| | Yg F | Yg F | | | | | | | | | | | | | | | | | | | | | | | |
| MONTH | 4 Feb - 5 Mar | | 6 Mar - 4 Apr | | 5 Apr - 5 May | | 6 May - 5 June | | 6 June - 6 Jul | | 7 Jul - 7 Aug | | 8 Aug - 7 Sep | | 8 Sep - 8 Oct | | 9 Oct - 7 Nov | | 8 Nov - 6 Dec | | 7 Dec - 5 Jan | | 6 Jan - 3 Feb | | |
| | Yg M | Yg Wd | Yn M | Yn Wd | Yg W | Yg E1 | Yn W | Yn F | Yg Wd | Yg F | Yn Wd | Yn E2 | Yg F | Yg M | Yn F | Yn M | Yg E | Yg E3 | Yn E | Yn W | Yg M | Yg W | Yn M | Yn E4 | |
| Starting time | 1st day | Mid-pt | 1st day | Mid-pt | 1st day | Mid-pt | 1st day | Mid-pt | 1st day | Mid-pt | 1st day | Mid-pt | 1st day | Mid-pt | 1st day | Mid-pt | 1st day | Mid-pt | 1st day | Mid-pt | 1st day | Mid-pt | 1st day | Mid-pt | |
| Date | 4 | 19 | 6 | 21 | 5 | 20 | 6 | 21 | 6 | 22 | 7 | 23 | 8 | 23 | 8 | 23 | 9 | 24 | 8 | 23 | 7 | 22 | 6 | 21 | |
| Hour | 1438 | 1038 | 0851 | 0953 | 1357 | 2112 | 0731 | 2032 | 1150 | 0434 | 2207 | 1523 | 0749 | 2218 | 1032 | 1943 | 0157 | 0451 | 0456 | 0214 | 2138 | 1528 | 0848 | 0208 | |
| DATE 4 | Yg Wd | Yg F | | | | | | | | | | | | | | | | | | | | | | | 4 |
| 5 | Yn Wd | Yn E2 | | | Yg Wd | Yg F | | | | | | | | | | | | | | | | | | | 5 |
| 6 | Yg F | Yg M | Yg Wd | Yg W | Yn Wd | Yn E2 | Yn Wd | Yn E4 | Yg F | Yg M | | | | | | | | | | | | | Yg M | Yg F | 6 |
| 7 | Yn F | Yn M | Yn Wd | Yn E4 | Yg F | Yg M | Yg F | Yg Wd | Yn F | Yn M | Yn F | Yn Wd | | | | | | | | | Yg M | Yg W | Yn M | Yn E2 | 7 |
| 8 | Yg E | Yg E3 | Yg F | Yg Wd | Yn F | Yn M | Yn F | Yn Wd | Yg E | Yg E3 | Yg E | Yg E1 | Yn E | Yn W | Yg M | Yg F | | | Yn M | Yn E2 | Yn M | Yn E4 | Yg W | Yg M | 8 |
| 9 | Yn E | Yn W | Yn F | Yn Wd | Yg E | Yg E3 | Yg E | Yg E1 | Yn E | Yn W | Yn E | Yn F | Yg M | Yg W | Yn M | Yn E2 | Yn M | Yn E4 | Yg W | Yg M | Yg W | Yg Wd | Yn W | Yn M | 9 |
| 10 | Yg M | Yg W | Yg E | Yg E1 | Yn E | Yn W | Yn E | Yn F | Yg M | Yg W | Yg M | Yg F | Yn M | Yn E4 | Yg W | Yg M | Yg W | Yg Wd | Yn W | Yn M | Yn W | Yn Wd | Yg Wd | Yg E3 | 10 |
| 11 | Yn M | Yn E4 | Yn E | Yn F | Yg M | Yg W | Yg M | Yg F | Yn M | Yn E4 | Yn M | Yn E2 | Yg W | Yg Wd | Yn W | Yn M | Yn W | Yn Wd | Yg Wd | Yg E3 | Yg Wd | Yg E1 | Yn Wd | Yn W | 11 |
| 12 | Yg W | Yg Wd | Yg M | Yg F | Yn M | Yn E4 | Yn M | Yn E2 | Yg W | Yg Wd | Yg W | Yg M | Yn W | Yn Wd | Yg Wd | Yg E3 | Yg Wd | Yg E1 | Yn Wd | Yn W | Yn Wd | Yn F | Yg F | Yg W | 12 |
| 13 | Yn W | Yn Wd | Yn M | Yn E2 | Yg W | Yg Wd | Yg W | Yg M | Yn W | Yn Wd | Yn W | Yn M | Yg Wd | Yg E1 | Yn Wd | Yn W | Yn Wd | Yn F | Yg F | Yg W | Yg F | Yg F | Yn F | Yn E4 | 13 |
| 14 | Yg Wd | Yg E1 | Yg W | Yg M | Yn W | Yn Wd | Yn W | Yn M | Yg Wd | Yg E1 | Yg Wd | Yg E3 | Yn Wd | Yn F | Yg F | Yg W | Yg F | Yg F | Yn F | Yn E4 | Yn F | Yn E2 | Yg E | Yg Wd | 14 |
| 15 | Yn Wd | Yn F | Yn W | Yn M | Yg Wd | Yg E1 | Yg Wd | Yg E3 | Yn Wd | Yn F | Yn Wd | Yn W | Yg F | Yg F | Yn F | Yn E4 | Yn F | Yn E2 | Yg E | Yg Wd | Yg E | Yg M | Yn E | Yn Wd | 15 |
| 16 | Yg F | Yg F | Yg Wd | Yg E3 | Yn Wd | Yn F | Yn Wd | Yn W | Yg F | Yg F | Yg F | Yg W | Yn F | Yn E2 | Yg E | Yg Wd | Yg E | Yg M | Yn E | Yn Wd | Yn E | Yn M | Yg M | Yg E1 | 16 |
| 17 | Yn F | Yn E2 | Yn Wd | Yn W | Yg F | Yg F | Yg F | Yg W | Yn F | Yn E2 | Yn F | Yn E4 | Yg E | Yg M | Yn E | Yn Wd | Yn E | Yn M | Yg M | Yg E1 | Yg M | Yg E3 | Yn M | Yn F | 17 |
| 18 | Yg E | Yg M | Yg F | Yg W | Yn F | Yn E2 | Yn F | Yn E4 | Yg E | Yg M | Yg E | Yg Wd | Yn E | Yn M | Yg M | Yg E1 | Yg M | Yg E3 | Yn M | Yn F | Yn M | Yn W | Yg W | Yg F | 18 |
| 19 | Yn E | Yn M | Yn F | Yn E4 | Yg E | Yg M | Yg E | Yg Wd | Yn E | Yn M | Yn E | Yn Wd | Yg M | Yg E3 | Yn M | Yn F | Yn M | Yn W | Yg W | Yg F | Yg W | Yg W | Yn W | Yn E2 | 19 |
| 20 | Yg M | Yg E3 | Yg E | Yg Wd | Yn E | Yn M | Yn E | Yn Wd | Yg M | Yg E3 | Yg M | Yg E1 | Yn M | Yn W | Yg W | Yg F | Yg W | Yg W | Yn W | Yn E2 | Yn W | Yn E4 | Yg Wd | Yg M | 20 |
| 21 | Yn M | Yn W | Yn E | Yn Wd | Yg M | Yg E3 | Yg M | Yg E1 | Yn M | Yn W | Yn M | Yn F | Yg W | Yg W | Yn W | Yn E2 | Yn W | Yn E4 | Yg Wd | Yg M | Yg Wd | Yg Wd | Yn Wd | Yn M | 21 |
| 22 | Yg W | Yg W | Yg M | Yg E1 | Yn M | Yn W | Yn M | Yn F | Yg W | Yg W | Yg W | Yg F | Yn W | Yn E4 | Yg Wd | Yg M | Yg Wd | Yg Wd | Yn Wd | Yn M | Yn Wd | Yn Wd | Yg F | Yg E3 | 22 |
| 23 | Yn W | Yn E4 | Yn M | Yn F | Yg W | Yg W | Yg W | Yg F | Yn W | Yn E4 | Yn W | Yn E2 | Yg Wd | Yg Wd | Yn Wd | Yn M | Yn Wd | Yn Wd | Yg F | Yg E3 | Yg F | Yg E1 | Yn F | Yn W | 23 |
| 24 | Yg Wd | Yg Wd | Yg W | Yg F | Yn W | Yn E4 | Yn W | Yn E2 | Yg Wd | Yg Wd | Yg Wd | Yg M | Yn Wd | Yn Wd | Yg F | Yg E3 | Yg F | Yg E1 | Yn F | Yn W | Yn F | Yn F | Yg E | Yg W | 24 |
| 25 | Yn Wd | Yn Wd | Yn W | Yn E2 | Yg Wd | Yg Wd | Yg Wd | Yg M | Yn Wd | Yn Wd | Yn Wd | Yn M | Yg F | Yg E1 | Yn F | Yn W | Yn F | Yn F | Yg E | Yg W | Yg E | Yg F | Yn E | Yn E4 | 25 |
| 26 | Yg F | Yg E1 | Yg Wd | Yg M | Yn Wd | Yn Wd | Yn Wd | Yn M | Yg F | Yg E1 | Yg F | Yg E3 | Yn F | Yn F | Yg E | Yg W | Yg E | Yg F | Yn E | Yn E4 | Yn E | Yn E2 | Yg M | Yg Wd | 26 |
| 27 | Yn F | Yn F | Yn Wd | Yn M | Yg F | Yg E1 | Yg F | Yg E3 | Yn F | Yn F | Yn F | Yn W | Yg E | Yg F | Yn E | Yn E4 | Yn E | Yn E2 | Yg M | Yg Wd | Yg M | Yg M | Yn M | Yn Wd | 27 |
| 28 | Yg E | Yg F | Yg F | Yg E3 | Yn F | Yn F | Yn F | Yn W | Yg E | Yg F | Yg E | Yg W | Yn E | Yn E2 | Yg M | Yg Wd | Yg M | Yg M | Yn M | Yn Wd | Yn M | Yn M | Yg W | Yg E1 | 28 |
| 29 | | | Yn F | Yn W | Yg E | Yg F | Yg E | Yg W | Yn E | Yn E2 | Yn E | Yn E4 | Yg M | Yg M | Yn M | Yn Wd | Yn M | Yn M | Yg W | Yg E1 | Yg W | Yg E3 | Yn W | Yn F | 29 |
| 30 | | | Yg E | Yg W | Yn E | Yn E2 | Yn E | Yn E4 | Yg M | Yg M | Yg M | Yg Wd | Yn M | Yn M | Yg W | Yg E1 | Yg W | Yg E3 | Yn W | Yn F | Yn W | Yn W | Yg Wd | Yg F | 30 |
| 31 | | | Yn E | Yn E4 | | | Yg M | Yg Wd | | | Yn M | Yn Wd | Yg W | Yg E3 | | | Yn W | Yn W | | | Yg Wd | Yg W | Yn Wd | Yn E2 | 31 |
| 1 | Yn E | Yn E2 | Yg M | Yg Wd | Yg M | Yg M | Yn M | Yn Wd | Yn M | Yn M | Yg W | Yg E1 | Yn W | Yn W | Yn W | Yn F | Yg Wd | Yg W | Yg Wd | Yg F | Yn Wd | Yn E4 | Yg F | Yg M | 1 |
| 2 | Yg M | Yg M | Yn M | Yn Wd | Yn M | Yn M | Yg W | Yg E1 | Yg W | Yg E3 | Yn W | Yn F | Yg Wd | Yg W | Yg Wd | Yg F | Yn Wd | Yn E4 | Yn Wd | Yn E2 | Yg F | Yg Wd | Yn F | Yn M | 2 |
| 3 | Yn M | Yn M | Yg W | Yg E1 | Yg W | Yg E3 | Yn W | Yn F | Yn W | Yn W | Yg Wd | Yg F | Yn Wd | Yn E4 | Yn Wd | Yn E2 | Yg F | Yg Wd | Yg F | Yg M | Yn F | Yn Wd | Yg E | Yg E3 | 3 |
| 4 | Yg W | Yg E3 | Yn W | Yn F | Yn W | Yn W | Yg Wd | Yg F | Yg Wd | Yg W | Yn Wd | Yn E2 | Yg F | Yg Wd | Yg F | Yg M | Yn F | Yn Wd | Yn F | Yn M | Yg E | Yg E1 | | | 4 |
| 5 | Yn W | Yn W | | | Yg Wd | Yg W | Yn Wd | Yn E2 | Yn Wd | Yn E4 | Yg F | Yg M | Yn F | Yn Wd | Yn F | Yn M | Yg E | Yg E1 | Yg E | Yg E3 | Yn E | Yn F | | | 5 |
| 6 | | | | | | | | | Yg F | Yg Wd | Yn F | Yn M | Yg E | Yg E1 | Yg E | Yg E3 | Yn E | Yn F | Yn E | Yn W | | | | | 6 |
| 7 | | | | | | | | | | | Yg E | Yg E3 | Yn E | Yn F | Yn E | Yn W | Yg M | Yg F | | | | | | | 7 |
| 8 | | | | | | | | | | | | | | | Yg M | Yg W | | | | | | | | | 8 |

# YEAR OF THE GOAT

| | H | E | H | E | H | E | H | E | H | E | H | E | H | E | H | E | H | E | H | E | H | E | H | E | |
|---|---|---|---|---|---|---|---|---|---|---|---|---|---|---|---|---|---|---|---|---|---|---|---|---|---|
| YEAR | YEAR Yn F | Yn E2 | 1967 | | | | | | | | | | | | | | | | | | | | 1968 | | |
| MONTH | 4 Feb - 5 Mar | | 6 Mar - 4 Apr | | 5 Apr - 5 May | | 6 May - 5 June | | 6 June - 7 Jul | | 8 Jul - 7 Aug | | 8 Aug - 7 Sep | | 8 Sep - 8 Oct | | 9 Oct - 7 Nov | | 8 Nov - 7 Dec | | 8 Dec - 5 Jan | | 6 Jan - 4 Feb | | |
| | Yg W | Yg Wd | Yn W | Yn Wd | Yg Wd | Yg E1 | Yn Wd | Yn F | Yg F | Yg F | Yn F | Yn E2 | Yg E | Yg M | Yn E | Yn M | Yg M | Yg E3 | Yn M | Yn W | Yg W | Yg W | Yn W | Yn E4 | |
| Starting time | 1st day | Mid-pt | 1st day | Mid-pt | 1st day | Mid-pt | 1st day | Mid-pt | 1st day | Mid-pt | 1st day | Mid-pt | 1st day | Mid-pt | 1st day | Mid-pt | 1st day | Mid-pt | 1st day | Mid-pt | 1st day | Mid-pt | 1st day | Mid-pt | |
| Date | 4 | 19 | 6 | 21 | 5 | 21 | 6 | 22 | 6 | 22 | 8 | 23 | 8 | 24 | 8 | 24 | 9 | 24 | 8 | 23 | 8 | 22 | 6 | 21 | |
| Hour | 2031 | 1624 | 1442 | 1537 | 1945 | 0255 | 1318 | 0218 | 1736 | 1023 | 0354 | 2116 | 1335 | 0413 | 1618 | 0138 | 0742 | 1044 | 1038 | 0805 | 0318 | 2117 | 1426 | 0754 | |
| DATE 4 | Yn E | Yn W | | | | | | | | | | | | | | | | | | | | | | | 4 |
| 5 | Yg M | Yg W | | | Yn E | Yn W | | | | | | | | | | | | | | | | | | | 5 |
| 6 | Yn M | Yn E4 | Yn E | Yn F | Yg M | Yg W | Yg M | Yg F | Yn M | Yn E4 | | | | | | | | | | | | | Yn Wd | Yn W | 6 |
| 7 | Yg W | Yg Wd | Yn M | Yg F | Yn M | Yn E4 | Yn M | Yn E2 | Yg W | Yg Wd | | | | | | | | | | | | | Yg F | Yg W | 7 |
| 8 | Yn W | Yn Wd | Yn M | Yn E2 | Yg W | Yg Wd | Yg W | Yg M | Yn W | Yn Wd | Yn W | Yn M | Yg Wd | Yg E1 | Yn Wd | Yn W | | | Yg F | Yg W | Yg F | Yg F | Yn F | Yn E4 | 8 |
| 9 | Yg Wd | Yg E1 | Yg W | Yg M | Yn W | Yn Wd | Yn W | Yn M | Yg Wd | Yg E1 | Yg Wd | Yg E3 | Yn Wd | Yn F | Yg F | Yg W | Yg F | Yg F | Yn F | Yn E4 | Yn F | Yn E2 | Yg E | Yg Wd | 9 |
| 10 | Yn Wd | Yn F | Yn W | Yn M | Yg Wd | Yg E1 | Yg Wd | Yg E3 | Yn Wd | Yn F | Yn Wd | Yn W | Yg F | Yg F | Yn F | Yn E4 | Yn F | Yn E2 | Yg E | Yg Wd | Yg E | Yg M | Yn E | Yn Wd | 10 |
| 11 | Yg F | Yg F | Yg Wd | Yg E3 | Yn Wd | Yn F | Yn Wd | Yn W | Yg F | Yg F | Yg F | Yg W | Yn F | Yn E2 | Yg E | Yg Wd | Yg E | Yg M | Yn E | Yn Wd | Yn E | Yn M | Yg M | Yg E1 | 11 |
| 12 | Yn F | Yn E2 | Yn Wd | Yn W | Yg F | Yg F | Yg F | Yg W | Yn F | Yn E2 | Yn F | Yn E4 | Yg E | Yg M | Yn E | Yn Wd | Yn E | Yn M | Yg M | Yg E1 | Yg M | Yg E3 | Yn M | Yn F | 12 |
| 13 | Yg E | Yg M | Yg F | Yg W | Yn F | Yn E2 | Yn F | Yn E4 | Yg E | Yg M | Yg E | Yg Wd | Yn E | Yn M | Yg M | Yg E1 | Yg M | Yg E3 | Yn M | Yn F | Yn M | Yn W | Yg W | Yg F | 13 |
| 14 | Yn E | Yn M | Yn F | Yn E4 | Yg E | Yg M | Yg E | Yg Wd | Yn E | Yn M | Yn E | Yn Wd | Yg M | Yg E3 | Yn M | Yn F | Yn M | Yn W | Yg W | Yg F | Yg W | Yg W | Yn W | Yn E2 | 14 |
| 15 | Yg M | Yg E3 | Yg E | Yg Wd | Yn E | Yn M | Yn E | Yn Wd | Yg M | Yg E3 | Yg M | Yg E1 | Yn M | Yn W | Yg W | Yg F | Yg W | Yg W | Yn W | Yn E2 | Yn W | Yn E4 | Yg Wd | Yg M | 15 |
| 16 | Yn M | Yn W | Yn E | Yn Wd | Yg M | Yg E3 | Yg M | Yg E1 | Yn M | Yn W | Yn M | Yn F | Yg W | Yg W | Yn W | Yn E2 | Yn W | Yn E4 | Yg Wd | Yg M | Yg Wd | Yg Wd | Yn Wd | Yn M | 16 |
| 17 | Yg W | Yg W | Yg M | Yg E1 | Yn M | Yn W | Yn M | Yn F | Yg W | Yg W | Yg W | Yg F | Yn W | Yn E4 | Yg Wd | Yg M | Yg Wd | Yg Wd | Yn Wd | Yn M | Yn Wd | Yn Wd | Yg F | Yg E3 | 17 |
| 18 | Yn W | Yn E4 | Yn M | Yn F | Yg W | Yg W | Yg W | Yg F | Yn W | Yn E4 | Yn W | Yn E2 | Yg Wd | Yg Wd | Yn Wd | Yn M | Yn Wd | Yn Wd | Yg F | Yg E3 | Yg F | Yg E1 | Yn F | Yn W | 18 |
| 19 | Yg Wd | Yg Wd | Yg W | Yg F | Yn W | Yn E4 | Yn W | Yn E2 | Yg Wd | Yg Wd | Yg Wd | Yg M | Yn Wd | Yn Wd | Yg F | Yg E3 | Yg F | Yg E1 | Yn F | Yn W | Yn F | Yn F | Yg E | Yg W | 19 |
| 20 | Yn Wd | Yn Wd | Yn W | Yn E2 | Yg Wd | Yg Wd | Yg Wd | Yg M | Yn Wd | Yn Wd | Yn Wd | Yn M | Yg F | Yg E1 | Yn F | Yn W | Yn F | Yn F | Yg E | Yg W | Yg E | Yg F | Yn E | Yn E4 | 20 |
| 21 | Yg F | Yg E1 | Yg Wd | Yg M | Yn Wd | Yn Wd | Yn Wd | Yn M | Yg F | Yg E1 | Yg F | Yg E3 | Yn F | Yn F | Yg E | Yg W | Yg E | Yg F | Yn E | Yn E4 | Yn E | Yn E2 | Yg M | Yg Wd | 21 |
| 22 | Yn F | Yn F | Yn Wd | Yn M | Yg F | Yg E1 | Yg F | Yg E3 | Yn F | Yn F | Yn F | Yn W | Yg E | Yg F | Yn E | Yn E4 | Yn E | Yn E2 | Yg M | Yg Wd | Yg M | Yg M | Yn M | Yn Wd | 22 |
| 23 | Yg E | Yg F | Yg F | Yg E3 | Yn F | Yn F | Yn F | Yn W | Yg E | Yg F | Yg E | Yg W | Yn E | Yn E2 | Yg M | Yg Wd | Yg M | Yg M | Yn M | Yn Wd | Yn M | Yn M | Yg W | Yg E1 | 23 |
| 24 | Yn E | Yn E2 | Yn F | Yn W | Yg E | Yg F | Yg E | Yg W | Yn E | Yn E2 | Yn E | Yn E4 | Yg M | Yg M | Yn M | Yn Wd | Yn M | Yn M | Yg W | Yg E1 | Yg W | Yg E3 | Yn W | Yn F | 24 |
| 25 | Yg M | Yg M | Yg E | Yg W | Yn E | Yn E2 | Yn E | Yn E4 | Yg M | Yg M | Yg M | Yg Wd | Yn M | Yn M | Yg W | Yg E1 | Yg W | Yg E3 | Yn W | Yn F | Yn W | Yn W | Yg Wd | Yg F | 25 |
| 26 | Yn M | Yn M | Yn E | Yn E4 | Yg M | Yg M | Yg M | Yg Wd | Yn M | Yn M | Yn M | Yn Wd | Yg W | Yg E3 | Yn W | Yn F | Yn W | Yn W | Yg Wd | Yg F | Yg Wd | Yg W | Yn Wd | Yn E2 | 26 |
| 27 | Yg W | Yg E3 | Yg M | Yg Wd | Yn M | Yn M | Yn M | Yn Wd | Yg W | Yg E3 | Yg W | Yg E1 | Yn W | Yn W | Yg Wd | Yg F | Yg Wd | Yg W | Yn Wd | Yn E2 | Yn Wd | Yn E4 | Yg F | Yg M | 27 |
| 28 | Yn W | Yn W | Yn M | Yn Wd | Yg W | Yg E3 | Yg W | Yg E1 | Yn W | Yn W | Yn W | Yn F | Yg Wd | Yg W | Yn Wd | Yn E2 | Yn Wd | Yn E4 | Yg F | Yg M | Yg F | Yg Wd | Yn F | Yn M | 28 |
| 29 | | | Yg W | Yg E1 | Yn W | Yn W | Yn W | Yn F | Yg Wd | Yg W | Yg Wd | Yg F | Yn Wd | Yn E4 | Yg F | Yg M | Yg F | Yg Wd | Yn F | Yn M | Yn F | Yn Wd | Yg E | Yg E3 | 29 |
| 30 | | | Yn W | Yn F | Yg Wd | Yg W | Yg Wd | Yg F | Yn Wd | Yn E4 | Yn Wd | Yn E2 | Yg F | Yg Wd | Yn F | Yn M | Yn F | Yn Wd | Yg E | Yg E3 | Yg E | Yg E1 | Yn E | Yn W | 30 |
| 31 | | | Yg Wd | Yg F | | | Yn Wd | Yn E2 | | | Yg F | Yg M | Yn F | Yn Wd | | | Yg E | Yg E1 | | | Yn E | Yn F | Yg M | Yg W | 31 |
| 1 | Yg Wd | Yg W | Yn Wd | Yn E2 | Yn Wd | Yn E4 | Yg F | Yg M | Yg F | Yg Wd | Yn F | Yn M | Yg E | Yg E1 | Yg E | Yg E3 | Yn E | Yn F | Yn E | Yn W | Yg M | Yg F | Yn M | Yn E4 | 1 |
| 2 | Yn Wd | Yn E4 | Yg F | Yg M | Yg F | Yg Wd | Yn F | Yn M | Yn F | Yn Wd | Yg E | Yg E3 | Yn E | Yn F | Yn E | Yn W | Yg M | Yg F | Yg M | Yg W | Yn M | Yn E2 | Yg W | Yg Wd | 2 |
| 3 | Yg F | Yg Wd | Yn F | Yn M | Yn F | Yn Wd | Yg E | Yg E3 | Yg E | Yg E1 | Yn E | Yn W | Yg M | Yg F | Yg M | Yg W | Yn M | Yn E2 | Yn M | Yn E4 | Yg W | Yg M | Yn W | Yn Wd | 3 |
| 4 | Yn F | Yn Wd | Yg E | Yg E3 | Yg E | Yg E1 | Yn E | Yn W | Yn E | Yn F | Yg M | Yg W | Yn M | Yn E2 | Yn M | Yn E4 | Yg W | Yg M | Yg W | Yg Wd | Yn W | Yn M | Yg Wd | Yg E1 | 4 |
| 5 | Yg E | Yg E1 | | | Yn E | Yn F | Yg M | Yg W | Yg M | Yg F | Yn M | Yn E4 | Yg W | Yg M | Yg W | Yg Wd | Yn W | Yn M | Yn W | Yn Wd | Yg Wd | Yg E3 | | | 5 |
| 6 | | | | | | | | | Yn M | Yn E2 | Yg W | Yg Wd | Yn W | Yn M | Yn W | Yn Wd | Yg Wd | Yg E3 | Yg Wd | Yg E1 | | | | | 6 |
| 7 | | | | | | | | | Yg W | Yg M | Yn W | Yn Wd | Yg Wd | Yg E3 | Yg Wd | Yg E1 | Yn Wd | Yn W | Yn Wd | Yn F | | | | | 7 |
| 8 | | | | | | | | | | | | | | | Yn Wd | Yn F | | | | | | | | | 8 |

# YEAR OF THE MONKEY

| | H | E | H | E | H | E | H | E | H | E | H | E | H | E | H | E | H | E | H | E | H | E | H | E | |
|---|---|---|---|---|---|---|---|---|---|---|---|---|---|---|---|---|---|---|---|---|---|---|---|---|---|
| YEAR | YEAR<br>Yg E | Yg M | 1968 | | | | | | | | | | | | | | | | | | | | 1969 | | |
| MONTH | 5 Feb - 4 Mar | | 5 Mar - 4 Apr | | 5 Apr - 4 May | | 5 May - 4 June | | 5 June - 6 Jul | | 7 Jul - 6 Aug | | 7 Aug - 6 Sep | | 7 Sep - 7 Oct | | 8 Oct - 6 Nov | | 7 Nov - 6 Dec | | 7 Dec - 4 Jan | | 5 Jan - 3 Feb | | |
| | Yg Wd | Yg Wd | Yn Wd | Yn Wd | Yg F | Yg E1 | Yn F | Yn F | Yg E | Yg F | Yn E | Yn E2 | Yg M | Yg M | Yn M | Yn M | Yg W | Yg E3 | Yn W | Yn W | Yg Wd | Yg W | Yn Wd | Yn E4 | |
| Starting time | 1st day | Mid-pt | 1st day | Mid-pt | 1st day | Mid-pt | 1st day | Mid-pt | 1st day | Mid-pt | 1st day | Mid-pt | 1st day | Mid-pt | 1st day | Mid-pt | 1st day | Mid-pt | 1st day | Mid-pt | 1st day | Mid-pt | 1st day | Mid-pt | |
| Date | 5 | 19 | 5 | 20 | 5 | 20 | 5 | 21 | 5 | 21 | 7 | 23 | 7 | 23 | 7 | 23 | 8 | 23 | 7 | 22 | 7 | 22 | 5 | 20 | |
| Hour | 0208 | 2209 | 2018 | 2122 | 0121 | 0841 | 1856 | 0806 | 2319 | 1613 | 0942 | 0308 | 1927 | 1003 | 2212 | 0726 | 1335 | 1630 | 1629 | 1349 | 0909 | 0300 | 2017 | 1338 | |
| DATE 4 | | | | | | | | | | | | | | | | | | | | | | | | | 4 |
| 5 | Yn Wd | Yn F | Yg Wd | Yg E3 | Yn Wd | Yn F | Yn Wd | Yn W | Yg F | Yg F | | | | | | | | | | | | | Yg M | Yg E1 | 5 |
| 6 | Yg F | Yg F | Yn Wd | Yn W | Yg F | Yg F | Yg F | Yg W | Yn F | Yn E2 | | | | | | | | | | | | | Yn M | Yn F | 6 |
| 7 | Yn F | Yn E2 | Yg F | Yg W | Yn F | Yn E2 | Yn F | Yn E4 | Yg E | Yg M | Yg E | Yg Wd | Yn E | Yn M | Yg M | Yg E1 | | | Yn M | Yn F | Yn M | Yn W | Yg W | Yg F | 7 |
| 8 | Yg E | Yg M | Yn F | Yn E4 | Yg E | Yg M | Yg E | Yg Wd | Yn E | Yn M | Yn E | Yn Wd | Yg M | Yg E3 | Yn M | Yn F | Yn M | Yn W | Yg W | Yg F | Yg W | Yg W | Yn W | Yn E2 | 8 |
| 9 | Yn E | Yn M | Yg E | Yg Wd | Yn E | Yn M | Yn E | Yn Wd | Yg M | Yg E3 | Yg M | Yg E1 | Yn M | Yn W | Yg W | Yg F | Yg W | Yg W | Yn W | Yn E2 | Yn W | Yn E4 | Yg Wd | Yg M | 9 |
| 10 | Yg M | Yg E3 | Yn E | Yn Wd | Yg M | Yg E3 | Yg M | Yg E1 | Yn M | Yn W | Yn M | Yn F | Yg W | Yg W | Yn W | Yn E2 | Yn W | Yn E4 | Yg Wd | Yg M | Yg Wd | Yg Wd | Yn Wd | Yn M | 10 |
| 11 | Yn M | Yn W | Yg M | Yg E1 | Yn M | Yn W | Yn M | Yn F | Yg W | Yg W | Yg W | Yg F | Yn W | Yn E4 | Yg Wd | Yg M | Yg Wd | Yg Wd | Yn Wd | Yn M | Yn Wd | Yn Wd | Yg F | Yg E3 | 11 |
| 12 | Yg W | Yg W | Yn M | Yn F | Yg W | Yg W | Yg W | Yg F | Yn W | Yn E4 | Yn W | Yn E2 | Yg Wd | Yg Wd | Yn Wd | Yn M | Yn Wd | Yn Wd | Yg F | Yg E3 | Yg F | Yg E1 | Yn F | Yn W | 12 |
| 13 | Yn W | Yn E4 | Yg W | Yg F | Yn W | Yn E4 | Yn W | Yn E2 | Yg Wd | Yg Wd | Yg Wd | Yg M | Yn Wd | Yn Wd | Yg F | Yg E3 | Yg F | Yg E1 | Yn F | Yn W | Yn F | Yn F | Yg E | Yg W | 13 |
| 14 | Yg Wd | Yg Wd | Yn W | Yn E2 | Yg Wd | Yg Wd | Yg Wd | Yg M | Yn Wd | Yn Wd | Yn Wd | Yn M | Yg F | Yg E1 | Yn F | Yn W | Yn F | Yn F | Yg E | Yg W | Yg E | Yg F | Yn E | Yn E4 | 14 |
| 15 | Yn Wd | Yn Wd | Yg Wd | Yg M | Yn Wd | Yn Wd | Yn Wd | Yn M | Yg F | Yg E1 | Yg F | Yg E3 | Yn F | Yn F | Yg E | Yg W | Yg E | Yg F | Yn E | Yn E4 | Yn E | Yn E2 | Yg M | Yg Wd | 15 |
| 16 | Yg F | Yg E1 | Yn Wd | Yn M | Yg F | Yg E1 | Yg F | Yg E3 | Yn F | Yn F | Yn F | Yn W | Yg E | Yg F | Yn E | Yn E4 | Yn E | Yn E2 | Yg M | Yg Wd | Yg M | Yg M | Yn M | Yn Wd | 16 |
| 17 | Yn F | Yn F | Yg F | Yg E3 | Yn F | Yn F | Yn F | Yn W | Yg E | Yg F | Yg E | Yg W | Yn E | Yn E2 | Yg M | Yg Wd | Yg M | Yg M | Yn M | Yn Wd | Yn M | Yn M | Yg W | Yg E1 | 17 |
| 18 | Yg E | Yg F | Yn F | Yn W | Yg E | Yg F | Yg E | Yg W | Yn E | Yn E2 | Yn E | Yn E4 | Yg M | Yg M | Yn M | Yn Wd | Yn M | Yn M | Yg W | Yg E1 | Yg W | Yg E3 | Yn W | Yn F | 18 |
| 19 | Yn E | Yn E2 | Yg E | Yg W | Yn E | Yn E2 | Yn E | Yn E4 | Yg M | Yg M | Yg M | Yg Wd | Yn M | Yn M | Yg W | Yg E1 | Yg W | Yg E3 | Yn W | Yn F | Yn W | Yn W | Yg Wd | Yg F | 19 |
| 20 | Yg M | Yg M | Yn E | Yn E4 | Yg M | Yg M | Yg M | Yg Wd | Yn M | Yn M | Yn M | Yn Wd | Yg W | Yg E3 | Yn W | Yn F | Yn W | Yn W | Yg Wd | Yg F | Yg Wd | Yg W | Yn Wd | Yn E2 | 20 |
| 21 | Yn M | Yn M | Yg M | Yg Wd | Yn M | Yn M | Yn M | Yn Wd | Yg W | Yg E3 | Yg W | Yg E1 | Yn W | Yn W | Yg Wd | Yg F | Yg Wd | Yg W | Yn Wd | Yn E2 | Yn Wd | Yn E4 | Yg F | Yg M | 21 |
| 22 | Yg W | Yg E3 | Yn M | Yn Wd | Yg W | Yg E3 | Yg W | Yg E1 | Yn W | Yn W | Yn W | Yn F | Yg Wd | Yg W | Yn Wd | Yn E2 | Yn Wd | Yn E4 | Yg F | Yg M | Yg F | Yg Wd | Yn F | Yn M | 22 |
| 23 | Yn W | Yn W | Yg W | Yg E1 | Yn W | Yn W | Yn W | Yn F | Yg Wd | Yg W | Yg Wd | Yg F | Yn Wd | Yn E4 | Yg F | Yg M | Yg F | Yg Wd | Yn F | Yn M | Yn F | Yn Wd | Yg E | Yg E3 | 23 |
| 24 | Yg Wd | Yg W | Yn W | Yn F | Yg Wd | Yg W | Yg Wd | Yg F | Yn Wd | Yn E4 | Yn Wd | Yn E2 | Yg F | Yg Wd | Yn F | Yn M | Yn F | Yn Wd | Yg E | Yg E3 | Yg E | Yg E1 | Yn E | Yn W | 24 |
| 25 | Yn Wd | Yn E4 | Yg Wd | Yg F | Yn Wd | Yn E4 | Yn Wd | Yn E2 | Yg F | Yg Wd | Yg F | Yg M | Yn F | Yn Wd | Yg E | Yg E3 | Yg E | Yg E1 | Yn E | Yn W | Yn E | Yn F | Yg M | Yg W | 25 |
| 26 | Yg F | Yg Wd | Yn Wd | Yn E2 | Yg F | Yg Wd | Yg F | Yg M | Yn F | Yn Wd | Yn F | Yn M | Yg E | Yg E1 | Yn E | Yn W | Yn E | Yn F | Yg M | Yg W | Yg M | Yg F | Yn M | Yn E4 | 26 |
| 27 | Yn F | Yn Wd | Yg F | Yg M | Yn F | Yn Wd | Yn F | Yn M | Yg E | Yg E1 | Yg E | Yg E3 | Yn E | Yn F | Yg M | Yg W | Yg M | Yg F | Yn M | Yn E4 | Yn M | Yn E2 | Yg W | Yg Wd | 27 |
| 28 | Yg E | Yg E1 | Yn F | Yn M | Yg E | Yg E1 | Yg E | Yg E3 | Yn E | Yn F | Yn E | Yn W | Yg M | Yg F | Yn M | Yn E4 | Yn M | Yn E2 | Yg W | Yg Wd | Yg W | Yg M | Yn W | Yn Wd | 28 |
| 29 | Yn E | Yn F | Yg E | Yg E3 | Yn E | Yn F | Yn E | Yn W | Yg M | Yg F | Yg M | Yg W | Yn M | Yn E2 | Yg W | Yg Wd | Yg W | Yg M | Yn W | Yn Wd | Yn W | Yn M | Yg Wd | Yg E1 | 29 |
| 30 | | | Yn E | Yn W | Yg M | Yg F | Yg M | Yg W | Yn M | Yn E2 | Yn M | Yn E4 | Yg W | Yg M | Yn W | Yn Wd | Yn W | Yn M | Yg Wd | Yg E1 | Yg Wd | Yg E3 | Yn Wd | Yn F | 30 |
| 31 | | | Yg M | Yg W | | | Yn M | Yn E4 | | | Yg W | Yg Wd | Yn W | Yn M | | | Yg Wd | Yg E3 | | | Yn Wd | Yn W | Yg F | Yg F | 31 |
| 1 | Yg M | Yg F | Yn M | Yn E4 | Yn M | Yn E2 | Yg W | Yg Wd | Yg W | Yg M | Yn W | Yn Wd | Yg Wd | Yg E3 | Yg Wd | Yg E1 | Yn Wd | Yn W | Yn Wd | Yn F | Yg F | Yg W | Yn F | Yn E2 | 1 |
| 2 | Yn M | Yn E2 | Yg W | Yg Wd | Yg W | Yg M | Yn W | Yn Wd | Yn W | Yn M | Yg Wd | Yg E1 | Yn Wd | Yn W | Yn Wd | Yn F | Yg F | Yg W | Yg F | Yg F | Yn F | Yn E4 | Yg E | Yg M | 2 |
| 3 | Yg W | Yg M | Yn W | Yn Wd | Yn W | Yn M | Yg Wd | Yg E1 | Yg Wd | Yg E3 | Yn Wd | Yn F | Yg F | Yg W | Yg F | Yg F | Yn F | Yn E4 | Yn F | Yn E2 | Yg E | Yg Wd | Yn E | Yn M | 3 |
| 4 | Yn W | Yn M | Yg Wd | Yg E1 | Yg Wd | Yg E3 | Yn Wd | Yn F | Yn Wd | Yn W | Yg F | Yg F | Yn F | Yn E4 | Yn F | Yn E2 | Yg E | Yg Wd | Yg E | Yg M | Yn E | Yn Wd | | | 4 |
| 5 | | | | | | | | | Yg F | Yg W | Yn F | Yn E2 | Yg E | Yg Wd | Yg E | Yg M | Yn E | Yn Wd | Yn E | Yn M | | | | | 5 |
| 6 | | | | | | | | | Yn F | Yn E4 | Yg E | Yg M | Yn E | Yn Wd | Yn E | Yn M | Yg M | Yg E1 | Yg M | Yg E3 | | | | | 6 |
| 7 | | | | | | | | | | | | | | | Yg M | Yg E3 | | | | | | | | | 7 |
| 8 | | | | | | | | | | | | | | | | | | | | | | | | | 8 |

# YEAR OF THE ROOSTER

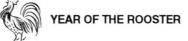

|  | H | E | H | E | H | E | H | E | H | E | H | E | H | E | H | E | H | E | H | E | H | E | H | E |  |
|---|---|---|---|---|---|---|---|---|---|---|---|---|---|---|---|---|---|---|---|---|---|---|---|---|---|
| YEAR | YEAR YnE | YnM | 1969 |  |  |  |  |  |  |  |  |  |  |  |  |  |  |  |  |  |  |  | 1970 |  |  |
| MONTH | 4 Feb - 5 Mar |  | 6 Mar - 4 Apr |  | 5 Apr - 5 May |  | 6 May - 5 June |  | 6 June - 6 Jul |  | 7 Jul - 7 Aug |  | 8 Aug - 7 Sep |  | 8 Sep - 7 Oct |  | 8 Oct - 6 Nov |  | 7 Nov - 6 Dec |  | 7 Dec - 5 Jan |  | 6 Jan - 3 Feb |  |  |
|  | Yg F | Yg Wd | Yn F | Yn Wd | Yg E | Yg E1 | Yn E | Yn F | Yg M | Yg F | Yn M | Yn E2 | Yg W | Yg M | Yn W | Yn M | Yg Wd | Yg E3 | Yn Wd | Yn W | Yg F | Yg W | Yn F | Yn E4 |  |
| Starting time | 1st day | Mid-pt | 1st day | Mid-pt | 1st day | Mid-pt | 1st day | Mid-pt | 1st day | Mid-pt | 1st day | Mid-pt | 1st day | Mid-pt | 1st day | Mid-pt | 1st day | Mid-pt | 1st day | Mid-pt | 1st day | Mid-pt | 1st day | Mid-pt |  |
| Date | 4 | 19 | 6 | 21 | 5 | 20 | 6 | 21 | 6 | 21 | 7 | 23 | 8 | 23 | 8 | 23 | 8 | 23 | 7 | 22 | 7 | 22 | 6 | 20 |  |
| Hour | 0759 | 0355 | 0211 | 0308 | 0715 | 1427 | 0050 | 1350 | 0512 | 2155 | 1532 | 0848 | 0114 | 1543 | 0356 | 1307 | 1917 | 2211 | 2212 | 1931 | 1451 | 0844 | 0202 | 1924 |  |
| DATE 4 | Yg M | Yg E3 |  |  |  |  |  |  |  |  |  |  |  |  |  |  |  |  |  |  |  |  |  |  | 4 |
| 5 | Yn M | Yn W |  |  | Yg M | Yg E3 |  |  |  |  |  |  |  |  |  |  |  |  |  |  |  |  |  |  | 5 |
| 6 | Yg W | Yg W | Yg M | Yg E1 | Yn M | Yn W | Yn M | Yn F | Yg W | Yg W |  |  |  |  |  |  |  |  |  |  |  |  | Yg F | Yg E3 | 6 |
| 7 | Yn W | Yn E4 | Yn M | Yn F | Yg W | Yg W | Yg W | Yg F | Yn W | Yn E4 | Yn W | Yn E2 |  |  |  |  |  |  | Yg F | Yg E3 | Yg F | Yg E1 | Yn F | Yn W | 7 |
| 8 | Yg Wd | Yg Wd | Yg W | Yg F | Yn W | Yn E4 | Yn W | Yn E2 | Yg Wd | Yg Wd | Yg Wd | Yg M | Yn Wd | Yn Wd | Yg F | Yg E3 | Yg F | Yg E1 | Yn F | Yn W | Yn F | Yn F | Yg E | Yg W | 8 |
| 9 | Yn Wd | Yn Wd | Yn W | Yn E2 | Yg Wd | Yg Wd | Yg Wd | Yg M | Yn Wd | Yn Wd | Yn Wd | Yn M | Yg F | Yg E1 | Yn F | Yn W | Yn F | Yn F | Yg E | Yg W | Yg E | Yg F | Yn E | Yn E4 | 9 |
| 10 | Yg F | Yg E1 | Yg Wd | Yg M | Yn Wd | Yn Wd | Yn Wd | Yn M | Yg F | Yg E1 | Yg F | Yg E3 | Yn F | Yn F | Yg E | Yg W | Yg E | Yg F | Yn E | Yn E4 | Yn E | Yn E2 | Yg M | Yg Wd | 10 |
| 11 | Yn F | Yn F | Yn Wd | Yn M | Yg F | Yg E1 | Yg F | Yg E3 | Yn F | Yn F | Yn F | Yn W | Yg E | Yg F | Yn E | Yn E4 | Yn E | Yn E2 | Yg M | Yg Wd | Yg M | Yg M | Yn M | Yn Wd | 11 |
| 12 | Yg E | Yg F | Yg F | Yg E3 | Yn F | Yn F | Yn F | Yn W | Yg E | Yg F | Yg E | Yg W | Yn E | Yn E2 | Yg M | Yg Wd | Yg M | Yg M | Yn M | Yn Wd | Yn M | Yn M | Yg W | Yg E1 | 12 |
| 13 | Yn E | Yn E2 | Yn F | Yn W | Yg E | Yg F | Yg E | Yg W | Yn E | Yn E2 | Yn E | Yn E4 | Yg M | Yg M | Yn M | Yn Wd | Yn M | Yn M | Yg W | Yg E1 | Yg W | Yg E3 | Yn W | Yn F | 13 |
| 14 | Yg M | Yg M | Yg E | Yg W | Yn E | Yn E2 | Yn E | Yn E4 | Yg M | Yg M | Yg M | Yg Wd | Yn M | Yn M | Yg W | Yg E1 | Yg W | Yg E3 | Yn W | Yn F | Yn W | Yn W | Yg Wd | Yg F | 14 |
| 15 | Yn M | Yn M | Yn E | Yn E4 | Yg M | Yg M | Yg M | Yg Wd | Yn M | Yn M | Yn M | Yn Wd | Yg W | Yg E3 | Yn W | Yn F | Yn W | Yn W | Yg Wd | Yg F | Yg Wd | Yg W | Yn Wd | Yn E2 | 15 |
| 16 | Yg W | Yg E3 | Yg M | Yg Wd | Yn M | Yn M | Yn M | Yn Wd | Yg W | Yg E3 | Yg W | Yg E1 | Yn W | Yn W | Yg Wd | Yg F | Yg Wd | Yg W | Yn Wd | Yn E2 | Yn Wd | Yn E4 | Yg F | Yg M | 16 |
| 17 | Yn W | Yn W | Yn M | Yn Wd | Yg W | Yg E3 | Yg W | Yg E1 | Yn W | Yn W | Yn W | Yn F | Yg Wd | Yg W | Yn Wd | Yn E2 | Yn Wd | Yn E4 | Yg F | Yg M | Yg F | Yg Wd | Yn F | Yn M | 17 |
| 18 | Yg Wd | Yg W | Yg W | Yg E1 | Yn W | Yn W | Yn W | Yn F | Yg Wd | Yg W | Yg Wd | Yg F | Yn Wd | Yn E4 | Yg F | Yg M | Yg F | Yg Wd | Yn F | Yn M | Yn F | Yn Wd | Yg E | Yg E3 | 18 |
| 19 | Yn Wd | Yn E4 | Yn W | Yn F | Yg Wd | Yg W | Yg Wd | Yg F | Yn Wd | Yn E4 | Yn Wd | Yn E2 | Yg F | Yg Wd | Yn F | Yn M | Yn F | Yn Wd | Yg E | Yg E3 | Yg E | Yg E1 | Yn E | Yn W | 19 |
| 20 | Yg F | Yg Wd | Yg Wd | Yg F | Yn Wd | Yn E4 | Yn Wd | Yn E2 | Yg F | Yg Wd | Yg F | Yg M | Yn F | Yn Wd | Yg E | Yg E3 | Yg E | Yg E1 | Yn E | Yn W | Yn E | Yn F | Yg M | Yg W | 20 |
| 21 | Yn F | Yn Wd | Yn Wd | Yn E2 | Yg F | Yg Wd | Yg F | Yg M | Yn F | Yn Wd | Yn F | Yn M | Yg E | Yg E1 | Yn E | Yn W | Yn E | Yn F | Yg M | Yg W | Yg M | Yg F | Yn M | Yn E4 | 21 |
| 22 | Yg E | Yg E1 | Yg F | Yg M | Yn F | Yn Wd | Yn F | Yn M | Yg E | Yg E1 | Yg E | Yg E3 | Yn E | Yn F | Yg M | Yg W | Yg M | Yg F | Yn M | Yn E4 | Yn M | Yn E2 | Yg W | Yg Wd | 22 |
| 23 | Yn E | Yn F | Yn F | Yn M | Yg E | Yg E1 | Yg E | Yg E3 | Yn E | Yn F | Yn E | Yn W | Yg M | Yg F | Yn M | Yn E4 | Yn M | Yn E2 | Yg W | Yg Wd | Yg W | Yg M | Yn W | Yn Wd | 23 |
| 24 | Yg M | Yg F | Yg E | Yg E3 | Yn E | Yn F | Yn E | Yn W | Yg M | Yg F | Yg M | Yg W | Yn M | Yn E2 | Yg W | Yg Wd | Yg W | Yg M | Yn W | Yn Wd | Yn W | Yn M | Yg Wd | Yg E1 | 24 |
| 25 | Yn M | Yn E2 | Yn E | Yn W | Yg M | Yg F | Yg M | Yg W | Yn M | Yn E2 | Yn M | Yn E4 | Yg W | Yg M | Yn W | Yn Wd | Yn W | Yn M | Yg Wd | Yg E1 | Yg Wd | Yg E3 | Yn Wd | Yn F | 25 |
| 26 | Yg W | Yg M | Yg M | Yg W | Yn M | Yn E2 | Yn M | Yn E4 | Yg W | Yg M | Yg W | Yg Wd | Yn W | Yn M | Yg Wd | Yg E1 | Yg Wd | Yg E3 | Yn Wd | Yn F | Yn Wd | Yn W | Yg F | Yg F | 26 |
| 27 | Yn W | Yn M | Yn M | Yn E4 | Yg W | Yg M | Yg W | Yg Wd | Yn W | Yn M | Yn W | Yn Wd | Yg Wd | Yg E3 | Yn Wd | Yn F | Yn Wd | Yn W | Yg F | Yg F | Yg F | Yg W | Yn F | Yn E2 | 27 |
| 28 | Yg Wd | Yg E3 | Yg W | Yg Wd | Yn W | Yn M | Yn W | Yn Wd | Yg Wd | Yg E3 | Yg Wd | Yg E1 | Yn Wd | Yn W | Yg F | Yg F | Yg F | Yg W | Yn F | Yn E2 | Yn F | Yn E4 | Yg E | Yg M | 28 |
| 29 |  |  | Yn W | Yn Wd | Yg Wd | Yg E3 | Yg Wd | Yg E1 | Yn Wd | Yn W | Yn Wd | Yn F | Yg F | Yg W | Yn F | Yn E2 | Yn F | Yn E4 | Yg E | Yg M | Yg E | Yg Wd | Yn E | Yn M | 29 |
| 30 |  |  | Yg Wd | Yg E1 | Yn Wd | Yn W | Yn Wd | Yn F | Yg F | Yg W | Yg F | Yg F | Yn F | Yn E4 | Yg E | Yg M | Yg E | Yg Wd | Yn E | Yn M | Yn E | Yn Wd | Yg M | Yg E3 | 30 |
| 31 |  |  | Yn Wd | Yn F |  |  | Yg F | Yg F |  |  | Yn F | Yn E2 | Yg E | Yg Wd |  |  | Yn E | Yn Wd |  |  | Yg M | Yg E1 | Yn M | Yn W | 31 |
| 1 | Yn Wd | Yn W | Yg F | Yg F | Yg F | Yg W | Yn F | Yn E2 | Yn F | Yn E4 | Yg E | Yg M | Yn E | Yn Wd | Yn E | Yn M | Yg M | Yg E1 | Yg M | Yg E3 | Yn M | Yn F | Yg W | Yg W | 1 |
| 2 | Yg F | Yg W | Yn F | Yn E2 | Yn F | Yn E4 | Yg E | Yg M | Yg E | Yg Wd | Yn E | Yn M | Yg M | Yg E1 | Yg M | Yg E3 | Yn M | Yn F | Yn M | Yn W | Yg W | Yg F | Yn W | Yn E4 | 2 |
| 3 | Yn F | Yn E4 | Yg E | Yg M | Yg E | Yg Wd | Yn E | Yn M | Yn E | Yn Wd | Yg M | Yg E3 | Yn M | Yn F | Yn M | Yn W | Yg W | Yg F | Yg W | Yg W | Yn W | Yn E2 | Yg Wd | Yg Wd | 3 |
| 4 | Yg E | Yg Wd | Yn E | Yn M | Yn E | Yn Wd | Yg M | Yg E3 | Yg M | Yg E1 | Yn M | Yn W | Yg W | Yg F | Yg W | Yg W | Yn W | Yn E2 | Yn W | Yn E4 | Yg Wd | Yg M |  |  | 4 |
| 5 | Yn E | Yn Wd |  |  | Yg M | Yg E1 | Yn M | Yn W | Yn M | Yn F | Yg W | Yg W | Yn W | Yn E2 | Yn W | Yn E4 | Yg Wd | Yg M | Yg Wd | Yg Wd | Yn Wd | Yn M |  |  | 5 |
| 6 |  |  |  |  |  |  |  |  | Yg W | Yg F | Yn W | Yn E4 | Yg Wd | Yg M | Yg Wd | Yg Wd | Yn Wd | Yn M | Yn Wd | Yn Wd |  |  |  |  | 6 |
| 7 |  |  |  |  |  |  |  |  |  |  | Yg Wd | Yg Wd | Yn Wd | Yn M | Yn Wd | Yn Wd |  |  |  |  |  |  |  |  | 7 |
| 8 |  |  |  |  |  |  |  |  |  |  |  |  |  |  |  |  |  |  |  |  |  |  |  |  | 8 |

# YEAR OF THE DOG

| | H | E | H | E | H | E | H | E | H | E | H | E | H | E | H | E | H | E | H | E | H | E | H | E | |
|---|---|---|---|---|---|---|---|---|---|---|---|---|---|---|---|---|---|---|---|---|---|---|---|---|---|
| YEAR | YEAR Yg M | Yg E3 | | | | | | | | | | 1970 | | | | | | | | | | | 1971 | | |
| MONTH | 4 Feb - 5 Mar | | 6 Mar - 4 Apr | | 5 Apr - 5 May | | 6 May - 5 June | | 6 June - 6 Jul | | 7 Jul - 7 Aug | | 8 Aug - 7 Sep | | 8 Sep - 8 Oct | | 9 Oct - 7 Nov | | 8 Nov - 6 Dec | | 7 Dec - 5 Jan | | 6 Jan - 3 Feb | | |
| | Yg E | Yg Wd | Yn E | Yn Wd | Yg M | Yg E1 | Yn M | Yn F | Yg W | Yg F | Yn W | Yn E2 | Yg Wd | Yg M | Yn Wd | Yn M | Yg F | Yg E3 | Yn F | Yn W | Yg E | Yg W | Yn E | Yn E4 | |
| Starting time | 1st day | Mid-pt | 1st day | Mid-pt | 1st day | Mid-pt | 1st day | Mid-pt | 1st day | Mid-pt | 1st day | Mid-pt | 1st day | Mid-pt | 1st day | Mid-pt | 1st day | Mid-pt | 1st day | Mid-pt | 1st day | Mid-pt | 1st day | Mid-pt | |
| Date | 4 | 19 | 6 | 21 | 5 | 20 | 6 | 21 | 6 | 22 | 7 | 23 | 8 | 23 | 8 | 23 | 9 | 24 | 8 | 23 | 7 | 22 | 6 | 21 | |
| Hour | 1346 | 0942 | 0759 | 0856 | 1302 | 2015 | 0634 | 1938 | 1052 | 0343 | 2111 | 1437 | 0654 | 2134 | 0938 | 1859 | 0102 | 0404 | 0358 | 0125 | 2038 | 1436 | 0745 | 0113 | |
| DATE 4 | Yn Wd | Yn Wd | | | | | | | | | | | | | | | | | | | | | | | 4 |
| 5 | Yg F | Yg E1 | | | Yn Wd | Yn Wd | | | | | | | | | | | | | | | | | | | 5 |
| 6 | Yn F | Yn F | Yn Wd | Yn M | Yg F | Yg E1 | Yg F | Yg E3 | Yn F | Yn F | | | | | | | | | | | | | Yn M | Yn Wd | 6 |
| 7 | Yg E | Yg F | Yg F | Yg E3 | Yn F | Yn F | Yn F | Yn W | Yg E | Yg F | Yg E | Yg W | | | | | | | | | Yn M | Yn M | Yg W | Yg E1 | 7 |
| 8 | Yn E | Yn E2 | Yn F | Yn W | Yg E | Yg F | Yg E | Yg W | Yn E | Yn E2 | Yn E | Yn E4 | Yg M | Yg M | Yn M | Yn Wd | | | Yg W | Yg E1 | Yg W | Yg E3 | Yn W | Yn F | 8 |
| 9 | Yg M | Yg M | Yg E | Yg W | Yn E | Yn E2 | Yn E | Yn E4 | Yg M | Yg M | Yg M | Yg Wd | Yn M | Yn M | Yg W | Yg E1 | Yg W | Yg E3 | Yn W | Yn F | Yn W | Yn W | Yg Wd | Yg F | 9 |
| 10 | Yn M | Yn M | Yn E | Yn E4 | Yg M | Yg M | Yg M | Yg Wd | Yn M | Yn M | Yn M | Yn Wd | Yg W | Yg E3 | Yn W | Yn F | Yn W | Yn W | Yg Wd | Yg F | Yg Wd | Yg W | Yn Wd | Yn E2 | 10 |
| 11 | Yg W | Yg E3 | Yg M | Yg Wd | Yn M | Yn M | Yn M | Yn Wd | Yg W | Yg E3 | Yg W | Yg E1 | Yn W | Yn W | Yg Wd | Yg F | Yg Wd | Yg W | Yn Wd | Yn E2 | Yn Wd | Yn E4 | Yg F | Yg M | 11 |
| 12 | Yn W | Yn W | Yn M | Yn Wd | Yg W | Yg E3 | Yg W | Yg E1 | Yn W | Yn W | Yn W | Yn F | Yg Wd | Yg W | Yn Wd | Yn E2 | Yn Wd | Yn E4 | Yg F | Yg M | Yg F | Yg Wd | Yn F | Yn M | 12 |
| 13 | Yg Wd | Yg W | Yg W | Yg E1 | Yn W | Yn W | Yn W | Yn F | Yg Wd | Yg W | Yg Wd | Yg F | Yn Wd | Yn E4 | Yg F | Yg M | Yg F | Yg Wd | Yn F | Yn M | Yn F | Yn Wd | Yg E | Yg E3 | 13 |
| 14 | Yn Wd | Yn E4 | Yn W | Yn F | Yg Wd | Yg W | Yg Wd | Yg F | Yn Wd | Yn E4 | Yn Wd | Yn E2 | Yg F | Yg Wd | Yn F | Yn M | Yn F | Yn Wd | Yg E | Yg E3 | Yg E | Yg E1 | Yn E | Yn W | 14 |
| 15 | Yg F | Yg Wd | Yg Wd | Yg F | Yn Wd | Yn E4 | Yn Wd | Yn E2 | Yg F | Yg Wd | Yg F | Yg M | Yn F | Yn Wd | Yg E | Yg E3 | Yg E | Yg E1 | Yn E | Yn W | Yn E | Yn F | Yg M | Yg W | 15 |
| 16 | Yn F | Yn Wd | Yn Wd | Yn E2 | Yg F | Yg Wd | Yg F | Yg M | Yn F | Yn Wd | Yn F | Yn M | Yg E | Yg E1 | Yn E | Yn W | Yn E | Yn F | Yg M | Yg W | Yg M | Yg F | Yn M | Yn E4 | 16 |
| 17 | Yg E | Yg E1 | Yg F | Yg M | Yn F | Yn Wd | Yn F | Yn M | Yg E | Yg E1 | Yg E | Yg E3 | Yn E | Yn F | Yg M | Yg W | Yg M | Yg F | Yn M | Yn E4 | Yn M | Yn E2 | Yg W | Yg Wd | 17 |
| 18 | Yn E | Yn F | Yn F | Yn M | Yg E | Yg E1 | Yg E | Yg E3 | Yn E | Yn F | Yn E | Yn W | Yg M | Yg F | Yn M | Yn E4 | Yn M | Yn E2 | Yg W | Yg Wd | Yg W | Yg M | Yn W | Yn Wd | 18 |
| 19 | Yg M | Yg F | Yg E | Yg E3 | Yn E | Yn F | Yn E | Yn W | Yg M | Yg F | Yg M | Yg W | Yn M | Yn E2 | Yg W | Yg Wd | Yg W | Yg M | Yn W | Yn Wd | Yn W | Yn M | Yg Wd | Yg E1 | 19 |
| 20 | Yn M | Yn E2 | Yn E | Yn W | Yg M | Yg F | Yg M | Yg W | Yn M | Yn E2 | Yn M | Yn E4 | Yg W | Yg M | Yn W | Yn Wd | Yn W | Yn M | Yg Wd | Yg E1 | Yg Wd | Yg E3 | Yn Wd | Yn F | 20 |
| 21 | Yg W | Yg M | Yg M | Yg W | Yn M | Yn E2 | Yn M | Yn E4 | Yg W | Yg M | Yg W | Yg Wd | Yn W | Yn M | Yg Wd | Yg E1 | Yg Wd | Yg E3 | Yn Wd | Yn F | Yn Wd | Yn W | Yg F | Yg F | 21 |
| 22 | Yn W | Yn M | Yn M | Yn E4 | Yg W | Yg M | Yg W | Yg Wd | Yn W | Yn M | Yn W | Yn Wd | Yg Wd | Yg E3 | Yn Wd | Yn F | Yn Wd | Yn W | Yg F | Yg F | Yg F | Yg W | Yn F | Yn E2 | 22 |
| 23 | Yg Wd | Yg E3 | Yg W | Yg Wd | Yn W | Yn M | Yn W | Yn Wd | Yg Wd | Yg E3 | Yg Wd | Yg E1 | Yn Wd | Yn W | Yg F | Yg F | Yg F | Yg W | Yn F | Yn E2 | Yn F | Yn E4 | Yg E | Yg M | 23 |
| 24 | Yn Wd | Yn W | Yn W | Yn Wd | Yg Wd | Yg E3 | Yg Wd | Yg E1 | Yn Wd | Yn W | Yn Wd | Yn F | Yg F | Yg W | Yn F | Yn E2 | Yn F | Yn E4 | Yg E | Yg M | Yg E | Yg Wd | Yn E | Yn M | 24 |
| 25 | Yg F | Yg W | Yg Wd | Yg E1 | Yn Wd | Yn W | Yn Wd | Yn F | Yg F | Yg W | Yg F | Yg F | Yn F | Yn E4 | Yg E | Yg M | Yg E | Yg Wd | Yn E | Yn M | Yn E | Yn Wd | Yg M | Yg E3 | 25 |
| 26 | Yn F | Yn E4 | Yn Wd | Yn F | Yg F | Yg W | Yg F | Yg F | Yn F | Yn E4 | Yn F | Yn E2 | Yg E | Yg Wd | Yn E | Yn M | Yn E | Yn Wd | Yg M | Yg E3 | Yg M | Yg E1 | Yn M | Yn W | 26 |
| 27 | Yg E | Yg Wd | Yg F | Yg F | Yn F | Yn E4 | Yn F | Yn E2 | Yg E | Yg Wd | Yg E | Yg M | Yn E | Yn Wd | Yg M | Yg E3 | Yg M | Yg E1 | Yn M | Yn W | Yn M | Yn F | Yg W | Yg W | 27 |
| 28 | Yn E | Yn Wd | Yn F | Yn E2 | Yg E | Yg Wd | Yg E | Yg M | Yn E | Yn Wd | Yn E | Yn M | Yg M | Yg E1 | Yn M | Yn W | Yn M | Yn F | Yg W | Yg W | Yg W | Yg F | Yn W | Yn E4 | 28 |
| 29 | | | Yg E | Yg M | Yn E | Yn Wd | Yn E | Yn M | Yg M | Yg E1 | Yg M | Yg E3 | Yn M | Yn F | Yg W | Yg W | Yg W | Yg F | Yn W | Yn E4 | Yn W | Yn E2 | Yg Wd | Yg Wd | 29 |
| 30 | | | Yn E | Yn M | Yg M | Yg E1 | Yg M | Yg E3 | Yn M | Yn F | Yn M | Yn W | Yg W | Yg F | Yn W | Yn E4 | Yn W | Yn E2 | Yg Wd | Yg Wd | Yg Wd | Yg M | Yn Wd | Yn Wd | 30 |
| 31 | | | Yg M | Yg E3 | | | Yn M | Yn W | | | Yg W | Yg W | Yn W | Yn E2 | | | Yg Wd | Yg M | | | Yn Wd | Yn M | Yg F | Yg E1 | 31 |
| 1 | Yg M | Yg E1 | Yn M | Yn W | Yn M | Yn F | Yg W | Yg W | Yg W | Yg F | Yn W | Yn E4 | Yg Wd | Yg M | Yg Wd | Yg Wd | Yn Wd | Yn M | Yn Wd | Yn Wd | Yg F | Yg E3 | Yn F | Yn F | 1 |
| 2 | Yn M | Yn F | Yg W | Yg W | Yg W | Yg F | Yn W | Yn E4 | Yn W | Yn E2 | Yg Wd | Yg Wd | Yn Wd | Yn M | Yn Wd | Yn Wd | Yg F | Yg E3 | Yg F | Yg E1 | Yn F | Yn W | Yg E | Yg F | 2 |
| 3 | Yg W | Yg F | Yn W | Yn E4 | Yn W | Yn E2 | Yg Wd | Yg Wd | Yg Wd | Yg M | Yn Wd | Yn Wd | Yg F | Yg E3 | Yg F | Yg E1 | Yn F | Yn W | Yn F | Yn F | Yg E | Yg W | Yn E | Yn E2 | 3 |
| 4 | Yn W | Yn E2 | Yg Wd | Yg Wd | Yg Wd | Yg M | Yn Wd | Yn Wd | Yn Wd | Yn M | Yg F | Yg E1 | Yn F | Yn W | Yn F | Yn F | Yg E | Yg W | Yg E | Yg F | Yn E | Yn E4 | | | 4 |
| 5 | Yg Wd | Yg M | | | Yn Wd | Yn M | Yg F | Yg E1 | Yg F | Yg E3 | Yn F | Yn F | Yg E | Yg W | Yg E | Yg F | Yn E | Yn E4 | Yn E | Yn E2 | Yg M | Yg Wd | | | 5 |
| 6 | | | | | | | | | Yn F | Yn W | Yg E | Yg F | Yn E | Yn E4 | Yn E | Yn E2 | Yg M | Yg Wd | Yg M | Yg M | | | | | 6 |
| 7 | | | | | | | | | | | Yn E | Yn E2 | Yg M | Yg Wd | Yg M | Yg M | Yn M | Yn Wd | | | | | | | 7 |
| 8 | | | | | | | | | | | | | | | Yn M | Yn M | | | | | | | | | 8 |

# YEAR OF THE PIG

| | H | E | H | E | H | E | H | E | H | E | H | E | H | E | H | E | H | E | H | E | H | E | H | E | |
|---|---|---|---|---|---|---|---|---|---|---|---|---|---|---|---|---|---|---|---|---|---|---|---|---|---|
| YEAR | YEAR YnM | YnW | 1971 | | | | | | | | | | | | | | | | | | | | 1972 | | |
| MONTH | 4 Feb - 5 Mar YgM | YgWd | 6 Mar - 4 Apr YnM | YnWd | 5 Apr - 5 May YgW | YgE1 | 6 May - 5 June YnW | YnF | 6 June - 7 Jul YgWd | YgF | 8 Jul - 7 Aug YnWd | YnE2 | 8 Aug - 7 Sep YgF | YgM | 8 Sep - 8 Oct YnF | YnM | 9 Oct - 7 Nov YgE | YgE3 | 8 Nov - 7 Dec YnE | YnW | 8 Dec - 5 Jan YgM | YgW | 6 Jan - 4 Feb YnM | YnE4 | |
| Starting time | 1st day | Mid-pt | 1st day | Mid-pt | 1st day | Mid-pt | 1st day | Mid-pt | 1st day | Mid-pt | 1st day | Mid-pt | 1st day | Mid-pt | 1st day | Mid-pt | 1st day | Mid-pt | 1st day | Mid-pt | 1st day | Mid-pt | 1st day | Mid-pt | |
| Date | 4 | 19 | 6 | 21 | 5 | 21 | 6 | 22 | 6 | 22 | 8 | 23 | 8 | 24 | 8 | 24 | 9 | 24 | 8 | 23 | 8 | 22 | 6 | 21 | |
| Hour | 1926 | 1527 | 1335 | 1438 | 1836 | 0154 | 1208 | 0115 | 1629 | 0920 | 0251 | 2015 | 1240 | 0315 | 1530 | 0045 | 0659 | 0953 | 0957 | 0714 | 0236 | 2024 | 1342 | 0659 | |
| DATE 4 | YgM | YgM | | | | | | | | | | | | | | | | | | | | | | | 4 |
| 5 | YnM | YnM | | | YgM | YgM | | | | | | | | | | | | | | | | | | | 5 |
| 6 | YgW | YgE3 | YgM | YgWd | YnM | YnM | YnM | YnWd | YgW | YgE3 | | | | | | | | | | | | | YgF | YgM | 6 |
| 7 | YnW | YnW | YnM | YnWd | YgW | YgE3 | YgW | YgE1 | YnW | YnW | | | | | | | | | | | | | YnF | YnM | 7 |
| 8 | YgWd | YgW | YgW | YgE1 | YnW | YnW | YnW | YnF | YgWd | YgW | YgWd | YgF | YnWd | YnE4 | YgF | YgM | | | YnF | YnM | YnF | YnWd | YgE | YgE3 | 8 |
| 9 | YnWd | YnE4 | YnW | YnF | YgWd | YgW | YgWd | YgF | YnWd | YnE4 | YnWd | YnE2 | YgF | YgWd | YnF | YnM | YnF | YnWd | YgE | YgE3 | YgE | YgE1 | YnE | YnW | 9 |
| 10 | YgF | YgWd | YgWd | YgF | YnWd | YnE4 | YnWd | YnE2 | YgF | YgWd | YgF | YgM | YnF | YnWd | YgE | YgE3 | YgE | YgE1 | YnE | YnW | YnE | YnF | YgM | YgW | 10 |
| 11 | YnF | YnWd | YnWd | YnE2 | YgF | YgWd | YgF | YgM | YnF | YnWd | YnF | YnM | YgE | YgE1 | YnE | YnW | YnE | YnF | YgM | YgW | YgM | YgF | YnM | YnE4 | 11 |
| 12 | YgE | YgE1 | YgF | YgM | YnF | YnWd | YnF | YnM | YgE | YgE1 | YgE | YgE3 | YnE | YnF | YgM | YgW | YgM | YgF | YnM | YnE4 | YnM | YnE2 | YgW | YgWd | 12 |
| 13 | YnE | YnF | YnF | YnM | YgE | YgE1 | YgE | YgE3 | YnE | YnF | YnE | YnW | YgM | YgF | YnM | YnE4 | YnM | YnE2 | YgW | YgWd | YgW | YgM | YnW | YnWd | 13 |
| 14 | YgM | YgF | YgE | YgE3 | YnE | YnF | YnE | YnW | YgM | YgF | YgM | YgW | YnM | YnE2 | YgW | YgWd | YgW | YgM | YnW | YnWd | YnW | YnM | YgWd | YgE1 | 14 |
| 15 | YnM | YnE2 | YnE | YnW | YgM | YgF | YgM | YgW | YnM | YnE2 | YnM | YnE4 | YgW | YgM | YnW | YnWd | YnW | YnM | YgWd | YgE1 | YgWd | YgE3 | YnWd | YnF | 15 |
| 16 | YgW | YgM | YgM | YgW | YnM | YnE2 | YnM | YnE4 | YgW | YgM | YgW | YgWd | YnW | YnM | YgWd | YgE1 | YgWd | YgE3 | YnWd | YnF | YnWd | YnW | YgF | YgF | 16 |
| 17 | YnW | YnM | YnM | YnE4 | YgW | YgM | YgW | YgWd | YnW | YnM | YnW | YnWd | YgWd | YgE3 | YnWd | YnF | YnWd | YnW | YgF | YgF | YgF | YgW | YnF | YnE2 | 17 |
| 18 | YgWd | YgE3 | YgW | YgWd | YnW | YnM | YnW | YnWd | YgWd | YgE3 | YgWd | YgE1 | YnWd | YnW | YgF | YgF | YgF | YgW | YnF | YnE2 | YnF | YnE4 | YgE | YgM | 18 |
| 19 | YnWd | YnW | YnW | YnWd | YgWd | YgE3 | YgWd | YgE1 | YnWd | YnW | YnWd | YnF | YgF | YgW | YnF | YnE2 | YnF | YnE4 | YgE | YgM | YgE | YgWd | YnE | YnM | 19 |
| 20 | YgF | YgW | YgWd | YgE1 | YnWd | YnW | YnWd | YnF | YgF | YgW | YgF | YgF | YnF | YnE4 | YgE | YgM | YgE | YgWd | YnE | YnM | YnE | YnWd | YgM | YgE3 | 20 |
| 21 | YnF | YnE4 | YnWd | YnF | YgF | YgW | YgF | YgF | YnF | YnE4 | YnF | YnE2 | YgE | YgWd | YnE | YnM | YnE | YnWd | YgM | YgE3 | YgM | YgE1 | YnM | YnW | 21 |
| 22 | YgE | YgWd | YgF | YgF | YnF | YnE4 | YnF | YnE2 | YgE | YgWd | YgE | YgM | YnE | YnWd | YgM | YgE3 | YgM | YgE1 | YnM | YnW | YnM | YnF | YgW | YgW | 22 |
| 23 | YnE | YnWd | YnF | YnE2 | YgE | YgWd | YgE | YgM | YnE | YnWd | YnE | YnM | YgM | YgE1 | YnM | YnW | YnM | YnF | YgW | YgW | YgW | YgF | YnW | YnE4 | 23 |
| 24 | YgM | YgE1 | YgE | YgM | YnE | YnWd | YnE | YnM | YgM | YgE1 | YgM | YgE3 | YnM | YnF | YgW | YgW | YgW | YgF | YnW | YnE4 | YnW | YnE2 | YgWd | YgWd | 24 |
| 25 | YnM | YnF | YnE | YnM | YgM | YgE1 | YgM | YgE3 | YnM | YnF | YnM | YnW | YgW | YgF | YnW | YnE4 | YnW | YnE2 | YgWd | YgWd | YgWd | YgM | YnWd | YnWd | 25 |
| 26 | YgW | YgF | YgM | YgE3 | YnM | YnF | YnM | YnW | YgW | YgF | YgW | YgW | YnW | YnE2 | YgWd | YgWd | YgWd | YgM | YnWd | YnWd | YnWd | YnM | YgF | YgE1 | 26 |
| 27 | YnW | YnE2 | YnM | YnW | YgW | YgF | YgW | YgW | YnW | YnE2 | YnW | YnE4 | YgWd | YgM | YnWd | YnWd | YnWd | YnM | YgF | YgE1 | YgF | YgE3 | YnF | YnF | 27 |
| 28 | YgWd | YgM | YgW | YgW | YnW | YnE2 | YnW | YnE4 | YgWd | YgM | YgWd | YgWd | YnWd | YnM | YgF | YgE1 | YgF | YgE3 | YnF | YnF | YnF | YnW | YgE | YgF | 28 |
| 29 | | | YnW | YnE4 | YgWd | YgM | YgWd | YgWd | YnWd | YnM | YnWd | YnWd | YgF | YgE3 | YnF | YnF | YnF | YnW | YgE | YgF | YgE | YgW | YnE | YnE2 | 29 |
| 30 | | | YgWd | YgWd | YnWd | YnM | YnWd | YnWd | YgF | YgE3 | YgF | YgE1 | YnF | YnW | YgE | YgF | YgE | YgW | YnE | YnE2 | YnE | YnE4 | YgM | YgM | 30 |
| 31 | | | YnWd | YnWd | | | YgF | YgE1 | | | YnF | YnF | YgE | YgW | | | YnE | YnE4 | | | YgM | YgWd | YnM | YnM | 31 |
| 1 | YnWd | YnM | YgF | YgE1 | YgF | YgE3 | YnF | YnF | YnF | YnW | YgE | YgF | YnE | YnE4 | YnE | YnE2 | YgM | YgWd | YgM | YgM | YnM | YnWd | YgW | YgE3 | 1 |
| 2 | YgF | YgE3 | YnF | YnF | YnF | YnW | YgE | YgF | YgE | YgW | YnE | YnE2 | YgM | YgWd | YgM | YgM | YnM | YnWd | YnM | YnM | YgW | YgE1 | YnW | YnW | 2 |
| 3 | YnF | YnW | YgE | YgF | YgE | YgW | YnE | YnE2 | YnE | YnE4 | YgM | YgM | YnM | YnWd | YnM | YnM | YgW | YgE1 | YgW | YgE3 | YnW | YnF | YgWd | YgW | 3 |
| 4 | YgE | YgW | YnE | YnE2 | YnE | YnE4 | YgM | YgM | YgM | YgWd | YnM | YnM | YgW | YgE1 | YgW | YgE3 | YnW | YnF | YnW | YnW | YgWd | YgF | YnWd | YnE4 | 4 |
| 5 | YnE | YnE4 | | | YgM | YgWd | YnM | YnM | YnM | YnWd | YgW | YgE3 | YnW | YnF | YnW | YnW | YgWd | YgF | YgWd | YgW | YnWd | YnE2 | | | 5 |
| 6 | | | | | | | | | YgW | YgE1 | YnW | YnW | YgWd | YgF | YgWd | YgW | YnWd | YnE2 | YnWd | YnE4 | | | | | 6 |
| 7 | | | | | | | | | YnW | YnF | YgWd | YgW | YnWd | YnE2 | YnWd | YnE4 | YgF | YgM | YgF | YgWd | | | | | 7 |
| 8 | | | | | | | | | | | | | | | YgF | YgWd | | | | | | | | | 8 |

# YEAR OF THE RAT

| | H | E | H | E | H | E | H | E | H | E | H | E | H | E | H | E | H | E | H | E | H | E | H | E | |
|---|---|---|---|---|---|---|---|---|---|---|---|---|---|---|---|---|---|---|---|---|---|---|---|---|---|
| YEAR | YEAR<br>Yg W | Yg W | 1972 | | | | | | | | | | | | | | | | | | | | 1973 | | |
| MONTH | 5 Feb - 4 Mar | | 5 Mar - 4 Apr | | 5 Apr - 4 May | | 5 May - 4 June | | 5 June - 6 Jul | | 7 Jul - 6 Aug | | 7 Aug - 6 Sep | | 7 Sep - 7 Oct | | 8 Oct - 6 Nov | | 7 Nov - 6 Dec | | 7 Dec - 4 Jan | | 5 Jan - 3 Feb | | |
| | Yg W | Yg Wd | Yn W | Yn Wd | Yg Wd | Yg E1 | Yn Wd | Yn F | Yg F | Yg F | Yn F | Yn E2 | Yg E | Yg M | Yn E | Yn M | Yg M | Yg E3 | Yn M | Yn W | Yg W | Yg W | Yn W | Yn E4 | |
| Starting time | 1st day | Mid-pt | 1st day | Mid-pt | 1st day | Mid-pt | 1st day | Mid-pt | 1st day | Mid-pt | 1st day | Mid-pt | 1st day | Mid-pt | 1st day | Mid-pt | 1st day | Mid-pt | 1st day | Mid-pt | 1st day | Mid-pt | 1st day | Mid-pt | |
| Date | 5 | 19 | 5 | 20 | 5 | 20 | 5 | 21 | 5 | 21 | 7 | 23 | 7 | 23 | 7 | 23 | 8 | 23 | 7 | 22 | 7 | 22 | 5 | 20 | |
| Hour | 0120 | 2112 | 1928 | 2022 | 0029 | 0738 | 1801 | 0700 | 2222 | 1506 | 0843 | 0203 | 1829 | 0903 | 2115 | 0633 | 1242 | 1542 | 1540 | 1303 | 0819 | 0213 | 1926 | 1248 | |
| DATE 4 | | | | | | | | | | | | | | | | | | | | | | | | | 4 |
| 5 | Yg F | Yg Wd | Yn Wd | Yn E2 | Yg F | Yg Wd | Yg F | Yg M | Yn F | Yn Wd | | | | | | | | | | | | | Yn M | Yn E4 | 5 |
| 6 | Yn F | Yn Wd | Yg F | Yg M | Yn F | Yn Wd | Yn F | Yn M | Yg E | Yg E1 | | | | | | | | | | | | | Yg W | Yg Wd | 6 |
| 7 | Yg E | Yg E1 | Yn F | Yn M | Yg E | Yg E1 | Yg E | Yg E3 | Yn E | Yn F | Yn E | Yn W | Yg M | Yg F | Yn M | Yn E4 | | | Yg W | Yg Wd | Yg W | Yg M | Yn W | Yn Wd | 7 |
| 8 | Yn E | Yn F | Yg E | Yg E3 | Yn E | Yn F | Yn E | Yn W | Yg M | Yg F | Yg M | Yg W | Yn M | Yn E2 | Yg W | Yg Wd | Yg W | Yg M | Yn W | Yn Wd | Yn W | Yn M | Yg Wd | Yg E1 | 8 |
| 9 | Yg M | Yg F | Yn E | Yn W | Yg M | Yg F | Yg M | Yg W | Yn M | Yn E2 | Yn M | Yn E4 | Yg W | Yg M | Yn W | Yn Wd | Yn W | Yn M | Yg Wd | Yg E1 | Yg Wd | Yg E3 | Yn Wd | Yn F | 9 |
| 10 | Yn M | Yn E2 | Yg M | Yg W | Yn M | Yn E2 | Yn M | Yn E4 | Yg W | Yg M | Yg W | Yg Wd | Yn W | Yn M | Yg Wd | Yg E1 | Yg Wd | Yg E3 | Yn Wd | Yn F | Yn Wd | Yn W | Yg F | Yg F | 10 |
| 11 | Yg W | Yg M | Yn M | Yn E4 | Yg W | Yg M | Yg W | Yg Wd | Yn W | Yn M | Yn W | Yn Wd | Yg Wd | Yg E3 | Yn Wd | Yn F | Yn Wd | Yn W | Yg F | Yg F | Yg F | Yg W | Yn F | Yn E2 | 11 |
| 12 | Yn W | Yn M | Yg W | Yg Wd | Yn W | Yn M | Yn W | Yn Wd | Yg Wd | Yg E3 | Yg Wd | Yg E1 | Yn Wd | Yn W | Yg F | Yg F | Yg F | Yg W | Yn F | Yn E2 | Yn F | Yn E4 | Yg E | Yg M | 12 |
| 13 | Yg Wd | Yg E3 | Yn W | Yn Wd | Yg Wd | Yg E3 | Yg Wd | Yg E1 | Yn Wd | Yn W | Yn Wd | Yn F | Yg F | Yg W | Yn F | Yn E2 | Yn F | Yn E4 | Yg E | Yg M | Yg E | Yg Wd | Yn E | Yn M | 13 |
| 14 | Yn Wd | Yn W | Yg Wd | Yg E1 | Yn Wd | Yn W | Yn Wd | Yn F | Yg F | Yg W | Yg F | Yg F | Yn F | Yn E4 | Yg E | Yg M | Yg E | Yg Wd | Yn E | Yn M | Yn E | Yn Wd | Yg M | Yg E3 | 14 |
| 15 | Yg F | Yg W | Yn Wd | Yn F | Yg F | Yg W | Yg F | Yg F | Yn F | Yn E4 | Yn F | Yn E2 | Yg E | Yg Wd | Yn E | Yn M | Yn E | Yn Wd | Yg M | Yg E3 | Yg M | Yg E1 | Yn M | Yn W | 15 |
| 16 | Yn F | Yn E4 | Yg F | Yg F | Yn F | Yn E4 | Yn F | Yn E2 | Yg E | Yg Wd | Yg E | Yg M | Yn E | Yn Wd | Yg M | Yg E3 | Yg M | Yg E1 | Yn M | Yn W | Yn M | Yn F | Yg W | Yg W | 16 |
| 17 | Yg E | Yg Wd | Yn F | Yn E2 | Yg E | Yg Wd | Yg E | Yg M | Yn E | Yn Wd | Yn E | Yn M | Yg M | Yg E1 | Yn M | Yn W | Yn M | Yn F | Yg W | Yg W | Yg W | Yg F | Yn W | Yn E4 | 17 |
| 18 | Yn E | Yn Wd | Yg E | Yg M | Yn E | Yn Wd | Yn E | Yn M | Yg M | Yg E1 | Yg M | Yg E3 | Yn M | Yn F | Yg W | Yg W | Yg W | Yg F | Yn W | Yn E4 | Yn W | Yn E2 | Yg Wd | Yg Wd | 18 |
| 19 | Yg M | Yg E1 | Yn E | Yn M | Yg M | Yg E1 | Yg M | Yg E3 | Yn M | Yn F | Yn M | Yn W | Yg W | Yg F | Yn W | Yn E4 | Yn W | Yn E2 | Yg Wd | Yg Wd | Yg Wd | Yg M | Yn Wd | Yn Wd | 19 |
| 20 | Yn M | Yn F | Yg M | Yg E3 | Yn M | Yn F | Yn M | Yn W | Yg W | Yg F | Yg W | Yg W | Yn W | Yn E2 | Yg Wd | Yg Wd | Yg Wd | Yg M | Yn Wd | Yn Wd | Yn Wd | Yn M | Yg F | Yg E1 | 20 |
| 21 | Yg W | Yg F | Yn M | Yn W | Yg W | Yg F | Yg W | Yg W | Yn W | Yn E2 | Yn W | Yn E4 | Yg Wd | Yg M | Yn Wd | Yn Wd | Yn Wd | Yn M | Yg F | Yg E1 | Yg F | Yg E3 | Yn F | Yn F | 21 |
| 22 | Yn W | Yn E2 | Yg W | Yg W | Yn W | Yn E2 | Yn W | Yn E4 | Yg Wd | Yg M | Yg Wd | Yg Wd | Yn Wd | Yn M | Yg F | Yg E1 | Yg F | Yg E3 | Yn F | Yn F | Yn F | Yn W | Yg E | Yg F | 22 |
| 23 | Yg Wd | Yg M | Yn W | Yn E4 | Yg Wd | Yg M | Yg Wd | Yg Wd | Yn Wd | Yn M | Yn Wd | Yn Wd | Yg F | Yg E3 | Yn F | Yn F | Yn F | Yn W | Yg E | Yg F | Yg E | Yg W | Yn E | Yn E2 | 23 |
| 24 | Yn Wd | Yn M | Yg Wd | Yg Wd | Yn Wd | Yn M | Yn Wd | Yn Wd | Yg F | Yg E3 | Yg F | Yg E1 | Yn F | Yn W | Yg E | Yg F | Yg E | Yg W | Yn E | Yn E2 | Yn E | Yn E4 | Yg M | Yg M | 24 |
| 25 | Yg F | Yg E3 | Yn Wd | Yn Wd | Yg F | Yg E3 | Yg F | Yg E1 | Yn F | Yn W | Yn F | Yn F | Yg E | Yg W | Yn E | Yn E2 | Yn E | Yn E4 | Yg M | Yg M | Yg M | Yg Wd | Yn M | Yn M | 25 |
| 26 | Yn F | Yn W | Yg F | Yg E1 | Yn F | Yn W | Yn F | Yn F | Yg E | Yg W | Yg E | Yg F | Yn E | Yn E4 | Yg M | Yg M | Yg M | Yg Wd | Yn M | Yn M | Yn M | Yn Wd | Yg W | Yg E3 | 26 |
| 27 | Yg E | Yg W | Yn F | Yn F | Yg E | Yg W | Yg E | Yg F | Yn E | Yn E4 | Yn E | Yn E2 | Yg M | Yg Wd | Yn M | Yn M | Yn M | Yn Wd | Yg W | Yg E3 | Yg W | Yg E1 | Yn W | Yn W | 27 |
| 28 | Yn E | Yn E4 | Yg E | Yg F | Yn E | Yn E4 | Yn E | Yn E2 | Yg M | Yg Wd | Yg M | Yg M | Yn M | Yn Wd | Yg W | Yg E3 | Yg W | Yg E1 | Yn W | Yn W | Yn W | Yn F | Yg Wd | Yg W | 28 |
| 29 | Yg M | Yg Wd | Yn E | Yn E2 | Yg M | Yg Wd | Yg M | Yg M | Yn M | Yn Wd | Yn M | Yn M | Yg W | Yg E1 | Yn W | Yn W | Yn W | Yn F | Yg Wd | Yg W | Yg Wd | Yg F | Yn Wd | Yn E4 | 29 |
| 30 | | | Yg M | Yg M | Yn M | Yn Wd | Yn M | Yn M | Yg W | Yg E1 | Yg W | Yg E3 | Yn W | Yn F | Yg Wd | Yg W | Yg Wd | Yg F | Yn Wd | Yn E4 | Yn Wd | Yn E2 | Yg F | Yg Wd | 30 |
| 31 | | | Yn M | Yn M | | | Yg W | Yg E3 | | | Yn W | Yn W | Yg Wd | Yg F | | | Yn Wd | Yn E2 | | | Yg F | Yg M | Yn F | Yn Wd | 31 |
| 1 | Yn M | Yn Wd | Yg W | Yg E3 | Yg W | Yg E1 | Yn W | Yn W | Yn W | Yn F | Yg Wd | Yg W | Yn Wd | Yn E2 | Yn Wd | Yn E4 | Yg F | Yg M | Yg F | Yg Wd | Yn F | Yn M | Yg E | Yg E1 | 1 |
| 2 | Yg W | Yg E1 | Yn W | Yn W | Yn W | Yn F | Yg Wd | Yg W | Yg Wd | Yg F | Yn Wd | Yn E4 | Yg F | Yg M | Yg F | Yg Wd | Yn F | Yn M | Yn F | Yn Wd | Yg E | Yg E3 | Yn E | Yn F | 2 |
| 3 | Yn W | Yn F | Yg Wd | Yg W | Yg Wd | Yg F | Yn Wd | Yn E4 | Yn Wd | Yn E2 | Yg F | Yg Wd | Yn F | Yn M | Yn F | Yn Wd | Yg E | Yg E3 | Yg E | Yg E1 | Yn E | Yn W | Yg M | Yg F | 3 |
| 4 | Yg Wd | Yg F | Yn Wd | Yn E4 | Yn Wd | Yn E2 | Yg F | Yg Wd | Yg F | Yg M | Yn F | Yn Wd | Yg E | Yg E3 | Yg E | Yg E1 | Yn E | Yn W | Yn E | Yn F | Yg M | Yg W | | | 4 |
| 5 | | | | | | | | | Yn F | Yn M | Yg E | Yg E1 | Yn E | Yn W | Yn E | Yn F | Yg M | Yg W | Yg M | Yg F | | | | | 5 |
| 6 | | | | | | | | | Yg E | Yg E3 | Yn E | Yn F | Yg M | Yg W | Yg M | Yg F | Yn M | Yn E4 | Yn M | Yn E2 | | | | | 6 |
| 7 | | | | | | | | | | | | | | | Yn M | Yn E2 | | | | | | | | | 7 |
| 8 | | | | | | | | | | | | | | | | | | | | | | | | | 8 |

# YEAR OF THE OX

| | H | E | H | E | H | E | H | E | H | E | H | E | H | E | H | E | H | E | H | E | H | E | H | E | |
|---|---|---|---|---|---|---|---|---|---|---|---|---|---|---|---|---|---|---|---|---|---|---|---|---|---|
| YEAR | YEAR<br>Yn W | Yn E4 | 1973 | | | | | | | | | | | | | | | | | | | | 1974 | | |
| MONTH | 4 Feb - 5 Mar | | 6 Mar - 4 Apr | | 5 Apr - 4 May | | 5 May - 5 June | | 6 June - 6 Jul | | 7 Jul - 7 Aug | | 8 Aug - 7 Sep | | 8 Sep - 7 Oct | | 8 Oct - 6 Nov | | 7 Nov - 6 Dec | | 7 Dec - 5 Jan | | 6 Jan - 3 Feb | | |
| | Yg Wd | Yg Wd | Yn Wd | Yn Wd | Yg F | Yg E1 | Yn F | Yn F | Yg E | Yg F | Yn E | Yn E2 | Yg M | Yg M | Yn M | Yn M | Yg W | Yg E3 | Yn W | Yn W | Yg Wd | Yg W | Yn Wd | Yn E4 | |
| Starting time | 1st day | Mid-pt | 1st day | Mid-pt | 1st day | Mid-pt | 1st day | Mid-pt | 1st day | Mid-pt | 1st day | Mid-pt | 1st day | Mid-pt | 1st day | Mid-pt | 1st day | Mid-pt | 1st day | Mid-pt | 1st day | Mid-pt | 1st day | Mid-pt | |
| Date | 4 | 19 | 6 | 21 | 5 | 20 | 5 | 21 | 6 | 21 | 7 | 23 | 8 | 23 | 8 | 23 | 8 | 23 | 7 | 22 | 7 | 22 | 6 | 20 | |
| Hour | 0704 | 0301 | 0113 | 0213 | 0614 | 1330 | 2347 | 1254 | 0407 | 2101 | 1428 | 0756 | 0013 | 1454 | 0300 | 1221 | 1827 | 2130 | 2128 | 1854 | 1411 | 0808 | 0120 | 1846 | |
| DATE 4 | Yn M | Yn E2 | | | | | | | | | | | | | | | | | | | | | | | 4 |
| 5 | Yg W | Yg M | | | Yn M | Yn E2 | Yn M | Yn E4 | | | | | | | | | | | | | | | | | 5 |
| 6 | Yn W | Yn M | Yn M | Yn E4 | Yg W | Yg M | Yg W | Yg Wd | Yn W | Yn M | | | | | | | | | | | | | Yn F | Yn E2 | 6 |
| 7 | Yg Wd | Yg E3 | Yg W | Yg Wd | Yn W | Yn M | Yn W | Yn Wd | Yg Wd | Yg E3 | Yg Wd | Yg E1 | | | | | | | Yn F | Yn E2 | Yn F | Yn E4 | Yg E | Yg M | 7 |
| 8 | Yn Wd | Yn W | Yn W | Yn Wd | Yg Wd | Yg E3 | Yg Wd | Yg E1 | Yn Wd | Yn W | Yn Wd | Yn F | Yg F | Yg W | Yn F | Yn E2 | Yn F | Yn E4 | Yg E | Yg M | Yg E | Yg Wd | Yn E | Yn M | 8 |
| 9 | Yg F | Yg W | Yg Wd | Yg E1 | Yn Wd | Yn W | Yn Wd | Yn F | Yg F | Yg W | Yg F | Yg F | Yn F | Yn E4 | Yg E | Yg M | Yg E | Yg Wd | Yn E | Yn M | Yn E | Yn Wd | Yg M | Yg E3 | 9 |
| 10 | Yn F | Yn E4 | Yn Wd | Yn F | Yg F | Yg W | Yg F | Yg F | Yn F | Yn E4 | Yn F | Yn E2 | Yg E | Yg Wd | Yn E | Yn M | Yn E | Yn Wd | Yg M | Yg E3 | Yg M | Yg E1 | Yn M | Yn W | 10 |
| 11 | Yg E | Yg Wd | Yg F | Yg F | Yn F | Yn E4 | Yn F | Yn E2 | Yg E | Yg Wd | Yg E | Yg M | Yn E | Yn Wd | Yg M | Yg E3 | Yg M | Yg E1 | Yn M | Yn W | Yn M | Yn F | Yg W | Yg W | 11 |
| 12 | Yn E | Yn Wd | Yn F | Yn E2 | Yg E | Yg Wd | Yg E | Yg M | Yn E | Yn Wd | Yn E | Yn M | Yg M | Yg E1 | Yn M | Yn W | Yn M | Yn F | Yg W | Yg W | Yg W | Yg F | Yn W | Yn E4 | 12 |
| 13 | Yg M | Yg E1 | Yg E | Yg M | Yn E | Yn Wd | Yn E | Yn M | Yg M | Yg E1 | Yg M | Yg E3 | Yn M | Yn F | Yg W | Yg W | Yg W | Yg F | Yn W | Yn E4 | Yn W | Yn E2 | Yg Wd | Yg Wd | 13 |
| 14 | Yn M | Yn F | Yn E | Yn M | Yg M | Yg E1 | Yg M | Yg E3 | Yn M | Yn F | Yn M | Yn W | Yg W | Yg F | Yn W | Yn E4 | Yn W | Yn E2 | Yg Wd | Yg Wd | Yg Wd | Yg M | Yn Wd | Yn Wd | 14 |
| 15 | Yg W | Yg F | Yg M | Yg E3 | Yn M | Yn F | Yn M | Yn W | Yg W | Yg F | Yg W | Yg W | Yn W | Yn E2 | Yg Wd | Yg Wd | Yg Wd | Yg M | Yn Wd | Yn Wd | Yn Wd | Yn M | Yg F | Yg E1 | 15 |
| 16 | Yn W | Yn E2 | Yn M | Yn W | Yg W | Yg F | Yg W | Yg W | Yn W | Yn E2 | Yn W | Yn E4 | Yg Wd | Yg M | Yn Wd | Yn Wd | Yn Wd | Yn M | Yg F | Yg E1 | Yg F | Yg E3 | Yn F | Yn F | 16 |
| 17 | Yg Wd | Yg M | Yg W | Yg W | Yn W | Yn E2 | Yn W | Yn E4 | Yg Wd | Yg M | Yg Wd | Yg Wd | Yn Wd | Yn M | Yg F | Yg E1 | Yg F | Yg E3 | Yn F | Yn F | Yn F | Yn W | Yg E | Yg F | 17 |
| 18 | Yn Wd | Yn M | Yn W | Yn E4 | Yg Wd | Yg M | Yg Wd | Yg Wd | Yn Wd | Yn M | Yn Wd | Yn Wd | Yg F | Yg E3 | Yn F | Yn F | Yn F | Yn W | Yg E | Yg F | Yg E | Yg W | Yn E | Yn E2 | 18 |
| 19 | Yg F | Yg E3 | Yg Wd | Yg Wd | Yn Wd | Yn M | Yn Wd | Yn Wd | Yg F | Yg E3 | Yg F | Yg E1 | Yn F | Yn W | Yg E | Yg F | Yg E | Yg W | Yn E | Yn E2 | Yn E | Yn E4 | Yg M | Yg M | 19 |
| 20 | Yn F | Yn W | Yn Wd | Yn Wd | Yg F | Yg E3 | Yg F | Yg E1 | Yn F | Yn W | Yn F | Yn F | Yg E | Yg W | Yn E | Yn E2 | Yn E | Yn E4 | Yg M | Yg M | Yg M | Yg Wd | Yn M | Yn M | 20 |
| 21 | Yg E | Yg W | Yg F | Yg E1 | Yn F | Yn W | Yn F | Yn F | Yg E | Yg W | Yg E | Yg F | Yn E | Yn E4 | Yg M | Yg M | Yg M | Yg Wd | Yn M | Yn M | Yn M | Yn Wd | Yg W | Yg E3 | 21 |
| 22 | Yn E | Yn E4 | Yn F | Yn F | Yg E | Yg W | Yg E | Yg F | Yn E | Yn E4 | Yn E | Yn E2 | Yg M | Yg Wd | Yn M | Yn M | Yn M | Yn Wd | Yg W | Yg E3 | Yg W | Yg E1 | Yn W | Yn W | 22 |
| 23 | Yg M | Yg Wd | Yg E | Yg F | Yn E | Yn E4 | Yn E | Yn E2 | Yg M | Yg Wd | Yg M | Yg M | Yn M | Yn Wd | Yg W | Yg E3 | Yg W | Yg E1 | Yn W | Yn W | Yn W | Yn F | Yg Wd | Yg W | 23 |
| 24 | Yn M | Yn Wd | Yn E | Yn E2 | Yg M | Yg Wd | Yg M | Yg M | Yn M | Yn Wd | Yn M | Yn M | Yg W | Yg E1 | Yn W | Yn W | Yn W | Yn F | Yg Wd | Yg W | Yg Wd | Yg F | Yn Wd | Yn E4 | 24 |
| 25 | Yg W | Yg E1 | Yg M | Yg M | Yn M | Yn Wd | Yn M | Yn M | Yg W | Yg E1 | Yg W | Yg E3 | Yn W | Yn F | Yg Wd | Yg W | Yg Wd | Yg F | Yn Wd | Yn E4 | Yn Wd | Yn E2 | Yg F | Yg Wd | 25 |
| 26 | Yn W | Yn F | Yn M | Yn M | Yg W | Yg E1 | Yg W | Yg E3 | Yn W | Yn F | Yn W | Yn W | Yg Wd | Yg F | Yn Wd | Yn E4 | Yn Wd | Yn E2 | Yg F | Yg Wd | Yg F | Yg M | Yn F | Yn Wd | 26 |
| 27 | Yg Wd | Yg F | Yg W | Yg E3 | Yn W | Yn F | Yn W | Yn W | Yg Wd | Yg F | Yg Wd | Yg W | Yn Wd | Yn E2 | Yg F | Yg Wd | Yg F | Yg M | Yn F | Yn Wd | Yn F | Yn M | Yg E | Yg E1 | 27 |
| 28 | Yn Wd | Yn E2 | Yn W | Yn W | Yg Wd | Yg F | Yg Wd | Yg W | Yn Wd | Yn E2 | Yn Wd | Yn E4 | Yg F | Yg M | Yn F | Yn Wd | Yn F | Yn M | Yg E | Yg E1 | Yg E | Yg E3 | Yn E | Yn F | 28 |
| 29 | | | Yg Wd | Yg W | Yn Wd | Yn E2 | Yn Wd | Yn E4 | Yg F | Yg M | Yg F | Yg Wd | Yn F | Yn M | Yg E | Yg E1 | Yg E | Yg E3 | Yn E | Yn F | Yn E | Yn W | Yg M | Yg F | 29 |
| 30 | | | Yn Wd | Yn E4 | Yg F | Yg M | Yg F | Yg Wd | Yn F | Yn M | Yn F | Yn Wd | Yg E | Yg E3 | Yn E | Yn F | Yn E | Yn W | Yg M | Yg F | Yg M | Yg W | Yn M | Yn E2 | 30 |
| 31 | | | Yg F | Yg Wd | | | Yn F | Yn Wd | | | Yg E | Yg E1 | Yn E | Yn W | | | Yg M | Yg W | | | Yn M | Yn E4 | Yg W | Yg M | 31 |
| 1 | Yg F | Yg M | Yn F | Yn Wd | Yn F | Yn M | Yg E | Yg E1 | Yg E | Yg E3 | Yn E | Yn F | Yg M | Yg W | Yg M | Yg F | Yn M | Yn E4 | Yn M | Yn E2 | Yg W | Yg Wd | Yn W | Yn M | 1 |
| 2 | Yn F | Yn M | Yg E | Yg E1 | Yg E | Yg E3 | Yn E | Yn F | Yn E | Yn W | Yg M | Yg F | Yn M | Yn E4 | Yn M | Yn E2 | Yg W | Yg Wd | Yg W | Yg M | Yn W | Yn Wd | Yg Wd | Yg E3 | 2 |
| 3 | Yg E | Yg E3 | Yn E | Yn F | Yn E | Yn W | Yg M | Yg F | Yg M | Yg W | Yn M | Yn E2 | Yg W | Yg Wd | Yg W | Yg M | Yn W | Yn Wd | Yn W | Yn M | Yg Wd | Yg E1 | Yn Wd | Yn W | 3 |
| 4 | Yn E | Yn W | Yg M | Yg F | Yg M | Yg W | Yn M | Yn E2 | Yn M | Yn E4 | Yg W | Yg M | Yn W | Yn Wd | Yn W | Yn M | Yg Wd | Yg E1 | Yg Wd | Yg E3 | Yn Wd | Yn F | | | 4 |
| 5 | Yg M | Yg W | | | | | Yg W | Yg M | Yg W | Yg Wd | Yn W | Yn M | Yg Wd | Yg E1 | Yg Wd | Yg E3 | Yn Wd | Yn F | Yn Wd | Yn W | Yg F | Yg F | | | 5 |
| 6 | | | | | | | | | Yn W | Yn Wd | Yg Wd | Yg E3 | Yn Wd | Yn F | Yn Wd | Yn W | Yg F | Yg F | Yg F | Yg W | | | | | 6 |
| 7 | | | | | | | | | | | Yn Wd | Yn W | Yg F | Yg F | Yg F | Yg W | | | | | | | | | 7 |
| 8 | | | | | | | | | | | | | | | | | | | | | | | | | 8 |

# YEAR OF THE TIGER

| | H | E | H | E | H | E | H | E | H | E | H | E | H | E | H | E | H | E | H | E | H | E | H | E | |
|---|---|---|---|---|---|---|---|---|---|---|---|---|---|---|---|---|---|---|---|---|---|---|---|---|---|
| YEAR | YEAR<br>Yg Wd | Yg Wd | 1974 | | | | | | | | | | | | | | | | | | | | 1975 | | |
| MONTH | 4 Feb - 5 Mar | | 6 Mar - 4 Apr | | 5 Apr - 5 May | | 6 May - 5 June | | 6 June - 6 Jul | | 7 Jul - 7 Aug | | 8 Aug - 7 Sep | | 8 Sep - 8 Oct | | 9 Oct - 7 Nov | | 8 Nov - 6 Dec | | 7 Dec - 5 Jan | | 6 Jan - 3 Feb | | |
| | Yg F | Yg Wd | Yn F | Yn Wd | Yg E | Yg E1 | Yn E | Yn F | Yg M | Yg F | Yn M | Yn E2 | Yg W | Yg M | Yn W | Yn M | Yg Wd | Yg E3 | Yn Wd | Yn W | Yg F | Yg W | Yn F | Yn E4 | |
| Starting time | 1st day | Mid-pt | 1st day | Mid-pt | 1st day | Mid-pt | 1st day | Mid-pt | 1st day | Mid-pt | 1st day | Mid-pt | 1st day | Mid-pt | 1st day | Mid-pt | 1st day | Mid-pt | 1st day | Mid-pt | 1st day | Mid-pt | 1st day | Mid-pt | |
| Date | 4 | 19 | 6 | 21 | 5 | 20 | 6 | 21 | 6 | 22 | 7 | 23 | 8 | 23 | 8 | 23 | 9 | 24 | 8 | 23 | 7 | 22 | 6 | 21 | |
| Hour | 1300 | 0859 | 0707 | 0807 | 1205 | 1919 | 0534 | 1836 | 0952 | 0238 | 2013 | 1330 | 0557 | 2029 | 0845 | 1759 | 0015 | 0311 | 0318 | 0039 | 2005 | 1356 | 0718 | 0036 | |
| DATE 4 | Yg F | Yg W | | | | | | | | | | | | | | | | | | | | | | | 4 |
| 5 | Yn F | Yn E4 | | | Yg F | Yg W | | | | | | | | | | | | | | | | | | | 5 |
| 6 | Yg E | Yg Wd | Yg F | Yg F | Yn F | Yn E4 | Yn F | Yn E2 | Yg E | Yg Wd | | | | | | | | | | | | | Yg W | Yg W | 6 |
| 7 | Yn E | Yn Wd | Yn F | Yn E2 | Yg E | Yg Wd | Yg E | Yg M | Yn E | Yn Wd | Yn E | Yn M | | | | | | | | | Yg W | Yg F | Yn W | Yn E4 | 7 |
| 8 | Yg M | Yg E1 | Yg E | Yg M | Yn E | Yn Wd | Yn E | Yn M | Yg M | Yg E1 | Yg M | Yg E3 | Yn M | Yn F | Yg W | Yg W | | | Yn W | Yn E4 | Yn W | Yn E2 | Yg Wd | Yg Wd | 8 |
| 9 | Yn M | Yn F | Yn E | Yn M | Yg M | Yg E1 | Yg M | Yg E3 | Yn M | Yn F | Yn M | Yn W | Yg W | Yg F | Yn W | Yn E4 | Yn W | Yn E2 | Yg Wd | Yg Wd | Yg Wd | Yg M | Yn Wd | Yn Wd | 9 |
| 10 | Yg W | Yg F | Yg M | Yg E3 | Yn M | Yn F | Yn M | Yn W | Yg W | Yg F | Yg W | Yg W | Yn W | Yn E2 | Yg Wd | Yg Wd | Yg Wd | Yg M | Yn Wd | Yn Wd | Yn Wd | Yn M | Yg F | Yg E1 | 10 |
| 11 | Yn W | Yn E2 | Yn M | Yn W | Yg W | Yg F | Yg W | Yg W | Yn W | Yn E2 | Yn W | Yn E4 | Yg Wd | Yg M | Yn Wd | Yn Wd | Yn Wd | Yn M | Yg F | Yg E1 | Yg F | Yg E3 | Yn F | Yn F | 11 |
| 12 | Yg Wd | Yg M | Yg W | Yg W | Yn W | Yn E2 | Yn W | Yn E4 | Yg Wd | Yg M | Yg Wd | Yg Wd | Yn Wd | Yn M | Yg F | Yg E1 | Yg F | Yg E3 | Yn F | Yn F | Yn F | Yn W | Yg E | Yg F | 12 |
| 13 | Yn Wd | Yn M | Yn W | Yn E4 | Yg Wd | Yg M | Yg Wd | Yg Wd | Yn Wd | Yn M | Yn Wd | Yn Wd | Yg F | Yg E3 | Yn F | Yn F | Yn F | Yn W | Yg E | Yg F | Yg E | Yg W | Yn E | Yn E2 | 13 |
| 14 | Yg F | Yg E3 | Yg Wd | Yg Wd | Yn Wd | Yn M | Yn Wd | Yn Wd | Yg F | Yg E3 | Yg F | Yg E1 | Yn F | Yn W | Yg E | Yg F | Yg E | Yg W | Yn E | Yn E2 | Yn E | Yn E4 | Yg M | Yg M | 14 |
| 15 | Yn F | Yn W | Yn Wd | Yn Wd | Yg F | Yg E3 | Yg F | Yg E1 | Yn F | Yn W | Yn F | Yn F | Yg E | Yg W | Yn E | Yn E2 | Yn E | Yn E4 | Yg M | Yg M | Yg M | Yg Wd | Yn M | Yn M | 15 |
| 16 | Yg E | Yg W | Yg F | Yg E1 | Yn F | Yn W | Yn F | Yn F | Yg E | Yg W | Yg E | Yg F | Yn E | Yn E4 | Yg M | Yg M | Yg M | Yg Wd | Yn M | Yn M | Yn M | Yn Wd | Yg W | Yg E3 | 16 |
| 17 | Yn E | Yn E4 | Yn F | Yn F | Yg E | Yg W | Yg E | Yg F | Yn E | Yn E4 | Yn E | Yn E2 | Yg M | Yg Wd | Yn M | Yn M | Yn M | Yn Wd | Yg W | Yg E3 | Yg W | Yg E1 | Yn W | Yn W | 17 |
| 18 | Yg M | Yg Wd | Yg E | Yg F | Yn E | Yn E4 | Yn E | Yn E2 | Yg M | Yg Wd | Yg M | Yg M | Yn M | Yn Wd | Yg W | Yg E3 | Yg W | Yg E1 | Yn W | Yn W | Yn W | Yn F | Yg Wd | Yg W | 18 |
| 19 | Yn M | Yn Wd | Yn E | Yn E2 | Yg M | Yg Wd | Yg M | Yg M | Yn M | Yn Wd | Yn M | Yn M | Yg W | Yg E1 | Yn W | Yn W | Yn W | Yn F | Yg Wd | Yg W | Yg Wd | Yg F | Yn Wd | Yn E4 | 19 |
| 20 | Yg W | Yg E1 | Yg M | Yg M | Yn M | Yn Wd | Yn M | Yn M | Yg W | Yg E1 | Yg W | Yg E3 | Yn W | Yn F | Yg Wd | Yg W | Yg Wd | Yg F | Yn Wd | Yn E4 | Yn Wd | Yn E2 | Yg F | Yg Wd | 20 |
| 21 | Yn W | Yn F | Yn M | Yn M | Yg W | Yg E1 | Yg W | Yg E3 | Yn W | Yn F | Yn W | Yn W | Yg Wd | Yg F | Yn Wd | Yn E4 | Yn Wd | Yn E2 | Yg F | Yg Wd | Yg F | Yg M | Yn F | Yn Wd | 21 |
| 22 | Yg Wd | Yg F | Yg W | Yg E3 | Yn W | Yn F | Yn W | Yn W | Yg Wd | Yg F | Yg Wd | Yg W | Yn Wd | Yn E2 | Yg F | Yg Wd | Yg F | Yg M | Yn F | Yn Wd | Yn F | Yn M | Yg E | Yg E1 | 22 |
| 23 | Yn Wd | Yn E2 | Yn W | Yn W | Yg Wd | Yg F | Yg Wd | Yg W | Yn Wd | Yn E2 | Yn Wd | Yn E4 | Yg F | Yg M | Yn F | Yn Wd | Yn F | Yn M | Yg E | Yg E1 | Yg E | Yg E3 | Yn E | Yn F | 23 |
| 24 | Yg F | Yg M | Yg Wd | Yg W | Yn Wd | Yn E2 | Yn Wd | Yn E4 | Yg F | Yg M | Yg F | Yg Wd | Yn F | Yn M | Yg E | Yg E1 | Yg E | Yg E3 | Yn E | Yn F | Yn E | Yn W | Yg M | Yg F | 24 |
| 25 | Yn F | Yn M | Yn Wd | Yn E4 | Yg F | Yg M | Yg F | Yg Wd | Yn F | Yn M | Yn F | Yn Wd | Yg E | Yg E3 | Yn E | Yn F | Yn E | Yn W | Yg M | Yg F | Yg M | Yg W | Yn M | Yn E2 | 25 |
| 26 | Yg E | Yg E3 | Yg F | Yg Wd | Yn F | Yn M | Yn F | Yn Wd | Yg E | Yg E3 | Yg E | Yg E1 | Yn E | Yn W | Yg M | Yg F | Yg M | Yg W | Yn M | Yn E2 | Yn M | Yn E4 | Yg W | Yg M | 26 |
| 27 | Yn E | Yn W | Yn F | Yn Wd | Yg E | Yg E3 | Yg E | Yg E1 | Yn E | Yn W | Yn E | Yn F | Yg M | Yg W | Yn M | Yn E2 | Yn M | Yn E4 | Yg W | Yg M | Yg W | Yg Wd | Yn W | Yn M | 27 |
| 28 | Yg M | Yg W | Yg E | Yg E1 | Yn E | Yn W | Yn E | Yn F | Yg M | Yg W | Yg M | Yg F | Yn M | Yn E4 | Yg W | Yg M | Yg W | Yg Wd | Yn W | Yn M | Yn W | Yn Wd | Yg Wd | Yg E3 | 28 |
| 29 | | | Yn E | Yn F | Yg M | Yg W | Yg M | Yg F | Yn M | Yn E4 | Yn M | Yn E2 | Yg W | Yg Wd | Yn W | Yn M | Yn W | Yn Wd | Yg Wd | Yg E3 | Yg Wd | Yg E1 | Yn Wd | Yn W | 29 |
| 30 | | | Yg M | Yg F | Yn M | Yn E4 | Yn M | Yn E2 | Yg W | Yg Wd | Yg W | Yg M | Yn W | Yn Wd | Yg Wd | Yg E3 | Yg Wd | Yg E1 | Yn Wd | Yn W | Yn Wd | Yn F | Yg F | Yg W | 30 |
| 31 | | | Yn M | Yn E2 | | | Yg W | Yg M | | | Yn W | Yn M | Yg Wd | Yg E1 | | | Yn Wd | Yn F | | | Yg F | Yg F | Yn F | Yn E4 | 31 |
| 1 | Yn M | Yn E4 | Yg W | Yg M | Yg W | Yg Wd | Yn W | Yn M | Yn W | Yn Wd | Yg Wd | Yg E3 | Yn Wd | Yn F | Yn Wd | Yn W | Yg F | Yg F | Yg F | Yg W | Yn F | Yn E2 | Yg E | Yg Wd | 1 |
| 2 | Yg W | Yg Wd | Yn W | Yn M | Yn W | Yn Wd | Yg Wd | Yg E3 | Yg Wd | Yg E1 | Yn Wd | Yn W | Yg F | Yg F | Yg F | Yg W | Yn F | Yn E2 | Yn F | Yn E4 | Yg E | Yg M | Yn E | Yn Wd | 2 |
| 3 | Yn W | Yn Wd | Yg Wd | Yg E3 | Yg Wd | Yg E1 | Yn Wd | Yn W | Yn Wd | Yn F | Yg F | Yg W | Yn F | Yn E2 | Yn F | Yn E4 | Yg E | Yg M | Yg E | Yg Wd | Yn E | Yn M | Yg M | Yg E1 | 3 |
| 4 | Yg Wd | Yg E1 | Yn Wd | Yn W | Yn Wd | Yn F | Yg F | Yg W | Yg F | Yg F | Yn F | Yn E4 | Yg E | Yg M | Yg E | Yg Wd | Yn E | Yn M | Yn E | Yn Wd | Yg M | Yg E3 | | | 4 |
| 5 | Yn Wd | Yn F | | | Yg F | Yg F | Yn F | Yn E4 | Yn F | Yn E2 | Yg E | Yg Wd | Yn E | Yn M | Yn E | Yn Wd | Yg M | Yg E3 | Yg M | Yg E1 | Yn M | Yn W | | | 5 |
| 6 | | | | | | | | | Yg E | Yg M | Yn E | Yn Wd | Yg M | Yg E3 | Yg M | Yg E1 | Yn M | Yn W | Yn M | Yn F | | | | | 6 |
| 7 | | | | | | | | | | | Yg M | Yg E1 | Yn M | Yn W | Yn M | Yn F | Yg W | Yg W | | | | | | | 7 |
| 8 | | | | | | | | | | | | | | | Yg W | Yg F | | | | | | | | | 8 |

# YEAR OF THE RABBIT

| | H | E | H | E | H | E | H | E | H | E | H | E | H | E | H | E | H | E | H | E | H | E | H | E | |
|---|---|---|---|---|---|---|---|---|---|---|---|---|---|---|---|---|---|---|---|---|---|---|---|---|---|
| YEAR | YEAR Yn Wd | Yn Wd | 1975 | | | | | | | | | | | | | | | | | | 1976 | | | | |
| MONTH | 4 Feb - 5 Mar | | 6 Mar - 4 Apr | | 5 Apr - 5 May | | 6 May - 5 June | | 6 June - 7 Jul | | 8 Jul - 7 Aug | | 8 Aug - 7 Sep | | 8 Sep - 8 Oct | | 9 Oct - 7 Nov | | 8 Nov - 7 Dec | | 8 Dec - 5 Jan | | 6 Jan - 4 Feb | | |
| | Yg E | Yg Wd | Yn E | Yn Wd | Yg M | Yg E1 | Yn M | Yn F | Yg W | Yg F | Yn W | Yn E2 | Yg Wd | Yg M | Yn Wd | Yn M | Yg F | Yg E3 | Yn F | Yn W | Yg E | Yg W | Yn E | Yn E4 | |
| Starting time | 1st day | Mid-pt | 1st day | Mid-pt | 1st day | Mid-pt | 1st day | Mid-pt | 1st day | Mid-pt | 1st day | Mid-pt | 1st day | Mid-pt | 1st day | Mid-pt | 1st day | Mid-pt | 1st day | Mid-pt | 1st day | Mid-pt | 1st day | Mid-pt | |
| Date | 4 | 19 | 6 | 21 | 5 | 21 | 6 | 22 | 6 | 22 | 8 | 23 | 8 | 24 | 8 | 23 | 9 | 24 | 8 | 23 | 8 | 22 | 6 | 21 | |
| Hour | 1859 | 1450 | 1306 | 1357 | 1802 | 0107 | 1127 | 0024 | 1542 | 0827 | 0200 | 1922 | 1145 | 0224 | 1433 | 2355 | 0602 | 0906 | 0903 | 0631 | 0146 | 1946 | 1258 | 0625 | |
| DATE 4 | Yn M | Yn F | | | | | | | | | | | | | | | | | | | | | | | 4 |
| 5 | Yg W | Yg F | | | Yn M | Yn F | | | | | | | | | | | | | | | | | | | 5 |
| 6 | Yn W | Yn E2 | Yn M | Yn W | Yg W | Yg F | Yg W | Yg W | Yn W | Yn E2 | | | | | | | | | | | | | Yn F | Yn F | 6 |
| 7 | Yg Wd | Yg M | Yg W | Yg W | Yn W | Yn E2 | Yn W | Yn E4 | Yg Wd | Yg M | | | | | | | | | | | | | Yg E | Yg F | 7 |
| 8 | Yn Wd | Yn M | Yn W | Yn E4 | Yg Wd | Yg M | Yg Wd | Yg Wd | Yn Wd | Yn M | Yn Wd | Yn Wd | Yg F | Yg E3 | Yn F | Yn F | | | Yg E | Yg F | Yg E | Yg W | Yn E | Yn E2 | 8 |
| 9 | Yg F | Yg E3 | Yg Wd | Yg Wd | Yn Wd | Yn M | Yn Wd | Yn Wd | Yg F | Yg E3 | Yg F | Yg E1 | Yn F | Yn W | Yg E | Yg F | Yg E | Yg W | Yn E | Yn E2 | Yn E | Yn E4 | Yg M | Yg M | 9 |
| 10 | Yn F | Yn W | Yn Wd | Yn Wd | Yg F | Yg E3 | Yg F | Yg E1 | Yn F | Yn W | Yn F | Yn F | Yg E | Yg W | Yn E | Yn E2 | Yn E | Yn E4 | Yg M | Yg M | Yg M | Yg Wd | Yn M | Yn M | 10 |
| 11 | Yg E | Yg W | Yg F | Yg E1 | Yn F | Yn W | Yn F | Yn F | Yg E | Yg W | Yg E | Yg F | Yn E | Yn E4 | Yg M | Yg M | Yg M | Yg Wd | Yn M | Yn M | Yn M | Yn Wd | Yg W | Yg E3 | 11 |
| 12 | Yn E | Yn E4 | Yn F | Yn F | Yg E | Yg W | Yg E | Yg F | Yn E | Yn E4 | Yn E | Yn E2 | Yg M | Yg Wd | Yn M | Yn M | Yn M | Yn Wd | Yg W | Yg E3 | Yg W | Yg E1 | Yn W | Yn W | 12 |
| 13 | Yg M | Yg Wd | Yg E | Yg F | Yn E | Yn E4 | Yn E | Yn E2 | Yg M | Yg Wd | Yg M | Yg M | Yn M | Yn Wd | Yg W | Yg E3 | Yg W | Yg E1 | Yn W | Yn W | Yn W | Yn F | Yg Wd | Yg W | 13 |
| 14 | Yn M | Yn Wd | Yn E | Yn E2 | Yg M | Yg Wd | Yg M | Yg M | Yn M | Yn Wd | Yn M | Yn M | Yg W | Yg E1 | Yn W | Yn W | Yn W | Yn F | Yg Wd | Yg W | Yg Wd | Yg F | Yn Wd | Yn E4 | 14 |
| 15 | Yg W | Yg E1 | Yg M | Yg M | Yn M | Yn Wd | Yn M | Yn M | Yg W | Yg E1 | Yg W | Yg E3 | Yn W | Yn F | Yg Wd | Yg W | Yg Wd | Yg F | Yn Wd | Yn E4 | Yn Wd | Yn E2 | Yg F | Yg Wd | 15 |
| 16 | Yn W | Yn F | Yn M | Yn M | Yg W | Yg E1 | Yg W | Yg E3 | Yn W | Yn F | Yn W | Yn W | Yg Wd | Yg F | Yn Wd | Yn E4 | Yn Wd | Yn E2 | Yg F | Yg Wd | Yg F | Yg M | Yn F | Yn Wd | 16 |
| 17 | Yg Wd | Yg F | Yg W | Yg E3 | Yn W | Yn F | Yn W | Yn W | Yg Wd | Yg F | Yg Wd | Yg W | Yn Wd | Yn E2 | Yg F | Yg Wd | Yg F | Yg M | Yn F | Yn Wd | Yn F | Yn M | Yg E | Yg E1 | 17 |
| 18 | Yn Wd | Yn E2 | Yn W | Yn W | Yg Wd | Yg F | Yg Wd | Yg W | Yn Wd | Yn E2 | Yn Wd | Yn E4 | Yg F | Yg M | Yn F | Yn Wd | Yn F | Yn M | Yg E | Yg E1 | Yg E | Yg E3 | Yn E | Yn F | 18 |
| 19 | Yg F | Yg M | Yg Wd | Yg W | Yn Wd | Yn E2 | Yn Wd | Yn E4 | Yg F | Yg M | Yg F | Yg Wd | Yn F | Yn M | Yg E | Yg E1 | Yg E | Yg E3 | Yn E | Yn F | Yn E | Yn W | Yg M | Yg F | 19 |
| 20 | Yn F | Yn M | Yn Wd | Yn E4 | Yg F | Yg M | Yg F | Yg Wd | Yn F | Yn M | Yn F | Yn Wd | Yg E | Yg E3 | Yn E | Yn F | Yn E | Yn W | Yg M | Yg F | Yg M | Yg W | Yn M | Yn E2 | 20 |
| 21 | Yg E | Yg E3 | Yg F | Yg Wd | Yn F | Yn M | Yn F | Yn Wd | Yg E | Yg E3 | Yg E | Yg E1 | Yn E | Yn W | Yg M | Yg F | Yg M | Yg W | Yn M | Yn E2 | Yn M | Yn E4 | Yg W | Yg M | 21 |
| 22 | Yn E | Yn W | Yn F | Yn Wd | Yg E | Yg E3 | Yg E | Yg E1 | Yn E | Yn W | Yn E | Yn F | Yg M | Yg W | Yn M | Yn E2 | Yn M | Yn E4 | Yg W | Yg M | Yg W | Yg Wd | Yn W | Yn M | 22 |
| 23 | Yg M | Yg W | Yg E | Yg E1 | Yn E | Yn W | Yn E | Yn F | Yg M | Yg W | Yg M | Yg F | Yn M | Yn E4 | Yg W | Yg M | Yg W | Yg Wd | Yn W | Yn M | Yn W | Yn Wd | Yg Wd | Yg E3 | 23 |
| 24 | Yn M | Yn E4 | Yn E | Yn F | Yg M | Yg W | Yg M | Yg F | Yn M | Yn E4 | Yn M | Yn E2 | Yg W | Yg Wd | Yn W | Yn M | Yn W | Yn Wd | Yg Wd | Yg E3 | Yg Wd | Yg E1 | Yn Wd | Yn W | 24 |
| 25 | Yg W | Yg Wd | Yg M | Yg F | Yn M | Yn E4 | Yn M | Yn E2 | Yg W | Yg Wd | Yg W | Yg M | Yn W | Yn Wd | Yg Wd | Yg E3 | Yg Wd | Yg E1 | Yn Wd | Yn W | Yn Wd | Yn F | Yg F | Yg W | 25 |
| 26 | Yn W | Yn Wd | Yn M | Yn E2 | Yg W | Yg Wd | Yg W | Yg M | Yn W | Yn Wd | Yn W | Yn M | Yg Wd | Yg E1 | Yn Wd | Yn W | Yn Wd | Yn F | Yg F | Yg W | Yg F | Yg F | Yn F | Yn E4 | 26 |
| 27 | Yg Wd | Yg E1 | Yg W | Yg M | Yn W | Yn Wd | Yn W | Yn M | Yg Wd | Yg E1 | Yg Wd | Yg E3 | Yn Wd | Yn F | Yg F | Yg W | Yg F | Yg F | Yn F | Yn E4 | Yn F | Yn E2 | Yg E | Yg Wd | 27 |
| 28 | Yn Wd | Yn F | Yn W | Yn M | Yg Wd | Yg E1 | Yg Wd | Yg E3 | Yn Wd | Yn F | Yn Wd | Yn W | Yg F | Yg F | Yn F | Yn E4 | Yn F | Yn E2 | Yg E | Yg Wd | Yg E | Yg M | Yn E | Yn Wd | 28 |
| 29 | | | Yg Wd | Yg E3 | Yn Wd | Yn F | Yn Wd | Yn W | Yg F | Yg F | Yg F | Yg W | Yn F | Yn E2 | Yg E | Yg Wd | Yg E | Yg M | Yn E | Yn Wd | Yn E | Yn M | Yg M | Yg E1 | 29 |
| 30 | | | Yn Wd | Yn W | Yg F | Yg F | Yg F | Yg W | Yn F | Yn E2 | Yn F | Yn E4 | Yg E | Yg M | Yn E | Yn Wd | Yn E | Yn M | Yg M | Yg E1 | Yg M | Yg E3 | Yn M | Yn F | 30 |
| 31 | | | Yg F | Yg W | | | Yn F | Yn E4 | | | Yg E | Yg Wd | Yn E | Yn M | | | Yg M | Yg E3 | | | Yn M | Yn W | Yg W | Yg F | 31 |
| 1 | Yg F | Yg F | Yn F | Yn E4 | Yn F | Yn E2 | Yg E | Yg Wd | Yg E | Yg M | Yn E | Yn Wd | Yg M | Yg E3 | Yg M | Yg E1 | Yn M | Yn W | Yn M | Yn F | Yg W | Yg W | Yn W | Yn E2 | 1 |
| 2 | Yn F | Yn E2 | Yg E | Yg Wd | Yg E | Yg M | Yn E | Yn Wd | Yn E | Yn M | Yg M | Yg E1 | Yn M | Yn W | Yn M | Yn F | Yg W | Yg W | Yg W | Yg F | Yn W | Yn E4 | Yg Wd | Yg M | 2 |
| 3 | Yg E | Yg M | Yn E | Yn Wd | Yn E | Yn M | Yg M | Yg E1 | Yg M | Yg E3 | Yn M | Yn F | Yg W | Yg W | Yg W | Yg F | Yn W | Yn E4 | Yn W | Yn E2 | Yg Wd | Yg Wd | Yn Wd | Yn M | 3 |
| 4 | Yn E | Yn M | Yg M | Yg E1 | Yg M | Yg E3 | Yn M | Yn F | Yn M | Yn W | Yg W | Yg F | Yn W | Yn E4 | Yn W | Yn E2 | Yg Wd | Yg Wd | Yg Wd | Yg M | Yn Wd | Yn Wd | Yg F | Yg E3 | 4 |
| 5 | Yg M | Yg E3 | | | Yn M | Yn W | Yg W | Yg F | Yg W | Yg W | Yn W | Yn E2 | Yg Wd | Yg Wd | Yg Wd | Yg M | Yn Wd | Yn Wd | Yn Wd | Yn M | Yg F | Yg E1 | | | 5 |
| 6 | | | | | | | | | Yn W | Yn E4 | Yg Wd | Yg M | Yn Wd | Yn Wd | Yn Wd | Yn M | Yg F | Yg E1 | Yg F | Yg E3 | | | | | 6 |
| 7 | | | | | | | | | Yg Wd | Yg Wd | Yn Wd | Yn M | Yg F | Yg E1 | Yg F | Yg E3 | Yn F | Yn F | Yn F | Yn W | | | | | 7 |
| 8 | | | | | | | | | | | | | | | Yn F | Yn W | | | | | | | | | 8 |

# YEAR OF THE DRAGON

| | H | E | H | E | H | E | H | E | H | E | H | E | H | E | H | E | H | E | H | E | H | E | H | E | |
|---|---|---|---|---|---|---|---|---|---|---|---|---|---|---|---|---|---|---|---|---|---|---|---|---|---|
| YEAR | YEAR | | 1976 | | | | | | | | | | | | | | | | | | | | 1977 | | |
| | Yg F | Yg E1 | | | | | | | | | | | | | | | | | | | | | | | |
| MONTH | 5 Feb - 4 Mar | | 5 Mar - 3 Apr | | 4 Apr - 4 May | | 5 May - 4 June | | 5 June - 6 Jul | | 7 Jul - 6 Aug | | 7 Aug - 6 Sep | | 7 Sep - 7 Oct | | 8 Oct - 6 Nov | | 7 Nov - 6 Dec | | 7 Dec - 4 Jan | | 5 Jan - 3 Feb | | |
| | Yg M | Yg Wd | Yn M | Yn Wd | Yg W | Yg E1 | Yn W | Yn F | Yg Wd | Yg F | Yn Wd | Yn E2 | Yg F | Yg M | Yn F | Yn M | Yg E | Yg E3 | Yn E | Yn W | Yg M | Yg W | Yn M | Yn E4 | |
| Starting time | 1st day | Mid-pt | 1st day | Mid-pt | 1st day | Mid-pt | 1st day | Mid-pt | 1st day | Mid-pt | 1st day | Mid-pt | 1st day | Mid-pt | 1st day | Mid-pt | 1st day | Mid-pt | 1st day | Mid-pt | 1st day | Mid-pt | 1st day | Mid-pt | |
| Date | 5 | 19 | 5 | 20 | 4 | 20 | 5 | 21 | 5 | 21 | 7 | 23 | 7 | 23 | 7 | 23 | 8 | 23 | 7 | 22 | 7 | 22 | 5 | 20 | |
| Hour | 0040 | 2040 | 1848 | 1950 | 2347 | 0703 | 1715 | 0621 | 2131 | 1424 | 0751 | 0119 | 1739 | 0819 | 2028 | 0548 | 1158 | 1458 | 1459 | 1222 | 0741 | 0135 | 1851 | 1215 | |
| DATE 4 | | | | | Yg F | Yg E3 | | | | | | | | | | | | | | | | | | | 4 |
| 5 | Yn F | Yn W | Yg F | Yg E1 | Yn F | Yn W | Yn F | Yn F | Yg E | Yg W | | | | | | | | | | | | | Yg W | Yg E3 | 5 |
| 6 | Yg E | Yg W | Yn F | Yn F | Yg E | Yg W | Yg E | Yg F | Yn E | Yn E4 | | | | | | | | | | | | | Yn W | Yn W | 6 |
| 7 | Yn E | Yn E4 | Yg E | Yg F | Yn E | Yn E4 | Yn E | Yn E2 | Yg M | Yg Wd | Yg M | Yg M | Yn M | Yn Wd | Yg W | Yg E3 | | | Yn W | Yn W | Yn W | Yn F | Yg Wd | Yg W | 7 |
| 8 | Yg M | Yg Wd | Yn E | Yn E2 | Yg M | Yg Wd | Yg M | Yg M | Yn M | Yn Wd | Yn M | Yn M | Yg W | Yg E1 | Yn W | Yn W | Yn W | Yn F | Yg Wd | Yg W | Yg Wd | Yg F | Yn Wd | Yn E4 | 8 |
| 9 | Yn M | Yn Wd | Yg M | Yg M | Yn M | Yn Wd | Yn M | Yn M | Yg W | Yg E1 | Yg W | Yg E3 | Yn W | Yn F | Yg Wd | Yg W | Yg Wd | Yg F | Yn Wd | Yn E4 | Yn Wd | Yn E2 | Yg F | Yg Wd | 9 |
| 10 | Yg W | Yg E1 | Yn M | Yn M | Yg W | Yg E1 | Yg W | Yg E3 | Yn W | Yn F | Yn W | Yn W | Yg Wd | Yg F | Yn Wd | Yn E4 | Yn Wd | Yn E2 | Yg F | Yg Wd | Yg F | Yg M | Yn F | Yn Wd | 10 |
| 11 | Yn W | Yn F | Yg W | Yg E3 | Yn W | Yn F | Yn W | Yn W | Yg Wd | Yg F | Yg Wd | Yg W | Yn Wd | Yn E2 | Yg F | Yg Wd | Yg F | Yg M | Yn F | Yn Wd | Yn F | Yn M | Yg E | Yg E1 | 11 |
| 12 | Yg Wd | Yg F | Yn W | Yn W | Yg Wd | Yg F | Yg Wd | Yg W | Yn Wd | Yn E2 | Yn Wd | Yn E4 | Yg F | Yg M | Yn F | Yn Wd | Yn F | Yn M | Yg E | Yg E1 | Yg E | Yg E3 | Yn E | Yn F | 12 |
| 13 | Yn Wd | Yn E2 | Yg Wd | Yg W | Yn Wd | Yn E2 | Yn Wd | Yn E4 | Yg F | Yg M | Yg F | Yg Wd | Yn F | Yn M | Yg E | Yg E1 | Yg E | Yg E3 | Yn E | Yn F | Yn E | Yn W | Yg M | Yg F | 13 |
| 14 | Yg F | Yg M | Yn Wd | Yn E4 | Yg F | Yg M | Yg F | Yg Wd | Yn F | Yn M | Yn F | Yn Wd | Yg E | Yg E3 | Yn E | Yn F | Yn E | Yn W | Yg M | Yg F | Yg M | Yg W | Yn M | Yn E2 | 14 |
| 15 | Yn F | Yn M | Yg F | Yg Wd | Yn F | Yn M | Yn F | Yn Wd | Yg E | Yg E3 | Yg E | Yg E1 | Yn E | Yn W | Yg M | Yg F | Yg M | Yg W | Yn M | Yn E2 | Yn M | Yn E4 | Yg W | Yg M | 15 |
| 16 | Yg E | Yg E3 | Yn F | Yn Wd | Yg E | Yg E3 | Yg E | Yg E1 | Yn E | Yn W | Yn E | Yn F | Yg M | Yg W | Yn M | Yn E2 | Yn M | Yn E4 | Yg W | Yg M | Yg W | Yg Wd | Yn W | Yn M | 16 |
| 17 | Yn E | Yn W | Yg E | Yg E1 | Yn E | Yn W | Yn E | Yn F | Yg M | Yg W | Yg M | Yg F | Yn M | Yn E4 | Yg W | Yg M | Yg W | Yg Wd | Yn W | Yn M | Yn W | Yn Wd | Yg Wd | Yg E3 | 17 |
| 18 | Yg M | Yg W | Yn E | Yn F | Yg M | Yg W | Yg M | Yg F | Yn M | Yn E4 | Yn M | Yn E2 | Yg W | Yg Wd | Yn W | Yn M | Yn W | Yn Wd | Yg Wd | Yg E3 | Yg Wd | Yg E1 | Yn Wd | Yn W | 18 |
| 19 | Yn M | Yn E4 | Yg M | Yg F | Yn M | Yn E4 | Yn M | Yn E2 | Yg W | Yg Wd | Yg W | Yg M | Yn W | Yn Wd | Yg Wd | Yg E3 | Yg Wd | Yg E1 | Yn Wd | Yn W | Yn Wd | Yn F | Yg F | Yg W | 19 |
| 20 | Yg W | Yg Wd | Yn M | Yn E2 | Yg W | Yg Wd | Yg W | Yg M | Yn W | Yn Wd | Yn W | Yn M | Yg Wd | Yg E1 | Yn Wd | Yn W | Yn Wd | Yn F | Yg F | Yg W | Yg F | Yg F | Yn F | Yn E4 | 20 |
| 21 | Yn W | Yn Wd | Yg W | Yg M | Yn W | Yn Wd | Yn W | Yn M | Yg Wd | Yg E1 | Yg Wd | Yg E3 | Yn Wd | Yn F | Yg F | Yg W | Yg F | Yg F | Yn F | Yn E4 | Yn F | Yn E2 | Yg E | Yg Wd | 21 |
| 22 | Yg Wd | Yg E1 | Yn W | Yn M | Yg Wd | Yg E1 | Yg Wd | Yg E3 | Yn Wd | Yn F | Yn Wd | Yn W | Yg F | Yg F | Yn F | Yn E4 | Yn F | Yn E2 | Yg E | Yg Wd | Yg E | Yg M | Yn E | Yn Wd | 22 |
| 23 | Yn Wd | Yn F | Yg Wd | Yg E3 | Yn Wd | Yn F | Yn Wd | Yn W | Yg F | Yg F | Yg F | Yg W | Yn F | Yn E2 | Yg E | Yg Wd | Yg E | Yg M | Yn E | Yn Wd | Yn E | Yn M | Yg M | Yg E1 | 23 |
| 24 | Yg F | Yg F | Yn Wd | Yn W | Yg F | Yg F | Yg F | Yg W | Yn F | Yn E2 | Yn F | Yn E4 | Yg E | Yg M | Yn E | Yn Wd | Yn E | Yn M | Yg M | Yg E1 | Yg M | Yg E3 | Yn M | Yn F | 24 |
| 25 | Yn F | Yn E2 | Yg F | Yg W | Yn F | Yn E2 | Yn F | Yn E4 | Yg E | Yg M | Yg E | Yg Wd | Yn E | Yn M | Yg M | Yg E1 | Yg M | Yg E3 | Yn M | Yn F | Yn M | Yn W | Yg W | Yg F | 25 |
| 26 | Yg E | Yg M | Yn F | Yn E4 | Yg E | Yg M | Yg E | Yg Wd | Yn E | Yn M | Yn E | Yn Wd | Yg M | Yg E3 | Yn M | Yn F | Yn M | Yn W | Yg W | Yg F | Yg W | Yg W | Yn W | Yn E2 | 26 |
| 27 | Yn E | Yn M | Yg E | Yg Wd | Yn E | Yn M | Yn E | Yn Wd | Yg M | Yg E3 | Yg M | Yg E1 | Yn M | Yn W | Yg W | Yg F | Yg W | Yg W | Yn W | Yn E2 | Yn W | Yn E4 | Yg Wd | Yg M | 27 |
| 28 | Yg M | Yg E3 | Yn E | Yn Wd | Yg M | Yg E3 | Yg M | Yg E1 | Yn M | Yn W | Yn M | Yn F | Yg W | Yg W | Yn W | Yn E2 | Yn W | Yn E4 | Yg Wd | Yg M | Yg Wd | Yg Wd | Yn Wd | Yn M | 28 |
| 29 | Yn M | Yn W | Yg M | Yg E1 | Yn M | Yn W | Yn M | Yn F | Yg W | Yg W | Yg W | Yg F | Yn W | Yn E4 | Yg Wd | Yg M | Yg Wd | Yg Wd | Yn Wd | Yn M | Yn Wd | Yn Wd | Yg F | Yg E3 | 29 |
| 30 | | | Yn M | Yn F | Yg W | Yg W | Yg W | Yg F | Yn W | Yn E4 | Yn W | Yn E2 | Yg Wd | Yg Wd | Yn Wd | Yn M | Yn Wd | Yn Wd | Yg F | Yg E3 | Yg F | Yg E1 | Yn F | Yn W | 30 |
| 31 | | | Yg W | Yg F | | | Yn W | Yn E2 | | | Yg Wd | Yg M | Yn Wd | Yn Wd | | | Yg F | Yg E1 | | | Yn F | Yn F | Yg E | Yg W | 31 |
| 1 | Yg W | Yg W | Yn W | Yn E2 | Yn W | Yn E4 | Yg Wd | Yg M | Yg Wd | Yg Wd | Yn Wd | Yn M | Yg F | Yg E1 | Yg F | Yg E3 | Yn F | Yn F | Yn F | Yn W | Yg E | Yg F | Yn E | Yn E4 | 1 |
| 2 | Yn W | Yn E4 | Yg Wd | Yg M | Yg Wd | Yg Wd | Yn Wd | Yn M | Yn Wd | Yn Wd | Yg F | Yg E3 | Yn F | Yn F | Yn F | Yn W | Yg E | Yg F | Yg E | Yg W | Yn E | Yn E2 | Yg M | Yg Wd | 2 |
| 3 | Yg Wd | Yg Wd | Yn Wd | Yn M | Yn Wd | Yn Wd | Yg F | Yg E3 | Yg F | Yg E1 | Yn F | Yn W | Yg E | Yg F | Yg E | Yg W | Yn E | Yn E2 | Yn E | Yn E4 | Yg M | Yg M | Yn M | Yn Wd | 3 |
| 4 | Yn Wd | Yn Wd | | | Yg F | Yg E1 | Yn F | Yn W | Yn F | Yn F | Yg E | Yg W | Yn E | Yn E2 | Yn E | Yn E4 | Yg M | Yg M | Yg M | Yg Wd | Yn M | Yn M | | | 4 |
| 5 | | | | | | | | | Yg E | Yg F | Yn E | Yn E4 | Yg M | Yg M | Yg M | Yg Wd | Yn M | Yn M | Yn M | Yn Wd | | | | | 5 |
| 6 | | | | | | | | | Yn E | Yn E2 | Yg M | Yg Wd | Yn M | Yn M | Yn M | Yn Wd | Yg W | Yg E3 | Yg W | Yg E1 | | | | | 6 |
| 7 | | | | | | | | | | | | | | | Yg W | Yg E1 | | | | | | | | | 7 |
| 8 | | | | | | | | | | | | | | | | | | | | | | | | | 8 |

# YEAR OF THE SNAKE

| | H | E | H | E | H | E | H | E | H | E | H | E | H | E | H | E | H | E | H | E | H | E | H | E | |
|---|---|---|---|---|---|---|---|---|---|---|---|---|---|---|---|---|---|---|---|---|---|---|---|---|---|
| YEAR | YEAR Yn F | Yn F | 1977 | | | | | | | | | | | | | | | | | | | | 1978 | | |
| MONTH | 4 Feb - 5 Mar | | 6 Mar - 4 Apr | | 5 Apr - 4 May | | 5 May - 5 June | | 6 June - 6 Jul | | 7 Jul - 6 Aug | | 7 Aug - 7 Sep | | 8 Sep - 7 Oct | | 8 Oct - 6 Nov | | 7 Nov - 6 Dec | | 7 Dec - 5 Jan | | 6 Jan - 3 Feb | | |
| | Yg W | Yg Wd | Yn W | Yn Wd | Yg Wd | Yg E1 | Yn Wd | Yn F | Yg F | Yg F | Yn F | Yn E2 | Yg E | Yg M | Yn E | Yn M | Yg M | Yg E3 | Yn M | Yn W | Yg W | Yg W | Yn W | Yn E4 | |
| Starting time | 1st day | Mid-pt | 1st day | Mid-pt | 1st day | Mid-pt | 1st day | Mid-pt | 1st day | Mid-pt | 1st day | Mid-pt | 1st day | Mid-pt | 1st day | Mid-pt | 1st day | Mid-pt | 1st day | Mid-pt | 1st day | Mid-pt | 1st day | Mid-pt | |
| Date | 4 | 19 | 6 | 21 | 5 | 20 | 5 | 21 | 6 | 21 | 7 | 23 | 7 | 23 | 8 | 23 | 8 | 23 | 7 | 22 | 7 | 22 | 6 | 20 | |
| Hour | 0634 | 0231 | 0044 | 0143 | 0546 | 1257 | 2316 | 1215 | 0332 | 2014 | 1348 | 0704 | 2330 | 1400 | 0216 | 1130 | 1744 | 2041 | 2046 | 1807 | 1331 | 0724 | 0043 | 1804 | |
| DATE 4 | Yg W | Yg E1 | | | | | | | | | | | | | | | | | | | | | | | 4 |
| 5 | Yn W | Yn F | | | Yg W | Yg E1 | Yg W | Yg E3 | | | | | | | | | | | | | | | | | 5 |
| 6 | Yg Wd | Yg F | Yg W | Yg E3 | Yn W | Yn F | Yn W | Yn W | Yg Wd | Yg F | | | | | | | | | | | | | Yg E | Yg E1 | 6 |
| 7 | Yn Wd | Yn E2 | Yn W | Yn W | Yg Wd | Yg F | Yg Wd | Yg W | Yn Wd | Yn E2 | Yn Wd | Yn E4 | Yg F | Yg M | | | | | Yg E | Yg E1 | Yg E | Yg E3 | Yn E | Yn F | 7 |
| 8 | Yg F | Yg M | Yg Wd | Yg W | Yn Wd | Yn E2 | Yn Wd | Yn E4 | Yg F | Yg M | Yg F | Yg Wd | Yn F | Yn M | Yg E | Yg E1 | Yg E | Yg E3 | Yn E | Yn F | Yn E | Yn W | Yg M | Yg F | 8 |
| 9 | Yn F | Yn M | Yn Wd | Yn E4 | Yg F | Yg M | Yg F | Yg Wd | Yn F | Yn M | Yn F | Yn Wd | Yg E | Yg E3 | Yn E | Yn F | Yn E | Yn W | Yg M | Yg F | Yg M | Yg W | Yn M | Yn E2 | 9 |
| 10 | Yg E | Yg E3 | Yg F | Yg Wd | Yn F | Yn M | Yn F | Yn Wd | Yg E | Yg E3 | Yg E | Yg E1 | Yn E | Yn W | Yg M | Yg F | Yg M | Yg W | Yn M | Yn E2 | Yn M | Yn E4 | Yg W | Yg M | 10 |
| 11 | Yn E | Yn W | Yn F | Yn Wd | Yg E | Yg E3 | Yg E | Yg E1 | Yn E | Yn W | Yn E | Yn F | Yg M | Yg W | Yn M | Yn E2 | Yn M | Yn E4 | Yg W | Yg M | Yg W | Yg Wd | Yn W | Yn M | 11 |
| 12 | Yg M | Yg W | Yg E | Yg E1 | Yn E | Yn W | Yn E | Yn F | Yg M | Yg W | Yg M | Yg F | Yn M | Yn E4 | Yg W | Yg M | Yg W | Yg Wd | Yn W | Yn M | Yn W | Yn Wd | Yg Wd | Yg E3 | 12 |
| 13 | Yn M | Yn E4 | Yn E | Yn F | Yg M | Yg W | Yg M | Yg F | Yn M | Yn E4 | Yn M | Yn E2 | Yg W | Yg Wd | Yn W | Yn M | Yn W | Yn Wd | Yg Wd | Yg E3 | Yg Wd | Yg E1 | Yn Wd | Yn W | 13 |
| 14 | Yg W | Yg Wd | Yg M | Yg F | Yn M | Yn E4 | Yn M | Yn E2 | Yg W | Yg Wd | Yg W | Yg M | Yn W | Yn Wd | Yg Wd | Yg E3 | Yg Wd | Yg E1 | Yn Wd | Yn W | Yn Wd | Yn F | Yg F | Yg W | 14 |
| 15 | Yn W | Yn Wd | Yn M | Yn E2 | Yg W | Yg Wd | Yg W | Yg M | Yn W | Yn Wd | Yn W | Yn M | Yg Wd | Yg E1 | Yn Wd | Yn W | Yn Wd | Yn F | Yg F | Yg W | Yg F | Yg F | Yn F | Yn E4 | 15 |
| 16 | Yg Wd | Yg E1 | Yg W | Yg M | Yn W | Yn Wd | Yn W | Yn M | Yg Wd | Yg E1 | Yg Wd | Yg E3 | Yn Wd | Yn F | Yg F | Yg W | Yg F | Yg F | Yn F | Yn E4 | Yn F | Yn E2 | Yg E | Yg Wd | 16 |
| 17 | Yn Wd | Yn F | Yn W | Yn M | Yg Wd | Yg E1 | Yg Wd | Yg E3 | Yn Wd | Yn F | Yn Wd | Yn W | Yg F | Yg F | Yn F | Yn E4 | Yn F | Yn E2 | Yg E | Yg Wd | Yg E | Yg M | Yn E | Yn Wd | 17 |
| 18 | Yg F | Yg F | Yg Wd | Yg E3 | Yn Wd | Yn F | Yn Wd | Yn W | Yg F | Yg F | Yg F | Yg W | Yn F | Yn E2 | Yg E | Yg Wd | Yg E | Yg M | Yn E | Yn Wd | Yn E | Yn M | Yg M | Yg E1 | 18 |
| 19 | Yn F | Yn E2 | Yn Wd | Yn W | Yg F | Yg F | Yg F | Yg W | Yn F | Yn E2 | Yn F | Yn E4 | Yg E | Yg M | Yn E | Yn Wd | Yn E | Yn M | Yg M | Yg E1 | Yg M | Yg E3 | Yn M | Yn F | 19 |
| 20 | Yg E | Yg M | Yg F | Yg W | Yn F | Yn E2 | Yn F | Yn E4 | Yg E | Yg M | Yg E | Yg Wd | Yn E | Yn M | Yg M | Yg E1 | Yg M | Yg E3 | Yn M | Yn F | Yn M | Yn W | Yg W | Yg F | 20 |
| 21 | Yn E | Yn M | Yn F | Yn E4 | Yg E | Yg M | Yg E | Yg Wd | Yn E | Yn M | Yn E | Yn Wd | Yg M | Yg E3 | Yn M | Yn F | Yn M | Yn W | Yg W | Yg F | Yg W | Yg W | Yn W | Yn E2 | 21 |
| 22 | Yg M | Yg E3 | Yg E | Yg Wd | Yn E | Yn M | Yn E | Yn Wd | Yg M | Yg E3 | Yg M | Yg E1 | Yn M | Yn W | Yg W | Yg F | Yg W | Yg W | Yn W | Yn E2 | Yn W | Yn E4 | Yg Wd | Yg M | 22 |
| 23 | Yn M | Yn W | Yn E | Yn Wd | Yg M | Yg E3 | Yg M | Yg E1 | Yn M | Yn W | Yn M | Yn F | Yg W | Yg W | Yn W | Yn E2 | Yn W | Yn E4 | Yg Wd | Yg M | Yg Wd | Yg Wd | Yn Wd | Yn M | 23 |
| 24 | Yg W | Yg W | Yg M | Yg E1 | Yn M | Yn W | Yn M | Yn F | Yg W | Yg W | Yg W | Yg F | Yn W | Yn E4 | Yg Wd | Yg M | Yg Wd | Yg Wd | Yn Wd | Yn M | Yn Wd | Yn Wd | Yg F | Yg E3 | 24 |
| 25 | Yn W | Yn E4 | Yn M | Yn F | Yg W | Yg W | Yg W | Yg F | Yn W | Yn E4 | Yn W | Yn E2 | Yg Wd | Yg Wd | Yn Wd | Yn M | Yn Wd | Yn Wd | Yg F | Yg E3 | Yg F | Yg E1 | Yn F | Yn W | 25 |
| 26 | Yg Wd | Yg Wd | Yg W | Yg F | Yn W | Yn E4 | Yn W | Yn E2 | Yg Wd | Yg Wd | Yg Wd | Yg M | Yn Wd | Yn Wd | Yg F | Yg E3 | Yg F | Yg E1 | Yn F | Yn W | Yn F | Yn F | Yg E | Yg W | 26 |
| 27 | Yn Wd | Yn Wd | Yn W | Yn E2 | Yg Wd | Yg Wd | Yg Wd | Yg M | Yn Wd | Yn Wd | Yn Wd | Yn M | Yg F | Yg E1 | Yn F | Yn W | Yn F | Yn F | Yg E | Yg W | Yg E | Yg F | Yn E | Yn E4 | 27 |
| 28 | Yg F | Yg E1 | Yg Wd | Yg M | Yn Wd | Yn Wd | Yn Wd | Yn M | Yg F | Yg E1 | Yg F | Yg E3 | Yn F | Yn F | Yg E | Yg W | Yg E | Yg F | Yn E | Yn E4 | Yn E | Yn E2 | Yg M | Yg Wd | 28 |
| 29 | | | Yn Wd | Yn M | Yg F | Yg E1 | Yg F | Yg E3 | Yn F | Yn F | Yn F | Yn W | Yg E | Yg F | Yn E | Yn E4 | Yn E | Yn E2 | Yg M | Yg Wd | Yg M | Yg M | Yn M | Yn Wd | 29 |
| 30 | | | Yg F | Yg E3 | Yn F | Yn F | Yn F | Yn W | Yg E | Yg F | Yg E | Yg W | Yn E | Yn E2 | Yg M | Yg Wd | Yg M | Yg M | Yn M | Yn Wd | Yn M | Yn M | Yg W | Yg E1 | 30 |
| 31 | | | Yn F | Yn W | | | Yg E | Yg W | | | Yn E | Yn E4 | Yg M | Yg M | | | Yn M | Yn M | | | Yg W | Yg E3 | Yn W | Yn F | 31 |
| 1 | Yn F | Yn F | Yg E | Yg W | Yg E | Yg F | Yn E | Yn E4 | Yn E | Yn E2 | Yg M | Yg Wd | Yn M | Yn M | Yn M | Yn Wd | Yg W | Yg E3 | Yg W | Yg E1 | Yn W | Yn W | Yg Wd | Yg F | 1 |
| 2 | Yg E | Yg F | Yn E | Yn E4 | Yn E | Yn E2 | Yg M | Yg Wd | Yg M | Yg M | Yn M | Yn Wd | Yg W | Yg E3 | Yg W | Yg E1 | Yn W | Yn W | Yn W | Yn F | Yg Wd | Yg W | Yn Wd | Yn E2 | 2 |
| 3 | Yn E | Yn E2 | Yg M | Yg Wd | Yg M | Yg M | Yn M | Yn Wd | Yn M | Yn M | Yg W | Yg E1 | Yn W | Yn W | Yn W | Yn F | Yg Wd | Yg W | Yg Wd | Yg F | Yn Wd | Yn E4 | Yg F | Yg M | 3 |
| 4 | Yg M | Yg M | Yn M | Yn Wd | Yn M | Yn M | Yg W | Yg E1 | Yg W | Yg E3 | Yn W | Yn F | Yg Wd | Yg W | Yg Wd | Yg F | Yn Wd | Yn E4 | Yn Wd | Yn E2 | Yg F | Yg Wd | | | 4 |
| 5 | Yn M | Yn M | | | | | Yn W | Yn F | Yn W | Yn W | Yg Wd | Yg F | Yn Wd | Yn E4 | Yn Wd | Yn E2 | Yg F | Yg Wd | Yg F | Yg M | Yn F | Yn Wd | | | 5 |
| 6 | | | | | | | | | Yg Wd | Yg W | Yn Wd | Yn E2 | Yg F | Yg Wd | Yg F | Yg M | Yn F | Yn Wd | Yn F | Yn M | | | | | 6 |
| 7 | | | | | | | | | | | | | Yn F | Yn Wd | Yn F | Yn M | | | | | | | | | 7 |
| 8 | | | | | | | | | | | | | | | | | | | | | | | | | 8 |

# YEAR OF THE HORSE

| | H | E | H | E | H | E | H | E | H | E | H | E | H | E | H | E | H | E | H | E | H | E | H | E |
|---|---|---|---|---|---|---|---|---|---|---|---|---|---|---|---|---|---|---|---|---|---|---|---|---|
| YEAR | YEAR YgE | YgF | 1978 | | | | | | | | | | | | | | | | | | | | 1979 | |
| MONTH | 4 Feb - 5 Mar | | 6 Mar - 4 Apr | | 5 Apr - 5 May | | 6 May - 5 June | | 6 June - 6 Jul | | 7 Jul - 7 Aug | | 8 Aug - 7 Sep | | 8 Sep - 7 Oct | | 8 Oct - 7 Nov | | 8 Nov - 6 Dec | | 7 Dec - 5 Jan | | 6 Jan - 3 Feb | |
| | Yg Wd | Yg Wd | Yn Wd | Yn Wd | Yg F | Yg E1 | Yn F | Yn F | Yg E | Yg F | Yn E | Yn E2 | Yg M | Yg M | Yn M | Yn M | Yg W | Yg E3 | Yn W | Yn W | Yg Wd | Yg W | Yn Wd | Yn E4 |
| Starting time | 1st day | Mid-pt | 1st day | Mid-pt | 1st day | Mid-pt | 1st day | Mid-pt | 1st day | Mid-pt | 1st day | Mid-pt | 1st day | Mid-pt | 1st day | Mid-pt | 1st day | Mid-pt | 1st day | Mid-pt | 1st day | Mid-pt | 1st day | Mid-pt |
| Date | 4 | 19 | 6 | 21 | 5 | 20 | 6 | 21 | 6 | 22 | 7 | 23 | 8 | 23 | 8 | 23 | 8 | 24 | 8 | 23 | 7 | 22 | 6 | 21 |
| Hour | 1227 | 0821 | 0638 | 0734 | 1139 | 1850 | 0509 | 1809 | 0923 | 0210 | 1937 | 1300 | 0518 | 1957 | 0803 | 1726 | 2331 | 0237 | 0234 | 0005 | 1920 | 1321 | 0632 | 0000 |
| DATE 4 | Yn F | Yn M | | | | | | | | | | | | | | | | | | | | | | |
| 5 | Yg E | Yg E3 | | | Yn F | Yn M | | | | | | | | | | | | | | | | | | |
| 6 | Yn E | Yn W | Yn F | Yn Wd | Yg E | Yg E3 | Yg E | Yg E1 | Yn E | Yn W | | | | | | | | | | | | | Yn W | Yn M |
| 7 | Yg M | Yg W | Yg E | Yg E1 | Yn E | Yn W | Yn E | Yn F | Yg M | Yg W | Yg M | Yg F | | | | | | | | | Yn W | Yn Wd | Yg Wd | Yg E3 |
| 8 | Yn M | Yn E4 | Yn E | Yn F | Yg M | Yg W | Yg M | Yg F | Yn M | Yn E4 | Yn M | Yn E2 | Yg W | Yg Wd | Yn W | Yn M | Yn W | Yn Wd | Yg Wd | Yg E3 | Yg Wd | Yg E1 | Yn Wd | Yn W |
| 9 | Yg W | Yg Wd | Yg M | Yg F | Yn M | Yn E4 | Yn M | Yn E2 | Yg W | Yg Wd | Yg W | Yg M | Yn W | Yn Wd | Yg Wd | Yg E3 | Yg Wd | Yg E1 | Yn Wd | Yn W | Yn Wd | Yn F | Yg F | Yg W |
| 10 | Yn W | Yn Wd | Yn M | Yn E2 | Yg W | Yg Wd | Yg W | Yg M | Yn W | Yn Wd | Yn W | Yn M | Yg Wd | Yg E1 | Yn Wd | Yn W | Yn Wd | Yn F | Yg F | Yg W | Yg F | Yg F | Yn F | Yn E4 |
| 11 | Yg Wd | Yg E1 | Yg W | Yg M | Yn W | Yn Wd | Yn W | Yn M | Yg Wd | Yg E1 | Yg Wd | Yg E3 | Yn Wd | Yn F | Yg F | Yg W | Yg F | Yg F | Yn F | Yn E4 | Yn F | Yn E2 | Yg E | Yg Wd |
| 12 | Yn Wd | Yn F | Yn W | Yn M | Yg Wd | Yg E1 | Yg Wd | Yg E3 | Yn Wd | Yn F | Yn Wd | Yn W | Yg F | Yg F | Yn F | Yn E4 | Yn F | Yn E2 | Yg E | Yg Wd | Yg E | Yg M | Yn E | Yn Wd |
| 13 | Yg F | Yg F | Yg Wd | Yg E3 | Yn Wd | Yn F | Yn Wd | Yn W | Yg F | Yg F | Yg F | Yg W | Yn F | Yn E2 | Yg E | Yg Wd | Yg E | Yg M | Yn E | Yn Wd | Yn E | Yn M | Yg M | Yg E1 |
| 14 | Yn F | Yn E2 | Yn Wd | Yn W | Yg F | Yg F | Yg F | Yg W | Yn F | Yn E2 | Yn F | Yn E4 | Yg E | Yg M | Yn E | Yn Wd | Yn E | Yn M | Yg M | Yg E1 | Yg M | Yg E3 | Yn M | Yn F |
| 15 | Yg E | Yg M | Yg F | Yg W | Yn F | Yn E2 | Yn F | Yn E4 | Yg E | Yg M | Yg E | Yg Wd | Yn E | Yn M | Yg M | Yg E1 | Yg M | Yg E3 | Yn M | Yn F | Yn M | Yn W | Yg W | Yg F |
| 16 | Yn E | Yn M | Yn F | Yn E4 | Yg E | Yg M | Yg E | Yg Wd | Yn E | Yn M | Yn E | Yn Wd | Yg M | Yg E3 | Yn M | Yn F | Yn M | Yn W | Yg W | Yg F | Yg W | Yg W | Yn W | Yn E2 |
| 17 | Yg M | Yg E3 | Yg E | Yg Wd | Yn E | Yn M | Yn E | Yn Wd | Yg M | Yg E3 | Yg M | Yg E1 | Yn M | Yn W | Yg W | Yg F | Yg W | Yg W | Yn W | Yn E2 | Yn W | Yn E4 | Yg Wd | Yg M |
| 18 | Yn M | Yn W | Yn E | Yn Wd | Yg M | Yg E3 | Yg M | Yg E1 | Yn M | Yn W | Yn M | Yn F | Yg W | Yg W | Yn W | Yn E2 | Yn W | Yn E4 | Yg Wd | Yg M | Yg Wd | Yg Wd | Yn Wd | Yn M |
| 19 | Yg W | Yg W | Yg M | Yg E1 | Yn M | Yn W | Yn M | Yn F | Yg W | Yg W | Yg W | Yg F | Yn W | Yn E4 | Yg Wd | Yg M | Yg Wd | Yg Wd | Yn Wd | Yn M | Yn Wd | Yn Wd | Yg F | Yg E3 |
| 20 | Yn W | Yn E4 | Yn M | Yn F | Yg W | Yg W | Yg W | Yg F | Yn W | Yn E4 | Yn W | Yn E2 | Yg Wd | Yg Wd | Yn Wd | Yn M | Yn Wd | Yn Wd | Yg F | Yg E3 | Yg F | Yg E1 | Yn F | Yn W |
| 21 | Yg Wd | Yg Wd | Yg W | Yg F | Yn W | Yn E4 | Yn W | Yn E2 | Yg Wd | Yg Wd | Yg Wd | Yg M | Yn Wd | Yn Wd | Yg F | Yg E3 | Yg F | Yg E1 | Yn F | Yn W | Yn F | Yn F | Yg E | Yg W |
| 22 | Yn Wd | Yn Wd | Yn W | Yn E2 | Yg Wd | Yg Wd | Yg Wd | Yg M | Yn Wd | Yn Wd | Yn Wd | Yn M | Yg F | Yg E1 | Yn F | Yn W | Yn F | Yn F | Yg E | Yg W | Yg E | Yg F | Yn E | Yn E4 |
| 23 | Yg F | Yg E1 | Yg Wd | Yg M | Yn Wd | Yn Wd | Yn Wd | Yn M | Yg F | Yg E1 | Yg F | Yg E3 | Yn F | Yn F | Yg E | Yg W | Yg E | Yg F | Yn E | Yn E4 | Yn E | Yn E2 | Yg M | Yg Wd |
| 24 | Yn F | Yn F | Yn Wd | Yn M | Yg F | Yg E1 | Yg F | Yg E3 | Yn F | Yn F | Yn F | Yn W | Yg E | Yg F | Yn E | Yn E4 | Yn E | Yn E2 | Yg M | Yg Wd | Yg M | Yg M | Yn M | Yn Wd |
| 25 | Yg E | Yg F | Yg F | Yg E3 | Yn F | Yn F | Yn F | Yn W | Yg E | Yg F | Yg E | Yg W | Yn E | Yn E2 | Yg M | Yg Wd | Yg M | Yg M | Yn M | Yn Wd | Yn M | Yn M | Yg W | Yg E1 |
| 26 | Yn E | Yn E2 | Yn F | Yn W | Yg E | Yg F | Yg E | Yg W | Yn E | Yn E2 | Yn E | Yn E4 | Yg M | Yg M | Yn M | Yn Wd | Yn M | Yn M | Yg W | Yg E1 | Yg W | Yg E3 | Yn W | Yn F |
| 27 | Yg M | Yg M | Yg E | Yg W | Yn E | Yn E2 | Yn E | Yn E4 | Yg M | Yg M | Yg M | Yg Wd | Yn M | Yn M | Yg W | Yg E1 | Yg W | Yg E3 | Yn W | Yn F | Yn W | Yn W | Yg Wd | Yg F |
| 28 | Yn M | Yn M | Yn E | Yn E4 | Yg M | Yg M | Yg M | Yg Wd | Yn M | Yn M | Yn M | Yn Wd | Yg W | Yg E3 | Yn W | Yn F | Yn W | Yn W | Yg Wd | Yg F | Yg Wd | Yg W | Yn Wd | Yn E2 |
| 29 | | | Yg M | Yg Wd | Yn M | Yn M | Yn M | Yn Wd | Yg W | Yg E3 | Yg W | Yg E1 | Yn W | Yn W | Yg Wd | Yg F | Yg Wd | Yg W | Yn Wd | Yn E2 | Yn Wd | Yn E4 | Yg F | Yg M |
| 30 | | | Yn M | Yn Wd | Yg W | Yg E3 | Yg W | Yg E1 | Yn W | Yn W | Yn W | Yn F | Yg Wd | Yg W | Yn Wd | Yn E2 | Yn Wd | Yn E4 | Yg F | Yg M | Yg F | Yg Wd | Yn F | Yn M |
| 31 | | | Yg W | Yg E1 | | | Yn W | Yn F | | | Yg Wd | Yg F | Yn Wd | Yn E4 | | | Yg F | Yg Wd | | | Yn F | Yn Wd | Yg E | Yg E3 |
| 1 | Yg W | Yg E3 | Yn W | Yn F | Yn W | Yn W | Yg Wd | Yg F | Yg Wd | Yg W | Yn Wd | Yn E2 | Yg F | Yg Wd | Yg F | Yg M | Yn F | Yn Wd | Yn F | Yn M | Yg E | Yg E1 | Yn E | Yn W |
| 2 | Yn W | Yn W | Yg Wd | Yg F | Yg Wd | Yg W | Yn Wd | Yn E2 | Yn Wd | Yn E4 | Yg F | Yg M | Yn F | Yn Wd | Yn F | Yn M | Yg E | Yg E1 | Yg E | Yg E3 | Yn E | Yn F | Yg M | Yg W |
| 3 | Yg Wd | Yg W | Yn Wd | Yn E2 | Yn Wd | Yn E4 | Yg F | Yg M | Yg F | Yg Wd | Yn F | Yn M | Yg E | Yg E1 | Yg E | Yg E3 | Yn E | Yn F | Yn E | Yn W | Yg M | Yg F | Yn M | Yn E4 |
| 4 | Yn Wd | Yn E4 | Yg F | Yg M | Yg F | Yg Wd | Yn F | Yn M | Yn F | Yn Wd | Yg E | Yg E3 | Yn E | Yn F | Yn E | Yn W | Yg M | Yg F | Yg M | Yg W | Yn M | Yn E2 | | |
| 5 | Yg F | Yg Wd | | | Yn F | Yn Wd | Yg E | Yg E3 | Yg E | Yg E1 | Yn E | Yn W | Yg M | Yg F | Yg M | Yg W | Yn M | Yn E2 | Yn M | Yn E4 | Yg W | Yg M | | |
| 6 | | | | | | | | | Yn E | Yn F | Yg M | Yg W | Yn M | Yn E2 | Yn M | Yn E4 | Yg W | Yg M | Yg W | Yg Wd | | | | |
| 7 | | | | | | | | | | | Yn M | Yn E4 | Yg W | Yg M | Yg W | Yg Wd | Yn W | Yn M | | | | | | |
| 8 | | | | | | | | | | | | | | | | | | | | | | | | |

# YEAR OF THE GOAT

| | H | E | H | E | H | E | H | E | H | E | H | E | H | E | H | E | H | E | H | E | H | E | H | E | |
|---|---|---|---|---|---|---|---|---|---|---|---|---|---|---|---|---|---|---|---|---|---|---|---|---|---|
| YEAR | YEAR<br>Yn E | <br>Yn E2 | 1979 | | | | | | | | | | | | | | | | | | | | 1980 | | |
| MONTH | 4 Feb - 5 Mar | | 6 Mar - 4 Apr | | 5 Apr - 5 May | | 6 May - 5 June | | 6 June - 7 Jul | | 8 Jul - 7 Aug | | 8 Aug - 7 Sep | | 8 Sep - 8 Oct | | 9 Oct - 7 Nov | | 8 Nov - 7 Dec | | 8 Dec - 5 Jan | | 6 Jan - 4 Feb | | |
| | Yg F | Yg Wd | Yn F | Yn Wd | Yg E | Yg E1 | Yn E | Yn F | Yg M | Yg F | Yn M | Yn E2 | Yg W | Yg M | Yn W | Yn M | Yg Wd | Yg E3 | Yn Wd | Yn W | Yg F | Yg W | Yn F | Yn E4 | |
| Starting time | 1st day | Mid-pt | 1st day | Mid-pt | 1st day | Mid-pt | 1st day | Mid-pt | 1st day | Mid-pt | 1st day | Mid-pt | 1st day | Mid-pt | 1st day | Mid-pt | 1st day | Mid-pt | 1st day | Mid-pt | 1st day | Mid-pt | 1st day | Mid-pt | |
| Date | 4 | 19 | 6 | 21 | 5 | 21 | 6 | 21 | 6 | 22 | 8 | 23 | 8 | 24 | 8 | 23 | 9 | 24 | 8 | 23 | 8 | 22 | 6 | 21 | |
| Hour | 1813 | 1413 | 1220 | 1322 | 1718 | 0036 | 1047 | 2354 | 1505 | 0756 | 0125 | 1849 | 1111 | 0147 | 1400 | 2317 | 0530 | 0828 | 0833 | 0554 | 0118 | 1910 | 1229 | 0549 | |
| DATE 4 | Yg W | Yg Wd | | | | | | | | | | | | | | | | | | | | | | | 4 |
| 5 | Yn W | Yn Wd | | | Yg W | Yg Wd | | | | | | | | | | | | | | | | | | | 5 |
| 6 | Yg Wd | Yg E1 | Yg W | Yg M | Yn W | Yn Wd | Yn W | Yn M | Yg Wd | Yg E1 | | | | | | | | | | | | | Yg E | Yg Wd | 6 |
| 7 | Yn Wd | Yn F | Yn W | Yn M | Yg Wd | Yg E1 | Yg Wd | Yg E3 | Yn Wd | Yn F | | | | | | | | | | | | | Yn E | Yn Wd | 7 |
| 8 | Yg F | Yg F | Yg Wd | Yg E3 | Yn Wd | Yn F | Yn Wd | Yn W | Yg F | Yg F | Yg F | Yg W | Yn F | Yn E2 | Yg E | Yg Wd | | | Yn E | Yn Wd | Yn E | Yn M | Yg M | Yg E1 | 8 |
| 9 | Yn F | Yn E2 | Yn Wd | Yn W | Yg F | Yg F | Yg F | Yg W | Yn F | Yn E2 | Yn F | Yn E4 | Yg E | Yg M | Yn E | Yn Wd | Yn E | Yn M | Yg M | Yg E1 | Yg M | Yg E3 | Yn M | Yn F | 9 |
| 10 | Yg E | Yg M | Yg F | Yg W | Yn F | Yn E2 | Yn F | Yn E4 | Yg E | Yg M | Yg E | Yg Wd | Yn E | Yn M | Yg M | Yg E1 | Yg M | Yg E3 | Yn M | Yn F | Yn M | Yn W | Yg W | Yg F | 10 |
| 11 | Yn E | Yn M | Yn F | Yn E4 | Yg E | Yg M | Yg E | Yg Wd | Yn E | Yn M | Yn E | Yn Wd | Yg M | Yg E3 | Yn M | Yn F | Yn M | Yn W | Yg W | Yg F | Yg W | Yg W | Yn W | Yn E2 | 11 |
| 12 | Yg M | Yg E3 | Yg E | Yg Wd | Yn E | Yn M | Yn E | Yn Wd | Yg M | Yg E3 | Yg M | Yg E1 | Yn M | Yn W | Yg W | Yg F | Yg W | Yg W | Yn W | Yn E2 | Yn W | Yn E4 | Yg Wd | Yg M | 12 |
| 13 | Yn M | Yn W | Yn E | Yn Wd | Yg M | Yg E3 | Yg M | Yg E1 | Yn M | Yn W | Yn M | Yn F | Yg W | Yg W | Yn W | Yn E2 | Yn W | Yn E4 | Yg Wd | Yg M | Yg Wd | Yg Wd | Yn Wd | Yn M | 13 |
| 14 | Yg W | Yg W | Yg M | Yg E1 | Yn M | Yn W | Yn M | Yn F | Yg W | Yg W | Yg W | Yg F | Yn W | Yn E4 | Yg Wd | Yg M | Yg Wd | Yg Wd | Yn Wd | Yn M | Yn Wd | Yn Wd | Yg F | Yg E3 | 14 |
| 15 | Yn W | Yn E4 | Yn M | Yn F | Yg W | Yg W | Yg W | Yg F | Yn W | Yn E4 | Yn W | Yn E2 | Yg Wd | Yg Wd | Yn Wd | Yn M | Yn Wd | Yn Wd | Yg F | Yg E3 | Yg F | Yg E1 | Yn F | Yn W | 15 |
| 16 | Yg Wd | Yg Wd | Yg W | Yg F | Yn W | Yn E4 | Yn W | Yn E2 | Yg Wd | Yg Wd | Yg Wd | Yg M | Yn Wd | Yn Wd | Yg F | Yg E3 | Yg F | Yg E1 | Yn F | Yn W | Yn F | Yn F | Yg E | Yg W | 16 |
| 17 | Yn Wd | Yn Wd | Yn W | Yn E2 | Yg Wd | Yg Wd | Yg Wd | Yg M | Yn Wd | Yn Wd | Yn Wd | Yn M | Yg F | Yg E1 | Yn F | Yn W | Yn F | Yn F | Yg E | Yg W | Yg E | Yg F | Yn E | Yn E4 | 17 |
| 18 | Yg F | Yg E1 | Yg Wd | Yg M | Yn Wd | Yn Wd | Yn Wd | Yn M | Yg F | Yg E1 | Yg F | Yg E3 | Yn F | Yn F | Yg E | Yg W | Yg E | Yg F | Yn E | Yn E4 | Yn E | Yn E2 | Yg M | Yg Wd | 18 |
| 19 | Yn F | Yn F | Yn Wd | Yn M | Yg F | Yg E1 | Yg F | Yg E3 | Yn F | Yn F | Yn F | Yn W | Yg E | Yg F | Yn E | Yn E4 | Yn E | Yn E2 | Yg M | Yg Wd | Yg M | Yg M | Yn M | Yn Wd | 19 |
| 20 | Yg E | Yg F | Yg F | Yg E3 | Yn F | Yn F | Yn F | Yn W | Yg E | Yg F | Yg E | Yg W | Yn E | Yn E2 | Yg M | Yg Wd | Yg M | Yg M | Yn M | Yn Wd | Yn M | Yn M | Yg W | Yg E1 | 20 |
| 21 | Yn E | Yn E2 | Yn F | Yn W | Yg E | Yg F | Yg E | Yg W | Yn E | Yn E2 | Yn E | Yn E4 | Yg M | Yg M | Yn M | Yn Wd | Yn M | Yn M | Yg W | Yg E1 | Yg W | Yg E3 | Yn W | Yn F | 21 |
| 22 | Yg M | Yg M | Yg E | Yg W | Yn E | Yn E2 | Yn E | Yn E4 | Yg M | Yg M | Yg M | Yg Wd | Yn M | Yn M | Yg W | Yg E1 | Yg W | Yg E3 | Yn W | Yn F | Yn W | Yn W | Yg Wd | Yg F | 22 |
| 23 | Yn M | Yn M | Yn E | Yn E4 | Yg M | Yg M | Yg M | Yg Wd | Yn M | Yn M | Yn M | Yn Wd | Yg W | Yg E3 | Yn W | Yn F | Yn W | Yn W | Yg Wd | Yg F | Yg Wd | Yg W | Yn Wd | Yn E2 | 23 |
| 24 | Yg W | Yg E3 | Yg M | Yg Wd | Yn M | Yn M | Yn M | Yn Wd | Yg W | Yg E3 | Yg W | Yg E1 | Yn W | Yn W | Yg Wd | Yg F | Yg Wd | Yg W | Yn Wd | Yn E2 | Yn Wd | Yn E4 | Yg F | Yg M | 24 |
| 25 | Yn W | Yn W | Yn M | Yn Wd | Yg W | Yg E3 | Yg W | Yg E1 | Yn W | Yn W | Yn W | Yn F | Yg Wd | Yg W | Yn Wd | Yn E2 | Yn Wd | Yn E4 | Yg F | Yg M | Yg F | Yg Wd | Yn F | Yn M | 25 |
| 26 | Yg Wd | Yg W | Yg W | Yg E1 | Yn W | Yn W | Yn W | Yn F | Yg Wd | Yg W | Yg Wd | Yg F | Yn Wd | Yn E4 | Yg F | Yg M | Yg F | Yg Wd | Yn F | Yn M | Yn F | Yn Wd | Yg E | Yg E3 | 26 |
| 27 | Yn Wd | Yn E4 | Yn W | Yn F | Yg Wd | Yg W | Yg Wd | Yg F | Yn Wd | Yn E4 | Yn Wd | Yn E2 | Yg F | Yg Wd | Yn F | Yn M | Yn F | Yn Wd | Yg E | Yg E3 | Yg E | Yg E1 | Yn E | Yn W | 27 |
| 28 | Yg F | Yg Wd | Yg Wd | Yg F | Yn Wd | Yn E4 | Yn Wd | Yn E2 | Yg F | Yg Wd | Yg F | Yg M | Yn F | Yn Wd | Yg E | Yg E3 | Yg E | Yg E1 | Yn E | Yn W | Yn E | Yn F | Yg M | Yg W | 28 |
| 29 | | | Yn Wd | Yn E2 | Yg F | Yg Wd | Yg F | Yg M | Yn F | Yn Wd | Yn F | Yn M | Yg E | Yg E1 | Yn E | Yn W | Yn E | Yn F | Yg M | Yg W | Yg M | Yg F | Yn M | Yn E4 | 29 |
| 30 | | | Yg F | Yg M | Yn F | Yn Wd | Yn F | Yn M | Yg E | Yg E1 | Yg E | Yg E3 | Yn E | Yn F | Yg M | Yg W | Yg M | Yg F | Yn M | Yn E4 | Yn M | Yn E2 | Yg W | Yg Wd | 30 |
| 31 | | | Yn F | Yn M | | | Yg E | Yg E3 | | | Yn E | Yn W | Yg M | Yg F | | | Yn M | Yn E2 | | | Yg W | Yg M | Yn W | Yn Wd | 31 |
| 1 | Yn F | Yn Wd | Yg E | Yg E3 | Yg E | Yg E1 | Yn E | Yn W | Yn E | Yn F | Yg M | Yg W | Yn M | Yn E2 | Yn M | Yn E4 | Yg W | Yg M | Yg W | Yg Wd | Yn W | Yn M | Yg Wd | Yg E1 | 1 |
| 2 | Yg E | Yg E1 | Yn E | Yn W | Yn E | Yn F | Yg M | Yg W | Yg M | Yg F | Yn M | Yn E4 | Yg W | Yg M | Yg W | Yg Wd | Yn W | Yn M | Yn W | Yn Wd | Yg Wd | Yg E3 | Yn Wd | Yn F | 2 |
| 3 | Yn E | Yn F | Yg M | Yg W | Yg M | Yg F | Yn M | Yn E4 | Yn M | Yn E2 | Yg W | Yg Wd | Yn W | Yn M | Yn W | Yn Wd | Yg Wd | Yg E3 | Yg Wd | Yg E1 | Yn Wd | Yn W | Yg F | Yg F | 3 |
| 4 | Yg M | Yg F | Yn M | Yn E4 | Yn M | Yn E2 | Yg W | Yg Wd | Yg W | Yg M | Yn W | Yn Wd | Yg Wd | Yg E3 | Yg Wd | Yg E1 | Yn Wd | Yn W | Yn Wd | Yn F | Yg F | Yg W | Yn F | Yn E2 | 4 |
| 5 | Yn M | Yn E2 | | | Yg W | Yg M | Yn W | Yn Wd | Yn W | Yn M | Yg Wd | Yg E1 | Yn Wd | Yn W | Yn Wd | Yn F | Yg F | Yg W | Yg F | Yg F | Yn F | Yn E4 | | | 5 |
| 6 | | | | | | | | | Yg Wd | Yg E3 | Yn Wd | Yn F | Yg F | Yg W | Yg F | Yg F | Yn F | Yn E4 | Yn F | Yn E2 | | | | | 6 |
| 7 | | | | | | | | | Yn Wd | Yn W | Yg F | Yg F | Yn F | Yn E4 | Yn F | Yn E2 | Yg E | Yg Wd | Yg E | Yg M | | | | | 7 |
| 8 | | | | | | | | | | | | | | | Yg E | Yg M | | | | | | | | | 8 |

# YEAR OF THE MONKEY

| | H | E | H | E | H | E | H | E | H | E | H | E | H | E | H | E | H | E | H | E | H | E | H | E | |
|---|---|---|---|---|---|---|---|---|---|---|---|---|---|---|---|---|---|---|---|---|---|---|---|---|---|
| YEAR | YEAR Yg M | Yg M | 1980 | | | | | | | | | | | | | | | | | | | | 1981 | | |
| MONTH | 5 Feb - 4 Mar | | 5 Mar - 3 Apr | | 4 Apr - 4 May | | 5 May - 4 June | | 5 June - 6 Jul | | 7 Jul - 6 Aug | | 7 Aug - 6 Sep | | 7 Sep - 7 Oct | | 8 Oct - 6 Nov | | 7 Nov - 6 Dec | | 7 Dec - 4 Jan | | 5 Jan - 3 Feb | | |
| | Yg E | Yg Wd | Yn E | Yn Wd | Yg M | Yg E1 | Yn M | Yn F | Yg W | Yg F | Yn W | Yn E2 | Yg Wd | Yg M | Yn Wd | Yn M | Yg F | Yg E3 | Yn F | Yn W | Yg E | Yg W | Yn E | Yn E4 | |
| Starting time | 1st day | Mid-pt | 1st day | Mid-pt | 1st day | Mid-pt | 1st day | Mid-pt | 1st day | Mid-pt | 1st day | Mid-pt | 1st day | Mid-pt | 1st day | Mid-pt | 1st day | Mid-pt | 1st day | Mid-pt | 1st day | Mid-pt | 1st day | Mid-pt | |
| Date | 5 | 19 | 5 | 20 | 4 | 20 | 5 | 21 | 5 | 21 | 7 | 23 | 7 | 23 | 7 | 23 | 8 | 23 | 7 | 22 | 7 | 22 | 5 | 20 | |
| Hour | 0010 | 2002 | 1817 | 1910 | 2315 | 0623 | 1645 | 0542 | 2104 | 1347 | 0724 | 0042 | 1709 | 0741 | 1954 | 0509 | 1119 | 1418 | 1418 | 1142 | 0702 | 0056 | 1813 | 1136 | |
| DATE 4 | | | | | Yn F | Yn E2 | | | | | | | | | | | | | | | | | | | 4 |
| 5 | Yg E | Yg M | Yn F | Yn E4 | Yg E | Yg M | Yg E | Yg Wd | Yn E | Yn M | | | | | | | | | | | | | Yn W | Yn E2 | 5 |
| 6 | Yn E | Yn M | Yg E | Yg Wd | Yn E | Yn M | Yn E | Yn Wd | Yg M | Yg E3 | | | | | | | | | | | | | Yg Wd | Yg M | 6 |
| 7 | Yg M | Yg E3 | Yn E | Yn Wd | Yg M | Yg E3 | Yg M | Yg E1 | Yn M | Yn W | Yn M | Yn F | Yg W | Yg W | Yn W | Yn E2 | | | Yg Wd | Yg M | Yg Wd | Yg Wd | Yn Wd | Yn M | 7 |
| 8 | Yn M | Yn W | Yg M | Yg E1 | Yn M | Yn W | Yn M | Yn F | Yg W | Yg W | Yg W | Yg F | Yn W | Yn E4 | Yg Wd | Yg M | Yg Wd | Yg Wd | Yn Wd | Yn M | Yn Wd | Yn Wd | Yg F | Yg E3 | 8 |
| 9 | Yg W | Yg W | Yn M | Yn F | Yg W | Yg W | Yg W | Yg F | Yn W | Yn E4 | Yn W | Yn E2 | Yg Wd | Yg Wd | Yn Wd | Yn M | Yn Wd | Yn Wd | Yg F | Yg E3 | Yg F | Yg E1 | Yn F | Yn W | 9 |
| 10 | Yn W | Yn E4 | Yg W | Yg F | Yn W | Yn E4 | Yn W | Yn E2 | Yg Wd | Yg Wd | Yg Wd | Yg M | Yn Wd | Yn Wd | Yg F | Yg E3 | Yg F | Yg E1 | Yn F | Yn W | Yn F | Yn F | Yg E | Yg W | 10 |
| 11 | Yg Wd | Yg Wd | Yn W | Yn E2 | Yg Wd | Yg Wd | Yg Wd | Yg M | Yn Wd | Yn Wd | Yn Wd | Yn M | Yg F | Yg E1 | Yn F | Yn W | Yn F | Yn F | Yg E | Yg W | Yg E | Yg F | Yn E | Yn E4 | 11 |
| 12 | Yn Wd | Yn Wd | Yg Wd | Yg M | Yn Wd | Yn Wd | Yn Wd | Yn M | Yg F | Yg E1 | Yg F | Yg E3 | Yn F | Yn F | Yg E | Yg W | Yg E | Yg F | Yn E | Yn E4 | Yn E | Yn E2 | Yg M | Yg Wd | 12 |
| 13 | Yg F | Yg E1 | Yn Wd | Yn M | Yg F | Yg E1 | Yg F | Yg E3 | Yn F | Yn F | Yn F | Yn W | Yg E | Yg F | Yn E | Yn E4 | Yn E | Yn E2 | Yg M | Yg Wd | Yg M | Yg M | Yn M | Yn Wd | 13 |
| 14 | Yn F | Yn F | Yg F | Yg E3 | Yn F | Yn F | Yn F | Yn W | Yg E | Yg F | Yg E | Yg W | Yn E | Yn E2 | Yg M | Yg Wd | Yg M | Yg M | Yn M | Yn Wd | Yn M | Yn M | Yg W | Yg E1 | 14 |
| 15 | Yg E | Yg F | Yn F | Yn W | Yg E | Yg F | Yg E | Yg W | Yn E | Yn E2 | Yn E | Yn E4 | Yg M | Yg M | Yn M | Yn Wd | Yn M | Yn M | Yg W | Yg E1 | Yg W | Yg E3 | Yn W | Yn F | 15 |
| 16 | Yn E | Yn E2 | Yg E | Yg W | Yn E | Yn E2 | Yn E | Yn E4 | Yg M | Yg M | Yg M | Yg Wd | Yn M | Yn M | Yg W | Yg E1 | Yg W | Yg E3 | Yn W | Yn F | Yn W | Yn W | Yg Wd | Yg F | 16 |
| 17 | Yg M | Yg M | Yn E | Yn E4 | Yg M | Yg M | Yg M | Yg Wd | Yn M | Yn M | Yn M | Yn Wd | Yg W | Yg E3 | Yn W | Yn F | Yn W | Yn W | Yg Wd | Yg F | Yg Wd | Yg W | Yn Wd | Yn E2 | 17 |
| 18 | Yn M | Yn M | Yg M | Yg Wd | Yn M | Yn M | Yn M | Yn Wd | Yg W | Yg E3 | Yg W | Yg E1 | Yn W | Yn W | Yg Wd | Yg F | Yg Wd | Yg W | Yn Wd | Yn E2 | Yn Wd | Yn E4 | Yg F | Yg M | 18 |
| 19 | Yg W | Yg E3 | Yn M | Yn Wd | Yg W | Yg E3 | Yg W | Yg E1 | Yn W | Yn W | Yn W | Yn F | Yg Wd | Yg W | Yn Wd | Yn E2 | Yn Wd | Yn E4 | Yg F | Yg M | Yg F | Yg Wd | Yn F | Yn M | 19 |
| 20 | Yn W | Yn W | Yg W | Yg E1 | Yn W | Yn W | Yn W | Yn F | Yg Wd | Yg W | Yg Wd | Yg F | Yn Wd | Yn E4 | Yg F | Yg M | Yg F | Yg Wd | Yn F | Yn M | Yn F | Yn Wd | Yg E | Yg E3 | 20 |
| 21 | Yg Wd | Yg W | Yn W | Yn F | Yg Wd | Yg W | Yg Wd | Yg F | Yn Wd | Yn E4 | Yn Wd | Yn E2 | Yg F | Yg Wd | Yn F | Yn M | Yn F | Yn Wd | Yg E | Yg E3 | Yg E | Yg E1 | Yn E | Yn W | 21 |
| 22 | Yn Wd | Yn E4 | Yg Wd | Yg F | Yn Wd | Yn E4 | Yn Wd | Yn E2 | Yg F | Yg Wd | Yg F | Yg M | Yn F | Yn Wd | Yg E | Yg E3 | Yg E | Yg E1 | Yn E | Yn W | Yn E | Yn F | Yg M | Yg W | 22 |
| 23 | Yg F | Yg Wd | Yn Wd | Yn E2 | Yg F | Yg Wd | Yg F | Yg M | Yn F | Yn Wd | Yn F | Yn M | Yg E | Yg E1 | Yn E | Yn W | Yn E | Yn F | Yg M | Yg W | Yg M | Yg F | Yn M | Yn E4 | 23 |
| 24 | Yn F | Yn Wd | Yg F | Yg M | Yn F | Yn Wd | Yn F | Yn M | Yg E | Yg E1 | Yg E | Yg E3 | Yn E | Yn F | Yg M | Yg W | Yg M | Yg F | Yn M | Yn E4 | Yn M | Yn E2 | Yg W | Yg Wd | 24 |
| 25 | Yg E | Yg E1 | Yn F | Yn M | Yg E | Yg E1 | Yg E | Yg E3 | Yn E | Yn F | Yn E | Yn W | Yg M | Yg F | Yn M | Yn E4 | Yn M | Yn E2 | Yg W | Yg Wd | Yg W | Yg M | Yn W | Yn Wd | 25 |
| 26 | Yn E | Yn F | Yg E | Yg E3 | Yn E | Yn F | Yn E | Yn W | Yg M | Yg F | Yg M | Yg W | Yn M | Yn E2 | Yg W | Yg Wd | Yg W | Yg M | Yn W | Yn Wd | Yn W | Yn M | Yg Wd | Yg E1 | 26 |
| 27 | Yg M | Yg F | Yn E | Yn W | Yg M | Yg F | Yg M | Yg W | Yn M | Yn E2 | Yn M | Yn E4 | Yg W | Yg M | Yn W | Yn Wd | Yn W | Yn M | Yg Wd | Yg E1 | Yg Wd | Yg E3 | Yn Wd | Yn F | 27 |
| 28 | Yn M | Yn E2 | Yg M | Yg W | Yn M | Yn E2 | Yn M | Yn E4 | Yg W | Yg M | Yg W | Yg Wd | Yn W | Yn M | Yg Wd | Yg E1 | Yg Wd | Yg E3 | Yn Wd | Yn F | Yn Wd | Yn W | Yg F | Yg F | 28 |
| 29 | Yg W | Yg M | Yn M | Yn E4 | Yg W | Yg M | Yg W | Yg Wd | Yn W | Yn M | Yn W | Yn Wd | Yg Wd | Yg E3 | Yn Wd | Yn F | Yn Wd | Yn W | Yg F | Yg F | Yg F | Yg W | Yn F | Yn E2 | 29 |
| 30 | | | Yg W | Yg Wd | Yn W | Yn M | Yn W | Yn Wd | Yg Wd | Yg E3 | Yg Wd | Yg E1 | Yn Wd | Yn W | Yg F | Yg F | Yg F | Yg W | Yn F | Yn E2 | Yn F | Yn E4 | Yg E | Yg M | 30 |
| 31 | | | Yn W | Yn Wd | | | Yg Wd | Yg E1 | | | Yn Wd | Yn F | Yg F | Yg W | | | Yn F | Yn E4 | | | Yg E | Yg Wd | Yn E | Yn M | 31 |
| 1 | Yn W | Yn M | Yg Wd | Yg E1 | Yg Wd | Yg E3 | Yn Wd | Yn F | Yn Wd | Yn W | Yg F | Yg F | Yn F | Yn E4 | Yn F | Yn E2 | Yg E | Yg Wd | Yg E | Yg M | Yn E | Yn Wd | Yg M | Yg E3 | 1 |
| 2 | Yg Wd | Yg E3 | Yn Wd | Yn F | Yn Wd | Yn W | Yg F | Yg F | Yg F | Yg W | Yn F | Yn E2 | Yg E | Yg Wd | Yg E | Yg M | Yn E | Yn Wd | Yn E | Yn M | Yg M | Yg E1 | Yn M | Yn W | 2 |
| 3 | Yn Wd | Yn W | Yg F | Yg F | Yg F | Yg W | Yn F | Yn E2 | Yn F | Yn E4 | Yg E | Yg M | Yn E | Yn Wd | Yn E | Yn M | Yg M | Yg E1 | Yg M | Yg E3 | Yn M | Yn F | Yg W | Yg W | 3 |
| 4 | Yg F | Yg W | | | Yn F | Yn E4 | Yg E | Yg M | Yg E | Yg Wd | Yn E | Yn M | Yg M | Yg E1 | Yg M | Yg E3 | Yn M | Yn F | Yn M | Yn W | Yg W | Yg F | | | 4 |
| 5 | | | | | | | | | Yn E | Yn Wd | Yg M | Yg E3 | Yn M | Yn F | Yn M | Yn W | Yg W | Yg F | Yg W | Yg W | | | | | 5 |
| 6 | | | | | | | | | Yg M | Yg E1 | Yn M | Yn W | Yg W | Yg F | Yg W | Yg W | Yn W | Yn E2 | Yn W | Yn E4 | | | | | 6 |
| 7 | | | | | | | | | | | | | | | Yn W | Yn E4 | | | | | | | | | 7 |
| 8 | | | | | | | | | | | | | | | | | | | | | | | | | 8 |

# YEAR OF THE ROOSTER

| | H | E | H | E | H | E | H | E | H | E | H | E | H | E | H | E | H | E | H | E | H | E | H | E | |
|---|---|---|---|---|---|---|---|---|---|---|---|---|---|---|---|---|---|---|---|---|---|---|---|---|---|
| YEAR | YEAR YnM | YnM | 1981 | | | | | | | | | | | | | | | | | | | | 1982 | | |
| MONTH | 4 Feb - 5 Mar | | 6 Mar - 4 Apr | | 5 Apr - 4 May | | 5 May - 5 June | | 6 June - 6 Jul | | 7 Jul - 6 Aug | | 7 Aug - 7 Sep | | 8 Sep - 7 Oct | | 8 Oct - 6 Nov | | 7 Nov - 6 Dec | | 7 Dec - 5 Jan | | 6 Jan - 3 Feb | | |
| | Yg M | Yg Wd | Yn M | Yn Wd | Yg W | Yg E1 | Yn W | Yn F | Yg Wd | Yg F | Yn Wd | Yn E2 | Yg F | Yg M | Yn F | Yn M | Yg E | Yg E3 | Yn E | Yn W | Yg M | Yg W | Yn M | Yn E4 | |
| Starting time | 1st day | Mid-pt | 1st day | Mid-pt | 1st day | Mid-pt | 1st day | Mid-pt | 1st day | Mid-pt | 1st day | Mid-pt | 1st day | Mid-pt | 1st day | Mid-pt | 1st day | Mid-pt | 1st day | Mid-pt | 1st day | Mid-pt | 1st day | Mid-pt | |
| Date | 4 | 19 | 6 | 21 | 5 | 20 | 5 | 21 | 6 | 21 | 7 | 23 | 7 | 23 | 8 | 23 | 8 | 23 | 7 | 22 | 7 | 22 | 6 | 21 | |
| Hour | 0556 | 0152 | 0005 | 0003 | 0505 | 1219 | 2235 | 1140 | 0253 | 1945 | 1312 | 0640 | 2257 | 1338 | 0143 | 1105 | 1710 | 2013 | 2009 | 1736 | 1251 | 0651 | 0006 | 1715 | |
| DATE 4 | Yn W | Yn E4 | | | | | | | | | | | | | | | | | | | | | | | 4 |
| 5 | Yg Wd | Yg Wd | | | Yn W | Yn E4 | Yn W | Yn E2 | | | | | | | | | | | | | | | | | 5 |
| 6 | Yn Wd | Yn Wd | Yn W | Yn E2 | Yg Wd | Yg Wd | Yg Wd | Yg M | Yn Wd | Yn Wd | | | | | | | | | | | | | Yn E | Yn E4 | 6 |
| 7 | Yg F | Yg E1 | Yg Wd | Yg M | Yn Wd | Yn Wd | Yn Wd | Yn M | Yg F | Yg E1 | Yg F | Yg E3 | Yn F | Yn F | | | | | Yn E | Yn E4 | Yn E | Yn E2 | Yg M | Yg Wd | 7 |
| 8 | Yn F | Yn F | Yn Wd | Yn M | Yg F | Yg E1 | Yg F | Yg E3 | Yn F | Yn F | Yn F | Yn W | Yg E | Yg F | Yn E | Yn E4 | Yn E | Yn E2 | Yg M | Yg Wd | Yg M | Yg M | Yn M | Yn Wd | 8 |
| 9 | Yg E | Yg F | Yg F | Yg E3 | Yn F | Yn F | Yn F | Yn W | Yg E | Yg F | Yg E | Yg W | Yn E | Yn E2 | Yg M | Yg Wd | Yg M | Yg M | Yn M | Yn Wd | Yn M | Yn M | Yg W | Yg E1 | 9 |
| 10 | Yn E | Yn E2 | Yn F | Yn W | Yg E | Yg F | Yg E | Yg W | Yn E | Yn E2 | Yn E | Yn E4 | Yg M | Yg M | Yn M | Yn Wd | Yn M | Yn M | Yg W | Yg E1 | Yg W | Yg E3 | Yn W | Yn F | 10 |
| 11 | Yg M | Yg M | Yg E | Yg W | Yn E | Yn E2 | Yn E | Yn E4 | Yg M | Yg M | Yg M | Yg Wd | Yn M | Yn M | Yg W | Yg E1 | Yg W | Yg E3 | Yn W | Yn F | Yn W | Yn W | Yg Wd | Yg F | 11 |
| 12 | Yn M | Yn M | Yn E | Yn E4 | Yg M | Yg M | Yg M | Yg Wd | Yn M | Yn M | Yn M | Yn Wd | Yg W | Yg E3 | Yn W | Yn F | Yn W | Yn W | Yg Wd | Yg F | Yg Wd | Yg W | Yn Wd | Yn E2 | 12 |
| 13 | Yg W | Yg E3 | Yg M | Yg Wd | Yn M | Yn M | Yn M | Yn Wd | Yg W | Yg E3 | Yg W | Yg E1 | Yn W | Yn W | Yg Wd | Yg F | Yg Wd | Yg W | Yn Wd | Yn E2 | Yn Wd | Yn E4 | Yg F | Yg M | 13 |
| 14 | Yn W | Yn W | Yn M | Yn Wd | Yg W | Yg E3 | Yg W | Yg E1 | Yn W | Yn W | Yn W | Yn F | Yg Wd | Yg W | Yn Wd | Yn E2 | Yn Wd | Yn E4 | Yg F | Yg M | Yg F | Yg Wd | Yn F | Yn M | 14 |
| 15 | Yg Wd | Yg W | Yg W | Yg E1 | Yn W | Yn W | Yn W | Yn F | Yg Wd | Yg W | Yg Wd | Yg F | Yn Wd | Yn E4 | Yg F | Yg M | Yg F | Yg Wd | Yn F | Yn M | Yn F | Yn Wd | Yg E | Yg E3 | 15 |
| 16 | Yn Wd | Yn E4 | Yn W | Yn F | Yg Wd | Yg W | Yg Wd | Yg F | Yn Wd | Yn E4 | Yn Wd | Yn E2 | Yg F | Yg Wd | Yn F | Yn M | Yn F | Yn Wd | Yg E | Yg E3 | Yg E | Yg E1 | Yn E | Yn W | 16 |
| 17 | Yg F | Yg Wd | Yg Wd | Yg F | Yn Wd | Yn E4 | Yn Wd | Yn E2 | Yg F | Yg Wd | Yg F | Yg M | Yn F | Yn Wd | Yg E | Yg E3 | Yg E | Yg E1 | Yn E | Yn W | Yn E | Yn F | Yg M | Yg W | 17 |
| 18 | Yn F | Yn Wd | Yn Wd | Yn E2 | Yg F | Yg Wd | Yg F | Yg M | Yn F | Yn Wd | Yn F | Yn M | Yg E | Yg E1 | Yn E | Yn W | Yn E | Yn F | Yg M | Yg W | Yg M | Yg F | Yn M | Yn E4 | 18 |
| 19 | Yg E | Yg E1 | Yg F | Yg M | Yn F | Yn Wd | Yn F | Yn M | Yg E | Yg E1 | Yg E | Yg E3 | Yn E | Yn F | Yg M | Yg W | Yg M | Yg F | Yn M | Yn E4 | Yn M | Yn E2 | Yg W | Yg Wd | 19 |
| 20 | Yn E | Yn F | Yn F | Yn M | Yg E | Yg E1 | Yg E | Yg E3 | Yn E | Yn F | Yn E | Yn W | Yg M | Yg F | Yn M | Yn E4 | Yn M | Yn E2 | Yg W | Yg Wd | Yg W | Yg M | Yn W | Yn Wd | 20 |
| 21 | Yg M | Yg F | Yg E | Yg E3 | Yn E | Yn F | Yn E | Yn W | Yg M | Yg F | Yg M | Yg W | Yn M | Yn E2 | Yg W | Yg Wd | Yg W | Yg M | Yn W | Yn Wd | Yn W | Yn M | Yg Wd | Yg E1 | 21 |
| 22 | Yn M | Yn E2 | Yn E | Yn W | Yg M | Yg F | Yg M | Yg W | Yn M | Yn E2 | Yn M | Yn E4 | Yg W | Yg M | Yn W | Yn Wd | Yn W | Yn M | Yg Wd | Yg E1 | Yg Wd | Yg E3 | Yn Wd | Yn F | 22 |
| 23 | Yg W | Yg M | Yg M | Yg W | Yn M | Yn E2 | Yn M | Yn E4 | Yg W | Yg M | Yg W | Yg Wd | Yn W | Yn M | Yg Wd | Yg E1 | Yg Wd | Yg E3 | Yn Wd | Yn F | Yn Wd | Yn W | Yg F | Yg F | 23 |
| 24 | Yn W | Yn M | Yn M | Yn E4 | Yg W | Yg M | Yg W | Yg Wd | Yn W | Yn M | Yn W | Yn Wd | Yg Wd | Yg E3 | Yn Wd | Yn F | Yn Wd | Yn W | Yg F | Yg F | Yg F | Yg W | Yn F | Yn E2 | 24 |
| 25 | Yg Wd | Yg E3 | Yg W | Yg Wd | Yn W | Yn M | Yn W | Yn Wd | Yg Wd | Yg E3 | Yg Wd | Yg E1 | Yn Wd | Yn W | Yg F | Yg F | Yg F | Yg W | Yn F | Yn E2 | Yn F | Yn E4 | Yg E | Yg M | 25 |
| 26 | Yn Wd | Yn W | Yn W | Yn Wd | Yg Wd | Yg E3 | Yg Wd | Yg E1 | Yn Wd | Yn W | Yn Wd | Yn F | Yg F | Yg W | Yn F | Yn E2 | Yn F | Yn E4 | Yg E | Yg M | Yg E | Yg Wd | Yn E | Yn M | 26 |
| 27 | Yg F | Yg W | Yg Wd | Yg E1 | Yn Wd | Yn W | Yn Wd | Yn F | Yg F | Yg W | Yg F | Yg F | Yn F | Yn E4 | Yg E | Yg M | Yg E | Yg Wd | Yn E | Yn M | Yn E | Yn Wd | Yg M | Yg E3 | 27 |
| 28 | Yn F | Yn E4 | Yn Wd | Yn F | Yg F | Yg W | Yg F | Yg F | Yn F | Yn E4 | Yn F | Yn E2 | Yg E | Yg Wd | Yn E | Yn M | Yn E | Yn Wd | Yg M | Yg E3 | Yg M | Yg E1 | Yn M | Yn W | 28 |
| 29 | | | Yg F | Yg F | Yn F | Yn E4 | Yn F | Yn E2 | Yg E | Yg Wd | Yg E | Yg M | Yn E | Yn Wd | Yg M | Yg E3 | Yg M | Yg E1 | Yn M | Yn W | Yn M | Yn F | Yg W | Yg W | 29 |
| 30 | | | Yn F | Yn E2 | Yg E | Yg Wd | Yg E | Yg M | Yn E | Yn Wd | Yn E | Yn M | Yg M | Yg E1 | Yn M | Yn W | Yn M | Yn F | Yg W | Yg W | Yg W | Yg F | Yn W | Yn E4 | 30 |
| 31 | | | Yg E | Yg M | | | Yn E | Yn M | | | Yg M | Yg E3 | Yn M | Yn F | | | Yg W | Yg F | | | Yn W | Yn E2 | Yg Wd | Yg Wd | 31 |
| 1 | Yg E | Yg Wd | Yn E | Yn M | Yn E | Yn Wd | Yg M | Yg E3 | Yg M | Yg E1 | Yn M | Yn W | Yg W | Yg F | Yg W | Yg W | Yn W | Yn E2 | Yn W | Yn E4 | Yg Wd | Yg M | Yn Wd | Yn Wd | 1 |
| 2 | Yn E | Yn Wd | Yg M | Yg E3 | Yg M | Yg E1 | Yn M | Yn W | Yn M | Yn F | Yg W | Yg W | Yn W | Yn E2 | Yn W | Yn E4 | Yg Wd | Yg M | Yg Wd | Yg Wd | Yn Wd | Yn M | Yg F | Yg E1 | 2 |
| 3 | Yg M | Yg E1 | Yn M | Yn W | Yn M | Yn F | Yg W | Yg W | Yg W | Yg F | Yn W | Yn E4 | Yg Wd | Yg M | Yg Wd | Yg Wd | Yn Wd | Yn M | Yn Wd | Yn Wd | Yg F | Yg E3 | Yn F | Yn F | 3 |
| 4 | Yn M | Yn F | Yg W | Yg W | Yg W | Yg F | Yn W | Yn E4 | Yn W | Yn E2 | Yg Wd | Yg Wd | Yn Wd | Yn M | Yn Wd | Yn Wd | Yg F | Yg E3 | Yg F | Yg E1 | Yn F | Yn W | | | 4 |
| 5 | Yg W | Yg F | | | | | Yg Wd | Yg Wd | Yg Wd | Yg M | Yn Wd | Yn Wd | Yg F | Yg E3 | Yg F | Yg E1 | Yn F | Yn W | Yn F | Yn F | Yg E | Yg W | | | 5 |
| 6 | | | | | | | | | Yn Wd | Yn M | Yg F | Yg E1 | Yn F | Yn W | Yn F | Yn F | Yg E | Yg W | Yg E | Yg F | | | | | 6 |
| 7 | | | | | | | | | | | | | Yg E | Yg W | Yg E | Yg F | | | | | | | | | 7 |
| 8 | | | | | | | | | | | | | | | | | | | | | | | | | 8 |

# YEAR OF THE DOG

| | H | E | H | E | H | E | H | E | H | E | H | E | H | E | H | E | H | E | H | E | H | E | H | E | |
|---|---|---|---|---|---|---|---|---|---|---|---|---|---|---|---|---|---|---|---|---|---|---|---|---|---|
| **YEAR** | YEAR Yg W | Yg E3 | 1982 | | | | | | | | | | | | | | | | | | | | 1983 | | |
| **MONTH** | 4 Feb - 5 Mar | | 6 Mar - 4 Apr | | 5 Apr - 5 May | | 6 May - 5 June | | 6 June - 6 Jul | | 7 Jul - 7 Aug | | 8 Aug - 7 Sep | | 8 Sep - 7 Oct | | 8 Oct - 7 Nov | | 8 Nov - 6 Dec | | 7 Dec - 5 Jan | | 6 Jan - 3 Feb | | |
| | Yg W | Yg Wd | Yn W | Yn Wd | Yg Wd | Yg E1 | Yn Wd | Yn F | Yg F | Yg F | Yn F | Yn E2 | Yg E | Yg M | Yn E | Yn M | Yg M | Yg E3 | Yn M | Yn W | Yg W | Yg W | Yn W | Yn E4 | |
| **Starting time** | 1st day | Mid-pt | 1st day | Mid-pt | 1st day | Mid-pt | 1st day | Mid-pt | 1st day | Mid-pt | 1st day | Mid-pt | 1st day | Mid-pt | 1st day | Mid-pt | 1st day | Mid-pt | 1st day | Mid-pt | 1st day | Mid-pt | 1st day | Mid-pt | |
| Date | 4 | 19 | 6 | 21 | 5 | 20 | 6 | 21 | 6 | 22 | 7 | 23 | 8 | 23 | 8 | 23 | 8 | 24 | 8 | 22 | 7 | 22 | 6 | 20 | |
| Hour | 1145 | 0733 | 0555 | 0646 | 1058 | 1805 | 0432 | 1727 | 0837 | 0123 | 1856 | 1225 | 0442 | 1921 | 0745 | 1645 | 2309 | 0151 | 0204 | 2313 | 1844 | 1226 | 0553 | 2314 | |
| **DATE** 4 | Yg E | Yg F | | | | | | | | | | | | | | | | | | | | | | | 4 |
| 5 | Yn E | Yn E2 | | | Yg E | Yg F | | | | | | | | | | | | | | | | | | | 5 |
| 6 | Yg M | Yg M | Yg E | Yg W | Yn E | Yn E2 | Yn E | Yn E4 | Yg M | Yg M | | | | | | | | | | | | | Yg Wd | Yg F | 6 |
| 7 | Yn M | Yn M | Yn E | Yn E4 | Yg M | Yg M | Yg M | Yg Wd | Yn M | Yn M | Yn M | Yn Wd | | | | | | | | | Yg Wd | Yg W | Yn Wd | Yn E2 | 7 |
| 8 | Yg W | Yg E3 | Yg M | Yg Wd | Yn M | Yn M | Yn M | Yn Wd | Yg W | Yg E3 | Yg W | Yg E1 | Yn W | Yn W | Yg Wd | Yg F | Yg Wd | Yg W | Yn Wd | Yn E2 | Yn Wd | Yn E4 | Yg F | Yg M | 8 |
| 9 | Yn W | Yn W | Yn M | Yn Wd | Yg W | Yg E3 | Yg W | Yg E1 | Yn W | Yn W | Yn W | Yn F | Yg Wd | Yg W | Yn Wd | Yn E2 | Yn Wd | Yn E4 | Yg F | Yg M | Yg F | Yg Wd | Yn F | Yn M | 9 |
| 10 | Yg Wd | Yg W | Yg W | Yg E1 | Yn W | Yn W | Yn W | Yn F | Yg Wd | Yg W | Yg Wd | Yg F | Yn Wd | Yn E4 | Yg F | Yg M | Yg F | Yg Wd | Yn F | Yn M | Yn F | Yn Wd | Yg E | Yg E3 | 10 |
| 11 | Yn Wd | Yn E4 | Yn W | Yn F | Yg Wd | Yg W | Yg Wd | Yg F | Yn Wd | Yn E4 | Yn Wd | Yn E2 | Yg F | Yg Wd | Yn F | Yn M | Yn F | Yn Wd | Yg E | Yg E3 | Yg E | Yg E1 | Yn E | Yn W | 11 |
| 12 | Yg F | Yg Wd | Yg Wd | Yg F | Yn Wd | Yn E4 | Yn Wd | Yn E2 | Yg F | Yg Wd | Yg F | Yg M | Yn F | Yn Wd | Yg E | Yg E3 | Yg E | Yg E1 | Yn E | Yn W | Yn E | Yn F | Yg M | Yg W | 12 |
| 13 | Yn F | Yn Wd | Yn Wd | Yn E2 | Yg F | Yg Wd | Yg F | Yg M | Yn F | Yn Wd | Yn F | Yn M | Yg E | Yg E1 | Yn E | Yn W | Yn E | Yn F | Yg M | Yg W | Yg M | Yg F | Yn M | Yn E4 | 13 |
| 14 | Yg E | Yg E1 | Yg F | Yg M | Yn F | Yn Wd | Yn F | Yn M | Yg E | Yg E1 | Yg E | Yg E3 | Yn E | Yn F | Yg M | Yg W | Yg M | Yg F | Yn M | Yn E4 | Yn M | Yn E2 | Yg W | Yg Wd | 14 |
| 15 | Yn E | Yn F | Yn F | Yn M | Yg E | Yg E1 | Yg E | Yg E3 | Yn E | Yn F | Yn E | Yn W | Yg M | Yg F | Yn M | Yn E4 | Yn M | Yn E2 | Yg W | Yg Wd | Yg W | Yg M | Yn W | Yn Wd | 15 |
| 16 | Yg M | Yg F | Yg E | Yg E3 | Yn E | Yn F | Yn E | Yn W | Yg M | Yg F | Yg M | Yg W | Yn M | Yn E2 | Yg W | Yg Wd | Yg W | Yg M | Yn W | Yn Wd | Yn W | Yn M | Yg Wd | Yg E1 | 16 |
| 17 | Yn M | Yn E2 | Yn E | Yn W | Yg M | Yg F | Yg M | Yg W | Yn M | Yn E2 | Yn M | Yn E4 | Yg W | Yg M | Yn W | Yn Wd | Yn W | Yn M | Yg Wd | Yg E1 | Yg Wd | Yg E3 | Yn Wd | Yn F | 17 |
| 18 | Yg W | Yg M | Yg M | Yg W | Yn M | Yn E2 | Yn M | Yn E4 | Yg W | Yg M | Yg W | Yg Wd | Yn W | Yn M | Yg Wd | Yg E1 | Yg Wd | Yg E3 | Yn Wd | Yn F | Yn Wd | Yn W | Yg F | Yg F | 18 |
| 19 | Yn W | Yn M | Yn M | Yn E4 | Yg W | Yg M | Yg W | Yg Wd | Yn W | Yn M | Yn W | Yn Wd | Yg Wd | Yg E3 | Yn Wd | Yn F | Yn Wd | Yn W | Yg F | Yg F | Yg F | Yg W | Yn F | Yn E2 | 19 |
| 20 | Yg Wd | Yg E3 | Yg W | Yg Wd | Yn W | Yn M | Yn W | Yn Wd | Yg Wd | Yg E3 | Yg Wd | Yg E1 | Yn Wd | Yn W | Yg F | Yg F | Yg F | Yg W | Yn F | Yn E2 | Yn F | Yn E4 | Yg E | Yg M | 20 |
| 21 | Yn Wd | Yn W | Yn W | Yn Wd | Yg Wd | Yg E3 | Yg Wd | Yg E1 | Yn Wd | Yn W | Yn Wd | Yn F | Yg F | Yg W | Yn F | Yn E2 | Yn F | Yn E4 | Yg E | Yg M | Yg E | Yg Wd | Yn E | Yn M | 21 |
| 22 | Yg F | Yg W | Yg Wd | Yg E1 | Yn Wd | Yn W | Yn Wd | Yn F | Yg F | Yg W | Yg F | Yg F | Yn F | Yn E4 | Yg E | Yg M | Yg E | Yg Wd | Yn E | Yn M | Yn E | Yn Wd | Yg M | Yg E3 | 22 |
| 23 | Yn F | Yn E4 | Yn Wd | Yn F | Yg F | Yg W | Yg F | Yg F | Yn F | Yn E4 | Yn F | Yn E2 | Yg E | Yg Wd | Yn E | Yn M | Yn E | Yn Wd | Yg M | Yg E3 | Yg M | Yg E1 | Yn M | Yn W | 23 |
| 24 | Yg E | Yg Wd | Yg F | Yg F | Yn F | Yn E4 | Yn F | Yn E2 | Yg E | Yg Wd | Yg E | Yg M | Yn E | Yn Wd | Yg M | Yg E3 | Yg M | Yg E1 | Yn M | Yn W | Yn M | Yn F | Yg W | Yg W | 24 |
| 25 | Yn E | Yn Wd | Yn F | Yn E2 | Yg E | Yg Wd | Yg E | Yg M | Yn E | Yn Wd | Yn E | Yn M | Yg M | Yg E1 | Yn M | Yn W | Yn M | Yn F | Yg W | Yg W | Yg W | Yg F | Yn W | Yn E4 | 25 |
| 26 | Yg M | Yg E1 | Yg E | Yg M | Yn E | Yn Wd | Yn E | Yn M | Yg M | Yg E1 | Yg M | Yg E3 | Yn M | Yn F | Yg W | Yg W | Yg W | Yg F | Yn W | Yn E4 | Yn W | Yn E2 | Yg Wd | Yg Wd | 26 |
| 27 | Yn M | Yn F | Yn E | Yn M | Yg M | Yg E1 | Yg M | Yg E3 | Yn M | Yn F | Yn M | Yn W | Yg W | Yg F | Yn W | Yn E4 | Yn W | Yn E2 | Yg Wd | Yg Wd | Yg Wd | Yg M | Yn Wd | Yn Wd | 27 |
| 28 | Yg W | Yg F | Yg M | Yg E3 | Yn M | Yn F | Yn M | Yn W | Yg W | Yg F | Yg W | Yg W | Yn W | Yn E2 | Yg Wd | Yg Wd | Yg Wd | Yg M | Yn Wd | Yn Wd | Yn Wd | Yn M | Yg F | Yg E1 | 28 |
| 29 | | | Yn M | Yn W | Yg W | Yg F | Yg W | Yg W | Yn W | Yn E2 | Yn W | Yn E4 | Yg Wd | Yg M | Yn Wd | Yn Wd | Yn Wd | Yn M | Yg F | Yg E1 | Yg F | Yg E3 | Yn F | Yn F | 29 |
| 30 | | | Yg W | Yg W | Yn W | Yn E2 | Yn W | Yn E4 | Yg Wd | Yg M | Yg Wd | Yg Wd | Yn Wd | Yn M | Yg F | Yg E1 | Yg F | Yg E3 | Yn F | Yn F | Yn F | Yn W | Yg E | Yg F | 30 |
| 31 | | | Yn W | Yn E4 | | | Yg Wd | Yg Wd | | | Yn Wd | Yn Wd | Yg F | Yg E3 | | | Yn F | Yn W | | | Yg E | Yg W | Yn E | Yn E2 | 31 |
| 1 | Yn W | Yn E2 | Yg Wd | Yg Wd | Yg Wd | Yg M | Yn Wd | Yn Wd | Yn Wd | Yn M | Yg F | Yg E1 | Yn F | Yn W | Yn F | Yn F | Yg E | Yg W | Yg E | Yg F | Yn E | Yn E4 | Yg M | Yg M | 1 |
| 2 | Yg Wd | Yg M | Yn Wd | Yn Wd | Yn Wd | Yn M | Yg F | Yg E1 | Yg F | Yg E3 | Yn F | Yn F | Yg E | Yg W | Yg E | Yg F | Yn E | Yn E4 | Yn E | Yn E2 | Yg M | Yg Wd | Yn M | Yn M | 2 |
| 3 | Yn Wd | Yn M | Yg F | Yg E1 | Yg F | Yg E3 | Yn F | Yn F | Yn F | Yn W | Yg E | Yg F | Yn E | Yn E4 | Yn E | Yn E2 | Yg M | Yg Wd | Yg M | Yg M | Yn M | Yn Wd | Yg W | Yg E3 | 3 |
| 4 | Yg F | Yg E3 | Yn F | Yn F | Yn F | Yn W | Yg E | Yg F | Yg E | Yg W | Yn E | Yn E2 | Yg M | Yg Wd | Yg M | Yg M | Yn M | Yn Wd | Yn M | Yn M | Yg W | Yg E1 | | | 4 |
| 5 | Yn F | Yn W | | | Yg E | Yg W | Yn E | Yn E2 | Yn E | Yn E4 | Yg M | Yg M | Yn M | Yn Wd | Yn M | Yn M | Yg W | Yg E1 | Yg W | Yg E3 | Yn W | Yn F | | | 5 |
| 6 | | | | | | | | | Yg M | Yg Wd | Yn M | Yn M | Yg W | Yg E1 | Yg W | Yg E3 | Yn W | Yn F | Yn W | Yn W | | | | | 6 |
| 7 | | | | | | | | | | | Yg W | Yg E3 | Yn W | Yn F | Yn W | Yn W | Yg Wd | Yg F | | | | | | | 7 |
| 8 | | | | | | | | | | | | | | | | | | | | | | | | | 8 |

# YEAR OF THE PIG

| | H | E | H | E | H | E | H | E | H | E | H | E | H | E | H | E | H | E | H | E | H | E | H | E | |
|---|---|---|---|---|---|---|---|---|---|---|---|---|---|---|---|---|---|---|---|---|---|---|---|---|---|
| YEAR | YEAR<br>Yn W | Yn W | 1983 | | | | | | | | | | | | | | | | | | 1984 | | | | |
| MONTH | 4 Feb - 5 Mar | | 6 Mar - 4 Apr | | 5 Apr - 5 May | | 6 May - 5 June | | 6 June - 7 Jul | | 8 Jul - 7 Aug | | 8 Aug - 7 Sep | | 8 Sep - 8 Oct | | 9 Oct - 7 Nov | | 8 Nov - 7 Dec | | 8 Dec - 5 Jan | | 6 Jan - 3 Feb | | |
| | Yg Wd | Yg Wd | Yn Wd | Yn Wd | Yg F | Yg E1 | Yn F | Yn F | Yg E | Yg F | Yn E | Yn E2 | Yg M | Yg M | Yn M | Yn M | Yg W | Yg E3 | Yn W | Yn W | Yg Wd | Yg W | Yn Wd | Yn E4 | |
| Starting time | 1st day | Mid-pt | 1st day | Mid-pt | 1st day | Mid-pt | 1st day | Mid-pt | 1st day | Mid-pt | 1st day | Mid-pt | 1st day | Mid-pt | 1st day | Mid-pt | 1st day | Mid-pt | 1st day | Mid-pt | 1st day | Mid-pt | 1st day | Mid-pt | |
| Date | 4 | 19 | 6 | 21 | 5 | 20 | 6 | 21 | 6 | 22 | 8 | 23 | 8 | 24 | 8 | 23 | 9 | 24 | 8 | 23 | 8 | 22 | 6 | 21 | |
| Hour | 1735 | 1331 | 1145 | 1238 | 1648 | 2352 | 1013 | 2308 | 1427 | 0709 | 0043 | 1814 | 1030 | 0110 | 1320 | 2241 | 0457 | 0756 | 0754 | 0519 | 0034 | 1830 | 1143 | 0506 | |
| DATE 4 | Yn W | Yn W | | | | | | | | | | | | | | | | | | | | | | | 4 |
| 5 | Yg Wd | Yg W | | | Yn W | Yn W | | | | | | | | | | | | | | | | | | | 5 |
| 6 | Yn Wd | Yn E4 | Yn W | Yn F | Yg Wd | Yg W | Yg Wd | Yg F | Yn Wd | Yn E4 | | | | | | | | | | | | | Yn E | Yn W | 6 |
| 7 | Yg F | Yg Wd | Yg Wd | Yg F | Yn Wd | Yn E4 | Yn Wd | Yn E2 | Yg F | Yg Wd | | | | | | | | | | | | | Yg M | Yg W | 7 |
| 8 | Yn F | Yn Wd | Yn Wd | Yn E2 | Yg F | Yg Wd | Yg F | Yg M | Yn F | Yn Wd | Yn F | Yn M | Yg E | Yg E1 | Yn E | Yn W | | | Yg M | Yg W | Yg M | Yg F | Yn M | Yn E4 | 8 |
| 9 | Yg E | Yg E1 | Yg F | Yg M | Yn F | Yn Wd | Yn F | Yn M | Yg E | Yg E1 | Yg E | Yg E3 | Yn E | Yn F | Yg M | Yg W | Yg M | Yg F | Yn M | Yn E4 | Yn M | Yn E2 | Yg W | Yg Wd | 9 |
| 10 | Yn E | Yn F | Yn F | Yn M | Yg E | Yg E1 | Yg E | Yg E3 | Yn E | Yn F | Yn E | Yn W | Yg M | Yg F | Yn M | Yn E4 | Yn M | Yn E2 | Yg W | Yg Wd | Yg W | Yg M | Yn W | Yn Wd | 10 |
| 11 | Yg M | Yg F | Yg E | Yg E3 | Yn E | Yn F | Yn E | Yn W | Yg M | Yg F | Yg M | Yg W | Yn M | Yn E2 | Yg W | Yg Wd | Yg W | Yg M | Yn W | Yn Wd | Yn W | Yn M | Yg Wd | Yg E1 | 11 |
| 12 | Yn M | Yn E2 | Yn E | Yn W | Yg M | Yg F | Yg M | Yg W | Yn M | Yn E2 | Yn M | Yn E4 | Yg W | Yg M | Yn W | Yn Wd | Yn W | Yn M | Yg Wd | Yg E1 | Yg Wd | Yg E3 | Yn Wd | Yn F | 12 |
| 13 | Yg W | Yg M | Yg M | Yg W | Yn M | Yn E2 | Yn M | Yn E4 | Yg W | Yg M | Yg W | Yg Wd | Yn W | Yn M | Yg Wd | Yg E1 | Yg Wd | Yg E3 | Yn Wd | Yn F | Yn Wd | Yn W | Yg F | Yg F | 13 |
| 14 | Yn W | Yn M | Yn M | Yn E4 | Yg W | Yg M | Yg W | Yg Wd | Yn W | Yn M | Yn W | Yn Wd | Yg Wd | Yg E3 | Yn Wd | Yn F | Yn Wd | Yn W | Yg F | Yg F | Yg F | Yg W | Yn F | Yn E2 | 14 |
| 15 | Yg Wd | Yg E3 | Yg W | Yg Wd | Yn W | Yn M | Yn W | Yn Wd | Yg Wd | Yg E3 | Yg Wd | Yg E1 | Yn Wd | Yn W | Yg F | Yg F | Yg F | Yg W | Yn F | Yn E2 | Yn F | Yn E4 | Yg E | Yg M | 15 |
| 16 | Yn Wd | Yn W | Yn W | Yn Wd | Yg Wd | Yg E3 | Yg Wd | Yg E1 | Yn Wd | Yn W | Yn Wd | Yn F | Yg F | Yg W | Yn F | Yn E2 | Yn F | Yn E4 | Yg E | Yg M | Yg E | Yg Wd | Yn E | Yn M | 16 |
| 17 | Yg F | Yg W | Yg Wd | Yg E1 | Yn Wd | Yn W | Yn Wd | Yn F | Yg F | Yg W | Yg F | Yg F | Yn F | Yn E4 | Yg E | Yg M | Yg E | Yg Wd | Yn E | Yn M | Yn E | Yn Wd | Yg M | Yg E3 | 17 |
| 18 | Yn F | Yn E4 | Yn Wd | Yn F | Yg F | Yg W | Yg F | Yg F | Yn F | Yn E4 | Yn F | Yn E2 | Yg E | Yg Wd | Yn E | Yn M | Yn E | Yn Wd | Yg M | Yg E3 | Yg M | Yg E1 | Yn M | Yn W | 18 |
| 19 | Yg E | Yg Wd | Yg F | Yg F | Yn F | Yn E4 | Yn F | Yn E2 | Yg E | Yg Wd | Yg E | Yg M | Yn E | Yn Wd | Yg M | Yg E3 | Yg M | Yg E1 | Yn M | Yn W | Yn M | Yn F | Yg W | Yg W | 19 |
| 20 | Yn E | Yn Wd | Yn F | Yn E2 | Yg E | Yg Wd | Yg E | Yg M | Yn E | Yn Wd | Yn E | Yn M | Yg M | Yg E1 | Yn M | Yn W | Yn M | Yn F | Yg W | Yg W | Yg W | Yg F | Yn W | Yn E4 | 20 |
| 21 | Yg M | Yg E1 | Yg E | Yg M | Yn E | Yn Wd | Yn E | Yn M | Yg M | Yg E1 | Yg M | Yg E3 | Yn M | Yn F | Yg W | Yg W | Yg W | Yg F | Yn W | Yn E4 | Yn W | Yn E2 | Yg Wd | Yg Wd | 21 |
| 22 | Yn M | Yn F | Yn E | Yn M | Yg M | Yg E1 | Yg M | Yg E3 | Yn M | Yn F | Yn M | Yn W | Yg W | Yg F | Yn W | Yn E4 | Yn W | Yn E2 | Yg Wd | Yg Wd | Yg Wd | Yg M | Yn Wd | Yn Wd | 22 |
| 23 | Yg W | Yg F | Yg M | Yg E3 | Yn M | Yn F | Yn M | Yn W | Yg W | Yg F | Yg W | Yg W | Yn W | Yn E2 | Yg Wd | Yg Wd | Yg Wd | Yg M | Yn Wd | Yn Wd | Yn Wd | Yn M | Yg F | Yg E1 | 23 |
| 24 | Yn W | Yn E2 | Yn M | Yn W | Yg W | Yg F | Yg W | Yg W | Yn W | Yn E2 | Yn W | Yn E4 | Yg Wd | Yg M | Yn Wd | Yn Wd | Yn Wd | Yn M | Yg F | Yg E1 | Yg F | Yg E3 | Yn F | Yn F | 24 |
| 25 | Yg Wd | Yg M | Yg W | Yg W | Yn W | Yn E2 | Yn W | Yn E4 | Yg Wd | Yg M | Yg Wd | Yg Wd | Yn Wd | Yn M | Yg F | Yg E1 | Yg F | Yg E3 | Yn F | Yn F | Yn F | Yn W | Yg E | Yg F | 25 |
| 26 | Yn Wd | Yn M | Yn W | Yn E4 | Yg Wd | Yg M | Yg Wd | Yg Wd | Yn Wd | Yn M | Yn Wd | Yn Wd | Yg F | Yg E3 | Yn F | Yn F | Yn F | Yn W | Yg E | Yg F | Yg E | Yg W | Yn E | Yn E2 | 26 |
| 27 | Yg F | Yg E3 | Yg Wd | Yg Wd | Yn Wd | Yn M | Yn Wd | Yn Wd | Yg F | Yg E3 | Yg F | Yg E1 | Yn F | Yn W | Yg E | Yg F | Yg E | Yg W | Yn E | Yn E2 | Yn E | Yn E4 | Yg M | Yg M | 27 |
| 28 | Yn F | Yn W | Yn Wd | Yn Wd | Yg F | Yg E3 | Yg F | Yg E1 | Yn F | Yn W | Yn F | Yn F | Yg E | Yg W | Yn E | Yn E2 | Yn E | Yn E4 | Yg M | Yg M | Yg M | Yg Wd | Yn M | Yn M | 28 |
| 29 | | | Yg F | Yg E1 | Yn F | Yn W | Yn F | Yn F | Yg E | Yg W | Yg E | Yg F | Yn E | Yn E4 | Yg M | Yg M | Yg M | Yg Wd | Yn M | Yn M | Yn M | Yn Wd | Yg W | Yg E3 | 29 |
| 30 | | | Yn F | Yn F | Yg E | Yg W | Yg E | Yg F | Yn E | Yn E4 | Yn E | Yn E2 | Yg M | Yg Wd | Yn M | Yn M | Yn M | Yn Wd | Yg W | Yg E3 | Yg W | Yg E1 | Yn W | Yn W | 30 |
| 31 | | | Yg E | Yg F | | | Yn E | Yn E2 | | | Yg M | Yg M | Yn M | Yn Wd | | | Yg W | Yg E1 | | | Yn W | Yn F | Yg Wd | Yg W | 31 |
| 1 | Yg E | Yg W | Yn E | Yn E2 | Yn E | Yn E4 | Yg M | Yg M | Yg M | Yg Wd | Yn M | Yn M | Yg W | Yg E1 | Yg W | Yg E3 | Yn W | Yn F | Yn W | Yn W | Yg Wd | Yg F | Yn Wd | Yn E4 | 1 |
| 2 | Yn E | Yn E4 | Yg M | Yg M | Yg M | Yg Wd | Yn M | Yn M | Yn M | Yn Wd | Yg W | Yg E3 | Yn W | Yn F | Yn W | Yn W | Yg Wd | Yg F | Yg Wd | Yg W | Yn Wd | Yn E2 | Yg F | Yg Wd | 2 |
| 3 | Yg M | Yg Wd | Yn M | Yn M | Yn M | Yn Wd | Yg W | Yg E3 | Yg W | Yg E1 | Yn W | Yn W | Yg Wd | Yg F | Yg Wd | Yg W | Yn Wd | Yn E2 | Yn Wd | Yn E4 | Yg F | Yg M | Yn F | Yn Wd | 3 |
| 4 | Yn M | Yn Wd | Yg W | Yg E3 | Yg W | Yg E1 | Yn W | Yn W | Yn W | Yn F | Yg Wd | Yg W | Yn Wd | Yn E2 | Yn Wd | Yn E4 | Yg F | Yg M | Yg F | Yg Wd | Yn F | Yn M | | | 4 |
| 5 | Yg W | Yg E1 | | | Yn W | Yn F | Yg Wd | Yg W | Yg Wd | Yg F | Yn Wd | Yn E4 | Yg F | Yg M | Yg F | Yg Wd | Yn F | Yn M | Yn F | Yn Wd | Yg E | Yg E3 | | | 5 |
| 6 | | | | | | | | | Yn Wd | Yn E2 | Yg F | Yg Wd | Yn F | Yn M | Yn F | Yn Wd | Yg E | Yg E3 | Yg E | Yg E1 | | | | | 6 |
| 7 | | | | | | | | | Yg F | Yg M | Yn F | Yn Wd | Yg E | Yg E3 | Yg E | Yg E1 | Yn E | Yn W | Yn E | Yn F | | | | | 7 |
| 8 | | | | | | | | | | | | | | | Yn E | Yn F | | | | | | | | | 8 |

# YEAR OF THE RAT

| | H | E | H | E | H | E | H | E | H | E | H | E |
|---|---|---|---|---|---|---|---|---|---|---|---|---|
| YEAR | YEAR Yg Wd | Yg W | 1984 | | | | | | | | | |
| MONTH | 4 Feb - 4 Mar | | 5 Mar - 3 Apr | | 4 Apr - 4 May | | 5 May - 4 June | | 5 June - 6 Jul | | 7 Jul - 6 Aug | |
| | Yg F | Yg Wd | Yn F | Yn Wd | Yg E | Yg E1 | Yn E | Yn F | Yg M | Yg F | Yn M | Yn E2 |
| Starting time | 1st day | Mid-pt | 1st day | Mid-pt | 1st day | Mid-pt | 1st day | Mid-pt | 1st day | Mid-pt | 1st day | Mid-pt |
| Date | 4 | 19 | 5 | 20 | 4 | 20 | 5 | 21 | 5 | 21 | 7 | 23 |
| Hour | 2320 | 1910 | 1726 | 1823 | 2223 | 0542 | 1552 | 0500 | 2009 | 1303 | 0629 | 0003 |
| DATE 4 | Yg E | Yg E1 | | | Yg E | Yg E1 | | | | | | |
| 5 | Yn E | Yn F | Yg E | Yg E3 | Yn E | Yn F | Yn E | Yn W | Yg M | Yg F | | |
| 6 | Yg M | Yg F | Yn E | Yn W | Yg M | Yg F | Yg M | Yg W | Yn M | Yn E2 | | |
| 7 | Yn M | Yn E2 | Yg M | Yg W | Yn M | Yn E2 | Yn M | Yn E4 | Yg W | Yg M | Yg W | Yg Wd |
| 8 | Yg W | Yg M | Yn M | Yn E4 | Yg W | Yg M | Yg W | Yg Wd | Yn W | Yn M | Yn W | Yn Wd |
| 9 | Yn W | Yn M | Yg W | Yg Wd | Yn W | Yn M | Yn W | Yn Wd | Yg Wd | Yg E3 | Yg Wd | Yg E1 |
| 10 | Yg Wd | Yg E3 | Yn W | Yn Wd | Yg Wd | Yg E3 | Yg Wd | Yg E1 | Yn Wd | Yn W | Yn Wd | Yn F |
| 11 | Yn Wd | Yn W | Yg Wd | Yg E1 | Yn Wd | Yn W | Yn Wd | Yn F | Yg F | Yg W | Yg F | Yg F |
| 12 | Yg F | Yg W | Yn Wd | Yn F | Yg F | Yg W | Yg F | Yg F | Yn F | Yn E4 | Yn F | Yn E2 |
| 13 | Yn F | Yn E4 | Yg F | Yg F | Yn F | Yn E4 | Yn F | Yn E2 | Yg E | Yg Wd | Yg E | Yg M |
| 14 | Yg E | Yg Wd | Yn F | Yn E2 | Yg E | Yg Wd | Yg E | Yg M | Yn E | Yn Wd | Yn E | Yn M |
| 15 | Yn E | Yn Wd | Yg E | Yg M | Yn E | Yn Wd | Yn E | Yn M | Yg M | Yg E1 | Yg M | Yg E3 |
| 16 | Yg M | Yg E1 | Yn E | Yn M | Yg M | Yg E1 | Yg M | Yg E3 | Yn M | Yn F | Yn M | Yn W |
| 17 | Yn M | Yn F | Yg M | Yg E3 | Yn M | Yn F | Yn M | Yn W | Yg W | Yg F | Yg W | Yg W |
| 18 | Yg W | Yg F | Yn M | Yn W | Yg W | Yg F | Yg W | Yg W | Yn W | Yn E2 | Yn W | Yn E4 |
| 19 | Yn W | Yn E2 | Yg W | Yg W | Yn W | Yn E2 | Yn W | Yn E4 | Yg Wd | Yg M | Yg Wd | Yg Wd |
| 20 | Yg Wd | Yg M | Yn W | Yn E4 | Yg Wd | Yg M | Yg Wd | Yg Wd | Yn Wd | Yn M | Yn Wd | Yn Wd |
| 21 | Yn Wd | Yn M | Yg Wd | Yg Wd | Yn Wd | Yn M | Yn Wd | Yn Wd | Yg F | Yg E3 | Yg F | Yg E1 |
| 22 | Yg F | Yg E3 | Yn Wd | Yn Wd | Yg F | Yg E3 | Yg F | Yg E1 | Yn F | Yn W | Yn F | Yn F |
| 23 | Yn F | Yn W | Yg F | Yg E1 | Yn F | Yn W | Yn F | Yn F | Yg E | Yg W | Yg E | Yg F |
| 24 | Yg E | Yg W | Yn F | Yn F | Yg E | Yg W | Yg E | Yg F | Yn E | Yn E4 | Yn E | Yn E2 |
| 25 | Yn E | Yn E4 | Yg E | Yg F | Yn E | Yn E4 | Yn E | Yn E2 | Yg M | Yg Wd | Yg M | Yg M |
| 26 | Yg M | Yg Wd | Yn E | Yn E2 | Yg M | Yg Wd | Yg M | Yg M | Yn M | Yn Wd | Yn M | Yn M |
| 27 | Yn M | Yn Wd | Yg M | Yg M | Yn M | Yn Wd | Yn M | Yn M | Yg W | Yg E1 | Yg W | Yg E3 |
| 28 | Yg W | Yg E1 | Yn M | Yn M | Yg W | Yg E1 | Yg W | Yg E3 | Yn W | Yn F | Yn W | Yn W |
| 29 | Yn W | Yn F | Yg W | Yg E3 | Yn W | Yn F | Yn W | Yn W | Yg Wd | Yg F | Yg Wd | Yg W |
| 30 | | | Yn W | Yn W | Yg Wd | Yg F | Yg Wd | Yg W | Yn Wd | Yn E2 | Yn Wd | Yn E4 |
| 31 | | | Yg Wd | Yg W | | | Yn Wd | Yn E4 | | | Yg F | Yg Wd |
| 1 | Yg Wd | Yg F | Yn Wd | Yn E4 | Yn Wd | Yn E2 | Yg F | Yg Wd | Yg F | Yg M | Yn F | Yn Wd |
| 2 | Yn Wd | Yn E2 | Yg F | Yg Wd | Yg F | Yg M | Yn F | Yn Wd | Yn F | Yn M | Yg E | Yg E1 |
| 3 | Yg F | Yg M | Yn F | Yn Wd | Yn F | Yn M | Yg E | Yg E1 | Yg E | Yg E3 | Yn E | Yn F |
| 4 | Yn F | Yn M | | | Yg E | Yg E3 | Yn E | Yn F | Yn E | Yn W | Yg M | Yg F |
| 5 | | | | | | | | | Yg M | Yg W | Yn M | Yn E2 |
| 6 | | | | | | | | | Yn M | Yn E4 | Yg W | Yg M |
| 7 | | | | | | | | | | | | |
| 8 | | | | | | | | | | | | |

| | H | E | H | E | H | E | H | E | H | E | H | E | |
|---|---|---|---|---|---|---|---|---|---|---|---|---|---|
| YEAR | 1984 | | | | | | | | | | 1985 | | |
| MONTH | 7 Aug - 6 Sep | | 7 Sep - 7 Oct | | 8 Oct - 6 Nov | | 7 Nov - 6 Dec | | 7 Dec - 4 Jan | | 5 Jan - 3 Feb | | |
| | Yg W | Yg M | Yn W | Yn M | Yg Wd | Yg E3 | Yn Wd | Yn W | Yg F | Yg W | Yn F | Yn E4 | |
| Starting time | 1st day | Mid-pt | 1st day | Mid-pt | 1st day | Mid-pt | 1st day | Mid-pt | 1st day | Mid-pt | 1st day | Mid-pt | |
| Date | 7 | 23 | 7 | 23 | 8 | 23 | 7 | 22 | 7 | 22 | 5 | 20 | |
| Hour | 1619 | 0701 | 1910 | 0425 | 1049 | 1331 | 1347 | 1111 | 0624 | 2306 | 1733 | 1044 | |
| DATE 4 | | | | | | | | | | | | | 4 |
| 5 | | | | | | | | | | | Yg Wd | Yg E1 | 5 |
| 6 | | | | | | | | | | | Yn Wd | Yn F | 6 |
| 7 | Yn W | Yn M | Yg Wd | Yg E1 | | | Yn Wd | Yn F | Yn Wd | Yn W | Yg F | Yg F | 7 |
| 8 | Yg Wd | Yg E3 | Yn Wd | Yn F | Yn Wd | Yn W | Yg F | Yg F | Yg F | Yg W | Yn F | Yn E2 | 8 |
| 9 | Yn Wd | Yn W | Yg F | Yg F | Yg F | Yg W | Yn F | Yn E2 | Yn F | Yn E4 | Yg E | Yg M | 9 |
| 10 | Yg F | Yg W | Yn F | Yn E2 | Yn F | Yn E4 | Yg E | Yg M | Yg E | Yg Wd | Yn E | Yn M | 10 |
| 11 | Yn F | Yn E4 | Yg E | Yg M | Yg E | Yg Wd | Yn E | Yn M | Yn E | Yn Wd | Yg M | Yg E3 | 11 |
| 12 | Yg E | Yg Wd | Yn E | Yn M | Yn E | Yn Wd | Yg M | Yg E3 | Yg M | Yg E1 | Yn M | Yn W | 12 |
| 13 | Yn E | Yn Wd | Yg M | Yg E3 | Yg M | Yg E1 | Yn M | Yn W | Yn M | Yn F | Yg W | Yg W | 13 |
| 14 | Yg M | Yg E1 | Yn M | Yn W | Yn M | Yn F | Yg W | Yg W | Yg W | Yg F | Yn W | Yn E4 | 14 |
| 15 | Yn M | Yn F | Yg W | Yg W | Yg W | Yg F | Yn W | Yn E4 | Yn W | Yn E2 | Yg Wd | Yg Wd | 15 |
| 16 | Yg W | Yg F | Yn W | Yn E4 | Yn W | Yn E2 | Yg Wd | Yg Wd | Yg Wd | Yg M | Yn Wd | Yn Wd | 16 |
| 17 | Yn W | Yn E2 | Yg Wd | Yg Wd | Yg Wd | Yg M | Yn Wd | Yn Wd | Yn Wd | Yn M | Yg F | Yg E1 | 17 |
| 18 | Yg Wd | Yg M | Yn Wd | Yn Wd | Yn Wd | Yn M | Yg F | Yg E1 | Yg F | Yg E3 | Yn F | Yn F | 18 |
| 19 | Yn Wd | Yn M | Yg F | Yg E1 | Yg F | Yg E3 | Yn F | Yn F | Yn F | Yn W | Yg E | Yg F | 19 |
| 20 | Yg F | Yg E3 | Yn F | Yn F | Yn F | Yn W | Yg E | Yg F | Yg E | Yg W | Yn E | Yn E2 | 20 |
| 21 | Yn F | Yn W | Yg E | Yg F | Yg E | Yg W | Yn E | Yn E2 | Yn E | Yn E4 | Yg M | Yg M | 21 |
| 22 | Yg E | Yg W | Yn E | Yn E2 | Yn E | Yn E4 | Yg M | Yg M | Yg M | Yg Wd | Yn M | Yn M | 22 |
| 23 | Yn E | Yn E4 | Yg M | Yg M | Yg M | Yg Wd | Yn M | Yn M | Yn M | Yn Wd | Yg W | Yg E3 | 23 |
| 24 | Yg M | Yg Wd | Yn M | Yn M | Yn M | Yn Wd | Yg W | Yg E3 | Yg W | Yg E1 | Yn W | Yn W | 24 |
| 25 | Yn M | Yn Wd | Yg W | Yg E3 | Yg W | Yg E1 | Yn W | Yn W | Yn W | Yn F | Yg Wd | Yg W | 25 |
| 26 | Yg W | Yg E1 | Yn W | Yn W | Yn W | Yn F | Yg Wd | Yg W | Yg Wd | Yg F | Yn Wd | Yn E4 | 26 |
| 27 | Yn W | Yn F | Yg Wd | Yg W | Yg Wd | Yg F | Yn Wd | Yn E4 | Yn Wd | Yn E2 | Yg F | Yg Wd | 27 |
| 28 | Yg Wd | Yg F | Yn Wd | Yn E4 | Yn Wd | Yn E2 | Yg F | Yg Wd | Yg F | Yg M | Yn F | Yn Wd | 28 |
| 29 | Yn Wd | Yn E2 | Yg F | Yg Wd | Yg F | Yg M | Yn F | Yn Wd | Yn F | Yn M | Yg E | Yg E1 | 29 |
| 30 | Yg F | Yg M | Yn F | Yn Wd | Yn F | Yn M | Yg E | Yg E1 | Yg E | Yg E3 | Yn E | Yn F | 30 |
| 31 | Yn F | Yn M | | | Yg E | Yg E3 | | | Yn E | Yn W | Yg M | Yg F | 31 |
| 1 | Yg E | Yg E3 | Yg E | Yg E1 | Yn E | Yn W | Yn E | Yn F | Yg M | Yg W | Yn M | Yn E2 | 1 |
| 2 | Yn E | Yn W | Yn E | Yn F | Yg M | Yg W | Yg M | Yg F | Yn M | Yn E4 | Yg W | Yg M | 2 |
| 3 | Yg M | Yg W | Yg M | Yg F | Yn M | Yn E4 | Yn M | Yn E2 | Yg W | Yg Wd | Yn W | Yn M | 3 |
| 4 | Yn M | Yn E4 | Yn M | Yn E2 | Yg W | Yg Wd | Yg W | Yg M | Yn W | Yn Wd | | | 4 |
| 5 | Yg W | Yg Wd | Yg W | Yg M | Yn W | Yn Wd | Yn W | Yn M | | | | | 5 |
| 6 | Yn W | Yn Wd | Yn W | Yn M | Yg Wd | Yg E1 | Yg Wd | Yg E3 | | | | | 6 |
| 7 | | | Yg Wd | Yg E3 | | | | | | | | | 7 |
| 8 | | | | | | | | | | | | | 8 |

# YEAR OF THE OX

| | H | E | H | E | H | E | H | E | H | E | H | E | H | E | H | E | H | E | H | E | H | E | H | E | |
|---|---|---|---|---|---|---|---|---|---|---|---|---|---|---|---|---|---|---|---|---|---|---|---|---|---|
| YEAR | YEAR Yn Wd | Yn E4 | 1985 | | | | | | | | | | | | | | | | | | 1986 | | | | |
| MONTH | 4 Feb - 4 Mar | | 5 Mar - 4 Apr | | 5 Apr - 4 May | | 5 May - 5 June | | 6 June - 6 Jul | | 7 Jul - 6 Aug | | 7 Aug - 7 Sep | | 8 Sep - 7 Oct | | 8 Oct - 6 Nov | | 7 Nov - 6 Dec | | 7 Dec - 4 Jan | | 5 Jan - 3 Feb | | |
| | Yg E | Yg Wd | Yn E | Yn Wd | Yg M | Yg E1 | Yn M | Yn F | Yg W | Yg F | Yn W | Yn E2 | Yg Wd | Yg M | Yn Wd | Yn M | Yg F | Yg E3 | Yn F | Yn W | Yg E | Yg W | Yn E | Yn E4 | |
| Starting time | 1st day | Mid-pt | 1st day | Mid-pt | 1st day | Mid-pt | 1st day | Mid-pt | 1st day | Mid-pt | 1st day | Mid-pt | 1st day | Mid-pt | 1st day | Mid-pt | 1st day | Mid-pt | 1st day | Mid-pt | 1st day | Mid-pt | 1st day | Mid-pt | |
| Date | 4 | 19 | 5 | 21 | 5 | 20 | 5 | 21 | 6 | 21 | 7 | 23 | 7 | 23 | 8 | 23 | 8 | 23 | 7 | 22 | 7 | 22 | 5 | 20 | |
| Hour | 0515 | 0014 | 2325 | 0021 | 0428 | 1134 | 2202 | 1045 | 0224 | 1902 | 1247 | 0554 | 2229 | 1250 | 0113 | 1014 | 1637 | 1920 | 1932 | 1642 | 1212 | 0555 | 2321 | 1633 | |
| DATE 4 | Yg Wd | Yg E3 | | | | | | | | | | | | | | | | | | | | | | | 4 |
| 5 | Yn Wd | Yn W | Yn W | Yn Wd | Yg Wd | Yg E3 | Yg Wd | Yg E1 | | | | | | | | | | | | | | | Yn E | Yn M | 5 |
| 6 | Yg F | Yg W | Yg Wd | Yg E1 | Yn Wd | Yn W | Yn Wd | Yn F | Yg F | Yg W | | | | | | | | | | | | | Yg M | Yg E3 | 6 |
| 7 | Yn F | Yn E4 | Yn Wd | Yn F | Yg F | Yg W | Yg F | Yg F | Yn F | Yn E4 | Yn F | Yn E2 | Yg E | Yg Wd | | | | | Yg M | Yg E3 | Yg M | Yg E1 | Yn M | Yn W | 7 |
| 8 | Yg E | Yg Wd | Yg F | Yg F | Yn F | Yn E4 | Yn F | Yn E2 | Yg E | Yg Wd | Yg E | Yg M | Yn E | Yn Wd | Yg M | Yg E3 | Yg M | Yg E1 | Yn M | Yn W | Yn M | Yn F | Yg W | Yg W | 8 |
| 9 | Yn E | Yn Wd | Yn F | Yn E2 | Yg E | Yg Wd | Yg E | Yg M | Yn E | Yn Wd | Yn E | Yn M | Yg M | Yg E1 | Yn M | Yn W | Yn M | Yn F | Yg W | Yg W | Yg W | Yg F | Yn W | Yn E4 | 9 |
| 10 | Yg M | Yg E1 | Yg E | Yg M | Yn E | Yn Wd | Yn E | Yn M | Yg M | Yg E1 | Yg M | Yg E3 | Yn M | Yn F | Yg W | Yg W | Yg W | Yg F | Yn W | Yn E4 | Yn W | Yn E2 | Yg Wd | Yg Wd | 10 |
| 11 | Yn M | Yn F | Yn E | Yn M | Yg M | Yg E1 | Yg M | Yg E3 | Yn M | Yn F | Yn M | Yn W | Yg W | Yg F | Yn W | Yn E4 | Yn W | Yn E2 | Yg Wd | Yg Wd | Yg Wd | Yg M | Yn Wd | Yn Wd | 11 |
| 12 | Yg W | Yg F | Yg M | Yg E3 | Yn M | Yn F | Yn M | Yn W | Yg W | Yg F | Yg W | Yg W | Yn W | Yn E2 | Yg Wd | Yg Wd | Yg Wd | Yg M | Yn Wd | Yn Wd | Yn Wd | Yn M | Yg F | Yg E1 | 12 |
| 13 | Yn W | Yn E2 | Yn M | Yn W | Yg W | Yg F | Yg W | Yg W | Yn W | Yn E2 | Yn W | Yn E4 | Yg Wd | Yg M | Yn Wd | Yn Wd | Yn Wd | Yn M | Yg F | Yg E1 | Yg F | Yg E3 | Yn F | Yn F | 13 |
| 14 | Yg Wd | Yg M | Yg W | Yg W | Yn W | Yn E2 | Yn W | Yn E4 | Yg Wd | Yg M | Yg Wd | Yg Wd | Yn Wd | Yn M | Yg F | Yg E1 | Yg F | Yg E3 | Yn F | Yn F | Yn F | Yn W | Yg E | Yg F | 14 |
| 15 | Yn Wd | Yn M | Yn W | Yn E4 | Yg Wd | Yg M | Yg Wd | Yg Wd | Yn Wd | Yn M | Yn Wd | Yn Wd | Yg F | Yg E3 | Yn F | Yn F | Yn F | Yn W | Yg E | Yg F | Yg E | Yg W | Yn E | Yn E2 | 15 |
| 16 | Yg F | Yg E3 | Yg Wd | Yg Wd | Yn Wd | Yn M | Yn Wd | Yn Wd | Yg F | Yg E3 | Yg F | Yg E1 | Yn F | Yn W | Yg E | Yg F | Yg E | Yg W | Yn E | Yn E2 | Yn E | Yn E4 | Yg M | Yg M | 16 |
| 17 | Yn F | Yn W | Yn Wd | Yn Wd | Yg F | Yg E3 | Yg F | Yg E1 | Yn F | Yn W | Yn F | Yn F | Yg E | Yg W | Yn E | Yn E2 | Yn E | Yn E4 | Yg M | Yg M | Yg M | Yg Wd | Yn M | Yn M | 17 |
| 18 | Yg E | Yg W | Yg F | Yg E1 | Yn F | Yn W | Yn F | Yn F | Yg E | Yg W | Yg E | Yg F | Yn E | Yn E4 | Yg M | Yg M | Yg M | Yg Wd | Yn M | Yn M | Yn M | Yn Wd | Yg W | Yg E3 | 18 |
| 19 | Yn E | Yn E4 | Yn F | Yn F | Yg E | Yg W | Yg E | Yg F | Yn E | Yn E4 | Yn E | Yn E2 | Yg M | Yg Wd | Yn M | Yn M | Yn M | Yn Wd | Yg W | Yg E3 | Yg W | Yg E1 | Yn W | Yn W | 19 |
| 20 | Yg M | Yg Wd | Yg E | Yg F | Yn E | Yn E4 | Yn E | Yn E2 | Yg M | Yg Wd | Yg M | Yg M | Yn M | Yn Wd | Yg W | Yg E3 | Yg W | Yg E1 | Yn W | Yn W | Yn W | Yn F | Yg Wd | Yg W | 20 |
| 21 | Yn M | Yn Wd | Yn E | Yn E2 | Yg M | Yg Wd | Yg M | Yg M | Yn M | Yn Wd | Yn M | Yn M | Yg W | Yg E1 | Yn W | Yn W | Yn W | Yn F | Yg Wd | Yg W | Yg Wd | Yg F | Yn Wd | Yn E4 | 21 |
| 22 | Yg W | Yg E1 | Yg M | Yg M | Yn M | Yn Wd | Yn M | Yn M | Yg W | Yg E1 | Yg W | Yg E3 | Yn W | Yn F | Yg Wd | Yg W | Yg Wd | Yg F | Yn Wd | Yn E4 | Yn Wd | Yn E2 | Yg F | Yg Wd | 22 |
| 23 | Yn W | Yn F | Yn M | Yn M | Yg W | Yg E1 | Yg W | Yg E3 | Yn W | Yn F | Yn W | Yn W | Yg Wd | Yg F | Yn Wd | Yn E4 | Yn Wd | Yn E2 | Yg F | Yg Wd | Yg F | Yg M | Yn F | Yn Wd | 23 |
| 24 | Yg Wd | Yg F | Yg W | Yg E3 | Yn W | Yn F | Yn W | Yn W | Yg Wd | Yg F | Yg Wd | Yg W | Yn Wd | Yn E2 | Yg F | Yg Wd | Yg F | Yg M | Yn F | Yn Wd | Yn F | Yn M | Yg E | Yg E1 | 24 |
| 25 | Yn Wd | Yn E2 | Yn W | Yn W | Yg Wd | Yg F | Yg Wd | Yg W | Yn Wd | Yn E2 | Yn Wd | Yn E4 | Yg F | Yg M | Yn F | Yn Wd | Yn F | Yn M | Yg E | Yg E1 | Yg E | Yg E3 | Yn E | Yn F | 25 |
| 26 | Yg F | Yg M | Yg Wd | Yg W | Yn Wd | Yn E2 | Yn Wd | Yn E4 | Yg F | Yg M | Yg F | Yg Wd | Yn F | Yn M | Yg E | Yg E1 | Yg E | Yg E3 | Yn E | Yn F | Yn E | Yn W | Yg M | Yg F | 26 |
| 27 | Yn F | Yn M | Yn Wd | Yn E4 | Yg F | Yg M | Yg F | Yg Wd | Yn F | Yn M | Yn F | Yn Wd | Yg E | Yg E3 | Yn E | Yn F | Yn E | Yn W | Yg M | Yg F | Yg M | Yg W | Yn M | Yn E2 | 27 |
| 28 | Yg E | Yg E3 | Yg F | Yg Wd | Yn F | Yn M | Yn F | Yn Wd | Yg E | Yg E3 | Yg E | Yg E1 | Yn E | Yn W | Yg M | Yg F | Yg M | Yg W | Yn M | Yn E2 | Yn M | Yn E4 | Yg W | Yg M | 28 |
| 29 | | | Yn F | Yn Wd | Yg E | Yg E3 | Yg E | Yg E1 | Yn E | Yn W | Yn E | Yn F | Yg M | Yg W | Yn M | Yn E2 | Yn M | Yn E4 | Yg W | Yg M | Yg W | Yg Wd | Yn W | Yn M | 29 |
| 30 | | | Yg E | Yg E1 | Yn E | Yn W | Yn E | Yn F | Yg M | Yg W | Yg M | Yg F | Yn M | Yn E4 | Yg W | Yg M | Yg W | Yg Wd | Yn W | Yn M | Yn W | Yn Wd | Yg Wd | Yg E3 | 30 |
| 31 | | | Yn E | Yn F | | | Yg M | Yg F | | | Yn M | Yn E2 | Yg W | Yg Wd | | | Yn W | Yn Wd | | | Yg Wd | Yg E1 | Yn Wd | Yn W | 31 |
| 1 | Yn E | Yn W | Yg M | Yg F | Yg M | Yg W | Yn M | Yn E2 | Yn M | Yn E4 | Yg W | Yg M | Yn W | Yn Wd | Yn W | Yn M | Yg Wd | Yg E1 | Yg Wd | Yg E3 | Yn Wd | Yn F | Yg F | Yg W | 1 |
| 2 | Yg M | Yg W | Yn M | Yn E2 | Yn M | Yn E4 | Yg W | Yg M | Yg W | Yg Wd | Yn W | Yn M | Yg Wd | Yg E1 | Yg Wd | Yg E3 | Yn Wd | Yn F | Yn Wd | Yn W | Yg F | Yg F | Yn F | Yn E4 | 2 |
| 3 | Yn M | Yn E4 | Yg W | Yg M | Yg W | Yg Wd | Yn W | Yn M | Yn W | Yn Wd | Yg Wd | Yg E3 | Yn Wd | Yn F | Yn Wd | Yn W | Yg F | Yg F | Yg F | Yg W | Yn F | Yn E2 | Yg E | Yg Wd | 3 |
| 4 | Yg W | Yg Wd | Yn W | Yn M | Yn W | Yn Wd | Yg Wd | Yg E3 | Yg Wd | Yg E1 | Yn Wd | Yn W | Yg F | Yg F | Yg F | Yg W | Yn F | Yn E2 | Yn F | Yn E4 | Yg E | Yg M | | | 4 |
| 5 | | | | | | | Yn Wd | Yn W | Yn Wd | Yn F | Yg F | Yg W | Yn F | Yn E2 | Yn F | Yn E4 | Yg E | Yg M | Yg E | Yg Wd | | | | | 5 |
| 6 | | | | | | | | | Yg F | Yg F | Yn F | Yn E4 | Yg E | Yg M | Yg E | Yg Wd | Yn E | Yn M | Yn E | Yn Wd | | | | | 6 |
| 7 | | | | | | | | | | | | | Yn E | Yn M | Yn E | Yn Wd | | | | | | | | | 7 |
| 8 | | | | | | | | | | | | | | | | | | | | | | | | | 8 |

# YEAR OF THE TIGER

| | H | E | H | E | H | E | H | E | H | E | H | E | H | E | H | E | H | E | H | E | H | E | H | E |
|---|---|---|---|---|---|---|---|---|---|---|---|---|---|---|---|---|---|---|---|---|---|---|---|---|
| YEAR | YEAR Yg F | Yg Wd | 1986 | | | | | | | | | | | | | | | | | | | | 1987 | |
| MONTH | 4 Feb - 5 Mar | | 6 Mar - 4 Apr | | 5 Apr - 5 May | | 6 May - 5 June | | 6 June - 6 Jul | | 7 Jul - 7 Aug | | 8 Aug - 7 Sep | | 8 Sep - 7 Oct | | 8 Oct - 7 Nov | | 8 Nov - 6 Dec | | 7 Dec - 5 Jan | | 6 Jan - 3 Feb | |
| | Yg M | Yg Wd | Yn M | Yn Wd | Yg W | Yg E1 | Yn W | Yn F | Yg Wd | Yg F | Yn Wd | Yn E2 | Yg F | Yg M | Yn F | Yn M | Yg E | Yg E3 | Yn E | Yn W | Yg M | Yg W | Yn M | Yn E4 |
| Starting time | 1st day | Mid-pt | 1st day | Mid-pt | 1st day | Mid-pt | 1st day | Mid-pt | 1st day | Mid-pt | 1st day | Mid-pt | 1st day | Mid-pt | 1st day | Mid-pt | 1st day | Mid-pt | 1st day | Mid-pt | 1st day | Mid-pt | 1st day | Mid-pt |
| Date | 4 | 19 | 6 | 21 | 5 | 20 | 6 | 21 | 6 | 22 | 7 | 23 | 8 | 23 | 8 | 23 | 8 | 24 | 8 | 22 | 7 | 22 | 6 | 20 |
| Hour | 1116 | 0650 | 0513 | 0604 | 1016 | 1727 | 0350 | 1645 | 0812 | 0041 | 1835 | 1143 | 0417 | 1839 | 0701 | 1603 | 2225 | 0109 | 0120 | 2231 | 1801 | 1144 | 0509 | 2222 |
| DATE 4 | Yn E | Yn Wd | | | | | | | | | | | | | | | | | | | | | | |
| 5 | Yg M | Yg E1 | | | Yn E | Yn Wd | | | | | | | | | | | | | | | | | | |
| 6 | Yn M | Yn F | Yn E | Yn M | Yg M | Yg E1 | Yg M | Yg E3 | Yn M | Yn F | | | | | | | | | | | | | Yn Wd | Yn Wd |
| 7 | Yg W | Yg F | Yg M | Yg E3 | Yn M | Yn F | Yn M | Yn W | Yg W | Yg F | Yg W | Yg W | | | | | | | | | Yn Wd | Yn M | Yg F | Yg E1 |
| 8 | Yn W | Yn E2 | Yn M | Yn W | Yg W | Yg F | Yg W | Yg W | Yn W | Yn E2 | Yn W | Yn E4 | Yg Wd | Yg M | Yn Wd | Yn Wd | Yn Wd | Yn M | Yg F | Yg E1 | Yg F | Yg E3 | Yn F | Yn F |
| 9 | Yg Wd | Yg M | Yg W | Yg W | Yn W | Yn E2 | Yn W | Yn E4 | Yg Wd | Yg M | Yg Wd | Yg Wd | Yn Wd | Yn M | Yg F | Yg E1 | Yg F | Yg E3 | Yn F | Yn F | Yn F | Yn W | Yg E | Yg F |
| 10 | Yn Wd | Yn M | Yn W | Yn E4 | Yg Wd | Yg M | Yg Wd | Yg Wd | Yn Wd | Yn M | Yn Wd | Yn Wd | Yg F | Yg E3 | Yn F | Yn F | Yn F | Yn W | Yg E | Yg F | Yg E | Yg W | Yn E | Yn E2 |
| 11 | Yg F | Yg E3 | Yg Wd | Yg Wd | Yn Wd | Yn M | Yn Wd | Yn Wd | Yg F | Yg E3 | Yg F | Yg E1 | Yn F | Yn W | Yg E | Yg F | Yg E | Yg W | Yn E | Yn E2 | Yn E | Yn E4 | Yg M | Yg M |
| 12 | Yn F | Yn W | Yn Wd | Yn Wd | Yg F | Yg E3 | Yg F | Yg E1 | Yn F | Yn W | Yn F | Yn F | Yg E | Yg W | Yn E | Yn E2 | Yn E | Yn E4 | Yg M | Yg M | Yg M | Yg Wd | Yn M | Yn M |
| 13 | Yg E | Yg W | Yg F | Yg E1 | Yn F | Yn W | Yn F | Yn F | Yg E | Yg W | Yg E | Yg F | Yn E | Yn E4 | Yg M | Yg M | Yg M | Yg Wd | Yn M | Yn M | Yn M | Yn Wd | Yg W | Yg E3 |
| 14 | Yn E | Yn E4 | Yn F | Yn F | Yg E | Yg W | Yg E | Yg F | Yn E | Yn E4 | Yn E | Yn E2 | Yg M | Yg Wd | Yn M | Yn M | Yn M | Yn Wd | Yg W | Yg E3 | Yg W | Yg E1 | Yn W | Yn W |
| 15 | Yg M | Yg Wd | Yg E | Yg F | Yn E | Yn E4 | Yn E | Yn E2 | Yg M | Yg Wd | Yg M | Yg M | Yn M | Yn Wd | Yg W | Yg E3 | Yg W | Yg E1 | Yn W | Yn W | Yn W | Yn F | Yg Wd | Yg W |
| 16 | Yn M | Yn Wd | Yn E | Yn E2 | Yg M | Yg Wd | Yg M | Yg M | Yn M | Yn Wd | Yn M | Yn M | Yg W | Yg E1 | Yn W | Yn W | Yn W | Yn F | Yg Wd | Yg W | Yg Wd | Yg F | Yn Wd | Yn E4 |
| 17 | Yg W | Yg E1 | Yg M | Yg M | Yn M | Yn Wd | Yn M | Yn M | Yg W | Yg E1 | Yg W | Yg E3 | Yn W | Yn F | Yg Wd | Yg W | Yg Wd | Yg F | Yn Wd | Yn E4 | Yn Wd | Yn E2 | Yg F | Yg Wd |
| 18 | Yn W | Yn F | Yn M | Yn M | Yg W | Yg E1 | Yg W | Yg E3 | Yn W | Yn F | Yn W | Yn W | Yg Wd | Yg F | Yn Wd | Yn E4 | Yn Wd | Yn E2 | Yg F | Yg Wd | Yg F | Yg M | Yn F | Yn Wd |
| 19 | Yg Wd | Yg F | Yg W | Yg E3 | Yn W | Yn F | Yn W | Yn W | Yg Wd | Yg F | Yg Wd | Yg W | Yn Wd | Yn E2 | Yg F | Yg Wd | Yg F | Yg M | Yn F | Yn Wd | Yn F | Yn M | Yg E | Yg E1 |
| 20 | Yn Wd | Yn E2 | Yn W | Yn W | Yg Wd | Yg F | Yg Wd | Yg W | Yn Wd | Yn E2 | Yn Wd | Yn E4 | Yg F | Yg M | Yn F | Yn Wd | Yn F | Yn M | Yg E | Yg E1 | Yg E | Yg E3 | Yn E | Yn F |
| 21 | Yg F | Yg M | Yg Wd | Yg W | Yn Wd | Yn E2 | Yn Wd | Yn E4 | Yg F | Yg M | Yg F | Yg Wd | Yn F | Yn M | Yg E | Yg E1 | Yg E | Yg E3 | Yn E | Yn F | Yn E | Yn W | Yg M | Yg F |
| 22 | Yn F | Yn M | Yn Wd | Yn E4 | Yg F | Yg M | Yg F | Yg Wd | Yn F | Yn M | Yn F | Yn Wd | Yg E | Yg E3 | Yn E | Yn F | Yn E | Yn W | Yg M | Yg F | Yg M | Yg W | Yn M | Yn E2 |
| 23 | Yg E | Yg E3 | Yg F | Yg Wd | Yn F | Yn M | Yn F | Yn Wd | Yg E | Yg E3 | Yg E | Yg E1 | Yn E | Yn W | Yg M | Yg F | Yg M | Yg W | Yn M | Yn E2 | Yn M | Yn E4 | Yg W | Yg M |
| 24 | Yn E | Yn W | Yn F | Yn Wd | Yg E | Yg E3 | Yg E | Yg E1 | Yn E | Yn W | Yn E | Yn F | Yg M | Yg W | Yn M | Yn E2 | Yn M | Yn E4 | Yg W | Yg M | Yg W | Yg Wd | Yn W | Yn M |
| 25 | Yg M | Yg W | Yg E | Yg E1 | Yn E | Yn W | Yn E | Yn F | Yg M | Yg W | Yg M | Yg F | Yn M | Yn E4 | Yg W | Yg M | Yg W | Yg Wd | Yn W | Yn M | Yn W | Yn Wd | Yg Wd | Yg E3 |
| 26 | Yn M | Yn E4 | Yn E | Yn F | Yg M | Yg W | Yg M | Yg F | Yn M | Yn E4 | Yn M | Yn E2 | Yg W | Yg Wd | Yn W | Yn M | Yn W | Yn Wd | Yg Wd | Yg E3 | Yg Wd | Yg E1 | Yn Wd | Yn W |
| 27 | Yg W | Yg Wd | Yg M | Yg F | Yn M | Yn E4 | Yn M | Yn E2 | Yg W | Yg Wd | Yg W | Yg M | Yn W | Yn Wd | Yg Wd | Yg E3 | Yg Wd | Yg E1 | Yn Wd | Yn W | Yn Wd | Yn F | Yg F | Yg W |
| 28 | Yn W | Yn Wd | Yn M | Yn E2 | Yg W | Yg Wd | Yg W | Yg M | Yn W | Yn Wd | Yn W | Yn M | Yg Wd | Yg E1 | Yn Wd | Yn W | Yn Wd | Yn F | Yg F | Yg W | Yg F | Yg F | Yn F | Yn E4 |
| 29 | | | Yg W | Yg M | Yn W | Yn Wd | Yn W | Yn M | Yg Wd | Yg E1 | Yg Wd | Yg E3 | Yn Wd | Yn F | Yg F | Yg W | Yg F | Yg F | Yn F | Yn E4 | Yn F | Yn E2 | Yg E | Yg Wd |
| 30 | | | Yn W | Yn M | Yg Wd | Yg E1 | Yg Wd | Yg E3 | Yn Wd | Yn F | Yn Wd | Yn W | Yg F | Yg F | Yn F | Yn E4 | Yn F | Yn E2 | Yg E | Yg Wd | Yg E | Yg M | Yn E | Yn Wd |
| 31 | | | Yg Wd | Yg E3 | | | Yn Wd | Yn W | | | Yg F | Yg W | Yn F | Yn E2 | | | Yg E | Yg M | | | Yn E | Yn M | Yg M | Yg E1 |
| 1 | Yg Wd | Yg E1 | Yn Wd | Yn W | Yn Wd | Yn F | Yg F | Yg W | Yg F | Yg F | Yn F | Yn E4 | Yg E | Yg M | Yg E | Yg Wd | Yn E | Yn M | Yn E | Yn Wd | Yg M | Yg E3 | Yn M | Yn F |
| 2 | Yn Wd | Yn F | Yg F | Yg W | Yg F | Yg F | Yn F | Yn E4 | Yn F | Yn E2 | Yg E | Yg Wd | Yn E | Yn M | Yn E | Yn Wd | Yg M | Yg E3 | Yg M | Yg E1 | Yn M | Yn W | Yg W | Yg F |
| 3 | Yg F | Yg F | Yn F | Yn E4 | Yn F | Yn E2 | Yg E | Yg Wd | Yg E | Yg M | Yn E | Yn Wd | Yg M | Yg E3 | Yg M | Yg E1 | Yn M | Yn W | Yn M | Yn F | Yg W | Yg W | Yn W | Yn E2 |
| 4 | Yn F | Yn E2 | Yg E | Yg Wd | Yg E | Yg M | Yn E | Yn Wd | Yn E | Yn M | Yg M | Yg E1 | Yn M | Yn W | Yn M | Yn F | Yg W | Yg W | Yg W | Yg F | Yn W | Yn E4 | | |
| 5 | Yg E | Yg M | | | Yn E | Yn M | Yg M | Yg E1 | Yg M | Yg E3 | Yn M | Yn F | Yg W | Yg W | Yg W | Yg F | Yn W | Yn E4 | Yn W | Yn E2 | Yg Wd | Yg Wd | | |
| 6 | | | | | | | | | Yn M | Yn W | Yg W | Yg F | Yn W | Yn E4 | Yn W | Yn E2 | Yg Wd | Yg Wd | Yg Wd | Yg M | | | | |
| 7 | | | | | | | | | | | Yn W | Yn E2 | Yg Wd | Yg Wd | Yg Wd | Yg M | Yn Wd | Yn Wd | | | | | | |
| 8 | | | | | | | | | | | | | | | | | | | | | | | | |

# YEAR OF THE RABBIT

| | H | E | H | E | H | E | H | E | H | E | H | E |
|---|---|---|---|---|---|---|---|---|---|---|---|---|
| YEAR | YEAR Yn F | Yn Wd | 1987 | | | | | | | | | |
| MONTH | 4 Feb - 5 Mar | | 6 Mar - 4 Apr | | 5 Apr - 5 May | | 6 May - 5 June | | 6 June - 7 Jul | | 8 Jul - 7 Aug | |
| | Yg W | Yg Wd | Yn W | Yn Wd | Yg Wd | Yg E1 | Yn Wd | Yn F | Yg F | Yg F | Yn F | Yn E2 |
| Starting time | 1st day | Mid-pt | 1st day | Mid-pt | 1st day | Mid-pt | 1st day | Mid-pt | 1st day | Mid-pt | 1st day | Mid-pt |
| Date | 4 | 19 | 6 | 21 | 5 | 20 | 6 | 21 | 6 | 22 | 8 | 23 |
| Hour | 1650 | 1239 | 1059 | 1152 | 1603 | 2314 | 0937 | 2233 | 1359 | 0639 | 0022 | 1732 |
| DATE 4 | Yg Wd | Yg M | | | | | | | | | | |
| 5 | Yn Wd | Yn M | | | Yg Wd | Yg M | | | | | | |
| 6 | Yg F | Yg E3 | Yg Wd | Yg Wd | Yn Wd | Yn M | Yn Wd | Yn Wd | Yg F | Yg E3 | | |
| 7 | Yn F | Yn W | Yn Wd | Yn Wd | Yg F | Yg E3 | Yg F | Yg E1 | Yn F | Yn W | | |
| 8 | Yg E | Yg W | Yg F | Yg E1 | Yn F | Yn W | Yn F | Yn F | Yg E | Yg W | Yg E | Yg F |
| 9 | Yn E | Yn E4 | Yn F | Yn F | Yg E | Yg W | Yg E | Yg F | Yn E | Yn E4 | Yn E | Yn E2 |
| 10 | Yg M | Yg Wd | Yg E | Yg F | Yn E | Yn E4 | Yn E | Yn E2 | Yg M | Yg Wd | Yg M | Yg M |
| 11 | Yn M | Yn Wd | Yn E | Yn E2 | Yg M | Yg Wd | Yg M | Yg M | Yn M | Yn Wd | Yn M | Yn M |
| 12 | Yg W | Yg E1 | Yg M | Yg M | Yn M | Yn Wd | Yn M | Yn M | Yg W | Yg E1 | Yg W | Yg E3 |
| 13 | Yn W | Yn F | Yn M | Yn M | Yg W | Yg E1 | Yg W | Yg E3 | Yn W | Yn F | Yn W | Yn W |
| 14 | Yg Wd | Yg F | Yg W | Yg E3 | Yn W | Yn F | Yn W | Yn W | Yg Wd | Yg F | Yg Wd | Yg W |
| 15 | Yn Wd | Yn E2 | Yn W | Yn W | Yg Wd | Yg F | Yg Wd | Yg W | Yn Wd | Yn E2 | Yn Wd | Yn E4 |
| 16 | Yg F | Yg M | Yg Wd | Yg W | Yn Wd | Yn E2 | Yn Wd | Yn E4 | Yg F | Yg M | Yg F | Yg Wd |
| 17 | Yn F | Yn M | Yn Wd | Yn E4 | Yg F | Yg M | Yg F | Yg Wd | Yn F | Yn M | Yn F | Yn Wd |
| 18 | Yg E | Yg E3 | Yg F | Yg Wd | Yn F | Yn M | Yn F | Yn Wd | Yg E | Yg E3 | Yg E | Yg E1 |
| 19 | Yn E | Yn W | Yn F | Yn Wd | Yg E | Yg E3 | Yg E | Yg E1 | Yn E | Yn W | Yn E | Yn F |
| 20 | Yg M | Yg W | Yg E | Yg E1 | Yn E | Yn W | Yn E | Yn F | Yg M | Yg W | Yg M | Yg F |
| 21 | Yn M | Yn E4 | Yn E | Yn F | Yg M | Yg W | Yg M | Yg F | Yn M | Yn E4 | Yn M | Yn E2 |
| 22 | Yg W | Yg Wd | Yg M | Yg F | Yn M | Yn E4 | Yn M | Yn E2 | Yg W | Yg Wd | Yg W | Yg M |
| 23 | Yn W | Yn Wd | Yn M | Yn E2 | Yg W | Yg Wd | Yg W | Yg M | Yn W | Yn Wd | Yn W | Yn M |
| 24 | Yg Wd | Yg E1 | Yg W | Yg M | Yn W | Yn Wd | Yn W | Yn M | Yg Wd | Yg E1 | Yg Wd | Yg E3 |
| 25 | Yn Wd | Yn F | Yn W | Yn M | Yg Wd | Yg E1 | Yg Wd | Yg E3 | Yn Wd | Yn F | Yn Wd | Yn W |
| 26 | Yg F | Yg F | Yg Wd | Yg E3 | Yn Wd | Yn F | Yn Wd | Yn W | Yg F | Yg F | Yg F | Yg W |
| 27 | Yn F | Yn E2 | Yn Wd | Yn W | Yg F | Yg F | Yg F | Yg W | Yn F | Yn E2 | Yn F | Yn E4 |
| 28 | Yg E | Yg M | Yg F | Yg W | Yn F | Yn E2 | Yn F | Yn E4 | Yg E | Yg M | Yg E | Yg Wd |
| 29 | | | Yn F | Yn E4 | Yg E | Yg M | Yg E | Yg Wd | Yn E | Yn M | Yn E | Yn Wd |
| 30 | | | Yg E | Yg Wd | Yn E | Yn M | Yn E | Yn Wd | Yg M | Yg E3 | Yg M | Yg E1 |
| 31 | | | Yn E | Yn Wd | | | Yg M | Yg E1 | | | Yn M | Yn F |
| 1 | Yn E | Yn M | Yg M | Yg E1 | Yg M | Yg E3 | Yn M | Yn F | Yn M | Yn W | Yg W | Yg F |
| 2 | Yg M | Yg E3 | Yn M | Yn F | Yn M | Yn W | Yg W | Yg F | Yg W | Yg W | Yn W | Yn E2 |
| 3 | Yn M | Yn W | Yg W | Yg F | Yg W | Yg W | Yn W | Yn E2 | Yn W | Yn E4 | Yg Wd | Yg M |
| 4 | Yg W | Yg W | Yn W | Yn E2 | Yn W | Yn E4 | Yg Wd | Yg M | Yg Wd | Yg Wd | Yn Wd | Yn M |
| 5 | Yn W | Yn E4 | | | Yg Wd | Yg Wd | Yn Wd | Yn M | Yn Wd | Yn Wd | Yg F | Yg E3 |
| 6 | | | | | | | | | Yg F | Yg E1 | Yn F | Yn W |
| 7 | | | | | | | | | Yn F | Yn F | Yg E | Yg W |
| 8 | | | | | | | | | | | | |

| | H | E | H | E | H | E | H | E | H | E | H | E | |
|---|---|---|---|---|---|---|---|---|---|---|---|---|---|
| YEAR | 1987 | | | | | | | | | | 1988 | | |
| MONTH | 8 Aug - 7 Sep | | 8 Sep - 8 Oct | | 9 Oct - 7 Nov | | 8 Nov - 6 Dec | | 7 Dec - 5 Jan | | 6 Jan - 3 Feb | | |
| | Yg E | Yg M | Yn E | Yn M | Yg M | Yg E3 | Yn M | Yn W | Yg W | Yg W | Yn W | Yn E4 | |
| Starting time | 1st day | Mid-pt | 1st day | Mid-pt | 1st day | Mid-pt | 1st day | Mid-pt | 1st day | Mid-pt | 1st day | Mid-pt | |
| Date | 8 | 24 | 8 | 23 | 9 | 24 | 8 | 23 | 7 | 22 | 6 | 21 | |
| Hour | 1004 | 0028 | 1248 | 2152 | 0412 | 0658 | 0707 | 0420 | 2347 | 1733 | 1056 | 0411 | |
| DATE 4 | | | | | | | | | | | | | 4 |
| 5 | | | | | | | | | | | | | 5 |
| 6 | | | | | | | | | | | Yg M | Yg M | 6 |
| 7 | | | | | | | | | Yg M | Yg Wd | Yn M | Yn M | 7 |
| 8 | Yn E | Yn E4 | Yg M | Yg M | | | Yn M | Yn M | Yn M | Yn Wd | Yg W | Yg E3 | 8 |
| 9 | Yg M | Yg Wd | Yn M | Yn M | Yn M | Yn Wd | Yg W | Yg E3 | Yg W | Yg E1 | Yn W | Yn W | 9 |
| 10 | Yn M | Yn Wd | Yg W | Yg E3 | Yg W | Yg E1 | Yn W | Yn W | Yn W | Yn F | Yg Wd | Yg W | 10 |
| 11 | Yg W | Yg E1 | Yn W | Yn W | Yn W | Yn F | Yg Wd | Yg W | Yg Wd | Yg F | Yn Wd | Yn E4 | 11 |
| 12 | Yn W | Yn F | Yg Wd | Yg W | Yg Wd | Yg F | Yn Wd | Yn E4 | Yn Wd | Yn E2 | Yg F | Yg Wd | 12 |
| 13 | Yg Wd | Yg F | Yn Wd | Yn E4 | Yn Wd | Yn E2 | Yg F | Yg Wd | Yg F | Yg M | Yn F | Yn Wd | 13 |
| 14 | Yn Wd | Yn E2 | Yg F | Yg Wd | Yg F | Yg M | Yn F | Yn Wd | Yn F | Yn M | Yg E | Yg E1 | 14 |
| 15 | Yg F | Yg M | Yn F | Yn Wd | Yn F | Yn M | Yg E | Yg E1 | Yg E | Yg E3 | Yn E | Yn F | 15 |
| 16 | Yn F | Yn M | Yg E | Yg E1 | Yg E | Yg E3 | Yn E | Yn F | Yn E | Yn W | Yg M | Yg F | 16 |
| 17 | Yg E | Yg E3 | Yn E | Yn F | Yn E | Yn W | Yg M | Yg F | Yg M | Yg W | Yn M | Yn E2 | 17 |
| 18 | Yn E | Yn W | Yg M | Yg F | Yg M | Yg W | Yn M | Yn E2 | Yn M | Yn E4 | Yg W | Yg M | 18 |
| 19 | Yg M | Yg W | Yn M | Yn E2 | Yn M | Yn E4 | Yg W | Yg M | Yg W | Yg Wd | Yn W | Yn M | 19 |
| 20 | Yn M | Yn E4 | Yg W | Yg M | Yg W | Yg Wd | Yn W | Yn M | Yn W | Yn Wd | Yg Wd | Yg E3 | 20 |
| 21 | Yg W | Yg Wd | Yn W | Yn M | Yn W | Yn Wd | Yg Wd | Yg E3 | Yg Wd | Yg E1 | Yn Wd | Yn W | 21 |
| 22 | Yn W | Yn Wd | Yg Wd | Yg E3 | Yg Wd | Yg E1 | Yn Wd | Yn W | Yn Wd | Yn F | Yg F | Yg W | 22 |
| 23 | Yg Wd | Yg E1 | Yn Wd | Yn W | Yn Wd | Yn F | Yg F | Yg W | Yg F | Yg F | Yn F | Yn E4 | 23 |
| 24 | Yn Wd | Yn F | Yg F | Yg W | Yg F | Yg F | Yn F | Yn E4 | Yn F | Yn E2 | Yg E | Yg Wd | 24 |
| 25 | Yg F | Yg F | Yn F | Yn E4 | Yn F | Yn E2 | Yg E | Yg Wd | Yg E | Yg M | Yn E | Yn Wd | 25 |
| 26 | Yn F | Yn E2 | Yg E | Yg Wd | Yg E | Yg M | Yn E | Yn Wd | Yn E | Yn M | Yg M | Yg E1 | 26 |
| 27 | Yg E | Yg M | Yn E | Yn Wd | Yn E | Yn M | Yg M | Yg E1 | Yg M | Yg E3 | Yn M | Yn F | 27 |
| 28 | Yn E | Yn M | Yg M | Yg E1 | Yg M | Yg E3 | Yn M | Yn F | Yn M | Yn W | Yg W | Yg F | 28 |
| 29 | Yg M | Yg E3 | Yn M | Yn F | Yn M | Yn W | Yg W | Yg F | Yg W | Yg W | Yn W | Yn E2 | 29 |
| 30 | Yn M | Yn W | Yg W | Yg F | Yg W | Yg W | Yn W | Yn E2 | Yn W | Yn E4 | Yg Wd | Yg M | 30 |
| 31 | Yg W | Yg W | | | Yn W | Yn E4 | | | Yg Wd | Yg Wd | Yn Wd | Yn M | 31 |
| 1 | Yn W | Yn E4 | Yn W | Yn E2 | Yg Wd | Yg Wd | Yg Wd | Yg M | Yn Wd | Yn Wd | Yg F | Yg E3 | 1 |
| 2 | Yg Wd | Yg Wd | Yg Wd | Yg M | Yn Wd | Yn Wd | Yn Wd | Yn M | Yg F | Yg E1 | Yn F | Yn W | 2 |
| 3 | Yn Wd | Yn Wd | Yn Wd | Yn M | Yg F | Yg E1 | Yg F | Yg E3 | Yn F | Yn F | Yg E | Yg W | 3 |
| 4 | Yg F | Yg E1 | Yg F | Yg E3 | Yn F | Yn F | Yn F | Yn W | Yg E | Yg F | | | 4 |
| 5 | Yn F | Yn F | Yn F | Yn W | Yg E | Yg F | Yg E | Yg W | Yn E | Yn E2 | | | 5 |
| 6 | Yg E | Yg F | Yg E | Yg W | Yn E | Yn E2 | Yn E | Yn E4 | | | | | 6 |
| 7 | Yn E | Yn E2 | Yn E | Yn E4 | Yg M | Yg M | | | | | | | 7 |
| 8 | | | Yg M | Yg Wd | | | | | | | | | 8 |

# YEAR OF THE DRAGON

| | H | E | H | E | H | E | H | E | H | E | H | E | H | E | H | E | H | E | H | E | H | E | H | E | |
|---|---|---|---|---|---|---|---|---|---|---|---|---|---|---|---|---|---|---|---|---|---|---|---|---|---|
| YEAR | YEAR Yg E | Yg E1 | 1988 | | | | | | | | | | | | | | | | | | | | 1989 | | |
| MONTH | 4 Feb - 4 Mar | | 5 Mar - 3 Apr | | 4 Apr - 4 May | | 5 May - 4 June | | 5 June - 6 Jul | | 7 Jul - 6 Aug | | 7 Aug - 6 Sep | | 7 Sep - 7 Oct | | 8 Oct - 6 Nov | | 7 Nov - 6 Dec | | 7 Dec - 4 Jan | | 5 Jan - 3 Feb | | |
| | Yg Wd | Yg Wd | Yn Wd | Yn Wd | Yg F | Yg E1 | Yn F | Yn F | Yg E | Yg F | Yn E | Yn E2 | Yg M | Yg M | Yn M | Yn M | Yg W | Yg E3 | Yn W | Yn W | Yg Wd | Yg W | Yn Wd | Yn E4 | |
| Starting time | 1st day | Mid-pt | 1st day | Mid-pt | 1st day | Mid-pt | 1st day | Mid-pt | 1st day | Mid-pt | 1st day | Mid-pt | 1st day | Mid-pt | 1st day | Mid-pt | 1st day | Mid-pt | 1st day | Mid-pt | 1st day | Mid-pt | 1st day | Mid-pt | |
| Date | 4 | 19 | 5 | 20 | 4 | 20 | 5 | 21 | 5 | 21 | 7 | 22 | 7 | 23 | 7 | 23 | 8 | 23 | 7 | 22 | 7 | 21 | 5 | 20 | |
| Hour | 2238 | 1828 | 1648 | 1741 | 2151 | 0459 | 1525 | 0422 | 1947 | 1228 | 0610 | 2321 | 1552 | 0617 | 1836 | 0341 | 1000 | 1247 | 1256 | 1009 | 0535 | 2322 | 1644 | 1001 | |
| DATE 4 | Yn E | Yn E4 | | | Yn E | Yn E4 | | | | | | | | | | | | | | | | | | | 4 |
| 5 | Yg M | Yg Wd | Yn E | Yn E2 | Yg M | Yg Wd | Yg M | Yg M | Yn M | Yn Wd | | | | | | | | | | | | | Yn Wd | Yn E4 | 5 |
| 6 | Yn M | Yn Wd | Yg M | Yg M | Yn M | Yn Wd | Yn M | Yn M | Yg W | Yg E1 | | | | | | | | | | | | | Yg F | Yg Wd | 6 |
| 7 | Yg W | Yg E1 | Yn M | Yn M | Yg W | Yg E1 | Yg W | Yg E3 | Yn W | Yn F | Yn W | Yn W | Yg Wd | Yg F | Yn Wd | Yn E4 | | | Yg F | Yg Wd | Yg F | Yg M | Yn F | Yn Wd | 7 |
| 8 | Yn W | Yn F | Yg W | Yg E3 | Yn W | Yn F | Yn W | Yn W | Yg Wd | Yg F | Yg Wd | Yg W | Yn Wd | Yn E2 | Yg F | Yg Wd | Yg F | Yg M | Yn F | Yn Wd | Yn F | Yn M | Yg E | Yg E1 | 8 |
| 9 | Yg Wd | Yg F | Yn W | Yn W | Yg Wd | Yg F | Yg Wd | Yg W | Yn Wd | Yn E2 | Yn Wd | Yn E4 | Yg F | Yg M | Yn F | Yn Wd | Yn F | Yn M | Yg E | Yg E1 | Yg E | Yg E3 | Yn E | Yn F | 9 |
| 10 | Yn Wd | Yn E2 | Yg Wd | Yg W | Yn Wd | Yn E2 | Yn Wd | Yn E4 | Yg F | Yg M | Yg F | Yg Wd | Yn F | Yn M | Yg E | Yg E1 | Yg E | Yg E3 | Yn E | Yn F | Yn E | Yn W | Yg M | Yg F | 10 |
| 11 | Yg F | Yg M | Yn Wd | Yn E4 | Yg F | Yg M | Yg F | Yg Wd | Yn F | Yn M | Yn F | Yn Wd | Yg E | Yg E3 | Yn E | Yn F | Yn E | Yn W | Yg M | Yg F | Yg M | Yg W | Yn M | Yn E2 | 11 |
| 12 | Yn F | Yn M | Yg F | Yg Wd | Yn F | Yn M | Yn F | Yn Wd | Yg E | Yg E3 | Yg E | Yg E1 | Yn E | Yn W | Yg M | Yg F | Yg M | Yg W | Yn M | Yn E2 | Yn M | Yn E4 | Yg W | Yg M | 12 |
| 13 | Yg E | Yg E3 | Yn F | Yn Wd | Yg E | Yg E3 | Yg E | Yg E1 | Yn E | Yn W | Yn E | Yn F | Yg M | Yg W | Yn M | Yn E2 | Yn M | Yn E4 | Yg W | Yg M | Yg W | Yg Wd | Yn W | Yn M | 13 |
| 14 | Yn E | Yn W | Yg E | Yg E1 | Yn E | Yn W | Yn E | Yn F | Yg M | Yg W | Yg M | Yg F | Yn M | Yn E4 | Yg W | Yg M | Yg W | Yg Wd | Yn W | Yn M | Yn W | Yn Wd | Yg Wd | Yg E3 | 14 |
| 15 | Yg M | Yg W | Yn E | Yn F | Yg M | Yg W | Yg M | Yg F | Yn M | Yn E4 | Yn M | Yn E2 | Yg W | Yg Wd | Yn W | Yn M | Yn W | Yn Wd | Yg Wd | Yg E3 | Yg Wd | Yg E1 | Yn Wd | Yn W | 15 |
| 16 | Yn M | Yn E4 | Yg M | Yg F | Yn M | Yn E4 | Yn M | Yn E2 | Yg W | Yg Wd | Yg W | Yg M | Yn W | Yn Wd | Yg Wd | Yg E3 | Yg Wd | Yg E1 | Yn Wd | Yn W | Yn Wd | Yn F | Yg F | Yg W | 16 |
| 17 | Yg W | Yg Wd | Yn M | Yn E2 | Yg W | Yg Wd | Yg W | Yg M | Yn W | Yn Wd | Yn W | Yn M | Yg Wd | Yg E1 | Yn Wd | Yn W | Yn Wd | Yn F | Yg F | Yg W | Yg F | Yg F | Yn F | Yn E4 | 17 |
| 18 | Yn W | Yn Wd | Yg W | Yg M | Yn W | Yn Wd | Yn W | Yn M | Yg Wd | Yg E1 | Yg Wd | Yg E3 | Yn Wd | Yn F | Yg F | Yg W | Yg F | Yg F | Yn F | Yn E4 | Yn F | Yn E2 | Yg E | Yg Wd | 18 |
| 19 | Yg Wd | Yg E1 | Yn W | Yn M | Yg Wd | Yg E1 | Yg Wd | Yg E3 | Yn Wd | Yn F | Yn Wd | Yn W | Yg F | Yg F | Yn F | Yn E4 | Yn F | Yn E2 | Yg E | Yg Wd | Yg E | Yg M | Yn E | Yn Wd | 19 |
| 20 | Yn Wd | Yn F | Yg Wd | Yg E3 | Yn Wd | Yn F | Yn Wd | Yn W | Yg F | Yg F | Yg F | Yg W | Yn F | Yn E2 | Yg E | Yg Wd | Yg E | Yg M | Yn E | Yn Wd | Yn E | Yn M | Yg M | Yg E1 | 20 |
| 21 | Yg F | Yg F | Yn Wd | Yn W | Yg F | Yg F | Yg F | Yg W | Yn F | Yn E2 | Yn F | Yn E4 | Yg E | Yg M | Yn E | Yn Wd | Yn E | Yn M | Yg M | Yg E1 | Yg M | Yg E3 | Yn M | Yn F | 21 |
| 22 | Yn F | Yn E2 | Yg F | Yg W | Yn F | Yn E2 | Yn F | Yn E4 | Yg E | Yg M | Yg E | Yg Wd | Yn E | Yn M | Yg M | Yg E1 | Yg M | Yg E3 | Yn M | Yn F | Yn M | Yn W | Yg W | Yg F | 22 |
| 23 | Yg E | Yg M | Yn F | Yn E4 | Yg E | Yg M | Yg E | Yg Wd | Yn E | Yn M | Yn E | Yn Wd | Yg M | Yg E3 | Yn M | Yn F | Yn M | Yn W | Yg W | Yg F | Yg W | Yg W | Yn W | Yn E2 | 23 |
| 24 | Yn E | Yn M | Yg E | Yg Wd | Yn E | Yn M | Yn E | Yn Wd | Yg M | Yg E3 | Yg M | Yg E1 | Yn M | Yn W | Yg W | Yg F | Yg W | Yg W | Yn W | Yn E2 | Yn W | Yn E4 | Yg Wd | Yg M | 24 |
| 25 | Yg M | Yg E3 | Yn E | Yn Wd | Yg M | Yg E3 | Yg M | Yg E1 | Yn M | Yn W | Yn M | Yn F | Yg W | Yg W | Yn W | Yn E2 | Yn W | Yn E4 | Yg Wd | Yg M | Yg Wd | Yg Wd | Yn Wd | Yn M | 25 |
| 26 | Yn M | Yn W | Yg M | Yg E1 | Yn M | Yn W | Yn M | Yn F | Yg W | Yg W | Yg W | Yg F | Yn W | Yn E4 | Yg Wd | Yg M | Yg Wd | Yg Wd | Yn Wd | Yn M | Yn Wd | Yn Wd | Yg F | Yg E3 | 26 |
| 27 | Yg W | Yg W | Yn M | Yn F | Yg W | Yg W | Yg W | Yg F | Yn W | Yn E4 | Yn W | Yn E2 | Yg Wd | Yg Wd | Yn Wd | Yn M | Yn Wd | Yn Wd | Yg F | Yg E3 | Yg F | Yg E1 | Yn F | Yn W | 27 |
| 28 | Yn W | Yn E4 | Yg W | Yg F | Yn W | Yn E4 | Yn W | Yn E2 | Yg Wd | Yg Wd | Yg Wd | Yg M | Yn Wd | Yn Wd | Yg F | Yg E3 | Yg F | Yg E1 | Yn F | Yn W | Yn F | Yn F | Yg E | Yg W | 28 |
| 29 | Yg Wd | Yg Wd | Yn W | Yn E2 | Yg Wd | Yg Wd | Yg Wd | Yg M | Yn Wd | Yn Wd | Yn Wd | Yn M | Yg F | Yg E1 | Yn F | Yn W | Yn F | Yn F | Yg E | Yg W | Yg E | Yg F | Yn E | Yn E4 | 29 |
| 30 | | | Yg Wd | Yg M | Yn Wd | Yn Wd | Yn Wd | Yn M | Yg F | Yg E1 | Yg F | Yg E3 | Yn F | Yn F | Yg E | Yg W | Yg E | Yg F | Yn E | Yn E4 | Yn E | Yn E2 | Yg M | Yg Wd | 30 |
| 31 | | | Yn Wd | Yn M | | | Yg F | Yg E3 | | | Yn F | Yn W | Yg E | Yg F | | | Yn E | Yn E2 | | | Yg M | Yg M | Yn M | Yn Wd | 31 |
| 1 | Yn Wd | Yn Wd | Yg F | Yg E3 | Yg F | Yg E1 | Yn F | Yn W | Yn F | Yn F | Yg E | Yg W | Yn E | Yn E2 | Yn E | Yn E4 | Yg M | Yg M | Yg M | Yg Wd | Yn M | Yn M | Yg W | Yg E1 | 1 |
| 2 | Yg F | Yg E1 | Yn F | Yn W | Yn F | Yn F | Yg E | Yg W | Yg E | Yg F | Yn E | Yn E4 | Yg M | Yg M | Yg M | Yg Wd | Yn M | Yn M | Yn M | Yn Wd | Yg W | Yg E3 | Yn W | Yn F | 2 |
| 3 | Yn F | Yn F | Yg E | Yg W | Yg E | Yg F | Yn E | Yn E4 | Yn E | Yn E2 | Yg M | Yg Wd | Yn M | Yn M | Yn M | Yn Wd | Yg W | Yg E3 | Yg W | Yg E1 | Yn W | Yn W | Yg Wd | Yg F | 3 |
| 4 | Yg E | Yg F | | | Yn E | Yn E2 | Yg M | Yg Wd | Yg M | Yg M | Yn M | Yn Wd | Yg W | Yg E3 | Yg W | Yg E1 | Yn W | Yn W | Yn W | Yn F | Yg Wd | Yg W | | | 4 |
| 5 | | | | | | | | | Yn M | Yn M | Yg W | Yg E1 | Yn W | Yn W | Yn W | Yn F | Yg Wd | Yg W | Yg Wd | Yg F | | | | | 5 |
| 6 | | | | | | | | | Yg W | Yg E3 | Yn W | Yn F | Yg Wd | Yg W | Yg Wd | Yg F | Yn Wd | Yn E4 | Yn Wd | Yn E2 | | | | | 6 |
| 7 | | | | | | | | | | | | | | | Yn Wd | Yn E2 | | | | | | | | | 7 |
| 8 | | | | | | | | | | | | | | | | | | | | | | | | | 8 |

# YEAR OF THE SNAKE

| | H | E | H | E | H | E | H | E | H | E | H | E | H | E | H | E | H | E | H | E | H | E | H | E | |
|---|---|---|---|---|---|---|---|---|---|---|---|---|---|---|---|---|---|---|---|---|---|---|---|---|---|
| YEAR | YEAR YnE | YnF | 1989 | | | | | | | | | | | | | | | | | | | | 1990 | | |
| MONTH | 4 Feb - 4 Mar | | 5 Mar - 4 Apr | | 5 Apr - 4 May | | 5 May - 5 June | | 6 June - 6 Jul | | 7 Jul - 6 Aug | | 7 Aug - 7 Sep | | 8 Sep - 7 Oct | | 8 Oct - 6 Nov | | 7 Nov - 6 Dec | | 7 Dec - 4 Jan | | 5 Jan - 3 Feb | | |
| | Yg F | Yg Wd | Yn F | Yn Wd | Yg E | Yg E1 | Yn E | Yn F | Yg M | Yg F | Yn M | Yn E2 | Yg W | Yg M | Yn W | Yn M | Yg Wd | Yg E3 | Yn Wd | Yn W | Yg F | Yg W | Yn F | Yn E4 | |
| Starting time | 1st day | Mid-pt | 1st day | Mid-pt | 1st day | Mid-pt | 1st day | Mid-pt | 1st day | Mid-pt | 1st day | Mid-pt | 1st day | Mid-pt | 1st day | Mid-pt | 1st day | Mid-pt | 1st day | Mid-pt | 1st day | Mid-pt | 1st day | Mid-pt | |
| Date | 4 | 19 | 5 | 20 | 5 | 20 | 5 | 21 | 6 | 21 | 7 | 23 | 7 | 23 | 8 | 23 | 8 | 23 | 7 | 22 | 7 | 22 | 5 | 20 | |
| Hour | 0426 | 0019 | 2236 | 2332 | 0339 | 1051 | 2113 | 1013 | 0135 | 1819 | 1158 | 0512 | 2141 | 1208 | 0025 | 0932 | 1549 | 1838 | 1844 | 1001 | 1124 | 0514 | 2233 | 1552 | |
| DATE 4 | Yn Wd | Yn E2 | | | | | | | | | | | | | | | | | | | | | | | 4 |
| 5 | Yg F | Yg M | Yg Wd | Yg W | Yn Wd | Yn E2 | Yn Wd | Yn E4 | | | | | | | | | | | | | | | Yg M | Yg F | 5 |
| 6 | Yn F | Yn M | Yn Wd | Yn E4 | Yg F | Yg M | Yg F | Yg Wd | Yn F | Yn M | | | | | | | | | | | | | Yn M | Yn E2 | 6 |
| 7 | Yg E | Yg E3 | Yg F | Yg Wd | Yn F | Yn M | Yn F | Yn Wd | Yg E | Yg E3 | Yg E | Yg E1 | Yn E | Yn W | | | | | Yn M | Yn E2 | Yn M | Yn E4 | Yg W | Yg M | 7 |
| 8 | Yn E | Yn W | Yn F | Yn Wd | Yg E | Yg E3 | Yg E | Yg E1 | Yn E | Yn W | Yn E | Yn F | Yg M | Yg W | Yn M | Yn E2 | Yn M | Yn E4 | Yg W | Yg M | Yg W | Yg Wd | Yn W | Yn M | 8 |
| 9 | Yg M | Yg W | Yg E | Yg E1 | Yn E | Yn W | Yn E | Yn F | Yg M | Yg W | Yg M | Yg F | Yn M | Yn E4 | Yg W | Yg M | Yg W | Yg Wd | Yn W | Yn M | Yn W | Yn Wd | Yg Wd | Yg E3 | 9 |
| 10 | Yn M | Yn E4 | Yn E | Yn F | Yg M | Yg W | Yg M | Yg F | Yn M | Yn E4 | Yn M | Yn E2 | Yg W | Yg Wd | Yn W | Yn M | Yn W | Yn Wd | Yg Wd | Yg E3 | Yg Wd | Yg E1 | Yn Wd | Yn W | 10 |
| 11 | Yg W | Yg Wd | Yg M | Yg F | Yn M | Yn E4 | Yn M | Yn E2 | Yg W | Yg Wd | Yg W | Yg M | Yn W | Yn Wd | Yg Wd | Yg E3 | Yg Wd | Yg E1 | Yn Wd | Yn W | Yn Wd | Yn F | Yg F | Yg W | 11 |
| 12 | Yn W | Yn Wd | Yn M | Yn E2 | Yg W | Yg Wd | Yg W | Yg M | Yn W | Yn Wd | Yn W | Yn M | Yg Wd | Yg E1 | Yn Wd | Yn W | Yn Wd | Yn F | Yg F | Yg W | Yg F | Yg F | Yn F | Yn E4 | 12 |
| 13 | Yg Wd | Yg E1 | Yg W | Yg M | Yn W | Yn Wd | Yn W | Yn M | Yg Wd | Yg E1 | Yg Wd | Yg E3 | Yn Wd | Yn F | Yg F | Yg W | Yg F | Yg F | Yn F | Yn E4 | Yn F | Yn E2 | Yg E | Yg Wd | 13 |
| 14 | Yn Wd | Yn F | Yn W | Yn M | Yg Wd | Yg E1 | Yg Wd | Yg E3 | Yn Wd | Yn F | Yn Wd | Yn W | Yg F | Yg F | Yn F | Yn E4 | Yn F | Yn E2 | Yg E | Yg Wd | Yg E | Yg M | Yn E | Yn Wd | 14 |
| 15 | Yg F | Yg F | Yg Wd | Yg E3 | Yn Wd | Yn F | Yn Wd | Yn W | Yg F | Yg F | Yg F | Yg W | Yn F | Yn E2 | Yg E | Yg Wd | Yg E | Yg M | Yn E | Yn Wd | Yn E | Yn M | Yg M | Yg E1 | 15 |
| 16 | Yn F | Yn E2 | Yn Wd | Yn W | Yg F | Yg F | Yg F | Yg W | Yn F | Yn E2 | Yn F | Yn E4 | Yg E | Yg M | Yn E | Yn Wd | Yn E | Yn M | Yg M | Yg E1 | Yg M | Yg E3 | Yn M | Yn F | 16 |
| 17 | Yg E | Yg M | Yg F | Yg W | Yn F | Yn E2 | Yn F | Yn E4 | Yg E | Yg M | Yg E | Yg Wd | Yn E | Yn M | Yg M | Yg E1 | Yg M | Yg E3 | Yn M | Yn F | Yn M | Yn W | Yg W | Yg F | 17 |
| 18 | Yn E | Yn M | Yn F | Yn E4 | Yg E | Yg M | Yg E | Yg Wd | Yn E | Yn M | Yn E | Yn Wd | Yg M | Yg E3 | Yn M | Yn F | Yn M | Yn W | Yg W | Yg F | Yg W | Yg W | Yn W | Yn E2 | 18 |
| 19 | Yg M | Yg E3 | Yg E | Yg Wd | Yn E | Yn M | Yn E | Yn Wd | Yg M | Yg E3 | Yg M | Yg E1 | Yn M | Yn W | Yg W | Yg F | Yg W | Yg W | Yn W | Yn E2 | Yn W | Yn E4 | Yg Wd | Yg M | 19 |
| 20 | Yn M | Yn W | Yn E | Yn Wd | Yg M | Yg E3 | Yg M | Yg E1 | Yn M | Yn W | Yn M | Yn F | Yg W | Yg W | Yn W | Yn E2 | Yn W | Yn E4 | Yg Wd | Yg M | Yg Wd | Yg Wd | Yn Wd | Yn M | 20 |
| 21 | Yg W | Yg W | Yg M | Yg E1 | Yn M | Yn W | Yn M | Yn F | Yg W | Yg W | Yg W | Yg F | Yn W | Yn E4 | Yg Wd | Yg M | Yg Wd | Yg Wd | Yn Wd | Yn M | Yn Wd | Yn Wd | Yg F | Yg E3 | 21 |
| 22 | Yn W | Yn E4 | Yn M | Yn F | Yg W | Yg W | Yg W | Yg F | Yn W | Yn E4 | Yn W | Yn E2 | Yg Wd | Yg Wd | Yn Wd | Yn M | Yn Wd | Yn Wd | Yg F | Yg E3 | Yg F | Yg E1 | Yn F | Yn W | 22 |
| 23 | Yg Wd | Yg Wd | Yg W | Yg F | Yn W | Yn E4 | Yn W | Yn E2 | Yg Wd | Yg Wd | Yg Wd | Yg M | Yn Wd | Yn Wd | Yg F | Yg E3 | Yg F | Yg E1 | Yn F | Yn W | Yn F | Yn F | Yg E | Yg W | 23 |
| 24 | Yn Wd | Yn Wd | Yn W | Yn E2 | Yg Wd | Yg Wd | Yg Wd | Yg M | Yn Wd | Yn Wd | Yn Wd | Yn M | Yg F | Yg E1 | Yn F | Yn W | Yn F | Yn F | Yg E | Yg W | Yg E | Yg F | Yn E | Yn E4 | 24 |
| 25 | Yg F | Yg E1 | Yg Wd | Yg M | Yn Wd | Yn Wd | Yn Wd | Yn M | Yg F | Yg E1 | Yg F | Yg E3 | Yn F | Yn F | Yg E | Yg W | Yg E | Yg F | Yn E | Yn E4 | Yn E | Yn E2 | Yg M | Yg Wd | 25 |
| 26 | Yn F | Yn F | Yn Wd | Yn M | Yg F | Yg E1 | Yg F | Yg E3 | Yn F | Yn F | Yn F | Yn W | Yg E | Yg F | Yn E | Yn E4 | Yn E | Yn E2 | Yg M | Yg Wd | Yg M | Yg M | Yn M | Yn Wd | 26 |
| 27 | Yg E | Yg F | Yg F | Yg E3 | Yn F | Yn F | Yn F | Yn W | Yg E | Yg F | Yg E | Yg W | Yn E | Yn E2 | Yg M | Yg Wd | Yg M | Yg M | Yn M | Yn Wd | Yn M | Yn M | Yg W | Yg E1 | 27 |
| 28 | Yn E | Yn E2 | Yn F | Yn W | Yg E | Yg F | Yg E | Yg W | Yn E | Yn E2 | Yn E | Yn E4 | Yg M | Yg M | Yn M | Yn Wd | Yn M | Yn M | Yg W | Yg E1 | Yg W | Yg E3 | Yn W | Yn F | 28 |
| 29 | | | Yg E | Yg W | Yn E | Yn E2 | Yn E | Yn E4 | Yg M | Yg M | Yg M | Yg Wd | Yn M | Yn M | Yg W | Yg E1 | Yg W | Yg E3 | Yn W | Yn F | Yn W | Yn W | Yg Wd | Yg F | 29 |
| 30 | | | Yn E | Yn E4 | Yg M | Yg M | Yg M | Yg Wd | Yn M | Yn M | Yn M | Yn Wd | Yg W | Yg E3 | Yn W | Yn F | Yn W | Yn W | Yg Wd | Yg F | Yg Wd | Yg W | Yn Wd | Yn E2 | 30 |
| 31 | | | Yg M | Yg Wd | | | Yn M | Yn Wd | | | Yg W | Yg E1 | Yn W | Yn W | | | Yg Wd | Yg W | | | Yn Wd | Yn E4 | Yg F | Yg M | 31 |
| 1 | Yg M | Yg M | Yn M | Yn Wd | Yn M | Yn M | Yg W | Yg E1 | Yg W | Yg E3 | Yn W | Yn F | Yg Wd | Yg W | Yg Wd | Yg F | Yn Wd | Yn E4 | Yn Wd | Yn E2 | Yg F | Yg Wd | Yn F | Yn M | 1 |
| 2 | Yn M | Yn M | Yg W | Yg E1 | Yg W | Yg E3 | Yn W | Yn F | Yn W | Yn W | Yg Wd | Yg F | Yn Wd | Yn E4 | Yn Wd | Yn E2 | Yg F | Yg Wd | Yg F | Yg M | Yn F | Yn Wd | Yg E | Yg E3 | 2 |
| 3 | Yg W | Yg E3 | Yn W | Yn F | Yn W | Yn W | Yg Wd | Yg F | Yg Wd | Yg W | Yn Wd | Yn E2 | Yg F | Yg Wd | Yg F | Yg M | Yn F | Yn Wd | Yn F | Yn M | Yg E | Yg E1 | Yn E | Yn W | 3 |
| 4 | Yn W | Yn W | Yg Wd | Yg F | Yg Wd | Yg W | Yn Wd | Yn E2 | Yn Wd | Yn E4 | Yg F | Yg M | Yn F | Yn Wd | Yn F | Yn M | Yg E | Yg E1 | Yg E | Yg E3 | Yn E | Yn F | | | 4 |
| 5 | | | | | | | Yg F | Yg M | Yg F | Yg Wd | Yn F | Yn M | Yg E | Yg E1 | Yg E | Yg E3 | Yn E | Yn F | Yn E | Yn W | | | | | 5 |
| 6 | | | | | | | | | Yn F | Yn Wd | Yg E | Yg E3 | Yn E | Yn F | Yn E | Yn W | Yg M | Yg F | Yg M | Yg W | | | | | 6 |
| 7 | | | | | | | | | | | | | Yg M | Yg F | Yg M | Yg W | | | | | | | | | 7 |
| 8 | | | | | | | | | | | | | | | | | | | | | | | | | 8 |

# YEAR OF THE HORSE

| | H | E | H | E | H | E | H | E | H | E | H | E | H | E | H | E | H | E | H | E | H | E | H | E | |
|---|---|---|---|---|---|---|---|---|---|---|---|---|---|---|---|---|---|---|---|---|---|---|---|---|---|
| YEAR | YEAR YgM | YgF | 1990 | | | | | | | | | | | | | | | | | | | | 1991 | | |
| MONTH | 4 Feb - 5 Mar | | 6 Mar - 4 Apr | | 5 Apr - 5 May | | 6 May - 5 June | | 6 June - 6 Jul | | 7 Jul - 7 Aug | | 8 Aug - 7 Sep | | 8 Sep - 7 Oct | | 8 Oct - 7 Nov | | 8 Nov - 6 Dec | | 7 Dec - 5 Jan | | 6 Jan - 3 Feb | | |
| | YgE | YgWd | YnE | YnWd | YgM | YgE1 | YnM | YnF | YgW | YgF | YnW | YnE2 | YgWd | YgM | YnWd | YnM | YgF | YgE3 | YnF | YnW | YgE | YgW | YnE | YnE4 | |
| Starting time | 1st day | Mid-pt | 1st day | Mid-pt | 1st day | Mid-pt | 1st day | Mid-pt | 1st day | Mid-pt | 1st day | Mid-pt | 1st day | Mid-pt | 1st day | Mid-pt | 1st day | Mid-pt | 1st day | Mid-pt | 1st day | Mid-pt | 1st day | Mid-pt | |
| Date | 4 | 19 | 6 | 21 | 5 | 20 | 6 | 21 | 6 | 22 | 7 | 23 | 8 | 23 | 8 | 23 | 8 | 24 | 8 | 22 | 7 | 22 | 6 | 20 | |
| Hour | 1015 | 0609 | 0425 | 0522 | 0928 | 1641 | 0302 | 1601 | 0724 | 0009 | 1747 | 1102 | 0330 | 1758 | 0614 | 1522 | 2138 | 0028 | 0033 | 2150 | 1713 | 1103 | 0501 | 2141 | |
| DATE 4 | YgM | YgW | | | | | | | | | | | | | | | | | | | | | | | 4 |
| 5 | YnM | YnE4 | | | YgM | YgW | | | | | | | | | | | | | | | | | | | 5 |
| 6 | YgW | YgWd | YgM | YgF | YnM | YnE4 | YnM | YnE2 | YgW | YgWd | | | | | | | | | | | | | YgF | YgW | 6 |
| 7 | YnW | YnWd | YnM | YnE2 | YgW | YgWd | YgW | YgM | YnW | YnWd | YnW | YnM | | | | | | | | | YgF | YgF | YnF | YnE4 | 7 |
| 8 | YgWd | YgE1 | YgW | YgM | YnW | YnWd | YnW | YnM | YgWd | YgE1 | YgWd | YgE3 | YnWd | YnF | YgF | YgW | YgF | YgF | YnF | YnE4 | YnF | YnE2 | YgE | YgWd | 8 |
| 9 | YnWd | YnF | YnW | YnM | YgWd | YgE1 | YgWd | YgE3 | YnWd | YnF | YnWd | YnW | YgF | YgF | YnF | YnE4 | YnF | YnE2 | YgE | YgWd | YgE | YgM | YnE | YnWd | 9 |
| 10 | YgF | YgF | YgWd | YgE3 | YnWd | YnF | YnWd | YnW | YgF | YgF | YgF | YgW | YnF | YnE2 | YgE | YgWd | YgE | YgM | YnE | YnWd | YnE | YnM | YgM | YgE1 | 10 |
| 11 | YnF | YnE2 | YnWd | YnW | YgF | YgF | YgF | YgW | YnF | YnE2 | YnF | YnE4 | YgE | YgM | YnE | YnWd | YnE | YnM | YgM | YgE1 | YgM | YgE3 | YnM | YnF | 11 |
| 12 | YgE | YgM | YgF | YgW | YnF | YnE2 | YnF | YnE4 | YgE | YgM | YgE | YgWd | YnE | YnM | YgM | YgE1 | YgM | YgE3 | YnM | YnF | YnM | YnW | YgW | YgF | 12 |
| 13 | YnE | YnM | YnF | YnE4 | YgE | YgM | YgE | YgWd | YnE | YnM | YnE | YnWd | YgM | YgE3 | YnM | YnF | YnM | YnW | YgW | YgF | YgW | YgW | YnW | YnE2 | 13 |
| 14 | YgM | YgE3 | YgE | YgWd | YnE | YnM | YnE | YnWd | YgM | YgE3 | YgM | YgE1 | YnM | YnW | YgW | YgF | YgW | YgW | YnW | YnE2 | YnW | YnE4 | YgWd | YgM | 14 |
| 15 | YnM | YnW | YnE | YnWd | YgM | YgE3 | YgM | YgE1 | YnM | YnW | YnM | YnF | YgW | YgW | YnW | YnE2 | YnW | YnE4 | YgWd | YgM | YgWd | YgWd | YnWd | YnM | 15 |
| 16 | YgW | YgW | YgM | YgE1 | YnM | YnW | YnM | YnF | YgW | YgW | YgW | YgF | YnW | YnE4 | YgWd | YgM | YgWd | YgWd | YnWd | YnM | YnWd | YnWd | YgF | YgE3 | 16 |
| 17 | YnW | YnE4 | YnM | YnF | YgW | YgW | YgW | YgF | YnW | YnE4 | YnW | YnE2 | YgWd | YgWd | YnWd | YnM | YnWd | YnWd | YgF | YgE3 | YgF | YgE1 | YnF | YnW | 17 |
| 18 | YgWd | YgWd | YgW | YgF | YnW | YnE4 | YnW | YnE2 | YgWd | YgWd | YgWd | YgM | YnWd | YnWd | YgF | YgE3 | YgF | YgE1 | YnF | YnW | YnF | YnF | YgE | YgW | 18 |
| 19 | YnWd | YnWd | YnW | YnE2 | YgWd | YgWd | YgWd | YgM | YnWd | YnWd | YnWd | YnM | YgF | YgE1 | YnF | YnW | YnF | YnF | YgE | YgW | YgE | YgF | YnE | YnE4 | 19 |
| 20 | YgF | YgE1 | YgWd | YgM | YnWd | YnWd | YnWd | YnM | YgF | YgE1 | YgF | YgE3 | YnF | YnF | YgE | YgW | YgE | YgF | YnE | YnE4 | YnE | YnE2 | YgM | YgWd | 20 |
| 21 | YnF | YnF | YnWd | YnM | YgF | YgE1 | YgF | YgE3 | YnF | YnF | YnF | YnW | YgE | YgF | YnE | YnE4 | YnE | YnE2 | YgM | YgWd | YgM | YgM | YnM | YnWd | 21 |
| 22 | YgE | YgF | YgF | YgE3 | YnF | YnF | YnF | YnW | YgE | YgF | YgE | YgW | YnE | YnE2 | YgM | YgWd | YgM | YgM | YnM | YnWd | YnM | YnM | YgW | YgE1 | 22 |
| 23 | YnE | YnE2 | YnF | YnW | YgE | YgF | YgE | YgW | YnE | YnE2 | YnE | YnE4 | YgM | YgM | YnM | YnWd | YnM | YnM | YgW | YgE1 | YgW | YgE3 | YnW | YnF | 23 |
| 24 | YgM | YgM | YgE | YgW | YnE | YnE2 | YnE | YnE4 | YgM | YgM | YgM | YgWd | YnM | YnM | YgW | YgE1 | YgW | YgE3 | YnW | YnF | YnW | YnW | YgWd | YgF | 24 |
| 25 | YnM | YnM | YnE | YnE4 | YgM | YgM | YgM | YgWd | YnM | YnM | YnM | YnWd | YgW | YgE3 | YnW | YnF | YnW | YnW | YgWd | YgF | YgWd | YgW | YnWd | YnE2 | 25 |
| 26 | YgW | YgE3 | YgM | YgWd | YnM | YnM | YnM | YnWd | YgW | YgE3 | YgW | YgE1 | YnW | YnW | YgWd | YgF | YgWd | YgW | YnWd | YnE2 | YnWd | YnE4 | YgF | YgM | 26 |
| 27 | YnW | YnW | YnM | YnWd | YgW | YgE3 | YgW | YgE1 | YnW | YnW | YnW | YnF | YgWd | YgW | YnWd | YnE2 | YnWd | YnE4 | YgF | YgM | YgF | YgWd | YnF | YnM | 27 |
| 28 | YgWd | YgW | YgW | YgE1 | YnW | YnW | YnW | YnF | YgWd | YgW | YgWd | YgF | YnWd | YnE4 | YgF | YgM | YgF | YgWd | YnF | YnM | YnF | YnWd | YgE | YgE3 | 28 |
| 29 | | | YnW | YnF | YgWd | YgW | YgWd | YgF | YnWd | YnE4 | YnWd | YnE2 | YgF | YgWd | YnF | YnM | YnF | YnWd | YgE | YgE3 | YgE | YgE1 | YnE | YnW | 29 |
| 30 | | | YgWd | YgF | YnWd | YnE4 | YnWd | YnE2 | YgF | YgWd | YgF | YgM | YnF | YnWd | YgE | YgE3 | YgE | YgE1 | YnE | YnW | YnE | YnF | YgM | YgW | 30 |
| 31 | | | YnWd | YnE2 | | | YgF | YgM | | | YnF | YnM | YgE | YgE1 | | | YnE | YnF | | | YgM | YgF | YnM | YnE4 | 31 |
| 1 | YnWd | YnE4 | YgF | YgM | YgF | YgWd | YnF | YnM | YnF | YnWd | YgE | YgE3 | YnE | YnF | YnE | YnW | YgM | YgF | YgM | YgW | YnM | YnE2 | YgW | YgWd | 1 |
| 2 | YgF | YgWd | YnF | YnM | YnF | YnWd | YgE | YgE3 | YgE | YgE1 | YnE | YnW | YgM | YgF | YgM | YgW | YnM | YnE2 | YnM | YnE4 | YgW | YgM | YnW | YnWd | 2 |
| 3 | YnF | YnWd | YgE | YgE3 | YgE | YgE1 | YnE | YnW | YnE | YnF | YgM | YgW | YnM | YnE2 | YnM | YnE4 | YgW | YgM | YgW | YgWd | YnW | YnM | YgWd | YgE1 | 3 |
| 4 | YgE | YgE1 | YnE | YnW | YnE | YnF | YgM | YgW | YgM | YgF | YnM | YnE4 | YgW | YgM | YgW | YgWd | YnW | YnM | YnW | YnWd | YgWd | YgE3 | | | 4 |
| 5 | YnE | YnF | | | YgM | YgF | YnM | YnE4 | YnM | YnE2 | YgW | YgWd | YnW | YnM | YnW | YnWd | YgWd | YgE3 | YgWd | YgE1 | YnWd | YnW | | | 5 |
| 6 | | | | | | | | | YgW | YgM | YnW | YnWd | YgWd | YgE3 | YgWd | YgE1 | YnWd | YnW | YnWd | YnF | | | | | 6 |
| 7 | | | | | | | | | | | YgWd | YgE1 | YnWd | YnW | YnWd | YnF | YgF | YgW | | | | | | | 7 |
| 8 | | | | | | | | | | | | | | | | | | | | | | | | | 8 |

# YEAR OF THE GOAT

| | H | E | H | E | H | E | H | E | H | E | H | E | H | E | H | E | H | E | H | E | H | E | H | E | |
|---|---|---|---|---|---|---|---|---|---|---|---|---|---|---|---|---|---|---|---|---|---|---|---|---|---|
| YEAR | YEAR | | | | | | | | | | | 1991 | | | | | | | | | | | 1992 | | |
| | YnM | Yn E2 | | | | | | | | | | | | | | | | | | | | | | | |
| MONTH | 4 Feb - 5 Mar | | 6 Mar - 4 Apr | | 5 Apr - 5 May | | 6 May - 5 June | | 6 June - 6 Jul | | 7 Jul - 7 Aug | | 8 Aug - 7 Sep | | 8 Sep - 8 Oct | | 9 Oct - 7 Nov | | 8 Nov - 6 Dec | | 7 Dec - 5 Jan | | 6 Jan - 3 Feb | | |
| | Yg M | Yg Wd | Yn M | Yn Wd | Yg W | Yg E1 | Yn W | Yn F | Yg Wd | Yg F | Yn Wd | Yn E2 | Yg F | Yg M | Yn F | Yn M | Yg E | Yg E3 | Yn E | Yn W | Yg M | Yg W | Yn M | Yn E4 | |
| Starting time | 1st day | Mid-pt | 1st day | Mid-pt | 1st day | Mid-pt | 1st day | Mid-pt | 1st day | Mid-pt | 1st day | Mid-pt | 1st day | Mid-pt | 1st day | Mid-pt | 1st day | Mid-pt | 1st day | Mid-pt | 1st day | Mid-pt | 1st day | Mid-pt | |
| Date | 4 | 19 | 6 | 21 | 5 | 20 | 6 | 21 | 6 | 22 | 7 | 23 | 8 | 23 | 8 | 23 | 9 | 24 | 8 | 23 | 7 | 22 | 6 | 21 | |
| Hour | 1604 | 1158 | 1014 | 1111 | 1517 | 2230 | 0851 | 2152 | 1314 | 0558 | 2337 | 1651 | 0920 | 2347 | 1204 | 2111 | 0328 | 0616 | 0623 | 0339 | 2305 | 1652 | 1012 | 0330 | |
| DATE 4 | Yn Wd | Yn F | | | | | | | | | | | | | | | | | | | | | | | 4 |
| 5 | Yg F | Yg F | | | Yn Wd | Yn F | | | | | | | | | | | | | | | | | | | 5 |
| 6 | Yn F | Yn E2 | Yn Wd | Yn W | Yg F | Yg F | Yg F | Yg W | Yn F | Yn E2 | | | | | | | | | | | | | Yn M | Yn F | 6 |
| 7 | Yg E | Yg M | Yg F | Yg W | Yn F | Yn E2 | Yn F | Yn E4 | Yg E | Yg M | Yg E | Yg Wd | | | | | | | | | Yn M | Yn W | Yg W | Yg F | 7 |
| 8 | Yn E | Yn M | Yn F | Yn E4 | Yg E | Yg M | Yg E | Yg Wd | Yn E | Yn M | Yn E | Yn Wd | Yg M | Yg E3 | Yn M | Yn F | | | Yg W | Yg F | Yg W | Yg W | Yn W | Yn E2 | 8 |
| 9 | Yg M | Yg E3 | Yg E | Yg Wd | Yn E | Yn M | Yn E | Yn Wd | Yg M | Yg E3 | Yg M | Yg E1 | Yn M | Yn W | Yg W | Yg F | Yg W | Yg W | Yn W | Yn E2 | Yn W | Yn E4 | Yg Wd | Yg M | 9 |
| 10 | Yn M | Yn W | Yn E | Yn Wd | Yg M | Yg E3 | Yg M | Yg E1 | Yn M | Yn W | Yn M | Yn F | Yg W | Yg W | Yn W | Yn E2 | Yn W | Yn E4 | Yg Wd | Yg M | Yg Wd | Yg Wd | Yn Wd | Yn M | 10 |
| 11 | Yg W | Yg W | Yg M | Yg E1 | Yn M | Yn W | Yn M | Yn F | Yg W | Yg W | Yg W | Yg F | Yn W | Yn E4 | Yg Wd | Yg M | Yg Wd | Yg Wd | Yn Wd | Yn M | Yn Wd | Yn Wd | Yg F | Yg E3 | 11 |
| 12 | Yn W | Yn E4 | Yn M | Yn F | Yg W | Yg W | Yg W | Yg F | Yn W | Yn E4 | Yn W | Yn E2 | Yg Wd | Yg Wd | Yn Wd | Yn M | Yn Wd | Yn Wd | Yg F | Yg E3 | Yg F | Yg E1 | Yn F | Yn W | 12 |
| 13 | Yg Wd | Yg Wd | Yg W | Yg F | Yn W | Yn E4 | Yn W | Yn E2 | Yg Wd | Yg Wd | Yg Wd | Yg M | Yn Wd | Yn Wd | Yg F | Yg E3 | Yg F | Yg E1 | Yn F | Yn W | Yn F | Yn F | Yg E | Yg W | 13 |
| 14 | Yn Wd | Yn Wd | Yn W | Yn E2 | Yg Wd | Yg Wd | Yg Wd | Yg M | Yn Wd | Yn Wd | Yn Wd | Yn M | Yg F | Yg E1 | Yn F | Yn W | Yn F | Yn F | Yg E | Yg W | Yg E | Yg F | Yn E | Yn E4 | 14 |
| 15 | Yg F | Yg E1 | Yg Wd | Yg M | Yn Wd | Yn Wd | Yn Wd | Yn M | Yg F | Yg E1 | Yg F | Yg E3 | Yn F | Yn F | Yg E | Yg W | Yg E | Yg F | Yn E | Yn E4 | Yn E | Yn E2 | Yg M | Yg Wd | 15 |
| 16 | Yn F | Yn F | Yn Wd | Yn M | Yg F | Yg E1 | Yg F | Yg E3 | Yn F | Yn F | Yn F | Yn W | Yg E | Yg F | Yn E | Yn E4 | Yn E | Yn E2 | Yg M | Yg Wd | Yg M | Yg M | Yn M | Yn Wd | 16 |
| 17 | Yg E | Yg F | Yg F | Yg E3 | Yn F | Yn F | Yn F | Yn W | Yg E | Yg F | Yg E | Yg W | Yn E | Yn E2 | Yg M | Yg Wd | Yg M | Yg M | Yn M | Yn Wd | Yn M | Yn M | Yg W | Yg E1 | 17 |
| 18 | Yn E | Yn E2 | Yn F | Yn W | Yg E | Yg F | Yg E | Yg W | Yn E | Yn E2 | Yn E | Yn E4 | Yg M | Yg M | Yn M | Yn Wd | Yn M | Yn M | Yg W | Yg E1 | Yg W | Yg E3 | Yn W | Yn F | 18 |
| 19 | Yg M | Yg M | Yg E | Yg W | Yn E | Yn E2 | Yn E | Yn E4 | Yg M | Yg M | Yg M | Yg Wd | Yn M | Yn M | Yg W | Yg E1 | Yg W | Yg E3 | Yn W | Yn F | Yn W | Yn W | Yg Wd | Yg F | 19 |
| 20 | Yn M | Yn M | Yn E | Yn E4 | Yg M | Yg M | Yg M | Yg Wd | Yn M | Yn M | Yn M | Yn Wd | Yg W | Yg E3 | Yn W | Yn F | Yn W | Yn W | Yg Wd | Yg F | Yg Wd | Yg W | Yn Wd | Yn E2 | 20 |
| 21 | Yg W | Yg E3 | Yg M | Yg Wd | Yn M | Yn M | Yn M | Yn Wd | Yg W | Yg E3 | Yg W | Yg E1 | Yn W | Yn W | Yg Wd | Yg F | Yg Wd | Yg W | Yn Wd | Yn E2 | Yn Wd | Yn E4 | Yg F | Yg M | 21 |
| 22 | Yn W | Yn W | Yn M | Yn Wd | Yg W | Yg E3 | Yg W | Yg E1 | Yn W | Yn W | Yn W | Yn F | Yg Wd | Yg W | Yn Wd | Yn E2 | Yn Wd | Yn E4 | Yg F | Yg M | Yg F | Yg Wd | Yn F | Yn M | 22 |
| 23 | Yg Wd | Yg W | Yg W | Yg E1 | Yn W | Yn W | Yn W | Yn F | Yg Wd | Yg W | Yg Wd | Yg F | Yn Wd | Yn E4 | Yg F | Yg M | Yg F | Yg Wd | Yn F | Yn M | Yn F | Yn Wd | Yg E | Yg E3 | 23 |
| 24 | Yn Wd | Yn E4 | Yn W | Yn F | Yg Wd | Yg W | Yg Wd | Yg F | Yn Wd | Yn E4 | Yn Wd | Yn E2 | Yg F | Yg Wd | Yn F | Yn M | Yn F | Yn Wd | Yg E | Yg E3 | Yg E | Yg E1 | Yn E | Yn W | 24 |
| 25 | Yg F | Yg Wd | Yg Wd | Yg F | Yn Wd | Yn E4 | Yn Wd | Yn E2 | Yg F | Yg Wd | Yg F | Yg M | Yn F | Yn Wd | Yg E | Yg E3 | Yg E | Yg E1 | Yn E | Yn W | Yn E | Yn F | Yg M | Yg W | 25 |
| 26 | Yn F | Yn Wd | Yn Wd | Yn E2 | Yg F | Yg Wd | Yg F | Yg M | Yn F | Yn Wd | Yn F | Yn M | Yg E | Yg E1 | Yn E | Yn W | Yn E | Yn F | Yg M | Yg W | Yg M | Yg F | Yn M | Yn E4 | 26 |
| 27 | Yg E | Yg E1 | Yg F | Yg M | Yn F | Yn Wd | Yn F | Yn M | Yg E | Yg E1 | Yg E | Yg E3 | Yn E | Yn F | Yg M | Yg W | Yg M | Yg F | Yn M | Yn E4 | Yn M | Yn E2 | Yg W | Yg Wd | 27 |
| 28 | Yn E | Yn F | Yn F | Yn M | Yg E | Yg E1 | Yg E | Yg E3 | Yn E | Yn F | Yn E | Yn W | Yg M | Yg F | Yn M | Yn E4 | Yn M | Yn E2 | Yg W | Yg Wd | Yg W | Yg M | Yn W | Yn Wd | 28 |
| 29 | | | Yg E | Yg E3 | Yn E | Yn F | Yn E | Yn W | Yg M | Yg F | Yg M | Yg W | Yn M | Yn E2 | Yg W | Yg Wd | Yg W | Yg M | Yn W | Yn Wd | Yn W | Yn M | Yg Wd | Yg E1 | 29 |
| 30 | | | Yn E | Yn W | Yg M | Yg F | Yg M | Yg W | Yn M | Yn E2 | Yn M | Yn E4 | Yg W | Yg M | Yn W | Yn Wd | Yn W | Yn M | Yg Wd | Yg E1 | Yg Wd | Yg E3 | Yn Wd | Yn F | 30 |
| 31 | | | Yg M | Yg W | | | Yn M | Yn E4 | | | Yg W | Yg Wd | Yn W | Yn M | | | Yg Wd | Yg E3 | | | Yn Wd | Yn W | Yg F | Yg F | 31 |
| 1 | Yg M | Yg F | Yn M | Yn E4 | Yn M | Yn E2 | Yg W | Yg Wd | Yg W | Yg M | Yn W | Yn Wd | Yg Wd | Yg E3 | Yg Wd | Yg E1 | Yn Wd | Yn W | Yn Wd | Yn F | Yg F | Yg W | Yn F | Yn E2 | 1 |
| 2 | Yn M | Yn E2 | Yg W | Yg Wd | Yg W | Yg M | Yn W | Yn Wd | Yn W | Yn M | Yg Wd | Yg E1 | Yn Wd | Yn W | Yn Wd | Yn F | Yg F | Yg W | Yg F | Yg F | Yn F | Yn E4 | Yg E | Yg M | 2 |
| 3 | Yg W | Yg M | Yn W | Yn Wd | Yn W | Yn M | Yg Wd | Yg E1 | Yg Wd | Yg E3 | Yn Wd | Yn F | Yg F | Yg W | Yg F | Yg F | Yn F | Yn E4 | Yn F | Yn E2 | Yg E | Yg Wd | Yn E | Yn M | 3 |
| 4 | Yn W | Yn M | Yg Wd | Yg E1 | Yg Wd | Yg E3 | Yn Wd | Yn F | Yn Wd | Yn W | Yg F | Yg F | Yn F | Yn E4 | Yn F | Yn E2 | Yg E | Yg Wd | Yg E | Yg M | Yn E | Yn Wd | | | 4 |
| 5 | Yg Wd | Yg E3 | | | Yn Wd | Yn W | Yg F | Yg F | Yg F | Yg W | Yn F | Yn E2 | Yg E | Yg Wd | Yg E | Yg M | Yn E | Yn Wd | Yn E | Yn M | Yg M | Yg E1 | | | 5 |
| 6 | | | | | | | | | Yn F | Yn E4 | Yg E | Yg M | Yn E | Yn Wd | Yn E | Yn M | Yg M | Yg E1 | Yg M | Yg E3 | | | | | 6 |
| 7 | | | | | | | | | | | Yn E | Yn M | Yg M | Yg E1 | Yg M | Yg E3 | Yn M | Yn F | | | | | | | 7 |
| 8 | | | | | | | | | | | | | | | Yn M | Yn W | | | | | | | | | 8 |

# YEAR OF THE MONKEY

| | H | E | H | E | H | E | H | E | H | E | H | E | H | E | H | E | H | E | H | E | H | E | H | E | |
|---|---|---|---|---|---|---|---|---|---|---|---|---|---|---|---|---|---|---|---|---|---|---|---|---|---|
| YEAR | YEAR Yg W | Yg M | 1992 | | | | | | | | | | | | | | | | | | 1993 | | | | |
| MONTH | 4 Feb - 4 Mar | | 5 Mar - 3 Apr | | 4 Apr - 4 May | | 5 May - 4 June | | 5 June - 6 Jul | | 7 Jul - 6 Aug | | 7 Aug - 6 Sep | | 7 Sep - 7 Oct | | 8 Oct - 6 Nov | | 7 Nov - 6 Dec | | 7 Dec - 4 Jan | | 5 Jan - 3 Feb | | |
| | Yg W | Yg Wd | Yn W | Yn Wd | Yg Wd | Yg E1 | Yn Wd | Yn F | Yg F | Yg F | Yn F | Yn E2 | Yg E | Yg M | Yn E | Yn M | Yg M | Yg E3 | Yn M | Yn W | Yg W | Yg W | Yn W | Yn E4 | |
| Starting time | 1st day | Mid-pt | 1st day | Mid-pt | 1st day | Mid-pt | 1st day | Mid-pt | 1st day | Mid-pt | 1st day | Mid-pt | 1st day | Mid-pt | 1st day | Mid-pt | 1st day | Mid-pt | 1st day | Mid-pt | 1st day | Mid-pt | 1st day | Mid-pt | |
| Date | 4 | 19 | 5 | 20 | 4 | 20 | 5 | 21 | 5 | 21 | 7 | 22 | 7 | 23 | 7 | 23 | 8 | 23 | 7 | 22 | 7 | 21 | 5 | 20 | |
| Hour | 2154 | 1747 | 1604 | 1659 | 2107 | 0418 | 1441 | 0340 | 1918 | 1146 | 0526 | 2239 | 1509 | 0535 | 1753 | 0259 | 0917 | 1205 | 1212 | 0927 | 0452 | 2240 | 1601 | 0918 | |
| DATE 4 | Yg M | Yg E3 | | | Yg M | Yg E3 | | | | | | | | | | | | | | | | | | | 4 |
| 5 | Yn M | Yn W | Yg M | Yg E1 | Yn M | Yn W | Yn M | Yn F | Yg W | Yg W | | | | | | | | | | | | | Yg F | Yg E3 | 5 |
| 6 | Yg W | Yg W | Yn M | Yn F | Yg W | Yg W | Yg W | Yg F | Yn W | Yn E4 | | | | | | | | | | | | | Yn F | Yn W | 6 |
| 7 | Yn W | Yn E4 | Yg W | Yg F | Yn W | Yn E4 | Yn W | Yn E2 | Yg Wd | Yg Wd | Yg Wd | Yg M | Yn Wd | Yn Wd | Yg F | Yg E3 | | | Yn F | Yn W | Yn F | Yn F | Yg E | Yg W | 7 |
| 8 | Yg Wd | Yg Wd | Yn W | Yn E2 | Yg Wd | Yg Wd | Yg Wd | Yg M | Yn Wd | Yn Wd | Yn Wd | Yn M | Yg F | Yg E1 | Yn F | Yn W | Yn F | Yn F | Yg E | Yg W | Yg E | Yg F | Yn E | Yn E4 | 8 |
| 9 | Yn Wd | Yn Wd | Yg Wd | Yg M | Yn Wd | Yn Wd | Yn Wd | Yn M | Yg F | Yg E1 | Yg F | Yg E3 | Yn F | Yn F | Yg E | Yg W | Yg E | Yg F | Yn E | Yn E4 | Yn E | Yn E2 | Yg M | Yg Wd | 9 |
| 10 | Yg F | Yg E1 | Yn Wd | Yn M | Yg F | Yg E1 | Yg F | Yg E3 | Yn F | Yn F | Yn F | Yn W | Yg E | Yg F | Yn E | Yn E4 | Yn E | Yn E2 | Yg M | Yg Wd | Yg M | Yg M | Yn M | Yn Wd | 10 |
| 11 | Yn F | Yn F | Yg F | Yg E3 | Yn F | Yn F | Yn F | Yn W | Yg E | Yg F | Yg E | Yg W | Yn E | Yn E2 | Yg M | Yg Wd | Yg M | Yg M | Yn M | Yn Wd | Yn M | Yn M | Yg W | Yg E1 | 11 |
| 12 | Yg E | Yg F | Yn F | Yn W | Yg E | Yg F | Yg E | Yg W | Yn E | Yn E2 | Yn E | Yn E4 | Yg M | Yg M | Yn M | Yn Wd | Yn M | Yn M | Yg W | Yg E1 | Yg W | Yg E3 | Yn W | Yn F | 12 |
| 13 | Yn E | Yn E2 | Yg E | Yg W | Yn E | Yn E2 | Yn E | Yn E4 | Yg M | Yg M | Yg M | Yg Wd | Yn M | Yn M | Yg W | Yg E1 | Yg W | Yg E3 | Yn W | Yn F | Yn W | Yn W | Yg Wd | Yg F | 13 |
| 14 | Yg M | Yg M | Yn E | Yn E4 | Yg M | Yg M | Yg M | Yg Wd | Yn M | Yn M | Yn M | Yn Wd | Yg W | Yg E3 | Yn W | Yn F | Yn W | Yn W | Yg Wd | Yg F | Yg Wd | Yg W | Yn Wd | Yn E2 | 14 |
| 15 | Yn M | Yn M | Yg M | Yg Wd | Yn M | Yn M | Yn M | Yn Wd | Yg W | Yg E3 | Yg W | Yg E1 | Yn W | Yn W | Yg Wd | Yg F | Yg Wd | Yg W | Yn Wd | Yn E2 | Yn Wd | Yn E4 | Yg F | Yg M | 15 |
| 16 | Yg W | Yg E3 | Yn M | Yn Wd | Yg W | Yg E3 | Yg W | Yg E1 | Yn W | Yn W | Yn W | Yn F | Yg Wd | Yg W | Yn Wd | Yn E2 | Yn Wd | Yn E4 | Yg F | Yg M | Yg F | Yg Wd | Yn F | Yn M | 16 |
| 17 | Yn W | Yn W | Yg W | Yg E1 | Yn W | Yn W | Yn W | Yn F | Yg Wd | Yg W | Yg Wd | Yg F | Yn Wd | Yn E4 | Yg F | Yg M | Yg F | Yg Wd | Yn F | Yn M | Yn F | Yn Wd | Yg E | Yg E3 | 17 |
| 18 | Yg Wd | Yg W | Yn W | Yn F | Yg Wd | Yg W | Yg Wd | Yg F | Yn Wd | Yn E4 | Yn Wd | Yn E2 | Yg F | Yg Wd | Yn F | Yn M | Yn F | Yn Wd | Yg E | Yg E3 | Yg E | Yg E1 | Yn E | Yn W | 18 |
| 19 | Yn Wd | Yn E4 | Yg Wd | Yg F | Yn Wd | Yn E4 | Yn Wd | Yn E2 | Yg F | Yg Wd | Yg F | Yg M | Yn F | Yn Wd | Yg E | Yg E3 | Yg E | Yg E1 | Yn E | Yn W | Yn E | Yn F | Yg M | Yg W | 19 |
| 20 | Yg F | Yg Wd | Yn Wd | Yn E2 | Yg F | Yg Wd | Yg F | Yg M | Yn F | Yn Wd | Yn F | Yn M | Yg E | Yg E1 | Yn E | Yn W | Yn E | Yn F | Yg M | Yg W | Yg M | Yg F | Yn M | Yn E4 | 20 |
| 21 | Yn F | Yn Wd | Yg F | Yg M | Yn F | Yn Wd | Yn F | Yn M | Yg E | Yg E1 | Yg E | Yg E3 | Yn E | Yn F | Yg M | Yg W | Yg M | Yg F | Yn M | Yn E4 | Yn M | Yn E2 | Yg W | Yg Wd | 21 |
| 22 | Yg E | Yg E1 | Yn F | Yn M | Yg E | Yg E1 | Yg E | Yg E3 | Yn E | Yn F | Yn E | Yn W | Yg M | Yg F | Yn M | Yn E4 | Yn M | Yn E2 | Yg W | Yg Wd | Yg W | Yg M | Yn W | Yn Wd | 22 |
| 23 | Yn E | Yn F | Yg E | Yg E3 | Yn E | Yn F | Yn E | Yn W | Yg M | Yg F | Yg M | Yg W | Yn M | Yn E2 | Yg W | Yg Wd | Yg W | Yg M | Yn W | Yn Wd | Yn W | Yn M | Yg Wd | Yg E1 | 23 |
| 24 | Yg M | Yg F | Yn E | Yn W | Yg M | Yg F | Yg M | Yg W | Yn M | Yn E2 | Yn M | Yn E4 | Yg W | Yg M | Yn W | Yn Wd | Yn W | Yn M | Yg Wd | Yg E1 | Yg Wd | Yg E3 | Yn Wd | Yn F | 24 |
| 25 | Yn M | Yn E2 | Yg M | Yg W | Yn M | Yn E2 | Yn M | Yn E4 | Yg W | Yg M | Yg W | Yg Wd | Yn W | Yn M | Yg Wd | Yg E1 | Yg Wd | Yg E3 | Yn Wd | Yn F | Yn Wd | Yn W | Yg F | Yg F | 25 |
| 26 | Yg W | Yg M | Yn M | Yn E4 | Yg W | Yg M | Yg W | Yg Wd | Yn W | Yn M | Yn W | Yn Wd | Yg Wd | Yg E3 | Yn Wd | Yn F | Yn Wd | Yn W | Yg F | Yg F | Yg F | Yg W | Yn F | Yn E2 | 26 |
| 27 | Yn W | Yn M | Yg W | Yg Wd | Yn W | Yn M | Yn W | Yn Wd | Yg Wd | Yg E3 | Yg Wd | Yg E1 | Yn Wd | Yn W | Yg F | Yg F | Yg F | Yg W | Yn F | Yn E2 | Yn F | Yn E4 | Yg E | Yg M | 27 |
| 28 | Yg Wd | Yg E3 | Yn W | Yn Wd | Yg Wd | Yg E3 | Yg Wd | Yg E1 | Yn Wd | Yn W | Yn Wd | Yn F | Yg F | Yg W | Yn F | Yn E2 | Yn F | Yn E4 | Yg E | Yg M | Yg E | Yg Wd | Yn E | Yn M | 28 |
| 29 | Yn Wd | Yn W | Yg Wd | Yg E1 | Yn Wd | Yn W | Yn Wd | Yn F | Yg F | Yg W | Yg F | Yg F | Yn F | Yn E4 | Yg E | Yg M | Yg E | Yg Wd | Yn E | Yn M | Yn E | Yn Wd | Yg M | Yg E3 | 29 |
| 30 | | | Yn Wd | Yn F | Yg F | Yg W | Yg F | Yg F | Yn F | Yn E4 | Yn F | Yn E2 | Yg E | Yg Wd | Yn E | Yn M | Yn E | Yn Wd | Yg M | Yg E3 | Yg M | Yg E1 | Yn M | Yn W | 30 |
| 31 | | | Yg F | Yg F | | | Yn F | Yn E2 | | | Yg E | Yg M | Yn E | Yn Wd | | | Yg M | Yg E1 | | | Yn M | Yn F | Yg W | Yg W | 31 |
| 1 | Yg F | Yg W | Yn F | Yn E2 | Yn F | Yn E4 | Yg E | Yg M | Yg E | Yg Wd | Yn E | Yn M | Yg M | Yg E1 | Yg M | Yg E3 | Yn M | Yn F | Yn M | Yn W | Yg W | Yg F | Yn W | Yn E4 | 1 |
| 2 | Yn F | Yn E4 | Yg E | Yg M | Yg E | Yg Wd | Yn E | Yn M | Yn E | Yn Wd | Yg M | Yg E3 | Yn M | Yn F | Yn M | Yn W | Yg W | Yg F | Yg W | Yg W | Yn W | Yn E2 | Yg Wd | Yg Wd | 2 |
| 3 | Yg E | Yg Wd | Yn E | Yn M | Yn E | Yn Wd | Yg M | Yg E3 | Yg M | Yg E1 | Yn M | Yn W | Yg W | Yg F | Yg W | Yg W | Yn W | Yn E2 | Yn W | Yn E4 | Yg Wd | Yg M | Yn Wd | Yn Wd | 3 |
| 4 | Yn E | Yn Wd | | | Yg M | Yg E1 | Yn M | Yn W | Yn M | Yn F | Yg W | Yg W | Yn W | Yn E2 | Yn W | Yn E4 | Yg Wd | Yg M | Yg Wd | Yg Wd | Yn Wd | Yn M | | | 4 |
| 5 | | | | | | | | | Yg W | Yg F | Yn W | Yn E4 | Yg Wd | Yg M | Yg Wd | Yg Wd | Yn Wd | Yn M | Yn Wd | Yn Wd | | | | | 5 |
| 6 | | | | | | | | | Yn W | Yn E2 | Yg Wd | Yg Wd | Yn Wd | Yn M | Yn Wd | Yn Wd | Yg F | Yg E3 | Yg F | Yg E1 | | | | | 6 |
| 7 | | | | | | | | | | | | | | | Yg F | Yg E1 | | | | | | | | | 7 |
| 8 | | | | | | | | | | | | | | | | | | | | | | | | | 8 |

# YEAR OF THE ROOSTER

| YEAR | H | E | H | E | H | E | H | E | H | E | H | E |
|---|---|---|---|---|---|---|---|---|---|---|---|---|
| YEAR | YEAR<br>Yn W | Yn M | 1993 | | | | | | | | | |
| MONTH | 4 Feb - 4 Mar<br>Yg Wd | Yg Wd | 5 Mar - 4 Apr<br>Yn Wd | Yn Wd | 5 Apr - 4 May<br>Yg F | Yg E1 | 5 May - 5 June<br>Yn F | Yn F | 6 June - 6 Jul<br>Yg E | Yg F | 7 Jul - 6 Aug<br>Yn E | Yn E2 |
| Starting time | 1st day | Mid-pt | 1st day | Mid-pt | 1st day | Mid-pt | 1st day | Mid-pt | 1st day | Mid-pt | 1st day | Mid-pt |
| Date | 4 | 18 | 5 | 20 | 5 | 20 | 5 | 21 | 6 | 21 | 7 | 23 |
| Hour | 0343 | 2335 | 2153 | 2248 | 0256 | 1007 | 2034 | 0929 | 0052 | 1735 | 1115 | 0428 |
| DATE 4 | Yg F | Yg E1 | | | | | | | | | | |
| 5 | Yn F | Yn F | Yn Wd | Yn M | Yg F | Yg E1 | Yg F | Yg E3 | | | | |
| 6 | Yg E | Yg F | Yg F | Yg E3 | Yn F | Yn F | Yn F | Yn W | Yg E | Yg F | | |
| 7 | Yn E | Yn E2 | Yn F | Yn W | Yg E | Yg F | Yg E | Yg W | Yn E | Yn E2 | Yn E | Yn E4 |
| 8 | Yg M | Yg M | Yg E | Yg W | Yn E | Yn E2 | Yn E | Yn E4 | Yg M | Yg M | Yg M | Yg Wd |
| 9 | Yn M | Yn M | Yn E | Yn E4 | Yg M | Yg M | Yg M | Yg Wd | Yn M | Yn M | Yn M | Yn Wd |
| 10 | Yg W | Yg E3 | Yg M | Yg Wd | Yn M | Yn M | Yn M | Yn Wd | Yg W | Yg E3 | Yg W | Yg E1 |
| 11 | Yn W | Yn W | Yn M | Yn Wd | Yg W | Yg E3 | Yg W | Yg E1 | Yn W | Yn W | Yn W | Yn F |
| 12 | Yg Wd | Yg W | Yg W | Yg E1 | Yn W | Yn W | Yn W | Yn F | Yg Wd | Yg W | Yg Wd | Yg F |
| 13 | Yn Wd | Yn E4 | Yn W | Yn F | Yg Wd | Yg W | Yg Wd | Yg F | Yn Wd | Yn E4 | Yn Wd | Yn E2 |
| 14 | Yg F | Yg Wd | Yg Wd | Yg F | Yn Wd | Yn E4 | Yn Wd | Yn E2 | Yg F | Yg Wd | Yg F | Yg M |
| 15 | Yn F | Yn Wd | Yn Wd | Yn E2 | Yg F | Yg Wd | Yg F | Yg M | Yn F | Yn Wd | Yn F | Yn M |
| 16 | Yg E | Yg E1 | Yg F | Yg M | Yn F | Yn Wd | Yn F | Yn M | Yg E | Yg E1 | Yg E | Yg E3 |
| 17 | Yn E | Yn F | Yn F | Yn M | Yg E | Yg E1 | Yg E | Yg E3 | Yn E | Yn F | Yn E | Yn W |
| 18 | Yg M | Yg F | Yg E | Yg E3 | Yn E | Yn F | Yn E | Yn W | Yg M | Yg F | Yg M | Yg W |
| 19 | Yn M | Yn E2 | Yn E | Yn W | Yg M | Yg F | Yg M | Yg W | Yn M | Yn E2 | Yn M | Yn E4 |
| 20 | Yg W | Yg M | Yg M | Yg W | Yn M | Yn E2 | Yn M | Yn E4 | Yg W | Yg M | Yg W | Yg Wd |
| 21 | Yn W | Yn M | Yn M | Yn E4 | Yg W | Yg M | Yg W | Yg Wd | Yn W | Yn M | Yn W | Yn Wd |
| 22 | Yg Wd | Yg E3 | Yg W | Yg Wd | Yn W | Yn M | Yn W | Yn Wd | Yg Wd | Yg E3 | Yg Wd | Yg E1 |
| 23 | Yn Wd | Yn W | Yn W | Yn Wd | Yg Wd | Yg E3 | Yg Wd | Yg E1 | Yn Wd | Yn W | Yn Wd | Yn F |
| 24 | Yg F | Yg W | Yg Wd | Yg E1 | Yn Wd | Yn W | Yn Wd | Yn F | Yg F | Yg W | Yg F | Yg F |
| 25 | Yn F | Yn E4 | Yn Wd | Yn F | Yg F | Yg W | Yg F | Yg F | Yn F | Yn E4 | Yn F | Yn E2 |
| 26 | Yg E | Yg Wd | Yg F | Yg F | Yn F | Yn E4 | Yn F | Yn E2 | Yg E | Yg Wd | Yg E | Yg M |
| 27 | Yn E | Yn Wd | Yn F | Yn E2 | Yg E | Yg Wd | Yg E | Yg M | Yn E | Yn Wd | Yn E | Yn M |
| 28 | Yg M | Yg E1 | Yg E | Yg M | Yn E | Yn Wd | Yn E | Yn M | Yg M | Yg E1 | Yg M | Yg E3 |
| 29 | | | Yn E | Yn M | Yg M | Yg E1 | Yg M | Yg E3 | Yn M | Yn F | Yn M | Yn W |
| 30 | | | Yg M | Yg E3 | Yn M | Yn F | Yn M | Yn W | Yg W | Yg F | Yg W | Yg W |
| 31 | | | Yn M | Yn W | | | Yg W | Yg W | | | Yn W | Yn E4 |
| 1 | Yn M | Yn F | Yg W | Yg W | Yg W | Yg F | Yn W | Yn E4 | Yn W | Yn E2 | Yg Wd | Yg Wd |
| 2 | Yg W | Yg F | Yn W | Yn E4 | Yn W | Yn E2 | Yg Wd | Yg Wd | Yg Wd | Yg M | Yn Wd | Yn Wd |
| 3 | Yn W | Yn E2 | Yg Wd | Yg Wd | Yg Wd | Yg M | Yn Wd | Yn Wd | Yn Wd | Yn M | Yg F | Yg E1 |
| 4 | Yg Wd | Yg M | Yn Wd | Yn Wd | Yn Wd | Yn M | Yg F | Yg E1 | Yg F | Yg E3 | Yn F | Yn F |
| 5 | | | | | | | Yn F | Yn F | Yn F | Yn W | Yg E | Yg F |
| 6 | | | | | | | | | Yg E | Yg W | Yn E | Yn E2 |
| 7 | | | | | | | | | | | | |
| 8 | | | | | | | | | | | | |

| H | E | H | E | H | E | H | E | H | E | H | E | |
|---|---|---|---|---|---|---|---|---|---|---|---|---|
| 1993 | | | | | | | | | | 1994 | | |
| 7 Aug - 6 Sep<br>Yg M | Yg M | 7 Sep - 7 Oct<br>Yn M | Yn M | 8 Oct - 6 Nov<br>Yg W | Yg E3 | 7 Nov - 6 Dec<br>Yn W | Yn W | 7 Dec - 4 Jan<br>Yg Wd | Yg W | 5 Jan - 3 Feb<br>Yn Wd | Yn E4 | |
| 1st day | Mid-pt | 1st day | Mid-pt | 1st day | Mid-pt | 1st day | Mid-pt | 1st day | Mid-pt | 1st day | Mid-pt | |
| 7 | 23 | 7 | 23 | 8 | 23 | 7 | 22 | 7 | 22 | 5 | 20 | |
| 2059 | 1124 | 2343 | 0848 | 1507 | 1754 | 1802 | 1516 | 1042 | 0429 | 2151 | 1507 | |
| | | | | | | | | | | | | 4 |
| | | | | | | | | | | Yn M | Yn Wd | 5 |
| | | | | | | | | | | Yg W | Yg E1 | 6 |
| Yg M | Yg M | Yn M | Yn Wd | | | Yg W | Yg E1 | Yg W | Yg E3 | Yn W | Yn F | 7 |
| Yn M | Yn M | Yg W | Yg E1 | Yg W | Yg E3 | Yn W | Yn F | Yn W | Yn W | Yg Wd | Yg F | 8 |
| Yg W | Yg E3 | Yn W | Yn F | Yn W | Yn W | Yg Wd | Yg F | Yg Wd | Yg W | Yn Wd | Yn E2 | 9 |
| Yn W | Yn W | Yg Wd | Yg F | Yg Wd | Yg W | Yn Wd | Yn E2 | Yn Wd | Yn E4 | Yg F | Yg M | 10 |
| Yg Wd | Yg W | Yn Wd | Yn E2 | Yn Wd | Yn E4 | Yg F | Yg M | Yg F | Yg Wd | Yn F | Yn M | 11 |
| Yn Wd | Yn E4 | Yg F | Yg M | Yg F | Yg Wd | Yn F | Yn M | Yn F | Yn Wd | Yg E | Yg E3 | 12 |
| Yg F | Yg Wd | Yn F | Yn M | Yn F | Yn Wd | Yg E | Yg E3 | Yg E | Yg E1 | Yn E | Yn W | 13 |
| Yn F | Yn Wd | Yg E | Yg E3 | Yg E | Yg E1 | Yn E | Yn W | Yn E | Yn F | Yg M | Yg W | 14 |
| Yg E | Yg E1 | Yn E | Yn W | Yn E | Yn F | Yg M | Yg W | Yg M | Yg F | Yn M | Yn E4 | 15 |
| Yn E | Yn F | Yg M | Yg W | Yg M | Yg F | Yn M | Yn E4 | Yn M | Yn E2 | Yg W | Yg Wd | 16 |
| Yg M | Yg F | Yn M | Yn E4 | Yn M | Yn E2 | Yg W | Yg Wd | Yg W | Yg M | Yn W | Yn Wd | 17 |
| Yn M | Yn E2 | Yg W | Yg Wd | Yg W | Yg M | Yn W | Yn Wd | Yn W | Yn M | Yg Wd | Yg E1 | 18 |
| Yg W | Yg M | Yn W | Yn Wd | Yn W | Yn M | Yg Wd | Yg E1 | Yg Wd | Yg E3 | Yn Wd | Yn F | 19 |
| Yn W | Yn M | Yg Wd | Yg E1 | Yg Wd | Yg E3 | Yn Wd | Yn F | Yn Wd | Yn W | Yg F | Yg F | 20 |
| Yg Wd | Yg E3 | Yn Wd | Yn F | Yn Wd | Yn W | Yg F | Yg F | Yg F | Yg W | Yn F | Yn E2 | 21 |
| Yn Wd | Yn W | Yg F | Yg F | Yg F | Yg W | Yn F | Yn E2 | Yn F | Yn E4 | Yg E | Yg M | 22 |
| Yg F | Yg W | Yn F | Yn E2 | Yn F | Yn E4 | Yg E | Yg M | Yg E | Yg Wd | Yn E | Yn M | 23 |
| Yn F | Yn E4 | Yg E | Yg M | Yg E | Yg Wd | Yn E | Yn M | Yn E | Yn Wd | Yg M | Yg E3 | 24 |
| Yg E | Yg Wd | Yn E | Yn M | Yn E | Yn Wd | Yg M | Yg E3 | Yg M | Yg E1 | Yn M | Yn W | 25 |
| Yn E | Yn Wd | Yg M | Yg E3 | Yg M | Yg E1 | Yn M | Yn W | Yn M | Yn F | Yg W | Yg W | 26 |
| Yg M | Yg E1 | Yn M | Yn W | Yn M | Yn F | Yg W | Yg W | Yg W | Yg F | Yn W | Yn E4 | 27 |
| Yn M | Yn F | Yg W | Yg W | Yg W | Yg F | Yn W | Yn E4 | Yn W | Yn E2 | Yg Wd | Yg Wd | 28 |
| Yg W | Yg F | Yn W | Yn E4 | Yn W | Yn E2 | Yg Wd | Yg Wd | Yg Wd | Yg M | Yn Wd | Yn Wd | 29 |
| Yn W | Yn E2 | Yg Wd | Yg Wd | Yg Wd | Yg M | Yn Wd | Yn Wd | Yn Wd | Yn M | Yg F | Yg E1 | 30 |
| Yg Wd | Yg M | | | Yn Wd | Yn M | | | Yg F | Yg E3 | Yn F | Yn F | 31 |
| Yn Wd | Yn M | Yn Wd | Yn Wd | Yg F | Yg E3 | Yg F | Yg E1 | Yn F | Yn W | Yg E | Yg F | 1 |
| Yg F | Yg E3 | Yg F | Yg E1 | Yn F | Yn W | Yn F | Yn F | Yg E | Yg W | Yn E | Yn E2 | 2 |
| Yn F | Yn W | Yn F | Yn F | Yg E | Yg W | Yg E | Yg F | Yn E | Yn E4 | Yg M | Yg M | 3 |
| Yg E | Yg W | Yg E | Yg F | Yn E | Yn E4 | Yn E | Yn E2 | Yg M | Yg Wd | | | 4 |
| Yn E | Yn E4 | Yn E | Yn E2 | Yg M | Yg Wd | Yg M | Yg M | | | | | 5 |
| Yg M | Yg Wd | Yg M | Yg M | Yn M | Yn Wd | Yn M | Yn M | | | | | 6 |
| | | Yn M | Yn M | | | | | | | | | 7 |
| | | | | | | | | | | | | 8 |

# YEAR OF THE DOG

| | H | E | H | E | H | E | H | E | H | E | H | E | H | E | H | E | H | E | H | E | H | E | H | E |
|---|---|---|---|---|---|---|---|---|---|---|---|---|---|---|---|---|---|---|---|---|---|---|---|---|
| YEAR | YEAR Yg Wd | Yg E3 | 1994 | | | | | | | | | | | | | | | | | | | | 1995 | |
| MONTH | 4 Feb - 5 Mar | | 6 Mar - 4 Apr | | 5 Apr - 5 May | | 6 May - 5 June | | 6 June - 6 Jul | | 7 Jul - 7 Aug | | 8 Aug - 7 Sep | | 8 Sep - 7 Oct | | 8 Oct - 6 Nov | | 7 Nov - 6 Dec | | 7 Dec - 5 Jan | | 6 Jan - 3 Feb | |
| | Yg F | Yg Wd | Yn F | Yn Wd | Yg E | Yg E1 | Yn E | Yn F | Yg M | Yg F | Yn M | Yn E2 | Yg W | Yg M | Yn W | Yn M | Yg Wd | Yg E3 | Yn Wd | Yn W | Yg F | Yg W | Yn F | Yn E4 |
| Starting time | 1st day | Mid-pt | 1st day | Mid-pt | 1st day | Mid-pt | 1st day | Mid-pt | 1st day | Mid-pt | 1st day | Mid-pt | 1st day | Mid-pt | 1st day | Mid-pt | 1st day | Mid-pt | 1st day | Mid-pt | 1st day | Mid-pt | 1st day | Mid-pt |
| Date | 4 | 19 | 6 | 21 | 5 | 20 | 6 | 21 | 6 | 21 | 7 | 23 | 8 | 23 | 8 | 23 | 8 | 23 | 7 | 22 | 7 | 22 | 6 | 20 |
| Hour | 0933 | 0524 | 0343 | 0437 | 0846 | 1556 | 0220 | 1519 | 0643 | 2325 | 1716 | 1018 | 0250 | 1714 | 0534 | 1438 | 2050 | 2344 | 2353 | 2106 | 1633 | 1019 | 0342 | 2057 |
| DATE 4 | Yn M | Yn M | | | | | | | | | | | | | | | | | | | | | | |
| 5 | Yg W | Yg E3 | | | Yn M | Yn M | | | | | | | | | | | | | | | | | | |
| 6 | Yn W | Yn W | Yn M | Yn Wd | Yg W | Yg E3 | Yg W | Yg E1 | Yn W | Yn W | | | | | | | | | | | | | Yn F | Yn M |
| 7 | Yg Wd | Yg W | Yg W | Yg E1 | Yn W | Yn W | Yn W | Yn F | Yg Wd | Yg W | Yg Wd | Yg F | | | | | | | Yn F | Yn M | Yn F | Yn Wd | Yg E | Yg E3 |
| 8 | Yn Wd | Yn E4 | Yn W | Yn F | Yg Wd | Yg W | Yg Wd | Yg F | Yn Wd | Yn E4 | Yn Wd | Yn E2 | Yg F | Yg Wd | Yn F | Yn M | Yn F | Yn Wd | Yg E | Yg E3 | Yg E | Yg E1 | Yn E | Yn W |
| 9 | Yg F | Yg Wd | Yg Wd | Yg F | Yn Wd | Yn E4 | Yn Wd | Yn E2 | Yg F | Yg Wd | Yg F | Yg M | Yn F | Yn Wd | Yg E | Yg E3 | Yg E | Yg E1 | Yn E | Yn W | Yn E | Yn F | Yg M | Yg W |
| 10 | Yn F | Yn Wd | Yn Wd | Yn E2 | Yg F | Yg Wd | Yg F | Yg M | Yn F | Yn Wd | Yn F | Yn M | Yg E | Yg E1 | Yn E | Yn W | Yn E | Yn F | Yg M | Yg W | Yg M | Yg F | Yn M | Yn E4 |
| 11 | Yg E | Yg E1 | Yg F | Yg M | Yn F | Yn Wd | Yn F | Yn M | Yg E | Yg E1 | Yg E | Yg E3 | Yn E | Yn F | Yg M | Yg W | Yg M | Yg F | Yn M | Yn E4 | Yn M | Yn E2 | Yg W | Yg Wd |
| 12 | Yn E | Yn F | Yn F | Yn M | Yg E | Yg E1 | Yg E | Yg E3 | Yn E | Yn F | Yn E | Yn W | Yg M | Yg F | Yn M | Yn E4 | Yn M | Yn E2 | Yg W | Yg Wd | Yg W | Yg M | Yn W | Yn Wd |
| 13 | Yg M | Yg F | Yg E | Yg E3 | Yn E | Yn F | Yn E | Yn W | Yg M | Yg F | Yg M | Yg W | Yn M | Yn E2 | Yg W | Yg Wd | Yg W | Yg M | Yn W | Yn Wd | Yn W | Yn M | Yg Wd | Yg E1 |
| 14 | Yn M | Yn E2 | Yn E | Yn W | Yg M | Yg F | Yg M | Yg W | Yn M | Yn E2 | Yn M | Yn E4 | Yg W | Yg M | Yn W | Yn Wd | Yn W | Yn M | Yg Wd | Yg E1 | Yg Wd | Yg E3 | Yn Wd | Yn F |
| 15 | Yg W | Yg M | Yg M | Yg W | Yn M | Yn E2 | Yn M | Yn E4 | Yg W | Yg M | Yg W | Yg Wd | Yn W | Yn M | Yg Wd | Yg E1 | Yg Wd | Yg E3 | Yn Wd | Yn F | Yn Wd | Yn W | Yg F | Yg F |
| 16 | Yn W | Yn M | Yn M | Yn E4 | Yg W | Yg M | Yg W | Yg Wd | Yn W | Yn M | Yn W | Yn Wd | Yg Wd | Yg E3 | Yn Wd | Yn F | Yn Wd | Yn W | Yg F | Yg F | Yg F | Yg W | Yn F | Yn E2 |
| 17 | Yg Wd | Yg E3 | Yg W | Yg Wd | Yn W | Yn M | Yn W | Yn Wd | Yg Wd | Yg E3 | Yg Wd | Yg E1 | Yn Wd | Yn W | Yg F | Yg F | Yg F | Yg W | Yn F | Yn E2 | Yn F | Yn E4 | Yg E | Yg M |
| 18 | Yn Wd | Yn W | Yn W | Yn Wd | Yg Wd | Yg E3 | Yg Wd | Yg E1 | Yn Wd | Yn W | Yn Wd | Yn F | Yg F | Yg W | Yn F | Yn E2 | Yn F | Yn E4 | Yg E | Yg M | Yg E | Yg Wd | Yn E | Yn M |
| 19 | Yg F | Yg W | Yg Wd | Yg E1 | Yn Wd | Yn W | Yn Wd | Yn F | Yg F | Yg W | Yg F | Yg F | Yn F | Yn E4 | Yg E | Yg M | Yg E | Yg Wd | Yn E | Yn M | Yn E | Yn Wd | Yg M | Yg E3 |
| 20 | Yn F | Yn E4 | Yn Wd | Yn F | Yg F | Yg W | Yg F | Yg F | Yn F | Yn E4 | Yn F | Yn E2 | Yg E | Yg Wd | Yn E | Yn M | Yn E | Yn Wd | Yg M | Yg E3 | Yg M | Yg E1 | Yn M | Yn W |
| 21 | Yg E | Yg Wd | Yg F | Yg F | Yn F | Yn E4 | Yn F | Yn E2 | Yg E | Yg Wd | Yg E | Yg M | Yn E | Yn Wd | Yg M | Yg E3 | Yg M | Yg E1 | Yn M | Yn W | Yn M | Yn F | Yg W | Yg W |
| 22 | Yn E | Yn Wd | Yn F | Yn E2 | Yg E | Yg Wd | Yg E | Yg M | Yn E | Yn Wd | Yn E | Yn M | Yg M | Yg E1 | Yn M | Yn W | Yn M | Yn F | Yg W | Yg W | Yg W | Yg F | Yn W | Yn E4 |
| 23 | Yg M | Yg E1 | Yg E | Yg M | Yn E | Yn Wd | Yn E | Yn M | Yg M | Yg E1 | Yg M | Yg E3 | Yn M | Yn F | Yg W | Yg W | Yg W | Yg F | Yn W | Yn E4 | Yn W | Yn E2 | Yg Wd | Yg Wd |
| 24 | Yn M | Yn F | Yn E | Yn M | Yg M | Yg E1 | Yg M | Yg E3 | Yn M | Yn F | Yn M | Yn W | Yg W | Yg F | Yn W | Yn E4 | Yn W | Yn E2 | Yg Wd | Yg Wd | Yg Wd | Yg M | Yn Wd | Yn Wd |
| 25 | Yg W | Yg F | Yg M | Yg E3 | Yn M | Yn F | Yn M | Yn W | Yg W | Yg F | Yg W | Yg W | Yn W | Yn E2 | Yg Wd | Yg Wd | Yg Wd | Yg M | Yn Wd | Yn Wd | Yn Wd | Yn M | Yg F | Yg E1 |
| 26 | Yn W | Yn E2 | Yn M | Yn W | Yg W | Yg F | Yg W | Yg W | Yn W | Yn E2 | Yn W | Yn E4 | Yg Wd | Yg M | Yn Wd | Yn Wd | Yn Wd | Yn M | Yg F | Yg E1 | Yg F | Yg E3 | Yn F | Yn F |
| 27 | Yg Wd | Yg M | Yg W | Yg W | Yn W | Yn E2 | Yn W | Yn E4 | Yg Wd | Yg M | Yg Wd | Yg Wd | Yn Wd | Yn M | Yg F | Yg E1 | Yg F | Yg E3 | Yn F | Yn F | Yn F | Yn W | Yg E | Yg F |
| 28 | Yn Wd | Yn M | Yn W | Yn E4 | Yg Wd | Yg M | Yg Wd | Yg Wd | Yn Wd | Yn M | Yn Wd | Yn Wd | Yg F | Yg E3 | Yn F | Yn F | Yn F | Yn W | Yg E | Yg F | Yg E | Yg W | Yn E | Yn E2 |
| 29 | | | Yg Wd | Yg Wd | Yn Wd | Yn M | Yn Wd | Yn Wd | Yg F | Yg E3 | Yg F | Yg E1 | Yn F | Yn W | Yg E | Yg F | Yg E | Yg W | Yn E | Yn E2 | Yn E | Yn E4 | Yg M | Yg M |
| 30 | | | Yn Wd | Yn Wd | Yg F | Yg E3 | Yg F | Yg E1 | Yn F | Yn W | Yn F | Yn F | Yg E | Yg W | Yn E | Yn E2 | Yn E | Yn E4 | Yg M | Yg M | Yg M | Yg Wd | Yn M | Yn M |
| 31 | | | Yg F | Yg E1 | | | Yn F | Yn F | | | Yg E | Yg F | Yn E | Yn E4 | | | Yg M | Yg Wd | | | Yn M | Yn Wd | Yg W | Yg E3 |
| 1 | Yg F | Yg E3 | Yn F | Yn F | Yn F | Yn W | Yg E | Yg F | Yg E | Yg W | Yn E | Yn E2 | Yg M | Yg Wd | Yg M | Yg M | Yn M | Yn Wd | Yn M | Yn M | Yg W | Yg E1 | Yn W | Yn W |
| 2 | Yn F | Yn W | Yg E | Yg F | Yg E | Yg W | Yn E | Yn E2 | Yn E | Yn E4 | Yg M | Yg M | Yn M | Yn Wd | Yn M | Yn M | Yg W | Yg E1 | Yg W | Yg E3 | Yn W | Yn F | Yg Wd | Yg W |
| 3 | Yg E | Yg W | Yn E | Yn E2 | Yn E | Yn E4 | Yg M | Yg M | Yg M | Yg Wd | Yn M | Yn M | Yg W | Yg E1 | Yg W | Yg E3 | Yn W | Yn F | Yn W | Yn W | Yg Wd | Yg F | Yn Wd | Yn E4 |
| 4 | Yn E | Yn E4 | Yg M | Yg M | Yg M | Yg Wd | Yn M | Yn M | Yn M | Yn Wd | Yg W | Yg E3 | Yn W | Yn F | Yn W | Yn W | Yg Wd | Yg F | Yg Wd | Yg W | Yn Wd | Yn E2 | | |
| 5 | Yg M | Yg Wd | | | Yn M | Yn Wd | Yg W | Yg E3 | Yg W | Yg E1 | Yn W | Yn W | Yg Wd | Yg F | Yg Wd | Yg W | Yn Wd | Yn E2 | Yn Wd | Yn E4 | Yg F | Yg M | | |
| 6 | | | | | | | | | Yn W | Yn F | Yg Wd | Yg W | Yn Wd | Yn E2 | Yn Wd | Yn E4 | Yg F | Yg M | Yg F | Yg Wd | | | | |
| 7 | | | | | | | | | | | Yn Wd | Yn E4 | Yg F | Yg M | Yg F | Yg Wd | | | | | | | | |
| 8 | | | | | | | | | | | | | | | | | | | | | | | | |

# YEAR OF THE PIG

| | H | E | H | E | H | E | H | E | H | E | H | E |
|---|---|---|---|---|---|---|---|---|---|---|---|---|
| YEAR | YEAR Yn Wd | Yn W | 1995 | | | | | | | | | |
| MONTH | 4 Feb - 5 Mar | | 6 Mar - 4 Apr | | 5 Apr - 5 May | | 6 May - 5 June | | 6 June - 6 Jul | | 7 Jul - 7 Aug | |
| | Yg E | Yg Wd | Yn E | Yn Wd | Yg M | Yg E1 | Yn M | Yn F | Yg W | Yg F | Yn W | Yn E2 |
| Starting time | 1st day | Mid-pt | 1st day | Mid-pt | 1st day | Mid-pt | 1st day | Mid-pt | 1st day | Mid-pt | 1st day | Mid-pt |
| Date | 4 | 19 | 6 | 21 | 5 | 20 | 6 | 21 | 6 | 22 | 7 | 23 |
| Hour | 1524 | 1114 | 0934 | 1013 | 1437 | 2146 | 0811 | 2108 | 1234 | 0514 | 2257 | 1607 |
| DATE 4 | Yg F | Yg Wd | | | | | | | | | | |
| 5 | Yn F | Yn Wd | | | Yg F | Yg Wd | | | | | | |
| 6 | Yg E | Yg E1 | Yg F | Yg M | Yn F | Yn Wd | Yn F | Yn M | Yg E | Yg E1 | | |
| 7 | Yn E | Yn F | Yn F | Yn M | Yg E | Yg E1 | Yg E | Yg E3 | Yn E | Yn F | Yn E | Yn W |
| 8 | Yg M | Yg F | Yg E | Yg E3 | Yn E | Yn F | Yn E | Yn W | Yg M | Yg F | Yg M | Yg W |
| 9 | Yn M | Yn E2 | Yn E | Yn W | Yg M | Yg F | Yg M | Yg W | Yn M | Yn E2 | Yn M | Yn E4 |
| 10 | Yg W | Yg M | Yg M | Yg W | Yn M | Yn E2 | Yn M | Yn E4 | Yg W | Yg M | Yg W | Yg Wd |
| 11 | Yn W | Yn M | Yn M | Yn E4 | Yg W | Yg M | Yg W | Yg Wd | Yn W | Yn M | Yn W | Yn Wd |
| 12 | Yg Wd | Yg E3 | Yg W | Yg Wd | Yn W | Yn M | Yn W | Yn Wd | Yg Wd | Yg E3 | Yg Wd | Yg E1 |
| 13 | Yn Wd | Yn W | Yn W | Yn Wd | Yg Wd | Yg E3 | Yg Wd | Yg E1 | Yn Wd | Yn W | Yn Wd | Yn F |
| 14 | Yg F | Yg W | Yg Wd | Yg E1 | Yn Wd | Yn W | Yn Wd | Yn F | Yg F | Yg W | Yg F | Yg F |
| 15 | Yn F | Yn E4 | Yn Wd | Yn F | Yg F | Yg W | Yg F | Yg F | Yn F | Yn E4 | Yn F | Yn E2 |
| 16 | Yg E | Yg Wd | Yg F | Yg F | Yn F | Yn E4 | Yn F | Yn E2 | Yg E | Yg Wd | Yg E | Yg M |
| 17 | Yn E | Yn Wd | Yn F | Yn E2 | Yg E | Yg Wd | Yg E | Yg M | Yn E | Yn Wd | Yn E | Yn M |
| 18 | Yg M | Yg E1 | Yg E | Yg M | Yn E | Yn Wd | Yn E | Yn M | Yg M | Yg E1 | Yg M | Yg E3 |
| 19 | Yn M | Yn F | Yn E | Yn M | Yg M | Yg E1 | Yg M | Yg E3 | Yn M | Yn F | Yn M | Yn W |
| 20 | Yg W | Yg F | Yg M | Yg E3 | Yn M | Yn F | Yn M | Yn W | Yg W | Yg F | Yg W | Yg W |
| 21 | Yn W | Yn E2 | Yn M | Yn W | Yg W | Yg F | Yg W | Yg W | Yn W | Yn E2 | Yn W | Yn E4 |
| 22 | Yg Wd | Yg M | Yg W | Yg W | Yn W | Yn E2 | Yn W | Yn E4 | Yg Wd | Yg M | Yg Wd | Yg Wd |
| 23 | Yn Wd | Yn M | Yn W | Yn E4 | Yg Wd | Yg M | Yg Wd | Yg Wd | Yn Wd | Yn M | Yn Wd | Yn Wd |
| 24 | Yg F | Yg E3 | Yg Wd | Yg Wd | Yn Wd | Yn M | Yn Wd | Yn Wd | Yg F | Yg E3 | Yg F | Yg E1 |
| 25 | Yn F | Yn W | Yn Wd | Yn Wd | Yg F | Yg E3 | Yg F | Yg E1 | Yn F | Yn W | Yn F | Yn F |
| 26 | Yg E | Yg W | Yg F | Yg E1 | Yn F | Yn W | Yn F | Yn F | Yg E | Yg W | Yg E | Yg F |
| 27 | Yn E | Yn E4 | Yn F | Yn F | Yg E | Yg W | Yg E | Yg F | Yn E | Yn E4 | Yn E | Yn E2 |
| 28 | Yg M | Yg Wd | Yg E | Yg F | Yn E | Yn E4 | Yn E | Yn E2 | Yg M | Yg Wd | Yg M | Yg M |
| 29 | | | Yn E | Yn E2 | Yg M | Yg Wd | Yg M | Yg M | Yn M | Yn Wd | Yn M | Yn M |
| 30 | | | Yg M | Yg M | Yn M | Yn Wd | Yn M | Yn M | Yg W | Yg E1 | Yg W | Yg E3 |
| 31 | | | Yn M | Yn M | | | Yg W | Yg E3 | | | Yn W | Yn W |
| 1 | Yn M | Yn Wd | Yg W | Yg E3 | Yg W | Yg E1 | Yn W | Yn W | Yn W | Yn F | Yg Wd | Yg W |
| 2 | Yg W | Yg E1 | Yn W | Yn W | Yn W | Yn F | Yg Wd | Yg W | Yg Wd | Yg F | Yn Wd | Yn E4 |
| 3 | Yn W | Yn F | Yg Wd | Yg W | Yg Wd | Yg F | Yn Wd | Yn E4 | Yn Wd | Yn E2 | Yg F | Yg Wd |
| 4 | Yg Wd | Yg F | Yn Wd | Yn E4 | Yn Wd | Yn E2 | Yg F | Yg Wd | Yg F | Yg M | Yn F | Yn Wd |
| 5 | Yn Wd | Yn E2 | | | Yg F | Yg M | Yn F | Yn Wd | Yn F | Yn M | Yg E | Yg E1 |
| 6 | | | | | | | | | Yg E | Yg E3 | Yn E | Yn F |
| 7 | | | | | | | | | | | Yg M | Yg F |
| 8 | | | | | | | | | | | | |

| | H | E | H | E | H | E | H | E | H | E | H | E | |
|---|---|---|---|---|---|---|---|---|---|---|---|---|---|
| YEAR | 1995 | | | | | | | | | | 1996 | | |
| MONTH | 8 Aug - 7 Sep | | 8 Sep - 8 Oct | | 9 Oct - 7 Nov | | 8 Nov - 6 Dec | | 7 Dec - 5 Jan | | 6 Jan - 3 Feb | | |
| | Yg Wd | Yg M | Yn Wd | Yn M | Yg F | Yg E3 | Yn F | Yn W | Yg E | Yg W | Yn E | Yn E4 | |
| Starting time | 1st day | Mid-pt | 1st day | Mid-pt | 1st day | Mid-pt | 1st day | Mid-pt | 1st day | Mid-pt | 1st day | Mid-pt | |
| Date | 8 | 23 | 8 | 23 | 9 | 24 | 8 | 23 | 7 | 23 | 6 | 21 | |
| Hour | 0841 | 2304 | 1125 | 2028 | 0249 | 0534 | 0544 | 0256 | 2224 | 1609 | 0933 | 0247 | |
| DATE 4 | | | | | | | | | | | | | 4 |
| 5 | | | | | | | | | | | | | 5 |
| 6 | | | | | | | | | | | Yg W | Yg Wd | 6 |
| 7 | | | | | | | | | Yg W | Yg M | Yn W | Yn Wd | 7 |
| 8 | Yn M | Yn E2 | Yg W | Yg Wd | | | Yn W | Yn Wd | Yn W | Yn M | Yg Wd | Yg E1 | 8 |
| 9 | Yg W | Yg M | Yn W | Yn Wd | Yn W | Yn M | Yg Wd | Yg E1 | Yg Wd | Yg E3 | Yn Wd | Yn F | 9 |
| 10 | Yn W | Yn M | Yg Wd | Yg E1 | Yg Wd | Yg E3 | Yn Wd | Yn F | Yn Wd | Yn W | Yg F | Yg F | 10 |
| 11 | Yg Wd | Yg E3 | Yn Wd | Yn F | Yn Wd | Yn W | Yg F | Yg F | Yg F | Yg W | Yn F | Yn E2 | 11 |
| 12 | Yn Wd | Yn W | Yg F | Yg F | Yg F | Yg W | Yn F | Yn E2 | Yn F | Yn E4 | Yg E | Yg M | 12 |
| 13 | Yg F | Yg W | Yn F | Yn E2 | Yn F | Yn E4 | Yg E | Yg M | Yg E | Yg Wd | Yn E | Yn M | 13 |
| 14 | Yn F | Yn E4 | Yg E | Yg M | Yg E | Yg Wd | Yn E | Yn M | Yn E | Yn Wd | Yg M | Yg E3 | 14 |
| 15 | Yg E | Yg Wd | Yn E | Yn M | Yn E | Yn Wd | Yg M | Yg E3 | Yg M | Yg E1 | Yn M | Yn W | 15 |
| 16 | Yn E | Yn Wd | Yg M | Yg E3 | Yg M | Yg E1 | Yn M | Yn W | Yn M | Yn F | Yg W | Yg W | 16 |
| 17 | Yg M | Yg E1 | Yn M | Yn W | Yn M | Yn F | Yg W | Yg W | Yg W | Yg F | Yn W | Yn E4 | 17 |
| 18 | Yn M | Yn F | Yg W | Yg W | Yg W | Yg F | Yn W | Yn E4 | Yn W | Yn E2 | Yg Wd | Yg Wd | 18 |
| 19 | Yg W | Yg F | Yn W | Yn E4 | Yn W | Yn E2 | Yg Wd | Yg Wd | Yg Wd | Yg M | Yn Wd | Yn Wd | 19 |
| 20 | Yn W | Yn E2 | Yg Wd | Yg Wd | Yg Wd | Yg M | Yn Wd | Yn Wd | Yn Wd | Yn M | Yg F | Yg E1 | 20 |
| 21 | Yg Wd | Yg M | Yn Wd | Yn Wd | Yn Wd | Yn M | Yg F | Yg E1 | Yg F | Yg E3 | Yn F | Yn F | 21 |
| 22 | Yn Wd | Yn M | Yg F | Yg E1 | Yg F | Yg E3 | Yn F | Yn F | Yn F | Yn W | Yg E | Yg F | 22 |
| 23 | Yg F | Yg E3 | Yn F | Yn F | Yn F | Yn W | Yg E | Yg F | Yg E | Yg W | Yn E | Yn E2 | 23 |
| 24 | Yn F | Yn W | Yg E | Yg F | Yg E | Yg W | Yn E | Yn E2 | Yn E | Yn E4 | Yg M | Yg M | 24 |
| 25 | Yg E | Yg W | Yn E | Yn E2 | Yn E | Yn E4 | Yg M | Yg M | Yg M | Yg Wd | Yn M | Yn M | 25 |
| 26 | Yn E | Yn E4 | Yg M | Yg M | Yg M | Yg Wd | Yn M | Yn M | Yn M | Yn Wd | Yg W | Yg E3 | 26 |
| 27 | Yg M | Yg Wd | Yn M | Yn M | Yn M | Yn Wd | Yg W | Yg E3 | Yg W | Yg E1 | Yn W | Yn W | 27 |
| 28 | Yn M | Yn Wd | Yg W | Yg E3 | Yg W | Yg E1 | Yn W | Yn W | Yn W | Yn F | Yg Wd | Yg W | 28 |
| 29 | Yg W | Yg E1 | Yn W | Yn W | Yn W | Yn F | Yg Wd | Yg W | Yg Wd | Yg F | Yn Wd | Yn E4 | 29 |
| 30 | Yn W | Yn F | Yg Wd | Yg W | Yg Wd | Yg F | Yn Wd | Yn E4 | Yn Wd | Yn E2 | Yg F | Yg Wd | 30 |
| 31 | Yg Wd | Yg F | | | Yn Wd | Yn E2 | | | Yg F | Yg M | Yn F | Yn Wd | 31 |
| 1 | Yn Wd | Yn E2 | Yn Wd | Yn E4 | Yg F | Yg M | Yg F | Yg Wd | Yn F | Yn M | Yg E | Yg E1 | 1 |
| 2 | Yg F | Yg M | Yg F | Yg Wd | Yn F | Yn M | Yn F | Yn Wd | Yg E | Yg E3 | Yn E | Yn F | 2 |
| 3 | Yn F | Yn M | Yn F | Yn Wd | Yg E | Yg E3 | Yg E | Yg E1 | Yn E | Yn W | Yg M | Yg F | 3 |
| 4 | Yg E | Yg E3 | Yg E | Yg E1 | Yn E | Yn W | Yn E | Yn F | Yg M | Yg W | | | 4 |
| 5 | Yn E | Yn W | Yn E | Yn F | Yg M | Yg W | Yg M | Yg F | Yn M | Yn E4 | | | 5 |
| 6 | Yg M | Yg W | Yg M | Yg F | Yn M | Yn E4 | Yn M | Yn E2 | | | | | 6 |
| 7 | Yn M | Yn E4 | Yn M | Yn E2 | Yg W | Yg Wd | | | | | | | 7 |
| 8 | | | Yg W | Yg M | | | | | | | | | 8 |

# YEAR OF THE RAT

| | H | E | H | E | H | E | H | E | H | E | H | E | H | E | H | E | H | E | H | E | H | E | H | E | |
|---|---|---|---|---|---|---|---|---|---|---|---|---|---|---|---|---|---|---|---|---|---|---|---|---|---|
| YEAR | YEAR Yg F | Yg W | 1996 | | | | | | | | | | | | | | | | | | | | 1997 | | |
| MONTH | 4 Feb - 4 Mar | | 5 Mar - 3 Apr | | 4 Apr - 4 May | | 5 May - 4 June | | 5 June - 6 Jul | | 7 Jul - 6 Aug | | 7 Aug - 6 Sep | | 7 Sep - 7 Oct | | 8 Oct - 6 Nov | | 7 Nov - 6 Dec | | 7 Dec - 4 Jan | | 5 Jan - 3 Feb | | |
| | Yg M | Yg Wd | Yn M | Yn Wd | Yg W | Yg E1 | Yn W | Yn F | Yg Wd | Yg F | Yn Wd | Yn E2 | Yg F | Yg M | Yn F | Yn M | Yg E | Yg E3 | Yn E | Yn W | Yg M | Yg W | Yn M | Yn E4 | |
| Starting time | 1st day | Mid-pt | 1st day | Mid-pt | 1st day | Mid-pt | 1st day | Mid-pt | 1st day | Mid-pt | 1st day | Mid-pt | 1st day | Mid-pt | 1st day | Mid-pt | 1st day | Mid-pt | 1st day | Mid-pt | 1st day | Mid-pt | 1st day | Mid-pt | |
| Date | 4 | 19 | 5 | 20 | 4 | 20 | 5 | 21 | 5 | 21 | 7 | 22 | 7 | 23 | 7 | 23 | 8 | 23 | 7 | 22 | 7 | 21 | 5 | 20 | |
| Hour | 2115 | 1704 | 1525 | 1617 | 2028 | 0336 | 1402 | 0258 | 1824 | 1104 | 0447 | 2157 | 1430 | 0453 | 1714 | 0217 | 0836 | 1123 | 1133 | 0845 | 0411 | 2158 | 1522 | 0836 | |
| DATE 4 | Yn M | Yn E2 | | | Yn M | Yn E2 | | | | | | | | | | | | | | | | | | | 4 |
| 5 | Yg W | Yg M | Yn M | Yn E4 | Yg W | Yg M | Yg W | Yg Wd | Yn W | Yn M | | | | | | | | | | | | | Yn F | Yn E2 | 5 |
| 6 | Yn W | Yn M | Yg W | Yg Wd | Yn W | Yn M | Yn W | Yn Wd | Yg Wd | Yg E3 | | | | | | | | | | | | | Yg E | Yg M | 6 |
| 7 | Yg Wd | Yg E3 | Yn W | Yn Wd | Yg Wd | Yg E3 | Yg Wd | Yg E1 | Yn Wd | Yn W | Yn Wd | Yn F | Yg F | Yg W | Yn F | Yn E2 | | | Yg E | Yg M | Yg E | Yg Wd | Yn E | Yn M | 7 |
| 8 | Yn Wd | Yn W | Yg Wd | Yg E1 | Yn Wd | Yn W | Yn Wd | Yn F | Yg F | Yg W | Yg F | Yg F | Yn F | Yn E4 | Yg E | Yg M | Yg E | Yg Wd | Yn E | Yn M | Yn E | Yn Wd | Yg M | Yg E3 | 8 |
| 9 | Yg F | Yg W | Yn Wd | Yn F | Yg F | Yg W | Yg F | Yg F | Yn F | Yn E4 | Yn F | Yn E2 | Yg E | Yg Wd | Yn E | Yn M | Yn E | Yn Wd | Yg M | Yg E3 | Yg M | Yg E1 | Yn M | Yn W | 9 |
| 10 | Yn F | Yn E4 | Yg F | Yg F | Yn F | Yn E4 | Yn F | Yn E2 | Yg E | Yg Wd | Yg E | Yg M | Yn E | Yn Wd | Yg M | Yg E3 | Yg M | Yg E1 | Yn M | Yn W | Yn M | Yn F | Yg W | Yg W | 10 |
| 11 | Yg E | Yg Wd | Yn F | Yn E2 | Yg E | Yg Wd | Yg E | Yg M | Yn E | Yn Wd | Yn E | Yn M | Yg M | Yg E1 | Yn M | Yn W | Yn M | Yn F | Yg W | Yg W | Yg W | Yg F | Yn W | Yn E4 | 11 |
| 12 | Yn E | Yn Wd | Yg E | Yg M | Yn E | Yn Wd | Yn E | Yn M | Yg M | Yg E1 | Yg M | Yg E3 | Yn M | Yn F | Yg W | Yg W | Yg W | Yg F | Yn W | Yn E4 | Yn W | Yn E2 | Yg Wd | Yg Wd | 12 |
| 13 | Yg M | Yg E1 | Yn E | Yn M | Yg M | Yg E1 | Yg M | Yg E3 | Yn M | Yn F | Yn M | Yn W | Yg W | Yg F | Yn W | Yn E4 | Yn W | Yn E2 | Yg Wd | Yg Wd | Yg Wd | Yg M | Yn Wd | Yn Wd | 13 |
| 14 | Yn M | Yn F | Yg M | Yg E3 | Yn M | Yn F | Yn M | Yn W | Yg W | Yg F | Yg W | Yg W | Yn W | Yn E2 | Yg Wd | Yg Wd | Yg Wd | Yg M | Yn Wd | Yn Wd | Yn Wd | Yn M | Yg F | Yg E1 | 14 |
| 15 | Yg W | Yg F | Yn M | Yn W | Yg W | Yg F | Yg W | Yg W | Yn W | Yn E2 | Yn W | Yn E4 | Yg Wd | Yg M | Yn Wd | Yn Wd | Yn Wd | Yn M | Yg F | Yg E1 | Yg F | Yg E3 | Yn F | Yn F | 15 |
| 16 | Yn W | Yn E2 | Yg W | Yg W | Yn W | Yn E2 | Yn W | Yn E4 | Yg Wd | Yg M | Yg Wd | Yg Wd | Yn Wd | Yn M | Yg F | Yg E1 | Yg F | Yg E3 | Yn F | Yn F | Yn F | Yn W | Yg E | Yg F | 16 |
| 17 | Yg Wd | Yg M | Yn W | Yn E4 | Yg Wd | Yg M | Yg Wd | Yg Wd | Yn Wd | Yn M | Yn Wd | Yn Wd | Yg F | Yg E3 | Yn F | Yn F | Yn F | Yn W | Yg E | Yg F | Yg E | Yg W | Yn E | Yn E2 | 17 |
| 18 | Yn Wd | Yn M | Yg Wd | Yg Wd | Yn Wd | Yn M | Yn Wd | Yn Wd | Yg F | Yg E3 | Yg F | Yg E1 | Yn F | Yn W | Yg E | Yg F | Yg E | Yg W | Yn E | Yn E2 | Yn E | Yn E4 | Yg M | Yg M | 18 |
| 19 | Yg F | Yg E3 | Yn Wd | Yn Wd | Yg F | Yg E3 | Yg F | Yg E1 | Yn F | Yn W | Yn F | Yn F | Yg E | Yg W | Yn E | Yn E2 | Yn E | Yn E4 | Yg M | Yg M | Yg M | Yg Wd | Yn M | Yn M | 19 |
| 20 | Yn F | Yn W | Yg F | Yg E1 | Yn F | Yn W | Yn F | Yn F | Yg E | Yg W | Yg E | Yg F | Yn E | Yn E4 | Yg M | Yg M | Yg M | Yg Wd | Yn M | Yn M | Yn M | Yn Wd | Yg W | Yg E3 | 20 |
| 21 | Yg E | Yg W | Yn F | Yn F | Yg E | Yg W | Yg E | Yg F | Yn E | Yn E4 | Yn E | Yn E2 | Yg M | Yg Wd | Yn M | Yn M | Yn M | Yn Wd | Yg W | Yg E3 | Yg W | Yg E1 | Yn W | Yn W | 21 |
| 22 | Yn E | Yn E4 | Yg E | Yg F | Yn E | Yn E4 | Yn E | Yn E2 | Yg M | Yg Wd | Yg M | Yg M | Yn M | Yn Wd | Yg W | Yg E3 | Yg W | Yg E1 | Yn W | Yn W | Yn W | Yn F | Yg Wd | Yg W | 22 |
| 23 | Yg M | Yg Wd | Yn E | Yn E2 | Yg M | Yg Wd | Yg M | Yg M | Yn M | Yn Wd | Yn M | Yn M | Yg W | Yg E1 | Yn W | Yn W | Yn W | Yn F | Yg Wd | Yg W | Yg Wd | Yg F | Yn Wd | Yn E4 | 23 |
| 24 | Yn M | Yn Wd | Yg M | Yg M | Yn M | Yn Wd | Yn M | Yn M | Yg W | Yg E1 | Yg W | Yg E3 | Yn W | Yn F | Yg Wd | Yg W | Yg Wd | Yg F | Yn Wd | Yn E4 | Yn Wd | Yn E2 | Yg F | Yg Wd | 24 |
| 25 | Yg W | Yg E1 | Yn M | Yn M | Yg W | Yg E1 | Yg W | Yg E3 | Yn W | Yn F | Yn W | Yn W | Yg Wd | Yg F | Yn Wd | Yn E4 | Yn Wd | Yn E2 | Yg F | Yg Wd | Yg F | Yg M | Yn F | Yn Wd | 25 |
| 26 | Yn W | Yn F | Yg W | Yg E3 | Yn W | Yn F | Yn W | Yn W | Yg Wd | Yg F | Yg Wd | Yg W | Yn Wd | Yn E2 | Yg F | Yg Wd | Yg F | Yg M | Yn F | Yn Wd | Yn F | Yn M | Yg E | Yg E1 | 26 |
| 27 | Yg Wd | Yg F | Yn W | Yn W | Yg Wd | Yg F | Yg Wd | Yg W | Yn Wd | Yn E2 | Yn Wd | Yn E4 | Yg F | Yg M | Yn F | Yn Wd | Yn F | Yn M | Yg E | Yg E1 | Yg E | Yg E3 | Yn E | Yn F | 27 |
| 28 | Yn Wd | Yn E2 | Yg Wd | Yg W | Yn Wd | Yn E2 | Yn Wd | Yn E4 | Yg F | Yg M | Yg F | Yg Wd | Yn F | Yn M | Yg E | Yg E1 | Yg E | Yg E3 | Yn E | Yn F | Yn E | Yn W | Yg M | Yg F | 28 |
| 29 | Yg F | Yg M | Yn Wd | Yn E4 | Yg F | Yg M | Yg F | Yg Wd | Yn F | Yn M | Yn F | Yn Wd | Yg E | Yg E3 | Yn E | Yn F | Yn E | Yn W | Yg M | Yg F | Yg M | Yg W | Yn M | Yn E2 | 29 |
| 30 | | | Yg F | Yg Wd | Yn F | Yn M | Yn F | Yn Wd | Yg E | Yg E3 | Yg E | Yg E1 | Yn E | Yn W | Yg M | Yg F | Yg M | Yg W | Yn M | Yn E2 | Yn M | Yn E4 | Yg W | Yg M | 30 |
| 31 | | | Yn F | Yn Wd | | | Yg E | Yg E1 | | | Yn E | Yn F | Yg M | Yg W | | | Yn M | Yn E4 | | | Yg W | Yg Wd | Yn W | Yn M | 31 |
| 1 | Yn F | Yn M | Yg E | Yg E1 | Yg E | Yg E3 | Yn E | Yn F | Yn E | Yn W | Yg M | Yg F | Yn M | Yn E4 | Yn M | Yn E2 | Yg W | Yg Wd | Yg W | Yg M | Yn W | Yn Wd | Yg Wd | Yg E3 | 1 |
| 2 | Yg E | Yg E3 | Yn E | Yn F | Yn E | Yn W | Yg M | Yg F | Yg M | Yg W | Yn M | Yn E2 | Yg W | Yg Wd | Yg W | Yg M | Yn W | Yn Wd | Yn W | Yn M | Yg Wd | Yg E1 | Yn Wd | Yn W | 2 |
| 3 | Yn E | Yn W | Yg M | Yg F | Yg M | Yg W | Yn M | Yn E2 | Yn M | Yn E4 | Yg W | Yg M | Yn W | Yn Wd | Yn W | Yn M | Yg Wd | Yg E1 | Yg Wd | Yg E3 | Yn Wd | Yn F | Yg F | Yg W | 3 |
| 4 | Yg M | Yg W | | | Yn M | Yn E4 | Yg W | Yg M | Yg W | Yg Wd | Yn W | Yn M | Yg Wd | Yg E1 | Yg Wd | Yg E3 | Yn Wd | Yn F | Yn Wd | Yn W | Yg F | Yg F | | | 4 |
| 5 | | | | | | | | | Yn W | Yn Wd | Yg Wd | Yg E3 | Yn Wd | Yn F | Yn Wd | Yn W | Yg F | Yg F | Yg F | Yg W | | | | | 5 |
| 6 | | | | | | | | | Yg Wd | Yg E1 | Yn Wd | Yn W | Yg F | Yg F | Yg F | Yg W | Yn F | Yn E2 | Yn F | Yn E4 | | | | | 6 |
| 7 | | | | | | | | | | | | | | | Yn F | Yn E4 | | | | | | | | | 7 |
| 8 | | | | | | | | | | | | | | | | | | | | | | | | | 8 |

# YEAR OF THE OX

| | H | E | H | E | H | E | H | E | H | E | H | E | H | E | H | E | H | E | H | E | H | E | H | E | |
|---|---|---|---|---|---|---|---|---|---|---|---|---|---|---|---|---|---|---|---|---|---|---|---|---|---|
| YEAR | YEAR Yn F | Yn E4 | 1997 | | | | | | | | | | | | | | | | | | | | 1998 | | |
| MONTH | 4 Feb - 4 Mar | | 5 Mar - 4 Apr | | 5 Apr - 4 May | | 5 May - 5 June | | 6 June - 6 Jul | | 7 Jul - 6 Aug | | 7 Aug - 6 Sep | | 7 Sep - 7 Oct | | 8 Oct - 6 Nov | | 7 Nov - 6 Dec | | 7 Dec - 4 Jan | | 5 Jan - 3 Feb | | |
| | Yg W | Yg Wd | Yn W | Yn Wd | Yg Wd | Yg E1 | Yn Wd | Yn F | Yg F | Yg F | Yn F | Yn E2 | Yg E | Yg M | Yn E | Yn M | Yg M | Yg E3 | Yn M | Yn W | Yg W | Yg W | Yn W | Yn E4 | |
| Starting time | 1st day | Mid-pt | 1st day | Mid-pt | 1st day | Mid-pt | 1st day | Mid-pt | 1st day | Mid-pt | 1st day | Mid-pt | 1st day | Mid-pt | 1st day | Mid-pt | 1st day | Mid-pt | 1st day | Mid-pt | 1st day | Mid-pt | 1st day | Mid-pt | |
| Date | 4 | 18 | 5 | 20 | 5 | 20 | 5 | 21 | 6 | 21 | 7 | 23 | 7 | 23 | 7 | 23 | 8 | 23 | 7 | 22 | 7 | 22 | 5 | 20 | |
| Hour | 0304 | 2253 | 2114 | 2206 | 0217 | 0925 | 1951 | 0818 | 0013 | 1654 | 1036 | 0347 | 2019 | 1043 | 2303 | 0807 | 1427 | 1713 | 1722 | 1435 | 1002 | 0348 | 2111 | 1426 | |
| DATE 4 | Yn F | Yn E4 | | | | | | | | | | | | | | | | | | | | | | | 4 |
| 5 | Yg E | Yg Wd | Yg F | Yg F | Yn F | Yn E4 | Yn F | Yn E2 | | | | | | | | | | | | | | | Yg W | Yg W | 5 |
| 6 | Yn E | Yn Wd | Yn F | Yn E2 | Yg E | Yg Wd | Yg E | Yg M | Yn E | Yn Wd | | | | | | | | | | | | | Yn W | Yn E4 | 6 |
| 7 | Yg M | Yg E1 | Yg E | Yg M | Yn E | Yn Wd | Yn E | Yn M | Yg M | Yg E1 | Yg M | Yg E3 | Yn M | Yn F | Yg W | Yg W | | | Yn W | Yn E4 | Yn W | Yn E2 | Yg Wd | Yg Wd | 7 |
| 8 | Yn M | Yn F | Yn E | Yn M | Yg M | Yg E1 | Yg M | Yg E3 | Yn M | Yn F | Yn M | Yn W | Yg W | Yg F | Yn W | Yn E4 | Yn W | Yn E2 | Yg Wd | Yg Wd | Yg Wd | Yg M | Yn Wd | Yn Wd | 8 |
| 9 | Yg W | Yg F | Yg M | Yg E3 | Yn M | Yn F | Yn M | Yn W | Yg W | Yg F | Yg W | Yg W | Yn W | Yn E2 | Yg Wd | Yg Wd | Yg Wd | Yg M | Yn Wd | Yn Wd | Yn Wd | Yn M | Yg F | Yg E1 | 9 |
| 10 | Yn W | Yn E2 | Yn M | Yn W | Yg W | Yg F | Yg W | Yg W | Yn W | Yn E2 | Yn W | Yn E4 | Yg Wd | Yg M | Yn Wd | Yn Wd | Yn Wd | Yn M | Yg F | Yg E1 | Yg F | Yg E3 | Yn F | Yn F | 10 |
| 11 | Yg Wd | Yg M | Yg W | Yg W | Yn W | Yn E2 | Yn W | Yn E4 | Yg Wd | Yg M | Yg Wd | Yg Wd | Yn Wd | Yn M | Yg F | Yg E1 | Yg F | Yg E3 | Yn F | Yn F | Yn F | Yn W | Yg E | Yg F | 11 |
| 12 | Yn Wd | Yn M | Yn W | Yn E4 | Yg Wd | Yg M | Yg Wd | Yg Wd | Yn Wd | Yn M | Yn Wd | Yn Wd | Yg F | Yg E3 | Yn F | Yn F | Yn F | Yn W | Yg E | Yg F | Yg E | Yg W | Yn E | Yn E2 | 12 |
| 13 | Yg F | Yg E3 | Yg Wd | Yg Wd | Yn Wd | Yn M | Yn Wd | Yn Wd | Yg F | Yg E3 | Yg F | Yg E1 | Yn F | Yn W | Yg E | Yg F | Yg E | Yg W | Yn E | Yn E2 | Yn E | Yn E4 | Yg M | Yg M | 13 |
| 14 | Yn F | Yn W | Yn Wd | Yn Wd | Yg F | Yg E3 | Yg F | Yg E1 | Yn F | Yn W | Yn F | Yn F | Yg E | Yg W | Yn E | Yn E2 | Yn E | Yn E4 | Yg M | Yg M | Yg M | Yg Wd | Yn M | Yn M | 14 |
| 15 | Yg E | Yg W | Yg F | Yg E1 | Yn F | Yn W | Yn F | Yn F | Yg E | Yg W | Yg E | Yg F | Yn E | Yn E4 | Yg M | Yg M | Yg M | Yg Wd | Yn M | Yn M | Yn M | Yn Wd | Yg W | Yg E3 | 15 |
| 16 | Yn E | Yn E4 | Yn F | Yn F | Yg E | Yg W | Yg E | Yg F | Yn E | Yn E4 | Yn E | Yn E2 | Yg M | Yg Wd | Yn M | Yn M | Yn M | Yn Wd | Yg W | Yg E3 | Yg W | Yg E1 | Yn W | Yn W | 16 |
| 17 | Yg M | Yg Wd | Yg E | Yg F | Yn E | Yn E4 | Yn E | Yn E2 | Yg M | Yg Wd | Yg M | Yg M | Yn M | Yn Wd | Yg W | Yg E3 | Yg W | Yg E1 | Yn W | Yn W | Yn W | Yn F | Yg Wd | Yg W | 17 |
| 18 | Yn M | Yn Wd | Yn E | Yn E2 | Yg M | Yg Wd | Yg M | Yg M | Yn M | Yn Wd | Yn M | Yn M | Yg W | Yg E1 | Yn W | Yn W | Yn W | Yn F | Yg Wd | Yg W | Yg Wd | Yg F | Yn Wd | Yn E4 | 18 |
| 19 | Yg W | Yg E1 | Yg M | Yg M | Yn M | Yn Wd | Yn M | Yn M | Yg W | Yg E1 | Yg W | Yg E3 | Yn W | Yn F | Yg Wd | Yg W | Yg Wd | Yg F | Yn Wd | Yn E4 | Yn Wd | Yn E2 | Yg F | Yg Wd | 19 |
| 20 | Yn W | Yn F | Yn M | Yn M | Yg W | Yg E1 | Yg W | Yg E3 | Yn W | Yn F | Yn W | Yn W | Yg Wd | Yg F | Yn Wd | Yn E4 | Yn Wd | Yn E2 | Yg F | Yg Wd | Yg F | Yg M | Yn F | Yn Wd | 20 |
| 21 | Yg Wd | Yg F | Yg W | Yg E3 | Yn W | Yn F | Yn W | Yn W | Yg Wd | Yg F | Yg Wd | Yg W | Yn Wd | Yn E2 | Yg F | Yg Wd | Yg F | Yg M | Yn F | Yn Wd | Yn F | Yn M | Yg E | Yg E1 | 21 |
| 22 | Yn Wd | Yn E2 | Yn W | Yn W | Yg Wd | Yg F | Yg Wd | Yg W | Yn Wd | Yn E2 | Yn Wd | Yn E4 | Yg F | Yg M | Yn F | Yn Wd | Yn F | Yn M | Yg E | Yg E1 | Yg E | Yg E3 | Yn E | Yn F | 22 |
| 23 | Yg F | Yg M | Yg Wd | Yg W | Yn Wd | Yn E2 | Yn Wd | Yn E4 | Yg F | Yg M | Yg F | Yg Wd | Yn F | Yn M | Yg E | Yg E1 | Yg E | Yg E3 | Yn E | Yn F | Yn E | Yn W | Yg M | Yg F | 23 |
| 24 | Yn F | Yn M | Yn Wd | Yn E4 | Yg F | Yg M | Yg F | Yg Wd | Yn F | Yn M | Yn F | Yn Wd | Yg E | Yg E3 | Yn E | Yn F | Yn E | Yn W | Yg M | Yg F | Yg M | Yg W | Yn M | Yn E2 | 24 |
| 25 | Yg E | Yg E3 | Yg F | Yg Wd | Yn F | Yn M | Yn F | Yn Wd | Yg E | Yg E3 | Yg E | Yg E1 | Yn E | Yn W | Yg M | Yg F | Yg M | Yg W | Yn M | Yn E2 | Yn M | Yn E4 | Yg W | Yg M | 25 |
| 26 | Yn E | Yn W | Yn F | Yn Wd | Yg E | Yg E3 | Yg E | Yg E1 | Yn E | Yn W | Yn E | Yn F | Yg M | Yg W | Yn M | Yn E2 | Yn M | Yn E4 | Yg W | Yg M | Yg W | Yg Wd | Yn W | Yn M | 26 |
| 27 | Yg M | Yg W | Yg E | Yg E1 | Yn E | Yn W | Yn E | Yn F | Yg M | Yg W | Yg M | Yg F | Yn M | Yn E4 | Yg W | Yg M | Yg W | Yg Wd | Yn W | Yn M | Yn W | Yn Wd | Yg Wd | Yg E3 | 27 |
| 28 | Yn M | Yn E4 | Yn E | Yn F | Yg M | Yg W | Yg M | Yg F | Yn M | Yn E4 | Yn M | Yn E2 | Yg W | Yg Wd | Yn W | Yn M | Yn W | Yn Wd | Yg Wd | Yg E3 | Yg Wd | Yg E1 | Yn Wd | Yn W | 28 |
| 29 | | | Yg M | Yg F | Yn M | Yn E4 | Yn M | Yn E2 | Yg W | Yg Wd | Yg W | Yg M | Yn W | Yn Wd | Yg Wd | Yg E3 | Yg Wd | Yg E1 | Yn Wd | Yn W | Yn Wd | Yn F | Yg F | Yg W | 29 |
| 30 | | | Yn M | Yn E2 | Yg W | Yg Wd | Yg W | Yg M | Yn W | Yn Wd | Yn W | Yn M | Yg Wd | Yg E1 | Yn Wd | Yn W | Yn Wd | Yn F | Yg F | Yg W | Yg F | Yg F | Yn F | Yn E4 | 30 |
| 31 | | | Yg W | Yg M | | | Yn W | Yn M | | | Yg Wd | Yg E3 | Yn Wd | Yn F | | | Yg F | Yg F | | | Yn F | Yn E2 | Yg E | Yg Wd | 31 |
| 1 | Yg W | Yg Wd | Yn W | Yn M | Yn W | Yn Wd | Yg Wd | Yg E3 | Yg Wd | Yg E1 | Yn Wd | Yn W | Yg F | Yg F | Yg F | Yg W | Yn F | Yn E2 | Yn F | Yn E4 | Yg E | Yg M | Yn E | Yn Wd | 1 |
| 2 | Yn W | Yn Wd | Yg Wd | Yg E3 | Yg Wd | Yg E1 | Yn Wd | Yn W | Yn Wd | Yn F | Yg F | Yg W | Yn F | Yn E2 | Yn F | Yn E4 | Yg E | Yg M | Yg E | Yg Wd | Yn E | Yn M | Yg M | Yg E1 | 2 |
| 3 | Yg Wd | Yg E1 | Yn Wd | Yn W | Yn Wd | Yn F | Yg F | Yg W | Yg F | Yg F | Yn F | Yn E4 | Yg E | Yg M | Yg E | Yg Wd | Yn E | Yn M | Yn E | Yn Wd | Yg M | Yg E3 | Yn M | Yn F | 3 |
| 4 | Yn Wd | Yn F | Yg F | Yg W | Yg F | Yg F | Yn F | Yn E4 | Yn F | Yn E2 | Yg E | Yg Wd | Yn E | Yn M | Yn E | Yn Wd | Yg M | Yg E3 | Yg M | Yg E1 | Yn M | Yn W | | | 4 |
| 5 | | | | | | | Yg E | Yg Wd | Yg E | Yg M | Yn E | Yn Wd | Yg M | Yg E3 | Yg M | Yg E1 | Yn M | Yn W | Yn M | Yn F | | | | | 5 |
| 6 | | | | | | | | | Yn E | Yn M | Yg M | Yg E1 | Yn M | Yn W | Yn M | Yn F | Yg W | Yg W | Yg W | Yg F | | | | | 6 |
| 7 | | | | | | | | | | | | | | | Yg W | Yg F | | | | | | | | | 7 |
| 8 | | | | | | | | | | | | | | | | | | | | | | | | | 8 |

# YEAR OF THE TIGER

| | H | E | H | E | H | E | H | E | H | E | H | E | H | E | H | E | H | E | H | E | H | E | H | E | |
|---|---|---|---|---|---|---|---|---|---|---|---|---|---|---|---|---|---|---|---|---|---|---|---|---|---|
| YEAR | YEAR YgE | YgWd | | | | | | | | | 1998 | | | | | | | | | | | | 1999 | | |
| MONTH | 4 Feb - 5 Mar | | 6 Mar - 4 Apr | | 5 Apr - 5 May | | 6 May - 5 June | | 6 June - 6 Jul | | 7 Jul - 7 Aug | | 8 Aug - 7 Sep | | 8 Sep - 7 Oct | | 8 Oct - 6 Nov | | 7 Nov - 6 Dec | | 7 Dec - 5 Jan | | 6 Jan - 3 Feb | | |
| | Yg Wd | Yg Wd | Yn Wd | Yn Wd | Yg F | Yg E1 | Yn F | Yn F | Yg E | Yg F | Yn E | Yn E2 | Yg M | Yg M | Yn M | Yn M | Yg W | Yg E3 | Yn W | Yn W | Yg Wd | Yg W | Yn Wd | Yn E4 | |
| Starting time | 1st day | Mid-pt | 1st day | Mid-pt | 1st day | Mid-pt | 1st day | Mid-pt | 1st day | Mid-pt | 1st day | Mid-pt | 1st day | Mid-pt | 1st day | Mid-pt | 1st day | Mid-pt | 1st day | Mid-pt | 1st day | Mid-pt | 1st day | Mid-pt | |
| Date | 4 | 19 | 6 | 21 | 5 | 20 | 6 | 21 | 6 | 21 | 7 | 23 | 8 | 23 | 8 | 23 | 8 | 23 | 7 | 22 | 7 | 22 | 6 | 20 | |
| Hour | 0853 | 0443 | 0303 | 0357 | 0806 | 1516 | 0140 | 1438 | 0602 | 2244 | 1625 | 0937 | 0208 | 1633 | 0452 | 1408 | 2016 | 2303 | 2311 | 2025 | 1551 | 0938 | 0300 | 2016 | |
| DATE 4 | Yg W | Yg F | | | | | | | | | | | | | | | | | | | | | | | 4 |
| 5 | Yn W | Yn E2 | | | Yg W | Yg F | | | | | | | | | | | | | | | | | | | 5 |
| 6 | Yg Wd | Yg M | Yg W | Yg W | Yn W | Yn E2 | Yn W | Yn E4 | Yg Wd | Yg M | | | | | | | | | | | | | Yg E | Yg F | 6 |
| 7 | Yn Wd | Yn M | Yn W | Yn E4 | Yg Wd | Yg M | Yg Wd | Yg Wd | Yn Wd | Yn M | Yn Wd | Yn Wd | | | | | | | Yg E | Yg F | Yg E | Yg W | Yn E | Yn E2 | 7 |
| 8 | Yg F | Yg E3 | Yg Wd | Yg Wd | Yn Wd | Yn M | Yn Wd | Yn Wd | Yg F | Yg E3 | Yg F | Yg E1 | Yn F | Yn W | Yg E | Yg F | Yg E | Yg W | Yn E | Yn E2 | Yn E | Yn E4 | Yg M | Yg M | 8 |
| 9 | Yn F | Yn W | Yn Wd | Yn Wd | Yg F | Yg E3 | Yg F | Yg E1 | Yn F | Yn W | Yn F | Yn F | Yg E | Yg W | Yn E | Yn E2 | Yn E | Yn E4 | Yg M | Yg M | Yg M | Yg Wd | Yn M | Yn M | 9 |
| 10 | Yg E | Yg W | Yg F | Yg E1 | Yn F | Yn W | Yn F | Yn F | Yg E | Yg W | Yg E | Yg F | Yn E | Yn E4 | Yg M | Yg M | Yg M | Yg Wd | Yn M | Yn M | Yn M | Yn Wd | Yg W | Yg E3 | 10 |
| 11 | Yn E | Yn E4 | Yn F | Yn F | Yg E | Yg W | Yg E | Yg F | Yn E | Yn E4 | Yn E | Yn E2 | Yg M | Yg Wd | Yn M | Yn M | Yn M | Yn Wd | Yg W | Yg E3 | Yg W | Yg E1 | Yn W | Yn W | 11 |
| 12 | Yg M | Yg Wd | Yg E | Yg F | Yn E | Yn E4 | Yn E | Yn E2 | Yg M | Yg Wd | Yg M | Yg M | Yn M | Yn Wd | Yg W | Yg E3 | Yg W | Yg E1 | Yn W | Yn W | Yn W | Yn F | Yg Wd | Yg W | 12 |
| 13 | Yn M | Yn Wd | Yn E | Yn E2 | Yg M | Yg Wd | Yg M | Yg M | Yn M | Yn Wd | Yn M | Yn M | Yg W | Yg E1 | Yn W | Yn W | Yn W | Yn F | Yg Wd | Yg W | Yg Wd | Yg F | Yn Wd | Yn E4 | 13 |
| 14 | Yg W | Yg E1 | Yg M | Yg M | Yn M | Yn Wd | Yn M | Yn M | Yg W | Yg E1 | Yg W | Yg E3 | Yn W | Yn F | Yg Wd | Yg W | Yg Wd | Yg F | Yn Wd | Yn E4 | Yn Wd | Yn E2 | Yg F | Yg Wd | 14 |
| 15 | Yn W | Yn F | Yn M | Yn M | Yg W | Yg E1 | Yg W | Yg E3 | Yn W | Yn F | Yn W | Yn W | Yg Wd | Yg F | Yn Wd | Yn E4 | Yn Wd | Yn E2 | Yg F | Yg Wd | Yg F | Yg M | Yn F | Yn Wd | 15 |
| 16 | Yg Wd | Yg F | Yg W | Yg E3 | Yn W | Yn F | Yn W | Yn W | Yg Wd | Yg F | Yg Wd | Yg W | Yn Wd | Yn E2 | Yg F | Yg Wd | Yg F | Yg M | Yn F | Yn Wd | Yn F | Yn M | Yg E | Yg E1 | 16 |
| 17 | Yn Wd | Yn E2 | Yn W | Yn W | Yg Wd | Yg F | Yg Wd | Yg W | Yn Wd | Yn E2 | Yn Wd | Yn E4 | Yg F | Yg M | Yn F | Yn Wd | Yn F | Yn M | Yg E | Yg E1 | Yg E | Yg E3 | Yn E | Yn F | 17 |
| 18 | Yg F | Yg M | Yg Wd | Yg W | Yn Wd | Yn E2 | Yn Wd | Yn E4 | Yg F | Yg M | Yg F | Yg Wd | Yn F | Yn M | Yg E | Yg E1 | Yg E | Yg E3 | Yn E | Yn F | Yn E | Yn W | Yg M | Yg F | 18 |
| 19 | Yn F | Yn M | Yn Wd | Yn E4 | Yg F | Yg M | Yg F | Yg Wd | Yn F | Yn M | Yn F | Yn Wd | Yg E | Yg E3 | Yn E | Yn F | Yn E | Yn W | Yg M | Yg F | Yg M | Yg W | Yn M | Yn E2 | 19 |
| 20 | Yg E | Yg E3 | Yg F | Yg Wd | Yn F | Yn M | Yn F | Yn Wd | Yg E | Yg E3 | Yg E | Yg E1 | Yn E | Yn W | Yg M | Yg F | Yg M | Yg W | Yn M | Yn E2 | Yn M | Yn E4 | Yg W | Yg M | 20 |
| 21 | Yn E | Yn W | Yn F | Yn Wd | Yg E | Yg E3 | Yg E | Yg E1 | Yn E | Yn W | Yn E | Yn F | Yg M | Yg W | Yn M | Yn E2 | Yn M | Yn E4 | Yg W | Yg M | Yg W | Yg Wd | Yn W | Yn M | 21 |
| 22 | Yg M | Yg W | Yg E | Yg E1 | Yn E | Yn W | Yn E | Yn F | Yg M | Yg W | Yg M | Yg F | Yn M | Yn E4 | Yg W | Yg M | Yg W | Yg Wd | Yn W | Yn M | Yn W | Yn Wd | Yg Wd | Yg E3 | 22 |
| 23 | Yn M | Yn E4 | Yn E | Yn F | Yg M | Yg W | Yg M | Yg F | Yn M | Yn E4 | Yn M | Yn E2 | Yg W | Yg Wd | Yn W | Yn M | Yn W | Yn Wd | Yg Wd | Yg E3 | Yg Wd | Yg E1 | Yn Wd | Yn W | 23 |
| 24 | Yg W | Yg Wd | Yg M | Yg F | Yn M | Yn E4 | Yn M | Yn E2 | Yg W | Yg Wd | Yg W | Yg M | Yn W | Yn Wd | Yg Wd | Yg E3 | Yg Wd | Yg E1 | Yn Wd | Yn W | Yn Wd | Yn F | Yg F | Yg W | 24 |
| 25 | Yn W | Yn Wd | Yn M | Yn E2 | Yg W | Yg Wd | Yg W | Yg M | Yn W | Yn Wd | Yn W | Yn M | Yg Wd | Yg E1 | Yn Wd | Yn W | Yn Wd | Yn F | Yg F | Yg W | Yg F | Yg F | Yn F | Yn E4 | 25 |
| 26 | Yg Wd | Yg E1 | Yg W | Yg M | Yn W | Yn Wd | Yn W | Yn M | Yg Wd | Yg E1 | Yg Wd | Yg E3 | Yn Wd | Yn F | Yg F | Yg W | Yg F | Yg F | Yn F | Yn E4 | Yn F | Yn E2 | Yg E | Yg Wd | 26 |
| 27 | Yn Wd | Yn F | Yn W | Yn M | Yg Wd | Yg E1 | Yg Wd | Yg E3 | Yn Wd | Yn F | Yn Wd | Yn W | Yg F | Yg F | Yn F | Yn E4 | Yn F | Yn E2 | Yg E | Yg Wd | Yg E | Yg M | Yn E | Yn Wd | 27 |
| 28 | Yg F | Yg F | Yg Wd | Yg E3 | Yn Wd | Yn F | Yn Wd | Yn W | Yg F | Yg F | Yg F | Yg W | Yn F | Yn E2 | Yg E | Yg Wd | Yg E | Yg M | Yn E | Yn Wd | Yn E | Yn M | Yg M | Yg E1 | 28 |
| 29 | | | Yn Wd | Yn W | Yg F | Yg F | Yg F | Yg W | Yn F | Yn E2 | Yn F | Yn E4 | Yg E | Yg M | Yn E | Yn Wd | Yn E | Yn M | Yg M | Yg E1 | Yg M | Yg E3 | Yn M | Yn F | 29 |
| 30 | | | Yg F | Yg W | Yn F | Yn E2 | Yn F | Yn E4 | Yg E | Yg M | Yg E | Yg Wd | Yn E | Yn M | Yg M | Yg E1 | Yg M | Yg E3 | Yn M | Yn F | Yn M | Yn W | Yg W | Yg F | 30 |
| 31 | | | Yn F | Yn E4 | | | Yg E | Yg Wd | | | Yn E | Yn Wd | Yg M | Yg E3 | | | Yn M | Yn W | | | Yg W | Yg W | Yn W | Yn E2 | 31 |
| 1 | Yn F | Yn E2 | Yg E | Yg Wd | Yg E | Yg M | Yn E | Yn Wd | Yn E | Yn M | Yg M | Yg E1 | Yn M | Yn W | Yn M | Yn F | Yg W | Yg W | Yg W | Yg F | Yn W | Yn E4 | Yg Wd | Yg M | 1 |
| 2 | Yg E | Yg M | Yn E | Yn Wd | Yn E | Yn M | Yg M | Yg E1 | Yg M | Yg E3 | Yn M | Yn F | Yg W | Yg W | Yg W | Yg F | Yn W | Yn E4 | Yn W | Yn E2 | Yg Wd | Yg Wd | Yn Wd | Yn M | 2 |
| 3 | Yn E | Yn M | Yg M | Yg E1 | Yg M | Yg E3 | Yn M | Yn F | Yn M | Yn W | Yg W | Yg F | Yn W | Yn E4 | Yn W | Yn E2 | Yg Wd | Yg Wd | Yg Wd | Yg M | Yn Wd | Yn Wd | Yg F | Yg E3 | 3 |
| 4 | Yg M | Yg E3 | Yn M | Yn F | Yn M | Yn W | Yg W | Yg F | Yg W | Yg W | Yn W | Yn E2 | Yg Wd | Yg Wd | Yg Wd | Yg M | Yn Wd | Yn Wd | Yn Wd | Yn M | Yg F | Yg E1 | | | 4 |
| 5 | Yn M | Yn W | | | Yg W | Yg W | Yn W | Yn E2 | Yn W | Yn E4 | Yg Wd | Yg M | Yn Wd | Yn Wd | Yn Wd | Yn M | Yg F | Yg E1 | Yg F | Yg E3 | Yn F | Yn F | | | 5 |
| 6 | | | | | | | | | Yg Wd | Yg Wd | Yn Wd | Yn M | Yg F | Yg E1 | Yg F | Yg E3 | Yn F | Yn F | Yn F | Yn W | | | | | 6 |
| 7 | | | | | | | | | | | Yg F | Yg E3 | Yn F | Yn F | Yn F | Yn W | | | | | | | | | 7 |
| 8 | | | | | | | | | | | | | | | | | | | | | | | | | 8 |

# YEAR OF THE RABBIT

| | H | E | H | E | H | E | H | E | H | E | H | E | H | E | H | E | H | E | H | E | H | E | H | E | |
|---|---|---|---|---|---|---|---|---|---|---|---|---|---|---|---|---|---|---|---|---|---|---|---|---|---|
| YEAR | YEAR<br>YnE | YnWd | 1999 | | | | | | | | | | | | | | | | | | 2000 | | | | |
| MONTH | 4 Feb - 5 Mar | | 6 Mar - 4 Apr | | 5 Apr - 5 May | | 6 May - 5 June | | 6 June - 6 Jul | | 7 Jul - 7 Aug | | 8 Aug - 7 Sep | | 8 Sep - 8 Oct | | 9 Oct - 7 Nov | | 8 Nov - 6 Dec | | 7 Dec - 5 Jan | | 6 Jan - 3 Feb | | |
| | Yg F | Yg Wd | Yn F | Yn Wd | Yg E | Yg E1 | Yn E | Yn F | Yg M | Yg F | Yn M | Yn E2 | Yg W | Yg M | Yn W | Yn M | Yg Wd | Yg E3 | Yn Wd | Yn W | Yg F | Yg W | Yn F | Yn E4 | |
| Starting time | 1st day | Mid-pt | 1st day | Mid-pt | 1st day | Mid-pt | 1st day | Mid-pt | 1st day | Mid-pt | 1st day | Mid-pt | 1st day | Mid-pt | 1st day | Mid-pt | 1st day | Mid-pt | 1st day | Mid-pt | 1st day | Mid-pt | 1st day | Mid-pt | |
| Date | 4 | 19 | 6 | 21 | 5 | 20 | 6 | 21 | 6 | 22 | 7 | 23 | 8 | 23 | 8 | 23 | 9 | 24 | 8 | 23 | 7 | 22 | 6 | 21 | |
| Hour | 1442 | 1033 | 0852 | 0946 | 1355 | 2055 | 0729 | 2027 | 1151 | 0433 | 2226 | 1526 | 0757 | 2222 | 1041 | 1946 | 0205 | 0452 | 0521 | 0214 | 2114 | 1527 | 0850 | 0205 | |
| DATE 4 | Yn F | Yn W | | | | | | | | | | | | | | | | | | | | | | | 4 |
| 5 | Yg E | Yg W | | | Yn F | Yn W | | | | | | | | | | | | | | | | | | | 5 |
| 6 | Yn E | Yn E4 | Yn F | Yn F | Yg E | Yg W | Yg E | Yg F | Yn E | Yn E4 | | | | | | | | | | | | | Yn W | Yn W | 6 |
| 7 | Yg M | Yg Wd | Yg E | Yg F | Yn E | Yn E4 | Yn E | Yn E2 | Yg M | Yg Wd | Yg M | Yg M | | | | | | | | | Yn W | Yn F | Yg Wd | Yg W | 7 |
| 8 | Yn M | Yn Wd | Yn E | Yn E2 | Yg M | Yg Wd | Yg M | Yg M | Yn M | Yn Wd | Yn M | Yn M | Yg W | Yg E1 | Yn W | Yn W | | | Yg Wd | Yg W | Yg Wd | Yg F | Yn Wd | Yn E4 | 8 |
| 9 | Yg W | Yg E1 | Yg M | Yg M | Yn M | Yn Wd | Yn M | Yn M | Yg W | Yg E1 | Yg W | Yg E3 | Yn W | Yn F | Yg Wd | Yg W | Yg Wd | Yg F | Yn Wd | Yn E4 | Yn Wd | Yn E2 | Yg F | Yg Wd | 9 |
| 10 | Yn W | Yn F | Yn M | Yn M | Yg W | Yg E1 | Yg W | Yg E3 | Yn W | Yn F | Yn W | Yn W | Yg Wd | Yg F | Yn Wd | Yn E4 | Yn Wd | Yn E2 | Yg F | Yg Wd | Yg F | Yg M | Yn F | Yn Wd | 10 |
| 11 | Yg Wd | Yg F | Yg W | Yg E3 | Yn W | Yn F | Yn W | Yn W | Yg Wd | Yg F | Yg Wd | Yg W | Yn Wd | Yn E2 | Yg F | Yg Wd | Yg F | Yg M | Yn F | Yn Wd | Yn F | Yn M | Yg E | Yg E1 | 11 |
| 12 | Yn Wd | Yn E2 | Yn W | Yn W | Yg Wd | Yg F | Yg Wd | Yg W | Yn Wd | Yn E2 | Yn Wd | Yn E4 | Yg F | Yg M | Yn F | Yn Wd | Yn F | Yn M | Yg E | Yg E1 | Yg E | Yg E3 | Yn E | Yn F | 12 |
| 13 | Yg F | Yg M | Yg Wd | Yg W | Yn Wd | Yn E2 | Yn Wd | Yn E4 | Yg F | Yg M | Yg F | Yg Wd | Yn F | Yn M | Yg E | Yg E1 | Yg E | Yg E3 | Yn E | Yn F | Yn E | Yn W | Yg M | Yg F | 13 |
| 14 | Yn F | Yn M | Yn Wd | Yn E4 | Yg F | Yg M | Yg F | Yg Wd | Yn F | Yn M | Yn F | Yn Wd | Yg E | Yg E3 | Yn E | Yn F | Yn E | Yn W | Yg M | Yg F | Yg M | Yg W | Yn M | Yn E2 | 14 |
| 15 | Yg E | Yg E3 | Yg F | Yg Wd | Yn F | Yn M | Yn F | Yn Wd | Yg E | Yg E3 | Yg E | Yg E1 | Yn E | Yn W | Yg M | Yg F | Yg M | Yg W | Yn M | Yn E2 | Yn M | Yn E4 | Yg W | Yg M | 15 |
| 16 | Yn E | Yn W | Yn F | Yn Wd | Yg E | Yg E3 | Yg E | Yg E1 | Yn E | Yn W | Yn E | Yn F | Yg M | Yg W | Yn M | Yn E2 | Yn M | Yn E4 | Yg W | Yg M | Yg W | Yg Wd | Yn W | Yn M | 16 |
| 17 | Yg M | Yg W | Yg E | Yg E1 | Yn E | Yn W | Yn E | Yn F | Yg M | Yg W | Yg M | Yg F | Yn M | Yn E4 | Yg W | Yg M | Yg W | Yg Wd | Yn W | Yn M | Yn W | Yn Wd | Yg Wd | Yg E3 | 17 |
| 18 | Yn M | Yn E4 | Yn E | Yn F | Yg M | Yg W | Yg M | Yg F | Yn M | Yn E4 | Yn M | Yn E2 | Yg W | Yg Wd | Yn W | Yn M | Yn W | Yn Wd | Yg Wd | Yg E3 | Yg Wd | Yg E1 | Yn Wd | Yn W | 18 |
| 19 | Yg W | Yg Wd | Yg M | Yg F | Yn M | Yn E4 | Yn M | Yn E2 | Yg W | Yg Wd | Yg W | Yg M | Yn W | Yn Wd | Yg Wd | Yg E3 | Yg Wd | Yg E1 | Yn Wd | Yn W | Yn Wd | Yn F | Yg F | Yg W | 19 |
| 20 | Yn W | Yn Wd | Yn M | Yn E2 | Yg W | Yg Wd | Yg W | Yg M | Yn W | Yn Wd | Yn W | Yn M | Yg Wd | Yg E1 | Yn Wd | Yn W | Yn Wd | Yn F | Yg F | Yg W | Yg F | Yg F | Yn F | Yn E4 | 20 |
| 21 | Yg Wd | Yg E1 | Yg W | Yg M | Yn W | Yn Wd | Yn W | Yn M | Yg Wd | Yg E1 | Yg Wd | Yg E3 | Yn Wd | Yn F | Yg F | Yg W | Yg F | Yg F | Yn F | Yn E4 | Yn F | Yn E2 | Yg E | Yg Wd | 21 |
| 22 | Yn Wd | Yn F | Yn W | Yn M | Yg Wd | Yg E1 | Yg Wd | Yg E3 | Yn Wd | Yn F | Yn Wd | Yn W | Yg F | Yg F | Yn F | Yn E4 | Yn F | Yn E2 | Yg E | Yg Wd | Yg E | Yg M | Yn E | Yn Wd | 22 |
| 23 | Yg F | Yg F | Yg Wd | Yg E3 | Yn Wd | Yn F | Yn Wd | Yn W | Yg F | Yg F | Yg F | Yg W | Yn F | Yn E2 | Yg E | Yg Wd | Yg E | Yg M | Yn E | Yn Wd | Yn E | Yn M | Yg M | Yg E1 | 23 |
| 24 | Yn F | Yn E2 | Yn Wd | Yn W | Yg F | Yg F | Yg F | Yg W | Yn F | Yn E2 | Yn F | Yn E4 | Yg E | Yg M | Yn E | Yn Wd | Yn E | Yn M | Yg M | Yg E1 | Yg M | Yg E3 | Yn M | Yn F | 24 |
| 25 | Yg E | Yg M | Yg F | Yg W | Yn F | Yn E2 | Yn F | Yn E4 | Yg E | Yg M | Yg E | Yg Wd | Yn E | Yn M | Yg M | Yg E1 | Yg M | Yg E3 | Yn M | Yn F | Yn M | Yn W | Yg W | Yg F | 25 |
| 26 | Yn E | Yn M | Yn F | Yn E4 | Yg E | Yg M | Yg E | Yg Wd | Yn E | Yn M | Yn E | Yn Wd | Yg M | Yg E3 | Yn M | Yn F | Yn M | Yn W | Yg W | Yg F | Yg W | Yg W | Yn W | Yn E2 | 26 |
| 27 | Yg M | Yg E3 | Yg E | Yg Wd | Yn E | Yn M | Yn E | Yn Wd | Yg M | Yg E3 | Yg M | Yg E1 | Yn M | Yn W | Yg W | Yg F | Yg W | Yg W | Yn W | Yn E2 | Yn W | Yn E4 | Yg Wd | Yg M | 27 |
| 28 | Yn M | Yn W | Yn E | Yn Wd | Yg M | Yg E3 | Yg M | Yg E1 | Yn M | Yn W | Yn M | Yn F | Yg W | Yg W | Yn W | Yn E2 | Yn W | Yn E4 | Yg Wd | Yg M | Yg Wd | Yg Wd | Yn Wd | Yn M | 28 |
| 29 | | | Yg M | Yg E1 | Yn M | Yn W | Yn M | Yn F | Yg W | Yg W | Yg W | Yg F | Yn W | Yn E4 | Yg Wd | Yg M | Yg Wd | Yg Wd | Yn Wd | Yn M | Yn Wd | Yn Wd | Yg F | Yg E3 | 29 |
| 30 | | | Yn M | Yn F | Yg W | Yg W | Yg W | Yg F | Yn W | Yn E4 | Yn W | Yn E2 | Yg Wd | Yg Wd | Yn Wd | Yn M | Yn Wd | Yn Wd | Yg F | Yg E3 | Yg F | Yg E1 | Yn F | Yn W | 30 |
| 31 | | | Yg W | Yg F | | | Yn W | Yn E2 | | | Yg Wd | Yg M | Yn Wd | Yn Wd | | | Yg F | Yg E1 | | | Yn F | Yn F | Yg E | Yg W | 31 |
| 1 | Yg W | Yg W | Yn W | Yn E2 | Yn W | Yn E4 | Yg Wd | Yg M | Yg Wd | Yg Wd | Yn Wd | Yn M | Yg F | Yg E1 | Yg F | Yg E3 | Yn F | Yn F | Yn F | Yn W | Yg E | Yg F | Yn E | Yn E4 | 1 |
| 2 | Yn W | Yn E4 | Yg Wd | Yg M | Yg Wd | Yg Wd | Yn Wd | Yn M | Yn Wd | Yn Wd | Yg F | Yg E3 | Yn F | Yn F | Yn F | Yn W | Yg E | Yg F | Yg E | Yg W | Yn E | Yn E2 | Yg M | Yg Wd | 2 |
| 3 | Yg Wd | Yg Wd | Yn Wd | Yn M | Yn Wd | Yn Wd | Yg F | Yg E3 | Yg F | Yg E1 | Yn F | Yn W | Yg E | Yg F | Yg E | Yg W | Yn E | Yn E2 | Yn E | Yn E4 | Yg M | Yg M | Yn M | Yn Wd | 3 |
| 4 | Yn Wd | Yn Wd | Yg F | Yg E3 | Yg F | Yg E1 | Yn F | Yn W | Yn F | Yn F | Yg E | Yg W | Yn E | Yn E2 | Yn E | Yn E4 | Yg M | Yg M | Yg M | Yg Wd | Yn M | Yn M | | | 4 |
| 5 | Yg F | Yg E1 | | | Yn F | Yn F | Yg E | Yg W | Yg E | Yg F | Yn E | Yn E4 | Yg M | Yg M | Yg M | Yg Wd | Yn M | Yn M | Yn M | Yn Wd | Yg W | Yg E3 | | | 5 |
| 6 | | | | | | | | | Yn E | Yn E2 | Yg M | Yg Wd | Yn M | Yn M | Yn M | Yn Wd | Yg W | Yg E3 | Yg W | Yg E1 | | | | | 6 |
| 7 | | | | | | | | | | | Yn M | Yn Wd | Yg W | Yg E3 | Yg W | Yg E1 | Yn W | Yn W | | | | | | | 7 |
| 8 | | | | | | | | | | | | | | | Yn W | Yn F | | | | | | | | | 8 |

# YEAR OF THE DRAGON

| | H | E | H | E | H | E | H | E | H | E | H | E | H | E | H | E | H | E | H | E | H | E | H | E | |
|---|---|---|---|---|---|---|---|---|---|---|---|---|---|---|---|---|---|---|---|---|---|---|---|---|---|
| YEAR | YEAR<br>YgM | YgE1 | 2000 | | | | | | | | | | | | | | | | | | | | 2001 | | |
| MONTH | 4 Feb - 4 Mar | | 5 Mar - 3 Apr | | 4 Apr - 4 May | | 5 May - 4 June | | 5 June - 6 Jul | | 7 Jul - 6 Aug | | 7 Aug - 6 Sep | | 7 Sep - 7 Oct | | 8 Oct - 6 Nov | | 7 Nov - 6 Dec | | 7 Dec - 4 Jan | | 5 Jan - 3 Feb | | |
| | YgE | YgWd | YnE | YnWd | YgM | YgE1 | YnM | YnF | YgW | YgF | YnW | YnE2 | YgWd | YgM | YnWd | YnM | YgF | YgE3 | YnF | YnW | YgE | YgW | YnE | YnE4 | |
| Starting time | 1st day | Mid-pt | 1st day | Mid-pt | 1st day | Mid-pt | 1st day | Mid-pt | 1st day | Mid-pt | 1st day | Mid-pt | 1st day | Mid-pt | 1st day | Mid-pt | 1st day | Mid-pt | 1st day | Mid-pt | 1st day | Mid-pt | 1st day | Mid-pt | |
| Date | 4 | 19 | 5 | 20 | 4 | 20 | 5 | 21 | 5 | 21 | 7 | 22 | 7 | 23 | 7 | 23 | 8 | 23 | 7 | 22 | 7 | 21 | 5 | 20 | |
| Hour | 2032 | 1622 | 1442 | 1535 | 1945 | 0254 | 1319 | 0216 | 1741 | 1022 | 0404 | 2115 | 1336 | 0411 | 1630 | 0135 | 0745 | 1041 | 1049 | 0803 | 0329 | 2116 | 1438 | 0754 | |
| DATE 4 | YgW | YgE1 | | | YgW | YgE1 | | | | | | | | | | | | | | | | | | | 4 |
| 5 | YnW | YnF | YgW | YgE3 | YnW | YnF | YnW | YnW | YgWd | YgF | | | | | | | | | | | | | YgE | YgE1 | 5 |
| 6 | YgWd | YgF | YnW | YnW | YgWd | YgF | YgWd | YgW | YnWd | YnE2 | | | | | | | | | | | | | YnE | YnF | 6 |
| 7 | YnWd | YnE2 | YgWd | YgW | YnWd | YnE2 | YnWd | YnE4 | YgF | YgM | YgF | YgWd | YnF | YnM | YgE | YgE1 | | | YnE | YnF | YnE | YnW | YgM | YgF | 7 |
| 8 | YgF | YgM | YnWd | YnE4 | YgF | YgM | YgF | YgWd | YnF | YnM | YnF | YnWd | YgE | YgE3 | YnE | YnF | YnE | YnW | YgM | YgF | YgM | YgW | YnM | YnE2 | 8 |
| 9 | YnF | YnM | YgF | YgWd | YnF | YnM | YnF | YnWd | YgE | YgE3 | YgE | YgE1 | YnE | YnW | YgM | YgF | YgM | YgW | YnM | YnE2 | YnM | YnE4 | YgW | YgM | 9 |
| 10 | YgE | YgE3 | YnF | YnWd | YgE | YgE3 | YgE | YgE1 | YnE | YnW | YnE | YnF | YgM | YgW | YnM | YnE2 | YnM | YnE4 | YgW | YgM | YgW | YgWd | YnW | YnM | 10 |
| 11 | YnE | YnW | YgE | YgE1 | YnE | YnW | YnE | YnF | YgM | YgW | YgM | YgF | YnM | YnE4 | YgW | YgM | YgW | YgWd | YnW | YnM | YnW | YnWd | YgWd | YgE3 | 11 |
| 12 | YgM | YgW | YnE | YnF | YgM | YgW | YgM | YgF | YnM | YnE4 | YnM | YnE2 | YgW | YgWd | YnW | YnM | YnW | YnWd | YgWd | YgE3 | YgWd | YgE1 | YnWd | YnW | 12 |
| 13 | YnM | YnE4 | YgM | YgF | YnM | YnE4 | YnM | YnE2 | YgW | YgWd | YgW | YgM | YnW | YnWd | YgWd | YgE3 | YgWd | YgE1 | YnWd | YnW | YnWd | YnF | YgF | YgW | 13 |
| 14 | YgW | YgWd | YnM | YnE2 | YgW | YgWd | YgW | YgM | YnW | YnWd | YnW | YnM | YgWd | YgE1 | YnWd | YnW | YnWd | YnF | YgF | YgW | YgF | YgF | YnF | YnE4 | 14 |
| 15 | YnW | YnWd | YgW | YgM | YnW | YnWd | YnW | YnM | YgWd | YgE1 | YgWd | YgE3 | YnWd | YnF | YgF | YgW | YgF | YgF | YnF | YnE4 | YnF | YnE2 | YgE | YgWd | 15 |
| 16 | YgWd | YgE1 | YnW | YnM | YgWd | YgE1 | YgWd | YgE3 | YnWd | YnF | YnWd | YnW | YgF | YgF | YnF | YnE4 | YnF | YnE2 | YgE | YgWd | YgE | YgM | YnE | YnWd | 16 |
| 17 | YnWd | YnF | YgWd | YgE3 | YnWd | YnF | YnWd | YnW | YgF | YgF | YgF | YgW | YnF | YnE2 | YgE | YgWd | YgE | YgM | YnE | YnWd | YnE | YnM | YgM | YgE1 | 17 |
| 18 | YgF | YgF | YnWd | YnW | YgF | YgF | YgF | YgW | YnF | YnE2 | YnF | YnE4 | YgE | YgM | YnE | YnWd | YnE | YnM | YgM | YgE1 | YgM | YgE3 | YnM | YnF | 18 |
| 19 | YnF | YnE2 | YgF | YgW | YnF | YnE2 | YnF | YnE4 | YgE | YgM | YgE | YgWd | YnE | YnM | YgM | YgE1 | YgM | YgE3 | YnM | YnF | YnM | YnW | YgW | YgF | 19 |
| 20 | YgE | YgM | YnF | YnE4 | YgE | YgM | YgE | YgWd | YnE | YnM | YnE | YnWd | YgM | YgE3 | YnM | YnF | YnM | YnW | YgW | YgF | YgW | YgW | YnW | YnE2 | 20 |
| 21 | YnE | YnM | YgE | YgWd | YnE | YnM | YnE | YnWd | YgM | YgE3 | YgM | YgE1 | YnM | YnW | YgW | YgF | YgW | YgW | YnW | YnE2 | YnW | YnE4 | YgWd | YgM | 21 |
| 22 | YgM | YgE3 | YnE | YnWd | YgM | YgE3 | YgM | YgE1 | YnM | YnW | YnM | YnF | YgW | YgW | YnW | YnE2 | YnW | YnE4 | YgWd | YgM | YgWd | YgWd | YnWd | YnM | 22 |
| 23 | YnM | YnW | YgM | YgE1 | YnM | YnW | YnM | YnF | YgW | YgW | YgW | YgF | YnW | YnE4 | YgWd | YgM | YgWd | YgWd | YnWd | YnM | YnWd | YnWd | YgF | YgE3 | 23 |
| 24 | YgW | YgW | YnM | YnF | YgW | YgW | YgW | YgF | YnW | YnE4 | YnW | YnE2 | YgWd | YgWd | YnWd | YnM | YnWd | YnWd | YgF | YgE3 | YgF | YgE1 | YnF | YnW | 24 |
| 25 | YnW | YnE4 | YgW | YgF | YnW | YnE4 | YnW | YnE2 | YgWd | YgWd | YgWd | YgM | YnWd | YnWd | YgF | YgE3 | YgF | YgE1 | YnF | YnW | YnF | YnF | YgE | YgW | 25 |
| 26 | YgWd | YgWd | YnW | YnE2 | YgWd | YgWd | YgWd | YgM | YnWd | YnWd | YnWd | YnM | YgF | YgE1 | YnF | YnW | YnF | YnF | YgE | YgW | YgE | YgF | YnE | YnE4 | 26 |
| 27 | YnWd | YnWd | YgWd | YgM | YnWd | YnWd | YnWd | YnM | YgF | YgE1 | YgF | YgE3 | YnF | YnF | YgE | YgW | YgE | YgF | YnE | YnE4 | YnE | YnE2 | YgM | YgWd | 27 |
| 28 | YgF | YgE1 | YnWd | YnM | YgF | YgE1 | YgF | YgE3 | YnF | YnF | YnF | YnW | YgE | YgF | YnE | YnE4 | YnE | YnE2 | YgM | YgWd | YgM | YgM | YnM | YnWd | 28 |
| 29 | YnF | YnF | YgF | YgE3 | YnF | YnF | YnF | YnW | YgE | YgF | YgE | YgW | YnE | YnE2 | YgM | YgWd | YgM | YgM | YnM | YnWd | YnM | YnM | YgW | YgE1 | 29 |
| 30 | | | YnF | YnW | YgE | YgF | YgE | YgW | YnE | YnE2 | YnE | YnE4 | YgM | YgM | YnM | YnWd | YnM | YnM | YgW | YgE1 | YgW | YgE3 | YnW | YnF | 30 |
| 31 | | | YgE | YgW | | | YnE | YnE4 | | | YgM | YgWd | YnM | YnM | | | YgW | YgE3 | | | YnW | YnW | YgWd | YgF | 31 |
| 1 | YgE | YgF | YnE | YnE4 | YnE | YnE2 | YgM | YgWd | YgM | YgM | YnM | YnWd | YgW | YgE3 | YgW | YgE1 | YnW | YnW | YnW | YnF | YgWd | YgW | YnWd | YnE2 | 1 |
| 2 | YnE | YnE2 | YgM | YgWd | YgM | YgM | YnM | YnWd | YnM | YnM | YgW | YgE1 | YnW | YnW | YnW | YnF | YgWd | YgW | YgWd | YgF | YnWd | YnE4 | YgF | YgM | 2 |
| 3 | YgM | YgM | YnM | YnWd | YnM | YnM | YgW | YgE1 | YgW | YgE3 | YnW | YnF | YgWd | YgW | YgWd | YgF | YnWd | YnE4 | YnWd | YnE2 | YgF | YgWd | YnF | YnM | 3 |
| 4 | YnM | YnM | | | YgW | YgE3 | YnW | YnF | YnW | YnW | YgWd | YgF | YnWd | YnE4 | YnWd | YnE2 | YgF | YgWd | YgF | YgM | YnF | YnWd | | | 4 |
| 5 | | | | | | | | | YgWd | YgW | YnWd | YnE2 | YgF | YgWd | YgF | YgM | YnF | YnWd | YnF | YnM | | | | | 5 |
| 6 | | | | | | | | | YnWd | YnE4 | YgF | YgM | YnF | YnWd | YnF | YnM | YgE | YgE1 | YgE | YgE3 | | | | | 6 |
| 7 | | | | | | | | | | | | | | | YgE | YgE3 | | | | | | | | | 7 |
| 8 | | | | | | | | | | | | | | | | | | | | | | | | | 8 |

# YEAR OF THE SNAKE

| | H | E | H | E | H | E | H | E | H | E | H | E | H | E | H | E | H | E | H | E | H | E | H | E | |
|---|---|---|---|---|---|---|---|---|---|---|---|---|---|---|---|---|---|---|---|---|---|---|---|---|---|
| YEAR | YEAR YnM | YnF | 2001 | | | | | | | | | | | | | | | | | | | | 2002 | | |
| MONTH | 4 Feb - 4 Mar | | 5 Mar - 4 Apr | | 5 Apr - 4 May | | 5 May - 4 June | | 5 June - 6 Jul | | 7 Jul - 6 Aug | | 7 Aug - 6 Sep | | 7 Sep - 7 Oct | | 8 Oct - 6 Nov | | 7 Nov - 6 Dec | | 7 Dec - 4 Jan | | 5 Jan - 3 Feb | | |
| | YgM | YgWd | YnM | YnWd | YgW | YgE1 | YnW | YnF | YgWd | YgF | YnWd | YnE2 | YgF | YgM | YnF | YnM | YgE | YgE3 | YnE | YnW | YgM | YgW | YnM | YnE4 | |
| Starting time | 1st day | Mid-pt | 1st day | Mid-pt | 1st day | Mid-pt | 1st day | Mid-pt | 1st day | Mid-pt | 1st day | Mid-pt | 1st day | Mid-pt | 1st day | Mid-pt | 1st day | Mid-pt | 1st day | Mid-pt | 1st day | Mid-pt | 1st day | Mid-pt | |
| Date | 4 | 18 | 5 | 20 | 5 | 20 | 5 | 21 | 5 | 21 | 7 | 23 | 7 | 23 | 7 | 23 | 8 | 23 | 7 | 22 | 7 | 22 | 5 | 20 | |
| Hour | 0220 | 2211 | 2030 | 2124 | 0133 | 0843 | 1907 | 0806 | 2319 | 1612 | 0952 | 0305 | 1934 | 1001 | 2218 | 0725 | 1342 | 1631 | 1631 | 1353 | 0917 | 0308 | 2026 | 1344 | |
| DATE 4 | YgE | YgE3 | | | | | | | | | | | | | | | | | | | | | | | 4 |
| 5 | YnE | YnW | YnF | YnWd | YgE | YgE3 | YgE | YgE1 | YnE | YnW | | | | | | | | | | | | | YnW | YnM | 5 |
| 6 | YgM | YgW | YgE | YgE1 | YnE | YnW | YnE | YnF | YgM | YgW | | | | | | | | | | | | | YgWd | YgE3 | 6 |
| 7 | YnM | YnE4 | YnE | YnF | YgM | YgW | YgM | YgF | YnM | YnE4 | YnM | YnE2 | YgW | YgWd | YnW | YnM | | | YgWd | YgE3 | YgWd | YgE1 | YnWd | YnW | 7 |
| 8 | YgW | YgWd | YgM | YgF | YnM | YnE4 | YnM | YnE2 | YgW | YgWd | YgW | YgM | YnW | YnWd | YgWd | YgE3 | YgWd | YgE1 | YnWd | YnW | YnWd | YnF | YgF | YgW | 8 |
| 9 | YnW | YnWd | YnM | YnE2 | YgW | YgWd | YgW | YgM | YnW | YnWd | YnW | YnM | YgWd | YgE1 | YnWd | YnW | YnWd | YnF | YgF | YgW | YgF | YgF | YnF | YnE4 | 9 |
| 10 | YgWd | YgE1 | YgW | YgM | YnW | YnWd | YnW | YnM | YgWd | YgE1 | YgWd | YgE3 | YnWd | YnF | YgF | YgW | YgF | YgF | YnF | YnE4 | YnF | YnE2 | YgE | YgWd | 10 |
| 11 | YnWd | YnF | YnW | YnM | YgWd | YgE1 | YgWd | YgE3 | YnWd | YnF | YnWd | YnW | YgF | YgF | YnF | YnE4 | YnF | YnE2 | YgE | YgWd | YgE | YgM | YnE | YnWd | 11 |
| 12 | YgF | YgF | YgWd | YgE3 | YnWd | YnF | YnWd | YnW | YgF | YgF | YgF | YgW | YnF | YnE2 | YgE | YgWd | YgE | YgM | YnE | YnWd | YnE | YnM | YgM | YgE1 | 12 |
| 13 | YnF | YnE2 | YnWd | YnW | YgF | YgF | YgF | YgW | YnF | YnE2 | YnF | YnE4 | YgE | YgM | YnE | YnWd | YnE | YnM | YgM | YgE1 | YgM | YgE3 | YnM | YnF | 13 |
| 14 | YgE | YgM | YgF | YgW | YnF | YnE2 | YnF | YnE4 | YgE | YgM | YgE | YgWd | YnE | YnM | YgM | YgE1 | YgM | YgE3 | YnM | YnF | YnM | YnW | YgW | YgF | 14 |
| 15 | YnE | YnM | YnF | YnE4 | YgE | YgM | YgE | YgWd | YnE | YnM | YnE | YnWd | YgM | YgE3 | YnM | YnF | YnM | YnW | YgW | YgF | YgW | YgW | YnW | YnE2 | 15 |
| 16 | YgM | YgE3 | YgE | YgWd | YnE | YnM | YnE | YnWd | YgM | YgE3 | YgM | YgE1 | YnM | YnW | YgW | YgF | YgW | YgW | YnW | YnE2 | YnW | YnE4 | YgWd | YgM | 16 |
| 17 | YnM | YnW | YnE | YnWd | YgM | YgE3 | YgM | YgE1 | YnM | YnW | YnM | YnF | YgW | YgW | YnW | YnE2 | YnW | YnE4 | YgWd | YgM | YgWd | YgWd | YnWd | YnM | 17 |
| 18 | YgW | YgW | YgM | YgE1 | YnM | YnW | YnM | YnF | YgW | YgW | YgW | YgF | YnW | YnE4 | YgWd | YgM | YgWd | YgWd | YnWd | YnM | YnWd | YnWd | YgF | YgE3 | 18 |
| 19 | YnW | YnE4 | YnM | YnF | YgW | YgW | YgW | YgF | YnW | YnE4 | YnW | YnE2 | YgWd | YgWd | YnWd | YnM | YnWd | YnWd | YgF | YgE3 | YgF | YgE1 | YnF | YnW | 19 |
| 20 | YgWd | YgWd | YgW | YgF | YnW | YnE4 | YnW | YnE2 | YgWd | YgWd | YgWd | YgM | YnWd | YnWd | YgF | YgE3 | YgF | YgE1 | YnF | YnW | YnF | YnF | YgE | YgW | 20 |
| 21 | YnWd | YnWd | YnW | YnE2 | YgWd | YgWd | YgWd | YgM | YnWd | YnWd | YnWd | YnM | YgF | YgE1 | YnF | YnW | YnF | YnF | YgE | YgW | YgE | YgF | YnE | YnE4 | 21 |
| 22 | YgF | YgE1 | YgWd | YgM | YnWd | YnWd | YnWd | YnM | YgF | YgE1 | YgF | YgE3 | YnF | YnF | YgE | YgW | YgE | YgF | YnE | YnE4 | YnE | YnE2 | YgM | YgWd | 22 |
| 23 | YnF | YnF | YnWd | YnM | YgF | YgE1 | YgF | YgE3 | YnF | YnF | YnF | YnW | YgE | YgF | YnE | YnE4 | YnE | YnE2 | YgM | YgWd | YgM | YgM | YnM | YnWd | 23 |
| 24 | YgE | YgF | YgF | YgE3 | YnF | YnF | YnF | YnW | YgE | YgF | YgE | YgW | YnE | YnE2 | YgM | YgWd | YgM | YgM | YnM | YnWd | YnM | YnM | YgW | YgE1 | 24 |
| 25 | YnE | YnE2 | YnF | YnW | YgE | YgF | YgE | YgW | YnE | YnE2 | YnE | YnE4 | YgM | YgM | YnM | YnWd | YnM | YnM | YgW | YgE1 | YgW | YgE3 | YnW | YnF | 25 |
| 26 | YgM | YgM | YgE | YgW | YnE | YnE2 | YnE | YnE4 | YgM | YgM | YgM | YgWd | YnM | YnM | YgW | YgE1 | YgW | YgE3 | YnW | YnF | YnW | YnW | YgWd | YgF | 26 |
| 27 | YnM | YnM | YnE | YnE4 | YgM | YgM | YgM | YgWd | YnM | YnM | YnM | YnWd | YgW | YgE3 | YnW | YnF | YnW | YnW | YgWd | YgF | YgWd | YgW | YnWd | YnE2 | 27 |
| 28 | YgW | YgE3 | YgM | YgWd | YnM | YnM | YnM | YnWd | YgW | YgE3 | YgW | YgE1 | YnW | YnW | YgWd | YgF | YgWd | YgW | YnWd | YnE2 | YnWd | YnE4 | YgF | YgM | 28 |
| 29 | | | YnM | YnWd | YgW | YgE3 | YgW | YgE1 | YnW | YnW | YnW | YnF | YgWd | YgW | YnWd | YnE2 | YnWd | YnE4 | YgF | YgM | YgF | YgWd | YnF | YnM | 29 |
| 30 | | | YgW | YgE1 | YnW | YnW | YnW | YnF | YgWd | YgW | YgWd | YgF | YnWd | YnE4 | YgF | YgM | YgF | YgWd | YnF | YnM | YnF | YnWd | YgE | YgE3 | 30 |
| 31 | | | YnW | YnF | | | YgWd | YgF | | | YnWd | YnE2 | YgF | YgWd | | | YnF | YnWd | | | YgE | YgE1 | YnE | YnW | 31 |
| 1 | YnW | YnW | YgWd | YgF | YgWd | YgW | YnWd | YnE2 | YnWd | YnE4 | YgF | YgM | YnF | YnWd | YnF | YnM | YgE | YgE1 | YgE | YgE3 | YnE | YnF | YgM | YgW | 1 |
| 2 | YgWd | YgW | YnWd | YnE2 | YnWd | YnE4 | YgF | YgM | YgF | YgWd | YnF | YnM | YgE | YgE1 | YgE | YgE3 | YnE | YnF | YnE | YnW | YgM | YgF | YnM | YnE4 | 2 |
| 3 | YnWd | YnE4 | YgF | YgM | YgF | YgWd | YnF | YnM | YnF | YnWd | YgE | YgE3 | YnE | YnF | YnE | YnW | YgM | YgF | YgM | YgW | YnM | YnE2 | YgW | YgWd | 3 |
| 4 | YgF | YgWd | YnF | YnM | YnF | YnWd | YgE | YgE3 | YgE | YgE1 | YnE | YnW | YgM | YgF | YgM | YgW | YnM | YnE2 | YnM | YnE4 | YgW | YgM | | | 4 |
| 5 | | | | | | | | | YnE | YnF | YgM | YgW | YnM | YnE2 | YnM | YnE4 | YgW | YgM | YgW | YgWd | | | | | 5 |
| 6 | | | | | | | | | YgM | YgF | YnM | YnE4 | YgW | YgM | YgW | YgWd | YnW | YnM | YnW | YnWd | | | | | 6 |
| 7 | | | | | | | | | | | | | | | YnW | YnWd | | | | | | | | | 7 |
| 8 | | | | | | | | | | | | | | | | | | | | | | | | | 8 |

# YEAR OF THE HORSE

| | H | E | H | E | H | E | H | E | H | E | H | E | H | E | H | E | H | E | H | E | H | E | H | E | |
|---|---|---|---|---|---|---|---|---|---|---|---|---|---|---|---|---|---|---|---|---|---|---|---|---|---|
| YEAR | YEAR Yg W | Yg F | 2002 | | | | | | | | | | | | | | | | | | | | 2003 | | |
| MONTH | 4 Feb - 5 Mar | | 6 Mar - 4 Apr | | 5 Apr - 5 May | | 6 May - 5 June | | 6 June - 6 Jul | | 7 Jul - 7 Aug | | 8 Aug - 7 Sep | | 8 Sep - 7 Oct | | 8 Oct - 6 Nov | | 7 Nov - 6 Dec | | 7 Dec - 5 Jan | | 6 Jan - 3 Feb | | |
| | Yg W | Yg Wd | Yn W | Yn Wd | Yg Wd | Yg E1 | Yn Wd | Yn F | Yg F | Yg F | Yn F | Yn E2 | Yg E | Yg M | Yn E | Yn M | Yg M | Yg E3 | Yn M | Yn W | Yg W | Yg W | Yn W | Yn E4 | |
| Starting time | 1st day | Mid-pt | 1st day | Mid-pt | 1st day | Mid-pt | 1st day | Mid-pt | 1st day | Mid-pt | 1st day | Mid-pt | 1st day | Mid-pt | 1st day | Mid-pt | 1st day | Mid-pt | 1st day | Mid-pt | 1st day | Mid-pt | 1st day | Mid-pt | |
| Date | 4 | 19 | 6 | 21 | 5 | 20 | 6 | 21 | 6 | 21 | 7 | 23 | 8 | 23 | 8 | 23 | 8 | 23 | 7 | 22 | 7 | 22 | 6 | 21 | |
| Hour | 0808 | 0401 | 0218 | 0314 | 0718 | 1433 | 0055 | 1355 | 0517 | 2203 | 1540 | 1554 | 0123 | 1548 | 0407 | 1314 | 1931 | 2220 | 2226 | 1942 | 1508 | 0855 | 0215 | 1933 | |
| DATE 4 | Yn W | Yn Wd | | | | | | | | | | | | | | | | | | | | | | | 4 |
| 5 | Yg Wd | Yg E1 | | | Yn W | Yn Wd | | | | | | | | | | | | | | | | | | | 5 |
| 6 | Yn Wd | Yn F | Yn W | Yn M | Yg Wd | Yg E1 | Yg Wd | Yg E3 | Yn Wd | Yn F | | | | | | | | | | | | | Yn E | Yn Wd | 6 |
| 7 | Yg F | Yg F | Yg Wd | Yg E3 | Yn Wd | Yn F | Yn Wd | Yn W | Yg F | Yg F | Yg F | Yg W | | | | | | | Yn E | Yn Wd | Yn E | Yn M | Yg M | Yg E1 | 7 |
| 8 | Yn F | Yn E2 | Yn Wd | Yn W | Yg F | Yg F | Yg F | Yg W | Yn F | Yn E2 | Yn F | Yn E4 | Yg E | Yg M | Yn E | Yn Wd | Yn E | Yn M | Yg M | Yg E1 | Yg M | Yg E3 | Yn M | Yn F | 8 |
| 9 | Yg E | Yg M | Yg F | Yg W | Yn F | Yn E2 | Yn F | Yn E4 | Yg E | Yg M | Yg E | Yg Wd | Yn E | Yn M | Yg M | Yg E1 | Yg M | Yg E3 | Yn M | Yn F | Yn M | Yn W | Yg W | Yg F | 9 |
| 10 | Yn E | Yn M | Yn F | Yn E4 | Yg E | Yg M | Yg E | Yg Wd | Yn E | Yn M | Yn E | Yn Wd | Yg M | Yg E3 | Yn M | Yn F | Yn M | Yn W | Yg W | Yg F | Yg W | Yg W | Yn W | Yn E2 | 10 |
| 11 | Yg M | Yg E3 | Yg E | Yg Wd | Yn E | Yn M | Yn E | Yn Wd | Yg M | Yg E3 | Yg M | Yg E1 | Yn M | Yn W | Yg W | Yg F | Yg W | Yg W | Yn W | Yn E2 | Yn W | Yn E4 | Yg Wd | Yg M | 11 |
| 12 | Yn M | Yn W | Yn E | Yn Wd | Yg M | Yg E3 | Yg M | Yg E1 | Yn M | Yn W | Yn M | Yn F | Yg W | Yg W | Yn W | Yn E2 | Yn W | Yn E4 | Yg Wd | Yg M | Yg Wd | Yg Wd | Yn Wd | Yn M | 12 |
| 13 | Yg W | Yg W | Yg M | Yg E1 | Yn M | Yn W | Yn M | Yn F | Yg W | Yg W | Yg W | Yg F | Yn W | Yn E4 | Yg Wd | Yg M | Yg Wd | Yg Wd | Yn Wd | Yn M | Yn Wd | Yn Wd | Yg F | Yg E3 | 13 |
| 14 | Yn W | Yn E4 | Yn M | Yn F | Yg W | Yg W | Yg W | Yg F | Yn W | Yn E4 | Yn W | Yn E2 | Yg Wd | Yg Wd | Yn Wd | Yn M | Yn Wd | Yn Wd | Yg F | Yg E3 | Yg F | Yg E1 | Yn F | Yn W | 14 |
| 15 | Yg Wd | Yg Wd | Yg W | Yg F | Yn W | Yn E4 | Yn W | Yn E2 | Yg Wd | Yg Wd | Yg Wd | Yg M | Yn Wd | Yn Wd | Yg F | Yg E3 | Yg F | Yg E1 | Yn F | Yn W | Yn F | Yn F | Yg E | Yg W | 15 |
| 16 | Yn Wd | Yn Wd | Yn W | Yn E2 | Yg Wd | Yg Wd | Yg Wd | Yg M | Yn Wd | Yn Wd | Yn Wd | Yn M | Yg F | Yg E1 | Yn F | Yn W | Yn F | Yn F | Yg E | Yg W | Yg E | Yg F | Yn E | Yn E4 | 16 |
| 17 | Yg F | Yg E1 | Yg Wd | Yg M | Yn Wd | Yn Wd | Yn Wd | Yn M | Yg F | Yg E1 | Yg F | Yg E3 | Yn F | Yn F | Yg E | Yg W | Yg E | Yg F | Yn E | Yn E4 | Yn E | Yn E2 | Yg M | Yg Wd | 17 |
| 18 | Yn F | Yn F | Yn Wd | Yn M | Yg F | Yg E1 | Yg F | Yg E3 | Yn F | Yn F | Yn F | Yn W | Yg E | Yg F | Yn E | Yn E4 | Yn E | Yn E2 | Yg M | Yg Wd | Yg M | Yg M | Yn M | Yn Wd | 18 |
| 19 | Yg E | Yg F | Yg F | Yg E3 | Yn F | Yn F | Yn F | Yn W | Yg E | Yg F | Yg E | Yg W | Yn E | Yn E2 | Yg M | Yg Wd | Yg M | Yg M | Yn M | Yn Wd | Yn M | Yn M | Yg W | Yg E1 | 19 |
| 20 | Yn E | Yn E2 | Yn F | Yn W | Yg E | Yg F | Yg E | Yg W | Yn E | Yn E2 | Yn E | Yn E4 | Yg M | Yg M | Yn M | Yn Wd | Yn M | Yn M | Yg W | Yg E1 | Yg W | Yg E3 | Yn W | Yn F | 20 |
| 21 | Yg M | Yg M | Yg E | Yg W | Yn E | Yn E2 | Yn E | Yn E4 | Yg M | Yg M | Yg M | Yg Wd | Yn M | Yn M | Yg W | Yg E1 | Yg W | Yg E3 | Yn W | Yn F | Yn W | Yn W | Yg Wd | Yg F | 21 |
| 22 | Yn M | Yn M | Yn E | Yn E4 | Yg M | Yg M | Yg M | Yg Wd | Yn M | Yn M | Yn M | Yn Wd | Yg W | Yg E3 | Yn W | Yn F | Yn W | Yn W | Yg Wd | Yg F | Yg Wd | Yg W | Yn Wd | Yn E2 | 22 |
| 23 | Yg W | Yg E3 | Yg M | Yg Wd | Yn M | Yn M | Yn M | Yn Wd | Yg W | Yg E3 | Yg W | Yg E1 | Yn W | Yn W | Yg Wd | Yg F | Yg Wd | Yg W | Yn Wd | Yn E2 | Yn Wd | Yn E4 | Yg F | Yg M | 23 |
| 24 | Yn W | Yn W | Yn M | Yn Wd | Yg W | Yg E3 | Yg W | Yg E1 | Yn W | Yn W | Yn W | Yn F | Yg Wd | Yg W | Yn Wd | Yn E2 | Yn Wd | Yn E4 | Yg F | Yg M | Yg F | Yg Wd | Yn F | Yn M | 24 |
| 25 | Yg Wd | Yg W | Yg W | Yg E1 | Yn W | Yn W | Yn W | Yn F | Yg Wd | Yg W | Yg Wd | Yg F | Yn Wd | Yn E4 | Yg F | Yg M | Yg F | Yg Wd | Yn F | Yn M | Yn F | Yn Wd | Yg E | Yg E3 | 25 |
| 26 | Yn Wd | Yn E4 | Yn W | Yn F | Yg Wd | Yg W | Yg Wd | Yg F | Yn Wd | Yn E4 | Yn Wd | Yn E2 | Yg F | Yg Wd | Yn F | Yn M | Yn F | Yn Wd | Yg E | Yg E3 | Yg E | Yg E1 | Yn E | Yn W | 26 |
| 27 | Yg F | Yg Wd | Yg Wd | Yg F | Yn Wd | Yn E4 | Yn Wd | Yn E2 | Yg F | Yg Wd | Yg F | Yg M | Yn F | Yn Wd | Yg E | Yg E3 | Yg E | Yg E1 | Yn E | Yn W | Yn E | Yn F | Yg M | Yg W | 27 |
| 28 | Yn F | Yn Wd | Yn Wd | Yn E2 | Yg F | Yg Wd | Yg F | Yg M | Yn F | Yn Wd | Yn F | Yn M | Yg E | Yg E1 | Yn E | Yn W | Yn E | Yn F | Yg M | Yg W | Yg M | Yg F | Yn M | Yn E4 | 28 |
| 29 | | | Yg F | Yg M | Yn F | Yn Wd | Yn F | Yn M | Yg E | Yg E1 | Yg E | Yg E3 | Yn E | Yn F | Yg M | Yg W | Yg M | Yg F | Yn M | Yn E4 | Yn M | Yn E2 | Yg W | Yg Wd | 29 |
| 30 | | | Yn F | Yn M | Yg E | Yg E1 | Yg E | Yg E3 | Yn E | Yn F | Yn E | Yn W | Yg M | Yg F | Yn M | Yn E4 | Yn M | Yn E2 | Yg W | Yg Wd | Yg W | Yg M | Yn W | Yn Wd | 30 |
| 31 | | | Yg E | Yg E3 | | | Yn E | Yn W | | | Yg M | Yg W | Yn M | Yn E2 | | | Yg W | Yg M | | | Yn W | Yn M | Yg Wd | Yg E1 | 31 |
| 1 | Yg E | Yg E1 | Yn E | Yn W | Yn E | Yn F | Yg M | Yg W | Yg M | Yg F | Yn M | Yn E4 | Yg W | Yg M | Yg W | Yg Wd | Yn W | Yn M | Yn W | Yn Wd | Yg Wd | Yg E3 | Yn Wd | Yn F | 1 |
| 2 | Yn E | Yn F | Yg M | Yg W | Yg M | Yg F | Yn M | Yn E4 | Yn M | Yn E2 | Yg W | Yg Wd | Yn W | Yn M | Yn W | Yn Wd | Yg Wd | Yg E3 | Yg Wd | Yg E1 | Yn Wd | Yn W | Yg F | Yg F | 2 |
| 3 | Yg M | Yg F | Yn M | Yn E4 | Yn M | Yn E2 | Yg W | Yg Wd | Yg W | Yg M | Yn W | Yn Wd | Yg Wd | Yg E3 | Yg Wd | Yg E1 | Yn Wd | Yn W | Yn Wd | Yn F | Yg F | Yg W | Yn F | Yn E2 | 3 |
| 4 | Yn M | Yn E2 | Yg W | Yg Wd | Yg W | Yg M | Yn W | Yn Wd | Yn W | Yn M | Yg Wd | Yg E1 | Yn Wd | Yn W | Yn Wd | Yn F | Yg F | Yg W | Yg F | Yg F | Yn F | Yn E4 | | | 4 |
| 5 | Yg W | Yg M | | | Yn W | Yn M | Yg Wd | Yg E1 | Yg Wd | Yg E3 | Yn Wd | Yn F | Yg F | Yg W | Yg F | Yg F | Yn F | Yn E4 | Yn F | Yn E2 | Yg E | Yg Wd | | | 5 |
| 6 | | | | | | | | | Yn Wd | Yn W | Yg F | Yg F | Yn F | Yn E4 | Yn F | Yn E2 | Yg E | Yg Wd | Yg E | Yg M | | | | | 6 |
| 7 | | | | | | | | | | | Yn F | Yn E2 | Yg E | Yg Wd | Yg E | Yg M | | | | | | | | | 7 |
| 8 | | | | | | | | | | | | | | | | | | | | | | | | | 8 |

# YEAR OF THE GOAT

| | H | E | H | E | H | E | H | E | H | E | H | E | H | E | H | E | H | E | H | E | H | E | H | E | |
|---|---|---|---|---|---|---|---|---|---|---|---|---|---|---|---|---|---|---|---|---|---|---|---|---|---|
| YEAR | YEAR Yn W | Yn E2 | 2003 | | | | | | | | | | | | | | | | | | | | 2004 | | |
| MONTH | 4 Feb - 5 Mar | | 6 Mar - 4 Apr | | 5 Apr - 5 May | | 6 May - 5 June | | 6 June - 6 Jul | | 7 Jul - 7 Aug | | 8 Aug - 7 Sep | | 8 Sep - 8 Oct | | 9 Oct - 7 Nov | | 8 Nov - 6 Dec | | 7 Dec - 5 Jan | | 6 Jan - 3 Feb | | |
| | Yg Wd | Yg Wd | Yn Wd | Yn Wd | Yg F | Yg E1 | Yn F | Yn F | Yg E | Yg F | Yn E | Yn E2 | Yg M | Yg M | Yn M | Yn M | Yg W | Yg E3 | Yn W | Yn W | Yg Wd | Yg W | Yn Wd | Yn E4 | |
| Starting time | 1st day | Mid-pt | 1st day | Mid-pt | 1st day | Mid-pt | 1st day | Mid-pt | 1st day | Mid-pt | 1st day | Mid-pt | 1st day | Mid-pt | 1st day | Mid-pt | 1st day | Mid-pt | 1st day | Mid-pt | 1st day | Mid-pt | 1st day | Mid-pt | |
| Date | 4 | 19 | 6 | 21 | 5 | 20 | 6 | 21 | 6 | 22 | 7 | 23 | 8 | 23 | 8 | 23 | 9 | 24 | 8 | 23 | 7 | 22 | 6 | 21 | |
| Hour | 1357 | 0950 | 0807 | 0913 | 1310 | 2022 | 0644 | 1944 | 1106 | 0350 | 2129 | 1443 | 0712 | 2139 | 0956 | 1903 | 0120 | 0409 | 0415 | 0131 | 2055 | 1444 | 0804 | 0122 | |
| DATE 4 | Yg E | Yg M | | | | | | | | | | | | | | | | | | | | | | | 4 |
| 5 | Yn E | Yn M | | | Yg E | Yg M | | | | | | | | | | | | | | | | | | | 5 |
| 6 | Yg M | Yg E3 | Yg E | Yg Wd | Yn E | Yn M | Yn E | Yn Wd | Yg M | Yg E3 | | | | | | | | | | | | | Yg Wd | Yg M | 6 |
| 7 | Yn M | Yn W | Yn E | Yn Wd | Yg M | Yg E3 | Yg M | Yg E1 | Yn M | Yn W | Yn M | Yn F | | | | | | | | | Yg Wd | Yg Wd | Yn Wd | Yn M | 7 |
| 8 | Yg W | Yg W | Yg M | Yg E1 | Yn M | Yn W | Yn M | Yn F | Yg W | Yg W | Yg W | Yg F | Yn W | Yn E4 | Yg Wd | Yg M | | | Yn Wd | Yn M | Yn Wd | Yn Wd | Yg F | Yg E3 | 8 |
| 9 | Yn W | Yn E4 | Yn M | Yn F | Yg W | Yg W | Yg W | Yg F | Yn W | Yn E4 | Yn W | Yn E2 | Yg Wd | Yg Wd | Yn Wd | Yn M | Yn Wd | Yn Wd | Yg F | Yg E3 | Yg F | Yg E1 | Yn F | Yn W | 9 |
| 10 | Yg Wd | Yg Wd | Yg W | Yg F | Yn W | Yn E4 | Yn W | Yn E2 | Yg Wd | Yg Wd | Yg Wd | Yg M | Yn Wd | Yn Wd | Yg F | Yg E3 | Yg F | Yg E1 | Yn F | Yn W | Yn F | Yn F | Yg E | Yg W | 10 |
| 11 | Yn Wd | Yn Wd | Yn W | Yn E2 | Yg Wd | Yg Wd | Yg Wd | Yg M | Yn Wd | Yn Wd | Yn Wd | Yn M | Yg F | Yg E1 | Yn F | Yn W | Yn F | Yn F | Yg E | Yg W | Yg E | Yg F | Yn E | Yn E4 | 11 |
| 12 | Yg F | Yg E1 | Yg Wd | Yg M | Yn Wd | Yn Wd | Yn Wd | Yn M | Yg F | Yg E1 | Yg F | Yg E3 | Yn F | Yn F | Yg E | Yg W | Yg E | Yg F | Yn E | Yn E4 | Yn E | Yn E2 | Yg M | Yg Wd | 12 |
| 13 | Yn F | Yn F | Yn Wd | Yn M | Yg F | Yg E1 | Yg F | Yg E3 | Yn F | Yn F | Yn F | Yn W | Yg E | Yg F | Yn E | Yn E4 | Yn E | Yn E2 | Yg M | Yg Wd | Yg M | Yg M | Yn M | Yn Wd | 13 |
| 14 | Yg E | Yg F | Yg F | Yg E3 | Yn F | Yn F | Yn F | Yn W | Yg E | Yg F | Yg E | Yg W | Yn E | Yn E2 | Yg M | Yg Wd | Yg M | Yg M | Yn M | Yn Wd | Yn M | Yn M | Yg W | Yg E1 | 14 |
| 15 | Yn E | Yn E2 | Yn F | Yn W | Yg E | Yg F | Yg E | Yg W | Yn E | Yn E2 | Yn E | Yn E4 | Yg M | Yg M | Yn M | Yn Wd | Yn M | Yn M | Yg W | Yg E1 | Yg W | Yg E3 | Yn W | Yn F | 15 |
| 16 | Yg M | Yg M | Yg E | Yg W | Yn E | Yn E2 | Yn E | Yn E4 | Yg M | Yg M | Yg M | Yg Wd | Yn M | Yn M | Yg W | Yg E1 | Yg W | Yg E3 | Yn W | Yn F | Yn W | Yn W | Yg Wd | Yg F | 16 |
| 17 | Yn M | Yn M | Yn E | Yn E4 | Yg M | Yg M | Yg M | Yg Wd | Yn M | Yn M | Yn M | Yn Wd | Yg W | Yg E3 | Yn W | Yn F | Yn W | Yn W | Yg Wd | Yg F | Yg Wd | Yg W | Yn Wd | Yn E2 | 17 |
| 18 | Yg W | Yg E3 | Yg M | Yg Wd | Yn M | Yn M | Yn M | Yn Wd | Yg W | Yg E3 | Yg W | Yg E1 | Yn W | Yn W | Yg Wd | Yg F | Yg Wd | Yg W | Yn Wd | Yn E2 | Yn Wd | Yn E4 | Yg F | Yg M | 18 |
| 19 | Yn W | Yn W | Yn M | Yn Wd | Yg W | Yg E3 | Yg W | Yg E1 | Yn W | Yn W | Yn W | Yn F | Yg Wd | Yg W | Yn Wd | Yn E2 | Yn Wd | Yn E4 | Yg F | Yg M | Yg F | Yg Wd | Yn F | Yn M | 19 |
| 20 | Yg Wd | Yg W | Yg W | Yg E1 | Yn W | Yn W | Yn W | Yn F | Yg Wd | Yg W | Yg Wd | Yg F | Yn Wd | Yn E4 | Yg F | Yg M | Yg F | Yg Wd | Yn F | Yn M | Yn F | Yn Wd | Yg E | Yg E3 | 20 |
| 21 | Yn Wd | Yn E4 | Yn W | Yn F | Yg Wd | Yg W | Yg Wd | Yg F | Yn Wd | Yn E4 | Yn Wd | Yn E2 | Yg F | Yg Wd | Yn F | Yn M | Yn F | Yn Wd | Yg E | Yg E3 | Yg E | Yg E1 | Yn E | Yn W | 21 |
| 22 | Yg F | Yg Wd | Yg Wd | Yg F | Yn Wd | Yn E4 | Yn Wd | Yn E2 | Yg F | Yg Wd | Yg F | Yg M | Yn F | Yn Wd | Yg E | Yg E3 | Yg E | Yg E1 | Yn E | Yn W | Yn E | Yn F | Yg M | Yg W | 22 |
| 23 | Yn F | Yn Wd | Yn Wd | Yn E2 | Yg F | Yg Wd | Yg F | Yg M | Yn F | Yn Wd | Yn F | Yn M | Yg E | Yg E1 | Yn E | Yn W | Yn E | Yn F | Yg M | Yg W | Yg M | Yg F | Yn M | Yn E4 | 23 |
| 24 | Yg E | Yg E1 | Yg F | Yg M | Yn F | Yn Wd | Yn F | Yn M | Yg E | Yg E1 | Yg E | Yg E3 | Yn E | Yn F | Yg M | Yg W | Yg M | Yg F | Yn M | Yn E4 | Yn M | Yn E2 | Yg W | Yg Wd | 24 |
| 25 | Yn E | Yn F | Yn F | Yn M | Yg E | Yg E1 | Yg E | Yg E3 | Yn E | Yn F | Yn E | Yn W | Yg M | Yg F | Yn M | Yn E4 | Yn M | Yn E2 | Yg W | Yg Wd | Yg W | Yg M | Yn W | Yn Wd | 25 |
| 26 | Yg M | Yg F | Yg E | Yg E3 | Yn E | Yn F | Yn E | Yn W | Yg M | Yg F | Yg M | Yg W | Yn M | Yn E2 | Yg W | Yg Wd | Yg W | Yg M | Yn W | Yn Wd | Yn W | Yn M | Yg Wd | Yg E1 | 26 |
| 27 | Yn M | Yn E2 | Yn E | Yn W | Yg M | Yg F | Yg M | Yg W | Yn M | Yn E2 | Yn M | Yn E4 | Yg W | Yg M | Yn W | Yn Wd | Yn W | Yn M | Yg Wd | Yg E1 | Yg Wd | Yg E3 | Yn Wd | Yn F | 27 |
| 28 | Yg W | Yg M | Yg M | Yg W | Yn M | Yn E2 | Yn M | Yn E4 | Yg W | Yg M | Yg W | Yg Wd | Yn W | Yn M | Yg Wd | Yg E1 | Yg Wd | Yg E3 | Yn Wd | Yn F | Yn Wd | Yn W | Yg F | Yg F | 28 |
| 29 | | | Yn M | Yn E4 | Yg W | Yg M | Yg W | Yg Wd | Yn W | Yn M | Yn W | Yn Wd | Yg Wd | Yg E3 | Yn Wd | Yn F | Yn Wd | Yn W | Yg F | Yg F | Yg F | Yg W | Yn F | Yn E2 | 29 |
| 30 | | | Yg W | Yg Wd | Yn W | Yn M | Yn W | Yn Wd | Yg Wd | Yg E3 | Yg Wd | Yg E1 | Yn Wd | Yn W | Yg F | Yg F | Yg F | Yg W | Yn F | Yn E2 | Yn F | Yn E4 | Yg E | Yg M | 30 |
| 31 | | | Yn W | Yn Wd | | | Yg Wd | Yg E1 | | | Yn Wd | Yn F | Yg F | Yg W | | | Yn F | Yn E4 | | | Yg E | Yg Wd | Yn E | Yn M | 31 |
| 1 | Yn W | Yn M | Yg Wd | Yg E1 | Yg Wd | Yg E3 | Yn Wd | Yn F | Yn Wd | Yn W | Yg F | Yg F | Yn F | Yn E4 | Yn F | Yn E2 | Yg E | Yg Wd | Yg E | Yg M | Yn E | Yn Wd | Yg M | Yg E3 | 1 |
| 2 | Yg Wd | Yg E3 | Yn Wd | Yn F | Yn Wd | Yn W | Yg F | Yg F | Yg F | Yg W | Yn F | Yn E2 | Yg E | Yg Wd | Yg E | Yg M | Yn E | Yn Wd | Yn E | Yn M | Yg M | Yg E1 | Yn M | Yn W | 2 |
| 3 | Yn Wd | Yn W | Yg F | Yg F | Yg F | Yg W | Yn F | Yn E2 | Yn F | Yn E4 | Yg E | Yg M | Yn E | Yn Wd | Yn E | Yn M | Yg M | Yg E1 | Yg M | Yg E3 | Yn M | Yn F | Yg W | Yg W | 3 |
| 4 | Yg F | Yg W | Yn F | Yn E2 | Yn F | Yn E4 | Yg E | Yg M | Yg E | Yg Wd | Yn E | Yn M | Yg M | Yg E1 | Yg M | Yg E3 | Yn M | Yn F | Yn M | Yn W | Yg W | Yg F | | | 4 |
| 5 | Yn F | Yn E4 | | | Yg E | Yg Wd | Yn E | Yn M | Yn E | Yn Wd | Yg M | Yg E3 | Yn M | Yn F | Yn M | Yn W | Yg W | Yg F | Yg W | Yg W | Yn W | Yn E2 | | | 5 |
| 6 | | | | | | | | | Yg M | Yg E1 | Yn M | Yn W | Yg W | Yg F | Yg W | Yg W | Yn W | Yn E2 | Yn W | Yn E4 | | | | | 6 |
| 7 | | | | | | | | | | | Yg W | Yg W | Yn W | Yn E2 | Yn W | Yn E4 | Yg Wd | Yg M | | | | | | | 7 |
| 8 | | | | | | | | | | | | | | | Yg Wd | Yg Wd | | | | | | | | | 8 |

# YEAR OF THE MONKEY

| | H | E | H | E | H | E | H | E | H | E | H | E | H | E | H | E | H | E | H | E | H | E | H | E | |
|---|---|---|---|---|---|---|---|---|---|---|---|---|---|---|---|---|---|---|---|---|---|---|---|---|---|
| YEAR | YEAR Yg Wd | Yg M | 2004 | | | | | | | | | | | | | | | | | | | | 2005 | | |
| MONTH | 4 Feb - 4 Mar | | 5 Mar - 3 Apr | | 4 Apr - 4 May | | 5 May - 4 June | | 5 June - 6 Jul | | 7 Jul - 6 Aug | | 7 Aug - 6 Sep | | 7 Sep - 7 Oct | | 8 Oct - 6 Nov | | 7 Nov - 6 Dec | | 7 Dec - 4 Jan | | 5 Jan - 3 Feb | | |
| | Yg F | Yg Wd | Yn F | Yn Wd | Yg E | Yg E1 | Yn E | Yn F | Yg M | Yg F | Yn M | Yn E2 | Yg W | Yg M | Yn W | Yn M | Yg Wd | Yg E3 | Yn Wd | Yn W | Yg F | Yg W | Yn F | Yn E4 | |
| Starting time | 1st day | Mid-pt | 1st day | Mid-pt | 1st day | Mid-pt | 1st day | Mid-pt | 1st day | Mid-pt | 1st day | Mid-pt | 1st day | Mid-pt | 1st day | Mid-pt | 1st day | Mid-pt | 1st day | Mid-pt | 1st day | Mid-pt | 1st day | Mid-pt | |
| Date | 4 | 19 | 5 | 20 | 4 | 20 | 5 | 21 | 5 | 21 | 7 | 22 | 7 | 23 | 7 | 23 | 8 | 23 | 7 | 22 | 7 | 21 | 5 | 20 | |
| Hour | 1946 | 1539 | 1356 | 1452 | 1844 | 0211 | 1233 | 0133 | 1655 | 0939 | 0318 | 2032 | 1259 | 0328 | 1544 | 0052 | 0708 | 0958 | 1003 | 0720 | 0243 | 2033 | 1352 | 0709 | |
| DATE 4 | Yn W | Yn E4 | | | Yn W | Yn E4 | | | | | | | | | | | | | | | | | | | 4 |
| 5 | Yg Wd | Yg Wd | Yn W | Yn E2 | Yg Wd | Yg Wd | Yg Wd | Yg M | Yn Wd | Yn Wd | | | | | | | | | | | | | Yn E | Yn E4 | 5 |
| 6 | Yn Wd | Yn Wd | Yg Wd | Yg M | Yn Wd | Yn Wd | Yn Wd | Yn M | Yg F | Yg E1 | | | | | | | | | | | | | Yg M | Yg Wd | 6 |
| 7 | Yg F | Yg E1 | Yn Wd | Yn M | Yg F | Yg E1 | Yg F | Yg E3 | Yn F | Yn F | Yn F | Yn W | Yg E | Yg F | Yn E | Yn E4 | | | Yg M | Yg Wd | Yg M | Yg M | Yn M | Yn Wd | 7 |
| 8 | Yn F | Yn F | Yg F | Yg E3 | Yn F | Yn F | Yn F | Yn W | Yg E | Yg F | Yg E | Yg W | Yn E | Yn E2 | Yg M | Yg Wd | Yg M | Yg M | Yn M | Yn Wd | Yn M | Yn M | Yg W | Yg E1 | 8 |
| 9 | Yg E | Yg F | Yn F | Yn W | Yg E | Yg F | Yg E | Yg W | Yn E | Yn E2 | Yn E | Yn E4 | Yg M | Yg M | Yn M | Yn Wd | Yn M | Yn M | Yg W | Yg E1 | Yg W | Yg E3 | Yn W | Yn F | 9 |
| 10 | Yn E | Yn E2 | Yg E | Yg W | Yn E | Yn E2 | Yn E | Yn E4 | Yg M | Yg M | Yg M | Yg Wd | Yn M | Yn M | Yg W | Yg E1 | Yg W | Yg E3 | Yn W | Yn F | Yn W | Yn W | Yg Wd | Yg F | 10 |
| 11 | Yg M | Yg M | Yn E | Yn E4 | Yg M | Yg M | Yg M | Yg Wd | Yn M | Yn M | Yn M | Yn Wd | Yg W | Yg E3 | Yn W | Yn F | Yn W | Yn W | Yg Wd | Yg F | Yg Wd | Yg W | Yn Wd | Yn E2 | 11 |
| 12 | Yn M | Yn M | Yg M | Yg Wd | Yn M | Yn M | Yn M | Yn Wd | Yg W | Yg E3 | Yg W | Yg E1 | Yn W | Yn W | Yg Wd | Yg F | Yg Wd | Yg W | Yn Wd | Yn E2 | Yn Wd | Yn E4 | Yg F | Yg M | 12 |
| 13 | Yg W | Yg E3 | Yn M | Yn Wd | Yg W | Yg E3 | Yg W | Yg E1 | Yn W | Yn W | Yn W | Yn F | Yg Wd | Yg W | Yn Wd | Yn E2 | Yn Wd | Yn E4 | Yg F | Yg M | Yg F | Yg Wd | Yn F | Yn M | 13 |
| 14 | Yn W | Yn W | Yg W | Yg E1 | Yn W | Yn W | Yn W | Yn F | Yg Wd | Yg W | Yg Wd | Yg F | Yn Wd | Yn E4 | Yg F | Yg M | Yg F | Yg Wd | Yn F | Yn M | Yn F | Yn Wd | Yg E | Yg E3 | 14 |
| 15 | Yg Wd | Yg W | Yn W | Yn F | Yg Wd | Yg W | Yg Wd | Yg F | Yn Wd | Yn E4 | Yn Wd | Yn E2 | Yg F | Yg Wd | Yn F | Yn M | Yn F | Yn Wd | Yg E | Yg E3 | Yg E | Yg E1 | Yn E | Yn W | 15 |
| 16 | Yn Wd | Yn E4 | Yg Wd | Yg F | Yn Wd | Yn E4 | Yn Wd | Yn E2 | Yg F | Yg Wd | Yg F | Yg M | Yn F | Yn Wd | Yg E | Yg E3 | Yg E | Yg E1 | Yn E | Yn W | Yn E | Yn F | Yg M | Yg W | 16 |
| 17 | Yg F | Yg Wd | Yn Wd | Yn E2 | Yg F | Yg Wd | Yg F | Yg M | Yn F | Yn Wd | Yn F | Yn M | Yg E | Yg E1 | Yn E | Yn W | Yn E | Yn F | Yg M | Yg W | Yg M | Yg F | Yn M | Yn E4 | 17 |
| 18 | Yn F | Yn Wd | Yg F | Yg M | Yn F | Yn Wd | Yn F | Yn M | Yg E | Yg E1 | Yg E | Yg E3 | Yn E | Yn F | Yg M | Yg W | Yg M | Yg F | Yn M | Yn E4 | Yn M | Yn E2 | Yg W | Yg Wd | 18 |
| 19 | Yg E | Yg E1 | Yn F | Yn M | Yg E | Yg E1 | Yg E | Yg E3 | Yn E | Yn F | Yn E | Yn W | Yg M | Yg F | Yn M | Yn E4 | Yn M | Yn E2 | Yg W | Yg Wd | Yg W | Yg M | Yn W | Yn Wd | 19 |
| 20 | Yn E | Yn F | Yg E | Yg E3 | Yn E | Yn F | Yn E | Yn W | Yg M | Yg F | Yg M | Yg W | Yn M | Yn E2 | Yg W | Yg Wd | Yg W | Yg M | Yn W | Yn Wd | Yn W | Yn M | Yg Wd | Yg E1 | 20 |
| 21 | Yg M | Yg F | Yn E | Yn W | Yg M | Yg F | Yg M | Yg W | Yn M | Yn E2 | Yn M | Yn E4 | Yg W | Yg M | Yn W | Yn Wd | Yn W | Yn M | Yg Wd | Yg E1 | Yg Wd | Yg E3 | Yn Wd | Yn F | 21 |
| 22 | Yn M | Yn E2 | Yg M | Yg W | Yn M | Yn E2 | Yn M | Yn E4 | Yg W | Yg M | Yg W | Yg Wd | Yn W | Yn M | Yg Wd | Yg E1 | Yg Wd | Yg E3 | Yn Wd | Yn F | Yn Wd | Yn W | Yg F | Yg F | 22 |
| 23 | Yg W | Yg M | Yn M | Yn E4 | Yg W | Yg M | Yg W | Yg Wd | Yn W | Yn M | Yn W | Yn Wd | Yg Wd | Yg E3 | Yn Wd | Yn F | Yn Wd | Yn W | Yg F | Yg F | Yg F | Yg W | Yn F | Yn E2 | 23 |
| 24 | Yn W | Yn M | Yg W | Yg Wd | Yn W | Yn M | Yn W | Yn Wd | Yg Wd | Yg E3 | Yg Wd | Yg E1 | Yn Wd | Yn W | Yg F | Yg F | Yg F | Yg W | Yn F | Yn E2 | Yn F | Yn E4 | Yg E | Yg M | 24 |
| 25 | Yg Wd | Yg E3 | Yn W | Yn Wd | Yg Wd | Yg E3 | Yg Wd | Yg E1 | Yn Wd | Yn W | Yn Wd | Yn F | Yg F | Yg W | Yn F | Yn E2 | Yn F | Yn E4 | Yg E | Yg M | Yg E | Yg Wd | Yn E | Yn M | 25 |
| 26 | Yn Wd | Yn W | Yg Wd | Yg E1 | Yn Wd | Yn W | Yn Wd | Yn F | Yg F | Yg W | Yg F | Yg F | Yn F | Yn E4 | Yg E | Yg M | Yg E | Yg Wd | Yn E | Yn M | Yn E | Yn Wd | Yg M | Yg E3 | 26 |
| 27 | Yg F | Yg W | Yn Wd | Yn F | Yg F | Yg W | Yg F | Yg F | Yn F | Yn E4 | Yn F | Yn E2 | Yg E | Yg Wd | Yn E | Yn M | Yn E | Yn Wd | Yg M | Yg E3 | Yg M | Yg E1 | Yn M | Yn W | 27 |
| 28 | Yn F | Yn E4 | Yg F | Yg F | Yn F | Yn E4 | Yn F | Yn E2 | Yg E | Yg Wd | Yg E | Yg M | Yn E | Yn Wd | Yg M | Yg E3 | Yg M | Yg E1 | Yn M | Yn W | Yn M | Yn F | Yg W | Yg W | 28 |
| 29 | Yg E | Yg Wd | Yn F | Yn E2 | Yg E | Yg Wd | Yg E | Yg M | Yn E | Yn Wd | Yn E | Yn M | Yg M | Yg E1 | Yn M | Yn W | Yn M | Yn F | Yg W | Yg W | Yg W | Yg F | Yn W | Yn E4 | 29 |
| 30 | | | Yg E | Yg M | Yn E | Yn Wd | Yn E | Yn M | Yg M | Yg E1 | Yg M | Yg E3 | Yn M | Yn F | Yg W | Yg W | Yg W | Yg F | Yn W | Yn E4 | Yn W | Yn E2 | Yg Wd | Yg Wd | 30 |
| 31 | | | Yn E | Yn M | | | Yg M | Yg E3 | | | Yn M | Yn W | Yg W | Yg F | | | Yn W | Yn E2 | | | Yg Wd | Yg M | Yn Wd | Yn Wd | 31 |
| 1 | Yn E | Yn Wd | Yg M | Yg E3 | Yg M | Yg E1 | Yn M | Yn W | Yn M | Yn F | Yg W | Yg W | Yn W | Yn E2 | Yn W | Yn E4 | Yg Wd | Yg M | Yg Wd | Yg Wd | Yn Wd | Yn M | Yg F | Yg E1 | 1 |
| 2 | Yg M | Yg E1 | Yn M | Yn W | Yn M | Yn F | Yg W | Yg W | Yg W | Yg F | Yn W | Yn E4 | Yg Wd | Yg M | Yg Wd | Yg Wd | Yn Wd | Yn M | Yn Wd | Yn Wd | Yg F | Yg E3 | Yn F | Yn F | 2 |
| 3 | Yn M | Yn F | Yg W | Yg W | Yg W | Yg F | Yn W | Yn E4 | Yn W | Yn E2 | Yg Wd | Yg Wd | Yn Wd | Yn M | Yn Wd | Yn Wd | Yg F | Yg E3 | Yg F | Yg E1 | Yn F | Yn W | Yg E | Yg F | 3 |
| 4 | Yg W | Yg F | | | Yn W | Yn E2 | Yg Wd | Yg Wd | Yg Wd | Yg M | Yn Wd | Yn Wd | Yg F | Yg E3 | Yg F | Yg E1 | Yn F | Yn W | Yn F | Yn F | Yg E | Yg W | | | 4 |
| 5 | | | | | | | | | Yn Wd | Yn M | Yg F | Yg E1 | Yn F | Yn W | Yn F | Yn F | Yg E | Yg W | Yg E | Yg F | | | | | 5 |
| 6 | | | | | | | | | Yg F | Yg E3 | Yn F | Yn F | Yg E | Yg W | Yg E | Yg F | Yn E | Yn E4 | Yn E | Yn E2 | | | | | 6 |
| 7 | | | | | | | | | | | | | | | Yn E | Yn E2 | | | | | | | | | 7 |
| 8 | | | | | | | | | | | | | | | | | | | | | | | | | 8 |

# YEAR OF THE ROOSTER

| | H | E | H | E | H | E | H | E | H | E | H | E | H | E | H | E | H | E | H | E | H | E | H | E | |
|---|---|---|---|---|---|---|---|---|---|---|---|---|---|---|---|---|---|---|---|---|---|---|---|---|---|
| YEAR | YEAR Yn Wd | Yn M | 2005 | | | | | | | | | | | | | | | | | | | | 2006 | | |
| MONTH | 4 Feb - 4 Mar | | 5 Mar - 4 Apr | | 5 Apr - 4 May | | 5 May - 4 June | | 5 June - 6 Jul | | 7 Jul - 6 Aug | | 7 Aug - 6 Sep | | 7 Sep - 7 Oct | | 8 Oct - 6 Nov | | 7 Nov - 6 Dec | | 7 Dec - 4 Jan | | 5 Jan - 3 Feb | | |
| | Yg E | Yg Wd | Yn E | Yn Wd | Yg M | Yg E1 | Yn M | Yn F | Yg W | Yg F | Yn W | Yn E2 | Yg Wd | Yg M | Yn Wd | Yn M | Yg F | Yg E3 | Yn F | Yn W | Yg E | Yg W | Yn E | Yn E4 | |
| Starting time | 1st day | Mid-pt | 1st day | Mid-pt | 1st day | Mid-pt | 1st day | Mid-pt | 1st day | Mid-pt | 1st day | Mid-pt | 1st day | Mid-pt | 1st day | Mid-pt | 1st day | Mid-pt | 1st day | Mid-pt | 1st day | Mid-pt | 1st day | Mid-pt | |
| Date | 4 | 18 | 5 | 20 | 5 | 20 | 5 | 21 | 5 | 21 | 7 | 23 | 7 | 23 | 7 | 23 | 8 | 23 | 7 | 22 | 7 | 22 | 5 | 20 | |
| Hour | 0134 | 2128 | 1945 | 2041 | 0048 | 0800 | 1823 | 0722 | 2245 | 1517 | 0908 | 0221 | 1851 | 0917 | 2135 | 0641 | 1259 | 1547 | 1554 | 1309 | 0834 | 0222 | 0943 | 1300 | |
| DATE 4 | Yn E | Yn E2 | | | | | | | | | | | | | | | | | | | | | | | 4 |
| 5 | Yg M | Yg M | Yg E | Yg W | Yn E | Yn E2 | Yn E | Yn E4 | Yg M | Yg M | | | | | | | | | | | | | Yg Wd | Yg F | 5 |
| 6 | Yn M | Yn M | Yn E | Yn E4 | Yg M | Yg M | Yg M | Yg Wd | Yn M | Yn M | | | | | | | | | | | | | Yn Wd | Yn E2 | 6 |
| 7 | Yg W | Yg E3 | Yg M | Yg Wd | Yn M | Yn M | Yn M | Yn Wd | Yg W | Yg E3 | Yg W | Yg E1 | Yn W | Yn W | Yg Wd | Yg F | | | Yn Wd | Yn E2 | Yn Wd | Yn E4 | Yg F | Yg M | 7 |
| 8 | Yn W | Yn W | Yn M | Yn Wd | Yg W | Yg E3 | Yg W | Yg E1 | Yn W | Yn W | Yn W | Yn F | Yg Wd | Yg W | Yn Wd | Yn E2 | Yn Wd | Yn E4 | Yg F | Yg M | Yg F | Yg Wd | Yn F | Yn M | 8 |
| 9 | Yg Wd | Yg W | Yg W | Yg E1 | Yn W | Yn W | Yn W | Yn F | Yg Wd | Yg W | Yg Wd | Yg F | Yn Wd | Yn E4 | Yg F | Yg M | Yg F | Yg Wd | Yn F | Yn M | Yn F | Yn Wd | Yg E | Yg E3 | 9 |
| 10 | Yn Wd | Yn E4 | Yn W | Yn F | Yg Wd | Yg W | Yg Wd | Yg F | Yn Wd | Yn E4 | Yn Wd | Yn E2 | Yg F | Yg Wd | Yn F | Yn M | Yn F | Yn Wd | Yg E | Yg E3 | Yg E | Yg E1 | Yn E | Yn W | 10 |
| 11 | Yg F | Yg Wd | Yg Wd | Yg F | Yn Wd | Yn E4 | Yn Wd | Yn E2 | Yg F | Yg Wd | Yg F | Yg M | Yn F | Yn Wd | Yg E | Yg E3 | Yg E | Yg E1 | Yn E | Yn W | Yn E | Yn F | Yg M | Yg W | 11 |
| 12 | Yn F | Yn Wd | Yn Wd | Yn E2 | Yg F | Yg Wd | Yg F | Yg M | Yn F | Yn Wd | Yn F | Yn M | Yg E | Yg E1 | Yn E | Yn W | Yn E | Yn F | Yg M | Yg W | Yg M | Yg F | Yn M | Yn E4 | 12 |
| 13 | Yg E | Yg E1 | Yg F | Yg M | Yn F | Yn Wd | Yn F | Yn M | Yg E | Yg E1 | Yg E | Yg E3 | Yn E | Yn F | Yg M | Yg W | Yg M | Yg F | Yn M | Yn E4 | Yn M | Yn E2 | Yg W | Yg Wd | 13 |
| 14 | Yn E | Yn F | Yn F | Yn M | Yg E | Yg E1 | Yg E | Yg E3 | Yn E | Yn F | Yn E | Yn W | Yg M | Yg F | Yn M | Yn E4 | Yn M | Yn E2 | Yg W | Yg Wd | Yg W | Yg M | Yn W | Yn Wd | 14 |
| 15 | Yg M | Yg F | Yg E | Yg E3 | Yn E | Yn F | Yn E | Yn W | Yg M | Yg F | Yg M | Yg W | Yn M | Yn E2 | Yg W | Yg Wd | Yg W | Yg M | Yn W | Yn Wd | Yn W | Yn M | Yg Wd | Yg E1 | 15 |
| 16 | Yn M | Yn E2 | Yn E | Yn W | Yg M | Yg F | Yg M | Yg W | Yn M | Yn E2 | Yn M | Yn E4 | Yg W | Yg M | Yn W | Yn Wd | Yn W | Yn M | Yg Wd | Yg E1 | Yg Wd | Yg E3 | Yn Wd | Yn F | 16 |
| 17 | Yg W | Yg M | Yg M | Yg W | Yn M | Yn E2 | Yn M | Yn E4 | Yg W | Yg M | Yg W | Yg Wd | Yn W | Yn M | Yg Wd | Yg E1 | Yg Wd | Yg E3 | Yn Wd | Yn F | Yn Wd | Yn W | Yg F | Yg F | 17 |
| 18 | Yn W | Yn M | Yn M | Yn E4 | Yg W | Yg M | Yg W | Yg Wd | Yn W | Yn M | Yn W | Yn Wd | Yg Wd | Yg E3 | Yn Wd | Yn F | Yn Wd | Yn W | Yg F | Yg F | Yg F | Yg W | Yn F | Yn E2 | 18 |
| 19 | Yg Wd | Yg E3 | Yg W | Yg Wd | Yn W | Yn M | Yn W | Yn Wd | Yg Wd | Yg E3 | Yg Wd | Yg E1 | Yn Wd | Yn W | Yg F | Yg F | Yg F | Yg W | Yn F | Yn E2 | Yn F | Yn E4 | Yg E | Yg M | 19 |
| 20 | Yn Wd | Yn W | Yn W | Yn Wd | Yg Wd | Yg E3 | Yg Wd | Yg E1 | Yn Wd | Yn W | Yn Wd | Yn F | Yg F | Yg W | Yn F | Yn E2 | Yn F | Yn E4 | Yg E | Yg M | Yg E | Yg Wd | Yn E | Yn M | 20 |
| 21 | Yg F | Yg W | Yg Wd | Yg E1 | Yn Wd | Yn W | Yn Wd | Yn F | Yg F | Yg W | Yg F | Yg F | Yn F | Yn E4 | Yg E | Yg M | Yg E | Yg Wd | Yn E | Yn M | Yn E | Yn Wd | Yg M | Yg E3 | 21 |
| 22 | Yn F | Yn E4 | Yn Wd | Yn F | Yg F | Yg W | Yg F | Yg F | Yn F | Yn E4 | Yn F | Yn E2 | Yg E | Yg Wd | Yn E | Yn M | Yn E | Yn Wd | Yg M | Yg E3 | Yg M | Yg E1 | Yn M | Yn W | 22 |
| 23 | Yg E | Yg Wd | Yg F | Yg F | Yn F | Yn E4 | Yn F | Yn E2 | Yg E | Yg Wd | Yg E | Yg M | Yn E | Yn Wd | Yg M | Yg E3 | Yg M | Yg E1 | Yn M | Yn W | Yn M | Yn F | Yg W | Yg W | 23 |
| 24 | Yn E | Yn Wd | Yn F | Yn E2 | Yg E | Yg Wd | Yg E | Yg M | Yn E | Yn Wd | Yn E | Yn M | Yg M | Yg E1 | Yn M | Yn W | Yn M | Yn F | Yg W | Yg W | Yg W | Yg F | Yn W | Yn E4 | 24 |
| 25 | Yg M | Yg E1 | Yg E | Yg M | Yn E | Yn Wd | Yn E | Yn M | Yg M | Yg E1 | Yg M | Yg E3 | Yn M | Yn F | Yg W | Yg W | Yg W | Yg F | Yn W | Yn E4 | Yn W | Yn E2 | Yg Wd | Yg Wd | 25 |
| 26 | Yn M | Yn F | Yn E | Yn M | Yg M | Yg E1 | Yg M | Yg E3 | Yn M | Yn F | Yn M | Yn W | Yg W | Yg F | Yn W | Yn E4 | Yn W | Yn E2 | Yg Wd | Yg Wd | Yg Wd | Yg M | Yn Wd | Yn Wd | 26 |
| 27 | Yg W | Yg F | Yg M | Yg E3 | Yn M | Yn F | Yn M | Yn W | Yg W | Yg F | Yg W | Yg W | Yn W | Yn E2 | Yg Wd | Yg Wd | Yg Wd | Yg M | Yn Wd | Yn Wd | Yn Wd | Yn M | Yg F | Yg E1 | 27 |
| 28 | Yn W | Yn E2 | Yn M | Yn W | Yg W | Yg F | Yg W | Yg W | Yn W | Yn E2 | Yn W | Yn E4 | Yg Wd | Yg M | Yn Wd | Yn Wd | Yn Wd | Yn M | Yg F | Yg E1 | Yg F | Yg E3 | Yn F | Yn F | 28 |
| 29 | | | Yg W | Yg W | Yn W | Yn E2 | Yn W | Yn E4 | Yg Wd | Yg M | Yg Wd | Yg Wd | Yn Wd | Yn M | Yg F | Yg E1 | Yg F | Yg E3 | Yn F | Yn F | Yn F | Yn W | Yg E | Yg F | 29 |
| 30 | | | Yn W | Yn E4 | Yg Wd | Yg M | Yg Wd | Yg Wd | Yn Wd | Yn M | Yn Wd | Yn Wd | Yg F | Yg E3 | Yn F | Yn F | Yn F | Yn W | Yg E | Yg F | Yg E | Yg W | Yn E | Yn E2 | 30 |
| 31 | | | Yg Wd | Yg Wd | | | Yn Wd | Yn Wd | | | Yg F | Yg E1 | Yn F | Yn W | | | Yg E | Yg W | | | Yn E | Yn E4 | Yg M | Yg M | 31 |
| 1 | Yg Wd | Yg M | Yn Wd | Yn Wd | Yn Wd | Yn M | Yg F | Yg E1 | Yg F | Yg E3 | Yn F | Yn F | Yg E | Yg W | Yg E | Yg F | Yn E | Yn E4 | Yn E | Yn E2 | Yg M | Yg Wd | Yn M | Yn M | 1 |
| 2 | Yn Wd | Yn M | Yg F | Yg E1 | Yg F | Yg E3 | Yn F | Yn F | Yn F | Yn W | Yg E | Yg F | Yn E | Yn E4 | Yn E | Yn E2 | Yg M | Yg Wd | Yg M | Yg M | Yn M | Yn Wd | Yg W | Yg E3 | 2 |
| 3 | Yg F | Yg E3 | Yn F | Yn F | Yn F | Yn W | Yg E | Yg F | Yg E | Yg W | Yn E | Yn E2 | Yg M | Yg Wd | Yg M | Yg M | Yn M | Yn Wd | Yn M | Yn M | Yg W | Yg E1 | Yn W | Yn W | 3 |
| 4 | Yn F | Yn W | Yg E | Yg F | Yg E | Yg W | Yn E | Yn E2 | Yn E | Yn E4 | Yg M | Yg M | Yn M | Yn Wd | Yn M | Yn M | Yg W | Yg E1 | Yg W | Yg E3 | Yn W | Yn F | | | 4 |
| 5 | | | | | | | | | Yg M | Yg Wd | Yn M | Yn M | Yg W | Yg E1 | Yg W | Yg E3 | Yn W | Yn F | Yn W | Yn W | | | | | 5 |
| 6 | | | | | | | | | Yn M | Yn Wd | Yg W | Yg E3 | Yn W | Yn F | Yn W | Yn W | Yg Wd | Yg F | Yg Wd | Yg W | | | | | 6 |
| 7 | | | | | | | | | | | | | | | Yg Wd | Yg W | | | | | | | | | 7 |
| 8 | | | | | | | | | | | | | | | | | | | | | | | | | 8 |

# YEAR OF THE DOG

| | H | E | H | E | H | E | H | E | H | E | H | E | H | E | H | E | H | E | H | E | H | E | H | E | |
|---|---|---|---|---|---|---|---|---|---|---|---|---|---|---|---|---|---|---|---|---|---|---|---|---|---|
| YEAR | YEAR Yg F | Yg E3 | 2006 | | | | | | | | | | | | | | | | | | | | 2007 | | |
| MONTH | 4 Feb - 5 Mar | | 6 Mar - 4 Apr | | 5 Apr - 5 May | | 6 May - 5 June | | 6 June - 6 Jul | | 7 Jul - 7 Aug | | 8 Aug - 7 Sep | | 8 Sep - 7 Oct | | 8 Oct - 6 Nov | | 7 Nov - 6 Dec | | 7 Dec - 5 Jan | | 6 Jan - 3 Feb | | |
| | Yg M | Yg Wd | Yn M | Yn Wd | Yg W | Yg E1 | Yn W | Yn F | Yg Wd | Yg F | Yn Wd | Yn E2 | Yg F | Yg M | Yn F | Yn M | Yg E | Yg E3 | Yn E | Yn W | Yg M | Yg W | Yn M | Yn E4 | |
| Starting time | 1st day | Mid-pt | 1st day | Mid-pt | 1st day | Mid-pt | 1st day | Mid-pt | 1st day | Mid-pt | 1st day | Mid-pt | 1st day | Mid-pt | 1st day | Mid-pt | 1st day | Mid-pt | 1st day | Mid-pt | 1st day | Mid-pt | 1st day | Mid-pt | |
| Date | 4 | 19 | 6 | 21 | 5 | 20 | 6 | 21 | 6 | 21 | 7 | 23 | 8 | 23 | 8 | 23 | 8 | 23 | 7 | 22 | 7 | 22 | 6 | 20 | |
| Hour | 0725 | 0317 | 0135 | 0230 | 0638 | 1349 | 0011 | 1312 | 0434 | 2118 | 1457 | 0811 | 0040 | 1507 | 0324 | 1231 | 1848 | 2137 | 2143 | 1900 | 1423 | 0813 | 0132 | 1851 | |
| DATE 4 | Yg Wd | Yg W | | | | | | | | | | | | | | | | | | | | | | | 4 |
| 5 | Yn Wd | Yn E4 | | | Yg Wd | Yg W | | | | | | | | | | | | | | | | | | | 5 |
| 6 | Yg F | Yg Wd | Yg Wd | Yg F | Yn Wd | Yn E4 | Yn Wd | Yn E2 | Yg F | Yg Wd | | | | | | | | | | | | | Yg M | Yg W | 6 |
| 7 | Yn F | Yn Wd | Yn Wd | Yn E2 | Yg F | Yg Wd | Yg F | Yg M | Yn F | Yn Wd | Yn F | Yn M | | | | | | | Yg M | Yg W | Yg M | Yg F | Yn M | Yn E4 | 7 |
| 8 | Yg E | Yg E1 | Yg F | Yg M | Yn F | Yn Wd | Yn F | Yn M | Yg E | Yg E1 | Yg E | Yg E3 | Yn E | Yn F | Yg M | Yg W | Yg M | Yg F | Yn M | Yn E4 | Yn M | Yn E2 | Yg W | Yg Wd | 8 |
| 9 | Yn E | Yn F | Yn F | Yn M | Yg E | Yg E1 | Yg E | Yg E3 | Yn E | Yn F | Yn E | Yn W | Yg M | Yg F | Yn M | Yn E4 | Yn M | Yn E2 | Yg W | Yg Wd | Yg W | Yg M | Yn W | Yn Wd | 9 |
| 10 | Yg M | Yg F | Yg E | Yg E3 | Yn E | Yn F | Yn E | Yn W | Yg M | Yg F | Yg M | Yg W | Yn M | Yn E2 | Yg W | Yg Wd | Yg W | Yg M | Yn W | Yn Wd | Yn W | Yn M | Yg Wd | Yg E1 | 10 |
| 11 | Yn M | Yn E2 | Yn E | Yn W | Yg M | Yg F | Yg M | Yg W | Yn M | Yn E2 | Yn M | Yn E4 | Yg W | Yg M | Yn W | Yn Wd | Yn W | Yn M | Yg Wd | Yg E1 | Yg Wd | Yg E3 | Yn Wd | Yn F | 11 |
| 12 | Yg W | Yg M | Yg M | Yg W | Yn M | Yn E2 | Yn M | Yn E4 | Yg W | Yg M | Yg W | Yg Wd | Yn W | Yn M | Yg Wd | Yg E1 | Yg Wd | Yg E3 | Yn Wd | Yn F | Yn Wd | Yn W | Yg F | Yg F | 12 |
| 13 | Yn W | Yn M | Yn M | Yn E4 | Yg W | Yg M | Yg W | Yg Wd | Yn W | Yn M | Yn W | Yn Wd | Yg Wd | Yg E3 | Yn Wd | Yn F | Yn Wd | Yn W | Yg F | Yg F | Yg F | Yg W | Yn F | Yn E2 | 13 |
| 14 | Yg Wd | Yg E3 | Yg W | Yg Wd | Yn W | Yn M | Yn W | Yn Wd | Yg Wd | Yg E3 | Yg Wd | Yg E1 | Yn Wd | Yn W | Yg F | Yg F | Yg F | Yg W | Yn F | Yn E2 | Yn F | Yn E4 | Yg E | Yg M | 14 |
| 15 | Yn Wd | Yn W | Yn W | Yn Wd | Yg Wd | Yg E3 | Yg Wd | Yg E1 | Yn Wd | Yn W | Yn Wd | Yn F | Yg F | Yg W | Yn F | Yn E2 | Yn F | Yn E4 | Yg E | Yg M | Yg E | Yg Wd | Yn E | Yn M | 15 |
| 16 | Yg F | Yg W | Yg Wd | Yg E1 | Yn Wd | Yn W | Yn Wd | Yn F | Yg F | Yg W | Yg F | Yg F | Yn F | Yn E4 | Yg E | Yg M | Yg E | Yg Wd | Yn E | Yn M | Yn E | Yn Wd | Yg M | Yg E3 | 16 |
| 17 | Yn F | Yn E4 | Yn Wd | Yn F | Yg F | Yg W | Yg F | Yg F | Yn F | Yn E4 | Yn F | Yn E2 | Yg E | Yg Wd | Yn E | Yn M | Yn E | Yn Wd | Yg M | Yg E3 | Yg M | Yg E1 | Yn M | Yn W | 17 |
| 18 | Yg E | Yg Wd | Yg F | Yg F | Yn F | Yn E4 | Yn F | Yn E2 | Yg E | Yg Wd | Yg E | Yg M | Yn E | Yn Wd | Yg M | Yg E3 | Yg M | Yg E1 | Yn M | Yn W | Yn M | Yn F | Yg W | Yg W | 18 |
| 19 | Yn E | Yn Wd | Yn F | Yn E2 | Yg E | Yg Wd | Yg E | Yg M | Yn E | Yn Wd | Yn E | Yn M | Yg M | Yg E1 | Yn M | Yn W | Yn M | Yn F | Yg W | Yg W | Yg W | Yg F | Yn W | Yn E4 | 19 |
| 20 | Yg M | Yg E1 | Yg E | Yg M | Yn E | Yn Wd | Yn E | Yn M | Yg M | Yg E1 | Yg M | Yg E3 | Yn M | Yn F | Yg W | Yg W | Yg W | Yg F | Yn W | Yn E4 | Yn W | Yn E2 | Yg Wd | Yg Wd | 20 |
| 21 | Yn M | Yn F | Yn E | Yn M | Yg M | Yg E1 | Yg M | Yg E3 | Yn M | Yn F | Yn M | Yn W | Yg W | Yg F | Yn W | Yn E4 | Yn W | Yn E2 | Yg Wd | Yg Wd | Yg Wd | Yg M | Yn Wd | Yn Wd | 21 |
| 22 | Yg W | Yg F | Yg M | Yg E3 | Yn M | Yn F | Yn M | Yn W | Yg W | Yg F | Yg W | Yg W | Yn W | Yn E2 | Yg Wd | Yg Wd | Yg Wd | Yg M | Yn Wd | Yn Wd | Yn Wd | Yn M | Yg F | Yg E1 | 22 |
| 23 | Yn W | Yn E2 | Yn M | Yn W | Yg W | Yg F | Yg W | Yg W | Yn W | Yn E2 | Yn W | Yn E4 | Yg Wd | Yg M | Yn Wd | Yn Wd | Yn Wd | Yn M | Yg F | Yg E1 | Yg F | Yg E3 | Yn F | Yn F | 23 |
| 24 | Yg Wd | Yg M | Yg W | Yg W | Yn W | Yn E2 | Yn W | Yn E4 | Yg Wd | Yg M | Yg Wd | Yg Wd | Yn Wd | Yn M | Yg F | Yg E1 | Yg F | Yg E3 | Yn F | Yn F | Yn F | Yn W | Yg E | Yg F | 24 |
| 25 | Yn Wd | Yn M | Yn W | Yn E4 | Yg Wd | Yg M | Yg Wd | Yg Wd | Yn Wd | Yn M | Yn Wd | Yn Wd | Yg F | Yg E3 | Yn F | Yn F | Yn F | Yn W | Yg E | Yg F | Yg E | Yg W | Yn E | Yn E2 | 25 |
| 26 | Yg F | Yg E3 | Yg Wd | Yg Wd | Yn Wd | Yn M | Yn Wd | Yn Wd | Yg F | Yg E3 | Yg F | Yg E1 | Yn F | Yn W | Yg E | Yg F | Yg E | Yg W | Yn E | Yn E2 | Yn E | Yn E4 | Yg M | Yg M | 26 |
| 27 | Yn F | Yn W | Yn Wd | Yn Wd | Yg F | Yg E3 | Yg F | Yg E1 | Yn F | Yn W | Yn F | Yn F | Yg E | Yg W | Yn E | Yn E2 | Yn E | Yn E4 | Yg M | Yg M | Yg M | Yg Wd | Yn M | Yn M | 27 |
| 28 | Yg E | Yg W | Yg F | Yg E1 | Yn F | Yn W | Yn F | Yn F | Yg E | Yg W | Yg E | Yg F | Yn E | Yn E4 | Yg M | Yg M | Yg M | Yg Wd | Yn M | Yn M | Yn M | Yn Wd | Yg W | Yg E3 | 28 |
| 29 | | | Yn F | Yn F | Yg E | Yg W | Yg E | Yg F | Yn E | Yn E4 | Yn E | Yn E2 | Yg M | Yg Wd | Yn M | Yn M | Yn M | Yn Wd | Yg W | Yg E3 | Yg W | Yg E1 | Yn W | Yn W | 29 |
| 30 | | | Yg E | Yg F | Yn E | Yn E4 | Yn E | Yn E2 | Yg M | Yg Wd | Yg M | Yg M | Yn M | Yn Wd | Yg W | Yg E3 | Yg W | Yg E1 | Yn W | Yn W | Yn W | Yn F | Yg Wd | Yg W | 30 |
| 31 | | | Yn E | Yn E2 | | | Yg M | Yg M | | | Yn M | Yn M | Yg W | Yg E1 | | | Yn W | Yn F | | | Yg Wd | Yg F | Yn Wd | Yn E4 | 31 |
| 1 | Yn E | Yn E4 | Yg M | Yg M | Yg M | Yg Wd | Yn M | Yn M | Yn M | Yn Wd | Yg W | Yg E3 | Yn W | Yn F | Yn W | Yn W | Yg Wd | Yg F | Yg Wd | Yg W | Yn Wd | Yn E2 | Yg F | Yg Wd | 1 |
| 2 | Yg M | Yg Wd | Yn M | Yn M | Yn M | Yn Wd | Yg W | Yg E3 | Yg W | Yg E1 | Yn W | Yn W | Yg Wd | Yg F | Yg Wd | Yg W | Yn Wd | Yn E2 | Yn Wd | Yn E4 | Yg F | Yg M | Yn F | Yn Wd | 2 |
| 3 | Yn M | Yn Wd | Yg W | Yg E3 | Yg W | Yg E1 | Yn W | Yn W | Yn W | Yn F | Yg Wd | Yg W | Yn Wd | Yn E2 | Yn Wd | Yn E4 | Yg F | Yg M | Yg F | Yg Wd | Yn F | Yn M | Yg E | Yg E1 | 3 |
| 4 | Yg W | Yg E1 | Yn W | Yn W | Yn W | Yn F | Yg Wd | Yg W | Yg Wd | Yg F | Yn Wd | Yn E4 | Yg F | Yg M | Yg F | Yg Wd | Yn F | Yn M | Yn F | Yn Wd | Yg E | Yg E3 | | | 4 |
| 5 | Yn W | Yn F | | | Yg Wd | Yg F | Yn Wd | Yn E4 | Yn Wd | Yn E2 | Yg F | Yg Wd | Yn F | Yn M | Yn F | Yn Wd | Yg E | Yg E3 | Yg E | Yg E1 | Yn E | Yn W | | | 5 |
| 6 | | | | | | | | | Yg F | Yg M | Yn F | Yn Wd | Yg E | Yg E3 | Yg E | Yg E1 | Yn E | Yn W | Yn E | Yn F | | | | | 6 |
| 7 | | | | | | | | | | | Yg E | Yg E1 | Yn E | Yn W | Yn E | Yn F | | | | | | | | | 7 |
| 8 | | | | | | | | | | | | | | | | | | | | | | | | | 8 |

# YEAR OF THE PIG

| | H | E | H | E | H | E | H | E | H | E | H | E | H | E | H | E | H | E | H | E | H | E | H | E | |
|---|---|---|---|---|---|---|---|---|---|---|---|---|---|---|---|---|---|---|---|---|---|---|---|---|---|
| YEAR | YEAR<br>Yn F | Yn W | 2007 | | | | | | | | | | | | | | | | | | | | 2008 | | |
| MONTH | 4 Feb - 5 Mar | | 6 Mar - 4 Apr | | 5 Apr - 5 May | | 6 May - 5 June | | 6 June - 6 Jul | | 7 Jul - 7 Aug | | 8 Aug - 7 Sep | | 8 Sep - 8 Oct | | 9 Oct - 7 Nov | | 8 Nov - 6 Dec | | 7 Dec - 5 Jan | | 6 Jan - 3 Feb | | |
| | Yg W | Yg Wd | Yn W | Yn Wd | Yg Wd | Yg E1 | Yn Wd | Yn F | Yg F | Yg F | Yn F | Yn E2 | Yg E | Yg M | Yn E | Yn M | Yg M | Yg E3 | Yn M | Yn W | Yg W | Yg W | Yn W | Yn E4 | |
| Starting time | 1st day | Mid-pt | 1st day | Mid-pt | 1st day | Mid-pt | 1st day | Mid-pt | 1st day | Mid-pt | 1st day | Mid-pt | 1st day | Mid-pt | 1st day | Mid-pt | 1st day | Mid-pt | 1st day | Mid-pt | 1st day | Mid-pt | 1st day | Mid-pt | |
| Date | 4 | 19 | 6 | 21 | 5 | 20 | 6 | 21 | 6 | 22 | 7 | 23 | 8 | 23 | 8 | 23 | 9 | 24 | 8 | 23 | 7 | 22 | 6 | 21 | |
| Hour | 1314 | 0908 | 0724 | 0821 | 1227 | 1940 | 0601 | 1902 | 1023 | 0308 | 2046 | 1401 | 0629 | 2057 | 0913 | 1821 | 0037 | 0327 | 0332 | 0049 | 2012 | 1402 | 0721 | 0040 | |
| DATE 4 | Yn E | Yn F | | | | | | | | | | | | | | | | | | | | | | | 4 |
| 5 | Yg M | Yg F | | | Yn E | Yn F | | | | | | | | | | | | | | | | | | | 5 |
| 6 | Yn M | Yn E2 | Yn E | Yn W | Yg M | Yg F | Yg M | Yg W | Yn M | Yn E2 | | | | | | | | | | | | | Yn Wd | Yn F | 6 |
| 7 | Yg W | Yg M | Yg M | Yg W | Yn M | Yn E2 | Yn M | Yn E4 | Yg W | Yg M | Yg W | Yg Wd | | | | | | | | | Yn Wd | Yn W | Yg F | Yg F | 7 |
| 8 | Yn W | Yn M | Yn M | Yn E4 | Yg W | Yg M | Yg W | Yg Wd | Yn W | Yn M | Yn W | Yn Wd | Yg Wd | Yg E3 | Yn Wd | Yn F | | | Yg F | Yg F | Yg F | Yg W | Yn F | Yn E2 | 8 |
| 9 | Yg Wd | Yg E3 | Yg W | Yg Wd | Yn W | Yn M | Yn W | Yn Wd | Yg Wd | Yg E3 | Yg Wd | Yg E1 | Yn Wd | Yn W | Yg F | Yg F | Yg F | Yg W | Yn F | Yn E2 | Yn F | Yn E4 | Yg E | Yg M | 9 |
| 10 | Yn Wd | Yn W | Yn W | Yn Wd | Yg Wd | Yg E3 | Yg Wd | Yg E1 | Yn Wd | Yn W | Yn Wd | Yn F | Yg F | Yg W | Yn F | Yn E2 | Yn F | Yn E4 | Yg E | Yg M | Yg E | Yg Wd | Yn E | Yn M | 10 |
| 11 | Yg F | Yg W | Yg Wd | Yg E1 | Yn Wd | Yn W | Yn Wd | Yn F | Yg F | Yg W | Yg F | Yg F | Yn F | Yn E4 | Yg E | Yg M | Yg E | Yg Wd | Yn E | Yn M | Yn E | Yn Wd | Yg M | Yg E3 | 11 |
| 12 | Yn F | Yn E4 | Yn Wd | Yn F | Yg F | Yg W | Yg F | Yg F | Yn F | Yn E4 | Yn F | Yn E2 | Yg E | Yg Wd | Yn E | Yn M | Yn E | Yn Wd | Yg M | Yg E3 | Yg M | Yg E1 | Yn M | Yn W | 12 |
| 13 | Yg E | Yg Wd | Yg F | Yg F | Yn F | Yn E4 | Yn F | Yn E2 | Yg E | Yg Wd | Yg E | Yg M | Yn E | Yn Wd | Yg M | Yg E3 | Yg M | Yg E1 | Yn M | Yn W | Yn M | Yn F | Yg W | Yg W | 13 |
| 14 | Yn E | Yn Wd | Yn F | Yn E2 | Yg E | Yg Wd | Yg E | Yg M | Yn E | Yn Wd | Yn E | Yn M | Yg M | Yg E1 | Yn M | Yn W | Yn M | Yn F | Yg W | Yg W | Yg W | Yg F | Yn W | Yn E4 | 14 |
| 15 | Yg M | Yg E1 | Yg E | Yg M | Yn E | Yn Wd | Yn E | Yn M | Yg M | Yg E1 | Yg M | Yg E3 | Yn M | Yn F | Yg W | Yg W | Yg W | Yg F | Yn W | Yn E4 | Yn W | Yn E2 | Yg Wd | Yg Wd | 15 |
| 16 | Yn M | Yn F | Yn E | Yn M | Yg M | Yg E1 | Yg M | Yg E3 | Yn M | Yn F | Yn M | Yn W | Yg W | Yg F | Yn W | Yn E4 | Yn W | Yn E2 | Yg Wd | Yg Wd | Yg Wd | Yg M | Yn Wd | Yn Wd | 16 |
| 17 | Yg W | Yg F | Yg M | Yg E3 | Yn M | Yn F | Yn M | Yn W | Yg W | Yg F | Yg W | Yg W | Yn W | Yn E2 | Yg Wd | Yg Wd | Yg Wd | Yg M | Yn Wd | Yn Wd | Yn Wd | Yn M | Yg F | Yg E1 | 17 |
| 18 | Yn W | Yn E2 | Yn M | Yn W | Yg W | Yg F | Yg W | Yg W | Yn W | Yn E2 | Yn W | Yn E4 | Yg Wd | Yg M | Yn Wd | Yn Wd | Yn Wd | Yn M | Yg F | Yg E1 | Yg F | Yg E3 | Yn F | Yn F | 18 |
| 19 | Yg Wd | Yg M | Yg W | Yg W | Yn W | Yn E2 | Yn W | Yn E4 | Yg Wd | Yg M | Yg Wd | Yg Wd | Yn Wd | Yn M | Yg F | Yg E1 | Yg F | Yg E3 | Yn F | Yn F | Yn F | Yn W | Yg E | Yg F | 19 |
| 20 | Yn Wd | Yn M | Yn W | Yn E4 | Yg Wd | Yg M | Yg Wd | Yg Wd | Yn Wd | Yn M | Yn Wd | Yn Wd | Yg F | Yg E3 | Yn F | Yn F | Yn F | Yn W | Yg E | Yg F | Yg E | Yg W | Yn E | Yn E2 | 20 |
| 21 | Yg F | Yg E3 | Yg Wd | Yg Wd | Yn Wd | Yn M | Yn Wd | Yn Wd | Yg F | Yg E3 | Yg F | Yg E1 | Yn F | Yn W | Yg E | Yg F | Yg E | Yg W | Yn E | Yn E2 | Yn E | Yn E4 | Yg M | Yg M | 21 |
| 22 | Yn F | Yn W | Yn Wd | Yn Wd | Yg F | Yg E3 | Yg F | Yg E1 | Yn F | Yn W | Yn F | Yn F | Yg E | Yg W | Yn E | Yn E2 | Yn E | Yn E4 | Yg M | Yg M | Yg M | Yg Wd | Yn M | Yn M | 22 |
| 23 | Yg E | Yg W | Yg F | Yg E1 | Yn F | Yn W | Yn F | Yn F | Yg E | Yg W | Yg E | Yg F | Yn E | Yn E4 | Yg M | Yg M | Yg M | Yg Wd | Yn M | Yn M | Yn M | Yn Wd | Yg W | Yg E3 | 23 |
| 24 | Yn E | Yn E4 | Yn F | Yn F | Yg E | Yg W | Yg E | Yg F | Yn E | Yn E4 | Yn E | Yn E2 | Yg M | Yg Wd | Yn M | Yn M | Yn M | Yn Wd | Yg W | Yg E3 | Yg W | Yg E1 | Yn W | Yn W | 24 |
| 25 | Yg M | Yg Wd | Yg E | Yg F | Yn E | Yn E4 | Yn E | Yn E2 | Yg M | Yg Wd | Yg M | Yg M | Yn M | Yn Wd | Yg W | Yg E3 | Yg W | Yg E1 | Yn W | Yn W | Yn W | Yn F | Yg Wd | Yg W | 25 |
| 26 | Yn M | Yn Wd | Yn E | Yn E2 | Yg M | Yg Wd | Yg M | Yg M | Yn M | Yn Wd | Yn M | Yn M | Yg W | Yg E1 | Yn W | Yn W | Yn W | Yn F | Yg Wd | Yg W | Yg Wd | Yg F | Yn Wd | Yn E4 | 26 |
| 27 | Yg W | Yg E1 | Yg M | Yg M | Yn M | Yn Wd | Yn M | Yn M | Yg W | Yg E1 | Yg W | Yg E3 | Yn W | Yn F | Yg Wd | Yg W | Yg Wd | Yg F | Yn Wd | Yn E4 | Yn Wd | Yn E2 | Yg F | Yg Wd | 27 |
| 28 | Yn W | Yn F | Yn M | Yn M | Yg W | Yg E1 | Yg W | Yg E3 | Yn W | Yn F | Yn W | Yn W | Yg Wd | Yg F | Yn Wd | Yn E4 | Yn Wd | Yn E2 | Yg F | Yg Wd | Yg F | Yg M | Yn F | Yn Wd | 28 |
| 29 | | | Yg W | Yg E3 | Yn W | Yn F | Yn W | Yn W | Yg Wd | Yg F | Yg Wd | Yg W | Yn Wd | Yn E2 | Yg F | Yg Wd | Yg F | Yg M | Yn F | Yn Wd | Yn F | Yn M | Yg E | Yg E1 | 29 |
| 30 | | | Yn W | Yn W | Yg Wd | Yg F | Yg Wd | Yg W | Yn Wd | Yn E2 | Yn Wd | Yn E4 | Yg F | Yg M | Yn F | Yn Wd | Yn F | Yn M | Yg E | Yg E1 | Yg E | Yg E3 | Yn E | Yn F | 30 |
| 31 | | | Yg Wd | Yg W | | | Yn Wd | Yn E4 | | | Yg F | Yg Wd | Yn F | Yn M | | | Yg E | Yg E3 | | | Yn E | Yn W | Yg M | Yg F | 31 |
| 1 | Yg Wd | Yg F | Yn Wd | Yn E4 | Yn Wd | Yn E2 | Yg F | Yg Wd | Yg F | Yg M | Yn F | Yn Wd | Yg E | Yg E3 | Yg E | Yg E1 | Yn E | Yn W | Yn E | Yn F | Yg M | Yg W | Yn M | Yn E2 | 1 |
| 2 | Yn Wd | Yn E2 | Yg F | Yg Wd | Yg F | Yg M | Yn F | Yn Wd | Yn F | Yn M | Yg E | Yg E1 | Yn E | Yn W | Yn E | Yn F | Yg M | Yg W | Yg M | Yg F | Yn M | Yn E4 | Yg W | Yg M | 2 |
| 3 | Yg F | Yg M | Yn F | Yn Wd | Yn F | Yn M | Yg E | Yg E1 | Yg E | Yg E3 | Yn E | Yn F | Yg M | Yg W | Yg M | Yg F | Yn M | Yn E4 | Yn M | Yn E2 | Yg W | Yg Wd | Yn W | Yn M | 3 |
| 4 | Yn F | Yn M | Yg E | Yg E1 | Yg E | Yg E3 | Yn E | Yn F | Yn E | Yn W | Yg M | Yg F | Yn M | Yn E4 | Yn M | Yn E2 | Yg W | Yg Wd | Yg W | Yg M | Yn W | Yn Wd | | | 4 |
| 5 | Yg E | Yg E3 | | | Yn E | Yn W | Yg M | Yg F | Yg M | Yg W | Yn M | Yn E2 | Yg W | Yg Wd | Yg W | Yg M | Yn W | Yn Wd | Yn W | Yn M | Yg Wd | Yg E1 | | | 5 |
| 6 | | | | | | | | | Yn M | Yn E4 | Yg W | Yg M | Yn W | Yn Wd | Yn W | Yn M | Yg Wd | Yg E1 | Yg Wd | Yg E3 | | | | | 6 |
| 7 | | | | | | | | | | | Yn W | Yn M | Yg Wd | Yg E1 | Yg Wd | Yg E3 | Yn Wd | Yn F | | | | | | | 7 |
| 8 | | | | | | | | | | | | | | | Yn Wd | Yn W | | | | | | | | | 8 |

# YEAR OF THE RAT

| | H | E | H | E | H | E | H | E | H | E | H | E | H | E | H | E | H | E | H | E | H | E | H | E | |
|---|---|---|---|---|---|---|---|---|---|---|---|---|---|---|---|---|---|---|---|---|---|---|---|---|---|
| YEAR | YEAR<br>Yg E | <br>Yg W | 2008 | | | | | | | | | | | | | | | | | | | | 2009 | | |
| MONTH | 4 Feb - 4 Mar | | 5 Mar - 3 Apr | | 4 Apr - 4 May | | 5 May - 4 June | | 5 June - 6 Jul | | 7 Jul - 6 Aug | | 7 Aug - 6 Sep | | 7 Sep - 7 Oct | | 8 Oct - 6 Nov | | 7 Nov - 6 Dec | | 7 Dec - 4 Jan | | 5 Jan - 3 Feb | | |
| | Yg Wd | Yg Wd | Yn Wd | Yn Wd | Yg F | Yg E1 | Yn F | Yn F | Yg E | Yg F | Yn E | Yn E2 | Yg M | Yg M | Yn M | Yn M | Yg W | Yg E3 | Yn W | Yn W | Yg Wd | Yg W | Yn Wd | Yn E4 | |
| Starting time | 1st day | Mid-pt | 1st day | Mid-pt | 1st day | Mid-pt | 1st day | Mid-pt | 1st day | Mid-pt | 1st day | Mid-pt | 1st day | Mid-pt | 1st day | Mid-pt | 1st day | Mid-pt | 1st day | Mid-pt | 1st day | Mid-pt | 1st day | Mid-pt | |
| Date | 4 | 19 | 5 | 20 | 4 | 20 | 5 | 21 | 5 | 21 | 7 | 22 | 7 | 23 | 7 | 23 | 8 | 23 | 7 | 22 | 7 | 21 | 5 | 20 | |
| Hour | 1903 | 1457 | 1313 | 1410 | 1816 | 0139 | 1150 | 0051 | 1612 | 0857 | 0235 | 1950 | 1218 | 0246 | 1502 | 0010 | 0626 | 0916 | 0921 | 0638 | 0201 | 1951 | 1310 | 0629 | |
| DATE 4 | Yg Wd | Yg E3 | | | Yg Wd | Yg E3 | | | | | | | | | | | | | | | | | | | 4 |
| 5 | Yn Wd | Yn W | Yg Wd | Yg E1 | Yn Wd | Yn W | Yn Wd | Yn F | Yg F | Yg W | | | | | | | | | | | | | Yg M | Yg E3 | 5 |
| 6 | Yg F | Yg W | Yn Wd | Yn F | Yg F | Yg W | Yg F | Yg F | Yn F | Yn E4 | | | | | | | | | | | | | Yn M | Yn W | 6 |
| 7 | Yn F | Yn E4 | Yg F | Yg F | Yn F | Yn E4 | Yn F | Yn E2 | Yg E | Yg Wd | Yg E | Yg M | Yn E | Yn Wd | Yg M | Yg E3 | | | Yn M | Yn W | Yn M | Yn F | Yg W | Yg W | 7 |
| 8 | Yg E | Yg Wd | Yn F | Yn E2 | Yg E | Yg Wd | Yg E | Yg M | Yn E | Yn Wd | Yn E | Yn M | Yg M | Yg E1 | Yn M | Yn W | Yn M | Yn F | Yg W | Yg W | Yg W | Yg F | Yn W | Yn E4 | 8 |
| 9 | Yn E | Yn Wd | Yg E | Yg M | Yn E | Yn Wd | Yn E | Yn M | Yg M | Yg E1 | Yg M | Yg E3 | Yn M | Yn F | Yn W | Yg W | Yg W | Yg F | Yn W | Yn E4 | Yn W | Yn E2 | Yg Wd | Yg Wd | 9 |
| 10 | Yg M | Yg E1 | Yn E | Yn M | Yg M | Yg E1 | Yg M | Yg E3 | Yn M | Yn F | Yn M | Yn W | Yg W | Yg F | Yn W | Yn E4 | Yn W | Yn E2 | Yg Wd | Yg Wd | Yg Wd | Yg M | Yn Wd | Yn Wd | 10 |
| 11 | Yn M | Yn F | Yg M | Yg E3 | Yn M | Yn F | Yn M | Yn W | Yg W | Yg F | Yg W | Yg W | Yn W | Yn E2 | Yg Wd | Yg Wd | Yg Wd | Yg M | Yn Wd | Yn Wd | Yn Wd | Yn M | Yg F | Yg E1 | 11 |
| 12 | Yg W | Yg F | Yn M | Yn W | Yg W | Yg F | Yg W | Yg W | Yn W | Yn E2 | Yn W | Yn E4 | Yg Wd | Yg M | Yn Wd | Yn Wd | Yn Wd | Yn M | Yg F | Yg E1 | Yg F | Yg E3 | Yn F | Yn F | 12 |
| 13 | Yn W | Yn E2 | Yg W | Yg W | Yn W | Yn E2 | Yn W | Yn E4 | Yg Wd | Yg M | Yg Wd | Yg Wd | Yn Wd | Yn M | Yg F | Yg E1 | Yg F | Yg E3 | Yn F | Yn F | Yn F | Yn W | Yg E | Yg F | 13 |
| 14 | Yg Wd | Yg M | Yn W | Yn E4 | Yg Wd | Yg M | Yg Wd | Yg Wd | Yn Wd | Yn M | Yn Wd | Yn Wd | Yg F | Yg E3 | Yn F | Yn F | Yn F | Yn W | Yg E | Yg F | Yg E | Yg W | Yn E | Yn E2 | 14 |
| 15 | Yn Wd | Yn M | Yg Wd | Yg Wd | Yn Wd | Yn M | Yn Wd | Yn Wd | Yg F | Yg E3 | Yg F | Yg E1 | Yn F | Yn W | Yg E | Yg F | Yg E | Yg W | Yn E | Yn E2 | Yn E | Yn E4 | Yg M | Yg M | 15 |
| 16 | Yg F | Yg E3 | Yn Wd | Yn Wd | Yg F | Yg E3 | Yg F | Yg E1 | Yn F | Yn W | Yn F | Yn F | Yg E | Yg W | Yn E | Yn E2 | Yn E | Yn E4 | Yg M | Yg M | Yg M | Yg Wd | Yn M | Yn M | 16 |
| 17 | Yn F | Yn W | Yg F | Yg E1 | Yn F | Yn W | Yn F | Yn F | Yg E | Yg W | Yg E | Yg F | Yn E | Yn E4 | Yg M | Yg M | Yg M | Yg Wd | Yn M | Yn M | Yn M | Yn Wd | Yg W | Yg E3 | 17 |
| 18 | Yg E | Yg W | Yn F | Yn F | Yg E | Yg W | Yg E | Yg F | Yn E | Yn E4 | Yn E | Yn E2 | Yg M | Yg Wd | Yn M | Yn M | Yn M | Yn Wd | Yg W | Yg E3 | Yg W | Yg E1 | Yn W | Yn W | 18 |
| 19 | Yn E | Yn E4 | Yg E | Yg F | Yn E | Yn E4 | Yn E | Yn E2 | Yg M | Yg Wd | Yg M | Yg M | Yn M | Yn Wd | Yg W | Yg E3 | Yg W | Yg E1 | Yn W | Yn W | Yn W | Yn F | Yg Wd | Yg W | 19 |
| 20 | Yg M | Yg Wd | Yn E | Yn E2 | Yg M | Yg Wd | Yg M | Yg M | Yn M | Yn Wd | Yn M | Yn M | Yg W | Yg E1 | Yn W | Yn W | Yn W | Yn F | Yg Wd | Yg W | Yg Wd | Yg F | Yn Wd | Yn E4 | 20 |
| 21 | Yn M | Yn Wd | Yg M | Yg M | Yn M | Yn Wd | Yn M | Yn M | Yg W | Yg E1 | Yg W | Yg E3 | Yn W | Yn F | Yg Wd | Yg W | Yg Wd | Yg F | Yn Wd | Yn E4 | Yn Wd | Yn E2 | Yg F | Yg Wd | 21 |
| 22 | Yg W | Yg E1 | Yn M | Yn M | Yg W | Yg E1 | Yg W | Yg E3 | Yn W | Yn F | Yn W | Yn W | Yg Wd | Yg F | Yn Wd | Yn E4 | Yn Wd | Yn E2 | Yg F | Yg Wd | Yg F | Yg M | Yn F | Yn Wd | 22 |
| 23 | Yn W | Yn F | Yg W | Yg E3 | Yn W | Yn F | Yn W | Yn W | Yg Wd | Yg F | Yg Wd | Yg W | Yn Wd | Yn E2 | Yg F | Yg Wd | Yg F | Yg M | Yn F | Yn Wd | Yn F | Yn M | Yg E | Yg E1 | 23 |
| 24 | Yg Wd | Yg F | Yn W | Yn W | Yg Wd | Yg F | Yg Wd | Yg W | Yn Wd | Yn E2 | Yn Wd | Yn E4 | Yg F | Yg M | Yn F | Yn Wd | Yn F | Yn M | Yg E | Yg E1 | Yg E | Yg E3 | Yn E | Yn F | 24 |
| 25 | Yn Wd | Yn E2 | Yg Wd | Yg W | Yn Wd | Yn E2 | Yn Wd | Yn E4 | Yg F | Yg M | Yg F | Yg Wd | Yn F | Yn M | Yg E | Yg E1 | Yg E | Yg E3 | Yn E | Yn F | Yn E | Yn W | Yg M | Yg F | 25 |
| 26 | Yg F | Yg M | Yn Wd | Yn E4 | Yg F | Yg M | Yg F | Yg Wd | Yn F | Yn M | Yn F | Yn Wd | Yg E | Yg E3 | Yn E | Yn F | Yn E | Yn W | Yg M | Yg F | Yg M | Yg W | Yn M | Yn E2 | 26 |
| 27 | Yn F | Yn M | Yg F | Yg Wd | Yn F | Yn M | Yn F | Yn Wd | Yg E | Yg E3 | Yg E | Yg E1 | Yn E | Yn W | Yg M | Yg F | Yg M | Yg W | Yn M | Yn E2 | Yn M | Yn E4 | Yg W | Yg M | 27 |
| 28 | Yg E | Yg E3 | Yn F | Yn Wd | Yg E | Yg E3 | Yg E | Yg E1 | Yn E | Yn W | Yn E | Yn F | Yg M | Yg W | Yn M | Yn E2 | Yn M | Yn E4 | Yg W | Yg M | Yg W | Yg Wd | Yn W | Yn M | 28 |
| 29 | Yn E | Yn W | Yg E | Yg E1 | Yn E | Yn W | Yn E | Yn F | Yg M | Yg W | Yg M | Yg F | Yn M | Yn E4 | Yg W | Yg M | Yg W | Yg Wd | Yn W | Yn M | Yn W | Yn Wd | Yg Wd | Yg E3 | 29 |
| 30 | | | Yn E | Yn F | Yg M | Yg W | Yg M | Yg F | Yn M | Yn E4 | Yn M | Yn E2 | Yg W | Yg Wd | Yn W | Yn M | Yn W | Yn Wd | Yg Wd | Yg E3 | Yg Wd | Yg E1 | Yn Wd | Yn W | 30 |
| 31 | | | Yg M | Yg F | | | Yn M | Yn E2 | | | Yg W | Yg M | Yn W | Yn Wd | | | Yg Wd | Yg E1 | | | Yn Wd | Yn F | Yg F | Yg W | 31 |
| 1 | Yg M | Yg W | Yn M | Yn E2 | Yn M | Yn E4 | Yg W | Yg M | Yg W | Yg Wd | Yn W | Yn M | Yg Wd | Yg E1 | Yg Wd | Yg E3 | Yn Wd | Yn F | Yn Wd | Yn W | Yg F | Yg F | Yn F | Yn E4 | 1 |
| 2 | Yn M | Yn E4 | Yg W | Yg M | Yg W | Yg Wd | Yn W | Yn M | Yn W | Yn Wd | Yg Wd | Yg E3 | Yn Wd | Yn F | Yn Wd | Yn W | Yg F | Yg F | Yg F | Yg W | Yn F | Yn E2 | Yg E | Yg Wd | 2 |
| 3 | Yg W | Yg Wd | Yn W | Yn M | Yn W | Yn Wd | Yg Wd | Yg E3 | Yg Wd | Yg E1 | Yn Wd | Yn W | Yg F | Yg F | Yg F | Yg W | Yn F | Yn E2 | Yn F | Yn E4 | Yg E | Yg M | Yn E | Yn Wd | 3 |
| 4 | Yn W | Yn Wd | | | Yg Wd | Yg E1 | Yn Wd | Yn W | Yn Wd | Yn F | Yg F | Yg W | Yn F | Yn E2 | Yn F | Yn E4 | Yg E | Yg M | Yg E | Yg Wd | Yn E | Yn M | | | 4 |
| 5 | | | | | | | | | Yg F | Yg F | Yn F | Yn E4 | Yg E | Yg M | Yg E | Yg Wd | Yn E | Yn M | Yn E | Yn Wd | | | | | 5 |
| 6 | | | | | | | | | Yn F | Yn E2 | Yg E | Yg Wd | Yn E | Yn M | Yn E | Yn Wd | Yg M | Yg E3 | Yg M | Yg E1 | | | | | 6 |
| 7 | | | | | | | | | | | | | | | Yg M | Yg E1 | | | | | | | | | 7 |
| 8 | | | | | | | | | | | | | | | | | | | | | | | | | 8 |

# YEAR OF THE OX

| | H | E | H | E | H | E | H | E | H | E | H | E | H | E | H | E | H | E | H | E | H | E. | H | E | |
|---|---|---|---|---|---|---|---|---|---|---|---|---|---|---|---|---|---|---|---|---|---|---|---|---|---|
| YEAR | YEAR YnE | Yn E4 | 2009 | | | | | | | | | | | | | | | | | | | | 2010 | | |
| MONTH | 4 Feb - 4 Mar | | 5 Mar - 4 Apr | | 5 Apr - 4 May | | 5 May - 4 June | | 5 June - 6 Jul | | 7 Jul - 6 Aug | | 7 Aug - 6 Sep | | 7 Sep - 7 Oct | | 8 Oct - 6 Nov | | 7 Nov - 6 Dec | | 7 Dec - 4 Jan | | 5 Jan - 3 Feb | | |
| | Yg F | Yg Wd | Yn F | Yn Wd | Yg E | Yg E1 | Yn E | Yn F | Yg M | Yg F | Yn M | Yn E2 | Yg W | Yg M | Yn W | Yn M | Yg Wd | Yg E3 | Yn Wd | Yn W | Yg F | Yg W | Yn F | Yn E4 | |
| Starting time | 1st day | Mid-pt | 1st day | Mid-pt | 1st day | Mid-pt | 1st day | Mid-pt | 1st day | Mid-pt | 1st day | Mid-pt | 1st day | Mid-pt | 1st day | Mid-pt | 1st day | Mid-pt | 1st day | Mid-pt | 1st day | Mid-pt | 1st day | Mid-pt | |
| Date | 4 | 18 | 5 | 20 | 5 | 20 | 5 | 21 | 5 | 21 | 7 | 23 | 7 | 23 | 7 | 23 | 8 | 23 | 7 | 22 | 7 | 22 | 5 | 20 | |
| Hour | 0052 | 2046 | 1902 | 1959 | 0005 | 0718 | 1739 | 0640 | 2217 | 1446 | 0824 | 0139 | 1807 | 0835 | 2051 | 0559 | 1215 | 1505 | 1510 | 1227 | 0705 | 0140 | 1900 | 1218 | |
| DATE 4 | Yg M | Yg E1 | | | | | | | | | | | | | | | | | | | | | | | 4 |
| 5 | Yn M | Yn F | Yn E | Yn M | Yg M | Yg E1 | Yg M | Yg E3 | Yn M | Yn F | | | | | | | | | | | | | Yn Wd | Yn Wd | 5 |
| 6 | Yg W | Yg F | Yg M | Yg E3 | Yn M | Yn F | Yn M | Yn W | Yg W | Yg F | | | | | | | | | | | | | Yg F | Yg E1 | 6 |
| 7 | Yn W | Yn E2 | Yn M | Yn W | Yg W | Yg F | Yg W | Yg W | Yn W | Yn E2 | Yn W | Yn E4 | Yg Wd | Yg M | Yn Wd | Yn Wd | | | Yg F | Yg E1 | Yg F | Yg E3 | Yn F | Yn F | 7 |
| 8 | Yg Wd | Yg M | Yg W | Yg W | Yn W | Yn E2 | Yn W | Yn E4 | Yg Wd | Yg M | Yg Wd | Yg Wd | Yn Wd | Yn M | Yg F | Yg E1 | Yg F | Yg E3 | Yn F | Yn F | Yn F | Yn W | Yg E | Yg F | 8 |
| 9 | Yn Wd | Yn M | Yn W | Yn E4 | Yg Wd | Yg M | Yg Wd | Yg Wd | Yn Wd | Yn M | Yn Wd | Yn Wd | Yg F | Yg E3 | Yn F | Yn F | Yn F | Yn W | Yg E | Yg F | Yg E | Yg W | Yn E | Yn E2 | 9 |
| 10 | Yg F | Yg E3 | Yg Wd | Yg Wd | Yn Wd | Yn M | Yn Wd | Yn Wd | Yg F | Yg E3 | Yg F | Yg E1 | Yn F | Yn W | Yg E | Yg F | Yg E | Yg W | Yn E | Yn E2 | Yn E | Yn E4 | Yg M | Yg M | 10 |
| 11 | Yn F | Yn W | Yn Wd | Yn Wd | Yg F | Yg E3 | Yg F | Yg E1 | Yn F | Yn W | Yn F | Yn F | Yg E | Yg W | Yn E | Yn E2 | Yn E | Yn E4 | Yg M | Yg M | Yg M | Yg Wd | Yn M | Yn M | 11 |
| 12 | Yg E | Yg W | Yg F | Yg E1 | Yn F | Yn W | Yn F | Yn F | Yg E | Yg W | Yg E | Yg F | Yn E | Yn E4 | Yg M | Yg M | Yg M | Yg Wd | Yn M | Yn M | Yn M | Yn Wd | Yg W | Yg E3 | 12 |
| 13 | Yn E | Yn E4 | Yn F | Yn F | Yg E | Yg W | Yg E | Yg F | Yn E | Yn E4 | Yn E | Yn E2 | Yg M | Yg Wd | Yn M | Yn M | Yn M | Yn Wd | Yg W | Yg E3 | Yg W | Yg E1 | Yn W | Yn W | 13 |
| 14 | Yg M | Yg Wd | Yg E | Yg F | Yn E | Yn E4 | Yn E | Yn E2 | Yg M | Yg Wd | Yg M | Yg M | Yn M | Yn Wd | Yg W | Yg E3 | Yg W | Yg E1 | Yn W | Yn W | Yn W | Yn F | Yg Wd | Yg W | 14 |
| 15 | Yn M | Yn Wd | Yn E | Yn E2 | Yg M | Yg Wd | Yg M | Yg M | Yn M | Yn Wd | Yn M | Yn M | Yg W | Yg E1 | Yn W | Yn W | Yn W | Yn F | Yg Wd | Yg W | Yg Wd | Yg F | Yn Wd | Yn E4 | 15 |
| 16 | Yg W | Yg E1 | Yg M | Yg M | Yn M | Yn Wd | Yn M | Yn M | Yg W | Yg E1 | Yg W | Yg E3 | Yn W | Yn F | Yg Wd | Yg W | Yg Wd | Yg F | Yn Wd | Yn E4 | Yn Wd | Yn E2 | Yg F | Yg Wd | 16 |
| 17 | Yn W | Yn F | Yn M | Yn M | Yg W | Yg E1 | Yg W | Yg E3 | Yn W | Yn F | Yn W | Yn W | Yg Wd | Yg F | Yn Wd | Yn E4 | Yn Wd | Yn E2 | Yg F | Yg Wd | Yg F | Yg M | Yn F | Yn Wd | 17 |
| 18 | Yg Wd | Yg F | Yg W | Yg E3 | Yn W | Yn F | Yn W | Yn W | Yg Wd | Yg F | Yg Wd | Yg W | Yn Wd | Yn E2 | Yg F | Yg Wd | Yg F | Yg M | Yn F | Yn Wd | Yn F | Yn M | Yg E | Yg E1 | 18 |
| 19 | Yn Wd | Yn E2 | Yn W | Yn W | Yg Wd | Yg F | Yg Wd | Yg W | Yn Wd | Yn E2 | Yn Wd | Yn E4 | Yg F | Yg M | Yn F | Yn Wd | Yn F | Yn M | Yg E | Yg E1 | Yg E | Yg E3 | Yn E | Yn F | 19 |
| 20 | Yg F | Yg M | Yg Wd | Yg W | Yn Wd | Yn E2 | Yn Wd | Yn E4 | Yg F | Yg M | Yg F | Yg Wd | Yn F | Yn M | Yg E | Yg E1 | Yg E | Yg E3 | Yn E | Yn F | Yn E | Yn W | Yg M | Yg F | 20 |
| 21 | Yn F | Yn M | Yn Wd | Yn E4 | Yg F | Yg M | Yg F | Yg Wd | Yn F | Yn M | Yn F | Yn Wd | Yg E | Yg E3 | Yn E | Yn F | Yn E | Yn W | Yg M | Yg F | Yg M | Yg W | Yn M | Yn E2 | 21 |
| 22 | Yg E | Yg E3 | Yg F | Yg Wd | Yn F | Yn M | Yn F | Yn Wd | Yg E | Yg E3 | Yg E | Yg E1 | Yn E | Yn W | Yg M | Yg F | Yg M | Yg W | Yn M | Yn E2 | Yn M | Yn E4 | Yg W | Yg M | 22 |
| 23 | Yn E | Yn W | Yn F | Yn Wd | Yg E | Yg E3 | Yg E | Yg E1 | Yn E | Yn W | Yn E | Yn F | Yg M | Yg W | Yn M | Yn E2 | Yn M | Yn E4 | Yg W | Yg M | Yg W | Yg Wd | Yn W | Yn M | 23 |
| 24 | Yg M | Yg W | Yg E | Yg E1 | Yn E | Yn W | Yn E | Yn F | Yg M | Yg W | Yg M | Yg F | Yn M | Yn E4 | Yg W | Yg M | Yg W | Yg Wd | Yn W | Yn M | Yn W | Yn Wd | Yg Wd | Yg E3 | 24 |
| 25 | Yn M | Yn E4 | Yn E | Yn F | Yg M | Yg W | Yg M | Yg F | Yn M | Yn E4 | Yn M | Yn E2 | Yg W | Yg Wd | Yn W | Yn M | Yn W | Yn Wd | Yg Wd | Yg E3 | Yg Wd | Yg E1 | Yn Wd | Yn W | 25 |
| 26 | Yg W | Yg Wd | Yg M | Yg F | Yn M | Yn E4 | Yn M | Yn E2 | Yg W | Yg Wd | Yg W | Yg M | Yn W | Yn Wd | Yg Wd | Yg E3 | Yg Wd | Yg E1 | Yn Wd | Yn W | Yn Wd | Yn F | Yg F | Yg W | 26 |
| 27 | Yn W | Yn Wd | Yn M | Yn E2 | Yg W | Yg Wd | Yg W | Yg M | Yn W | Yn Wd | Yn W | Yn M | Yg Wd | Yg E1 | Yn Wd | Yn W | Yn Wd | Yn F | Yg F | Yg W | Yg F | Yg F | Yn F | Yn E4 | 27 |
| 28 | Yg Wd | Yg E1 | Yg W | Yg M | Yn W | Yn Wd | Yn W | Yn M | Yg Wd | Yg E1 | Yg Wd | Yg E3 | Yn Wd | Yn F | Yg F | Yg W | Yg F | Yg F | Yn F | Yn E4 | Yn F | Yn E2 | Yg E | Yg Wd | 28 |
| 29 | | | Yn W | Yn M | Yg Wd | Yg E1 | Yg Wd | Yg E3 | Yn Wd | Yn F | Yn Wd | Yn W | Yg F | Yg F | Yn E | Yn E4 | Yn F | Yn E2 | Yg E | Yg Wd | Yg E | Yg M | Yn E | Yn Wd | 29 |
| 30 | | | Yg Wd | Yg E3 | Yn Wd | Yn F | Yn Wd | Yn W | Yg F | Yg F | Yg F | Yg W | Yn F | Yn E2 | Yg E | Yg Wd | Yg E | Yg M | Yn E | Yn Wd | Yn E | Yn M | Yg M | Yg E1 | 30 |
| 31 | | | Yn Wd | Yn W | | | Yg F | Yg W | | | Yn F | Yn E4 | Yg E | Yg M | | | Yn E | Yn M | | | Yg M | Yg E3 | Yn M | Yn F | 31 |
| 1 | Yn Wd | Yn F | Yg F | Yg W | Yg F | Yg F | Yn F | Yn E4 | Yn F | Yn E2 | Yg E | Yg Wd | Yn E | Yn M | Yn E | Yn Wd | Yg M | Yg E3 | Yg M | Yg E1 | Yn M | Yn W | Yg W | Yg F | 1 |
| 2 | Yg F | Yg F | Yn F | Yn E4 | Yn F | Yn E2 | Yg E | Yg Wd | Yg E | Yg M | Yn E | Yn Wd | Yg M | Yg E3 | Yg M | Yg E1 | Yn M | Yn W | Yn M | Yn F | Yg W | Yg W | Yn W | Yn E2 | 2 |
| 3 | Yn F | Yn E2 | Yg E | Yg Wd | Yg E | Yg M | Yn E | Yn Wd | Yn E | Yn M | Yg M | Yg E1 | Yn M | Yn W | Yn M | Yn F | Yg W | Yg W | Yg W | Yg F | Yn W | Yn E4 | Yg Wd | Yg M | 3 |
| 4 | Yg E | Yg M | Yn E | Yn Wd | Yn E | Yn M | Yg M | Yg E1 | Yg M | Yg E3 | Yn M | Yn F | Yg W | Yg W | Yg W | Yg F | Yn W | Yn E4 | Yn W | Yn E2 | Yg Wd | Yg Wd | | | 4 |
| 5 | | | | | | | | | Yn M | Yn W | Yg W | Yg F | Yn W | Yn E4 | Yn W | Yn E2 | Yg Wd | Yg Wd | Yg Wd | Yg M | | | | | 5 |
| 6 | | | | | | | | | Yg W | Yg W | Yn W | Yn E2 | Yg Wd | Yg Wd | Yg Wd | Yg M | Yn Wd | Yn Wd | Yn Wd | Yn M | | | | | 6 |
| 7 | | | | | | | | | | | | | | | Yn Wd | Yn M | | | | | | | | | 7 |
| 8 | | | | | | | | | | | | | | | | | | | | | | | | | 8 |

# YEAR OF THE TIGER

| | H | E | H | E | H | E | H | E | H | E | H | E | H | E | H | E | H | E | H | E | H | E | H | E | |
|---|---|---|---|---|---|---|---|---|---|---|---|---|---|---|---|---|---|---|---|---|---|---|---|---|---|
| YEAR | YEAR<br>Yg M | Yg Wd | 2010 | | | | | | | | | | | | | | | | | | | | 2011 | | |
| MONTH | 4 Feb - 5 Mar<br>Yg E | Yg Wd | 6 Mar - 4 Apr<br>Yn E | Yn Wd | 5 Apr - 4 May<br>Yg M | Yg E1 | 5 May - 5 June<br>Yn M | Yn F | 6 June - 6 Jul<br>Yg W | Yg F | 7 Jul - 6 Aug<br>Yn W | Yn E2 | 7 Aug - 7 Sep<br>Yg Wd | Yg M | 8 Sep - 7 Oct<br>Yn Wd | Yn M | 8 Oct - 6 Nov<br>Yg F | Yg E3 | 7 Nov - 6 Dec<br>Yn F | Yn W | 7 Dec - 5 Jan<br>Yg E | Yg W | 6 Jan - 3 Feb<br>Yn E | Yn E4 | |
| Starting time | 1st day | Mid-pt | 1st day | Mid-pt | 1st day | Mid-pt | 1st day | Mid-pt | 1st day | Mid-pt | 1st day | Mid-pt | 1st day | Mid-pt | 1st day | Mid-pt | 1st day | Mid-pt | 1st day | Mid-pt | 1st day | Mid-pt | 1st day | Mid-pt | |
| Date | 4 | 19 | 6 | 21 | 5 | 20 | 5 | 21 | 6 | 21 | 7 | 23 | 7 | 23 | 8 | 23 | 8 | 23 | 7 | 22 | 7 | 22 | 6 | 20 | |
| Hour | 0642 | 0235 | 0052 | 0148 | 0555 | 1307 | 2329 | 1229 | 0351 | 2035 | 1414 | 0728 | 2357 | 1424 | 0241 | 1148 | 1805 | 2054 | 2103 | 1816 | 1341 | 0728 | 0050 | 1807 | |
| DATE 4 | Yn Wd | Yn M | | | | | | | | | | | | | | | | | | | | | | | 4 |
| 5 | Yg F | Yg E3 | | | Yn Wd | Yn M | Yn Wd | Yn Wd | | | | | | | | | | | | | | | | | 5 |
| 6 | Yn F | Yn W | Yn Wd | Yn Wd | Yg F | Yg E3 | Yg F | Yg E1 | Yn F | Yn W | | | | | | | | | | | | | Yn M | Yn M | 6 |
| 7 | Yg E | Yg W | Yg F | Yg E1 | Yn F | Yn W | Yn F | Yn F | Yg E | Yg W | Yg E | Yg F | Yn E | Yn E4 | | | | | Yn M | Yn M | Yn M | Yn Wd | Yg W | Yg E3 | 7 |
| 8 | Yn E | Yn E4 | Yn F | Yn F | Yg E | Yg W | Yg E | Yg F | Yn E | Yn E4 | Yn E | Yn E2 | Yg M | Yg Wd | Yn M | Yn M | Yn M | Yn Wd | Yg W | Yg E3 | Yg W | Yg E1 | Yn W | Yn W | 8 |
| 9 | Yg M | Yg Wd | Yg E | Yg F | Yn E | Yn E4 | Yn E | Yn E2 | Yg M | Yg Wd | Yg M | Yg M | Yn M | Yn Wd | Yg W | Yg E3 | Yg W | Yg E1 | Yn W | Yn W | Yn W | Yn F | Yg Wd | Yg W | 9 |
| 10 | Yn M | Yn Wd | Yn E | Yn E2 | Yg M | Yg Wd | Yg M | Yg M | Yn M | Yn Wd | Yn M | Yn M | Yg W | Yg E1 | Yn W | Yn W | Yn W | Yn F | Yg Wd | Yg W | Yg Wd | Yg F | Yn Wd | Yn E4 | 10 |
| 11 | Yg W | Yg E1 | Yg M | Yg M | Yn M | Yn Wd | Yn M | Yn M | Yg W | Yg E1 | Yg W | Yg E3 | Yn W | Yn F | Yg Wd | Yg W | Yg Wd | Yg F | Yn Wd | Yn E4 | Yn Wd | Yn E2 | Yg F | Yg Wd | 11 |
| 12 | Yn W | Yn F | Yn M | Yn M | Yg W | Yg E1 | Yg W | Yg E3 | Yn W | Yn F | Yn W | Yn W | Yg Wd | Yg F | Yn Wd | Yn E4 | Yn Wd | Yn E2 | Yg F | Yg Wd | Yg F | Yg M | Yn F | Yn Wd | 12 |
| 13 | Yg Wd | Yg F | Yg W | Yg E3 | Yn W | Yn F | Yn W | Yn W | Yg Wd | Yg F | Yg Wd | Yg W | Yn Wd | Yn E2 | Yg F | Yg Wd | Yg F | Yg M | Yn F | Yn Wd | Yn F | Yn M | Yg E | Yg E1 | 13 |
| 14 | Yn Wd | Yn E2 | Yn W | Yn W | Yg Wd | Yg F | Yg Wd | Yg W | Yn Wd | Yn E2 | Yn Wd | Yn E4 | Yg F | Yg M | Yn F | Yn Wd | Yn F | Yn M | Yg E | Yg E1 | Yg E | Yg E3 | Yn E | Yn F | 14 |
| 15 | Yg F | Yg M | Yg Wd | Yg W | Yn Wd | Yn E2 | Yn Wd | Yn E4 | Yg F | Yg M | Yg F | Yg Wd | Yn F | Yn M | Yg E | Yg E1 | Yg E | Yg E3 | Yn E | Yn F | Yn E | Yn W | Yg M | Yg F | 15 |
| 16 | Yn F | Yn M | Yn Wd | Yn E4 | Yg F | Yg M | Yg F | Yg Wd | Yn F | Yn M | Yn F | Yn Wd | Yg E | Yg E3 | Yn E | Yn F | Yn E | Yn W | Yg M | Yg F | Yg M | Yg W | Yn M | Yn E2 | 16 |
| 17 | Yg E | Yg E3 | Yg F | Yg Wd | Yn F | Yn M | Yn F | Yn Wd | Yg E | Yg E3 | Yg E | Yg E1 | Yn E | Yn W | Yg M | Yg F | Yg M | Yg W | Yn M | Yn E2 | Yn M | Yn E4 | Yg W | Yg M | 17 |
| 18 | Yn E | Yn W | Yn F | Yn Wd | Yg E | Yg E3 | Yg E | Yg E1 | Yn E | Yn W | Yn E | Yn F | Yg M | Yg W | Yn M | Yn E2 | Yn M | Yn E4 | Yg W | Yg M | Yg W | Yg Wd | Yn W | Yn M | 18 |
| 19 | Yg M | Yg W | Yg E | Yg E1 | Yn E | Yn W | Yn E | Yn F | Yg M | Yg W | Yg M | Yg F | Yn M | Yn E4 | Yg W | Yg M | Yg W | Yg Wd | Yn W | Yn M | Yn W | Yn Wd | Yg Wd | Yg E3 | 19 |
| 20 | Yn M | Yn E4 | Yn E | Yn F | Yg M | Yg W | Yg M | Yg F | Yn M | Yn E4 | Yn M | Yn E2 | Yg W | Yg Wd | Yn W | Yn M | Yn W | Yn Wd | Yg Wd | Yg E3 | Yg Wd | Yg E1 | Yn Wd | Yn W | 20 |
| 21 | Yg W | Yg Wd | Yg M | Yg F | Yn M | Yn E4 | Yn M | Yn E2 | Yg W | Yg Wd | Yg W | Yg M | Yn W | Yn Wd | Yg Wd | Yg E3 | Yg Wd | Yg E1 | Yn Wd | Yn W | Yn Wd | Yn F | Yg F | Yg W | 21 |
| 22 | Yn W | Yn Wd | Yn M | Yn E2 | Yg W | Yg Wd | Yg W | Yg M | Yn W | Yn Wd | Yn W | Yn M | Yg Wd | Yg E1 | Yn Wd | Yn W | Yn Wd | Yn F | Yg F | Yg W | Yg F | Yg F | Yn F | Yn E4 | 22 |
| 23 | Yg Wd | Yg E1 | Yg W | Yg M | Yn W | Yn Wd | Yn W | Yn M | Yg Wd | Yg E1 | Yg Wd | Yg E3 | Yn Wd | Yn F | Yg F | Yg W | Yg F | Yg F | Yn F | Yn E4 | Yn F | Yn E2 | Yg E | Yg Wd | 23 |
| 24 | Yn Wd | Yn F | Yn W | Yn M | Yg Wd | Yg E1 | Yg Wd | Yg E3 | Yn Wd | Yn F | Yn Wd | Yn W | Yg F | Yg F | Yn F | Yn E4 | Yn F | Yn E2 | Yg E | Yg Wd | Yg E | Yg M | Yn E | Yn Wd | 24 |
| 25 | Yg F | Yg F | Yg Wd | Yg E3 | Yn Wd | Yn F | Yn Wd | Yn W | Yg F | Yg F | Yg F | Yg W | Yn F | Yn E2 | Yg E | Yg Wd | Yg E | Yg M | Yn E | Yn Wd | Yn E | Yn M | Yg M | Yg E1 | 25 |
| 26 | Yn F | Yn E2 | Yn Wd | Yn W | Yg F | Yg F | Yg F | Yg W | Yn F | Yn E2 | Yn F | Yn E4 | Yg E | Yg M | Yn E | Yn Wd | Yn E | Yn M | Yg M | Yg E1 | Yg M | Yg E3 | Yn M | Yn F | 26 |
| 27 | Yg E | Yg M | Yg F | Yg W | Yn F | Yn E2 | Yn F | Yn E4 | Yg E | Yg M | Yg E | Yg Wd | Yn E | Yn M | Yg M | Yg E1 | Yg M | Yg E3 | Yn M | Yn F | Yn M | Yn W | Yg W | Yg F | 27 |
| 28 | Yn E | Yn M | Yn F | Yn E4 | Yg E | Yg M | Yg E | Yg Wd | Yn E | Yn M | Yn E | Yn Wd | Yg M | Yg E3 | Yn M | Yn F | Yn M | Yn W | Yg W | Yg F | Yg W | Yg W | Yn W | Yn E2 | 28 |
| 29 | | | Yg E | Yg Wd | Yn E | Yn M | Yn E | Yn Wd | Yg M | Yg E3 | Yg M | Yg E1 | Yn M | Yn W | Yg W | Yg F | Yg W | Yg W | Yn W | Yn E2 | Yn W | Yn E4 | Yg Wd | Yg M | 29 |
| 30 | | | Yn E | Yn Wd | Yg M | Yg E3 | Yg M | Yg E1 | Yn M | Yn W | Yn M | Yn F | Yg W | Yg W | Yn W | Yn E2 | Yn W | Yn E4 | Yg Wd | Yg M | Yg Wd | Yg Wd | Yn Wd | Yn M | 30 |
| 31 | | | Yg M | Yg E1 | | | Yn M | Yn F | | | Yg W | Yg F | Yn W | Yn E4 | | | Yg Wd | Yg Wd | | | Yn Wd | Yn Wd | Yg F | Yg E3 | 31 |
| 1 | Yg M | Yg E3 | Yn M | Yn F | Yn M | Yn W | Yg W | Yg F | Yg W | Yg W | Yn W | Yn E2 | Yg Wd | Yg Wd | Yg Wd | Yg M | Yn Wd | Yn Wd | Yn Wd | Yn M | Yg F | Yg E1 | Yn F | Yn W | 1 |
| 2 | Yn M | Yn W | Yg W | Yg F | Yg W | Yg W | Yn W | Yn E2 | Yn W | Yn E4 | Yg Wd | Yg M | Yn Wd | Yn Wd | Yn Wd | Yn M | Yg F | Yg E1 | Yg F | Yg E3 | Yn F | Yn F | Yg E | Yg W | 2 |
| 3 | Yg W | Yg W | Yn W | Yn E2 | Yn W | Yn E4 | Yg Wd | Yg M | Yg Wd | Yg Wd | Yn Wd | Yn M | Yg F | Yg E1 | Yg F | Yg E3 | Yn F | Yn F | Yn F | Yn W | Yg E | Yg F | Yn E | Yn E4 | 3 |
| 4 | Yn W | Yn E4 | Yg Wd | Yg M | Yg Wd | Yg Wd | Yn Wd | Yn M | Yn Wd | Yn Wd | Yg F | Yg E3 | Yn F | Yn F | Yn F | Yn W | Yg E | Yg F | Yg E | Yg W | Yn E | Yn E2 | | | 4 |
| 5 | Yg Wd | Yg Wd | | | | | Yg F | Yg E3 | Yg F | Yg E1 | Yn F | Yn W | Yg E | Yg F | Yg E | Yg W | Yn E | Yn E2 | Yn E | Yn E4 | Yg M | Yg M | | | 5 |
| 6 | | | | | | | | | Yn F | Yn F | Yg E | Yg W | Yn E | Yn E2 | Yn E | Yn E4 | Yg M | Yg M | Yg M | Yg Wd | | | | | 6 |
| 7 | | | | | | | | | | | | | Yg M | Yg M | Yg M | Yg Wd | | | | | | | | | 7 |
| 8 | | | | | | | | | | | | | | | | | | | | | | | | | 8 |

# YEAR OF THE RABBIT

| | H | E | H | E | H | E | H | E | H | E | H | E | H | E | H | E | H | E | H | E | H | E | H | E | |
|---|---|---|---|---|---|---|---|---|---|---|---|---|---|---|---|---|---|---|---|---|---|---|---|---|---|
| YEAR | YEAR<br>Yn M | Yn Wd | 2011 | | | | | | | | | | | | | | | | | | | | 2012 | | |
| MONTH | 4 Feb - 5 Mar<br>Yg M | Yg Wd | 6 Mar - 4 Apr<br>Yn M | Yn Wd | 5 Apr - 5 May<br>Yg W | Yg E1 | 6 May - 5 June<br>Yn W | Yn F | 6 June - 6 Jul<br>Yg Wd | Yg F | 7 Jul - 7 Aug<br>Yn Wd | Yn E2 | 8 Aug - 7 Sep<br>Yg F | Yg M | 8 Sep - 7 Oct<br>Yn F | Yn M | 8 Oct - 7 Nov<br>Yg E | Yg E3 | 8 Nov - 6 Dec<br>Yn E | Yn W | 7 Dec - 5 Jan<br>Yg M | Yg W | 6 Jan - 3 Feb<br>Yn M | Yn E4 | |
| Starting time | 1st day | Mid-pt | 1st day | Mid-pt | 1st day | Mid-pt | 1st day | Mid-pt | 1st day | Mid-pt | 1st day | Mid-pt | 1st day | Mid-pt | 1st day | Mid-pt | 1st day | Mid-pt | 1st day | Mid-pt | 1st day | Mid-pt | 1st day | Mid-pt | |
| Date | 4 | 19 | 6 | 21 | 5 | 20 | 6 | 21 | 6 | 22 | 7 | 23 | 8 | 23 | 8 | 23 | 8 | 24 | 8 | 23 | 7 | 22 | 6 | 20 | |
| Hour | 1232 | 0824 | 0643 | 0737 | 1146 | 1856 | 0524 | 1818 | 0943 | 0224 | 2006 | 1317 | 0549 | 2013 | 0833 | 1737 | 2357 | 0243 | 0252 | 0008 | 1932 | 1318 | 0641 | 2356 | |
| DATE 4 | Yg M | Yg Wd | | | | | | | | | | | | | | | | | | | | | | | 4 |
| 5 | Yn M | Yn Wd | | | Yg M | Yg Wd | | | | | | | | | | | | | | | | | | | 5 |
| 6 | Yg W | Yg E1 | Yg M | Yg M | Yn M | Yn Wd | Yn M | Yn M | Yg W | Yg E1 | | | | | | | | | | | | | Yg F | Yg Wd | 6 |
| 7 | Yn W | Yn F | Yn M | Yn M | Yg W | Yg E1 | Yg W | Yg E3 | Yn W | Yn F | Yn W | Yn W | | | | | | | | | Yg F | Yg M | Yn F | Yn Wd | 7 |
| 8 | Yg Wd | Yg F | Yg W | Yg E3 | Yn W | Yn F | Yn W | Yn W | Yg Wd | Yg F | Yg Wd | Yg W | Yn Wd | Yn E2 | Yg F | Yg Wd | Yg F | Yg M | Yn F | Yn Wd | Yn F | Yn M | Yg E | Yg E1 | 8 |
| 9 | Yn Wd | Yn E2 | Yn W | Yn W | Yg Wd | Yg F | Yg Wd | Yg W | Yn Wd | Yn E2 | Yn Wd | Yn E4 | Yg F | Yg M | Yn F | Yn Wd | Yn F | Yn M | Yg E | Yg E1 | Yg E | Yg E3 | Yn E | Yn F | 9 |
| 10 | Yg F | Yg M | Yg Wd | Yg W | Yn Wd | Yn E2 | Yn Wd | Yn E4 | Yg F | Yg M | Yg F | Yg Wd | Yn F | Yn M | Yg E | Yg E1 | Yg E | Yg E3 | Yn E | Yn F | Yn E | Yn W | Yg M | Yg F | 10 |
| 11 | Yn F | Yn M | Yn Wd | Yn E4 | Yg F | Yg M | Yg F | Yg Wd | Yn F | Yn M | Yn F | Yn Wd | Yg E | Yg E3 | Yn E | Yn F | Yn E | Yn W | Yg M | Yg F | Yg M | Yg W | Yn M | Yn E2 | 11 |
| 12 | Yg E | Yg E3 | Yg F | Yg Wd | Yn F | Yn M | Yn F | Yn Wd | Yg E | Yg E3 | Yg E | Yg E1 | Yn E | Yn W | Yg M | Yg F | Yg M | Yg W | Yn M | Yn E2 | Yn M | Yn E4 | Yg W | Yg M | 12 |
| 13 | Yn E | Yn W | Yn F | Yn Wd | Yg E | Yg E3 | Yg E | Yg E1 | Yn E | Yn W | Yn E | Yn F | Yg M | Yg W | Yn M | Yn E2 | Yn M | Yn E4 | Yg W | Yg M | Yg W | Yg Wd | Yn W | Yn M | 13 |
| 14 | Yg M | Yg W | Yg E | Yg E1 | Yn E | Yn W | Yn E | Yn F | Yg M | Yg W | Yg M | Yg F | Yn M | Yn E4 | Yg W | Yg M | Yg W | Yg Wd | Yn W | Yn M | Yn W | Yn Wd | Yg Wd | Yg E3 | 14 |
| 15 | Yn M | Yn E4 | Yn E | Yn F | Yg M | Yg W | Yg M | Yg F | Yn M | Yn E4 | Yn M | Yn E2 | Yg W | Yg Wd | Yn W | Yn M | Yn W | Yn Wd | Yg Wd | Yg E3 | Yg Wd | Yg E1 | Yn Wd | Yn W | 15 |
| 16 | Yg W | Yg Wd | Yg M | Yg F | Yn M | Yn E4 | Yn M | Yn E2 | Yg W | Yg Wd | Yg W | Yg M | Yn W | Yn Wd | Yg Wd | Yg E3 | Yg Wd | Yg E1 | Yn Wd | Yn W | Yn Wd | Yn F | Yg F | Yg W | 16 |
| 17 | Yn W | Yn Wd | Yn M | Yn E2 | Yg W | Yg Wd | Yg W | Yg M | Yn W | Yn Wd | Yn W | Yn M | Yg Wd | Yg E1 | Yn Wd | Yn W | Yn Wd | Yn F | Yg F | Yg W | Yg F | Yg F | Yn F | Yn E4 | 17 |
| 18 | Yg Wd | Yg E1 | Yg W | Yg M | Yn W | Yn Wd | Yn W | Yn M | Yg Wd | Yg E1 | Yg Wd | Yg E3 | Yn Wd | Yn F | Yg F | Yg W | Yg F | Yg F | Yn F | Yn E4 | Yn F | Yn E2 | Yg E | Yg Wd | 18 |
| 19 | Yn Wd | Yn F | Yn W | Yn M | Yg Wd | Yg E1 | Yg Wd | Yg E3 | Yn Wd | Yn F | Yn Wd | Yn W | Yg F | Yg F | Yn F | Yn E4 | Yn F | Yn E2 | Yg E | Yg Wd | Yg E | Yg M | Yn E | Yn Wd | 19 |
| 20 | Yg F | Yg F | Yg Wd | Yg E3 | Yn Wd | Yn F | Yn Wd | Yn W | Yg F | Yg F | Yg F | Yg W | Yn F | Yn E2 | Yg E | Yg Wd | Yg E | Yg M | Yn E | Yn Wd | Yn E | Yn M | Yg M | Yg E1 | 20 |
| 21 | Yn F | Yn E2 | Yn Wd | Yn W | Yg F | Yg F | Yg F | Yg W | Yn F | Yn E2 | Yn F | Yn E4 | Yg E | Yg M | Yn E | Yn Wd | Yn E | Yn M | Yg M | Yg E1 | Yg M | Yg E3 | Yn M | Yn F | 21 |
| 22 | Yg E | Yg M | Yg F | Yg W | Yn F | Yn E2 | Yn F | Yn E4 | Yg E | Yg M | Yg E | Yg Wd | Yn E | Yn M | Yg M | Yg E1 | Yg M | Yg E3 | Yn M | Yn F | Yn M | Yn W | Yg W | Yg F | 22 |
| 23 | Yn E | Yn M | Yn F | Yn E4 | Yg E | Yg M | Yg E | Yg Wd | Yn E | Yn M | Yn E | Yn Wd | Yg M | Yg E3 | Yn M | Yn F | Yn M | Yn W | Yg W | Yg F | Yg W | Yg W | Yn W | Yn E2 | 23 |
| 24 | Yg M | Yg E3 | Yg E | Yg Wd | Yn E | Yn M | Yn E | Yn Wd | Yg M | Yg E3 | Yg M | Yg E1 | Yn M | Yn W | Yg W | Yg F | Yg W | Yg W | Yn W | Yn E2 | Yn W | Yn E4 | Yg Wd | Yg M | 24 |
| 25 | Yn M | Yn W | Yn E | Yn Wd | Yg M | Yg E3 | Yg M | Yg E1 | Yn M | Yn W | Yn M | Yn F | Yg W | Yg W | Yn W | Yn E2 | Yn W | Yn E4 | Yg Wd | Yg M | Yg Wd | Yg Wd | Yn Wd | Yn M | 25 |
| 26 | Yg W | Yg W | Yg M | Yg E1 | Yn M | Yn W | Yn M | Yn F | Yg W | Yg W | Yg W | Yg F | Yn W | Yn E4 | Yg Wd | Yg M | Yg Wd | Yg Wd | Yn Wd | Yn M | Yn Wd | Yn Wd | Yg F | Yg E3 | 26 |
| 27 | Yn W | Yn E4 | Yn M | Yn F | Yg W | Yg W | Yg W | Yg F | Yn W | Yn E4 | Yn W | Yn E2 | Yg Wd | Yg Wd | Yn Wd | Yn M | Yn Wd | Yn Wd | Yg F | Yg E3 | Yg F | Yg E1 | Yn F | Yn W | 27 |
| 28 | Yg Wd | Yg Wd | Yg W | Yg F | Yn W | Yn E4 | Yn W | Yn E2 | Yg Wd | Yg Wd | Yg Wd | Yg M | Yn Wd | Yn Wd | Yg F | Yg E3 | Yg F | Yg E1 | Yn F | Yn W | Yn F | Yn F | Yg E | Yg W | 28 |
| 29 | | | Yn W | Yn E2 | Yg Wd | Yg Wd | Yg Wd | Yg M | Yn Wd | Yn Wd | Yn Wd | Yn M | Yg F | Yg E1 | Yn F | Yn W | Yn F | Yn F | Yg E | Yg W | Yg E | Yg F | Yn E | Yn E4 | 29 |
| 30 | | | Yg Wd | Yg M | Yn Wd | Yn Wd | Yn Wd | Yn M | Yg F | Yg E1 | Yg F | Yg E3 | Yn F | Yn F | Yg E | Yg W | Yg E | Yg F | Yn E | Yn E4 | Yn E | Yn E2 | Yg M | Yg Wd | 30 |
| 31 | | | Yn Wd | Yn M | | | Yg F | Yg E3 | | | Yn F | Yn W | Yg E | Yg F | | | Yn E | Yn E2 | | | Yg M | Yg M | Yn M | Yn Wd | 31 |
| 1 | Yn Wd | Yn Wd | Yg F | Yg E3 | Yg F | Yg E1 | Yn F | Yn W | Yn F | Yn F | Yg E | Yg W | Yn E | Yn E2 | Yn E | Yn E4 | Yg M | Yg M | Yg M | Yg Wd | Yn M | Yn M | Yg W | Yg E1 | 1 |
| 2 | Yg F | Yg E1 | Yn F | Yn W | Yn F | Yn F | Yg E | Yg W | Yg E | Yg F | Yn E | Yn E4 | Yg M | Yg M | Yg M | Yg Wd | Yn M | Yn M | Yn M | Yn Wd | Yg W | Yg E3 | Yn W | Yn F | 2 |
| 3 | Yn F | Yn F | Yg E | Yg W | Yg E | Yg F | Yn E | Yn E4 | Yn E | Yn E2 | Yg M | Yg Wd | Yn M | Yn M | Yn M | Yn Wd | Yg W | Yg E3 | Yg W | Yg E1 | Yn W | Yn W | Yg Wd | Yg F | 3 |
| 4 | Yg E | Yg F | Yn E | Yn E4 | Yn E | Yn E2 | Yg M | Yg Wd | Yg M | Yg M | Yn M | Yn Wd | Yg W | Yg E3 | Yg W | Yg E1 | Yn W | Yn W | Yn W | Yn F | Yg Wd | Yg W | | | 4 |
| 5 | Yn E | Yn E2 | | | Yg M | Yg M | Yn M | Yn Wd | Yn M | Yn M | Yg W | Yg E1 | Yn W | Yn W | Yn W | Yn F | Yg Wd | Yg W | Yg Wd | Yg F | Yn Wd | Yn E4 | | | 5 |
| 6 | | | | | | | | | Yg W | Yg E3 | Yn W | Yn F | Yg Wd | Yg W | Yg Wd | Yg F | Yn Wd | Yn E4 | Yn Wd | Yn E2 | | | | | 6 |
| 7 | | | | | | | | | | | Yg Wd | Yg F | Yn Wd | Yn E4 | Yn Wd | Yn E2 | Yg F | Yg Wd | | | | | | | 7 |
| 8 | | | | | | | | | | | | | | | | | | | | | | | | | 8 |

# YEAR OF THE DRAGON

| | H | E | H | E | H | E | H | E | H | E | H | E | H | E | H | E | H | E | H | E | H | E | H | E | |
|---|---|---|---|---|---|---|---|---|---|---|---|---|---|---|---|---|---|---|---|---|---|---|---|---|---|
| YEAR | YEAR | | 2012 | | | | | | | | | | | | | | | | | | | | 2013 | | |
| | Yg W | Yg E1 | | | | | | | | | | | | | | | | | | | | | | | |
| MONTH | 4 Feb - 4 Mar | | 5 Mar - 3 Apr | | 4 Apr - 4 May | | 5 May - 4 June | | 5 June - 6 Jul | | 7 Jul - 6 Aug | | 7 Aug - 6 Sep | | 7 Sep - 7 Oct | | 8 Oct - 6 Nov | | 7 Nov - 6 Dec | | 7 Dec - 4 Jan | | 5 Jan - 3 Feb | | |
| | Yg W | Yg Wd | Yn W | Yn Wd | Yg Wd | Yg E1 | Yn Wd | Yn F | Yg F | Yg F | Yn F | Yn E2 | Yg E | Yg M | Yn E | Yn M | Yg M | Yg E3 | Yn M | Yn W | Yg W | Yg W | Yn W | Yn E4 | |
| Starting time | 1st day | Mid-pt | 1st day | Mid-pt | 1st day | Mid-pt | 1st day | Mid-pt | 1st day | Mid-pt | 1st day | Mid-pt | 1st day | Mid-pt | 1st day | Mid-pt | 1st day | Mid-pt | 1st day | Mid-pt | 1st day | Mid-pt | 1st day | Mid-pt | |
| Date | 4 | 19 | 5 | 20 | 4 | 20 | 5 | 20 | 5 | 21 | 7 | 22 | 7 | 23 | 7 | 23 | 8 | 23 | 7 | 22 | 7 | 21 | 5 | 20 | |
| Hour | 1840 | 1425 | 1228 | 1320 | 1716 | 0025 | 1043 | 2340 | 1443 | 0745 | 0121 | 1851 | 1126 | 0216 | 1444 | 0018 | 0642 | 0952 | 0956 | 0720 | 0232 | 2016 | 1316 | 0626 | |
| DATE 4 | Yn Wd | Yn E2 | | | Yn Wd | Yn E2 | | | | | | | | | | | | | | | | | | | 4 |
| 5 | Yg F | Yg M | Yn Wd | Yn E4 | Yg F | Yg M | Yg F | Yg Wd | Yn F | Yn M | | | | | | | | | | | | | Yn M | Yn E2 | 5 |
| 6 | Yn F | Yn M | Yg F | Yg Wd | Yn F | Yn M | Yn F | Yn Wd | Yg E | Yg E3 | | | | | | | | | | | | | Yg W | Yg M | 6 |
| 7 | Yg E | Yg E3 | Yn F | Yn Wd | Yg E | Yg E3 | Yg E | Yg E1 | Yn E | Yn W | Yn E | Yn F | Yg M | Yg W | Yn M | Yn E2 | | | Yg W | Yg M | Yg W | Yg Wd | Yn W | Yn M | 7 |
| 8 | Yn E | Yn W | Yg E | Yg E1 | Yn E | Yn W | Yn E | Yn F | Yg M | Yg W | Yg M | Yg F | Yn M | Yn E4 | Yg W | Yg M | Yg W | Yg Wd | Yn W | Yn M | Yn W | Yn Wd | Yg Wd | Yg E3 | 8 |
| 9 | Yg M | Yg W | Yn E | Yn F | Yg M | Yg W | Yg M | Yg F | Yn M | Yn E4 | Yn M | Yn E2 | Yg W | Yg Wd | Yn W | Yn M | Yn W | Yn Wd | Yg Wd | Yg E3 | Yg Wd | Yg E1 | Yn Wd | Yn W | 9 |
| 10 | Yn M | Yn E4 | Yg M | Yg F | Yn M | Yn E4 | Yn M | Yn E2 | Yg W | Yg Wd | Yg W | Yg M | Yn W | Yn Wd | Yg Wd | Yg E3 | Yg Wd | Yg E1 | Yn Wd | Yn W | Yn Wd | Yn F | Yg F | Yg W | 10 |
| 11 | Yg W | Yg Wd | Yn M | Yn E2 | Yg W | Yg Wd | Yg W | Yg M | Yn W | Yn Wd | Yn W | Yn M | Yg Wd | Yg E1 | Yn Wd | Yn W | Yn Wd | Yn F | Yg F | Yg W | Yg F | Yg F | Yn F | Yn E4 | 11 |
| 12 | Yn W | Yn Wd | Yg W | Yg M | Yn W | Yn Wd | Yn W | Yn M | Yg Wd | Yg E1 | Yg Wd | Yg E3 | Yn Wd | Yn F | Yg F | Yg W | Yg F | Yg F | Yn F | Yn E4 | Yn F | Yn E2 | Yg E | Yg Wd | 12 |
| 13 | Yg Wd | Yg E1 | Yn W | Yn M | Yg Wd | Yg E1 | Yg Wd | Yg E3 | Yn Wd | Yn F | Yn Wd | Yn W | Yg F | Yg F | Yn F | Yn E4 | Yn F | Yn E2 | Yg E | Yg Wd | Yg E | Yg M | Yn E | Yn Wd | 13 |
| 14 | Yn Wd | Yn F | Yg Wd | Yg E3 | Yn Wd | Yn F | Yn Wd | Yn W | Yg F | Yg F | Yg F | Yg W | Yn F | Yn E2 | Yg E | Yg Wd | Yg E | Yg M | Yn E | Yn Wd | Yn E | Yn M | Yg M | Yg E1 | 14 |
| 15 | Yg F | Yg F | Yn Wd | Yn W | Yg F | Yg F | Yg F | Yg W | Yn F | Yn E2 | Yn F | Yn E4 | Yg E | Yg M | Yn E | Yn Wd | Yn E | Yn M | Yg M | Yg E1 | Yg M | Yg E3 | Yn M | Yn F | 15 |
| 16 | Yn F | Yn E2 | Yg F | Yg W | Yn F | Yn E2 | Yn F | Yn E4 | Yg E | Yg M | Yg E | Yg Wd | Yn E | Yn M | Yg M | Yg E1 | Yg M | Yg E3 | Yn M | Yn F | Yn M | Yn W | Yg W | Yg F | 16 |
| 17 | Yg E | Yg M | Yn F | Yn E4 | Yg E | Yg M | Yg E | Yg Wd | Yn E | Yn M | Yn E | Yn Wd | Yg M | Yg E3 | Yn M | Yn F | Yn M | Yn W | Yg W | Yg F | Yg W | Yg W | Yn W | Yn E2 | 17 |
| 18 | Yn E | Yn M | Yg E | Yg Wd | Yn E | Yn M | Yn E | Yn Wd | Yg M | Yg E3 | Yg M | Yg E1 | Yn M | Yn W | Yg W | Yg F | Yg W | Yg W | Yn W | Yn E2 | Yn W | Yn E4 | Yg Wd | Yg M | 18 |
| 19 | Yg M | Yg E3 | Yn E | Yn Wd | Yg M | Yg E3 | Yg M | Yg E1 | Yn M | Yn W | Yn M | Yn F | Yg W | Yg W | Yn W | Yn E2 | Yn W | Yn E4 | Yg Wd | Yg M | Yg Wd | Yg Wd | Yn Wd | Yn M | 19 |
| 20 | Yn M | Yn W | Yg M | Yg E1 | Yn M | Yn W | Yn M | Yn F | Yg W | Yg W | Yg W | Yg F | Yn W | Yn E4 | Yg Wd | Yg M | Yg Wd | Yg Wd | Yn Wd | Yn M | Yn Wd | Yn Wd | Yg F | Yg E3 | 20 |
| 21 | Yg W | Yg W | Yn M | Yn F | Yg W | Yg W | Yg W | Yg F | Yn W | Yn E4 | Yn W | Yn E2 | Yg Wd | Yg Wd | Yn Wd | Yn M | Yn Wd | Yn Wd | Yg F | Yg E3 | Yg F | Yg E1 | Yn F | Yn W | 21 |
| 22 | Yn W | Yn E4 | Yg W | Yg F | Yn W | Yn E4 | Yn W | Yn E2 | Yg Wd | Yg Wd | Yg Wd | Yg M | Yn Wd | Yn Wd | Yg F | Yg E3 | Yg F | Yg E1 | Yn F | Yn W | Yn F | Yn F | Yg E | Yg W | 22 |
| 23 | Yg Wd | Yg Wd | Yn W | Yn E2 | Yg Wd | Yg Wd | Yg Wd | Yg M | Yn Wd | Yn Wd | Yn Wd | Yn M | Yg F | Yg E1 | Yn F | Yn W | Yn F | Yn F | Yg E | Yg W | Yg E | Yg F | Yn E | Yn E4 | 23 |
| 24 | Yn Wd | Yn Wd | Yg Wd | Yg M | Yn Wd | Yn Wd | Yn Wd | Yn M | Yg F | Yg E1 | Yg F | Yg E3 | Yn F | Yn F | Yg E | Yg W | Yg E | Yg F | Yn E | Yn E4 | Yn E | Yn E2 | Yg M | Yg Wd | 24 |
| 25 | Yg F | Yg E1 | Yn Wd | Yn M | Yg F | Yg E1 | Yg F | Yg E3 | Yn F | Yn F | Yn F | Yn W | Yg E | Yg F | Yn E | Yn E4 | Yn E | Yn E2 | Yg M | Yg Wd | Yg M | Yg M | Yn M | Yn Wd | 25 |
| 26 | Yn F | Yn F | Yg F | Yg E3 | Yn F | Yn F | Yn F | Yn W | Yg E | Yg F | Yg E | Yg W | Yn E | Yn E2 | Yg M | Yg Wd | Yg M | Yg M | Yn M | Yn Wd | Yn M | Yn M | Yg W | Yg E1 | 26 |
| 27 | Yg E | Yg F | Yn F | Yn W | Yg E | Yg F | Yg E | Yg W | Yn E | Yn E2 | Yn E | Yn E4 | Yg M | Yg M | Yn M | Yn Wd | Yn M | Yn M | Yg W | Yg E1 | Yg W | Yg E3 | Yn W | Yn F | 27 |
| 28 | Yn E | Yn E2 | Yg E | Yg W | Yn E | Yn E2 | Yn E | Yn E4 | Yg M | Yg M | Yg M | Yg Wd | Yn M | Yn M | Yg W | Yg E1 | Yg W | Yg E3 | Yn W | Yn F | Yn W | Yn W | Yg Wd | Yg F | 28 |
| 29 | Yg M | Yg M | Yn E | Yn E4 | Yg M | Yg M | Yg M | Yg Wd | Yn M | Yn M | Yn M | Yn Wd | Yg W | Yg E3 | Yn W | Yn F | Yn W | Yn W | Yg Wd | Yg F | Yg Wd | Yg W | Yn Wd | Yn E2 | 29 |
| 30 | | | Yg M | Yg Wd | Yn M | Yn M | Yn M | Yn Wd | Yg W | Yg E3 | Yg W | Yg E1 | Yn W | Yn W | Yg Wd | Yg F | Yg Wd | Yg W | Yn Wd | Yn E2 | Yn Wd | Yn E4 | Yg F | Yg M | 30 |
| 31 | | | Yn M | Yn Wd | | | Yg W | Yg E1 | | | Yn W | Yn F | Yg Wd | Yg W | | | Yn Wd | Yn E4 | | | Yg F | Yg Wd | Yn F | Yn M | 31 |
| 1 | Yn M | Yn M | Yg W | Yg E1 | Yg W | Yg E3 | Yn W | Yn F | Yn W | Yn W | Yg Wd | Yg F | Yn Wd | Yn E4 | Yn Wd | Yn E2 | Yg F | Yg Wd | Yg F | Yg M | Yn F | Yn Wd | Yg E | Yg E3 | 1 |
| 2 | Yg W | Yg E3 | Yn W | Yn F | Yn W | Yn W | Yg Wd | Yg F | Yg Wd | Yg W | Yn Wd | Yn E2 | Yg F | Yg Wd | Yg F | Yg M | Yn F | Yn Wd | Yn F | Yn M | Yg E | Yg E1 | Yn E | Yn W | 2 |
| 3 | Yn W | Yn W | Yg Wd | Yg F | Yg Wd | Yg W | Yn Wd | Yn E2 | Yn Wd | Yn E4 | Yg F | Yg M | Yn F | Yn Wd | Yn F | Yn M | Yg E | Yg E1 | Yg E | Yg E3 | Yn E | Yn F | Yg M | Yg W | 3 |
| 4 | Yg Wd | Yg W | | | Yn Wd | Yn E4 | Yg F | Yg M | Yg F | Yg Wd | Yn F | Yn M | Yg E | Yg E1 | Yg E | Yg E3 | Yn E | Yn F | Yn E | Yn W | Yg M | Yg F | | | 4 |
| 5 | | | | | | | | | Yn F | Yn Wd | Yg E | Yg E3 | Yn E | Yn F | Yn E | Yn W | Yg M | Yg F | Yg M | Yg W | | | | | 5 |
| 6 | | | | | | | | | Yg E | Yg E1 | Yn E | Yn W | Yg M | Yg F | Yg M | Yg W | Yn M | Yn E2 | Yn M | Yn E4 | | | | | 6 |
| 7 | | | | | | | | | | | | | | | Yn M | Yn E4 | | | | | | | | | 7 |
| 8 | | | | | | | | | | | | | | | | | | | | | | | | | 8 |

## YEAR OF THE SNAKE

| | H | E | H | E | H | E | H | E | H | E | H | E | H | E | H | E | H | E | H | E | H | E | H | E | |
|---|---|---|---|---|---|---|---|---|---|---|---|---|---|---|---|---|---|---|---|---|---|---|---|---|---|
| YEAR | YEAR<br>Yn W | Yn F | 2013 | | | | | | | | | | | | | | | | | | | | 2014 | | |
| MONTH | 4 Feb - 4 Mar<br>Yg Wd | Yg Wd | 5 Mar - 3 Apr<br>Yn Wd | Yn Wd | 4 Apr - 4 May<br>Yg F | Yg E1 | 5 May - 4 June<br>Yn F | Yn F | 5 June - 6 Jul<br>Yg E | Yg F | 7 Jul - 6 Aug<br>Yn E | Yn E2 | 7 Aug - 6 Sep<br>Yg M | Yg M | 7 Sep - 7 Oct<br>Yn M | Yn M | 8 Oct - 6 Nov<br>Yg W | Yg E3 | 7 Nov - 6 Dec<br>Yn W | Yn W | 7 Dec - 5 Jan<br>Yg Wd | Yg W | 6 Jan - 3 Feb<br>Yn Wd | Yn E4 | |
| Starting time | 1st day | Mid-pt | 1st day | Mid-pt | 1st day | Mid-pt | 1st day | Mid-pt | 1st day | Mid-pt | 1st day | Mid-pt | 1st day | Mid-pt | 1st day | Mid-pt | 1st day | Mid-pt | 1st day | Mid-pt | 1st day | Mid-pt | 1st day | Mid-pt | |
| Date | 4 | 18 | 5 | 20 | 4 | 20 | 5 | 21 | 5 | 21 | 7 | 23 | 7 | 23 | 7 | 23 | 8 | 23 | 7 | 22 | 7 | 22 | 6 | 20 | |
| Hour | 0019 | 2015 | 1819 | 1909 | 2305 | 0614 | 1628 | 0529 | 2044 | 1333 | 0709 | 0040 | 1714 | 0805 | 2033 | 0622 | 1231 | 1541 | 1545 | 1308 | 0821 | 0205 | 2007 | 1215 | |
| DATE 4 | Yn M | Yn E4 | | | Yg M | Yg W | | | | | | | | | | | | | | | | | | | 4 |
| 5 | Yg W | Yg Wd | Yg M | Yg F | Yn M | Yn E4 | Yn M | Yn E2 | Yg W | Yg Wd | | | | | | | | | | | | | | | 5 |
| 6 | Yn W | Yn Wd | Yn M | Yn E2 | Yg W | Yg Wd | Yg W | Yg M | Yn W | Yn Wd | | | | | | | | | | | | | Yn F | Yn E4 | 6 |
| 7 | Yg Wd | Yg E1 | Yg W | Yg M | Yn W | Yn Wd | Yn W | Yn M | Yg Wd | Yg E1 | Yg Wd | Yg E3 | Yn Wd | Yn F | Yg F | Yg W | | | Yn F | Yn E4 | Yn F | Yn E2 | Yg E | Yg Wd | 7 |
| 8 | Yn Wd | Yn F | Yn W | Yn M | Yg Wd | Yg E1 | Yg Wd | Yg E3 | Yn Wd | Yn F | Yn Wd | Yn W | Yg F | Yg F | Yn F | Yn E4 | Yn F | Yn E2 | Yg E | Yg Wd | Yg E | Yg M | Yn E | Yn Wd | 8 |
| 9 | Yg F | Yg F | Yg Wd | Yg E3 | Yn Wd | Yn F | Yn Wd | Yn W | Yg F | Yg F | Yg F | Yg W | Yn F | Yn E2 | Yg E | Yg Wd | Yg E | Yg M | Yn E | Yn Wd | Yn E | Yn M | Yg M | Yg E1 | 9 |
| 10 | Yn F | Yn E2 | Yn Wd | Yn W | Yg F | Yg F | Yg F | Yg W | Yn F | Yn E2 | Yn F | Yn E4 | Yg E | Yg M | Yn E | Yn Wd | Yn E | Yn M | Yg M | Yg E1 | Yg M | Yg E3 | Yn M | Yn F | 10 |
| 11 | Yg E | Yg M | Yg F | Yg W | Yn F | Yn E2 | Yn F | Yn E4 | Yg E | Yg M | Yg E | Yg Wd | Yn E | Yn M | Yg M | Yg E1 | Yg M | Yg E3 | Yn M | Yn F | Yn M | Yn W | Yg W | Yg F | 11 |
| 12 | Yn E | Yn M | Yn F | Yn E4 | Yg E | Yg M | Yg E | Yg Wd | Yn E | Yn M | Yn E | Yn Wd | Yg M | Yg E3 | Yn M | Yn F | Yn M | Yn W | Yg W | Yg F | Yg W | Yg W | Yn W | Yn E2 | 12 |
| 13 | Yg M | Yg E3 | Yg E | Yg Wd | Yn E | Yn M | Yn E | Yn Wd | Yg M | Yg E3 | Yg M | Yg E1 | Yn M | Yn W | Yg W | Yg F | Yg W | Yg W | Yn W | Yn E2 | Yn W | Yn E4 | Yg Wd | Yg M | 13 |
| 14 | Yn M | Yn W | Yn E | Yn Wd | Yg M | Yg E3 | Yg M | Yg E1 | Yn M | Yn W | Yn M | Yn F | Yg W | Yg W | Yn W | Yn E2 | Yn W | Yn E4 | Yg Wd | Yg M | Yg Wd | Yg Wd | Yn Wd | Yn M | 14 |
| 15 | Yg W | Yg W | Yg M | Yg E1 | Yn M | Yn W | Yn M | Yn F | Yg W | Yg W | Yg W | Yg F | Yn W | Yn E4 | Yg Wd | Yg M | Yg Wd | Yg Wd | Yn Wd | Yn M | Yn Wd | Yn Wd | Yg F | Yg E3 | 15 |
| 16 | Yn W | Yn E4 | Yn M | Yn F | Yg W | Yg W | Yg W | Yg F | Yn W | Yn E4 | Yn W | Yn E2 | Yg Wd | Yg Wd | Yn Wd | Yn M | Yn Wd | Yn Wd | Yg F | Yg E3 | Yg F | Yg E1 | Yn F | Yn W | 16 |
| 17 | Yg Wd | Yg Wd | Yg W | Yg F | Yn W | Yn E4 | Yn W | Yn E2 | Yg Wd | Yg Wd | Yg Wd | Yg M | Yn Wd | Yn Wd | Yg F | Yg E3 | Yg F | Yg E1 | Yn F | Yn W | Yn F | Yn F | Yg E | Yg W | 17 |
| 18 | Yn Wd | Yn Wd | Yn W | Yn E2 | Yg Wd | Yg Wd | Yg Wd | Yg M | Yn Wd | Yn Wd | Yn Wd | Yn M | Yg F | Yg E1 | Yn F | Yn W | Yn F | Yn F | Yg E | Yg W | Yg E | Yg F | Yn E | Yn E4 | 18 |
| 19 | Yg F | Yg E1 | Yg Wd | Yg M | Yn Wd | Yn Wd | Yn Wd | Yn M | Yg F | Yg E1 | Yg F | Yg E3 | Yn F | Yn F | Yg E | Yg W | Yg E | Yg F | Yn E | Yn E4 | Yn E | Yn E2 | Yg M | Yg Wd | 19 |
| 20 | Yn F | Yn F | Yn Wd | Yn M | Yg F | Yg E1 | Yg F | Yg E3 | Yn F | Yn F | Yn F | Yn W | Yg E | Yg F | Yn E | Yn E4 | Yn E | Yn E2 | Yg M | Yg Wd | Yg M | Yg M | Yn M | Yn Wd | 20 |
| 21 | Yg E | Yg F | Yg F | Yg E3 | Yn F | Yn F | Yn F | Yn W | Yg E | Yg F | Yg E | Yg W | Yn E | Yn E2 | Yg M | Yg Wd | Yg M | Yg M | Yn M | Yn Wd | Yn M | Yn M | Yg W | Yg E1 | 21 |
| 22 | Yn E | Yn E2 | Yn F | Yn W | Yg E | Yg F | Yg E | Yg W | Yn E | Yn E2 | Yn E | Yn E4 | Yg M | Yg M | Yn M | Yn Wd | Yn M | Yn M | Yg W | Yg E1 | Yg W | Yg E3 | Yn W | Yn F | 22 |
| 23 | Yg M | Yg M | Yg E | Yg W | Yn E | Yn E2 | Yn E | Yn E4 | Yg M | Yg M | Yg M | Yg Wd | Yn M | Yn M | Yg W | Yg E1 | Yg W | Yg E3 | Yn W | Yn F | Yn W | Yn W | Yg Wd | Yg F | 23 |
| 24 | Yn M | Yn M | Yn E | Yn E4 | Yg M | Yg M | Yg M | Yg Wd | Yn M | Yn M | Yn M | Yn Wd | Yg W | Yg E3 | Yn W | Yn F | Yn W | Yn W | Yg Wd | Yg F | Yg Wd | Yg W | Yn Wd | Yn E2 | 24 |
| 25 | Yg W | Yg E3 | Yg M | Yg Wd | Yn M | Yn M | Yn M | Yn Wd | Yg W | Yg E3 | Yg W | Yg E1 | Yn W | Yn W | Yg Wd | Yg F | Yg Wd | Yg W | Yn Wd | Yn E2 | Yn Wd | Yn E4 | Yg F | Yg M | 25 |
| 26 | Yn W | Yn W | Yn M | Yn Wd | Yg W | Yg E3 | Yg W | Yg E1 | Yn W | Yn W | Yn W | Yn F | Yg Wd | Yg W | Yn Wd | Yn E2 | Yn Wd | Yn E4 | Yg F | Yg M | Yg F | Yg Wd | Yn F | Yn M | 26 |
| 27 | Yg Wd | Yg W | Yg W | Yg E1 | Yn W | Yn W | Yn W | Yn F | Yg Wd | Yg W | Yg Wd | Yg F | Yn Wd | Yn E4 | Yg F | Yg M | Yg F | Yg Wd | Yn F | Yn M | Yn F | Yn Wd | Yg E | Yg E3 | 27 |
| 28 | Yn Wd | Yn E4 | Yn W | Yn F | Yg Wd | Yg W | Yg Wd | Yg F | Yn Wd | Yn E4 | Yn Wd | Yn E2 | Yg F | Yg Wd | Yn F | Yn M | Yn F | Yn Wd | Yg E | Yg E3 | Yg E | Yg E1 | Yn E | Yn W | 28 |
| 29 | | | Yg Wd | Yg F | Yn Wd | Yn E4 | Yn Wd | Yn E2 | Yg F | Yg Wd | Yg F | Yg M | Yn F | Yn Wd | Yg E | Yg E3 | Yg E | Yg E1 | Yn E | Yn W | Yn E | Yn F | Yg M | Yg W | 29 |
| 30 | | | Yn Wd | Yn E2 | Yg F | Yg Wd | Yg F | Yg M | Yn F | Yn Wd | Yn F | Yn M | Yg E | Yg E1 | Yn E | Yn W | Yn E | Yn F | Yg M | Yg W | Yg M | Yg F | Yn M | Yn E4 | 30 |
| 31 | | | Yg F | Yg M | | | Yn F | Yn M | | | Yg E | Yg E3 | Yn E | Yn F | | | Yg M | Yg F | | | Yn M | Yn E2 | Yg W | Yg Wd | 31 |
| 1 | Yg F | Yg Wd | Yn F | Yn M | Yn F | Yn Wd | Yg E | Yg E3 | Yg E | Yg E1 | Yn E | Yn W | Yg M | Yg F | Yg M | Yg W | Yn M | Yn E2 | Yn M | Yn E4 | Yg W | Yg M | Yn W | Yn Wd | 1 |
| 2 | Yn F | Yn Wd | Yg E | Yg E3 | Yg E | Yg E1 | Yn E | Yn W | Yn E | Yn F | Yg M | Yg W | Yn M | Yn E2 | Yn M | Yn E4 | Yg W | Yg M | Yg W | Yg Wd | Yn W | Yn M | Yg Wd | Yg E1 | 2 |
| 3 | Yg E | Yg E1 | Yn E | Yn W | Yn E | Yn F | Yg M | Yg W | Yg M | Yg F | Yn M | Yn E4 | Yg W | Yg M | Yg W | Yg Wd | Yn W | Yn M | Yn W | Yn Wd | Yg Wd | Yg E3 | Yn Wd | Yn F | 3 |
| 4 | Yn E | Yn F | | | Yg M | Yg F | Yn M | Yn E4 | Yn M | Yn E2 | Yg W | Yg Wd | Yn W | Yn M | Yn W | Yn Wd | Yg Wd | Yg E3 | Yg Wd | Yg E1 | Yn Wd | Yn W | | | 4 |
| 5 | | | | | | | | | Yg W | Yg M | Yn W | Yn Wd | Yg Wd | Yg E3 | Yg Wd | Yg E1 | Yn Wd | Yn W | Yn Wd | Yn F | Yg F | Yg W | | | 5 |
| 6 | | | | | | | | | Yn W | Yn M | Yg Wd | Yg E1 | Yn Wd | Yn W | Yn Wd | Yn F | Yg F | Yg W | Yg F | Yg F | | | | | 6 |
| 7 | | | | | | | | | | | | | | | Yg F | Yg F | | | | | | | | | 7 |
| 8 | | | | | | | | | | | | | | | | | | | | | | | | | 8 |

# YEAR OF THE HORSE

| | H | E | H | E | H | E | H | E | H | E | H | E | H | E | H | E | H | E | H | E | H | E | H | E | |
|---|---|---|---|---|---|---|---|---|---|---|---|---|---|---|---|---|---|---|---|---|---|---|---|---|---|
| YEAR | YEAR Yg Wd | Yg F | 2014 | | | | | | | | | | | | | | | | | | | | 2015 | | |
| MONTH | 4 Feb - 5 Mar | | 6 Mar - 4 Apr | | 5 Apr - 4 May | | 5 May - 5 June | | 6 June - 6 Jul | | 7 Jul - 6 Aug | | 7 Aug - 7 Sep | | 8 Sep - 7 Oct | | 8 Oct - 6 Nov | | 7 Nov - 6 Dec | | 7 Dec - 5 Jan | | 6 Jan - 3 Feb | | |
| | Yg F | Yg Wd | Yn F | Yn Wd | Yg E | Yg E1 | Yn E | Yn F | Yg M | Yg F | Yn M | Yn E2 | Yg W | Yg M | Yn W | Yn M | Yg Wd | Yg E3 | Yn Wd | Yn W | Yg F | Yg W | Yn F | Yn E4 | |
| Starting time | 1st day | Mid-pt | 1st day | Mid-pt | 1st day | Mid-pt | 1st day | Mid-pt | 1st day | Mid-pt | 1st day | Mid-pt | 1st day | Mid-pt | 1st day | Mid-pt | 1st day | Mid-pt | 1st day | Mid-pt | 1st day | Mid-pt | 1st day | Mid-pt | |
| Date | 4 | 19 | 6 | 21 | 5 | 20 | 5 | 21 | 6 | 21 | 7 | 23 | 7 | 23 | 8 | 23 | 8 | 23 | 7 | 22 | 7 | 22 | 6 | 20 | |
| Hour | 0621 | 0204 | 0009 | 0057 | 0454 | 1212 | 1216 | 1217 | 0232 | 1921 | 1257 | 0627 | 2302 | 1353 | 0221 | 1151 | 1820 | 2130 | 2136 | 1858 | 1411 | 0750 | 0057 | 1805 | |
| DATE 4 | Yg F | Yg F | | | | | | | | | | | | | | | | | | | | | | | 4 |
| 5 | Yn F | Yn E2 | | | Yg F | Yg F | Yg F | Yg W | | | | | | | | | | | | | | | | | 5 |
| 6 | Yg E | Yg M | Yg F | Yg W | Yn F | Yn E2 | Yn F | Yn E4 | Yg E | Yg M | | | | | | | | | | | | | Yg W | Yg F | 6 |
| 7 | Yn E | Yn M | Yn F | Yn E4 | Yg E | Yg M | Yg E | Yg Wd | Yn E | Yn M | Yn E | Yn Wd | Yg M | Yg E3 | | | | | Yg W | Yg F | Yg W | Yg W | Yn W | Yn E2 | 7 |
| 8 | Yg M | Yg E3 | Yg E | Yg Wd | Yn E | Yn M | Yn E | Yn Wd | Yg M | Yg E3 | Yg M | Yg E1 | Yn M | Yn W | Yg W | Yg F | Yg W | Yg W | Yn W | Yn E2 | Yn W | Yn E4 | Yg Wd | Yg M | 8 |
| 9 | Yn M | Yn W | Yn E | Yn Wd | Yg M | Yg E3 | Yg M | Yg E1 | Yn M | Yn W | Yn M | Yn F | Yg W | Yg W | Yn W | Yn E2 | Yn W | Yn E4 | Yg Wd | Yg M | Yg Wd | Yg Wd | Yn Wd | Yn M | 9 |
| 10 | Yg W | Yg W | Yg M | Yg E1 | Yn M | Yn W | Yn M | Yn F | Yg W | Yg W | Yg W | Yg F | Yn W | Yn E4 | Yg Wd | Yg M | Yg Wd | Yg Wd | Yn Wd | Yn M | Yn Wd | Yn Wd | Yg F | Yg E3 | 10 |
| 11 | Yn W | Yn E4 | Yn M | Yn F | Yg W | Yg W | Yg W | Yg F | Yn W | Yn E4 | Yn W | Yn E2 | Yg Wd | Yg Wd | Yn Wd | Yn M | Yn Wd | Yn Wd | Yg F | Yg E3 | Yg F | Yg E1 | Yn F | Yn W | 11 |
| 12 | Yg Wd | Yg Wd | Yg W | Yg F | Yn W | Yn E4 | Yn W | Yn E2 | Yg Wd | Yg Wd | Yg Wd | Yg M | Yn Wd | Yn Wd | Yg F | Yg E3 | Yg F | Yg E1 | Yn F | Yn W | Yn F | Yn F | Yg E | Yg W | 12 |
| 13 | Yn Wd | Yn Wd | Yn W | Yn E2 | Yg Wd | Yg Wd | Yg Wd | Yg M | Yn Wd | Yn Wd | Yn Wd | Yn M | Yg F | Yg E1 | Yn F | Yn W | Yn F | Yn F | Yg E | Yg W | Yg E | Yg F | Yn E | Yn E4 | 13 |
| 14 | Yg F | Yg E1 | Yg Wd | Yg M | Yn Wd | Yn Wd | Yn Wd | Yn M | Yg F | Yg E1 | Yg F | Yg E3 | Yn F | Yn F | Yg E | Yg W | Yg E | Yg F | Yn E | Yn E4 | Yn E | Yn E2 | Yg M | Yg Wd | 14 |
| 15 | Yn F | Yn F | Yn Wd | Yn M | Yg F | Yg E1 | Yg F | Yg E3 | Yn F | Yn F | Yn F | Yn W | Yg E | Yg F | Yn E | Yn E4 | Yn E | Yn E2 | Yg M | Yg Wd | Yg M | Yg M | Yn M | Yn Wd | 15 |
| 16 | Yg E | Yg F | Yg F | Yg E3 | Yn F | Yn F | Yn F | Yn W | Yg E | Yg F | Yg E | Yg W | Yn E | Yn E2 | Yg M | Yg Wd | Yg M | Yg M | Yn M | Yn Wd | Yn M | Yn M | Yg W | Yg E1 | 16 |
| 17 | Yn E | Yn E2 | Yn F | Yn W | Yg E | Yg F | Yg E | Yg W | Yn E | Yn E2 | Yn E | Yn E4 | Yg M | Yg M | Yn M | Yn Wd | Yn M | Yn M | Yg W | Yg E1 | Yg W | Yg E3 | Yn W | Yn F | 17 |
| 18 | Yg M | Yg M | Yg E | Yg W | Yn E | Yn E2 | Yn E | Yn E4 | Yg M | Yg M | Yg M | Yg Wd | Yn M | Yn M | Yg W | Yg E1 | Yg W | Yg E3 | Yn W | Yn F | Yn W | Yn W | Yg Wd | Yg F | 18 |
| 19 | Yn M | Yn M | Yn E | Yn E4 | Yg M | Yg M | Yg M | Yg Wd | Yn M | Yn M | Yn M | Yn Wd | Yg W | Yg E3 | Yn W | Yn F | Yn W | Yn W | Yg Wd | Yg F | Yg Wd | Yg W | Yn Wd | Yn E2 | 19 |
| 20 | Yg W | Yg E3 | Yg M | Yg Wd | Yn M | Yn M | Yn M | Yn Wd | Yg W | Yg E3 | Yg W | Yg E1 | Yn W | Yn W | Yg Wd | Yg F | Yg Wd | Yg W | Yn Wd | Yn E2 | Yn Wd | Yn E4 | Yg F | Yg M | 20 |
| 21 | Yn W | Yn W | Yn M | Yn Wd | Yg W | Yg E3 | Yg W | Yg E1 | Yn W | Yn W | Yn W | Yn F | Yg Wd | Yg W | Yn Wd | Yn E2 | Yn Wd | Yn E4 | Yg F | Yg M | Yg F | Yg Wd | Yn F | Yn M | 21 |
| 22 | Yg Wd | Yg W | Yg W | Yg E1 | Yn W | Yn W | Yn W | Yn F | Yg Wd | Yg W | Yg Wd | Yg F | Yn Wd | Yn E4 | Yg F | Yg M | Yg F | Yg Wd | Yn F | Yn M | Yn F | Yn Wd | Yg E | Yg E3 | 22 |
| 23 | Yn Wd | Yn E4 | Yn W | Yn F | Yg Wd | Yg W | Yg Wd | Yg F | Yn Wd | Yn E4 | Yn Wd | Yn E2 | Yg F | Yg Wd | Yn F | Yn M | Yn F | Yn Wd | Yg E | Yg E3 | Yg E | Yg E1 | Yn E | Yn W | 23 |
| 24 | Yg F | Yg Wd | Yg Wd | Yg F | Yn Wd | Yn E4 | Yn Wd | Yn E2 | Yg F | Yg Wd | Yg F | Yg M | Yn F | Yn Wd | Yg E | Yg E3 | Yg E | Yg E1 | Yn E | Yn W | Yn E | Yn F | Yg M | Yg W | 24 |
| 25 | Yn F | Yn Wd | Yn Wd | Yn E2 | Yg F | Yg Wd | Yg F | Yg M | Yn F | Yn Wd | Yn F | Yn M | Yg E | Yg E1 | Yn E | Yn W | Yn E | Yn F | Yg M | Yg W | Yg M | Yg F | Yn M | Yn E4 | 25 |
| 26 | Yg E | Yg E1 | Yg F | Yg M | Yn F | Yn Wd | Yn F | Yn M | Yg E | Yg E1 | Yg E | Yg E3 | Yn E | Yn F | Yg M | Yg W | Yg M | Yg F | Yn M | Yn E4 | Yn M | Yn E2 | Yg W | Yg Wd | 26 |
| 27 | Yn E | Yn F | Yn F | Yn M | Yg E | Yg E1 | Yg E | Yg E3 | Yn E | Yn F | Yn E | Yn W | Yg M | Yg F | Yn M | Yn E4 | Yn M | Yn E2 | Yg W | Yg Wd | Yg W | Yg M | Yn W | Yn Wd | 27 |
| 28 | Yg M | Yg F | Yg E | Yg E3 | Yn E | Yn F | Yn E | Yn W | Yg M | Yg F | Yg M | Yg W | Yn M | Yn E2 | Yg W | Yg Wd | Yg W | Yg M | Yn W | Yn Wd | Yn W | Yn M | Yg Wd | Yg E1 | 28 |
| 29 | | | Yn E | Yn W | Yg M | Yg F | Yg M | Yg W | Yn M | Yn E2 | Yn M | Yn E4 | Yg W | Yg M | Yn W | Yn Wd | Yn W | Yn M | Yg Wd | Yg E1 | Yg Wd | Yg E3 | Yn Wd | Yn F | 29 |
| 30 | | | Yg M | Yg W | Yn M | Yn E2 | Yn M | Yn E4 | Yg W | Yg M | Yg W | Yg Wd | Yn W | Yn M | Yg Wd | Yg E1 | Yg Wd | Yg E3 | Yn Wd | Yn F | Yn Wd | Yn W | Yg F | Yg F | 30 |
| 31 | | | Yn M | Yn E4 | | | Yg W | Yg Wd | | | Yn W | Yn Wd | Yg Wd | Yg E3 | | | Yn Wd | Yn W | | | Yg F | Yg W | Yn F | Yn E2 | 31 |
| 1 | Yn M | Yn E2 | Yg W | Yg Wd | Yg W | Yg M | Yn W | Yn Wd | Yn W | Yn M | Yg Wd | Yg E1 | Yn Wd | Yn W | Yn Wd | Yn F | Yg F | Yg W | Yg F | Yg F | Yn F | Yn E4 | Yg E | Yg M | 1 |
| 2 | Yg W | Yg M | Yn W | Yn Wd | Yn W | Yn M | Yg Wd | Yg E1 | Yg Wd | Yg E3 | Yn Wd | Yn F | Yg F | Yg W | Yg F | Yg F | Yn F | Yn E4 | Yn F | Yn E2 | Yg E | Yg Wd | Yn E | Yn M | 2 |
| 3 | Yn W | Yn M | Yg Wd | Yg E1 | Yg Wd | Yg E3 | Yn Wd | Yn F | Yn Wd | Yn W | Yg F | Yg F | Yn F | Yn E4 | Yn F | Yn E2 | Yg E | Yg Wd | Yg E | Yg M | Yn E | Yn Wd | Yg M | Yg E3 | 3 |
| 4 | Yg Wd | Yg E3 | Yn Wd | Yn F | Yn Wd | Yn W | Yg F | Yg F | Yg F | Yg W | Yn F | Yn E2 | Yg E | Yg Wd | Yg E | Yg M | Yn E | Yn Wd | Yn E | Yn M | Yg M | Yg E1 | | | 4 |
| 5 | Yn Wd | Yn W | | | | | Yn F | Yn E2 | Yn F | Yn E4 | Yg E | Yg M | Yn E | Yn Wd | Yn E | Yn M | Yg M | Yg E1 | Yg M | Yg E3 | Yn M | Yn F | | | 5 |
| 6 | | | | | | | | | Yg E | Yg Wd | Yn E | Yn M | Yg M | Yg E1 | Yg M | Yg E3 | Yn M | Yn F | Yn M | Yn W | | | | | 6 |
| 7 | | | | | | | | | | | | | Yn M | Yn F | Yn M | Yn W | | | | | | | | | 7 |
| 8 | | | | | | | | | | | | | | | | | | | | | | | | | 8 |

# YEAR OF THE GOAT

| | H | E | H | E | H | E | H | E | H | E | H | E | H | E | H | E | H | E | H | E | H | E | H | E | |
|---|---|---|---|---|---|---|---|---|---|---|---|---|---|---|---|---|---|---|---|---|---|---|---|---|---|
| YEAR | YEAR<br>Yn Wd | <br>Yn E2 | 2015 | | | | | | | | | | | | | | | | | | 2016 | | | | |
| MONTH | 4 Feb - 5 Mar | | 6 Mar - 4 Apr | | 5 Apr - 5 May | | 6 May - 5 June | | 6 June - 6 Jul | | 7 Jul - 7 Aug | | 8 Aug - 7 Sep | | 8 Sep - 8 Oct | | 9 Oct - 7 Nov | | 8 Nov - 6 Dec | | 7 Dec - 5 Jan | | 6 Jan - 3 Feb | | |
| | Yg E | Yg Wd | Yn E | Yn Wd | Yg M | Yg E1 | Yn M | Yn F | Yg W | Yg F | Yn W | Yn E2 | Yg Wd | Yg M | Yn Wd | Yn M | Yg F | Yg E3 | Yn F | Yn W | Yg E | Yg W | Yn E | Yn E4 | |
| Starting time | 1st day | Mid-pt | 1st day | Mid-pt | 1st day | Mid-pt | 1st day | Mid-pt | 1st day | Mid-pt | 1st day | Mid-pt | 1st day | Mid-pt | 1st day | Mid-pt | 1st day | Mid-pt | 1st day | Mid-pt | 1st day | Mid-pt | 1st day | Mid-pt | |
| Date | 4 | 19 | 6 | 21 | 5 | 20 | 6 | 21 | 6 | 22 | 7 | 23 | 8 | 23 | 8 | 23 | 9 | 24 | 8 | 23 | 7 | 22 | 6 | 21 | |
| Hour | 1209 | 0754 | 0556 | 0647 | 1058 | 1752 | 0411 | 1708 | 0820 | 0209 | 1830 | 1216 | 0451 | 1951 | 0810 | 1745 | 0009 | 0320 | 0325 | 0048 | 2001 | 1345 | 0647 | 2350 | |
| DATE 4 | Yn M | Yn W | | | | | | | | | | | | | | | | | | | | | | | 4 |
| 5 | Yg W | Yg W | | | Yn M | Yn W | | | | | | | | | | | | | | | | | | | 5 |
| 6 | Yn W | Yn E4 | Yn M | Yn F | Yg W | Yg W | Yg W | Yg F | Yn W | Yn E4 | | | | | | | | | | | | | Yn F | Yn W | 6 |
| 7 | Yg Wd | Yg Wd | Yg W | Yg F | Yn W | Yn E4 | Yn W | Yn E2 | Yg Wd | Yg Wd | Yg Wd | Yg M | | | | | | | | | Yn F | Yn F | Yg E | Yg W | 7 |
| 8 | Yn Wd | Yn Wd | Yn W | Yn E2 | Yg Wd | Yg Wd | Yg Wd | Yg M | Yn Wd | Yn Wd | Yn Wd | Yn M | Yg F | Yg E1 | Yn F | Yn W | | | Yg E | Yg W | Yg E | Yg F | Yn E | Yn E4 | 8 |
| 9 | Yg F | Yg E1 | Yg Wd | Yg M | Yn Wd | Yn Wd | Yn Wd | Yn M | Yg F | Yg E1 | Yg F | Yg E3 | Yn F | Yn F | Yg E | Yg W | Yg E | Yg F | Yn E | Yn E4 | Yn E | Yn E2 | Yg M | Yg Wd | 9 |
| 10 | Yn F | Yn F | Yn Wd | Yn M | Yg F | Yg E1 | Yg F | Yg E3 | Yn F | Yn F | Yn F | Yn W | Yg E | Yg F | Yn E | Yn E4 | Yn E | Yn E2 | Yg M | Yg Wd | Yg M | Yg M | Yn M | Yn Wd | 10 |
| 11 | Yg E | Yg F | Yg F | Yg E3 | Yn F | Yn F | Yn F | Yn W | Yg E | Yg F | Yg E | Yg W | Yn E | Yn E2 | Yg M | Yg Wd | Yg M | Yg M | Yn M | Yn Wd | Yn M | Yn M | Yg W | Yg E1 | 11 |
| 12 | Yn E | Yn E2 | Yn F | Yn W | Yg E | Yg F | Yg E | Yg W | Yn E | Yn E2 | Yn E | Yn E4 | Yg M | Yg M | Yn M | Yn Wd | Yn M | Yn M | Yg W | Yg E1 | Yg W | Yg E3 | Yn W | Yn F | 12 |
| 13 | Yg M | Yg M | Yg E | Yg W | Yn E | Yn E2 | Yn E | Yn E4 | Yg M | Yg M | Yg M | Yg Wd | Yn M | Yn M | Yg W | Yg E1 | Yg W | Yg E3 | Yn W | Yn F | Yn W | Yn W | Yg Wd | Yg F | 13 |
| 14 | Yn M | Yn M | Yn E | Yn E4 | Yg M | Yg M | Yg M | Yg Wd | Yn M | Yn M | Yn M | Yn Wd | Yg W | Yg E3 | Yn W | Yn F | Yn W | Yn W | Yg Wd | Yg F | Yg Wd | Yg W | Yn Wd | Yn E2 | 14 |
| 15 | Yg W | Yg E3 | Yg M | Yg Wd | Yn M | Yn M | Yn M | Yn Wd | Yg W | Yg E3 | Yg W | Yg E1 | Yn W | Yn W | Yg Wd | Yg F | Yg Wd | Yg W | Yn Wd | Yn E2 | Yn Wd | Yn E4 | Yg F | Yg M | 15 |
| 16 | Yn W | Yn W | Yn M | Yn Wd | Yg W | Yg E3 | Yg W | Yg E1 | Yn W | Yn W | Yn W | Yn F | Yg Wd | Yg W | Yn Wd | Yn E2 | Yn Wd | Yn E4 | Yg F | Yg M | Yg F | Yg Wd | Yn F | Yn M | 16 |
| 17 | Yg Wd | Yg W | Yg W | Yg E1 | Yn W | Yn W | Yn W | Yn F | Yg Wd | Yg W | Yg Wd | Yg F | Yn Wd | Yn E4 | Yg F | Yg M | Yg F | Yg Wd | Yn F | Yn M | Yn F | Yn Wd | Yg E | Yg E3 | 17 |
| 18 | Yn Wd | Yn E4 | Yn W | Yn F | Yg Wd | Yg W | Yg Wd | Yg F | Yn Wd | Yn E4 | Yn Wd | Yn E2 | Yg F | Yg Wd | Yn F | Yn M | Yn F | Yn Wd | Yg E | Yg E3 | Yg E | Yg E1 | Yn E | Yn W | 18 |
| 19 | Yg F | Yg Wd | Yg Wd | Yg F | Yn Wd | Yn E4 | Yn Wd | Yn E2 | Yg F | Yg Wd | Yg F | Yg M | Yn F | Yn Wd | Yg E | Yg E3 | Yg E | Yg E1 | Yn E | Yn W | Yn E | Yn F | Yg M | Yg W | 19 |
| 20 | Yn F | Yn Wd | Yn Wd | Yn E2 | Yg F | Yg Wd | Yg F | Yg M | Yn F | Yn Wd | Yn F | Yn M | Yg E | Yg E1 | Yn E | Yn W | Yn E | Yn F | Yg M | Yg W | Yg M | Yg F | Yn M | Yn E4 | 20 |
| 21 | Yg E | Yg E1 | Yg F | Yg M | Yn F | Yn Wd | Yn F | Yn M | Yg E | Yg E1 | Yg E | Yg E3 | Yn E | Yn F | Yg M | Yg W | Yg M | Yg F | Yn M | Yn E4 | Yn M | Yn E2 | Yg W | Yg Wd | 21 |
| 22 | Yn E | Yn F | Yn F | Yn M | Yg E | Yg E1 | Yg E | Yg E3 | Yn E | Yn F | Yn E | Yn W | Yg M | Yg F | Yn M | Yn E4 | Yn M | Yn E2 | Yg W | Yg Wd | Yg W | Yg M | Yn W | Yn Wd | 22 |
| 23 | Yg M | Yg F | Yg E | Yg E3 | Yn E | Yn F | Yn E | Yn W | Yg M | Yg F | Yg M | Yg W | Yn M | Yn E2 | Yg W | Yg Wd | Yg W | Yg M | Yn W | Yn Wd | Yn W | Yn M | Yg Wd | Yg E1 | 23 |
| 24 | Yn M | Yn E2 | Yn E | Yn W | Yg M | Yg F | Yg M | Yg W | Yn M | Yn E2 | Yn M | Yn E4 | Yg W | Yg M | Yn W | Yn Wd | Yn W | Yn M | Yg Wd | Yg E1 | Yg Wd | Yg E3 | Yn Wd | Yn F | 24 |
| 25 | Yg W | Yg M | Yg M | Yg W | Yn M | Yn E2 | Yn M | Yn E4 | Yg W | Yg M | Yg W | Yg Wd | Yn W | Yn M | Yg Wd | Yg E1 | Yg Wd | Yg E3 | Yn Wd | Yn F | Yn Wd | Yn W | Yg F | Yg F | 25 |
| 26 | Yn W | Yn M | Yn M | Yn E4 | Yg W | Yg M | Yg W | Yg Wd | Yn W | Yn M | Yn W | Yn Wd | Yg Wd | Yg E3 | Yn Wd | Yn F | Yn Wd | Yn W | Yg F | Yg F | Yg F | Yg W | Yn F | Yn E2 | 26 |
| 27 | Yg Wd | Yg E3 | Yg W | Yg Wd | Yn W | Yn M | Yn W | Yn Wd | Yg Wd | Yg E3 | Yg Wd | Yg E1 | Yn Wd | Yn W | Yg F | Yg F | Yg F | Yg W | Yn F | Yn E2 | Yn F | Yn E4 | Yg E | Yg M | 27 |
| 28 | Yn Wd | Yn W | Yn W | Yn Wd | Yg Wd | Yg E3 | Yg Wd | Yg E1 | Yn Wd | Yn W | Yn Wd | Yn F | Yg F | Yg W | Yn F | Yn E2 | Yn F | Yn E4 | Yg E | Yg M | Yg E | Yg Wd | Yn E | Yn M | 28 |
| 29 | | | Yg Wd | Yg E1 | Yn Wd | Yn W | Yn Wd | Yn F | Yg F | Yg W | Yg F | Yg F | Yn F | Yn E4 | Yg E | Yg M | Yg E | Yg Wd | Yn E | Yn M | Yn E | Yn Wd | Yg M | Yg E3 | 29 |
| 30 | | | Yn Wd | Yn F | Yg F | Yg W | Yg F | Yg F | Yn F | Yn E4 | Yn F | Yn E2 | Yg E | Yg Wd | Yn E | Yn M | Yn E | Yn Wd | Yg M | Yg E3 | Yg M | Yg E1 | Yn M | Yn W | 30 |
| 31 | | | Yg F | Yg F | | | Yn F | Yn E2 | | | Yg E | Yg M | Yn E | Yn Wd | | | Yg M | Yg E1 | | | Yn M | Yn F | Yg W | Yg W | 31 |
| 1 | Yg F | Yg W | Yn F | Yn E2 | Yn F | Yn E4 | Yg E | Yg M | Yg E | Yg Wd | Yn E | Yn M | Yg M | Yg E1 | Yg M | Yg E3 | Yn M | Yn F | Yn M | Yn W | Yg W | Yg F | Yn W | Yn E4 | 1 |
| 2 | Yn F | Yn E4 | Yg E | Yg M | Yg E | Yg Wd | Yn E | Yn M | Yn E | Yn Wd | Yg M | Yg E3 | Yn M | Yn F | Yn M | Yn W | Yg W | Yg F | Yg W | Yg W | Yn W | Yn E2 | Yg Wd | Yg Wd | 2 |
| 3 | Yg E | Yg Wd | Yn E | Yn M | Yn E | Yn Wd | Yg M | Yg E3 | Yg M | Yg E1 | Yn M | Yn W | Yg W | Yg F | Yg W | Yg W | Yn W | Yn E2 | Yn W | Yn E4 | Yg Wd | Yg M | Yn Wd | Yn Wd | 3 |
| 4 | Yn E | Yn Wd | Yg M | Yg E3 | Yg M | Yg E1 | Yn M | Yn W | Yn M | Yn F | Yg W | Yg W | Yn W | Yn E2 | Yn W | Yn E4 | Yg Wd | Yg M | Yg Wd | Yg Wd | Yn Wd | Yn M | | | 4 |
| 5 | Yg M | Yg E1 | | | Yn M | Yn F | Yg W | Yg W | Yg W | Yg F | Yn W | Yn E4 | Yg Wd | Yg M | Yg Wd | Yg Wd | Yn Wd | Yn M | Yn Wd | Yn Wd | Yg F | Yg E3 | | | 5 |
| 6 | | | | | | | | | Yn W | Yn E2 | Yg Wd | Yg Wd | Yn Wd | Yn M | Yn Wd | Yn Wd | Yg F | Yg E3 | Yg F | Yg E1 | | | | | 6 |
| 7 | | | | | | | | | | | Yn Wd | Yn Wd | Yg F | Yg E3 | Yg F | Yg E1 | Yn F | Yn W | | | | | | | 7 |
| 8 | | | | | | | | | | | | | | | Yn F | Yn F | | | | | | | | | 8 |

# YEAR OF THE MONKEY

| | H | E | H | E | H | E | H | E | H | E | H | E | H | E | H | E | H | E | H | E | H | E | H | E | |
|---|---|---|---|---|---|---|---|---|---|---|---|---|---|---|---|---|---|---|---|---|---|---|---|---|---|
| YEAR | YEAR<br>Yg F | Yg M | 2016 | | | | | | | | | | | | | | | | | | 2017 | | | | |
| MONTH | 4 Feb - 4 Mar | | 5 Mar - 3 Apr | | 4 Apr - 4 May | | 5 May - 4 June | | 5 June - 6 Jul | | 7 Jul - 6 Aug | | 7 Aug - 6 Sep | | 7 Sep - 7 Oct | | 8 Oct - 6 Nov | | 7 Nov - 6 Dec | | 7 Dec - 4 Jan | | 5 Jan - 2 Feb | | |
| | Yg M | Yg Wd | Yn M | Yn Wd | Yg W | Yg E1 | Yn W | Yn F | Yg Wd | Yg F | Yn Wd | Yn E2 | Yg F | Yg M | Yn F | Yn M | Yg E | Yg E3 | Yn E | Yn W | Yg M | Yg W | Yn M | Yn E4 | |
| Starting time | 1st day | Mid-pt | 1st day | Mid-pt | 1st day | Mid-pt | 1st day | Mid-pt | 1st day | Mid-pt | 1st day | Mid-pt | 1st day | Mid-pt | 1st day | Mid-pt | 1st day | Mid-pt | 1st day | Mid-pt | 1st day | Mid-pt | 1st day | Mid-pt | |
| Date | 4 | 19 | 5 | 20 | 4 | 19 | 5 | 20 | 5 | 21 | 7 | 22 | 7 | 23 | 7 | 22 | 8 | 23 | 7 | 22 | 7 | 21 | 5 | 20 | |
| Hour | 1814 | 1344 | 1146 | 1237 | 1632 | 2330 | 0954 | 2254 | 1409 | 0657 | 0033 | 1803 | 1039 | 0130 | 1348 | 2334 | 0559 | 0909 | 0934 | 0638 | 0154 | 1935 | 1236 | 0545 | |
| DATE 4 | Yg F | Yg E1 | | | Yg F | Yg E1 | | | | | | | | | | | | | | | | | | | 4 |
| 5 | Yn F | Yn F | Yg F | Yg E3 | Yn F | Yn F | Yn F | Yn W | Yg E | Yg F | | | | | | | | | | | | | Yg W | Yg E1 | 5 |
| 6 | Yg E | Yg F | Yn F | Yn W | Yg E | Yg F | Yg E | Yg W | Yn E | Yn E2 | | | | | | | | | | | | | Yn W | Yn F | 6 |
| 7 | Yn E | Yn E2 | Yg E | Yg W | Yn E | Yn E2 | Yn E | Yn E4 | Yg M | Yg M | Yg M | Yg Wd | Yn M | Yn M | Yg W | Yg E1 | | | Yn W | Yn F | Yn W | Yn W | Yg Wd | Yg F | 7 |
| 8 | Yg M | Yg M | Yn E | Yn E4 | Yg M | Yg M | Yg M | Yg Wd | Yn M | Yn M | Yn M | Yn Wd | Yg W | Yg E3 | Yn W | Yn F | Yn W | Yn W | Yg Wd | Yg F | Yg Wd | Yg W | Yn Wd | Yn E2 | 8 |
| 9 | Yn M | Yn M | Yg M | Yg Wd | Yn M | Yn M | Yn M | Yn Wd | Yg W | Yg E3 | Yg W | Yg E1 | Yn W | Yn W | Yg Wd | Yg F | Yg Wd | Yg W | Yn Wd | Yn E2 | Yn Wd | Yn E4 | Yg F | Yg M | 9 |
| 10 | Yg W | Yg E3 | Yn M | Yn Wd | Yg W | Yg E3 | Yg W | Yg E1 | Yn W | Yn W | Yn W | Yn F | Yg Wd | Yg W | Yn Wd | Yn E2 | Yn Wd | Yn E4 | Yg F | Yg M | Yg F | Yg Wd | Yn F | Yn M | 10 |
| 11 | Yn W | Yn W | Yg W | Yg E1 | Yn W | Yn W | Yn W | Yn F | Yg Wd | Yg W | Yg Wd | Yg F | Yn Wd | Yn E4 | Yg F | Yg M | Yg F | Yg Wd | Yn F | Yn M | Yn F | Yn Wd | Yg E | Yg E3 | 11 |
| 12 | Yg Wd | Yg W | Yn W | Yn F | Yg Wd | Yg W | Yg Wd | Yg F | Yn Wd | Yn E4 | Yn Wd | Yn E2 | Yg F | Yg Wd | Yn F | Yn M | Yn F | Yn Wd | Yg E | Yg E3 | Yg E | Yg E1 | Yn E | Yn W | 12 |
| 13 | Yn Wd | Yn E4 | Yg Wd | Yg F | Yn Wd | Yn E4 | Yn Wd | Yn E2 | Yg F | Yg Wd | Yg F | Yg M | Yn F | Yn Wd | Yg E | Yg E3 | Yg E | Yg E1 | Yn E | Yn W | Yn E | Yn F | Yg M | Yg W | 13 |
| 14 | Yg F | Yg Wd | Yn Wd | Yn E2 | Yg F | Yg Wd | Yg F | Yg M | Yn F | Yn Wd | Yn F | Yn M | Yg E | Yg E1 | Yn E | Yn W | Yn E | Yn F | Yg M | Yg W | Yg M | Yg F | Yn M | Yn E4 | 14 |
| 15 | Yn F | Yn Wd | Yg F | Yg M | Yn F | Yn Wd | Yn F | Yn M | Yg E | Yg E1 | Yg E | Yg E3 | Yn E | Yn F | Yg M | Yg W | Yg M | Yg F | Yn M | Yn E4 | Yn M | Yn E2 | Yg W | Yg Wd | 15 |
| 16 | Yg E | Yg E1 | Yn F | Yn M | Yg E | Yg E1 | Yg E | Yg E3 | Yn E | Yn F | Yn E | Yn W | Yg M | Yg F | Yn M | Yn E4 | Yn M | Yn E2 | Yg W | Yg Wd | Yg W | Yg M | Yn W | Yn Wd | 16 |
| 17 | Yn E | Yn F | Yg E | Yg E3 | Yn E | Yn F | Yn E | Yn W | Yg M | Yg F | Yg M | Yg W | Yn M | Yn E2 | Yg W | Yg Wd | Yg W | Yg M | Yn W | Yn Wd | Yn W | Yn M | Yg Wd | Yg E1 | 17 |
| 18 | Yg M | Yg F | Yn E | Yn W | Yg M | Yg F | Yg M | Yg W | Yn M | Yn E2 | Yn M | Yn E4 | Yg W | Yg M | Yn W | Yn Wd | Yn W | Yn M | Yg Wd | Yg E1 | Yg Wd | Yg E3 | Yn Wd | Yn F | 18 |
| 19 | Yn M | Yn E2 | Yg M | Yg W | Yn M | Yn E2 | Yn M | Yn E4 | Yg W | Yg M | Yg W | Yg Wd | Yn W | Yn M | Yg Wd | Yg E1 | Yg Wd | Yg E3 | Yn Wd | Yn F | Yn Wd | Yn W | Yg F | Yg F | 19 |
| 20 | Yg W | Yg M | Yn M | Yn E4 | Yg W | Yg M | Yg W | Yg Wd | Yn W | Yn M | Yn W | Yn Wd | Yg Wd | Yg E3 | Yn Wd | Yn F | Yn Wd | Yn W | Yg F | Yg F | Yg F | Yg W | Yn F | Yn E2 | 20 |
| 21 | Yn W | Yn M | Yg W | Yg Wd | Yn W | Yn M | Yn W | Yn Wd | Yg Wd | Yg E3 | Yg Wd | Yg E1 | Yn Wd | Yn W | Yg F | Yg F | Yg F | Yg W | Yn F | Yn E2 | Yn F | Yn E4 | Yg E | Yg M | 21 |
| 22 | Yg Wd | Yg E3 | Yn W | Yn Wd | Yg Wd | Yg E3 | Yg Wd | Yg E1 | Yn Wd | Yn W | Yn Wd | Yn F | Yg F | Yg W | Yn F | Yn E2 | Yn F | Yn E4 | Yg E | Yg M | Yg E | Yg Wd | Yn E | Yn M | 22 |
| 23 | Yn Wd | Yn W | Yg Wd | Yg E1 | Yn Wd | Yn W | Yn Wd | Yn F | Yg F | Yg W | Yg F | Yg F | Yn F | Yn E4 | Yg E | Yg M | Yg E | Yg Wd | Yn E | Yn M | Yn E | Yn Wd | Yg M | Yg E3 | 23 |
| 24 | Yg F | Yg W | Yn Wd | Yn F | Yg F | Yg W | Yg F | Yg F | Yn F | Yn E4 | Yn F | Yn E2 | Yg E | Yg Wd | Yn E | Yn M | Yn E | Yn Wd | Yg M | Yg E3 | Yg M | Yg E1 | Yn M | Yn W | 24 |
| 25 | Yn F | Yn E4 | Yg F | Yg F | Yn F | Yn E4 | Yn F | Yn E2 | Yg E | Yg Wd | Yg E | Yg M | Yn E | Yn Wd | Yg M | Yg E3 | Yg M | Yg E1 | Yn M | Yn W | Yn M | Yn F | Yg W | Yg W | 25 |
| 26 | Yg E | Yg Wd | Yn F | Yn E2 | Yg E | Yg Wd | Yg E | Yg M | Yn E | Yn Wd | Yn E | Yn M | Yg M | Yg E1 | Yn M | Yn W | Yn M | Yn F | Yg W | Yg W | Yg W | Yg F | Yn W | Yn E4 | 26 |
| 27 | Yn E | Yn Wd | Yg E | Yg M | Yn E | Yn Wd | Yn E | Yn M | Yg M | Yg E1 | Yg M | Yg E3 | Yn M | Yn F | Yg W | Yg W | Yg W | Yg F | Yn W | Yn E4 | Yn W | Yn E2 | Yg Wd | Yg Wd | 27 |
| 28 | Yg M | Yg E1 | Yn E | Yn M | Yg M | Yg E1 | Yg M | Yg E3 | Yn M | Yn F | Yn M | Yn W | Yg W | Yg F | Yn W | Yn E4 | Yn W | Yn E2 | Yg Wd | Yg Wd | Yg Wd | Yg M | Yn Wd | Yn Wd | 28 |
| 29 | Yn M | Yn F | Yg M | Yg E3 | Yn M | Yn F | Yn M | Yn W | Yg W | Yg F | Yg W | Yg W | Yn W | Yn E2 | Yg Wd | Yg Wd | Yg Wd | Yg M | Yn Wd | Yn Wd | Yn Wd | Yn M | Yg F | Yg E1 | 29 |
| 30 | | | Yn M | Yn W | Yg W | Yg F | Yg W | Yg W | Yn W | Yn E2 | Yn W | Yn E4 | Yg Wd | Yg M | Yn Wd | Yn Wd | Yn Wd | Yn M | Yg F | Yg E1 | Yg F | Yg E3 | Yn F | Yn F | 30 |
| 31 | | | Yg W | Yg W | | | Yn W | Yn E4 | | | Yg Wd | Yg Wd | Yn Wd | Yn M | | | Yg F | Yg E3 | | | Yn F | Yn W | Yg E | Yg F | 31 |
| 1 | Yg W | Yg F | Yn W | Yn E4 | Yn W | Yn E2 | Yg Wd | Yg Wd | Yg Wd | Yg M | Yn Wd | Yn Wd | Yg F | Yg E3 | Yg F | Yg E1 | Yn F | Yn W | Yn F | Yn F | Yg E | Yg W | Yn E | Yn E2 | 1 |
| 2 | Yn W | Yn E2 | Yg Wd | Yg Wd | Yg Wd | Yg M | Yn Wd | Yn Wd | Yn Wd | Yn M | Yg F | Yg E1 | Yn F | Yn W | Yn F | Yn F | Yg E | Yg W | Yg E | Yg F | Yn E | Yn E4 | Yg M | Yg M | 2 |
| 3 | Yg Wd | Yg M | Yn Wd | Yn Wd | Yn Wd | Yn M | Yg F | Yg E1 | Yg F | Yg E3 | Yn F | Yn F | Yg E | Yg W | Yg E | Yg F | Yn E | Yn E4 | Yn E | Yn E2 | Yg M | Yg Wd | | | 3 |
| 4 | Yn Wd | Yn M | | | Yg F | Yg E3 | Yn F | Yn F | Yn F | Yn W | Yg E | Yg F | Yn E | Yn E4 | Yn E | Yn E2 | Yg M | Yg Wd | Yg M | Yg M | Yn M | Yn Wd | | | 4 |
| 5 | | | | | | | | | Yg E | Yg W | Yn E | Yn E2 | Yg M | Yg Wd | Yg M | Yg M | Yn M | Yn Wd | Yn M | Yn M | | | | | 5 |
| 6 | | | | | | | | | Yn E | Yn E4 | Yg M | Yg M | Yn M | Yn Wd | Yn M | Yn M | Yg W | Yg E1 | Yg W | Yg E3 | | | | | 6 |
| 7 | | | | | | | | | | | | | | | Yg W | Yg E3 | | | | | | | | | 7 |
| 8 | | | | | | | | | | | | | | | | | | | | | | | | | 8 |

# YEAR OF THE ROOSTER

| | H | E | H | E | H | E | H | E | H | E | H | E | H | E | H | E | H | E | H | E | H | E | H | E | |
|---|---|---|---|---|---|---|---|---|---|---|---|---|---|---|---|---|---|---|---|---|---|---|---|---|---|
| YEAR | YEAR<br>Yn F | Yn M | 2017 | | | | | | | | | | | | | | | | | | | | 2018 | | |
| MONTH | 3 Feb - 4 Mar | | 5 Mar - 3 Apr | | 4 Apr - 4 May | | 5 May - 4 June | | 5 June - 6 Jul | | 7 Jul - 6 Aug | | 7 Aug - 6 Sep | | 7 Sep - 7 Oct | | 8 Oct - 6 Nov | | 7 Nov - 6 Dec | | 7 Dec - 4 Jan | | 5 Jan - 3 Feb | | |
| | Yg W | Yg Wd | Yn W | Yn Wd | Yg Wd | Yg E1 | Yn Wd | Yn F | Yg F | Yg F | Yn F | Yn E2 | Yg E | Yg M | Yn E | Yn M | Yg M | Yg E3 | Yn M | Yn W | Yg W | Yg W | Yn W | Yn E4 | |
| Starting time | 1st day | Mid-pt | 1st day | Mid-pt | 1st day | Mid-pt | 1st day | Mid-pt | 1st day | Mid-pt | 1st day | Mid-pt | 1st day | Mid-pt | 1st day | Mid-pt | 1st day | Mid-pt | 1st day | Mid-pt | 1st day | Mid-pt | 1st day | Mid-pt | |
| Date | 3 | 18 | 5 | 20 | 4 | 20 | 5 | 21 | 5 | 21 | 7 | 22 | 7 | 23 | 7 | 23 | 8 | 23 | 7 | 22 | 7 | 22 | 5 | 22 | |
| Hour | 2349 | 1931 | 1736 | 1825 | 2214 | 0529 | 1542 | 0442 | 1957 | 1246 | 0621 | 2351 | 1527 | 0718 | 1946 | 0522 | 1147 | 1458 | 1503 | 1226 | 0740 | 0124 | 1826 | 1134 | |
| DATE 3 | Yn M | Yn M | | | | | | | | | | | | | | | | | | | | | | | 3 |
| 4 | Yg W | Yg E3 | | | Yn M | Yn M | | | | | | | | | | | | | | | | | | | 4 |
| 5 | Yn W | Yn W | Yn M | Yn Wd | Yg W | Yg E3 | Yg W | Yg E1 | Yn W | Yn W | | | | | | | | | | | | | Yn F | Yn M | 5 |
| 6 | Yg Wd | Yg W | Yg W | Yg E1 | Yn W | Yn W | Yn W | Yn F | Yg Wd | Yg W | | | | | | | | | | | | | Yg E | Yg E3 | 6 |
| 7 | Yn Wd | Yn E4 | Yn W | Yn F | Yg Wd | Yg W | Yg Wd | Yg F | Yn Wd | Yn E4 | Yn Wd | Yn E2 | Yg F | Yg Wd | Yn F | Yn M | | | Yg E | Yg E3 | Yg E | Yg E1 | Yn E | Yn W | 7 |
| 8 | Yg F | Yg Wd | Yg Wd | Yg F | Yn Wd | Yn E4 | Yn Wd | Yn E2 | Yg F | Yg Wd | Yg F | Yg M | Yn F | Yn Wd | Yg E | Yg E3 | Yg E | Yg E1 | Yn E | Yn W | Yn E | Yn F | Yg M | Yg W | 8 |
| 9 | Yn F | Yn Wd | Yn Wd | Yn E2 | Yg F | Yg Wd | Yg F | Yg M | Yn F | Yn Wd | Yn F | Yn M | Yg E | Yg E1 | Yn E | Yn W | Yn E | Yn F | Yg M | Yg W | Yg M | Yg F | Yn M | Yn E4 | 9 |
| 10 | Yg E | Yg E1 | Yg F | Yg M | Yn F | Yn Wd | Yn F | Yn M | Yg E | Yg E1 | Yg E | Yg E3 | Yn E | Yn F | Yg M | Yg W | Yg M | Yg F | Yn M | Yn E4 | Yn M | Yn E2 | Yg W | Yg Wd | 10 |
| 11 | Yn E | Yn F | Yn F | Yn M | Yg E | Yg E1 | Yg E | Yg E3 | Yn E | Yn F | Yn E | Yn W | Yg M | Yg F | Yn M | Yn E4 | Yn M | Yn E2 | Yg W | Yg Wd | Yg W | Yg M | Yn W | Yn Wd | 11 |
| 12 | Yg M | Yg F | Yg E | Yg E3 | Yn E | Yn F | Yn E | Yn W | Yg M | Yg F | Yg M | Yg W | Yn M | Yn E2 | Yg W | Yg Wd | Yg W | Yg M | Yn W | Yn Wd | Yn W | Yn M | Yg Wd | Yg E1 | 12 |
| 13 | Yn M | Yn E2 | Yn E | Yn W | Yg M | Yg F | Yg M | Yg W | Yn M | Yn E2 | Yn M | Yn E4 | Yg W | Yg M | Yn W | Yn Wd | Yn W | Yn M | Yg Wd | Yg E1 | Yg Wd | Yg E3 | Yn Wd | Yn F | 13 |
| 14 | Yg W | Yg M | Yg M | Yg W | Yn M | Yn E2 | Yn M | Yn E4 | Yg W | Yg M | Yg W | Yg Wd | Yn W | Yn M | Yg Wd | Yg E1 | Yg Wd | Yg E3 | Yn Wd | Yn F | Yn Wd | Yn W | Yg F | Yg F | 14 |
| 15 | Yn W | Yn M | Yn M | Yn E4 | Yg W | Yg M | Yg W | Yg Wd | Yn W | Yn M | Yn W | Yn Wd | Yg Wd | Yg E3 | Yn Wd | Yn F | Yn Wd | Yn W | Yg F | Yg F | Yg F | Yg W | Yn F | Yn E2 | 15 |
| 16 | Yg Wd | Yg E3 | Yg W | Yg Wd | Yn W | Yn M | Yn W | Yn Wd | Yg Wd | Yg E3 | Yg Wd | Yg E1 | Yn Wd | Yn W | Yg F | Yg F | Yg F | Yg W | Yn F | Yn E2 | Yn F | Yn E4 | Yg E | Yg M | 16 |
| 17 | Yn Wd | Yn W | Yn W | Yn Wd | Yg Wd | Yg E3 | Yg Wd | Yg E1 | Yn Wd | Yn W | Yn Wd | Yn F | Yg F | Yg W | Yn F | Yn E2 | Yn F | Yn E4 | Yg E | Yg M | Yg E | Yg Wd | Yn E | Yn M | 17 |
| 18 | Yg F | Yg W | Yg Wd | Yg E1 | Yn Wd | Yn W | Yn Wd | Yn F | Yg F | Yg W | Yg F | Yg F | Yn F | Yn E4 | Yg E | Yg M | Yg E | Yg Wd | Yn E | Yn M | Yn E | Yn Wd | Yg M | Yg E3 | 18 |
| 19 | Yn F | Yn E4 | Yn Wd | Yn F | Yg F | Yg W | Yg F | Yg F | Yn F | Yn E4 | Yn F | Yn E2 | Yg E | Yg Wd | Yn E | Yn M | Yn E | Yn Wd | Yg M | Yg E3 | Yg M | Yg E1 | Yn M | Yn W | 19 |
| 20 | Yg E | Yg Wd | Yg F | Yg F | Yn F | Yn E4 | Yn F | Yn E2 | Yg E | Yg Wd | Yg E | Yg M | Yn E | Yn Wd | Yg M | Yg E3 | Yg M | Yg E1 | Yn M | Yn W | Yn M | Yn F | Yg W | Yg W | 20 |
| 21 | Yn E | Yn Wd | Yn F | Yn E2 | Yg E | Yg Wd | Yg E | Yg M | Yn E | Yn Wd | Yn E | Yn M | Yg M | Yg E1 | Yn M | Yn W | Yn M | Yn F | Yg W | Yg W | Yg W | Yg F | Yn W | Yn E4 | 21 |
| 22 | Yg M | Yg E1 | Yg E | Yg M | Yn E | Yn Wd | Yn E | Yn M | Yg M | Yg E1 | Yg M | Yg E3 | Yn M | Yn F | Yg W | Yg W | Yg W | Yg F | Yn W | Yn E4 | Yn W | Yn E2 | Yg Wd | Yg Wd | 22 |
| 23 | Yn M | Yn F | Yn E | Yn M | Yg M | Yg E1 | Yg M | Yg E3 | Yn M | Yn F | Yn M | Yn W | Yg W | Yg F | Yn W | Yn E4 | Yn W | Yn E2 | Yg Wd | Yg Wd | Yg Wd | Yg M | Yn Wd | Yn Wd | 23 |
| 24 | Yg W | Yg F | Yg M | Yg E3 | Yn M | Yn F | Yn M | Yn W | Yg W | Yg F | Yg W | Yg W | Yn W | Yn E2 | Yg Wd | Yg Wd | Yg Wd | Yg M | Yn Wd | Yn Wd | Yn Wd | Yn M | Yg F | Yg E1 | 24 |
| 25 | Yn W | Yn E2 | Yn M | Yn W | Yg W | Yg F | Yg W | Yg W | Yn W | Yn E2 | Yn W | Yn E4 | Yg Wd | Yg M | Yn Wd | Yn Wd | Yn Wd | Yn M | Yg F | Yg E1 | Yg F | Yg E3 | Yn F | Yn F | 25 |
| 26 | Yg Wd | Yg M | Yg W | Yg W | Yn W | Yn E2 | Yn W | Yn E4 | Yg Wd | Yg M | Yg Wd | Yg Wd | Yn Wd | Yn M | Yg F | Yg E1 | Yg F | Yg E3 | Yn F | Yn F | Yn F | Yn W | Yg E | Yg F | 26 |
| 27 | Yn Wd | Yn M | Yn W | Yn E4 | Yg Wd | Yg M | Yg Wd | Yg Wd | Yn Wd | Yn M | Yn Wd | Yn Wd | Yg F | Yg E3 | Yn F | Yn F | Yn F | Yn W | Yg E | Yg F | Yg E | Yg W | Yn E | Yn E2 | 27 |
| 28 | Yg F | Yg E3 | Yg Wd | Yg Wd | Yn Wd | Yn M | Yn Wd | Yn Wd | Yg F | Yg E3 | Yg F | Yg E1 | Yn F | Yn W | Yg E | Yg F | Yg E | Yg W | Yn E | Yn E2 | Yn E | Yn E4 | Yg M | Yg M | 28 |
| 29 | | | Yn Wd | Yn Wd | Yg F | Yg E3 | Yg F | Yg E1 | Yn F | Yn W | Yn F | Yn F | Yg E | Yg W | Yn E | Yn E2 | Yn E | Yn E4 | Yg M | Yg M | Yg M | Yg Wd | Yn M | Yn M | 29 |
| 30 | | | Yg F | Yg E1 | Yn F | Yn W | Yn F | Yn F | Yg E | Yg W | Yg E | Yg F | Yn E | Yn E4 | Yg M | Yg M | Yg M | Yg Wd | Yn M | Yn M | Yn M | Yn Wd | Yg W | Yg E3 | 30 |
| 31 | | | Yn F | Yn F | | | Yg E | Yg F | | | Yn E | Yn E2 | Yg M | Yg Wd | | | Yn M | Yn Wd | | | Yg W | Yg E1 | Yn W | Yn W | 31 |
| 1 | Yn F | Yn W | Yg E | Yg F | Yg E | Yg W | Yn E | Yn E2 | Yn E | Yn E4 | Yg M | Yg M | Yn M | Yn Wd | Yn M | Yn M | Yg W | Yg E1 | Yg W | Yg E3 | Yn W | Yn F | Yg Wd | Yg W | 1 |
| 2 | Yg E | Yg W | Yn E | Yn E2 | Yn E | Yn E4 | Yg M | Yg M | Yg M | Yg Wd | Yn M | Yn M | Yg W | Yg E1 | Yg W | Yg E3 | Yn W | Yn F | Yn W | Yn W | Yg Wd | Yg F | Yn Wd | Yn E4 | 2 |
| 3 | Yn E | Yn E4 | Yg M | Yg M | Yg M | Yg Wd | Yn M | Yn M | Yn M | Yn Wd | Yg W | Yg E3 | Yn W | Yn F | Yn W | Yn W | Yg Wd | Yg F | Yg Wd | Yg W | Yn Wd | Yn E2 | Yg F | Yg Wd | 3 |
| 4 | Yg M | Yg Wd | | | Yn M | Yn Wd | Yg W | Yg E3 | Yg W | Yg E1 | Yn W | Yn W | Yg Wd | Yg F | Yg Wd | Yg W | Yn Wd | Yn E2 | Yn Wd | Yn E4 | Yg F | Yg M | | | 4 |
| 5 | | | | | | | | | Yn W | Yn F | Yg Wd | Yg W | Yn Wd | Yn E2 | Yn Wd | Yn E4 | Yg F | Yg M | Yg F | Yg Wd | | | | | 5 |
| 6 | | | | | | | | | Yg Wd | Yg F | Yn Wd | Yn E4 | Yg F | Yg M | Yg F | Yg Wd | Yn F | Yn M | Yn F | Yn Wd | | | | | 6 |
| 7 | | | | | | | | | | | | | | | Yn F | Yn Wd | | | | | | | | | 7 |
| 8 | | | | | | | | | | | | | | | | | | | | | | | | | 8 |

# YEAR OF THE DOG

| | H | E | H | E | H | E | H | E | H | E | H | E | H | E | H | E | H | E | H | E | H | E | H | E | |
|---|---|---|---|---|---|---|---|---|---|---|---|---|---|---|---|---|---|---|---|---|---|---|---|---|---|
| YEAR | YEAR<br>Yg E | Yg E3 | 2018 | | | | | | | | | | | | | | | | | | | | 2019 | | |
| MONTH | 4 Feb - 4 Mar<br>Yg Wd | Yg Wd | 5 Mar - 4 Apr<br>Yn Wd | Yn Wd | 5 Apr - 4 May<br>Yg F | Yg E1 | 5 May - 5 June<br>Yn F | Yn F | 6 June - 6 Jul<br>Yg E | Yg F | 7 Jul - 6 Aug<br>Yn E | Yn E2 | 7 Aug - 7 Sep<br>Yg M | Yg M | 8 Sep - 7 Oct<br>Yn M | Yn M | 8 Oct - 6 Nov<br>Yg W | Yg E3 | 7 Nov - 6 Dec<br>Yn W | Yn W | 7 Dec - 5 Jan<br>Yg Wd | Yg W | 6 Jan - 3 Feb<br>Yn Wd | Yn E4 | |
| Starting time | 1st day | Mid-pt | 1st day | Mid-pt | 1st day | Mid-pt | 1st day | Mid-pt | 1st day | Mid-pt | 1st day | Mid-pt | 1st day | Mid-pt | 1st day | Mid-pt | 1st day | Mid-pt | 1st day | Mid-pt | 1st day | Mid-pt | 1st day | Mid-pt | |
| Date | 4 | 19 | 5 | 21 | 5 | 20 | 5 | 21 | 6 | 21 | 7 | 23 | 7 | 23 | 8 | 23 | 8 | 23 | 7 | 22 | 7 | 22 | 6 | 20 | |
| Hour | 0538 | 0122 | 2325 | 0028 | 0420 | 1118 | 2131 | 1030 | 0129 | 1833 | 1216 | 0540 | 2215 | 1307 | 0135 | 1111 | 1736 | 2047 | 2054 | 1817 | 1330 | 0714 | 0009 | 1728 | |
| DATE 3 | | | | | | | | | | | | | | | | | | | | | | | | | 3 |
| 4 | Yn F | Yn Wd | | | | | | | | | | | | | | | | | | | | | | | 4 |
| 5 | Yg E | Yg E1 | Yg F | Yg M | Yn F | Yn Wd | Yn F | Yn M | | | | | | | | | | | | | | | | | 5 |
| 6 | Yn E | Yn F | Yn F | Yn M | Yg E | Yg E1 | Yg E | Yg E3 | Yn E | Yn F | | | | | | | | | | | | | Yn W | Yn Wd | 6 |
| 7 | Yg M | Yg F | Yg E | Yg E3 | Yn E | Yn F | Yn E | Yn W | Yg M | Yg F | Yg M | Yg W | Yn M | Yn E2 | | | | | Yn W | Yn Wd | Yn W | Yn M | Yg Wd | Yg E1 | 7 |
| 8 | Yn M | Yn E2 | Yn E | Yn W | Yg M | Yg F | Yg M | Yg W | Yn M | Yn E2 | Yn M | Yn E4 | Yg W | Yg M | Yn W | Yn Wd | Yn W | Yn M | Yg Wd | Yg E1 | Yg Wd | Yg E3 | Yn Wd | Yn F | 8 |
| 9 | Yg W | Yg M | Yg M | Yg W | Yn M | Yn E2 | Yn M | Yn E4 | Yg W | Yg M | Yg W | Yg Wd | Yn W | Yn M | Yg Wd | Yg E1 | Yg Wd | Yg E3 | Yn Wd | Yn F | Yn Wd | Yn W | Yg F | Yg F | 9 |
| 10 | Yn W | Yn M | Yn M | Yn E4 | Yg W | Yg M | Yg W | Yg Wd | Yn W | Yn M | Yn W | Yn Wd | Yg Wd | Yg E3 | Yn Wd | Yn F | Yn Wd | Yn W | Yg F | Yg F | Yg F | Yg W | Yn F | Yn E2 | 10 |
| 11 | Yg Wd | Yg E3 | Yg W | Yg Wd | Yn W | Yn M | Yn W | Yn Wd | Yg Wd | Yg E3 | Yg Wd | Yg E1 | Yn Wd | Yn W | Yg F | Yg F | Yg F | Yg W | Yn F | Yn E2 | Yn F | Yn E4 | Yg E | Yg M | 11 |
| 12 | Yn Wd | Yn W | Yn W | Yn Wd | Yg Wd | Yg E3 | Yg Wd | Yg E1 | Yn Wd | Yn W | Yn Wd | Yn F | Yg F | Yg W | Yn F | Yn E2 | Yn F | Yn E4 | Yg E | Yg M | Yg E | Yg Wd | Yn E | Yn M | 12 |
| 13 | Yg F | Yg W | Yg Wd | Yg E1 | Yn Wd | Yn W | Yn Wd | Yn F | Yg F | Yg W | Yg F | Yg F | Yn F | Yn E4 | Yg E | Yg M | Yg E | Yg Wd | Yn E | Yn M | Yn E | Yn Wd | Yg M | Yg E3 | 13 |
| 14 | Yn F | Yn E4 | Yn Wd | Yn F | Yg F | Yg W | Yg F | Yg F | Yn F | Yn E4 | Yn F | Yn E2 | Yg E | Yg Wd | Yn E | Yn M | Yn E | Yn Wd | Yg M | Yg E3 | Yg M | Yg E1 | Yn M | Yn W | 14 |
| 15 | Yg E | Yg Wd | Yg F | Yg F | Yn F | Yn E4 | Yn F | Yn E2 | Yg E | Yg Wd | Yg E | Yg M | Yn E | Yn Wd | Yg M | Yg E3 | Yg M | Yg E1 | Yn M | Yn W | Yn M | Yn F | Yg W | Yg W | 15 |
| 16 | Yn E | Yn Wd | Yn F | Yn E2 | Yg E | Yg Wd | Yg E | Yg M | Yn E | Yn Wd | Yn E | Yn M | Yg M | Yg E1 | Yn M | Yn W | Yn M | Yn F | Yg W | Yg W | Yg W | Yg F | Yn W | Yn E4 | 16 |
| 17 | Yg M | Yg E1 | Yg E | Yg M | Yn E | Yn Wd | Yn E | Yn M | Yg M | Yg E1 | Yg M | Yg E3 | Yn M | Yn F | Yg W | Yg W | Yg W | Yg F | Yn W | Yn E4 | Yn W | Yn E2 | Yg Wd | Yg Wd | 17 |
| 18 | Yn M | Yn F | Yn E | Yn M | Yg M | Yg E1 | Yg M | Yg E3 | Yn M | Yn F | Yn M | Yn W | Yg W | Yg F | Yn W | Yn E4 | Yn W | Yn E2 | Yg Wd | Yg Wd | Yg Wd | Yg M | Yn Wd | Yn Wd | 18 |
| 19 | Yg W | Yg F | Yg M | Yg E3 | Yn M | Yn F | Yn M | Yn W | Yg W | Yg F | Yg W | Yg W | Yn W | Yn E2 | Yg Wd | Yg Wd | Yg Wd | Yg M | Yn Wd | Yn Wd | Yn Wd | Yn M | Yg F | Yg E1 | 19 |
| 20 | Yn W | Yn E2 | Yn M | Yn W | Yg W | Yg F | Yg W | Yg W | Yn W | Yn E2 | Yn W | Yn E4 | Yg Wd | Yg M | Yn Wd | Yn Wd | Yn Wd | Yn M | Yg F | Yg E1 | Yg F | Yg E3 | Yn F | Yn F | 20 |
| 21 | Yg Wd | Yg M | Yg W | Yg W | Yn W | Yn E2 | Yn W | Yn E4 | Yg Wd | Yg M | Yg Wd | Yg Wd | Yn Wd | Yn M | Yg F | Yg E1 | Yg F | Yg E3 | Yn F | Yn F | Yn F | Yn W | Yg E | Yg F | 21 |
| 22 | Yn Wd | Yn M | Yn W | Yn E4 | Yg Wd | Yg M | Yg Wd | Yg Wd | Yn Wd | Yn M | Yn Wd | Yn Wd | Yg F | Yg E3 | Yn F | Yn F | Yn F | Yn W | Yg E | Yg F | Yg E | Yg W | Yn E | Yn E2 | 22 |
| 23 | Yg F | Yg E3 | Yg Wd | Yg Wd | Yn Wd | Yn M | Yn Wd | Yn Wd | Yg F | Yg E3 | Yg F | Yg E1 | Yn F | Yn W | Yg E | Yg F | Yg E | Yg W | Yn E | Yn E2 | Yn E | Yn E4 | Yg M | Yg M | 23 |
| 24 | Yn F | Yn W | Yn Wd | Yn Wd | Yg F | Yg E3 | Yg F | Yg E1 | Yn F | Yn W | Yn F | Yn F | Yg E | Yg W | Yn E | Yn E2 | Yn E | Yn E4 | Yg M | Yg M | Yg M | Yg Wd | Yn M | Yn M | 24 |
| 25 | Yg E | Yg W | Yg F | Yg E1 | Yn F | Yn W | Yn F | Yn F | Yg E | Yg W | Yg E | Yg F | Yn E | Yn E4 | Yg M | Yg M | Yg M | Yg Wd | Yn M | Yn M | Yn M | Yn Wd | Yg W | Yg E3 | 25 |
| 26 | Yn E | Yn E4 | Yn F | Yn F | Yg E | Yg W | Yg E | Yg F | Yn E | Yn E4 | Yn E | Yn E2 | Yg M | Yg Wd | Yn M | Yn M | Yn M | Yn Wd | Yg W | Yg E3 | Yg W | Yg E1 | Yn W | Yn W | 26 |
| 27 | Yg M | Yg Wd | Yg E | Yg F | Yn E | Yn E4 | Yn E | Yn E2 | Yg M | Yg Wd | Yg M | Yg M | Yn M | Yn Wd | Yg W | Yg E3 | Yg W | Yg E1 | Yn W | Yn W | Yn W | Yn F | Yg Wd | Yg W | 27 |
| 28 | Yn M | Yn Wd | Yn E | Yn E2 | Yg M | Yg Wd | Yg M | Yg M | Yn M | Yn Wd | Yn M | Yn M | Yg W | Yg E1 | Yn W | Yn W | Yn W | Yn F | Yg Wd | Yg W | Yg Wd | Yg F | Yn Wd | Yn E4 | 28 |
| 29 | | | Yg M | Yg M | Yn M | Yn Wd | Yn M | Yn M | Yg W | Yg E1 | Yg W | Yg E3 | Yn W | Yn F | Yg Wd | Yg W | Yg Wd | Yg F | Yn Wd | Yn E4 | Yn Wd | Yn E2 | Yg F | Yg Wd | 29 |
| 30 | | | Yn M | Yn M | Yg W | Yg E1 | Yg W | Yg E3 | Yn W | Yn F | Yn W | Yn W | Yg Wd | Yg F | Yn Wd | Yn E4 | Yn Wd | Yn E2 | Yg F | Yg Wd | Yg F | Yg M | Yn F | Yn Wd | 30 |
| 31 | | | Yg W | Yg E3 | | | Yn W | Yn W | | | Yg Wd | Yg W | Yn Wd | Yn E2 | | | Yg F | Yg M | | | Yn F | Yn M | Yg E | Yg E1 | 31 |
| 1 | Yg W | Yg E1 | Yn W | Yn W | Yn W | Yn F | Yg Wd | Yg W | Yg Wd | Yg F | Yn Wd | Yn E4 | Yg F | Yg M | Yg F | Yg Wd | Yn F | Yn M | Yn F | Yn Wd | Yg E | Yg E3 | Yn E | Yn F | 1 |
| 2 | Yn W | Yn F | Yg Wd | Yg W | Yg Wd | Yg F | Yn Wd | Yn E4 | Yn Wd | Yn E2 | Yg F | Yg Wd | Yn F | Yn M | Yn F | Yn Wd | Yg E | Yg E3 | Yg E | Yg E1 | Yn E | Yn W | Yg M | Yg F | 2 |
| 3 | Yg Wd | Yg F | Yn Wd | Yn E4 | Yn Wd | Yn E2 | Yg F | Yg Wd | Yg F | Yg M | Yn F | Yn Wd | Yg E | Yg E3 | Yg E | Yg E1 | Yn E | Yn W | Yn E | Yn F | Yg M | Yg W | Yn M | Yn E2 | 3 |
| 4 | Yn Wd | Yn E2 | Yg F | Yg Wd | Yg F | Yg M | Yn F | Yn Wd | Yn F | Yn M | Yg E | Yg E1 | Yn E | Yn W | Yn E | Yn F | Yg M | Yg W | Yg M | Yg F | Yn M | Yn E4 | | | 4 |
| 5 | | | | | | | Yg E | Yg E1 | Yg E | Yg E3 | Yn E | Yn F | Yg M | Yg W | Yg M | Yg F | Yn M | Yn E4 | Yn M | Yn E2 | Yg W | Yg Wd | | | 5 |
| 6 | | | | | | | | | Yn E | Yn W | Yg M | Yg F | Yn M | Yn E4 | Yn M | Yn E2 | Yg W | Yg Wd | Yg W | Yg M | | | | | 6 |
| 7 | | | | | | | | | | | | | Yg W | Yg Wd | Yg W | Yg M | | | | | | | | | 7 |
| 8 | | | | | | | | | | | | | | | | | | | | | | | | | 8 |

# YEAR OF THE PIG

| | H | E | H | E | H | E | H | E | H | E | H | E | H | E | H | E | H | E | H | E | H | E | H | E | |
|---|---|---|---|---|---|---|---|---|---|---|---|---|---|---|---|---|---|---|---|---|---|---|---|---|---|
| YEAR | YEAR<br>YnE | YnW | 2019 | | | | | | | | | | | | | | | | | | 2020 | | | | |
| MONTH | 4 Feb - 5 Mar | | 6 Mar - 4 Apr | | 5 Apr - 5 May | | 6 May - 5 June | | 6 June - 6 Jul | | 7 Jul - 7 Aug | | 8 Aug - 7 Sep | | 8 Sep - 7 Oct | | 8 Oct - 7 Nov | | 8 Nov - 6 Dec | | 7 Dec - 6 Jan | | 7 Jan - 3 Feb | | |
| | Yg F | Yg Wd | Yn F | Yn Wd | Yg E | Yg E1 | Yn E | Yn F | Yg M | Yg F | Yn M | Yn E2 | Yg W | Yg M | Yn W | Yn M | Yg Wd | Yg E3 | Yn Wd | Yn W | Yg F | Yg W | Yn F | Yn E4 | |
| Starting time | 1st day | Mid-pt | 1st day | Mid-pt | 1st day | Mid-pt | 1st day | Mid-pt | 1st day | Mid-pt | 1st day | Mid-pt | 1st day | Mid-pt | 1st day | Mid-pt | 1st day | Mid-pt | 1st day | Mid-pt | 1st day | Mid-pt | 1st day | Mid-pt | |
| Date | 4 | 19 | 6 | 21 | 5 | 20 | 6 | 21 | 6 | 22 | 7 | 23 | 8 | 23 | 8 | 23 | 8 | 24 | 8 | 23 | 7 | 22 | 7 | 20 | |
| Hour | 1128 | 0712 | 0514 | 0604 | 0959 | 1707 | 0328 | 1619 | 0733 | 0022 | 1757 | 1128 | 0403 | 1855 | 0724 | 1700 | 2325 | 0236 | 0242 | 0006 | 1920 | 1304 | 0606 | 2310 | |
| DATE 3 | | | | | | | | | | | | | | | | | | | | | | | | | 3 |
| 4 | Yg W | Yg M | | | | | | | | | | | | | | | | | | | | | | | 4 |
| 5 | Yn W | Yn M | | | Yg W | Yg M | | | | | | | | | | | | | | | | | | | 5 |
| 6 | Yg Wd | Yg E3 | Yg W | Yg Wd | Yn W | Yn M | Yn W | Yn Wd | Yg Wd | Yg E3 | | | | | | | | | | | | | | | 6 |
| 7 | Yn Wd | Yn W | Yn W | Yn Wd | Yg Wd | Yg E3 | Yg Wd | Yg E1 | Yn Wd | Yn W | Yn Wd | Yn F | | | | | | | | | Yg E | Yg Wd | Yn E | Yn M | 7 |
| 8 | Yg F | Yg W | Yg Wd | Yg E1 | Yn Wd | Yn W | Yn Wd | Yn F | Yg F | Yg W | Yg F | Yg F | Yn F | Yn E4 | Yg E | Yg M | Yg E | Yg Wd | Yn E | Yn M | Yn E | Yn Wd | Yg M | Yg E3 | 8 |
| 9 | Yn F | Yn E4 | Yn Wd | Yn F | Yg F | Yg W | Yg F | Yg F | Yn F | Yn E4 | Yn F | Yn E2 | Yg E | Yg Wd | Yn E | Yn M | Yn E | Yn Wd | Yg M | Yg E3 | Yg M | Yg E1 | Yn M | Yn W | 9 |
| 10 | Yg E | Yg Wd | Yg F | Yg F | Yn F | Yn E4 | Yn F | Yn E2 | Yg E | Yg Wd | Yg E | Yg M | Yn E | Yn Wd | Yg M | Yg E3 | Yg M | Yg E1 | Yn M | Yn W | Yn M | Yn F | Yg W | Yg W | 10 |
| 11 | Yn E | Yn Wd | Yn F | Yn E2 | Yg E | Yg Wd | Yg E | Yg M | Yn E | Yn Wd | Yn E | Yn M | Yg M | Yg E1 | Yn M | Yn W | Yn M | Yn F | Yg W | Yg W | Yg W | Yg F | Yn W | Yn E4 | 11 |
| 12 | Yg M | Yg E1 | Yg E | Yg M | Yn E | Yn Wd | Yn E | Yn M | Yg M | Yg E1 | Yg M | Yg E3 | Yn M | Yn F | Yg W | Yg W | Yg W | Yg F | Yn W | Yn E4 | Yn W | Yn E2 | Yg Wd | Yg Wd | 12 |
| 13 | Yn M | Yn F | Yn E | Yn M | Yg M | Yg E1 | Yg M | Yg E3 | Yn M | Yn F | Yn M | Yn W | Yg W | Yg F | Yn W | Yn E4 | Yn W | Yn E2 | Yg Wd | Yg Wd | Yg Wd | Yg M | Yn Wd | Yn Wd | 13 |
| 14 | Yg W | Yg F | Yg M | Yg E3 | Yn M | Yn F | Yn M | Yn W | Yg W | Yg F | Yg W | Yg W | Yn W | Yn E2 | Yg Wd | Yg Wd | Yg Wd | Yg M | Yn Wd | Yn Wd | Yn Wd | Yn M | Yg F | Yg E1 | 14 |
| 15 | Yn W | Yn E2 | Yn M | Yn W | Yg W | Yg F | Yg W | Yg W | Yn W | Yn E2 | Yn W | Yn E4 | Yg Wd | Yg M | Yn Wd | Yn Wd | Yn Wd | Yn M | Yg F | Yg E1 | Yg F | Yg E3 | Yn F | Yn F | 15 |
| 16 | Yg Wd | Yg M | Yg W | Yg W | Yn W | Yn E2 | Yn W | Yn E4 | Yg Wd | Yg M | Yg Wd | Yg Wd | Yn Wd | Yn M | Yg F | Yg E1 | Yg F | Yg E3 | Yn F | Yn F | Yn F | Yn W | Yg E | Yg F | 16 |
| 17 | Yn Wd | Yn M | Yn W | Yn E4 | Yg Wd | Yg M | Yg Wd | Yg Wd | Yn Wd | Yn M | Yn Wd | Yn Wd | Yg F | Yg E3 | Yn F | Yn F | Yn F | Yn W | Yg E | Yg F | Yg E | Yg W | Yn E | Yn E2 | 17 |
| 18 | Yg F | Yg E3 | Yg Wd | Yg Wd | Yn Wd | Yn M | Yn Wd | Yn Wd | Yg F | Yg E3 | Yg F | Yg E1 | Yn F | Yn W | Yg E | Yg F | Yg E | Yg W | Yn E | Yn E2 | Yn E | Yn E4 | Yg M | Yg M | 18 |
| 19 | Yn F | Yn W | Yn Wd | Yn Wd | Yg F | Yg E3 | Yg F | Yg E1 | Yn F | Yn W | Yn F | Yn F | Yg E | Yg W | Yn E | Yn E2 | Yn E | Yn E4 | Yg M | Yg M | Yg M | Yg Wd | Yn M | Yn M | 19 |
| 20 | Yg E | Yg W | Yg F | Yg E1 | Yn F | Yn W | Yn F | Yn F | Yg E | Yg W | Yg E | Yg F | Yn E | Yn E4 | Yg M | Yg M | Yg M | Yg Wd | Yn M | Yn M | Yn M | Yn Wd | Yg W | Yg E3 | 20 |
| 21 | Yn E | Yn E4 | Yn F | Yn F | Yg E | Yg W | Yg E | Yg F | Yn E | Yn E4 | Yn E | Yn E2 | Yg M | Yg Wd | Yn M | Yn M | Yn M | Yn Wd | Yg W | Yg E3 | Yg W | Yg E1 | Yn W | Yn W | 21 |
| 22 | Yg M | Yg Wd | Yg E | Yg F | Yn E | Yn E4 | Yn E | Yn E2 | Yg M | Yg Wd | Yg M | Yg M | Yn M | Yn Wd | Yg W | Yg E3 | Yg W | Yg E1 | Yn W | Yn W | Yn W | Yn F | Yg Wd | Yg W | 22 |
| 23 | Yn M | Yn Wd | Yn E | Yn E2 | Yg M | Yg Wd | Yg M | Yg M | Yn M | Yn Wd | Yn M | Yn M | Yg W | Yg E1 | Yn W | Yn W | Yn W | Yn F | Yg Wd | Yg W | Yg Wd | Yg F | Yn Wd | Yn E4 | 23 |
| 24 | Yg W | Yg E1 | Yg M | Yg M | Yn M | Yn Wd | Yn M | Yn M | Yg W | Yg E1 | Yg W | Yg E3 | Yn W | Yn F | Yg Wd | Yg W | Yg Wd | Yg F | Yn Wd | Yn E4 | Yn Wd | Yn E2 | Yg F | Yg Wd | 24 |
| 25 | Yn W | Yn F | Yn M | Yn M | Yg W | Yg E1 | Yg W | Yg E3 | Yn W | Yn F | Yn W | Yn W | Yg Wd | Yg F | Yn Wd | Yn E4 | Yn Wd | Yn E2 | Yg F | Yg Wd | Yg F | Yg M | Yn F | Yn Wd | 25 |
| 26 | Yg Wd | Yg F | Yg W | Yg E3 | Yn W | Yn F | Yn W | Yn W | Yg Wd | Yg F | Yg Wd | Yg W | Yn Wd | Yn E2 | Yg F | Yg Wd | Yg F | Yg M | Yn F | Yn Wd | Yn F | Yn M | Yg E | Yg E1 | 26 |
| 27 | Yn Wd | Yn E2 | Yn W | Yn W | Yg Wd | Yg F | Yg Wd | Yg W | Yn Wd | Yn E2 | Yn Wd | Yn E4 | Yg F | Yg M | Yn F | Yn Wd | Yn F | Yn M | Yg E | Yg E1 | Yg E | Yg E3 | Yn E | Yn F | 27 |
| 28 | Yg F | Yg M | Yg Wd | Yg W | Yn Wd | Yn E2 | Yn Wd | Yn E4 | Yg F | Yg M | Yg F | Yg Wd | Yn F | Yn M | Yg E | Yg E1 | Yg E | Yg E3 | Yn E | Yn F | Yn E | Yn W | Yg M | Yg F | 28 |
| 29 | | | Yn Wd | Yn E4 | Yg F | Yg M | Yg F | Yg Wd | Yn F | Yn M | Yn F | Yn Wd | Yg E | Yg E3 | Yn E | Yn F | Yn E | Yn W | Yg M | Yg F | Yg M | Yg W | Yn M | Yn E2 | 29 |
| 30 | | | Yg F | Yg Wd | Yn F | Yn M | Yn F | Yn Wd | Yg E | Yg E3 | Yg E | Yg E1 | Yn E | Yn W | Yg M | Yg F | Yg M | Yg W | Yn M | Yn E2 | Yn M | Yn E4 | Yg W | Yg M | 30 |
| 31 | | | Yn F | Yn Wd | | | Yg E | Yg E1 | | | Yn E | Yn F | Yg M | Yg W | | | Yn M | Yn E4 | | | Yg W | Yg Wd | Yn W | Yn M | 31 |
| 1 | Yn F | Yn M | Yg E | Yg E1 | Yg E | Yg E3 | Yn E | Yn F | Yn E | Yn W | Yg M | Yg F | Yn M | Yn E4 | Yn M | Yn E2 | Yg W | Yg Wd | Yg W | Yg M | Yn W | Yn Wd | Yg Wd | Yg E3 | 1 |
| 2 | Yg E | Yg E3 | Yn E | Yn F | Yn E | Yn W | Yg M | Yg F | Yg M | Yg W | Yn M | Yn E2 | Yg W | Yg Wd | Yg W | Yg M | Yn W | Yn Wd | Yn W | Yn M | Yg Wd | Yg E1 | Yn Wd | Yn W | 2 |
| 3 | Yn E | Yn W | Yg M | Yg F | Yg M | Yg W | Yn M | Yn E2 | Yn M | Yn E4 | Yg W | Yg M | Yn W | Yn Wd | Yn W | Yn M | Yg Wd | Yg E1 | Yg Wd | Yg E3 | Yn Wd | Yn F | Yg F | Yg W | 3 |
| 4 | Yg M | Yg W | Yn M | Yn E2 | Yn M | Yn E4 | Yg W | Yg M | Yg W | Yg Wd | Yn W | Yn M | Yg Wd | Yg E1 | Yg Wd | Yg E3 | Yn Wd | Yn F | Yn Wd | Yn W | Yg F | Yg F | | | 4 |
| 5 | Yn M | Yn E4 | | | Yg W | Yg Wd | Yn W | Yn M | Yn W | Yn Wd | Yg Wd | Yg E3 | Yn Wd | Yn F | Yn Wd | Yn W | Yg F | Yg F | Yg F | Yg W | Yn F | Yn E2 | | | 5 |
| 6 | | | | | | | | | Yg Wd | Yg E1 | Yn Wd | Yn W | Yg F | Yg F | Yg F | Yg W | Yn F | Yn E2 | Yn F | Yn E4 | Yg E | Yg M | | | 6 |
| 7 | | | | | | | | | | | Yg F | Yg W | Yn F | Yn E2 | Yn F | Yn E4 | Yg E | Yg M | | | | | | | 7 |
| 8 | | | | | | | | | | | | | | | | | | | | | | | | | 8 |

# YEAR OF THE RAT

| | H | E | H | E | H | E | H | E | H | E | H | E | H | E | H | E | H | E | H | E | H | E | H | E | |
|---|---|---|---|---|---|---|---|---|---|---|---|---|---|---|---|---|---|---|---|---|---|---|---|---|---|
| YEAR | YEAR YgM | YgW | 2020 | | | | | | | | | | | | | | | | | | | | 2021 | | |
| MONTH | 4 Feb - 4 Mar | | 5 Mar - 3 Apr | | 4 Apr - 4 May | | 5 May - 4 June | | 5 June - 5 Jul | | 6 Jul - 6 Aug | | 7 Aug - 6 Sep | | 7 Sep - 7 Oct | | 8 Oct - 6 Nov | | 7 Nov - 6 Dec | | 7 Dec - 4 Jan | | 5 Jan - 2 Feb | | |
| | YgE | YgWd | YnE | YnWd | YgM | YgE1 | YnM | YnF | YgW | YgF | YnW | YnE2 | YgWd | YgM | YnWd | YnM | YgF | YgE3 | YnF | YnW | YgE | YgW | YnE | YnE4 | |
| Starting time | 1st day | Mid-pt | 1st day | Mid-pt | 1st day | Mid-pt | 1st day | Mid-pt | 1st day | Mid-pt | 1st day | Mid-pt | 1st day | Mid-pt | 1st day | Mid-pt | 1st day | Mid-pt | 1st day | Mid-pt | 1st day | Mid-pt | 1st day | Mid-pt | |
| Date | 4 | 19 | 5 | 20 | 4 | 19 | 5 | 20 | 5 | 21 | 6 | 22 | 7 | 23 | 7 | 22 | 8 | 23 | 7 | 22 | 7 | 21 | 5 | 20 | |
| Hour | 1718 | 1302 | 1103 | 1153 | 1548 | 2255 | 0908 | 2007 | 1349 | 0610 | 2346 | 1716 | 0951 | 0043 | 1312 | 2049 | 0515 | 0826 | 0831 | 0556 | 0109 | 1854 | 1155 | 0504 | |
| DATE 3 | | | | | | | | | | | | | | | | | | | | | | | | | 3 |
| 4 | YnF | YnE4 | | | YnF | YnE4 | | | | | | | | | | | | | | | | | | | 4 |
| 5 | YgE | YgWd | YnF | YnE2 | YgE | YgWd | YgE | YgM | YnE | YnWd | | | | | | | | | | | | | YnW | YnE4 | 5 |
| 6 | YnE | YnWd | YgE | YgM | YnE | YnWd | YnE | YnM | YgM | YgE1 | YgM | YgE3 | | | | | | | | | | | YgWd | YgWd | 6 |
| 7 | YgM | YgE1 | YnE | YnM | YgM | YgE1 | YgM | YgE3 | YnM | YnF | YnM | YnW | YgW | YgF | YnW | YnE4 | | | YgWd | YgWd | YgWd | YgM | YnWd | YnWd | 7 |
| 8 | YnM | YnF | YgM | YgE3 | YnM | YnF | YnM | YnW | YgW | YgF | YgW | YgW | YnW | YnE2 | YgWd | YgWd | YgWd | YgM | YnWd | YnWd | YnWd | YnM | YgF | YgE1 | 8 |
| 9 | YgW | YgF | YnM | YnW | YgW | YgF | YgW | YgW | YnW | YnE2 | YnW | YnE4 | YgWd | YgM | YnWd | YnWd | YnWd | YnM | YgF | YgE1 | YgF | YgE3 | YnF | YnF | 9 |
| 10 | YnW | YnE2 | YgW | YgW | YnW | YnE2 | YnW | YnE4 | YgWd | YgM | YgWd | YgWd | YnWd | YnM | YgF | YgE1 | YgF | YgE3 | YnF | YnF | YnF | YnW | YgE | YgF | 10 |
| 11 | YgWd | YgM | YnW | YnE4 | YgWd | YgM | YgWd | YgWd | YnWd | YnM | YnWd | YnWd | YgF | YgE3 | YnF | YnF | YnF | YnW | YgE | YgF | YgE | YgW | YnE | YnE2 | 11 |
| 12 | YnWd | YnM | YgWd | YgWd | YnWd | YnM | YnWd | YnWd | YgF | YgE3 | YgF | YgE1 | YnF | YnW | YgE | YgF | YgE | YgW | YnE | YnE2 | YnE | YnE4 | YgM | YgM | 12 |
| 13 | YgF | YgE3 | YnWd | YnWd | YgF | YgE3 | YgF | YgE1 | YnF | YnW | YnF | YnF | YgE | YgW | YnE | YnE2 | YnE | YnE4 | YgM | YgM | YgM | YgWd | YnM | YnM | 13 |
| 14 | YnF | YnW | YgF | YgE1 | YnF | YnW | YnF | YnF | YgE | YgW | YgE | YgF | YnE | YnE4 | YgM | YgM | YgM | YgWd | YnM | YnM | YnM | YnWd | YgW | YgE3 | 14 |
| 15 | YgE | YgW | YnF | YnF | YgE | YgW | YgE | YgF | YnE | YnE4 | YnE | YnE2 | YgM | YgWd | YnM | YnM | YnM | YnWd | YgW | YgE3 | YgW | YgE1 | YnW | YnW | 15 |
| 16 | YnE | YnE4 | YgE | YgF | YnE | YnE4 | YnE | YnE2 | YgM | YgWd | YgM | YgM | YnM | YnWd | YgW | YgE3 | YgW | YgE1 | YnW | YnW | YnW | YnF | YgWd | YgW | 16 |
| 17 | YgM | YgWd | YnE | YnE2 | YgM | YgWd | YgM | YgM | YnM | YnWd | YnM | YnM | YgW | YgE1 | YnW | YnW | YnW | YnF | YgWd | YgW | YgWd | YgF | YnWd | YnE4 | 17 |
| 18 | YnM | YnWd | YgM | YgM | YnM | YnWd | YnM | YnM | YgW | YgE1 | YgW | YgE3 | YnW | YnF | YgWd | YgW | YgWd | YgF | YnWd | YnE4 | YnWd | YnE2 | YgF | YgWd | 18 |
| 19 | YgW | YgE1 | YnM | YnM | YgW | YgE1 | YgW | YgE3 | YnW | YnF | YnW | YnW | YgWd | YgF | YnWd | YnE4 | YnWd | YnE2 | YgF | YgWd | YgF | YgM | YnF | YnWd | 19 |
| 20 | YnW | YnF | YgW | YgE3 | YnW | YnF | YnW | YnW | YgWd | YgF | YgWd | YgW | YnWd | YnE2 | YgF | YgWd | YgF | YgM | YnF | YnWd | YnF | YnM | YgE | YgE1 | 20 |
| 21 | YgWd | YgF | YnW | YnW | YgWd | YgF | YgWd | YgW | YnWd | YnE2 | YnWd | YnE4 | YgF | YgM | YnF | YnWd | YnF | YnM | YgE | YgE1 | YgE | YgE3 | YnE | YnF | 21 |
| 22 | YnWd | YnE2 | YgWd | YgW | YnWd | YnE2 | YnWd | YnE4 | YgF | YgM | YgF | YgWd | YnF | YnM | YgE | YgE1 | YgE | YgE3 | YnE | YnF | YnE | YnW | YgM | YgF | 22 |
| 23 | YgF | YgM | YnWd | YnE4 | YgF | YgM | YgF | YgWd | YnF | YnM | YnF | YnWd | YgE | YgE3 | YnE | YnF | YnE | YnW | YgM | YgF | YgM | YgW | YnM | YnE2 | 23 |
| 24 | YnF | YnM | YgF | YgWd | YnF | YnM | YnF | YnWd | YgE | YgE3 | YgE | YgE1 | YnE | YnW | YgM | YgF | YgM | YgW | YnM | YnE2 | YnM | YnE4 | YgW | YgM | 24 |
| 25 | YgE | YgE3 | YnF | YnWd | YgE | YgE3 | YgE | YgE1 | YnE | YnW | YnE | YnF | YgM | YgW | YnM | YnE2 | YnM | YnE4 | YgW | YgM | YgW | YgWd | YnW | YnM | 25 |
| 26 | YnE | YnW | YgE | YgE1 | YnE | YnW | YnE | YnF | YgM | YgW | YgM | YgF | YnM | YnE4 | YgW | YgM | YgW | YgWd | YnW | YnM | YnW | YnWd | YgWd | YgE3 | 26 |
| 27 | YgM | YgW | YnE | YnF | YgM | YgW | YgM | YgF | YnM | YnE4 | YnM | YnE2 | YgW | YgWd | YnW | YnM | YnW | YnWd | YgWd | YgE3 | YgWd | YgE1 | YnWd | YnW | 27 |
| 28 | YnM | YnE4 | YgM | YgF | YnM | YnE4 | YnM | YnE2 | YgW | YgWd | YgW | YgM | YnW | YnWd | YgWd | YgE3 | YgWd | YgE1 | YnWd | YnW | YnWd | YnF | YgF | YgW | 28 |
| 29 | YgW | YgWd | YnM | YnE2 | YgW | YgWd | YgW | YgM | YnW | YnWd | YnW | YnM | YgWd | YgE1 | YnWd | YnW | YnWd | YnF | YgF | YgW | YgF | YgF | YnF | YnE4 | 29 |
| 30 | | | YgW | YgM | YnW | YnWd | YnW | YnM | YgWd | YgE1 | YgWd | YgE3 | YnWd | YnF | YgF | YgW | YgF | YgF | YnF | YnE4 | YnF | YnE2 | YgE | YgWd | 30 |
| 31 | | | YnW | YnM | | | YgWd | YgE3 | | | YnWd | YnW | YgF | YgF | | | YnF | YnE2 | | | YgE | YgM | YnE | YnWd | 31 |
| 1 | YnW | YnWd | YgWd | YgE3 | YgWd | YgE1 | YnWd | YnW | YnWd | YnF | YgF | YgW | YnF | YnE2 | YnF | YnE4 | YgE | YgM | YgE | YgWd | YnE | YnM | YgM | YgE1 | 1 |
| 2 | YgWd | YgE1 | YnWd | YnW | YnWd | YnF | YgF | YgW | YgF | YgF | YnF | YnE4 | YgE | YgM | YgE | YgWd | YnE | YnM | YnE | YnWd | YgM | YgE3 | YnM | YnF | 2 |
| 3 | YnWd | YnF | YgF | YgW | YgF | YgF | YnF | YnE4 | YnF | YnE2 | YgE | YgWd | YnE | YnM | YnE | YnWd | YgM | YgE3 | YgM | YgE1 | YnM | YnW | | | 3 |
| 4 | YgF | YgF | | | YnF | YnE2 | YgE | YgWd | YgE | YgM | YnE | YnWd | YgM | YgE3 | YgM | YgE1 | YnM | YnW | YnM | YnF | YgW | YgW | | | 4 |
| 5 | | | | | | | | | YnE | YnM | YgM | YgE1 | YnM | YnW | YnM | YnF | YgW | YgW | YgW | YgF | | | | | 5 |
| 6 | | | | | | | | | | | YnM | YnF | YgW | YgW | YgW | YgF | YnW | YnE4 | YnW | YnE2 | | | | | 6 |
| 7 | | | | | | | | | | | | | | | YnW | YnE2 | | | | | | | | | 7 |
| 8 | | | | | | | | | | | | | | | | | | | | | | | | | 8 |

# YEAR OF THE OX

| | H | E | H | E | H | E | H | E | H | E | H | E | H | E | H | E | H | E | H | E | H | E | H | E | |
|---|---|---|---|---|---|---|---|---|---|---|---|---|---|---|---|---|---|---|---|---|---|---|---|---|---|
| **YEAR** | YEAR Yn M | Yn E4 | 2021 | | | | | | | | | | | | | | | | | | | 2022 | | | |
| **MONTH** | 3 Feb - 4 Mar | | 5 Mar - 3 Apr | | 4 Apr - 4 May | | 5 May - 4 June | | 5 June - 6 Jul | | 7 Jul - 6 Aug | | 7 Aug - 6 Sep | | 7 Sep - 7 Oct | | 8 Oct - 6 Nov | | 7 Nov - 6 Dec | | 7 Dec - 4 Jan | | 5 Jan - 3 Feb | | |
| | Yg M | Yg Wd | Yn M | Yn Wd | Yg W | Yg E1 | Yn W | Yn F | Yg Wd | Yg F | Yn Wd | Yn E2 | Yg F | Yg M | Yn F | Yn M | Yg E | Yg E3 | Yn E | Yn W | Yg M | Yg W | Yn M | Yn E4 | |
| **Starting time** | 1st day | Mid-pt | 1st day | Mid-pt | 1st day | Mid-pt | 1st day | Mid-pt | 1st day | Mid-pt | 1st day | Mid-pt | 1st day | Mid-pt | 1st day | Mid-pt | 1st day | Mid-pt | 1st day | Mid-pt | 1st day | Mid-pt | 1st day | Mid-pt | |
| Date | 3 | 18 | 5 | 20 | 4 | 20 | 5 | 21 | 5 | 21 | 7 | 22 | 7 | 23 | 7 | 23 | 8 | 23 | 7 | 22 | 7 | 22 | 5 | 20 | |
| Hour | 2308 | 1851 | 1654 | 1742 | 2137 | 0444 | 1457 | 0356 | 1909 | 1158 | 0553 | 2305 | 1540 | 0632 | 1901 | 0437 | 1104 | 1415 | 1421 | 1146 | 0700 | 0044 | 1746 | 1054 | |
| **DATE** 3 | Yg W | Yg F | | | | | | | | | | | | | | | | | | | | | | | 3 |
| 4 | Yn W | Yn E2 | | | Yg W | Yg F | | | | | | | | | | | | | | | | | | | 4 |
| 5 | Yg Wd | Yg M | Yg W | Yg W | Yn W | Yn E2 | Yn W | Yn E4 | Yg Wd | Yg M | | | | | | | | | | | | | Yg E | Yg F | 5 |
| 6 | Yn Wd | Yn M | Yn W | Yn E4 | Yg Wd | Yg M | Yg Wd | Yg Wd | Yn Wd | Yn M | | | | | | | | | | | | | Yn E | Yn E2 | 6 |
| 7 | Yg F | Yg E3 | Yg Wd | Yg Wd | Yn Wd | Yn M | Yn Wd | Yn Wd | Yg F | Yg E3 | Yg F | Yg E1 | Yn F | Yn W | Yg E | Yg F | | | Yn E | Yn E2 | Yn E | Yn E4 | Yg M | Yg M | 7 |
| 8 | Yn F | Yn W | Yn Wd | Yn Wd | Yg F | Yg E3 | Yg F | Yg E1 | Yn F | Yn W | Yn F | Yn F | Yg E | Yg W | Yn E | Yn E2 | Yn E | Yn E4 | Yg M | Yg M | Yg M | Yg Wd | Yn M | Yn M | 8 |
| 9 | Yg E | Yg W | Yg F | Yg E1 | Yn F | Yn W | Yn F | Yn F | Yg E | Yg W | Yg E | Yg F | Yn E | Yn E4 | Yg M | Yg M | Yg M | Yg Wd | Yn M | Yn M | Yn M | Yn Wd | Yg W | Yg E3 | 9 |
| 10 | Yn E | Yn E4 | Yn F | Yn F | Yg E | Yg W | Yg E | Yg F | Yn E | Yn E4 | Yn E | Yn E2 | Yg M | Yg Wd | Yn M | Yn M | Yn M | Yn Wd | Yg W | Yg E3 | Yg W | Yg E1 | Yn W | Yn W | 10 |
| 11 | Yg M | Yg Wd | Yg E | Yg F | Yn E | Yn E4 | Yn E | Yn E2 | Yg M | Yg Wd | Yg M | Yg M | Yn M | Yn Wd | Yg W | Yg E3 | Yg W | Yg E1 | Yn W | Yn W | Yn W | Yn F | Yg Wd | Yg W | 11 |
| 12 | Yn M | Yn Wd | Yn E | Yn E2 | Yg M | Yg Wd | Yg M | Yg M | Yn M | Yn Wd | Yn M | Yn M | Yg W | Yg E1 | Yn W | Yn W | Yn W | Yn F | Yg Wd | Yg W | Yg Wd | Yg F | Yn Wd | Yn E4 | 12 |
| 13 | Yg W | Yg E1 | Yg M | Yg M | Yn M | Yn Wd | Yn M | Yn M | Yg W | Yg E1 | Yg W | Yg E3 | Yn W | Yn F | Yg Wd | Yg W | Yg Wd | Yg F | Yn Wd | Yn E4 | Yn Wd | Yn E2 | Yg F | Yg Wd | 13 |
| 14 | Yn W | Yn F | Yn M | Yn M | Yg W | Yg E1 | Yg W | Yg E3 | Yn W | Yn F | Yn W | Yn W | Yg Wd | Yg F | Yn Wd | Yn E4 | Yn Wd | Yn E2 | Yg F | Yg Wd | Yg F | Yg M | Yn F | Yn Wd | 14 |
| 15 | Yg Wd | Yg F | Yg W | Yg E3 | Yn W | Yn F | Yn W | Yn W | Yg Wd | Yg F | Yg Wd | Yg W | Yn Wd | Yn E2 | Yg F | Yg Wd | Yg F | Yg M | Yn F | Yn Wd | Yn F | Yn M | Yg E | Yg E1 | 15 |
| 16 | Yn Wd | Yn E2 | Yn W | Yn W | Yg Wd | Yg F | Yg Wd | Yg W | Yn Wd | Yn E2 | Yn Wd | Yn E4 | Yg F | Yg M | Yn F | Yn Wd | Yn F | Yn M | Yg E | Yg E1 | Yg E | Yg E3 | Yn E | Yn F | 16 |
| 17 | Yg F | Yg M | Yg Wd | Yg W | Yn Wd | Yn E2 | Yn Wd | Yn E4 | Yg F | Yg M | Yg F | Yg Wd | Yn F | Yn M | Yg E | Yg E1 | Yg E | Yg E3 | Yn E | Yn F | Yn E | Yn W | Yg M | Yg F | 17 |
| 18 | Yn F | Yn M | Yn Wd | Yn E4 | Yg F | Yg M | Yg F | Yg Wd | Yn F | Yn M | Yn F | Yn Wd | Yg E | Yg E3 | Yn E | Yn F | Yn E | Yn W | Yg M | Yg F | Yg M | Yg W | Yn M | Yn E2 | 18 |
| 19 | Yg E | Yg E3 | Yg F | Yg Wd | Yn F | Yn M | Yn F | Yn Wd | Yg E | Yg E3 | Yg E | Yg E1 | Yn E | Yn W | Yg M | Yg F | Yg M | Yg W | Yn M | Yn E2 | Yn M | Yn E4 | Yg W | Yg M | 19 |
| 20 | Yn E | Yn W | Yn F | Yn Wd | Yg E | Yg E3 | Yg E | Yg E1 | Yn E | Yn W | Yn E | Yn F | Yg M | Yg W | Yn M | Yn E2 | Yn M | Yn E4 | Yg W | Yg M | Yg W | Yg Wd | Yn W | Yn M | 20 |
| 21 | Yg M | Yg W | Yg E | Yg E1 | Yn E | Yn W | Yn E | Yn F | Yg M | Yg W | Yg M | Yg F | Yn M | Yn E4 | Yg W | Yg M | Yg W | Yg Wd | Yn W | Yn M | Yn W | Yn Wd | Yg Wd | Yg E3 | 21 |
| 22 | Yn M | Yn E4 | Yn E | Yn F | Yg M | Yg W | Yg M | Yg F | Yn M | Yn E4 | Yn M | Yn E2 | Yg W | Yg Wd | Yn W | Yn M | Yn W | Yn Wd | Yg Wd | Yg E3 | Yg Wd | Yg E1 | Yn Wd | Yn W | 22 |
| 23 | Yg W | Yg Wd | Yg M | Yg F | Yn M | Yn E4 | Yn M | Yn E2 | Yg W | Yg Wd | Yg W | Yg M | Yn W | Yn Wd | Yg Wd | Yg E3 | Yg Wd | Yg E1 | Yn Wd | Yn W | Yn Wd | Yn F | Yg F | Yg W | 23 |
| 24 | Yn W | Yn Wd | Yn M | Yn E2 | Yg W | Yg Wd | Yg W | Yg M | Yn W | Yn Wd | Yn W | Yn M | Yg Wd | Yg E1 | Yn Wd | Yn W | Yn Wd | Yn F | Yg F | Yg W | Yg F | Yg F | Yn F | Yn E4 | 24 |
| 25 | Yg Wd | Yg E1 | Yg W | Yg M | Yn W | Yn Wd | Yn W | Yn M | Yg Wd | Yg E1 | Yg Wd | Yg E3 | Yn Wd | Yn F | Yg F | Yg W | Yg F | Yg F | Yn F | Yn E4 | Yn F | Yn E2 | Yg E | Yg Wd | 25 |
| 26 | Yn Wd | Yn F | Yn W | Yn M | Yg Wd | Yg E1 | Yg Wd | Yg E3 | Yn Wd | Yn F | Yn Wd | Yn W | Yg F | Yg F | Yn F | Yn E4 | Yn F | Yn E2 | Yg E | Yg Wd | Yg E | Yg M | Yn E | Yn Wd | 26 |
| 27 | Yg F | Yg F | Yg Wd | Yg E3 | Yn Wd | Yn F | Yn Wd | Yn W | Yg F | Yg F | Yg F | Yg W | Yn F | Yn E2 | Yg E | Yg Wd | Yg E | Yg M | Yn E | Yn Wd | Yn E | Yn M | Yg M | Yg E1 | 27 |
| 28 | Yn F | Yn E2 | Yn Wd | Yn W | Yg F | Yg F | Yg F | Yg W | Yn F | Yn E2 | Yn F | Yn E4 | Yg E | Yg M | Yn E | Yn Wd | Yn E | Yn M | Yg M | Yg E1 | Yg M | Yg E3 | Yn M | Yn F | 28 |
| 29 | | | Yg F | Yg W | Yn F | Yn E2 | Yn F | Yn E4 | Yg E | Yg M | Yg E | Yg Wd | Yn E | Yn M | Yg M | Yg E1 | Yg M | Yg E3 | Yn M | Yn F | Yn M | Yn W | Yg W | Yg F | 29 |
| 30 | | | Yn F | Yn E4 | Yg E | Yg M | Yg E | Yg Wd | Yn E | Yn M | Yn E | Yn Wd | Yg M | Yg E3 | Yn M | Yn F | Yn M | Yn W | Yg W | Yg F | Yg W | Yg W | Yn W | Yn E2 | 30 |
| 31 | | | Yg E | Yg Wd | | | Yn E | Yn Wd | | | Yg M | Yg E1 | Yn M | Yn W | | | Yg W | Yg W | | | Yn W | Yn E4 | Yg Wd | Yg M | 31 |
| 1 | Yg E | Yg M | Yn E | Yn Wd | Yn E | Yn M | Yg M | Yg E1 | Yg M | Yg E3 | Yn M | Yn F | Yg W | Yg W | Yg W | Yg F | Yn W | Yn E4 | Yn W | Yn E2 | Yg Wd | Yg Wd | Yn Wd | Yn M | 1 |
| 2 | Yn E | Yn M | Yg M | Yg E1 | Yg M | Yg E3 | Yn M | Yn F | Yn M | Yn W | Yg W | Yg F | Yn W | Yn E4 | Yn W | Yn E2 | Yg Wd | Yg Wd | Yg Wd | Yg M | Yn Wd | Yn Wd | Yg F | Yg E3 | 2 |
| 3 | Yg M | Yg E3 | Yn M | Yn F | Yn M | Yn W | Yg W | Yg F | Yg W | Yg W | Yn W | Yn E2 | Yg Wd | Yg Wd | Yg Wd | Yg M | Yn Wd | Yn Wd | Yn Wd | Yn M | Yg F | Yg E1 | Yn F | Yn W | 3 |
| 4 | Yn M | Yn W | | | Yg W | Yg W | Yn W | Yn E2 | Yn W | Yn E4 | Yg Wd | Yg M | Yn Wd | Yn Wd | Yn Wd | Yn M | Yg F | Yg E1 | Yg F | Yg E3 | Yn F | Yn F | | | 4 |
| 5 | | | | | | | | | Yg Wd | Yg Wd | Yn Wd | Yn M | Yg F | Yg E1 | Yg F | Yg E3 | Yn F | Yn F | Yn F | Yn W | | | | | 5 |
| 6 | | | | | | | | | Yn Wd | Yn Wd | Yg F | Yg E3 | Yn F | Yn F | Yn F | Yn W | Yg E | Yg F | Yg E | Yg W | | | | | 6 |
| 7 | | | | | | | | | | | | | | | Yg E | Yg W | | | | | | | | | 7 |
| 8 | | | | | | | | | | | | | | | | | | | | | | | | | 8 |

# YEAR OF THE TIGER

| | H | E | H | E | H | E | H | E | H | E | H | E | H | E | H | E | H | E | H | E | H | E | H | E | |
|---|---|---|---|---|---|---|---|---|---|---|---|---|---|---|---|---|---|---|---|---|---|---|---|---|---|
| YEAR | YEAR<br>Yg W | Yg Wd | 2022 | | | | | | | | | | | | | | | | | | | | 2023 | | |
| MONTH | 4 Feb - 4 Mar<br>Yg W | Yg Wd | 5 Mar - 4 Apr<br>Yn W | Yn Wd | 5 Apr - 4 May<br>Yg Wd | Yg E1 | 5 May - 5 June<br>Yn Wd | Yn F | 6 June - 6 Jul<br>Yg F | Yg F | 7 Jul - 6 Aug<br>Yn F | Yn E2 | 7 Aug - 7 Sep<br>Yg E | Yg M | 8 Sep - 7 Oct<br>Yn E | Yn M | 8 Oct - 6 Nov<br>Yg M | Yg E3 | 7 Nov - 6 Dec<br>Yn M | Yn W | 7 Dec - 4 Jan<br>Yg W | Yg W | 5 Jan - 3 Feb<br>Yn W | Yn E4 | |
| Starting time | 1st day | Mid-pt | 1st day | Mid-pt | 1st day | Mid-pt | 1st day | Mid-pt | 1st day | Mid-pt | 1st day | Mid-pt | 1st day | Mid-pt | 1st day | Mid-pt | 1st day | Mid-pt | 1st day | Mid-pt | 1st day | Mid-pt | 1st day | Mid-pt | |
| Date | 4 | 19 | 5 | 20 | 5 | 20 | 5 | 21 | 6 | 21 | 7 | 23 | 7 | 23 | 8 | 23 | 8 | 23 | 7 | 22 | 7 | 22 | 5 | 20 | |
| Hour | 0458 | 0045 | 2242 | 2332 | 0322 | 1033 | 2045 | 0944 | 0058 | 1746 | 1122 | 0452 | 2128 | 1220 | 0050 | 1027 | 1653 | 2004 | 2011 | 1735 | 1249 | 0633 | 2335 | 1643 | |
| DATE 3 | | | | | | | | | | | | | | | | | | | | | | | | | 3 |
| 4 | Yg E | Yg W | | | | | | | | | | | | | | | | | | | | | | | 4 |
| 5 | Yn E | Yn E4 | Yn F | Yn F | Yg E | Yg W | Yg E | Yg F | | | | | | | | | | | | | | | Yn W | Yn W | 5 |
| 6 | Yg M | Yg Wd | Yg E | Yg F | Yn E | Yn E4 | Yn E | Yn E2 | Yg M | Yg Wd | | | | | | | | | | | | | Yg Wd | Yg W | 6 |
| 7 | Yn M | Yn Wd | Yn E | Yn E2 | Yg M | Yg Wd | Yg M | Yg M | Yn M | Yn Wd | Yn M | Yn M | Yg W | Yg E1 | | | | | Yg Wd | Yg W | Yg Wd | Yg F | Yn Wd | Yn E4 | 7 |
| 8 | Yg W | Yg E1 | Yg M | Yg M | Yn M | Yn Wd | Yn M | Yn M | Yg W | Yg E1 | Yg W | Yg E3 | Yn W | Yn F | Yg Wd | Yg W | Yg Wd | Yg F | Yn Wd | Yn E4 | Yn Wd | Yn E2 | Yg F | Yg Wd | 8 |
| 9 | Yn W | Yn F | Yn M | Yn M | Yg W | Yg E1 | Yg W | Yg E3 | Yn W | Yn F | Yn W | Yn W | Yg Wd | Yg F | Yn Wd | Yn E4 | Yn Wd | Yn E2 | Yg F | Yg Wd | Yg F | Yg M | Yn F | Yn Wd | 9 |
| 10 | Yg Wd | Yg F | Yg W | Yg E3 | Yn W | Yn F | Yn W | Yn W | Yg Wd | Yg F | Yg Wd | Yg W | Yn Wd | Yn E2 | Yg F | Yg Wd | Yg F | Yg M | Yn F | Yn Wd | Yn F | Yn M | Yg E | Yg E1 | 10 |
| 11 | Yn Wd | Yn E2 | Yn W | Yn W | Yg Wd | Yg F | Yg Wd | Yg W | Yn Wd | Yn E2 | Yn Wd | Yn E4 | Yg F | Yg M | Yn F | Yn Wd | Yn F | Yn M | Yg E | Yg E1 | Yg E | Yg E3 | Yn E | Yn F | 11 |
| 12 | Yg F | Yg M | Yg Wd | Yg W | Yn Wd | Yn E2 | Yn Wd | Yn E4 | Yg F | Yg M | Yg F | Yg Wd | Yn F | Yn M | Yg E | Yg E1 | Yg E | Yg E3 | Yn E | Yn F | Yn E | Yn W | Yg M | Yg F | 12 |
| 13 | Yn F | Yn M | Yn Wd | Yn E4 | Yg F | Yg M | Yg F | Yg Wd | Yn F | Yn M | Yn F | Yn Wd | Yg E | Yg E3 | Yn E | Yn F | Yn E | Yn W | Yg M | Yg F | Yg M | Yg W | Yn M | Yn E2 | 13 |
| 14 | Yg E | Yg E3 | Yg F | Yg Wd | Yn F | Yn M | Yn F | Yn Wd | Yg E | Yg E3 | Yg E | Yg E1 | Yn E | Yn W | Yg M | Yg F | Yg M | Yg W | Yn M | Yn E2 | Yn M | Yn E4 | Yg W | Yg M | 14 |
| 15 | Yn E | Yn W | Yn F | Yn Wd | Yg E | Yg E3 | Yg E | Yg E1 | Yn E | Yn W | Yn E | Yn F | Yg M | Yg W | Yn M | Yn E2 | Yn M | Yn E4 | Yg W | Yg M | Yg W | Yg Wd | Yn W | Yn M | 15 |
| 16 | Yg M | Yg W | Yg E | Yg E1 | Yn E | Yn W | Yn E | Yn F | Yg M | Yg W | Yg M | Yg F | Yn M | Yn E4 | Yg W | Yg M | Yg W | Yg Wd | Yn W | Yn M | Yn W | Yn Wd | Yg Wd | Yg E3 | 16 |
| 17 | Yn M | Yn E4 | Yn E | Yn F | Yg M | Yg W | Yg M | Yg F | Yn M | Yn E4 | Yn M | Yn E2 | Yg W | Yg Wd | Yn W | Yn M | Yn W | Yn Wd | Yg Wd | Yg E3 | Yg Wd | Yg E1 | Yn Wd | Yn W | 17 |
| 18 | Yg W | Yg Wd | Yg M | Yg F | Yn M | Yn E4 | Yn M | Yn E2 | Yg W | Yg Wd | Yg W | Yg M | Yn W | Yn Wd | Yg Wd | Yg E3 | Yg Wd | Yg E1 | Yn Wd | Yn W | Yn Wd | Yn F | Yg F | Yg W | 18 |
| 19 | Yn W | Yn Wd | Yn M | Yn E2 | Yg W | Yg Wd | Yg W | Yg M | Yn W | Yn Wd | Yn W | Yn M | Yg Wd | Yg E1 | Yn Wd | Yn W | Yn Wd | Yn F | Yg F | Yg W | Yg F | Yg F | Yn F | Yn E4 | 19 |
| 20 | Yg Wd | Yg E1 | Yg W | Yg M | Yn W | Yn Wd | Yn W | Yn M | Yg Wd | Yg E1 | Yg Wd | Yg E3 | Yn Wd | Yn F | Yg F | Yg W | Yg F | Yg F | Yn F | Yn E4 | Yn F | Yn E2 | Yg E | Yg Wd | 20 |
| 21 | Yn Wd | Yn F | Yn W | Yn M | Yg Wd | Yg E1 | Yg Wd | Yg E3 | Yn Wd | Yn F | Yn Wd | Yn W | Yg F | Yg F | Yn F | Yn E4 | Yn F | Yn E2 | Yg E | Yg Wd | Yg E | Yg M | Yn E | Yn Wd | 21 |
| 22 | Yg F | Yg F | Yg Wd | Yg E3 | Yn Wd | Yn F | Yn Wd | Yn W | Yg F | Yg F | Yg F | Yg W | Yn F | Yn E2 | Yg E | Yg Wd | Yg E | Yg M | Yn E | Yn Wd | Yn E | Yn M | Yg M | Yg E1 | 22 |
| 23 | Yn F | Yn E2 | Yn Wd | Yn W | Yg F | Yg F | Yg F | Yg W | Yn F | Yn E2 | Yn F | Yn E4 | Yg E | Yg M | Yn E | Yn Wd | Yn E | Yn M | Yg M | Yg E1 | Yg M | Yg E3 | Yn M | Yn F | 23 |
| 24 | Yg E | Yg M | Yg F | Yg W | Yn F | Yn E2 | Yn F | Yn E4 | Yg E | Yg M | Yg E | Yg Wd | Yn E | Yn M | Yg M | Yg E1 | Yg M | Yg E3 | Yn M | Yn F | Yn M | Yn W | Yg W | Yg F | 24 |
| 25 | Yn E | Yn M | Yn F | Yn E4 | Yg E | Yg M | Yg E | Yg Wd | Yn E | Yn M | Yn E | Yn Wd | Yg M | Yg E3 | Yn M | Yn F | Yn M | Yn W | Yg W | Yg F | Yg W | Yg W | Yn W | Yn E2 | 25 |
| 26 | Yg M | Yg E3 | Yg E | Yg Wd | Yn E | Yn M | Yn E | Yn Wd | Yg M | Yg E3 | Yg M | Yg E1 | Yn M | Yn W | Yg W | Yg F | Yg W | Yg W | Yn W | Yn E2 | Yn W | Yn E4 | Yg Wd | Yg M | 26 |
| 27 | Yn M | Yn W | Yn E | Yn Wd | Yg M | Yg E3 | Yg M | Yg E1 | Yn M | Yn W | Yn M | Yn F | Yg W | Yg W | Yn W | Yn E2 | Yn W | Yn E4 | Yg Wd | Yg M | Yg Wd | Yg Wd | Yn Wd | Yn M | 27 |
| 28 | Yg W | Yg W | Yg M | Yg E1 | Yn M | Yn W | Yn M | Yn F | Yg W | Yg W | Yg W | Yg F | Yn W | Yn E4 | Yg Wd | Yg M | Yg Wd | Yg Wd | Yn Wd | Yn M | Yn Wd | Yn Wd | Yg F | Yg E3 | 28 |
| 29 | | | Yn M | Yn F | Yg W | Yg W | Yg W | Yg F | Yn W | Yn E4 | Yn W | Yn E2 | Yg Wd | Yg Wd | Yn Wd | Yn M | Yn Wd | Yn Wd | Yg F | Yg E3 | Yg F | Yg E1 | Yn F | Yn W | 29 |
| 30 | | | Yg W | Yg F | Yn W | Yn E4 | Yn W | Yn E2 | Yg Wd | Yg Wd | Yg Wd | Yg M | Yn Wd | Yn Wd | Yg F | Yg E3 | Yg F | Yg E1 | Yn F | Yn W | Yn F | Yn F | Yg E | Yg W | 30 |
| 31 | | | Yn W | Yn E2 | | | Yg Wd | Yg M | | | Yn Wd | Yn M | Yg F | Yg E1 | | | Yn F | Yn F | | | Yg E | Yg F | Yn E | Yn E4 | 31 |
| 1 | Yn W | Yn E4 | Yg Wd | Yg M | Yg Wd | Yg Wd | Yn Wd | Yn M | Yn Wd | Yn Wd | Yg F | Yg E3 | Yn F | Yn F | Yn F | Yn W | Yg E | Yg F | Yg E | Yg W | Yn E | Yn E2 | Yg M | Yg Wd | 1 |
| 2 | Yg Wd | Yg Wd | Yn Wd | Yn M | Yn Wd | Yn Wd | Yg F | Yg E3 | Yg F | Yg E1 | Yn F | Yn W | Yg E | Yg F | Yg E | Yg W | Yn E | Yn E2 | Yn E | Yn E4 | Yg M | Yg M | Yn M | Yn Wd | 2 |
| 3 | Yn Wd | Yn Wd | Yg F | Yg E3 | Yg F | Yg E1 | Yn F | Yn W | Yn F | Yn F | Yg E | Yg W | Yn E | Yn E2 | Yn E | Yn E4 | Yg M | Yg M | Yg M | Yg Wd | Yn M | Yn M | Yg W | Yg E1 | 3 |
| 4 | Yg F | Yg E1 | Yn F | Yn W | Yn F | Yn F | Yg E | Yg W | Yg E | Yg F | Yn E | Yn E4 | Yg M | Yg M | Yg M | Yg Wd | Yn M | Yn M | Yn M | Yn Wd | Yg W | Yg E3 | | | 4 |
| 5 | | | | | | | Yn E | Yn E4 | Yn E | Yn E2 | Yg M | Yg Wd | Yn M | Yn M | Yn M | Yn Wd | Yg W | Yg E3 | Yg W | Yg E1 | | | | | 5 |
| 6 | | | | | | | | | Yg M | Yg M | Yn M | Yn Wd | Yg W | Yg E3 | Yg W | Yg E1 | Yn W | Yn W | Yn W | Yn F | | | | | 6 |
| 7 | | | | | | | | | | | | | Yn W | Yn W | Yn W | Yn F | | | | | | | | | 7 |
| 8 | | | | | | | | | | | | | | | | | | | | | | | | | 8 |

# YEAR OF THE RABBIT

| | H | E | H | E | H | E | H | E | H | E | H | E | H | E | H | E | H | E | H | E | H | E | H | E | |
|---|---|---|---|---|---|---|---|---|---|---|---|---|---|---|---|---|---|---|---|---|---|---|---|---|---|
| **YEAR** | **YEAR** Yn W | Yn Wd | 2023 | | | | | | | | | | | | | | | | | | | | 2024 | | |
| **MONTH** | 4 Feb - 5 Mar | | 6 Mar - 4 Apr | | 5 Apr - 5 May | | 6 May - 5 June | | 6 June - 6 Jul | | 7 Jul - 7 Aug | | 8 Aug - 7 Sep | | 8 Sep - 7 Oct | | 8 Oct - 7 Nov | | 8 Nov - 6 Dec | | 7 Dec - 5 Jan | | 6 Jan - 3 Feb | | |
| | Yg Wd | Yg Wd | Yn Wd | Yn Wd | Yg F | Yg E1 | Yn F | Yn F | Yg E | Yg F | Yn E | Yn E2 | Yg M | Yg M | Yn M | Yn M | Yg W | Yg E3 | Yn W | Yn W | Yg Wd | Yg W | Yn Wd | Yn E4 | |
| **Starting time** | 1st day | Mid-pt | 1st day | Mid-pt | 1st day | Mid-pt | 1st day | Mid-pt | 1st day | Mid-pt | 1st day | Mid-pt | 1st day | Mid-pt | 1st day | Mid-pt | 1st day | Mid-pt | 1st day | Mid-pt | 1st day | Mid-pt | 1st day | Mid-pt | |
| Date | 4 | 19 | 6 | 21 | 5 | 20 | 6 | 21 | 6 | 21 | 7 | 23 | 8 | 23 | 8 | 23 | 8 | 24 | 8 | 22 | 7 | 22 | 6 | 20 | |
| Hour | 1047 | 0630 | 0431 | 0520 | 0921 | 1621 | 0233 | 1532 | 0646 | 2335 | 1810 | 1040 | 0316 | 0223 | 0638 | 1615 | 2241 | 0153 | 0200 | 2324 | 1838 | 1223 | 0511 | 2233 | |
| **DATE** 3 | | | | | | | | | | | | | | | | | | | | | | | | | 3 |
| 4 | Yn W | Yn F | | | | | | | | | | | | | | | | | | | | | | | 4 |
| 5 | Yg Wd | Yg F | | | Yn W | Yn F | | | | | | | | | | | | | | | | | | | 5 |
| 6 | Yn Wd | Yn E2 | Yn W | Yn W | Yg Wd | Yg F | Yg Wd | Yg W | Yn Wd | Yn E2 | | | | | | | | | | | | | Yn E | Yn F | 6 |
| 7 | Yg F | Yg M | Yg Wd | Yg W | Yn Wd | Yn E2 | Yn Wd | Yn E4 | Yg F | Yg M | Yg F | Yg Wd | | | | | | | | | Yn E | Yn W | Yg M | Yg F | 7 |
| 8 | Yn F | Yn M | Yn Wd | Yn E4 | Yg F | Yg M | Yg F | Yg Wd | Yn F | Yn M | Yn F | Yn Wd | Yg E | Yg E3 | Yn E | Yn F | Yn E | Yn W | Yg M | Yg F | Yg M | Yg W | Yn M | Yn E2 | 8 |
| 9 | Yg E | Yg E3 | Yg F | Yg Wd | Yn F | Yn M | Yn F | Yn Wd | Yg E | Yg E3 | Yg E | Yg E1 | Yn E | Yn W | Yg M | Yg F | Yg M | Yg W | Yn M | Yn E2 | Yn M | Yn E4 | Yg W | Yg M | 9 |
| 10 | Yn E | Yn W | Yn F | Yn Wd | Yg E | Yg E3 | Yg E | Yg E1 | Yn E | Yn W | Yn E | Yn F | Yg M | Yg W | Yn M | Yn E2 | Yn M | Yn E4 | Yg W | Yg M | Yg W | Yg Wd | Yn W | Yn M | 10 |
| 11 | Yg M | Yg W | Yg E | Yg E1 | Yn E | Yn W | Yn E | Yn F | Yg M | Yg W | Yg M | Yg F | Yn M | Yn E4 | Yg W | Yg M | Yg W | Yg Wd | Yn W | Yn M | Yn W | Yn Wd | Yg Wd | Yg E3 | 11 |
| 12 | Yn M | Yn E4 | Yn E | Yn F | Yg M | Yg W | Yg M | Yg F | Yn M | Yn E4 | Yn M | Yn E2 | Yg W | Yg Wd | Yn W | Yn M | Yn W | Yn Wd | Yg Wd | Yg E3 | Yg Wd | Yg E1 | Yn Wd | Yn W | 12 |
| 13 | Yg W | Yg Wd | Yg M | Yg F | Yn M | Yn E4 | Yn M | Yn E2 | Yg W | Yg Wd | Yg W | Yg M | Yn W | Yn Wd | Yg Wd | Yg E3 | Yg Wd | Yg E1 | Yn Wd | Yn W | Yn Wd | Yn F | Yg F | Yg W | 13 |
| 14 | Yn W | Yn Wd | Yn M | Yn E2 | Yg W | Yg Wd | Yg W | Yg M | Yn W | Yn Wd | Yn W | Yn M | Yg Wd | Yg E1 | Yn Wd | Yn W | Yn Wd | Yn F | Yg F | Yg W | Yg F | Yg F | Yn F | Yn E4 | 14 |
| 15 | Yg Wd | Yg E1 | Yg W | Yg M | Yn W | Yn Wd | Yn W | Yn M | Yg Wd | Yg E1 | Yg Wd | Yg E3 | Yn Wd | Yn F | Yg F | Yg W | Yg F | Yg F | Yn F | Yn E4 | Yn F | Yn E2 | Yg E | Yg Wd | 15 |
| 16 | Yn Wd | Yn F | Yn W | Yn M | Yg Wd | Yg E1 | Yg Wd | Yg E3 | Yn Wd | Yn F | Yn Wd | Yn W | Yg F | Yg F | Yn F | Yn E4 | Yn F | Yn E2 | Yg E | Yg Wd | Yg E | Yg M | Yn E | Yn Wd | 16 |
| 17 | Yg F | Yg F | Yg Wd | Yg E3 | Yn Wd | Yn F | Yn Wd | Yn W | Yg F | Yg F | Yg F | Yg W | Yn F | Yn E2 | Yg E | Yg Wd | Yg E | Yg M | Yn E | Yn Wd | Yn E | Yn M | Yg M | Yg E1 | 17 |
| 18 | Yn F | Yn E2 | Yn Wd | Yn W | Yg F | Yg F | Yg F | Yg W | Yn F | Yn E2 | Yn F | Yn E4 | Yg E | Yg M | Yn E | Yn Wd | Yn E | Yn M | Yg M | Yg E1 | Yg M | Yg E3 | Yn M | Yn F | 18 |
| 19 | Yg E | Yg M | Yg F | Yg W | Yn F | Yn E2 | Yn F | Yn E4 | Yg E | Yg M | Yg E | Yg Wd | Yn E | Yn M | Yg M | Yg E1 | Yg M | Yg E3 | Yn M | Yn F | Yn M | Yn W | Yg W | Yg F | 19 |
| 20 | Yn E | Yn M | Yn F | Yn E4 | Yg E | Yg M | Yg E | Yg Wd | Yn E | Yn M | Yn E | Yn Wd | Yg M | Yg E3 | Yn M | Yn F | Yn M | Yn W | Yg W | Yg F | Yg W | Yg W | Yn W | Yn E2 | 20 |
| 21 | Yg M | Yg E3 | Yg E | Yg Wd | Yn E | Yn M | Yn E | Yn Wd | Yg M | Yg E3 | Yg M | Yg E1 | Yn M | Yn W | Yg W | Yg F | Yg W | Yg W | Yn W | Yn E2 | Yn W | Yn E4 | Yg Wd | Yg M | 21 |
| 22 | Yn M | Yn W | Yn E | Yn Wd | Yg M | Yg E3 | Yg M | Yg E1 | Yn M | Yn W | Yn M | Yn F | Yg W | Yg W | Yn W | Yn E2 | Yn W | Yn E4 | Yg Wd | Yg M | Yg Wd | Yg Wd | Yn Wd | Yn M | 22 |
| 23 | Yg W | Yg W | Yg M | Yg E1 | Yn M | Yn W | Yn M | Yn F | Yg W | Yg W | Yg W | Yg F | Yn W | Yn E4 | Yg Wd | Yg M | Yg Wd | Yg Wd | Yn Wd | Yn M | Yn Wd | Yn Wd | Yg F | Yg E3 | 23 |
| 24 | Yn W | Yn E4 | Yn M | Yn F | Yg W | Yg W | Yg W | Yg F | Yn W | Yn E4 | Yn W | Yn E2 | Yg Wd | Yg Wd | Yn Wd | Yn M | Yn Wd | Yn Wd | Yg F | Yg E3 | Yg F | Yg E1 | Yn F | Yn W | 24 |
| 25 | Yg Wd | Yg Wd | Yg W | Yg F | Yn W | Yn E4 | Yn W | Yn E2 | Yg Wd | Yg Wd | Yg Wd | Yg M | Yn Wd | Yn Wd | Yg F | Yg E3 | Yg F | Yg E1 | Yn F | Yn W | Yn F | Yn F | Yg E | Yg W | 25 |
| 26 | Yn Wd | Yn Wd | Yn W | Yn E2 | Yg Wd | Yg Wd | Yg Wd | Yg M | Yn Wd | Yn Wd | Yn Wd | Yn M | Yg F | Yg E1 | Yn F | Yn W | Yn F | Yn F | Yg E | Yg W | Yg E | Yg F | Yn E | Yn E4 | 26 |
| 27 | Yg F | Yg E1 | Yg Wd | Yg M | Yn Wd | Yn Wd | Yn Wd | Yn M | Yg F | Yg E1 | Yg F | Yg E3 | Yn F | Yn F | Yg E | Yg W | Yg E | Yg F | Yn E | Yn E4 | Yn E | Yn E2 | Yg M | Yg Wd | 27 |
| 28 | Yn F | Yn F | Yn Wd | Yn M | Yg F | Yg E1 | Yg F | Yg E3 | Yn F | Yn F | Yn F | Yn W | Yg E | Yg F | Yn E | Yn E4 | Yn E | Yn E2 | Yg M | Yg Wd | Yg M | Yg M | Yn M | Yn Wd | 28 |
| 29 | | | Yg F | Yg E3 | Yn F | Yn F | Yn F | Yn W | Yg E | Yg F | Yg E | Yg W | Yn E | Yn E2 | Yg M | Yg Wd | Yg M | Yg M | Yn M | Yn Wd | Yn M | Yn M | Yg W | Yg E1 | 29 |
| 30 | | | Yn F | Yn W | Yg E | Yg F | Yg E | Yg W | Yn E | Yn E2 | Yn E | Yn E4 | Yg M | Yg M | Yn M | Yn Wd | Yn M | Yn M | Yg W | Yg E1 | Yg W | Yg E3 | Yn W | Yn F | 30 |
| 31 | | | Yg E | Yg W | | | Yn E | Yn E4 | | | Yg M | Yg Wd | Yn M | Yn M | | | Yg W | Yg E3 | | | Yn W | Yn W | Yg Wd | Yg F | 31 |
| 1 | Yg E | Yg F | Yn E | Yn E4 | Yn E | Yn E2 | Yg M | Yg Wd | Yg M | Yg M | Yn M | Yn Wd | Yg W | Yg E3 | Yg W | Yg E1 | Yn W | Yn W | Yn W | Yn F | Yg Wd | Yg W | Yn Wd | Yn E2 | 1 |
| 2 | Yn E | Yn E2 | Yg M | Yg Wd | Yg M | Yg M | Yn M | Yn Wd | Yn M | Yn M | Yg W | Yg E1 | Yn W | Yn W | Yn W | Yn F | Yg Wd | Yg W | Yg Wd | Yg F | Yn Wd | Yn E4 | Yg F | Yg M | 2 |
| 3 | Yg M | Yg M | Yn M | Yn Wd | Yn M | Yn M | Yg W | Yg E1 | Yg W | Yg E3 | Yn W | Yn F | Yg Wd | Yg W | Yg Wd | Yg F | Yn Wd | Yn E4 | Yn Wd | Yn E2 | Yg F | Yg Wd | Yn F | Yn M | 3 |
| 4 | Yn M | Yn M | Yg W | Yg E1 | Yg W | Yg E3 | Yn W | Yn F | Yn W | Yn W | Yg Wd | Yg F | Yn Wd | Yn E4 | Yn Wd | Yn E2 | Yg F | Yg Wd | Yg F | Yg M | Yn F | Yn Wd | | | 4 |
| 5 | Yg W | Yg E3 | | | Yn W | Yn W | Yg Wd | Yg F | Yg Wd | Yg W | Yn Wd | Yn E2 | Yg F | Yg Wd | Yg F | Yg M | Yn F | Yn Wd | Yn F | Yn M | Yg E | Yg E1 | | | 5 |
| 6 | | | | | | | | | Yn Wd | Yn E4 | Yg F | Yg M | Yn F | Yn Wd | Yn F | Yn M | Yg E | Yg E1 | Yg E | Yg E3 | | | | | 6 |
| 7 | | | | | | | | | | | Yn F | Yn M | Yg E | Yg E1 | Yg E | Yg E3 | Yn E | Yn F | | | | | | | 7 |
| 8 | | | | | | | | | | | | | | | | | | | | | | | | | 8 |

# YEAR OF THE DRAGON

| | H | E | H | E | H | E | H | E | H | E | H | E | H | E | H | E | H | E | H | E | H | E | H | E | |
|---|---|---|---|---|---|---|---|---|---|---|---|---|---|---|---|---|---|---|---|---|---|---|---|---|---|
| YEAR | YEAR Yg Wd | Yg E1 | 2024 | | | | | | | | | | | | | | | | | | | | 2025 | | |
| MONTH | 4 Feb - 4 Mar | | 5 Mar - 3 Apr | | 4 Apr - 4 May | | 5 May - 4 June | | 5 June - 5 Jul | | 6 Jul - 6 Aug | | 7 Aug - 6 Sep | | 7 Sep - 7 Oct | | 8 Oct - 6 Nov | | 7 Nov - 6 Dec | | 7 Dec - 4 Jan | | 5 Jan - 2 Feb | | |
| | Yg F | Yg Wd | Yn F | Yn Wd | Yg E | Yg E1 | Yn E | Yn F | Yg M | Yg F | Yn M | Yn E2 | Yg W | Yg M | Yn W | Yn M | Yg Wd | Yg E3 | Yn Wd | Yn W | Yg F | Yg W | Yn F | Yn E4 | |
| Starting time | 1st day | Mid-pt | 1st day | Mid-pt | 1st day | Mid-pt | 1st day | Mid-pt | 1st day | Mid-pt | 1st day | Mid-pt | 1st day | Mid-pt | 1st day | Mid-pt | 1st day | Mid-pt | 1st day | Mid-pt | 1st day | Mid-pt | 1st day | Mid-pt | |
| Date | 4 | 19 | 5 | 20 | 4 | 19 | 5 | 20 | 5 | 21 | 6 | 22 | 7 | 22 | 7 | 22 | 8 | 23 | 7 | 22 | 7 | 21 | 5 | 20 | |
| Hour | 1637 | 1203 | 1021 | 1110 | 1503 | 2210 | 0822 | 2120 | 1234 | 0522 | 2258 | 1629 | 0905 | 2357 | 1227 | 2204 | 0431 | 0743 | 0749 | 0514 | 0029 | 1813 | 1115 | 0419 | |
| DATE 3 | | | | | | | | | | | | | | | | | | | | | | | | | 3 |
| 4 | Yg E | Yg E3 | | | Yg E | Yg E3 | | | | | | | | | | | | | | | | | | | 4 |
| 5 | Yn E | Yn W | Yg E | Yg E1 | Yn E | Yn W | Yn E | Yn F | Yg M | Yg W | | | | | | | | | | | | | Yg Wd | Yg E3 | 5 |
| 6 | Yg M | Yg W | Yn E | Yn F | Yg M | Yg W | Yg M | Yg F | Yn M | Yn E4 | Yn M | Yn E2 | | | | | | | | | | | Yn Wd | Yn W | 6 |
| 7 | Yn M | Yn E4 | Yg M | Yg F | Yn M | Yn E4 | Yn M | Yn E2 | Yg W | Yg Wd | Yg W | Yg M | Yn W | Yn Wd | Yg Wd | Yg E3 | | | Yn Wd | Yn W | Yn Wd | Yn F | Yg F | Yg W | 7 |
| 8 | Yg W | Yg Wd | Yn M | Yn E2 | Yg W | Yg Wd | Yg W | Yg M | Yn W | Yn Wd | Yn W | Yn M | Yg Wd | Yg E1 | Yn Wd | Yn W | Yn Wd | Yn F | Yg F | Yg W | Yg F | Yg F | Yn F | Yn E4 | 8 |
| 9 | Yn W | Yn Wd | Yg W | Yg M | Yn W | Yn Wd | Yn W | Yn M | Yg Wd | Yg E1 | Yg Wd | Yg E3 | Yn Wd | Yn F | Yg F | Yg W | Yg F | Yg F | Yn F | Yn E4 | Yn F | Yn E2 | Yg E | Yg Wd | 9 |
| 10 | Yg Wd | Yg E1 | Yn W | Yn M | Yg Wd | Yg E1 | Yg Wd | Yg E3 | Yn Wd | Yn F | Yn Wd | Yn W | Yg F | Yg F | Yn F | Yn E4 | Yn F | Yn E2 | Yg E | Yg Wd | Yg E | Yg M | Yn E | Yn Wd | 10 |
| 11 | Yn Wd | Yn F | Yg Wd | Yg E3 | Yn Wd | Yn F | Yn Wd | Yn W | Yg F | Yg F | Yg F | Yg W | Yn F | Yn E2 | Yg E | Yg Wd | Yg E | Yg M | Yn E | Yn Wd | Yn E | Yn M | Yg M | Yg E1 | 11 |
| 12 | Yg F | Yg F | Yn Wd | Yn W | Yg F | Yg F | Yg F | Yg W | Yn F | Yn E2 | Yn F | Yn E4 | Yg E | Yg M | Yn E | Yn Wd | Yn E | Yn M | Yg M | Yg E1 | Yg M | Yg E3 | Yn M | Yn F | 12 |
| 13 | Yn F | Yn E2 | Yg F | Yg W | Yn F | Yn E2 | Yn F | Yn E4 | Yg E | Yg M | Yg E | Yg Wd | Yn E | Yn M | Yg M | Yg E1 | Yg M | Yg E3 | Yn M | Yn F | Yn M | Yn W | Yg W | Yg F | 13 |
| 14 | Yg E | Yg M | Yn F | Yn E4 | Yg E | Yg M | Yg E | Yg Wd | Yn E | Yn M | Yn E | Yn Wd | Yg M | Yg E3 | Yn M | Yn F | Yn M | Yn W | Yg W | Yg F | Yg W | Yg W | Yn W | Yn E2 | 14 |
| 15 | Yn E | Yn M | Yg E | Yg Wd | Yn E | Yn M | Yn E | Yn Wd | Yg M | Yg E3 | Yg M | Yg E1 | Yn M | Yn W | Yg W | Yg F | Yg W | Yg W | Yn W | Yn E2 | Yn W | Yn E4 | Yg Wd | Yg M | 15 |
| 16 | Yg M | Yg E3 | Yn E | Yn Wd | Yg M | Yg E3 | Yg M | Yg E1 | Yn M | Yn W | Yn M | Yn F | Yg W | Yg W | Yn W | Yn E2 | Yn W | Yn E4 | Yg Wd | Yg M | Yg Wd | Yg Wd | Yn Wd | Yn M | 16 |
| 17 | Yn M | Yn W | Yg M | Yg E1 | Yn M | Yn W | Yn M | Yn F | Yg W | Yg W | Yg W | Yg F | Yn W | Yn E4 | Yg Wd | Yg M | Yg Wd | Yg Wd | Yn Wd | Yn M | Yn Wd | Yn Wd | Yg F | Yg E3 | 17 |
| 18 | Yg W | Yg W | Yn M | Yn F | Yg W | Yg W | Yg W | Yg F | Yn W | Yn E4 | Yn W | Yn E2 | Yg Wd | Yg Wd | Yn Wd | Yn M | Yn Wd | Yn Wd | Yg F | Yg E3 | Yg F | Yg E1 | Yn F | Yn W | 18 |
| 19 | Yn W | Yn E4 | Yg W | Yg F | Yn W | Yn E4 | Yn W | Yn E2 | Yg Wd | Yg Wd | Yg Wd | Yg M | Yn Wd | Yn Wd | Yg F | Yg E3 | Yg F | Yg E1 | Yn F | Yn W | Yn F | Yn F | Yg E | Yg W | 19 |
| 20 | Yg Wd | Yg Wd | Yn W | Yn E2 | Yg Wd | Yg Wd | Yg Wd | Yg M | Yn Wd | Yn Wd | Yn Wd | Yn M | Yg F | Yg E1 | Yn F | Yn W | Yn F | Yn F | Yg E | Yg W | Yg E | Yg F | Yn E | Yn E4 | 20 |
| 21 | Yn Wd | Yn Wd | Yg Wd | Yg M | Yn Wd | Yn Wd | Yn Wd | Yn M | Yg F | Yg E1 | Yg F | Yg E3 | Yn F | Yn F | Yg E | Yg W | Yg E | Yg F | Yn E | Yn E4 | Yn E | Yn E2 | Yg M | Yg Wd | 21 |
| 22 | Yg F | Yg E1 | Yn Wd | Yn M | Yg F | Yg E1 | Yg F | Yg E3 | Yn F | Yn F | Yn F | Yn W | Yg E | Yg F | Yn E | Yn E4 | Yn E | Yn E2 | Yg M | Yg Wd | Yg M | Yg M | Yn M | Yn Wd | 22 |
| 23 | Yn F | Yn F | Yg F | Yg E3 | Yn F | Yn F | Yn F | Yn W | Yg E | Yg F | Yg E | Yg W | Yn E | Yn E2 | Yg M | Yg Wd | Yg M | Yg M | Yn M | Yn Wd | Yn M | Yn M | Yg W | Yg E1 | 23 |
| 24 | Yg E | Yg F | Yn F | Yn W | Yg E | Yg F | Yg E | Yg W | Yn E | Yn E2 | Yn E | Yn E4 | Yg M | Yg M | Yn M | Yn Wd | Yn M | Yn M | Yg W | Yg E1 | Yg W | Yg E3 | Yn W | Yn F | 24 |
| 25 | Yn E | Yn E2 | Yg E | Yg W | Yn E | Yn E2 | Yn E | Yn E4 | Yg M | Yg M | Yg M | Yg Wd | Yn M | Yn M | Yg W | Yg E1 | Yg W | Yg E3 | Yn W | Yn F | Yn W | Yn W | Yg Wd | Yg F | 25 |
| 26 | Yg M | Yg M | Yn E | Yn E4 | Yg M | Yg M | Yg M | Yg Wd | Yn M | Yn M | Yn M | Yn Wd | Yg W | Yg E3 | Yn W | Yn F | Yn W | Yn W | Yg Wd | Yg F | Yg Wd | Yg W | Yn Wd | Yn E2 | 26 |
| 27 | Yn M | Yn M | Yg M | Yg Wd | Yn M | Yn M | Yn M | Yn Wd | Yg W | Yg E3 | Yg W | Yg E1 | Yn W | Yn W | Yg Wd | Yg F | Yg Wd | Yg W | Yn Wd | Yn E2 | Yn Wd | Yn E4 | Yg F | Yg M | 27 |
| 28 | Yg W | Yg E3 | Yn M | Yn Wd | Yg W | Yg E3 | Yg W | Yg E1 | Yn W | Yn W | Yn W | Yn F | Yg Wd | Yg W | Yn Wd | Yn E2 | Yn Wd | Yn E4 | Yg F | Yg M | Yg F | Yg Wd | Yn F | Yn M | 28 |
| 29 | Yn W | Yn W | Yg W | Yg E1 | Yn W | Yn W | Yn W | Yn F | Yg Wd | Yg W | Yg Wd | Yg F | Yn Wd | Yn E4 | Yg F | Yg M | Yg F | Yg Wd | Yn F | Yn M | Yn F | Yn Wd | Yg E | Yg E3 | 29 |
| 30 | | | Yn W | Yn F | Yg Wd | Yg W | Yg Wd | Yg F | Yn Wd | Yn E4 | Yn Wd | Yn E2 | Yg F | Yg Wd | Yn F | Yn M | Yn F | Yn Wd | Yg E | Yg E3 | Yg E | Yg E1 | Yn E | Yn W | 30 |
| 31 | | | Yg Wd | Yg F | | | Yn Wd | Yn E2 | | | Yg F | Yg M | Yn F | Yn Wd | | | Yg E | Yg E1 | | | Yn E | Yn F | Yg M | Yg W | 31 |
| 1 | Yg Wd | Yg W | Yn Wd | Yn E2 | Yn Wd | Yn E4 | Yg F | Yg M | Yg F | Yg Wd | Yn F | Yn M | Yg E | Yg E1 | Yg E | Yg E3 | Yn E | Yn F | Yn E | Yn W | Yg M | Yg F | Yn M | Yn E4 | 1 |
| 2 | Yn Wd | Yn E4 | Yg F | Yg M | Yg F | Yg Wd | Yn F | Yn M | Yn F | Yn Wd | Yg E | Yg E3 | Yn E | Yn F | Yn E | Yn W | Yg M | Yg F | Yg M | Yg W | Yn M | Yn E2 | Yg W | Yg Wd | 2 |
| 3 | Yg F | Yg Wd | Yn F | Yn M | Yn F | Yn Wd | Yg E | Yg E3 | Yg E | Yg E1 | Yn E | Yn W | Yg M | Yg F | Yg M | Yg W | Yn M | Yn E2 | Yn M | Yn E4 | Yg W | Yg M | | | 3 |
| 4 | Yn F | Yn Wd | | | Yg E | Yg E1 | Yn E | Yn W | Yn E | Yn F | Yg M | Yg W | Yn M | Yn E2 | Yn M | Yn E4 | Yg W | Yg M | Yg W | Yg Wd | Yn W | Yn M | | | 4 |
| 5 | | | | | | | | | Yg M | Yg F | Yn M | Yn E4 | Yg W | Yg M | Yg W | Yg Wd | Yn W | Yn M | Yn W | Yn Wd | | | | | 5 |
| 6 | | | | | | | | | | | Yg W | Yg Wd | Yn W | Yn M | Yn W | Yn Wd | Yg Wd | Yg E3 | Yg Wd | Yg E1 | | | | | 6 |
| 7 | | | | | | | | | | | | | | | Yg Wd | Yg E1 | | | | | | | | | 7 |
| 8 | | | | | | | | | | | | | | | | | | | | | | | | | 8 |

# YEAR OF THE SNAKE

| | H | E | H | E | H | E | H | E | H | E | H | E | H | E | H | E | H | E | H | E | H | E | H | E |
|---|---|---|---|---|---|---|---|---|---|---|---|---|---|---|---|---|---|---|---|---|---|---|---|---|
| **YEAR** | **YEAR** | | 2025 | | | | | | | | | | | | | | | | | | | | 2026 | |
| | Yn Wd | Yn F | | | | | | | | | | | | | | | | | | | | | | |
| **MONTH** | 3 Feb - 4 Mar | | 5 Mar - 3 Apr | | 4 Apr - 4 May | | 5 May - 4 June | | 5 June - 6 Jul | | 7 Jul - 6 Aug | | 7 Aug - 6 Sep | | 7 Sep - 7 Oct | | 8 Oct - 6 Nov | | 7 Nov - 6 Dec | | 7 Dec - 4 Jan | | 5 Jan - 3 Feb | |
| | Yg E | Yg Wd | Yn E | Yn Wd | Yg M | Yg E1 | Yn M | Yn F | Yg W | Yg F | Yn W | Yn E2 | Yg Wd | Yg M | Yn Wd | Yn M | Yg F | Yg E3 | Yn F | Yn W | Yg E | Yg W | Yn E | Yn E4 |
| **Starting time** | 1st day | Mid-pt | 1st day | Mid-pt | 1st day | Mid-pt | 1st day | Mid-pt | 1st day | Mid-pt | 1st day | Mid-pt | 1st day | Mid-pt | 1st day | Mid-pt | 1st day | Mid-pt | 1st day | Mid-pt | 1st day | Mid-pt | 1st day | Mid-pt |
| Date | 3 | 18 | 5 | 20 | 4 | 20 | 5 | 21 | 5 | 21 | 7 | 22 | 7 | 23 | 7 | 23 | 8 | 23 | 7 | 22 | 7 | 22 | 5 | 20 |
| Hour | 2227 | 1810 | 1611 | 1659 | 2052 | 0336 | 1411 | 0309 | 1822 | 1111 | 0446 | 2217 | 1453 | 0545 | 1815 | 0353 | 1019 | 1332 | 1340 | 1114 | 0618 | 0003 | 1705 | 1013 |
| **DATE** 3 | Yn W | Yn Wd | | | | | | | | | | | | | | | | | | | | | | |
| 4 | Yg Wd | Yg E1 | | | Yn W | Yn Wd | | | | | | | | | | | | | | | | | | |
| 5 | Yn Wd | Yn F | Yn W | Yn M | Yg Wd | Yg E1 | Yg Wd | Yg E3 | Yn Wd | Yn F | | | | | | | | | | | | | Yn E | Yn Wd |
| 6 | Yg F | Yg F | Yg Wd | Yg E3 | Yn Wd | Yn F | Yn Wd | Yn W | Yg F | Yg F | | | | | | | | | | | | | Yg M | Yg E1 |
| 7 | Yn F | Yn E2 | Yn Wd | Yn W | Yg F | Yg F | Yg F | Yg W | Yn F | Yn E2 | Yn F | Yn E4 | Yg E | Yg M | Yn E | Yn Wd | | | Yg M | Yg E1 | Yg M | Yg E3 | Yn M | Yn F |
| 8 | Yg E | Yg M | Yg F | Yg W | Yn F | Yn E2 | Yn F | Yn E4 | Yg E | Yg M | Yg E | Yg Wd | Yn E | Yn M | Yg M | Yg E1 | Yg M | Yg E3 | Yn M | Yn F | Yn M | Yn W | Yg W | Yg F |
| 9 | Yn E | Yn M | Yn F | Yn E4 | Yg E | Yg M | Yg E | Yg Wd | Yn E | Yn M | Yn E | Yn Wd | Yg M | Yg E3 | Yn M | Yn F | Yn M | Yn W | Yg W | Yg F | Yg W | Yg W | Yn W | Yn E2 |
| 10 | Yg M | Yg E3 | Yg E | Yg Wd | Yn E | Yn M | Yn E | Yn Wd | Yg M | Yg E3 | Yg M | Yg E1 | Yn M | Yn W | Yg W | Yg F | Yg W | Yg W | Yn W | Yn E2 | Yn W | Yn E4 | Yg Wd | Yg M |
| 11 | Yn M | Yn W | Yn E | Yn Wd | Yg M | Yg E3 | Yg M | Yg E1 | Yn M | Yn W | Yn M | Yn F | Yg W | Yg W | Yn W | Yn E2 | Yn W | Yn E4 | Yg Wd | Yg M | Yg Wd | Yg Wd | Yn Wd | Yn M |
| 12 | Yg W | Yg W | Yg M | Yg E1 | Yn M | Yn W | Yn M | Yn F | Yg W | Yg W | Yg W | Yg F | Yn W | Yn E4 | Yg Wd | Yg M | Yg Wd | Yg Wd | Yn Wd | Yn M | Yn Wd | Yn Wd | Yg F | Yg E3 |
| 13 | Yn W | Yn E4 | Yn M | Yn F | Yg W | Yg W | Yg W | Yg F | Yn W | Yn E4 | Yn W | Yn E2 | Yg Wd | Yg Wd | Yn Wd | Yn M | Yn Wd | Yn Wd | Yg F | Yg E3 | Yg F | Yg E1 | Yn F | Yn W |
| 14 | Yg Wd | Yg Wd | Yg W | Yg F | Yn W | Yn E4 | Yn W | Yn E2 | Yg Wd | Yg Wd | Yg Wd | Yg M | Yn Wd | Yn Wd | Yg F | Yg E3 | Yg F | Yg E1 | Yn F | Yn W | Yn F | Yn F | Yg E | Yg W |
| 15 | Yn Wd | Yn Wd | Yn W | Yn E2 | Yg Wd | Yg Wd | Yg Wd | Yg M | Yn Wd | Yn Wd | Yn Wd | Yn M | Yg F | Yg E1 | Yn F | Yn W | Yn F | Yn F | Yg E | Yg W | Yg E | Yg F | Yn E | Yn E4 |
| 16 | Yg F | Yg E1 | Yg Wd | Yg M | Yn Wd | Yn Wd | Yn Wd | Yn M | Yg F | Yg E1 | Yg F | Yg E3 | Yn F | Yn F | Yg E | Yg W | Yg E | Yg F | Yn E | Yn E4 | Yn E | Yn E2 | Yg M | Yg Wd |
| 17 | Yn F | Yn F | Yn Wd | Yn M | Yg F | Yg E1 | Yg F | Yg E3 | Yn F | Yn F | Yn F | Yn W | Yg E | Yg F | Yn E | Yn E4 | Yn E | Yn E2 | Yg M | Yg Wd | Yg M | Yg M | Yn M | Yn Wd |
| 18 | Yg E | Yg F | Yg F | Yg E3 | Yn F | Yn F | Yn F | Yn W | Yg E | Yg F | Yg E | Yg W | Yn E | Yn E2 | Yg M | Yg Wd | Yg M | Yg M | Yn M | Yn Wd | Yn M | Yn M | Yg W | Yg E1 |
| 19 | Yn E | Yn E2 | Yn F | Yn W | Yg E | Yg F | Yg E | Yg W | Yn E | Yn E2 | Yn E | Yn E4 | Yg M | Yg M | Yn M | Yn Wd | Yn M | Yn M | Yg W | Yg E1 | Yg W | Yg E3 | Yn W | Yn F |
| 20 | Yg M | Yg M | Yg E | Yg W | Yn E | Yn E2 | Yn E | Yn E4 | Yg M | Yg M | Yg M | Yg Wd | Yn M | Yn M | Yg W | Yg E1 | Yg W | Yg E3 | Yn W | Yn F | Yn W | Yn W | Yg Wd | Yg F |
| 21 | Yn M | Yn M | Yn E | Yn E4 | Yg M | Yg M | Yg M | Yg Wd | Yn M | Yn M | Yn M | Yn Wd | Yg W | Yg E3 | Yn W | Yn F | Yn W | Yn W | Yg Wd | Yg F | Yg Wd | Yg W | Yn Wd | Yn E2 |
| 22 | Yg W | Yg E3 | Yg M | Yg Wd | Yn M | Yn M | Yn M | Yn Wd | Yg W | Yg E3 | Yg W | Yg E1 | Yn W | Yn W | Yg Wd | Yg F | Yg Wd | Yg W | Yn Wd | Yn E2 | Yn Wd | Yn E4 | Yg F | Yg M |
| 23 | Yn W | Yn W | Yn M | Yn Wd | Yg W | Yg E3 | Yg W | Yg E1 | Yn W | Yn W | Yn W | Yn F | Yg Wd | Yg W | Yn Wd | Yn E2 | Yn Wd | Yn E4 | Yg F | Yg M | Yg F | Yg Wd | Yn F | Yn M |
| 24 | Yg Wd | Yg W | Yg W | Yg E1 | Yn W | Yn W | Yn W | Yn F | Yg Wd | Yg W | Yg Wd | Yg F | Yn Wd | Yn E4 | Yg F | Yg M | Yg F | Yg Wd | Yn F | Yn M | Yn F | Yn Wd | Yg E | Yg E3 |
| 25 | Yn Wd | Yn E4 | Yn W | Yn F | Yg Wd | Yg W | Yg Wd | Yg F | Yn Wd | Yn E4 | Yn Wd | Yn E2 | Yg F | Yg Wd | Yn F | Yn M | Yn F | Yn Wd | Yg E | Yg E3 | Yg E | Yg E1 | Yn E | Yn W |
| 26 | Yg F | Yg Wd | Yg Wd | Yg F | Yn Wd | Yn E4 | Yn Wd | Yn E2 | Yg F | Yg Wd | Yg F | Yg M | Yn F | Yn Wd | Yg E | Yg E3 | Yg E | Yg E1 | Yn E | Yn W | Yn E | Yn F | Yg M | Yg W |
| 27 | Yn F | Yn Wd | Yn Wd | Yn E2 | Yg F | Yg Wd | Yg F | Yg M | Yn F | Yn Wd | Yn F | Yn M | Yg E | Yg E1 | Yn E | Yn W | Yn E | Yn F | Yg M | Yg W | Yg M | Yg F | Yn M | Yn E4 |
| 28 | Yg E | Yg E1 | Yg F | Yg M | Yn F | Yn Wd | Yn F | Yn M | Yg E | Yg E1 | Yg E | Yg E3 | Yn E | Yn F | Yg M | Yg W | Yg M | Yg F | Yn M | Yn E4 | Yn M | Yn E2 | Yg W | Yg Wd |
| 29 | | | Yn F | Yn M | Yg E | Yg E1 | Yg E | Yg E3 | Yn E | Yn F | Yn E | Yn W | Yg M | Yg F | Yn M | Yn E4 | Yn M | Yn E2 | Yg W | Yg Wd | Yg W | Yg M | Yn W | Yn Wd |
| 30 | | | Yg E | Yg E3 | Yn E | Yn F | Yn E | Yn W | Yg M | Yg F | Yg M | Yg W | Yn M | Yn E2 | Yg W | Yg Wd | Yg W | Yg M | Yn W | Yn Wd | Yn W | Yn M | Yg Wd | Yg E1 |
| 31 | | | Yn E | Yn W | | | Yg M | Yg W | | | Yn M | Yn E4 | Yg W | Yg M | | | Yn W | Yn M | | | Yg Wd | Yg E3 | Yn Wd | Yn F |
| 1 | Yn E | Yn F | Yg M | Yg W | Yg M | Yg F | Yn M | Yn E4 | Yn M | Yn E2 | Yg W | Yg Wd | Yn W | Yn M | Yn W | Yn Wd | Yg Wd | Yg E3 | Yg Wd | Yg E1 | Yn Wd | Yn W | Yg F | Yg F |
| 2 | Yg M | Yg F | Yn M | Yn E4 | Yn M | Yn E2 | Yg W | Yg Wd | Yg W | Yg M | Yn W | Yn Wd | Yg Wd | Yg E3 | Yg Wd | Yg E1 | Yn Wd | Yn W | Yn Wd | Yn F | Yg F | Yg W | Yn F | Yn E2 |
| 3 | Yn M | Yn E2 | Yg W | Yg Wd | Yg W | Yg M | Yn W | Yn Wd | Yn W | Yn M | Yg Wd | Yg E1 | Yn Wd | Yn W | Yn Wd | Yn F | Yg F | Yg W | Yg F | Yg F | Yn F | Yn E4 | Yg E | Yg M |
| 4 | Yg W | Yg M | | | Yn W | Yn M | Yg Wd | Yg E1 | Yg Wd | Yg E3 | Yn Wd | Yn F | Yg F | Yg W | Yg F | Yg F | Yn F | Yn E4 | Yn F | Yn E2 | Yg E | Yg Wd | | |
| 5 | | | | | | | | | Yn Wd | Yn W | Yg F | Yg F | Yn F | Yn E4 | Yn F | Yn E2 | Yg E | Yg Wd | Yg E | Yg M | | | | |
| 6 | | | | | | | | | Yg F | Yg W | Yn F | Yn E2 | Yg E | Yg Wd | Yg E | Yg M | Yn E | Yn Wd | Yn E | Yn M | | | | |
| 7 | | | | | | | | | | | | | | | Yn E | Yn M | | | | | | | | |
| 8 | | | | | | | | | | | | | | | | | | | | | | | | |

# YEAR OF THE HORSE

| | H | E | H | E | H | E | H | E | H | E | H | E | H | E | H | E | H | E | H | E | H | E | H | E | |
|---|---|---|---|---|---|---|---|---|---|---|---|---|---|---|---|---|---|---|---|---|---|---|---|---|---|
| YEAR | YEAR Yg F | Yg F | 2026 | | | | | | | | | | | | | | | | | | | | 2027 | | |
| MONTH | 4 Feb - 4 Mar | | 5 Mar - 4 Apr | | 5 Apr - 4 May | | 5 May - 5 June | | 6 June - 6 Jul | | 7 Jul - 6 Aug | | 7 Aug - 7 Sep | | 8 Sep - 7 Oct | | 8 Oct - 6 Nov | | 7 Nov - 6 Dec | | 7 Dec - 4 Jan | | 5 Jan - 3 Feb | | |
| | Yg M | Yg Wd | Yn M | Yn Wd | Yg W | Yg E1 | Yn W | Yn F | Yg Wd | Yg F | Yn Wd | Yn E2 | Yg F | Yg M | Yn F | Yn M | Yg E | Yg E3 | Yn E | Yn W | Yg M | Yg W | Yn M | Yn E4 | |
| Starting time | 1st day | Mid-pt | 1st day | Mid-pt | 1st day | Mid-pt | 1st day | Mid-pt | 1st day | Mid-pt | 1st day | Mid-pt | 1st day | Mid-pt | 1st day | Mid-pt | 1st day | Mid-pt | 1st day | Mid-pt | 1st day | Mid-pt | 1st day | Mid-pt | |
| Date | 4 | 18 | 5 | 20 | 5 | 20 | 5 | 21 | 6 | 21 | 7 | 23 | 7 | 23 | 8 | 23 | 8 | 23 | 7 | 22 | 7 | 22 | 5 | 20 | |
| Hour | 0416 | 2359 | 2200 | 2248 | 0216 | 0948 | 1959 | 0857 | 0011 | 1659 | 1034 | 0405 | 2041 | 1134 | 0004 | 0942 | 1608 | 1921 | 1929 | 1653 | 1208 | 0552 | 2255 | 1629 | |
| DATE 3 | | | | | | | | | | | | | | | | | | | | | | | | | 3 |
| 4 | Yn E | Yn M | | | | | | | | | | | | | | | | | | | | | | | 4 |
| 5 | Yg M | Yg E3 | Yg E | Yg Wd | Yn E | Yn M | Yn E | Yn Wd | | | | | | | | | | | | | | | Yg Wd | Yg M | 5 |
| 6 | Yn M | Yn W | Yn E | Yn Wd | Yg M | Yg E3 | Yg M | Yg E1 | Yn M | Yn W | | | | | | | | | | | | | Yn Wd | Yn M | 6 |
| 7 | Yg W | Yg W | Yg M | Yg E1 | Yn M | Yn W | Yn M | Yn F | Yg W | Yg W | Yg W | Yg F | Yn W | Yn E4 | | | | | Yn Wd | Yn M | Yn Wd | Yn Wd | Yg F | Yg E3 | 7 |
| 8 | Yn W | Yn E4 | Yn M | Yn F | Yg W | Yg W | Yg W | Yg F | Yn W | Yn E4 | Yn W | Yn E2 | Yg Wd | Yg Wd | Yn Wd | Yn M | Yn Wd | Yn Wd | Yg F | Yg E3 | Yg F | Yg E1 | Yn F | Yn W | 8 |
| 9 | Yg Wd | Yg Wd | Yg W | Yg F | Yn W | Yn E4 | Yn W | Yn E2 | Yg Wd | Yg Wd | Yg Wd | Yg M | Yn Wd | Yn Wd | Yg F | Yg E3 | Yg F | Yg E1 | Yn F | Yn W | Yn F | Yn F | Yg E | Yg W | 9 |
| 10 | Yn Wd | Yn Wd | Yn W | Yn E2 | Yg Wd | Yg Wd | Yg Wd | Yg M | Yn Wd | Yn Wd | Yn Wd | Yn M | Yg F | Yg E1 | Yn F | Yn W | Yn F | Yn F | Yg E | Yg W | Yg E | Yg F | Yn E | Yn E4 | 10 |
| 11 | Yg F | Yg E1 | Yg Wd | Yg M | Yn Wd | Yn Wd | Yn Wd | Yn M | Yg F | Yg E1 | Yg F | Yg E3 | Yn F | Yn F | Yg E | Yg W | Yg E | Yg F | Yn E | Yn E4 | Yn E | Yn E2 | Yg M | Yg Wd | 11 |
| 12 | Yn F | Yn F | Yn Wd | Yn M | Yg F | Yg E1 | Yg F | Yg E3 | Yn F | Yn F | Yn F | Yn W | Yg E | Yg F | Yn E | Yn E4 | Yn E | Yn E2 | Yg M | Yg Wd | Yg M | Yg M | Yn M | Yn Wd | 12 |
| 13 | Yg E | Yg F | Yg F | Yg E3 | Yn F | Yn F | Yn F | Yn W | Yg E | Yg F | Yg E | Yg W | Yn E | Yn E2 | Yg M | Yg Wd | Yg M | Yg M | Yn M | Yn Wd | Yn M | Yn M | Yg W | Yg E1 | 13 |
| 14 | Yn E | Yn E2 | Yn F | Yn W | Yg E | Yg F | Yg E | Yg W | Yn E | Yn E2 | Yn E | Yn E4 | Yg M | Yg M | Yn M | Yn Wd | Yn M | Yn M | Yg W | Yg E1 | Yg W | Yg E3 | Yn W | Yn F | 14 |
| 15 | Yg M | Yg M | Yg E | Yg W | Yn E | Yn E2 | Yn E | Yn E4 | Yg M | Yg M | Yg M | Yg Wd | Yn M | Yn M | Yg W | Yg E1 | Yg W | Yg E3 | Yn W | Yn F | Yn W | Yn W | Yg Wd | Yg F | 15 |
| 16 | Yn M | Yn M | Yn E | Yn E4 | Yg M | Yg M | Yg M | Yg Wd | Yn M | Yn M | Yn M | Yn Wd | Yg W | Yg E3 | Yn W | Yn F | Yn W | Yn W | Yg Wd | Yg F | Yg Wd | Yg W | Yn Wd | Yn E2 | 16 |
| 17 | Yg W | Yg E3 | Yg M | Yg Wd | Yn M | Yn M | Yn M | Yn Wd | Yg W | Yg E3 | Yg W | Yg E1 | Yn W | Yn W | Yg Wd | Yg F | Yg Wd | Yg W | Yn Wd | Yn E2 | Yn Wd | Yn E4 | Yg F | Yg M | 17 |
| 18 | Yn W | Yn W | Yn M | Yn Wd | Yg W | Yg E3 | Yg W | Yg E1 | Yn W | Yn W | Yn W | Yn F | Yg Wd | Yg W | Yn Wd | Yn E2 | Yn Wd | Yn E4 | Yg F | Yg M | Yg F | Yg Wd | Yn F | Yn M | 18 |
| 19 | Yg Wd | Yg W | Yg W | Yg E1 | Yn W | Yn W | Yn W | Yn F | Yg Wd | Yg W | Yg Wd | Yg F | Yn Wd | Yn E4 | Yg F | Yg M | Yg F | Yg Wd | Yn F | Yn M | Yn F | Yn Wd | Yg E | Yg E3 | 19 |
| 20 | Yn Wd | Yn E4 | Yn W | Yn F | Yg Wd | Yg W | Yg Wd | Yg F | Yn Wd | Yn E4 | Yn Wd | Yn E2 | Yg F | Yg Wd | Yn F | Yn M | Yn F | Yn Wd | Yg E | Yg E3 | Yg E | Yg E1 | Yn E | Yn W | 20 |
| 21 | Yg F | Yg Wd | Yg Wd | Yg F | Yn Wd | Yn E4 | Yn Wd | Yn E2 | Yg F | Yg Wd | Yg F | Yg M | Yn F | Yn Wd | Yg E | Yg E3 | Yg E | Yg E1 | Yn E | Yn W | Yn E | Yn F | Yg M | Yg W | 21 |
| 22 | Yn F | Yn Wd | Yn Wd | Yn E2 | Yg F | Yg Wd | Yg F | Yg M | Yn F | Yn Wd | Yn F | Yn M | Yg E | Yg E1 | Yn E | Yn W | Yn E | Yn F | Yg M | Yg W | Yg M | Yg F | Yn M | Yn E4 | 22 |
| 23 | Yg E | Yg E1 | Yg F | Yg M | Yn F | Yn Wd | Yn F | Yn M | Yg E | Yg E1 | Yg E | Yg E3 | Yn E | Yn F | Yg M | Yg W | Yg M | Yg F | Yn M | Yn E4 | Yn M | Yn E2 | Yg W | Yg Wd | 23 |
| 24 | Yn E | Yn F | Yn F | Yn M | Yg E | Yg E1 | Yg E | Yg E3 | Yn E | Yn F | Yn E | Yn W | Yg M | Yg F | Yn M | Yn E4 | Yn M | Yn E2 | Yg W | Yg Wd | Yg W | Yg M | Yn W | Yn Wd | 24 |
| 25 | Yg M | Yg F | Yg E | Yg E3 | Yn E | Yn F | Yn E | Yn W | Yg M | Yg F | Yg M | Yg W | Yn M | Yn E2 | Yg W | Yg Wd | Yg W | Yg M | Yn W | Yn Wd | Yn W | Yn M | Yg Wd | Yg E1 | 25 |
| 26 | Yn M | Yn E2 | Yn E | Yn W | Yg M | Yg F | Yg M | Yg W | Yn M | Yn E2 | Yn M | Yn E4 | Yg W | Yg M | Yn W | Yn Wd | Yn W | Yn M | Yg Wd | Yg E1 | Yg Wd | Yg E3 | Yn Wd | Yn F | 26 |
| 27 | Yg W | Yg M | Yg M | Yg W | Yn M | Yn E2 | Yn M | Yn E4 | Yg W | Yg M | Yg W | Yg Wd | Yn W | Yn M | Yg Wd | Yg E1 | Yg Wd | Yg E3 | Yn Wd | Yn F | Yn Wd | Yn W | Yg F | Yg F | 27 |
| 28 | Yn W | Yn M | Yn M | Yn E4 | Yg W | Yg M | Yg W | Yg Wd | Yn W | Yn M | Yn W | Yn Wd | Yg Wd | Yg E3 | Yn Wd | Yn F | Yn Wd | Yn W | Yg F | Yg F | Yg F | Yg W | Yn F | Yn E2 | 28 |
| 29 | | | Yg W | Yg Wd | Yn W | Yn M | Yn W | Yn Wd | Yg Wd | Yg E3 | Yg Wd | Yg E1 | Yn Wd | Yn W | Yg F | Yg F | Yg F | Yg W | Yn F | Yn E2 | Yn F | Yn E4 | Yg E | Yg M | 29 |
| 30 | | | Yn W | Yn Wd | Yg Wd | Yg E3 | Yg Wd | Yg E1 | Yn Wd | Yn W | Yn Wd | Yn F | Yg F | Yg W | Yn F | Yn E2 | Yn F | Yn E4 | Yg E | Yg M | Yg E | Yg Wd | Yn E | Yn M | 30 |
| 31 | | | Yg Wd | Yg E1 | | | Yn Wd | Yn F | | | Yg F | Yg F | Yn F | Yn E4 | | | Yg E | Yg Wd | | | Yn E | Yn Wd | Yg M | Yg E3 | 31 |
| 1 | Yg Wd | Yg E3 | Yn Wd | Yn F | Yn Wd | Yn W | Yg F | Yg F | Yg F | Yg W | Yn F | Yn E2 | Yg E | Yg Wd | Yg E | Yg M | Yn E | Yn Wd | Yn E | Yn M | Yg M | Yg E1 | Yn M | Yn W | 1 |
| 2 | Yn Wd | Yn W | Yg F | Yg F | Yg F | Yg W | Yn F | Yn E2 | Yn F | Yn E4 | Yg E | Yg M | Yn E | Yn Wd | Yn E | Yn M | Yg M | Yg E1 | Yg M | Yg E3 | Yn M | Yn F | Yg W | Yg W | 2 |
| 3 | Yg F | Yg W | Yn F | Yn E2 | Yn F | Yn E4 | Yg E | Yg M | Yg E | Yg Wd | Yn E | Yn M | Yg M | Yg E1 | Yg M | Yg E3 | Yn M | Yn F | Yn M | Yn W | Yg W | Yg F | Yn W | Yn E4 | 3 |
| 4 | Yn F | Yn E4 | Yg E | Yg M | Yg E | Yg Wd | Yn E | Yn M | Yn E | Yn Wd | Yg M | Yg E3 | Yn M | Yn F | Yn M | Yn W | Yg W | Yg F | Yg W | Yg W | Yn W | Yn E2 | | | 4 |
| 5 | | | | | | | Yg M | Yg E3 | Yg M | Yg E1 | Yn M | Yn W | Yg W | Yg F | Yg W | Yg W | Yn W | Yn E2 | Yn W | Yn E4 | | | | | 5 |
| 6 | | | | | | | | | Yn M | Yn F | Yg W | Yg W | Yn W | Yn E2 | Yn W | Yn E4 | Yg Wd | Yg M | Yg Wd | Yg Wd | | | | | 6 |
| 7 | | | | | | | | | | | | | Yg Wd | Yg M | Yg Wd | Yg Wd | | | | | | | | | 7 |
| 8 | | | | | | | | | | | | | | | | | | | | | | | | | 8 |

# YEAR OF THE GOAT

| | H | E | H | E | H | E | H | E | H | E | H | E | H | E | H | E | H | E | H | E | H | E | H | E | |
|---|---|---|---|---|---|---|---|---|---|---|---|---|---|---|---|---|---|---|---|---|---|---|---|---|---|
| YEAR | YEAR Yn F | Yn E2 | 2027 | | | | | | | | | | | | | | | | | | | | 2028 | | |
| MONTH | 4 Feb - 5 Mar | | 6 Mar - 4 Apr | | 5 Apr - 5 May | | 6 May - 5 June | | 6 June - 6 Jul | | 7 Jul - 7 Aug | | 8 Aug - 7 Sep | | 8 Sep - 7 Oct | | 8 Oct - 7 Nov | | 8 Nov - 6 Dec | | 7 Dec - 5 Jan | | 6 Jan - 3 Feb | | |
| | Yg W | Yg Wd | Yn W | Yn Wd | Yg Wd | Yg E1 | Yn Wd | Yn F | Yg F | Yg F | Yn F | Yn E2 | Yg E | Yg M | Yn E | Yn M | Yg M | Yg E3 | Yn M | Yn W | Yg W | Yg W | Yn W | Yn E4 | |
| Starting time | 1st day | Mid-pt | 1st day | Mid-pt | 1st day | Mid-pt | 1st day | Mid-pt | 1st day | Mid-pt | 1st day | Mid-pt | 1st day | Mid-pt | 1st day | Mid-pt | 1st day | Mid-pt | 1st day | Mid-pt | 1st day | Mid-pt | 1st day | Mid-pt | |
| Date | 4 | 19 | 6 | 21 | 5 | 20 | 6 | 21 | 6 | 21 | 7 | 23 | 8 | 23 | 8 | 23 | 8 | 24 | 8 | 22 | 7 | 22 | 6 | 20 | |
| Hour | 1006 | 0549 | 0349 | 0437 | 0831 | 1511 | 0148 | 1446 | 0558 | 2247 | 1622 | 0954 | 0230 | 1722 | 0552 | 1533 | 2158 | 0110 | 0118 | 2243 | 1758 | 1143 | 0444 | 2152 | |
| DATE 3 | | | | | | | | | | | | | | | | | | | | | | | | | 3 |
| 4 | Yg Wd | Yg Wd | | | | | | | | | | | | | | | | | | | | | | | 4 |
| 5 | Yn Wd | Yn Wd | | | Yg Wd | Yg Wd | | | | | | | | | | | | | | | | | | | 5 |
| 6 | Yg F | Yg E1 | Yg Wd | Yg M | Yn Wd | Yn Wd | Yn Wd | Yn M | Yg F | Yg E1 | | | | | | | | | | | | | Yg M | Yg Wd | 6 |
| 7 | Yn F | Yn F | Yn Wd | Yn M | Yg F | Yg E1 | Yg F | Yg E3 | Yn F | Yn F | Yn F | Yn W | | | | | | | | | Yg M | Yg M | Yn M | Yn Wd | 7 |
| 8 | Yg E | Yg F | Yg F | Yg E3 | Yn F | Yn F | Yn F | Yn W | Yg E | Yg F | Yg E | Yg W | Yn E | Yn E2 | Yg M | Yg Wd | Yg M | Yg M | Yn M | Yn Wd | Yn M | Yn M | Yg W | Yg E1 | 8 |
| 9 | Yn E | Yn E2 | Yn F | Yn W | Yg E | Yg F | Yg E | Yg W | Yn E | Yn E2 | Yn E | Yn E4 | Yg M | Yg M | Yn M | Yn Wd | Yn M | Yn M | Yg W | Yg E1 | Yg W | Yg E3 | Yn W | Yn F | 9 |
| 10 | Yg M | Yg M | Yg E | Yg W | Yn E | Yn E2 | Yn E | Yn E4 | Yg M | Yg M | Yg M | Yg Wd | Yn M | Yn M | Yg W | Yg E1 | Yg W | Yg E3 | Yn W | Yn F | Yn W | Yn W | Yg Wd | Yg F | 10 |
| 11 | Yn M | Yn M | Yn E | Yn E4 | Yg M | Yg M | Yg M | Yg Wd | Yn M | Yn M | Yn M | Yn Wd | Yg W | Yg E3 | Yn W | Yn F | Yn W | Yn W | Yg Wd | Yg F | Yg Wd | Yg W | Yn Wd | Yn E2 | 11 |
| 12 | Yg W | Yg E3 | Yg M | Yg Wd | Yn M | Yn M | Yn M | Yn Wd | Yg W | Yg E3 | Yg W | Yg E1 | Yn W | Yn W | Yg Wd | Yg F | Yg Wd | Yg W | Yn Wd | Yn E2 | Yn Wd | Yn E4 | Yg F | Yg M | 12 |
| 13 | Yn W | Yn W | Yn M | Yn Wd | Yg W | Yg E3 | Yg W | Yg E1 | Yn W | Yn W | Yn W | Yn F | Yg Wd | Yg W | Yn Wd | Yn E2 | Yn Wd | Yn E4 | Yg F | Yg M | Yg F | Yg Wd | Yn F | Yn M | 13 |
| 14 | Yg Wd | Yg W | Yg W | Yg E1 | Yn W | Yn W | Yn W | Yn F | Yg Wd | Yg W | Yg Wd | Yg F | Yn Wd | Yn E4 | Yg F | Yg M | Yg F | Yg Wd | Yn F | Yn M | Yn F | Yn Wd | Yg E | Yg E3 | 14 |
| 15 | Yn Wd | Yn E4 | Yn W | Yn F | Yg Wd | Yg W | Yg Wd | Yg F | Yn Wd | Yn E4 | Yn Wd | Yn E2 | Yg F | Yg Wd | Yn F | Yn M | Yn F | Yn Wd | Yg E | Yg E3 | Yg E | Yg E1 | Yn E | Yn W | 15 |
| 16 | Yg F | Yg Wd | Yg Wd | Yg F | Yn Wd | Yn E4 | Yn Wd | Yn E2 | Yg F | Yg Wd | Yg F | Yg M | Yn F | Yn Wd | Yg E | Yg E3 | Yg E | Yg E1 | Yn E | Yn W | Yn E | Yn F | Yg M | Yg W | 16 |
| 17 | Yn F | Yn Wd | Yn Wd | Yn E2 | Yg F | Yg Wd | Yg F | Yg M | Yn F | Yn Wd | Yn F | Yn M | Yg E | Yg E1 | Yn E | Yn W | Yn E | Yn F | Yg M | Yg W | Yg M | Yg F | Yn M | Yn E4 | 17 |
| 18 | Yg E | Yg E1 | Yg F | Yg M | Yn F | Yn Wd | Yn F | Yn M | Yg E | Yg E1 | Yg E | Yg E3 | Yn E | Yn F | Yg M | Yg W | Yg M | Yg F | Yn M | Yn E4 | Yn M | Yn E2 | Yg W | Yg Wd | 18 |
| 19 | Yn E | Yn F | Yn F | Yn M | Yg E | Yg E1 | Yg E | Yg E3 | Yn E | Yn F | Yn E | Yn W | Yg M | Yg F | Yn M | Yn E4 | Yn M | Yn E2 | Yg W | Yg Wd | Yg W | Yg M | Yn W | Yn Wd | 19 |
| 20 | Yg M | Yg F | Yg E | Yg E3 | Yn E | Yn F | Yn E | Yn W | Yg M | Yg F | Yg M | Yg W | Yn M | Yn E2 | Yg W | Yg Wd | Yg W | Yg M | Yn W | Yn Wd | Yn W | Yn M | Yg Wd | Yg E1 | 20 |
| 21 | Yn M | Yn E2 | Yn E | Yn W | Yg M | Yg F | Yg M | Yg W | Yn M | Yn E2 | Yn M | Yn E4 | Yg W | Yg M | Yn W | Yn Wd | Yn W | Yn M | Yg Wd | Yg E1 | Yg Wd | Yg E3 | Yn Wd | Yn F | 21 |
| 22 | Yg W | Yg M | Yg M | Yg W | Yn M | Yn E2 | Yn M | Yn E4 | Yg W | Yg M | Yg W | Yg Wd | Yn W | Yn M | Yg Wd | Yg E1 | Yg Wd | Yg E3 | Yn Wd | Yn F | Yn Wd | Yn W | Yg F | Yg F | 22 |
| 23 | Yn W | Yn M | Yn M | Yn E4 | Yg W | Yg M | Yg W | Yg Wd | Yn W | Yn M | Yn W | Yn Wd | Yg Wd | Yg E3 | Yn Wd | Yn F | Yn Wd | Yn W | Yg F | Yg F | Yg F | Yg W | Yn F | Yn E2 | 23 |
| 24 | Yg Wd | Yg E3 | Yg W | Yg Wd | Yn W | Yn M | Yn W | Yn Wd | Yg Wd | Yg E3 | Yg Wd | Yg E1 | Yn Wd | Yn W | Yg F | Yg F | Yg F | Yg W | Yn F | Yn E2 | Yn F | Yn E4 | Yg E | Yg M | 24 |
| 25 | Yn Wd | Yn W | Yn W | Yn Wd | Yg Wd | Yg E3 | Yg Wd | Yg E1 | Yn Wd | Yn W | Yn Wd | Yn F | Yg F | Yg W | Yn F | Yn E2 | Yn F | Yn E4 | Yg E | Yg M | Yg E | Yg Wd | Yn E | Yn M | 25 |
| 26 | Yg F | Yg W | Yg Wd | Yg E1 | Yn Wd | Yn W | Yn Wd | Yn F | Yg F | Yg W | Yg F | Yg F | Yn F | Yn E4 | Yg E | Yg M | Yg E | Yg Wd | Yn E | Yn M | Yn E | Yn Wd | Yg M | Yg E3 | 26 |
| 27 | Yn F | Yn E4 | Yn Wd | Yn F | Yg F | Yg W | Yg F | Yg F | Yn F | Yn E4 | Yn F | Yn E2 | Yg E | Yg Wd | Yn E | Yn M | Yn E | Yn Wd | Yg M | Yg E3 | Yg M | Yg E1 | Yn M | Yn W | 27 |
| 28 | Yg E | Yg Wd | Yg F | Yg F | Yn F | Yn E4 | Yn F | Yn E2 | Yg E | Yg Wd | Yg E | Yg M | Yn E | Yn Wd | Yg M | Yg E3 | Yg M | Yg E1 | Yn M | Yn W | Yn M | Yn F | Yg W | Yg W | 28 |
| 29 | | | Yn F | Yn E2 | Yg E | Yg Wd | Yg E | Yg M | Yn E | Yn Wd | Yn E | Yn M | Yg M | Yg E1 | Yn M | Yn W | Yn M | Yn F | Yg W | Yg W | Yg W | Yg F | Yn W | Yn E4 | 29 |
| 30 | | | Yg E | Yg M | Yn E | Yn Wd | Yn E | Yn M | Yg M | Yg E1 | Yg M | Yg E3 | Yn M | Yn F | Yg W | Yg W | Yg W | Yg F | Yn W | Yn E4 | Yn W | Yn E2 | Yg Wd | Yg Wd | 30 |
| 31 | | | Yn E | Yn M | | | Yg M | Yg E3 | | | Yn M | Yn W | Yg W | Yg F | | | Yn W | Yn E2 | | | Yg Wd | Yg M | Yn Wd | Yn Wd | 31 |
| 1 | Yn E | Yn Wd | Yg M | Yg E3 | Yg M | Yg E1 | Yn M | Yn W | Yn M | Yn F | Yg W | Yg W | Yn W | Yn E2 | Yn W | Yn E4 | Yg Wd | Yg M | Yg Wd | Yg Wd | Yn Wd | Yn M | Yg F | Yg E1 | 1 |
| 2 | Yg M | Yg E1 | Yn M | Yn W | Yn M | Yn F | Yg W | Yg W | Yg W | Yg F | Yn W | Yn E4 | Yg Wd | Yg M | Yg Wd | Yg Wd | Yn Wd | Yn M | Yn Wd | Yn Wd | Yg F | Yg E3 | Yn F | Yn F | 2 |
| 3 | Yn M | Yn F | Yg W | Yg W | Yg W | Yg F | Yn W | Yn E4 | Yn W | Yn E2 | Yg Wd | Yg Wd | Yn Wd | Yn M | Yn Wd | Yn Wd | Yg F | Yg E3 | Yg F | Yg E1 | Yn F | Yn W | Yg E | Yg F | 3 |
| 4 | Yg W | Yg F | Yn W | Yn E4 | Yn W | Yn E2 | Yg Wd | Yg Wd | Yg Wd | Yg M | Yn Wd | Yn Wd | Yg F | Yg E3 | Yg F | Yg E1 | Yn F | Yn W | Yn F | Yn F | Yg E | Yg W | | | 4 |
| 5 | Yn W | Yn E2 | | | Yg Wd | Yg M | Yn Wd | Yn Wd | Yn Wd | Yn M | Yg F | Yg E1 | Yn F | Yn W | Yn F | Yn F | Yg E | Yg W | Yg E | Yg F | Yn E | Yn E4 | | | 5 |
| 6 | | | | | | | | | Yg F | Yg E3 | Yn F | Yn F | Yg E | Yg W | Yg E | Yg F | Yn E | Yn E4 | Yn E | Yn E2 | | | | | 6 |
| 7 | | | | | | | | | | | Yg E | Yg F | Yn E | Yn E4 | Yn E | Yn E2 | Yg M | Yg Wd | | | | | | | 7 |
| 8 | | | | | | | | | | | | | | | | | | | | | | | | | 8 |

# YEAR OF THE MONKEY

| | H | E | H | E | H | E | H | E | H | E | H | E | H | E | H | E | H | E | H | E | H | E | H | E | |
|---|---|---|---|---|---|---|---|---|---|---|---|---|---|---|---|---|---|---|---|---|---|---|---|---|---|
| YEAR | YEAR<br>YgE | YgM | 2028 | | | | | | | | | | | | | | | | | | | | 2029 | | |
| MONTH | 4 Feb - 4 Mar | | 5 Mar - 3 Apr | | 4 Apr - 4 May | | 5 May - 4 June | | 5 June - 5 Jul | | 6 Jul - 6 Aug | | 7 Aug - 6 Sep | | 7 Sep - 7 Oct | | 8 Oct - 6 Nov | | 7 Nov - 5 Dec | | 6 Dec - 4 Jan | | 5 Jan - 2 Feb | | |
| | Yg Wd | Yg Wd | Yn Wd | Yn Wd | Yg F | Yg E1 | Yn F | Yn F | Yg E | Yg F | Yn E | Yn E2 | Yg M | Yg M | Yn M | Yn M | Yg W | Yg E3 | Yn W | Yn W | Yg Wd | Yg W | Yn Wd | Yn E4 | |
| Starting time | 1st day | Mid-pt | 1st day | Mid-pt | 1st day | Mid-pt | 1st day | Mid-pt | 1st day | Mid-pt | 1st day | Mid-pt | 1st day | Mid-pt | 1st day | Mid-pt | 1st day | Mid-pt | 1st day | Mid-pt | 1st day | Mid-pt | 1st day | Mid-pt | |
| Date | 4 | 19 | 5 | 20 | 4 | 19 | 5 | 20 | 5 | 21 | 6 | 22 | 7 | 22 | 7 | 22 | 8 | 23 | 7 | 22 | 6 | 21 | 5 | 20 | |
| Hour | 1526 | 1138 | 0938 | 1027 | 1419 | 2125 | 0736 | 2034 | 1147 | 0435 | 2208 | 1541 | 0817 | 2310 | 1141 | 2119 | 0346 | 0659 | 0707 | 0429 | 2347 | 1732 | 1034 | 0342 | |
| DATE 3 | | | | | | | | | | | | | | | | | | | | | | | | | 3 |
| 4 | Yn E | Yn E2 | | | Yn E | Yn E2 | | | | | | | | | | | | | | | | | | | 4 |
| 5 | Yg M | Yg M | Yn E | Yn E4 | Yg M | Yg M | Yg M | Yg Wd | Yn M | Yn M | | | | | | | | | | | | | Yn Wd | Yn E2 | 5 |
| 6 | Yn M | Yn M | Yg M | Yg Wd | Yn M | Yn M | Yn M | Yn Wd | Yg W | Yg E3 | Yg W | Yg E1 | | | | | | | | | Yn Wd | Yn E4 | Yg F | Yg M | 6 |
| 7 | Yg W | Yg E3 | Yn M | Yn Wd | Yg W | Yg E3 | Yg W | Yg E1 | Yn W | Yn W | Yn W | Yn F | Yg Wd | Yg W | Yn Wd | Yn E2 | | | Yg F | Yg M | Yg F | Yg Wd | Yn F | Yn M | 7 |
| 8 | Yn W | Yn W | Yg W | Yg E1 | Yn W | Yn W | Yn W | Yn F | Yg Wd | Yg W | Yg Wd | Yg F | Yn Wd | Yn E4 | Yg F | Yg M | Yg F | Yg Wd | Yn F | Yn M | Yn F | Yn Wd | Yg E | Yg E3 | 8 |
| 9 | Yg Wd | Yg W | Yn W | Yn F | Yg Wd | Yg W | Yg Wd | Yg F | Yn Wd | Yn E4 | Yn Wd | Yn E2 | Yg F | Yg Wd | Yn F | Yn M | Yn F | Yn Wd | Yg E | Yg E3 | Yg E | Yg E1 | Yn E | Yn W | 9 |
| 10 | Yn Wd | Yn E4 | Yg Wd | Yg F | Yn Wd | Yn E4 | Yn Wd | Yn E2 | Yg F | Yg Wd | Yg F | Yg M | Yn F | Yn Wd | Yg E | Yg E3 | Yg E | Yg E1 | Yn E | Yn W | Yn E | Yn F | Yg M | Yg W | 10 |
| 11 | Yg F | Yg Wd | Yn Wd | Yn E2 | Yg F | Yg Wd | Yg F | Yg M | Yn F | Yn Wd | Yn F | Yn M | Yg E | Yg E1 | Yn E | Yn W | Yn E | Yn F | Yg M | Yg W | Yg M | Yg F | Yn M | Yn E4 | 11 |
| 12 | Yn F | Yn Wd | Yg F | Yg M | Yn F | Yn Wd | Yn F | Yn M | Yg E | Yg E1 | Yg E | Yg E3 | Yn E | Yn F | Yg M | Yg W | Yg M | Yg F | Yn M | Yn E4 | Yn M | Yn E2 | Yg W | Yg Wd | 12 |
| 13 | Yg E | Yg E1 | Yn F | Yn M | Yg E | Yg E1 | Yg E | Yg E3 | Yn E | Yn F | Yn E | Yn W | Yg M | Yg F | Yn M | Yn E4 | Yn M | Yn E2 | Yg W | Yg Wd | Yg W | Yg M | Yn W | Yn Wd | 13 |
| 14 | Yn E | Yn F | Yg E | Yg E3 | Yn E | Yn F | Yn E | Yn W | Yg M | Yg F | Yg M | Yg W | Yn M | Yn E2 | Yg W | Yg Wd | Yg W | Yg M | Yn W | Yn Wd | Yn W | Yn M | Yg Wd | Yg E1 | 14 |
| 15 | Yg M | Yg F | Yn E | Yn W | Yg M | Yg F | Yg M | Yg W | Yn M | Yn E2 | Yn M | Yn E4 | Yg W | Yg M | Yn W | Yn Wd | Yn W | Yn M | Yg Wd | Yg E1 | Yg Wd | Yg E3 | Yn Wd | Yn F | 15 |
| 16 | Yn M | Yn E2 | Yg M | Yg W | Yn M | Yn E2 | Yn M | Yn E4 | Yg W | Yg M | Yg W | Yg Wd | Yn W | Yn M | Yg Wd | Yg E1 | Yg Wd | Yg E3 | Yn Wd | Yn F | Yn Wd | Yn W | Yg F | Yg F | 16 |
| 17 | Yg W | Yg M | Yn M | Yn E4 | Yg W | Yg M | Yg W | Yg Wd | Yn W | Yn M | Yn W | Yn Wd | Yg Wd | Yg E3 | Yn Wd | Yn F | Yn Wd | Yn W | Yg F | Yg F | Yg F | Yg W | Yn F | Yn E2 | 17 |
| 18 | Yn W | Yn M | Yg W | Yg Wd | Yn W | Yn M | Yn W | Yn Wd | Yg Wd | Yg E3 | Yg Wd | Yg E1 | Yn Wd | Yn W | Yg F | Yg F | Yg F | Yg W | Yn F | Yn E2 | Yn F | Yn E4 | Yg E | Yg M | 18 |
| 19 | Yg Wd | Yg E3 | Yn W | Yn Wd | Yg Wd | Yg E3 | Yg Wd | Yg E1 | Yn Wd | Yn W | Yn Wd | Yn F | Yg F | Yg W | Yn F | Yn E2 | Yn F | Yn E4 | Yg E | Yg M | Yg E | Yg Wd | Yn E | Yn M | 19 |
| 20 | Yn Wd | Yn W | Yg Wd | Yg E1 | Yn Wd | Yn W | Yn Wd | Yn F | Yg F | Yg W | Yg F | Yg F | Yn F | Yn E4 | Yg E | Yg M | Yg E | Yg Wd | Yn E | Yn M | Yn E | Yn Wd | Yg M | Yg E3 | 20 |
| 21 | Yg F | Yg W | Yn Wd | Yn F | Yg F | Yg W | Yg F | Yg F | Yn F | Yn E4 | Yn F | Yn E2 | Yg E | Yg Wd | Yn E | Yn M | Yn E | Yn Wd | Yg M | Yg E3 | Yg M | Yg E1 | Yn M | Yn W | 21 |
| 22 | Yn F | Yn E4 | Yg F | Yg F | Yn F | Yn E4 | Yn F | Yn E2 | Yg E | Yg Wd | Yg E | Yg M | Yn E | Yn Wd | Yg M | Yg E3 | Yg M | Yg E1 | Yn M | Yn W | Yn M | Yn F | Yg W | Yg W | 22 |
| 23 | Yg E | Yg Wd | Yn F | Yn E2 | Yg E | Yg Wd | Yg E | Yg M | Yn E | Yn Wd | Yn E | Yn M | Yg M | Yg E1 | Yn M | Yn W | Yn M | Yn F | Yg W | Yg W | Yg W | Yg F | Yn W | Yn E4 | 23 |
| 24 | Yn E | Yn Wd | Yg E | Yg M | Yn E | Yn Wd | Yn E | Yn M | Yg M | Yg E1 | Yg M | Yg E3 | Yn M | Yn F | Yg W | Yg W | Yg W | Yg F | Yn W | Yn E4 | Yn W | Yn E2 | Yg Wd | Yg Wd | 24 |
| 25 | Yg M | Yg E1 | Yn E | Yn M | Yg M | Yg E1 | Yg M | Yg E3 | Yn M | Yn F | Yn M | Yn W | Yg W | Yg F | Yn W | Yn E4 | Yn W | Yn E2 | Yg Wd | Yg Wd | Yg Wd | Yg M | Yn Wd | Yn Wd | 25 |
| 26 | Yn M | Yn F | Yg M | Yg E3 | Yn M | Yn F | Yn M | Yn W | Yg W | Yg F | Yg W | Yg W | Yn W | Yn E2 | Yg Wd | Yg Wd | Yg Wd | Yg M | Yn Wd | Yn Wd | Yn Wd | Yn M | Yg F | Yg E1 | 26 |
| 27 | Yg W | Yg F | Yn M | Yn W | Yg W | Yg F | Yg W | Yg W | Yn W | Yn E2 | Yn W | Yn E4 | Yg Wd | Yg M | Yn Wd | Yn Wd | Yn Wd | Yn M | Yg F | Yg E1 | Yg F | Yg E3 | Yn F | Yn F | 27 |
| 28 | Yn W | Yn E2 | Yg W | Yg W | Yn W | Yn E2 | Yn W | Yn E4 | Yg Wd | Yg M | Yg Wd | Yg Wd | Yn Wd | Yn M | Yg F | Yg E1 | Yg F | Yg E3 | Yn F | Yn F | Yn F | Yn W | Yg E | Yg F | 28 |
| 29 | Yg Wd | Yg M | Yn W | Yn E4 | Yg Wd | Yg M | Yg Wd | Yg Wd | Yn Wd | Yn M | Yn Wd | Yn Wd | Yg F | Yg E3 | Yn F | Yn F | Yn F | Yn W | Yg E | Yg F | Yg E | Yg W | Yn E | Yn E2 | 29 |
| 30 | | | Yg Wd | Yg Wd | Yn Wd | Yn M | Yn Wd | Yn Wd | Yg F | Yg E3 | Yg F | Yg E1 | Yn F | Yn W | Yg E | Yg F | Yg E | Yg W | Yn E | Yn E2 | Yn E | Yn E4 | Yg M | Yg M | 30 |
| 31 | | | Yn Wd | Yn Wd | | | Yg F | Yg E1 | | | Yn F | Yn F | Yg E | Yg W | | | Yn E | Yn E4 | | | Yg M | Yg Wd | Yn M | Yn M | 31 |
| 1 | Yn Wd | Yn M | Yg F | Yg E1 | Yg F | Yg E3 | Yn F | Yn F | Yn F | Yn W | Yg E | Yg F | Yn E | Yn E4 | Yn E | Yn E2 | Yg M | Yg Wd | Yg M | Yg M | Yn M | Yn Wd | Yg W | Yg E3 | 1 |
| 2 | Yg F | Yg E3 | Yn F | Yn F | Yn F | Yn W | Yg E | Yg F | Yg E | Yg W | Yn E | Yn E2 | Yg M | Yg Wd | Yg M | Yg M | Yn M | Yn Wd | Yn M | Yn M | Yg W | Yg E1 | Yn W | Yn W | 2 |
| 3 | Yn F | Yn W | Yg E | Yg F | Yg E | Yg W | Yn E | Yn E2 | Yn E | Yn E4 | Yg M | Yg M | Yn M | Yn Wd | Yn M | Yn M | Yg W | Yg E1 | Yg W | Yg E3 | Yn W | Yn F | | | 3 |
| 4 | Yg E | Yg W | | | Yn E | Yn E4 | Yg M | Yg M | Yg M | Yg Wd | Yn M | Yn M | Yg W | Yg E1 | Yg W | Yg E3 | Yn W | Yn F | Yn W | Yn W | Yg Wd | Yg F | | | 4 |
| 5 | | | | | | | | | Yn M | Yn Wd | Yg W | Yg E3 | Yn W | Yn F | Yn W | Yn W | Yg Wd | Yg F | Yg Wd | Yg W | | | | | 5 |
| 6 | | | | | | | | | | | Yn W | Yn W | Yg Wd | Yg F | Yg Wd | Yg W | Yn Wd | Yn E2 | | | | | | | 6 |
| 7 | | | | | | | | | | | | | | | Yn Wd | Yn E4 | | | | | | | | | 7 |
| 8 | | | | | | | | | | | | | | | | | | | | | | | | | 8 |

# YEAR OF THE ROOSTER

| | H | E | H | E | H | E | H | E | H | E | H | E | H | E | H | E | H | E | H | E | H | E | H | E | |
|---|---|---|---|---|---|---|---|---|---|---|---|---|---|---|---|---|---|---|---|---|---|---|---|---|---|
| YEAR | YEAR YnE | YnM | 2029 | | | | | | | | | | | | | | | | | | 2030 | | | | |
| MONTH | 3 Feb - 4 Mar | | 5 Mar - 3 Apr | | 4 Apr - 4 May | | 5 May - 4 June | | 5 June - 6 Jul | | 7 Jul - 6 Aug | | 7 Aug - 6 Sep | | 7 Sep - 7 Oct | | 8 Oct - 6 Nov | | 7 Nov - 6 Dec | | 7 Dec - 4 Jan | | 5 Jan - 3 Feb | | |
| | Yg F | Yg Wd | Yn F | Yn Wd | Yg E | Yg E1 | Yn E | Yn F | Yg M | Yg F | Yn M | Yn E2 | Yg W | Yg M | Yn W | Yn M | Yg Wd | Yg E3 | Yn Wd | Yn W | Yg F | Yg W | Yn F | Yn E4 | |
| Starting time | 1st day | Mid-pt | 1st day | Mid-pt | 1st day | Mid-pt | 1st day | Mid-pt | 1st day | Mid-pt | 1st day | Mid-pt | 1st day | Mid-pt | 1st day | Mid-pt | 1st day | Mid-pt | 1st day | Mid-pt | 1st day | Mid-pt | 1st day | Mid-pt | |
| Date | 3 | 18 | 5 | 20 | 4 | 20 | 5 | 21 | 5 | 21 | 7 | 22 | 7 | 23 | 7 | 23 | 8 | 23 | 7 | 22 | 7 | 21 | 5 | 20 | |
| Hour | 2145 | 1728 | 1529 | 1616 | 2011 | 0314 | 1326 | 0244 | 1735 | 1023 | 0358 | 2129 | 1406 | 0459 | 1729 | 0308 | 0935 | 1233 | 1257 | 1022 | 0537 | 2322 | 1624 | 0931 | |
| DATE 3 | Yg Wd | Yg W | | | | | | | | | | | | | | | | | | | | | | | 3 |
| 4 | Yn Wd | Yn E4 | | | Yg Wd | Yg W | | | | | | | | | | | | | | | | | | | 4 |
| 5 | Yg F | Yg Wd | Yg Wd | Yg F | Yn Wd | Yn E4 | Yn Wd | Yn E2 | Yg F | Yg Wd | | | | | | | | | | | | | Yg M | Yg W | 5 |
| 6 | Yn F | Yn Wd | Yn Wd | Yn E2 | Yg F | Yg Wd | Yg F | Yg M | Yn F | Yn Wd | | | | | | | | | | | | | Yn M | Yn E4 | 6 |
| 7 | Yg E | Yg E1 | Yg F | Yg M | Yn F | Yn Wd | Yn F | Yn M | Yg E | Yg E1 | Yg E | Yg E3 | Yn E | Yn F | Yg M | Yg W | | | Yn M | Yn E4 | Yn M | Yn E2 | Yg W | Yg Wd | 7 |
| 8 | Yn E | Yn F | Yn F | Yn M | Yg E | Yg E1 | Yg E | Yg E3 | Yn E | Yn F | Yn E | Yn W | Yg M | Yg F | Yn M | Yn E4 | Yn M | Yn E2 | Yg W | Yg Wd | Yg W | Yg M | Yn W | Yn Wd | 8 |
| 9 | Yg M | Yg F | Yg E | Yg E3 | Yn E | Yn F | Yn E | Yn W | Yg M | Yg F | Yg M | Yg W | Yn M | Yn E2 | Yg W | Yg Wd | Yg W | Yg M | Yn W | Yn Wd | Yn W | Yn M | Yg Wd | Yg E1 | 9 |
| 10 | Yn M | Yn E2 | Yn E | Yn W | Yg M | Yg F | Yg M | Yg W | Yn M | Yn E2 | Yn M | Yn E4 | Yg W | Yg M | Yn W | Yn Wd | Yn W | Yn M | Yg Wd | Yg E1 | Yg Wd | Yg E3 | Yn Wd | Yn F | 10 |
| 11 | Yg W | Yg M | Yg M | Yg W | Yn M | Yn E2 | Yn M | Yn E4 | Yg W | Yg M | Yg W | Yg Wd | Yn W | Yn M | Yg Wd | Yg E1 | Yg Wd | Yg E3 | Yn Wd | Yn F | Yn Wd | Yn W | Yg F | Yg F | 11 |
| 12 | Yn W | Yn M | Yn M | Yn E4 | Yg W | Yg M | Yg W | Yg Wd | Yn W | Yn M | Yn W | Yn Wd | Yg Wd | Yg E3 | Yn Wd | Yn F | Yn Wd | Yn W | Yg F | Yg F | Yg F | Yg W | Yn F | Yn E2 | 12 |
| 13 | Yg Wd | Yg E3 | Yg W | Yg Wd | Yn W | Yn M | Yn W | Yn Wd | Yg Wd | Yg E3 | Yg Wd | Yg E1 | Yn Wd | Yn W | Yg F | Yg F | Yg F | Yg W | Yn F | Yn E2 | Yn F | Yn E4 | Yg E | Yg M | 13 |
| 14 | Yn Wd | Yn W | Yn W | Yn Wd | Yg Wd | Yg E3 | Yg Wd | Yg E1 | Yn Wd | Yn W | Yn Wd | Yn F | Yg F | Yg W | Yn F | Yn E2 | Yn F | Yn E4 | Yg E | Yg M | Yg E | Yg Wd | Yn E | Yn M | 14 |
| 15 | Yg F | Yg W | Yg Wd | Yg E1 | Yn Wd | Yn W | Yn Wd | Yn F | Yg F | Yg W | Yg F | Yg F | Yn F | Yn E4 | Yg E | Yg M | Yg E | Yg Wd | Yn E | Yn M | Yn E | Yn Wd | Yg M | Yg E3 | 15 |
| 16 | Yn F | Yn E4 | Yn Wd | Yn F | Yg F | Yg W | Yg F | Yg F | Yn F | Yn E4 | Yn F | Yn E2 | Yg E | Yg Wd | Yn E | Yn M | Yn E | Yn Wd | Yg M | Yg E3 | Yg M | Yg E1 | Yn M | Yn W | 16 |
| 17 | Yg E | Yg Wd | Yg F | Yg F | Yn F | Yn E4 | Yn F | Yn E2 | Yg E | Yg Wd | Yg E | Yg M | Yn E | Yn Wd | Yg M | Yg E3 | Yg M | Yg E1 | Yn M | Yn W | Yn M | Yn F | Yg W | Yg W | 17 |
| 18 | Yn E | Yn Wd | Yn F | Yn E2 | Yg E | Yg Wd | Yg E | Yg M | Yn E | Yn Wd | Yn E | Yn M | Yg M | Yg E1 | Yn M | Yn W | Yn M | Yn F | Yg W | Yg W | Yg W | Yg F | Yn W | Yn E4 | 18 |
| 19 | Yg M | Yg E1 | Yg E | Yg M | Yn E | Yn Wd | Yn E | Yn M | Yg M | Yg E1 | Yg M | Yg E3 | Yn M | Yn F | Yg W | Yg W | Yg W | Yg F | Yn W | Yn E4 | Yn W | Yn E2 | Yg Wd | Yg Wd | 19 |
| 20 | Yn M | Yn F | Yn E | Yn M | Yg M | Yg E1 | Yg M | Yg E3 | Yn M | Yn F | Yn M | Yn W | Yg W | Yg F | Yn W | Yn E4 | Yn W | Yn E2 | Yg Wd | Yg Wd | Yg Wd | Yg M | Yn Wd | Yn Wd | 20 |
| 21 | Yg W | Yg F | Yg M | Yg E3 | Yn M | Yn F | Yn M | Yn W | Yg W | Yg F | Yg W | Yg W | Yn W | Yn E2 | Yg Wd | Yg Wd | Yg Wd | Yg M | Yn Wd | Yn Wd | Yn Wd | Yn M | Yg F | Yg E1 | 21 |
| 22 | Yn W | Yn E2 | Yn M | Yn W | Yg W | Yg F | Yg W | Yg W | Yn W | Yn E2 | Yn W | Yn E4 | Yg Wd | Yg M | Yn Wd | Yn Wd | Yn Wd | Yn M | Yg F | Yg E1 | Yg F | Yg E3 | Yn F | Yn F | 22 |
| 23 | Yg Wd | Yg M | Yg W | Yg W | Yn W | Yn E2 | Yn W | Yn E4 | Yg Wd | Yg M | Yg Wd | Yg Wd | Yn Wd | Yn M | Yg F | Yg E1 | Yg F | Yg E3 | Yn F | Yn F | Yn F | Yn W | Yg E | Yg F | 23 |
| 24 | Yn Wd | Yn M | Yn W | Yn E4 | Yg Wd | Yg M | Yg Wd | Yg Wd | Yn Wd | Yn M | Yn Wd | Yn Wd | Yg F | Yg E3 | Yn F | Yn F | Yn F | Yn W | Yg E | Yg F | Yg E | Yg W | Yn E | Yn E2 | 24 |
| 25 | Yg F | Yg E3 | Yg Wd | Yg Wd | Yn Wd | Yn M | Yn Wd | Yn Wd | Yg F | Yg E3 | Yg F | Yg E1 | Yn F | Yn W | Yg E | Yg F | Yg E | Yg W | Yn E | Yn E2 | Yn E | Yn E4 | Yg M | Yg M | 25 |
| 26 | Yn F | Yn W | Yn Wd | Yn Wd | Yg F | Yg E3 | Yg F | Yg E1 | Yn F | Yn W | Yn F | Yn F | Yg E | Yg W | Yn E | Yn E2 | Yn E | Yn E4 | Yg M | Yg M | Yg M | Yg Wd | Yn M | Yn M | 26 |
| 27 | Yg E | Yg W | Yg F | Yg E1 | Yn F | Yn W | Yn F | Yn F | Yg E | Yg W | Yg E | Yg F | Yn E | Yn E4 | Yg M | Yg M | Yg M | Yg Wd | Yn M | Yn M | Yn M | Yn Wd | Yg W | Yg E3 | 27 |
| 28 | Yn E | Yn E4 | Yn F | Yn F | Yg E | Yg W | Yg E | Yg F | Yn E | Yn E4 | Yn E | Yn E2 | Yg M | Yg Wd | Yn M | Yn M | Yn M | Yn Wd | Yg W | Yg E3 | Yg W | Yg E1 | Yn W | Yn W | 28 |
| 29 | | | Yg E | Yg F | Yn E | Yn E4 | Yn E | Yn E2 | Yg M | Yg Wd | Yg M | Yg M | Yn M | Yn Wd | Yg W | Yg E3 | Yg W | Yg E1 | Yn W | Yn W | Yn W | Yn F | Yg Wd | Yg W | 29 |
| 30 | | | Yn E | Yn E2 | Yg M | Yg Wd | Yg M | Yg M | Yn M | Yn Wd | Yn M | Yn M | Yg W | Yg E1 | Yn W | Yn W | Yn W | Yn F | Yg Wd | Yg W | Yg Wd | Yg F | Yn Wd | Yn E4 | 30 |
| 31 | | | Yg M | Yg M | | | Yn M | Yn M | | | Yg W | Yg E3 | Yn W | Yn F | | | Yg Wd | Yg F | | | Yn Wd | Yn E2 | Yg F | Yg Wd | 31 |
| 1 | Yg M | Yg Wd | Yn M | Yn M | Yn M | Yn Wd | Yg W | Yg E3 | Yg W | Yg E1 | Yn W | Yn W | Yg Wd | Yg F | Yg Wd | Yg W | Yn Wd | Yn E2 | Yn Wd | Yn E4 | Yg F | Yg M | Yn F | Yn Wd | 1 |
| 2 | Yn M | Yn Wd | Yg W | Yg E3 | Yg W | Yg E1 | Yn W | Yn W | Yn W | Yn F | Yg Wd | Yg W | Yn Wd | Yn E2 | Yn Wd | Yn E4 | Yg F | Yg M | Yg F | Yg Wd | Yn F | Yn M | Yg E | Yg E1 | 2 |
| 3 | Yg W | Yg E1 | Yn W | Yn W | Yn W | Yn F | Yg Wd | Yg W | Yg Wd | Yg F | Yn Wd | Yn E4 | Yg F | Yg M | Yg F | Yg Wd | Yn F | Yn M | Yn F | Yn Wd | Yg E | Yg E3 | Yn E | Yn F | 3 |
| 4 | Yn W | Yn F | | | Yg Wd | Yg F | Yn Wd | Yn E4 | Yn Wd | Yn E2 | Yg F | Yg Wd | Yn F | Yn M | Yn F | Yn Wd | Yg E | Yg E3 | Yg E | Yg E1 | Yn E | Yn W | | | 4 |
| 5 | | | | | | | | | Yg F | Yg M | Yn F | Yn Wd | Yg E | Yg E3 | Yg E | Yg E1 | Yn E | Yn W | Yn E | Yn F | | | | | 5 |
| 6 | | | | | | | | | Yn F | Yn M | Yg E | Yg E1 | Yn E | Yn W | Yn E | Yn F | Yg M | Yg W | Yg M | Yg F | | | | | 6 |
| 7 | | | | | | | | | | | | | | | Yg M | Yg F | | | | | | | | | 7 |
| 8 | | | | | | | | | | | | | | | | | | | | | | | | | 8 |

# YEAR OF THE DOG

| | H | E | H | E | H | E | H | E | H | E | H | E | H | E | H | E | H | E | H | E | H | E | H | E | |
|---|---|---|---|---|---|---|---|---|---|---|---|---|---|---|---|---|---|---|---|---|---|---|---|---|---|
| YEAR | YEAR Yg M | Yg E3 | 2030 | | | | | | | | | | | | | | | | | | | | 2031 | | |
| MONTH | 4 Feb - 4 Mar | | 5 Mar - 4 Apr | | 5 Apr - 4 May | | 5 May - 4 June | | 5 June - 6 Jul | | 7 Jul - 6 Aug | | 7 Aug - 6 Sep | | 7 Sep - 7 Oct | | 8 Oct - 6 Nov | | 7 Nov - 6 Dec | | 7 Dec - 4 Jan | | 5 Jan - 3 Feb | | |
| | Yg E | Yg Wd | Yn E | Yn Wd | Yg M | Yg E1 | Yn M | Yn F | Yg W | Yg F | Yn W | Yn E2 | Yg Wd | Yg M | Yn Wd | Yn M | Yg F | Yg E3 | Yn F | Yn W | Yg E | Yg W | Yn E | Yn E4 | |
| Starting time | 1st day | Mid-pt | 1st day | Mid-pt | 1st day | Mid-pt | 1st day | Mid-pt | 1st day | Mid-pt | 1st day | Mid-pt | 1st day | Mid-pt | 1st day | Mid-pt | 1st day | Mid-pt | 1st day | Mid-pt | 1st day | Mid-pt | 1st day | Mid-pt | |
| Date | 4 | 18 | 5 | 20 | 5 | 20 | 5 | 21 | 5 | 21 | 7 | 23 | 7 | 23 | 7 | 23 | 8 | 23 | 7 | 22 | 7 | 22 | 5 | 20 | |
| Hour | 0335 | 2317 | 2118 | 2205 | 0157 | 0903 | 1913 | 0810 | 2323 | 1611 | 0946 | 0318 | 1954 | 1047 | 2318 | 0857 | 1524 | 1838 | 1847 | 1612 | 1127 | 0512 | 2214 | 1522 | |
| DATE 3 | | | | | | | | | | | | | | | | | | | | | | | | | 3 |
| 4 | Yg M | Yg F | | | | | | | | | | | | | | | | | | | | | | | 4 |
| 5 | Yn M | Yn E2 | Yn E | Yn W | Yg M | Yg F | Yg M | Yg W | Yn M | Yn E2 | | | | | | | | | | | | | Yn Wd | Yn F | 5 |
| 6 | Yg W | Yg M | Yg M | Yg W | Yn M | Yn E2 | Yn M | Yn E4 | Yg W | Yg M | | | | | | | | | | | | | Yg F | Yg F | 6 |
| 7 | Yn W | Yn M | Yn M | Yn E4 | Yg W | Yg M | Yg W | Yg Wd | Yn W | Yn M | Yn W | Yn Wd | Yg Wd | Yg E3 | Yn Wd | Yn F | | | Yg F | Yg F | Yg F | Yg W | Yn F | Yn E2 | 7 |
| 8 | Yg Wd | Yg E3 | Yg W | Yg Wd | Yn W | Yn M | Yn W | Yn Wd | Yg Wd | Yg E3 | Yg Wd | Yg E1 | Yn Wd | Yn W | Yg F | Yg F | Yg F | Yg W | Yn F | Yn E2 | Yn F | Yn E4 | Yg E | Yg M | 8 |
| 9 | Yn Wd | Yn W | Yn W | Yn Wd | Yg Wd | Yg E3 | Yg Wd | Yg E1 | Yn Wd | Yn W | Yn Wd | Yn F | Yg F | Yg W | Yn F | Yn E2 | Yn F | Yn E4 | Yg E | Yg M | Yg E | Yg Wd | Yn E | Yn M | 9 |
| 10 | Yg F | Yg W | Yg Wd | Yg E1 | Yn Wd | Yn W | Yn Wd | Yn F | Yg F | Yg W | Yg F | Yg F | Yn F | Yn E4 | Yg E | Yg M | Yg E | Yg Wd | Yn E | Yn M | Yn E | Yn Wd | Yg M | Yg E3 | 10 |
| 11 | Yn F | Yn E4 | Yn Wd | Yn F | Yg F | Yg W | Yg F | Yg F | Yn F | Yn E4 | Yn F | Yn E2 | Yg E | Yg Wd | Yn E | Yn M | Yn E | Yn Wd | Yg M | Yg E3 | Yg M | Yg E1 | Yn M | Yn W | 11 |
| 12 | Yg E | Yg Wd | Yg F | Yg F | Yn F | Yn E4 | Yn F | Yn E2 | Yg E | Yg Wd | Yg E | Yg M | Yn E | Yn Wd | Yg M | Yg E3 | Yg M | Yg E1 | Yn M | Yn W | Yn M | Yn F | Yg W | Yg W | 12 |
| 13 | Yn E | Yn Wd | Yn F | Yn E2 | Yg E | Yg Wd | Yg E | Yg M | Yn E | Yn Wd | Yn E | Yn M | Yg M | Yg E1 | Yn M | Yn W | Yn M | Yn F | Yg W | Yg W | Yg W | Yg F | Yn W | Yn E4 | 13 |
| 14 | Yg M | Yg E1 | Yg E | Yg M | Yn E | Yn Wd | Yn E | Yn M | Yg M | Yg E1 | Yg M | Yg E3 | Yn M | Yn F | Yg W | Yg W | Yg W | Yg F | Yn W | Yn E4 | Yn W | Yn E2 | Yg Wd | Yg Wd | 14 |
| 15 | Yn M | Yn F | Yn E | Yn M | Yg M | Yg E1 | Yg M | Yg E3 | Yn M | Yn F | Yn M | Yn W | Yg W | Yg F | Yn W | Yn E4 | Yn W | Yn E2 | Yg Wd | Yg Wd | Yg Wd | Yg M | Yn Wd | Yn Wd | 15 |
| 16 | Yg W | Yg F | Yg M | Yg E3 | Yn M | Yn F | Yn M | Yn W | Yg W | Yg F | Yg W | Yg W | Yn W | Yn E2 | Yg Wd | Yg Wd | Yg Wd | Yg M | Yn Wd | Yn Wd | Yn Wd | Yn M | Yg F | Yg E1 | 16 |
| 17 | Yn W | Yn E2 | Yn M | Yn W | Yg W | Yg F | Yg W | Yg W | Yn W | Yn E2 | Yn W | Yn E4 | Yg Wd | Yg M | Yn Wd | Yn Wd | Yn Wd | Yn M | Yg F | Yg E1 | Yg F | Yg E3 | Yn F | Yn F | 17 |
| 18 | Yg Wd | Yg M | Yg W | Yg W | Yn W | Yn E2 | Yn W | Yn E4 | Yg Wd | Yg M | Yg Wd | Yg Wd | Yn Wd | Yn M | Yg F | Yg E1 | Yg F | Yg E3 | Yn F | Yn F | Yn F | Yn W | Yg E | Yg F | 18 |
| 19 | Yn Wd | Yn M | Yn W | Yn E4 | Yg Wd | Yg M | Yg Wd | Yg Wd | Yn Wd | Yn M | Yn Wd | Yn Wd | Yg F | Yg E3 | Yn F | Yn F | Yn F | Yn W | Yg E | Yg F | Yg E | Yg W | Yn E | Yn E2 | 19 |
| 20 | Yg F | Yg E3 | Yg Wd | Yg Wd | Yn Wd | Yn M | Yn Wd | Yn Wd | Yg F | Yg E3 | Yg F | Yg E1 | Yn F | Yn W | Yg E | Yg F | Yg E | Yg W | Yn E | Yn E2 | Yn E | Yn E4 | Yg M | Yg M | 20 |
| 21 | Yn F | Yn W | Yn Wd | Yn Wd | Yg F | Yg E3 | Yg F | Yg E1 | Yn F | Yn W | Yn F | Yn F | Yg E | Yg W | Yn E | Yn E2 | Yn E | Yn E4 | Yg M | Yg M | Yg M | Yg Wd | Yn M | Yn M | 21 |
| 22 | Yg E | Yg W | Yg F | Yg E1 | Yn F | Yn W | Yn F | Yn F | Yg E | Yg W | Yg E | Yg F | Yn E | Yn E4 | Yg M | Yg M | Yg M | Yg Wd | Yn M | Yn M | Yn M | Yn Wd | Yg W | Yg E3 | 22 |
| 23 | Yn E | Yn E4 | Yn F | Yn F | Yg E | Yg W | Yg E | Yg F | Yn E | Yn E4 | Yn E | Yn E2 | Yg M | Yg Wd | Yn M | Yn M | Yn M | Yn Wd | Yg W | Yg E3 | Yg W | Yg E1 | Yn W | Yn W | 23 |
| 24 | Yg M | Yg Wd | Yg E | Yg F | Yn E | Yn E4 | Yn E | Yn E2 | Yg M | Yg Wd | Yg M | Yg M | Yn M | Yn Wd | Yg W | Yg E3 | Yg W | Yg E1 | Yn W | Yn W | Yn W | Yn F | Yg Wd | Yg W | 24 |
| 25 | Yn M | Yn Wd | Yn E | Yn E2 | Yg M | Yg Wd | Yg M | Yg M | Yn M | Yn Wd | Yn M | Yn M | Yg W | Yg E1 | Yn W | Yn W | Yn W | Yn F | Yg Wd | Yg W | Yg Wd | Yg F | Yn Wd | Yn E4 | 25 |
| 26 | Yg W | Yg E1 | Yg M | Yg M | Yn M | Yn Wd | Yn M | Yn M | Yg W | Yg E1 | Yg W | Yg E3 | Yn W | Yn F | Yg Wd | Yg W | Yg Wd | Yg F | Yn Wd | Yn E4 | Yn Wd | Yn E2 | Yg F | Yg Wd | 26 |
| 27 | Yn W | Yn F | Yn M | Yn M | Yg W | Yg E1 | Yg W | Yg E3 | Yn W | Yn F | Yn W | Yn W | Yg Wd | Yg F | Yn Wd | Yn E4 | Yn Wd | Yn E2 | Yg F | Yg Wd | Yg F | Yg M | Yn F | Yn Wd | 27 |
| 28 | Yg Wd | Yg F | Yg W | Yg E3 | Yn W | Yn F | Yn W | Yn W | Yg Wd | Yg F | Yg Wd | Yg W | Yn Wd | Yn E2 | Yg F | Yg Wd | Yg F | Yg M | Yn F | Yn Wd | Yn F | Yn M | Yg E | Yg E1 | 28 |
| 29 | | | Yn W | Yn W | Yg Wd | Yg F | Yg Wd | Yg W | Yn Wd | Yn E2 | Yn Wd | Yn E4 | Yg F | Yg M | Yn F | Yn Wd | Yn F | Yn M | Yg E | Yg E1 | Yg E | Yg E3 | Yn E | Yn F | 29 |
| 30 | | | Yg Wd | Yg W | Yn Wd | Yn E2 | Yn Wd | Yn E4 | Yg F | Yg M | Yg F | Yg Wd | Yn F | Yn M | Yg E | Yg E1 | Yg E | Yg E3 | Yn E | Yn F | Yn E | Yn W | Yg M | Yg F | 30 |
| 31 | | | Yn Wd | Yn E4 | | | Yg F | Yg Wd | | | Yn F | Yn Wd | Yg E | Yg E3 | | | Yn E | Yn W | | | Yg M | Yg W | Yn M | Yn E2 | 31 |
| 1 | Yn Wd | Yn E2 | Yg F | Yg Wd | Yg F | Yg M | Yn F | Yn Wd | Yn F | Yn M | Yg E | Yg E1 | Yn E | Yn W | Yn E | Yn F | Yg M | Yg W | Yg M | Yg F | Yn M | Yn E4 | Yg W | Yg M | 1 |
| 2 | Yg F | Yg M | Yn F | Yn Wd | Yn F | Yn M | Yg E | Yg E1 | Yg E | Yg E3 | Yn E | Yn F | Yg M | Yg W | Yg M | Yg F | Yn M | Yn E4 | Yn M | Yn E2 | Yg W | Yg Wd | Yn W | Yn M | 2 |
| 3 | Yn F | Yn M | Yg E | Yg E1 | Yg E | Yg E3 | Yn E | Yn F | Yn E | Yn W | Yg M | Yg F | Yn M | Yn E4 | Yn M | Yn E2 | Yg W | Yg Wd | Yg W | Yg M | Yn W | Yn Wd | Yg Wd | Yg E3 | 3 |
| 4 | Yg E | Yg E3 | Yn E | Yn F | Yn E | Yn W | Yg M | Yg F | Yg M | Yg W | Yn M | Yn E2 | Yg W | Yg Wd | Yg W | Yg M | Yn W | Yn Wd | Yn W | Yn M | Yg Wd | Yg E1 | | | 4 |
| 5 | | | | | | | | | Yn M | Yn E4 | Yg W | Yg M | Yn W | Yn Wd | Yn W | Yn M | Yg Wd | Yg E1 | Yg Wd | Yg E3 | | | | | 5 |
| 6 | | | | | | | | | Yg W | Yg Wd | Yn W | Yn M | Yg Wd | Yg E1 | Yg Wd | Yg E3 | Yn Wd | Yn F | Yn Wd | Yn W | | | | | 6 |
| 7 | | | | | | | | | | | | | | | Yn Wd | Yn W | | | | | | | | | 7 |
| 8 | | | | | | | | | | | | | | | | | | | | | | | | | 8 |

# YEAR OF THE PIG

| | H | E | H | E | H | E | H | E | H | E | H | E | H | E | H | E | H | E | H | E | H | E | H | E | |
|---|---|---|---|---|---|---|---|---|---|---|---|---|---|---|---|---|---|---|---|---|---|---|---|---|---|
| YEAR | YEAR<br>Yn M | Yn W | 2031 | | | | | | | | | | | | | | | | | | | | 2032 | | |
| MONTH | 4 Feb - 5 Mar | | 6 Mar - 4 Apr | | 5 Apr - 5 May | | 6 May - 5 June | | 6 June - 6 Jul | | 7 Jul - 7 Aug | | 8 Aug - 7 Sep | | 8 Sep - 7 Oct | | 8 Oct - 7 Nov | | 8 Nov - 6 Dec | | 7 Dec - 5 Jan | | 6 Jan - 3 Feb | | |
| | Yg M | Yg Wd | Yn M | Yn Wd | Yg W | Yg E1 | Yn W | Yn F | Yg Wd | Yg F | Yn Wd | Yn E2 | Yg F | Yg M | Yn F | Yn M | Yg E | Yg E3 | Yn E | Yn W | Yg M | Yg W | Yn M | Yn E4 | |
| Starting time | 1st day | Mid-pt | 1st day | Mid-pt | 1st day | Mid-pt | 1st day | Mid-pt | 1st day | Mid-pt | 1st day | Mid-pt | 1st day | Mid-pt | 1st day | Mid-pt | 1st day | Mid-pt | 1st day | Mid-pt | 1st day | Mid-pt | 1st day | Mid-pt | |
| Date | 4 | 19 | 6 | 21 | 5 | 20 | 6 | 21 | 6 | 21 | 7 | 23 | 8 | 23 | 8 | 23 | 8 | 24 | 8 | 22 | 7 | 22 | 6 | 20 | |
| Hour | 0909 | 0507 | 0309 | 0354 | 0746 | 1451 | 0107 | 1359 | 0511 | 2159 | 1535 | 0905 | 0142 | 1635 | 0507 | 1445 | 2113 | 0027 | 0035 | 2203 | 1716 | 1104 | 0408 | 2111 | |
| DATE 3 | | | | | | | | | | | | | | | | | | | | | | | | | 3 |
| 4 | Yn Wd | Yn W | | | | | | | | | | | | | | | | | | | | | | | 4 |
| 5 | Yg F | Yg W | | | Yn Wd | Yn W | | | | | | | | | | | | | | | | | | | 5 |
| 6 | Yn F | Yn E4 | Yn Wd | Yn F | Yg F | Yg W | Yg F | Yg F | Yn F | Yn E4 | | | | | | | | | | | | | Yn M | Yn W | 6 |
| 7 | Yg E | Yg Wd | Yg F | Yg F | Yn F | Yn E4 | Yn F | Yn E2 | Yg E | Yg Wd | Yg E | Yg M | | | | | | | | | Yn M | Yn F | Yg W | Yg W | 7 |
| 8 | Yn E | Yn Wd | Yn F | Yn E2 | Yg E | Yg Wd | Yg E | Yg M | Yn E | Yn Wd | Yn E | Yn M | Yg M | Yg E1 | Yn M | Yn W | Yn M | Yn F | Yg W | Yg W | Yg W | Yg F | Yn W | Yn E4 | 8 |
| 9 | Yg M | Yg E1 | Yg E | Yg M | Yn E | Yn Wd | Yn E | Yn M | Yg M | Yg E1 | Yg M | Yg E3 | Yn M | Yn F | Yg W | Yg W | Yg W | Yg F | Yn W | Yn E4 | Yn W | Yn E2 | Yg Wd | Yg Wd | 9 |
| 10 | Yn M | Yn F | Yn E | Yn M | Yg M | Yg E1 | Yg M | Yg E3 | Yn M | Yn F | Yn M | Yn W | Yg W | Yg F | Yn W | Yn E4 | Yn W | Yn E2 | Yg Wd | Yg Wd | Yg Wd | Yg M | Yn Wd | Yn Wd | 10 |
| 11 | Yg W | Yg F | Yg M | Yg E3 | Yn M | Yn F | Yn M | Yn W | Yg W | Yg F | Yg W | Yg W | Yn W | Yn E2 | Yg Wd | Yg Wd | Yg Wd | Yg M | Yn Wd | Yn Wd | Yn Wd | Yn M | Yg F | Yg E1 | 11 |
| 12 | Yn W | Yn E2 | Yn M | Yn W | Yg W | Yg F | Yg W | Yg W | Yn W | Yn E2 | Yn W | Yn E4 | Yg Wd | Yg M | Yn Wd | Yn Wd | Yn Wd | Yn M | Yg F | Yg E1 | Yg F | Yg E3 | Yn F | Yn F | 12 |
| 13 | Yg Wd | Yg M | Yg W | Yg W | Yn W | Yn E2 | Yn W | Yn E4 | Yg Wd | Yg M | Yg Wd | Yg Wd | Yn Wd | Yn M | Yg F | Yg E1 | Yg F | Yg E3 | Yn F | Yn F | Yn F | Yn W | Yg E | Yg F | 13 |
| 14 | Yn Wd | Yn M | Yn W | Yn E4 | Yg Wd | Yg M | Yg Wd | Yg Wd | Yn Wd | Yn M | Yn Wd | Yn Wd | Yg F | Yg E3 | Yn F | Yn F | Yn F | Yn W | Yg E | Yg F | Yg E | Yg W | Yn E | Yn E2 | 14 |
| 15 | Yg F | Yg E3 | Yg Wd | Yg Wd | Yn Wd | Yn M | Yn Wd | Yn Wd | Yg F | Yg E3 | Yg F | Yg E1 | Yn F | Yn W | Yg E | Yg F | Yg E | Yg W | Yn E | Yn E2 | Yn E | Yn E4 | Yg M | Yg M | 15 |
| 16 | Yn F | Yn W | Yn Wd | Yn Wd | Yg F | Yg E3 | Yg F | Yg E1 | Yn F | Yn W | Yn F | Yn F | Yg E | Yg W | Yn E | Yn E2 | Yn E | Yn E4 | Yg M | Yg M | Yg M | Yg Wd | Yn M | Yn M | 16 |
| 17 | Yg E | Yg W | Yg F | Yg E1 | Yn F | Yn W | Yn F | Yn F | Yg E | Yg W | Yg E | Yg F | Yn E | Yn E4 | Yg M | Yg M | Yg M | Yg Wd | Yn M | Yn M | Yn M | Yn Wd | Yg W | Yg E3 | 17 |
| 18 | Yn E | Yn E4 | Yn F | Yn F | Yg E | Yg W | Yg E | Yg F | Yn E | Yn E4 | Yn E | Yn E2 | Yg M | Yg Wd | Yn M | Yn M | Yn M | Yn Wd | Yg W | Yg E3 | Yg W | Yg E1 | Yn W | Yn W | 18 |
| 19 | Yg M | Yg Wd | Yg E | Yg F | Yn E | Yn E4 | Yn E | Yn E2 | Yg M | Yg Wd | Yg M | Yg M | Yn M | Yn Wd | Yg W | Yg E3 | Yg W | Yg E1 | Yn W | Yn W | Yn W | Yn F | Yg Wd | Yg W | 19 |
| 20 | Yn M | Yn Wd | Yn E | Yn E2 | Yg M | Yg Wd | Yg M | Yg M | Yn M | Yn Wd | Yn M | Yn M | Yg W | Yg E1 | Yn W | Yn W | Yn W | Yn F | Yg Wd | Yg W | Yg Wd | Yg F | Yn Wd | Yn E4 | 20 |
| 21 | Yg W | Yg E1 | Yg M | Yg M | Yn M | Yn Wd | Yn M | Yn M | Yg W | Yg E1 | Yg W | Yg E3 | Yn W | Yn F | Yg Wd | Yg W | Yg Wd | Yg F | Yn Wd | Yn E4 | Yn Wd | Yn E2 | Yg F | Yg Wd | 21 |
| 22 | Yn W | Yn F | Yn M | Yn M | Yg W | Yg E1 | Yg W | Yg E3 | Yn W | Yn F | Yn W | Yn W | Yg Wd | Yg F | Yn Wd | Yn E4 | Yn Wd | Yn E2 | Yg F | Yg Wd | Yg F | Yg M | Yn F | Yn Wd | 22 |
| 23 | Yg Wd | Yg F | Yg W | Yg E3 | Yn W | Yn F | Yn W | Yn W | Yg Wd | Yg F | Yg Wd | Yg W | Yn Wd | Yn E2 | Yg F | Yg Wd | Yg F | Yg M | Yn F | Yn Wd | Yn F | Yn M | Yg E | Yg E1 | 23 |
| 24 | Yn Wd | Yn E2 | Yn W | Yn W | Yg Wd | Yg F | Yg Wd | Yg W | Yn Wd | Yn E2 | Yn Wd | Yn E4 | Yg F | Yg M | Yn F | Yn Wd | Yn F | Yn M | Yg E | Yg E1 | Yg E | Yg E3 | Yn E | Yn F | 24 |
| 25 | Yg F | Yg M | Yg Wd | Yg W | Yn Wd | Yn E2 | Yn Wd | Yn E4 | Yg F | Yg M | Yg F | Yg Wd | Yn F | Yn M | Yg E | Yg E1 | Yg E | Yg E3 | Yn E | Yn F | Yn E | Yn W | Yg M | Yg F | 25 |
| 26 | Yn F | Yn M | Yn Wd | Yn E4 | Yg F | Yg M | Yg F | Yg Wd | Yn F | Yn M | Yn F | Yn Wd | Yg E | Yg E3 | Yn E | Yn F | Yn E | Yn W | Yg M | Yg F | Yg M | Yg W | Yn M | Yn E2 | 26 |
| 27 | Yg E | Yg E3 | Yg F | Yg Wd | Yn F | Yn M | Yn F | Yn Wd | Yg E | Yg E3 | Yg E | Yg E1 | Yn E | Yn W | Yg M | Yg F | Yg M | Yg W | Yn M | Yn E2 | Yn M | Yn E4 | Yg W | Yg M | 27 |
| 28 | Yn E | Yn W | Yn F | Yn Wd | Yg E | Yg E3 | Yg E | Yg E1 | Yn E | Yn W | Yn E | Yn F | Yg M | Yg W | Yn M | Yn E2 | Yn M | Yn E4 | Yg W | Yg M | Yg W | Yg Wd | Yn W | Yn M | 28 |
| 29 | | | Yg E | Yg E1 | Yn E | Yn W | Yn E | Yn F | Yg M | Yg W | Yg M | Yg F | Yn M | Yn E4 | Yg W | Yg M | Yg W | Yg Wd | Yn W | Yn M | Yn W | Yn Wd | Yg Wd | Yg E3 | 29 |
| 30 | | | Yn E | Yn F | Yg M | Yg W | Yg M | Yg F | Yn M | Yn E4 | Yn M | Yn E2 | Yg W | Yg Wd | Yn W | Yn M | Yn W | Yn Wd | Yg Wd | Yg E3 | Yg Wd | Yg E1 | Yn Wd | Yn W | 30 |
| 31 | | | Yg M | Yg F | | | Yn M | Yn E2 | | | Yg W | Yg M | Yn W | Yn Wd | | | Yg Wd | Yg E1 | | | Yn Wd | Yn F | Yg F | Yg W | 31 |
| 1 | Yg M | Yg W | Yn M | Yn E2 | Yn M | Yn E4 | Yg W | Yg M | Yg W | Yg Wd | Yn W | Yn M | Yg Wd | Yg E1 | Yg Wd | Yg E3 | Yn Wd | Yn F | Yn Wd | Yn W | Yg F | Yg F | Yn F | Yn E4 | 1 |
| 2 | Yn M | Yn E4 | Yg W | Yg M | Yg W | Yg Wd | Yn W | Yn M | Yn W | Yn Wd | Yg Wd | Yg E3 | Yn Wd | Yn F | Yn Wd | Yn W | Yg F | Yg F | Yg F | Yg W | Yn F | Yn E2 | Yg E | Yg Wd | 2 |
| 3 | Yg W | Yg Wd | Yn W | Yn M | Yn W | Yn Wd | Yg Wd | Yg E3 | Yg Wd | Yg E1 | Yn Wd | Yn W | Yg F | Yg F | Yg F | Yg W | Yn F | Yn E2 | Yn F | Yn E4 | Yg E | Yg M | Yn E | Yn Wd | 3 |
| 4 | Yn W | Yn Wd | Yg Wd | Yg E3 | Yg Wd | Yg E1 | Yn Wd | Yn W | Yn Wd | Yn F | Yg F | Yg W | Yn F | Yn E2 | Yn F | Yn E4 | Yg E | Yg M | Yg E | Yg Wd | Yn E | Yn M | | | 4 |
| 5 | Yg Wd | Yg E1 | | | Yn Wd | Yn F | Yg F | Yg W | Yg F | Yg F | Yn F | Yn E4 | Yg E | Yg M | Yg E | Yg Wd | Yn E | Yn M | Yn E | Yn Wd | Yg M | Yg E3 | | | 5 |
| 6 | | | | | | | | | Yn F | Yn E2 | Yg E | Yg Wd | Yn E | Yn M | Yn E | Yn Wd | Yg M | Yg E3 | Yg M | Yg E1 | | | | | 6 |
| 7 | | | | | | | | | | | Yn E | Yn Wd | Yg M | Yg E3 | Yg M | Yg E1 | Yn M | Yn W | | | | | | | 7 |
| 8 | | | | | | | | | | | | | | | | | | | | | | | | | 8 |

# THE AUTHOR

Hee Yin Fan was born in Pahang, Malaysia. She qualified as a Certified Public Accountant after completing her articleship with a local accounting firm in Kuantan. Ms Hee then worked in Malaysia for several years before moving to Singapore in 1990.

In 1993, she chanced upon a course conducted by Master Raymond Lo, a *feng shui* expert from Hong Kong. Since then, she has pursued the subject enthusiastically. After 18 years in accounting, Ms Hee switched careers. Understanding her own destiny gave her the courage to make the crossover. She is now a showroom manager with a company which provides interior design consultancy and project management.